KNOW IT ALL

KNOW IT ALL

Marsha Kranes
Fred Worth
Steve Temerius

Tess Press

Published by
Tess Press, an imprint of
Black Dog & Leventhal Publishers, Inc.
151 West 19th Street
New York, NY 10011

Designed by Sabrina Bowers
Cover design by Filip Zawodnik

Manufactured in the United States of America

ISBN 1-57912-405-4

h g f e d c b a

Contents

Arts, Comics & Literature

Questions

1. What do P. G. Wodehouse, Ezra Pound and William Joyce have in common?

2. What was the first published Sherlock Holmes story written by Sir Arthur Conan Doyle?

3. Who was Clark Kent's high school sweetheart?

4. What is the name of Dr. Seuss's egg-hatching elephant?

5. George G. Moppet was the father of what comic strip character?

6. John Clayton Jr. was the childhood name of what well-known fictional character?

7. What one word was intentionally left out of the movie version of Mario Puzo's novel, "The Godfather," even though this word was the working title of the book?

8. Ernest Hemingway once wrote that a man must do four things in his life to demonstrate his manhood. What were they?

9. What is the name of the poem which appears on the pedestal of the Statue of Liberty?

Answers

1. *They all made broadcasts for the enemy during World War II.*

2. *A Study In Scarlet, in 1887.*

3. *Lana Lang.*

4. *Horton.*

5. *Little Lulu.*

6. *Tarzan, whose title was Lord Greystoke.*

7. *"Mafia."*

8. *Plant a tree, fight a bull, write a book, and have a son.*

9. *"The New Colossus," by Emma Lazarus.*

10. In the comic strips, what was the name of Mandrake the Magician's giant partner?

11. *Men Against the Sea* and *Pitcairn's Island* were two sequels to what famous novel?

12. What novel contains the longest sentence in literature?

13. Where did Samuel Clemens get the idea for his pseudonym, Mark Twain?

14. In what comic strip would you have found an animal called the "Schmoo"?

15. What couple live next door to Dagwood and Blondie Bumstead in "Blondie"?

16. What is the only novel to top the best-seller lists for two consecutive years?

17. What classic gothic novel of 1818 was subtitled, *The Modern Prometheus*?

18. Who was the Lone Ranger's great grand-nephew?

19. Psychologist William Moulton Marston, inventor of the polygraph, or lie detector, also created a famous comic book heroine. Who was she?

20. The Max Fleischer cartoon character, Betty Boop, was based on which real-life actress?

21. "Last night I dreamt I went to Manderley again," was the first line of what Daphne du Maurier novel?

22. What is the actual title of Leonardo da Vinci's "Mona Lisa"?

23. Who did cartoonist Milton Caniff use as his inspiration for the Dragon Lady, in his "Terry and the Pirates" comic strip?

24. In Henry Wadsworth Longfellow's famous poem, *Hiawatha*, what was the name of Hiawatha's wife?

10. *Lothar.*

11. Mutiny On The Bounty *(Charles Nordoff and James Norman Hall co-wrote all three novels).*

12. Les Miserables, *by Victor Hugo, with 823 words.*

13. *It was the river call used by boatmen on the Mississippi to signify two fathoms of water.*

14. Li'l Abner. *The Schmoo gave milk, laid eggs and tasted similar to chicken or steak.*

15. *Herb and Tootsie Woodley.*

16. Jonathan Livingston Seagull, *by Richard Bach, in 1972 and 1973.*

17. Frankenstein, *by Mary Wollstonecraft Shelley.*

18. *The Green Hornet. The relationship was as follows: John Reid (the Lone Ranger) had a brother named Dan Reid, who had a son named Dan Jr., who had a son named Henry Reid, who had a son named Britt Reid (the Green Hornet).*

19. *Wonder Woman.*

20. *Helen Kane, known as the boop-boop-a-doop girl.*

21. Rebecca.

22. La Gioconda.

23. *Joan Crawford.*

24. *Minnehaha.*

25. Puddleburg was the hometown of what cartoon character?

26. "The temperature hit ninety degrees the day she arrived" was the opening line of one of the best-selling novels ever. What was it?

27. Who was the first writer to incorporate himself?

28. Tess Trueheart is the wife of what comic strip character?

29. What is the native country of Agatha Christie's detective Hercule Poirot?

30. What was the hometown of Sgt. Snorkel in *Beetle Bailey*?

31. In the Robin Hood stories, what was the real name of Little John?

32. What was Scarlett O'Hara's real first name?

33. Most of us are familiar with the faces of Dr. B. H. McKeeby and Nan Wood, but who are they and where have we seen them?

34. In the *Little Orphan Annie* comic strip, what was the name of Daddy Warbucks's giant bodyguard who wore a turban?

35. *The Last Of The Really Great Whangdoodles and Mandy* are children's books written by what well-known Oscar-winning actress?

36. Under what assumed name did Oscar Wilde live out the last three years of his life, in France?

37. By what pseudonym is writer Frederick Dannay Manfred Bennington Lee better known?

38. What was the name of the pig leader in George Orwell's *Animal Farm*?

39. What was the name of the girlfriend of Felix the Cat?

40. To whom did Herman Melville dedicate his novel, *Moby Dick*?

25. *Woody Woodpecker.*

26. The Valley of the Dolls *by Jacqueline Susann.*

27. *Edgar Rice Burroughs, the creator of Tarzan, who became a corporation in 1923.*

28. *Dick Tracy.*

29. *Belgium.*

30. *Pork Corners, Kansas.*

31. *John Little.*

32. *Katie.*

33. *The farmer and his wife in Grant Wood's classic painting,* American Gothic

34. *Punjab.*

35. *Julie Andrews.*

36. *Sebastian Melmoth.*

37. *Ellery Queen.*

38. *Napoleon.*

39. *Phyllis.*

40. *Nathaniel Hawthorne.*

41. What comic strip character was named after heavyweight boxing champion James J. Jeffries

42. What was Juliet's last name, in Shakespeare's *Romeo and Juliet* ?

43. *The Terror of the Monster* was an early title for a best-selling novel which inspired one of the highest-grossing movies of the mid-70's. Under what name did it eventually terrify the reading and filmgoing public.

44. *The Emerald City* was the working title of which classic novel?

45. What was the name of the gang that was always trying to steal Scrooge McDuck's money in the comics?

46. What famous writer named a dull-witted character in one of his plays Moron, introducing the word into the vocabulary?

47. What famous American poet penned the oft-quoted line "Into each life some rain must fall"?

48. Who is the only named dog to appear in a Shakespearean play?

49. What was strange about the watch worn by the Mad Hatter in the Lewis Carroll classic *Alice's Adventures in Wonderland*?

50. What was the favorite cocktail of Ian Fleming, creator of suave superspy James Bond?

51. What famous American writer's gravestone epitaph is this last line from one of his novels: "So we beat on, boats against the current, borne back ceaselessly into the past"?

52. To what famous architect do we attribute the dictum "Less is more"?

53. What unusual use did writer D. H. Lawrence make of his favorite horse, Aaron, after it died?

54. What popular comic strip has a concerto named in its honor by a contemporary composer?

41. Jeff, of Mutt and Jeff.

42. Capulet.

43. Jaws, *by Peter Benchley.*

44. The Wonderful Wizard of Oz, *by L. Frank Baum.*

45. The Beagle Boys.

46. Molière. The play was La Princesse d'Elide.

47. Henry Wadsworth Longfellow. The line is from his poem The Rainy Day, *written in 1842.*

48. Crab. The play is The Two Gentlemen of Verona. *Dogs are mentioned, but not by name, in several other Shakespearean plays.*

49. As Alice observed: "It tells the day of the month but doesn't tell what o'clock it is."

50. Pink gin—not Bond's famous vodka martini (shaken, not stirred).

51. F. Scott Fitzgerald's. The line quoted is from The Great Gatsby.

52. Ludwig Mies van der Rohe.

53. He had the hide made into a duffel bag.

54. Peanuts. The concerto is by Ellen Taaffe Zwilich.

55. What famous British poet and playwright had an m—for "murderer"—branded on his left thumb?

56. What famous character in literature was inspired by an Augustinian monk named Alonso Quixado.

57. What was popular author Louis L'Amour's real name?

58. The title of what poetic drama by Robert Browning was used to name a Kentucky town?

59. How many years did Robinson Crusoe spend shipwrecked on his island?

60. What did L. Frank Baum, author of *The Wonderful Wizard* of *Oz*, call his home in Hollywood?

61. What famous American poet was a West Point cadet for two weeks, but was forced to leave after failing arithmetic and grammar?

62. What is the real name of the evil Batman comic strip character known as the Riddler?

63. What were the names of the brothers Karamozov in the novel by Feodor Dostoevsky?

64. What exotic city was featured in *National Geographic* magazine's first photo story in 1905?

65. What was the name of Dick and Jane's baby sister in elementary school primers of old?

66. What was mystery writer Dashiell Hammett's first name?

67. How many exclamation points did author Tom Wolfe use in his blockbuster bestseller *The Bonfire of the Vanities?*

68. What is the literary source of the F. Scott Fitzgerald book title *Tender Is the Night?*

55. *Ben Jonson, for killing an actor in a duel in 1598. Jonson escaped the gallows by pleading benefit of clergy and forfeiting all his goods and chattels.*

56. Don Quixote. *Quixado was writer Miguel de Cervantes's great-uncle by marriage.*

57. *Louis LaMoore.*

58. Pippa Passes. *The name was suggested by a schoolteacher in 1915. Browning's play gave us the line: "God's in his heaven—/All's right with the world."*

59. *24.*

60. *Ozcot.*

61. *Carl Sandburg, in 1899. One of his classmates was general-to-be Douglas MacArthur.*

62. *E. Nigma. The E. is for Edward.*

63. *Dmitri (or Mitya), Ivan (or Vanya), Alexei (or Alyosha) and Smerdyakov.*

64. *Lhasa, Tibet.*

65. *Sally.*

66. *Samuel, or Sam—as in Sam Spade, his famous detective.*

67. *2,343.*

68. *Keats' poem* Ode to a Nightingale.

69. What well-known writer appeared in the 1981 movie *Ragtime* as Stanford White, the celebrated architect who was shot to death in the sensational *Girl in the Red Velvet Swing* murder?

70. What did Jughead, the buddy of comic strip character Archie, become when he grew up, according to a 1990 TV movie about the two Riverdale High School grads?

71. What was the name of the dog that was with Rip Van Winkle when he fell asleep for 20 years?

72. What was Dr. Frankenstein's first name in the famous novel by Mary Wollstonecraft Shelley?

73. What cartoon character's "racy lifestyle" once led to a ban on his comic books in youth club libraries in Helsinki, Finland?

74. How many references are there to crying in Tammy Faye Bakker's two books, *I Gotta Be Me* and *Run to the Roar*?

75. What was the title of Harpo Marx's 1985 autobiography?

76. What famous artist's first name means welcome in his native tongue?

77. What was the name of the cat Alice left behind when she fell down the rabbit hole in *Alice's Adventures in Wonderland* by Lewis Carroll?

78. What was Rembrandt's last name?

79. What American novel was the first to sell over one million copies?

80. What comic strip character was the first to grow up and age in the strip?

81. What is the name of the gypsy girl the hunchback Quasimodo falls in love with in Victor Hugo's *The Hunchback of Notre Dame*?

69. Norman Mailer.

70. A psychiatrist—known by his given name, Forsythe, rather than Jughead.

71. Wolf.

72. Victor.

73. Donald Duck's, in 1978. His questionable behavior included a 50-year engagement to Daisy Duck; the uncertain parentage of his nephews, Huey, Dewey and Louie; and his regular appearance in a sailor suit that failed to cover his feathery behind.

74. 60.

75. The zany, but silent Marx brother called his book Harpo Speaks!

76. Benvenuto Cellini's.

77. Dinah.

78. Van Ryn (or van Rijn).

79. Uncle Tom's Cabin, *or,* Life Among the Lowly, *by Harriet Beecher Stowe, which was published in 1852.*

80. Skeezix, who first appeared in the Gasoline Alley *comic strip as a baby left on bachelor Walt Wallet's doorstep.*

81. Esmeralda.

82. What was the ransom paid for the release of yeoman Geoffrey Chaucer after he was captured by the French in 1359 during the Hundred Years' War?

83. What famous American writer worked as an entertainer aboard a Swedish ocean liner cruising the Caribbean before being drafted to serve in World War II?

84. To whom did Helen Keller dedicate her autobiography, *The Story of My Life?*

85. What did famed architect Frank Lloyd Wright reply when an important client called to complain that water on the roof of his newly completed house was leaking onto a dinner guest?

86. What famous book begins: "Chug, chug, chug. Puff, puff, puff"?

87. What was the name of Don Quixote's worn-out old horse?

88. What were the first names of L'il Abner Yokum's parents in the popular Al Capp comic strip?

89. How many husbands did the Wife of Bath have, as reported in *Chaucer's Canterbury Tales?*

90. What were the first names of Robert Louis Stevenson's Dr. Jekyll and Mr. Hyde?

91. In what unusual way did writer Nathan Weinstein follow publisher Horace Greeley's advice to "Go west, young man"?

92. What was the name of the she-ape that rescued the infant Tarzan and raised him to be Lord of the Apes?

93. In what best-selling book did an author offer acknowledgment to a friend who later killed him?

94. What Pulitzer and Nobel Prize-winning American novelist worked on the screenplays of the movies *The Road to Glory, Gunga , To Have and Have Not* and *The Big Sleep?*

82. £16—*about $4,800 in today's currency.*

83. *J. D. Salinger.*

84. *To inventor Alexander Graham Bell, who helped direct her education and considered himself, first and foremost, a teacher of the deaf.*

85. *"Tell him to move his chair."*

86. *The children's book The Little Engine That Could," by Watty Piper.*

87. *Rosinante. Sidekick Sancho Panza's donkey was called Dapple.*

88. *Mammy was Pansy; Pappy, Lucifer.*

89. *Five.*

90. *The good doctor was Henry; the evil Mr. Hyde, Edward.*

91. *He changed his last name to West—and became famous as Nathanael West, author of "Miss Lonelyhearts" and "The Day of the Locust."*

92. *Kala.*

93. *"The Complete Scarsdale Medical Diet," in which Dr. Herman Tarnower thanked his friend Jean Harris.*

94. *William Faulkner.*

95. What is the origin of the expression "Cowabunga!"—the war cry of the Teenage Mutant Ninja Turtles?

96. How many times did Ernest Hemingway revise the last page of *A Farewell to Arms*?

97. What is the name of the elementary school attended by Lucy, Linus and Charlie Brown in Charles Schulz's *Peanuts* comic strip?

98. How many syllables are there in a Japanese haiku poem?

99. In Lewis Carroll's poem *The Hunting of the Snark*, what did the elusive, troublesome snark turn into to fool hunters?

100. In the novel *Shoeless Joe*—upon which the 1989 hit movie *Field of Dreams* was based—what real-life American writer was "kidnapped" by the hero, Iowa farmer Ray Kinsella?

101. What unflattering observation did poet Dylan Thomas make about writer T. S. Eliot's name?

102. In the original L. Frank Baum story *The Wonderful Wizard of Oz*, what color were Dorothy's slippers?

103. What was art-world guru Andy Warhol's name at birth?

104. What phrase did French impressionist artist Paul Cezanne teach his pet parrot to say over and over again?

105. What was the maiden name of Blondie Bumstead, the comic-strip wife of hapless Dagwood Bumstead?

106. Whose autobiography is entitled *The Wheel of Fortune*?

107. What famous comic strip character was inspired by the 1936 Henry Fonda film *Trail of the Lonesome Pine*?

108. What was the original name of the orphan created in 1924 by cartoonist Harold Gray in the comic strip we know as *Little Orphan Annie*?

109. In what comic strip did the onomatopoeia "ZAP" originate?

95. *It was the greeting exchanged by Buffalo Bob Smith and Chief Thunderthud on the "Howdy Doody" TV show in the 1950s. Its use spread through the "Gidget" surfer movies, and later the "Peanuts" comic strip.*

96. *39 times.*

97. *Birchwood.*

98. *17, arranged in 3 lines of 5, 7 and 5 syllables.*

99. *A boojum.*

100. *The reclusive J. D. Salinger. Because Salinger threatened to sue, he was replaced in the film by a fictitious writer named Terence Mann, who was portrayed by James Earl Jones.*

101. *Backward—but for one misplaced letter—it would spell toilets.*

102. *Silver.*

103. *Andrew Warhola.*

104. *"Cezanne is a great painter!"*

105. *Boopadoop. In the early days of the Chic Young cartoon "Blondie," she was a gold-digging flapper trailed by rich suitors, one of whom was playboy Dagwood.*

106. *The answer is not Vanna White, who was only eight years old when the book was published in 1965. Its author was French singer Edith Piaf.*

107. *Al Capp's Li'l Abner. Fonda played a backwoods mountaineer in the movie.*

108. *Otto. Gray was advised to "put a skirt on the kid and call it 'Little Orphan Annie'" by Chicago Tribune publisher Joseph Patterson.*

109. *In Buck Rogers, in 1929. Cartoonist Philip Francis Nowlan used it to describe the sound of Buck's paralyzing ray gun.*

110. Why was Clark Kent—alias Superman—rejected for military service during World War II?

111. What is the native language of English playwright Tom Stoppard, author of *Rosencrantz and Guildenstern Are Dead,* Travesties and *The Real Thing*?

112. What was Captain Queeg's first name and rank in the 1951 novel—and later movie—*The Caine Mutiny*?

113. Under what name did Italian artist Jocopo Robusti gain world renown?

114. What title did Russian author Leo Tolstoy originally give to the novel we know as *War and Peace*?

115. What classic adventure story did author William Styron reject when he was a reader for McGraw-Hill—a mistake he had his narrator, Stingo, repeat in his novel *Sophie's Choice*?

116. Vincent Van Gogh's painting *Sunflowers* was sold at auction for $39.9 million in 1987. How much did that come to per sunflower?

117. What famous character in English literature made his debut in *Beeton's Christmas Annual* in 1887?

118. How many medals and ribbons were awarded to comic strip hero Steve Canyon during his 41 years in the Air Force?

119. What was the title of the detective story by stripteaser Gypsy Rose Lee, published in 1941?

120. What headgear is named after the title character of a Robert Burns poem?

121. What is the last line of the Thomas Hood poem that begins:
> No sun—no moon!
> No morn—no noon
> No dawn—no dusk—no proper time of day.

122. How many names did Andy Warhol, the gossipy guru of the avant garde, drop in his diaries, which were published in 1989?.

110. *He failed the eye test portion of the Army physical. Because of his X-ray vision, he inadvertently read an eye chart in another room.*

111. *Czech. He was born Thomas Straussler in Zlin, Czechoslovakia, 1937. Stoppard is the name of the British Army officer his mother married in 1946.*

112. *First name, Philip; rank, lieutenant commander.*

113. *Tintorette. Robusti's nickname—Italian for "little dyer"—was bestowed on him because his father was a dyer, or tintore, of silk.*

114. All's Well That Ends Well.

115. Kon-Tiki *by Thor Heyerdahl.*

116. *$2.66 million. There are 15 sunflowers in the painting.*

117. *Sherlock Holmes. His first published exploit was* A Study in Scarlet, *for which Sir Arthur Conan Doyle was paid £25.*

118. *21—that's 13 medals and 8 ribbons. They're on display at Ohio State University, the alma mater of both Canyon and his creator, Milton Caniff*

119. The G-String Murders. *The book, ghost-written by Craig Rice, is about two striptease queens murdered with their own G-strings.*

120. *The tam-o'-shanter, or tam.*

121. *"November!" The poem's title is* No!

122. *According to "Fame" magazine, exactly 2,809—or more than three per page in the 807-page book.*

123. What Pulitzer Prize-winning novelist worked as a hod carrier, wheeling 100-pound barrows of concrete along scaffolding, during construction of New York's Madison Square Garden in the 1920s?

124. In what play does the title character have a son named Swiss Cheese?

125. How many grandchildren did artist Grandma Moses have?

126. In the early James Bond books, Agent 007 packed a Walther PPK. What weapon replaced it in his later appearances?

127. In what state was playwright Tennessee Williams born?

128. Who said "Nothing is so much to be feared as fear"?

129. What was the name of Elizabeth Barrett Browning's pet golden cocker spaniel?

130. What famous novel provided the basic story line for Francis Ford Coppola's 1979 Vietnam War film epic, *Apocalypse Now*?

131. What famous British literary figure wrote under the pseudonym S.P.A.M.?

132. What do the initials P. G. stand for in writer P. G. Wodehouse's name?

133. What 804-page book by a little-known zoologist became a best-seller in 1948 despite a reviewer's description of it as "so turgid, so repetitive, so full of nearly meaningless tables, that it will only be read by specialists..."?

134. Alexandra Ripley was paid $4.94 million in 1988 as an advance for the sequel to *Gone With the Wind*. What was Margaret Mitchell's advance for the best-selling, Pulitzer Prize-winning original?

135. In what language was the first complete Bible in America printed?

123. *John Steinbeck.*

124. Mother Courage and Her Children *by Bertolt Brecht.*

125. *11.*

126. *A German-made, 9-millimeter, Heckler and Koch semi-automatic pistol.*

127. *In Mississippi, as Thomas Lanier Williams. He took the name Tennessee after his father's home state.*

128. *Henry David Thoreau, in his 14-volume* Journal, *published posthumously in 1906.*

129. *Flush.*

130. The Heart of Darkness *by Joseph Conrad, published in 1902 and set in Africa.*

131. *Satirist Jonathan Swift. It was one of a series of pseudonyms he used—others were Isaac Bickerstaff, Martinus Scribberus, T. Tinker, Dr. Andrew Tripe and Simon Wagstaff.*

132. *Pelham Grenville.*

133. *The* Kinsey Report *by Alfred C. Kinsey, published as* Sexual Behavior in the Human Male.

134. *$500.*

135. *That of the Algonquin Indians of Massachusetts. It was translated into their language by the Rev. John Eliot and published in 1663.*

136. What famous American writer wrote a fictional biography of Joan of Arc that was published anonymously in *Harper's* magazine?

137. What was the title of Mae West's 1959 autobiography?

138. How many copies did Doubleday run off the presses in its first printing of Bill Cosby's 1987 book *Time Flies*?

139. Why did 70-year-old Miguel Ramirez sue writer Ernest Hemingway?

140. Complete this Biblical quotation: "It is easier for a camel to go through the eye of a needle, than..."

141. What is unusual about the 50,100-word novel *Gadsby*, written by Ernest Vincent Wright in 1937?

142. What words did Lewis Carroll combine to come up with the term "chortle" in *Through a Looking-Glass*?

143. What literary animals "dined on mince, and slices of quince, which they ate with a runcible spoon"? And just what is a runcible spoon?

144. Who wrote, "Oh, East is East, and West is West, and never the twain shall meet"?

145. Who was the subject of the 1968 biography *Always on Sunday*?

146. Where did mystery writer Agatha Christie acquire her extensive knowledge of poisons?

147. What was Truman Capote's last name before he was adopted by his stepfather?

148. What book knocked Henry Kissinger's *White House Years* out of first place on the best-seller list in November 1979?

149. Shakespeare wrote that "brevity is the soul of wit." What did noted wit Dorothy Parker say it was?

136. *Mark Twain, in 1896. It was called* Personal Recollections of Joan of Arc *and written under the pseudonym of The Sieur Louis de Conte, page and secretary to Joan of Arc* **137.** Goodness Had Nothing to Do With It.

138. *1.5 million.*

139. *The Cuban fisherman claimed Hemingway stole his story, the Pulitzer Prize-winning* The Old Man and the Sea. *The suit was thrown out.*

140. *"...for a rich man to enter into the kingdom of God." The words are those of Jesus, from Matthew 19:24.*

141. *It doesn't contain a single letter "e"—the most frequently used letter in the English alphabet. Wright made sure he didn't use it by tying down the "e" bar on his typewriter.*

142. *Chuckle and snort.*

143. *The Owl and the Pussy-Cat did the dining in the poem of the same name by Edward Lear. A runcible spoon is a three-pronged fork that's curved like a spoon and has a cutting edge.*

144. *Rudyard Kipling, in "The Ballad of East and West."*

145. *Ed Sullivan.*

146. *In a hospital dispensary—where she worked during World War I.*

147. *Persons.*

148. *"Aunt Erma's Cope Book," by Erma Bombeck.*

149. *"The soul of lingerie."*

150. The title of what artist's painting was used to name the Blue Rider (Blaue Reiter) school of German expressionist painters?

151. Who wrote the poem *The Pied Piper of Hamelin*?

152. By what pseudonym is novelist David John Moore Cornwell best known?

153. By what score was Mudville defeated in Ernest Thayer's classic poem *Casey at the Bat*?

154. For what career was Western writer Zane Grey trained?

155. What American literary classic was published in Russian 50 years ago under the title *Volshebnik Izumrudnovo Goroda*?

156. What famous play served as the inspiration for the 1956 science-fiction film *Forbidden Planet*?

157. What is the name of the town in which Thornton Wilder's Pulitzer Prize-winning play *Our Town* takes place?

158. What famous writer is believed to have made the first reference to tennis in English literature?

159. How much was poet John Milton paid for his epic poem *Paradise Lost*, which was first published in 1667?

160. In *Gulliver's Travels*, what was a professor at the Grand Academy in Lagado busily trying to extract from cucumbers?

161. What was the first name of supercapitalist war profiteer "Daddy" Warbucks in the *Little Orphan Annie* cartoon series?

162. What play opens with "Now is the winter of our discontent"?

163. What was the title of the biography of Thomas Crapper, the British sanitary engineer who invented the modern flush toilet in 1878?

164. What second career did nineteenth-century literary giants Nathaniel Hawthorne and William Dean Howells have in common?

150. *Russian Wassily Kandinsky.*

151. *Robert Browning, in 1842.*

152. *John Le Carré, which translated from the French means John the Square.*

153. *The score was 4 to 2.*

154. *Dentistry.*

155. The Wonderful Wizard of Oz.

156. *Shakespeare's* The Tempest.

157. *Grover's Corners, New Hampshire.*

158. *Geoffrey Chaucer, in 1380, when he wrote of "playen racket to and fro" in* Troilus and Criseyde.

159. *Ten pounds—five down and another five pounds when all 1,300 copies in the first printing were sold. After Milton's death, his widow gave up all future claims for an additional eight pounds.*

160. *Sunbeams.*

161. *Oliver.*

162. *Shakespeare's "The Tragedy of King Richard III."*

163. Flushed with Pride: The Story of Thomas Crapper.

164. *Both were diplomats: Hawthorne wrote a campaign biography of Franklin Pierce, earning himself the consul post in Liverpool; Howells' campaign biography of Abraham Lincoln won him the consul post in Venice.*

165. Who wrote the story upon which Alfred Hitchcock based his 1963 suspense film *The Birds*?

166. What famous American writer was granted a patent for a best-selling book that contained no words?

167. Where will you find a 24-foot-long, 3,500-pound aluminum lipstick tube mounted on a caterpillar tractor tread?

168. What foreign government did Rex Stout's fictional Sleuth Nero Wolfe serve as a secret agent when he was a young man?

169. What famous American writer called a volume of his short stories *Rolling Stones?*

170. What was the name of the life-saving pet mongoose in *The Jungle Book* by *Rudyard Kipling*?

171. What controversial painting caused an uproar at the New York Armory Show in 1913?

172. What are the four ghosts in Charles Dickens' *A Christmas Carol*?

173. What writer worked as a Pinkerton detective on cases involving movie comic Fatty Arbuckle and gambler Nicky Arnstein?

174. What book was Mark David Chapman carrying with him when he killed John Lennon on 12/8/80?

175. What writer was expelled from West Point for showing up for public parade wearing only a white belt and gloves?

176. What was the working title of Joseph Heller's best-selling *Catch 22*?

177. What Frenchman wrote about two fantastic space odysseys— one to the moon and one to the sun—more than 200 years before Jules Verne?

178. What kind of tree was Betty Smith referring to in her book "A Tree Grows in Brooklyn"?

165. *Daphne du Maurier, best known for* Rebecca.

166. *Mark Twain. It was a* Self-Pasting Scrapbook *containing blank pages coated with a gum veneer.*

167. *On the Yale University campus in New Haven, Connecticut—it's a sculpture donated by pop artist Claes Oldenburg.*

168. *Austria.*

169. *O. Henry (William Sydney Porter), in 1913. Earlier, he had founded a humorous weekly called* The Rolling Stone.

170. *Rikki-Tikki-Tavi.*

171. Nude Descending a Staircase No. 2, *by Marcel Duchamp.*

172. *The ghosts of Christmas Past, Christmas Present, Christmas Yet to Come, and Jacob Marley (Scrooge's partner).*

173. *Dashiell Hammett.*

174. *J. D. Salinger's* Catcher in the Rye.

175. *Edgar Allan Poe.*

176. Catch 18. *The title was changed because of the Leon Uris novel,* Mila 18, *published the same year, 1961.*

177. *Cyrano de Bergerac.*

178. *An ailanthus, known as "the tree of heaven."*

179. What nineteenth-century American literary classic was labeled "downright socialistic" and banned from U.S. Information Service libraries in 1954?

180. Who wrote:
> "Twinkle Twinkle little bat!
> How I wonder what you're at!
> Up above the world you fly!
> Like a tea tray in the sky!"

181. What great American writer ran rum because he couldn't sell his work?

182. Who was Little Lulu's boy companion in the comic strip created by Marjorie Henderson?

183. What major British literary figure served two years at hard labor after being found guilty of homosexuality?

184. What special commission did a French baron give to artists Georges Braque, Marc Chagall, Salvatore Dali, and Andy Warhol?

185. Sherlock Holmes' sidekick, Dr. Watson, suffered a war-time bullet wound. Where was it?

186. Dorothy Parker wrote:
> "Men seldom make passes
> At girls who wear glasses."
> Did she?

187. What was Huck Finn's remedy for warts?

188. What book was once banned by the Eldon, Missouri library because it contained 39 "objectionable" words?

189. William Sidney Porter, whom we know as O. Henry, spent some time in Honduras. What was he doing there?

190. What do mystery writers Gordon Ashe, Michael Halliday, J. J. Marric, and Kyle Hunt have in common?

191. What was *Jazz Age* writer F. Scott Fitzgerald's full name?

179. Walden, *by Henry David Thoreau.*

180. *Lewis Carroll, in* Alice in Wonderland. *It was sung by the Mad Hatter.*

181. *William Faulkner, creator of Yoknapatawpha County and two-time Pulitzer Prize winner for fiction (*A Fable *and* The Reivers*).*

182. *Tubby.*

183. *Oscar Wilde, who wrote* De Profundis *during his imprisonment.*

184. *Designing wine labels for Mouton Rothschild. The baron was Philippe de Rothschild.*

185. *On his shoulder, according to* A Study in Scarlet; *in the leg, according to* The Sign of Four.

186. *Yes.*

187. *Swinging a dead cat in a graveyard at midnight.*

188. *The American Heritage Dictionary.*

189. *Fleeing prosecution on embezzlement charges. When he returned to the U.S., he served time in jail—where he began writing the adventure stories that made him famous.*

190. *They're all the same man, John Creasey, who used 26 pseudonyms for his 600-plus books.*

191. *Francis Scott Key Fitzgerald. He was a distant relative of the man who wrote our national anthem.*

192. *Tattered Tom* and *Ragged Dick* were the heroes and titles of books written by what nineteenth century American author?

193. What are the names of Popeye's four nephews?

194. What writer-friend nicknamed T. S. Eliot "Old Possum"?

195. What American writer, while a war correspondent, is credited with capturing a town single-handedly during the Spanish-American War?

196. What cartoon character said, "The trouble with the rat race is there is never a finish line"?

197. What visual impairment do some experts believe influenced the styles of artists El Greco and Modigliani?

198. *All the King's Men* by Robert Penn Warren is a roman à clef about what American political figure?

199. What famous writer had several butterflies named after him?

200. In the novel *Futility*, published in 1898—fourteen years before the sinking of the Titanic—an "unsinkable" luxury liner was lost after hitting an iceberg on its maiden voyage. What was the ship's name?

201. What was the house in the background of Grant Wood's classic painting *American Gothic*?

202. Who wrote:
>"There was a little girl
>Who had a little curl
>Right in the middle of her forehead"?

203. What was the name of Frances Hodgson Burnett's character Little Lord Fauntleroy?

204. What was the first daily comic strip published in the U.S.?

205. What fellow artist did French impressionist Paul Gauguin refer to as "the little green chemist"?

192. *Horatio Alger, who wrote more than 100 rags-to-riches success stories about hardworking and honest young men.*

193. *Pipeye, Peepeye, Pupeye, and Poopeye.*

194. *Ezra Pound.*

195. *Stephen Crane. The town was Juana Di´az in Puerto Rico; the resistance was nonexistent.*

196. *Dagwood in the* Blondie *strip.*

197. *Astigmatism.*

198. *Louisiana governor and senator Huey Long.*

199. Lolita *author Vladimir Nabokov, who was also a lepidopterist.*

200. *The Titan. It was the creation of writer Morgan Robertson.*

201. *A brothel in Eldon, Iowa.*

202. *Henry Wadsworth Longfellow, in his 1883 poem* There Was a Little Girl.

203. *Cedric Errol.*

204. Mr. Mutt *by H.C. (Bud) Fisher, later called* Mutt and Jeff. *The strip first appeared in the San Francisco Chronicle in 1907.*

205. *Pointillist Georges Seurat.*

206. What skill won people high office in the land of Lilliput in Jonathan Swift's *Gulliver's Travels*?

207. When Goofy first appeared in a Mickey Mouse cartoon, what was his name?

208. What did Clark Kent's adoptive mother, Martha, use to make his Superman costume?

209. How many knights could be seated around King Arthur's Round Table?

210. Abstract expressionist painter Arshile Gorky plagiarized the work of sculptor Henri Gaudier-Brzeska, but it wasn't art that he copied. What was it?

211. What were Cinderella's slippers made of in Frenchman Charles Perrault's original version of the fairy tale classic?

212. In the cartoon *Hazel*, what is the name of the Baxter family cat?

213. William Shakespeare left his wife his second-best bed and willed the bulk of his estate to his two daughters. What were their names?

214. Where was Snoopy born in Charles Schulz' popular *Peanuts* comic strip?

215. Whose fortune was estimated at $1 multiplijillion, 9 obsquatumatillion?

216. In which of his plays did William Shakespeare include the stage direction "Exit, pursued by a bear"?

217. What was the name of the cat featured with Dick, Jane and their dog spot in the old school primer *Now We Read*?

218. The first western novel of what popular author was entitled *Hopalong Cassidy and the Riders of High Rock*?

206.   *Rope dancing.*

207.   *Dippy Dawg. He was renamed when he began costarring with Mickey in the mid-1930s.*

208.   *The swaddling clothes that protected him on his rocket journey from Krypton to Earth.*

209.   *The Round Table accommodated one hundred and fifty knights.*

210.   *The sculptor's love letters.*

211.   *Fur. The slippers became glass when the story was translated into English and pantoufle en vair (fur slipper) was mistaken for en verre (glass).*

212.   *Mostly, because she is mostly Siamese.*

213.   *Susanna and Judith.*

214.   *At the Daisy Hill Puppy Farm.*

215.   *Scrooge McDuck, Donald Duck's uncle.*

216.   The Winter's Tale *(Act III, Scene iii).*

217.   *Puff.*

218.   *Louis L'Amour, using the pseudonym Tex Burns in 1951.*

219. How many years after American expatriate Henry Miller's *Tropic of Cancer* was published in France did the novel become legal in the United States?

220. What does "rubaiyat" mean—as in the famous *Ruaiyat of Omar Khayyam?*

221. In the Disney version of *Snow White and the Seven Dwarfs*, the wicked Queen falls off a precipice and dies. How does she meet her end in the original Grimm brothers fairy tale?

222. What bizarre theory about Dr. Watson did mystery writer Rex Stout, an ardent Sherlock Holmes fan, once suggest to fellow members of the Baker Street Irregulars?

223. In H.G. Wells's science-fiction classic *War of the Worlds*, how did the Martian invaders get to Earth?

224. What best-selling author opened the first Saab auto dealership in the United States?

225. What was the inspiration for the title of the long-running TV mystery series *Murder, She Wrote* starring Angela Lansbury?

226. What is the first name of mystery writer Georges Simenon's celebrated Inspector Maigret?

227. What book was the best-seller of the year in America in 1794?

228. According to Howland Owl, the scienterrific genius of the *Pogo* comic strip, what would you get if you crossed a geranium plant and a baby yew tree?

229. To whom did writer John le Carré dedicate his 1991 spy thriller *The Secret Pilgrim?*

230. What are the names of Shakespeare's *Two Gentlemen of Verona?*

231. What was the name of Tarzan's pet chimpanzee in Edgar Rice Burroughs's books about the King of the Apes?

219. 27. *Published in France in 1934 with a dust jacket cautioning booksellers not to display it in their shop windows, the book was banned in the U.S. until 1961 on the grounds of obscenity.*

220. *Quatrains.*

221. *She was condemned to dance in red-hot iron shoes until she died.*

222. *That Watson was a woman.*

223. *They were shot to Earth in giant projectiles.*

224. *Kurt Vonnegut.*

225. *The 1961 movie* Murder She Said, *which was based on the Agatha Christie mystery "4:50 from Paddington."*

226. *Jules.*

227. *Benjamin Franklin's* Autobiography, *which had been published in England the year before—three years after his death.*

228. *A yew-ranium bush.*

229. *To actor Alec Guinness, who portrayed spymaster George Smiley in the TV versions of le Carré's earlier books* Tinker, Tailor, Soldier, Spy *and* Smiley's People.

230. *Valentine and Proteus.*

231. *Nkima. The chimp was renamed Cheeta for Johnny Weissmuller's film debut as* Tarzan the Ape Man *in 1932.*

232. Which is the only Shakespearean play to include a mention of America?

233. What was on the ceiling of the Vatican's Sistine Chapel before Michelangelo painted his famous fresco?

234. What famous writer claimed she did most of the plotting for her books while sitting in a bathtub munching on apples?

235. What famous nineteenth-century French novelist published a plagiarized nonfiction work under the pseudonym Bombet and, when the plagiarism was discovered, defended the nonexistent Bombet in letters signed by an equally nonexistent Bombet Jr.?

236. What kind of ship was the *U.S.S. Caine* in Herman Wouk's 1952 Pulitzer Prize-winning novel, *The Caine Mutiny*?

237. In what year was George Orwell's chilling political satire *Nineteen Eighty-four published*?

238. What was the title of the 1960 autobiography of the very first Fuller Brush man, Alfred Fuller?

239. In what writer's work did author Cicily Isabel Fairfield Andrews find her famous pseudonym—Rebecca West?

240. What famous artist designed shirts, hats, ashtrays, stamps, brandy bottles, coat hangers, bathing suits, crystal ware, tapestries and playing cards—among other things?

241. How many books with "rags to riches" success stories did Horatio Alger write?

242. What was the name of the seaport hometown of comic strip hero Popeye the Sailor?

243. What is the only building in the Western Hemisphere designed by famed British architect Sir Christopher Wren?

244. What is the Greek meaning of Utopia—the name of the perfect island society created by Sir Thomas More in his book of the same name?

232. The Comedy of Errors *(Act III, Scene ii).*

233. Silver stars on a plain blue field.

234. Agatha Christie.

235. Stendhal, who is best known for his novels The Red and the Black *and* The Charterhouse of Parma. *For his plagiarized work,* The Lives of Haydn, Mozart, and Metastasio, *he lifted from two biographies and a eulogy.*

236. A minesweeper.

237. In 1949.

238. A Foot in the Door.

239. Henrik Ibsen's. Rebecca West is the name of the strong-willed heroine in his play Rosmersholm.

240. Surrealist Salvador Dali.

241. 119.

242. Sweetwater.

243. The Wren Building at the College of William and Mary in Williamsburg, Virginia. It is the oldest academic building still in use in the United States.

244. It means nowhere, from the Greek ou, *meaning "not," and* topos, *meaning "a place."*

245. What Alfred Hitchcock movie title is drawn from Shakespeare's *Hamlet?*

246. Who was Sir Galahad's father?

247. What was the name of French writer Alexandre Dumas' palatial home in Paris?

248. What piece of tableware is upset in Leonardo da Vinci's famous painting of the Last Supper?

249. What was the estate tax paid to the French government by Pablo Picasso's heirs after the artist died in 1973 at age 91?

250. In the Ernest Hemingway classic *The Old Man and the Sea*, what famous athlete does the old man say he would like to take fishing?

251. What is the name of the principal city in Hell—"the high capital of Satan and his peers"—in John Milton's epic poem *Paradise Lost?*

252. What did writer Edgar Allan Poe and rock n' roller Jerry Lee Lewis have in common in their choice of wives?

253. Who was the inspiration for the popular sixteenth-century nursery rhyme *Little Miss Muffet?*

254. What was Goldilocks's name when the hungry little girl was first introduced in the famous children's fairy tale *The Three Little Bears* over a hundred years ago?

255. What were the names of Scarlett O'Hara's sisters in the Margaret Mitchell classic *Gone With the Wind?*

256. In May 1969 *Esquire* magazine featured a story about the decline of the American avant-garde. How was this illustrated on its cover?

257. What architect designed the Gateway Arch in St. Louis?

258. To whom did Abraham Lincoln say: "Is this the little woman whose book made such a war?"

245. *The 1959 thriller,* North by Northwest, *in which Cary Grant feigns madness. The title is taken from Hamlet's words: "I am but mad north-north-west; when the wind is southerly, I know a hawk from a handsaw.*

246. *Sir Lancelot.*

247. *Monte-Cristo, after his famous novel* The Count of Monte Cristo.

248. *A salt cellar near Judas Iscariot.*

249. *They paid $78.5 million. The value of the artwork, properties and investments he left was estimated for tax purposes at $312 million, but in reality they were worth well over $1 billion.*

250. The Great DiMaggio.

251. *Pandemonium.*

252. *Each married a 13-year-old cousin.*

253. *Patience Muffet, the daughter of the poem's creator, Dr. Thomas Muffet, an entomologist who wrote about spiders more often than he did about his little girl.*

254. *Silver Hair. From that she became Golden Hair, and finally Goldilocks.*

255. *Her two younger sisters were Careen, for Caroline Irene, and Suellen, for Susan Elinor.*

256. *By a picture of Andy Warhol drowning in a can of Campbell's tomato soup.*

257. *Eero Saarinen.*

258. *Harriet Beecher Stowe, author of* Uncle Tom's Cabin.

259. What French writer used Alcofribas Nasier—an anagram of his real name—as a pseudonym?

260. What was Dr. Frankenstein's first name in the Mary Shelley horror classic?

261. How many kinds of kisses are described in the Kama Sutra, the classical Indian text on eroticism?

262. Who attended the Mad Hatter's tea party in Lewis Carroll's Alice's Adventures in Wonderland?

263. What name did artist Doménikos TheotokÛpoulos sign on his paintings?

264. What twentieth-century English writer used the words hook, line and sinker in the titles of a three-book espionage series?

265. What American novelist's great-grandfather wrote a book in response to Harriet Beecher Stowe's *Uncle Tom's Cabin?*

266. What was the first painting by an American obtained by the world-famous Louvre Museum in Paris?

267. What famous writer was the as-told-to author of The Autobiography of Malcolm X?

268. What was the name of the ocean liner that provided the setting for Katherine Anne Porter's novel *A Ship of Fools?*

269. What famous author wrote the short story *Dry September* in 1931 and the novel Light in August in 1932?

270. What world-famous artist painted the historic Civil War sea battle between the Union sloop Kearsage and the Confederacy's corvette Alabama?

271. What popular table game does William Shakespeare have Cleopatra play in *Antony and Cleopatra?*

272. In Herman Melville's famous novel Moby Dick, what was Captain Ahab's peg leg made from?

259. *Francois Rabelais. He used the pseudonym for his satirical works.*

260. *Victor.*

261. *20.*

262. *The Mad Hatter, the March Hare, the Dormouse and Alice.*

263. *El Greco, which means "the Greek."*

264. *Len Deighton. The books were* Spy Hook, Spy Line *and* Spy Sinker.

265. *William Faulkner's great-grandfather William Clark Falkner (the family's original name). The book was entitled* The Little Brick Church. *The older Falkner also wrote a romantic novel,* The White Rose of Memphis, *and a book about his travels,* Rapid Ramblings in Europe.

266. *James Abbott McNeill Whistler's portrait of his elderly mother, formally known as* Arrangement in Grey and Black, No. 1: The Artist's Mother, *and popularly known as* Whistler's Mother.

267. *Alex Haley, best known for his 1976 epic* Roots.

268. *The Vera. It sailed from Veracruz, Mexico, to Bremerhaven, Germany.*

269. *William Faulkner.*

270. *French artist Edouard Manet. The battle, fought in French waters outside Cherbourg harbor on June 15, 1864, was watched from shore and small boats by more than 15,000 people—one of them, Manet. The naval engagement ended with the sinking of the Alabama, which had defeated more than 60 Union ships in prior battles.*

271. *Billiards.*

272. *The ivory from the jawbone of a whale. Ahab's leg had been snapped off during an encounter with the whale Moby Dick.*

273. What is the chief oil in the oil paints used by artists?

274. What Shakespearean character was based on a London doctor who served as Queen Elizabeth I's chief physician—until he was arrested and hanged for conspiring to kill her?

275. Hamlet—with 1,530 lines— is the longest speaking part in all of Shakespeare's plays. What is the second longest?

276. What popular American comic strip is known as Radishes in Denmark?

277. What happened to the parents of Batman's sidekick, Robin, a.k.a. Dick Grayson?

278. For what famous writer was the drink known as the Brandy Alexander named?

279. What was the name of the broken-down, partially blind old horse Ichabod Crane rode in Washington Irving's *Legend of Sleepy Hollow*?

280. What famous poet was known to his close friends by the nickname Junkets?

281. All told, how many novels did the Bronte sisters—Anne, Charlotte and Emily—write?

282. What was Jeeves's first name in humorist P. G. Wodehouse's stories about Bertie Wooster and his resourceful valet?

283. In the folk tale about Rumpelstiltskin, how long did it take the miller's daughter to guess his name?

284. What famous English writer, while living in Vermont, invented snow golf—painting his golf balls red so he could find them?

285. What is the name of Babar the Elephant's wife?

286. Who owned the land on Walden Pond, where Henry David Thoreau built a cabin and wrote the essays that became his book Walden, or Life in the Woods?

273. Linseed oil—made from the seed of the flax plant, Linum usitatissimum.

274. Shylock, the money-lender in The Merchant of Venice. The doctor's name was Roderigo Lopez.

275. Richard III, *with 1,164 lines.*

276. Peanuts.

277. The Boy Wonder's parents—circus performers known as The Flying Graysons—died in a trapeze accident.

278. Alexander Woollcott, drama and literary critic and Algonquin Round Table regular.

279. Gunpowder.

280. John Keats.

281. Seven. Emily wrote one, Wuthering Heights; *Anne wrote two,* Agnes Grey and The Tenant of Wildfell Hall; *and Charlotte wrote four,* Jane Eyre, The Professor, Villette, *and* Shirley.

282. Reginald.

283. Three days.

284. Rudyard Kipling.

285. Celeste.

286. Ralph Waldo Emerson.

287. What was Gulliver's first name in Jonathan Swift's *Gulliver's Travels*?

288. What famous American poet wrote the line that provided the title for the 1942 Bette Davis film *Now Voyager*?

289. What environmentally correct gesture did publisher Harper San Francisco make in 1990 in conjunction with its publication of the book 2 Minutes a Day for a Greener Planet?

290. What popular children's book was written by Ian Fleming, creator of British secret agent James Bond?

291. What early American writer used the pen names Geoffrey Crayon and Jonathan Oldstyle?

292. What famous entertainer wrote the bestsellers *The Man in Black* in 1975 and *Man in White* in 1986?

293. What is the title of the 1989 biography of cartoonist Charles Schulz?

294. What did the letters in the magic word SHAZAM represent in the Captain Marvel comics?

295. In what famous novel did physicist Murray Gell-Mann find the word quark—which he used to name the basic building block of matter in the early 1960s?

296. What famous American poet wrote: "My candle burns at both ends;/It will not last the night"?

297. What popular comic strip featured a character named Appassionata Von Climax?

298. How many sonnets did William Shakespeare write?

299. What river did artist Emanuel Leutze use as a model for the Delaware when he painted his famous historical work "Washington Crossing the Delaware" in 1851?

287. *Lemuel.*

288. *Walt Whitman. In his two-line poem* The Untold Want, *in Leaves of Grass, he wrote: "Now voyager sail thou forth to seek and find." The movie was based on the novel* Now Voyager *by Olive Higgins Prouty.*

289. *It planted 1,000 trees to replace those used in producing the book.*

290. Chitty Chitty Bang Bang, the Magical Car.

291. *Washington Irving.*

292. *Country singer Johnny Cash. Black is an autobiography; White, a novel about the apostle Saint Paul.*

293. *Good Grief. It was written by Rheta Grimsley Johnson.*

294. *Solomon's wisdom, Hercules' strength, Atlas' s stamina, Zeus' s power, Achilles' courage, and Mercury's speed.*

295. *In James Joyce's* Finnegan's Wake.

296. *Edna St. Vincent Millay. The lines are from her poem* First Fig.

297. Li'l Abner.

298. 154.

299. *The Rhine. Leutze was in his native Germany when he painted it.*

300. What famous rock star returned a $5 million advance on his memoirs, explaining that he "couldn't remember" significant details of his own life?

301. In *Mad* magazine's spoofs of Superman, what names were used for the Man of Steel and his newspaperman alter ego?

302. What did Robert Browning use to wean and cure his wife, Elizabeth Barrett Browning, from her addiction to laudanum?

303. Whose painting of a sunset gave the Impressionist school of art its name?

304. What two great writers died on the same day—April 23, 1616?

305. What American novelist was challenged to a duel and beaten by a woman he later married?

306. Whose autobiography is entitled *What's It All About?*

307. What sexually explicit novel banned as obscene in the U.S. and England for 30 years ówas originally called Tenderness by its author?

308. What novel is set in the year 632AF (for After Ford)?

309. What famous novel is set in Thornfield Hall?

310. Whose life story is told in the 1974 biography *Shooting Star?*

311. Who wrote the popular children's poem *The Pied Piper of Hamelin* ?

312. What was the medical specialty of Sherlock Holme's creator, Arthur Conan Doyle?

313. What sinister fictional killer was introduced to movie audiences in the 1986 film *Manhunter?*

314. What was the name of the Indian chief referred to in the title of James Fenimore Cooper's 1826 novel *The Last of the Mohicans?*

300. *Mick Jagger.*

301. *Superduperman and Clark Bent. Lois Lane was Lois Pain.*

302. *Chianti.*

303. *Claude Monet's. The painting was called "Impression: Sunrise." The first use of the term Impressionist came in 1874 in a satirical article ridiculing Monet and his artist friends.*

304. *Shakespeare and Cervantes.*

305. *Jack London. His duel with Charmian Kittredge was with foils, face masks and breast plates.*

306. *Actor Michael Caine. The book title was taken from the first line in the title song of Caine's first big movie, Alfie. The line is: "What's it all about, Alfie?"*

307. *Lawrence's Lady Chatterley's Lover. Before it was given its final name, it also was known as John Thomas and Lady Jane.*

308. Brave New World, *by Aldous Huxley.*

309. *Charlotte Bronte's* Jane Eyre.

310. *John Wayne's.*

311. *Robert Browning.*

312. *He was an ophthalmologist or eye doctor.*

313. *Hannibal Lecter, whom most moviegoers became acquainted with in the 1991 Academy Award-winning film* Silence of the Lambs. *Both films were based on Thomas Harris's novel* Red Dragon.

314. *Uncas.*

315. What book begins, "He came into the world in the middle of the thicket, in one of those little, hidden forest glades which seems to be entirely open, but are really screened in on all sides"?

316. What future playwright was expelled from Princeton University by Woodrow Wilson when the American president-to-be was president of the university?

317. What famous writer is credited with originating the expression "rain cats and dogs"?

318. What did artist Pablo Picasso reply when he was asked to name his favorite among all his paintings?

319. What unusual message was attached to all copies of Henry Miller's sex-packed novel *Tropic of Cancer* when it was first offered for sale in France in 1934?

320. On orders from Pope Pius IV, what did Italian artist Daniele de Volterra add to Michelangelo's Last Judgment on the west wall of the Sistine Chapel in the mid-sixteenth century.

321. What famous writer gave us the line, "Polly put the kettle on, we'll all have tea"?

322. According to Shakespeare, what was England's Henry VIII doing on the night his daughter, future Queen Elizabeth I, was born?

323. What satiric fifth-century B.C. play introduced the classic comedy team of the tall, thin, insulting straight man and the short, fat buffoon?

324. In Jonathan Swift's *Gulliver's Travels*, why were Lilliputian heretics known as Big-Enders?

325. What writer originated the phrase "Do not count your chickens before they are hatched" in a story about a farmer's daughter?

326. Who is the subject of the biography *Poison Pen*, published in 1991?

315. Bambi, *by Felix Salten.*

316. Eugene O'Neill. He was expelled for throwing a bottle of beer through Wilson's office window.

317. Jonathan Swift, in A Complete Collection of Polite and Ingenious Conversation, *which he originally had published under the pseudonym Simon Wagstaff, Esquire.*

318. "The next one."

319. A warning to book dealers—on a removable band—not to display the controversial novel in their shop windows.

320. Loincloths, to cover up the nudity that shocked church officials. The commission earned the artist the nickname Il Braghettone, "the breeches maker."

321. Charles Dickens, in Barnaby Rudge.

322. Playing cards. The game was primero, an early form of poker.

323. Lysistrata, *by Aristophanes.*

324. They believed eggs should be broken at the big end—as opposed to the traditionalist Little-Enders, who broke their eggs at the little end.

325. Aesop, in his story The Milkmaid and Her Pail.

326. Kitty Kelley, author of unauthorized biographies of Jacqueline Kennedy Onassis, Elizabeth Taylor, Frank Sinatra and Nancy Reagan.

327. Who serves as Dante's guide through Hell and Purgatory in his masterpiece *The Divine Comedy*?

328. The house of what famous Greek poet was the only home spared by Alexander the Great when he invaded and destroyed the city of Thebes in 335 B.C.?

329. How many self-portraits did Rembrandt paint?

330. The name of what Texas town came close to being changed in the late 1950s because of a controversial best-selling novel?

331. Who immortalized the world of American finance with a painting entitled *The New Orleans Cotton Exchange*?

332. What was the first career-girl comic strip?

333. What English literary classic was inspired by the adventures of Scottish pirate Andrew Selkirk?

334. What is the only sculpture on which Michelangelo is believed to have carved his name?

335. Did science fiction writer Jules Verne—who told of trips around the world and to the moon—ever fly?

336. What was the first book to vanish from the Association of American Publishers' display at the Moscow Book Fair in September 1985?

337. In the Nero Wolfe mysteries, what did Archie keep in his closet?

338. What was the name of Smilin' Jack's buddy in the comic strip about the dashing aviator?

339. Whose autobiography was entitled, *R.S.V.P.*?

340. What great writer, shortly before his death at age 90, successfully defended himself against senility charges by reading his latest work in court?

327. *The Roman poet Virgil.*

328. *Pindar.*

329. *Almost 100—that are known.*

330. *Lolita. The novel was* Lolita, *by Vladimir Nabokov. After much debate, the citizens of the small southeast Texas town decided to keep the name adopted by their forefathers in honor of early settler Lolita Reese.*

331. *French impressionist Edgar Degas. He did a painting of the exchange during an 1872-73 visit to New Orleans, where his uncle and two brothers were in the cotton business.*

332. Winnie Winkle, *by Martin Branner, which made its debut in 1920.*

333. Robinson Crusoe. *Daniel Defoe wrote the tale after hearing the story of Selkirk's four and a half years on uninhabited Juan Fernandez Island off the coast of Chile.*

334. *The Pieta. He reportedly did it after overhearing someone mistakenly attribute it to sculptor Christoforo Solari.*

335. *Yes, once. He made a balloon ascension in 1873.*

336. Jane Fonda's Workout Book. *The second was the Sears, Roebuck and Company catalog.*

337. *A bottle of rye, for the times when he was particularly frustrated with Nero Wolfe.*

338. *Downwind.*

339. *Professional party-giver Elsa Maxwell's.*

340. *Sophocles. The work was* Oedipus at Colonus.

341. *Lolly Willowes,* a novel about a spinster who realizes her vocation as a witch, won what unique honor when it was published in 1926?

342. How many lovers are named in Casanova's memoirs, *Story of My Life,* first published in their complete form in the early 1960s?

343. Who drew the first cartoon published in an American newspaper?

344. What famous American's 1952 autobiography is entitled *From Under My Hat* ?

345. Somerset Maugham's 1919 novel *The Moon and Sixpence* is a roman à clef about what great French artist?

346. What is the origin of the phrase, "United we stand, divided we fall"?

347. The first Encyclopedia Britannica, published in 1771, devoted its first volume to "A" and "B." How many additional volumes did it take to cover "C" through "Z"?

348. Whose marriage in March 1952 was featured in a "Life" magazine cover story?

349. The work of what famous French artist hung upside down in the Museum of Modern Art in New York for 47 days before someone realized it?

350. What comic-strip character started out in 1932 as a middle-aged woman who sold apples on street corners?

351. Who use the pen names Acton, Ellis and Currer Bell?

352. What book did Aristotle Onassis keep on his desk in his multimillion-dollar yacht Christina?

353. Who wrote the first modern ghost story in the English language?

341. *The book, by British author Sylvia Townsend Warner, was the first offering of the Book-of-the-Month Club.*

342. *Though he boasted about seducing thousands, the great lover named only 116.*

343. *Benjamin Franklin. His drawing of a severed snake—each piece representing one of the colonies—appeared with the motto "Unite or Die" in the* Pennsylvania Gazette *on May 9, 1754.*

344. *Hedda Hopper's—she was known for her exotic hats and juicy Hollywood gossip.*

345. *Paul Gauguin.*

346. *Aesop's fables. It's from* The Four Oxen and the Lion, *written in the sixth century B.C.*

347. *Only two.*

348. *Comic strip characters Daisy Mae Scragg and Li'l Abner of Dogpatch. Marryin' Sam performed the ceremony for $1.35, ending their 17-year courtship.*

349. *Henri Matisse, in 1961. The painting was* Le Bateau.

350. *"Mary Worth," who was originally known as "Apple Mary."*

351. *Anne, Emily and Charlotte Bronte.*

352. *A copy of J. Paul Getty's* How to be Rich.

353. *Daniel Defoe. It was* True Relation of the Apparition of One Mrs. Veal.

354. What American literary classic was made into a film called *I Married a Doctor*?

355. Who designed the red, yellow and dark blue Renaissance uniform worn by the Swiss Guard at the Vatican?

356. Who wrote: "All animals are equal, but some animals are more equal than others"?

357. How many paintings did Flemish Dutch artits Vincent Van Gogh sell during his lifetime?

358. Where did writer Ian Fleming find the name James Bond for his hero-spy?

359. Whose autobiography, published in 1977, is called *Grinding It Out*?

360. What book was the first submitted to a publisher as a typewritten manuscript?

361. In the *Mad Magazine* parody of the *Archie* comic book, what name was given to the teenage hero?

362. How little was Stuart Little, the mouse born into an otherwise human family in the E. B. White children's fantasy?

363. What famous American writer created the Cisco Kid?

364. Writer Kay Thompson's goddaughter provided the inspiration for her books about Eloise, the mischievous little girl who lived at the Plaza Hotel in New York. Who was she?

365. In Jules Verne's 1865 book *From Earth to the Moon,* three men are blasted to the moon by cannon. Their speed of departure has proven to be the earth's escape velocity. What is it?

366. Who were Miss Marple's next door neighbors in the Agatha Christie mysteries about the sleuthing senior citizen from St. Mary Mead?

367. Whom did Olive Oyl go out with before she met Popeye?

354. Main Street, *by Sinclair Lewis. Producer Jack Warner reportedly claimed that nobody would go to see "a picture about a street."*

355. Michelangelo. It's one of several costumes worn by the Gendarmeria Pontifica.

356. George Orwell in Animal Farm.

357. Only one.

358. On a coffee-table book, Birds of the West Indies, *by ornithologist James Bond.*

359. Ray Kroc's. He was the traveling salesman behind McDonald's franchising empire.

360. Mark Twain's The Adventures of Tom Sawyer. *The year was 1876; the typewriter, a Remington.*

361. Starchie. In the "Mad" parody, which appeared in June 1954 and cost 10 cents, Starchie ended up in jail for running a high school protection racket.

362. He was two inches high and slept in a bed made from a cigarette box and four clothespins.

363. *O.Henry, in his short story,* The Caballero's Way.

364. Liza Minnelli.

365. Seven miles a second. (Escape velocity is the minimum speed required to escape a planet's pull.)

366. Dr. Haydock and Miss Harnell.

367. Ham Gravy.

368. What British writer and noted wit claimed "America had often been discovered before Columbus, but it had always been hushed up"?

369. In the poem *Jabberwocky* in the *Alice in Wonderland* sequel *Through the Looking Glass,* what words did author Lewis Carroll combine to create the nonsense word slithy?

370. What novel provided the story line for the 1975 Robert Redford-Faye Dunaway movie *Three Days of the Condor*?

371. What famous American novelist has written several mysteries under the pen name Edgar Box?

372. What was the name of Joe and Frank Hardy's maiden aunt—and detective Fenton Hardy's sister—in the popular book series for boys?

373. What does Don Quixote's sidekick Sancho Panza's last name mean in Spanish?

374. What name did cartoonist Al Capp give the hero in his *Li'l Abner* parody of *Gone With the Wind*?

375. In the *Alley Oop* comic strip, who was the king of Moo?

376. The novel *Ulysses* takes place in Dublin on one day—June 16, 1904. What significance did that day have for writer James Joyce?

377. What do the initials J. D. stand for in author J. D. Salinger's name?

378. Who wrote, "A good education is the next best thing to a pushy mother"?

379. What first name did author Margaret Mitchell originally give her *Gone With the Wind* heroine, Scarlett O'Hara?

380. What does Rex Stout's cerebral sleuth Nero Wolfe do for exercise?

368. *Oscar Wilde.*

369. *Slimy and lithe.*

370. Six Days of the Condor, *by James Grady.*

371. *Gore Vidal.*

372. *Aunt Gertrude.*

373. *Panza means "paunch."*

374. *Wreck Butler.*

375. *King Guzzle.*

376. *It was the day of his first date with Nora Barnacle, the woman he eventually married.*

377. *Jerome David.*

378. *Charles Schulz, in* Peanuts.

379. *Pansy.*

380. *He plays javelins—darts as we know it—for 15 minutes a day.*

381. What American literary figure wrote his daughter: "Worry about cleanliness, courage, efficiency and horsemanship, but don't worry about the past, the future, boys, mosquitoes and popular opinion"?

382. Writer Robert Benchley demanded a stuntman's fee for his performance in the 1941 film comedy *Bedtime Story*. What was his "stunt"?

383. Who was the subject of the Auguste Rodin sculpture *The Thinker*?

384. What famous writer fought to ban Mark Twain's *Huckleberry Finn* from the public library, claiming it was inappropriate for "our pure-minded lads and lassies"?

385. How did writer L. Frank Baum pick Oz for the name of the fantasyland in his *Wizard of Oz* stories?

386. What is unusual about Mona Lisa's eyebrows in the famous Leonardo da Vinci painting?

387. Pinocchio had two pets. What were they and what were their names?

388. What was the name of Popeye's ship?

389. Pop artist Andy Warhol once declared that everyone would be famous for how long?

390. In what field is the Hugo Award given?

391. What popular American writer coined the word nerd?

392. What is the literal translation of Dada—the name given to the anti-traditionalist art movement begun in 1916?

393. In Spain, kids call them Pitufo; in Germany, Schlumpf. What do American kids call them?

394. What was the name of the last book written by Amelia Earhart?

381. *Scott Fitzgerald.*

382. *He drank 13 glasses of milk.*

383. *The poet Dante.*

384. Little Women *author Louisa May Alcott.*

385. *He spotted a file cabinet marked O-Z while he was making up the story for his children and their friends.*

386. *She has none.*

387. *A cat named Figaro and a goldfish named Cleo.*

388. *The Olive, in honor of his longtime girlfriend.*

389. *15 minutes.*

390. *Science fiction writing. The award was named for Hugo Gernsback, the "father of science fiction."*

391. *Dr. Seuss—whose real name was Theodor Seuss Geisel.*

392. *It means "hobby horse" in French. The name was chosen at random from a dictionary.*

393. *Smurfs.*

394. Last Flight. *It was published after she disappeared in the central Pacific in 1937 while attempting an around-the-world flight. Her husband, publisher George Putnam, put it together using her letters, diary entries, charts, cables, and phone conversations.*

395. Before settling on the name Tiny Tim for Bob Cratchit's crippled son in his book *A Christmas Carol,* what three alliterative names did Charles Dickens consider?

396. Why is the well-known chrome-and-leather chair designed by German-born architect Ludwig Mies van der Rohe called the Barcelona chair?

397. What famous writer bragged that he gave his talent to his work and saved his genius for his life?

398. What famous artist shocked the art world in 1919 by painting a mustache, eyebrows and a beard on a reproduction of the Mona Lisa and submitting it to a Paris art show?

399. What was the name of the orange-and-white kitten in the classic children's books that featured Dick and Jane and their dog Spot?

400. What title did William Burroughs intend to give his controversial, scatological book *Naked Lunch*?

401. What famous artist in 1953 erased an original abstract expressionist drawing by Willem de Kooning—with his consent—and then framed it and exhibited it as an original work of his own?

402. How did Madrid's famous art museum come to be named the Prado?

403. What famous American writer claimed that a brand of cigarettes was named after him?

404. Under what title do we know the book that was originally published as *Murder in the Calais Coach*?

405. What art form is known as xylography?

406. Where did the name Winnie, for Winnie the Pooh, come from?

407. What first name did Arthur Conan Doyle give to him famous detective before he came up with Sherlock?

395. *Little Larry, Puny Pete and Small Sam.*

396. *He created it for the International Exposition in Barcelona in 1929, to go in the German pavilion, which he also designed.*

397. *Oscar Wilde.*

398. *Marcel Duchamp.*

399. Puff. *The book series was called Now We Read.*

400. Naked Lust. *Its name was changed by accident. Fellow Beat Generation writer Allen Ginsberg misread Burroughs' handwriting, and the wrong title stuck.*

401. *Robert Rauschenberg. He called the work* Erased de Kooning.

402. *It was named for the meadow, or prado, that once surrounded it.*

403. *Truman Capote. The brand, True.*

404. *Agatha Christie's* Murder on the Orient Express. *The name was not changed until several editions had been printed.*

405. *Wood engraving. In Greek xylon means "wood," and graphe means "writing" or "drawing."*

406. *From a bear named Winnie in the London Zoo. The animal had been born in Winnipeg, Canada, and was brought to London in 1914 as the mascot of a Canadian regiment.*

407. *Sherringford. The name was used in a shott story Doyle wrote in 1886. Holmes's sidekick in the story was called Ormond Sacker—soon to be renamed Thomas Watson.*

408. What famous American author's grandfather was the model for Oliver Wendell Holmes' poem *The Last Leaf*, about an aged survivor of the Boston Tea Party?

409. What cultural phenomena did psychiatrist Fredric Wertheim link to juvenile delinquency in his 1954 book *Seduction of the Innocent?*

410. What artist had his wife pose for the face of Christ in his painting of the Last Supper?

411. Where was the sprawling family estate of early American novelist James Fenimore Cooper?

412. The novella Pal Joey by John O'Hara consists of a series of letters written by nightclub singer Pal Joey—to whom?

413. To whom did French painter Edgar Degas write, "Most women paint as though they are trimming hats....Not you"?

414. What was the name of the parrot that taught Dr. Dolittle to talk to the animals?

415. What French novelist inadvertently provided actress Ruth Davis with her stage name, Bette Davis?

416. Who is the subject of the unauthorized 1997 biography entitled *The Good, the Bad and the Very Ugly?*

417. What famous author wrote under the pen names Thomas Jefferson Snodgrass, Sergeant Fathom and W. Apaminondas Adrastus Blab before switching to the name with which he gained fame?

418. What famous woman entrepreneur provided the money to help artist Marc Chagall and his wife flee the Nazis and move to New York City in 1941?

419. When *The Joy of Cooking* was revised and republished in 1997, it contained 4,500 recipes. How many were in the original Joy, self-published by Irma Rombauer in 1931?

408. *Herman Melville's grandfather, Major Thomas Melvill. (Melvill was the original spelling of the family name.)*

409. *Comic books. His book led to Senate hearings and the establishment of the Comics Code Authority, which banned "all scenes of horror, excessive bloodshed, gory or gruesome crimes, depravity, lust, sadism [and] masochism."*

410. *Spanish surrealist Salvador Dali. The title of the painting is* Sacrament of the Last Supper.

411. *In Cooperstown, New York—it was the setting of his Leather Stocking Tales and is today the home of the Baseball Hall of Fame. William Cooper, the writer's father and one of the wealthiest landowners of his time, purchased the Cooperstown site in 1785.*

412. *Pal Ted, a bandleader.*

413. *American artist and Degas disciple Mary Cassatt.*

414. *Polynesia. The doctor's other pets in the popular series of children's books by Hugh Lofting were his duck, Dab Dab; his owl, Too Too; his baby pig, Gub Gub; his monkey, Chee Chee; and his dog, Jib.*

415. *Honorè de Balzac. Davis took her stage name from the title of his 1840 novel* Cousin Bette.

416. *Clint Eastwood. The bio was written by his ex-girlfriend Sondra Locke.*

417. *Samuel Clemens, who finally settled on the name Mark Twain.*

418. *Cosmetics queen Helena Rubinstein.*

419. *1,195. The original sold for $3; the new edition, the sixth, was priced at $30.*

420. Which book did Americans rate as their favorite—second only to the Bible in 1900?

421. What famous French dramatist, as a 20-year-old, served Louis XIII as valet-tapissier du roi—maker of the king's bed?

422. What famous novel opens with the line: "Once upon a time and a very good time it was there was a moocow coming down along the road..."?

423. What famous artist served as a war correspondent for *Harper's Weekly* magazine during the Civil War?

424. What American artist named most of his 17 children after famous artists—including Rembrandt, Titian, Rubens and Raphael?

425. How many of Shakespeare's heroines disguise themselves as males?

426. The first published drawings of what famous children's book author-illustrator appeared in a physics text entitled *Atomics for the Millions*?

427. In the book *Gone With the Wind,* how many months actually pass during Melanie's pregnancy?

Bonus Trivia

428. Poet Henry Wadsworth Longfellow was the first American to have plumbing installed in his house, in 1840.

420. *The Sears Roebuck catalog.*

421. *Molière.*

422. A Portrait of the Artist as a Young Man *by James Joyce.*

423. *Winslow Homer. As an artist-reporter for the magazine, he covered a number of campaigns with the Union Army.*

424. *Charles Wilson Peale. The four children named all achieved prominence as artists.*

425. *Five—Rosalind in* As You Like It; *Julia in* Two Gentlemen of Verona; *Portia in* The Merchant of Venice; *Viola in* Twelfth Night; *Imogen in* Cymbeline.

426. *Maurice Sendak. The text was written by one of his high-school teachers, who Sendak said gave him a passing grade and small fee for his illustrations.*

427. *21—based on the battles mentioned. When this was pointed out to author Margaret Mitchell, she reportedly replied that a Southerner's pace is slower than that of a Yankee.*

Sports & Games

Questions

429. What sport was the first to be filmed—and who filmed it?

430. What souvenir did New York Giant linebacker Lawrence Taylor request from a referee after he played his last game in January 1994?

431. How many games did Chicago Bears running back Walter Payton miss during his 13-year National Football League career?

432. What is the distance between bases on a Little League baseball field?

433. What was the first sport in which women were invited to compete at the Olympics?

434. What card game gave us the term bilk?

435. What college once had 22 members of the Phi Beta Kappa honor society on its football team?

436. How wide and high are the netted goals in ice hockey? How about field hockey?

429. *The sport was boxing; the man who did the filming, Thomas A. Edison; the year, 1894. Edison filmed a boxing match between Jack Cushing and Mike Leonard in a studio on the grounds of his laboratory complex in West Orange, New Jersey.*

430. *The referee's yellow flag. Taylor said he felt he deserved it because the refs "throw it against me often enough."*

431. *Only one. He carried the ball more often (3,838 times) for more yards (16,726) and scored more rushing touchdowns (110) than anyone else.*

432. *60 feet. In the major leagues, the distance is 90 feet.*

433. *Tennis, at the 1900 games in Paris. Charlotte Cooper of Great Britain was the first gold medalist.*

434. *Cribbage. Bilk, a variant of balk, originally meant "to defraud an opposing player of points through sharp, sly tactics." It now means "to cheat."*

435. *Dartmouth, in 1925.*

436. *Ice, 6 feet wide and 4 feet high; field, 4 yards wide and 7 feet high.*

437. How many home runs did baseball great Ty Cobb hit in the three World Series in which he played?

438. What career did Hawaiian swimming and surfing star Duke Kahanamoku pursue after playing Polynesian chiefs in Hollywood movies?

439. In cross-country bike racing, what do the initials BMX represent?

440. Under what name did Dr. Joshua Pim of Great Britain enter and win the Wimbledon tennis tournament in 1893?

441. In 1939, what famous American athlete starred on UCLA's undefeated football team and was the top scorer in the Pacific Coast Conference for basketball?

442. Which popular sport did Joe Sobek invent at the Greenwich, Connecticut, YMCA in 1950?

443. In blackjack, players try to get cards that add up to 21, and no higher. What is the count sought in baccarat?

444. Who was the first Olympic gold medalist to win a professional world boxing title?

445. What sports activity was originally known in England as "plank-gliding"?

446. Which was the first sport to have its top players named to an All-American team?

447. What was golfing great Ben Hogan's famous reply when he was asked how to improve one's game?

448. How many world records did swimmer Mark Spitz set when he won seven gold medals at the 1972 Olympics?

449. After retiring as a player, with what team did baseball great Babe Ruth spend one year as a coach?

437. *None. Cobb's overall World Series batting average—for 1907, 1908 and 1909—was .262. His team, the Detroit Tigers, lost the first two to the Chicago Cubs, the third to the Pittsburgh Pirates.*

438. *Kahanamoku, the inventor of windsurfing, was sheriff of Honolulu for 20 years.*

439. *Bicycle moto x (cross).*

440. *Mr. X. Because he feared that revealing his true identity would hurt his medical practice, Pim entered under the mystery name.*

441. *Jackie Robinson, who later gained national fame playing professional baseball. At UCLA, he earned letters in baseball, basketball, football and track.*

442. *Racquetball. Sobek designed a "strung paddle racquet" and handle, and combined the rules of squash and handball, to create the game he called "paddle rackets."*

443. *Nine.*

444. *Floyd Patterson, who won the Olympic gold medal as a middleweight in 1952, and the world championship as a heavyweight in 1956.*

445. *Waterskiing. The first recorded mention of the sport in England was in 1914.*

446. *Football, in 1889. The idea originated with famed football authority Walter Camp, who picked 36 All-American teams until his death in 1925.*

447. *"Hit the ball closer to the hole."*

448. *Seven—one in each of the races in which he competed.*

449. *The Brooklyn Dodgers in 1938.*

450. Which property represented as a railroad on the Monopoly game board was not actually a railroad?

451. In what year's Olympics were electric timing devices and a public-address system used for the first time?

452. What is the maximum weight permitted for calves in rodeo calf-roping competition?

453. How many different types of figure eights does the International Skating Union recognize in competition?

454. What Baseball Hall of Fame pitcher hit a home run in his first major league at-bat—and never hit another?

455. What baseball player hit the only home run of his 22-year major league career off his own brother?

456. What 1921 sporting event took up all of the first 13 pages of The New York Times—except for a little space on the front page devoted to the formal end of World War I?

457. In the National Football League, how many footballs is the home team required to provide for each game?

458. Brooks Robinson and Carl Yastrzemski hold the major league baseball record for playing the greatest number of seasons with the same team. How many years did they play—and with what teams?

459. How much liquid can the 27-inch-high silver America's Cup hold?

460. Why is the site of a boxing match called a ring when it's square?

461. In the very first Boston Marathon, 15 runners competed. How many finished?

462. How long is the average pool cue?

450. *Short Line. It was a bus company.*

451. *In 1912, in Stockholm*

452. *350 pounds. The minimum is 200 pounds.*

453. *48.*

454. *New York Giant knuckleballer Hoyt Wilhelm, in 1952.*

455. *Joe Niekro in 1976. Niekro, a pitcher with the Houston Astros, hit a four-bagger off his brother Phil, who was pitching for the Atlanta Braves. Houston won the game, 4-3.*

456. *The July 2nd heavyweight championship bout between Jack Dempsey and George Carpentier, the first fight to gross over $1 million in gate receipts. Dempsey won in a fourth-round knockout.*

457. *24—although from 8 to 12 are usually used.*

458. *23 years. Third baseman Robinson played with the Baltimore Orioles from 1955 to 1977; Carl Yastrzemski, outfielder/first baseman, played with the Boston Red Sox from 1961 to 1983.*

459. *None. It's bottomless.*

460. *Boxing rings were originally circular.*

461. *10.*

462. *57 inches.*

463. Under the rules outlined in the charter of the International Olympic Committee, how much pure gold must there be in each gold medal awarded to first-place winners?

464. What professional ice hockey star didn't hang up his skates until he was 52?

465. What is the state sport of Alaska?

466. Who was the first athlete to hit a major league home run and make a professional football touchdown in the same week?

467. Who was the famous great-great-great-grandfather of San Francisco 49er quarterback Steve Young?

468. Who was the first professional athlete to win championship rings in two major sports?

469. How long and wide is the balance beam used in Olympic gymnastic competition?

470. What sport besides football did famed fullback Jim Brown compete and excel in while he attended Syracuse University in the mid 1950s?

471. How much did a one-minute TV spot cost advertisers on the first Super Bowl broadcast in 1967?

472. How many of the four Grand Slam trophies in tennis are gold; how many are silver?

473. What pitcher made it into the Baseball Hall of Fame with a 28-31 major league win-loss record?

474. Who was the first sports great to have his number retired by his team?

475. How many points did Chicago Cardinals fullback Ernie Nevers rack up in a 1929 game to set the highest single-game scoring mark in National Football League history?

463. *At least 6 grams. Silver medals must be at least .925 sterling silver. There are no rules regarding the purity of bronze medals. All medals must be 60 millimeters in diameter and 3 millimeters thick.*

464. *Gordie Howe, who played in 1,687 games in the National Hockey League.*

465. *Dog-mushing.*

466. *Jim Thorpe, in 1917. He did it a second time in 1919. Deion Sanders was the second athlete to accomplish the feat—70 years later, in 1989.*

467. *Mormon leader Brigham Young.*

468. *Gene Conley. He pitched for the Milwaukee Braves team that won the 1957 World Series, and was on the Boston Celtic teams that won National Basketball Association championships in 1959, 1960 and 1961.*

469. *Length, 16 feet 3 inches; width, 4 inches.*

470. *Lacrosse. He made All-American.*

471. *$85,000. It now costs well over $1 million for a half-minute spot.*

472. *Only the Wimbledon trophy is gold; the others—for the U.S. Open, the French Open and the Australian Open—are silver.*

473. *The legendary Satchel Paige, who played pro ball for 22 years— reportedly winning more than 2,000 of the 2,500 games he pitched—before he joined the majors in 1949 at age 42.*

474. *Lou Gehrig. The New York Yankees retired his No. 4 from play on July 4, 1939.*

475. *40—which accounted for all his team's points in its 40-6 Thanksgiving Day victory over the Chicago Bears. Nevers scored six touchdowns and kicked four extra points.*

476. What is the standard width of a bowling alley—gutters not included?

477. What is par on the longest golf hole in the world—the 909-yard 7th hole at Japan's Sano Course at the Satsuki Golf Club?

478. What was Babe Ruth's won-lost record as a big-league pitcher?

479. Within what range must the water temperature be in competitive swimming events at the Olympics?

480. Why did Roberta Gibb Bingay wear a hooded sweatshirt to disguise her appearance when she ran in the Boston Marathon in 1966?

481. What subject did football legend Knute Rockne teach at Notre Dame before he was named head coach of the Fighting Irish in 1918?

482. In tennis, what is the difference—in width—between a singles court and a doubles court?

483. What was the fitting name of the first miniature golf course in the United States?

484. What is the given name of football coach Weeb Ewbank, the only coach to win championships in both the National and American Football Leagues?

485. In 1974, what sport banned all lefties—except those who had already been playing—from competing in sanctioned matches in the U.S.?

486. Why was world champion swimmer Eleanor Holm disqualified from competing in the 1936 Olympics in Berlin?

487. For how many years was the instant replay rule in effect in the National Football League?

488. What is the only track and field event for which a world record has never been set in Olympic competition?

476. *41½ inches, with a tolerance of plus or minus a half-inch permitted.*

477. *Seven.*

478. *94-46.*

479. *Between 78° and 80° Fahrenheit (25.5° to 26.6° Celsius).*

480. *Women were banned from the race until 1972. Bingay, of San Diego, California, was the first woman to complete the race. Her time—unofficial because she was an illegal participant—was 3 hours 20 minutes.*

481. *Chemistry.*

482. *9 feet. A singles court is 27 feet across. A 4½-foot-wide alley is added to each side for a doubles court, making it 36 feet across.*

483. *The Tom Thumb Golf Course. It was built in 1929 in Chattanooga, Tennessee, by John Garnet Carter.*

484. *Wilbur. The nickname Weeb originated with a younger brother's mispronunciation of his name.*

485. *Polo. The rule was imposed by the U.S. Polo Association to prevent collisions between lefties and righties.*

486. *"For sipping champagne with officials" en route to the competition.*

487. *Six—from 1986 to 1992.*

488. *The discus throw.*

489. What American sister and brother won the mixed doubles tennis championship at Wimbledon in 1980?

490. What was unique about the two no-hitters pitched by Cincinnati Red southpaw John Vandermeer?

491. In tennis, what is a golden set?

492. When American Eric Heiden swept all five men's speed-skating events at the 1980 Winter Olympics, his waist size was 32 inches. What did his thighs measure?

493. What popular sport was known in ancient Germany as Heidenwerfen?

494. In what sport is a stimpmeter used, and what does it measure?

495. In the game of Monopoly, how much is a player awarded for drawing the Community Chest card that announces, "You have just won second prize in a beauty contest"?

496. What basketball player racked up the greatest number of personal fouls during his professional career?

497. What major league baseball team was featured in the 1951 film Angels in the Outfield, starring Paul Douglas and Janet Leigh?

498. In what game do you find taws, bowlers, reelers and monnies?

499. What is the greatest distance the Olympic torch ever has been carried within a single country?

500. How many numbered sections is a standard roulette wheel divided into?

501. Who was the first professional football player to run for more than 2,000 yards in a season?

502. In gambling, what is an ambsace?

489. Tracy and John Austin.

490. They were consecutive—and the only no-hitters he ever threw. Vandermeer blanked both the Boston Braves and the Brooklyn Dodgers in June 1938. He's in the record books as the only pitcher in major league history to throw back-to-back no-hitters.

491. A set for which the score is 6-0, with the winner not losing a single point.

492. A muscular 29 inches according to published reports; 27 inches according to Heiden.

493. Bowling. Heidenwerfen means "strike down the heathens."

494. It's used in golf to measure the speed of the greens on a golf course. It's named for Ed Stimpson, the man who developed it in 1935.

495. $10.

496. Kareem Abdul-Jabbar—with 4,657. Other career records he holds include number of minutes played (57,446), points scored (38,387), and field goals scored (15,837). He played from 1969 to 1989.

497. The Pittsburgh Pirates. (When President Eisenhower was in office, he told an interviewer it was his favorite movie.)

498. Marbles. They're all slang for shooter marbles. Target marbles are known as ducks, stickers, dibs, hoodles, kimmies, immies, commies and mibs.

499. 11,222 miles—in Canada. The torch was carried from St. John's to Calgary for the 1988 Winter Olympics. Of the 11,222 miles, 5,088 were covered by foot, 4,419 by aircraft and ferry, 1,712 by snowmobile, and 3 by dogsled.

500. In the United States, 38; in Europe, 37. In the U.S., sections of the wheel are numbered 1 through 36, 0 and 00. In Europe, there's no 00.

501. O.J Simpson, who racked up 2,003 yards for Buffalo in 1973, breaking the previous record of 1,863 yards set 10 years earlier by Jim Brown.

502. Double aces—the lowest throw at dice. In general use, the term means bad luck.

503. How many baseball gloves can be made from one cow?

504. How far must the left and right field fences be from home plate in a major league baseball park?

505. What was the first U.S. city to host the Olympics?

506. Under what name did boxing great Walter Smith enjoy a 25-year ring career, winning both the welterweight and middleweight championship titles?

507. Who was the heaviest heavyweight boxer to compete in a title fight?

508. Who was baseball's first Rookie of the Year?

509. What is the average lifespan of an NBA basketball—in bounces?

510. Why did the Cincinnati Reds baseball team send an autographed second-base bag to cowboy movie star Roy Rogers?

511. Wood from what tree is used in making the bats used in major league baseball?

512. What tennis breakthrough was made by Lili de Alvarez on center court at Wimbledon in 1931?

513. What now-standard riding practice did turn-of-the-century jockey Tod Sloan popularize in horse racing?

514. To whom is the Lady Byng trophy awarded annually?

515. What baseball legend hit Yankee Stadium's first two World Series home runs?

516. Where was the Rose Bowl played in 1942—the only time it wasn't played in Pasadena, California?

503. Five.

504. 325 feet. The minimum distance was set in 1959.

505. St. Louis, Missouri—in 1904.

506. "Sugar Ray" Robinson. Born Walter Smith, he started boxing when he was too young to legally enter the ring—so he used the fight card of an older friend, Ray Robinson. He stuck with the name; a sportswriter added "Sugar" some years later.

507. Italy's Primo Carnera, who tipped the scales at 270 pounds when he successfully defended his title against 184-pound Tommy Loughran in March 1934. Carnera lost the title three months later to Max Baer, whom he outweighed 263¼ to 209½.

508. Brooklyn Dodger great Jackie Robinson, who was given the award in 1947. Forty years later, it was officially renamed the Jackie Robinson Award, although it's still widely called Rookie of the Year.

509. 10,000—according to the manufacturer, Spalding.

510. The red-brick tenement that was his boyhood home once stood on the site of second base at Cincinnati's Riverfront Stadium.

511. Ash.

512. She wore shorts—she was the first woman to do so at Wimbledon.

513. The "monkey crouch" position—knees tucked under chin, upper body lying along the horse's neck.

514. To the National Hockey League player who combines the highest degree of sportsmanship and gentlemanly behavior with a high standard of playing ability. Lady Byng was the wife of the governor-general of Canada when the award was first given in 1925.

515. Casey Stengel—in the 1923 World Series when he was playing for the New York Giants. The homers were hit in games one and three, the only two games the Giants won in the series.

516. In Durham, North Carolina. The reason: Pearl Harbor had been bombed less than a month earlier, and there were fears that California would be next.

517. Who was the only two-time winner of the Heisman Trophy?

518. Basketball star Kareem Abdul-Jabbar and singer Frank Sinatra had what in common?

519. Who was the first athlete to high jump over seven feet?

520. What future politician scored the only touchdown for Harvard when they played Yale in 1955?

521. Who was the only member of the College Football Hall of Fame to receive an Oscar?

522. Who was the only major league baseball player to have a brand of cigarettes named after him?

523. In 1999, who became only the fifth man to win all four major tennis tournaments-Wimbleton, the U.S Open, the Austrialian Open and the French Open-completing a career Grand Slam?

524. In 1927, when Babe Ruth hit his 60 home runs, two of those home runs were hit off a pitcher who was later elected to the Pro Football Hall of Fame. Who was this multi-talented individual?

525. Who was scheduled to be the next batter when Bobby Thomson hit his famous home run in the 1951 National League play-offs, winning the pennant for the New York Giants?

526. Who were the only three men to play for both the Milwaukee Braves and Milwaukee Brewers?

527. The legendary race horse, Man O'War, lost the only race of his illustrious career on August 13, 1919. To whom did "Big Red" lose?

528. "Daredevil Jack" is the title of a 1920 movie serial starring which heavyweight boxer?

529. What Cleveland Indians shortstop stopped Joe DiMaggio's record consecutive hitting streak at 56 games by snaring Joe's potential hit in the eighth inning of a night game July 17, 1941?

530. Who are the only brothers to hit All-Star game home runs?

517. Archie Griffin of Ohio State, who won the award in both 1974 and 1975.

518. They both weighed 13 pounds when born.

519. The American, Charlie Dumas, in 1956.

520. Edward M. Kennedy.

521. Irvine (Cotton) Warburton, who won the Best Film Editing award for "Mary Poppins," in 1964 and was an All-American at the University of Southern California.

522. Ty Cobb.

523. Andre Agassi. He was also the first to do it on three surfces (the French Open's clay, Wimbledon's grass and the concrete of the United States Open and the Austrialian Open). The four previous Grand Slam winners-Don Budge, Fred Perry, Rod Laver and Roy Emerson-won the French Open when it was still played on grass.

524. Ernie Nevers, who played baseball for the St. Louis Browns in 1926, '27 and '28; and football for the Duluth Eskimos in 1926 and '27, and the Chicago Cardinals in 1929, '30 and '31.

525. Rookie Willie Mays.

526. Hank Aaron, Phil Roof, and Felipe Alou.

527. To a horse named Upset, who at odds of 8-to-1, forced Man O'War into second place in the Sanford Memorial Stakes in Saratoga.

528. Jack Dempsey.

529. Lou Boudreau.

530. Joe and Vince DiMaggio. Joe hit his in 1939 for the American League and Vince reciprocated in 1943 for the National League.

531. What was the occupation of Joseph Cooper, the man with whom Billy Martin had the confrontation that cost him his job as manager of the New York Yankees in 1979?

532. Fred Cox, former Minnesota Viking kicker, holds the patent on what athletic toy?

533. Who was the first woman to ride in the Kentucky Derby?

534. Mickey Mantle wore number 7 throughout most of his career with the New York Yankees. What number did he wear as a rookie?

535. Who was the only man in major league history to bat over .400 during his official rookie season?

536. What former heavyweight boxing champion was rejected for the role of Apollo Creed in the 1976 film, *Rocky*, because he made Sylvester Stallone look too small?

537. Who, in 1954, was named *Sports Illustrated* magazine's first Sportsman of the Year?

538. Who was the first major league pitcher to be selected Most Valuable Player and win the Cy Young award in the same year?

539. Who was the only American to win a gold medal at the 1968 Winter Olympics?

540. Where would the 1940 Olympic Games have been held if World War II had not intervened?

541. Of what Colorado mining town was heavyweight boxing champion Jack Dempsey a native?

542. In the game of jacks, how many prongs are there are on each jack?

543. How many possible hands can a player be dealt in a game of bridge?

544. What are the odds against hitting the jackpot on a slot machine?

531. A marshmallow salesman.

532. The Nerf Ball.

533. Diane Crump, on May 2, 1970.

534. Number 6.

535. Shoeless Joe Jackson, who hit .408 for the Cleveland Indians in 1911.

536. Ken Norton.

537. Roger Bannister, who broke the four-minute mile.

538. Don Newcombe, with the Brooklyn Dodgers, in 1956.

539. Figure skater Peggy Fleming.

540. Tokyo, Japan.

541. Manassa—thus his nickname, the Manassa Mauler, coined by Damon Runyon.

542. Six. *543.* Over 600 billion—635,013,559,599 to be exact.

544. 889 to 1.

545. How many clues were there in the first crossword puzzle published in the United States?

546. How many bills does each player get at the beginning of a game of Monopoly?

547. How many dots are there on a pair of dice?

548. How did the French dice game known as hazards come to be called craps in the United States?

549. What popular board game did New Yorker Alfred Butta invent in 1931—and finally find someone to market in 1948?

550. What game featured ghosts named Inky, Blinky, Pinky and Clyde?

551. How many bedrooms are there in the detective board game Clue?

552. Who won five of the United States' six gold medals at the 1980 Winter Olympics at Lake Placid—becoming the first athlete in history to win five gold medals at a Winter Olympics?

553. How many Olympic gold medals in swimming did aquatic movie star Esther Williams win?

554. What is the meaning of basketball great Shaquille Rashaun O'Neal's given Islamic name?

555. In what major league ballpark was a pitcher charged with a balk when the wind blew him off the mound during an All-Star game?

556. How much is a tennis ball supposed to weigh?

557. In boxing, what is the top weight allowed a flyweight?

558. According to ancient chronicles, why were trainers required to be nude at the original Olympics?

559. In what sport do players scrummage?

545. *32. The puzzle appeared in the* New York World *in December 1913.*

546. *27. The bills add up to $1,500 (five $1s, $5s and $10s; two $50s, $100s and $500s; and six $20s).*

547. *42.*

548. *The game was introduced to the U.S. in New Orleans by a Creole in 1813—when the nickname for a Creole man was Johnny Crapaud. At first, the game was referred to as Crapaud's game, and later as craps.*

549. *Scrabble.*

550. *The Pac-Man video arcade game.*

551. *None. There's a ballroom billiard room, conservatory, dining room, kitchen, library, lounge, study and hall.*

552. *Skater Eric Heiden.*

553. *None. In 1940, the year in which she was to compete, the Olympic games scheduled for Finland were canceled because of World War II.*

554. *"Little Warrior." O'Neal is 7 feet 1 inch tall.*

555. *Candlestick Park, home of the San Francisco Giants, in 1961. The pitcher, Stu Miller of the Giants, ended up credited with the National League's 5-4 win. An All-Star record of 7 errors were committed during the 10-inning game.*

556. *Between 2 and 2¹⁄₁₆ ounces.*

557. *112 pounds.*

558. *To enforce the ban on women at the competition. The nude requirement for trainers went into effect after a mother attended the men-only event unnoticed, disguised as her son's trainer, until her robe fell open when she leaped over a barrier to congratulate him for winning.*

559. *English rugby. The term—used for the battle for possession of the ball—was changed to scrimmage and adopted by American football in 1880. Both scrimmage and scrummage are early versions of the word skirmish.*

560. How many times does a sprinter, running at top speed, make contact with the ground during a 100-meter (328-foot) race?

561. What error record did New York Yankee pitcher Tommy John set in a 1988 baseball game against the Milwaukee Brewers?

562. How many players are on a hurling team?

563. Who was the first sports figure to be featured on the covers of *Time, Sports Illustrated, Newsweek* and *U.S. News and World Report* on the same day?

564. How thick is a regulation ice hockey puck?

565. Who was the first American golfer to break 60 on 18 holes in a major tournament

566. How long did the longest wrestling match in Olympic history last?

567. What happens at a golf tournament when a competitor signs his card and it has the wrong score?

568. When Harvard and Yale competed in the first U.S. intercollegiate athletic contest, what was the event?

569. What is the only major sport created in the United States that did not have roots in another sport?

570. What is the world's fastest racquet sport?

571. How many of the 271 events at the 1996 Summer Olympics in Atlanta were open to both male and female competitors?

572. In the jargon of archery, what is a Robin Hood?

573. Who was the first major league baseball player to win a batting title in three different decades?

560. *Approximately 40.*

561. *He made three errors in a single play. He bobbled a slow roller and threw too late to get the batter at first base, his throw was wild and went into right field, then he cut off the throw to home plate and made a second wild throw. Despite all this, the Yankees won the game 16-3 and John had only four errors for the season.*

562. *15.*

563. *Basketball great Magic Johnson, on February 12, 1996—when he returned to the Los Angeles Lakers.*

564. *1 inch. It's 3 inches in diameter.*

565. *Sam Snead, who shot a 59 (31 out, 28 in), 11 strokes under par, in the 1959 Greenbrier Open at White Sulphur Springs, West Virginia. The competition has since been renamed the Sam Snead Festival Golf Tournament.*

566. *11 hours and 40 minutes. The match, a Greco-Roman middleweight bout at the 1912 Olympics, was between Estonian Martin Klein and Finn Alfred Asikainen. Klein won, but was too exhausted to compete in the final. He ended up with the silver medal; Asikainen with the bronze.*

567. *If the score on the card is lower than his actual score, he's disqualified. It it's higher, it replaces his score.*

568. *A boat race, in 1852.*

569. *Basketball.*

570. *Badminton. Shuttlecock speeds approach 200 mph.*

571. *11—mixed doubles badminton, four classes of yachting and all the equestrian events. Of the remaining events, 165 were for men only, and 95 for women only.*

572. *When the tip and shaft of an arrow is fired deep into the end of an arrow already in the bull's-eye.*

573. *George Brett, of the Kansas City Royals. Third baseman Brett won the title with a .333 average in 1976, a .390 average in 1980 and a .329 average in 1990.*

574. Who is the shortest player to lead the National Basketball Association in rebounding?

575. In 1988, Christa Rothenburger-Luding of East Germany became the only Olympic competitor to earn medals in winter and summer games of the same year. What events did she win?

576. What annual sports event was introduced in 1933 as an adjunct to the Chicago World's Fair?

577. In horseracing, what's a walkover?

578. What first name was shared by baseball managers Birdie Tebbetts and Sparky Anderson?

579. In 1996, how much of the $12.9 million earned by basketball oddball Dennis Rodman was compensation for playing for the Chicago Bulls?

580. How did Ernie Shore of the Boston Red Sox get to pitch the only perfect game thrown by a reliever?

581. How many players compete on an equestrian polo team? How about a water polo team?

582. To boost his chances of retrieving a home-run ball, what baseball-loving movie star paid $6,537 for several hundred seats behind the left-field fence for a 1996 game at Anaheim Stadium?

583. What item found in the pocket of pitcher Tom Seaver's New York Mets game jacket—worn from 1967 through 1969—brought $440 at auction?

584. What professional ice hockey star didn't hang up his skates until he was 52—and had played in 2,421 games?

585. What immodest two-word statement is on basketball great Michael Jordan's Illinois vanity license plate?

586. Why were there two kickoffs at the start of the second half of Superbowl I?

574. Charles Barkley, at 6 foot 5 inches. He led in rebounding, with a 14.6 per game average for the 1986-87 season, when he was with the Philadelphia 76ers.

575. Speed skating (gold and silver medals) and cycling (silver medal). Her feat cannot be duplicated because winter and summer games are now held in different years.

576. Baseball's All-Star Game. The first All-Star Game was played at Comiskey Park. The American League, managed by Connie Mack, defeated the National League, managed by John McGraw, 4-2.

577. A race in which a horse is uncontested and simply has to walk the course to win. Spectacular Bid won the 1980 Woodward Stakes at Belmont Raceway in a walkover.

578. George.

579. $3.9 million. Most of his earnings came from endorsements, and some came from his best-selling book, Bad as I Wanna Be.

580. Starting pitcher Babe Ruth was thrown out of the 1917 game for cussing out the umpire after throwing four balls to the lead-off batter. Shore took over on the mound and retired the next 27 batters.

581. Equestrian, 4; water, 7.

582. Charlie Sheen, who attended the game with three friends. They came up empty-handed—no homers were hit their way.

583. A toothpick.

584. Gordie Howe. He played for 32 seasons—26 in the National Hockey League and six in the World Hockey Association—racking up 1,071 goals, 1,518 assists and 2,418 penalty minutes.

585. RARE AIR.

586. NBC was running a commercial and missed the first kickoff. Officials nullified the play and had the half start over again. The 1967 game ended with the Green Bay Packers beating the Kansas City Chiefs, 35-10.

587. What two baseball players were named rookie of the year in 1964—the first time African-Americans won the coveted award in both leagues?

588. In what sport does competition generally take place on a triangular race course?

589. Who was tennis star Monica Seles playing in the 1993 Citizen's Cup Tournament in Hamburg, Germany, when she was stabbed in the back by a spectator?

590. What baseball era ended in 1894 with the retirement of infielder Jeremiah Denny, who had played with the Indianapolis Hoosiers and Louisville Colonels?

591. In bowling, what is the difference between the headpin and the kingpin?

592. What boxing great has been credited with inventing the left hook?

593. Who belted 43 home runs in 1973—matching Baseball Hall of Famer Roger Hornsby's record for the most home runs by a second baseman in one season?

594. Professional teams playing in St. Louis include the Blues (hockey) and the Cardinals (baseball). What big league sports teams has the city had and lost since World War II?

595. American horse racing's top three contests—the Kentucky Derby, the Preakness and the Belmont Stakes—are known as the Triple Crown. What are the three big races exclusively for fillies called?

596. What regulation about fighters' footwear is included in the 12 Marquis of Queensberry Rules, which have governed boxing for over 100 years?

597. With what football team did the huddle originate?

598. Saint Lydwina is the patron saint of what sport?

587. Richie Allen, third baseman for the Philadelphia Phillies, won in the National League; Tony Oliva, outfielder for the Minnesota Twins, won in the American League.

588. Sailing.

589. Magdalena Maleeva. The spectator wanted fellow German Steffi Graf to win the tournament—but she lost the final to Arantxa Sanchez Vicario.

590. The era of bare-handed fielding.

591. The headpin is pin number one, located at the head of the triangle of pins; the kingpin is pin number five, located in the center of all the other pins. Some bowlers and dictionaries mistakenly use both terms for the number one pin.

592. James "Gentleman Jim" Corbett—who came up with the powerful punch in 1889 after suffering two broken knuckles in a heavyweight bout.

593. Manager-to-be Davey Johnson, who was with the Atlanta Braves at the time.

594. The Browns (baseball); the Hawks (basketball); and the Cardinals (football).

595. The Triple Tiara—they are the Acorn, the Mother Goose and the Coaching Club-American Oaks.

596. "No shoes or boots with springs allowed."

597. With the deaf Gallaudet College team, in the 1890s. Members of the Washington, D.C., team went into a huddle to hide the hand signals they were using during a game against another deaf team.

598. Ice skating.

599. What was the championship seed-spitting distance set by John Wilkinson at the "11th Annual Watermelon Thump" held in Luling, Texas, in 1980?

600. What hockey first was achieved by Clarence "Taffy" Abel of the New York Rangers in 1929?

601. With what game did the expression "knuckle down" originate?

602. What action did temperamental relief pitcher Pedro Borbon take when the Cincinnati Reds traded him to the San Francisco Giants in 1979?

603. What National Football League team had its start as the Boston Braves in 1932?

604. What TV newsman was part of the Lancia car racing team that competed in the 1959 Sebring 12-hour race?

605. Ty Cobb's first name was Tyrus. What was the first name of that other baseball great Cy Young?

606. What are the periods of play in a polo match called?

607. Who coined the slogan, "You can't tell the players without a scorecard"?

608. What was boxing great Rocky Marciano's nickname for his deadly right hand?

609. What defensive end was named to the Pro Bowl squad in all but one of his 15 years in the game—a National Football League record?

610. "Lefty" historically has been the most common nickname in baseball. What were the real first names of Hall of Fame southpaws Lefty Grove and Lefty Gomez?

611. What great ballplayer played first base in high school and had pitched only one season in college when he was given a bonus to pitch in the major leagues?

599. *65 feet 4 inches.*

600. *He was the first American-born player to be on a Stanley Cup team.*

601. *Marbles—players put fist (knuckles) to the ground for their best shots.*

602. *He put a voodoo curse on the Reds.*

603. *The Washington Redskins. The team became the Boston Redskins a year later, and moved to Washington in 1937.*

604. *Walter Cronkite.*

605. *Denton. He was nicknamed Cy—for Cyclone—because of the destruction wrought by his famous fastball.*

606. *Chukkers. In U.S. competition there are six of them in a normal game, each seven and a half minutes long.*

607. *Baseball's first professional concessionaire, Harry M. Stevens, who used it when he started hawking ballpark programs in Columbus, Ohio, in the 1880s.*

608. *Suzi-Q.*

609. *Merlin Olsen, who played with the L.A. Rams. Olsen, now a sportscaster and actor, was bypassed for the Pro Bowl squad in 1976—his last season.*

610. *Robert and Vernon, respectively.*

611. *Sandy Koufax, who was 19 in 1954 when the Brooklyn Dodgers signed him up with a $14,000 bonus and an annual salary of $6,000.*

612. What baseball-playing brothers came in first and second in the race for the National League batting title in 1966?

613. Where were the first outdoor miniature golf courses in the United States built?

614. What fruit did early Greek Olympians eat for their health and sometimes even wear as medals?

615. What was baseball great Babe Ruth's response when he was asked why he deserved a higher salary than President Herbert Hoover?

616. What country established the modern tradition of having the Olympic torch carried from Greece to the site of the international games?

617. How long did England's Roger Bannister, the first athlete to run the long-elusive four-minute mile, hold the world title in the event?

618. Whose tennis serve was the fastest ever recorded?

619. What was the average weight of the legendary Four Horsemen—the gridiron greats who played for Notre Dame under Knute Rockne in 1924?

620. Basketball great Kareem Abdul-Jabbar wore number 33 during his 20-year career because it was the number of his favorite football player. Can you name that player?

621. Famed boxer Jack Dempsey was named after what American president?

622. Who was the only major league baseball player to hit a home run to win the seventh game of a World Series?

623. What was baseball great Stan Musial's advice to those trying to hit a spitball?

624. In what sport is a battledore used?

612. *The Alou brothers, Matty and Felipe. Matty's batting average with the Pittsburgh Pirates was .342; Felipe's average with the Atlanta Braves was .327.*

613. *On rooftops in New York City—in 1926.*

614. *Figs.*

615. *"Why not? I had a better year." Ruth's salary at the time (1931) was $80,000; Hoover's, $75,000.*

616. *Germany, in 1936—when the Olympics were held in Berlin.*

617. *For 46 days. Bannister's record of 3:59.4, set on May 6, 1954, was broken by Australia's John Landy, who hit the tape at 3:58.0 on June 21, 1954.*

618. *Bill Tilden's. It was measured at 163.6 miles per hour in 1931.*

619. *159 pounds. The breakdown: fullback Elmer Layden, 162; halfback Don Miller, 160; halfback James Crowley, 159; and quarterback Harry Stuhldreher, 155.*

620. *Former New York Giants running back Mel Triplett.*

621. *William Henry Harrison. The "Manassa Mauler" was named William Harrison Dempsey at birth.*

622. *Bill Mazeroski, who clinched the 1960 series for the Pittsburgh Pirates with his homer off Ralph Terry of the New York Yankees.*

623. *"Hit it on the dry side."*

624. *In badminton—it's the racket used to hit the shuttlecock. Originally the game was known as battledore and shuttlecock.*

625. How many times did the "Father of Baseball," Abner Doubleday, mention that sport in his 67 diaries?

626. How many players are there on a men's lacrosse team?

627. Who was the only rookie in baseball history to be honored as rookie of the year and most valuable player in the same season?

628. What baseball team introduced the sacrifice bunt, the squeeze play, the hit-and-run play, and double-steal?

629. Why did baseball manager Hal Lanier order all television sets removed from the Houston Astros clubhouse in 1986?

630. Who was the first black athlete to carry the American flag in the opening procession of the Olympics?

631. How much did premier jockey Eddie Arcaro earn in purses during his 30-year career?

632. In golfing slang, what is a Dolly Parton?

633. In 1950, baseball commissioner Ford Frick ordered New York Giant second baseman Eddie Stanky to stop performing "the Stanky maneuver." What was it?

634. What famous sports commentator announced his first major league baseball game without ever having seen one before?

635. The Kentucky Derby is named for its home state; the Belmont Stakes for its founder, August Belmont. How did the Preakness get its name?

636. What was the greatest number of home runs hit in a single season by baseball's "Georgia Peach," Ty Cobb?

637. What hard-hitting football great once said: "I wouldn't ever set out to hurt anybody deliberately unless it was, you know, important. Like a league game or something."

638. What well-known baseball pitcher is descended from a Hessian mercenary who fought for the British in the American Revolution?

625. *Not once.*

626. *Ten—three defensemen, three midfield players, three attackmen, and a goalkeeper.*

627. *Outfielder Fred Lynn, in 1975, when he helped the Boston Red Sox capture the American League pennant by batting .331.*

628. *The Baltimore Orioles—before the turn of the century.*

629. *The players were skipping infield practice to watch "Wheel of Fortune."*

630. *Decathlon champion Rafer Johnson, in Rome in 1960.*

631. *Exactly $30,039,543—of which his share was approximately 10 percent.*

632. *A putt on an especially hilly green. It's also known as a roller coaster.*

633. *Jumping up and down and waving wildly to distract batters. As one baseball executive said of Stanky: "He cannot hit, he cannot throw, and he cannot outrun his grandmother. But if there's a way to beat the other team, he'll find it."*

634. *Red Barber, in 1934 for the Cincinnati Reds.*

635. *From the colt that won the first stakes race ever held at Maryland's Pimlico Race Course.*

636. *12.*

637. *Hall of Fame linebacker Dick Butkus, who helped the Chicago Bears earn the title "monsters of the midway" in the late 1960s and early '70s.*

638. *Orel Hershiser, whose first name is Slavic for "eagle."*

639. How many points did basketball great Kareem Abdul-Jabbar score during his 20-season career?

640. Why was Russian pentathlon star Boris Onischenko disqualified for cheating at the 1976 Olympics in Montreal?

641. What was the name of the only National Football League team playing in Pennsylvania in 1943?

642. What is the width of a football field?

643. How big a cut did baseball's Gary Carter take in his base pay when he signed with the San Francisco Giants in 1990 after being dropped as a catcher by the New York Mets?

644. What was basketball great Wilt Chamberlain's record high for points scored in one half?

645. What sport has a sex allowance?

646. The New York Jets were beating the Oakland Raiders 32-29 with 75 seconds of play to go in November 1968 when the game was pre-empted by the children's classic "Heidi." What was the final score?

647. How did baseball superstar Leroy "Satchel" Paige get his nickname?

648. What is the diameter of the cup on a standard golf course putting green?

649. How old was boxer Archie Moore in 1952 when he won the light-heavyweight championship?

650. What does basketball great Kareem Abdul-Jabbar's name mean in English?

651. What two baseball-playing brothers hit home runs in the same World Series game?

652. What left-handed British head of state competed at Wimbledon—and lost in a first-round doubles match?

639. *A record 38,387—or 44,149 if you're counting playoffs.*

640. *He was caught using a rigged épée in the fencing competition. It had an electronic device in its handle that caused a "hit" to be registered on the electronic scoreboard when none had been made.*

641. *The Steagles—the Pittsburgh Steelers and Philadelphia Eagles merged during World War II when many players were serving overseas.*

642. *53⅓ yards.*

643. *Almost $2 million—he went from $2.2 million to $250,000.*

644. *He scored 59 points in one half; his game high was 100.*

645. *Thoroughbred horse racing. It's the number of pounds below the minimum—usually three to five pounds—that fillies are permitted to carry when running against males.*

646. *The Raiders won, 43-32, after making two last-minute touchdowns.*

647. *From his size-14 shoes, which were "as big as satchels."*

648. *Exactly 4¼ inches.*

649. *He was 39—and he held the NBA title from 1952 to 1961.*

650. *Generous Servant of Allah.*

651. *The Boyers, Ken and Clete, third basemen for the St. Louis Cardinals and New York Yankees, respectively. Their homers came in the seventh game of the 1964 Series.*

652. *King George VI—father of Queen Elizabeth II—in 1926 when he was the Duke of York.*

653. How many tiles are there in a game of dominoes?

654. What was the controversial name of the French yacht that competed in the 1987 America's Cup race?

655. What famous boxer once said: "I was never knocked out. I've been unconscious, but it's always been on my feet"?

656. Who was the first designated hitter in major league baseball history?

657. What was long-time Philadelphia Athletics baseball manager Connie Mack's name before he shortened it to fit on the scoreboard?

658. How did basketball get its name?

659. The Indianapolis 500 was begun in 1911. When was the first time the winning race car exceeded 100 mph?

660. What popular actor was part owner of the racehorse that placed third in the 1980 Kentucky Derby?

661. What sport did novelist Joyce Carol Oates write a book about?

662. Walter Alston, manager of the Brooklyn and L.A. Dodgers, appeared in only one major league game as a player. For what team did he go to bat and how did he do?

663. What are the odds of getting four of a kind in a five-card deal in poker?

664. What is the maximum length and thickness permitted for a major league baseball bat?

665. What two sports have telltales—and what are they?

666. What did tennis star Gussie Moran wear in a tournament in Egypt nine months after she stunned the staid Wimbledon crowd by wearing white lace-fringed panties?

653. There are 28.

654. French Kiss.

655. Floyd Patterson, world heavyweight champion from 1956 to 1959 and from 1960 to 1962.

656. Ron Blomberg of the New York Yankees. He drew a bases-loaded walk from Red Sox pitcher Luis Tiant in his historic April 6, 1973 at-bat at Boston's Fenway Park.

657. Cornelius McGillicuddy.

658. From the half-bushel peach baskets used as targets by the sport's originator, James A. Naismith, in the first game in December 1891.

659. In 1925, when Peter De Paolo averaged 101.13 mph in an 8-cylinder Duesenberg Special.

660. Jack ("Quincy" and "Oscar Madison") Klugman. The horse was named Jaklin Klugman.

661. Boxing. The book, published in 1987, is called "On Boxing."

662. In his sole at-bat for the 1936 St. Louis Cardinals, Alston struck out.

663. The odds are 4,164 to 1.

664. Length, 42 inches; thickness, 2¼ inches.

665. Squash and sailing. In squash, it is the narrow 17-inch-high metal strip the ball must clear on the front wall. In sailing, it's a small piece of cloth or yarn attached to the shroud or backstay to indicate the relative direction of the wind.

666. Black shorts. She explained that she made the change because she had gained 13 pounds and her white tennis attire no longer fit.

667. What is the maximum a horseshoe may weigh in the game of horseshoes?

668. Whom did Casey Stengel advise, "Kid, you're too small. You ought to go out and shine shoes"?

669. How long is a standard six-foot-wide shuffleboard court?

670. What is the average life span of a baseball—in pitches—in the major leagues?

671. How tall is former Dallas Cowboy defensive end Ed "Too Tall" Jones?

672. What major league pitcher was ordered to stop wearing hair curlers on the field during practice?

673. In the National Hockey League, how many members of a team are permitted to suit up for a game?

674. What former major league baseball player is the younger brother of tennis great Billie Jean King?

675. How many feathers are there on a standard badminton shuttlecock?

676. Who was the first woman to serve as grand marshal of the Tournament of Roses parade, first held in 1890?

677. What TV western star was once the highest paid, highest scoring professional lacrosse player in Canadian history?

678. How many pieces does each player start with in a chess game?

679. What sport was banned in Scotland in 1457 by King James II, and why?

680. What boxers competed in the first prize fight with a $1 million gate?

681. In what event did Dr. Benjamin Spock compete in the 1924 Paris Olympics?

667. The maximum is 2½ pounds. Those worn by horses vary, with thoroughbred racehorses wearing 4-ounce aluminum shoes and pleasure horses wearing 12-ounce steel shoes.

668. Phil Rizzuto, who went on to play with the New York Yankees as a shortstop under Stengel and later became the Yankees' broadcaster. Casey made the remark while he was managing the Brooklyn Dodgers.

669. It's 52 feet long.

670. Five.

671. He's 6 feet 9 inches tall.

672. Dock Ellis of the Pittsburgh Pirates, in 1973.

673. Twenty.

674. Randy Moffitt, who pitched for the San Francisco Giants and the Toronto Blue Jays.

675. Between 14 and 16, each from 2½ to 2¼ inches long, from its tip to the top of the shuttlecock's cork base.

676. Humorist and syndicated columnist Erma Bombeck, in 1986.

677. Jay Silverheels—Tonto on "The Lone Ranger."

678. Sixteen—a king, a queen, two knights, two bishops, two castles, and eight pawns.

679. Golf—he claimed it distracted people from the archery practice needed for national defense.

680. Heavyweights Jack Dempsey and George Carpentier. Dempsey won the 1921 bout, billed as "The Fight of the Century," with a fourth round knockout.

681. Rowing. He won a gold medal as a member of the Yale team.

682. How did poker's Dead Man's Hand—a pair of aces and a pair of eights—get its name?

683. What West Point cadet's football career came to an abrupt halt when he injured his knee tackling Jim Thorpe, who was playing for the Carlisle Indian School?

684. In 1882, who knocked out Paddy Ryan to become the last bareknuckle world's heavyweight boxing champion?

685. What pitcher's career spanned the greatest number of years—twenty-five seasons?

686. What are the three one-eyed face cards in a desk of cards?

687. What is the name of golfer Jack Nicklaus's international real-estate conglomerate?

688. Participants in the 1960 Olympics were asked what question concerning their early childhoods on an official questionnaire?

689. What Olympic requirement was waived for Princess Anne when she competed as an equestrian in the 1976 summer games in Montreal?

690. What does the O. J. in football star O. J. Simpson's name stand for?

691. In what game did William Shakespeare play against Henry Wadsworth Longfellow?

692. What St. Louis Cardinal pitchers won two games each to clinch the 1934 World Series against the Detroit Tigers?

693. What two-time Wimbledon champion became the first tennis millionaire in 1971?

694. Who were the swimming stars in Billy Rose's "Aquacade" at the 1939 New York World's Fair?

695. On what team did basketball greats Oscar Robertson, Jerry West, and John Havlicek play together?

682. It was the hand held by *Wild Bill Hickok* when he was gunned down.

683. *Dwight D. Eisenhower*, left halfback on the losing team. Score: 27 to 6.

684. *John L. Sullivan.*

685. *James L. Kaat*, who retired in 1983.

686. The king of diamonds, the jack of spades, and the jack of hearts.

687. *Golden Bear, Inc.*—inspired by his golf circuit nickname, *Golden Bear.*

688. They were asked if they had been bottle- or breast-fed.

689. She was the only female competitor not given a chromosome (sex) test.

690. *Orenthal James.*

691. Football—in 1935, Notre Dame's Shakespeare faced Northwestern's Longfellow. Longfellow's team won, 14 to 7.

692. Brothers *Dizzy* and *Daffy Dean.*

693. Australian *Rod Laver.*

694. American Olympic gold medal winners *Johnny Weissmuller, Eleanor Holm,* and *Gertrude Ederle,* the first woman to swim across the English Channel.

695. The winning 1960 U.S. Olympic basketball team.

696. In what sport did sailor Alvin "Shipwreck" Kelly rise to the top?

697. What game did the Duchess of Windsor teach TV interviewer Edward R. Murrow to play on "Person to Person"?

698. What American ballet star was a boxing champion in college?

699. Who asked: "Sin tax? Are them jokers down in Washington puttin' a tax on that, too?"

700. What number did baseball legend Ty Cobb wear?

701. Where are all baseballs used in the U.S. major leagues manufactured?

702. What is the origin of the winning term "checkmate" in chess?

703. What two college teams played the first football game in the U.S.?

704. What boxing champion-to-be was disqualified in the 1952 Olympic heavyweight finals for "inactivity in the ring"?

705. Outfielder Pete Gray played with the St. Louis Browns in 1945 despite a serious handicap. What was it?

706. What did the French Boxing Federation ban in an official edict in 1924?

707. What famous football coach had every member of his team take dancing lessons "to develop a sense of rhythm essential in the timing of shift plays"?

708. In bowling, what term describes the split in which the 5 and 10 pins are left standing?

709. How long was Muhammad Ali exiled from boxing for refusing to enter military service during the war in Vietnam?

710. What football teams were playing when TV made its first use of the instant replay 30 years ago?

696. *Flagpole sitting. He traveled the country setting records. His best time was 49 days; his lifetime total was 20,613 hours.*

697. *Jacks.*

698. *Edward Villella.*

699. *Baseball great turned sportscaster Dizzy Dean, when told that his syntax greatly distressed educators.*

700. *None. He played before numbers were used.*

701. *In Haiti, where cheap labor is used to handstitch the leather cover on each 369-yard roll of woolen yarn and cotton string. (The Rawlings Sporting Goods Co.'s exclusive contract expired in 1986.)*

702. *The Arabic phrase "shah mat," literally "the king is dead."*

703. *Princeton and Rutgers. Rutgers won the 1869 contest, 6 to 4.*

704. *Sweden's Ingemar Johansson. He was presented with the silver medal thirty years later.*

705. *He had only one arm.*

706. *The fighters' practice of kissing one another at the end of their bouts.*

707. *Notre Dame's Knute Rockne, in 1923.*

708. *Woolworth.*

709. *For 3½ years, from April 1967 to October 1970, when he returned to the ring and knocked out Jerry Quarry.*

710. *Army and Navy. The play shown was a touchdown by Army quarterback Carl "Rollie" Stichweh.*

711. What popular sport was called Sphairistikè when it was introduced in England in 1873?

712. How many pentagonal patches are there on a soccer ball?

713. What two well-known hockey figures teamed up to pay $451,000 for a rare Honus Wagner baseball card in 1991?

714. In golfing slang, what is a Volkswagen?

715. Who was the last major league baseball player to get on base more than 50 percent of the time during a season with at least 400 at-bats?

716. How much did CBS pay for the United States TV broadcast rights to the 1994 Winter Olympics in Lillehammer, Norway?

717. After what popular TV actor of the 1960s was football-baseball star Bo Jackson named?

718. What change did Charlie O. Finley, the colorful former owner of the Oakland Athletics, try but fail to make in the ball used in our national pastime?

719. Who holds the basketball record for the most free throws made in a game?

720. What message was on the T-shirt worn by New York Yankee pitcher Gaylord Perry—who was nicknamed the Great Expectorator—on the day he won his 300th game?

721. What famous American boxer was named Arnold Raymond Cream at birth?

722. What unusual—and quite revolutionary—track and field event was officially recognized by the Physical Culture and Sports Commission of Communist China in 1956?

723. What now standard boxing equipment did ringside newspaper-telegraph operator Stanley Taylor invent in a bid to upgrade the sport?

711. *Th modern game of tennis. Its creator was Major Walter C. Wingfield. Sphairistikè is a Greek word that means "to play."*

712. *12. They're usually black. The white patches are hexagons.*

713. *Wayne Gretzky and Los Angeles Kings owner Bruce McNall.*

714. *An awkward or bad shot that turns out well.*

715. *New York Yankee Mickey Mantle, in 1957, when his on-base average was .515. The Boston Red Sox's Ted Williams holds the record for the best on-base average ever, .551, achieved in 1941.*

716. *$300 million—$57 million more than it paid for the rights to broadcast the 1992 games held in Albertville, France.*

717. *Vince Edwards. Jackson, whose given name is Vincent Edward, was named after the actor who appeared in the title role on the "Ben Casey" show. The nickname Bo is a shortened version of Boar—the moniker Jackson's brother gave him when he was eight because he was as tough as a wild boar.*

718. *He wanted baseballs to be yellow.*

719. *Bob Cousy of the Boston Celtics, who made 30 of 32 free-throw attempts in a 1953 four-overtime playoff game against the Syracuse Nationals. Although he racked up 50 points, the Celtics lost 111-105.*

720. *"300 wins is nothing to spit at." The win came in May 1982. Perry retired the following year with a career record of 314 wins and 265 losses.*

721. *Jersey Joe Walcott.*

722. *The hand-grenade throw.*

723. *The protective cup. Taylor had seen too many losing boxers turn the tide of their bouts with low blows.*

724. Who was the first relief pitcher elected to baseball's Hall of Fame?

725. What is the maximum circumference of a standard bowling ball?

726. What was the name of the only horse to beat Man O'War in his incredible 21-race career?

727. What happens in major league baseball if an outfielder catches a fly ball with his hat instead of his glove?

728. Before wooden tees were introduced in the late 1920s, what did golfers use to elevate the ball for driving?

729. What famous American tennis player's father boxed for Iran in the 1948 and 1952 Olympics?

730. When they play trictrac in France, what game are they playing?

731. Who was the first black to play major league baseball with an American League team?

732. What did Japan's century-old Nintendo company manufacture before it made its mark in the world of computer games?

733. The winner of the Kentucky Derby is blanketed with roses. What flowers are used to adorn the winners of the Belmont Stakes and the Preakness?

734. What sport is named for the country estate of the English duke whose house guests helped devise and popularize it?

735. How many wickets and wooden stakes are used in playing tournament croquet?

736. Name the seven baseball greats who share the distinction of having been voted "most valuable player" three times.

737. What is unusual about the names boxer George Foreman has given his five sons?

724. *Right-handed knuckleball specialist Hoyt Wilhelm, in 1985.*

725. *27 inches—or 27.002 inches, to be exact.*

726. *Upset.*

727. *The batter gets three bases.*

728. *A small mound of sand.*

729. *Andre Agassi's Armenian-born father, Emmanuel Agassi, better known as Mike.*

730. *Backgammon.*

731. *Larry Doby, who joined the Cleveland Indians in July 1947—11 weeks after Jackie Robinson broke the major league color barrier by joining the Brooklyn Dodgers.*

732. *Playing cards.*

733. *At Belmont, white carnations are traditional. At the Preakness, yellow daisies are dabbed with black shoe polish to look like black-eyed Susans—the Maryland state flower, which doesn't bloom until a month after the big race.*

734. *Badminton. It was during a house party on a rainy day in 1873 at the Duke of Beaufort's home in Gloucestershire, that guests picked up the battledores and shuttlecock used in a children's game and began playing over a cord stretched across a hall.*

735. *Six wickets and one stake.*

736. *Jimmy Foxx, Joe DiMaggio, Stan Musial, Yogi Berra, Roy Campanella, Mickey Mantle and Mike Schmidt.*

737. *All are named George.*

738. How many sides are there on the grip of a standard tennis racket?

739. What vessels were used when the first regattas were held in the seventeenth century?

740. How many field goals and how many free throws did basketball great Wilt "The Stilt" Chamberlain make in his famous 100-point game in 1962?

741. By what name was Dimitrios Synodinos better known in the sporting world?

742. In what country did the card game canasta originate?

743. In what city did basketball's barnstorming Harlem Globetrotters get their start?

744. When the New York Knickerbockers became the first baseball club to adopt an official uniform in 1849, what did team members wear on their heads?

745. What was sports great Jesse Owens's real given name?

746. What is the name of the cookbook that Boston Red Sox third baseman Wade Boggs co-authored with his wife, Debbie, in 1984?

747. In golf, what is an albatross?

748. What were the first American and National League baseball teams to draw over one million fans in a season?

749. How many hits did the "Yankee Clipper," Joe DiMaggio, get during his 56-game batting streak in 1941?

750. In the earliest days of baseball, how many balls were required for a batter to draw a walk?

751. In bowling alley slang, what's a turkey?

752. When you hit a tennis ball, how much time does it spend in contact with your tennis racket?

738. *Eight.*

739. *Gondolas. The regattas were held on the Grand Canal in Venice.*

740. *Chamberlain, playing for the Philadelphia Warriors, scored 36 field goals and 28 free throws against the New York Knickerbockers in that historic game.*

741. *Jimmy "the Greek" Snyder—the famous Las Vegas oddsmaker.*

742. *In Uruguay, in the 1940s.*

743. *In Chicago—home of team organizer Abe Saperstein.*

744. *Straw hats. The rest of the uniform consisted of blue woolen pantaloons and white flannel shirts.*

745. *James Cleveland. He was known by his initials, J.C., until he was nine, when a teacher mistakenly called him Jesse—and a new nickname was born.*

746. *"Fowl Tips." It's a chicken cookbook. Boggs says he eats chicken every day.*

747. *Three under par—which also is known as a double eagle.*

748. *For the American League, the New York Yankees—1,289,422 in 1920; for the National League, the Chicago Cubs—1,159,168 in 1927.*

749. *He got 91 hits, knocked in 55 runs and reached home himself 56 times. Of his 91 hits, 56 were singles, 16 were doubles, 4 were triples and 15 were homers.*

750. *Nine. The number was reduced little by little until 1889, when it became four.*

751. *Three strikes in a row. The term dates back to the late 1800s, when bowling alley owners presented live turkeys around Thanksgiving and Christmas to the first member of a team to score three consecutive strikes.*

752. *$4/_{1,000}$ second.*

753. What is the minimum weight permitted for a baseball in the major leagues?

754. What was the name of the very first video game?

755. What did pentathlon and decathlon winner Jim Thorpe reply when Sweden's King Gustav V called him "the greatest athlete in the world" as he presented him with his gold medals at the 1912 Olympics?

756. What does zugzwang describe in the game of chess?

757. What was the original meaning of bogey—the golf term that now indicates one stroke over par?

758. Who was on the mound for the Brooklyn Dodgers when Yankee righthander Don Larsen pitched his perfect game in the 1956 World Series?

759. What dubious first did discus thrower Danuta Rosani of Poland achieve at the 1976 Olympics in Montreal?

760. Who was the first tennis player from an Iron Curtain country to win the United States Open?

761. According to the rules in effect at the first intercollegiate baseball game ever played—back in 1859—the first team to score 65 runs would be the winner. How long did the game last?

762. What are the five events in the modern Olympic pentathlon?

763. Under what weather conditions does a baseball travel farthest?

764. Who was the first driver to cover a mile in less than a minute in a gas-powered automobile?

765. In 1988 the Chicago Cubs became the last major league team to get lights for night baseball. What team was next to last?

766. In 1896 in Athens, Greece, Harvard student James B. Connolly became the first gold medal winner in modern Olympic history. What was his event?

753. The minimum is 5 ounces. (The maximum weight allowed is 5¼ ounces.)

754. Pong—which was introduced in 1972 by Noel Bushnell, who soon after created Atari.

755. "Thanks, King." Thorpe, who was later disqualified for alleged professionalism, was posthumously restored to the roster of Olympic champions in 1982.

756. A situation in which all possible moves are to the player's disadvantage.

757. It originally meant par—and still does in Great Britain.

758. Sal Maglie, who allowed only five hits in the 2-0 Dodger loss.

759. She failed the test for anabolic steroids and became the first Olympic athlete to be disqualified for taking drugs.

760. Romanian Ilie Nastase, in 1972.

761. It went 26 innings, or "rounds," with Amherst beating Williams 66-32.

762. The 5,000-meter cross-country horseback ride, 300-meter swim, 4,000-meter cross-country run, foil fencing and pistol shooting.

763. When it is hot and humid—because the air is less dense than when it is cold and dry.

764. Legendary race car driver Barney Oldfield in 1903. He did the mile in 59.6 seconds in a Ford 999.

765. The Detroit Tigers, 40 years earlier.

766. The hop, step and jump, now known as the triple jump. Connolly went a distance of 45 feet.

767. What are the usual dimensions of the professional boxing ring?

768. What baseball team got its name because of a second baseman named Louis Bierbauer?

769. In how many World Series did Babe Ruth play during his 22-year baseball career?

770. What was the final score of the $100,000, winner-take-all "Battle of the Sexes" tennis match between Billy Jean King and Bobby Riggs at the Houston Astrodome in 1973?

771. Who was the first American sports figure to earn $1 million during his career?

772. What are the ten events in the grueling Olympic decathlon competition?

773. How many homeruns did Mark McGwire hit in 1998—the year he broke Roger Maris's longstanding record?

774. Who directed the opening ceremonies at the 1960 Winter Olympics in Squaw Valley, California?

775. What is the distance from foul line to head pin on a bowling lane?

776. How many rounds did John L. Sullivan and Jake Kilrain go in America's last professional bare-knuckle heavyweight boxing bout?

777. How many fingers did Mordecai "Three Finger" Brown, the great right-handed Chicago Cub pitcher, have?

778. In modern day camel racing in Abu Dhabi, in the United Arab Emirates, what is used to keep jockeys on their mounts?

779. Who was the only tennis player to win the U.S. Open on three different surfaces—grass and clay at Forest Hills and hardcourt at Flushing Meadows?

780. Who was the first female athlete to appear in a Wheaties "Breakfast of Champions" television commercial?

767. *The professional ring is generally 20 feet square (although the size may vary from 16 to 24 feet square).*

768. *The Pittsburgh Pirates. The team—which had gone through a variety of names including the Alleghenies, Potato Bugs, Zulus and Smoked Italians— earned the name by "pirating" Bierbauer away from the Philadelphia Athletics.*

769. *Ten, with his team winning seven of them.*

770. *King (age 29) beat Riggs (age 55) in three sets, 6-4, 6-3, 6-3.*

771. *Heavyweight boxer John L. Sullivan.*

772. *The 100-meter, 400-meter and 1,500-meter races, the long jump, 16-pound shot put, high jump, 110-meter high hurdles, discus throw, pole vault and javelin throw.*

773. *70—nine more than Maris hit in 1961*

774. *Walt Disney.*

775. *Sixty feet.*

776. *The 1889 bout went 75 rounds—with Bat Masterson serving as timekeeper for loser Kilrain.*

777. *Nine and a half. He was missing the top half of his right index finger.*

778. *Velcro. It has replaced rope.*

779. *Jimmy Connors.*

780. *Pint-sized gymnast Mary Lou Retton, shortly after her gold medal triumph at the 1984 Summer Olympics.*

781. Where did the home run hit by Pittsburgh Pirate Hall of Famer Willie Stargell land in the 1965 All-Star baseball game in Minnesota?

782. Name the tallest shortstop in the history of major league baseball.

783. What physical deformity did American Kristi Yamaguchi, winner of a 1992 Olympic gold medal in figure-skating, have at birth and later overcome?

784. What was sports great Jim Thorpe's batting average during his 289-game career as a major league baseball player?

785. How many World Series championships did the New York Yankees win while baseball great Joe DiMaggio was on the team?

786. What union did players on basketball's Harlem Globetrotters become affiliated with in 1974?

787. In amateur boxing, how many cloth-wrapped strands of rope are required along the four sides of the boxing ring?

788. In golfing circles, what is a snowman?

789. How were numbers assigned when members of the 1929 New York Yankees became the first baseball players to have them on their uniforms?

790. What are the odds that a professional golfer will get a hole-in-one?

791. Which member of the legendary Tinker-to-Evers-to-Chance double-play team was the first to be elected to the Baseball Hall of Fame?

792. What ice-skating spin is named for Olympic gold medalist Dorothy Hamill?

793. What famous baseball player's older brother was runner-up to Jesse Owens in the 200-meter race at the 1936 Olympic Games in Berlin?

781. *Inside a tuba in the right field bullpen—where a marching band was practicing.*

782. *Cal Ripken Jr., of the Baltimore Orioles. His height is 6 feet 4.*

783. *Clubfeet—which were treated with corrective shoes.*

784. *Thorpe played the outfield in the National League from 1913 to 1919, when he went into football.*

785. *9—of the 10 he played in.*

786. *They joined a local of the Service Employees Union, which represents janitors, vendors, stagehands and others who work in arenas.*

787. *Four.*

788. *A score of 8 for a hole or 88 for a round. The name is derived from the number 8's resemblance to a snowman.*

789. *According to their position in the batting lineup. No. 1 was centerfielder Earl Combs, who batted first; No. 2, third baseman Mark Koenig, who batted second; No. 3, rightfielder Babe Ruth, who batted third; No. 4, first baseman Lou Gehrig, who batted fourth; and so on down the line.*

790. *One in 15,000.*

791. *They were elected as a unit in 1946. The three Chicago Cub infielders were Joe Tinker, Johnny Evers and Frank Chance.*

792. *Hamill's camel.*

793. *Jackie Robinson's. His brother Mack's time was 21.1 seconds to Owens's 20.7.*

794. What international sports competition is named for former president George Bush's grandfather?

795. What song did members of the "miracle" New York Mets baseball team sing on the Ed Sullivan TV show after they won the 1969 World Series?

796. In speed skating, what do the competitors wear to indicate which lane they start in?

797. What popular sport does the Fédération Internationale des Quilleurs (FIQ) oversee?

798. What American baseball team introduced the "high five"?

799. What sport—in its primitive form—gave us the word melee?

800. What major change was made in 1967 in the uniforms worn by major league baseball players?

801. How many home runs did Mickey Mantle hit in 1961, the year his New York Yankee teammate Roger Maris hit a then-record-setting 61?

802. What key word was eliminated from the Olympic Charter in 1971?

803. How many more career wins did major league pitcher Gaylord Perry have than his older brother Jim Perry?

804. In professional ice hockey, what is the maximum length permitted for the blade of a hockey stick?

805. What is the standard pitching distance in the game of horseshoes?

806. What did Boston Red Sox slugger Ted Williams do in his last major league at-bat in September 1960?

794. *Amateur golf's Walker Cup. It was named in honor of George Herbert Walker Bush's grandfather, George Herbert Walker, after he donated the tournament trophy for the first competition in 1922.*

795. *"You've Gotta Have Heart" from the musical Damn Yankees.*

796. *Colored armbands. White is worn by the skater starting in the inner lane; red by the skater starting in the outer lane. The skaters change lanes after each circuit of the track.*

797. *Bowling.*

798. *The Los Angeles Dodgers. Outfielder Glenn Burke is credited with originating it in 1977.*

799. *Soccer. In French, melée means "a confused mass," which was what the playing field looked like in Europe in the Middle Ages when towns competed using teams of up to a hundred players, with the goals a half-mile or so apart.*

800. *The fabric was switched from flannel to double knit.*

801. *54.*

802. *Amateur.*

803. *99. Gaylord had 314 wins; Jim, 215.*

804. *For all players except the goaltender, the blade is limited to 12½ inches in length; for a goaltender, it can be up to 15½ inches long.*

805. *40 feet for men; 30 feet for women and juniors.*

806. *He hit a home run off Baltimore's Jack Fisher. It was his 521st homer.*

807. A German named Hermann Ratjen claims the Nazis forced him to masquerade as a woman and compete in the women's high jump at the 1936 Olympics. How did "Dora Ratjen" rank in the event?

808. What two pitchers were baseball's first free agents?

809. What football player was the recipient of the biggest Super Bowl ring ever made?

810. In the 1992 America's Cup competition, what was the significance of the letters ENZA on the sails of the New Zealand yacht?

811. On the Professional Golf Association tour, how much time are players allotted for each shot?

812. What football teams were on the field in the 1977 film *Black Sunday*?

813. What teams competed in the first football Superbowl in 1967?

814. Who is the only man elected to both the Baseball and Football Halls of Fame?

815. Who was the youngest golfer to win the Masters Tournament?

816. What does the small printed label on the back of all National Football League helmets say?

817. Where does catgut—used in stringed instruments, surgical sutures and tennis rackets—come from?

818. Who said, "Show me a good loser and I'll show you a loser"?

819. Who played basketball with the Boston Celtics, hockey with the Boston Bruins, football with the Detroit Lions and soccer with the Tampa Bay Rowdies?

820. How high is a tennis ball supposed to bounce when it's dropped on concrete from a height of 100 inches?

807. Fourth.

808. Andy Messersmith and Dave McNally, in 1976.

809. Defensive tackle William "The Refrigerator" Perry of the Chicago Bears in 1986. The ring was a size 23.

810. They stood for Eat New Zealand Apples. The New Zealand Apple and Pear Marketing Board was a sponsor of New Zealand's entry in the prestigious regatta.

811. They get 45 seconds per shot—with a $500 fine after 4 violations in a round; an additional $1,000 fine after 8 violations; a two-stroke penalty after 10; and disqualification from the tournament for 12.

812. The Dallas Cowboys and the Pittsburgh Steelers. The game shown is Super Bowl X at the Orange Bowl, won by the Steelers, 21-17.

813. The Green Bay Packers and the Kansas City Chiefs. The Packers won the game, 35-10.

814. Cal Hubbard, the tackle for the Green Bay Packers and New York Giants who became an American League umpire after his retirement from football.

815. Tiger Woods, at the age of 21 in 1997. He won by a margin of twelve strokes—another Master's record.

816. It warns players. in 72 words, not to use the helmet "to butt, ram or spear an opposing player."

817. The intestines of sheep, horses and several other animals—but not from cats. Some believe the word is a shortened form of cattlegut.

818. Former Ohio State football coach Woody Hayes, who was fired for being a bad loser and attacking a Clemson player who intercepted a pass in the closing moments of the 1978 Gator Bowl. Ohio lost, 17-15.

819. Amateur athlete and professional writer George Plimpton.

820. Between 53 and 58 inches, measured from the bottom of the ball, according to the U.S. Lawn Tennis Association. The concrete surface should be a minimum of 4 inches thick.

821. Who was the first seven-footer to play professional basketball?

822. What did the umpires rule when Dave Kingman, batting for the Oakland Athletics in May 1984, smashed a ball 180 feet up into the fabric ceiling of the Minnesota Twins' Metrodome?

823. Who received the first perfect score ever—a 10—in Olympic gymnastic competition?

824. How much do the gloves worn by professional boxers weight. How about Golden Glovers?

825. Why is tennis scored 15, 30, 40 rather than the more traditional 1 point, 2 points, 3 points of other sports?

826. Who threw baseball's last legal spitball?

827. What American multimillionaire was knocked out during a sparring match with world heavyweight champion Jack Dempsey in the 1920s?

828. What baseball card is considered the most valuable?

829. Why was baseball great Charles Dillon Stengel nicknamed Casey?

830. How long does a cowboy have to hang on in a rodeo bull-riding competition?

831. In what direction—clockwise or counterclockwise—do horses race in Europe?

832. What do baseball fans have Reuben Berman to thank for?

833. Four players on the first New York Mets team became major-league managers. Name them.

834. How many characters are the names of registered thoroughbred horses limited to in the United States?

835. What baseball player said, "Some people give their bodies to science, I give mine to baseball"?

821. *Ralph (Sky) Siewert, who played with the St. Louis Bombers and Toronto Huskies. In his 21 games he scored a total of 20 points.*

822. *They called it a ground-rule double. The ball was removed from the ceiling and is now on display at the Baseball Hall of Fame.*

823. *Nadia Comaneci of Romania, in the 1976 Olympics. She was 14 years old at the time.*

824. *Professionals, 8 ounces; Golden Glovers, 10 ounces.*

825. *In its early days as an indoor sport, a tennis game's score was kept by moving the hands of a clock to 15, 30 and 45. Later, for reasons now obscure, the 45 became 40.*

826. *Hall of Famer Burleigh Grimes, for the New York Yankees in 1934. Although the pitch had been outlawed 14 years earlier, those already throwing it were permitted to continue.*

827. *Paul Getty.*

828. *The 1910 Piedmont cigarette card of Honus Wagner. The great Pittsburgh Pirate shortstop was a strict Southern Baptist who disapproved of smoking and asked that his card be discontinued. Only 20 are known to exist.*

829. *His hometown was Kansas City—which led first to the nickname K.C. and then to Casey.*

830. *Eight seconds. The same is true for bareback-bronc and saddle-bronc events.*

831. *Clockwise. In the United States they race counterclockwise.*

832. *His 1921 lawsuit against the New York Giants, which established a fan's right to keep a baseball hit into the stands.*

833. *Gil Hodges, Don Zimmer, Roger Craig and Jim Marshall were the four future managers on Casey Stengel's 1962 Mets.*

834. *Eighteen (including spaces).*

835. *Ron Hunt—who was hit by a record-setting 243 pitches during his career.*

836. What former baseball player, winner of the prestigious jewel-studded Hickok Belt as 1962's Professional Athlete of the Year, lost a court battle with the Internal Revenue Service after claiming the belt as non-taxable income?

837. While visiting Russia in the early 1970s, Phil Esposito and other North American hockey stars removed what they thought was an electronic bugging device from the floor of their Moscow hotel room. What happened?

838. In baseball, how wide is home plate?

839. In 1979 what golfers competed in the first sudden-death playoff in the history of the Masters Tournament?

840. What pitcher was baseball's first 200-game winner?

841. Which Triple Crown race is the shortest?

842. What are the six weapons available in the game of Clue?

843. When Pete Rose of the Cincinnati Reds broke baseball great Ty Cobb's 4,191-hit record on September 11, 1985, what famous ex-slugger said, "If I'd a hit that many singles, I'd a wore a dress"?

844. What baseball star was the first Little Leaguer voted Most Valuable Player of the Year in the big leagues?

845. What horses did jockey Eddie Arcaro ride to the winner's circle in his two Triple Crown victories?

846. How did the game of ninepins, brought to the U.S. by the Dutch in the 1600s, get changed to ten-pins, the popular bowling game of today?

847. Who threw New York Giant Bobby Thomson the pennant-winning home-run pitch in the 1951 National League playoffs?

848. In professional golf, how many clubs is a player limited to during a round?

836. Los Angeles Dodger shortstop Maury Wills, who was honored for stealing 104 bases.

837. They detached the chandelier in the room below and it went crashing to the floor.

838. Seventeen inches.

839. Frank "Fuzzy" Zoeller Jr., Tom Watson and Ed Sneed. Zoeller won.

840. Hall of Famer Albert G. Spalding, a founder, captain, manager and eventual owner of the Chicago White Stockings (now the Cubs) and the man who started the sporting goods company that still bears his name.

841. The Preakness, at 1³⁄₁₆ miles. The Kentucky Derby is 1¼ miles; the Belmont, 1½.

842. A knife, a rope, a candlestick, a lead pipe, a revolver and a wrench.

843. Mickey Mantle.

844. The Philadelphia Phillies' slugging infielder Mike Schmidt, in 1980. He won again in 1981.

845. Whirlaway in 1941; Citation in 1948.

846. Ninepins was outlawed by New York and Connecticut in the 1840s because of heavy gambling. Since the ban didn't forbid bowling in general, a tenth pin was added to circumvent the law.

847. Ralph Branca of the Brooklyn Dodgers, wearing number 13. He gave up the three-run homer in the bottom of the ninth after relieving Don Newcombe.

848. Fourteen.

849. What was the game of softball originally called when its rules were written down in Minneapolis in 1895?

850. What sports hall of fame is located in Ishpeming, Michigan?

851. What was unusual about Stanley Steamer, a five-year-old gelding that lost its one-and-only harness race at Florida's Pompano Park in 1974?

852. What baseball great frowned on exercise, saying, "I believe in training by rising gently up and down from the bench"?

853. Who was known as La Tulipe Noire in France, Il Re in Italy, O Vasilas in Greece and El Peligor in Chile?

854. How tall was 7-foot-2 Kareem Abdul-Jabbar at birth?

855. Among card players, what is a pone?

856. What was the World Series batting average of Shoeless Joe Jackson, one of the eight Chicago White Sox players convicted of accepting bribes to throw the 1919 world championship to the Cincinnati Reds?

857. What professional sport did Dave DeBusschere play before he decided to devote full attention to his basketball career in 1964?

858. Together, baseball-playing brothers Hank and Tommy Aaron hit 768 home runs. How many were Tommy's?

859. Who was the first heavyweight champion in history to lose his title and then regain it?

860. Why was Kansas City Royal slugger George Brett issued a driver's license in 1985 without being required to take a vision test?

861. What is Muhammad Ali's CB (citizens band) handle?

862. Why is nineteenth-century pitcher William Arthur "Candy" Cummings—who had a two-year, 21-22 win-loss record in the major leagues—in the Baseball Hall of Fame?

849. *Kitten ball. It became known as softball in 1926.*

850. *Skiing.*

851. *It was a zebra.*

852. *Hall of Fame pitcher Satchel Paige.*

853. *Brazilian soccer great Pele—who was born Edson Arantes de Nascimento.*

854. *Just a bit taller than the average newborn at 22½ inches, but he weighed a hefty 12 pounds 11 ounces.*

855. *The person who sits to the dealer's right.*

856. *He had the highest average in the series, .375, as well as a perfect fielding record.*

857. *Baseball. He pitched for the Chicago White Sox for two seasons, earning a 3-4 record and a 2.90 ERA in 36 games.*

858. *Thirteen.*

859. *American Floyd Patterson, who lost to Swede Ingemar Johansson in 1959 and then beat him to win the title back a year later.*

860. *According to a Kansas official, "If he can hit .350, we figured he could see."*

861. *Big Bopper.*

862. *He is credited with inventing the curveball in 1866. He got the idea while throwing clam shells on a Brooklyn, New York, beach.*

863. Why was the marathon, originally 26 miles long, increased by 385 yards in 1908?

864. Who was the last baseball player to have a season's batting average over .400?

865. How many games did the longest Wimbledon men's singles match on record last?

866. What unique player restriction is in effect in both polo and jai alai?

867. What was the winning speed when automobile designer Ray Harroun won the first Indianapolis 500 in 1911?

868. What baseball team was the first to introduce numbers as a permanent part of their players' uniforms?

869. What team always marches last in the opening procession of the Olympics?

870. Whose bat was San Francisco Giant slugger Willie Mays using when he slammed four home runs in a single game in April 1961?

871. Who said, "It took me 17 years to get 3,000 hits in baseball. I did it in one afternoon on the golf course"?

872. What football gear did Miami Dolphin running back Woody Bennett introduce and market in 1983?

873. Where can you find the world's largest collection of baseball cards—more than 200,000?

874. What famous American sports figure served as director of physical fitness for the Navy during World War II?

875. What colors were chosen for the five Olympic rings and why?

863. So that the race would finish in front of King Edward VII's royal box in the Olympic Stadium in London.

864. Boston Red Sox slugger Ted Williams, in 1941. His average was .406.

865. It went 112 games, with Pancho Gonzalez beating Charlie Pasarell 22-24, 1-6, 16-14, 6-3, 11-9. It took place in 1969—two years before the tie-breaker was introduced to the game.

866. Left-handers are barred from competition.

867. He averaged 74.59 miles per hour in his Marmon Wasp, the only single-seater in the race and the first car to have a rearview mirror.

868. The New York Yankees, in 1929.

869. The team representing the host nation.

870. Teammate Joe Amalfitano's.

871. Hank Aaron.

872. A lightweight padded girdle to cushion blows.

873. At the prestigious Metropolitan Museum of Art in New York City.

874. Undefeated world heavyweight boxing champion Gene Tunney.

875. The rings are blue, red, yellow, black and green. They were chosen because at least one of them appears in the flag of every nation in the world.

876. What was the bonus paid to players on the Chicago Bears for their 23-21 victory over the New York Giants in the first NFL East-West championship game in 1933?

877. What is the maximum weight permitted for a bowling ball?

878. On her record-breaking English Channel crossing in August 1926, how many miles did Gertrude Ederle have to swim to cover the 21-mile distance between Cape Gris-Nez and Dover?

879. What is the origin of the word furlong—used in horse racing to describe a distance of ⅛ mile?

880. What sport do we have to thank for the phrase "red herring"?

881. How did the axel—the difficult figure-skating jump-turn—get its name?

882. Where did the divining board game "Ouija" get its name?

883. What do the British call the game we know as checkers?

884. What popular game gave us the word "debut"?

885. In mountain-biking slang, what's a snakebite?

886. Members of what football team recorded the rap song "Super Bowl Shuffle" in November 1985—and went on to win Super Bowl XX two months later?

887. Who was the first Japanese-born player in major league baseball in the United States?

888. Which are the most frequently landed-upon properties in the game of Monopoly?

889. How many basic dives are listed on the official Olympic dive chart?

876. They received $210.34 each, plus a free overcoat if they scored a touchdown. The losers received $140.22 each.

877. Sixteen pounds.

878. Thirty-five, because of rough seas. Nevertheless she bettered the world record by an hour and 59 minutes making the crossing in 14 hours and 31 minutes.

879. It dates back to the days when a race was a furrow long—the length of a plowed field.

880. Fox-hunting. In seventeenth-century England, anti-hunt advocates would draw smelly, dried smoked herring across a fox's path to throw the pursuing hounds off the scent.

881. It's named for the Norwegian skater who invented it, Axel Paulsen.

882. From the French and German words for "yes"—oui and ja.

883. Draughts.

884. Billiards. Debut is derived from the French word debuter—to make the first stroke in billiards, to lead off.

885. A flat tire caused by hitting a hard object, resulting in the wheel rim piercing the inner tube, creating a two-hole puncture that resembles a snakebite.

886. The Chicago Bears.

887. Masanori Murakami. He pitched for the San Francisco Giants in 1964 and 1965, compiling a 5-1 record with nine saves. Thirty years later, Hideo Nomo joined the Los Angeles Dodgers as the second Japanese-born major leaguer and was named National League rookie of the year.

888. The four railroads—B & O, Reading, Shortline and Pennsylvania. A survey by Parker Brothers, the manufacturer, found that the odds are 64 percent that a player will land on one of the four in a single trip around the game board. The least landed-on properties—with 24 percent odds—are the dark purple-colored Mediterranean and Baltic avenues.

889. 87—with 348 variations based on body position (straight, pike, tuck or free).

890. What ancient sport gave us the phrase "turning point"?

891. What U.S. city was the first to have a team in the National Hockey League?

892. How many record-setting times was Don Baylor hit by a pitch during his 9 years as a major league baseball player?

893. What did Minnesota Twins players rub for good luck during the 1987 World Series?

894. What baseball great has had his uniform number retired by three teams?

895. How many points did the Denver Nuggets pile up in the 1983 game in which star Kiki Vandeweghe scored his career high of 51 points?

896. What is the maximum height allowed for a fence in equestrian horse-jumping competitions?

897. In 1904 William K. Vanderbilt II created the Vanderbilt Cup for auto racing; for what did Harold S. Vanderbilt establish a Vanderbilt Cup in 1928?

898. What system was used instead of rounds when boxing matches were introduced at the 23rd ancient Olympiad in 776 B.C.?

899. What team's baseball cap did Tom Selleck often wear in his title role in TV's *Magnum, P.I.*?

900. What is the meaning of TWIsM, the name of basketball great Shaquille O'Neals' record label and line of clothing?

901. What major league baseball player retired in 1980 after playing in five different decades?

902. Who was the first American Leaguer to hit four consecutive home runs in one game?

890. *Chariot racing. Turning points were the places where chariot drivers turned at each end of a stadium.*

891. *Boston, in 1924. The league was organized in 1917 with Canadian teams.*

892. *267.*

893. *Teammate Kirby Puckett's shaved head. The Twins defeated the St. Louis Cardinals, 4 games to 3, in the series.*

894. *Nolan Ryan, who pitched a record seven no-hitters during his career. His number, 34, has been retired by the California (Anaheim) Angels, the Texas Rangers and the Houston Astros.*

895. *Denver scored 184 and lost by two points to the Detroit Pistons in triple overtime. The December 13, 1983, contest was the highest-scoring game in NBA history.*

896. *5.6 feet.*

897. *Contract bridge.*

898. *None. Competitors boxed until one man either dropped or raised a fist, conceding defeat. There were no breaks or segments.*

899. *The Detroit Tigers. Selleck is a rabid Tigers fan.*

900. *It stands for "The world is mine," the slogan O'Neal has tattooed on his right biceps—encircling a globe held in the palm of a massive hand.*

901. *Outfielder Minnie Minoso, who started out with the Cleveland Indians in 1949, and ended his career as a pinch hitter for the Chicago White Sox.*

902. *Lou Gehrig, on June 3, 1932. Gehrig, playing for the New York Yankees, hit four-baggers in the first, fourth, fifth and seventh innings against Philadelphia. The Yankees won, 20-13.*

903. What is the fist size—in inches—of James "Big Cat" Williams, the 6-foot-7, 340-pound right tackle of the Chicago Bears?

904. How many bases do major league teams usually have ready for a regular-season game—home plate not included?

905. For what sport did Col. Meriwether Lewis Clark, Jr., develop most of the rules in the United States?

906. In the game of craps, what does the slang term "Little Phoebe" refer to?

907. In the 1950s, grass on golf putting greens was generally mowed to a height of one-quarter inch. What is the average grass height today?

908. What are Blue Professor, Bottle Imp, General Hooker, Tango Triumph, Walla Walls and Rat-Faced McDougal?

909. What baseball great holds the record for winning the greatest number of league batting titles?

910. Who was the only golfer to win three of the four major men's professional tournaments in the same year?

911. For what sport did baseball pitching great Sandy Koufax win a college athletic scholarship?

912. What did archers at the ancient Olympic Games use as targets?

913. What basketball great has been selected for more NBA All-Star teams than any other player?

914. Who was the first catcher in major league baseball history to win the Rookie of the Year award?

915. With what sport did the word "stymie" originate?

916. To what section did the Hollywood Wax Museum move boxer Mike Tyson's figure after his infamous 1997 ear-biting attack on Evander Holyfield?

903. *14½ inches. His biceps are 21 inches; neck, 23; waist, 44; chest, 54.*

904. *Nine.*

905. *Horse racing. He founded Churchill Downs, where the first Kentucky Derby was held in 1875.*

906. *A throw of 5 on the dice.*

907. *One-eighth of an inch. The height has gotten progressively lower through the years.*

908. *Flies used in trout fishing.*

909. *Ty Cobb—with 12 titles.*

910. *Ben Hogan, who won the U.S. Open, the Masters and the British Open in 1953. (The fourth major tournament is the PGA championship.)*

911. *Basketball. He tried out for the University of Cincinnati baseball team only after he learned that it was going on a trip to New Orleans.*

912. *Tethered doves.*

913. *Kareem Abdul-Jabbar. The former Los Angeles Laker was named to 19 All-Star teams.*

914. *Johnny Bench of the Cincinnati Reds, in 1968.*

915. *Golf. To be stymied meant to find an opponent's ball between your ball and the hole on the green. Until 1952, when the rules of golf were changed, the ball had to remain where it was, blocking yours, so that you had to loft your ball to reach the hole.*

916. *The Chamber of Horrors—he was relocated alongside Hannibal Lecter. Tyson's figure was originally in the museum's Sports Hall of Fame.*

917. Baseball fan Robert Heuer won $2,250,000 in the New York State lottery in 1987 with the numbers of his favorite players— DiMaggio, Ford, Mays, Marichal, Stengel and McCovey. What were his winning numbers?

918. To a competitive swimmer, what does the abbreviation d.p.s. mean?

919. What nonstandard item of football clothing did one-time New York Jet quarterback Joe Namath donate to Planet Hollywood?

920. How many cows does it take to make the 22,000 footballs used per season by the teams in the National Football League?

Bonus Trivia

921. The oldest individual to win a medal in the Olympics was Oscar Swahn, who won a silver medal in shooting for Sweden in 1920. He was 72.

922. John Heisman—whose name is commemorated by the award given to college football's best player, the Heisman Trophy—was the coach at Georgia Tech when they set a college football record on October 7, 1916: they slaughtered Cumberland, 222 to 0.

923. The oldest driver in the 1979 Le Mans 24-hour race was actor Paul Newman.

924. ABC-TV's "Monday Night Football" premiered in September, 1970. Its three original commentators were Keith Jackson, Don Meredith and Howard Cosell.

925. Boog Powell, former first baseman for the Baltimore Orioles, was the first baseball player to appear in both the Little League World Series (for Lakeland, Florida) and the Major League World Series.

917. *5, 16, 24, 27, 37 and 44, respectively.*

918. *Distance per stroke.*

919. *The pantyhose he wore on the playing field on chilly days.*

920. *3,000.*

War & the Military

Questions

926. What was the only U.S. battleship to be present at both the Japanese attack on Pearl Harbor, on December 7, 1941, and at the D-Day invasion, on June 6, 1944?

927. What organization has the motto, "Peace Is Our Profession"?

928. How were the height and width of modern American battleships originally determined?

929. What was the first U.S. Navy ship named in honor of a black person?

930. What was the name of the Japanese destroyer that sank PT-109, commanded by Lt. John F. Kennedy, on August 2, 1943?

931. The 7th Earl of Cardigan led the charge of the Light Brigade during the Crimean War. What was the name of the British commander who ordered the ill-fated attack?

932. After German flying ace Manfred von Richthofen was killed in action in World War I, who became commander of his "Flying Circus" fighter squadron?

Answers

926. *The* U.S.S. Nevada.

927. *The U.S. Air Force Strategic Air Command (SAC).*

928. *The ships had to be able to go beneath the Brooklyn Bridge and through the Panama Canal.*

929. *The* U.S.S. Harmon, *named after Leonard Roy Harmon, a mess attendant who was killed at Guadalcanal on July 25, 1943.*

930. *Amigiri.*

931. *Lord Raglan. Both men are better remembered for fashions they introduced during the war—Cardigan for the woolen jacket he designed for his troops, and Raglan for the unique sleeves on the coat he wore.*

932. *Hermann Goering, who went on to become one of Adolf Hitler's closest associates.*

933. What type of aircraft was used to drop bombs in the first German air raids on London in 1915?

934. What is the meaning of the Comanche phrase posah-tai-vo, the term Indian code-talkers in the Army Signal Corps used on the battlefield during World War II to refer to Adolf Hitler?

935. In 1996, which country's army became the last in the world to disband its carrier pigeon service?

936. What were the code names for the five beachheads invaded by the Allies on D-Day, June 6, 1944?

937. What message was transmitted to the French resistance during World War II with the first line of the Paul Verlaine poem *Autumn Song*?

938. In World War II American army slang, what was a GI Moe?

939. Which of the U.S. service academies was the first to admit women?

940. How many times did the nuclear submarine USS Triton surface during its historic 1960 underwater circumnavigation of the globe?

941. In what war was the color khaki first used for uniforms?

942. How many crewmembers and officers were required to run the Britannia, Great Britain's 412-foot royal yacht?

943. Where is Yalta—the city where President Franklin D. Roosevelt met with Russia's Joseph Stalin and England's Winston Churchill in 1945 to plan the final defeat of Nazi Germany?

944. Who was issued ID number 01 when the U.S. military started issuing dog tags in 1918?

945. What animal did the Carthaginians use to defeat the Romans at sea during the third century B.C.?

946. Who was the first to use the term "atomic bomb"?

933. A zeppelin.

934. Crazy white man.

935. Switzerland's. Its army owned 7,000 pigeons and had another 23,000 privately owned birds on standby in case of a national emergency. The pigeon service was disbanded in hopes of saving money and instituting a more modern communications system.

936. Utah, Omaha, Gold, Juno and Sword.

937. That the D-Day landings were about to begin. The line from Verlaine was: "The long sobs / Of the violins of autumnÖ"

938. An army mule.

939. The Coast Guard Academy, in July 1976.

940. Twice—once to remove a sick crew member, and once to pay tribute to Ferdinand Magellan on the island of Mactan in the Philippines, where the explorer was killed in 1521 during his circumnavigation of the globe.

941. The Afghan War in 1880—the color was considered good camouflage.

942. Crew, 230; officers, 20. The yacht, christened by Queen Elizabeth II in 1953 and decommissioned in 1997 was costing $18.5 million a year to operate.

943. In the Crimea, in the Soviet Union.

944. General John J. Pershing.

945. Snakes. The Carthaginians catapulted earthenware pots of poisonous snakes onto the decks of the Roman ships.

946. Science fiction writer H.G. Wells, in the story The World Set Free, written in 1914.

947. What was the cause of the brief undeclared war that broke out between Honduras and El Salvador in July 1969?

948. What did the famous backstage mother of actress Ginger Rogers do during World War I?

949. How did wartime conservation efforts affect the Oscars handed out at Academy Award ceremonies during World War II?

950. Soldiers of what nation do not have to salute officers and are paid overtime for KP and other undesirable assignments?

951. How did Napoleon Bonaparte finance his invasion of Russia in 1812?

952. What bathtub-bathing edict did England's King George VI issue for Buckingham Palace and Windsor Castle to cut down on the use of fuel during World War II?

953. When World War II ended in 1945, how many enlisted men and women were in the nation's armed services?

954. What is a military contractor referring to when talking about a "manually powered fastener-driving impact device"?

955. For what expenditure did the tiny European principality of Andorra allocate its entire national defense budget of $5 twenty years ago?

956. What utensil were British sailors forbidden to use until the very late nineteenth century because it was considered both unmanly and harmful to discipline?

957. Who beat out Frank Sinatra as the favorite singer of American servicemen in Europe in a poll taken during World War II?

958. As a young naval officer serving in World War II, what famous American set up the only hamburger stand in the South Pacific?

959. In a military contract, what item is referred to as a "portable, hand-held communications inscriber"?

947. El Salvador's victory over Honduras in the three-game World Cup soccer play-off. The war is known as the Soccer War.

948. Lela Rogers was a Marine sergeant.

949. They were made out of wood—gilded wood, of course. After the war, they were replaced by real Oscars.

950. The Netherlands, whose army was fully unionized in the 1960s.

951. With counterfeit money. After printing it at a factory he set up in Paris, he used it to purchase military supplies.

952. He decreed that tubs could be filled with no more than five inches of water—and had lines painted at the five-inch level to make the depth of his commitment clear.

953. Almost eleven million (10,795,775).

954. A hammer.

955. For bullets (blanks), for ceremonial salutes to guest dignitaries.

956. The fork.

957. Country singer Ray Acuff. During the war, correspondent Ernie Pyle wrote of a Japanese attack that was preceded by the battle cry: "To hell with Roosevelt! To hell with Babe Ruth! To hell with Roy Acuff!"

958. President-to-be Richard M. Nixon, who was a Navy lieutenant at the time. At Nixon's Snack Shack, he served free hamburgers and Australian beer to flight crews.

959. A pencil.

960. How long did the Battle of Waterloo last?

961. When during World War II did Russia declare war on Japan?

962. How many oarsmen were carried aboard triremes—the fast-moving warships that helped the Greeks rule the Mediterranean during the fifth century B.C.?

963. How many pounds of feed were consumed daily by the 5,000 horses that pulled the artillery for Napoleon's Army of the North in 1815?

964. For whom was Italian dictator Benito Mussolini named?

965. How many inmates were liberated from the Bastille after it was stormed by an angry mob on July 14, 1789, at the start of the French Revolution?

966. How did the Dutch in Amsterdam mobilize to defeat the invading Spanish during the winter of 1572-73?

967. What did the real Butch Cassidy do after escaping to Bolivia with his partner-in-crime, the Sundance Kid?

968. What problem in expressing themselves did Aristotle, Sir Isaac Newton, Moses and Charles Darwin have in common?

969. Where did Adolf Hitler's sister-in-law work during World War II?

970. Who was the first American congressman to don a uniform following the Japanese attack on Pearl Harbor on December 7, 1941?

971. The U.S. government entered the nuclear arms race in 1940 when it issued a grant for research into an atomic bomb. How much was allocated?

972. What famous former public figure commanded the squadron of torpedo boats in which John F. Kennedy served as a skipper during World War II?

960. *About nine and a half hours.*

961. *On August 8, 1945—two days after the U.S. bombed Hiroshima.*

962. *170—they were seated at banks of 31, 27 and 27 oars on each side of the ship.*

963. *10,000 pounds—or 50 tons. That comes to 20 pounds per horse.*

964. *Mexican liberator Benito Juarez.*

965. *Seven.*

966. *The ice-locked Dutch routed the Spanish on skates.*

967. *Cassidy, whose real name was Robert LeRoy Parker, reportedly returned to the U.S. and went into the adding machine manufacturing business.*

968. *They all stuttered.*

969. *For British War Relief in New York City. Bridget Hitler was the Irish-born wife of Hitler's older half-brother, Alois.*

970. *President-to-be Lyndon Johnson, who served in the Navy.*

971. *$6,000.*

972. *John N. Mitchell, who went on to become U.S. attorney general in the Nixon administration.*

973. Why did U.S. secret agents abandon plans—approved by President Franklin D. Roosevelt—to drop live bats from airplanes to frighten the Japanese during World War II?

974. What unsung role did William Dawes and Samuel Prescott play in American history?

975. Why was infantryman (and actor-to-be) James Arness picked to go first when the troops aboard his landing craft splashed ashore during the Allied attack at Anzio during World War II?

976. How much money in U.S. humanitarian aid did the Nicaraguan contras spend on deodorant in 1985 and 1986?

977. What was the profession of Hitler's mistress, Eva Braun?

978. During the Civil War, how many states fought for the Union; how many for the Confederacy?

979. What two nations were involved in a year-long conflict that was popularly known as the Pastry War?

980. What president ordered the integration of America's armed forces?

981. What famous American signed the Treaty of Kanagawa?

982. Adolf Hitler called his country home Eagle's Nest. What name did Winston Churchill give to his?

983. What American billionaire tried to airlift 28 tons of medicine and Christmas gifts to American POWs in North Vietnam in 1969?

984. Charles de Gaulle served as ghost-writer of the book "The Soldier" for what famous World War I military hero?

985. How does Lockheed, manufacturer of the Trident missile, transmit data from its Sunnyvale, California, headquarters to its plant thirty miles away in Santa Cruz?

986. During whose presidency was the U.S. War Dept. replaced by the Defense Dept.?

973. *The bats froze at high altitudes, before they could be released.*

974. *They accompanied Paul Revere on his celebrated midnight ride to warn their countrymen that "the British are coming."*

975. *At 6 feet 6, he was the tallest man in his outfit—and his commanding officer wanted to know just how deep the water was.*

976. *$5,760—the expenditure was approved by the State Department's Nicaraguan Humanitarian Assistance Office.*

977. *Photographer's assistant.*

978. *For the Union, 23; for the Confederacy, 11.*

979. *France and Mexico, in 1838. It was triggered by Mexico's refusal to pay for damage done by Mexican army officers to a restaurant run by a French pastry chef in Tacubaya, now a section of Mexico City.*

980. *Harry S. Truman, in 1948.*

981. *Commodore Matthew C. Perry, on March 31, 1854. The treaty opened Japan to western trade.*

982. *Cosy Pig, although it was formally known as Chartwell.*

983. *Ross Perot.*

984. *Marshal Philippe Pétain, whose 1945 death sentence for collaboration during WWII was commuted by de Gaulle to life imprisonment.*

985. *By carrier pigeon.*

986. *Harry S. Truman's, in 1947.*

987. What famous American patriot served as a rear admiral in the Russian navy?

988. What actress obtained a patent as co-inventor of a radar-controlled system to direct torpedoes at moving ships?

989. When the British garrison at Khartoum was under siege in 1884, who organized the 1,500-boat flotilla of troops and supplies that came to its rescue?

990. Where was the Battle of Bunker Hill actually fought in June 1775?

991. What was the Allies' password on D-Day?

992. What American military leader said, "Lafayette we are here," and on what occasion?

993. What physical ailment is said to have contributed to Napoleon's defeat at Waterloo?

994. What war was the first to have authorized film coverage?

995. "GI Joe" won the Dickins Medal for saving a thousand British solders from a bombing attack in Italy during World War II. Who was he and what's the Dickins Medal?

996. In 1969 the Navy spent $375,000 on an "aerodynamic analysis of the self-suspended flare." What was the study's conclusion?

997. Why did Caedwalla, King of Gwynedd (north Wales), order his soldiers to wear leeks fastened to their helmets when they battled the troops of King Edwin of Northumbria in 632 A.D.?

998. During World War I, what famous American directed U.S. Navy research in torpedo mechanisms and anti-submarine devices?

999. What sport had been played on the court at Stagg Field in Chicago that was converted into the Manhattan Project laboratory where scientists achieved the first self-sustaining nuclear chain reaction in history?

987. *John Paul Jones, who won several naval victories in Russian encounters with the Turks in 1788.*

988. *Hedy Lamarr. Her co-inventor was composer George Antheil.*

989. *The travel agency Thomas Cook & Son, for a fee of $15 million.*

990. *On Breed's Hill, southeast of Bunker Hill.*

991. *"Mickey Mouse."*

992. *Gen. Black Jack Pershing, arriving in France in 1917 after the U.S. entered WWI.*

993. *Hemorrhoids, which prevented him from surveying the battlefield on horseback.*

994. *The Boer War (1899-1902).*

995. *He was a pigeon, one of thirty-one WWII pigeons to receive Britain's "Animal Victoria Cross."*

996. *The Frisbee isn't feasible as military hardware.*

997. *So he could tell his men from the enemy. Caedwalla was victorious, Edwin was slain, and the leek later became the national emblem of Wales.*

998. *Thomas Edison, who served as head of the Naval Consulting Board.*

999. *Squash.*

1000. What military firsts were achieved by Benjamin O. Davis Sr. and Benjamin O. Davis Jr.?

1001. What actor has attained the highest U.S. military rank in history for an entertainer?

1002. Before the U.S. Navy adopted the standard 21-gun salute in 1841, how many blasts did its warships fire when they sailed into foreign ports?

1003. What was a tenth-century Chinese alchemist trying to discover when he accidentally produced gunpowder?

1004. On what side did British-born newspaperman-explorer Henry Morton Stanley (of "Dr. Livingston, I presume" fame) fight in the American Civil War?

1005. What rank did Russian czar Peter the Great give himself in the Russian Army?

1006. In the military world, what is EGADS?

1007. Who was Andrea Doria—the person for whom the famous passenger ship was named?

1008. You may remember the Alamo, but do you know what the word means in Spanish?

1009. What did the Marquis de Lafayette, America's Revolutionary War ally, name his only son?

1010. Who were Michael Strank, Harlon H. Block, Franklin R. Sousley, Ira Hayes, Rene Gagnon and John H. Bradley, and how have they been memorialized?

1011. Why was actor Paul Newman disqualified from the Navy's pilot-training program during World War II?

1012. What was the name of the barbaric German tribe that overran Gaul, Spain and North Africa and sacked Rome in the fifth century?

1000. *In 1940, Davis Sr. became the first black general in U.S. Army history; in 1954, his son Davis Jr. became the first black general in U.S. Air Force history.*

1001. *James Stewart, who rose to the rank of brigadier general in the U.S. Air Force Reserve.*

1002. *One for each state in the Union.*

1003. *A formula for immortality.*

1004. *Both. He first joined the Confederate Army, but after being captured at Shiloh, he enlisted in the Union Navy to avoid imprisonment.*

1005. *None. He served as a common soldier in the artillery.*

1006. *The signal used when it's necessary to destroy a missile in flight. EGADS is an acronym for Electronic Ground Automatic Destruct System.*

1007. *He was a sixteenth-century Genoese admiral who was known as the "Father of Peace" and the "Liberator of Genoa."*

1008. *Cottonwood.*

1009. *George Washington Lafayette.*

1010. *They were the six servicemen who raised the American flag on Mount Suribachi on Iwo Jima during World War II—and who are memorialized in the dramatic 78-foot-high Iwo Jima Monument in Arlington, Virginia.*

1011. *Newman's dazzling blue eyes are colorblind.*

1012. *The Vandals.*

1013. Lt. Col. George Armstrong Custer paid a $127.80 premium for a life insurance policy in 1874, two years before the Battle of Little Bighorn. How much was his coverage?

1014. By what name did Chief Crazy Horse know the Little Bighorn River, the scene of Custer's last stand?

1015. At a 1986 auction, what was the winning bid for two arrows from the Battle of Little Bighorn?

1016. What state was the setting of the Battle of the Little Bighorn, where George Armstrong Custer made his infamous last stand?

1017. What was George Armstrong Custer's rank when he was killed at Little Bighorn in 1876?

1018. Who fired the first Union shot of the Civil War?

1019. What nation was the first to use frogmen in warfare?

1020. What did the U.S. military name in honor of American physiologist Ancel Keys?

1021. What major Japanese company made the famous Zero fighter plane during World War II?

1022. How long—in days—did the 1991 Persian Gulf War last?

1023. Translated from Pentagon doublespeak, what is a "combat emplacement evacuator"?

1024. The site of what state capital was given to the Marquis de Lafayette for his services during the Revolutionary War?

1025. When Adolf Hitler declared himself ruler of the Third Reich, what did he view as Germany's first and second reichs?

1026. To celebrate the patriots' success in getting the British to evacuate Boston on this day in 1776, Gen. George Washington chose "Boston" as his army's password of the day. What did he pick as the proper response?

1013. *It was for $5,000.*

1014. *The Greasy Grass River.*

1015. *$17,000.*

1016. *Montana.*

1017. *Lieutenant Colonel.*

1018. *Gen. Abner Doubleday, in 1861, at Fort Sumter. He is the same Abner Doubleday who is often incorrectly given credit for inventing baseball.*

1019. *Italy, in December 1941, against the British in the Mediterranean. Three frogmen disabled the British battleships Valiant and Queen Elizabeth, as well as a tanker and a destroyer, in Alexandria harbor.*

1020. *The K ration—the small packet of food, containing all the essential nutrients, that served as emergency rations for soldiers in the field.*

1021. *Mitsubishi. The company now known for its cars, TVs and hundreds of other products, was prohibited from producing aircraft for seven years after the war.*

1022. *42 days from January 16 to February 27.*

1023. *A shovel.*

1024. *Tallahassee, Florida. Lafayette never occupied the then-wilderness site, but one of the city's early residents was a nephew of Napoleon Bonaparte, Prince Napoleon Achille Murat, who married a grandniece of George Washington.*

1025. *The first was the Holy Roman Empire of Charlemagne; the second was Bismarck's united Germany, declared in 1871 and known as the German Empire.*

1026. *St. Patrick.*

1027. What childhood name was shared by Gen. George A. Custer and Chief Crazy Horse, the Oglala Sioux leader he faced at the Battle of the Little Bighorn?

1028. How long did it take Napoleon to send a message from Rome to Paris—almost 700 miles—using a semaphore system to signal from mountaintop to mountaintop?

1029. The walls of what structure—made entirely of natural material—stand up better to modern artillery than a concrete barricade, according to tests conducted by the Swedish army?

1030. What film was based on the Civil War exploits of the 54th Massachusetts Infantry Regiment?

1031. Where did Napoleon Bonaparte bid farewell to his imperial guard in 1814?

1032. In World War II Navy slang, what was an airdale?

1033. What was the daily ration of hard liquor for soldiers in the Continental Army during the Revolutionary War?

1034. During World War II, what wearing apparel were American women encouraged to turn in for use in making parachutes?

1035. What army did the Greeks defeat at the battle of Marathon in 490 B.C.?

1036. How many members of Lt. Col. George Armstrong Custer's family were killed at the Battle of Little Big Horn?

1037. A pin-up photo of what actress adorned the first test bomb dropped on Bikini atoll in the Marshall Islands in July 1946?

1038. What European country—the last surviving monarchy of the Holy Roman Empire—hasn't had an army since 1868?

1039. What was the name of Japanese propagandist Tokyo Rose's World War II radio show for U.S. servicemen in the Pacific?

1027. *Curly.*

1028. *Four hours.*

1029. *The igloo. Not only do its walls absorb an artillery blast, but they are almost invisible from the air and can't be spotted by the infrared sensors that guide today's missiles.*

1030. *Glory. The 54th was one of two black regiments formed by Massachusetts in 1862. Massachusetts was the first state to have blacks in its organized militia.*

1031. *In the courtyard at Fontainebleau Palace—which is now known as the Adieux Courtyard. In French, adieux means "farewell."*

1032. *A naval aviation recruit.*

1033. *Four ounces—when available.*

1034. *Their nylon stockings—which were melted down and turned into parachute fabric.*

1035. *The Persian army. The marathon race commemorates the run a Greek courier made from the battlefield to Athens to deliver news of the victory before collapsing and dying of exhaustion.*

1036. *Five, counting Custer. Those who died with him were his half-brothers, Tom and Boston; a nephew, Harry Armstrong Reed; and a brother-in-law, James Calhoun.*

1037. *Rita Hayworth.*

1038. *Liechtenstein.*

1039. *Zero Hour.*

1040. Why did the British Broadcasting Company (BBC) play the opening bars of Beethoven's Fifth Symphony in all its broadcasts to Europe during World War II?

1041. What was the name of General Robert E. Lee's favorite horse before he bought it for $175 and rechristened it Traveller?

1042. Before going into battle, what did the notorious pirate Blackbeard put under his tricorn to frighten those he was attacking?

1043. What were the names of the horses ridden by Napoleon Bonaparte and the Duke of Wellington at the Battle of Waterloo?

1044. What bird's name has been given to the U.S. Marine tilt-rotor transport that takes off and lands like a helicopter, but flies like an airplane?

1045. What were the Q-ships put to sea by the United States and Britain during World War I?

1046. Who lead the U.S. marine detachment that captured abolitionist John Brown following his 1859 raid on the federal arsenal at Harper's Ferry?

1047. What was the full name of the V-2 rocket developed by Wernher von Braun for the Germans during World War II?

1048. What was the only southern town to remain in Union hands throughout the Civil War?

1049. Who was the führer of Germany when World War II ended?

1050. In the event of a nuclear holocaust, what artifact did architect Frank Lloyd Wright believe would be excavated in great quantity from the ruins of twentieth-century civilization?

1051. What entertainer sold more U.S. war bonds than anyone else during World War II?

1040. *Because its familiar "dah-dah-dah-DAAAAH" opening is the same as Morse code for the letter v (dot-dot-dot-dash)—the symbol adopted for "victory."*

1041. *Jeff Davis.*

1042. *Slow-burning fuses that would wreath his head in black smoke.*

1043. *Napoleon rode the white stallion Marengo; Wellington, the chestnut Copenhagen. Both men named their mounts after famous battle sites where they had been victorious.*

1044. *Osprey. The aircraft is also known as the V-22.*

1045. *They were heavily armed warships camouflaged as harmless merchant vessels, which were used to lure German U-boats to their destruction. When a German submarine surfaced to attack (saving its torpedoes for armed vessels), the Q-ship dropped its dummy bulwarks and opened fire.*

1046. *Robert E. Lee, then a colonel.*

1047. *Vergeltungswaffe Zwei—Revenge Weapon Two.*

1048. *Key West, Florida, the southernmost city in the continental United States.*

1049. *Grand Admiral Karl Doenitz. Hitler appointed Doenitz before taking his own life a week before the Nazi surrender.*

1050. *The vitreous china toilet bowl.*

1051. *Kate "God Bless America" Smith. She sold $600 million worth.*

1052. What American actor was given the British Distinguished Service Cross for commanding a flotilla of raiding craft for Admiral Louis Mountbatten's commandos during World War II

1053. What great military leader was an accomplished yo-yo player?

1054. Who was Emil R. Goldfus of Brooklyn, New York?

1055. What was the first war in which soldiers wore machine-made uniforms?

1056. At the Battle of the Marne in 1914, how were French reinforcements rushed from Paris to the front in order to help fend off the advancing Germans?

1057. Who signed Major Clark Gable's army discharge papers in 1944?

1058. How did the army of Persian king Xerxes I cross the Hellespont—the strait between Europe and Asia—in 480 B.C.?

1059. Who was the youngest U.S. Army officer ever to be promoted to general?

1060. How many stars were on the American flag during the Spanish-American War in 1898?

1061. For what did General John J. "Black Jack" Pershing win a Pulitzer Prize in 1932?

1062. Following the British defeat at Dunkirk in June 1940, who made the stirring broadcast vowing that "we shall fight in the fields and in the streets...we shall never surrender"?

1063. What was the inspiration for the name Rough Riders—the name of the elite fighting unit Theodore Roosevelt organized for the Spanish-American War?

1064. How many years did Hyman Rickover, the man credited with propelling the Navy into the nuclear age, serve on active duty÷

1052. *Douglas Fairbanks Jr.*

1053. *Napoleon's nemesis, the Duke of Wellington. At the time, the yo-yo was known as a bandalore.*

1054. *Colonel Rudolf Abel, the Soviet intelligence agent convicted of spying in 1957, who was exchanged for downed American U-2 reconnaissance pilot Francis Gary Powers in 1962.*

1055. *The American Civil War.*

1056. *In commandeered Renault taxis. Each cabbie was paid a 27-percent tip on top of his metered fare.*

1057. *President-to-be Ronald Reagan, then a captain.*

1058. *On two bridges of boats. Alexander the Great duplicated the feat 146 years later.*

1059. *George Custer, a graduate of West Point, who became a general at age 23—14 years before his infamous battle of Little Big Horn.*

1060. *Forty-five. The five states not yet admitted to the Union and not represented on the flag were Oklahoma, New Mexico, Arizona, Alaska and Hawaii.*

1061. *History, for his book* My Experiences in the World War.

1062. *British actor Norman Shelley. He sounded just like Winston Churchill and read the address so that the prime minister could deal with pressing matters of state.*

1063. *The Rough Riders Hotel in Medora, North Dakota, where Roosevelt had tried ranching.*

1064. *Sixty—he was forced to retire at age 82 by President Ronald Reagan.*

1065. Who were the two servicemen who carried the American flag as Jeanette MacDonald sang the national anthem at the wartime Oscar awards ceremony in 1943?

1066. How many volumes made up the Pentagon Papers, the Defense Department's study of U.S. involvement in the Vietnam War?

1067. How did the MiG, the famous Soviet jet fighter, get its name?

1068. What did Dutch-born German spy Mata Hari wear to her firing squad execution in October 1917?

1069. In Air Force slang, what is the meaning of the term "laundry bag"?

1070. How many pushups do young female recruits have to do in two minutes to pass U.S. Army basic training? How about their male counterparts?

1071. What was the first enemy fighting ship captured by the U.S. Navy after the War of 1812?

1072. What is the meaning of the U.S. Coast Guard motto, semper paratus?

1073. What Revolutionary War figure laid the cornerstone of the Bunker Hill Monument on June 17, 1825—the 50th anniversary of the famous battle?

1074. How many masts are on the *U.S.S. Constitution*, the historic square-rigged flagship of the U.S. Navy popularly known as "Old Ironsides"?

1075. What insect served as Napoleon Bonaparte's official emblem?

1076. Where would a soldier wear a havelock?

1077. In which state is the Wyoming Battle Monument located?

1065. *Marine private Tyrone Power and Army private Alan Ladd.*

1066. *Forty-seven—they included 3,000 pages of text, 4,000 pages of documents and weighed 60 pounds.*

1067. *From the names of the plane's designers, Artem Mikoyan and Mikhail I. Gurevich.*

1068. *Black—black velvet, fur-trimmed cape; black silk stockings; black kid gloves; and large floppy black hat with a black silk ribbon.*

1069. *It's a parachute.*

1070. *Women, a minimum of 17; men, a minimum of 40.*

1071. *The U-505, a World War II German submarine. It was captured in the Atlantic off the coast of French West Africa in 1944 and is now on exhibit at the Museum of Science and Industry in Chicago.*

1072. *Always prepared.*

1073. *The Marquis de Lafayette, who was visiting the U.S. at the time. Daniel Webster made the key address.*

1074. *Three. The warship, first launched in 1797, was restored at a cost of $12 million and is now on exhibit in Boston.*

1075. *The bumblebee.*

1076. *On his head, in the desert. It's the light cloth covering, attached to a military cap, that protects the back of a soldier's neck from the sun. It was named for Sir Henry Havelock, a British officer who served in India.*

1077. *In Pennsylvania. The monument commemorates a July 1778 Revolutionary War battle in which a group of Loyalists and Indians massacred settlers in Wyoming Valley in northeastern Pennsylvania.*

1078. What auto maker built the first armored tanks used by U.S. troops in battle?

1079. What baseball Hall of Famer was court-martialed for refusing to take a seat in the back of a U.S. Army bus?

1080. What future U.S. Army general participated in the 1912 Olympics in Stockholm, Sweden?

1081. Which controversial hero graduated at the bottom of his West Point class in 1861?

1082. What twentieth-century American general had a grandfather who was a Confederate brigadier general in the Civil War, and a great-great-great-grandfather who was a general in the Revolutionary War?

1083. What was the name of Adolf Hitler's favorite dog—the Alsatian he used to make sure his cyanide capsules were lethal?

1078. *Renault. The French-made tanks first saw service in the Battle of St. Mihiel on September 12, 1918. No American-made tanks were used in World War I.*

1079. *Jackie Robinson, in 1944, while a second lieutenant. He was acquitted.*

1080. *George S. Patton, who was a contestant in the pentathlon.*

1081. *Gen. George Armstrong Custer.*

1082. *George S. Patton.*

1083. *Blondi. Hitler used the cyanide to commit suicide after seeing that it worked on Blondi.*

Television & Radio

Questions

1084. What was the name of ventriloquist Edgar Bergen's female dummy?

1085. What actress was the high-school girlfriend of Judge Joseph A. Wapner of TV's *The People's Court*?

1086. Who turned down the role of Columbo before Peter Falk was signed up for the TV detective series?

1087. What TV newsman lived with a tribe of headhunters for a month after bailing out of a crippled military plane in the Himalayas during World War II?

1088. What TV personality had four skywriting planes draw a three-mile-wide Valentine's Day heart for his wife?

1089. What is the name of Oscar the Grouch's pet worm on TV's *Street Street*?

1090. Two members of TV's *A Team* had names with initials— B.A. Baracus and H.M. Murdock. What do the initials represent?

1091. Why does Mr. Spock of TV's *Star Trek* have green skin?

Answers

1084. *Effie Klinker.*

1085. *Lana Turner.*

1086. *Bing Crosby.*

1087. *Eric Sevareid.*

1088. *Garry Moore. The heart was pierced by a six-mile-long arrow and had the names "Garry & Nell"—written inside.*

1089. *Slimey.*

1090. *B.A. is for Bad Attitude; H.M., for Howling Mad.*

1091. *Because of traces of nickel and copper in his blood.*

1092. On whose 1932 talk and variety show did comedian Jack Benny make his radio debut?

1093. What was the radio show *Inner Sanctum* originally called?"

1094. What famous family comedy act started on the road to success as the Six Mascots, featuring brothers Leonard, Adolph, Julius, Milton, mother Minnie and aunt Hannah?

1095. How old was Clark Kent when he landed his job at the *Daily Planet* on the *Superman* TV series starring George Reeves?

1096. "You rang?" were the only words spoken by Lurch, the 7-foot-tall butler on TV's *The Addams Family*. What other TV sitcom character also popularized the phrase?

1097. What was the TV soap opera *One Life To Live* originally going to be called?

1098. On TV's *The Honeymooners*, who earned more money—bus driver Ralph Kramden or sewer worker Ed Norton?

1099. What was the first name of Lieutenant Columbo, portrayed on TV by Peter Falk?

1100. Who wrote "Johnny's Theme," the signature music of Johnny Carson's *Tonight Show*?

1101. What were the names of Woody Woodpecker's niece and nephew?

1102. What was the biggest jackpot ever won on TV's *The $64,000 Question*?

1103. Who was the television clown whose nose blinked the message *CBS Presents* and whose bald head proclaimed *The Big Top* from July 1950 to September 1957?

1104. Who was the first black entertainer to star in a dramatic TV series?

1092. *Ed Sullivan's. Others first heard on the radio on Sullivan's show included Irving Berlin and George M. Cohan.*

1093. The Squeaky Door.

1094. *The Marx brothers. Leonard later became Chico; Adolph, Harpo; Julius, Groucho; and Milton, Gummo.*

1095. *He was 25.*

1096. *Maynard G. Krebs on* The Many Loves of Dobie Gillis.

1097. Between Heaven and Hell. *The title was rejected as too racy by ABC-TV executives before its debut in July 1968.*

1098. *Their weekly pay was the same—$62.*

1099. *Phillip.*

1100. *Paul Anka, with Johnny Carson.*

1101. *Splinter was his niece; Knothead, his nephew.*

1102. *Three times $64,000—for a total of $192,000. The winner, a 10-year-old fifth-grader named Robert Strom, hit the jackpot on April 16, 1957.*

1103. *Johnny Carson's announcer-sidekick Ed McMahon.*

1104. *Bill Cosby, in* I Spy *in 1965.*

1105. What are the names of the two old codgers who wisecrack from their box seats on *The Muppet Show*?

1106. What was Johnny Carson's famous reply when a reporter asked what he would like his epitaph to be?

1107. What 1949 television program was the very first coast-to-coast network show?

1108. What great American tried to stump the celebrity panel on TV's *Masquerade Party* by showing up in a penguin costume?

1109. Who played Beau Maverick on the TV Western comedy series *Maverick*?

1110. Where did *M*A*S*H* army surgeon Hawkeye Pierce hail from?

1111. What did *Candid Camera* creator Alan Funt do before he started catching people off-guard with his hidden camera?

1112. In real life—and in TV script—who was married at the Byram River Beagle Club in Greenwich, Connecticut?

1113. What four actresses played Sid Caesar's wife during his run on *Your Show of Shows*?

1114. What was the waist size of the Ralph Kramden bus driver's uniform that Jackie Gleason gave to R.A.L.P.H. (Royal Association for the Longevity & Preservation of the Honeymooners)?

1115. Who provided Superman's radio voice in the 1940s?

1116. How many plumes were on the tail of the original NBC peacock?

1117. What were the only words spoken by Clarabell the Clown on *The Howdy Doody Show*?

1118. What popular television and movie actor served as senior director of news and special events for ABC-TV before launching his career as a performer?

1105. *Statler and Waldorf.*

1106. *"I'll be right back."*

1107. Kukla, Fan and Ollie.

1108. *Explorer Richard E. Byrd, who made the first flights over both the North and South Poles and established the* Little America *base in Antarctica.*

1109. *Roger Moore.*

1110. *Crab Apple Cove, Maine.*

1111. *He caught people off-guard with a hidden microphone on a successful radio show called* Candid Microphone.

1112. *Lucille Ball and Desi Arnaz.*

1113. *Imogene Coca, Nanette Fabray, Janet Blair and Gisele Mackenzie.*

1114. *It was 49¾ inches.*

1115. *TV emcee Bud Collyer, who also supplied the Man of Steel's voice for the animated television series in 1966.*

1116. *Eleven.*

1117. *"Good bye kids," on the 2,343rd-and-last episode of the popular kiddie show on September 30, 1960.*

1118. *Telly Savalas.*

1119. To what tribe did Jay Silverheels, who played Tonto on TV's *The Lone Ranger,* belong?

1120. What was the address of Big Bird's nest on TV's *Sesame Street?*

1121. How many fingers does Mickey Mouse have on each hand?

1122. Who portrayed Elvis Presley in the 1981 made-for-TV film *Elvis and the Beauty Queen?*

1123. What subject was actor Errol Flynn questioned about when he appeared as a contestant on the mid-1950s TV quiz show *The Big Surprise?*

1124. What popular stand-up comic turned down the role of Trapper John McIntyre in the TV sitcom *M*A*S*H* before Wayne Rogers signed on for the part?

1125. How many opening monologues did Johnny Carson deliver during his 30 years as host of *The Tonight Show?*

1126. What television personality appeared as a kiss-and-tell lothario who is murdered in the 1992 Perry Mason TV episode entitled *The Case of the Reckless Romeo* ?

1127. What American TV personality, while an art student in Italy, appeared as a dancing meatball in an Italian TV commercial and also was in the food orgy scene in Fellini's *Satyricon?*

1128. What was the number of the mobile hospital unit Hawkeye Pierce and Hot Lips Houlihan belonged to on TV's *M*A*S*H* ?

1129. What comic strip character did Gary Burghoff play off-Broadway before he became known to moviegoers and TV viewers as Corporal Radar O'Reilly of *M*A*S*H* ?

1130. On what early 1950s children's TV show did acting unknowns and future *Odd Couple* Tony Randall and Jack Klugman meet?

1131. What was the name of the church to which comedian Flip Wilson's character Reverend Leroy belonged?

1119. *Mohawk. He was born on the Six Nations Indian Reservation in Ontario, Canada.*

1120. *123½ Sesame Street.*

1121. *Four.*

1122. *Don Johnson.*

1123. *Sailing. Flynn won $30,000.*

1124. *Robert Klein.*

1125. *4,531.*

1126. *Tabloid TV star Geraldo Rivera.*

1127. *Fitness guru Richard Simmons.*

1128. *The 4077.*

1129. *He played Charlie Brown in the musical* You're a Good Man, Charlie Brown, *in 1967.*

1130. Captain Video and His Video Rangers.

1131. *The Church of What's Happening Now.*

1132. What was the name of the horse-ghost buddy of cartoon character Casper, the Friendly Ghost?

1133. What role did Art Carney play in Jackie Gleason's very first *Honeymooners* sketch?

1134. Who was the first mystery guest to appear on the TV quiz show *What's My Line* in 1950?

1135. In the TV sitcom *Mork and Mindy*, how far from Earth was Ork, Mork's home planet?

1136. What TV sitcom family lived at 1313 Mockingbird Lane?

1137. What was the theme song Jack Benny played off-key on his violin?

1138. What character actress provides the voice of mother Marge on TV's animated sitcom *The Simpsons* ?

1139. What is the only radio station in the United States with call letters that spell out the name of its home city?

1140. What famous American won $15,000 on the TV quiz show *Name That Tune* ? Hint: One of the 25 songs he named correctly was "Far Away Places."

1141. Who portrayed a wacky housewife in a 1948 radio series called *My Favorite Husband* ?

1142. What car did TV's Archie Bunker recall fondly in "Those Were the Days," the theme song of the sitcom *All in the Family* ?

1143. What actress, as a 12-year-old, won $32,000, on TV's *$64,000* Challenge" and later admitted she had been given the answers in advance?

1144. What was the name Walt Disney originally proposed for Mickey Mouse?

1145. What famous Hollywood star turned down the role of Marshal Matt Dillon on TV's *Gunsmoke* before James Arness was offered the part?

1132. *Nightmare.*

1133. *A policeman—it was a minor role. The sketch was part of a 1950 Cavalcade of Stars show.*

1134. *Yankee shortstop Phil Rizzuto.*

1135. *60 bleems—or 60 billion light-years.*

1136. *The Munsters.*

1137. *"Love in Bloom."*

1138. *Julie Kavner—who first came to the attention of TV audiences as Brenda Morgenstern, the awkward kid sister on "Rhoda."*

1139. *WACO in Waco, Texas.*

1140. *Former Ohio senator and astronaut John Glenn, who was a Marine major at the time.*

1141. *Lucille Ball, who is best known as the wacky housewife on TV's "I Love Lucy."*

1142. *The LaSalle. He sang, "Gee our old LaSalle ran great."*

1143. *Patty Duke, in 1958, shortly before she won acclaim for her portrayal of Helen Keller in "The Miracle Worker" on Broadway.*

1144. *Mortimer.*

1145. *John Wayne—who recommended his little-known actor-friend Arness for the role.*

1146. On what TV show did Robert Guillaume first portray the sharp-witted, sharp-tongued butler Benson?

1147. Who was the host of television's first telethon, which raised $1.1 million for cancer research?

1148. Who was the last mystery guest on the long-running TV show *What's My Line* when it went off the air in September 1967?

1149. What innovative TV show brought us the first joint Chinese-American television production?

1150. Who played Kato, the faithful Philippine valet-chauffeur, on the TV show *The Green Hornet* ?

1151. What actress was featured in the TV horror films *Satan's School for Girls*, *Killer Bees*, *Death Cruise* and *Death Scream* during the 1970s?

1152. Who portrayed Arnold Ziffel on *Green Acres*, the late 1960s TV sitcom that starred Eddie Albert and Eva Gabor?

1153. What building on Maxwell Street in Chicago should be familiar to most prime-time TV viewers?

1154. What famous person was interviewed in his pajamas on Ed Murrow's *Person to Person* TV show in 1959?

1155. What clever telegram message convinced a reluctant William F. BuckleyJr. to make a cameo TV appearance on Rowan and Martin's *Laugh-In* ?

1156. How did Larry Gelbart, the brilliant writer behind TV's *M*A*S*H* and Hollywood's *Tootsie*, get his start in show biz at age 16?

1157. TV talk show host and entrepreneur Merv Griffin sold his privately held entertainment company, Merv Griffin Enterprises, in 1986 for a reported $250 million. Who bought it?

1146. *On* Soap, *in 1977, two years before the spinoff series "Benson."*

1147. Mr. Television, *Milton Berle, in 1949.*

1148. *The show's moderator, John Charles Daly.*

1149. Sesame Street, *in 1983. The show that resulted was "Big Bird in China."*

1150. *Bruce Lee, before he became a kung fu movie star.*

1151. *Kate Jackson.*

1152. *A pig named Arnold.*

1153. *The former Maxwell Street police station, now headquarters for Chicago's vice squad. It's the setting of the exterior shots of the Hill Street stationhouse on* Hill Street Blues.

1154. *Cuban dictator Fidel Castro, who had just seized power.*

1155. *Buckley was asked, "Would you be on the show if we flew you on a plane with two right wings?"*

1156. *Through his father, who was comedian Danny Thomas' barber. Gelbart wrote his fist gags for Thomas, who delivered them on the Fanny Brice radio show.*

1157. *The Coca-Cola Company. Among the firm's holdings were the popular TV game shows* Wheel of Fortune *and* Jeopardy, *both of which were created by Griffin.*

1158. In the TV sitcom *All in the Family,* what did Edith Bunker claim Archie told her as he carried her over the threshold after their marriage?

1159. What did TV comic Red Skelton claim is the longest word?

1160. What TV series appeared opposite Judy Garland's musical variety show in 1963 and knocked the popular singer off the air after only one season?

1161. What was the name of the short-lived spin-off of TV's popular *Columbo* show, which featured Peter Falk as the rumpled, cigar-smoking sleuth?

1162. How many cases did Perry Mason lose in the nine seasons Raymond Bur appeared on TV as the ace defense lawyer?

1163. Whom did Mary Hartman's father, George Shumway, look like after an accident forced him to undergo plastic surgery on the satirical TV soap opera *Mary Hartman, Mary Hartman* ?

1164. What was the first name of mild-mannered bespectacled Mr. Peepers in the 1950s TV sitcom of that name starring Wally Cox?

1165. What musical instrument did Fibber McGee keep in his cluttered hall closet at 79 Wistful Vista on the popular radio show *Fibber McGee and Molly* ?

1166. Who was the only person ever shown smoking a cigar on *The Camel News Caravan,* the early TV news show sponsored by Camel cigarettes and starring John Cameron Swayze?

1167. What childhood word game was the inspiration for TV's very popular *Wheel of Fortune* ?

1168. What TV performer was described in 1955 by the Russian newspaper *Izvestia* as "a symbol of the American way of life...necessary in order that the average American should not look into reports on rising taxes and decreasing pay."?

1158. *"Watch your head dingbat, or you'll knock your brains out."*

1159. *The one that follows the announcement, "And now a word from our sponsor."*

1160. *Bonanza. Garland's hour-long show appeared on CBS Sundays at 9 P.M. from September 1963 to March 1964.*

1161. Mrs. Columbo. *The show, aired in 1979, starred Kate Mulgrew as Kate Columbo. Before it went off the air it went through two name changes—to* Kate the Detective *and* Kate Loves a Mystery—*and* Mrs. Columbo *became* Ms. Callahan.

1162. *Only one—but he later proved his client innocent and caught the guilty party.*

1163. *Actor Tab Hunter.*

1164. *Robinson.*

1165. *A mandolin.*

1166. *Winston Churchill.*

1167. *Hangman.*

1168. *Celebrity chimpanzee J. Fred Muggs, mascot of* The Today Show.

1169. What was the year and model of comedian Jack Benny's oft-mentioned automobile?

1170. On what TV show did comic Robin Williams first appear as the alien Mork?

1171. In what century does the 1979 film *Star Trek: The Motion Picture take place*?

1172. What was the address of the Bellamy family's London townhouse in the TV series *Upstairs, Downstairs*?

1173. What were the names of the three sons in the TV sitcom *My Three Sons*, which featured Fred MacMurray as widower Steve Douglas?

1174. What did the acronym UNCLE stand for on the TV spy series *The Man from U.N.C.L.E.*, starring Robert Vaughn and David McCallum?

1175. Who was the only cast member of the movie *M*A*S*H* to appear as a regular in the popular TV version.

1176. What is the meaning of kemo sabe—the words Tonto used to address the Lone Ranger?

1177. What town in the Ozarks was home to the Clampett clan on TV's *Beverly Hillbillies* ?

1178. Who was featured as comedian Jimmy Durante's sidekick on his popular radio show from 1943 to 1948?

1179. What hours are considered prime time on television?

1180. What famous entertainer was offered the role of Archie Bunker in the TV pilot for *All in the Family* before Carroll O'Connor was signed for the role?

1181. What was the name of Baby Snooks' baby brother in the popular radio show that starred Fanny Brice?

1182. Who starred in the title role of TV's kiddie space program *Rod Brown of the Rocket Rangers* in 1953?

1169. It was a 1924 Maxwell.

1170. On "Happy Days"—in a dream of Richie Cunningham's.

1171. The twenty-third century.

1172. 165 Eaton Place.

1173. Chip, Mike and Robbie in the show's first five years. When Mike married and moved away, Chip's orphaned buddy, Ernie, was adopted to keep the show's title valid.

1174. United Network Command for Law Enforcement.

1175. Gary Burghoff, who appeared as Corporal Radar O'Reilly in both.

1176. Trusty scout.

1177. Hooterville, which served as the setting for the spinoff series Petticoat Junction and Green Acres.

1178. Garry Moore.

1179. From 8 to 11 P.M. weekdays and Saturdays; from 7 to 11 P.M. on Sundays.

1180. Mickey Rooney.

1181. Robespierre.

1182. Actor Cliff Robertson.

1183. What was the first opera written especially for television?

1184. How did the TV sitcom *Sanford and Son* get its name?

1185. What first in radio history occurred on December 24, 1906, thanks to electrical engineer Reginald Fessenden?

1186. What sitcom was the most popular show on television in 1963?

1187. Under what name did show biz entrepreneur Merv Griffin originally try to sell the TV game show we know as *Jeopardy* ?

1188. What actor seen munching a carrot in a movie inspired cartoonist Bob Clampett to create Bugs Bunny?

1189. Which of TV's *Golden Girls* was the oldest—Beatrice Arthur (Dorothy), Estelle Getty (Sophia), Rue McClanahan (Blanche) or Betty White (Rose)?

1190. What actress's unpublished home telephone number did comedienne Joan Rivers give out on national TV in 1986 when she was hosting *The Late Show Starring Joan Rivers* ?

1191. Shots were fired only once in the 1970 movie *M*A*S*H*. What were they for?

1192. What was used to power the engines of the starship Enterprise in the *Star Trek* television series?

1193. In the Arab world, what popular TV show is known as "Iftah Ya Simsim" ?

1194. What television show featured fictional Russian spies Boris Badenov and Natasha Fatale?

1195. How many freckles did early TV puppet Howdy Doody have?

1196. What male TV heartthrob appeared nude in *The Harrad Experiment*, a 1973 film about a college experiment in premarital sex?

1183. Amahl and the Night Visitors, *by Gian-Carlo Menotti. It was first presented in 1951.*

1184. *From it's star, Redd Foxx, who was born John Elroy Sanford.*

1185. *The airwaves were used for entertainment for the first time, with Fessenden performing "O Holy Night" on his violin, playing some records and reading from the Bible—all from his transmitter in Brant Rock, Massachusetts.*

1186. The Beverly Hillbillies.

1187. What's the Question?

1188. *Clark Gable—the movie was the 1934 comedy classic* It Happened One Night. *Bugs made his film debut in 1940 in* A Wild Hare.

1189. *Betty White. The youngest was Rue McClanahan.*

1190. *Victoria Principal's. The two had feuded earlier, when Rivers was guest-hosting on* The Tonight Show.

1191. *Timekeeping at a football game.*

1192. *Antimatter.*

1193. Sesame Street.

1194. The Bullwinkle Show. *In the satirical cartoon series, Natasha's last name sometimes was given as Nogoodnik.*

1195. *48—one for each state in the Union at the time.*

1196. *Don Johnson, who portrayed the campus stud.*

1197. What TV sitcom couple was the first to share a double bed?

1198. What actor—best known for his straight-man TV sitcom role as a befuddled husband—appeared on Broadway with Deborah Kerr in *Tea and Sympathy* and with Kim Stanley in *Bus Stop* ?

1199. Who was the first entertainer shown diapering a baby in full view on television?

1200. On what popular TV sitcom were the two female stars pregnant at the same time—although the story line only acknowledged one of the pregnancies?

1201. What was the name of the *U.S.S. Enterprise* in the original draft for the *Star Trek* TV series?

1202. What popular TV and movie actor once appeared in a television commercial as a package of lemon chiffon pie mix, all decked out in a yellow box and matching yellow tights and flanked by actors playing chocolate, vanilla and butterscotch pie mix?

1203. Who played Oscar Madison's secretary, Myrna Turner, on the TV sitcom *The Odd Couple* ?

1204. What title role did Norman Lloyd—best known as the cranky but good-hearted Dr. Daniel Auschlander on TV's *St. Elsewhere*—play in an Alfred Hitchcock thriller more than 50 years ago?

1205. Whose photo did Michael J. Fox, in his role as Alex P. Keaton, keep on his nightstand in the popular TV sitcom *Family Ties* ?

1206. What popular 1960s TV sitcom was based on the novel *The Fifteenth Pelican* by Tere Ross?

1207. How often is it necessary for Mr. Spock of *Star Trek* to have sex?

1208. On TV's *Petticoat Junction,* what were the names of the three Bradley girls and their uncle?

1197. *The Munsters, Lily and Herman, played by Yvonne De Carlo and Fred Gwynne, during the 1964-65 season of the mock-horror show.*

1198. *Dick York, who played Darrin Stephens in* Bewitched.

1199. *Carroll O'Connor, as Archie Bunker, in the sitcom* All in the Family. *The baby was his TV grandson, Joey Stivic.*

1200. Cheers. *In its third season (1984-85), both Shelley Long (Diane Chambers) and Rhea Perlman (Carla Tortelli) were expecting. Long's pregnancy was concealed on camera while Perlman's was worked into the script.*

1201. *The* U.S.S. Yorktown.

1202. *Ted Danson, who's much better known for his portrayal of Sam Malone in the TV sitcom* Cheers.

1203. *Penny Marshall—who went on to make a name for herself as Laverne in the sitcom* Laverne & Shirley, *and as the director of such movies as* Big *and* Awakenings.

1204. *The saboteur who falls from the Statue of Liberty at the climax of Hitchcock's 1942 film* Saboteur, *starring Robert Cummings and Priscilla Lane.*

1205. *Richard Nixon's. A poster of William F. Buckley, Jr., was over Alex's bed.*

1206. The Flying Nun, *which starred Sally Field in the title role.*

1207. *Once every seven years.*

1208. *Billie Jo, Betty Jo, Bobbie Jo, and Uncle Joe.*

1209. Whose TV contract stipulated that she stay overweight and wear dumpy dresses so she'd look frumpier than the show's star?

1210. What role did mystery writer Erle Stanley Gardner, creator of the character of Perry Mason, play in the last TV episode of *The Perry Mason Show*?

1211. What was the "line" of the very first contestant on *What's My Line*, which premiered on February 16, 1950?

1212. What was the name of Col. Sherman Potter's horse in the *M*A*S*H* TV series?

1213. How did the last episode of TV's *Mary Tyler Moore Show* end?

1214. Where did Rocket J. Squirrel and Bullwinkle Moose live in the animated TV mock adventure series *Rocky and His Friends* ?

1215. What was Archie Bunker's address in the TV sitcom *All in the Family* ?

1216. Gore Vidal wrote a satirical TV comedy called *State of Confusion* for what comedian?

1217. On *The Andy Griffith Show*, what did deputy sheriff Barney Fife keep in his shirt pocket?

1218. What was Groucho Marx's real first name?

1219. What TV sitcom did Carl Reiner write and hope to star in?

1220. Who danced a pas de deux from "Swine Lake" with Miss Piggy on TV's The Muppet Show ?

1221. Who played Ronnie Burns, son of George Burns and Gracie Allen, on their TV show?

1222. On what TV show did Nancy Walker get her training for the maid's job on *McMillan and Wife*?

1209. *Vivian Vance's contract—to play Ethel Mertz on the* I Love Lucy *show.*

1210. *He played the judge.*

1211. *Hat check girl at the Stork Club.*

1212. *Sophie.*

1213. *Everyone but incompetent newscaster Ted Baxter was fired.*

1214. *Frostbite Falls, Minnesota.*

1215. *Archie resided at 704 Houser St., in the Corona section of Queens, New York City.*

1216. *Milton Berle, in 1955.*

1217. *His one bullet.*

1218. *Julius.*

1219. The Dick Van Dyke Show, *in which he ended up playing boss Alan Brady.*

1220. *Rudolf Nureyev.*

1221. *Ronnie Burns, their son.*

1222. *She portrayed a part-time maid on* Family Affair.

1223. What was the name of the lawyer who never lost a case on TV's cartoon sitcom *The Flintstones*?

1224. What was the name of TV detective Baretta's pet cockatoo?

1225. What TV character did *Time* magazine describe as a "human oil slick"?

1226. On the TV sitcom *My Mother, the Car*, who was the voice of the car?

1227. As a struggling young actor, James Dean helped support himself by testing stunts for what TV game show?

1228. What was the name of Phyllis Diller's short-lived 1968 TV variety show?

1229. The producer of what TV series once said that sometimes his actors' "faces get so green you can't shoot them"?

1230. Why did the fourteenth screen Tarzan, former LA Rams linebacker Mike Henry, sue for physical and mental injury following his third and final film?

1231. What was the name of the lurid novel written by Det. Ron Harris on the *Barney Miller TV* show?

1232. How much were Dean Martin and Jerry Lewis paid for their appearance on the first *Ed Sullivan Show* in June 1948?

1233. What was Maxwell Smart's cover on the TV spy comedy *Get Smart*?

1234. What was the Skipper's full name on TV's *Gilligan's Island*?

1235. For what film role did Telly Savalas first shave his head?

1236. What popular actor once noted, "I am a slob, but nobody will believe it"?

1237. Comedienne Joan Rivers has a registered trademark. What is it?

1223. *Perry Masonry.*

1224. *Fred.*

1225. Dallas *villain J. R. Ewing.*

1226. *Ann Southern.*

1227. Beat the Clock.

1228. The Beautiful Phyllis Diller Show.

1229. Sea Hunt—*he was referring to his regularly seasick cast.*

1230. *Dinky the Chimp bit him.*

1231. Blood on the Badge.

1232. *They shared $200.*

1233. *Salesman for the Pontiac Greeting Card Co.*

1234. *Jonas Grumby, played by Alan Hale Jr.*

1235. *Pontius Pilate, in* The Greatest Story Ever Told, *in 1965.*

1236. *Tony Randall, who portrayed Felix Unger, the fussy roommate in the* Odd Couple *television series.*

1237. *Her famous line: "Can we talk?"*

1238. What were the names of cartoon superstars Tom and Jerry when they made their debut in 1940 in *Puss Gets the Boot*?

1239. What television soap opera was the very first to use plastic surgery to explain a cast change?

1240. What was the working title of the TV series "Dynasty" before it went on TV in 1981?

1241. What television personality won America's Junior Miss crown in 1963?

1242. What TV sex symbol appeared as a contestant on "The Dating Game"—and wasn't chosen?

1243. Debbie Allen, who portrayed dance teacher Lydia Grant on TV's "Fame," has a sister who also became well-known through a popular television series. Who is she?

1244. Who appeared on the TV soap "All My Children" as Verla Grubbs, daughter of a carnival snake charmer, who was searching for her long-lost father?

1245. What is the apartment number of "The Jeffersons" on the popular television series?

1246. What was the name of the first female member of TV's "Mission Impossible" team?

1247. What famous cowboy's horse had its own TV series?

1248. In May 1977 Bill Cosby was awarded a doctor of education degree by the University of Massachusetts. What was the subject of his 242-page dissertation?

1249. At what age did Lucille Ball become a redhead?

1250. Who played Mr. Spock's mother in both film and television episodes of "Star Trek"?

1251. Why was Simon Templar—portrayed on television by Roger Moore—called "The Saint"?

1238. *Tom, the cat, was called Jasper; Jerry, the mouse, was unnamed.*

1239. One Life to Live, *in 1969 when Michael Storm replaced his brother Jim as Dr. Larry Wolek.*

1240. *"Oil."*

1241. *News show host Diane Sawyer.*

1242. *Tom "Magnum, P.I." Selleck.*

1243. *Phylicia Raschad, better known as Clair Huxtable on* The Cosby Show.

1244. *Comedienne and former TV regular Carol Burnett, in 1983.*

1245. *Apartment 12-D.*

1246. *Cinnamon Carter. She was portrayed by Barbara Bain.*

1247. *Gene Autry's Champion, the* Wonder Horse. *Autry produced but never appeared in the series,* The Adventures of Champion, *which ran from September 1955 to February 1956.*

1248. *Fat Albert and the Cosby Kids. It was called "An Integration of the Visual Media via Fat Albert and the Cosby Kids into the Elementary School Curriculum as a Teaching Aid and Vehicle to Achieve Increased Learning."*

1249. *At age 30, after 12 years as a platinum blonde and 18 as a natural brunette.*

1250. *Jane Wyatt, who prepared for Trekkie motherhood by playing Margaret Anderson on TV's* Father Knows Best.

1251. *Because of his initials, S.T.*

1252. On what TV sitcom did the schnauzer-cocker-poodle mix we know as Benji appear before he made it big in the movies?

1253. What popular TV personality claims he was once fired as a weekend TV weatherman for describing a storm as having "hailstones the size of canned hams"?

1254. What famous actress had a plumbing fixture named after her?

1255. On what TV program did Johnny Carson first team up with Ed McMahon?

1256. What was the first Hollywood film shown on TV after the U.S. movie industry ended its ban and started selling television rights to its films in late 1955?

1257. What was the radio classic *Amos 'n' Andy* originally called when it went on the air in Chicago in 1926?

1258. What actor-comedian, before attaining stardom, performed with a popular folksinging group called The Tarriers?

1259. What female entertainer, as a five-year-old kindergarten student in 1953, appeared regularly on television on the *Horn & Hardart Children's Hour*?

1260. What famous actor, offered the role of the Penguin in the *Batman* TV series, said he would only take the part if he could kill Batman?

1261. Remember all the promotional hoopla in 1980 about "Who shot J.R." on TV's *Dallas*? Well, who did?

1262. How did Batman disguise the lever that opened the secret panel hiding the bat slides he and Robin used to get to the bat cave?

1263. What is the diameter of TV's famous *Wheel of Fortune*?

1264. Bob Hope had a reputation for delivering six punch lines a minute. How many a minute has Phyllis Diller been known to reel off?

1252. *On* Petticoat Junction, *as Uncle Joe's dog. At the time Benji was known as Higgins.*

1253. *David Letterman.*

1254. *Farrah Fawcett. The fixture was the gold-plated "Farrah faucet."*

1255. *On the daytime quiz show* Who Do You Trust, *in 1958.*

1256. King Kong, *starring Fay Wray.*

1257. Sam 'n' Henry.

1258. *Alan Arkin.*

1259. *Bernadette Peters, who was Bernadette Lazzara at the time.*

1260. *Spencer Tracy.*

1261. *Ewing's pregnant mistress, his sister-in-law Kristin Shepard, played by Mary Frances Crosby.*

1262. *As a bust of Shakespeare.*

1263. *Eight and a half feet.*

1264. *Twelve.*

1265. Which of Jim Henson's Muppets was the first to become a regular on national television?

1266. What well-known actor has been known to carry a small battery-powered fan to blow cigarette and cigar smoke back at the offending source?

1267. What famous couple appeared in the 1958 television play *A Turkey for the President* ?

1268. In what film did actor Leonard Nimoy—best known as Mr. Spock on *Star Trek*—first appear as an alien from outer space?

1269. What TV series did David Hartman star in before he became the host of *Good Morning America* in 1975?

1270. What fellow performer's Congressional candidacy did Beverly Hillbilly Buddy Ebsen oppose in a 1984 radio commercial?

1271. Name the third baseman in the Bud Abbott-Lou Costello *Who's on First* comedy routine.

1272. On what television show did Julie Newmar portray a robot?

1273. Actor Robert Blake worked with a cockatoo named Fred on the *Baretta* TV series. With what famous animal did he share credits much earlier in his career?

1274. Before he legally changed his name, what was strongman-actor Mr. T's name?

1275. Where did actor Jim Backus' radio character Hubert Updyke III (a fabulously wealthy forerunner of his Thurston Howell III on TV's *Gilligan's Island*) claim his ancestors landed when they arrived in America?

1276. How did Lauren Bacall entertain the audience when she made her television debut on in 1954?

1277. Which of TV's card-carrying private eyes was an indirect namesake of Dashiell Hammett's Sam Spade?

1265. *Rowlf the Dog. The Muppet hound, created for a dog food commercial, appeared for three seasons on* The Jimmy Dean Show.

1266. *Larry (J. R. Ewing) Hagman.*

1267. *President-to-be Ronald Reagan and his wife Nancy. The dramatization was the Thanksgiving feature on* General Electric Theater, *which Reagan hosted.*

1268. *In* The Zombie Vanguard, *the first of 12 episodes in the serial* Zombies of the Stratosphere. *Nimoy, 20 at the time, played a Martian in the zombie army.*

1269. Lucas Tanner, *in which he played the title role.*

1270. *That of Nancy Kulp, who played homely Jane Hathaway on* The Beverly Hillbillies. *She lost her bid for the Pennsylvania seat.*

1271. *"I Don't Know."*

1272. *On* My Living Doll, *starring Robert Cummings. The show ran from September 1964 to September 1965.*

1273. *Rin Tin Tin III—in the 1947 film* The Return of Rin Tin Tin.

1274. *Lawrence Tero.*

1275. *On Cadillac Rock.*

1276. *She recited the poem* Casey at the Bat.

1277. *Richard Diamond, played by David Janssen. His name was taken from another suit of cards.*

1278. What was the first American television series acquired for screening in the Soviet Union?

1279. What was the name of the 1973 TV movie that co-starred twice-wed, twice-divorced entertainers Elizabeth Taylor and Richard Burton?

1280. Why did gunslinger Matt Paladin on TV's *Have Gun, Will Travel* have a knight chesspiece inscribed on his calling card?

1281. How did Kukla, the bubble-nosed puppet featured on the TV kiddie show *Kukla, Fran and Ollie*, get his name?

1282. What was wacky *Today Show* weatherman Willard Scott's first television job?

1283. How many miles per gallon did the 19 ½-foot long, 8-foot-wide crime-fighting Batmobile get on the campy *Batman* TV show starring Adam West?

1284. How many 25-foot mobile vans did TV's traveling newscaster Charles Kuralt wear out in logging a million miles for his *On the Road* show?

1285. What were the names of Johnny Carson's first three wives?

1286. Where did Captain Benjamin Franklin Pierce, the irreverent doctor portrayed by Alan Alda on the popular *M*A*S*H* TV series, get his nickname, Hawkeye?

1287. What was the name of Buffalo Bob Smith's replacement on the *Howdy Doody Show* during the 1954-55 TV season when the puppet's best pal was incapacitated by a heart attack?

1288. What percentage of the episodes of TV's Gilligan's Island dealt with getting off the island?

1289. Who showed up disguised as a man at a stag Friars Club roast for Sid Caesar in 1983—and got through the entire evening undetected by any of the 2,200 male guests?

1290. What popular television series was originally going to be called *The Alley Cats* ?

1278. Fraggle Rock, *the children's educational show developed by Muppet creator Jim Henson. The Soviets bought 24 half-hour episodes.*

1279. Divorce His/Divorce Hers.

1280. *Because paladin is another word for knight.*

1281. *Kukla means "puppet" in Russian.*

1282. *He appeared as Bozo the clown on TV in Washington, D.C., in 1959.*

1283. *Four miles per gallon.*

1284. *Seven.*

1285. *From first to third: Joan, Joanne and Joanna.*

1286. *From James Fenimore Cooper's 1826 novel, "The Last of the Mohicans," in which the principal character, frontier scout Natty Bumppo, is known as Hawkeye.*

1287. *Bison Bill—Buffalo Bob's brother. He was played by Ted Brown, who went on to become a leading New York City disc jockey.*

1288. *32 percent.*

1289. *Phyllis Diller, who attended the roast under the alias Phillip Downey.*

1290. *"Charlie's Angels."*

1291. Who got his big break on TV when he filled in at the last minute for Red Skelton after the slapstick comic was injured during rehearsal?

1292. Why was madcap comedienne Lucille Ball kicked out of drama school in New York City when she was 15?

1293. What did Bugs Bunny drink to become invisible?

1294. What heavyweight actor portrayed Marshall Matt Dillon in the long-running 1950's radio version of *Gunsmoke* ?

1295. Who was the left fielder in the Bud Abbott and Lou Costello comedy skit *Who's on First* ?

1296. What was the original theme song of the *Happy Days* TV series, starring Ron Howard and Henry Winkler?

1297. What was Oprah Winfrey's first name supposed to be—before it was misspelled on her birth certificate?

1298. In the TV sitcom *Cheers*, what was the legal capacity of the popular Boston bar?

1299. On the TV kiddie show *Howdy Doody*, to what tribe did Chief Thunderthud belong? Hint: It's the name of an animal spelled backward.

1300. What is the name of the production company Tom Arnold formed after he and Roseanne Barr split?

1301. On the hit TV sitcom *Seinfeld,*what role did Kramer land on the "Murphy Brown" show when he moved to Hollywood to pursue an acting career?

1302. What is the significance of the name actor Michael J. Fox gave his production company, Snowback Productions?

1303. Who played Don Johnson's partner in the pilot for the hip TV police drama *Miami Vice* ?

1304. What popular movie star appeared as Michael J. Fox's alcoholic uncle on the TV sitcom *Family Ties* ?

1291. *Johnny Carson, in 1954. He was a staff writer for Skelton's network variety show at the time.*

1292. *Her teacher thought she was too quiet and shy.*

1293. *Hare remover.*

1294. *William Conrad, best known to TV viewers for his title roles in the* Cannon *and* Jake and the Fatman *series.*

1295. *Why.*

1296. *"Rock Around The Clock," by Bill Haley and the Comets.*

1297. *Orpah, after Ruth's sister-in-law in the Bible. (Ruth 1:4) The midwife transposed the second and third letters when she filled out Winfrey's birth certificate.*

1298. *75. The number was in a notice posted over the front door.*

1299. *Ooragnak—that's kangaroo spelled backward.*

1300. *Clean Break Productions.*

1301. *He played one of Murphy's many short-term secretaries. Kramer is played by Michael Richards.*

1302. *Snowback is Canadian slang for a native who crosses the border into the United States. Fox was born in Canada.*

1303. *Jimmy Smits, before he achieved fame as lawyer Victor Sifuentes in* L.A. Law. *Philip Michael Thomas ended up playing Johnson's partner, Det. Ricardo Tubbs, on* Miami Vice.

1304. *Tom Hanks.*

1305. What was the name of the newspaper started by cross-dressing corporal Max Klinger on the hit TV sitcom *M*A*S*H*?

1306. What famous catchphrase delivered by Peter Falk indicated that Columbo, TV's rumpled detective, was closing in on the criminal?

1307. What one-time TV Western star got his acting start in college when someone strong was needed to carry bodies in a student production of Arsenic and Old Lace?

1308. What new career did actor Jay Silverheels, best known for his portrayal of the Lone Ranger's faithful companion, Tonto, launch after retiring from show business in 1984?

1309. What TV show featured radio station KBHR? How about radio station KJCM?

1310. On the TV sitcom *The Munsters,* what was Lily Munster's maiden name?

1311. What did the American Lung Association call the "awards" it issued in 1996 to TV dramas it felt wrongly glamorized smoking?

1312. In what role did Helen Hunt, star of the TV sitcom *Mad About You*, appear on *The Mary Tyler Moore Show* when she was seven years old?

1313. What Hollywood sexpot played the wicked Siren on the *Batman* television series?

1314. Who plays Captain Kangaroo, and what other well-known television character did he play?

1315. The only time Ralph Edwards did not host *This Is Your Life*, was on January 30, 1957. Who was the substitute host that night?

1316. What actress, appearing in the TV series *Dynasty*, made her television debut in 1957 in *Bachelor Father* with her *Dynasty* co-star John Forsythe?

1305. *M*A*S*H Notes.*

1306. *"Oh, one more thing."*

1307. *Dan Blocker, who played Hoss Cartwright on* Bonanza.

1308. *He became a harness-racing driver.*

1309. *KBHR was on* Northern Exposure; *KJCM, on* Midnight Caller.

1310. *Dracula.*

1311. *Phlemmys. The big winners were* Chicago Hope *and* NYPD Blue.

1312. *The daughter of head newswriter Murray Slaughter.*

1313. *Joan Collins.*

1314. *Bob Keeshan, who was also the first Clarabell the Clown on* The Howdy Doody Show.

1315. *Ronald Reagan.*

1316. *Linda Evans.*

1317. CBS-TV's *60 Minutes* ran a feature called "Point Counterpoint" from 1971 to 1979, in which conservative James L. Kilpatrick debated two liberal adversaries. Can you name them?

1318. To what fraternal organization did Ralph Kramden and Ed Norton belong in the TV series, *The Honeymooners* ?

1319. Who was the four-foot-tall, hairy character in the TV series, *The Addams Family* ?

1320. What was the first film released in CinemaScope?

1321. "Man-woman-birth-death-infinity" were the opening words of what television series and who said them?

1322. Who commanded the *U.S.S. Enterprise* in TV's *Star Trek* before Capt. James T. Kirk came on board?

1323. What well-known movie actor once played the role of Ben Harper on the TV soap opera, *Love of Life* ?

1324. *Laverne and Shirley*, *Mork and Mindy* and Joanie *Loves Chachi* were spin-offs of the more successful TV series, *Happy Days*. From what series was *Happy Days* itself a spin-off?

1325. In the Walt Disney cartoons, what was the name of Goofy's brilliant nephew?

1326. In the old *Mickey Mouse Club* TV series, each day of the week had a theme. What were the themes for Monday through Friday?

1327. What school did Beaver Cleaver attend in the television series, *Leave It To Beaver* ?

1328. What TV cartoon characters belonged to the Royal Order of Water Buffaloes?

1329. Who was the first black person to host a network television game show?

1317. *Nicholas Von Hoffman (in the 1971—74 seasons), and Shana Alexander (from 1975 to 1979).*

1318. *The Royal Order of Raccoons, also known as the International Order of Friendly Raccoons.*

1319. *Cousin Itt, played by Felix Silla.*

1320. The Robe, *in 1953.*

1321. *"Ben Casey," spoken by Sam Jaffe.*

1322. *Capt. Christopher Pike, played by Jeffrey Hunter.*

1323. *Christopher Reeve.*

1324. Love, American Style.

1325. *Gilbert.*

1326. *Fun With Music Day, Guest Star Day, Anything Can Happen Day, Circus Day, and Talent Roundup Day.*

1327. *Grant Avenue Grammar School.*

1328. *Fred Flintstone and Barney Rubble of* The Flintstones.

1329. *Singer Adam Wade, who hosted* Musical Chairs *(1975).*

1330. What brand of stopwatch is seen in the TV program, *60 Minutes*?

1331. Humphrey Bogart acted for television only once—in a 1955 live production of what play?

1332. Ferdy and Morty are the two mischievous nephews of what well-known cartoon figure?

1333. In the TV series, *Wild Bill Hickok*, what was the name of Wild Bill's horse?

1334. In the TV series, *Three's Company*, what was the full name of Chrissy, played by Suzanne Somers?

1335. What is the name of the television series which began: "There is nothing wrong with your television set; do not attempt to adjust the picture. We are controlling transmission"?

1336. What was the working title of the TV series, *Dallas*?

1337. Who was the only Dumont television network star ever to win an Emmy Award?

1338. On the television series *Batman*, who played Batman and Robin's nemesis, Chandell?

1339. *Primrose Lane* was the theme song of what TV series starring Henry Fonda?

1340. What company always supplied the numerous devices used by Wile E. Coyote in his efforts to capture the Road Runner?

1341. In the TV series, *Mork and Mindy*, what was the capital city of Mork's home planet, Ork?

1342. Two actors who played high school students on the TV series, *The Many Loves of Dobie Gillis*, went on to become big stars, both renowned for "many loves" of their own. Who are they?

1330. Heuer.

1331. The Petrified Forest, in which he played Duke Mantee.

1332. Mickey Mouse.

1333. Buckshot.

1334. Christmas Snow.

1335. The Outer Limits. The introduction and closing words were spoken by Vic Perrin.

1336. Houston.

1337. Bishop Fulton J. Sheen, who was voted the Most Outstanding Personality for the 1952 season.

1338. Liberace.

1339. The Smith Family.

1340. Acme.

1341. Kork.

1342. Warren Beatty and Ryan O'Neal.

1343. When Elizabeth Montgomery played the dual roles of Samantha Stevens and her cousin, Serena, in the TV series, *Bewitched*, she was credited by what name for the role of Serena?

1344. Which well-known newsman narrated the TV series, *The Untouchables*?

1345. On the TV series, *M*A*S*H*, B. J. Hunnicutt was often pining for his wife and daughter back home. What were their names?

1346. Mayor La Trivia, Wallace Wimple and Myrt, the telephone operator, were characters on what classic radio program?

1347. Who was the first guest host of NBC-TV's *Saturday Night Live* ?

1348. What was the longtime sponsor of the radio series, *Jack Armstrong, the All-American Boy*, and where did Jack go to school?

1349. The NBC-TV game show, *Hollywood Squares*, first aired on October 17, 1966. Who occupied the center square on that telecast?

1350. Identify the father, mother and brother of Olive Oyl, Popeye's girlfriend.

1351. What was the name of the dirty old man, played by Arte Johnson, who always offered a Walnetto to Gladys Ormphby (played by Ruth Buzzi) in TV's *Laugh-In* ?

1352. Husband and wife Martin Landau and Barbara Bain starred together in which two television series?

1353. Vinko Bogataj has been seen once a week on ABC-TV for several years. What does he do?

1354. Which actress won the top prize on the TV quiz show, *The $64,000 Question*, by answering questions on Shakespeare?

1343. *Pandora Sparks.*

1344. *Walter Winchell.*

1345. *Peg and Erin, respectively.*

1346. Fibber McGee and Molly.

1347. *Comedian George Carlin, on October 10, 1975.*

1348. *Wheaties, and Hudson High, respectively.*

1349. *Ernest Borgnine. (For the record, the other squares housed Nick Adams, Abby Dalton, Charlie Weaver, Wally Cox, Sally Field, Morey Amsterdam, Agnes Moorehead and Rose Marie.)*

1350. *Cole Oyl, Nana Oyl and Castor Oyl, respectively.*

1351. *Tyrone F. Horneigh.*

1352. Mission: Impossible *and* Space: 1999.

1353. *He is the skier shown going off the side of the ski jump in the introduction to* Wide World of Sports.

1354. *Barbara Feldon.*

1355. What was Laverne De Fazio's favorite drink in the TV series, *Laverne & Shirley*?

1356. What was the first ABC-TV series to be rated number one for an entire season?

1357. "All aboard for Anaheim, Azusa and Cucamonga." Who uttered that phrase and on what program?

1358. Who was Johnny Carson's first guest when he took over the *Tonight Show* on October 1, 1962?

1359. *The Mary Tyler Moore Show* spawned three successful spin-off series. What were they?

1360. Who sings the theme song of the TV series, *The Love Boat* ?

1361. In the late 1950's, Steve McQueen played the bounty hunter, Josh Randall, in what western TV series?

1362. The British television program, *Till Death Us Do Part*, inspired what extremely popular American TV series?

1363. What was the name of Tonto's horse in the TV series of *The Lone Ranger* ?

1364. Jessica Tandy and Hume Cronyn were the stars of a 1954 NBC-TV situation comedy called, *The Marriage*—an otherwise unremarkable series, were it not for what pioneering distinction?

1365. On December 31, 1970, something disappeared from television. What was it?

1366. Whom did actress Joan Crawford replace in four episodes of the TV soap opera The Secret Storm in 1968?

1367. What word did censors ban from I Love Lucy scripts during the 1952-53 TV season?

1355.   *Pepsi and milk.*

1356.   Marcus Welby, M.D., *in 1970-71.*

1357.   *Mel Blanc, on both the radio and television versions of* The Jack Benny Program.

1358.   *Groucho Marx.*

1359.   Rhoda, Phyllis *and* Lou Grant.

1360.   *Jack Jones.*

1361.   Wanted: Dead Or Alive.

1362.   All In The Family.

1363.   *Scout.*

1364.   *It was the first network show to telecast regularly in color.*

1365.   *The cigarette commercial.*

1366.   *Her adopted daughter, Christina—who later poison-penned the bestseller* Mommie Dearest. *Christina appeared as Joann Kane on the show. Her mother filled in for her while she was hospitalized.*

1367.   *The word* pregnant—*even though Lucy was obviously expecting and the birth of her son was the highlight of the season.*

1368. By what more popular name do TV viewers know fictional Old West hero Don Diego de la Vega?

1369. What is the name of the more famous actor-brother of TV's Steve Forrest, who appeared as Hondo in *S.W.A.T.* and as Ben Stivers on *Dallas* ?

1370. What popular actor's father appeared as Clem, the deputy sheriff, on TV's long-running Western series *Bonanza* ?

1371. How did TV's Emmy Awards get their name?

1372. What popular actor fell in love with a woman he saw in a Maxwell House commercial—and married her?

1373. What was the name of the baby born to Ted Baxter and his wife Georgette on the popular TV sitcom *The Mary Tyler Moore Show* ?

1374. What burly character actor provided the voices of Charlie the Tuna and the Jolly Green Giant in television commercials?

1375. What famous entertainer appeared on educational TV in the 1970s as the milkman on *The Electric Company* ?

1376. Whom did actor John Forsythe replace as multimillionaire Blake Carrington on TV's *Dynasty* 16 days after filming had begun?

1377. In the Abbott and Costello *Who's on First* routine, what was the pitcher's name?

1378. Why was the *Muppet Show* banned from TV in Saudi Arabia?

1379. Meredith Baxter-Birney played the mother, Elyse Keaton, on the hit TV sitcom *Family Ties*. On what sitcom did her mother play a mother?

1380. What popular actress was once a regular in the Peanut Gallery of TV's *The Howdy Doody Show* ?

1368. *Zorro.*

1369. *Dana Andrews.*

1370. *Kurt Russell's father, Bing Russell.*

1371. *From the feminized form of "immy", a nickname for the image orthicon—the TV camera tube in wide use when the awards were first given in 1949.*

1372. *Michael Caine. His wife is Shakira Baksh.*

1373. *Mary Lou—for Mary Richards and Lou Grant, the show's two leading characters.*

1374. *Herschel Bernardi.*

1375. *Bill Cosby.*

1376. *George Peppard, who disagreed with the producers on how the part should be played. He ended up on* The A-Team.

1377. *Tomorrow.*

1378. *Because one of its stars was a pig.*

1379. *On* Hazel—*her mother, Whitney Blake, appeared as Dorothy Baxter.*

1380. *Sigourney Weaver—whose father, Pat Weaver, was president of NBC.*

1381. What actress-comedienne was a dancer until she was spotted in the chorus line of an Andy Griffith TV special in 1966 and became a regular on a popular TV show?

1382. How large a crew did *Star Trek's* Captain Kirk command?

1383. What size pumps did cross-dressing Corporal Max Klinger wear on the TV sitcom *M*A*S*H* ?

1384. What question did TV quiz show contestant Herb Stempel answer incorrectly to set the stage for Charles Van Doren's reign as champion on *Twenty-One* ?

1385. Why did CBS-TV display a blank screen for seven minutes following its coverage of the women's tennis semi-finals at the 1987 U.S. Open?

1386. What is the Canadian equivalent of the Emmy?

1387. What popular entertainer portrayed the first openly homosexual character on a nationally broadcast TV series?

1388. What long-running TV series was based on the 1963 movie *Spencer's Mountain*, starring Henry Fonda and Maureen O'Hara?

1389. What was the name of Walt Disney's family dog?

1390. Actors Jack Klugman and Tony Randall played roommates in the TV sitcom *The Odd Couple*. What actor was Klugman's real-life roommate in New York City before both became stars?

1391. What entertainer, upset at the high decibel level of the commercials shown during the TV premiere of one of her movies, called NBC and ordered an engineer to lower the volume?

1392. What famous entertainer first appeared onstage under the name Earl Knight?

1381. *Goldie Hawn. Her first acting role wa*s as a gossipy neighbor in the one-season comedy series *Good Morning, World in 1967. From there she went to "Rowan and Martin's Laugh-In" and stardom.*

1382. *Kird's crew numbered 430. His successor, Captain Picard, had 1,012—in crew and civilians—under his command.*

1383. *Size 10.*

1384. *As shown in the 1994 film* Quiz Show, *Stempel was asked to name the 1955 Oscar winner for Best Picture. Following instructions to muff the question, he answered* On the Waterfront *instead of* Marty.

1385. *The* CBS Evening News *was scheduled to go on, but anchorman Dan Rather walked out of the studio, disturbed that the long match between Steffi Graf and Lori McNeil had pushed back the start of the show.*

1386. *The Nelly.*

1387. *Billy Crystal, who played Jodie Dallas in the prime-time sitcom Soap from 1977 to 1981.*

1388. The Waltons, *which was on TV from 1970 to 1981, featuring Richard Thomas as John-Boy. James MacArthur played the role in the movie—where the character was known as Clay-Boy.*

1389. *Lady. She was a poodle, not a cocker spaniel like Lady in Disney's 1955 film* Lady and the Tramp.

1390. *Charles Bronson.*

1391. *Barbra Striesand, in February 1995. The film was The Prince of Tides.*

1392. *Alan King, who was born Irwin Kniberg. As a teen he formed a combo called Earl Knight and His Musical Knights, which performed at weddings and bar mitzvahs—with Kniberg/Knight/King on the drums.*

1393. What was Kramer's first name on the TV sitcom *Seinfeld?*

1394. To what lodge do Fred and Barney of TV's *The Flintstones* belong?

1395. On *The Mary Tyler Moore Show,* how did Chuckles the Clown die?

1396. How many times were Madonna's remarks bleeped during her first appearance on *Late Night with David Letterman* ? How about her second appearance?

1397. Why was Merv Griffin dumped as a featured vocalist on Kate Smith's TV show in the early 1950s?

1398. How many fingers and toes do Fred Flintstone, Barney Rubble and their relatives have on the animated TV sitcom *The Flintstones* ?

1399. What was the name of the adult son born to Mork on the TV sitcom M*ork and Mindy,* starring Robin Williams and Pam Dawber?

1400. In TV's Bonanza series, how did each of Ben Cartwright's three wives die?

1401. What message is written on the tombstone of Mel Blanc, the Man of 1,000 Voices—including those of Bugs Bunny, Porky Pig, Sylvester the Cat, Tweetee pie and Jack Benny's Maxwell?

1402. On what TV show did Jim Dial, the uptight senior anchor on TV's *Murphy Brown,* begin this television career?

1403. What moneymaking scheme did bus driver Ralph Kramden, of TV's *The Honeymooners,* daim would cut down on electricity bills?

1404. Mailman Cliff Claven on the TV sitcom *Cheers* hated two things about his job. One was a dog on his route, what was the other?

1393. *Cosmo. Kramer, Seinfeld's eccentric next-door neighbor, was played by Michael Richards.*

1394. *The Loyal Order of Water Buffaloes.*

1395. *He was dressed as a peanut for a parade—and was killed when an elephant tried to shell him.*

1396. *12 the first time; once the second time.*

1397. *His last name was the same as one of the chief competing brands of the show's sponsor—Esquire Shoe Polish.*

1398. *Four fingers on each hand; three toes on each foot.*

1399. *Mearth.*

1400. *Adam's mother, Elizabeth, died after childbirth; Inger, Hoss's mother, was killed by Indians; and Marie, Little Joe's mother, was thrown from a horse and died. (Elizabeth was played by Geraldine Brooks, Inger by Inga Stevens, and Marie by Felicia Farr.)*

1401. *"That's all folks," the sign-off line of all Porky Pig cartoons. Blanc is buried in the Hollywood Memorial Park Cemetery.*

1402. *A local kiddie show called "Poop Deck Pete and Cartoons Ahoy," on which he served as host.*

1403. *Glow-in-the-dark üwallpaper. Jackie Gleason, of course, played Kramden.*

1404. *The day the Sears catalog came out.*

1405. How did a salt shaker serve as a prop in early episodes of TV's original *Star Trek* series?

1406. What was The Fonz's full name on the TV sitcom *Happy Days* ?

1407. In what city is the building whose exterior was used for Jerry Seinfeld's apartment house on the TV sitcom *Seinfeld* ?

1408. Who demonstrated a chin lock that left comedian Richard Belzer bloodied and unconscious on his cable TV show *Hot Properties* ?

1409. How many hours of television a day does the average person watch, according to Nielsen Media Research?

1410. What TV news anchor was once described in *Life* magazine as looking "eerily like a police composite made up of the best features of the more famous anchors"?

1411. What popular TV show is called *Rehov Sumsum* in Hebew and *Shaara Simsim* in Arabic?

1412. On TV game shows, what's a *Bambi*?

1413. What was the name of Porky Pig's father?

1414. In what TV sitcom town would you find Foley's Market, Floyd's Barbershop and the Bluebird Diner?

1415. Under federal law, how many minutes of advertising per hour are permitted during children's TV shows on weekdays? How about on weekends?

1416. What kind of feathers are used in making Big Bird's costume?

1417. What stands a in 1983 in the 20th Century-Fox parking lot in Hollywood?

1405. *It was used as Dr. McCoy's medical scanner.*

1406. *Arthur Herbert Fonzarelli. The part was played by Henry Winkler.*

1407. *Los Angeles—not New York City, which is the setting of the sitcom.*

1408. *Hulk Hogan.*

1409. *About 4 hours—or more precisely, 27 hours and 53 minutes a week.*

1410. *Peter Jennings, in 1983, when he replaced Frank Reynolds on ABC-TV.*

1411. Sesame Street.

1412. *A contestant who freezes in front of the camera—as deer do in the glare of headlights.*

1413. *Phineas Pig.*

1414. *Mayberry, North Carolina, the setting of The* Andy Griffith Show.

1415. *Weekdays, 10 minutes per hour; weekends, 10½. The time limits were set by the Children's Television Act of 1990.*

1416. *Turkey—dyed, of course.*

1417. *A Marriott Hotel. No marker was put on the site when the capsule—containing mementos from the show—was buried.*

1418. As a youngster, what popular TV show host won seven spelling-bee and four science-fair championships?

1419. What TV personality authored a cookbook entitled *Sweetie Pie*?

1420. What were the names of the seven castaways on TV's *Gilligan's Island*?

Bonus Trivia

1421. For many years, the globe on the *NBC Nightly News* spun in the wrong direction. On January 2, 1984, NBC finally set the world back in the proper direction.

1422. Before his comedian days, Bob Hope boxed, under the name of Packy East.

1423. On the night of October 31, 1938, Orson Welles and his Mercury Theatre troupe provided "the panic broadcast that shook the world," when they performed *The War of the Worlds* by H. G. Wells as a terrifying real-life episode.

1424. The doomed TV series, *Turn On*, hosted by Tim Conway, established a record on February 5, 1969: it was aired and canceled on the same day.

1425. Novelist Jacqueline Susann once hosted the TV game shows, *Your Surprise Store* and *Ring the Bell*.

1426. Actress Mary Tyler Moore made her television debut as Happy Hotpoint in a commercial. In an early acting role, she was Sam in *Richard Diamond, Private Detective*. Playing a woman at an answering service, you could only see her legs and hear her voice.

1418. *Alex Trebek, of* Jeopardy.

1419. *Diet guru Richard Simmons, in 1997.*

1420. *Gilligan; the Skipper (Jonas Grumby); the Professor (Roy Hinkley); Mary Ann (Summers); Ginger (Grant); Thurston Howell III and Lovey Howell.*

Business, Advertising & Inventions

Questions

1427. According to Raymond Loewy, the industrial designer who introduced streamlining to packaging, what are the two most perfectly designed containers ever made?

1428. What essential piece of office equipment did Johann Vaaler invent in 1900?

1429. What Scottish innkeeper's son invented the thermos bottle in 1892?

1430. Who started the first airship passenger service in 1910?

1431. Who invented the aerosol valve in 1949?

1432. Who invented the Johnny Mop, the disposable toilet bowl cleaner on a stick?

1433. What did Englishman Edwin Budding invent in 1830?

1434. On what wardrobe item did zipper inventor Whitcomb Judson use his first "clasp locker" in the late nineteenth century?

1435. Who invented charcoal briquettes?

1436. With what product did the term "brand name" originate?

Answers

1427. The old Coca-Cola bottle and the egg.

1428. The paper clip.

1429. Sir James Dewar, who later invented cordite, the first smokeless explosive.

1430. Ferdinand, Graf von Zeppelin, who flew passengers 300 miles between Düsseldorf and Friedrichshafen.

1431. Richard Nixon's buddy, Robert Abplanalp.

1432. Dorothy Rodgers, wife of composer Richard Rodgers.

1433. The lawn mower, or as he described it: "machinery for the purpose of cropping or shearing the vegetable surface of lawns."

1434. A pair of boots.

1435. Henry Ford, to make use of scrap wood left over in the manufacture of the Model T.

1436. Whiskey. Producers branded their names on the barrels they shipped out.

1437. What do the initials S.O.S. stand for in the brand of steel-wool soap pads marketed under that name?

1438. A certain Capt. Hanson Gregory is credited with a curious invention: It has neither weight nor density; it can be seen but not felt. What is it?

1439. What is the economic status of someone referred to by the acronym DINK?

1440. To a Wall Streeter, what is a shark repellent?

1441. For what is the NOW in NOW bank accounts an acronym?

1442. What is the derivation of the trademark name Velcro?

1443. In the world of economics, what does the acronym GATT represent?

1444. What do the letters represent in the over-the-counter stock market acronym NASDAQ?

1445. What did John Matthews do with all the scrap marble he bought from the St. Patrick's Cathedral construction site in New York City in 1879?

1446. What famous statesman sold 18 canvases to Hallmark cards for reproduction on greeting cards?

1447. How many years after the total assets of America's mutual funds hit $1 billion did it take for them to reach $1 trillion?

1448. What was megacorporation IBM known as before its name was changed in 1924?

1449. What did the George N. Pierce Co. manufacture before it began producing the Pierce-Arrow and other automobiles?

1450. What piece of modern office equipment was first developed in 1842 by Scottish clockmaker Alexander Bain?

1437. *Save Our Saucepans.*

1438. *The doughnut hole.*

1439. *Double income, no kids. The acronym is used to describe either half of a career couple.*

1440. *Any device or strategy used to ward off a hostile takeover.*

1441. *Negotiable order of withdrawal.*

1442. *It's from the words velvet and crochet, which means "hook" in French.*

1443. *General Agreement on Tariffs and Trade. GATT is an international organization, headquartered in Geneva and associated with the U. N. that was established in 1948 to reduce tariffs and other barriers to international trade.*

1444. *National Association of Securities Dealers Automated Quotations.*

1445. *Matthews, a manufacturer of soda fountain equipment, made 25 million gallons of soda water by dissolving the marble (calcium carbonate) with dilute acid.*

1446. *Winston Churchill, in 1950. He was paid an undisclosed sum, which he donated to Churchill College at Cambridge.*

1447. *45 years. They hit $1 billion in 1945, $1 trillion in 1990.*

1448. *C-T-R, for Computing-Tabulating-Recording Company.*

1449. *Bird cages.*

1450. *The facsimile machine—better known as the fax. Bain was granted a patent in 1843 for his electro-chemical duplicating telegraph system, which was capable of transmitting crude images short distances.*

1451. What unusual use did non-drinker Andy Warhol make of Absolut Vodka, the Swedish liquor for which he and other artists created a series of innovative print ads?

1452. What was the last 12-cylinder car produced ·in the United States?

1453. For whom was the Mercedes automobile named?

1454. What mother's aid did Marion Donovan patent in 1951?

1455. Why are the annual awards given for the best billboards called Obies by the Outdoor Advertising Association of American Marketing?

1456. What phrase is said to be the most oft-printed warning in the history of the printed word?

1457. What famous children's book author created an imaginative ad campaign for an insect spray called Flit?

1458. Where did Robert Fulton launch his first steamboat?

1459. Prior to 1953, what product was advertised with the slogan, "Just what the doctor ordered"?

1460. An illustration of what TV and movie "celebrity" appeared on the teal-blue bottle of a unisex fragrance called Amphibia in 1995?

1461. What American industry introduced the 5-day, 40-hour work week?

1462. What famous circus performer introduced the flying trapeze?

1463. What was the name of the car that followed Ford's 1932 Model B, the last in the automaker's series of cars known by letter designations?

1464. Who is second only to Thomas Edison in the number of U.S. patents granted for inventions?

1451. *He claimed he used it as perfume.*

1452. *The 1948 Lincoln Continental.*

1453. *Mercedes Daimler, the daughter of German automaker Gottlieb Daimler.*

1454. *The disposable diaper.*

1455. *They're named after the ancient obelisks of Egypt, which are considered by the association to be the precursors of today's outdoor advertising.*

1456. *"Close Cover Before Striking"—the words of caution that appear on most matchbooks.*

1457. *Dr. Seuss, whose real name was Theodor Seuss Geisel. He worked on the ad campaign—which featured his trademark bugs—for 17 years.*

1458. *In Paris, on the Seine, in 1803. It sank. But Fulton made history four years later when his steamboat Clermont traveled the Hudson River from New York City to Albany.*

1459. *L & M cigarettes.*

1460. *Kermit the Frog. The scent "pour homme, femme, et frog" was marketed by Jim Henson Productions, creator of the Muppets.*

1461. *The steel industry, in 1923. Henry Ford adopted it in 1926.*

1462. *French aerialist Jules Leotard, who also invented the tights we call leotards.*

1463. *The Model 18—the 8 indicated it had an eight-cylinder engine; the 1 that it was Ford's first V-8.*

1464. *Edwin Land, inventor of the Polaroid camera.*

1465. What state was the home of the U.S. auto industry before World War I and the rise of Michigan?

1466. How much did the first three minutes of a call cost when commercial telephone service was introduced between New York and London in 1927?

1467. What did a horse named Nita beat in a famous race in 1830?

1468. What is the blue crayon in Crayola's box Magic Scents crayons designed to smell like?

1469. What was Henry Ford's first mass-produced car?

1470. Who invented the coffee filter?

1471. What were the first products marketed in aerosol containers?

1472. What fast-food chain founded in 1964 was named for brothers Forrest and LeRoy Raffel?

1473. On the New York Stock Exchange, what is the ticker-tape symbol for the Anheuser-Busch company?

1474. Frank W. Woolworth started selling 5-cent goods in 1878 and added 10-cent items in 1880. When did he begin offering 20-cent items?

1475. What toy did American author John Dos Passos invent and have patented in 1959?

1476. What was produced when sewing machines were first set up in a French factory in 1841?

1477. What was Lifebuoy soap called when it was first introduced in 1897?

1478. In the 1925 edition of the Encyclopaedia Britannica, who was credited with writing the article on mass production?

1465. *Indiana, where there were once hundreds of automakers. The last, Studebaker, shut down its operations in 1963. The Indianapolis 500 auto race, held annually on Memorial Day weekend, dates back to 1911, when Indianapolis was an auto-manufacturing center.*

1466. *$75.*

1467. *Tom Thumb, the first locomotive built in America. Nita, a part-Mustang gray mare, outran the iron horse after its engine broke down.*

1468. *A new car. It was initially given a blueberry aroma, but Crayola changed all its scents after parents suggested that kids would be less likely to eat crayons that were not food-scented. The sepia crayon, formerly chocolate-scented, now smells like dirt; white went from coconut to baby powder; black, from licorice to leather; pink, from bubblegum to shampoo.*

1469. *The Model N—which sold for $500 in 1906.*

1470. *Melitta Bentz, in Germany in 1908. To improve the quality of coffee for her family, she pierced holes in a tin container, put a circular piece of absorbent paper in the bottom of it and put her creation over a coffee pot.*

1471. *Insecticides. The aerosol dispenser was developed and patented by American chemist Lyle D. Goodhue in 1941.*

1472. *Arby's. The name stands for RB—Raffel Brothers.*

1473. *BUD. The company manufactures Budweiser beer.*

1474. *In 1932.*

1475. *A "toy pistol that blows soap bubbles," which he coinvented with three friends. They designed it in Dos Passos's kitchen for his daughter, Lucy, when she was six years old.*

1476. *Uniforms for the French army. Rioting tailors—fearing they'd be put out of work—broke into the factory and destroyed the machines.*

1477. *Lifebudy soap.*

1478. *Henry Ford, although the entry was actually written by the Ford Motor Company's official spokesman, William Cameron.*

1479. How often did the spark plugs in the Model T Ford have to be cleaned—in miles driven?

1480. In the world of business, what is the meaning of the acronym IPO?

1481. What household appliance designed for Sears, Roebuck and Company by visionary engineer Raymond Loewy won first prize at the Paris International Exposition in 1937?

1482. For what product was the term twofers first used?

1483. Who invented the first hideaway bed ever patented in the United States?

1484. What common plastic product do we owe to Nathaniel C. Wyeth—son of artist N.C. Wyeth, brother of artists Andrew, Carolyn and Henriette Wyeth, and uncle of artist Jamie Wyeth?

1485. What role did Mrs. P.F.E. Albee of Winchester, New Hampshire—widow of a U.S. senator—play in American sales history?

1486. What was the only product ever promoted by Elvis Presley in a television commercial?

1487. How did secure, relatively high-yielding stocks get to be called blue chips?

1488. What century-old product was originally promoted with the advertising slogan "You press the button—we do the rest"?

1489. What company is both the oldest corporate enterprise still in existence and the largest corporate landowner in history?

1490. What product was first introduced in 1906 as Blibber-Blubber?

1491. What popular baby device was inspired by something former Peace Corps member Anne Moore saw while serving in West Africa?

1479. *Every 200 miles.*

1480. *Initial public offering—it's a company's first sale of stock to the public.*

1481. *The refrigerator.*

1482. *Cigars. The term was used as early as 1892 for two-for-a-nickel cigars. It's been used for selling two-for-the-price-of-one theater tickets since 1948.*

1483. *Thomas Jefferson. The bed was hoisted and secured to the ceiling when it wasn't in use.*

1484. *The now-ubiquitous plastic soda bottle. He developed it as an engineer for the DuPont Company.*

1485. *She was the first Avon lady—although the company she worked for before the turn of the century was not yet called Avon. Mrs. Albee sold Little Dot Perfume Sets door-to-door for Avon founder David McConnell and set up a door-to-door sales network for him by recruiting and training other women.*

1486. *Donuts—the commercial, for Southern Made Donuts, was aired in 1954.*

1487. *The term was taken from the game of poker, where blue chips are more valuable than white or red chips.*

1488. *The Kodak camera. The slogan was first used in 1888.*

1489. *The Hudson Bay Company. Founded in 1670, its realm once covered nearly 3 million square miles. The company now operates Canada's largest department store chain.*

1490. *Bubblegum. Developed and marketed by the Frank H. Fleer Corporation, it was soon abandoned because it was too sticky and brittle. In the 1920s the company came up with a winning formula, which it marketed under the name Dubble Bubble.*

1491. *The strap-on baby pouch known as the Snugli. Moore made the first one for herself when she had a baby shortly after returning to the United States from Africa in 1964.*

1492. Joan Collins, Elizabeth Taylor and Cher all have marketed perfumes. Can you name their scents?

1493. What is the maximum number of individual memberships—or seats—permitted on the New York Stock Exchange?

1494. In 1985 officials of a New York supermarket chain advertised for "part-time career associate scanning professionals." What job position were they trying to fill?

1495. In 1985 a Denver hotel published an ad offering guests a "Free Hotel Room" in large type. What was the catch in the fine print below?

1496. What hand-rolled device did Marvin Chester Stone of Washington, D.C., patent in 1888? Hint: although no longer hand rolled, it's still very much on the scene today.

1497. How many miles per gallon did the 22-horsepower, 4-cylinder Model T Ford get when it was introduced in 1908?

1498. What food industry innovator invented a recoilless harpoon for whaling and a fast process for converting sugar cane waste into paper pulp?

1499. Who invented the whistle for the railroad train?

1500. How many exposures were there on the roll of film sold with Kodak's first box camera in 1888?

1501. What was the source of billionaire recluse Howard Hughes' original fortune?

1502. The makers of Ivory soap claim their product is 99 and $^{44}/_{100}$ percent pure. What are the "impurities" in the remaining $^{56}/_{100}$ percent?

1503. In 1851, how much money did newspaper publisher Horace Greeley recommend that the average workingman set aside weekly for rent if he were supporting a family of five?

1504. What was the price of a gross of metal suspender buttons in the 1908 Sears, Roebuck and Co. catalog?

1492. *Collins, "Spectacular"; Taylor, "Passion"; and Cher, "Uninhibited."*

1493. *1,366. The number is set in the exchange's constitution.*

1494. *Checkout clerk.*

1495. *"Parking $55.00/night (Parking is mandatory)."*

1496. *The wax paper drinking straw.*

1497. *It got between 25 and 30 miles per gallon.*

1498. *Frozen food king Clarence Birdseye.*

1499. *George Washington Whistler—father of artist James Abbott McNeill Whistler.*

1500. *One hundred. The price of camera and film together was $25.*

1501. *His father's invention of an oil drill bit capable of boring through subterranean rock.*

1502. *Uncombined alkali, carbonates and mineral matter. Fatty acids and alkali make up the "pure" part of the soap.*

1503. *$3.*

1504. *Nine cents.*

1505. What was the dowry of Consuelo Vanderbilt, daughter of multimillionaire William Henry Vanderbilt, when she married the Duke of Marlborough in 1895?

1506. To celebrate its one-hundredth anniversary in 1860, what did the Lorillard Company put at random in packages of its Century brand of tobacco?

1507. Who invented flexible greasepaint—the first natural-looking cosmetic used in the movies?

1508. In what year was the first American car sold for export—and where was it shipped?

1509. What famous Christmas legend did a Montgomery Ward advertising man create as part of his job?

1510. In 1933, how much did a night's stay in a double room cost at the famous Waldorf-Astoria Hotel in New York City?

1511. What was the first consumer product purchased on the installment plan?

1512. What enduring advertising symbol was created by a Virginia schoolboy as part of a drawing competition held in 1916?

1513. What was plastic first used for in America?

1514. In 1937, an American company built the very first auto-airplane combination. What was it called?

1515. When Gillette first marketed its safety razor at the turn of the century, it sold 20 blades for $1. How much did the razor handle cost?

1516. What was the name of the first major deodorant company in the Untied States?

1517. Why was Sam Colt—inventor of the six-shooter—expelled from school at the age of 16?

1518. Who wrote the Ford Motor Co., "While I still have got breath in my lungs, I will tell you what a dandy car you make"?

1505. *The duke received $2.5 million in railroad stock.*

1506. *$100 bills.*

1507. *Russian-born makeup expert Max Factor.*

1508. *In 1893. An Olds gasoline steam carriage was shipped to Bombay, India, for use by the branch office of a British patent medicine company. It's price: $400.*

1509. *Rudolph, the Red-Nosed Reindeer. Adman Robert May first wrote of the now famous reindeer in a pamphlet distributed to children by store Santas in 1939.*

1510. *In 1933, a double cost $9; a single, $6; a suite, $20.*

1511. *A Singer sewing machine, in 1856. It was purchased by Margaret Hellmuth of New York for $50 down, with the remaining $100 paid in six monthly installments. Later customers were able to buy machines for $5 down and payments of $3 a month.*

1512. *Mr. Peanut—the trademark of Planters Peanuts. Schoolboy Antonio Gentile of Suffolk, Virginia, received $5 for his winning entry.*

1513. *Billiard balls. Brothers Isaiah and John Wesley Hyatt developed celluloid in 1869 while competing for a $10,000 prize offered by a company looking for a substitute for ivory in billiard balls.*

1514. *The Arrowbile.*

1515. *$5.*

1516. *Odorono—its magazine ad mentioning underarm odor in 1919 led hundreds of offended women to cancel their subscriptions to the "Ladies' Home Journal."*

1517. *For experimenting with explosives.*

1518. *Killer Clyde Barrow, who added, "I have drove Fords exclusively when I could get away with one." Lawmen killed him during an ambush—in the last Ford he stole.*

1519. What actress was billed as "Miss Deepfreeze" when she toured the country demonstrating refrigerators?

1520. On a February afternoon in 1959, the TV game show "Haggis Baggis" was interrupted with the announcement, "Ladies and gentlemen, Mrs. Franklin D. Roosevelt." What followed?

1521. How many shades of blue are there in the 64-crayon box sold by Crayola?

1522. "She kissed the hairbrush by mistake. She thought it was her husband Jake." What is the origin of this rhyme?

1523. All automaker Henry Ford's cars were black until 1925, when he introduced two new colors. What were they?

1524. One hundred years ago today Griswold "Grizzy" Lorillard wore the first tailless dinner coat for men in the U.S. Where did he wear it and what did it come to be called?

1525. How did the term "the 400" come to mean the wealthiest and most fashionable members of society in 1892?

1526. What are the street lights in Hershey, Pennsylvania designed to look like?

1527. What U.S. department store was the first to install electric lighting?

1528. What was sold in the Burpee mail-order catalog when it was introduced by 17-year-old Washington Atlee Burpee in 1876?

1529. What product used Bobby Darin's 1958 hit song "Splish Splash" in its commercials?

1530. What American innovation did Walter Scott of Providence, Rhode Island, introduce in a converted horse-drawn freight wagon in 1872?

1531. What famous American, in a bid to show the commercial potential of the soybean, appeared at a convention in 1939 outfitted in clothes made entirely from that very versatile vegetable?

1519. Kim Novak.

1520. A commercial for Good Luck Margarine delivered by the former First Lady.

1521. Eleven: aquamarine, blue, cadet blue, cornflower, green blue, midnight blue, navy blue, periwinkle, sky blue, turquoise blue, and violet blue. (Not counted: blue gray, blue green, and blue violet.)

1522. Burma Shave roadside jingle, 1940.

1523. Green and maroon.

1524. He wore it to New York City's exclusive Tuxedo Park Club, from which it took its name—tuxedo.

1525. It was the number of people Mrs. William Astor's ballroom could accommodate.

1526. Foil-wrapped Hershey's chocolate kisses.

1527. Wanamaker's of Philadelphia, in 1878.

1528. Chickens. Burpee soon added chicken feed and then the vegetable and flower seeds the catalog has long been famous for.

1529. Drano.

1530. The diner.

1531. Henry Ford. His shoes were the only part of his wardrobe not made from soybeans.

1532. The first paid radio commercial ever aired promoted a cooperative apartment house in New York City in 1922. The ad cost $100. How long did it last?

1533. What legendary American folk hero was popularized in pamphlets written and illustrated by adman W. B. Laughead in the early twentieth century?

1534. Where did Uniroyal get the steel frame for the 80-foot-tall tire that stands near Detroit's Edsel Ford Freeway?

1535. What was unusual about the Sexto-Auto manufactured by the Reeves Manufacturing Company of Columbus, Indiana, in 1912?

1536. The Ford Motor Company manufactured one million cars for the first time in 1922. In what year did it hit the two-million mark?

1537. What were Kleenex tissues marketed as when they were first introduced in 1924?

1538. What did the Jacuzzi brothers manufacture when they first opened up shop in 1915—long before their grandchildren gave the bathtub business a whirl?

1539. What product was the first to use animated characters in its television commercials?

1540. Woolworth's 5-and-10-cent store chain was founded in 1879. For how long did 10 cents remain its top price?

1541. How many buildings are there in the landmark Rockefeller Center complex in New York City?

1542. What American city bills itself as the home of the first push-button car radio, the first canned tomato juice, the first mechanical corn picker and the first commercially built car?

1543. Who was the only American to have two cars named after him?

1544. What is the full name of Barbie, the doll?

1532. 10 minutes.

1533. Giant lumberjack Paul Bunyan. The pamphlets were for the Red River Lumber Company of Minnesota.

1534. It was the Ferris wheel at the 1964 New York World's Fair.

1535. It had six wheels—two in front and four in the rear. The same company previously had manufactured the eight-wheel Octo-Auto.

1536. In 1923.

1537. A cold-cream remover.

1538. Farm pumps.

1539. Ajax cleanser. The Ajax pixies used to tell us, "You'll stop paying the elbow tax when you start cleaning with Ajax."

1540. For 53 years, until 1932—but only in its U.S. stores east of the Missouri River. Prices west of the Missouri and in Canada were higher because of greater freight costs.

1541. 19.

1542. Kokomo, Indiana, which calls itself the "city of firsts."

1543. Ransom E. Olds—who gave us the Oldsmobile and the long-discontinued Reo, which was produced from 1904 to 1936 and got its name from its manufacturer's initials.

1544. Barbara Millicent Roberts.

1545. What famous American showman had his obituary published before his death?

1546. What is the largest American corporation named for an owner's daughter?

1547. Which were the only four of the contiguous 48 states that never had rhyming Burma-Shave signs on their highways?

1548. What was the longest flight ever made by aviation pioneer Wilbur Wright?

1549. What American bank adopted its cable address as its official name?

1550. What did the first vending machines in the United States dispense?

1551. How tall is the Barbie doll?

1552. Largelamb, an anagram pseudonym of a famous inventor, was one of the founders of "National Geographic" magazine. Who was he?

1553. How was Coca-Cola originally billed when it appeared on the market in 1886?

1554. Where does the Barbie Doll get its name?

1555. Where did Levi Strauss come from, and what did his blue jeans first sell for in 1850?

1556. In 1937, the grocery business was revolutionized by Sylvan Goldman's simple invention. What was it?

1557. What is the name of the camel on the Camel cigarettes pack?

1558. What was the original name of the Bank of America?

1559. What children's product does Binney and Smith manufacture?

1545. *P.T. Barnum.*

1546. *The Sara Lee Corp. It's named for the daughter of Chicago bakery owner Charles Lubin, who first named a cheesecake after his daughter and then, in 1951, his company, which was originally known as the Kitchens of Sara Lee.*

1547. *Arizona, Massachusetts, Nevada and New Mexico.*

1548. *77 miles. He made the flight in 1908 (five years after Kitty Hawk) from Camp d'Auvours, France, setting a world record and winning the Michelin Prize of 20,000 francs.*

1549. *Citibank, which originally was the City Bank of New York.*

1550. *Chewing gum. The machines were installed on New York City train platforms in 1888.*

1551. *11½ inches.*

1552. *Alexander Graham Bell.*

1553. *As an "Esteemed Brain Tonic and Intellectual Beverage."*

1554. *It was named after Barbara Handler, the daughter of its designer, Ruth Handler.*

1555. *He came from Bavaria, and the original price was $13.50.*

1556. *The shopping cart.*

1557. *Old Joe.*

1558. *The Bank of Italy.*

1559. *Crayola Crayons.*

1560. What cigarette company first used a woman in its advertisements, and what was the headline?

1561. What do J.C. Penney's initials stand for?

1562. Where did the soft drink Dr. Pepper get its name?

1563. What western hero was featured in comic book advertisements for Daisy air rifles?

1564. What was the name of multimillionaire fur trader John Jacob Astor's hometown in Germany?

1565. What was the original source of the Hearst publishing family's fortune?

1566. How much did supermarket "coupon queen" Susan Samtur pay for $130 in groceries when she went shopping with a TV consumer reporter in 1978?

1567. What did eccentric Texas businessman Stanley Marsh have planted in an Amarillo cornfield?

1568. Who sent the next message after the historic words "What hath God wrought" were transmitted over Samuel F. B. Morse's telegraph in 1844?

1569. What husband did two of the richest women in the world—five-and-dime heiress Barbara Hutton and tobacco heiress Doris Duke—have in common?

1570. How long did it take Robert Fulton's steamboat, the Clermont, to make its historic 150-mile maiden voyage up the Hudson River from New York City to Albany in 1807?

1571. What famous American inventor ran twice for mayor of New York City—in 1836 and 1841—and lost both times?

1572. Who uttered the famous words, "Mr. Watson, come here. I want you"?

1573. In how many articles did the word "recession" appear in *The Wall Street Journal* in 1990?

1560. Chesterfield, with the caption, "Blow some my way."

1561. James Cash.

1562. Chemist Charles Alderton named his drink after the father of a girl he was dating, Dr. Charles Kenneth Pepper.

1563. Red Ryder.

1564. Waldorf—which explains both halves of the name of the Waldorf-Astoria Hotel.

1565. Gold mining. George Hearst struck it rich in Nevada in 1859, nine years after crossing the plains from Missouri to join the California gold rush.

1566. Only $7 in cash—coupons covered the rest.

1567. Ten Cadillacs—half-buried, nose-down, each slanted toward California at the same angle as one side of the Great Pyramid in Egypt. Marsh dubbed the sculpture "The Great American Dream."

1568. Dolly Madison. The words: "Message from Mrs. Madison. She sends her love to Mrs. Wethered." Mrs. Wethered was a friend of the 76-year-old former First Lady.

1569. Dominican playboy-diplomat Porfirio Rubirosa. He was the fifth of Hutton's seven husbands; the second of Duke's two.

1570. 32 hours.

1571. Samuel F. B. Morse.

1572. Alexander Graham Bell—not Sherlock Holmes. This was the first complete sentence heard over the newly invented telephone. Blurted out by Bell on March 10, 1876, when he spilled acid on his trousers, the words were picked up by his assistant, Thomas A. Watson, at the other end of the line.

1573. 1,583, by the paper's own count.

1574. What fuel did Stuart Perry of New York City use in the engine he invented in 1844—the very first gasoline engine patented in the United States?

1575. The title of what film classic was used in the *Variety* headline reporting the stock market crash of October 29, 1987—a day now known as Black Monday?

1576. What famous American actress was the first woman to run a U.S. airline?

1577. The Dow Jones average closed at over 3,000 for the first time in 1991. When did it first top 2,000? How about 1,000?

1578. What was the horsepower of the four-cylinder engine in the Flyer, the plane piloted by Orville Wright in his historic flight on December 17, 1903?

1579. In 1884, what enterprising American helped squelch doubts about the stability of the Brooklyn Bridge—and how?

1580. Who invented rubber dental plates in 1855?

1581. Who kept Thomas Edison's dying breath in a bottle?

1582. What automobile made the first U.S. cross-country journey in 1903?

1583. In March 1981 students at an Allentown, Pennsylvania high school got into trouble for a money-making extracurricular venture. What was it?

1584. What colonial American devised the first wet suit for divers as well as a primitive version of today's flippers?

1585. In what city was the world's first electric traffic light installed 75 years ago?

1586. By how much did "steel-driving man" John Henry best a steam drill in the legendary face-off?

1587. When was power steering first offered in an automobile?

1574. *Turpentine.*

1575. Gone With the Wind. *The headline was* Bull Market Gone With the Wind.

1576. *Maureen O'Hara. From 1978 to 1981, she was president of 27-plane Antilles Air Boats, an airline based in the Virgin Islands that had been operated by her pilot husband until his death.*

1577. *It passed 2,000 in 1987; 1,000 in 1972.*

1578. *12 horsepower.*

1579. *P. T Barnum—he led a herd of twenty-one elephants over it.*

1580. *Charles Goodyear, who accidentally discovered how to vulcanize rubber in 1839 when he dropped a mixture of rubber and sulfur on a hot stove.*

1581. *Henry Ford. It's now on display at the Ford Museum in Greenfield Village, Michigan.*

1582. *A chauffeur-driven 1903 Winton touring car. It left San Francisco on May 23, 1903 and arrived in New York City on July 26.*

1583. *They were manufacturing counterfeit $1 and $5 bills on the school's offset printing press.*

1584. *Benjamin Franklin.*

1585. *In Cleveland, Ohio—at the intersection of Euclid Avenue and East 105th Street.*

1586. *By 5 feet—John Henry drove his 20-pound hammer 14 feet while the steam drill went only 9.*

1587. *In 1895, in the Sweany Steam Carriage manufactured by the C. S. Caffre Company. The first mass-produced gas-powered automobiles with power steering were marketed by Chrysler and Buick in 1951.*

1588. Where did pioneering American newspaperwoman Elizabeth Cochrane get her pseudonym Nellie Bly, the name she made famous when she circled the globe faster than Phileas Fogg, hero of *Around the World in 80 Days* ?

1589. Who issued the first mail-order catalog in the United States?

1590. During his most creative years, how often did Thomas Edison believe he should come up with a new invention?

1591. Who was aviatrix Amelia Earhart's wealthy husband?

1592. What nicknames did inventor Thomas A. Edison give to his first two children, Marion and Thomas Jr.?

1593. What stock exchange was the first in the United States to be completely computerized, with all transactions handled without benefit of a physical trading floor?

1594. When Charles Lindbergh made his pioneering transatlantic flight on May 20-21, 1927, he covered 3,610 miles in 33½ hours. How long did it take Amelia Earhart to make her solo crossing exactly five years later?

1595. In 1989, who became the first foreign monarch to patent an invention in the United States?

1596. What was the average yearly salary of an American public school teacher at the turn of the century?

1597. What would have been Charles Lindbergh's name if his paternal grandfather hadn't changed it when he fled to the United States to escape being jailed in Sweden for his political beliefs?

1598. In what year was the first mutual fund introduced in the United States?

1599. Why was there a big uproar about the 12-foot-high statue honoring steelworkers that was unveiled at a Pittsburgh arts festival in 1990?

1600. How much did Levi Strauss get for his first pair of jeans in 1850?

1588. From a Stephen Foster song called "Nellie Bly."

1589. Benjamin Franklin, in 1744. He was selling books.

1590. In his own words: "A minor invention every 10 days and a big thing every 6 months or so."

1591. Publisher G. P. Putnam.

1592. Dot and Dash—in honor of telegraphy. Edison married twice and had six children.

1593. The Cincinnati Stock Exchange (CSE), in 1978.

1594. Just under 15 hours—14 hours and 56 minutes, to be exact. But Earhart's crossing covered fewer miles (2,026).

1595. King Hassan II of Morocco, who was issued patent No. 4,805,631 for an invention that combines videotape and an electrocardiogram to study heart performance.

1596. $325.

1597. Charles Mannson.

1598. In 1924—it was the Massachusetts Investors Trust and had no set minimum investment.

1599. It wasn't made of steel. Sculptor Luis Jimenez used fiberglass, claiming that "it holds up better than steel."

1600. Six dollars—in gold dust.

1601. What was financier J. P. Morgan's reply when a journalist asked, "Mr. Morgan, will the market go up or down"?

1602. Who was the first person to officially walk across the Brooklyn Bridge when it opened on May 24, 1883?

1603. What famous American roasted a turkey on a rotating electric spit—in 1749?

1604. How did Robert S. Brookings amass the fortune that enabled him to found and underwrite the work of the Brookings Institution, the highly respected Washington, D.C., think tank?

1605. In what year did the New York Stock Exchange have its first million-share trading day?

1606. What was the nickname of the Lockheed Electra in which Amelia Earhart was flying when she disappeared over the Pacific in 1937?

1607. Which record-setting aviation mechanic was the godfather of Robert Cummings, the actor?

1608. How fast—in miles per hour—did the Wright brothers' Model A biplane fly in test flights conducted for the U.S. Army in 1909?

1609. What was Charles Lindbergh's average speed on his historic, 3,610-mile, nonstop flight across the Atlantic in 1927?

1610. When the first home TV set was demonstrated in 1928, what was the size of the screen?

1611. What life-saving device did Philip Drinker and Louis Agassiz Shaw build with two vacuum cleaners at Harvard University in 1927?

1612. What product did Armenian-born Sarkis Colombosian introduce to the United States in 1929?

1613. Where did American drivers buy gasoline for their automobiles before 1912, when the first gasoline stations were opened?

1601. *"Yes."*

1602. *President Chester A. Arthur.*

1603. *Benjamin Franklin, in a cooking experiment he conducted on the banks of the Schuylkill River in Philadelphia.*

1604. *He manufactured clothespins.*

1605. *1886.*

1606. *The Flying Laboratory.*

1607. *Orville Wright.*

1608. *42 mph. The price the army paid for the plane was based on its speed in the test flight. The base price was $25,000 plus a 10 percent bonus for every mile per hour over 40—so the Wright brothers were paid $30,000.*

1609. *About 108 mph.*

1610. *3 inches by 4 inches.*

1611. *The first iron lung. Iron lungs are known as Drinker respirators.*

1612. *Yogurt. Colombosian produced it at his Colombo dairy in Methuen, Massachusetts.*

1613. *From coal merchants, lumberyards and hardware stores.*

1614. What company's stock has been included in the Dow Jones Transportation Average ever since the index was created more than a century ago?

1615. What was the first Japanese car imported to the United States?

1616. What significant event occurred at 5 Exeter Place in Boston, in 1876?

1617. There were 15,700,003 of them manufactured, all in black. What were they?

1618. Who established what is believed to be America's first department store?

1619. Who designed the original 1936 Volkswagen?

1620. Asa Griggs Candler purchased the formula for Coca-Cola from fellow pharmacist John Pemberton for $2,300 in 1887. How much did Candler's sons get when they sold out in 1916?

1621. What singing commercial became a Top 10 hit in 1972?

1622. How much did Eastman Kodak's Brownie camera cost when it was introduced in 1900?

1623. How did denim, the fabric used for blue jeans, get its name?

1624. What department-store chain marketed its own car in 1952 and 1953?

1625. What modern convenience owes its discovery to a melted Hershey bar in scientist Percy LeBaron Spencer's pocket?

1626. Why did Proctor and Gamble decide to drop its century-old moon and stars trademark from its packaging in 1985?

1627. Which was the first well-known auto company to install steering wheels in its cars?

1628. The U.S. record for the greatest number of patented inventions is 1,093. Who holds it?

1614. *Union Pacific's.*

1615. *The Datsun, in 1958. A total of 83 were sold in the U.S. that year.*

1616. *The first telephone conversation. On March 10, Alexander Graham Bell spoke the first sentence transmitted directly over wire when he yelled to his assistant in another room, "Mr. Watson, come here; I want you."*

1617. *Model T Ford's.*

1618. *Mormon leader Brigham Young, in 1868. His Zion's Co-operative Mercantile Institution still exists in Salt Lake City, Utah, where it is known as ZCMI.*

1619. *Ferdinand Porsche, who later went on to build sports cars bearing his name.*

1620. *They were paid $25 million.*

1621. *The New Seekers' "I'd Love to Teach the World to Sing," which originated as a Coca-Cola ad.*

1622. *Just $1.*

1623. *From the city in which it originated—Nimes, France. It's a shortened version of serge de Nimes, or serge of Nimes.*

1624. *Sears, Roebuck & Company. The car, the Allstate, was built by the Kaiser-Frazer Corporation.*

1625. *The microwave oven. The Raytheon Company, where he worked, developed the oven after Spencer saw what a microwave signal had done to the chocolate.*

1626. *There was a rumor circulating nationwide that the logo—showing a man in the moon and 13 stars—was the mark of the devil.*

1627. *Packard. In 1900 it replaced the tiller with a steering wheel, mounting it on the right side.*

1628. *Thomas Alva Edison.*

1629. What was the inspiration for Campbell's red-and-white soup can?

1630. What is believed to be the first coin-operated machine ever designed?

1631. What famous American appeared in a 1947 soft-drink advertisement boasting, "My wife is a pretty smart Jane"?

1632. How long did Thomas Alva Edison's first incandescent lightbulb burn when he tested it in 1879?

1633. Why were featherless chickens—developed by avian scientists in 1975—a commercial failure?

1634. What did David Dunbar Buick build before he began manufacturing automobiles in 1901?

1635. What popular TV star appeared in Salem cigarette commercials for four years—with his green eyes colored blue?

1636. What was the original name of the Xerox Corporation?

1637. What did Christopher Cockerell invent with his wife's vacuum cleaner in 1950?

1638. What special payment arrangement was made in 1973 when Pepsi-Cola became the first American company to market a consumer product in Russia?

1639. *Garbo Talks* was the famous ad that promoted the reclusive screen star's first talkie, *Anna Christie*. What film did the later *Garbo Laughs* ad boost?

1640. What letter designations did Henry Ford use for his cars before he introduced the Model T in 1909?

1641. What was the name of the plane in which Orville Wright made his historic 12-second flight 85 years ago today?

1642. What was the Pennsylvania Fireplace?

1629. *The Cornell University football team uniform. Campbell's company treasurer was inspired by the brilliant Cornell colors when he attended a Penn-Cornell football game on Thanksgiving Day in 1898.*

1630. *A holy-water dispenser that required a five-drachma piece to operate. It was the brainchild of the Greek scientist Hero in the first century A.D.*

1631. *Ronald Reagan. The magazine ad, for Royal Crown Cola, also featured his former wife, actress Jane Wyman.*

1632. *Forty hours.*

1633. *It cost more to heat their houses than to defeather them.*

1634. *Bathtubs and other plumbing fixtures.*

1635. *Tom ("Magnum PI") Selleck.*

1636. *The Haloid Company.*

1637. *The Hovercraft. He created his air-cushion boat by reversing the vacuum's blower so it blew air out instead of sucking it in.*

1638. *Pepsi accepted payment in Stolichnaya vodka.*

1639. *"Ninotchka."*

1640. *Models A, B, C, F, K, N, R and S. He built nearly 29,000 of them between 1903 and 1909.*

1641. *Flyer I—now popularly known as Kitty Hawk I, after its North Carolina takeoff site.*

1642. *The original name of the Franklin stove, invented by Benjamin Franklin.*

1643. On October 21, 1929, inventor Thomas Edison returned to his laboratory to reenact the moment he created the incandescent lightbulb. Where was he?

1644. What did London blacksmith Charles Moncke invent?

1645. From what crop did agricultural genius George Washington Carver produce tapioca, ink, synthetic rubber and postage stamp mucilage?

1646. What American engineer supervised construction of a rail link between Moscow and St. Petersburg for Russia's Czar Nicholas I in 1842?

1647. What startling creation did French engineer-designer Louis Reard unveil in June 1946?

1648. Who invented the power lawn mower?

1649. Who invented waxed paper, an electric pen and a process that turned goldenrod plants into synthetic rubber?

1650. When was the rocket first invented?

1651. When searching for a manufacturing hub, what city had the Ford Company originally favored as center of its operations?

1652. What America merchandising pioneer used to shoplift from his own stores to check the alertness of his employees?

1653. What did Joseph C. Gayetty invent in 1857?

1654. How much did the first ballpoint pens cost when they were offered for sale in 1945?

1655. What was the Schwimmwagen?

1656. How much did the first Rolls-Royce sell for when the opulent auto was first marketed in 1906?

1643. In Dearborn, Michigan's Greenfield Park—where his Menlo Park, New Jersey, lab had been reassembled, stick by stick, by Henry Ford.

1644. The monkey wrench, which was originally called Moncke's wrench.

1645. The sweet potato.

1646. Artist James Abbot McNeill Whistler's father, George Washington Whistler. The famous portrait of his wife hangs in the Musée d'Dorsay in Paris.

1647. The bikini—which he named after Bikini atoll, where the U.S. had just conducted a nuclear test.

1648. Car maker Ransom E. Olds (of Oldsmobile fame), in 1915.

1649. Thomas Edison.

1650. In the thirteenth century, by the Chinese. Bamboo tubes stuffed with gunpowder were used against the Mongols in 1232 at the Battle of K'ai-fung-fu.

1651. Oswego, New York. Due to complications Ford encountered with the local government, the site was switched to Detroit—which would later become known as "The Motor City."

1652. Woolworth.

1653. Toilet paper.

1654. $12.

1655. An amphibious Volkswagen with a retractable propeller that the Germans used during World War II.

1656. $600. The cheapest model now goes for close to $200,000.

1657. Which oil company opened the first drive-in service station in the United States?

1658. On Wall Street, what's a "quack"?

1659. Which American passenger car was the first to pass the one-million production mark in a single year?

1660. What did manufacturers add to wood cement to discourage glue-sniffing by people seeking highs in the 1970s?

1661. What was the first automobile to have air-conditioning?

1662. How many copies per minute did the first Xerox machine produce when it was marketed 40 years ago?

1663. What is traded on NYMEX, the New York Mercantile Exchange?

1664. What is the oldest registered food trademark still in use in the United States?

1665. What was unique about the wristwatch for which Zeppo Marx obtained a patent?

1666. What are Hoot the Owl, Tabasco the Bull, Peanut the Elephant, Rex the Tyrannosaurus and Peking the Panda?

1667. How many burgers were there to a pound at the original McDonald's drive-in opened by brothers Maurice and Richard McDonald in San Bernardino, California in 1948?

1668. How did Swedish immigrant John W. Nordstrom make the fortune with which he founded the shoe store that grew into today's Nordstrom fashion-retail empire?

1669. What color is Martha Stewart's "Himalayan Eyes" paint?

1670. What does "cutting a melon" mean to a Wall Streeter?

1657. *Gulf—on December 1, 1913, in Pittsburgh, Pennsylvania.*

1658. *A quarter-point change in a stock's price.*

1659. *Chevrolet, 1949, when a record 1,109,958 were manufactured.*

1660. *Pungent oil of mustard.*

1661. *The Packard, in 1939.*

1662. *Seven. At the time, the company that developed and manufactured the copying machine was known as Haloid. It later took on the name of its breakthrough process.*

1663. *Metal and energy futures. The exchange is also known as the Merc.*

1664. *The red devil on cans of Underwood's deviled ham. It dates back to 1866.*

1665. *It included a heartbeat monitor.*

1666. *Beanie Babies—among the many seven-inch-long, plush-covered polyvinyl-chloride-pellet-stuffed animals first introduced in 1993 by Ty Inc.*

1667. *10. Ray Kroc established the nationwide chain in 1955 and introduced the quarter-pounder in 1972.*

1668. *He struck gold during the Klondike Gold Rush in 1897.*

1669. *Blue—dusty blue. It's one of the hundreds of colors produced by Sherwin-Williams bearing the imprimatur of the queen of the domestic scene.*

1670. *The declaration of an extra-large dividend by a company.*

1671. What roadside signs did the Burma-Shave admen erect a short time after they made the tempting offer: "Free, free, a trip to Mars for 900 empty jars"?

1672. What automobile company produced a car called the Dictator from 1927 to 1936?

1673. What was William Wrigley selling when he started handing out free packages of chewing gum to his customers as a premium?

Bonus Trivia

1674. On July 28, 1933, the first singing telegram was delivered to Rudy Vallee on the occasion of his birthday.

1671. *Signs cautioning, "If a trip to Mars you'd earn, remember friend there's no return."*

1672. *Studebaker.*

1673. *Baking powder—a product he soon abandoned when he realized his customers were more interested in his sticks of gum.*

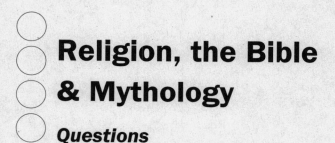

Religion, the Bible & Mythology

Questions

1675. Can you name the nine daughters of Zeus and Mnemosyne—the nine Muses of Greek mythology?

1676. How much time did Jonah spend in the belly of the whale?

1677. Why did a Bible published in London in 1632 become known as the Wicked Bible?

1678. The name of God is not mentioned in only one book of the Bible. Which one?

1679. What kind of wood was used to make Noah's Ark?

1680. Who was the only Englishman to become Pope?

1681. If you lived as long as Methuselah, what age would you live to?

1682. What sculpted bird sits atop the Mormon temple in Salt Lake City—and why?

1683. What mythological beast has the head of a man, the body of a lion, and the tail and feet of a dragon?

Answers

1675. *Calliope, Clio, Erato, Euterpe, Melpomene, Polyhymnia, Terpischore, Thalia, and Urania.*

1676. *Three days and three nights.*

1677. *Because "not" was missing from the seventh commandment, making it "Thou shalt commit adultery."*

1678. *The Book of Esther.*

1679. *Gopher wood, according to Genesis 6:14.*

1680. *Nicholas Breakspear, who was Adrian IV from 1154 to 1159.*

1681. *According to Genesis 5:27, you'd be 969 years old.*

1682. *A seagull—honored for devouring an 1848 plague of crickets in that city.*

1683. *A manticore.*

1684. For what event in February 1964 did evangelist Billy Graham break his strict rule against watching TV on Sunday?

1685. What celebrated evangelist baptized a little girl named Norma Jeane Mortensen, and by what name was that girl later known?

1686. According to the Bible, what substance was used to caulk Noah's ark and to seal the basket in which the infant Moses was set adrift on the Nile?

1687. The diet of what mythical monster periodically included seven youths and seven maidens?

1688. How old was Moses when he died?

1689. In Greek mythology, who was the goddess of the rainbow?

1690. How tall was Goliath, the Philistine giant slain by David with a stone hurled from a sling?

1691. In ancient Athens, what tree was considered sacred—with all its fruit belonging to the state, and death the penalty for anyone caught cutting one down?

1692. What Biblical Babylonian king cast Daniel into the lion's den for praying to God in defiance of a royal decree?

1693. What is the longest name in the Bible?

1694. What day of the week is the sabbath for Muslims?

1695. What legendary fire-breathing female monster had a lion's head, a goat's body and a dragon's tail?

1696. What famous structure in Greek mythology was built by a man named Epeius?

1697. According to legend, who fired the arrow that hit Achilles in the heel, his only vulnerable spot?

1684. *The Beatles' first appearance on "The Ed Sullivan Show."*

1685. *Aimee Semple McPherson christened the child who would be Marilyn Monroe, in December 1926.*

1686. *Pitch, or natural asphalt.*

1687. *The Minotaur's.*

1688. *He was 120 years old, according to the Bible (Deuteronomy 34:7).*

1689. *Iris.*

1690. *"Six cubits and a span," according to the Bible (I Samuel 17:4). That would put Goliath's height somewhere between 9 feet 3 inches and 11 feet 9 inches. The cubit measure (the distance from the elbow to the end of the middle finger) varied from about 17 to 22 inches, and the span (the distance from the thumb to the little finger when extended) was approximately 9 inches.*

1691. *The olive tree.*

1692. *Darius the Mede (Book of Daniel, Chapter 6).*

1693. *Mahershalalhashbaz, which is also written Maher-shalal-hash-baz (Isaiah 8:1).*

1694. *Friday.*

1695. *The chimera.*

1696. *The Trojan Horse. According to the legend, Epeius was a skilled woodworker commissioned by Odysseus to build the huge gift horse.*

1697. *Paris.*

1698. What mythological god was portrayed as the Colossus of Rhodes, the more than 100-foot-high sculpture that was one of the Seven Wonders of the World?

1699. In Greek mythology, who was the queen of the underworld and wife of Hades?

1700. In the Bible, which of the four horsemen of the Apocalypse rides a red horse?

1701. In Greek mythology, who were Arges, Brontes and Steropes?

1702. How many books of the Bible are named for women?

1703. Who was the ancient Greek god of dreams?

1704. What bird was credited with saving Rome from attack by the Gauls in 390 B.C.?

1705. What is the latest day in the year on which Easter Sunday can fall in Western Christian churches?

1706. What language is Jesus believed to have spoken?

1707. In the Bible, for what "price" did Esau sell his birthright to his younger twin brother, Jacob?

1708. According to classical mythology, who was the first mortal woman?

1709. Janus—the ancient Roman god of good beginnings for whom January is named—is pictured on early coins with two faces looking in opposite directions. What did the faces represent?

1710. What did the lords of the Philistines offer Delilah for revealing the secret of Samson's strength?

1711. In the Old Testament, who was Jezebel's husband?

1712. How were Noah and Methuselah related?

1713. What bird is named for the apostle Peter?

1698. *Helios, the sun god. The statue was destroyed by an earthquake in 224 B.C.*

1699. *Persephone.*

1700. *War (Book of Revelation).*

1701. *Cyclopes.*

1702. *Two—Ruth and Esther.*

1703. *Morpheus. (Hypnus was the god of sleep.)*

1704. *The goose. According to legend, the honking of geese alerted the Romans to a night raid by the Gauls.*

1705. *April 25th. The earliest is March 22nd. Under guidelines established by the Council of Nicaea in 325 A.D., Easter Sunday is the first Sunday after the first full moon that occurs on the day of the vernal equinox or on one of the next 28 days.*

1706. *Aramaic—an ancient language in use on the north Arabian Peninsula at the time of Christ. A modern version of the language is spoken today in Syria and among Assyrians in Azerbaijan.*

1707. *Pottage of lentils (Genesis 25:29-34).*

1708. *Pandora.*

1709. *The future and the past.*

1710. *They promised the sum of 1,100 pieces of silver each, according to the Bible (Judges 16:5).*

1711. *Ahab, King of Israel (I Kings 16:28-31).*

1712. *Methuselah was Noah's paternal grandfather (Genesis 5:25-29).*

1713. *The petrel, from a diminutive form of Petrus, or "Peter," in Latin. The reason—it appears to walk on water when it hunts for food, reminiscent of St. Peter's walking on water (Matthew 14:29).*

1714. What political-religious movement is named after former Ethiopian emperor Haile Selassie?

1715. What is the name of the imaginary city built in the air in *The Birds,* the comedy written by the Greek playwright Aristophanes in 414 B.C.?

1716. In Greek mythology, what were the names of Oedipus's parents?

1717. According to legend, what is the color of the horn in the middle of the unicorn's forehead?

1718. What was comic W. C. Fields's explanation when actor Thomas Mitchell caught him thumbing through a Bible?

1719. According to early Christian theologians, how many grades of angels are there?

1720. How many locks of hair did Delilah have cut from the mighty Samson's head to render him powerless?

1721. What was the first town in the United States to be given a biblical name? Hint: Its name is the most common biblical place name in the country.

1722. In the Bible, who did the sun and moon stand still before?

1723. According to Norse legend, what animals pulled Thor's chariot across the sky?

1724. What Biblical name did writer Dorothy Parker give to her pet canary?

1725. What country was the world's first constitutionally atheistic state?

1726. Who is the only woman whose age is mentioned in the Bible?

1727. Why is the egg a symbol of Easter?

1714. The Rastafarians. The movement gets its name from Selassie's title before his coronation—Ras Tafari, or Prince Tafari.

1715. Cloud-Cuckoo-Land—or Nephelococcygia in Greek.

1716. Laius, King of Thebes, and his queen, Jocasta.

1717. White at the base, black in the middle and red at the tip.

1718. "Looking for loopholes."

1719. Nine. The hierarchy of angels, from highest rank to lowest, is seraphim, cherubim, thrones, dominions, virtues, powers, principalities, archangels and angels.

1720. Seven, according to the Bible (Judges 16:19).

1721. Salem, Massachusetts. Salem is the shortened form of Jerusalem, which means "the city of peace" in Hebrew.

1722. Joshua. The passage is in Joshua 10:12-13.

1723. Two goats. Thor was the god of thunder.

1724. Onan. He was so named, she said, because he spilled his seed.

1725. Albania, between 1967 and 1990, when all churches and mosques were closed and religious observances were banned.

1726. Sarah. Her age is mentioned twice: In Genesis 17:17, when she is 90 and Abraham is told that she will bear him a child (Isaac); and in Genesis 23:1, when she dies at age 127.

1727. As an ancient symbol of new life, it's considered a fitting symbol for the Resurrection.

1728. What is the most common name in the Bible—shared by 32 people in the Old Testament and one in the New Testament?

1729. According to legend, what Hindu god died as Achilles did—from an arrow shot into his heel?

1730. The name of what brave Trojan warrior once was a synonym for hero, but now means bully?

1731. Along what body of water is there a low salt mountain some believe is the pillar of salt that Lot's wife was turned into after the destruction of the cities of Sodom and Gomorrah?

1732. In Greek mythology, who were the parents of the love child Harmonia?

1733. What was the Bedouin Muhammad adh-Dhib looking for when he discovered the Dead Sea Scrolls in 1947?

1734. According to the Bible, what weapons was the Philistine giant Goliath carrying when he was slain by David?

1735. In Greek mythology, what sea did Jason sail across in search of the legendary Golden Fleece?

1736. What is the meaning of orbium phonographicorum theca, one of the words the Vatican has added to the Latin language in a bid to keep it up to date?

1737. In the heavens above, at what constellation is the archer Sagittarius aiming his arrow?

1738. According to Roman mythology, in what volcano's crater did Vulcan, the god of fire, work at his forge?

1739. How did the Vatican's Sistine Chapel get its name?

1740. What does the word "amen" mean?

1741. What two constellations are named for mythical centaurs?

1742. Who was the founder of the International Church of the Foursquare Gospel?

1728. Zechariah.

1729. Krishna. He was shot by a hunter who mistook him for a deer. His heel was his only vulnerable spot.

1730. Hector, the eldest son of Priam. The present meaning of the name can be traced back to a seventeenth-century London street gang whose members called themselves hectors—or heroes.

1731. The Dead Sea—which is known for its high salt content. The Arabs call it the Sea of Lot; the Israelis, the Salt Sea.

1732. Aphrodite and Ares.

1733. A lost goat.

1734. A sword and a spear, according to I Samuel 17:45.

1735. The Black Sea.

1736. "Discotheque."

1737. Scorpius—to avenge the death of fellow hunter Orion, who, according to legend, died of a scorpion sting.

1738. Mount Etna's, in Sicily.

1739. From the fifteenth-century pope who had it built as a private papal chapel—Pope Sixtus IV.

1740. "So be it," or "Let it be."

1741. Centaurus and Sagittarius.

1742. Evangelist Aimee Semple McPherson, in 1927.

1743. How wide and deep was the moat dug around the famous 21-foot-high wall that protected the biblical city of Jericho in 7000 B.C.?

1744. In what language was the New Testament originally written?

1745. How many of the 150 psalms in the Bible's Book of Psalms are attributed to Moses?

1746. According to the Bible, on what day did God divide land and water?

1747. In Norse mythology, who was Ull?

1748. What was the playing time of the Bible when the American Foundation for the Blind recorded the entire 774,000-word King James version in 1944?

1749. In classical Greek mythology, who was the third and better-known sister of the trio of siblings that included Stheno and Euryale?

1750. According to the Bible, how many pearly gates are there?

1751. What was the total population of the world at the time of Christ?

1752. According to the Bible, in what city were the disciples of Jesus first called Christians?

1753. In the Bible, who saw the handwriting on the wall?

1754. Who was the only ugly male god among the immortals in Roman mythology?

1755. According to legend, what tragedian died when an eagle, looking for a stone on which to smash a tortoise shell, mistakenly dropped the shell on his bald head?

1756. What were the names of the three wise men?

1757. How high were the walls of Jericho before they came tumbling down?

1743. *It was 15 feet wide and 9 feet deep.*

1744. *In Greek.*

1745. *One—Psalm 90, "A Prayer of Moses, the man of God."*

1746. *On the third day (Genesis 1:9).*

1747. *The god of snowshoes.*

1748. *84½ hours.*

1749. *Medusa. The three were Gorgons—monstrously ugly women with serpents for hair and tusks for teeth.*

1750. *12 (Revelation 21:12-21).*

1751. *About 200 million.*

1752. *In Antioch, one of the earliest centers of Christianity (Acts 11:26).*

1753. *The Babylonian king Belshazzar (Daniel 5:1-5).*

1754. *Vulcan, the god of fire (known as Hephaestus in Greek mythology).*

1755. *The Greek tragic dramatist Aeschylus, who lived from 525 to 456 B.C.*

1756. *Balthazar, Caspar and Melchior.*

1757. *Twenty-one feet. They enclosed a 10-acre area.*

1758. How many people were on Noah's Ark?

1759. How did the ancient Greeks spread word about the winners of Olympic Games held between 776 B.C. and A.D. 393?

1760. What are the seven cardinal virtues?

1761. What are the seven deadly sins?

1762. How many decks were there on Noah's Ark?

1763. "Salt of the earth."
"Feet of clay."
"Apple of my eye."
All are clichés. What is their common source?

1764. Who were the parents of King Solomon?

1765. What was the first imprisonment recorded in the Bible?

1766. How many times a day do observant Muslims pray?

1767. According to Indian legend, how did the sacred thunderbird produce thunder and lightning?

Bonus Trivia

1768. Pope John Paul II's talents extend beyond the realm of his calling: He is also a gifted writer and musician. His 1979 record album, "At the Festival of the Sacro Song," sold over a million copies.

1758. *Eight—Noah, his wife; and his sons, Shem, Ham and Japheth, and their wives.*

1759. *By carrier pigeon.*

1760. *Prudence, temperance, fortitude, justice, faith, love, and hope.*

1761. *Pride, covetousness, lust, gluttony, anger, envy and sloth.*

1762. *Three, according to Genesis 6:16.*

1763. *The King James Version of the Bible.*

1764. *David and Bathsheba.*

1765. *The jailing of Joseph by Potiphar, the captain of the Egyptian pharoah's guards, after Joseph was falsely accused of trying to seduce Potiphar's wife (Genesis 39:6-20).*

1766. *Five—at daybreak, noon, midafternoon, sunset and evening.*

1767. *It produced thunder by beating its wings; lightning by blinking its eyes.*

America— Past & Present

Questions

1769. What room in the average American home is the scene of the greatest number of arguments?

1770. How much does the 555-foot-5-⅛-inch-high Washington Monument in Washington, D.C., weigh?

1771. What does Separation Creek in Oregon separate?

1772. How many figures were tattooed on the body of Captain George Costentenus, one of the human curiosities put on exhibit by legendary showman P. T. Barnum in 1876?

1773. In what year did motor vehicle registrations in the United States pass the million mark?

1774. How many hours a year are Americans expected to spend waiting in traffic jams by the year 2005?

1775. What is the length and width of the dollar bill?

1776. Under California law, what fish may only be caught using bare hands?

Answers

1769. *The kitchen.*

1770. *90,854 tons.*

1771. *Two mountains known as The Husband and The Wife.*

1772. *From head to toe, 386—including fish, animals, birds, mummies and hieroglyphics.*

1773. *In 1913, when there were 1,258,070 vehicles registered—1,190,393 of them passenger cars; 67,677 of them trucks and buses.*

1774. *8.1 billion, according to the Federal Highway Administration.*

1775. *Length, 6.14 inches; width, 2.61 inches.*

1776. *The tiny grunion, which comes ashore to spawn.*

1777. In 1960, the citizens of Hot Springs, New Mexico, voted to rename their town in honor of a popular radio show. What is it now called?

1778. What are the names of the two landmark stone lions sitting in front of the New York Public Library at Fifth Avenue and 42nd Street in New York City?

1779. How many windows are there on the 102-story Empire State Building?

1780. How much time—in months—does the average American motorist spend during his lifetime waiting for red lights to turn green?

1781. Borden is the name of a county in Texas. What is the name of its county seat?

1782. Two states bill themselves as the "Sunshine State." Can you name them?

1783. In 1954 the Pennsylvania coalmining communities of Maunch Chunk and East Maunch Chunk merged and adopted a new name in honor of a famous athlete. What was it?

1784. What are school teams nicknamed at Jack Benny Junior High, the school the citizens of Waukegan, Illinois, named after their most famous son?

1785. What was the name of the first series of U.S. postage stamps ever produced outside the country?

1786. What employee-grooming regulation at Disney World would prevent the hiring of Walt Disney—if he were alive and job hunting today?

1787. What was put between the steel framework and the copper skin of the restored Statue of Liberty to prevent corrosion?

1788. On the reverse side of the $100 bill, what time is shown on the Independence Hall clock?

1777. *Truth or Consequences—known as T or C for short. The change was made after radio (and later TV) show host Ralph Edwards promised to hold a program there annually.*

1778. *Patience and Fortitude, names given them by Mayor Fiorello LaGuardia.*

1779. *6,000.*

1780. *Six months.*

1781. *Gail, for Gail Borden, the man who brought us condensed milk—but only after drawing the first topographical map of Texas and surveying and laying out the city of Galveston.*

1782. *Florida and South Dakota.*

1783. *Jim Thorpe, after the great Oklahoma Indian athlete. The renaming was part of a plan to establish the town as a shrine to Thorpe, who was buried there.*

1784. *The 39ers—39 was the age comedian Benny claimed for more than 39 years of his life.*

1785. *Great Americans. The series, introduced in 1991, was printed in Canada.*

1786. *The ban on facial hair. Disney had a mustache.*

1787. *Teflon.*

1788. *4:10.*

1789. In what state can you find the towns of Romance, Sweet Home and Success?

1790. Where are the only remaining free-roaming panthers in North America?

1791. Why was the entire village of Hibbing, Minnesota, relocated?

1792. What physical handicap afflicted Juliette Low, founder of the Girl Scouts of America?

1793. Where did Samuel McPherson Hunt, gangster Al Capone's feared hitman, carry his submachine gun when he went out on a job?

1794. In what unusual manner did Ashrita Furman retrace the 13 ¼-mile route taken by Paul Revere on his historic 1775 ride?

1795. What U.S. city is at almost the same latitude as Mexico City?

1796. In what state can you visit Athens, Carthage, Damascus, Egypt, England, Formosa, Hamburg, Havana, Holland, Jerusalem, London, Manila, Melbourne, Oxford, Palestine, Paris, Scotland and Stuttgart?

1797. What was the first poll ever taken by national pulse-taker George Gallup?

1798. What famous gangster, posing as a reporter for a detective magazine, convinced some cops to take him on a tour of the weapons arsenal in their police station—and later returned to steal everything in it?

1799. What state is most dependent on tourism, with almost 30 percent of its jobs tourist related?

1800. To whom was columnist Grantland Rice referring when he wrote: "Outlined against the blue-gray October sky, the Four Horsemen rode again"?

1801. American naturalist George B. Grinnell founded the Audubon Society. What did his middle initial stand for?

1789. Arkansas.

1790. In Southern Florida—in the Everglades and Big Cypress Swamp.

1791. The village was sitting atop huge beds of iron ore. After it was moved south, the original site became one of the largest open-pit iron mines in the world—covering over 1,600 acres and running 535 feet deep.

1792. She was deaf.

1793. In a golf bag, rather than in the traditional violin case. His nickname was Golf Bag.

1794. She somersaulted the entire way.

1795. Hilo, on the Big Island of Hawaii. It's at 19°42´ north; Mexico City is at 19°25´ north.

1796. Arkansas—which has towns with all of those names.

1797. A survey to find the prettiest girl on campus at the University of Iowa, where he was editor of the student newspaper in the early 1920s. Gallup ended up marrying the winner, Ophelia Smith.

1798. John Dillinger, in 1934. The police station was in Peru, Indiana.

1799. The state of Nevada.

1800. Notre Dame's undefeated 1924 backfield, Elmer Layden, Harry Stuhldreher, Don Miller, and Jim Crowley.

1801. Bird.

1802. Who gave his red hand-knitted cardigan sweater, size 38, to the Smithsonian Institution in 1984?

1803. What's on the flip side of the Susan B. Anthony $1 coin?

1804. How many Ringling Brothers were there?

1805. Which is the smallest of New York City's five boroughs—with a total area of 22.6 square miles?

1806. What unique distinction does Maine's 5,268-foot Mt. Katahdin enjoy?

1807. What is the only car that consumer crusader Ralph Nader has ever owned?

1808. What oft-played American song's tune, meter, and verse form were borrowed from an English drinking song?

1809. Mistletoe is the state flower of what state?

1810. The names of 48 states are engraved on the frieze of the Lincoln Memorial, which was completed in 1922. How many are in the etching of the memorial on the back of the $5 bill?

1811. What U.S. canyon is the deepest gorge on the North American continent?

1812. What was the official New York City weather forecast on the day of the Great Blizzard of 1888?

1813. What inland state has the longest shoreline?

1814. What are the only four states to share a common boundary?

1815. How did John Luther Jones, the engineer of the "Cannonball Express" whose death in a collision with a freight train is memorialized in ballad and legend, get his nickname "Casey"?

1816. What three national parks does the Continental Divide pass through?

1802. Fred Rogers of public television's "Mister Rogers' Neighborhood."

1803. An eagle landing on the moon, commemorating the Apollo II moon landing on July 20, 1969.

1804. Seven: John, who headed the circus empire, and brothers Albert, Otto, Alfred, Charles, August, and Henry.

1805. Manhattan. (Queens is the largest borough with 118.6 square miles.)

1806. It is the first spot in the U.S. to be touched by the rays of the rising sun.

1807. A 1949 Studebaker, which he sold thirty years ago when he was a Harvard Law School student.

1808. "The Star Spangled Banner," which was based on the song "Anacreon in Heaven."

1809. Rhode Island.

1810. Twenty-six. Use a magnifying glass to check—they're in two rows on the frieze above the colonnade.

1811. Hell's Canyon, also known as the Grand Canyon of the Snake River, which reaches a depth of 7,900 feet.

1812. "Clearing and colder, preceded by light snow." The city was hit with 20.9 inches of snow and a temperature of -6 °F.

1813. Michigan. Its more than 3,100 miles of freshwater shoreline includes four of the five Great Lakes—Michigan, Superior, Huron and Erie.

1814. Arizona, Colorado, New Mexico, and Utah.

1815. From his hometown: Cayce, Kentucky.

1816. Yellowstone, Rocky Mountain and Glacier national parks.

1817. According to the folklore of the early American lumber camp, how was the Grand Canyon created?

1818. How much does the Liberty Bell weigh?

1819. What unearthly attraction can visitors find in Coconino National Forest, outside Flagstaff, Arizona?

1820. How many islands are there in the Hawaiian Islands?

1821. What is the origin of the name Baton Rouge, the capital of Louisiana?

1822. What is the size of automobile license plates issued by the 50 states, Canada, and Mexico?

1823. What is the name of the island on which Newport, Rhode Island, is located?

1824. How long is the Grand Canyon of the Colorado River?

1825. How did the town of Snowflake, Arizona, get its name?

1826. How much does it cost the U.S. government to produce a quarter?

1827. How much does Plymouth Rock weigh?

1828. What U.S. government agencies are known as Freddie Mac and Sallie Mae?

1829. The Algonquin Hotel is a famous New York literary landmark. What is the name of the hotel down the street where the struggling young James Dean once lived?

1830. How did Goon Dip Mountain, in Alaska, get its name?

1831. What does verdigris have to do with the Statue of Liberty?

1832. How many crayons does the average American child wear down in his or her coloring lifetime (ages 2 to 8)?

1833. Where are the oldest church bells in the United States?

1817. By Paul Bunyan dragging his pick behind him.

1818. Just over a ton—2,080 pounds.

1819. A 640,000-square-foot re-creation of the lunar landscape blasted in the volcanic ash and cinders of a dry lake bed.

1820. There are 132—8 major islands and 124 islets.

1821. The name, translated from French, means "red stick"—for the red cypress tree that once marked the boundary between local Indian tribes.

1822. They're 12 inches wide by 6 inches high.

1823. Rhode Island—formerly Aquidneck. It gave its name to the state.

1824. 217 miles.

1825. From two early settlers—Erastus Snow and William J. Flake.

1826. 2½ cents—which gives Uncle Sam a profit (or seigniorage) of 22½ cents.

1827. Approximately four tons.

1828. Freddie is the Federal Home Loan Mortgage Corporation; Sallie, the Student Loan Marketing Association.

1829. The Iroquois.

1830. It was named in 1939 for Goon Dip, who had been the Chinese consul in Seattle.

1831. It's the green patina on her copper body.

1832. 730, according to the folks at Crayola.

1833. In Boston's Old North Church. They were made in England in 1744 and shipped to Boston.

1834. Where in the U.S. will you find both Neon and Krypton?

1835. How did the town of Disco, Michigan, get its name?

1836. What are the numbers of the three interstate highways that run from coast-to-coast?

1837. How many elevators are there in the Empire State Building in New York City?

1838. How many windows are there in the Pentagon, the world's largest office building?

1839. What was the given name of Doc Holliday, the frontier dentist, gambler and gunman who befriended Wyatt Earp and was at his side during the shootout at the O.K. Corral?

1840. Which American city was the first to establish a police department?

1841. What comic strip character did the grateful farmers of Crystal City, Texas, honor with a six-foot-high stone mountain in 1937?

1842. Who came in second to Eleanor Roosevelt in a 1945 *Fortune* magazine poll taken to determine the most famous woman in America?

1843. Who once said: "The hardest thing in the world to understand is the income tax?"

1844. Whose appearance in a nearly transparent white fishnet bathing suit in the 1978 *Sports Illustrated* swimsuit issue led an editor to promise, "We never have, and never will, run anything so revealing again"?

1845. What was the average amount of money left per visit by the tooth fairy in 1950?

1846. Why did Trinity College in Durham, North Carolina, change its name to Duke University in 1924?

1834. In Kentucky. They're small towns named after the two elements.

1835. From a school once located there that was called Disco—which in Latin means "I learn."

1836. I-10, I-80 and I-90.

1837. 73.

1838. 7,754.

1839. John Henry.

1840. Boston. Regular-duty officers were appointed on May 5, 1838.

1841. Popeye—for his role in popularizing spinach, their main crop.

1842. The fictitious Betty Crocker, the symbol created in 1921 for General Mills' baking products.

1843. Albert Einstein.

1844. Cheryl Tiegs.

1845. A quarter.

1846. To honor its leading benefactor, tobacco tycoon James Buchanan Duke, and his family.

1847. How many official time zones are there in the United States—including Puerto Rico, the Virgin Islands and American Samoa?

1848. Who owns the 45.52-carat Hope diamond?

1849. What is the most frequently stolen street sign in New York City?

1850. What was the total weight of the identical Dionne quintuplets—Annette, Cecile, Emilie, Marie and Yvonne—when they were born on May 28, 1934?

1851. Prior to their complete 1998 redesign, how did $20 bills differ from those printed before 1948?

1852. What name was originally spelled out in the huge mountainside sign that welcomes visitors in Hollywood?

1853. Why is Arizona sometimes referred to as the Valentine State?

1854. When you translate "revenue enhancement" from government doublespeak, what have you got?

1855. What is the name of the tiny pond in New York's Adirondack Mountains where the 315-mile-long Hudson River originates?

1856. What four state capitals are named after cities in England?

1857. What was the name of pioneer Daniel Boone's family cat?

1858. What words appear on the front of the penny, nickel, dime and quarter—alongside the likenesses of Presidents Lincoln, Jefferson, Franklin D. Roosevelt and Washington, respectively?

1859. What is the name of the periodical published by the Procrastinators Club of America?

1860. How deep is Oregon's Crater Lake, the deepest lake in the United States?

1847. *Eight. From Puerto Rico to Samoa, they are Atlantic, Eastern, Central, Mountain, Pacific, Alaska Standard, Hawaii-Aleutian and Samoa Standard.*

1848. *The United States. It was given to the Smithsonian Institution by jeweler Harry Winston in 1958.*

1849. *Hooker Place.*

1850. *13½ pounds.*

1851. *The engraving of the White House on the back of the bill was changed in 1948 to include structural alterations made during Harry S. Truman's presidency. Additions include a balcony on the front portico and two more chimneys. Also different on the revised bill are the words below the engraving, which were changed from "White House" to "The White House."*

1852. *Hollywoodland, the name of a real-estate subdivision on the site of what is now the nation's film capital.*

1853. *It joined the Union as the 48th state on February 14, 1912.*

1854. *A tax increase.*

1855. *Lake Tear of the Clouds.*

1856. *Hartford, Connecticut; Dover, Delaware, Boston, Massachusetts; and Richmond, Virginia.*

1857. *Bluegrass—which is also the nickname of Kentucky, the state he helped found.*

1858. *"LIBERTY" and "IN GOD WE TRUST."*

1859. *"Last Month's Newsletter"*

1860. *1,932 feet deep. The lake is in the crater of Mount Mazama, an extinct volcano.*

1861. What car is shown in front of the U.S. Treasury Building on the back of the $10 bill?

1862. How much garbage—in tons—is generated daily in the twin towers of the World Trade Center in New York City?

1863. Which is the only state on the eastern seaboard to fall partially in the central time zone?

1864. What city—more than 2½ times the size of Rhode Island—is America's largest in area?

1865. Through how many states does U.S. 80—the main northern route from New York to California—pass?

1866. Which two states have neighboring towns named for explorers Meriwether Lewis and William Clark?

1867. Which of the 50 states takes in the least amount of tourist dollars?

1868. What animals—besides horses—accompanied Buffalo Bill Cody when he sailed his Wild West Show to London in 1887 to appear before Queen Victoria?

1869. What are roller coasters classified as by the U.S. Patent Office?

1870. What is the name of the boulevard on which Fort Knox is located?

1871. Which of the states uses the Napoleonic code rather than English common law as the basis of its civil law?

1872. How many U.S. states and their capital cities have names that begin with the same letter?

1873. What major vegetable crop was grown in Beverly Hills, California, before it became home to the rich and famous?

1874. What is the only place below sea level in the United States that is not in the California desert? Hint: It's a major city.

1861. *A 1926 Hupmobile.*

1862. *65—of which about 37½ tons are waste paper.*

1863. *Florida.*

1864. *Juneau, Alaska. It covers an area of 3,108 square miles. Rhode Island covers 1,214 square miles.*

1865. *12—from east to west: New York, New Jersey, Pennsylvania, Ohio, Indiana, Illinois, Iowa, Nebraska, Wyoming, Utah, Nevada, California.*

1866. *Idaho and Washington. The towns—Lewiston, Idaho, and Clarkston, Washington—are separated by the Snake River. Lewiston was a Lewis and Clark campsite.*

1867. *Rhode Island. California takes in the greatest amount.*

1868. *Buffalo (18), elk (10), mules (10), steers (5), donkeys (4) and deer (2). His cowboy-and-Indian entourage also included 180 horses.*

1869. *Scenic railways. The classification was first used for roller coasters in 1886.*

1870. *Bullion Boulevard.*

1871. *Louisiana.*

1872. *Four. Dover, Delaware; Indianapolis, Indiana; Oklahoma City, Oklahoma; and Honolulu, Hawaii.*

1873. *Lima beans.*

1874. *New Orleans.*

1875. What aptly named village has the highest post office in the United States?

1876. What newspaper, launched in 1982, was dubbed the *McPaper* because it provided its readers with "McNuggets" of news?

1877. How fast—in words per minute—does the average American adult read?

1878. How many steps are there to the top of the Empire State Building?

1879. What is the best-selling magazine in the United States, and who founded it?

1880. In 1949, Mrs. Ralph E. Smafield of Rockford, Ill., won first prize in what event with her Water-Rising Twists?

1881. Who appeared on the cover of the maiden issue of *People* magazine on March 4, 1974?

1882. What was Walt Disney's original title for his dream world, Disneyland?

1883. Between 1835 and 1837 a now perennial feature of American life was blissfully absent. What was it?

1884. Where is it illegal for a portrait of a living person to appear in the United States.

1885. Who was *Time* magazine's Man of the Year for 1952?

1886. In what connection is Anne Reese Jarvis remembered today?

1887. Where is the longest street in the United States?

1888. How was the three-mile territorial limit from the U.S. coastline determined?

1889. What was the working title of Hugh Hefner's *Playboy* magazine, before it made its debut in December 1953?

1875.   *Climax, Colorado. It's located in the Rockies at 11,320 feet above sea level.*

1876.   *USA Today.*

1877.   *275 words per minute.*

1878.   *1,575.*

1879.   *"TV Guide," first published in 1953 by Walter Annenberg.*

1880.   *The first annual Pillsbury Bake-Off.*

1881.   *Mia Farrow.*

1882.   *Mickey Mouse Park.*

1883.   *The national debt.*

1884.   *On our postage stamps.*

1885.   *Queen Elizabeth II of Great Britain. It was her coronation year.*

1886.   *She was the inspiration for Mother's Day, which was dreamed up by her daughter, Anna M. Jarvis.*

1887.   *Los Angeles, where Figueroa Street runs for 30 miles.*

1888.   *It was the distance that coastal cannons could fire a shell.*

1889.   *"Stag Party."*

1890. What was the full name of the 8-year-old girl, Virginia, who wrote to the *New York Sun*, asking if there really is a Santa Claus?

1891. In what city did Will Rogers serve as honorary mayor?

1892. Eighty-seven-year-old Democrat Rebecca Latimer Selton held what distinction in the political arena?

1893. In 1992, the governor of Hawaii received a 30,000-signature petition to change the name of the island of Maui—to what?

1894. Which territory in North America did Detroit's founder, Antoine Laumet de la Mothe Cadillac, the man for whom the car is named, serve as governor from 1713 to 1716?

1895. Whose body was the first to lie in state in the rotunda of the Capitol Building in Washington, D.C.?

1896. What country benefited from the first foreign aid bill approved by the United States Congress?

1897. What was the first building erected by the federal government in Washington, D.C.?

1898. In a 1989 newspaper survey, only 9 percent of those polled knew William Rehnquist was chief justice of the U.S. Supreme Court. What judge was identified by 54 percent of those polled?

1899. Of the 32 civil rights cases Thurgood Marshall argued before the U.S. Supreme Court as the lawyer for the National Association for the Advancement of Colored People, how many did he win?

1900. Who was the first black American to win the Nobel Prize for Peace?

1901. Which American colony was the first to enact anti-slavery legislation?

1902. To what amount did Congress vote to raise the minimum wage on October 26, 1949?

1890. *Virginia O'Hanlon.*

1891. *Beverly Hills.*

1892. *She was the first woman to become a U.S. Senator, when she was appointed by the governor of Georgia to serve the remaining day of a vacated Senate seat, November 21-22, 1922.*

1893. *Gilligan's Island, in honor of the TV sitcom. Needless to say, the island is still called Maui.*

1894. *Louisiana.*

1895. *Senator Henry Clay's. He died in 1852.*

1896. *Venezuela. In May 1812, Congress appropriated $50,000 for relief following an earthquake in Venezuela.*

1897. *The executive mansion—later known as the White House. It was first occupied in 1800 by John Adams.*

1898. *Retired California judge Joseph Wapner, of television's "The People's Court."*

1899. *29.*

1900. *American statesman and United Nations official Ralph Bunche, in 1950, for his mediation of the 1948-49 Arab-Israeli War. Dr. Martin Luther King, Jr., whose birth we celebrate today, won the coveted award in 1964.*

1901. *Massachusetts, in 1641, in its "Body of Liberties."*

1902. *They raised it to 75 cents an hour; it had been 40 cents.*

1903. What did the U.S. government buy for Alaska's Eskimos in 1891?

1904. What state was the last to adopt the secret ballot?

1905. Uncle Sam made his first appearance—beardless—in 1852. When did he acquire whiskers?

1906. What state abolished its personal income tax in 1980 and refunded $185 million already collected to its taxpayers?

1907. What senator gave the longest filibuster on record—24 hours, 18 minutes?

1908. How many years of schooling did Benjamin Franklin have?

1909. John Jay, John Marshall, Roger B. Taney, and Salmon P. Chase were all chief justices of the U.S. Supreme Court. What other distinction did they share?

1910. What was the name of the father of Sioux Indian leader Sitting Bull?

1911. In 1812 New York City's Federal Hall—the site of America's first presidential inauguration—was torn down and sold for scrap at auction. How much did the city get for it?

1912. What was Martin Luther King, Jrs.'s name at birth?

1913. Did Captain Miles Standish ever marry? You remember Standish, the Pilgrim leader who, according to legend, sought Priscilla Mullins' hand in marriage by having John Alden do the asking for him.

1914. Who was the first civilian astronaut launched into space by the U.S.?

1915. French daredevil aerialist Philippe Petit walked a tightrope linking the twin towers of New York's World Trade Center in 1974. How did he attach his 270-pound steel cable tightrope between the towers?

1903. *Sixteen Siberian reindeer—the start of the state's herd.*

1904. *South Carolina, in 1950.*

1905. *In his seventeenth year, in 1869, in "Harper's Weekly" magazine.*

1906. *Alaska, which has the highest per capita income in the country.*

1907. *South Carolina Republican Strom Thurmond. He was opposing the 1957 voting rights bill.*

1908. *Two—one year in grammar school and one with a private teacher.*

1909. *They never went to law school.*

1910. *Jumping Bull.*

1911. *$425.*

1912. *Michael Luther King Jr.*

1913. *Standish married twice. Rose, his first wife, died during the Pilgrims' first winter in the New World. Barbara, whom he married in 1624, bore him six children. Standish was between wives when John supposedly spoke for himself and married Priscilla.*

1914. *Neil Armstrong. The former Navy pilot went into space twice: in 1966 as commander of Gemini 8; in 1969 as commander of Apollo 11.*

1915. *Friends used a bow and arrow to shoot a fishing line across the 131-foot gap—and then used the fishing line to pull the cable across.*

1916. What is the significance of latitude 39°43' N in American history?

1917. How long did America's first space flight, made by astronaut Alan ShepardJr., last?

1918. Who wrote "Fish and visitors smell in three days"?

1919. What was the name of the huge Newfoundland dog that accompanied explorers Meriwether Lewis and William Clark on their famous expedition to the Pacific northwest in the early nineteenth century?

1920. What did Thomas Jefferson smuggle out of Italy in 1784 to help boost America's post-Revolution economy?

1921. How many states were created—in part or in their entirety—from the Louisiana Territory, purchased from France in 1803?

1922. How many cherry trees had to be cut down to prepare the site for the Jefferson Memorial in Washington, D.C., in 1938?

1923. Who gained fame as Richard Saunders during America's colonial days?

1924. Who was the last man on the moon?

1925. How many chests of tea were dumped overboard at the Boston Tea Party on December 16, 1773.

1926. How long did the black boycott against the Montgomery, Alabama, bus system last?

1927. What crime led to Billy the Kid's first run-in with the law?

1928. When and where was the first recorded report of a UFO sighting made in the United States?

1929. Which were the only four states to vote against the Sixteenth Amendment, the amendment ratified 80 years ago that gave Congress the power to "lay and collect taxes on incomes, from whatever sources derived"?

1916. It's the location of the Mason-Dixon Line, surveyed in the mid-eighteenth century to settle a boundary dispute between Pennsylvania and Maryland and considered the dividing line between North and South.

1917. Shepard's suborbital flight in a 6-by-9-foot capsule lasted 15 minutes and 22 seconds.

1918. Benjamin Franklin, in his wisdom-packed "Poor Richard's Almanack."

1919. Scammon.

1920. Jefferson snuck out two sacks of an improved strain of rice—despite a ban on its export from Italy—to help revitalize the Georgia and Carolina rice crops destroyed by the British during the Revolution.

1921. Thirteen: the entire states of Arkansas, Missouri, Iowa and Nebraska; and parts of Louisiana, Oklahoma, Kansas, Colorado, Wyoming, Montana, North Dakota, South Dakota and Minnesota.

1922. 171.

1923. Benjamin Franklin. Richard Saunders was the pen name he used in his "Poor Richard's Almanack" between 1732 and 1757.

1924. Astronaut Eugene Cernan, commander of Apollo 17—in December 1972.

1925. 342.

1926. The boycott, led by the Rev. Martin Luther King, Jr., lasted 382 days. It ended when the city of Montgomery began integrated bus service on December 21, 1956.

1927. The theft of some butter. His second known offense was receiving stolen property—clothes taken from a Chinese laundry.

1928. In June 1947, near Mount Rainier, Washington. Idaho businessman Kenneth Arnold reported seeing nine silvery, saucer-shaped disks flying in formation at very high speed.

1929. Connecticut, Florida, Rhode Island and Utah.

1930. What article of clothing were women required to wear on the beach at New Jersey's Atlantic City until 1907—along with their standard attire of long bathing dresses, bathing shoes and straw hats?

1931. How did Massachusetts sea captain Joshua Slocum—the first man to sail solo around the world—fight off pirates attacking his sloop?

1932. What famous American's father headed the investigation into the Lindbergh kidnapping in 1932?

1933. What triggered the legendary feud between the hillbilly Hatfields and McCoys in 1873?

1934. What was the powder used by America's Founding Fathers to keep their wigs white?

1935. Judge Roy Bean gained fame as the Law West of the Pecos. What was his brother, Josh, known for?

1936. What was astronaut Neil Armstrong's total annual salary when he walked on the moon on July 20, 1969?

1937. What was the name of the prospector who discovered gold in the Alaska panhandle in 1880?

1938. In what year did the average American salary pass $100 a week?

1939. Which state was the first in the nation to recognize Labor Day as a legal holiday?

1940. What famous Cherokee Indian was known to the Americans of his time as George Guess?

1941. What famous words did Francis Bellamy write to commemorate the 400th anniversary of Columbus's discovery of America?

1942. What was the name of the very first ocean-going vessel built by Englishmen in the New World?

1930. Stockings.

1931. He turned away the barefoot pirates by spreading carpet tacks on the deck of his boat. Slocum completed his historic 46,000-mile, 38-month voyage in 1898.

1932. General H. Norman Schwarzkopf's. The senior Schwarzkopf was a retired brigadier general who was New Jersey's state chief of police at the time of the kidnapping.

1933. The alleged theft of a pig.

1934. Ground rice.

1935. He was the first mayor of the city of San Diego, California.

1936. Just over $30,000.

1937. Joseph Juneau—the man for whom the capital of Alaska is named.

1938. In 1963.

1939. Oregon, in February 1887—followed later the same year by Colorado, Massachusetts, New Jersey and New York.

1940. Sequoya.

1941. "The Pledge of Allegiance"—which was published in "The Youth's Companion" magazine. Bellamy was on the magazine's staff.

1942. Virginia. The 30-ton ship was built by settlers who landed in Maine in 1607, established a colony, but found life and the winter weather so harsh that they built a ship to escape a second winter.

1943. What was the name of the first permanent settlement in Kentucky, established in 1775 by frontiersman Daniel Boone?

1944. What role did the ships "Discovery," "Sarah Constant" and "Goodspeed" play in American history?

1945. What house is the second-most-visited American home in the United States—outdrawn only by the White House?

1946. In 1784 American settlers established an independent state named Franklin, in honor of Benjamin Franklin. Where was it?

1947. How much expense money did Congress allot Meriwether Lewis and William Clark for their expedition across America that lasted from May 1804 to September 1806?

1948. What famous frontierswoman was buried in Deadwood, South Dakota, wearing a white dress and holding a gun in each hand?

1949. Who designed the Statue of Liberty's iron skeleton for French sculptor Frédéric Auguste Bartholdi?

1950. What fashion was introduced by and named after Civil War Gen. Ambrose Burnside?

1951. Why couldn't surgeon Charles Richard Drew, who organized the first blood bank in the U.S., donate his own blood?

1952. What foreign government contributed the greatest amount of money for the relief of victims of the 1906 San Francisco earthquake?

1953. What famous Northern publisher signed the bail bond for Confederate leader Jefferson Davis in 1867?

1954. In 1867, how much per acre did the U.S. pay Russia for what is now the state of Alaska?

1955. What movie had John Dillinger just seen when federal agents gunned him down outside the Biograph Theater in Chicago?

1943. *Boonesborough.*

1944. *They landed in what is now Jamestown, Virginia, in 1607, carrying the colonists who established the first permanent English settlement in the United States.*

1945. *Graceland, the home of Elvis Presley in Memphis, Tennessee.*

1946. *In what is now eastern Tennessee. The territory had been ceded to the federal government by North Carolina.*

1947. *The sum of $2,500.*

1948. *Calamity Jane, aka Martha Jane Burke.*

1949. *Alexandre Gustave Eiffel, who is best known for the tower that bears his name.*

1950. *Sideburns—an anagram of his name.*

1951. *Segregation laws in 1941 prohibited it—he was black.*

1952. *Japan.*

1953. *Horace Greeley, editor of the "New York Tribune."*

1954. *Just under 2 cents, compared to 4 cents an acre paid for the Louisiana Territory in 1803.*

1955. *"Manhattan Melodrama," in which "gangster" Clark Gable dies in the electric chair.*

1956. Who gave the "in" party for the Black Panthers that inspired the phrase "Radical Chic"?

1957. What American institution did Napoleon's grandnephew Charles Bonaparte found in 1908?

1958. Who was the first U.S. citizen to be canonized as a saint?

1959. Which state was the first to pass a right-to-die law?

1960. The U.S. bought the Virgin Islands for $25 million in 1917—from what country?

1961. What concession earned $862,000 in just five months at the Chicago World's Fair in 1933?

1962. What was the Mayflower's cargo before it was chartered to carry the pilgrims to America in 1620?

1963. What speed limit was set by Connecticut in 1901 in the first statewide automobile legislation passed in the U.S.?

1964. What state was the first to proclaim Christmas a holiday?

1965. What sentence did Patty Hearst receive in 1976 for the bank robbery she participated in while she was with the Symbionese Liberation Army?

1966. What event was precipitated by a book entitled "Civic Biology"?

1967. What historical trial gave birth to the phrase "sharp as a Philadelphia lawyer"?

1968. With what story did the tiny German-language newspaper "Philadelphische Staatshote" scoop the world?

1969. What famous early American once boasted: "I can't say I was ever lost, but I was bewildered once for three days"?

1970. How did the town of Showlow, Arizona, get its name?

1956. *Conductor-composer Leonard Bernstein.*

1957. *The F.B. I. He was attorney general of the U.S. at the time.*

1958. *Mother Frances Xavier Cabrini, in 1946.*

1959. *California, in 1976.*

1960. *Denmark, which had established its first settlement there in 1672.*

1961. *The rest room, at 5 cents a visit.*

1962. *Wine. Just prior to its Atlantic crossing, the Mayflower transported 153 tuns and 16 hogsheads (39,564 gallons) of wine from Bordeaux to London.*

1963. *On country highways, 15 mph; on highways within city limits, 12 mph.*

1964. *Alabama, 150 years ago.*

1965. *Seven years, but she served only 22 months—President Carter commuted her sentence.*

1966. *The 1925 "Monkey Trial." "Civic Biology" was the text science teacher John Scopes read to his students in defiance of a Tennessee law banning the teaching of evolution.*

1967. *The landmark 1735 libel trial of New York newspaperman John Peter Zenger, who was defended by Philadelphia lawyer Andrew Hamilton. Zenger was acquitted when the jury found his charges against the colonial governor were based on fact.*

1968. *The adoption of the Declaration of Independence. The Staatshote (which, translated, means "Messenger of the State") was the only Philadelphia newspaper published on Fridays—and July 5th fell on a Friday in 1776.*

1969. *Frontiersman Daniel Boone.*

1970. *From the card draw held to pick the mayor of the mining town. The player who drew and showed the low card became mayor—giving the town its name. Its main street is called Deuce of Clubs in honor of the winning low card.*

1971. From what European country did the ancestors of the people we call Pennsylvania Dutch originally come?

1972. What were Robert E. Lee's dying words?

1973. How many bullet holes did lawmen put in Clyde Barrow's car when they ambushed and killed him and his gangster girlfriend Bonnie Parker in 1934?

1974. Which of the contiguous 48 states was the last to be explored?

1975. What are the six flags that have flown over Texas?

1976. Columbus had three ships on his first exploration of America. How many were under his command on his second expedition?

1977. How did the American Indian brave shave?

1978. How did the Pilgrims celebrate New Year's Day?

1979. How many days did the historic civil rights march from Selma to Montgomery, Alabama, take?

1980. According to poetic legend, Lizzie Borden used her ax to give her mother 40 whacks and her father 41. How many whacks did the police actually accuse her of delivering?

1981. What does Apache chief Geronimo's Indian name—Goyathlay—mean in English?

1982. How long did the April 18, 1906, earthquake in San Francisco last?

1983. What were the dimensions of the "Star Spangled Banner" Francis Scott Key saw flying over Baltimore's Fort McHenry "by the dawn's early light" almost 185 years ago?

1984. What size was the first footprint on the moon—the one made by astronaut Neil Armstrong when he took his historic "one small step for man" on July 20, 1969?

1971. From Germany—the Dutch designation comes from the word Deutsch, meaning "German."

1972. "Strike the tent."

1973. They counted 106.

1974. Idaho, which was first visited by Meriwether Lewis and William Clark in 1805 during their famous expedition across America.

1975. The flags of Spain, France, Mexico, the Republic of Texas, the Confederacy, and the U.S.

1976. Seventeen.

1977. With clam shells, which he used as tweezers.

1978. They didn't. They considered it a blasphemous reverence for the Roman god Janus, for whom the month of January is named. The pilgrims referred to January as First Month.

1979. Five days.

1980. Dad, 10; stepmom, 19. But Lizzie was acquitted at her trial for the 1892 double slaying.

1981. One who yawns. He was given the name Geronimo—Spanish for Jerome—by Mexicans.

1982. 48 seconds. The San Francisco earthquake of 1989 lasted 15 seconds.

1983. 30 feet by 42 feet. The fort's commander had it made that large so "the British will have no difficulty in seeing it from a distance."

1984. It was 13 inches by 6 inches—the dimensions of Armstrong's boot. The exterior shell is the same size for all the astronauts' boots.

1985. What were the police in Atlantic City, New Jersey, cracking down on when they arrested 42 men on the beach in 1935?

1986. What is Mary E. Surratt's significance in U.S. history?

1987. What did famed bank robber Charles Arthur "Pretty Boy" Floyd do whenever he pulled off a job, which made him a hero to many people?

1988. How many children did Mormon leader Brigham Young have?

1989. How many crates did it take to transport the Statue of Liberty from France to New York in 1885?

1990. What did gangster Al Capone's oldest brother, Jim—who went by the name Richard "Two Gun" Hart—do for a living?

1991. In an effort to avoid recapture, how did convicted bank robber Robert Alan Litchfield change his features after his 1989 escape from Fort Leavenworth, where he was serving a 140-year term?

1992. Why didn't the anti-porn law passed by the town council of Winchester, Indiana, ever take effect?

1993. What plant's leaves did American colonists use to brew a tea substitute following their Boston Tea Party tax protest?

1994. When police and federal agents finally decoded the notation "K1,P2,CO8,K5" found in a Seattle woman's little black book in 1942, what did it turn out to be?

1995. What was the name of the ship that was supposed to accompany the Mayflower on its historic journey across the Atlantic in 1620?

1996. What well-known millionaire died when the Titanic sank?

1997. What song was the band playing while the Titanic was sinking?

1998. Who gave our country the name, the United States of America?

1985.   *Topless swimsuits on men.*

1986.   *She was the first woman executed by hanging. A military panel convicted her of conspiracy in the assassination of President Abraham Lincoln. Her guilt, however, is still in question.*

1987.   *He destroyed all first mortgages he could find on the chance they had not been recorded, and tossed money out the window of his getaway car.*

1988.   *57, with 16 of his 27 wives.*

1989.   *214.*

1990.   *He was a lawman in Nebraska—serving as a town marshal and a state sheriff.*

1991.   *He underwent plastic surgery so he would look like actor Robert DeNiro.*

1992.   *The editors of the only newspaper in town refused to publish it, claiming the law itself was pornographic. Under local statutes, no law could take effect until published in a newspaper.*

1993.   *The goldenrod's—the drink it yielded was known as "liberty tea."*

1994.   *Knitting instructions: "Knit one, purl two, cast on eight, knit five."*

1995.   *The Speedwell. It was left behind in Plymouth, England, when it started taking on water.*

1996.   *John Jacob Astor.*

1997.   *Not "Nearer My God To Thee," as is popularly believed, but the hymn "Autumn," by Francois Barthelemon.*

1998.   *Thomas Paine.*

1999. Who was the only U.S. astronaut to fly in the Mercury, Gemini and Apollo programs?

2000. What exactly did the Apollo II crew declare on a U.S. Customs form upon their return from the moon on July 24, 1969?

2001. Who is infamous for staging the first train robbery?

2002. What was the name of the ship on which Francis Scott Key composed "The Star Spangled Banner" in Baltimore Harbor, in 1814?

2003. French architect Pierre L'Enfant is best remembered in American history for what?

2004. What was the name of the first child born of English parents in the New World?

2005. John Glenn was the first American to orbit the earth. Who was the second?

2006. How many women were among the first 105 colonists to settle in Jamestown, Virginia, in 1607?

2007. When the first census of the United States was taken in 1790, what percentage of the population was African-American?

2008. What was the name of the man who shot frontier legend Wild Bill Hickok in the back while he was playing poker in a Deadwood, South Dakota, saloon in 1876.

2009. On what day of the week in 1492 did Christopher Columbus set sail for the New World?

2010. What was originally on the site of America's first mint, the Philadelphia mint, which opened in 1792?

2011. What bird was imported to the United States from England in 1850 to protect shade trees from voracious, foliage-eating caterpillars?

2012. What were the five tribes in the Iroquois League when it was formed around 1600?

1999. *Walter Shirra.*

2000. *"Moon walk and moon dust samples."*

2001. *Jesse James, at Adair, Iowa, on July 21, 1873.*

2002. *The Minden.*

2003. *He planned the city of Washington, D.C. in 1791. It was known at the time as Federal City.*

2004. *Virginia Dare, who was born in 1587 on Roanoke Island.*

2005. *Scott Carpenter, on May 24, 1962.*

2006. *None. The first two women settlers arrived in 1609.*

2007. *19.3 percent—of which 59,557 were free blacks and 697,624 were slaves.*

2008. *Jack McCall. He was acquitted at a trial the day after the shooting, then retried and hanged.*

2009. *Friday.*

2010. *A distillery.*

2011. *The English (or house) sparrow. Eight pairs were imported by the Brooklyn Institute in New York. They multiplied so prolifically that in 1890, New York City imported starlings to prey on the sparrows in Central Park.*

2012. *The Mohawk, Seneca, Onondaga, Oneida and Cayuga. The league later expanded to six tribes when it admitted the Tuscarora.*

2013. How many stripes were on the official American flag in 1818 before Congress passed a law forever setting the number at 13?

2014. How many signatures are on the Declaration of Independence?

2015. How was Martha's Vineyard spelled on official U.S. government maps before 1933?

2016. Who was the first European explorer to see and cross the Mississippi River?

2017. What famous Old West town was known as Goose Flats before a prospector named Ed Schieffelin discovered silver there?

2018. How much did the multi-layered space suits worn by astronauts on the Apollo moon landings weigh—life-support system included?

2019. What city was the center of gold mining in the United States before the discovery of gold at Sutter's Mill in 1848 triggered the California gold rush?

2020. How many children did Pocahontas and her husband John Rolfe have?

2021. A likeness of what famous legendary figure was on the prow of the first ship to bring Dutch settlers to America?

2022. How many states were there in the United States at the turn of the century?

2023. What is the diameter of each of the two main cables on San Francisco's Golden Gate Bridge?

2024. For what famous historic figure was Marietta, Ohio, named?

2025. What role did the ships Dartmouth, Beaver and Eleanor play in American history?

2026. Which American state capital was originally incorporated as the town of Marthasville?

2013. 15. The number had been increased to 15 in 1795 to include Kentucky and Vermont. But with more and more states joining the Union, the number was reduced to 13 as of July 4, 1818, to represent the original 13 states.

2014. 56.

2015. Marthas Vineyard. The apostrophe making the name possessive was the first apostrophe sanctioned by the U.S. Board on Geographic Names.

2016. Hernando de Soto of Spain, in 1541. He died the following year.

2017. Tombstone, Arizona. Schieffelin picked the name because soldiers laughingly told him all he'd find there would be his tombstone when he set out to prospect in the area in the 1870s.

2018. On earth, 180 pounds; on the moon, with the reduced lunar gravity, 30 pounds.

2019. Charlotte, North Carolina. From 1800 to 1848, gold mines in the Charlotte area were the main source of U.S. gold.

2020. One, a son named Thomas, who was born and educated in England but settled in Virginia.

2021. Sinterklass—a predecessor of Saint Nicholas, better known to us as Santa Claus.

2022. 45. Oklahoma became the 46th state in 1907; followed by New Mexico and Arizona in 1912; and Alaska and Hawaii in 1959.

2023. 3 feet—or 36.5 inches, to be exact. There are 25,572 wires contained in each of the cables.

2024. Marie Antoinette.

2025. They were the three ships targeted by American colonists at the Boston Tea Party on December 16, 1773. Together the three ships had 342 casks of the tea dumped into Boston Harbor by colonists who disguised themselves as Mohawks to carry out their historic protest of the British tax on tea.

2026. Atlanta, Georgia, in 1843—in honor of Martha Lumpkin, daughter of the governor of the state. A railroad official changed the name two years later to Atlanta, the feminine of Atlantic, after the Western and Atlantic Railroad, which had selected the town as the last stop on its line.

2027. What famous Englishman gave us the expression, "Keep your powder dry"?

2028. How long—in days—did the Pilgrims' first Thanksgiving in 1621 last?

2029. How much was suffragette Susan B. Anthony fined for voting in 1872?

2030. What was the source of E pluribus unum—Latin for "one from many"—the motto the Second Continental Congress adopted for the Great Seal of the newly named United States?

2031. How many times does each newly produced U.S. dollar bill have to go through the printing press?

2032. According to the Census Bureau, what are the five most common surnames in the United States?

2033. Where were the Library of Congress's original copies of the U.S. Constitution and the Declaration of Independence kept during World War II?

2034. Which state is America's flattest, with a difference of only 345 feet between its highest and lowest points?

2035. Which state is the most thickly forested, with 89.8 percent of its land area classified as wooded by the U.S. Forest Service?

2036. How many jurors were dismissed during the course of O. J. Simpson's double-murder trial?

2037. How many ballots in the House of Representatives did it take to break the deadlocked presidential election between Thomas Jefferson and Aaron Burr in February 1801?

2038. How fast—in miles per hour—do the fastest roller coasters in the U.S. go?

2039. How many signers of the Declaration of Independence went on to serve as president of the United States?

2040. What was the country of origin of the greatest number of immigrants to pass through Ellis Island between 1892 and 1924?

2027. *Oliver Cromwell. In 1642 at the Battle of Edgehill, he told his troops, "Put your trust in God, but keep your powder dry."*

2028. *Three. It featured bountiful meals, demonstrations by the Plymouth militia, traditional Indian dancing by the native guests, and foot races and other athletic contests.*

2029. *$100.*

2030. *It was from a recipe for salad in a poem entitled "Moretum," attributed to Virgil. The words, chosen by Benjamin Franklin, John Adams and Thomas Jefferson, were known at the time because they appeared as a motto on the cover of Gentlemen's Magazine.*

2031. *Three. First the front is printed in black, then the back is printed in green, and finally, the front is overprinted with the serial number and Treasury Department seal in green.*

2032. *Smith, Johnson, Williams, Jones and Brown, in that order.*

2033. *At Fort Knox, Kentucky*

2034. *Florida. Delaware is the second flattest state, with an elevation range of 442 feet.*

2035. *Maine. It's followed by New Hampshire, at 88.1 percent, and West Virginia, with 77.5 percent.*

2036. *10.*

2037. *36.*

2038. *The two fastest—the Steel Phantom in West Mifflin, Pennsylvania, and the Desperado in Jean, Nevada—reach a speed of 82 miles an hour.*

2039. *Two—John Adams and Thomas Jefferson.*

2040. *Italy, with 2.5 million. It was followed by Austria-Hungary, 2.2 million; Russia, 1.9 million; and Germany, 633,000.*

2041. How many states border an ocean?

2042. Where is the Superman Museum located?

2043. What words did Thomas Jefferson use in his final draft of the Declaration of Independence to describe the truths we now hold to be "self-evident"?

2044. What interest rate was charged when the U.S. government took out its first loan in September 1789 to help pay the salaries of the president and Congress?

2045. How much—in pounds and shillings—did Paul Revere charge in expenses for his ride to New York and Philadelphia to deliver news of the Boston Tea Party in December 1773?

2046. What motto was inscribed on the 1787 Fugio cent, the first coin issued by authority of the United States?

2047. After what famous eatery did railroad innovator George Pullman name his first luxury dining car in 1832?

2048. How many male justices had been appointed to the U.S. Supreme Court before Sandra Day O'Connor became the first woman named to the nation's highest court?

2049. What are the eight Rocky Mountain states?

2050. How long did it take aerialist Philippe Petit to make his 1,350-foot-long tightrope walk between the twin towers of the World Trade Center in New York City in 1974?

2051. What state capital was originally called Pig's Eye?

2052. What famous Indian chief's name was Goyakla or Goyathlay, which means One Who Yawns in his native tongue?

2053. In the early years of America's celebration of Mother's Day, what flower was customarily worn by those honoring their moms?

2054. What did "Little Miss Sure Shot" Annie Oakley do with all her gold shooting medals?

2055. What percent of a newly minted dime is silver?

2041. *23. They are: Maine, New Hampshire, Massachusetts, Rhode Island, Connecticut, New York, New Jersey, Delaware, Maryland, Virginia, North Carolina, South Carolina, Georgia, Florida, Alabama, Mississippi, Louisiana, Texas, California, Oregon, Washington, Alaska and Hawaii.*

2042. *In Metropolis, Illinois. The comic book superhero lived and worked as Clark Kent in a fictional city named Metropolis.*

2043. *Jefferson wrote "sacred and undeniable," but Benjamin Franklin, acting as his editor, changed the wording to "self-evident." In all, 86 changes were made to the draft submitted by Jefferson.*

2044. *Six percent. The loan, for $200,000, was from the Bank of New York. A similar loan was obtained from the Bank of North America.*

2045. *14 pounds, 2 shillings. The trip took him 11 days. His bill, endorsed by John Hancock, was sold at auction in 1978 for $70,000.*

2046. *"Mind your business." The motto was suggested by Benjamin Franklin. Fugio is Latin for "I am fleeing"—meaning time flies.*

2047. *Delmonico's, the fashionable New York restaurant.*

2048. *104. She was nominated to the Supreme Court in 1981 by Ronald Reagan.*

2049. *Idaho, Montana, Wyoming, Nevada, Utah, Colorado, Arizona and New Mexico.*

2050. *50 minutes.*

2051. *St. Paul, Minnesota. Pig's Eye was the nickname of one of the town's first settlers, a French-Canadian trader named Pierre Parrant.*

2052. *The Apache we know as Geronimo, Spanish for Jerome.* **2053.** *The carnation. Pink carnations were worn by those whose mothers were alive; white by those whose mothers had died.*

2054. *She had them melted down, then sold the gold and gave the money to charity.*

2055. *None. As of 1965, the U.S. Mint stopped putting silver in dimes. They contain 75 percent copper and 25 percent nickel, bonded to an inner core of pure copper. Previously, dimes were 90 percent silver and 10 percent copper.*

2056. For what is the telephone number 800-555-0199 reserved?

2057. What three names were given to more than half the females christened in the Massachusetts Bay Colony in the 1600s?

2058. What group of Americans speak a dialect they call Mudderschprooch?

2059. What shipboard position did John Washington, George Washington's grandfather, hold when he sailed from England to Virginia aboard the ketch Sea Horse of London in 1657?

2060. What Ivy League college was the last to go coed?

2061. What Old West city was named after a biblical city that drew its name from the Hebrew word for "grassy plain."

2062. How many U.S. states are there with only four letters in their names? Watch out, this is a trick question.

2063. What American city claims to have the only authentic Dutch windmill in the country?

2064. How long must a person be dead before he or she can be honored with a U.S. commemorative stamp?

2065. In airport code, LAX stands for Los Angeles International Airport and JFK for Kennedy International Airport. What airport is represented by the initials IAD?

2066. What weekly periodical was the first magazine in history to sell a billion copies in a year?

2056. *The movies. It's the 800 number set aside for use in films.*

2057. *Sarah, Elizabeth and Mary.*

2058. *The Amish. The language is Pennsylvania Dutch.*

2059. *He was a ship's mate. Although Washington intended to return to England with the ketch and a cargo of tobacco, the ship sank and he stayed in the colonies.*

2060. *Dartmouth, in 1972.*

2061. *Abilene, Kansas, which was entirely grassland when it was named in the mid-nineteenth century and served as the end of the famous Chisholm Trail. The biblical Abilene (from the Hebrew word abel) is mentioned in Luke 3:1 and was in ancient Syria.*

2062. *Nine. The easy ones are Iowa and Utah. The tough ones are Alabama, Alaska, Hawaii, Indiana, Kansas, Mississippi and Tennessee.*

2063. *Aptly named Holland, Michigan, founded in 1847 by Dutch immigrants and site of an annual tulip festival. The city's centuries-old windmill was dismantled in Vinkel, Holland, and reassembled there in 1965.*

2064. *At least 10 years—except for U.S. presidents. Commemorative stamps can be issued for a deceased president on the first birthday anniversary following his death, or anytime thereafter.*

2065. *Dulles International Airport in Washington, D.C.*

2066. *TV Guide, in 1974.*

2067. What was the dark blue Crayola crayon called before its name was changed to midnight blue in 1958?

2068. What did Wild Bill Hickok toss around his bed so he wouldn't be surprised by anyone sneaking up on him while he slept?

2069. What state has an average of 124 tornadoes a year—more than any other?

2070. What name was given to the largest diamond ever found in the U.S.?

2071. What did the middle initial O stand for in the late Supreme Court Justice William O. Douglas's name?

2072. What number iron did astronaut Alan Shepard use when he took his famous swing at a golf ball on the moon?

2073. What is the flickertail, from which North Dakota gets its official state nickname, the Flickertail State?

2074. What did Robert LeRoy Ripley, creator of the Believe It or Not newspaper cartoons, call his oddity-filled 27-room home?

2075. How many of the ships involved in Columbus's historic 1492 expedition made return voyages to the New World?

2076. American dollar bills are not printed on paper as many believe—what are they printed on?

2077. What famous American statesman made three appearances on national TV as a weather forecaster?

2078. According to Senate tradition, who is assigned the desk once occupied by Daniel Webster?

2079. What famous Old West lawman was appointed deputy U.S. marshal for New York by Theodore Roosevelt?

2080. What state's official bird is the roadrunner?

2081. How many terms did American frontiersman Davy Crockett serve in Congress?

2067. Prussian blue. It was the first crayon renamed by Binney & Smith, which started producing crayons in 1903.

2068. Crumpled newspapers.

2069. Texas. In second place is Oklahoma, which averages 56 tornadoes a year.

2070. The Uncle Sam diamond. It was 40.23 carats in the rough when it was found in Murfreesboro, Arkansas, in 1924, and it yielded a 12.42-carat gem.

2071. Orville.

2072. A six. The club actually was a 6-iron head attached to a jointed astronaut tool used to scoop soil.

2073. A squirrel—the Richardson ground squirrel—widely found in North Dakota.

2074. Bion—for Believe It or Not.

2075. Only one—the Niña. The Santa Maria, Columbus's flagship, ran aground off Hispaniola and was abandoned on the first expedition; the Pinta sailed home from the New World and disappeared from history.

2076. Fabric—a cotton linen blend.

2077. Former secretary of state and national security advisor Henry Kissinger, in 1991.

2078. The senior senator from New Hampshire. The tradition was established by New Hampshire Senator Styles Bridges, who discovered the desk in the basement of the Capitol. (Webster, who represented Massachusetts in the Senate, was born in New Hampshire.)

2079. Bat Masterson.

2080. New Mexico's.

2081. Three.

2082. What figure in American history is believed to have inspired the exclamation "Great Scott"?

2083. How fast was New York City cabbie Jacob German driving when he became the first motorist arrested in the U.S. for speeding?

2084. What was the first word spoken on the moon?

2085. What was Benjamin Franklin explaining when he said, "An ounce of prevention is worth a pound of cure"?

2086. How many banks and trains did the notorious Jesse James rob?

2087. What was the name of De Tour Village, Michigan, before it was changed?

2088. What was the first country to which the United States sent a woman as ambassador?

2089. Of the 14 states bordering on the Atlantic, which has the least oceanfront—only 13 miles?

2090. What did the town of Ismay, Montana, change its name to in 1993?

2091. How did Embarrass, Wisconsin, get its name?

2092. What was the weekly salary paid to Chief Sitting Bull when he was part of Buffalo Bill Cody's traveling Wild West Show?

2093. What is the only crime defined in the U.S. Constitution?

2094. When the first U.S. Congress set the president's pay at $25,000 a year, what salary did it establish for the vice president?

2082. *Gen. Winfield Scott—the hero of the Mexican War and the losing candidate for president in 1852.*

2083. *12 miles an hour. The year was 1899, and the arresting officer was on a bicycle.*

2084. *"Houston." Astronaut Neil Armstrong's first message on July 20, 1969, was: "Houston, Tranquillity Base here. The Eagle has landed."*

2085. *Why he had just attached a lightning rod to his house.*

2086. *Banks, 12; trains, 7.*

2087. *Detour. It was changed to avoid confusion with road signs. The village is located on Lake Huron at the eastern tip of Michigan's Upper Peninsula.*

2088. *Denmark, in 1933. Ruth Bryan Owen, a two-term congresswoman and the daughter of William Jennings Bryan, served until 1936 when she married Danish citizen Borge Rohde.*

2089. *New Hampshire. Florida has the most, 580 miles.*

2090. *Joe, Montana, in honor of the star quarterback.*

2091. *The village's founding fathers weren't commemorating an event that left them red-faced. They took the name from a local river that lumberjacks often found impassable—and embarras is French for "hindrance" or "obstacle."*

2092. *$50.*

2093. *Treason—in Article III, Section 3.*

2094. *$5,000.*

2095. What state owes its name to its having been discovered during Eastertime?

2096. In what state was the Battle of Tippecanoe fought in November 1811?

2097. El Paso is known as the Four C City. What attractions do the four C's represent?

2098. Under the rules of the Senate Ethics Committee, what is the maximum number of times a senator's name can appear in a newsletter to his or her constituents?

2099. Who represented Aaron Burr's wife, Eliza Jumel, when she sued her 80-year-old husband for divorce on grounds of adultery in 1836?

2100. What was the name of Paul Bunyan's pet moosehound?

2101. What state has official neckwear?

2102. In what year did the F. B. I, established in 1908 as the Bureau of Investigation, start hiring women as special agents?

2103. The flag of what American state was designed by a 13-year-old- boy?

2104. At what constant speed does the cable that pulls San Francisco's famous cable cars move—in miles per hour?

2105. Who was the first African-American to have his portrait engraved on a U.S. coin?

2106. What was the late Supreme Court Justice Thurgood Marshall's first name at birth?

2107. What was the featured attraction between the Indian elephant act and the ape-man act at the Barnum & Bailey Circus in 1896?

2108. Where was Billy the Kid, the notorious Wild West outlaw, born?

2109. In what city did the high-kicking Rockettes of New York's Radio City Music Hall get their start?

2095. *Florida. Spanish explorer Juan Ponce de Leon named the land Pascua Florida— "flowery Easter"—when he discovered it in 1513.*

2096. *Indiana.*

2097. *Cattle, climate, copper and cotton.*

2098. *An average of eight times per page. The rule applies to franked (postage-exempt) mail.*

2099. *Alexander Hamilton, Jr., son of the man Burr killed in his famous duel. Jumel was granted a legal divorce on the day of Burr's death.*

2100. *Elmer.*

2101. *Arizona—the bolo tie.*

2102. *In 1972—after the death of longtime director J. Edgar Hoover, who had banned women agents.*

2103. *Alaska. Seventh-grader Benny Benson entered the design—of the Big Dipper and the North Star on a field of blue—in an American Legion contest in 1927. It was adopted as the territorial flag, and later as the state flag.*

2104. *9 mph.*

2105. *Booker T. Washington, on a commemorative silver half-dollar issued from 1946 to 1951.*

2106. *Thoroughgood—he shortened it when he was in the second grade.*

2107. *An automobile. American auto pioneer Charles Duryea drove around in one of the 13 autos his Duryea Motor Wagon Company produced that year.*

2108. *In New York City, as Henry McCarty, in 1859. He later changed his name to Henry Antrim, then to William (Billy the Kid) Bonney.*

2109. *In St. Louis. The dancing group was organized there in 1925 as the Missouri Rockets. After changing the name to the Roxyettes, the group moved to Radio City, becoming the Rockettes in 1932.*

2110. How has American veterinarian and U.S. Agriculture Department inspector Daniel E. Salmon (1850-1914) been immortalized?

2111. What was the last institution of higher learning in the United States established by royal decree?

2112. What mountain has the most extensive glacial system of any single peak in the contiguous 48 states?

2113. What was the Declaration of Sentiments, drafted in Seneca Falls, New York, in 1848?

2114. What was the name of strongman-bodybuilder Charles Atlas's son?

2115. What was Benjamin Franklin's last official act?

2116. What body of water did the early American settlers describe as "too thick to drink, too thin to plow"?

2117. What is the name of the 600-mile-long California trail that the Spanish blazed from mission to mission from San Diego to Sonoma?

2118. What role did Garret A. Hobart play in American history?

2119. In what city was the first stock exchange in the United States established?

2120. Who wrote the unofficial anthem of Hawaii, "Aloha Oe"?

2121. What famous early Americans named North America's whistling swan?

2122. How many single-serving jars of baby food does the average American baby eat in one year?

2123. In 1910 there were 32 million Americans living on farms. How many were living on farms in 1990?

2124. How was a man named Fred Ott immortalized by Thomas Edison?

2110. *Salmonella—the sometimes deadly bacteria—is named for him.*

2111. *Dartmouth College, which received its royal charter from England's King George III in 1769.*

2112. *Mount Rainier, in Washington State. It has a total of 26 named glaciers.*

2113. *A treatise, patterned after the Declaration of Independence, that declared "All men and women are created equal." It was signed by 100 people— 68 women and 32 men—at the nation's first women's rights convention.*

2114. *Hercules. He grew up to become a math teacher.*

2115. *Two months before his death in 1790, he signed a petition to Congress calling for the abolition of slavery. He did so as president of the Pennsylvania Society for Promoting the Abolition of Slavery.*

2116. *The Mississippi River, which is nicknamed the Big Muddy.*

2117. *El Camino Real. It linked 21 missions and 4 forts.*

2118. *Vice president (1897-99) to William McKinley—Hobart died while in office.*

2119. *In Philadelphia, in 1790—two years before a New York exchange was set up.*

2120. *Queen Liliuokalani—the last royal ruler of the Hawaiian Islands.*

2121. *Explorers Meriwether Lewis and William Clark, who discovered the swan and named it for its song during their expedition to the West Coast.*

2122. *630, according to the folks at Gerber Products.*

2123. *4.6 million.*

2124. *Edison filmed him sneezing in the first copyrighted film in history.*

2125. What late Nobel Peace Prize-winning world leader was once a wanted terrorist with a $50,000 bounty on his head?

2126. How did Charles Lindbergh's Spirit of St. Louis get back to the U.S. after its historic 1927 transatlantic flight to Paris?

2127. Where was the flower known as the Yellow Rose of Texas first found in the United States?

2128. How wide are the stars from point to point on the flag that inspired Francis Scott Key to write "The Star-Spangled Banner"?

2129. What two changes have been made in the wording of the U.S. Pledge of Allegiance since it was first published in 1892?

2130. How many birthday cards does the average person receive annually?

2131. What magazine regularly publishes a column called "Streetwalker"?

2132. The name of what American state capital means "sheltered harbor."

2133. Why were many private clubs able to serve alcoholic beverages legally during Prohibition?

2134. What is the waist size of the Statue of Liberty?

2135. Who opened the first public aquarium in the United States?

2136. What group of Americans were the first to use the term rub out as a synonym for killing?

2125. *Israeli Prime Minister Menachem Begin. The bounty was offered by British authorities in 1946 when Begin led the Irgun underground guerrillas in their fight for Zionist homeland. He shared the Nobel Prize with Egyptian President Anwar Sadat in 1978.*

2126. *In a pine packing crate, measuring 27 by 12 by 9 feet, that was put aboard the cruiser USS Memphis.*

2127. *In New York City. A lawyer named George Harrison found it as a seedling in the 1830s on his farm near what is now Penn Station. The rose was brought out west by settlers and—according to legend—adopted by Texans after Mexican General Santa Anna was distracted by a beautiful woman wearing it in her hair.*

2128. *Two feet across. The flag is now on display at the Smithsonian Institute in Washington, D.C.*

2129. *The words "the flag of the United States of America" replaced the original words "my flag" in 1923; and the phrase "under God" was added in 1954.*

2130. *Eight, according to the folks at Hallmark.*

2131. *Forbes. The street referred to, of course, is Wall Street.*

2132. *Honolulu.*

2133. *Their alcohol had been purchased before Prohibition went into effect. The Eighteenth Amendment didn't ban the purchase, possession or consumption of alcohol—it banned its manufacture, sale, transportation, importation or exportation.*

2134. *The statue measures 35 feet in diameter at the waist. But there is no real "waistline"—the robe forms the outer shell of the statue and there is no "torso" underneath.*

2135. *Showman P.T. Barnum, in New York City in 1856.*

2136. *Trappers—not gangsters—during the early nineteenth century. The term was derived from Plains Indian sign language, which used a rubbing motion to indicate killing.*

2137. What magazine did the Library of Congress cease publishing in braille in 1985 after Congress voted to withhold funding?

2138. Who was the first chairman of the Securities and Exchange Commission?

2139. For whom were Mount Wayne, Mount Powell and Mount Hughes named in Utah's Escalante Desert?

2140. What six Americans states were named after English kings or queens?

2141. Which is the only one of the original 48 states to have a fjord—a narrow sea inlet bordered by steep cliffs?

2142. What state's official motto has the capital of another state in it?

2143. What famous American was listed in the 1920 Chicago telephone directory as "second hand furniture dealer, 2220 S. Wabash Ave."?

2144. By law, how long must information collected in a U.S. census remain confidential?

2145. What is the unusual state gem of Washington?

2146. Who coined the word hello and introduced it as the proper way to answer a telephone call?

2147. How soon after gold was discovered at Sutter's mill in 1848 did the United States acquire California?

2148. What post office—zip code 33843—is the smallest in the country?

2149. What cities served as the seat of government for the fledgling U.S.A. before Washington, D.C., became the nation's capital in December 1800?

2137. *Playboy, which it had been publishing in braille—without ads or pictures—for 15 years. Publication resumed in 1986 after the courts ruled Congress's action illegal. At the time Playboy was the sixth most popular of the 36 publications the Library was printing in braille.*

2138. *Joseph P. Kennedy—father of President John F. Kennedy.*

2139. *John Wayne, Dick Powell and Howard Hughes. The three mountains were named in their honor after they filmed The Conqueror—about Mongol leader Genghis Khan—on location in the desert in 1954.*

2140. *Georgia, named for King George II; North Carolina and South Carolina, named for King Charles I (from Carolana, "land of Charles," in Latin); Maryland, for Queen Henrietta Maria, wife of Charles I; and Virginia and West Virginia, named for Elizabeth I (who was known as the Virgin Queen).*

2141. *Maine—its six-mile-long fjord, Somes Sound, is located at Mount Desert Island, the largest island in the state.*

2142. *Colorado's—Nothing without providence (Nil sine numine). Providence, of course, is the capital of Rhode Island.*

2143. *Alphonse Capone, better known to us as gangster Al Capone.*

2144. *For 72 years—which is considered a normal lifetime.*

2145. *Petrified wood.*

2146. *Thomas Edison. Alexander Graham Bell favored ahoy but lost out to Edison, whose hello was derived from halloo, the traditional call to rouse hounds to the chase.*

2147. *Nine days. California was part of the territory Mexico ceded to the U.S. in the Treaty of Guadalupe Hidalgo.*

2148. *The converted 8- by-7-foot fertilizer shed that serves the 200 families living in and around Ochopee, in the Florida Everglades.*

2149. *Philadelphia, York and Lancaster, Pennsylvania; Baltimore and Annapolis, Maryland; Princeton and Trenton, New Jersey; and New York City.*

2150. How did a postage stamp convince the U.S. Congress to build a canal across Panama rather than the original choice, Nicaragua?

2151. In June 1939 a New York City magistrate ruled nose-thumbing legal with one reservation. What was it?

2152. What two state flags include a Confederate flag in their design?

2153. Where did the prefabricated Quonset hut get its name?

2154. How did Manhattan get its name—and what does it mean?

2155. Who were Robert Leroy Parker and Henry Longbaugh?

2156. Why did Benjamin Franklin call himself "perhaps the loneliest man" attending the First Continental Congress in 1774?

2157. How did San Francisco policemen save important city records from the devastating fires sparked by the 1906 earthquake?

2158. What city has the country's highest zip code number—99950?

2159. How many crisp new dollar bills to the pound?

2160. In 1925 what did con man Arthur Ferguson "lease" to a wealthy cattle rancher for 99 years at $100,000 a year?

2161. In 1814 when Francis Scott Key wrote what is now our National Anthem, how many stars and stripes were on the flag flying over Fort McHenry in Baltimore Harbor?

2162. Who was Florence Nightingale Graham?

2163. How much did Texas millionaire H. Ross Perot pay for a copy of the Magna Carta in 1984?

2150. *The Nicaraguan postage stamp showed a belching volcano, triggering fears that an eruption might destroy the canal.*

2151. *That the "thumber" be at a safe distance— "about 10 feet"—from the "thumbee."*

2152. *Those of Georgia and Mississippi.*

2153. *From Quonset, Rhode Island, where it was first manufactured during World War II.*

2154. *It's a derivative of the Indian word Manahachtaniek, which means "the island where we all got drunk," apparently referring to a spirited encounter between the Native Americans and some newly arrived Dutchmen.*

2155. *The inspiration for "Butch Cassidy and the Sundance Kid," portrayed on film by Paul Newman and Robert Redford in 1969 and William Katt and Tom Berenger in 1979.*

2156. *He had chosen his country over his only son, William, who had pledged loyalty to the British crown.*

2157. *They hauled them to a downtown square and soaked them with beer from nearby saloons.*

2158. *Ketchikan, Alaska. The lowest 00401, belongs to the Reader's Digest company in Pleasantville, New York.*

2159. *Exactly 490, according to the Bureau of Engraving and Printing.*

2160. *The White House. He fled after collecting the first year's rent but got caught a short time later trying to sell the Statue of Liberty to an Australian.*

2161. *Fifteen each. They represented the original 13 states plus Vermont and Kentucky.*

2162. *Beauty entrepreneur Elizabeth Arden. (Consistent with her given name, she briefly pursued a nursing career.)*

2163. *He paid $1.5 million for a version issued in 1297 and believed to be the most complete of the 17 copies known to exist. The original was issued in 1215, and 4 copies of that still exist: 2 in the British Museum, 1 at Lincoln Cathedral and 1 at Salisbury Cathedral.*

2164. Which six states have more senators than representatives in Congress?

2165. Where did the family of Thomas Mellon, founder of the prosperous banking dynasty, settle after immigrating to the U.S. from northern Ireland?

2166. What state has designated "Home on the Range" its official song?

2167. When Charles Lindbergh soloed across the Atlantic in 1927, what did he bring along to keep him company?

2168. Podunk has come to mean Smalltown, U.S.A. Where is Podunk?

2169. What organization in 1972 began encouraging its members to learn how to treat rat bites and read subway maps?

2170. What two cities were linked by the Chisholm Trail, the cattle drivers' route first used in 1867?

2171. Which American state legislature is the only one to have a single chamber?

2172. What city promotes itself as the "air capital of the world" because it produces more aircraft than any other city?

2173. What special training was required of the first airline stewardesses, hired by United Airlines in 1930?

2174. What is the foggiest place in the United States?

2175. At 11:03 p.m. on February 28, 1983, why did water usage in New York City rise by an unprecedented 300 million gallons?

2176. In what year were FBI agents first allowed to carry guns?

2177. What American statesman, in his later years, regularly received mail deliveries at a park bench in Lafayette Square, opposite the White House?

2164. *Alaska, Delaware, North Dakota, South Dakota, Vermont and Wyoming have only one representative each.*

2165. *Poverty Point, Pennsylvania.*

2166. *Kansas.*

2167. *The "Lone Eagle" took a Feliz the Cat doll on his 33½-hour flight.*

2168. *In Massachusetts, near Worcester.*

2169. *The Boy Scouts, by offering merit badges in those two areas of achievement.*

2170. *San Antonio, Texas, and Abilene, Kansas.*

2171. *The Nebraska legislature.*

2172. *Wichita, Kansas.*

2173. *They had to be registered nurses. The requirement was dropped 12 years later.*

2174. *Cape Disappointment, Washington. It's foggy there an average of 2,552 hours a year—or 106 complete days.*

2175. *The final episode of M*A*S*H had just ended, and an estimated one million New Yorkers flushed their toilets in unison.*

2176. *In 1934—26 years after the agency was established, and the year in which the careers of John Dillinger, Pretty Boy Floyd and Baby Face Nelson came to abrupt and bloody ends.*

2177. *Financier Bernard Baruch, who became known as the "Park Bench Statesman" during World War II when he used the unpainted oak bench as his office.*

2178. How many children were born to the Mayflower's Priscilla Mullins and "Speak for yourself John" Alden, whose romance was immortalized in "The Courtship of Miles Standish" by Henry Wadsworth Longfellow?

2179. What unwanted distinction did the Red Lantern in Chicago gain on February 1, 1920?

2180. The motto "In God We Trust" first appeared on U.S. currency in 1864. What was the denomination of the coin?

2181. What was on the site of the Empire State Building before the 102-story skyscraper was erected in 1931?

2182. To whom was Santa Claus delivering Christmas gifts in the Thomas Nast cartoon that first depicted him with a sleigh and reindeer?

2183. What did the town of Lovelady, New Jersey, change its name to in 1962?

2184. When was "In God We Trust"—which first appeared on an American coin in 1864—adopted as the national motto?

2185. What are the vital statistics of the 72-foot-high Betty Boop balloon in the Macy's Thanksgiving Day Parade?

2186. What famous Old West duo threw an elegant five-course Thanksgiving dinner for their neighbors as a thank-you for not being turned in to the law?

2187. When television cameras moved into the Senate in 1986, who advised its members, "You learn your lines, don't bump into the furniture, and, in the kissing scenes, keep your mouth closed?"

2188. When was the site of the Washington Memorial—completed in 1885—first proposed?

2189. What was the real name of criminal George "Baby Face" Nelson, who was Public Enemy Number One when he was gunned down by F.B.I. agents in 1934?

2190. How many American astronauts have walked on the moon?

2178. *Ten. According to "Families of the Pilgrims," by the Massachusetts Society of Mayflower Descendants, there were six girls and four boys.*

2179. *It was the first speakeasy raided by federal agents during Prohibition.*

2180. *Two cents.*

2181. *The original Waldorf-Astoria Hotel.*

2182. *Soldiers fighting in the Civil War. The cartoon, entitled "Santa Claus in Camp," appeared on the cover of "Harper's Weekly" on January 3, 1863.*

2183. *Loveladies.*

2184. *In 1956.*

2185. *A shapely 34-24-36 (feet, that is).*

2186. *Butch Cassidy and the Sundance Kid. The dinner, from oysters to plum pudding with brandy sauce, took place in Brown's Park, a valley at the junction of Utah, Colorado and Wyoming.*

2187. *President Reagan, who said the advice came from his Hollywood days.*

2188. *In 1791, in Pierre L'Enfant's original master plan for the District of Columbia.*

2189. *Lester Gillis, who adopted his famous alias when he was arrested in his teens.*

2190. *Twelve, between July 1969 and December 1972. In order of their lunar visits: Neil Armstrong, Edwin Aldrin, Charles Conrad, Alan Bean, Alan Shepard, Edgar Mitchell, David Scott, James Irwin, John Young, Charles Duke, Eugene Cernan and Harrison Schmitt.*

2191. What was Montana's capital, Helena, called when it was a mining camp in the 1860s?

2192. What unique monetary service has the St. Francis Hotel in San Francisco provided for the past 60 years?

2193. Colonial New York paved its first street—using stones—in 1657. What was its name?

2194. How much was Tennessee schoolteacher John T. Scopes fined after he was found guilty of teaching evolution at his famous "monkey trial" in 1925?

2195. How did John Paul Scott, the only prisoner known to have survived an escape from Alcatraz, make it across the perilous waters of San Francisco Bay?

2196. What state, of the contiguous 48, touches only one other state?

2197. Where did Yale students find the name "Whiffenpoof" for their singing society and song?

2198. Congress established the nation's first minimum wage in 1938. What was it?

2199. Who is the source of the U.S. Post Office's unofficial motto: "Neither snow, nor rain, nor heat, nor gloom of night stays these couriers from the swift completion of their appointed rounds"?

2200. What American city was founded in 1733 as a haven for British debtors?

2201. The highest and lowest points in the contiguous 48 states are within 75 miles of one another. What are they?

2202. The sign in front of a building on George Washington Parkway in Langley, Virginia, used to say Fairbank Highway Research. What does it say now?

2203. What was the source of the green copper used to repair the Statue of Liberty for her 100th birthday in 1986?

2191. *Last Chance Gulch.*

2192. *Its guests are given only freshly washed coins. The hotel employs a full-time coin washer.*

2193. *Stone Street.*

2194. *He had to pay $100.*

2195. *With water wings he fashioned from surgical gloves. Although he survived, he was recaptured after a 2½-mile swim.*

2196. *Maine—it touches only New Hampshire.*

2197. *From an imaginary character in the 1908 Victor Herbert operetta "Little Nemo."*

2198. *Twenty-five cents an hour.*

2199. *Greek historian Herodotus, who was referring to the couriers of Persia's King Xerxes I in the fifth century B.C.*

2200. *Savannah, Georgia.*

2201. *Mount Whitney, which is 14,494 feet above sea level, and Death Valley, which drops to 282 feet below sea level at a spot known as Bad Water. Both are in California.*

2202. *CIA—it was changed in 1974 in a Nixon administration move toward more open government.*

2203. *A Bell Laboratory roof in Murray Hill, New Jersey. New copper would have been penny-bright.*

2204. How much did NASA charge for America's first paying space passenger, scientist Charles Walker, on his trip aboard the shuttle Challenger in August 1984?

2205. How much did industrialist-philanthropist John D. Rockefeller—America's first billionaire—give to charity during his 97-year lifetime?

2206. What was civil libertarian Henry David Thoreau's response when his friend Ralph Waldo Emerson visited him in jail and asked: "Why are you in there, Henry?"

2207. How many sisters and brothers did Benjamin Franklin have?

2208. According to legend, why did Betsy Ross suggest making the stars on the American flag five-pointed instead of six-pointed, as originally planned?

2209. By what names do we know twin sisters Pauline and Esther Friedman, born on the Fourth of July, 1918?

2210. Why was astronaut John Young reprimanded after returning from the first multi-manned space flight with Gus Grissom in March 1965?

2211. What American city boasts a Moon Walk?

2212. What American diversion did the London *Times* label a "menace" in 1924 for "making devastating inroads on the working hours of every rank of society"?

2213. How long was Prohibition in effect in the U.S.?

2214. What name did Pocahontas, the Indian princess who saved Captain John Smith, adopt after she married settler John Rolfe and converted to Christianity?

2215. Who is the only king to be included in the National Statuary Hall in the U.S. Capitol building?

2216. What is the English translation of Sputnik—the name Russia gave to the first artificial satellite to orbit the earth?

2204. *NASA was paid $80,000 by McDonnell Douglas, for whom Walker manufactured a batch of rare hormones at zero gravity.*

2205. *He gave away more than a half billion dollars—$531,326,842.*

2206. *"Why are you out there?" Thoreau, as a protest against slavery, had refused to pay his poll tax.*

2207. *Sixteen—seven sisters and nine brothers. He was the fifteenth child and youngest son.*

2208. *Because she could easily cut them with a single snip of the scissors after folding the fabric in a special way.*

2209. *We know Pauline as* Dear Abby, *advice columnist Abigail Van Buren; Esther as advice columnist Ann Landers.*

2210. *For eating a smuggled corned beef sandwich during the flight, creating crumbs that threatened the craft's sensitive machinery.*

2211. *New Orleans. The crescent-shaped promenade along the Mississippi River is named for a former city mayor, Moon Landrieu.*

2212. *The crossword puzzle, which the introduced as a Christmas treat in its Sunday supplement in 1913.*

2213. *Almost 14 years, from January 1920 to December 1933.*

2214. *Rebecca.*

2215. *Hawaii's King Kamehameha.*

2216. *"Traveler."*

2217. What were the first words spoken by aviation great Charles Lindbergh when he landed in Paris following his historic nonstop solo flight across the Atlantic?

2218. How long did it take news of the "shot heard 'round the world" at the Battle of Lexington on April 19, 1775, to reach New York City?

2219. How many Finger Lakes are there in central New York?

2220. To whom did "New York" magazine present its 1985 "More Clothes Than Nancy Reagan Award"?

2221. For what 1961 story did the Associated Press issue its first public apology since it prematurely announced the end of World War II?

2222. How did the town of Ink, Arkansas, get its name?

2223. In what special way did Chicago mayor Richard J. Daley commemorate St. Patrick's Day in 1965?

2224. Where were the first parking meters in the U.S. installed?

2225. How much was the tax on tea when the colonists held the Boston Tea Party in 1773?

2226. What four states have active volcanoes?

2227. According to Indian legend, Lake Itasca in northwest Minnesota is named for I-tesk-ka, daughter of Hiawatha. What is its other claim to fame?

2228. Who was Marie Joseph Paul Yves Roch Gilbert du Motier?

2229. Which state was the first to outlaw slavery?

2230. How much was black seamstress Rosa Parks fined for refusing to give up her bus seat to a white man in the incident that launched the Reverend Martin Luther King Jr.'s civil rights career?

2231. What did the high-living gastronomical giant Diamond Jim Brady buy when his doctor ordered him to get some exercise?

2217. *"Are there any mechanics here?" When he was unable to understand the flurry of replies in French, he shouted, "Does anyone here speak English?"*

2218. *Four days.*

2219. *Eleven. According to Indian legend, they are the water-filled fingerprints of the Great Spirit.*

2220. *Barbie, the doll—because of the 20 million designer fashions sold for her.*

2221. *A story that First Lady Jackie Kennedy had been spotted doing the twist in a Palm Beach nightclub.*

2222. *When the Post Office application for the community was being filled out, someone wrote "ink" where the form requested "Name of town (write in ink)."*

2223. *He had 100 pounds of emerald green dye poured into the Chicago River.*

2224. *In Oklahoma City, Oklahoma, in 1935. Motorists paid a nickel for a 20-foot space.*

2225. *Three pence per pound.*

2226. *Alaska, California, Hawaii and Washington.*

2227. *The 1.8-square-mile lake is the main source of the 2,348-mile-long "father of waters," the Mississippi River.*

2228. *America's Revolutionary War ally, the Marquis de Lafayette.*

2229. *Rhode Island, in 1774.*

2230. *She was fined $14.*

2231. *A gold-plated bicycle with diamonds and rubies embedded in the handlebars.*

2232. On what college campus was Phi Beta Kappa—the oldest Greek letter society in the U.S.—first established in 1776?

2233. What was the name of the 1,550-pound bison at the New York Zoo that served as a model for the buffalo nickel, introduced in 1913?

2234. What wood is most widely used in making pencils in the United States?

2235. What two states produce the greatest number of Christmas trees?

2236. What creature serves as the mascot of the University of California at Santa Cruz?

2237. What was the name of Yale University's original bulldog mascot—and all namesakes that have followed?

2238. What did philanthropist Andrew Carnegie contribute to Princeton University in 1906?

2239. With what word did most people answer the telephone when it was first introduced at the end of the nineteenth century?

2240. What is May Day known as in Hawaii?

2241. The name of what Florida city means "rodent mouth" in Spanish?

2242. Before it got its present name in 1847, what American city was known as Yerba Buena— "good herb" in Spanish—for an aromatic herb that grew in the area?

2243. What monument is the tallest in the United States—at 630 feet?

2244. Where was the first library in North America established in 1638?

2245. What percentage of the United States is officially designated wilderness?

2232. *The College of William and Mary in Williamsburg, Virginia.*

2233. *Black Diamond. It was sold for $700 in 1915 and turned into 750 pounds of usable meat.*

2234. *Cedar—more specifically, the incense cedar of the high Sierra Nevada in northern California. It has a straight grain and is soft enough to be sharpened without splintering. It replaced the red cedar of the southern U.S. after those forests were depleted.*

2235. *Oregon and Michigan.*

2236. *The banana slug.*

2237. *Handsome Dan.*

2238. *A 3½-mile-long lake to "take the young men's minds off football," a game he detested.*

2239. *"Ahoy." Thomas Edison later suggested replacing it with a simple "Hello."*

2240. *Lei Day. Ever since 1928, Hawaiians have dedicated the day to the garland of flowers that is their symbol of friendship—celebrating with Polynesian songs and pageantry.*

2241. *Boca Raton. The name is believed to come from the shape of the city's Atlantic Ocean shoreline.*

2242. *San Francisco.*

2243. *The Gateway Arch, in St. Louis, Missouri.*

2244. *At Harvard College. The initial collection consisted of 329 religious and philosophical texts.*

2245. *3.8 percent.*

2246. What was unusual about the hand-carved Great Seal of the U.S. that Soviet diplomats gave Averell Harriman in 1945 when he was U.S. ambassador to Moscow?

2247. How often can the design of an American coin be changed without Congressional approval?

2248. How many islands, reefs and shoals make up the Hawaiian archipelago?

2249. What city on the Virginia-North Carolina border is named for the two states?

2250. Who was the first U.S. citizen to cross the Continental Divide?

2251. How many shots were fired in the famous gunfight at the O.K. Corral?

2252. What building in Hayward, Wisconsin, is shaped like a muskie?

2253. The life expectancy of the average American born in 1990 is 72.7 years for males and 76.1 for females. What was it for the average American born in 1900?

2254. What animal served as Yale's mascot before the bulldog?

2255. How did Washington Post reporter Bob Woodward signal his anonymous Watergate source, Deep Throat, when he wanted to make contact?

2256. What major American city passed an ordinance in 1838 making it necessary to get a license before serenading a woman?

2257. What was the size of the standard lot in Levittown, New York, when it was developed as the first mass-housing suburb in the country following World War II?

2258. How many burglars were arrested inside the Democratic Party's national headquarters at the Watergate complex in Washington, D.C., on June 17, 1972?

2259. Who was the first American to get oil drilling concessions in Saudi Arabia and Kuwait?

2246. *It contained a listening device that enabled the Soviets to monitor all conversations in Harriman's private study, where the seal was displayed on the wall. The bug wasn't discovered until 1952.*

2247. *Once in 25 years.*

2248. *132.*

2249. *Virgilina.*

2250. *Meriwether Lewis, on August 12, 1805, during his historic expedition with William Clark.*

2251. *34—evenly split between the Earps and the Clantons. But the Earps were better marksmen, scoring 13 hits and killing three (Billy Clanton, and Frank and Tom McLowery). The Clantons had three hits, wounding two (Morgan and Virgil Earp) and ripping a hole in Wyatt Earp's coat.*

2252. *The National Fresh Water Fishing Hall of Fame.*

2253. *Males, 46.6; females, 48.7.*

2254. *A cat. The bulldog replaced the cat in the late 1800s.*

2255. *He put a red flag in a flowerpot on his apartment balcony.*

2256. *Los Angeles.*

2257. *60 by 100 feet. More than 17,000 one-story, two-bedroom, one-bath, wood-frame ranch houses were built—and sold for about $6,000 each.*

2258. *Five. They were adjusting wiretapping equipment that had been installed in May.*

2259. *John Paul Getty.*

2260. Whose statue stands in front of the headquarters of the Organization of American States in Washington, D.C.?

2261. Which state averages the greatest number of shark attacks annually?

2262. How much of the currency in circulation in the United States was believed to be counterfeit in 1865, when the Secret Service was established to combat counterfeiting?

2263. How many British bullets tore through the flag flying over Fort McHenry during the War of 1812 bombardment that inspired Francis Scott Key to write The Star-Spangled Banner?

2264. What state is nicknamed the Pelican State?

2265. The average shower Americans take lasts 10.4 minutes. How many gallons of water does it use up? Bonus: What's the most popular water temperature?

2266. What is the very appropriate state flower of Massachusetts?

2267. How old was Billy the Kid when he was shot to death by Sheriff Pat Garrett?

2268. How long did the jury deliberate at the sensational 1925 "Monkey Trial" of Tennessee science teacher John Scopes?

2269. What was the total weight—to the closest pound—of the septuplets born to Iowa parents Bobbi and Kenny McCaughey in 1997?

2270. What was the highest price ever paid by the United States for a territorial acquisition?

2271. What was the native tribe of Sacagawea, the Indian woman who helped guide Lewis and Clark on their historic 1804 journey of discovery?

2272. What was the name of the ship that carried the second group of colonists to Plymouth, Massachusetts?

2260. Queen Isabella I, who financed Christopher Columbus's expedition to America. The statue was a gift from Spain.

2261. Florida, with an average of 13 a year.

2262. One-third.

2263. 11.

2264. Louisiana. Its state bird is the pelican.

2265. Gallons, 12.4; temperature, 105°F.

2266. The mayflower.

2267. 21.

2268. Nine minutes. Scopes—whose trial was the setting for the play and film *Inherit The Wind*—was found guilty of violating a state law banning the teaching of evolution in public schools.

2269. 20 pounds—or to be precise, 19 pounds 14 ounces.

2270. $25 million—to Denmark in 1917 for what is now the U.S. Virgin Islands.

2271. Shoshone. She was captured by the Hidatsas and sold into marriage to French Canadian trader/trapper Toussaint Charbonneau, who subsequently joined the Lewis and Clark expedition as a paid interpreter.

2272. The Fortune. It landed at Plymouth with 30 settlers on December 13, 1621—just under a year after the colonists aboard the Mayflower disembarked there.

2273. How much did Baltimore seamstress Mary Young Pickersgill charge for materials and labor for the 30- by 42-foot woolen flag immortalized in Francis Scott Key's "The Star-Spangled Banner"?

2274. How high was the 1,340-foot-long wall that gave New York's Wall Street its name?

2275. Which U.S. Supreme Court justice wrote the greatest number of majority opinions?

2276. What historic name did Buffalo Bill Cody give to his buffalo gun?

2277. How many rest rooms are there along the 17½ miles of corridors in the Pentagon?

2278. Which is the only state ever to have two decorated Vietnam War combat veterans serving as U.S. senators at the same time?

2279. What was the municipal "cremator" built in New York City in 1885?

2280. When Benjamin Franklin was living in England, what stroke did he use in his regular swims across the Thames River?

2281. What is taught at the California Academy of Tauromaquia in San Diego?

2282. How many sides does a Navajo hogan have?

2283. What name was given to the baby born aboard the Mayflower during its historic voyage to the New World?

2284. Who was the first person honored as Man of the Year by Time magazine?

2285. In whose honor did the city of Modesto, California, erect a bronze sculpture of a teenage boy and girl sitting on the fender of a 1957 Chevrolet?

2286. Which state capital is situated on the Delaware River?

2287. What famous frontier outlaw once handed a press release to a robbery victim and told him to fill in the amount taken?

2273. $405.90.

2274. 12 feet. It was erected in 1653 by the Dutch colonists as protection against their enemies.

2275. Oliver Wendell Holmes. He wrote 873 majority opinions while serving on the Court from 1902 to 1932. Morrison H. Waite, chief justice from 1874 to 1888, wrote just one less-872.

2276. Lucrezia Borgia.

2277. 284.

2278. Nebraska. The two are Democrat Bob Kerrey and Republican Chuck Hagel.

2279. An incinerator—the first city-run incinerator in the U.S. The first one built in England, in 1894, was called a "destructor."

2280. The breast stroke—the same stroke used by Matthew Webb in 1875 when he became the first person to swim across the English Channel.

2281. Bullfighting.

2282. Six; the entry always faces east, toward the morning sun.

2283. Oceanus. A second baby, who was named Peregrine, was born aboard ship after the Mayflower set anchor. The full names of the two boys were Oceanus Hopkins and Peregrine White.

2284. Charles Lindbergh, in 1927.

2285. Director-producer George Lucas. The sculpture, erected in 1997 on a plot renamed Lucas Square, pays tribute to the Modesto-born filmmaker's 1973 movie classic American Graffiti.

2286. Trenton, New Jersey.

2287. Jesse James. The victim was a train conductor.

2288. How did Wisconsin come to be called the Badger State?

2289. On which holiday are the greatest number of collect calls generally made in the United States?

2290. What famous American inventor and diplomat compiled a list of more than 200 synonyms for "drunk," including cherry-merry, nimptopsical, and soaked?

2291. What did Paul Revere shout on his famous midnight ride from Boston to Lexington on April 18, 1775? Hint: Longfellow had it wrong in his poem.

2292. English ships once carried limes to protect sailors from scurvy; what did American vessels carry?

2293. What is the official state dessert of Massachusetts?

2294. How much was the tax per pound of tea that triggered the Boston Tea Party in 1773?

2295. How did Zilwaukee, Michigan, get its name?

2296. What American coin was the first to have nickel in it?

2297. Why do old firehouses have circular staircases?

Bonus Trivia

2298. General Henry "Lighthorse Harry" Lee, who said, "to the memory of the man, first in war, first in peace, and first in the hearts of his countrymen," in reference to George Washington, was the father of Confederate General Robert E. Lee.

2299. Ohio, known as the 17th state, technically did not become a state until August 7, 1953. Due to an oversight, Congress never voted on the resolution to admit Ohio to the Union until that date.

2300. Contrary to popular opinion, the "Saturday Evening Post" was not founded by Benjamin Franklin. It was founded by Charles Alexander and Samuel C. Atkinson in 1821. The "Saturday Evening Post" was, however, begun in the same building in which Franklin had published his "Pennsylvania Gazette."

2288. *"Badger"* was the nickname given to Wisconsin's early miners— mostly Cornish immigrants—who worked underground in lead mines and, like badgers, dug caves in hillsides to survive the coldest winter months.

2289. Father's Day.

2290. Benjamin Franklin.

2291. *"The Regulars are out!"* The Regulars were the British troops.

2292. Cranberries.

2293. Boston cream pie.

2294. 3 cents per pound.

2295. The owners of a local sawmill devised it, hoping German immigrants would confuse it with Milwaukee and settle in their town.

2296. The one-cent piece issued in 1857. It contained 12 percent nickel and 88 percent copper. It was not until 1866 that five-cent pieces containing nickel were put into circulation.

2297. Because in days of yore the horses that pulled fire engines were stabled on the ground floor of fire houses and figured out how to walk up straight staircases.

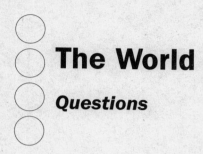

The World

Questions

2301. Where is Rock English spoken?

2302. In 1519 Portuguese navigator Ferdinand Magellan set out to circumnavigate the globe with five ships and 250 men. How many ships and men were left when the expedition ended in 1522?

2303. Where in the world is there a place called Disko Island?

2304. What recreational activity did Joseph Merlin of Belgium demonstrate for the first time in 1760 at a London masquerade party?

2305. What great thinker proved a lunar eclipse is the circular shadow of the earth on the moon?

2306. What is the longest strait in the world?

2307. In what country is the most remote weather station in the world located?

2308. How many members did the United Nations have when it celebrated its 50th anniversary in 1995?

Answers

2301. On Gibraltar, which is commonly known as the Rock. It is a mixed patois of Spanish and English spoken by the natives of the strategic Mediterranean island.

2302. One ship, the Victoria, and 18 men—Magellan not among them. He was killed during the expedition.

2303. In Greenland. Although it's been renamed Qeqertarsuup, it is still widely known by its old name.

2304. Roller skating. Unfortunately, Merlin crashed into a mirror and was seriously injured, discouraging others from giving skating a whirl. Another 103 years passed before the first modern four-wheeled skates were introduced.

2305. Aristotle.

2306. The Strait of Malacca, between the Malay Peninsula and the island of Sumatra. It's about 500 miles long and connects the Andaman and South China seas.

2307. Canada. Its Eureka weather station is 600 miles from the North Pole.

2308. 185. The last to join was the Pacific island chain of Palau, in December 1994.

2309. How many loincloths did archaeologists find in King Tut's tomb after it was discovered in 1922?

2310. What percentage of the earth's land has a temperate climate?

2311. Which European country has two elements on the Periodic Table named after it?

2312. The capitals of what two South American countries are located on the mouth of the same river—the Rio de la Plata?

2313. What famous geological feature was named for the man who headed the Great Trigonometrical Survey of India in the first half of the nineteenth century?

2314. What country produces the world's largest crop of soybeans?

2315. Why did the English call their gold coins guineas?

2316. In what country did the automat originate?

2317. What floral symbol do the state of Kansas and the country of Peru have in common?

2318. What famous statesman was known as Dizzy to his supporters?

2319. Why did the rulers of ancient Sparta mint large, unwieldy iron coins?

2320. On international automobile license plates, what country is represented by the letter E?

2321. What was the first colony in the New World put to agricultural use—with sugar cane plantations?

2322. Which continent is the highest—with more than half of it 6,562 feet above sea level?

2323. What was the name of the first public theater built in England?

2309. *145. The loincloths have been in storage in the Cairo Museum since 1939, along with Tut's jewel-encrusted sandals, beaded tunics, leopard skins and other items of apparel.*

2310. *Seven percent. But nearly half the earth's population lives in temperate zones.*

2311. *France. The elements are No. 31, gallium (Ga), and No. 87, francium (Fr). The name gallium is derived from Gallia, the Latin name for almost all the region we now know as France.*

2312. *Argentina's capital, Buenos Aires; and Uruguay's capital, Montevideo.*

2313. *Mount Everest, which was named for Sir George Everest.*

2314. *The United States. China is the second-largest producer.*

2315. *The gold used for the coins was originally mined in Guinea, in West Africa. Although the coins haven't been minted since 1813, the term guinea is still used to denote a value of 21 shillings.*

2316. *In Sweden. There had been automats there for half a century before Horn & Hardart opened the first U.S. automat in Philadelphia in 1902.*

2317. *The sunflower.*

2318. *Benjamin Disraeli, Queen Victoria's favorite prime minister.*

2319. *To make it difficult for citizens to take the coins with them when they left the country.*

2320. *Spain—the E is for España.*

2321. *Brazil, in the mid-1500s, under the Portuguese. By 1600, it was producing half the world's sugar supply.*

2322. *Antarctica.*

2323. *The Theatre. It was built in 1576, a half-mile outside London because the city fathers barred the performance of plays inside city limits.*

2324. Who was the first American to have a monument erected in his honor in India?

2325. What did Chinese businessmen in the third century B.C. use to put their personal seals on documents?

2326. What percentage of all English surnames are derived from animal names such as Lamb, Fox, Wolf, Hawk and Bird?

2327. How did the Red Sea get its name?

2328. What country is represented by the letters SF on international license plates?

2329. What California city is directly across the border from the Mexican city of Mexicali—and has a name to match it?

2330. How many writing systems appear on the Rosetta Stone, found near Rosetta, Egypt, in 1799 by a Napoleonic expedition?

2331. What article of clothing worn by Roman emperor Caligula as a child gave him his name?

2332. What famous seafarer called his ship the Adventure Galley?

2333. At what speed was the Titanic traveling when it hit an iceberg and sank on its maiden voyage in 1912?

2334. What are the three largest islands in the Mediterranean?

2335. The name of what part of the world is derived from a Latin verb that means "to rise"?

2336. What is the distance—in yards—between the corral and the bull ring at the famous bull runs held annually in Pamplona, Spain?

2337. How did Lake Itasca, the source of the Mississippi River, get its name?

2338. What is the largest desert in Europe?

2324. *George Washington Carver. The monument, erected in Bombay in 1947 by the peanut growers of India, honored Carver for his contributions in making the peanut a popular crop. India is the world's largest peanut-producing country.*

2325. *Their fingerprints. Chinese tablets dating back to 200 B.C. bear fingerprint impressions to prove their authenticity.*

2326. *Three percent.*

2327. *From the occasionally extensive blooms of algae that, upon dying, turn the Red Sea's normally intense blue-green waters red.*

2328. *Finland. SF stands for Suomi Finland.*

2329. *Calexico.*

2330. *Three. The inscription is written in the Greek alphabet, Egyptian hieroglyphics, and demotic script (a cursive form of Egyptian hieroglyphics). The stone is now housed in the British Museum.*

2331. *His sandals. He grew up among his father's soldiers and wore small shoes similar to their iron-nailed military sandals, called caligae in Latin. As a result, he became known by the diminutive Caligula, or Little Shoes. His real name was Gaius Caesar.*

2332. *Captain Kidd.*

2333. *22 knots—to landlubbers, a little over 25 miles per hour.*

2334. *Sicily, Sardinia and Cyprus.*

2335. *The Orient, so named because the sun rises in the east.*

2336. *825 yards.*

2337. *Not from an Indian tribe or word, but from Latin. An early explorer called it Lake Veritas Caput, meaning "true source" or "true head." His companion decided that was too long and chopped off letters at both ends.*

2338. *Europe has no deserts—it's the only continent without one.*

2339. Where is Hillary's Chimney?

2340. What city is the southernmost state capital in the United States?

2341. The region known as Lapland comprises parts of what four countries?

2342. What is the unit of currency of both North and South Korea?

2343. What is the average temperature at the South Pole?

2344. What country has a massive mountain chain known as the Southern Alps?

2345. What city was the first to mint its own gold coins?

2346. What was the name of the daughter Lady Emma Hamilton bore Admiral Horatio Nelson?

2347. How was the great lover and adventurer Casanova earning his livelihood when he died?

2348. What Asian countries are known in economic circles as the Four Tigers?

2349. After Faisal I was deposed as king of Syria in 1920, what country did he serve as king until his death in 1933?

2350. Geographically speaking, what is the area north of latitude 66(30'N called?

2351. How long is the standard single oar used by gondoliers in Venice?

2352. How many stone monoliths are there on Easter Island?

2353. What British statesman was born in a ladies' cloakroom?

2354. How many yards of silk and lace were used to make actress Grace Kelly's wedding gown for her 1956 marriage to Prince Rainier of Monaco?

2339. *On Mount Everest—it's a 40-foot vertical path near the summit of the world's highest mountain (29,028 feet), and the toughest obstacle for those attempting to scale it. It is named for Sir Edmund Hillary, who conquered the mountain in 1953 with Sherpa guide Tenzing Norgay.*

2340. *Austin, Texas—it's about 11 miles farther south than runner-up Tallahassee, Florida.*

2341. *Norway, Sweden, Finland and Russia.*

2342. *The won.*

2343. *-56° Fahrenheit. At the North Pole, the average temperature is -21° F.*

2344. *New Zealand. Located on South Island, the chain has 16 snow-covered peaks over 10,000 feet. The highest, Mount Cook, is named for the explorer who named the chain for its "prodigious height" in 1770.*

2345. *Florence, Italy, in 1252. The coin, the fiorino ("little flower"), became known as the florence, then florin—a name that has been used for coins in a number of countries.*

2346. *Horatia.*

2347. *As a librarian for a count in Bohemia.*

2348. *Hong Kong, Singapore, South Korea and Taiwan. All are major Asian exporting nations that, along with Japan, are responsible for a big part of the U.S. trade deficit.*

2349. *Iraq—the British installed him on the Iraqi throne in 1921.*

2350. *The Arctic Circle.*

2351. *14 feet.*

2352. *838.*

2353. *Winston Churchill, whose mother went into labor while attending a fancy-dress ball.*

2354. *450 yards.*

2355. What country has the world's oldest surviving parliament?

2356. What is the only country in Southeast Asia never ruled by a European nation?

2357. What did Agamemnon and the French revolutionary Jean Marat have in common?

2358. Where is the Louisiana Museum of Modern Art?

2359. What words are missing from this old Irish maxim: "Only two things in this world are too serious to be jested on: ___and___"?

2360. In what four European countries are motorists required to drive on the left-hand side of the road?

2361. What toll was American adventure writer Richard Halliburton charged when he swam the length of the Panama Canal in 1928?

2362. What Italian city receives about 1,000 letters addressed to Juliet every Valentine's Day?

2363. The Germans call it Donou; the Russians call it Dunay. What do people in English-speaking countries call it?

2364. What was the first European city to pave all its streets?

2365. Where was the first Neanderthal fossil excavated in 1856?

2366. How did the ancient Romans keep dry when it rained at the Colosseum?

2367. How did Venice's centuries-old Bridge of Sighs get its name?

2368. What European capital is located in the crater of an extinct volcano?

2369. How many baths did France's King Louis XIV take during his lifetime of almost 77 years?

2370. What is London's equivalent of Wall Street?

2355. *Iceland. Its parliament, the Althing, first met in 930 when Viking chieftains gathered at an open-air assembly to iron out their differences.*

2356. *Thailand.*

2357. *Each was slain in his bath—Agamemnon by his wife, Clytemnestra; Maaraat by Charlotte Corday.*

2358. *In Denmark, in the city of Humlebaek. The museum, established in 1958, features art from the mid-twentieth century to the present.*

2359. *Potatoes and matrimony.*

2360. *Great Britain, Ireland, Malta and Cyprus.*

2361. *36 cents. Halliburton, who weighted 140 pounds, was charged as though he were a vessel—in terms of cargo tonnage.*

2362. *Verona—the city in which Shakespeare's most famous lovers, Romeo and Juliet, lived.*

2363. *The Danube.*

2364. *Florence, Italy. All its streets were paved by 1339.*

2365. *In the Feldhofer Grotto of Germany's Neander Valley—from which the name Neanderthal is derived.*

2366. *An awning known as a velarium shielded them from both rain and sun. It was pulled across the great amphitheater by sailors operating an elaborate network of guy ropes.*

2367. *From the sighs of prisoners taken across the bridge from the judgment hall in the Doge's Palace to the dungeons and place of execution in the state prisons on the other side.*

2368. *Edinburgh.*

2369. *Only three—when he was baptized, when a mistress insisted, and when a doctor lanced a sore on his rear end and ordered him to soak in a tub of water.*

2370. *Throgmorton Street. It's where the London Stock Exchange is located.*

2371. In what country does Domino's Pizza have a reindeer sausage pie on its menu?

2372. Where is the White Sea?

2373. What cape is at the southernmost point of Africa?

2374. Which foreign airline has the longest record of continuous scheduled service?

2375. Why did Flemish artists once belong to the same guild as physicians and pharmacists?

2376. In the Bahamas, what's a banana wind?

2377. What city is the southernmost national capital in the world?

2378. How many judges are on the International Court of Justice, headquartered in The Hague, in the Netherlands?

2379. In what village was Leonardo da Vinci born?

2380. What company produced the world's first front-wheel-drive motor vehicle?

2381. What is the national bird of India?

2382. What is the official language of Andorra, the tiny Pyrenees principality on the French-Spanish border?

2383. What country boasts the highest per capita ownership of Rolls Royces in the world?

2384. What country includes the islands of New Britain and New Ireland?

2385. What group of people won the right to vote in India in 1994?

2386. Which is the only Central American nation that does not border the Caribbean Sea?

2387. What city is home to the International War Crimes Tribunal?

2371.   *Iceland.*

2372.   *In northern Russia. It's an almost-landlocked extension of the Arctic Ocean.*

2373.   *Cape Agulhas. It is about 100 miles southeast of the Cape of Good Hope, which many people mistakenly believe is the answer. The cape was named agulhas, Portuguese for "needles" for its many saw-edged reefs and sunken rocks.*

2374.   *Avianca (Aerovias Nacionales de Colombia SA). It was established in 1919.*

2375.   *Because they used the same grinding and mixing techniques in preparing their pigments and varnishes as doctors and pharmacists sued in preparing their salves and potions.*

2376.   *A strong wind—strong enough to blow fruit off the trees, but not as dangerous as a hurricane.*

2377.   *Wellington, New Zealand.*

2378.   *15. No country can have more than one citizen on the court. Judges are elected by the United Nations General Assembly and Security Council to nine-year terms and are eligible for reelection.*

2379.   *Vinci, in what is now Italy.*

2380.   *Citroen, in 1934.*

2381.   *The peacock.*

2382.   *Catalan.*

2383.   *Monaco. A survey in the early 1990s put the figure at one for every 65.1 people.*

2384.   *Papua New Guinea.*

2385.   *Eunuchs.*

2386.   *El Salvador.*

2387.   *The Hague, in the Netherlands.*

2388. Who was the first non-head of state—living or dead—to be depicted on a postage stamp?

2389. How did Russian leader Boris Yeltsin lose the thumb and forefinger of his left hand?

2390. Who is the only woman in history to have married the kings of both France and England?

2391. What river did Alexander the Great believe was the boundary of the universe?

2392. Where is the world's biggest airport—covering 91 square miles?

2393. What country, after the United States, has the world's greatest number of tornadoes?

2394. Who was the last czar of Russia?

2395. Where was the world's first boardwalk built?

2396. In England, how did a quarter of a penny come to be called a farthing?

2397. What country is the world's largest tobacco producer?

2398. What European country was founded by a German-born nobleman known as William the Silent?

2399. What country is the source of most of the blackthorn used to make shillelaghs?

2400. Who was the first living ruler to have his own face on a coin?

2401. What country is the largest importer of American cars?

2402. Which country established the world's first national theater in 1680? Hint: The theater is still in existence.

2388. *Benjamin Franklin, America's first postmaster general. He was on a U.S. 10-cent stamp issued in July 1847.*

2389. *In a hand-grenade explosion. As an 11-year-old, Yeltsin and some friends stole two grenades from a weapons warehouse. One of the grenades detonated when they tried to disassemble it.*

2390. *Eleanor of Aquitaine. Her husbands were Louis VII of France and Henry II of England.*

2391. *The Ganges, in India.*

2392. *In Saudi Arabia, near Riyadh. The King Khalid International Airport is more than four times the size of Bermuda.*

2393. *Australia. It has a few hundred a year—a distant second to the U.S., which has about 1,000 a year.*

2394. *Nicholas II, the last of the Romanov dynasty. He was executed by the Bolsheviks in 1918.*

2395. *In Atlantic City, New Jersey. Opened in June 1870, the mile-long boardwalk rested on the sand. It was built in 8-foot sections that were removed every September and stored for the winter.*

2396. *It was originally called a fourthing—when coins were cut into pieces to make change. Farthing is a corruption of fourthing.*

2397. *China. Brazil is the largest exporter.*

2398. *The Netherlands—which was established as the United Provinces of the Netherlands in 1579 by William, the prince of Orange.*

2399. *Germany. The wood is imported from the Black Forest.*

2400. *Ptolemy I of Egypt.*

2401. *Canada.*

2402. *France. Its national theater, the Comédie-Française, was created by Louis XIV.*

2403. What body of water was originally called the Strait of the Eleven Thousand Virgins?

2404. What is the lowest body of water on the earth?

2405. Where in the world was the bridge of San Luis Rey—immortalized by Thornton Wilder in his Pulitzer Prize-winning novel?

2406. Who was the first person other than royalty to be portrayed on a British stamp?

2407. What are the only two countries in the world whose names begin with the letter Z?

2408. What is the most common domestic animal on the African continent?

2409. What river is the muddiest in the world?

2410. What country was liberated by Bernardo O'Higgins in 1818?

2411. How tall is the Eiffel Tower?

2412. Halloween is a remnant of an ancient Druid celebration—of what?

2413. How many of the Great Lakes are in both the United States and Canada?

2414. What are the natives of Monaco called?

2415. What percentage of the Sahara Desert is covered by sand?

2416. Who was Roderigo de Triana?

2417. What English king died from a lethal dose of morphine and cocaine administered by his personal physician—with the royal family's approval?

2418. Of what land was Helen of Troy queen?

2419. What great ruler died of a nosebleed on his wedding night?

2403. The Strait of Magellan, the winding, 350-mile-long channel linking the Atlantic and Pacific oceans at the southern tip of South America. It was navigated by explorer Ferdinand Magellan in 1520 and given its original name by his crew. It also has been called Victoria Strait, Strait of All Saints, and Strait of the Patagonians.

2404. The Dead Sea. At its lowest point, it's 1,315 feet below sea level.

2405. In the Peruvian Andes, spanning the Apurimac River.

2406. William Shakespeare, in 1964.

2407. Zambia and Zimbabwe. Both countries are in Africa.

2408. The goat.

2409. The Yellow River, known as the Hwang Ho in China. It gets its name from the yellowish silt it carries to an arm of the Yellow Sea.

2410. Chile. O'Higgins, the son of a Spanish officer of Irish origin, served as Chile's head of state until 1823.

2411. 984 feet.

2412. New Year's Eve. The Druids' new year started on November 1.

2413. Four. Only one—Lake Michigan—is entirely within the United States.

2414. Monegasques.

2415. About 20 percent—the rest is comprised of barren rocks, rocky plateaus and gravel-covered plains.

2416. The sailor aboard Columbus's ship the Pinta, who made the first definite sighting of land in the New World on October 12, 1492.

2417. King George V—grandfather of Queen Elizabeth II—who was comatose and on his deathbed at the time.

2418. Sparta.

2419. Attila the Hun, in A.D. 453.

2420. What is the only country in the Middle East that does not have a desert?

2421. In what country was geothermal energy first harnessed to produce electricity?

2422. What animal was the symbol of liberty in ancient Rome?

2423. What are Rum, Eigg, Coll, Mull, Muck, and Canna?

2424. What do workers in the mangrove forests of West Bengal, India, wear to protect themselves from tiger attacks?

2425. Following the bridal tradition of wearing something old, new, borrowed and blue, what new item did divorcée Wallis Warfield Simpson have in her left shoe at her wedding to Edward VIII, who had abdicated the British throne to marry her?

2426. What was the first name of the Queen of Sheba, who visited King Solomon bearing great riches?

2427. In England, a citizen of Birmingham is called a Brummagem, and a student at Cambridge is called a Cantabrigian. What is a resident of Manchester called?

2428. In what country did India ink originate?

2429. When did the world's first daily newspaper begin publishing?

2430. Where was St. Patrick, the patronß saint of Ireland, born?

2431. In classical mythology, what god dressed as a woman, spun wool and performed other womanly tasks for three years to appease his fellow gods?

2432. The fictitious name John Doe was first used in British courts to represent the unknown plaintiff in a real—property suit. What fictitious name was used for the defendant?

2433. Split is an important seaport—in what European country?

2434. What is the Temple of the Tooth?

2420. *Lebanon.*

2421. *In Italy—at the Larderello hot springs in Tuscany, where steam has been producing electricity since 1904.*

2422. *The cat.*

2423. *Some of Scotland's Inner Hebrides islands.*

2424. *Rubber masks tied to the back of their heads—because tigers are known to attack humans only from behind.*

2425. *A gold coin minted just 18 months earlier for Edward's coronation.*

2426. *Balkis.*

2427. *A Mancunian.*

2428. *In China.*

2429. *In 59 B.C.—it was a government-controlled daily bulletin called Acta Diurna (Action Journal) that Julius Caesar had posted throughout Rome.*

2430. *In Scotland, in the town of Kilpatrick, near Dumbarton. He was captured at age 16 by Gaels and taken to Ireland, where he was sold as a slave.*

2431. *Hercules.*

2432. *Richard Roe.*

2433. *Yugoslavia. It's on the Adriatic Sea.*

2434. *A Buddhist temple in Kandy, in central Sri Lanka (formerly Ceylon), where a sacred relic reputed to be a tooth of the Buddha has been enshrined since the fourth century A.D.*

2435. What nation do we have to thank for Florida's orange crop?

2436. What rousing song was originally known as the "Battle Song of the Rhine Army"?

2437. How many time zones are there in China?

2438. What is the basic monetary unit of Zimbabwe called?

2439. On what island are one-third of the world's languages spoken?

2440. What two boundaries lie between Big Diomede Island and Little Diomede Island?

2441. What did 5-and-10-cent-store magnate F. W. Woolworth call the chain of stores he opened in England in 1909?

2442. What famous French landmark is named after a German city?

2443. Archaeologists believe they have located the burial site of Boudicca, the British queen who led a bloody revolt against Roman rule in the first century A.D. Where is it?

2444. When was the first kissaten—coffee shop—established in Tokyo?

2445. What piece of construction equipment is named after an early seventeenth-century British hangman?

2446. What island nation was named after a Dutch province?

2447. What river is the longest in Europe?

2435. *Spain. During the seventeenth century, every Spanish explorer was required to bring 100 orange seeds with him when he set sail for the New World.*

2436. *"La Marseillaise," the French national anthem.*

2437. *Only one. Although the country covers 3,691,521 square miles and geographically could be in five different zones, the government requires clocks throughout the nation to conform to those in the capital (Beijing).*

2438. *The dollar.*

2439. *On New Guinea, where more than 700 distinct native languages can be heard.*

2440. *The U.S.-U.S.S.R. border and the International Date Line. The islands, in the Bering Strait, are 2 miles apart and 25 miles from both mainland U.S. and mainland U.S.S.R. They were named by Danish explorer Vitus Bering, who discovered them on St. Diomede's Day (August 16) in 1728.*

2441. *"Three-and-Sixpence" stores.*

2442. *The Eiffel Tower. It was built by Gustave Eiffel, whose upholsterer grandfather moved to Paris from Eifel, Germany, and became known as Eifel because his friends couldn't pronounce his name, Boenickhausen. Eventually granddad added another "f" and legally changed his name to Eiffel.*

2443. *Under Platform 8 of the King's Cross Railway Station in London.*

2444. *In 1889.*

2445. *The derrick, which is named for Thomas Derrick—who carried out more than 3,000 executions during his career at Tyburn, near what is now the Marble Arch in London.*

2446. *New Zealand, which was discovered by Dutch explorer Abel Tasman in 1642 and named Nieuw Zeeland after Zeeland, a Dutch province bordering the North Sea.*

2447. *The Volga, the principal waterway in Russia, which is approximately 2,293 miles long.*

2448. What is the northernmost city in Europe?

2449. How are 99 percent of the buildings heated in Reykjavik, the capital of Iceland?

2450. In what country did the windmill originate?

2451. Parts of which existing European countries once were included in the nation known as Flanders?

2452. What famous philosopher said, "Children today are tyrants. They contradict their parents, gobble their food, and tyrannize their teachers"?

2453. What Middle Eastern country's name includes the name of its first ruler?

2454. What famous philosopher is known by the name given to him by his wrestling teacher?

2455. Where was Nero when Rome burned in 64 A.D.?

2456. What European country was once known as the Batavian Republic?

2457. How many children did Cleopatra have?

2458. According to Greek legend, who cut the Gordian Knot?

2459. How is the Balinese national holiday known as Njebi (pronounced nn-YEH-pee) celebrated?

2460. What was blamed for the deaths of Emperor Claudius and Tiberius, Czar Alexander I, Pope Clement VII and Charles V of France?

2461. What was Mahatma Gandhi's reply when he was asked what he thought of Western civilization?

2462. Lutetia, which means "mid-water dwelling" in Latin, is the original name of what European city?

2448. Hammerfest, Norway—which is at 70° 38' north.

2449. With geothermal power—from natural hot (140°F) water from an underground reservoir. The water (from Ice Age glaciers trapped by hardened lava from volcanic eruptions) is piped to radiators and hot-water tanks throughout the city.

2450. In Iran, in A.D. 644. It was used to grind grain.

2451. France, Belgium and the Netherlands.

2452. Socrates, who lived in Greece from 470 to 399 B.C.

2453. Saudi Arabia. Ruler Abd al-Aziz ibn Saud unified his dual kingdoms of Hejaz and Nejd and their dependencies under the name Saudi Arabia in 1932.

2454. Plato, who was originally named Aristocles. According to historians the nickname Plato, which means "broad" in Greek, referred to either his broad shoulders or broad forehead.

2455. At his villa at Antium (now Anxio), 35 miles from Rome. And he wasn't fiddling—the violin had not yet been invented.

2456. The Netherlands, between 1795 and 1806, during the French Revolutionary Wars. The name came from the Batavi, a Germanic tribe that originally inhabited the region.

2457. Four: with Julius Caesar a son, Caesarion; with Mark Antony twins, Alexander Helios and Cleopatra Selene, and a son, Ptolemy Philadelphus.

2458. Alexander the Great (356-323 B.C.).

2459. In silence. It is the national day of silence.

2460. Mushroom poisoning.

2461. "I think it would be a good idea."

2462. Paris. It was named Lutetia by the Romans in the first century B.C. after Julius Caesar's forces defeated the original settlers, a Gallic people known as the Parisii. The city became known as Paris in the early fourth century after the Romans were defeated by Barbarian invaders.

2463. According to Roman mythology, what was the name of the daughter born to Cupid and Psyche?

2464. American children get their Easter eggs from the Easter Bunny. Who delivers Easter eggs to Swiss youngsters?

2465. Where is Pushtu spoken?

2466. What nation has the city of Godthaab as its capital?

2467. What happened to the Latin inscription on the Blarney Stone?

2468. Russia's space station program is called Salyut, which means salute. To whom is it a salute?

2469. What are the Near Islands near?

2470. How many languages are spoken in the Republic of Sudan, the largest country on the African continent?

2471. The latitude of the North Pole is 90° north; what is its longitude?

2472. Haiti and the Dominican Republic are the only two independent nations in the world to be located on the same island. What is the island called?

2473. What is the most popular first name in the world?

2474. The Russian Czarevitch, Alexis, inherited Queen Victoria's hemophilia from his mother's side of the family. Did he eventually die from the disease?

2475. What is the name of Moscow's largest department store?

2476. What is London's Big Ben?

2477. How many diamonds are there on Britain's Imperial State Crown, which is worn by the reigning monarch on state occasions?

2478. How long did the Trojan War last?

2463. Pleasure—or *Volupta* in Latin.

2464. The Easter Cuckoo.

2465. In Afghanistan. It's one of the country's two official languages. The other is Dari Persian.

2466. Greenland.

2467. The words were rubbed off the stone after years of removing the lipstick left by women who kissed it.

2468. The first man in space, cosmonaut Yuri Gargarin, who died in a MiG-15 test in 1968.

2469. The Alaska mainland, although they were named for their relatively close proximity to Russia. They are part of the Aleutian chain off the southern tip of the Alaska peninsula and became part of the U.S. with the purchase of Alaska in 1867.

2470. 115—most of them tribal dialects.

2471. No longitude is given since all degrees of longitude pass through the North Pole.

2472. Hispaniola.

2473. Muhammad.

2474. No. He was executed with other members of the royal family in 1918.

2475. GUM.

2476. The bell in the clock tower of the Houses of Parliament; not the clock tower itself, as is usually supposed.

2477. There are 1,783—including the 309-carat Star of Africa. The crown also has 277 pearls, 17 sapphires, 11 emeralds, and 5 rubies.

2478. Ten years.

2479. Who was the first member of the English royal family to wear a pair of silk stockings?

2480. In Middle Eastern legend, what is widely considered to be the forbidden fruit?

2481. Which continent is the only one to have no glaciers?

2482. What world leader was originally known as Karl Herbert Frahm?

2483. What was the given name of the long-time Yugoslavian communist leader we knew as Marshal Tito?

2484. What was the source of the earliest eye glitter ever used— that devised by the ancient Egyptians?

2485. What country was once known as New Holland?

2486. What is the native language of the Fiji Islands?

2487. How was Queen Victoria trained to keep her chin up as a child?

2488. What Dutch colony was ceded to the British in 1667 in exchange for Dutch Guiana—the South American country now known as Suriname?

2489. What is the claim to fame of the Turkish site known as Hissarlik?

2490. Where do the Blue Nile and White Nile meet?

2491. Where were Panama hats—woven from jipijapa leaves— first made?

2492. Which ocean is the smallest and shallowest?

2493. How long is the Suez Canal, the water link between the Gulf of Suez and the Mediterranean Sea?

2494. Who was Somdetch Phra Paramendr Maha Mongkut?

2479. *Oft-married Henry VIII, in 1509. The stockings were a gift from Spain.*

2480. *The banana.*

2481. *Australia.*

2482. *Former German chancellor Willy Brandt. He changed his name to escape the Gestapo.*

2483. *Josip Broz.*

2484. *Iridescent beetle shells.*

2485. *Australia, in the mid-seventeenth century.*

2486. *Fijian.*

2487. *A sprig of holly was placed beneath her collar.*

2488. *New York—then known as Nieuw Amsterdam. The exchange was part of the Treaty of Breda.*

2489. *It is the site of ancient Troy.*

2490. *At Khartoum, the capital of Sudan.*

2491. *In Peru. They're also made in Colombia and Eucador—but not in Panama. They were misnamed after being discovered by North Americans in Panama.*

2492. *The Arctic Ocean.*

2493. *It's 105 miles long.*

2494. *The monarch immortalized by writer Margaret D. Langdon in her book "Anna and the King of Siam" and portrayed by Yul Brynner in stage and screen productions of "The King and I."*

2495. How long was the reign of Louis XIV, the French king who proclaimed, "L'état, c'est moi"—"I am the state"?

2496. What great discovery were Ooqueah, Ootah, Egingwah and Seegloo part of on April 6, 1909?

2497. Where do you have to go to find Le Restaurant de la Tour Eiffel, which was located on the first level of Paris' landmark Eiffel Tower from 1937 to 1981?

2498. In England, what are the five grades of peerage—or nobility—entitled to seats in the House of Lords?

2499. What major European country does not belong to the United Nations?

2500. Serendip was the early name for Ceylon. What is it now called?

2501. What are the Soo Locks and where are they located?

2502. Where was the world's first successful oil well drilled?

2503. Where is Interpol, the international police organization, headquartered?

2504. "Confound their politics. Frustrate their knavish tricks" is part of what country's national anthem?

2505. It took Fred Newton 742 hours over a six-month period to take the world's longest swim. He went 1,826 miles in what body of water?

2506. How did the world's highest waterfall—the Angel Falls in Venezuela—get its name?

2507. What lake, once part of a sea, has the only freshwater sharks in the world?

2508. What well-known scientist was offered the presidency of Israel, but turned it down, after the death of Chaim Weizmann in 1952?

2495. *Seventy-two years—he acceded to the throne at age 5, in the year 1643*

2496. *The discovery of the North Pole. The four Eskimos, with Robert Peary and his assistant Matthew Henson, were the first men to reach latitude 90 degrees north.*

2497. *To New Orleans, Louisiana, where the dismantled restaurant was reassembled and put back in business in 1986.*

2498. *In descending order: duke, marquess, earl, viscount and baron.*

2499. *Switzerland, on grounds that membership would jeopardize its neutrality.*

2500. *Sri Lanka.*

2501. *They are the busiest locks in the world, linking Lake Superior and 22-foot-lower Lake Huron in Sault Ste. Marie, Michigan.*

2502. *Titusville, Pennsylvania, in 1859.*

2503. *In Saint Cloud, a suburb of Paris. Its popular nickname comes from its cable designation.*

2504. *Great Britain's "God Save the Queen."*

2505. *The Mississippi River, from Minneapolis to New Orleans, in 1930.*

2506. *From American bush pilot Jimmy Angel, who crash-landed nearby in 1937.*

2507. *Lake Nicaragua, in Nicaragua.*

2508. *Albert Einstein.*

2509. In 1872 what three cities, located near the Danube, merged into one?

2510. What mountain is the largest on earth?

2511. In what year during this century did England have three kings?

2512. If you flew due east from Cape Horn where would you next pass over land?

2513. What kind of car did Communist leader Nikolai Lenin equip with skis and half-tracks in order to overcome Russia's heavy snows?

2514. What breed was Sir Winston Churchill's favorite pet dog, Rufus?

2515. During what war was the Battle of the Herrings fought?

2516. What kings were named by Egypt's King Farouk when he predicted, after being overthrown by Gamal Abdel Nasser, that "one day there will be only five kings left"?

2517. How was Kublai Khan related to Genghis Khan?

2518. What career was Casanova preparing for before he distinguished himself as a rogue and libertine?

2519. What great ruler's name at birth was Sophie Friederike Auguste?

2520. What unusual museum is located in Pontedassio, Italy?

2521. Who was the last British monarch to ascend to the throne as a teenager?

2522. How large—in acres—is the area in France where grapes for Champagne are grown?

2523. Chinese writings dating back to the fourth century B.C. mention fishing with a bamboo rod, silk line and a hook made from a needle. What was used for bait?

2509. *Buda, Obuda, and Pest joined to become Budapest.*

2510. *Mauna Loa (Long Mountain), Hawaii. A 13,680-foot-high volcano, its dome measures 75 miles by 64 miles.*

2511. *In 1936—when George V died, Edward VIII abdicated to marry divorcée Wally Simpson, and George VI began his sixteen-year reign.*

2512. *Cape Horn—there's no other land at the same latitude, 56° 00'S.*

2513. *A Rolls-Royce.*

2514. *Poodle.*

2515. *The Hundred Years' War. It took place on February 12, 1429, while the British were laying siege to Orléans and their Lenten rations of herring were intercepted by the French.*

2516. *"Hearts, spades, diamonds, clubs and England."*

2517. *He was the grandson of Genghis, the great Mongol conqueror.*

2518. *The priesthood.*

2519. *Catherine the Great's.*

2520. *The Museo Storico degli Spaghetti—or the Historical Museum of Spaghetti.*

2521. *Queen Victoria, who was 18 when she became queen in 1837. She went on to reign a record 63½ years.*

2522. *85,000 acres—in the Pernay-Reims region, 90 miles east of Paris.*

2523. *Cooked rice.*

2524. Where are the volcanoes Shira, Kibo and Mawenzi located?

2525. What famous explorer included a photograph of his nude mistress in a book about his travels?

2526. What does Chinese leader Deng Xiaoping's name mean in English?

2527. What is the meaning of the nickname Rasputin, bestowed upon Grigory Yefimovich Novykh, the notorious Siberian monk and mystic who wielded great influence over the Russian imperial family?

2528. The French knew the first ruler of the Holy Roman Empire as Charlemagne. What did the Germans call him?

2529. What was the name of the pug that shared Napoleon and Josephine's bed?

2530. What was the profession of Edmund Hillary, the New Zealander who conquered Mount Everest with Sherpa guide Tenzing Norkay in 1953?

2531. How many beds were listed in the palace inventories of France's King Louis XIV?

2532. The British prime minister's official residence is at Number 10 Downing Street. Whose official residence is at Number 11?

2533. What Middle Eastern capital was once known as Philadelphia?

2534. There was a major mistake in the 1968 film "Krakatoa, East of Java." What was it?

2535. In 1305, what did England's King Edward I decree should be used to determine the length of an inch in shoemaking and other trades?

2536. In what country was World War I German spy Mata Hari born?

2524. *In Tanzania—they are the three principal volcanoes that make up Mount Kilimanjaro.*

2525. *Robert Peary, discoverer of the North Pole. His Eskimo mistress, Aleqasina, was shown bathing.*

2526. *Little Peace. Born Kan Tse-kao, he began using the name Deng Xiaoping as an underground alias when he joined the Chinese Communist Party in 1924.*

2527. *Rasputin—derived from the Russian word rasputny—means "debauchee" or "libertine."*

2528. *Karl der Grosse—which, like Charlemagne, means Charles the Great.*

2529. *Fortunè.*

2530. *Beekeeper, or apiarist.*

2531. *413.*

2532. *The Chancellor of the Exchequer's.*

2533. *Amman, Jordan.*

2534. *The location given in the title. The famous volcano is west of Java. The mistake was remedied when the movie was released on videocassette under a new title, "Volcano."*

2535. *Barleycorns. According to his decree, three contiguous dried barleycorns were an inch.*

2536. *In Holland, as Margaretha Geertruida Zelle.*

2537. Four years after King Edward VIII abdicated the British throne, he became governor—of what?

2538. In what country is the austral the basic monetary unit?

2539. What country was the second in the world to adopt communism?

2540. What did the late King Prajadhipok, the last absolute ruler of Siam (now Thailand), do to prepare himself financially for life after his anticipated overthrow in the early 1930s?

2541. The name of what South American capital city means "I see a hill"?

2542. What is the highest large navigable lake in the world—at 12,500 feet above sea level?

2543. Where is the city of Batman?

2544. When the swallows return to California's Mission San Juan Capistrano every year, where are they coming from?

2545. What is the significance of the shamrock, the emblem of Ireland?

2546. How many icebergs are there in the world?

2547. If you weigh 154 pounds in America, how many stone do you weigh in England; how many kilograms in France?

2548. What did the Queen Mother say to Queen Elizabeth II when her elder daughter considered having a second glass of wine with lunch shortly after her coronation?

2549. In what country was the first English-language newspaper published?

2550. What country was the world's largest producer of potatoes in 1990?

2537. *The Bahamas. He retired after serving from 1940 to 1945.*

2538. *Argentina.*

2539. *Mongolia, in 1921—four years after the Bolshevik revolution in Russia. In 1990, Mongolia became the first Asian country to desert communism.*

2540. *Prajadhipok took out unemployment insurance with French and British insurance companies. He collected on the policies after his ouster, and lived comfortably in England for the remaining six years of his life.*

2541. *Montevideo, Uruguay.*

2542. *Lake Titicaca, which lies between Bolivia and Peru.*

2543. *In southeastern Turkey.*

2544. *Their winter home in Goya, Argentina.*

2545. *According to legend, St. Patrick chose the three-leaflet plant as the symbol of the Trinity. He is said to have used it to drive the snakes of Ireland into the sea. The word shamrock is derived from the Irish seamrog, meaning "trefoil."*

2546. *Approximately 320,000.*

2547. *You weigh 11 stone in England; and 70 kilograms in France. A stone is equal to 14 pounds; a kilogram to 2.2 pounds.*

2548. *"Don't forget, my dear, you have to reign all afternoon."*

2549. *In Holland, in 1620. The newspaper was published by Puritan refugees from England—the same community of Puritans that provided the Pilgrims who crossed the Atlantic on the Mayflower in 1620.*

2550. *The Soviet Union. The United States was fifth, after China, Poland and India.*

2551. What was the most common first name given to children born in China during the years of the Cultural Revolution (1966-1977)?

2552. What is the last remaining British colony in the South Pacific?

2553. What country was the first to produce lace?

2554. How many islands are there in the Indonesian archipelago?

2555. Why did the Coca-Cola Company change the name of its popular soft drink in China in 1986?

2556. Sir Laurence Olivier once held a press conference in London to complain about railroad service. What was his beef?

2557. Where was the first tunnel in recorded history?

2558. What political party emblem was the first to be used on a national flag?

2559. What is the origin of the Russian title czar for ruler?

2560. What common sight on the English street scene is named for Sir Robert Peel?

2561. What capital is the oldest continuously inhabited city in the world?

2562. What country was the first to produce the leather we know as suede?

2563. What is the traditional salute to a royal birth in Great Britain?

2564. What silver hood ornament does Queen Elizabeth II have installed on any car in which she is traveling?

2565. Who are the Hottentots?

2551. *Hong—which means "red" in Chinese.*

2552. *Pitcairn Island—made up of tiny, remote Pitcairn, where the nine mutineers from the HMS Bounty landed in 1790, and the uninhabited islands of Oeno, Henderson and Ducie.*

2553. *Italy, in the early sixteenth century.*

2554. *There are 13,677—most of which are uninhabited.*

2555. *Company officials learned that the phonetic equivalent, ke kou ke la, means "bite the wax tadpole" in Chinese.*

2556. *Kippers had been dropped from the dining car menu.*

2557. *In Babylon. Built by the Assyrians in about 2100 B.C., the secret 3,000-foot-long passageway linked the royal palace on one side of the Euphrates River with the Temple of Jupiter on the other side.*

2558. *The Nazi's swastika. The black swastika in a circle of white on a red background was introduced as the banner of Germany's National Socialist Party in 1919; it became the flag of the Third Reich in 1935.*

2559. *It was derived from Caesar, after Julius Caesar—as was kaiser, in Germany, and qaysar, in the Islamic world.*

2560. *English bobbies, or policemen—originally known as Bobby's boys. Peel is the man who organized the London police force in 1829.*

2561. *Damascus, Syria.*

2562. *Sweden, which is what Suède means in French. The name was first used in the phrase gants de Suède, or "gloves from Sweden."*

2563. *A 41-gun salute.*

2564. *A sculpture of St. George—the patron saint of England—slaying a dragon.*

2565. *Members of a semi-nomadic pastoral tribe, the Khoikhoin, living in southwestern South Africa. The name is a pejorative label the Dutch bestowed on them because of their clipped way of speaking.*

2566. How many children of England's oft-married King Henry VIII sat on the British throne?

2567. How many trunks and suitcases did the Duchess of Windsor take with her on her honeymoon with England's ex-king Edward XIII, who had abdicated to marry her?

2568. What is the basic monetary unit of Venezuela?

2569. What day followed September 2nd in Great Britain and its American colonies in 1752?

2570. How old was England's youngest monarch, Henry VI, when he ascended to the throne?

2571. The tallest wave ever observed was spotted in the North Pacific in 1933. How tall was it?

2572. Whose bowlegs inspired a furniture style?

2573. What country has the most phones per capita?

2574. What rare metal was used to make coins in Russia between 1818 and 1845?

2575. What financially ailing country's bid to be annexed by the United States failed to win passage in the Senate in 1870?

2576. The Isle of Man is in the Irish Sea, off the British coast. Where is the isle called Male?

2577. What French city was home to Anthelme Brillat-Savarin, the famous gastronome?

2578. In Persia, what is the color associated with mourning?

2579. What is the diameter of the earth at the equator?

2580. What did Ludwig I, King of Bavaria from 1825 to 1848, have stuffed inside his velvet-covered mattress?

2581. There are 12 locks on the Panama Canal. How many are there on the Suez Canal, which is twice as long?

2566. *Three—Edward VI (son of wife #3, Jane Seymour); Queen Mary I (daughter of wife #1, Catherine of Aragon); and Queen Elizabeth I (daughter of wife #2, Anne Boleyn).*

2567. *186 trunks and 83 suitcases.*

2568. *The bolivar—named for the nation's liberator, Simon Bolivar.*

2569. *September 14th. Parliament omitted 11 days from September that year when it adopted the new Gregorian calendar. Cutting the 11 days put the calendar and the seasons back in line with one another.*

2570. *He was just under nine months—269 days old to be exact.*

2571. *It was 112 feet high—a towering ten stories.*

2572. *England's Queen Anne.*

2573. *Sweden.*

2574. *Platinum—which wasn't highly valued at the time.*

2575. *The Dominican Republic's. The Senate vote was 28 to 28.*

2576. *In the Indian Ocean, off the coast of India. It's the capital of the Maldives.*

2577. *Belley.*

2578. *Pale brown, the color of withered leaves.*

2579. *7,926 miles. (The circumference is 24,902 miles.)*

2580. *The beards and mustaches of soldiers from his father's old Alsatian regiment.*

2581. *None.*

2582. Where did the umbrella originate?

2583. Who made it fashionable to leave undone the bottom button on the vest of a man's three-piece suit?

2584. What country has more volcanoes than any other?

2585. What is the destination of an airline passenger whose luggage tags are marked AZO? or YYZ?

2586. What historic leader was the first to be called the "Father of His Country"?

2587. What size were the 2,400 pairs of shoes Imelda Marcos left behind when she and her husband, deposed Philippine president Ferdinand Marcos, went into exile in 1986?

2588. On the Chinese lunar calendar, the year of the horse began January 27, 1990. Can you name the other eleven animals on the calendar?

2589. How much did Aga Khan III weigh in 1946 when his followers gave him his weight in diamonds in celebration of his sixtieth year as leader of the Ismaili sect of the Shiite Muslims?

2590. What sport did King Jigme Singye Wangchuck, then 34-year-old ruler of the isolated Himalayan nation of Bhutan, engage in daily in 1990?

2591. What unique wedding gift did Indian leader Mahatma Gandi send to England's Princess Elizabeth and Prince Philip when they wed in 1947?

2592. What country was the first to impose a general income tax?

2593. How many of Canada's 10 provinces do not border on the United States?

2594. Which is the only one of the Seven Wonders of the Ancient World still in existence today?

2595. What country has a glacier located on the Equator?

2582. In Mesopotamia, in 1400 B.C. It was used for shade, which is why its name is derived from the Latin word for a shade, umbra.

2583. The Prince of Wales (later King Edward VII), at the turn of the century—because he was too portly to button his bottom button.

2584. Indonesia—it has 167 of the 850 active volcanoes known in the world.

2585. AZO is Kalamazoo, Michigan; YYZ is Toronto, Canada.

2586. Augustus Caesar, earlier known as Octavian, grandnephew of Julius Caesar and the first Roman emperor. He was granted the title Pater Patriae in 2 B.C. by the Roman senate and people.

2587. There were size 8½.

2588. The sheep (or goat), monkey, hen (or rooster), dog, pig, rat, ox (or bull), tiger, rabbit (or hare or cat), snake and horse.

2589. He tipped the scale at 243¼ pounds, which translated into $2.5 million in diamonds. His followers contributed that amount in cash to charities he sponsored.

2590. Basketball.

2591. A hand-spun loincloth.

2592. Great Britain—in 1799. It was done to finance the Napoleonic Wars.

2593. Three—Newfoundland, Nova Scotia and Prince Edward Island.

2594. The Pyramids of Egypt at Giza. The other six wonders were the Hanging Gardens of Babylon, the Tomb of Mausolus at Helicarnassus, the Temple of Artemis (Diana) at Ephesus, the Colossus of Rhodes, the Statue of Zeus (Jupiter) by Phidias at Olympia, and the Pharos of Alexandria.

2595. Ecuador. The glacier is on a volcano known as Cayambe.

2596. Who was the only English king to be honored with the epithet "the great" after his name?

2597. What is the largest island in the South Pacific archipelago known as the Society Islands?

2598. Where in the world are there geological features known as ergs, regs and hamadas?

2599. How many countries joined the United Nations when it was formed in 1945?

2600. The United States is the oldest independent country in the Americas. What country is the second oldest?

2601. The name of what East African country means "land of sunburned faces" in Greek?

2602. What river divides the Dutch capital of Amsterdam in two?

2603. Where is the 1,300-mile-long Orange River?

2604. In what country are the natives known as Malagasy?

2605. What is the sacred animal of Thailand?

2606. What is Canada's highest city?

2607. What was Casablanca called when it was first built by the Portuguese in 1515?

2608. How much does the jewel-studded Crown of England—worn only at coronations—weigh?

2609. What is the largest river delta in the world?

2610. In the African version of the Hansel and Gretel story, what is the house of the wicked witch made of instead of gingerbread?

2611. Where is the iron key to the Bastille—the notorious French prison—kept today?

2612. What country's flag consists of a single solid color?

2596. *Alfred the Great, who ruled from 871 to 899.*

2597. *Tahiti. The French-controlled islands are named for the group of scientists from the Royal Society brought to visit some of the islands in 1769 by Lt. (later Capt.) James Cook.*

2598. *In the Sahara—where ergs are sandy expanses, regs are gravelly plains and hamadas are stony upland plateaus.*

2599. *51.*

2600. *Haiti, which gained its independence from France in 1804.*

2601. *Ethiopia.*

2602. *The Amstel. The city's name is derived from a dam built between dikes bordering the river.*

2603. *In South Africa.*

2604. *Madagascar. They're also called Madagascans.*

2605. *The white elephant.*

2606. *Kimberley, British Columbia.*

2607. *Casa Branca. Both names mean "white house"—for the city's many white houses.*

2608. *The crown, also known as St. Edward's Crown, weighs just under seven pounds.*

2609. *The Ganges Delta, or Ganges-Brahmaputra Delta, in India and Bangladesh. It extends for about 250 miles north to south, and ranges from 80 to 200 miles west to east.*

2610. *Salt, which is highly prized south of the Sahara.*

2611. *At George Washington's home, Mount Vernon, where it is on display in the central hallway. The key was sent to Washington by the Marquis de Lafayette, "as a missionary of liberty to its patriarch."*

2612. *Libya's. Its flag is green.*

2613. What is the state language of Luxembourg?

2614. What Canadian province is named for the Great Spirit of the Algonquin Indians?

2615. What country or countries would you be visiting if you traveled the length of the Mosquito Coast?

2616. What European country uses the initials CH on its automobile license plates and in its postal codes?

2617. The name of what former world leader, translated into English, means "Mr. Clean"?

2618. What is the heroine's name in the version of "Snow White" told to children in Africa, where snow is virtually unknown?

2619. Hot springs are known as geysers after the Great Geysir. In what country is it located?

2620. What famous woman, using a diamond, scratched the following message on her prison window: Much suspected of me, Nothing proved can be.

2621. What mammal do fishermen in China train to help them increase their catch?

2622. Where in the world is Spa, the resort town that gave its name to mineral springs everywhere?

2623. In 1512 why did France's King Louis XII order the removal of all the garbage that for years had been routinely tossed over the walls surrounding the city of Paris?

2624. What daily exercise routine did seventeenth-century French statesman Cardinal Richelieu perform to stay in shape?

2625. How did the Caribbean island of Curaçao get is name?

2626. What was the name of the space vehicle in which Yuri Gagarin, the Soviet Union's first cosmonaut, orbited Earth on April 12, 1961?

2613. *Luxembourgish, which is also known as Letzeburgesch. The language is used by most Luxembourgers in their daily lives. French, however, is Luxembourg's administrative language, and students are taught German in primary school. Many also study English.*

2614. *Manitoba. The Algonquin god is Manitou.*

2615. *Nicaragua and Honduras. The approximately 225-mile-long stretch of lowland skirting the Caribbean is named for the Miskito—or Mosquito—Indians.*

2616. *Switzerland.*

2617. *U Thant, the Burmese diplomat who served as secretary general of the United Nations from 1961 to 1971.*

2618. *Flower White.*

2619. *Iceland. Geysir is Icelandic for "gusher."*

2620. *England's Queen Elizabeth I, while she was confined at Woodstock in the mid-sixteenth century before she attained the throne.*

2621. *The otter. The Chinese train otters to chase fish under large nets, which are then dropped and pulled in.*

2622. *In Belgium.*

2623. *He feared invaders would climb the mounds of garbage and scale the walls.*

2624. *He jumped over furniture.*

2625. *From the word cure—for the cure for scurvy it unexpectedly provided to Portuguese sailors set ashore with the disease. When they were later picked up, all were in good health—having partaken of the island's abundant crop of citrus fruit.*

2626. *Vostok I.*

2627. The French were so taken with a particularly beautiful double pink rose back in 1797 that they named it Blushing Thigh of the Aroused Nymph. What was it renamed by the prim and proper English?

2628. What percentage of the world's land area is occupied by Asia, the largest continent?

2629. What was the name of Sir Walter Raleigh's black greyhound?

2630. What was the first continental European city to build a subway?

2631. How many vessels were in the Spanish Armada, the great fleet sent by Spain's King Philip II to conquer England in 1588?

2632. What nation's symbol is an eagle perched on a cactus with a writhing snake in its beak?

2633. How many republics were there in the Union of Soviet Socialist Republics before its dissolution in 1991?

2634. Where is the world's largest sculpted strawberry?

2635. What percentage of the world's ice is contained in the continental ice sheet that covers Antarctica?

2636. What famous royal rulers were the first in-laws of England's oft-married King Henry VIII?

2637. What three Italian cities have lent their names to reddish hues?

2638. How many women named Cleopatra served as rulers of ancient Egypt before the most famous one—the one linked romantically to Julius Caesar and Marc Antony?

2639. What colors do the flags of North Korea and South Korea have in common?

2640. Where was the world's first paper money used?

2627.   *Great Maiden's Blush.*

2628.   *About 30 percent.*

2629.   *Hamlet.*

2630.   *Budapest, Hungary—in the 1890s.*

2631.   *130.*

2632.   *Mexico's.*

2633.   *15.*

2634.   *In Strawberry Point, Iowa.*

2635.   *90 percent.*

2636.   *Spain's King Ferdinand and Queen Isabella. Their daughter Catherine of Aragon was the first of Henry's six wives.*

2637.   *Magenta, Siena and Venice (for Venetian red).*

2638.   *Six.*

2639.   *Red, white and blue. The South Korean flag also has a fourth color—black.*

2640.   *In China in the ninth century. It was introduced due to a scarcity of the copper used for coins.*

2641. What two cities were linked by the Orient Express?

2642. What two American entertainers believe that in a previous life they were Queen Hatshepsut, ruler of Egypt from 1503 to 1482 B.C.?

2643. What city was the first in the world to have a population over one million?

2644. Into how many standard time zones is the world divided?

2645. What country's language is composed of the dialects of Gheg and Tosk?

2646. What nation owns Easter Island, the Polynesian outpost in the eastern Pacific known for its mysterious 50-ton monolithic sculptures?

2647. What was the cargo of the Cutty Sark when the famous three-masted clipper ship returned to England on its maiden voyage in 1869?

2648. What is the only place in the world where alligators and crocodiles coexist?

2649. What was 21-year-old Captain Nathaniel Brown Palmer, of Stonington, Connecticut, credited with discovering while hunting for seals in 1820?

2650. What were Mexican revolutionary Pancho Villa's dying words?

2651. What is the oldest European settlement in the Americas?

2652. Where did the pawnbroker's symbol—three gold balls—originate?

2653. How many years did the Hundred Years War between England and France last?

2654. What wildlife gave the Canary Islands their name?

2641. *Paris and Istanbul.*

2642. *Hoofer Ann Miller and singer Tina Turner.*

2643. *London. It passed the million mark in 1811.*

2644. *Twenty-four.*

2645. *Albania. Its official language has been based on Tosk since 1945.*

2646. *Chile, which is 2,300 miles away.*

2647. *Tea from China. The ship, now restored, is on view in Greenwich, England.*

2648. *Southern Florida.*

2649. *The continent of Antarctica.*

2650. *"Don't let it end like this. Tell them I said something."*

2651. *Santo Domingo, in the Dominican Republic. It was founded in 1496 by Bartholomew Columbus, brother of Christopher.*

2652. *On the coat of arms of the Medici banking family.*

2653. *It went on for 116 years, from 1337 to 1453.*

2654. *Wild dogs—canis in Latin. The songbirds we call canaries were named after the islands.*

2655. Simon Bolivar was the liberator of five South American countries, one of them his native land. Can you name them?

2656. What noted Englishman did singer Texas Guinan rush into her nightclub kitchen and arm with a chef's hat and skillet, so he would escape arrest during a Prohibition raid?

2657. What did a man named George Harrison sell for $50 in 1886?

2658. What great act of courage brought scorn upon British philanthropist Jonas Hanaway in 1750?

2659. In what geological era are we living?

2660. How did the War of the Roses (1455-1485) get its name?

2661. What 10 European countries still have crowned heads of state?

2662. How old was Joan of Arc when she was burned at the stake?

2663. What popular children's rhyme was an outgrowth of the bubonic plague?

2664. What unique distinction is shared by Spain's Paseo del Prado, Germany's Schlossalle and France's Rue de la Paix?

2665. Whose Day-Glo orange-and-yellow striped mini-dress, with matching headband and tights, is on view at the Victoria and Albert Museum in London?

2666. Who was K'ung Fu-tzu?

2667. Lusitania was the Roman name for what country?

2668. When Ugandan officials rummaged through the home of deposed president Idi Amin in April 1979, they found a case of old film reels. What were they?

2669. What area of the world is the only place where the insect-eating Venus's-flytrap grows naturally?

2655. *Bolivia, Colombia, Ecuador, Peru and Venezuela, the last being his homeland.*

2656. *The Prince of Wales, who later became Edward VIII, the king who abdicated to marry divorcée Wallis Warfield Simpson.*

2657. *The Rand in South Africa—the world's major source of gold.*

2658. *He was the first man to carry an umbrella in public. Previously, only women carried them.*

2659. *The Cenozoic Era, which started 65 million years ago.*

2660. *It was fought between England's House of York, whose symbol was the white rose, and the House of Lancaster, whose symbol was the red rose. The Tudor rose, a combination of the two, is now England's floral emblem.*

2661. *Belgium, Denmark, England, Liechtenstein, Luxembourg, Monaco, the Netherlands, Norway, Spain and Sweden.*

2662. *The Maid of Orleans was 19 years old.*

2663. *"Ring-a-ring o'roses," which refers to the rosy red rash that was a symptom of the Black Death.*

2664. *Each, like Boardwalk in the U.S., is the most expensive property on its country's version of the Monopoly game board.*

2665. *Platinum-haired Deborah Harry's. She wore the outfit during Blondie's 1979 European tour.*

2666. *Chinese philosopher Confucius.*

2667. *Portugal.*

2668. *Segments of the "I Love Lucy" show and Tom and Jerry cartoons.*

2669. *A narrow, 100-mile-long strip of swampy coastland in the Carolinas.*

2670. What special device did Saudi Arabia's King Fahd have installed in the ceiling of each room in his $150-million "Flying Palace"?

2671. What three civilizations are believed to have been the only ones in history to invent the zero?

2672. What were the last words of Queen Elizabeth I when she died in 1603?

2673. Where are the highest tides in the world?

2674. What country is the only one to have been represented in all modern Olympic games—both summer and winter?

2675. What nation's flag has remained unchanged the longest?

2676. In the Indonesian village of Wirakan in 1985, what unusual payment were couples required to make in order to get married?

2677. What role did France's King Louis XIV play in a ballet written especially for him?

2678. At what age did Cleopatra take her first lover?

2679. What was the toll charged when the 66,851-ton, 963-foot Queen Elizabeth II traveled through the Panama Canal in January 1980?

2680. What was the name of the ill-fated Titanic's sister ship?

2681. What country has diverted roads to avoid disrupting "elf mounds"—communities of elves?

2682. What nation was in one continent in 1902 and another in 1903?

2683. Swat, once a principality, is now part of what country?

2684. Who was the first woman head of state in the Western Hemisphere?

2670. *A dial with a needle that automatically points to the holy city of Mecca.*

2671. *The Babylonian, Hindu and Mayan civilizations.*

2672. *"All my possessions for one moment of time."*

2673. *In the Bay of Fundy in southeastern Canada. Tides have reached 70 feet at the head of the bay.*

2674. *Great Britain.*

2675. *Denmark's.*

2676. *Ten rats—in a bid to combat a plague of rats threatening the rice harvest. Divorces cost 20 rats.*

2677. *The Sun King appeared as the sun.*

2678. *At the age of 12.*

2679. *Exactly $89,154.62.*

2680. *The Olympic. Launched on the same day as the Titanic, it collided with a Royal Navy warship on its maiden voyage two weeks later.*

2681. *Iceland.*

2682. *Panama. After winning its independence from Colombia in 1903, the new government decided to switch continents—from South America to North America.*

2683. *Pakistan.*

2684. *Isabel Peron, who succeeded her husband, Argentine dictator Juan Peron, after his death. She was ousted by a military junta in March 1976 after 20 months as president.*

2685. A hundredweight is 100 pounds in the U.S. How much is it in England?

2686. What happened to Captain William Bligh when he was governor of New South Wales in 1808—almost 20 years after he was set adrift in the famous mutiny on the Bounty?

2687. Who were the two women who joined Napoleon during his 10-month exile on the Italian island of Elba?

2688. Who coined the phrase "Third World"?

2689. What was Israeli prime minister Golda Meir's response when someone asked her how it felt to be a woman minister?

2690. What was the name of the cardinal in office in the Philippines in 1986 when strongman Ferdinand Marcos was ousted?

2691. How many member nations were there in NATO—the North Atlantic Treaty Organization—when it was founded in 1949?

2692. Who was the famous wife of Leofric, earl of Mercia and lord of Coventry?

2693. Where is the world's highest railway?

2694. What did 16-year-old Louis-Auguste, France's future King Louis XVI, write in his diary for the day of his wedding to Marie Antoinette in 1770?

2695. Where is the Valley of Ten Thousand Smokes?

2696. Why did Western Australia build a three-foot-high, 1000-mile-long fence between its northern and southern coasts in 1907?

2697. Whom did Catherine II of Russia keep in an iron cage in her bedroom for more than three years?

2698. What did Czar Nicholas II of Russia buy from Hammacher Schlemmer in 1914?

2685. *It's 112 pounds.*

2686. *Another mutiny. British Army officers rebelled, captured him and forced him to resign—for stifling the colony's rum trade.*

2687. *Maria Walenska, the Polish countess who bore him a son, and his mother, Letizia Ramolino Bonaparte.*

2688. *Indian leader Jawaharlal Nehru.*

2689. *"I don't know—I've never been a man minister."*

2690. *Cardinal Sin.*

2691. *Twelve: Belgium, Canada, Denmark, France, Iceland, Italy, Luxembourg, the Netherlands, Norway, Portugal, the United Kingdom and the U.S. Four others—Greece, Spain, Turkey and West Germany—joined later.*

2692. *Lady Godiva, who accepted her husband's challenge to ride naked through the marketplace in return for his vow to lower Coventry's taxes.*

2693. *In Peru. The Central Railway climbs to 15,694 feet in the Galera Tunnel, 108 miles from Lima. Tourists take it to get from Cuzco to the Inca ruins of Machu Picchu.*

2694. *He wrote just one word: "Nothing."*

2695. *In southwest Alaska—its name comes from the steam that rises from volcanic fissures.*

2696. *To keep its booming and destructive rabbit population from migrating from the east. The rabbits, however, were not stopped by the "No. 1 Rabbit-proof Fence."*

2697. *Her wig maker. She didn't want anyone to know her hair wasn't her own.*

2698. *One of everything the store offered.*

2699. What nation was the first to be represented on both U.S. and Russian space missions?

2700. What was the cost of a first-class ticket on the first and only around-the-world flight by an airship, made by the Graf Zeppelin in 1929?

2701. What South American country is named for an Italian city?

2702. How long did King Edward VIII sit on the English throne before he abdicated for the woman he loved?

2703. What are the citizens of Rio de Janeiro, Brazil, called?

2704. For what country did Florentine explorer Giovanni da Verrazano sail to the New World?

2705. What world-famous family changed its name from Wettin early in this century?

2706. What country's highest mountain is named for Thaddeus Kosciusko, the Polish general who fought in the American Revolution?

2707. What was Pago Pago, the administrative capital of American Samoa, formerly known as?

2708. What was 18-year-old Queen Victoria's first act after her coronation in 1838?

2709. In what country can you find Europe's last remaining herd of bison?

2710. What natural phenomenon did the ancient Egyptians use to mark the start of their New Year?

2711. Shang-tu in China was the summer palace of a great ruler. What name do we know it by?

2712. What two unique physical characteristics did Anne Boleyn—second wife of King Henry VIII—have?

2699. *France. It had representatives aboard a Soviet space flight in June 1982 and on an American flight in June 1985.*

2700. *The ticket for the 20,000 miles, 21-day trip was $9,000.*

2701. *Venezuela—which, translated, means "Little Venice."*

2702. *Eleven months, from January 20 to December 10, 1936.*

2703. *Cariocas.*

2704. *France.*

2705. *England's royal family. Wettin—the family name of Queen Victoria's German husband—was changed to Windsor when Great Britain was fighting Germany during World War I.*

2706. *Australia.*

2707. *Pango Pango, which is how Pago Pago is pronounced in the Samoan language, with "g" pronounced "ng."*

2708. *She had her bed moved from her mother's room to the very first room of her own.*

2709. *In Poland, in the Bialowieza Forest.*

2710. *The annual flooding of the Nile River.*

2711. *Xanadu, the "stately pleasure-dome" of Kubla Khan in the poem by Samuel Taylor Coleridge.*

2712. *Three breasts and an extra finger on one hand.*

2713. What distinctive emblem, descriptive of his family name, was on Dutchman Peter Minuit's coat of arms?

2714. What colors did Cleopatra paint her eyelids?

2715. Whom did Queen Elizabeth II name baron of Brighton, a peer of the realm, in 1970?

2716. In what city did Polish-born Helena Rubinstein launch her cosmetics and beauty-care business?

2717. What did the ancient Japanese use to get bricks to the top of the tall buildings they constructed?

2718. The fiber of what plant was used to make the fine linen sheets upon which Mary, Queen of Scots, slept?

2719. In 1653, what city became the first in the world to install an organized system of roadside mailboxes?

2720. According to legend, what did Cleopatra have her mattresses stuffed with every night?

2721. In England, what's a bap?

2722. What do the French refer to when they speak of "La Manche"?

2723. In the U.S. a pig says "oink." How do the French describe the sound?

2724. What's the British slang for white-collar worker?

2725. In the United States, a redcap is a baggage porter at an airport or a train or bus station. What's a redcap in Great Britain?

2726. What were the GPU, the NKVD and the MVD?

2727. Russian emperors were known as czars—but what was a czarevich?

2728. In medieval days, what were the narrow windows in thick castle walls called?

2713. *A bat—symbolizing midnight, which in French is minuit.*

2714. *Lower lids, green; upper lids, blue-black.*

2715. *Laurence Olivier—or, more appropriately, Lord Olivier of Brighton. He was the first actor in English history to reach the House of Lords.*

2716. *Melbourne, Australia, in 1902. She opened a salon in London in 1908, in Paris in 1912 and in New York in 1915.*

2717. *Kites.*

2718. *The stinging nettle.*

2719. *Paris. The boxes, used for mail bound for other parts of the city, were emptied three times a day. They were in use only briefly and then abandoned because of vandalism.*

2720. *Fresh roses.*

2721. *A hamburger bun.*

2722. *The English Channel. La manche means "the sleeve" in French.*

2723. *"Grwahng."*

2724. *Black-coat worker.*

2725. *A military policeman.*

2726. *Earlier names of the KGB, the secret political police of the now-dissolved Soviet Union.*

2727. *The eldest son of a czar. The czar's wife was a czarina.*

2728. *Loopholes. Modern-day loopholes are usually sought in contracts and laws.*

2729. In an ancient Roman amphitheater or stadium, what was a vomitory?

2730. The Romans had three words for kissing—basium, osculum and suavium. What were the distinctions among them?

2731. What topographical feature is known as elv in Danish, gang in Korean, and reka in Russian?

2732. In the German version of Monopoly, it's Goethestrasse; in the British, it's Piccadilly; and in the French, Rue Lafayette. What is this property in the American version?

2733. In Cockney rhyming slang, what is the meaning of the phrase "Would you Adam and Eve it"?

2734. How many islands are there in Hong Kong?

2735. During Napoleon's rule in France (1799-1815), what was the only year-long period he was not at war?

2736. Where in ancient Rome would you find a frigidarium?

2737. Which Caribbean island nation is closest to Mexico?

2738. What does Sinter Klaas, the Santa Claus of The Netherlands, ride when he delivers gifts to children on December 5th, St. Nicholas's Eve?

2739. What is the largest city north of the Arctic Circle?

2740. Future kings Louis XVII of France and George IV of England are both shown playing with what toy in boyhood portraits?

2741. The name Mesopotamia means "between two rivers" in Greek. What are the two rivers?

2742. What world leader-to-be lived in exile in England using the pseudonym Jacob Richter?

2743. What are the only two towns in England allowed to use the word "Royal" in their names?

2729. *A large opening that served as an entrance to or exißt from a tier of seats.*

2730. *Basium was the kiss exchanged by acquaintances; osculum, the kiss between close friends; and suavium, the kiss between lovers.*

2731. *A river.*

2732. *Marvin Gardens.*

2733. *Would you believe it?*

2734. *235 islands.*

2735. *1802-1803.*

2736. *In a Roman bath. The third of the three chambers in a Roman bath, it consisted of a cold bath and sometimes a swimming pool. The two other chambers were the caldarium (hot water bath) and the tepidarium (warm room).*

2737. *Cuba.*

2738. *A white horse. And instead of the white-trimmed red suit that Santa wears, Sinter is decked out in a red cape.*

2739. *Murmansk, in Russia.*

2740. *A yo-yo.*

2741. *The Tigris and Euphrates. Much of what was Mesopotamia is in present-day Iraq.*

2742. *Lenin, founder of the Russian Communist Party and premier of the first Soviet government.*

2743. *Royal Tunbridge Wells and Royal Leamington Spa. The right to use "Royal" as a prefix was granted to commemorate visits by Queen Victoria.*

2744. Who was Egypt's only woman pharaoh?

2745. What dog is named for an area along the coast of Croatia?

2746. The House of Windsor rules England. What house rules the Netherlands?

2747. By what means did Swedish explorer Salomon Andrée try to reach the North Pole with two companions in 1897?

2748. By what nickname is the infamous Ilich Ramirez Sanchez more commonly known?

2749. In what country is the historic city of Timbuktu located?

2750. What destination is indicated as MME in airport code?

2751. What country's thriving film industry has been nicknamed "Bollywood"?

2752. What famous teenager lived at 263 Prinsengracht?

2753. What common fate was shared by millionaires John Jacob Astor, Isidor Straus and Benjamin Guggenheim?

2754. If you saw a daibutsu in Japan, what would you be looking at?

2755. What country includes several groups of islands, including the Laccadives, the Andamans and the Nicobars?

2756. The flagship known as Queen Anne's Revenge belonged to what famous pirate?

2757. On what continent have more meteorites been discovered than have been found in all the rest of the world?

2758. How many rooms are there in Buckingham Palace?

2759. Where is the only recorded flying saucer pad on earth located?

2744. *Hatshepsut, who ruled from 1492 to 1458 B.C. The daughter and heiress of Thutmose I, who proclaimed her his successor, she ruled jointly with her half-brother, Thutmose III, whom she married.*

2745. *The dalmatian. The popular spotted dog is believed to have been originally bred along the Dalmatian coast.*

2746. *The House of Orange.*

2747. *By balloon. They failed and perished when their balloon became weighed down by ice and they were forced to land.*

2748. *Carlos the Jackal. He's the Cold War terrorist who claimed responsibility for 83 murders. His nom de guerre was Carlos, but he was dubbed "The Jackal" after a copy of the Frederick Forsyth best-seller The Day of the Jackal reportedly was found in one of his safe houses.*

2749. *Mali.*

2750. *Marseilles, France.*

2751. *India's. The bulk of the Indian film industry is based in Bombay.*

2752. *Anne Frank. The address is in Amsterdam, Holland.*

2753. *They all died when the Titanic hit an iceberg and sank on the night of April 14-15, 1912.*

2754. *A gigantic statue of Buddha.*

2755. *India. The Laccadives are in the Arabian Sea; the Andamans and Nicobars in the Bay of Bengal.*

2756. *Blackbeard, whose real name was Edward Teach. The ship sank in 1718 after it was attacked and hit a sandbar off the North Carolina coast.*

2757. *Antarctica. More than 6,000 have been found there.*

2758. *600.*

2759. *In Canada—in St. Paul, Alberta. It was built in 1967.*

2760. What formal wearing apparel—never before worn in public—led to the arrest of James Hetherington in England in 1797?

2761. What nation has an AK-47 assault rifle on its flag?

2762. Which European country was the first to establish a trading post and colony in India?

2763. What is the warmest month of the year in the Arctic?

2764. What is England's Queen Elizabeth II referring to when she mentions "Granny's chips"?

2765. Where is Mount Harvard?

2766. Where in the world are the Glasshouse Mountains?

2767. What did the Inuit use to waterproof the sea lion skins that covered their kayaks?

2768. Whose legs were banned from posters in the Paris Metro because they were considered too distracting for riders?

2769. What wood did Thor Heyerdahl use in building Kon-Tiki, the raft he sailed across the Pacific in 1947 to prove that Polynesian islanders originally came from South America?

2770. What does the dragonfly signify in Japan?

2771. Who was the first European to visit Cuba?

2772. Which national flag has the largest animal emblem?

2773. What gem served as Cleopatra's signet?

2774. In airport code, TYO stands for Tokyo. What does YTO stand for?

2775. What are the six official languages of the United Nations?

2776. To what Caribbean island territory do Bonaire, Curaçao, Saba, St. Eustatius and St. Maarten belong?

2760. *The top hat. The charge was that he "appeared on the public highway wearing upon his head a tall structure of shining luster and calculated to disturb timid people."*

2761. *Mozambique.*

2762. *Portugal, in 1502.*

2763. *July, when the average temperature is no more than 50°F 10°C.*

2764. *Her 94 and 63-carat diamonds. "Granny" was Queen Mary, wife of King George V.*

2765. *In Colorado, near Buena Vista, in the Sawatch Range of the Rocky Mountains. Its peak, at 14,399 feet, is the third highest in the state. Peaks to its south include 14,196-foot Mount Yale and 14,197-foot Mount Princeton.*

2766. *In Queensland, Australia. They were named in 1770 by explorer James Cook, who apparently observed that the volcanic mountains' smooth rock surface reflected the sun like glass.*

2767. *Whale fat.*

2768. *Marlene Dietrich's.*

2769. *Balsa. He lashed 12 giant balsa logs together.*

2770. *Good luck, courage, manliness. Japanese warriors wore the dragonfly emblem in battle.*

2771. *Christopher Columbus. He stepped ashore there on October 28, 1492, during his historic exploration of the New World.*

2772. *The flag of Sri Lanka. The animal is a lion.*

2773. *The amethyst. She believed it had magical powers.*

2774. *Toronto.*

2775. *English, French, Arabic, Chinese, Russian and Spanish.*

2776. *The Netherlands Antilles. A sixth island, Aruba, broke from the group in 1986.*

2777. Why do the natives of the Duke of York Islands in the South Pacific send a canoe adrift, once a year, loaded with money and decorated with green leaves?

2778. In what country will you find a city called Zagazig? How about a city called Wagga Wagga?

2779. What would happen if the Grimaldis, the ruling family of Monaco, should ever be without a male heir?

2780. What country once was plagued by a murderous religious sect whose members were called thugs?

2781. What is the largest city, in population, south of the Equator?

2782. What is the name of the highest mountain peak in the the former Soviet Union?

2783. In what year did Hong Kong lose its status as a Crown Colony of the United Kingdom to become a part of China again?

2784. What river is the only one that flows both north and south of the equator?

2785. What street is London's equivalent of New York's Wall Street?

2786. What was the name of polar explorer Admiral Richard Byrd's dog?

Bonus Trivia

2787. The Roman Emperor, Caligula, once wanted to appoint his favorite horse, Incitatus, a consul of Rome

2777. *To pay the fish for their relatives who were caught.*

2778. *Zagazig is in Egypt. It's a cotton and grain center in the Nile delta about 40 miles from Cairo. Wagga Wagga is in Australia, in New South Wales, 320 miles southwest of Sydney. It's an agricultural area and important livestock-selling center.*

2779. *Under a treaty that dates back to 1918, Monaco would cease to exist as a sovereign state and would become a self-governing French protectorate.*

2780. *India. The group was wiped out by the British in the nineteenth century, but its name is still used to describe criminals.*

2781. *Sao Paolo, Brazil.*

2782. *Communism Peak, or "Pik Kommunizma." The 24,590-foot-high mountain is in modern-day Tajikistan, in the Pamir Range.*

2783. *In 1997.*

2784. *The Congo River, which crosses the Equator twice.*

2785. *Lombard Street. It's named for the Lombard family, the first modern bankers of Europe, whose residence was once located there.*

2786. *Igloo.*

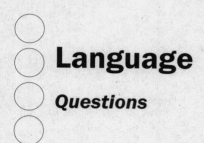

Language

Questions

2788. What is the last letter of the Greek alphabet?

2789. What is the measurement, "one foot," based on?

2790. What is the word "laser" an acronym for?

2791. Who invented the word, "carport"?

2792. What do the letters "Z", "I", and "P" stand for in zip codes?

2793. What ails you if you have a bilateral perorbital hematoma?

2794. In ballet, what's a promenade?

2795. A milligram is a thousandth of a gram. What's a picogram?

2796. What is the meaning of the Greek word kosmetikos, from which we get the word cosmetics?

2797. The first two letters of what three words were combined to form wohelo, the watchword of the Campfire Girls?

2798. What do noologists study?

Answers

2788. Omega.

2789. One third the length of the arm of King Henry I (1068-1135) of England.

2790. Light amplification by stimulated emission of radiation.

2791. Frank Lloyd Wright.

2792. Zone Improvement Plan.

2793. You have a black eye.

2794. A slow turn of the body, pivoting on the heel.

2795. A trillionth of a gram.

2796. Skilled in decorating.

2797. Work, health, and love.

2798. The mind.

2799. How fast is hypersonic?

2800. What are you afraid of if you have ergophobia?

2801. What is a dentiloquist?

2802. What does an ammeter measure?

2803. In the world of computers, what is spam?

2804. What kind of voice does someone have if he or she is oxyphonic?

2805. In the world of gardening, what is a clairvoyee?

2806. What are zoonoses?

2807. In weaving, what's the weft, or woof?

2808. What is a neuroblast?

2809. Synonyms are words with the same or nearly the same meaning. What are heteronyms?

2810. What words were combined to form the word contrail—the visible cloudlike streak left behind by jet airplanes?

2811. In Japan, what automobile accessory is known as a bakkumira?

2812. What is the meaning of the legal term involuntary conversion?

2813. What is a triolet?

2814. When it comes to waves in the ocean, what is a wavelength?

2815. SPAM is an acronym formed from what two words?

2816. What do the letters DC stand for in the airplane known as the DC-10?

2799. *More than five times the speed of sound—or above Mach 5. The speed of sound is about 740 miles an hour at sea level.*

2800. *Work.*

2801. *Someone who speaks through clenched teeth.*

2802. *Electric current—it measures the strength of an electric current in amperes.*

2803. *Junk e-mail.*

2804. *Unusually shrill.*

2805. *A windowlike hole cut in a hedge.*

2806. *Animal diseases communicable to man.*

2807. *The yarn that's threaded over and under the strands of yarn that run parallel along the length of the cloth. The parallel strands are known as the warp.*

2808. *A newly formed nerve cell.*

2809. *Words that are spelled the same but have different meanings and often different pronunciations—such as minute, meaning "60 seconds," and minute, meaning "tiny."*

2810. *Condensation and trail.*

2811. *The rear-view mirror. The Japanese word was drawn from two English words—back and mirror.*

2812. *Loss or destruction of property through theft, accident or condemnation.*

2813. *A poem. It's an eight-line poem having a rhyming scheme of ab aa ab ab, with its first line repeated as the fourth and seventh lines, and the second line repeated as the eighth line.*

2814. *The linear distance between the crests of two successive waves.*

2815. *Spiced ham.*

2816. *Douglas Commercial.*

2817. What is poliosis?

2818. What words were combined and shortened to form the radio code response "wilco"?

2819. What's the difference between a nook and a cranny?

2820. In business jargon, what does the term glocal mean?

2821. What part of an airplane is the empennage?

2822. What is a bicorn?

2823. In what profession is the scruple used as a measure?

2824. "En la komenco, Dio kreis le cielon kaj la teron." Can you translate this famous line from Esperanto into English?

2825. What is the chief symptom of someone suffering from oniomania?

2826. How did the duffel bag get its name?

2827. What does the word climax mean in Greek?

2828. In the field of accounting, what does the abbreviation "dr." signify?

2829. What is your problem if you have trichottilomania?

2830. Dublin theater manager James Daly was credited with inventing and introducing what word into the English language during the late eighteenth century by scrawling it in bathrooms and other public places?

2831. What sort of words does a sesquipedalian speaker use?

2832. What is the more common name we use for the physical affliction known as furfur?

2833. What is your problem if you have sitomania?

2817. The graying of the hair. It comes from *polios*, the Greek word for "gray." The disease *poliomyelitis* was so named because it involves the inflammation of the gray matter of the spinal cord.

2818. Will comply.

2819. A nook is a corner; a cranny is a crack.

2820. A combination of the words *global* and *local*, it means taking a global view of the market and adjusting it to local needs, or making global products fit the local market.

2821. The complete tail assembly. *Empennage* is a French word meaning "the feathers at the end of an arrow," which the tail unit resembles.

2822. The crescent-shaped hat worn by Napoleon. The three-cornered hat worn by early American colonists is known as a *tricorn*.

2823. Pharmacy—the *scruple* is an apothecary weight equal to 20 grains, or $\frac{1}{24}$ ounce.

2824. "In the beginning, God created the heaven and the earth," the first sentence of the Bible.

2825. An uncontrollable desire to buy things.

2826. From the Belgian town of Duffel, where the coarse, thicknapped woolen fabric used for the bags was manufactured.

2827. "Ladder." In Greece it is spelled *klimax*.

2828. Debtor.

2829. You have an overwhelming urge to tear your hair out.

2830. Quiz. Daly reportedly bet a friend he could introduce a new word into the language within 24 hours—and won.

2831. Long ones—like *sesquipedalian*.

2832. Dandruff.

2833. An abnormal craving for food.

2834. What are you afraid of if you have pogonophobia?

2835. What is the meaning of the oft-quoted Latin phrase "O tempora! O mores!"?

2836. Where does the expression "out of the mouths of babes" come from?

2837. What word originated as the nickname for an English insane asylum?

2838. In Gaelic, what is the literal meaning of the name Campbell?

2839. What is the origin of the word hoax?

2840. What is the meaning of the Latin word veto?

2841. What do we call a phrase that combines two contradictory words—such as pretty ugly, jumbo shrimp or unbiased opinion?

2842. When truck drivers talk about green stamps, what are they discussing?

2843. What game is known as ajedrez in Spain and Schachspiel in Germany?

2844. What are you suffering from if you have ozostomia?

2845. What do the letters in the computer-world acronym BASIC represent?

2846. What are you studying if you're into oology?

2847. What do the letters in the acronym LED stand for?

2848. In computerese, what are pixels?

2849. What was the original meaning of the Latin word musculus, meaning muscle?

2850. What language gave us the word honcho, for big shot or boss?

2834. *Beards, or men wearing beards.*

2835. *"What times! What manners!"—suggesting that both have changed for the worse. The line is from Cicero's "In Catilinam."*

2836. *The Bible, Psalms 8.2, which begins: "Out of the mouth of babes..."*

2837. *Bedlam. It was the nickname for the Hospital of St. Mary of Bethlehem in London.*

2838. *"Crooked Mouth."*

2839. *It's believed to be a contraction of "hocus," from the expression hocus pocus.*

2840. *"I forbid."*

2841. *An oxymoron.*

2842. *Speeding tickets.*

2843. *Chess.*

2844. *Halitosis—or bad breath.*

2845. *Beginner's all-purpose symbolic instruction code.*

2846. *Birds' eggs.*

2847. *Light-emitting diode. It's the light on a computer product that indicates the power is on.*

2848. *More formally known as picture, or pix, elements (pix-els), they are the individual dots on a computer monitor. In combination, they form characters as well as graphics. The more dots, the clearer the image.*

2849. *Little mouse.*

2850. *Japanese. Hancho means "squad commander" in Japanese. American flyers picked up the term during the American occupation of Japan following World War II and started using it to mean top boss.*

2851. What does the name Jonah mean when translated from Hebrew?

2852. How did April get its name?

2853. How did the ampersand become a symbol for the word "and"?

2854. What flower's name means nose-twitching in Latin—a name bestowed on it because of its pungent aroma?

2855. What is the meaning of katzenjammer, the German word used in the name of the early comic strip "The Katzenjammer Kids"?

2856. What is the name of the international association of women helicopter pilots?

2857. A bibliophile is a collector of rare books. What is a bibliopole?

2858. How did the paisley fabric design get its name?

2859. How did the airgun known as the BB gun get is name?

2860. What was the original meaning of the word clue?

2861. What do the letters in the abbreviation e.g. stand for?

2862. What is the origin of the expression "on the Q.T."?

2863. What is the origin of the word Thursday?

2864. How did Mrs. come to be the abbreviation for a married woman?

2865. What does Iwo Jima mean in Japanese?

2866. In the world of dolls, who is Midge Hadley?

2867. What are hackles—the things that get raised with anger or agitation?

2868. What do Eskimos mean when they refer to the "Big Nail"?

2851. Dove.

2852. From the Latin name of the month, Aprilis—derived from the verb aperire, "to open," signifying the time of the year buds begin to open.

2853. The symbol is a representation of the Latin word et, which means "and." It combines a capital "E" with a lowercase "t".

2854. The nasturtium.

2855. Hangover.

2856. Whirly-Girls.

2857. A seller of rare books.

2858. From the Scottish manufacturing town of Paisley, where copies were made of shawls sent home by soldiers serving in India.

2859. From the ball bearing pellets it fires.

2860. A ball of thread or yarn—which makes the concept of unraveling a clue all the more meaningful.

2861. Exempli gratia—which in Latin means "for example."

2862. The word quiet—from which it takes the first and last letters.

2863. It is the day of Thor, the god of thunder in Norse mythology. In the past it was sometimes called Thunderday.

2864. It's the abbreviation of Mistress, which originally was a title and form of address for a married woman and was always capitalized. It later became missus, and mistress lost both its capitalization and its respectability.

2865. Sulfur Island.

2866. The Barbie doll's best friend.

2867. They are the feathers on the neck of a rooster or hen.

2868. The North Pole.

2869. What is the origin of the expression "knock on wood"?

2870. What does the German word "bad" mean?

2871. In the international civil aviation alphabet used by airport control towers, the letters A, B, and C are represented by Alfa, Bravo, and Charlie. What about X,Y, Z?

2872. What is the literal translation of the pasta "vermicelli"?

2873. What are yurts?

2874. What is the origin of the word "flak"?

2875. What is the name of the layer of atmosphere between the stratosphere and the ionosphere?

2876. What letter was the last to be included in our alphabet?

2877. What is a funambulist?

2878. In computerese, what is the difference between a bit and a byte?

2879. How did the nautical measure of speed known as the knot get its name?

2880. What is the origin of "buck" in the phrase "passing the buck"?

2881. What is a gigaton?

2882. What is the origin of the word "radar"?

2883. What were the very first items referred to as gadgets?

2884. How many feet of fabric are there in a bolt of cloth?

2885. What does "Erin go bragh" mean?

2869. *It dates back to ancient European cultures whose members believed guardian spirits lived in trees and could be summoned to help with a little knocking.*

2870. *Bath.*

2871. *They're X-ray, Yankee, Zulu.*

2872. *"Little worms"—describing its shape.*

2873. *The domed, circular portable tents used by the nomads of Mongolia and Siberia.*

2874. *It's an acronym for the German Fliegerabwehrkanonen, an anti-aircraft gun.*

2875. *The mesosphere.*

2876. *The "j", which became the 26th letter during the fifteenth century. Before then, the "i" represented both the "i" and "j" sounds.*

2877. *A tightrope walker.*

2878. *A bit is a single, basic unit of information; a byte is generally eight bits.*

2879. *From sixteenth-century mariners who let out a line with knots tied at regular intervals and then counted the number of knots played out in a given time to determine their ship's approximate speed.*

2880. *A buckhorn-handled knife that was placed in front of the next card dealer. A card player who didn't want to deal would pass the knife—or buckhorn.*

2881. *The explosive force of a billion tons of TNT—or 1,000 megatons.*

2882. *It comes from radio detecting and ranging.*

2883. *Miniatures of the Statue of Liberty sold in Europe in 1886 to mark the statue's dedication. The word "gadget" came from the name of the man—Gaget—who came up with the replica idea.*

2884. *One hundred and twenty feet.*

2885. *"Ireland forever."*

2886. What are the alevin, parr, smolt and grilse?

2887. In soda fountain slang, what's a bucket of mud?

2888. Why was the Chevrolet Nova renamed the Caribe in Spanish-speaking countries?

2889. Where does the term "maverick" come from?

2890. What character in Richard Sheridan's comedy *The Rivals* has become part of the English language?

2891. How did bloomers—ladies pantaloons—get their name?

2892. Where did the term "strike" originate?

2893. When an Englishman refers to an "affiliation order," what is he talking about?

2894. A pony is a horse that measures 14.2 hands or less in height. How big is a hand?

2895. A "hairbreadth" away—just how close is that?

2896. Where did the term "the real McCoy" originate?

2897. What is a gluteusmaximusplasty?

2898. English poet John Philips wrote: "Lewd did I live & evil I did dwel." What is this an example of?

2899. What is arachibutyrophobia?

2900. What does the Japanese word "judo" mean?

2901. What is the meaning of the Latin phrase "annus mirabilis?"

2902. What word did critics of brilliant thirteenth-century Scottish philosopher-theologian John Duns Scotus contribute to the English language?

2903. What does the name Noah mean?

2886. *Names for a salmon at various stages in its life cycle.*

2887. *A dish of chocolate ice cream.*

2888. *In Spanish, no va means "does not go."*

2889. *Texas cattleman Sam Maverick's practice of not branding his calves.*

2890. *Mrs. Malaprop, whose misuse of words led to the word "malapropism."*

2891. *From suffragette Amelia Bloomer.*

2892. *With British sailors in 1768, who backed their refusal to work by striking (lowering) their sails.*

2893. *A paternity suit.*

2894. *Four inches.*

2895. *Exactly ¼₈ inch.*

2896. *In a nineteenth century advertisement for a McCoy sewing machine.*

2897. *A tush tuck.*

2898. *The palindrome—it reads the same backward and forward.*

2899. *Fear of peanut butter sticking to the roof of the mouth.*

2900. *The gentle way.*

2901. *"Wonderful year."*

2902. *Dunce. Two centuries after Scotus's death, during the Renaissance, his followers were labeled Dunsmen or Dunses—and, ultimately, Dunces—for resisting change.*

2903. *Rest.*

2904. What is the meaning of the Latin term ad hoc?

2905. What is the unfriendly meaning of the acronym NIMBY?

2906. In mining, what is a manway?

2907. How do the British pronounce the name Beauchamp?

2908. What is an undecennial?

2909. The Pennsylvania Dutch call it schmierkäse. What do most of us know it as?

2910. What is a parsec?

2911. In space lingo, what does the acronym EVA stand for?

2912. What is trokenbeerenauslese?

2913. What is a valetudinarian?

2914. How did the loosely woven fabric we know as gauze get its name?

2915. In agriculture, what is a windfall?

2916. What does a deltiologist collect?

2917. When a knight of yore sported a panache, what was he wearing?

2918. What is Guido's scale?

2919. What is the definition of "zax"—the highest-scoring three-letter word possible in the game Scrabble?

2920. In the radio communications alphabet that begins "Alpha, Bravo, Charlie," what names of Shakespearean characters are used to denote letters?

2921. What is "wagger pagger bagger" slang for in England?

2904. *"For this"—in the sense of "for this task only."*

2905. *Not in my backyard.*

2906. *A passage wide enough for just one person.*

2907. *BEE-cham.*

2908. *An eleventh anniversary.*

2909. *Cottage cheese.*

2910. *It's a unit equal to 3.26 light years, or 19.2 trillion miles, used in astronomy to measure interstellar space.*

2911. *Extra-vehicular activity, which refers to all movement outside the spacecraft.*

2912. *A German wine made from vine-dried grapes so rare that it can take a skilled picker a day to gather enough for a single bottle.*

2913. *A professional invalid—a sickly person who thinks constantly and anxiously about his or her health.*

2914. *From the city of Gaza, in Palestine, where it was first made.*

2915. *Ripening fruit knocked down from a tree by the wind.*

2916. *Postcards.*

2917. *Plumes of feathers atop his helmet.*

2918. *The musical exercise we know as do, re, mi, fa, sol, la—devised by eleventh-century Benedictine monk Guido d'Arezzo. The last two syllables-ti and do-were added later.*

2919. *A zax is a tool for cutting and trimming roof slates. In Scrabble, it earns a minimum score of 19 points—and much more if one or more of the consonants is placed on a bonus square.*

2920. *Romeo and Juliet.*

2921. *Wastepaper basket.*

2922. What are the only two words in the English language that contain all the vowels, including "y," in alphabetical order?

2923. What does dingbats mean in Australia?

2924. You've no doubt heard the French children's ditty "Alouette." Just what or who is alouette?

2925. What's a trilemma?

2926. What does dottle have to do with pipe smoking?

2927. What are descriptive word combinations such as brunch, motel and smog called?

2928. What is a chiromancer?

2929. How did lb. come to be the abbreviation for a pound?

2930. What does a vexillologist study?

2931. What is the origin of the popular dog's name Fido?

2932. What does volvo—the name of the Swedish automaker—mean in English?

2933. What is the occupational origin of the name Walker?

2934. What is sneet?

2935. What are you afraid of if you have stenophobia?

2936. In hospital slang, what is a GOMER?

2937. In America's horse-and-carriage days, what was a curricle?

2938. What was the original meaning of ezel, the name seventeenth-century Dutch artists gave to the three-legged stand we know today as an easel?

2939. What is pseudogyny?

2940. What is brontology the study of?

2922. *Facetiously and abstemiously.*

2923. *Delirium tremens.*

2924. *It's a skylark.*

2925. *It's similar to a dilemma, but involves three alternatives rather than two.*

2926. *It's the caked ash left in the bottom of the bowl after a pipe of tobacco has been smoked.*

2927. *Portmanteau words.*

2928. *A palm reader.*

2929. *It's the abbreviation for libra, from the Latin phrase libra pondo— libra meaning "a unit of measurement," and pondo meaning "by weight."*

2930. *Flags.*

2931. *It's from the Latin fidus, meaning "faithful."*

2932. *"I roll"—the name comes not from Swedish, but from Latin.*

2933. *In the Middle Ages a walker was someone who cleaned cloth.*

2934. *In California, where smoke and fog combine to become smog, a downpour of snow and sleet is known as sneet.*

2935. *Narrow places.*

2936. *A patient seeking emergency treatment for a minor complaint. The term is an acronym for Get Out of My Emergency Room.*

2937. *A two-wheeled chaise usually drawn by two horses running abreast.*

2938. *Ezel is Dutch for "donkey." The artist's stand was so named because like a donkey, it too carried a burden.*

2939. *The use of a woman's pen name by a male writer. When a female writer uses a man's pen name it's pseudandry.*

2940. *Thunder.*

2941. What does the acronym NOEL mean to those who test food additives on animals?

2942. In England, what is the hobby of people known as "twitchers"?

2943. What are you afraid of if you have siderodromophobia?

2944. What is a zeedonk?

2945. What is measured in nits?

2946. What did the term skyscraper originally mean—before it was used to describe a tall building?

2947. What's an ananym?

2948. What was the nautical origin of the expression, "not enough room to swing a cat"?

2949. In the newspaper business, the night staff is known as the lobster shift. What is it known as in mining?

2950. What is a squab?

2951. What is the ylang-ylang?

2952. In the world of computers, what are megaflops?

2953. What does the Australian slang word hooroo mean?

2954. Why is a car's instrument panel called a dashboard?

2955. When the bald eagle was first named, what was the meaning of the word bald?

2956. What does the word koala mean in Australia's Aborigine language?

2941. *No observed effect level. It means that no adverse effects were seen.*

2942. *Bird-watching. In the United States, they'd be called birders.*

2943. *Trains.*

2944. *The offspring of a zebra and a donkey.*

2945. *Luminance. A nit is a unit of brightness equal to one candela per square meter.*

2946. *It was the name of the small triangular sail set above the royals on square-riggers to catch wind in calm weather. It was later used to describe tall men and horses, and eventually buildings.*

2947. *A name spelled backwards that is sometimes used as a pseudonym. Oprah Winfrey uses an ananym of her first name for her production company—Harpo.*

2948. *The cat referred to was a cat-o'-nine-tails, which was used for lashings at sea.*

2949. *The hoot owl.*

2950. *A young pigeon that has not yet flown.*

2951. *A tree with fragrant flowers widely used in perfume making. The tree is found in southeast Asia; the scent from its blossoms is found in such popular perfumes as Chanel No. 5 and Arpège.*

2952. *Processing—or operating—speeds of a million floating-points per second. FLOPS is an acronym for floating-point operations per second.*

2953. *"Good-bye."*

2954. *The name dates back to horse-and-buggy days when dashing horses kicked up mud, splashing the passengers riding behind them. The dashboard was devised to protect them.*

2955. *White.*

2956. *It means "no drink." This Australian marsupial gets all the liquid it needs from the eucalyptus leaves it eats.*

2957. The word peninsula is derived from the Latin words paene and insula. What do they mean?

2958. What information is sought in a Schick test? How about a Dick test?

2959. How could the word mile be derived from the Latin phrase mille passuum, which means 1,000 paces, when it takes at least twice that many steps to walk a mile?

2960. What letter of the alphabet is the oldest?

2961. On sailboats, what are barnacles and binnacles?

2962. What is the only word in the English language that both begins and ends with the letters u-n-d?

2963. What two dances are among the words used in the radio communications alphabet that begins Alpha, Bravo, Charlie?

2964. What is the meaning of the word Siberia?

2965. What physical phenomenon are you experiencing if you have horripilation?

2966. What is the meaning of the legal term pro se?

2967. What is the meaning of the Huron-Iroquois Indian word kanata—from which Canada derives its name?

2968. How much does a bushel of apples weigh?

2969. What punctuation mark is derived from the Latin word for joy?

2970. What is the meaning of the word aprosexia?

2971. What astronomical term comes from the Greek word for milk?

2957. *Paene means "almost"; "insula," island.*

2958. *Both are skin tests—the first to determine an individual's susceptibility to diphtheria, and the second to determine susceptibility to scarlet fever.*

2959. *The 1,000 paces referred to were those of the Roman Legion, whose formal parade step consisted of two steps that covered a distance of 5.2 feet. That would make a mile 5,200 feet—very close to today's statute mile of 5,280 feet.*

2960. *The O.*

2961. *A barnacle is a marine animal that attaches itself to a boat's bottom; a binnacle is a covered, nonmagnetic case that contains a ship's compass and a light.*

2962. *Underground.*

2963. *Foxtrot and Tango.*

2964. *It's from sibir, which means "sleeping giant" in the language of the Tatars who once dwelled in the area.*

2965. *Gooseflesh—the bristling of hair on your head or body caused by fear, cold, or disease.*

2966. *"By oneself"—without a lawyer.*

2967. *The name of the world's second largest country comes from a word that means "small village." Explorer Jacques Cartier first used it for the area around what is now Quebec city.*

2968. *About 42 pounds.*

2969. *The exclamation point (!). Joy in Latin is io, which was abbreviated by putting the i above the o.*

2970. *"Abnormal inability to concentrate."*

2971. *Galaxy. In Greek, gala means "milk." The Greeks thought the Milky Way looked like milk spilled across the sky.*

2972. What is garbo slang for in Australia?

2973. What do the initials o.g. mean to a stamp collector?

2974. What is the meaning of the acronym GRAS when it is used by the U.S. Food and Drug Administration?

2975. What is the literal meaning of the word Eskimo?

2976. What is poliosis?

2977. When people in New Orleans speak about Mardi Grass, what are they talking about?

2978. What is a pulicologist's area of expertise?

2979. How many letters are there in the Hawaiian alphabet?

2980. How many words are given for the color yellow in the revised and updated Roget's International Thesaurus, published in 1992?

2981. What do you fear if you have nephophobia?

2982. What is Koninklijke Luchtvaart Maatschappij?

2983. What on earth is the lithosphere?

2984. What is a kakistocracy?

2985. Who wears an item of clothing known as a sporran?

2986. Feline means "catlike," bovine means "cowlike," but what does aquiline mean?

2987. What is cat ice?

2988. What is the arched handle of a bucket or kettle called?

2989. For whom was the fabric poplin named?

2990. From what phrase is the oath zounds derived?

2972. "Garbageman".

2973. "Original gum"—which indicates that the gum that was on the back of a stamp when it was first issued is still there.

2974. Generally recognized as safe.

2975. "Eaters of raw flesh." It's an Algonquin word, one the Eskimos themselves don't use. They call themselves Inuit, which means "The People."

2976. Premature graying of the hair.

2977. The artificial turf used at the Superdome.

2978. Fleas.

2979. 12—A, E, I, O, U, H, K, L, M, N, P and W.

2980. 58.

2981. Clouds.

2982. KLM—or Royal Dutch Airlines.

2983. The layer of hard rock that makes up the earth's outer shell.

2984. A government ruled by the worst people in the state.

2985. Scottish Highlanders. The sporran is the pouch, or purse, worn with a kilt.

2986. Eaglelike.

2987. Very thin ice, from which the water underneath has receded—making it unable to bear virtually any weight, even that of a cat.

2988. A bail.

2989. The pope. The name dates back to at least the sixteenth century, when Avignon, France—where the finely ribbed fabric originated—served as a papal seat.

2990. God's wounds.

2991. What do the lowercase initials U.S. stand for in England?

2992. What does the word yoga mean in Sanskirt?

2993. In postal circles, ZIP is an acronym for Zone Improvement Plan. What do the same letters mean to psychologists? How about bankers?

2994. What is the English translation of the Olympic motto, Citius—Altius—Fortius?

2995. What is pogonology the study of?

2996. What is a nightjar?

2997. What does the acronym LION stand for at the National Aeronautics and Space Administration (NASA)?

2998. What is a Nilometer?

2999. On what part of the body would a man wear a gibus?

3000. What is a callithump?

3001. In the days when last names were linked to a person's trade, what was the occupation of someone named Travers?

3002. What is philematology?

3003. What is the definition of the word manumission?

3004. What would you do if you found a sign written in Latin that said "Cave Canem"?

3005. How did Christmas become Xmas?

3006. Where did the word vamp—meaning seductress—originate?

3007. In political slang, what does it mean if you call a candidate drab?

3008. How did the phrase "cold shoulder" come to mean a polite snub?

2991. *Useless. The initials, originally used in the army, are derived from the word unserviceable.*

2992. *Union.*

2993. *To psychologists, ZIP means Zero Intelligence Potential—or a person of low intelligence; to bankers, Zero Interest Payment.*

2994. *Faster—Higher—Stronger.*

2995. *Beards.*

2996. *A nocturnal bird common to Europe and Asia. It's also known as a goatsucker.*

2997. *Lunar International Observer Network.*

2998. *A gauge devised by the ancient Egyptians to measure the water level of the Nile during flood time.*

2999. *On his head—it's a collapsible opera hat named for its inventor, Antoine Gibus, a nineteenth-century Parisian hat-maker.*

3000. *A noisy, boisterous serenade or parade.*

3001. *Toll bridge collector.*

3002. *The science of kissing.*

3003. *The liberation of a slave from bondage; emancipation.*

3004. *You would "beware of the dog."*

3005. *X is the Greek letter chi, the first letter of Christ's name written in Greek. It has been a symbol for Christ since the Middle Ages.*

3006. *With Theda Bara's arousing performance in the film* The Vampire.

3007. *Doesn't rock any boats.*

3008. *In medieval France a guest who had overstayed his welcome was served a cold shoulder of beef or mutton rather than a hot meal.*

3009. What is the origin of Mayday, the international radiotelephonic distress signal for ships and aircraft?

3010. What is the longest word in the *Oxford English Dictionary* ?

3011. How did the blimp get named?

3012. What is the literal meaning of "aloha"—the Hawaiian word of greeting and farewell?

3013. What is a tittle?

3014. How did detectives come to be called private eyes?

3015. Which is more, an American billion or a British billion?

3016. In computer slang, a byte is a group of bits. What do you call a group of bytes?

3017. What is the origin of the word "good-bye"?

3018. What is trinitrotoluene?

3019. In the Middle Ages, when last names such as Baker and Taylor reflected a person's occupation, what did "Webster" indicate?

3020. The Sherpa tribesmen of Nepal call the creature we know as the Abominable Snowman "Metohkangmi." What is the literal translation of the name?

3021. If you are taking a class in pistology, what are you studying?

3022. What are pilchards called in their younger schooldays?

3023. What are the plastic or metal tips on shoelaces called?

3024. What does a culicidologist study?

3025. What is a formicary?

3026. In citizens band (CB) slang, what's a bear bite?

3027. What's a long ton?

3009. *The French m'aidez—help me.*

3010. *Floccinaucinihilipilifacation, which is defined as "the act or habit of estimating as worthless."*

3011. *During World War II there were two categories of dirigibles: A-rigid and B-limp.*

3012. *Love.*

3013. *The dot over the letters "i" and "j."*

3014. *From the unblinking-eye logo of Pinkerton's detective agency which proclaimed "We Never Sleep."*

3015. *A British billion. It's 1,000,000,000,000—which is a trillion in the U.S. The American billion, 1,000,000,000, is known as a milliard in England.*

3016. *A gulp.*

3017. *It's a contraction of the sixteenth-century phrase "God be with ye."*

3018. *The chemical compound we know as TNT.*

3019. *A female weaver. A male weaver was called Webb.*

3020. *"The indescribably filthy man of the snow."*

3021. *Faith.*

3022. *Sardines.*

3023. *Aglets.*

3024. *The mosquito.*

3025. *An ant hill.*

3026. *A speeding ticket.*

3027. *It's a unit of weight in Great Britain, the equivalent of 2,240 pounds. America's 2,000-pound ton is known as a short ton.*

3028. What is the meaning of the Chinese phrase "gong hay fot choy"?

3029. What is the origin of the word "stentorian," meaning "extremely loud"?

3030. What are you afraid of if you have peccatophobia?

3031. How did the term "red-letter day" originate?

3032. What is the meaning of the Swahili word Kwanzaa—the name adopted for the annual celebration of African-American history and culture?

3033. When the State Department refers to "vertical transportation units," what is it describing?

3034. What is the meaning of deinos and sauros, the two Greek words paleontologists combined to name the long-extinct dinosaur?

3035. What is a dactylogram?

3036. What is vog?

3037. What is the meaning of the Sioux word tonka, which was adopted in 1947 as the name of the toy company known for its sturdy toy trucks?

3038. What is the origin of the expression "upper crust"?

3039. In logging slang, what's a "jackpot"?

3040. Why do we call seedy saloons "dives"?

3041. In trucking circles, what's meant by a "bumper sticker"?

3042. How many letters in our alphabet serve as Roman numerals?

3028. *"Wishing you a prosperous New Year."*

3029. *Stentor, a Greek herald during the Trojan War, whose "voice of bronze," according to Homer's "Iliad," was as "loud as the cry of 50 other men."*

3030. *Sinning.*

3031. *In the fifteenth century it became common practice to print important feast days, saints' days and holidays in red ink on ecclesiastical calendars and in almanacs. Since these were memorable, happy days, "red-letter day" came to mean any lucky day or day recalled with delight.*

3032. *It means "first fruits." The celebration, based on African harvest festivals, runs from December 26 to January 1.*

3033. *Elevators.*

3034. *Deinos means "terrible" or "terrifying"; sauros, "lizard."*

3035. *A fingerprint.*

3036. *A Hawaiian cousin of smog—it's a fog caused when sulfuric volcanic fumes mix with oxygen.*

3037. *Tonka means "great."*

3038. *Etiquette in days of yore required that the choice top crust of a loaf of bread be presented to the king or ranking noble at the table.*

3039. *A messy pile of logs.*

3040. *When the word "dive" first came into use in New York City in the mid-1800s, such an establishment was usually located below street level in a run-down row house, requiring patrons to descend into the building's depths.*

3041. *A tailgater; a driver who is following another vehicle too closely.*

3042. *Seven—I, V, X, L, C, D and M. (I=1; V=5; X=10; L=50; C=100; D=500; M=1,000.)*

3043. What is the British term for the maid of honor at a wedding?

3044. What does the word "bellwether" have to do with sheep?

3045. What are menhirs, cromlechs and dolmens?

3046. How did the term "in the buff" come to mean naked?

3047. What is the meaning of the Dutch word doop, which gave us the word "dope" as a synonym for illegal narcotics?

3048. What is a pilot talking about when he uses the term "cumulo-granite"?

3049. On what part of your body would you wear a shako?

3050. What is the only two-syllable word in the English language with no true vowels?

3051. What is a yoctosecond?

3043. *The chief bridesmaid.*

3044. *The word originated with sheep farmers. A shepherd would hang a bell from the neck of his lead sheep—generally a castrated ram known as a wether—so he would know where the flock was heading.*

3045. *Prehistoric monuments.*

3046. *Buff came to us via the buffalo—and was originally used to refer to the soft yellow leather of buffalo hides. The link between hide and skin eventually led to the term "in the buff," meaning naked, and the color buff.*

3047. *It means sauce or gravy. In English its meaning evolved to refer to any mixture of unknown or suspicious ingredients, and then to drugs.*

3048. *Clouds that obscure tall mountains.*

3049. *On your head. The shako is a tall, cylindrical military hat with a flat top, visor and feather cockade in front. It's often worn by members of marching bands.*

3050. *Rhythm.*

3051. *The smallest designated unit of time—equivalent to .00000000000000000000001 second (that's with 23 zeroes).*

Food

Questions

3052. How did pound cake get its name?

3053. How did the manufacturers of Old Grand-Dad bourbon get away with producing their whisky during Prohibition?

3054. What popular drink did a Dutch medical professor produce in his laboratory while trying to come up with a blood cleanser that could be sold in drugstores?

3055. What breakfast food gets its name from the German word for "stirrup"?

3056. What beverage did Pope Clement VIII officially recognize as a Christian drink in an edict issued in 1592?

3057. In wine making, what is the must?

3058. What animal is the source of the milk used in making Roquefort cheese?

3059. Why was the Animal Crackers box designed with a string handle?

Answers

3052. From the one-pound quantities of the key ingredients (sugar, butter, eggs and flour) in the original recipe.

3053. They marked the bottles "for medicinal purposes."

3054. Gin. The professor, Franciscus dele Boë Sylvius, was distilling pure laboratory alcohol with the essence of juniper berries when he ended up with the drink—which originally was known as Hollandsch genever (Dutch juniper).

3055. The bagel. Originally a horn-shaped roll known as a kipfel, it was reshaped to resemble a riding stirrup and renamed bügel—from the German steigbügel for "stirrup"—to honor Poland's King John III Sobiesky for driving Turkish invaders from Vienna in the late seventeenth century. Riding was the king's favorite hobby.

3056. Coffee, which had been introduced to Europe by Arab traders and was considered by many Roman Catholics to be the wine of infidels.

3057. The juice drawn from the grapes but not yet fermented into wine.

3058. The ewe, or female sheep.

3059. The animal-shaped cookie treats were introduced in 1902 as a Christmas novelty—and packaged so they could be hung from Christmas trees.

3060. What elaborate confection was inspired by St. Bride's Church in London?

3061. On what vegetable did an ancient Egyptian place his right hand when taking an oath?

3062. How was the dish we know as chicken à la king first listed when it was added to the menu at New York's Delmonico's restaurant in the 1880's?

3063. What American city produces most of the egg rolls sold in grocery stores in the United States?

3064. What drink is named for the wormwood plant?

3065. Italy leads the world in pasta consumption with 61.7 pounds eaten per person per year. What country is second?

3066. When Birdseye introduced the first frozen food in 1930, what did the company call it?

3067. What vegetables did the Iroquois plant together and refer to as the "three sisters"?

3068. With what did Queen Victoria mix her claret?

3069. What is the largest food-marketing cooperative in the United States?

3070. What novelty salt shakers did publishing czar William Randolph Hearst have on the refectory table in the dining room of his San Simeon estate?

3071. What two spices are derived from the fruit of the nutmeg tree?

3072. How many different animal shapes are there in the "Animal Crackers" cookie zoo?

3073. How many flowers are in the design stamped on each side of an Oreo cookie?

3060. The tiered wedding cake—which was based on the tiered spire of the church, designed by Sir Christopher Wren.

3061. The onion. Its round shape symbolized eternity.

3062. As chicken à la Keene—it was named in honor of Foxhall Keene, a regular at Delmonico's.

3063. Houston, Texas.

3064. Vermouth, which is flavored with wormwood (vermout in French; wermut in German)—so called because the bitter-tasting plant was once used as a cure for intestinal worms. Only the harmless blossoms of the plant, not its toxic leaves, are used in making vermouth.

3065. Venezuela, where the annual pasta consumption is 27.9 pounds. The United States, with 19.8 pounds of pasta consumed per person annually is sixth—after Argentina, Tunisia and Switzerland.

3066. Frosted food. Company officials feared the word frozen would suggest flesh burns. The name was changed to frozen soon after.

3067. Corn, beans and squash. Planted together on earthen hills, the corn stalks supported the vines of the bean plants and the broad-leafed squash plants blocked the growth of weeds.

3068. Whiskey—the mixture was her favorite alcoholic beverage.

3069. Land O'Lakes, which markets the products of more than 300,000 farmers and ranchers in 15 midwestern and northwestern states. The co-op, formed in 1921 with $1,375 in seed money from the U.S. Farm Bureau, is now America's top marketer of butter, butter blends and delicatessen cheeses.

3070. Mickey and Minnie Mouse shakers.

3071. Nutmeg, which is produced from the kernel; and mace, which is produced from the kernel's lacy covering.

3072. Eighteen—two bears (one walking, one seated), a bison, camel, cougar, elephant, giraffe, gorilla, hippopotamus, hyena, kangaroo, lion, monkey, rhinoceros, seal, sheep, tiger and zebra.

3073. Twelve. Each has four petals.

3074. What part of the strawberry plant is the true fruit?

3075. Peter Cooper, best known for inventing the locomotive "Tom Thumb," patented a dessert in 1845. What was it?

3076. What percentage of whole milk is water?

3077. In which American city is the greatest amount of ketchup consumed?

3078. How many kernels of durum wheat are used to make a pound of pasta?

3079. What is the official state beverage of Delaware?

3080. What part of the banana is used to make banana oil?

3081. From what part of the cinnamon tree do we get the spice?

3082. According to U.S. Agriculture Department grading regulations, how many ounces must a dozen "jumbo" eggs weigh?

3083. Black-eyed peas are not peas. What are they?

3084. What product was introduced in Japanese supermarkets after a survey showed half the country's young people weren't able to use chopsticks?

3085. The pretzel shape was created by French monks in 610 AD. What was it designed to resemble?

3086. What American brewery was the first to market beer in a bottle?

3087. Two states have official beverages. Florida's is orange juice. What's the other state and its beverage?

3088. In 1867 Emperor Napoleon III had a chemist develop a food product "for the army, navy, and the needy classes of the population." What was it?

3089. The father of what American poet invented peppermint Life Savers?

3090. In cooking, how many drops to a teaspoon?

3074. *The seed. The delicacy that we eat and call the fruit is actually the swollen end of the stem called a drupe.*

3075. *A gelatin treat that eventually became known as Jell-O when it was marketed in 1897.*

3076. *87 percent.*

3077. *New Orleans.*

3078. *Approximately 16,550.*

3079. *Milk.*

3080. *No part. Banana oil, a synthetic compound made with amyl alcohol, is named for its banana-like aroma. It is used primarily as a paint solvent and in artificial fruit flavoring.*

3081. *The inner bark of young wood.*

3082. *Thirty ounces.*

3083. *Beans.*

3084. *Trainer chopsticks, with loops to show users where to put their fingers.*

3085. *A little child's arms in prayer.*

3086. *F & M Schaefer.*

3087. *Ohio; tomato juice.*

3088. *Margarine.*

3089. *Hart Crane; his father's name was Clarence.*

3090. *Sixty.*

3091. Who invented evaporated milk in 1853?

3092. What was the first of H. J. Heinz' "57 varieties"?

3093. What word did Winston Churchill coin to describe Socialist nations where people have to wait in line for everything?

3094. What flavor ice cream did Dolly Madison serve at the inaugural festivities in 1812?

3095. Where was the first automated fortune cookie machine manufactured?

3096. How many pounds of roasted, ground coffee does one coffee tree yield annually?

3097. What does the word "pizza" mean in Italian?

3098. Who said: "Never eat more than you can lift"?

3099. Where does the name "Sanka" come from?

3100. What does VVSOP mean on a cognac bottle?

3101. What was the drink we know as the Bloody Mary originally called?

3102. What capital city is expected to be the most populous in the world—with more than thirty million residents—by the year 2000?

3103. What product did Mother Nature personified endorse in a television commercial, and who played the role?

3104. What is the traditional food served at Wimbledon each year?

3105. Who originally coined the phrase that has been appropriated as the slogan for Maxwell House coffee: "Good to the last drop"?

3106. Who first developed frozen foods?

3107. What was the first commercially-manufactured breakfast cereal?

3108. How tall is gourmet cook Julia Child?

3091. Gail Borden, who went on to invent a variety of juice concentrates and became known as "the father of the instant food industry."

3092. Horseradish, marketed in 1869.

3093. Queuetopias.

3094. Strawberry.

3095. In Japan, for Los Angeles' Hong Kong Noodle Co., which first introduced cookies with messages (written by a Presbyterian minister) in 1918.

3096. Just one.

3097. Pie, which makes the phrase "pizza pie" redundant.

3098. Miss Piggy.

3099. Sans caféine, French for without caffeine.

3100. Very Very Superior Old Pale.

3101. The Red Snapper, which was its name when it crossed the Atlantic from Harry's New York Bar in Paris.

3102. Mexico City, Mexico.

3103. Chiffon Margarine; Dena Dietrich played Mother Nature.

3104. Strawberries and cream.

3105. President Theodore Roosevelt.

3106. Clarence Birdseye, in 1930.

3107. Shredded Wheat, made by Henry Perky in 1882.

3108. 6 feet 2 inches.

3109. What is the name of the dog on the Cracker Jack box?

3110. Cleopatra used the juice of what common salad ingredient to preserve her skin?

3111. What did the homesick alien get drunk on in Steven Spielberg's 1982 hit film E.T.—The Extra-Terrestrial?

3112. What words are on the three rings on the Ballantine ale label?

3113. In what country did the beverage we know as punch originate?

3114. What seeds are used to flavor the Scandinavian liquor aquavit?

3115. What color did blue replace in 1995 when it was introduced to the standard package of M&Ms candies?

3116. What two tools were recommended in the instructions for opening a tin of roast veal that was taken on English explorer William Parry's third voyage to the Arctic in 1824?

3117. How many pounds of dried saffron does an acre of crocus plants yield?

3118. On average, how many calories a day are American astronauts given to eat while on missions in outer space?

3119. What do herring, cabbage and carrots represent at New Year's Eve feasts in Germany and Scandinavia?

3120. What is the American name for the British delicacy known as trotters?

3121. For whom was the surf 'n' turf meal originally created?

3122. What country boasts the highest per capita consumption of cereal in the world?

3123. How many lemons does the average lemon tree yield per year?

3109. Bingo.

3110. Cucumber, which is still used in skin care—in facial creams, lotions and cleansers.

3111. Coors beer.

3112. Purity, body, flavor.

3113. India. The British gave the refreshing drink the name punch, most likely from the Hindi word panch, for the number five, because it had five basic ingredients—alcohol, tea, lemon, sugar and water.

3114. Caraway.

3115. Tan. Blue was the overwhelming choice in a vote taken by Mars, Inc. The runner-up colors were purple and pink.

3116. Chisel and hammer. The can opener was not invented until 1858.

3117. 10 pounds. It takes about 75,000 flowers to produce a pound of saffron—which is why it's the most expensive spice in the world.

3118. 3,000.

3119. Herring represents good luck; cabbage, plenty of silver; and carrots, gold in the year ahead.

3120. Pigs' feet.

3121. Famous gastronome Diamond Jim Brady. It was served to him at a waterfront restaurant in Brooklyn, New York, in the late 1880s.

3122. Ireland, where the annual consumption is over 15 pounds per person.

3123. 1,500. The trees usually bloom throughout the year, with the fruit picked 6 to 10 times a year.

3124. What food product, marketed as Elijah's Manna in 1904, was renamed because of objections from the clergy?

3125. What name is shared by a citrus fruit and the citizens of an African capital?

3126. What is Bombay duck?

3127. What popular treat did 11-year-old Frank Epperson accidentally invent in 1905 and patent in 1924?

3128. Where did the pineapple plant originate?

3129. What was margarine called when it was first marketed in England?

3130. What American city lead all others in per capita consumption of pizza in 1990?

3131. How much did Weight Watchers founder Jean Nidetch weigh in 1963 when she came up with the concept that helped her shed pounds and make a fortune?

3132. Under what name did the Domino's Pizza chain get its start?

3133. What are the two top-selling spices in the world?

3134. What European nation consumes more spicy Mexican food than any other?

3135. Under U.S. government regulations, what percentage of peanut butter has to be peanuts?

3136. Drupes are a regular part of the American diet. What are they?

3137. What is the essential ingredient in a dish that's prepared à la DuBarry in honor of King Louis XV's mistress?

3138. What is the literal meaning of the Italian word linguine?

3139. Under federal food-labeling regulations, how much caffeine must be removed from coffee for it to be called decaffeinated?

3124. *Post Toasties cereal.*

3125. *Tangerine (Tangiers is the summer capital of Morocco.)*

3126. *Dried, salted fish. It's both a snack and a flavoring used in Indian cooking.*

3127. *The Popsicle, which he originally marketed as the Epsicle. Epperson inadvertently made the first one when he left a glass of lemonade with a spoon in it on a windowsill—and it froze overnight.*

3128. *In South America. It didn't reach Hawaii until the early nineteenth century.*

3129. *Butterine.*

3130. *Milwaukee.*

3131. *214 pounds. A year later, she weighed 142.*

3132. *DomiNick's.*

3133. *Pepper is the top seller; mustard is second.*

3134. *Norway.*

3135. *90 percent.*

3136. *Simple, succulent, usually single-pitted fruit—such as plums, apricots, peaches, cherries, almonds and olives.*

3137. *Cauliflower.*

3138. *"Little tongues."*

3139. *97 percent.*

3140. How many quarts of whole milk does it take to make one pound of butter?

3141. What shortbread cookie is named for the heroine of a nineteenth-century English novel?

3142. How much did Americans spend on pizzas in 1988?

3143. Christmas is the biggest candy-selling season in the U.S. What holiday ranks second?

3144. How much money did American Airlines claim it saved in 1987 by eliminating one olive from each of the salads served in first class?

3145. What is the hamburger we know as the Big Mac called in Russia?

3146. What was the name of the breakfast cereal Cheerios when it was first marketed 50 years ago?

3147. What famous dish was named after shipping magnate Ben Wenberg?

3148. Under federal regulation, how much caffeine must be removed from coffee for it to be labeled "decaffeinated"?

3149. What favorite recipe of her and her husband's did First Lady Jacqueline Kennedy have taped to the wall in the White House kitchen?

3150. What beverage was advertised as "good to the last drop" in 1907?

3151. How long would a 130-pound person have to walk at a leisurely pace to burn off the calories in a McDonald's Big Mac? How about a Burger King Double Beef Whopper with cheese?

3152. What popular soft drink contained the drug lithium—now available only by prescription—when it was introduced in 1929?

3153. How did the croissant get its name?

3140. *Almost 10—9.86 to be exact.*

3141. *The Lorna Doone. The novel* Lorna Doone, *by R. D. Blackmore, was published in 1869.*

3142. *$20 billion, according to the National Association of Pizza Operators.*

3143. *Easter—which surpasses Valentine's Day, Mother's Day and Halloween.*

3144. *$40,000.*

3145. *The Bolshoi Mak—bolshoi means "big" in Russian.*

3146. *Cherrioats. The name was changed the following year at the urging of the folks at Quaker Oats.*

3147. *Lobster Newburg. Wenberg, who had sampled the dish in South America, passed the recipe on to the chef at Delmonico's in New York in the late nineteenth century. The dish was named for him until he was involved in a drunken brawl and banned from the restaurant. Then it was altered to Newburg.*

3148. *97 percent.*

3149. *The recipe for the daiquiri.*

3150. *Coca-Cola. The slogan was long forgotten by the time the line was adopted by Maxwell House coffee.*

3151. *Two hours and one minute for the Big Mac; three hours and twenty-six minutes for the Double Whopper.*

3152. *7-Up, which originally was marketed under the name Bib-Label Lithiated Lemon-Lime soda. Lithium, now used to treat manic depression, was eliminated from the formula in the mid-1940s.*

3153. *From the crescent design (creissant in Old French) on the Turkish flag. Viennese bakers created the crescent-shaped rolls to mark their city's successful stand against Turkish invaders in 1683.*

3154. What recipe did Texas ice-cream maker Elmer Doolin buy for $100 from the owner of a San Antonio café in 1933—and use to make a fortune?

3155. What popular drink was marketed as Diastoid when it was first introduced in 1882?

3156. What did the Wrigley Company do to promote its chewing gum nationwide in 1914?

3157. What member of the British nobility received a special award from America's National Pickle Packers Association in 1956 in recognition of an ancestor's invention?

3158. What percentage of the grains used in making bourbon must be corn?

3159. What are the five most frequently consumed fruits in the United States?

3160. In the United States, we call a tall iced drink of gin, lemon or lime, club soda and sugar a Tom Collins. What do they call it in England?

3161. What flavor did Baskin-Robbins introduce to commemorate America's landing on the moon on July 20, 1969?

3162. What general introduced chicle—the main ingredient in chewing gum—to the United States?

3163. What eating utensil was first brought to America in 1630 by Massachusetts Bay Colony governor John Winthrop, who carried it around with him in a specially made, velvet-lined leather case?

3164. Where in a wine shop will you find coiffes?

3165. How long does it take to hard-boil a three-pound ostrich egg?

3166. A pound of ground coffee yields 50 cups. How many cups does a pound of tea yield?

3167. What popular fruit was named after a papal estate outside Rome?

3154. *The recipe for tasty corn chips that he marketed as Fritos. He made them at night in his mother's kitchen and peddled them from his Model-T Ford.*

3155. *The malted milk, which was first sold as a special food supplement for babies and sick people.*

3156. *It mailed Doublemint gum to everyone listed in U.S. phone books.*

3157. *The Earl of Sandwich, whose eighteenth-century ancestor—the fourth earl—is credited with having invented the sandwich. The pickle packers gave the award in appreciation of the sandwich's contribution to the consumption of pickles.*

3158. *51 percent.*

3159. *The banana, apple, watermelon, orange and cantaloupe—in order of their greatest consumption, according to the Food and Drug Administration.*

3160. *A John Collins.*

3161. *Lunar cheesecake.*

3162. *Mexican general Antonio López de Santa Anna, while he was living in exile in New York City more than 30 years after he guaranteed himself a place in American history by storming the Alamo. He enjoyed chewing unflavored chicle and brought it north with him.*

3163. *The fork.*

3164. *On champagne bottles. The coiffe is the metal wire contraption that holds the champagne cork in place.*

3165. *1 hour and 45 minutes.*

3166. *200.*

3167. *The cantaloupe, which was named after the Pope's summer residence of Cantalupo.*

3168. Currants—small seedless grapes—were named for their place of origin. Just where was that?

3169. In what country did the Jerusalem artichoke originate?

3170. What was Charles Elmer Hires originally going to call the drink we now know as root beer?

3171. What is the most widely eaten fish in the world?

3172. How long does it take a ginseng root to reach marketable size?

3173. What snack food commercial was pulled off the air in 1970 because of complaints from an outraged ethnic group?

3174. Vichyssoise—the cold potato and leek soup—was first created in 1917 by chef Louis Diat. Do you know where?

3175. What fruit did the Visigoths demand in ransom when they laid siege to Rome in 408?

3176. What ethnic food did Jeno Paulucci make available in supermarkets nationwide for the very first time in 1947?

3177. What recipe—first published 50 years ago—has been requested most frequently through the years by the readers of "Better Homes and Gardens"?

3178. What were guests at the Buckinghamshire estate of financier Alfred de Rothschild asked when they requested milk with their tea?

3179. Under standards established by the U.S. Food and Drug Administration, what is the minimum a gallon of ice cream must weigh?

3180. What food product is named after Hannibal's brother Mago?

3181. When was coffee first sold in sealed tin cans in the United States?

3168. *Corinth, Greece. They were originally known as raysons de Corauntz, or "raisins of Corinth."*

169. *In the United States. Its name has nothing to do with the biblical city, but is a corruption of the Italian word for sunflower, girasole.*

3170. *Root tea—but a friend convinced him the name would discourage sales.*

3171. *The herring.*

3172. *Seven years.*

3173. *The Frito Bandito commercial for Frito corn chips. The complaints came from Mexican-Americans.*

3174. *In New York City—in the kitchen of the Ritz-Carlton Hotel, where Diat was head chef.*

3175. *Peppercorns—3,000 pounds of them. Pepper was a highly valued spice at the time.*

3176. *Paulucci gave us Chinese food—under the Chun King label. He later brought us Jeno's pizza.*

3177. *The recipe for hamburger pie, which has been updated and republished a number of times over the years.*

3178. *"Jersey, Hereford and Shorthorn?"*

3179. *Four and one-half pounds.*

3180. *Mayonnaise—which is named after the Minorca Island port city of Mahon, which was named for Mago.*

3181. *In 1879—by Chase & Sanborn.*

3182. For over fifty years, Ann Turner Cook's portrait has been the symbol for what well-known food product?

3183. What was the first name of Dom Pérignon, the seventeenth-century French monk who gave us Champagne?

3184. What part of the traditional Thanksgiving dinner is the merrythought?

3185. What is the name of the evergreen shrub from which we get capers?

3186. What is the largest fruit crop on earth?

3187. A California vintner named a Napa Valley wine in honor of Marilyn Monroe. What was it called?

3188. What is the official state beverage of Massachusetts?

3189. What food product overtook ketchup as the top-selling condiment in the United States in 1991?

3190. What fruit was originally named the Chinese gooseberry?

3191. What common salad ingredient belongs to the aster family?

3192. What is Danish pastry known as in Denmark?

3193. What is the only essential vitamin not found in the white potato?

3194. Under federal guidelines, how much alcohol can there be in beer labeled "non-alcoholic"?

3195. What delicacy is named for the city of Cheriton, Virginia?

3196. What is the Asiatic cordial kumiss made from?

3197. Under U.S. Agriculture Department guidelines, what percentage of a meatball has to be meat?

3198. What popular lunch and snack food did an unidentified St. Louis doctor develop in 1890 for patients requiring an easily digested form of protein?

3182. Gerber's baby food.

3183. Pierre.

3184. The wishbone of the turkey.

3185. The caper, or caper bush.

3186. Grapes. Followed by bananas.

3187. Marilyn Merlot.

3188. Cranberry juice. The state's cranberry crop is the nation's largest.

3189. Salsa.

3190. The kiwi.

3191. Lettuce.

3192. Vienna bread—Wienerbrod, in Danish.

3193. Vitamin A.

3194. Up to .4999 percent.

3195. The cherrystone clam (the town was originally known as Cherry Stones).

3196. Fermented mare's or cow's milk.

3197. At least 65 percent.

3198. Peanut butter. Five years later, Dr. John Harvey Kellogg filed for a patent for the "process of preparing nut meal"—a spread of steamed peanuts that was not very popular with patients at his Battle Creek, Michigan, sanitarium.

3199. How did the ice-cream sundae get its name?

3200. Who introduced standardized level measurements to recipes?

3201. With whom did the shallow champagne glass originate?

3202. Who introduced table knives in the seventeenth century?

3203. What did blind cellarmaster Dom Perignon say when he discovered Champagne in 1668?

3204. What nation produces two thirds of the world's vanilla?

3205. What now famous chef joined the OSS (Office of Strategic Services) during World War II, hoping to become an American spy?

3206. How did the Gatorade fruit drink get its name?

3207. Why did candy maker Milton S. Hershey switch from making caramels to chocolate bars in 1903?

3208. What fruits were crossed to produce the nectarine?

3209. What was used to make the coffee substitute given to American soldiers during World War II?

3210. What food product was discovered because of a long camel ride?

3211. What does cookbook author Julia Child claim is "so beautifully arranged on the plate—you know someone's fingers have been all over it"?

3212. The peanut isn't a nut. What is it?

3213. Where were the first frankfurters sold in the United States?

3214. Wild rice isn't rice. What is it?

3215. Who is credited with having invented the Manhattan cocktail, a combination of sweet vermouth and rye whiskey?

3199. *The sundae was created in Evanston, Illinois, in the late nineteenth century to get around a Sabbath ban on selling ice-cream sodas. It was dubbed Sunday but spelled with an "e" instead of a "y" to avoid religious objections.*

3200. *Fannie Farmer.*

3201. *With Marie Antoinette, from wax molds made of her breasts.*

3202. *Cardinal Richelieu. Daggers were in fashion at the dinner table until he became disgusted with their use as toothpicks and ordered knives with rounded ends.*

3203. *"Oh, come quickly. I am drinking stars!"*

3204. *Madagascar, the world's fourth-largest island (after Greenland, New Guinea and Borneo).*

3205. *Julia Child.*

3206. *From the University of Florida football team—the Gators—after the team tested it.*

3207. *Caramels didn't retain the imprint of his name in summertime; chocolate did.*

3208. *None. The nectarine is a smooth-skinned variety of peach, and not— as many people believe—a cross between a peach and a plum.*

3209. *Peanuts. It was one of hundreds of peanut by-products developed by Tuskegee University scientist George Washington Carver.*

3210. *Cottage cheese. An Arab trader found that milk he was carrying in a goatskin bag had turned into tasty solid white curds.*

3211. *Nouvelle cuisine.*

3212. *A legume—a member of the pea family.*

3213. *At Coney Island, in Brooklyn, New York, in 1871. They were made by Charles Feltmann, a butcher from Frankfurt, Germany.*

3214. *A coarse, annual grass native to shallow, marshy lakes and streams.*

3215. *Winston Churchill's Brooklyn-born mother, Jennie Jerome.*

3216. What do Eskimos use to prevent their food from freezing?

3217. What animal's milk is used to make authentic Italian mozzarella cheese?

3218. What is the world's largest herb?

3219. If you order the 5 Bs for dinner in New England, what will you be served?

3220. In the world of food, what is pluck?

3221. What is a cluster or bunch of bananas called?

3222. What part of the orange is the albedo?

3223. What is the BRAT diet?

3224. Why are canned herring called sardines?

3225. Who introduced the gin and lime juice cocktail we know as the gimlet?

3226. What would you get if you ordered a Mae West in a diner?

3227. Which fruit has a variety known as Winter Banana?

3228. Which is the only U.S. state to produce coffee?

Bonus Trivia

3229. In the early nineteenth century, ketchup was sold in the United States as a medicine—Dr. Miles' Compound Extract of Tomato.

3216. Refrigerators.

3217. The water buffalo's.

3218. The banana.

3219. Boston baked beans and brown bread.

3220. An animal's heart, liver and lungs.

3221. A hand. Individual bananas are known as fingers.

3222. The bitter-tasting white tissue that makes the peel stick to the skin.

3223. A diet of bananas, rice, applesauce and toast that's often prescribed for infants with diarrhea.

3224. The canning process for herring was developed in Sardinia, and the fish were first canned there.

3225. Sir T.O. Gimlette, a British naval surgeon at the turn of the century who believed that drinking straight gin was unhealthy and impaired the efficiency of naval officers—so he began diluting it with lime juice.

3226. A figure-eight cruller.

3227. The apple.

3228. Hawaii.

Music & Theatre

Questions

3230. What is the Internal Revenue Service's "Dinah Shore ruling"?

3231. From what performer did Elvis Presley pick up his pelvic gyrations?

3232. What is Cher's real first name?

3233. What was the brand of pajamas manufactured in the factory in which the 1954 Broadway musical *The Pajama Game* was set?

3234. What American actor—nominated for more Tony Awards than any other—made his New York acting debut in 1947 as the rear end of a cow in a production of *Jack and the Beanstalk* ?

3235. Who was unexpectedly cast in *Hair* after he played the piano at his actor half-brother's unsuccessful audition for the West Coast production of the rock musical in 1969?

3236. What job did Geraldine Page leave to appear off-Broadway in Tennessee Williams' *Summer and Smoke* in 1952?

Answers

3230. *A dress can be deducted as a professional expense if it is too tight to sit down in. The ruling was issued after singer Shore deducted gowns worn in public appearances as business expenses and insisted, when challenged by the IRS, that they were only worn onstage while performing.*

3231. *Bo Diddley.*

3232. *Cherilyn. Her name at birth was Cherilyn Sarkisian.*

3233. *Sleep-Tite.*

3234. *Jason Robards Jr.*

3235. *Keith Carradine. The brother who didn't get the part was David.*

3236. *Clerk and negligee model in a New York City dress shop.*

3237. What actor—long since overshadowed by his celebrity son—won a Tony in 1951 for his portrayal of suave gambler Sky Masterson in the original Broadway production of *Guys and Dolls* ?

3238. What famous acting duo's off-stage bickering during a production of Shakespeare's *The Taming of the Shrew* was the inspiration for Cole Porter's musical comedy *Kiss Me Kate* ?

3239. Who was Alice Brock?

3240. What famous entertainer helped reimburse dissatisfied customers when an acne medicine he endorsed was found to be ineffective?

3241. What title did famed drama critic George Jean Nathan suggest for a magazine photograph of Mae West posing as the Statue of Liberty?

3242. What was the film inspiration for the Stephen Sondheim musical *A Little Night Music* ?

3243. In show biz slang, what's an *Annie Oakley*?

3244. What special imprint did Al Jolson make outside Grauman's Chinese Theatre?

3245. What famous American was code-named Napoleon by the Secret Service?

3246. In 1926, the police raided Mae West's Broadway show *Sex* and jailed her on vice charges. What did the wisecracking blonde sexpot claim when she was freed after serving 8 days of her 10-day sentence?

3247. What Beatles hits were on the first single recorded by the Fab Four on their Apple label?

3248. What business was Latin bombshell Carmen Miranda's father in back home in her native Brazil?

3249. What famous entertainer had two nicknames as a teenager: "Slacksey" because of his extensive wardrobe of trousers, and "Angles" because he was such a smart aleck?

3237. Robert Alda, father of Alan.

3238. Alfred Lunt and Lynn Fontanne.

3239. The owner of the Stockbridge, Massachusetts, restaurant of Arlo Guthrie's Alice's Restaurant, *an album popular in 1967, which in turn was the inspiration for the Arthur Penn movie of the same name.*

3240. Pat Boone, in 1979.

3241. The Statue of Libido.

3242. Ingmar Bergman's Smiles of a Summer Night.

3243. A free pass to the theater. The legendary sharpshooter would toss a playing card in the air and shoot so many holes in it that it resembled a punched ticket.

3244. His knees, commemorating the trademark pose he took whenever he sang "Mammy."

3245. Frank Sinatra.

3246. That it was the only time she ever got anything for good behavior.

3247. "Hey Jude" and "Revolution."

3248. He ran a wholesale fruit business—which might explain the fruit-laden headdresses that became her trademark.

3249. Frank Sinatra.

3250. Who was the first person ever awarded a gold record?

3251. For what famous entertainer was the Broadway musical *Hello Dolly!* written?

3252. Bing Crosby's recording of Irving Berlin's "White Christmas" is the best-selling pop record of all time. What rock 'n' roll single is in second place?

3253. What role did Dutch-born Andreas Cornelius van Kuijk play in Elvis Presley's life?

3254. What instrument did "King of Jazz" orchestra leader Paul Whiteman play when he launched his musical career with the Denver Symphony?

3255. Tenor Stefan Zucker held the longest-sustained high note on record during a Carnegie Hall performance in 1972. How long did he hold it?

3256. What distinctive vanity license plates did bandleader Lawrence Welk have in California?

3257. What are the three most frequently sung songs in the English language, according to the *Guinness Book of World Records* ?

3258. What was the record number of curtain calls ballet greats Margot Fonteyn and Rudolf Nureyev received following a 1964 performance of *Swan Lake* in Vienna?

3259. What hit song was banned on Canadian radio during a 1960 royal visit by Queen Elizabeth II?

3260. What was the only comedy written by American playwright Eugene O'Neill?

3261. What was Beatle John Lennon's middle name?

3262. Who was Meyer Boston?

3263. Who bought one of rock 'n' roll pioneer Buddy Holly's guitars at auction for $242,000 in 1990?

3250. *Glenn Miller, for "Chattanooga Choo-Choo."*

3251. *Ethel Merman. But she didn't star in the hit show until long after it opened—and only after Carol Channing, Ginger Rogers, Martha Raye, Betty Grable, Bibi Osterwald, Pearl Bailey and Phyllis Diller had appeared in the title role.*

3252. *"Rock Around the Clock," by Bill Haley and the Comets. The 1954 hit has sold 25 million copies to Crosby's 170 million plus.*

3253. *He was Elvis's manager, better known to us as "Colonel" Tom Parker. He changed his name in his teens after he fled to the U.S. and joined a traveling carnival as a salesman and publicity agent.*

3254. *The viola.*

3255. *3.8 seconds. It was an A in alt-altissimo.*

3256. *A1ANA2—his trademark phrase.*

3257. *"Happy Birthday," "For He's a Jolly Good Fellow" and "Auld Lang Syne."*

3258. *89.*

3259. *Johnny Horton's "The Battle of New Orleans," which celebrates the smashing defeat of the British by American troops led by Andrew Jackson in 1815.*

3260. Ah, Wilderness*!*

3261. *Winston, after Winston Churchill.*

3262. *The gambler after whom Damon Runyon modeled his character Nathan Detroit—best known to us as the operator of "the oldest established permanent floating crap game in New York" in the musical* Guys and Dolls.

3263. *Gary Busey, who won a best actor Oscar nomination for his portrayal of Holly in the 1978 film* The Buddy Holly Story.

3264. What record album was the first ever to be taken directly from a film's musical soundtrack?

3265. What city was the hometown of both Nellie Forbush in the musical *South Pacific* and Lorelei Lee in *Gentlemen Prefer Blondes*?

3266. What sticker message did Capitol Records add to a recording of Delibes' opera *Lakmé* in 1988 in a bid to boost sales among buyers not ordinarily interested in classical music?

3267. Who wrote Yale's "Bulldog" song?

3268. How many of the 107 musicians in the new York Philharmonic Orchestra play second violin?

3269. What singer—called Clara Ann Fowler at birth—adopted the name of the milk company that sponsored her first radio show?

3270. What recipe is recited in the play *Cyrano de Bergerac* ?

3271. Which of U2's songs is a tribute to Martin Luther King Jr.?

3272. What is the only sound heard on the record *The Best of Marcel Marceau* ?

3273. What popular band is named for a hallucinogenic treat made by a member's grandmother?

3274. What led jazz great Dizzy Gillespie to redesign his trumpet so it had an upturned bell?

3275. What stringed instrument was the first to have a keyboard?

3276. What famous entertainer was known as Annie Mae Bullock before she adopted a stage name?

3277. When he was six years old, what did country singer Chet Atkins use to string his first musical instrument—an old, discarded ukulele?

3278. What was American rock star Eddie Money's surname at birth?

3264. *Walt Disney's* Snow White and the Seven Dwarfs, *in 1937.*

3265. *Little Rock, Arkansas.*

3266. *"Includes the Flower Duet from the British Airways TV commercial."*

3267. *Cole Porter, in 1911, when he was a student there.*

3268. *16.*

3269. *Patti Page. The company was the Page Milk Company of Tulsa, Oklahoma.*

3270. *The recipe for tart almondine—it's recited by Ragueneau.*

3271. *Pride (In the Name Love).*

3272. *Clapping, after 40 minutes of silence.*

3273. *Pearl Jam. It's named for lead singer Eddie Vedder's grandmother Pearl and the hallucinogenic preserves she made from peyote.*

3274. *He liked the slightly muted sound of his trumpet after comic James "Stump" Cross fell on it, bending the bell to a 45-degree angle. After the accident, Gillespie had his trumpet custom-made—with an upturned bell.*

3275. *The clavichord, which was developed around 1400.*

3276. *Actress-singer Tina Turner.*

3277. *Wire from a screen door.*

3278. *Mahoney. He changed it in hopes the name Money would bring him fame and fortune.*

3279. What is the significance of the Bon Jovi album title 7800 Fahrenheit?

3280. What famous singer-songwriter met his future wife when he was working as a nightclub bouncer—and threw her out for fighting?

3281. Who was the first performer to win Grammy Awards for jazz and classical recordings in the same year?

3282. What flamboyant pop star auctioned off his costumes for $8.2 million in 1988, explaining "I don't want to go on stage looking like Tina Turner's grandmother anymore"?

3283. What was the color of the streetcar named Desire in Tennessee Williams's Pulitzer Prize-winning play?

3284. The rock group Electric Mayhem made an appearance in what 1979 film?

3285. Who was rumored to be the subject of Carly Simon's 1972 record, "You're So Vain"?

3286. Irving Berlin reworked one of his songs, "Smile and Show Your Dimple." What became the song's more memorable title?

3287. From what other singer did Elvis Presley borrow his characteristic hip-swinging?

3288. Max Born, winner of the 1954 Nobel Prize in Physics, is the grandfather of which well-known pop singer?

3289. The singing duo of Caesar and Cleo only achieved fame under another name. What was it?

3290. What pop singer-songwriter once played the piano at the Executive Lounge in Los Angeles under the name of William Martin?

3291. A song called "I Wish You Peace," recorded by The Eagles, was written by Bernie Leadon and Patti Davis. What is Ms. Davis's more obvious claim to fame?

3279. *It refers to the temperature of an exploding volcano.*

3280. *Garth Brooks. His wife, Sandy Mahl, was in the nightclub's ladies' room when she threw a punch at the jealous ex-girlfriend of a man she had dated—and her hand got stuck in the wall. Brooks, a college student at the time, freed her hand and threw her out. He later began dating her.*

3281. *Trumpet virtuoso Wynton Marsalis, in 1984. He won for the albums Trumpet Concertos and Think of One.*

3282. *Elton John.*

3283. *Green*

3284. The Muppet Movie—*it was the muppet rock band.*

3285. *Warren Beatty.*

3286. *"Easter Parade."*

3287. *Bo Diddley.*

3288. *Olivia Newton-John.*

3289. *Sonny and Cher.*

3290. *Billy Joel, who recalled those early days in the 1974 hit record,* Piano Man.

3291. *She is the younger daughter of former President Ronald Reagan.*

3292. What brand of apple was used as the symbol for the Beatles' record label, Apple Records?

3293. In 1948, Peter Goldmark introduced something for which people like Stevie Wonder, Pink Floyd and Fleetwood Mac would be forever grateful. What was it?

3294. "Anywhere the Bluebird Goes" was the original title of which very popular 1939 tune?

3295. In 1970, cult ringleader and convicted killer, Charles Manson recorded an album of his songs. What was its title?

3296. What were the names of the two gangs in *West Side Story*?

3297. Chip Taylor, the composer of such hit songs as "Wild Thing" and "Angel of the Morning," is the brother of which Oscar-winning actor?

3298. Country music comedienne Minnie Pearl always wears a hat with a price tag on it when she performs. What is the amount on the price tag?

3299. "Palisades Park" was a hit in 1962 for singer Freddy Cannon. Its composer, Chuck Barris, is better remembered for creating and hosting which excruciatingly bad TV show of the 70s?

3300. Radio station WSM in Nashville, Tennessee, has been broadcasting *The Grand Ole Opry* since November 1928. What do the call letters "WSM," stand for?

3301. What three Gershwin songs contain the phrase, "Who could ask for anything more"?

3302. In 1957, a group called The Scholars released the record, "Kan-gu-wa," which failed to hit the charts. Both the composer and the lead singer are probably grateful to be remembered for their other accomplishments—who are they?

3303. Although popularized in *Casablanca*, the song, "As Time Goes By," was introduced in what 1931 musical play?

3292. *Granny Smith.*

3293. *The long-playing, 33⅓ RPM record album.*

3294. *"Don't Sit Under the Apple Tree (With Anyone Else But Me)."*

3295. *"Lie."*

3296. *The Jets and the Sharks.*

3297. Jon Voight.

3298. *$1.98.*

3299. The Gong Show.

3300. *"We Shield Millions,"* the motto of the National Life and Accident Company, which originally owned the station.

3301. *"I Got Rhythm," "Nice Work if You Can Get it"* and *"I'm About to Become a Mother."*

3302. Gossip-columnist, Louella Parsons, who wrote the song; Kenny Rogers, who sang it.

3303. Everybody's Welcome.

3304. What role did Sarah Bernhardt play in *The Sleeping Beauty* when she was 62 years old?

3305. Which actress is thought to be the first woman to wear trousers?

3306. How did the 1950's instrumental group, The Champs, who had a number one hit with "Tequila" in 1958, get their name?

3307. Who was Pat Boone's famous father-in-law?

3308. What rich and famous singer-songwriter owns the publishing rights to *Stormy Weather* and *Hello Dolly*, as well as the soundtracks of *Grease, Mame, Annie* and *A Chorus Line*, among many others?

3309. In *Peter Pan*, if you traveled "second to the right and then straight on till morning," where would you emerge?

3310. What song, originally recorded in 1958 by Hank Ballard and The Midnighters, became the only recording in *Billboard* history to reach number one in two different years when it was recorded by another artist?

3311. Who was the first performer to sell over half-a-million copies of a quadradisc—a stereo, four-channel record?

3312. In April, 1971, what rock group became the first ever to appear at New York's Carnegie Hall?

3313. What song holds the record for the biggest leap to the number one position on *Billboard's* Hot 100 chart?

3314. An opera written to commemorate the opening of the Suez Canal was first performed on December 24, 1871. What was it?

3315. How much did RCA records pay Sun Records for Elvis Presley's contract in 1955?

3316. Who wrote and recorded the song "Beware of Young Girls" after her husband left her for a young woman?

3304. *Prince Charming.*

3305. *Sarah Bernhardt, in 1876.*

3306. *The group was named after Champion, Gene Autry's horse. (Autry owned Challenge Records, for which The Champs recorded.)*

3307. *Country singer Red Foley.*

3308. *Paul McCartney.*

3309. *Into Never Never Land.*

3310. *"The Twist," sung by Chubby Checker, which reached number one in 1960 and again in 1962.*

3311. *Elvis Presley, with "Elvis: Aloha From Hawaii Via Satellite," in 1973.*

3312. *Chicago, in April 1971.*

3313. *The Beatles' "Can't Buy Me Love." On March 28, 1964, it entered the chart at number 37, the next week, it was number 1.*

3314. *"Aida," by Giuseppe Verdi.*

3315. *RCA paid $35,000 plus a $5,000 bonus when Elvis signed.*

3316. *Dory Previn, ex-wife of composer-conductor Andre Previn. The younger woman was actress Mia Farrow.*

3317. In addition to singing superstar Michael Jackson, who were the original members of the Jackson Five?

3318. What is the name of the street in Charleston, South Carolina, that served as the prototype for Catfish Row in George Gershwin's opera *Porgy and Bess*?

3319. What was the musical theme of TV's *Captain Video and His Video Rangers* ?

3320. What rock star was christened William Broad?

3321. To whom did super-rocker Elton John pay tribute in his hit "Candle in the Wind"?

3322. How did British actor Charles Laughton, subbing as emcee for Ed Sullivan, introduce Elvis Presley when Elvis made his second appearance on TV's *The Toast of the Town* ?

3323. What was the musical theme played at the beginning of the *Green Hornet* radio series?

3324. Under what name was folksinger Joan Baez satirized in Al Capp's *Li'l Abner* cartoon?

3325. What Nobel Peace Prize-winning American vice-president composed the music for the song "It's All in the Game," which became a hit tune for Tommy Edwards in 1951 and again in 1958?

3326. When the roles in *The Odd Couple* were switched from male to female on Broadway, what names were used instead of Oscar and Felix?

3327. Who invented the saxophone?

3328. What is Fats Domino's real first name?

3329. What famous opera was inspired by a short story written in 1898 by Philadelphia lawyer John Luther Long?

3330. How tall is songwriter Randy Newman, the man who wrote the 1977 hit parody of bigotry *Short People*?

3317. *His brothers Jackie, Jermaine, Marlon and Tito.*

3318. *Cabbage Row.*

3319. *The overture to Richard Wagner's "Der Fliegende Holländer" (The Flying Dutchman).*

3320. *Billy Idol.*

3321. *Marilyn Monroe.*

3322. *As Elvin Presley.*

3323. *"Flight of the Bumble Bee," by Nikolai Rimsky-Korsakov.*

3324. *Joany Phoney.*

3325. *Charles G. Dawes, who served as vice-president to Calvin Coolidge from 1925 to 1929. He wrote the song in 1912.*

3326. *Olive and Florence. They were played by Rita Moreno and Sally Struthers, respectively.*

3327. *Adolphe Sax—he patented it in 1846.*

3328. *Antoine.*

3329. Madame Butterfly, *by Puccini.*

3330. *He's 5 feet 11 inches tall.*

3331. Who sang advertising jingles for McDonald's, Pepsi, Chevrolet, Kentucky Fried Chicken and others before making it big on the music scene?

3332. What popular stage and screen musical was based on *Green Grow the Lilacs*, a 1931 Broadway show starring Franchot Tone and singing cowboy Woodward "Tex" Ritter?

3333. What performer rocketed to stardom from the *Pajama Game* chorus line when star Carol Haney was sidelined by an ankle injury?

3334. How many Beatles songs were at the top of the *Billboard Hot 100* singles list in early April 1964?

3335. What did Buddy Holly originally call "Peggy Sue," the rock 'n' roll classic he recorded with the Crickets in 1957?

3336. What modern musical instrument is based on the medieval sackbut?

3337. Who was the only cast member of the hit rock musical *Hair* to refuse to shed her clothes in the closing number?

3338. What popular singer was heard on the first multi-track vocal—on a recording that was billed as a duet?

3339. Who wrote the title song for the 1973 James Bond film *Live and Let Die* ?

3340. How much did a piano cost in the 1900 Sears, Roebuck and Company catalog?

3341. Carole King's song "The Loco-Motion" was made into a hit record in 1962 by her maid. Who was she?

3342. What Broadway show put performers John Travolta, Richard Gere, Marilu Henner, Treat Williams and Barry Bostwick on the road to stardom?

3343. What are the names of the theme parks established by country singers Dolly Parton and Conway Twitty?

3331. *Singer-composer Barry Manilow.*

3332. Oklahoma*!*

3333. *Shirley MacLaine, in 1954.*

3334. *An unprecedented and never duplicated five. From No. 1 to No. 5 they were: "Can't Buy Me Love," "Twist and Shout," "She Loves You," "I Want to Hold Your Hand," and "Please Please Me."*

3335. *"Cindy Lou." Holly renamed it at the urging of Crickets drummer Jerry Allison, whose girlfriend's name was Peggy Sue.*

3336. *The trombone.*

3337. *Diane Keaton.*

3338. *Patti Page, in 1951. The song was "The Tennessee Waltz."*

3339. *Ex-Beatle Paul McCartney.*

3340. *It cost $98—FOB Chicago.*

3341. *Little Eva—Eva Narcissus Boyd.*

3342. *The 1972 rock musical* Grease.

3343. *Parton's is Dollywood (located in Pigeon Forge, Tennessee); Twitty's is Twitty City (in Hendersonville, Tennessee).*

3344. British songwriter-impresario Gordon Mills gave three rock stars their stage names. Can you name them?

3345. What were the last words of famed ballerina Anna Pavlova?

3346. What classical music inspired the theme music for TV's *Alfred Hitchcock Presents* ?

3347. What famous songwriter supported himself by writing *Topper* TV scripts?

3348. What TV personality asked Dolly Parton, "Is it all you?" and what was her reply?

3349. What song about a rat became a hit single?

3350. What's the name of theatrical rock musician David Bowie's son?

3351. Who wrote *The Coffee Cantata* ?

3352. What former Beatle was convicted of "unconscious plagiarism"?

3353. With what group did Linda Ronstadt launch her musical career as a lead singer in 1964?

3354. What was the site of the Beatles' last performance on August 29, 1966?

3355. What was the musical version of the Broadway show *The Rainmaker* called?

3356. What American songwriter could compose music and play the piano only in the key of F?

3357. What European theater legend resumed her stage career after having a leg amputated?

3358. What pop rock singer-songwriter helped launch Bette Midler's career?

3344. *Engelbert Humperdinck (Arnold George Dorsey), Tom Jones (Thomas Jones Woodward) and Gilbert O'Sullivan (Ray O'Sullivan).*

3345. *"Get my swan costume ready!"*

3346. *Gounod's "Funeral March of a Marionette."*

3347. *Stephen Sondheim, before his* West Side Story *success in 1957.*

3348. *Barbara Walters asked the question and was told: "If I hadn't had it on my own, I'm just the kind of person who would get it!"*

3349. *"Ben's Song"—performed by Michael Jackson—the title song from the movie* Ben, *which is about a rat.*

3350. *Originally Zowie, now renamed Joey.*

3351. *Johann Sebastian Bach.*

3352. *George Harrison, for "My Sweet Lord," which was similar to Phil Spector's "He's So Fine."*

3353. *The Stone Poneys.*

3354. *Candlestick Park, San Francisco.*

3355. 110 in the Shade.

3356. *Irving Berlin.*

3357. *Sarah Bernhardt.*

3358. *Barry "I Write the Songs" Manilow, who was the Divine Miss M's accompanist-arranger.*

3359. What musician was the first to write down blues music and the first to publish it?

3360. What Broadway musical was staged by a labor union in 1939?

3361. What inspired John, Paul, George, and Ringo to call themselves the Beatles?

3362. What famous actor made his Broadway debut in 1944, as Dagmar's brother Nels in *I Remember Mama* ?

3363. In December 1963, Frank Sinatra Jr. was kidnapped. What ransom did his father pay for his release?

3364. Brothers Jimmy and Tommy Dorsey were famous band leaders. Who is Arnold Dorsey?

3365. What teenaged rock 'n' roller appeared in the film *Hound Dog Man* wearing the same jeans and boots worn by Elvis Presley in "Love Me Tender" three years earlier?

3366. What performer's only Las Vegas booking was a two-week stint with the slapstick Honey Brothers at the Hotel Last Frontier in 1954?

3367. What singer subbed for Brian Wilson during the Beach Boys' 1965 tour?

3368. What rock superstar left $2,500 in her will for a farewell party "so my friends can have a ball after I'm gone"?

3369. What gold-plated 33-rpm record did the Apollo astronauts leave behind on the moon?

3370. What popular performer was named best female singer of the year a record 21 times by *Down Beat* magazine?

3359. *Handy, composer of "The St. Louis Blues," who is known as the "father of the blues."*

3360. Pins and Needles, *produced by and with International Ladies Garment Workers Union personnel.*

3361. *Buddy Holly's group, the Crickets. The "beat" spelling was intended as a musical pun.*

3362. *Marlon Brando.*

3363. *He paid $240,000.*

3364. *Pop singer Engelbert Humperdinck.*

3365. *Fabian, whose name in the film was Clint—the same as Elvis' in* Love Me Tender.

3366. *Ronald Reagan, who later became the 40th President of the United States.*

3367. *Glen Campbell.*

3368. *Janis Joplin.*

3369. Camelot—*a favorite of President John F. Kennedy.*

3370. *Ella Fitzgerald.*

3371. What did opera great Luciano Pavarotti do for a living before he became a professional tenor?

3372. Who is the famous clarinetist who performs with the New Orleans Funeral and Jazz Band?

3373. How long was the train on pianist-showman Liberace's 175-pound Norwegian blue shadow fox coat?

3374. What jazz great was known by the nicknames Dippermouth and Gatemouth?

3375. In disc jockey slang, what is a lunar rotation?

3376. What hat is named after a play written for the great Sarah Bernhardt?

3377. What famous country and western singer recorded under the pseudonym Luke the Drifter, as well as his real name?

3378. In the world of music, adagio is a direction to play slowly. What do the terms adagietto and adagissomo mean?

3379. What did Aretha Franklin wear on her head when she sang "Funny Girl" at the Academy Awards ceremony in 1969?

3380. What popular recording star's real name is Robert Van Winkle?

3381. What musical masterpiece commemorates a battle fought at a place called Borodino?

3382. In ballet, what is a fondu?

3383. What's the name of the Mississippi paddle-wheeler that provides the setting for the stage and movie musical *Show Boat*?

3384. What famous writer co-authored the lyrics to Rosemary Clooney's 1951 hit song "Come On-a My House"?

3385. How many children did Baron von Trapp have in the Broadway show and hit movie musical *The Sound of Music*?

3371. He taught in an elementary school and then sold insurance—because he found teaching too hard on his vocal cords.

3372. Woody Allen.

3373. 16 feet. The coat is on display at the Liberace Museum in Las Vegas.

3374. Louis Armstrong—who is better known as Satchmo, a shortened version of Satchelmouth.

3375. An infrequently played record.

3376. The fedora. The play Fédora, by French dramatist Victorien Sardou, features a Russian princess who wears a brimmed, soft felt hat with a creased crown.

3377. Hank Williams.

3378. Adagietto is a direction to play slightly faster than adagio; adagissomo, to play very slowly.

3379. Antlers.

3380. Vanilla Ice's.

3381. Tchaikovsky's "1812 Overture." Borodino is a village 70 miles west of Moscow. The battle was between Napoleon's troops and the Russian Army.

3382. A lowering of the body by bending the knee of the supporting leg.

3383. "Cotton Blossom."

3384. William Saroyan—with his cousin, songwriter-record producer Ross Bagdasarian (who used the professional name of David Seville to make Alvin and the Chipmunks records).

3385. Seven—Leisel, Friedrich, Louisa, Brigitta, Kurt, Marta and Gretl.

3386. What famous American composer has had two of his songs adopted as official state anthems?

3387. As a child, what famous opera singer was featured as an orphan—a singing orphan, of course—on a radio soap opera?

3388. Who was the first rock or pop performer to appear on the covers of *Time* and *Newsweek* magazines in the same week?

3389. The title of what Broadway show and popular movie was inspired by a painting by Marc Chagall?

3390. What top rock group took its name from a song by blues great Muddy Waters?

3391. What famous American singer-songwriter played the part of slick, name-dropping record-industry promoter Tony Lacey in Woody Allen's 1977 movie hit, *Annie Hall* ?

3392. What classical music served as the theme of the 1968 film " *2001: A Space Odyssey* ?

3393. Where is the Tallahatchie Bridge, the site of Billie Joe McAllister's suicide leap in the popular 1967 Bobbie Gentry folk ballad, "Ode to Billie Joe"?

3394. What rock band was the first to perform at New York's Metropolitan Opera House?

3395. Who designed the famous working-zipper album cover for the Rolling Stones' 1971 LP *Sticky Fingers* ?

3396. Who played Captain Hook and Mr. Darling opposite Jean Arthur in the 1950 Broadway production of Sir James M. Barrie's *Peter Pan* ?

3397. What famous performer is heard in the background on Harry Belafonte's 1961 LP *Midnight Special* ?

3398. Why did the members of the rock group Led Zeppelin perform under an alias—The Nobs—when they appeared in Copenhagen, Denmark, in 1970?

3386. *Stephen Foster. His "My Old Kentucky Home" is the state song of Kentucky, and his "Old Folks at Home" is the state song of Florida.*

3387. *Beverly Sills, who was known as the Nightingale of the Mountains on the radio serial* Our Gal Sunday.

3388. *Bruce Springsteen, in 1975—after the release of his third album,* Born to Run.

3389. Fiddler on the Roof. *The title came from the Russian-born artist's painting* The Green Violinist, *which depicts a violinist floating over village rooftops.*

3390. *The Rolling Stones. Waters song, of course, was "Rollin' Stone."*

3391. *Paul Simon.*

3392. *Richard Strauss' "Also sprach Zarathustra (Thus Spake Zarathustra)," written in 1896.*

3393. *In Greenwood, Mississippi.*

3394. *The Who, in 1970—for a performance of the rock opera* Tommy.

3395. *Pop artist Andy Warhol.*

3396. *Boris Karloff.*

3397. *Bob Dylan, playing the harmonica.*

3398. *Airship heiress Eva Von Zeppelin threatened legal action if the group performed under its real name.*

3399. Who was the subject of the 1944 song "Nancy (With the Laughing Face)"?

3400. Where did the British reggae band UB40 get its name?

3401. What famous classical musician was named Harvey Lavan Jr. at birth?

3402. What British rock group took its name from a character in the 1968 science-fiction film spoof *Barbarella*, which starred Jane Fonda?

3403. What is Max Yasgur's claim to fame in the world of music?

3404. What popular entertainer sang "Love Me Tender" on a 1960 TV special co-starring Elvis Presley?

3405. What three rock 'n' roll stars were featured in *The Longest Day*, the 1962 film epic about the Allies' D-Day invasion of Normandy?

3406. How old was country-western singer Loretta Lynn when she became a grandmother for the first time?

3407. What name did Chuck Berry originally use in his 1955 rock 'n' roll hit "Maybelline"?

3408. Why did Dame Edith Evans, the famous British actress, refuse to appear onstage as Lady Macbeth?

3409. Who replaced Chico Marx as the pianist at Manhattan's City Theatre in 1917?

3410. What famous entertainment figure once had a solo hit record called "I've Got a Lovely Bunch of Cocoanuts"?

3411. Under what name did New Wave singer-songwriter Declan McManus gain fame?

3412. What does Yoko Ono's first name mean when translated from Japanese?

3399. *Nancy Sinatra, who was four years old at the time. The song, introduced by her crooner father, Frank, was written by comedian Phil Silvers (lyrics) and Jimmy Van Heusen (music).*

3400. *From the code number on the British unemployment benefit card.*

3401. *Pianist Van Cliburn, who gained international renown in 1958 when he became the first American to win the Tchaikovsky Competition in Moscow.*

3402. *Duran Duran. In the movie, Duran Duran was portrayed by actor Milo O'Shea.*

3403. *He was the owner of the Bethel, New York, farm where the famous Woodstock rock festival was held in 1969.*

3404. *Frank Sinatra. Presley, in turn, sang Sinatra's hit "Witchcraft."*

3405. *Paul Anka, Tommy Sands and Fabian.*

3406. *She was 29 years old.*

3407. *"Ida Red." Maybelline was the name of a cow in a school reading book.*

3408. *She claimed, "I could never impersonate a woman who had such a peculiar notion of hospitality".*

3409. *George Gershwin. His salary was $25 a week, but he quit after one show.*

3410. *Merv Griffin.*

3411. *Elvis Costello.*

3412. *Ocean child.*

3413. What song, with a 21-word title, did Fred Astaire sing and dance to with Jane Powell in the 1951 Hollywood musical *Royal Wedding* ?

3414. What is the source of the lyrics of the Byrds' 1965 hit song "Turn! Turn! Turn!"?

3415. Who co-starred with pop singer Petula Clark in a 1969 musical remake of the 1939 film classic *Goodbye Mr. Chips* ?

3416. Who appeared in a Beatle wig on the cover of the July 1965 issue of *Esquire* magazine?

3417. In 1976 what famous singer snuck onto the grounds of Graceland, Elvis Presley's Memphis home, in an unsuccessful bid to meet his rock idol?

3418. What is the diameter of a compact disc, which holds up to three miles of playing track?

3419. What state was used for the location shots for the 1955 hit musical *Oklahoma!*?

3420. What is the origin of the do-si-do, the square dance call that instructs partners to pass each other right shoulder to right shoulder and circle back to back?

3421. What was playwright George S. Kaufman's reply when *Vanity* Fair magazine asked him to write his own epitaph?

3422. What onstage activity started the fire in 1613 that burned down England's first Globe Theatre, where Shakespeare's greatest plays were first performed?

3423. Who dubbed504

the fiddling in the 1971 film *Fiddler on the Roof?*

3424. What perfume is named after a musical term?

3425. What was the name of the first record label developed by entertainment mogul David Geffen?

3413. How Could You Believe Me When I Said I Love You When You Know I've Been a Liar All My Life *? Lyrics by Alan Jay Lerner; music by Burton Lane.*

3414. *The Bible. Composer Pete Seeger adapted the song from Chapter 3 of the Book of Ecclesiastes, which begins, "To every thing there is a season."*

3415. *Peter O'Toole.*

3416. *TV variety show host Ed Sullivan.*

3417. *Bruce Springsteen, who once said, "Anybody who sees Elvis Presley and doesn't want to be like Elvis Presley has got to have something wrong with him."*

3418. *4 ¾ inches.*

3419. *Arizona. There were too many oil derricks and noisy airplanes in Oklahoma at the time. The filming took place outside Nogales, Arizona, where a field of corn was planted long before shooting so it would get "as high as an elephant's eye."*

3420. *The French phrase dos à dos, which means "back to back."*

3421. *"Over my dead body!"*

3422. *A spark from a stage cannon accidentally set the theater's thatched roof ablaze during a performance of Shakespeare's* Henry VIII.

3423. *Isaac Stern*

3424. *Arpège. In music arpeggio is a chord in which the notes are played individually in quick succession. The perfume was named for it because its various floral essences are intended to strike the senses in a similar way.*

3425. *Asylum.*

3426. What popular crooner won a Grammy in 1992 for an album entitled *Perfectly Frank*?

3427. What famous play begins with the line, "Who's there?"

3428. What husband-and-wife acting duo spent more time in bed together onstage than any other theater couple?

3429. Under what name was Harpo Marx portrayed in the Moss Hart-George S. Kaufman play *The Man Who Came to Dinner*?

3430. What singer has recorded under the alias Apollo C. Vermouth?

3431. What is the meaning of the musical direction estinto?

3432. How old was Stevie Wonder when he signed his first record contract?

3433. What color was Elvis Presley's first Cadillac before he bought it and had it painted pink in 1955?

3434. Who provided the voice of the ghost of Hamlet's father when Richard Burton appeared on Broadway in the title role of *Hamlet* in 1964?

3435. Who is the only playwright to have won four Pulitzer Prizes?

3436. How did Bono, the lead singer and lyricist of the Irish rock band U2, get his name?

3437. What woman's name was originally used in the old barbershop quartet favorite "Sweet Adeline"?

3438. What is the name of the album Madonna released in 1990 to coincide with her appearance in the movie *Dick Tracy* with Warren Beatty?

3439. In the 1968 Beatles cartoon fantasy *Yellow Submarine*, what did Jeremy Boob, Ph.D., use to repair the sub's propeller, enabling the Fab Four to escape His Meaniness and the Blue Meanies?

3426. *Tony Bennett. The album contained songs identified with Frank Sinatra.*

3427. *Shakespeare's* Hamlet. *The line is spoken by the soldier Bernardo.*

3428. *Jessica Tandy and Hume Cronyn, who appeared together on Broadway and on tour in* The Fourposter, *a hilarious history of a 35-year marriage told through a series of bedroom scenes.*

3429. *Banjo. The usually mute Marx actually appeared onstage in the role— speaking his first lines as a performer in 25 years.*

3430. *Ex-Beatle Paul McCartney.*

3431. *As soft as possible—so soft it can hardly be heard.*

3432. *11—it was a five-year contract with Motown.*

3433. *Blue.*

3434. *Sir John Gielgud, who directed the highly acclaimed production.*

3435. *Eugene O'Neill. He won the drama prize for* Beyond the Horizon *in 1920, for* Anna Christie *in 1922, for* Strange Interlude *in 1928 and for* Long Day's Journey Into Night *in 1957.*

3436. *From a hearing aid store in Dublin called Bono Voz—an adaptation of a Latin phrase meaning "good voice," although Bono, who was named Paul Hewson at birth, says he didn't know what it meant.*

3437. *Rosalie. Written by Richard Gerard (music) and Henry Armstrong (words) in 1903, it was originally entitled "You're the Flower of My Heart, Sweet Rosalie." When the song didn't sell, they renamed it for popular Italian soprano Adelina Patti and shortened the title.*

3438. *I'm Breathless. Madonna played Breathless Mahoney in the film.*

3439. *Bubble gum.*

3440. What famous singer, after receiving an honorary degree from Georgetown University, enrolled as a freshman and earned a B.A. in theology?

3441. From what poetic source did Noel Coward get the title for his play *Blithe Spirit*?

3442. What musical instrument did bandleader-trumpeter Herb Alpert play during his brief appearance in Cecil B. DeMille's 1956 film spectacular *The Ten Commandments*?

3443. What country singer was given a part as an extra in the 1973 film *American Graffiti* after she was spotted driving her mother's 1957 Chevy in Hollywood?

3444. The premiere of what famous play by a Nobel Prize-winning writer was held in England's Canterbury Cathedral in 1935?

3445. What did Frank Sinatra give forever-39 Jack Benny on his 80th birthday?

3446. Who was the last act at the famous three-day Woodstock festival in 1969?

3447. What popular nursery rhyme provided Neil Simon with the title for his first play?

3448. Kurt Weil wrote the music for "September Song." What famous American playwright wrote the lyrics?

3449. What famous opera is based on the search for the Holy Grail?

3450. What famous American songwriter-entertainer recorded a song about Belgian surrealist painter René Magritte and his wife dancing to doo-wop?

3451. Why did musician Herb Alpert, founder of the Tijuana Brass, name his son Dore?

3452. What Grammy-winning 1959 hit—with music written by Hoagy Carmichael—is an official state song?

3440. *Pearl Bailey. She received her B.A. in 1985 after seven years as a part-time student.*

3441. *From Percy Bysshe Shelley's* To a Skylark, *which begins, "Hail to thee, blithe spirit!*

3442. *A drum, which Alpert beats while Moses, played by Charlton Heston, strides down Mount Sinai with the commandments.*

3443. *Wynonna Judd.*

3444. *Eliot's* Murder in the Cathedral. *Canterbury Cathedral was where the play's central character, Thomas `à Becket, was martyred.*

3445. *Two copies of the book* Life Begins at Forty.

3446. *Jimi Hendrix, who performed "The Star-Spangled Banner."*

3447. *"Little Boy Blue" gave him the title for* Come Blow Your Horn.

3448. *Maxwell Anderson. "September Song" was in their 1938 Broadway musical* Knickerbocker Holiday.

3449. Parsifal, *by Richard Wagner.*

3450. *Paul Simon. The song, "René and Georgette Magritte and Their Dog After the War," is on his 1983 album* Hearts and Bones.

3451. *The name contains the first two notes of the musical scale, do and re.*

3452. *"Georgia on My Mind." The lyrics are by Stuart Gorrell.*

3453. How many marches did John Philip Sousa write?

3454. In what famous person's bed did actress Anne Bancroft sleep (alone) in preparation for a Broadway role?

3455. How much does a 9-foot Steinway concert grand piano weigh? How about a 5-foot 1-inch baby grand?

3456. To whom did the Beatles dedicate the movie *Help!*?

3457. What was singer Ray Charles's name at birth?

3458. Who played Madonna's father in the 1986 music video the popular singer made for her recording of "Papa Don't Preach"?

3459. What former friend did singer Al Jolson knock out in a grudge prizefight in 1933?

3460. What musical instrument did Meredith Willson, author of *The Music Man,* play in his hometown band as well as with the John Philip Sousa band and the New York Philharmonic?

3461. What instrument did Dolly Parton play in her high-school marching band?

3462. What popular recording star owes his name to his resemblance to baseball great Hank Aaron?

3463. In the 1961 James Cagney spy comedy *One, Two, Three,* what American hit song did the East Germans use as a form of torture?

3464. Who composed the pop gospel standard "The Bible Tells Me So"?

3465. In music what is a hemidemisemiquaver?

3466. What was the inspiration for the Paul Simon song "Mother and Child Reunion"?

3467. Who composed the coronation anthem first played for England's King George II in 1727 and used at British coronations ever since?

3453. *136. He also wrote 15 operettas, 15 band suites and 70 songs.*

3454. *Golda Meir's. In 1977, Bancroft visited Meir in Israel and slept in her bed before appearing in the title role of* Golda, *a dramatization of Meir's autobiography,* My Life.

3455. *Grand, 990 pounds; baby, 540.*

3456. *To "Elias Howe who, in 1846, invented the sewing machine."*

3457. *Ray Charles Robinson. He dropped his surname early in his career to avoid confusion with boxer Sugar Ray Robinson.*

3458. *Actor Danny Aiello.*

3459. *Columnist Walter Winchell.*

3460. *The flute.*

3461. *The snare drum.*

3462. *Hammer, who was named Stanley Kirk Burrell at birth. He was nicknamed Little Hammer while a batboy for the Oakland Athletics because of his resemblance to Hammerin' Hank.*

3463. *"Itsy Bitsy Teenie Weenie Yellow Polkadot Bikini."*

3464. *Dale Evans, cowgirl wife of Roy Rogers. She also wrote their theme song, "Happy Trails."*

3465. *A sixty-fourth note.*

3466. *A chicken-and-egg dish of that name on the menu of a restaurant in New York City's Chinatown.*

3467. *George Frederic Handel.*

3468. What middle name did Reginald Kenneth Dwight give himself when he legally changed his name to Elton John in 1971?

3469. What is the name of the broomstick-riding witch in German composer Engelbert Humperdinck's opera Hansel and Gretel?

3470. How many pipes are there in a typical set of Scottish bagpipes?

3471. What did Elvis Presley have lining three walls, the floor and the ceiling of his "Jungle Room" at his Memphis mansion, Graceland?

3472. What is the full name of the theater named for singer Andy Williams in Branson, Missouri, the new country music mecca?

3473. What Irish-born Nobel Prize winner wrote music reviews for a London newspaper under the pseudonym Corno di Bassetto before he established himself as a dramatist?

3474. What famous Broadway show, later made into a movie, was based in part on a short story entitled The Idyll of *Miss Sarah Brown?*

3475. In *Peter and the Wolf,* Sergei Prokofiev's popular symphonic fairy tale for children, what instrument is used to represent the cat?

3476. What top band leader was the first to appear before paying audiences with black and white musicians performing side by side?

3477. What famous American songwriter—discouraged over the failure of his first musical comedy—briefly joined the Foreign Legion?

3478. What song was performed more than any other on TV's *The Hit Parade* during the show's 24-year run?

3479. What great pianist served as premier of his native land?

3480. What folk song was inspired by Laura Foster's death in North Carolina in 1866?

3468. *Hercules.*

3469. *Rosina Daintymouth, or Rosina Sweet Tooth, according to the translation.*

3470. *Five: the intake pipe, a valved tube connecting the bag to the player's mouth; the chanter, a pipe fitted with a double reed and pierced with eight sounding holes, used to play the melody; and three drones, pipes fitted with single reeds that provide the background.*

3471. *Green shag carpeting. The fourth wall of the room was covered with a fieldstone waterfall.*

3472. *The Andy Williams Moon River Theatre. "Moon River," of course, is his signature song.*

3473. *George Bernard Shaw.*

3474. Guys and Dolls. *The short story, of course, was written by Damon Runyon.*

3475. *The oboe.*

3476. *Benny Goodman, in 1936. Helping him break the color barrier while making music were pianist Teddy Wilson and vibraharpist Lionel Hampton.*

3477. *Cole Porter, in 1917. His musical flop was called* See America First.

3478. *"White Christmas." It was presented 32 times.*

3479. *Ignacy Jan Paderewski, in 1919. The country was Poland.*

3480. *"Tom Dooley." She was the woman ex-Confederate soldier Tom Dula "met up on the mountain" and stabbed with his knife.*

3481. If you dialed the title of the Glenn Miller song "Pennsylvania 6-5000" when he wrote it, who would have answered?

3482. How did singer Riley King get his stage name B.B. King?

3483. Who was the first American invited to conduct at La Scala in Milan?

3484. Who played solo guitar on "While My Guitar Gently Weeps" for the 1968 Beatles "White Album"?

3485. What famous composer wrote ballet music for elephants in the Ringling Brothers, Barnum and Bailey Circus?

3486. What real-life roommates were the inspiration for the Neil Simon play, *The Odd Couple* ?

3487. The melody of the song on TV's *The Hit Parade* in 1941, *Tonight We Love*, was drawn from what musical classic?

3488. What patriotic American song first appeared as a poem in the *Atlantic Monthly* in 1862?

3489. What popular singer worked in a pineapple cannery before getting her first taste of show business as an extra in the 1966 film *Hawaii* ?

3490. During a Metropolitan Opera tour of *Turandot*, soprano Birgit Nilsson held the high C in a duet longer than Franco Corelli. What did the temperamental tenor do to show his disapproval?

3491. What band leader started in show business at age 15 as a concert violinist with Enrico Caruso?

3492. What opera features characters named Ping, Pang and Pong.

3493. What world-famous ballerina was once jailed for participating in an unsuccessful coup attempt with her husband?

3494. Name the musicians and instruments featured in Benny Goodman's Swing Quartet?

3481. *The switchboard operator at New York's Pennsylvania Hotel—later the Statler Hilton and now the New York Penta.*

3482. *From the nickname Blues Boy, given to him during a stint as a disc jockey on a Memphis radio station.*

3483. *Leonard Bernstein.*

3484. *Eric Clapton.*

3485. *Igor Stravinsky in 1942. His "Circus Polka" was choreographed by George Balanchine.*

3486. *Simon and his director brother, Danny. Neil was the neat freak; his brother, the disorganized slob.*

3487. *Tchaikovsky's "First Piano Concerto (No. 1 in B-Flat Minor)".*

3488. *"The Battle Hymn of the Republic," written by Julia Ward Howe after she saw Union troops marching to "John Brown's Body," the music to which her poem was set.*

3489. *Bette Midler, who was paid $350 for portraying a Christian missionary in the screen adaptation of the James Michener novel.*

3490. *He bit her on the neck when he was supposed to give her a stage kiss.*

3491. *Cuban "Rhumba King" Xavier Cugat.*

3492. Turandot *by Puccini.*

3493. *Margot Fonteyn, in 1959. The country involved was Panama, her diplomat-husband's native land.*

3494. *Goodman on clarinet; Teddy Wilson at the piano; Gene Krupa on drums; and Lionel Hampton on the vibraphone.*

3495. What famous songwriter started his career as an accompanist for singer Vic Damone—and was fired?

3496. What rock group is named after the eighteenth-century English inventor of the seed drill?

3497. Antonio Stradivari made 1,116 violins, cellos and violas. How many are believed to still exist?

3498. What singer, when she was seven years old, won a $200 grand prize on Ted Mack's *Original Amateur Hour* with her renditions of "Too Young," "Because of You," and "Brahms' Lullaby"?

3499. What rock superstar sang backup on the Carly Simon hit "You're So Vain," the song supposedly written about Warren Beatty?

3500. What Elvis Presley hit was based on the Italian folk song, "O Sole Mio"?

3501. What actress portrayed a nude Christine Keeler—the call girl named in Britain's John Profumo sex scandal—in a review sponsored by the Royal Shakespeare Company?

3502. Whose romance inspired the sixteenth-century song, "A Frog Went A-Courting"?

3503. What Beatles song ends with a portion of Shakespeare's "King Lear"?

3504. How did jazz singer Anita O'Day, who was called Anita Colton at birth, pick her stage name?

3505. Composer Cole Porter inherited $250,000 from his wealthy grandfather, J. O. Cole. How did the older man earn his fortune?

3506. What song, written in the 1890s by Sunday school teachers Patty and Mildred Hill, do we still sing today?

3507. The first $1-million rockabilly recording was "Blue Suede Shoes." Who wrote and sang it?

3495. *Burt Bacharach.*

3496. *Jethro Tull.*

3497. *More than half—630 violins, 60 cellos and 15 violas.*

3498. *Gladys Knight, in 1951.*

3499. *Mick Jagger.*

3500. *"It's Now or Never," in 1960.*

3501. *Glenda Jackson, in 1963.*

3502. *The first Queen Elizabeth's romance with the Duc d'Alençon.*

3503. *"I Am the Walrus," recorded in 1967.*

3504. *From what she hoped her career would bring her— a lot of dough, or "ough-day" in Pig Latin.*

3505. *He sold water to thirsty miners in the California gold fields.*

3506. *"Happy Birthday to You," which the sisters rewrote from their earlier song, "Good Morning to All."*

3507. *Carl Perkins, in 1956. His rendition outsold that of Elvis Presley.*

3508. What musical instrument does bearded bandleader Mitch ("Sing Along") Miller play?

3509. Why did Al Jolson first take his trademark pose—singing on one knee with arms outstretched?

3510. What was the original name of the George M. Cohan song, "You're a Grand Old Flag"?

3511. On what show did Elvis Presley make his television debut singing "Heartbreak Hotel"?

3512. At a command performance for King George V of England, what great American musician bowed at the royal box and said, "This one's for you, Rex"?

3513. What was the first song to win the Academy Award when the category was introduced in 1934?

3514. The melody of what famous song is also known as "The Miller's Wedding"?

3515. To whom did Russian-born composer Sergei Rachmaninoff dedicate his "Second Piano Concerto (No. 2 in C Minor)" written in 1908?

3516. What Cole Porter classic was inspired by an Indonesian war dance that the songwriter heard during a world cruise?

3517. The music for what patriotic American song was adapted from an obscure operetta by French composer Jacques Offenbach?

3518. The play with the longest title on record was performed on Broadway in 1965 and called "Marat-Sade" for short. What was its full title?

3519. What singer, performing with the Blue Moon Boys, was turned down after auditioning for *Arthur Godfrey's Talent Scouts* TV show in 1955?

3520. Who wrote the musical score for the 1954 film classic *On the Waterfront*?

3508. *The oboe.*

3509. *He had a painful ingrown toenail and dropped to one knee to relieve the pressure.*

3510. *"You're a Grand Old Rag." Cohan wrote it for his 1906 musical* George Washington Jr., *inspired by a Gettysburg veteran's remark. He changed rag to flag following a public protest.*

3511. *On* Stage Show, *produced by Jackie Gleason and co-hosted by bandleader brothers Jimmy and Tommy Dorsey, on January 28, 1956. Presley didn't make his famous Ed Sullivan Show appearance until the fall of that year.*

3512. *Louis Armstrong, in 1934.*

3513. *"The Continental," from the Fred Astaire-Ginger Rogers film,* The Gay Divorcée.

3514. *"Auld Lang Syne," by Scottish poet Robert Burns.*

3515. *His psychoanalyst, Dr. Nikolai Dahl.*

3516. *"Begin the Beguine."*

3517. *The "Marines' Hymn." Its musical source, Offenbach's "Genevieve de Brambant," was first performed in Paris in 1859.*

3518. The Persecution and Assassination of Marat as Performed by the Inmates of the Asylum of Charenton under the Direction of the Marquis de Sade.

3519. *Elvis Presley.*

3520. *Conductor-composer Leonard Bernstein.*

3521. What award-winning 1979 Broadway offering, later made into an Oscar-winning movie, dealt with the same subject as an eighteenth-century play by Russia's Alexander Pushkin?

3522. What famous actress appeared in the title role in *Hamlet*?

3523. Whose put-down gave the heavy-metal rock group Led Zeppelin its name?

3524. What Broadway composer was first flutist with the New York Philharmonic when it was conducted by Arturo Toscanini?

3525. What 1963 hit song was recorded by Martha and the Vandellas in mid-winter, but not released until July?

3526. What was pop singer Boy George's name at birth?

3527. When Federico Fellini's autobiographical film "8½" was made into a Broadway musical in 1982, what new title was it given?

3528. What two opera stars have had food named after them?

3529. What famous pianist got his start in a Milwaukee piano bar playing under the name Walter Busterkeys?

3530. In what two Broadway hits did opera star Ezio Pinza appear?

3531. What famous baritone broke his contract with the Metropolitan Opera to appear in a movie called "Aaron Slick of Punkin Crick"?

3532. What was the name of the wife of Charles Ives, the avant-garde composer known for his atonal music?

3533. What was the original title of Leonard Bernstein's musical *West Side Story*?

3534. How did Gordon Sumner, the rock star and actor we know as Sting, get his stage name?

3521. Amadeus, *by Peter Schaffer. Pushkin's play was called* Mozart and Salieri.

3522. *Sarah Bernhardt.*

3523. *The Who's late drummer Keith Moon's—he told members of the group they'd go over like a lead balloon.*

3524. *"Music Man" Meredith Willson, who also wrote* The Unsinkable Molly Brown.

3525. *"Heat Wave."*

3526. *George O'Dowd.*

3527. Nine.

3528. *Nellie Melba (peach melba and melba toast) and Luisa Tetrazzini (chicken tetrazzini).*

3529. *Liberace.*

3530. South Pacific *and* Fanny.

3531. *Robert Merrill, in 1951.*

3532. *Harmony.*

3533. East Side Story.

3534. *From the yellow-and-black jerseys he used to wear, which fellow musicians thought made him look like a bumble bee.*

3535. Who did soprano Birgit Nilsson once list as a dependent on her U.S. income tax return, claiming he needed her?

3536. What enduring song was introduced on "Black Tuesday," the day the stock market crashed in 1929?

3537. Whose last words were, "I shall hear in heaven"?

3538. What song did the horn on singer Pat Boone's Ferrari play?

3539. On what label did the British rock trio Police cut its first single, the punk screamer "Fallout," in 1977?

3540. What was crooning bandleader Rudy Vallee's real first name?

3541. What famous actor, as a 14-year-old, played Kate in Shakespeare's *The Taming of the Shrew* at Stratford-upon-Avon, prompting a reviewer to remark, "I cannot remember any actress in the part who looked better?"

3542. What boxer appeared on the cover of the Beatles album "Sgt. Pepper's Lonely Hearts Club Band"?

3543. What was the original title of the song "Let Me Go, Lover," which was a million-record seller for Joan Weber in the mid-1950s?

3544. What is the origin of the musical term honky-tonk?

3545. What is the meaning of the expression "three-dog night"— which most of us know only as the name of a rock group?

3546. Under what name do we know Ferdinand Joseph La Menthe Morton?

3547. What country singer's first two hits were "Dumb Blonde" and "Something Fishy"?

3548. Who was the first entertainer to offer public bonds backed by his future music royalties?

3549. Who was featured on the cover of the very first issue of Rolling Stone magazine?

3535. Metropolitan Opera boss Rudolph Bing.

3536. "Happy Days Are Here Again." (It was played by band leader George Olsen at the Hotel Pennsylvania in New York City.)

3537. Ludwig von Beethoven's. The composer was totally deaf during the last eight years of his life.

3538. "April Love," the title song of the 1957 movie he made with Shirley Jones.

3539. Illegal Records.

3540. Hubert. He took the name Rudy in the 1920s from a saxophonist he admired.

3541. Laurence Olivier, in 1922.

3542. Sonny Liston.

3543. "Let Me Go, Devil."

3544. It was black slang for "gin mill"—but later was used to describe the spirited music that thrived in such places in the 1930s.

3545. The phrase, which originated with the Eskimos, means a very cold night—so cold that you'd have to bed down with three dogs to keep warm.

3546. "Jelly Roll" Morton, the jazz great.

3547. Dolly Parton. Both were recorded in 1967.

3548. David Bowie, in 1997. The 7.9 percent average-life bonds were rated single-A by Moody's.

3549. John Lennon.

3550. What famous country singer is the subject of more than a dozen musical tributes, including "Singing Teacher," "The Long Gone Lonesome Blues," "Midnight in Montgomery" and "The Ride"?

3551. What early rock 'n' roll group performed under the name "Saddle Pals" when it first started out—as singers of country music?

3552. What Polynesian island was the inspiration for Bali H'ai in the Rodgers and Hammerstein musical *South Pacific?*

3553. How many operas did Ludwig van Beethoven write?

3554. What show marked the Broadway debuts of Jerome Robbins, Leonard Bernstein, Betty Comden and Adolph Green?

3555. How much—in tons—does the sound system used on tour by the rock group U2 weigh?

3556. Which two woodwind orchestra instruments are classified as double reeds?

3557. What is the name of Madonna's pet Chihuahua?

3558. What song describes the young woman in its title as "a tomboy in lace"?

3559. Who is the famous sister of gospel singer Susie Luchsinger?

3560. In 1985 what four famous country singers recorded an album together as The Highwaymen?

3561. What song was Michael Jackson performing when he introduced his "moonwalk" to the world on a 1983 TV special?

3562. Who were the famous musicians who made up the original Benny Goodman Swing Quartet?

3563. The name of what musical instrument is derived from a French term meaning "high wood"?

3564. What category of performers do we have to thank for the term "hanky-panky"?

3550. Hank Williams. *The titles of most of the other tributes mention him by name.*

3551. Bill Haley and the Comets. *The group was originally called Bill Haley's Saddle Pals.*

3552. Bora Bora.

3553. Only one, Fidelio. *Its libretto was adapted from Jean Nicolas Bouilly's play* Léonore.

3554. On the Town. *It opened on Broadway on December 28, 1944.*

3555. 30 tons.

3556. The oboe and the bassoon.

3557. Chiquita.

3558. "Nancy (With the Laughing Face)." *The song was written by comedian Phil Silvers for Frank Sinatra's daughter Nancy.*

3559. Reba McEntire. *Susie, who is four years younger than her country-music superstar sister, is well known in Christian music circles. She has a number of albums to her credit as well as a book,* A Tender Road Home, *which was published in 1997.*

3560. Johnny Cash, Waylon Jennings, Kris Kristofferson and Willie Nelson. *Their album was called* The Highwaymen.

3561. "Billie Jean". *The TV show was* Motown 24: Yesterday, Today and Forever.

3562. Goodman (clarinet), Teddy Wilson (piano), Gene Krupa (drums) and Lionel Hampton (vibraphone).

3563. The oboe. *In French, "high wood" is hautbois—which the Italians transcribed into oboe.*

3564. Magicians. *The expression was inspired by their practice of using a handkerchief in one hand to distract the audience from noticing what they were doing with the other hand—with the rhyme influenced by the term hocus-pocus.*

3565. What famous composer always poured ice water over his head before he sat down to work?

3566. What instrument did Arturo Toscanini play before he switched to conducting?

3567. What popular band—led by a single-name star—was originally known as the Strontium 90?

3568. What was the stage name of actor Lincoln Theodore Monroe Andrew Perry?

3569. What names did Dolly Parton give her two dogs—both of them spitzes?

3570. What musical instrument was referred to as the "stomach Steinway" by Mark Twain?

3571. What is the stage name of heavy-metal bandleader Brian Warner?

3572. How much did Warner Communications pay in 1988 for the copyright to the song "Happy Birthday"?

3573. Before playwright Mary Chase created her imaginary 6-foot-1 rabbit named "Harvey," what make-believe animal had she planned on making the centerpiece of a new play?

3574. What singer, as a teenager, ended up in a juvenile detention center for shoplifting a Kiss T-shirt?

Bonus Trivia

3575. Most people know that Abraham Lincoln was shot while watching a performance of *Our American Cousin* at Ford's Theatre in Washington, D.C. The same play was also running at the McVerick Theatre in Chicago on May 18, 1860—the day Lincoln was nominated for president in that city.

3565. Beethoven. He believed it stimulated his brain.

3566. The cello.

3567. The Police. The band's lead singer was Sting.

3568. Stepin Fetchit.

3569. Mark Spitz (after the Olympic swimmer) and Lickety Spitz.

3570. The accordion.

3571. Marilyn Manson. He created the name by combining screen legend Marilyn Monroe's first name with serial killer Charles Manson's last name.

3572. $28 million.

3573. A 4-foot-tall canary named Daisy.

3574. Courtney Love.

3576. Lloyd Copeland invented the prototype of what we now call the microwave oven, but he might be enjoying better favor nowadays for another "creation": his granddaughter, Linda Ronstadt.

3577. Only two original TV show theme songs have reached the number one slot on "Billboard's" pop chart: "The Theme From S.W.A.T." by the Rhythm Heritage, in 1975, and "Welcome Back" (from *Welcome Back, Kotter*) by John Sebastian, in 1976.

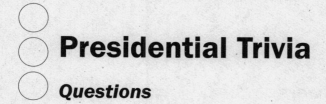

Presidential Trivia

Questions

3578. What is the only U.S. presidential landmark operated outside the country by the National Park Service?

3579. What four state capitals are named after American presidents?

3580. What was the Secret Service's code name for Barbara Bush?

3581. How many bathrooms are there in the White House?

3582. Who was president when running water was first installed in the White House?

3583. In which White House room did President Monroe play cards, Mrs. Theodore Roosevelt receive visitors, and President John F. Kennedy's casket lie in state?

3584. In 1973 what convicted felon was given a free half-hour of airtime on the three major television networks to declare his innocence?

3585. Which American president turned over 40 years of government paychecks to charity?

3586. Who was the first president to throw out the first ball of the season at a baseball game?

Answers

3578. Campobello, the summer home of Franklin Delano Roosevelt, in New Brunswick Province, Canada.

3579. Jackson, Mississippi; Jefferson City, Missouri; Lincoln, Nebraska; and Madison, Wisconsin

3580. "Tranquillity." President Bush was known as "Timberwolf."

3581. 34.

3582. Andrew Jackson.

3583. The Green Room.

3584. Just-resigned vice president Spiro Agnew, who had pleaded nolo contendere—no contest—to charges of tax evasion on bribes paid to him.

3585. Independently wealthy Herbert Hoover.

3586. William Howard Taft, in 1910. The Washington Senators beat the Philadelphia Athletics in the one-hit shutout pitched by baseball great Walter Johnson.

3587. John Tyler had more children than any other American president. How many did he have?

3588. What precipitated the $5.7-million renovation of the White House during the Truman administration?

3589. What did Woodrow Wilson, America's twenty-eighth president, denounce as a symbol of "the arrogance of wealth"?

3590. At what hour did presidential nominee George McGovern deliver his acceptance speech at the disorganized and discordant 1972 Democratic National Convention in Miami Beach?

3591. President Gerald Ford pardoned Iva D'Aquino in 1977. Who was she?

3592. Who was the only presidential candidate other than George Washington to run unopposed?

3593. What presidential wife was the first to be referred to as the First Lady?

3594. Which American president has the greatest number of cities and towns in the United States named after him?

3595. How many American presidents did not attend college?

3596. What did George Washington suggest building on the land that is now the site of the Washington Monument in Washington, D.C?

3597. What was the name of the horse Teddy Roosevelt rode in the famous Battle of San Juan Hill during the Spanish-American War?

3598. Who was the last of the eight American presidents to be born in Virginia—the state that claims the title Mother of Presidents?

3599. What salary did Benjamin Franklin advocate for the president of the United States during debates at the Constitutional Convention in 1787?

3587. *Fifteen. Married twice, he had a total of eight sons and seven daughters.*

3588. *A leg of Margaret Truman's grand piano broke through her sitting room floor into the family dining room below.*

3589. *The automobile.*

3590. *At 3:00 in the morning.*

3591. *Tokyo Rose—the seductive-voiced Japanese radio propagandist during World War II.*

3592. *James Monroe, for his second term in 1820, during the "Era of Good Feeling."*

3593. *Lucy Hayes, wife of Rutherford B. Hayes, in 1877.*

3594. *Madison, whose name is used in 27 states. He's followed in popularity by Washington (26), Monroe (22), Jackson and Jefferson (20 each), and Lincoln (16).*

3595. *Nine—Washington, Jackson, Van Buren, Taylor, Fillmore, Lincoln, Andrew Johnson, Cleveland and Truman.*

3596. *A monument to an unknown soldier of the American Revolution.*

3597. *Texas.*

3598. *Woodrow Wilson. The Virginians who preceded him were George Washington, Thomas Jefferson, James Madison, James Monroe, William Henry Harrison, John Tyler and Zachary Taylor.*

3599. *None. He felt that only the elite should serve as president and that they could do so without compensation.*

3600. The 1990-91 edition of "Who's Who in America" contained 10 lines about former president Ronald Reagan; how many were devoted to his wife, Nancy?

3601. What famous American explorer was the first presidential candidate of the Republican party?

3602. President Lyndon Johnson called his pet beagles Him and Her; what did President Franklin D. Roosevelt and his wife, Eleanor, name His and Hers?

3603. What position did president-to-be George Bush play on the Yale University baseball team?

3604. What equipment purchased by sixth president John Quincy Adams sparked accusations that he was installing "gaming furniture" in the White House?

3605. What was the presidential retreat in Maryland's Catoctin Mountains—now known as Camp David—originally called by President Franklin Delano Roosevelt?

3606. What presidential candidate coined the phrase, "The New Frontier"?

3607. In April 1793, George Washington attended the nation's first circus in Philadelphia and was paid $150. What was the money for?

3608. What President was ticketed for speeding in Washington, D.C., while he was in office?

3609. What President signed the first federal income tax law—3 percent on incomes over $600?

3610. What was the setting of the 1959 confrontation between Vice-President Richard Nixon and Soviet Premier Nikita Khrushchev?

3600. *28.*

3601. *John C. Frémont, in 1856. He lost to James Buchanan. Republican candidate Abraham Lincoln won the presidency four years later.*

3602. *The pistols they kept under their pillows.*

3603. *First base.*

3604. *A chess set and a billiard table.*

3605. *Shangri-La.*

3606. *Alf Landon, in 1936.*

3607. *Allowing Jack, the white charger he had ridden during the Revolutionary War, to be put on exhibit.*

3608. *Ulysses S. Grant, in his horse and buggy. He was fined $5.*

3609. *Abraham Lincoln.*

3610. *The model American kitchen of a U.S. exhibit in Moscow. The setting gave the encounter its name— "The Kitchen Debate."*

3611. In 1868 impeachment proceedings were initiated against President Andrew Johnson for his opposition to black rights and Congress' Reconstruction efforts. By what margin did he escape conviction?

3612. What U.S. President had a special bathtub—big enough to hold four men—installed in the White House to accommodate his great bulk?

3613. What kind of dogs were Nixon's Checkers and FDR's Fala?

3614. Who designed the pillbox hat that Jacqueline Kennedy made famous at her husband's inauguration in 1961?

3615. What did President John F. Kennedy commission Pierre Salinger to do on the eve of signing the Cuban trade embargo?

3616. Who was the smallest U.S. President?

3617. Who invented a metal-locating device to find the bullet lodged in President James Garfield's body after he was shot by assassin Charles Guiteau in 1881?

3618. Whose ghost did Queen Wilhelmina of the Netherlands claim she saw during a 1945 stay at the White House?

3619. What strange pets did John Quincy Adams and his wife, Louisa, bring with them to the White House?

3620. Which of our nation's chief executives could have been known as President King?

3621. How much did President Abraham Lincoln spend on a string of seed pearls and matching earrings purchased from Tiffany's for his wife, Mary?

3622. Who was the only American president to remain a bachelor his entire life?

3623. How short was George Washington's second inaugural address—the shortest in U.S. history?

3611. *One vote. The Senate voted 35 to 19 against Johnson, just shy of the two-thirds required to remove him from office.*

3612. *William Howard Taft, who weighed in at 325 pounds at the time.*

3613. *Checkers was a black-and-white cocker spaniel; Fala, a Scottish terrier.*

3614. *Halston, whose full name is Roy Halston Frowick.*

3615. *Buy and stockpile 1,500 Havana cigars.*

3616. *James Madison, the fourth President, who was 5 feet 4 inches tall and never weighed more than 100 pounds.*

3617. *Alexander Graham Bell. The device worked, but not on Garfield—because of interference from his steel-spring mattress.*

3618. *Abraham Lincoln's.*

3619. *Several hundred silkworms, which the First Lady fed and cared for while trying to make raw silk.*

3620. *Gerald R. Ford. He was named Leslie L. King at birth, but later assumed his stepfather's name.*

3621. *He paid $2,600.*

3622. *James Buchanan, who preceded Abraham Lincoln as the nation's chief executive, serving from 1857 to 1861.*

3623. *It contained only 135 words.*

PRESIDENTIAL TRIVIA—QUESTIONS

3624. What was the message on the one-word telegram Bob Hope sent to President Harry S. Truman after he stunned the oddsmakers and beat Thomas E. Dewey in 1948?

3625. How many times during his 12 years as president did Franklin Delano Roosevelt use the veto?

3626. Where did Herbert Hoover's 1932 campaign slogan "A chicken in every pot" originate?

3627. George Washington left America's shores only once. Where did he go?

3628. What did Richard M. Nixon's father raise on his ranch in Yorba Linda, California, before moving his family to Whittier when the future president was nine?

3629. What well-known American woman's maiden name was Elizabeth Anne Bloomer?

3630. Who was the first president paid a salary of $100,000?

3631. Who was president when electricity was installed in the White House?

3632. How much was architect James Horan awarded in 1792 for his winning design for the President's House—now known as the White House?

3633. Who once addressed the Mayflower-minded members of the Daughters of the American Revolution as "my fellow immigrants"?

3634. How many tons of jelly beans did the White House buy during Ronald Reagan's presidency?

3635. What unusual coincidence has been noted about the names of the secretaries who served Presidents Lincoln and Kennedy?

3636. Who said, "Let us begin by committing ourselves to the truth—to see it like it is, and tell it like it is—to find the truth, to speak the truth, and live the truth"?

3624. *"Unpack."*

3625. *He used it 635 times (372 regular vetoes; 263 pocket vetoes).*

3626. *With France's King Henry IV, who at his coronation said that he hoped "to make France so prosperous that every peasant will have a chicken in his pot on Sunday."*

3627. *To Barbados, in the West Indies, in 1751 with his ailing half-brother Lawrence. It was during his stay there that he was stricken with smallpox.*

3628. *Lemons.*

3629. *Former First Lady Betty Ford.*

3630. *Harry S. Truman.*

3631. *Benjamin Harrison. The year was 1889.*

3632. *Horan was given $500 and a lot in Washington, D.C.*

3633. *Eleanor Roosevelt.*

3634. *12 tons.*

3635. *Lincoln's secretary was named Kennedy (John); Kennedy's was named Lincoln (Evelyn).*

3636. *Richard M. Nixon, in accepting the Republican party's presidential nomination in 1968.*

3637. Who has been credited with writing George Washington's famous Farewell Address?

3638. Who gave Thomas Jefferson the fur-collared coat he's shown wearing in the famous statue of him at the Jefferson Memorial in Washington, D.C.?

3639. How many children did former President Jimmy Carter have besides his high-profile daughter, Amy?

3640. What famous American political figure worked during his teen years as a summer barker at the Slippery Gulch Carnival in Prescott, Arizona?

3641. What coincidence was there in the timing of the decisions of our two President Johnsons—Andrew and Lyndon—not to seek re-election?

3642. Who changed the presidential seal so that the American eagle faces the talon in which it's holding an olive branch of peace rather than the one in which it clasps arrows of war?

3643. What four American presidents ran unsuccessfully for re-election on third-party tickets?

3644. What national political experience did Abraham Lincoln have before he became president?

3645. What did President Franklin Delano Roosevelt have imprinted on White House matchbooks?

3646. What was George Washington's nickname for his wife, Martha?

3647. How many U.S. presidents had full beards?

3648. What prompted President Harry S. Truman to write a newspaper columnist, "Some day I hope to meet you. When that happens you'll need a new nose, a lot of beefsteak for black eyes, and perhaps a supporter below"?

3649. What is the average age at which America's presidents have taken office?

3637. *Alexander Hamilton.*

3638. *Polish patriot Thaddeus Kosciusko.*

3639. *Three—sons Jack (John William), Chip (James Earl), and Jeff (Donnel Jeffrey).*

3640. *Richard M. Nixon.*

3641. *Both took place in the year '68—Andrew's in 1868; Lyndon's in 1968.*

3642. *Harry S. Truman—but Franklin Delano Roosevelt had ordered the change before his death in 1945.*

3643. *John Tyler, who withdrew his candidacy before the election, Martin Van Buren, Millard Fillmore, and Theodore Roosevelt.*

3644. *He served a two-year term in the House of Representatives.*

3645. *"Stolen from the White House."*

3646. *Patsy.*

3647. *Five—Lincoln, Grant, Hayes, Garfield and Benjamin Harrison.*

3648. *A music review that panned daughter Margaret's singing ability. The letter was sent to* Washington Post *music critic Paul Hume.*

3649. *54.*

3650. What American president was First Lady Barbara Bush's great-great-great-uncle?

3651. What American president had an electric horse installed in his White House bedroom—and rode it almost daily?

3652. What is former Vice President Dan Quayle's first name?

3653. Who was the only U.S. president not to use the word "I" in his inaugural address?

3654. Who was the first president elected when women nationwide had the right to vote?

3655. How big a raise in his base pay did George Bush receive when he moved up from vice president to president?

3656. Which American president owned dogs named Drunkard, Tipler and Tipsy?

3657. What engraved gift did President Lyndon Johnson give to friends and acquaintances to make sure they thought of him "first thing in the morning and the last at night"?

3658. Who was the last governor to serve as vice president?

3659. Which two members of George Washington's cabinet were redheads?

3660. As a boy, what 20th-century American president was known as Tommy?

3661. Who was the first American president to hold an airplane pilot's license?

3662. Who was the first American president to have an inaugural ball?

3663. Who was the first American to win a Noble Prize?

3664. What was the name of Theodore Roosevelt's dog?

3650. *Democrat Franklin Pierce. Mrs. Bush's maiden name is Pierce.*

3651. *Calvin Coolidge.*

3652. *James.*

3653. *Theodore Roosevelt.*

3654. *Warren G. Harding, in 1920.*

3655. *$85,000—from $115,000 as vice president to $200,000 as president.*

3656. *George Washington. They were foxhounds.*

3657. *Electric toothbrushes.*

3658. *Nelson Rockefeller of New York. Gerald Ford nominated Rockefeller as vice president in August 1974 after Ford vacated the post to become president upon the resignation of Richard Nixon. (Spiro Agnew of Maryland was the last governor elected vice president, in 1972.)*

3659. *His secretary of state, Thomas Jefferson, and his treasury secretary, Alexander Hamilton.*

3660. *Woodrow Wilson, whose given names were Thomas Woodrow. He officially dropped his first name when he was 24.*

3661. *Dwight David Eisenhower, who was issued a license in November 1939. He learned to fly while a lieutenant colonel on Gen. Douglas MacArthur's staff in the Philippines.*

3662. *George Washington. He held his inaugural ball in New York City on May 7, 1789.*

3663. *Theodore Roosevelt. He won the coveted Noble Prize in 1906 for helping end the Russo-Japanese War with the Treaty of Portsmouth.*

3664. *Scamp.*

3665. Who was the first U.S. President born outside the 13 original states?

3666. What was the first moving picture ever to be shown at the White House?

3667. Where was the first Presidential mansion located?

3668. On a 1957 visit to Disneyland, Harry S. Truman refused to ride one of the attractions. Which one was it, and why?

3669. Franklin D. Roosevelt held the office of President of the United States of America for the longest period. Which President holds the record for longevity after leaving office?

3670. What was the nickname of the first official Presidential airplane (a C-45 piloted by Major Henry T. Myers in 1944)?

3671. What famous politician was nicknamed Gloomy Gus when he attended Duke University law school?

3672. What was the nickname of Jimmy Carter's campaign plane in 1976?

3673. Thelma Catherine Ryan is the real name of the wife of one of American's most controversial public figures from the 1970's. Who is she?

3674. Two books written by United States Presidents have been made into television series. What are they?

3675. Which First Lady was edited out of her movie debut?

3676. Who was the first woman Presidential candidate?

3677. Who were the only left-handed Presidents?

3678. President Richard M. Nixon kept a music box in his Oval Office desk. What tune did it play?

3679. Who was the only U.S. President to marry a woman from another country?

3665. *Abraham Lincoln, who was born in Kentucky, the 15th state.*

3666. *"The Birth of a Nation," on February 15, 1916.*

3667. *At 1 Cherry Street in New York City.*

3668. *Dumbo the Elephant, since he considered it the symbol of the Republican Party.*

3669. *John Adams, who was ex-President for 25 years and 4 months (March 1801 to July 1826).*

3670. *Sacred Cow.*

3671. *Richard M. Nixon.*

3672. *Peanut One, piloted by James Carter (no relation).*

3673. *Pat Nixon.*

3674. *"Crusade In Europe" by Dwight D. Eisenhower, and "Profiles In Courage" by John F. Kennedy.*

3675. *Pat Nixon, who had a walk-on in the 1935 film, "Becky Sharp," only to have her scenes end up on the cutting room floor.*

3676. *Victoria Claflin Woodhull, who, on May 10, 1872, was nominated by the Equal Rights Party.*

3677. *James Garfield, Harry Truman and Gerald Ford.*

3678. *"Hail to the Chief."*

3679. *John Quincy Adams, whose wife, Louisa, was born in London.*

3680. Who was the only U.S. president to serve as a member of the Congress of the Confederate States?

3681. What presidential candidate ran his campaign from prison, in 1920?

3682. Both President John Tyler Jr. and his father, John Tyler Sr. served as governor of what state?

3683. What name did George Washington use in addressing his friend the Marquis de Lafayette?

3684. What twentieth-century American president was so obsessed with secrecy that he often wrote "burn this" on personal letters?

3685. What famous American politician coined the phrase "lunatic fringe"?

3686. What crime was the U.S. Secret Service established to combat when it was created in 1865?

3687. How many doors are there in the 132-room White House?

3688. What three successive American presidents were Republicans, Union Army generals and born in Ohio?

3689. Who was the only president born in Illinois, the Land of Lincoln?

3690. What were the Four Freedoms outlined by President Franklin D. Roosevelt in his State of the Union message to Congress in January 1941?

3691. Who was the only American president to graduate from the U.S. Naval Academy?

3692. How many men named Johnson have served as vice president of the United States?

3693. How many presidents did J. Edgar Hoover serve under as chief of the Federal Bureau of Investigation?

3680. John Tyler.

3681. Eugene V. Debs, the Socialist Party candidate. Jailed for sedition, he received nearly one million votes.

3682. Virginia.

3683. Fayette.

3684. Lyndon Baines Johnson.

3685. Teddy Roosevelt. He used the term in 1913 to describe people of excessive zeal within the reform groups that supported him.

3686. Counterfeiting. It was not until 1901, after the assassinations of Presidents Abraham Lincoln, James A. Garfield and William McKinley, that the Secret Service was given the job of protecting American presidents.

3687. 412.

3688. Ulysses S. Grant, Rutherford B. Hayes and James A. Garfield.

3689. Ronald Reagan. He was born in Tampico, Illinois. Lincoln was born in Kentucky.

3690. Freedom of speech and worship, and freedom from want and fear.

3691. Jimmy Carter, who was in the class of 1946.

3692. Three—Richard Mentor Johnson, who served with Martin Van Buren; Andrew Johnson, who served with Abraham Lincoln and succeeded him as president; and Lyndon Baines Johnson, who served with John F. Kennedy and succeeded him as president.

3693. Eight—Calvin Coolidge, Herbert Hoover, Franklin D. Roosevelt, Harry S. Truman, Dwight D. Eisenhower, John F. Kennedy, Lyndon B. Johnson and Richard M. Nixon. Hoover headed the agency from 1924 until his death in 1972.

3694. How many animals did ex-president Theodore Roosevelt bag during his 11-month hunting expedition to Africa after leaving office in 1909?

3695. How many times did Abraham Lincoln and Stephen Douglas debate during their 1858 race for the U.S. Senate?

3696. What president's bid for reelection inspired the opposition slogan, "Let's get another deck"?

3697. What U.S. president was born on the Fourth of July?

3698. After Spiro Agnew resigned from office in disgrace in 1973, what entertainer loaned him $230,000 for living expenses and payment of Internal Revenue Service fines?

3699. What three animals were party symbols in the 1912 presidential race?

3700. What recipe offered by First Lady-to-be Florence Harding in the 1920 presidential race became a symbol of her husband's "return to normalcy" campaign?

3701. What U.S. president appointed the greatest number of Supreme Court justices?

3702. George Washington's second inaugural address was the shortest in U.S. history; what president gave the second-shortest?

3703. Why did President Millard Fillmore turn down a prestigious honorary degree from Oxford University?

3704. What valuables were found hidden in Mary Todd Lincoln's underwear when the president's widow was judged insane in 1875?

3705. According to a book co-authored by Sigmund Freud, what American president suffered from an unresolved Oedipus complex?

3706. What did President Andrew Jackson have installed on the second floor of the White House in 1835 to ensure that he had a steady supply of running water?

3694. *296—including 9 lions, 5 elephants, 13 rhinos and 7 hippos.*

3695. *Seven. They debated in each of Illinois' seven congressional districts. Douglas won the election—and Lincoln gained national prominence.*

3696. *Franklin Delano Roosevelt's—in 1936. The slogan was the Republican party's response to Roosevelt's New Deal.*

3697. *Calvin Coolidge—in 1872. (Three American presidents died on July 4th—Thomas Jefferson and John Adams in 1826, and James Monroe in 1831.)*

3698. *Frank Sinatra.*

3699. *The two old standards, the donkey and the elephant, and the bull moose, for Theodore Roosevelt's independent Bull Moose party.*

3700. *Her waffle recipe. It was the first recipe offered as a campaign tactic in a presidential election. Not coincidentally, 1920 was the year women got the vote.*

3701. *George Washington. He named ten during his eight years in office. The high court was composed of six members at the time.*

3702. *Franklin Delano Roosevelt—his fourth inaugural address was 559 words long. Other inaugural addresses under 1,000 words were Lincoln's second, with 698 words. Theodore Roosevelt's, 985; Zachary Taylor's, 996.*

3703. *Because it was written in Latin, a language he didn't understand. As he explained, "I have not the advantage of a classical education and no man should, in my judgment, accept a degree he cannot read."*

3704. *Bonds worth $56,000.*

3705. *Woodrow Wilson. In the book Thomas Woodrow Wilson, written with William Bullitt, Freud claimed Wilson's two wives served as mother substitutes.*

3706. *Free-standing water hydrants.*

3707. What American president banned Christmas trees in his home—even when he lived in the White House?

3708. What two brothers were nominated for president at the Republican Party convention in 1884?

3709. President Franklin D. Roosevelt appeared in the 1943 romantic comedy *Princess O'Rourke*—as what?

3710. What two rivers, bearing the names of the United States presidents, join the Gallatin River in Montana to form the Missouri?

3711. The campaign slogan of what presidential candidate is on the oldest printed T-shirt in the Smithsonian Institution's extensive T-shirt collection?

3712. Who was the first presidential jogger?

3713. Who was the first divorcée to live in the White House as First Lady of the United States?

3714. What is the minimum age set in the Constitution for the president of the United States?

3715. When all the paint was stripped from the outer walls of the White House for the very first time in the 1980's, how many coats were removed?

3716. How many presidents were among the eight great American leaders profiled by president-to-be John F. Kennedy in his 1956 Pulitzer Prize-winning book *Profiles in Courage*?

3717. How many U.S. presidents were British subjects at birth?

3718. What major American city is named for the man who served as vice president of the United States from 1845 to 1849?

3719. What American president signed an amnesty bill restoring citizenship to Jefferson Davis, retroactive to 1868?

3720. What were the Secret Service code names for Presidents Carter and Nixon?

3707. *Theodore Roosevelt, who was a staunch conservationist. Christmas trees did get into the White Hose during his presidency, though—his children smuggled them into their bedroom.*

3708. *General William Tecumseh Sherman and Senator John Sherman of Ohio. The general got 2 votes on the first ballot; the senator, 30. James G. Blaine won the party's nomination on the fourth ballot and lost the election to Grover Cleveland.*

3709. *Himself. The film featured Olivia de Havilland in the title role.*

3710. *The Jefferson and the Madison.*

3711. *Thomas E. Dewey. The slogan, "DEW-IT with DEWEY," is from his ill-fated 1948 presidential campaign against Harry S. Truman.*

3712. *Theodore Roosevelt. He jogged around the Washington Monument daily.*

3713. *Florence Harding, wife of Warren G. Harding.*

3714. *35—according to Article II, Section 1.*

3715. *42.*

3716. *One—John Quincy Adams. The other seven profiled were Daniel Webster, Thomas Hart Benton, Sam Houston, Edmund G. Ross, Lucius Quintus Cincinnatus Lamar, George Norris and Robert A. Taft.*

3717. *Eight. George Washington, John Adams, Thomas Jefferson, James Madison, James Monroe, John Quincy Adams, Andrew Jackson and William Henry Harrison. The first president born an American was Martin Van Buren, who served between Jackson and Harrison.*

3718. *Dallas, Texas. It was named for Pennsylvanian George M. Dallas, who was vice president under James Polk in 1846 when Big D was laid out.*

3719. *Jimmy Carter.*

3720. *Carter was Deacon; Nixon was Searchlight.*

3721. What historic presidential site was closed in 1985 because visitors balked at having to pass prison gates, gun towers and armed guards to get to it?

3722. What president won election after three unsuccessful bids for the nomination?

3723. Who was honored with the first toast ever made at a White House dinner?

3724. Which U.S. president has the greatest number of American communities named after him?

3725. What president was granted a patent for a device for lifting vessels over shoals?

3726. Presidents Jefferson, Tyler and Nixon played the violin; Truman and Nixon, the piano. What did "Silent" Calvin Coolidge play?

3727. What American president, in a bid to pay back $107,000 in debts, set up a lottery with his house as the prize?

3728. What president-to-be released the trap door on the gallows at two hangings?

3729. Who wrote the words to the American presidential anthem, "Hail to the Chief"?

3730. What jellybean flavors were Ronald Reagan's favorites?

3731. Who posed for the statue of Alexander Hamilton that stands in front of the Treasury Building in Washington, D.C.?

3732. The heads of four U.S. presidents were carved on Mount Rushmore to the scale of a man 465 feet tall. Who are they and how long are each of their noses?

3733. What were the names of Abe Lincoln's four sons?

3734. Which American president was the first to have a phone on his desk in the White House?

3721. *The house in Moreau, New York, where Ulysses S. Grant completed his memoirs and died. It's now part of Mt. McGregor Prison.*

3722. *James Buchanan, who won in 1856 after losing the nomination in 1844, 1848 and 1852.*

3723. *Lafayette. President John Quincy Adams proposed the toast on September 6, 1825, as the Marine Corps Band played the "Marseillaise."*

3724. *Thomas Jefferson, with 37. Lincoln and Washington are tied for second with 32 each.*

3725. *Abraham Lincoln, in 1849.*

3726. *The harmonica.*

3727. *Thomas Jefferson, in 1826. There were few takers, however, and the lottery was abandoned shortly before Jefferson's death later that year.*

3728. *Grover Cleveland, while he was sheriff of Buffalo, New York, in the early 1870s.*

3729. *Sir Walter Scott. They're from his poem, "The Lady of the Lake." English tunesmith James Sanderson set the words to music and the song was first performed in London in 1811.*

3730. *Coconut and licorice.*

3731. *Strongman Charles Atlas. The statue was unveiled on May 17, 1923.*

3732. *The noses of Washington, Jefferson, Lincoln and Theodore Roosevelt are each 20 feet long.*

3733. *Robert, Eddie, Willie and Tad. Only Robert lived to maturity.*

3734. *Herbert Hoover, in 1929. Previous presidents used an enclosed phone booth in the hallway outside the Oval Office.*

3735. Who were the five Civil War generals who went on to serve as president of the United States?

3736. Who was President Ronald Reagan quoting when he said "I forgot to duck" after he was shot by John W. HinckleyJr. in 1981?

3737. President Andrew Jackson's political advisers were nicknamed the Kitchen Cabinet. What label was given to President Warren G. Harding's advisers?

3738. Which president modeled winter sportswear for *Look* magazine in 1939?

3739. Which two presidents were Quakers?

3740. Which First Lady was known as Lemonade Lucy?

3741. What was Richard Nixon talking about when he told a TV audience, "I just want to say this, right now, that regardless of what they say about it, we are going to keep it"?

3742. John Quincy Adams, describing the first presidential inaugural ball, wrote: "The crowd was excessive—the heat excessive, and the entertainment bad." Whose ball was it?

3743. Which two presidents are buried at Arlington National Cemetery?

3744. What president installed the first bathtub in the White House?

3745. What was George Washington's shoe size?

3746. What are George Washington' s false teeth—stolen in 1981 from the Smithsonian Institution in Washington, D.C.—composed of?

3747. Why did the general and president we know as Ulysses Grant change his given name, Hiram Ulysses, to Ulysses Hiram?

3748. If the seated figure in the Lincoln Memorial in Washington, D.C., were to stand up, how tall would it be?

3735. *In order of their terms of office: Ulysses S. Grant, Rutherford B. Hayes, James A. Garfield, Chester A. Arthur and Benjamin Harrison.*

3736. *Jack Dempsey, who made the remark after Gene Tunney beat him in a world heavyweight championship bout in 1926.*

3737. *The Poker Cabinet.*

3738. *Gerald R. Ford, who was a Yale University law student at the time.*

3739. *Herbert Hoover and Richard M. Nixon.*

3740. *Rutherford B. Hayes's teetotaling wife, who permitted only soft drinks in the White House during her husband's term, from 1877 to 1881.*

3741. *His family dog, Checkers, given to him by a supporter. The TV address was his famous Checkers speech.*

3742. *James Madison's.*

3743. *William Howard Taft and John Fitzgerald Kennedy.*

3744. *Millard Fillmore, our thirteenth president, who served from 1850 until 1853.*

3745. *Thirteen.*

3746. *The uppers, gold and hippopotamus teeth; the lowers, elephant and hippopotamus teeth.*

3747. *He did not want his initials to be H.U.G. He became U.S. Grant when his congressman mistakenly nominated him for West Point as Ulysses Simpson Grant. (Simpson was his mother's maiden name.)*

3748. *It would be 28 feet tall. Lincoln himself stood 6 feet 4 inches.*

3749. Who was the first president to wear long trousers rather than knee breeches to his inauguration?

3750. Which president was the first to visit China?

3751. Who was the first president to have the name of his official residence, the White House, on his stationery?

3752. Into what three major categories did Thomas Jefferson organize the books in his library at Monticello?

3753. How many pages long was John F. Kennedy's will?

3754. Why was Franklin D. Roosevelt chosen to be portrayed on the dime in 1945?

3755. What future American First Lady's display of support helped save the Marquis de Lafayette's wife from the guillotine?

3756. Who was the first U.S. president to die in office?

3757. Who was the first presidential wife to be referred to as FLOTUS—for First Lady of the United States?

3758. What age were four of the first six U.S. presidents—George Washington, Thomas Jefferson, James Madison and John Quincy Adams—when they were inaugurated?

3759. What president's inaugural jacket was woven from the wool of sheep he was raising at home in Virginia?

3760. Which scandal-scarred official in the Nixon administration borrowed $4,850 from the White House safe to pay for his honeymoon?

3761. Which presidential library was the first to be established?

3762. What was the official presidential plane called during Harry S. Truman's presidency?

3763. During whose presidency were the greatest number of states admitted to the Union?

3749. *Our sixth president, John Quincy Adams, in 1825.*

3750. *Ulysses S. Grant, in 1879, two years after he left the White House.*

3751. *Teddy Roosevelt.*

3752. *Memory, reason and imagination. Memory covered history; reason included philosophy, law, science and geography; and imagination included architecture, music, literature and the leisure arts. Within each category, books were arranged according to size.*

3753. *16. In it he set up trusts for his wife and children.*

3754. *Because of his work on behalf of the March of Dimes and its battle against polio, the disease that crippled Roosevelt.*

3755. *Elizabeth Monroe, while James Monroe was serving as U.S. minister to France.*

3756. *William Henry Harrison. He died on April 4, 1841, a month after contracting pneumonia at his inauguration.*

3757. *Mary Todd Lincoln. FLOTUS (pronounced FLOW-tus) and POTUS (President of the United States) have long been acronyms for the First Couple used by White House staff.*

3758. *57. No other presidents have been inaugurated at that age.*

3759. *James Madison. He had imported the Merino sheep from Portugal.*

3760. *John Dean. He paid it all back.*

3761. *The Rutherford B. Hayes Presidential Library in Fremont, Ohio. It was dedicated in 1916.*

3762. *The Independence, after his hometown in Missouri. Truman's predecessor, Franklin D. Roosevelt, was the first White House occupant to have an official presidential plane. His was nicknamed "Sacred Cow" by reporters.*

3763. *Benjamin Harrison's. He served from 1889 to 1893 and saw six states added to the Union: North Dakota, South Dakota, Montana and Washington in 1889; Idaho and Wyoming in 1890.*

3764. Who gave Chelsea Clinton her cat, Socks?

3765. How was Martha Washington formally addressed during her husband's presidency?

3766. Who was the first U.S. presidential nominee to give his acceptance speech in person at his party's convention?

3767. Who piloted Eleanor Roosevelt, in evening dress, to Baltimore, just after she became First Lady?

3768. Who was the first black presidential candidate nominated at a national political convention?

3769. Who was the first rap artist to perform at a presidential inaugural gala? Bonus: Who was the president?

3770. What live trophy from the Lewis and Clark expedition to the American Northwest did President Thomas Jefferson keep on the grounds of the White House?

Bonus Trivia

3771. On his way home from Harvard one day, Robert Todd Lincoln, the son of President Abraham Lincoln, fell off the platform while waiting for his train. He was saved from possible death by Edwin Booth, the actor, and the brother of John Wilkes Booth—the man who, only a few week later, assassinated President Lincoln.

3764. Her piano teacher, who found Socks and his sister, Midnight, abandoned in a park in Little Rock, Arkansas, in 1990 and took them home. Chelsea fell in love with Socks during a piano lesson and adopted her.

3765. As Lady Washington.

3766. Franklin D. Roosevelt, in 1932.

3767. Amelia Earhart. Mrs. Roosevelt was so enthusiastic about the flight, she wanted Earhart to give her flying lessons, but the president said no.

3768. Frederick Douglass, in 1888. He received one vote at the Republican convention in Chicago that ultimately picked Benjamin Harrison as the party candidate. Douglass went on to become U.S. minister to Haiti.

3769. The performer was L.L. Cool J; the president, Bill Clinton; the year, 1993.

3770. A grizzly bear.

Science, Nature & Medicine

Questions

3772. If man had a jumping ability proportional to that of the minuscule flea—which can make a horizontal leap of over a foot—how far would one leap take him?

3773. When you cross cattle with buffalo, what do you get?

3774. What is the most plentiful metal in the earth's crust?

3775. An octopus has eight tentacles. How many does its relative the squid have?

3776. What reason did Sigmund Freud give for sitting behind his patients' couch during psychoanalytic sessions?

3777. How fast does lightning travel?

3778. What is the normal body temperature of a horse?

3779. What living creature is believed to enjoy more hours of daylight annually than any other?

3780. What male mammal has the greatest number of mates in a season?

3781. What gives the gemstone turquoise its distinctive color?

Answers

3772. Five city blocks.

3773. Beefalo.

3774. Aluminum, most of which is extracted from bauxite.

3775. Ten.

3776. Freud wrote: "I cannot bear to be gazed at eight hours a day."

3777. It travels 90,000 miles a second—almost half the speed of light (186,000 miles a second).

3778. 100.5 °F.

3779. The Arctic tern, which travels twice a year from pole to pole—covering more than 20,000 miles round-trip—to enjoy nearly four months of continuous daylight during the Arctic summer and another four months during the Antarctic summer.

3780. The northern fur seal, which averages 40 to 60 mates a season.

3781. Traces of copper.

3782. How fast do flying fish "fly"?

3783. Who was the first to suggest using contact lenses to improve vision?

3784. How many cubic feet of gas does a cow belch on an average day?

3785. When lions and tigers mate, what do you call their cubs?

3786. What are the seven colors of the rainbow?

3787. How many times a minute does the average adult elephant's heart beat?

3788. What animal always gives birth to identical quadruplets?

3789. How much does the heart of the average man weigh?

3790. How many sides are there to a snow crystal?

3791. Why could we call William Stewart Halsted the "Mr. Clean" of medicine?

3792. How many ribs does man have?

3793. What Nobel Prize winner admitted that he had contributed his sperm to a sperm bank in hopes of producing exceptionally gifted children?

3794. If seedless oranges don't have seeds, how are they propagated?

3795. What vaccine caused more death and illness than the disease it was intended to prevent?

3796. What distinction do the chevrotain (mouse deer) and dik-dik (antelope) share?

3797. What is the hardest part of the normal human body?

3798. What is the maximum lifespan of a goldfish in captivity?

3782. *They average 35 mph and have been known to go as fast as 45 mph.*

3783. *Leonardo da Vinci, in 1508.*

3784. *Thirty-five.*

3785. *Ligers when the father is a lion; tigons or tiglons when the father is a tiger.*

3786. *Red, orange, yellow, green, blue, indigo and violet.*

3787. *Only 25. In man, the average adult heartbeat is 70 to 80 times per minute.*

3788. *The nine-banded armadillo, known as* Dasypus novemcinctus— *the only armadillo native to the U.S.*

3789. *From 10 to 12 ounces. A woman's heart weighs from 8 to 10 ounces.*

3790. *Six.*

3791. *Halsted, developer of local anesthesia, was the first doctor to wear rubber gloves in surgery in 1890.*

3792. *Twenty-four.*

3793. *William Shockley, inventor of the transistor.*

3794. *By grafting. The original seedless orange was a mutant.*

3795. *The swine flu vaccine, 1976.*

3796. *They are among the world's tiniest-hoofed animals, reaching only 12 to 16 inches in height.*

3797. *Tooth enamel.*

3798. *Twenty-five years.*

3799. What did Dr. Alfred Kinsey study before he turned his attention to our sexual behavior?

3800. How many bee trips from flower to hive does it take to make a pound of honey?

3801. A baby kangaroo is called a joey. What are its parents called?

3802. What flower has more varieties than any other—at least 30,000—ranging in size from ¼ inch to 20 feet?

3803. What famous American hero—educated as a mechanical engineer—helped design a germ-proof "artificial heart" in the early 1930s?

3804. The mayfly lives six hours. How long do its eggs take to hatch?

3805. A female black bear weighs about 300 pounds. How much does one of its babies weigh at birth?

3806. What is the largest member of the dolphin family?

3807. How many of the average adult's 32 permanent teeth are molars?

3808. Approximately how many pounds of dung does the average elephant produce daily?

3809. How were the first written messages transmitted by air?

3810. How can you tell the age of a mountain goat?

3811. What is the most plentiful element in seawater?

3812. What device was introduced commercially in 1934 as a "portable superregenerative receiver and transmitter"?

3813. What mammal has the world's shortest sperm?

3814. What color is topaz in its pure state?

3815. Before the barometer was discovered, what animal did German meteorologists use to predict air pressure changes?

3799. *The gall wasp.*

3800. *Forty thousand.*

3801. *Mom's a flyer; Dad, a boomer.*

3802. *The orchid.*

3803. *Charles Lindbergh, working with surgeon Alexis Carrel.*

3804. *Three years.*

3805. *One-half pound.*

3806. *The killer whale.*

3807. *12. There are 3 per quadrant—top and bottom, on each side of the mouth.*

3808. *50.*

3809. *By arrow—in the fifth century B.C., during the siege of Potidaea during the Peloponnesian War.*

3810. *By the number of rings on its small, curved black horns. The first ring develops at age two, and another ring is added every spring thereafter. Both males and females grow horns.*

3811. *Chlorine.*

3812. *The walkie-talkie.*

3813. *The hippopotamus.*

3814. *It's colorless. Topaz takes on a variety of hues from trace elements, radiation and defects in its crystal structure. Pale gold-brown is its most common color.*

3815. *The frog. Frogs croak when the pressure drops.*

3816. How many points must a stag elk have on each of its antlers to be considered mature?

3817. The name of what dog breed, translated from German, means "monkey terrier"?

3818. The giant panda is a member of the bear family. To what family does the much smaller red panda belong?

3819. At what temperature does water boil at the top of Mount Everest?

3820. What dog carries the name of the English minister who first bred it?

3821. What is the most common transplant operation?

3822. What did a National Aeronautics and Space Administration employee buy at a Wal-Mart in 1995 to protect the space shuttle from woodpeckers?

3823. What is the largest rodent in North America?

3824. Where did Leonardo da Vinci advise the adventurous to test his design for a rudimentary helicopter?

3825. What mammal can starve to death, despite a plentiful supply of food, if there are too many cool, cloudy days in a row?

3826. At what standard level above ground—in feet—do meteorologists measure wind speed?

3827. How many eyes does a bee have?

3828. How much does a baby giraffe weigh at birth?

3829. What planet has the greatest number of known satellites?

3830. What is believed to be the largest of all the world's creatures with no backbone?

3831. How many domestic silkworm cocoons does it take to make a man's tie?

3816. *Six. The antlers drop off at the end of each mating season and usually gain a point every time they grow back.*

3817. *The Affenpinscher. In German, affe means "monkey" and pinscher means "terrier."*

3818. *The raccoon family.*

3819. *At 150°F (or 70°C). At sea level, the boiling point of water is 212°F (100°C). As you get higher, the atmospheric pressure drops, and with it the boiling point of water.*

3820. *The Jack Russell. It's named for the Rev. John Russell.*

3821. *The bone graft.*

3822. *Six plastic owls.*

3823. *The beaver. The porcupine is second.*

3824. *Over a body of water. He wrote: "You will experiment with this instrument on a lake, so that in falling you will come to no harm."*

3825. *The sloth, which has to sun itself daily to raise its body temperature so the bacteria in its stomach is warm enough to break down the leaves it eats. It often takes up to 100 hours to digest a stomachful of food.*

3826. *33 feet.*

3827. *Five. The two large compound eyes on either side of its head are complex visual organs; the three ocelli (primitive eyes) on top of its head are believed to primarily detect light intensity.*

3828. *About 150 pounds—and it's about 6 feet tall.*

3829. *Saturn, with 20. Close behind are Jupiter, with 16, and Uranus, with 15.*

3830. *The giant squid.*

3831. *110. It takes 630 to make a blouse.*

3832. What was the original purpose of ENIAC, the world's first "modern" computer?

3833. What gives the mineral turquoise its distinctive color?

3834. What creature was named walckvogel—"disgusting bird"— by the Dutch explorers who first spotted it in 1598?

3835. What percentage of the average human brain is water?

3836. What does eccentricity mean to an astronomer?

3837. What was the first human organ to be successfully transplanted?

3838. What is alloyed with steel to make it stainless?

3839. How long—in feet—is the trunk of the average full-grown elephant?

3840. An average human has 46 chromosomes. How many does a cabbage have?

3841. Which planet weighs over twice as much as all the other known planets combined?

3842. How many inkblots are on the standard Rorschach test?

3843. How many pounds of fish can a pelican hold in its pouch?

3844. On an average day, how many hours does an elephant spend sleeping? How about a giraffe?

3845. How fast—in miles per hour—do the fastest messages transmitted by the human nervous system travel?

3846. Some armadillos give birth to duodecuplets. How many offspring is that?

3847. What parts of the oleander plant are toxic?

3848. On average, how many peas are there in a pod?

3832. *To compute ballistic trajectories for artillery shells. ENIAC—an acronym for Electronic Numerical Integrator and Calculator—was introduced in 1946.*

3833. *Traces of copper.*

3834. *The flightless and now-extinct dodo. The Dutch saw it on the island of Mauritius.*

3835. *80 percent.*

3836. *The degree to which an orbit deviates from a circle. The eccentricity of Earth's orbit is 0.017 (or 0.016722, to be more precise).*

3837. *The kidney. Dr. Richard H. Lawler performed the transplant in 1956 in Chicago. His patient, Ruth Tucker, lived for five years with her new kidney.*

3838. *Chromium.*

3839. *8 feet.*

3840. *18.*

3841. *Jupiter, the largest planet in our solar system.*

3842. *10.*

3843. *About 25 pounds.*

3844. *Four hours for both.*

3845. *180 to 200 mph.*

3846. *12.*

3847. *All parts. The seeds of the ornamental bush are usually the most toxic, the leaves a little less and the flowers least—but still dangerous. Even the stems are toxic.*

3848. *Seven to nine.*

3849. How many frames—or pictures—per second are transmitted over American television?

3850. In years past what was used as transmission oil in Rolls-Royce automobiles?

3851. What breed of dog is particularly distinctive because of a genetic condition called achondroplasia?

3852. How many pointers were there on the first clocks with hands—made in the fourteenth century?

3853. What temperature does the tungsten filament in an electric light reach when the light is turned on?

3854. What bird has been spotted flying at 27,000 feet—higher than any other bird on record?

3855. An estimated five million Americans suffer from a recurring ailment known as SAD. For what is SAD an acronym?

3856. Why did German scientist Wilhelm Roentgen name the invisible rays he discovered X-rays?

3857. How small is a pygmy right whale?

3858. Who, long before Columbus, claimed the world was round, reasoning that if it were flat all the stars would be visible from all points on its surface?

3859. When did American sales of cassette recordings surpass those of long-playing records?

3860. What product was originally called the Soundabout when it was introduced in the U.S. in 1979?

3861. The wild pomegranate is said to contain as many seeds as there are commandments in the Old Testament. How many is that?

3862. What are zygodactyl feet?

3849. *30.*

3850. *Spermaceti oil—from the sperm whale.*

3851. *The dachshund. Achondroplasia causes dwarfism—in the dachshund's case, abnormally short legs.*

3852. *Only one—to tell the hour. Minute and second hands were added in the sixteenth and seventeenth centuries.*

3853. *2,577°C (4,664°F).*

3854. *The whooper swan. A flock of 30 was spotted by a pilot and picked up on radar at that altitude in 1967.*

3855. *Seasonal affective disorder. It's a wintertime syndrome that can be treated with light.*

3856. *Because he had no idea what the mysterious rays were.*

3857. *It's about 16 feet long.*

3858. *Aristotle, who offered as added proof the fact that the earth casts a spherical shadow on the moon during an eclipse.*

3859. *Eight years ago, in 1983.*

3860. *The Sony Walkman. It was called the Stowaway in England.*

3861. *613.*

3862. *Feet with two toes pointing forward and two pointing backward—which birds such as parakeets, parrots and woodpeckers have.*

3863. What do the letters represent in the acronym DNA—the protein substance inside each cell that transmits genetic information from parent to child?

3864. What is the larva of the ant lion called?

3865. How long does a nanosecond last?

3866. What animal is the source of the luxuriously soft wool known as cashmere?

3867. What are the berries that grow on the hawthorn tree called?

3868. What percentage of the world's food crops are pollinated by insects?

3869. What is the difference between a crawfish and a crayfish?

3870. If you're selecting a three-course meal from a menu that offers four appetizers, seven entrées and three desserts, how many different meals can you order?

3871. How many different chemical reactions occur in the normal human brain every second?

3872. Which is larger, a crocodile's egg or a duck's egg?

3873. In mathematics, what is the meaning of the term googol?

3874. What word defines sounds too low for human hearing?

3875. What reptile, according to ancient legend, was able to live in fire?

3876. How many eyes do most spiders have?

3877. Where are the grasshopper's "eardrums" located?

3878. How did the bird known as the Baltimore oriole get its name?

3879. How did the element strontium—also known by the symbol Sr and the atomic number 38—get its name?

3863. *Deoxyribonucleic acid.*

3864. *A doodlebug.*

3865. *One billionth of a second*

3866. *The Kashmir goat, which lives in mountainous regions of Kashmir (in India), China and Iran.*

3867. *Haws.*

3868. *80 percent.*

3869. *Nothing. Both names apply to the same freshwater crustacean.*

3870. *84 (that's 4 × 7 × 3).*

3871. *At least 100,000.*

3872. *They're about the same size—around three inches long.*

3873. *It represents the number 1 followed by 100 zeroes—or 10^{100}.*

3874. *Infrasonic.*

3875. *The salamander.*

3876. *Eight.*

3877. *Either on its forelegs or at the base of its abdomen, depending on the type of grasshopper.*

3878. *From its colors, orange and black—the same as those on the heraldic coat of arms of the House of Baltimore, the family that founded the colony of Maryland and gave the city of Baltimore its name.*

3879. *From Strontian, the Scottish mining village in which it was discovered.*

3880. What reply did newspaper tycoon William Randolph Hearst receive when he sent a telegram to a leading astronomer asking, "Is there life on Mars? Please cable one thousand words"?

3881. How many miles of arteries, capillaries and veins are there in the adult human body?

3882. What do beavers eat?

3883. How many pounds of lunar rock and soil were collected and brought back to Earth from America's six expeditions to the moon?

3884. What is the average lifespan of a human being's tastebud?

3885. What planet is most like earth in size, mass, density and gravity?

3886. Berkshire, Cheshire, Victoria and Poland China are breeds of what animal?

3887. What percentage of its body weight does the average bear lose during hibernation?

3888. What is the name of the computer program developed by the Los Angeles Police Department to help solve homicides?

3889. In the original Hippocratic oath, by whom did the individual doctor swear to uphold the standards of professional behavior?

3890. What do the bacteria Lactobacillus bulgaricus and Streptococcus thermophilus have in common?

3891. What heavenly bodies have astronomers named after Brahms, Beethoven, Bach, the four Beatles and Eric Clapton— among others?

3892. Where are sea horses hatched?

3893. What animal is believed to limit its breeding to Macquarie Island, the rocky crest of a submerged South Pacific mountain?

3894. How many pairs of legs does a shrimp have?

3880. *"Nobody knows"—repeated 500 times.*

3881. *62,000.*

3882. *The bark of hardwood trees, leaves, and aquatic and shore plants. Beavers are vegetarians—and do not eat fish, as is widely believed.*

3883. *841.6.*

3884. *From 7 to 10 days.*

3885. *Venus.*

3886. *The pig.*

3887. *Up to 25 percent.*

3888. *HITMAN—for Homicide Information Tracking Management Automation Network.*

3889. *Apollo.*

3890. *Both must be present in a product for it to be labeled yogurt under U.S. Food and Drug Administration regulations.*

3891. *Asteroids.*

3892. *In a pouch on the male parent's belly. Eggs are deposited there by the female.*

3893. *The royal penguin.*

3894. *Five.*

3895. What is the difference between poultry and fowl?

3896. The winter sleep of bears and other animals in cold climates is known as hibernation. What do we call the summer sleep of desert snails and other creatures in excessively warm or dry climates?

3897. How many eyes—or eye spots—do most starfish have?

3898. Fish travel in schools; what about whales?

3899. How many muscles are there in an elephant's trunk?

3900. How many beats per second does a bumblebee flap its wings?

3901. How long is a day on Mars?

3902. What distance can the average healthy slug cover in a day?

3903. Even with leap year, the average year is about 26 seconds longer than Earth's orbital period. How many years will it take for those seconds to build up into a single day?

3904. How many watts are there in one horsepower of energy?

3905. How many calories are consumed during an hour of typing?

3906. What bird is the only one to have nostrils at the tip of its bill?

3907. How many hairs does the average human scalp contain?

3908. Which celebrated chemist-inventor is credited with developing plywood?

3909. Do peacocks give birth to their young or do they lay eggs?

3910. What is the only food a koala bear will eat?

3911. What is cosmology?

3912. In the days when British sailors were given lime or lemon juice to prevent scurvy, what were Dutch sailors given?

3895. *Poultry is domesticated fowl.*

3896. *Estivation.*

3897. *Five—one at the tip of each of its arms.*

3898. *They get together in gams, or pods.*

3899. *100,000.*

3900. *160.*

3901. *24 hours, 37 minutes and 22 seconds.*

3902. *50 yards. Slug races generally are held on a 1-yard course.*

3903. *3,323.*

3904. *746.*

3905. *110—just 30 more an hour than the number consumed while sleeping.*

3906. *The kiwi.*

3907. *Between 120,000 and 150,000.*

3908. *Alfred Nobel, the inventor of dynamite and subsequent founder of the Nobel Prize.*

3909. *Neither—a peacock is male, but a peahen lays eggs.*

3910. *The leaves of the eucalyptus tree.*

3911. *The study of the origin and structure of the universe.*

3912. *Sauerkraut—or zourkool, as they called it.*

3913. How many milligrams of sodium are there in a teaspoon of salt?

3914. How many bones are there in the human wrist?

3915. To what plant family do the radish and turnip belong?

3916. What part of the poison hemlock plant is deadly?

3917. What are the colors of a primary rainbow, from inside to outside?

3918. In the world of fruit, what is the rag?

3919. What famous scientist was the first to figure out how to gauge the tidal effects of the moon and sun and how to calculate the exact path of a comet?

3920. How many toes does a rhinoceros have on each foot?

3921. What are the durian, cherimoya and mangosteen?

3922. To what plant family do rosemary, oregano, thyme and marjoram belong?

3923. A group of lions is a pride; a group of elephants, a herd; what is a group of leopards?

3924. What poisonous weed gets it name from a historic American village?

3925. What is a scalene triangle?

3926. How many miles of nerves are there in the adult human body?

3927. What diameter does a drop of liquid precipitation have to reach to graduate from drizzle to rain?

3928. How fast do microwaves travel?

3929. How many pints of air per minute does the average adult use during normal quiet breathing?

3913. *Approximately 2,000.*

3914. *Eight.*

3915. *The mustard family.*

3916. *All parts—the flowers, seeds, leaves, stem and roots.*

3917. *Violet, indigo, blue, green, yellow, orange and red.*

3918. *The white fibrous membrane inside the skin and around the sections of citrus fruit.*

3919. *Sir Isaac Newton.*

3920. *Three—encased in a hoof.*

3921. *Exotic fruits.*

3922. *The mint family.*

3923. *A leap.*

3924. *Jimson weed—which is a corruption of its original name, Jamestown weed, which was named for Jamestown, Virginia.*

3925. *A triangle with unequal sides and angles.*

3926. *45.*

3927. *It's a raindrop if it's over .02 inch in diameter.*

3928. *186,282 miles per second—the speed of light—as do all kinds of electromagnetic radiation including radio waves, infrared rays, visible light, ultraviolet light and X-rays.*

3929. *Almost 13 pints, or 6 liters.*

3930. For what therapeutic purpose have physicians used green blowfly maggots?

3931. How much farther from Earth does the moon's orbit move every year?

3932. What word was spelled out in the first neon sign?

3933. By definition, what is the lifting capacity of one unit of horsepower?

3934. What earthly creature has four "noses" and 3,000 tiny teeth?

3935. A beehive produces between 100 and 200 pounds of honey a year. How much does a single worker honeybee manufacture in its lifetime?

3936. How long does it take a whole fingernail to replace itself?

3937. How fast per second does Earth travel in its orbit around the sun?

3938. What is on the daily menu for an adult hippopotamus at the National Zoo in Washington, D.C.?

3939. How many toes does an ostrich have?

3940. What do you call the little bits of paper left over when holes are punched in data cards or tape?

3941. What part of the human body is named for its resemblance to the sea horse?

3942. How many eggs at a time do the most productive starfish release?

3943. How fast does the sound of thunder travel per second?

3944. How did the fish known as the guppy get its name?

3945. How many meteorites hit the earth each year?

3930. *To cleanse wounds. The maggots eat decaying flesh and release a natural antibiotic. This practice was most widely used during World War I.*

3931. *About 1.5 inches. Scientists believe the moon has been inching away from Earth for billions of years.*

3932. *Neon. The small bright red sign was created by Dr. Perley G. Nutting, a government scientist, and exhibited at the 1904 Louisiana Purchase Exposition in St. Louis, Missouri—15 years before neon signs became widely used commercially.*

3933. *The ability to raise 33,000 pounds one foot high in one minute.*

3934. *The slug.*

3935. *¹/₁₂ teaspoon.*

3936. *About three months. Our nails grow about 0.1 mm (.004 inch) per day.*

3937. *18.5 miles per second.*

3938. *About 10 pounds of kale, 3 gallons of high-protein cereal pellets and ¾ bale of alfalfa hay.*

3939. *Four—two on each of its feet.*

3940. *Chad.*

3941. *The hippocampus—the ridge along each lateral ventricle of the brain. Hippocampus is Latin for "sea horse."*

3942. *Up to 2.5 million.*

3943. *About 1,100 feet.*

3944. *From the man who discovered it and presented specimens to the British Museum—naturalist R . J .L. Guppy of Trinidad.*

3945. *About 500—most of them go unrecorded, falling into oceans, deserts and other uninhabited areas.*

3946. How often does the epidermis, the outer layer of our skin, replace itself?

3947. Modern computer chips consist of millions of transistors. How many transistors were on the first chips made in 1958?

3948. In 1988 what did a panel of 10 international design experts pick as the best-designed product costing less than $5?

3949. In computerese, what does wysiwyg mean?

3950. Before surgical dressings of gauze and cotton were introduced, what was commonly used to cover wounds in American hospitals?

3951. How did the magnolia get its name?

3952. To what plant family does the asparagus belong?

3953. What is a group of rhinoceroses called?

3954. What is the only member of the cat family that does not have retractable claws?

3955. Noble Prize-winning missionary Dr. Albert Schweitzer had a pet named Parsifal. What kind of animal was it?

3956. There are an estimated 10 trillion stars in our galaxy, the Milky Way. How many are visible to the naked eye from the earth?

3957. What is a geoduck?

3958. How can you tell the sex of a horse by its teeth?

3959. What animal is believed to have the best hearing?

3960. From what language do we get the two scientific terms used to describe hardened lava fields: aa and pahoehoe?

3961. What was the first human organ to be successfully transplanted?

3946. *About once every four weeks.*

3947. *Just two.*

3948. *The eightpenny finishing nail.*

3949. *It's shorthand for what you see is what you get.*

3950. *Pressed sawdust.*

3951. *From French botanist Pierre Magnol, who introduced it.*

3952. *It's a member of the lily family—as are the onion and garlic.*

3953. *A crash.*

3954. *The cheetah.*

3955. *A pelican.*

3956. *About 6,000.*

3957. *A large clam.*

3958. *Most males have 40 teeth; most females 36.*

3959. *The barn owl—even though its ears can't be seen. Its face is dish-shaped, enabling the owl to receive sounds like sonar.*

3960. *Hawaiian. Aa is lava that is rough and jumbled; pahoehoe is lava that is smooth and wavy.*

3961. *The kidney. Dr. Richard H. Lawler performed the transplant in 1956 in Chicago. His patient, Ruth Tucker, lived for five years with her new kidney.*

3962. How many pounds per day does a baby blue whale gain during its first seven months of life?

3963. What is the "lead" in a lead pencil?

3964. Why is the small shorebird Americans know as the red phalarope called the grey phalarope in England?

3965. By what popular name do we know the fluorine-based compound polytetrafluoro-ethylene, or PTFE?

3966. How many toes does a giraffe have on each foot?

3967. Where are a butterfly's tastebuds located?

3968. What popular dog was originally known as a waterside terrier?

3969. How long is the tongue of the giant anteater of South America?

3970. What is a horse called before it reaches age one and becomes a yearling?

3971. How long is the average adult's spinal cord?

3972. What bacterium is named for German pediatrician Theodor Escherich?

3973. What six elements make up over 95 percent of all living material?

3974. If a carnivore is a meat-eating animal, what's a frugivore?

3975. At what wind speed does a snowstorm become a blizzard?

3976. What part of a horse's anatomy is known as a stifle?

3977. Which is the largest order of mammals, with about 1,700 species?

3962. *At least 200 pounds. A baby blue whale—which is about 22 feet long at birth—grows 29 feet longer in its first seven months.*

3963. *Graphite and clay. Lead pencils never contained lead—but graphite was originally thought to be a type of lead.*

3964. *The bird is named for its summer plummage in America; for its winter plummage in England.*

3965. *Teflon.*

3966. *Two.*

3967. *On its legs. They are microscopic hairs, called sensilla, on the terminal part of the butterfly's legs.*

3968. *The airdale. It was renamed when a judge at the Airdale Agriculture Society Show in Bingley, Yorkshire—in the valley of the Aire River—suggested another name be found for the locally bred dog.*

3969. *22 to 24 inches. It uses its tongue to lap up ants—about 35,000 a day.*

3970. *A weanling. It remains a weanling until its first birthday, which is always on January 1.*

3971. *From 17 to 18 inches. It weight, minus membranes and nerves, is about 1½ ounces.*

3972. **E.** *coli. The E is for Escherichia, after its discoverer, who first identified the bacteria in 1885 and called it Bacterium coli commune. It was give its current name in 1919.*

3973. *Carbon, hydrogen, nitrogen, oxygen, phosphorus and sulfur.*

3974. *A fruit eater.*

3975. *In excess of 35 miles an hour.*

3976. *The joint on the hind leg—between the femur and the tibia—that corresponds anatomically to a human's knee. It's also know as the stifle joint.*

3977. *Rodents. Bats are second, with about 950 species.*

3978. How many vertebrae does a human being have?

3979. What is the body's largest organ—by weight?

3980. In the world of horses, what's a palomilla?

3981. What are the only two types of mammals that are poisonous?

3982. How many seeds from the giant sequoia tree—the most massive of all living things—are there in an ounce?

3983. Which is the longest muscle in the human body?

3984. How many mosquito-size insects is the one-ounce brown bat—the most common bat in North America—capable of eating in an hour of nighttime dining?

3985. What form of precipitation generally falls only from cumulonimbus clouds?

3986. What part of the body is the Brannock device used to measure?

3987. How wide an angle is the average person's field of vision?

3988. In what country did the French poodle originate?

3989. What mammal has the heaviest brain?

3990. What is your buccal cavity?

3991. How fast—in miles per hour—can a crocodile move on land? How about in water?

3992. How many times brighter is a full moon than a half moon?

3993. What does a mellivorous bird eat?

3994. With the exception of the whale, what animal has the largest mouth?

3978. 33—7 cervical, 12 thoracic (or dorsal), 5 lumbar, 5 sacral, and 4 caudal (or coccygeal).

3979. The lungs. Together they weigh about 42 ounces. The right lung is two ounces heavier than the left, and the male's lungs are heavier than the female's.

3980. A milk-white horse with white mane and tail.

3981. Shrews and platypuses. Some shrews have slightly poisonous bites, and male platypuses have poisonous spurs on their hind legs.

3982. 8,000. The seeds are ¼ inch long. The largest giant sequoia in existence, the General Sherman, is in California's Sequoia National Park.

3983. The sartorius, which runs from the pelvis across the front of the thigh to the top of the tibia below the knee.

3984. About 500.

3985. Hail. Cumulonimbus clouds are heavy, swelling, vertically developed clouds.

3986. The foot. It's the device used in shoe stores to determine your shoe size.

3987. About 200 degrees.

3988. In Germany, where it was known as the pudel, from a word meaning "to splash in the water." In France, it's known as the caniche, which is derived from "duck dog." Its Latin name is canis familiaris aquatius.

3989. The sperm whale. Its brain weighs up to 20 pounds—six times heavier than a human's.

3990. The inside of your mouth.

3991. On land, up to 30 mph; in water, 20.

3992. 10 times.

3993. Honey. Mell comes from a Greek word for "honey."

3994. The hippopotamus.

3995. How much does the skeleton of the average 160-pound body weigh?

3996. Pine wood ignites at 800°F. At what temperature does charcoal ignite?

3997. What creature produces sperm that are ⅔ inch long—the longest in the world?

3998. What planet's moon is the largest satellite in our solar system?

3999. How did scientist Louis Pasteur make sure the food he was served at the homes of his friends was safe to eat?

4000. Where in the human body is the only bone that is not connected to another bone?

4001. How can you tell a fish's age?

4002. What is the first bird mentioned in the Bible?

4003. What animal's skin is the source of true moroccan leather?

4004. How did the skeleton of the more-than-three-million-year-old female hominid discovered in Ethiopia in 1974 come to be called Lucy?

4005. What unpopular bird's Latin name is Sturnus vulgaris?

4006. What mammal is the only living member of its order?

4007. What two types of dogs were crossed to create the whippet?

4008. What is the only land mammal native to New Zealand?

4009. How fast can a sailfish swim—in miles per hour?

3995. *About 29 pounds.*

3996. *580°F.*

3997. *Some fruit flies of the genus Drosophila. Their sperm, more than 300 times longer than human sperm, are six times longer than the fly itself—but hair-thin and all balled up.*

3998. *Jupiter's moon Ganymede.*

3999. *He checked it with a portable microscope he carried with him.*

4000. *In the throat, at the back of the tongue. It's the horseshoe-shaped hyoid bone, which supports the tongue and its muscles. Also known as the lingual bone, it is suspended by ligaments from the base of the skull.*

4001. *From the number of growth rings on each of its scales. Each pair of rings represents a year—the dark narrow rings represent winter; the wider, lighter rings represent summer.*

4002. *The raven. It appears in Genesis 8:7, when it is sent out from the ark by Noah to see if the flood waters have abated.*

4003. *The goat.*

4004. *Donald Johanson, the anthropologist who found the skeleton, and his colleagues were listening to the Beatles' song "Lucy in the Sky with Diamonds" while they were discussing and celebrating the discovery—and they started referring to the skeleton by that name.*

4005. *The common, or European, starling, which is held in low esteem by bird-watchers because it takes the nest of domestic songbirds, and by farmers because it often damages fruit and grain crops.*

4006. *The aardvark. Its order is Tubulidentata*

4007. *The greyhound and the terrier.*

4008. *The bat.*

4009. *More than 60 mph, faster than any other known fish. Humans have been recorded swimming up to 5.19 mph.*

4010. What is the main food of mosquitoes?

4011. What wind speed does a storm have to exceed to be given a name by the National Hurricane Center?

4012. What plant's name—derived from the French—means "lion's tooth"?

4013. How many times per second does a mosquito beat its wings?

4014. What is the only female deer to grow antlers?

4015. What physical symptom is exhibited by those who suffer from blepharospasms?

4016. What does the chemical symbol Fe2O3 represent?

4017. A female pig is called a sow; what is a male pig called?

4018. How many legs does a spider have?

4019. How many true vocal cords does a normal person have?

4020. What is the wrinkled flesh that hangs from the neck of a turkey called?

4021. If the angles of a pentagon are equal, what are they—in degrees?

4022. Where in the world are you most likely to find lemurs in the wild?

4023. Where on the human face is there a muscle know as the corrugator?

4024. Before the advent of electricity, how did theatrical companies put their stars in the spotlight?

4025. What was the "dephlogisticated air" discovered by English scientist Joseph Priestley in 1774?

4026. What is the average minimum speed in miles per hour needed for a bird to remain aloft?

4010. *Nectar from flowers, not your blood. The blood we lose to mosquitoes—females only—is needed for protein to help them lay their eggs.*

4011. *39 mph.*

4012. *The dandelion. In French it's called dente de lion, for the toothlike points on its leaves.*

4013. *Up to 600.*

4014. *The reindeer.*

4015. *Uncontrollable winking.*

4016. *Rust.*

4017. *A boar. A baby is a piglet.*

4018. *Eight—four pairs, which is one of the features that distinguishes a spider from an insect, which has three pairs of legs.*

4019. *Two. They are called true (or inferior) vocal cords and are involved in the production of sound. We also have a pair of false (or superior) vocal cords that have no direct role in producing the voice.*

4020. *The wattle.*

4021. *108 degrees. Such a pentagon is called a regular pentagon.*

4022. *In Madagascar.*

4023. *On the forehead. It's the muscle that contract the forehead into wrinkles and pulls the eyebrows together.*

4024. *Lime was burned in a lamp, creating an intense white light that was directed at featured performers—and giving us the word limelight.*

4025. *Oxygen. At the time phlogiston was believed to be a chemical released during combustion.*

4026. *11 mph—or 16½ feet per second.*

4027. What planet has surface winds that have been measured at 1,500 mph—the strongest in the solar system?

4028. How many of an adult domestic cat's 30 teeth are canines?

4029. How much coal does it take to get the same amount of energy provided by burning one full cord of seasoned firewood?

4030. How tall is a baby giraffe at birth?

4031. How are all the workers of an African driver ant colony, numbering around 22 million, related?

4032. On what planet is the largest known mountain in the solar system?

4033. How fast can an ostrich run?

4034. How was the Tonkinese breed of cat developed?

4035. What animal's name means "earth pig"?

4036. If you hear thunder 10 seconds after you see lightning, how far away was the lightning?

4037. What was Sigmund Freud's fee—in U.S. dollars—for one session of psychoanalysis in 1925?

4038. How many bones are there in the human skull?

4039. How much does an adult giraffe's heart weigh?

4040. How many newborn opossums can fit in a teaspoon?

4041. How many constellations are there?

4042. The name of what flower means "fleshlike"?

4043. What part of the human body is the axilla?

4044. What is a diadromous fish?

4027. *Neptune.*

4028. *4. The cat also has 12 incisors, 10 premolars and 4 molars.*

4029. *One ton.*

4030. *About 6 feet.*

4031. *They're all sisters—although they have different fathers.*

4032. *On Mars. Called Olympus Mons, it's a volcano more than three times the height of Mount Everest.*

4033. *About 40 miles per hour—taking strides of 12 to 15 feet.*

4034. *By crossing a Burmese with a Siamese.*

4035. *The aardvark's—in the Afrikaans language.*

4036. *2 miles away. Sound travels about a mile in 5 seconds.*

4037. *$25—adjusted for inflation, that would be about $160 today.*

4038. *29—the cranium has 8; the face, 15 (including the lower jaw); the ears, 6.*

4039. *About 25 pounds. It's 2 feet long, with walls up to 3 inches thick. It has quite a job pumping blood to the brain—which is sometimes 12 feet above the heart.*

4040. *About 24. They're very small—about .07 ounce each—at birth.*

4041. *100,000.*

4042. *The carnation, which was named for a rosy pink color developed by artists during the sixteenth century. The first carnations were that color. In Latin, carnis means "flesh."*

4043. *The armpit.*

4044. *A fish—such as salmon or sturgeon—that can exist in both salt water and fresh water.*

4045. How many sweat glands are there on the skin of the average adult human being?

4046. How many toes does a pig have on each of its feet?

4047. The average adult takes 14 breaths a minute; how many does an infant take?

4048. How much horsepower does the typical horse provide?

4049. How fast can a swordfish swim?

4050. What animal has the largest eyes—each a foot or more in diameter?

4051. What contribution did Sarah Nelmes make to medicine in 1796?

4052. What are the odds of having an ear of corn with an odd number of rows of kernels?

4053. What is the gestation period for an elephant?

4054. What is the largest deer in the world?

4055. From where in nature do we get quinine, the medicine used to treat and prevent malaria?

4056. How much syrup does the average sugar maple tree yield each season?

4057. What animal, traveling at an average ground speed of six to eight feet per minute, is the slowest moving land mammal?

4058. In Space Age lingo, what is LOX?

4059. Which has more cervical vertebrae—a mouse, a man or a giraffe?

4060. How many average-size houses can you make from one giant sequoia—the biggest living thing on earth today?

4061. What bird strays as far as 2,500 miles from its nest to find food for its young?

4045. *More than 2 million—an estimated 2,381,248, according to Gray's Anatomy.*

4046. *Four—two of which touch the ground.*

4047. *33.*

4048. *About 24. Horsepower is the power needed to lift 33,000 pounds 1 foot in 1 minute. Scientists came up with the 24 horsepower figure based on a horse weighing about 1,320 pounds.*

4049. *More than 60 miles an hour. It and the sailfish are the fastest swimming fish.*

4050. *The giant squid. The largest creature without a backbone, it weighs up to 2.5 tons and grows up to 55 feet long.*

4051. *Edward Jenner used her cowpox lesions for the first smallpox vaccination.*

4052. *Zero. There are always an even number of rows.*

4053. *From 20 to 22 months. Baby weighs in at about 200 pounds.*

4054. *The Alaska bull moose, which has been known to reach a shoulder height of 7½ feet and a weight of up to 1,800 pounds.*

4055. *From the bark of the cinchona tree, a South American evergreen.*

4056. *One to one and a quarter quarts.*

4057. *The three-toed sloth, which spends 18 hours of every day sleeping.*

4058. *Liquid oxygen, a component of rocket fuel.*

4059. *All have the same number, seven.*

4060. *Fifty. The sequoia often exceeds 300 feet in height and 25 feet in diameter. Its seed weighs only ¹⁄₆₀₀₀ ounce.*

4061. *The albatross, which has the largest wingspan of any living bird—over 11 feet.*

4062. How old is the average 1½-pound lobster?

4063. What is the lightest substance known to science?

4064. What makes flamingos pink?

4065. How many muscles does a caterpillar have?

4066. The swallows traditionally return to San Juan Capistrano, California, on March 19. What birds return to Hinckley, Ohio, four days earlier?

4067. How did a Nebraska mule named Krause make news, first in 1984 and again in 1985?

4068. How many times a day does the average human heart beat?

4069. How many bones does the average human adult have?

4070. How many muscles do we use when we smile broadly?

4071. You get a geep when you cross what two animals?

4072. What is the world's tallest grass, which sometimes grows 130 feet or more?

4073. What is the only pouched animal found in North America—and the only one not found in Australia?

4074. In what direction do most cyclones whirl?

4075. What is the ermine known as during its off-seasons, when its fur isn't white?

4076. How many leaves does the average mature oak tree shed in the fall?

4077. What part of the human body is called the atlas?

4078. Who was the first person known to have died of radiation poisoning?

4079. What is the only breed of dog to have a black, rather than pink, tongue?

4062. *About 8 years old. If it avoids the lobster trap, it can live to about 50 and weigh up to 35 pounds.*

4063. *The element hydrogen, with a specific gravity of 0.0695 compared to air. Helium is the second lightest with a specific gravity of 0.139.*

4064. *Canthaxantin, a Vitamin A-like chemical found in the soda lakes where they feed. Away from the lakes, flamingos turn white.*

4065. *Four thousand—more than five times as many as a human.*

4066. *The turkey buzzards.*

4067. *Although mules are almost always infertile, Krause gave birth to baby mules in both years. Each birth was a billion-to-one shot.*

4068. *About 100,000—to pump five quarts of blood every minute.*

4069. *Two hundred and six.*

4070. *Seventeen.*

4071. *A sheep and a goat. Some prefer to call it a shoat.*

4072. *Bamboo.*

4073. *The opossum.*

4074. *Clockwise in the Southern Hemisphere; counterclockwise in the Northern Hemisphere.*

4075. *The short-tailed weasel, also known as a stoat.*

4076. *About 700,000.*

4077. *The first vertebra of the neck, which holds up your head—just as Atlas held up the world.*

4078. *Two-time Nobel Prize-winner Marie Curie.*

4079. *The chow.*

4080. What expensive fur do we get from an aquatic cat-sized rodent with orange teeth called the coypu?

4081. What element is named after a state?

4082. How long does it take light from the sun to travel to earth, a distance of about 93,000,000 miles?

4083. What part of the human body has the thinnest skin?

4084. Which is the only bird that can fly backward?

4085. An animal named Louise has helped West German police sniff out narcotics, explosives and other contraband. What kind of animal is she?

4086. What temperature do honey bees maintain in their hives year-round?

4087. How many bones are there in your big toe?

4088. What are the only two mammals that lay eggs rather than give birth to live offspring?

4089. How many teeth are there in our first set of teeth—our baby teeth?

4090. What important point did Scottish mathematician John Napier come up with in the early seventeenth century?

4091. What was the name of the first computer used for weather research?

4092. When is Halley's comet, first observed in 240 B.C. and last seen in 1986, expected to appear again?

4093. How much does the blue whale, the world's largest mammal, weigh at birth?

4094. For what operation was Antonio de Egas Moniz of Portugal awarded the Nobel Prize in medicine in 1949?

4095. How tall is a newborn giraffe?

4080. *Nutria.*

4081. *Californium, first produced in 1950 by scientists at the University of California at Berkeley.*

4082. *About eight minutes.*

4083. *The eyelid—it's less than ¹/₅₀₀ inch thick.*

4084. *The tiny hummingbird.*

4085. *A wild boar.*

4086. *An even 94 °F.*

4087. *Fourteen, the same as in your other toes.*

4088. *The duck-billed platypus and the spiny anteater.*

4089. *Twenty. Our second set has 32.*

4090. *The decimal point.*

4091. *MANIAC—an acronym for Mathematical Analyzer, Numerical Integrator and Computer.*

4092. *In the year 2061.*

4093. *Two tons. Fully grown, it will weigh as much as 150 tons.*

4094. *The now-discredited prefrontal lobotomy.*

4095. *Five and a half feet, head to hoof.*

4096. Do identical twins have identical fingerprints?

4097. What bird has the longest nestling life—taking up to nine months to fly?

4098. In geology, what is calving?

4099. What common chemical compound is represented by the formula NH3?

4100. In the animal kingdom, what is a glutton?

4101. How did the tarantula get its name?

4102. What is the name of the protein—the most abundant in the human body—that holds our skin together?

4103. How much saliva does the average human produce daily?

4104. How long are the antlers of the pudu, the smallest deer in the world?

4105. How many muscles are there in the human ear?

4106. What kind of creature do Australians call the tasseled wobbegong?

4107. How many teeth does a turtle have?

4108. What color are the eggs laid by the flightless emu, the largest bird alive today after the ostrich?

4109. What is the world's largest living fish?

4110. How many calories do hibernating bears burn daily?

4111. What is the average lifespan of a red blood cell in the normal human body?

4112. How many bones are there in the human hand?

4113. What is N2O—nitrous oxide—more commonly called?

4096. *No. No two sets of prints are alike, including those of identical twins.*

4097. *The wandering albatross.*

4098. *The breaking off or detachment of an iceberg from a glacier that has reached the sea, or the separation of a portion of a floating iceberg.*

4099. *Ammonia.*

4100. *A wolverine.*

4101. *From the Italian seaport city of Taranto, where the hairy, venomous wolf spider once abounded.*

4102. *Collagen.*

4103. *One quart.*

4104. *They grow to 3 inches long. The pudu, found in northwest and southwest South America, is about 14 inches tall to the shoulders and weighs about 20 pounds.*

4105. *Six.*

4106. *A shark found near Australia's Great Barrier Reef.*

4107. *None—turtles are toothless, although some have sharp, jagged edges on their horny jaws that function as teeth.*

4108. *Green.*

4109. *The harmless whale shark, which reaches up to 50 or more feet in length and weighs up to 20 tons.*

4110. *About 4,000.*

4111. *Four months.*

4112. *27.*

4113. *Laughing gas.*

4114. In what order do most pigs move their legs when walking normally?

4115. How many miles of blood vessels are there in the average human body?

4116. What is the softest mineral known?

4117. What is the largest living invertebrate?

4118. What color is the blood of an octopus?

4119. What is unique about the food-catching technique of the anhinga—also known as the snakebird, darter or water turkey?

4120. What were the first objects in the solar system discovered by means of a telescope?

4121. How many teeth does a normal adult dog have?

4122. How long is a Martian year in Earth days—a year being the length of time it takes the planet to revolve once around the Sun?

4123. How did the quarter horse get its name?

4124. What animal has more teeth than any other North American land mammal?

4125. What two elements comprise almost 100 percent of the matter in the universe?

4126. In the American system of mathematical progressions, what five denominations come after million, billion and trillion?

4127. In costume jewelry, when gold is electroplated to metal, how thick must the layer of gold be?

4128. What is present in the variety of quartz stone known as cat's-eye that gives it its unique glowing appearance?

4129. In what direction does the jet stream flow?

4130. What is the most abundant metallic element in the earth's surface?

4114. *Left front foot first, then right rear foot, right front foot, left rear foot.*

4115. *About 62,000.*

4116. *Talc.*

4117. *The giant squid, which achieves a length of more than 60 feet—tentacles included.*

4118. *Pale bluish-green.*

4119. *It spears fish with its long, straight, sharp bill—the only bird to do so. It has extra cervical vertebrae, which enable it to coil its neck and then release it with viper-like speed.*

4120. *The four largest satellites of Jupiter—Ganymede, Io, Callisto and Europa.*

4121. *42—that's 20 on the upper jaw and 22 on the lower jaw. The adult human has 32, evenly divided between upper and lower jaws.*

4122. *687 days.*

4123. *From its speed in running the quarter mile.*

4124. *The opossum, the only marsupial native to North America. It has 50 teeth.*

4125. *Hydrogen (approximately 75 percent) and helium (approximately 25 percent). The remaining, heavier elements constitute a mere fraction of existence.*

4126. *Quadrillion, quintillion, sextillion, septillion and octillion.*

4127. *At least seven millionths of an inch thick—and the gold must be at least 10-karat.*

4128. *Asbestos fibers. The glow is known as chatoyancy.*

4129. *From west to east.*

4130. *Aluminum—it accounts for an estimated 8 percent of the solid portion of the earth's crust.*

4131. What are the ornamental plumes of the male egret called?

4132. If you traveled at a snail's pace, how much ground would you cover in an hour?

4133. How many fat cells does the average adult have?

4134. Where are the pyramids of Malpighi and the pyramids of Ferrein?

4135. Bovine means cow-like. What does murine mean?

4136. What is a group of foxes called?

4137. A cob is a male swan; a cygnet is a baby. What is the female called?

4138. What is a female rabbit called?

4139. How did the horse chestnut tree get its name?

4140. What tree's name contains all five vowels?

4141. What are amberjack, cusk and pout?

4142. What are Shaggy Mane, Slimy Gomphidius, Inky Cap, Sulphur Top and Pig's Ears?

4143. What is the skin that peels off after a bad sunburn?

4144. What word best describes the snout of a pig?

4145. What is a group of owls called?

4146. What are baby beavers called?

4147. What is a perfusionist's role in a hospital operating room?

4148. There are two atria in the human body—where are they?

4149. What do the letters CAT represent in CAT scan—the three-dimensional composite image that can be taken of body, brain or lungs?

4131. *Aigrettes.*

4132. *25 feet—for a great many species.*

4133. *Between 40 and 50 billion.*

4134. *In the human body—in the kidneys.*

4135. *Mouse-like.*

4136. *A skulk.*

4137. *A pen.*

4138. *A doe. A male is a buck; a baby, a kit or kitten. The act of giving birth is known as kindling.*

4139. *From the early use of its chestnuts as a medicine for horses.*

4140. *The sequoia's.*

4141. *Fish.*

4142. *Mushrooms.*

4143. *Blype.*

4144. *Gruntle.*

4145. *A parliament.*

4146. *Kits or kittens.*

4147. *Running the heart-lung machine during open-heart surgery. The machine keeps the patient's heart pumping while it removes carbon dioxide from the blood and adds oxygen to it.*

4148. *In the heart. They are the two upper chambers (auricles) that receive the blood from the veins and pump it into the two lower chambers (ventricles).*

4149. *Computerized axial tomography.*

4150. What belief was Galileo forced to recant by the Inquisition in 1633?

4151. In astronomy, what is a white dwarf?

4152. Wild turkeys can run at speeds of at least 12 miles an hour. How fast can they fly?

4153. What does the acronym DSB mean to a hospital worker?

4154. What famous naturalist penned a book entitled, *The Formation of Vegetable Mold, Through the Action of Worms, With Observations on Their Habits?*

4155. What was the Calypso, Jacques-Yves Cousteau's ship, before he converted it into an oceanographic research vessel?

4156. Who was the first person to record that the number of rings in the cross section of a tree trunk reveals its age?

4157. What is the meaning of the word "lore" when it's used by an ornithologist?

4158. What's a winkle?

4159. In the world of living things, what are zebus? How about zebubs?

4160. What celestial body got its name from a Greek word meaning "long-haired"?

4161. How many compartments does a normal cow's stomach have?

4162. The discovery of what semiprecious stone often indicates that diamonds are nearby?

4163. To what animal family does the wolverine belong—as its largest member?

4164. Why are Mercury and Venus known as inferior planets?

4150. *That the earth revolved around a stationary sun. He was kept under house arrest for the last eight years of his life for debunking the traditional belief that the earth was the center of the universe.*

4151. *The dense, burned-out remains of a star; a stellar corpse.*

4152. *Up to 55 miles an hour.*

4153. *Drug-seeking behavior. The designation is used for a patient or wannabe patient who is complaining of a bogus ailment in an attempt to get narcotics.*

4154. *Charles Darwin, who is better known for his revolutionary tome,* Origin of the Species. *His book on worms, a pioneering work in the field of quantitative ecology published in 1881, was his last.*

4155. *A minesweeper.*

4156. *Leonardo da Vinci. He also discovered that the width between the rings indicates annual moisture.*

4157. *The space between a bird's eye and its bill.*

4158. *An edible sea snail.*

4159. *Zebus are humped cattle found in India, China and northern Africa; zebubs are tsetse-like flies found in Ethiopia.*

4160. *Comet. The name comes from the Greek* kom(t(s, *an adjective formed from the verb* koman, *"to wear long hair."*

4161. *Four. The rumen, reticulum (storage area), omasum (where water is absorbed), and abomasum (the only compartment with digestive juices).*

4162. *Garnet.*

4163. *The weasel family, Mustelidae.*

4164. *Their orbits are closer to the sun than Earth's orbit. Planets orbiting the sun beyond Earth are referred to as superior planets.*

4165. How much silver must an item contain to be considered sterling?

4166. What system of healing did Canadian-born grocer Daniel David Palmer formally introduce in Davenport, Iowa, in September 1895?

4167. What part of a horse is the pastern?

4168. What is unusual about the tail of the flightless kiwi bird?

4169. What is silviculture?

4170. How many times its own body weight can a worker ant carry?

4171. In Web site addresses on the Internet, what does http stand for?

4172. How many degrees can a great horned owl turn its head?

4165. *92.5 percent.*

4166. *Chiropractic medicine. Although new at the time, the principles upon which chiropractic medicine was based can be traced back to the earliest physicians—including Hippocrates (460-370 B.C.). Palmer created the name "chiropractic" by combining the Greek words for hand, cheir, and practical (or efficient), praktikos.*

4167. *The part of the foot between the fetlock and the hoof.*

4168. *It doesn't exist. The kiwi has no tail feathers.*

4169. *Forestry—the planting of trees for the preservation of forests. The Latin word silva means "forest."*

4170. *Up to 50 times its weight. Worker ants are always female.*

4171. *Hypertext transfer protocol.*

4172. *270 degrees.*

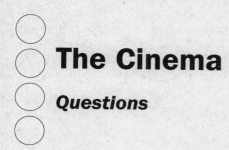

The Cinema

Questions

4173. What well-known Tasmanian-born leading lady launched her entertainment career under the name Queenie O'Brien?

4174. In what country was famous French actor Yves Montand born?

4175. What were the real first names of Beau Brummell and Beau Geste?

4176. What famous character actor prepared for a career in psychiatry—studying and working with pioneer psychoanalysts Sigmund Freud and Alfred Adler—before he turned to performing?

4177. In a charity pantomime performance in 1984, rocker Elton John was featured as "Mother Goose." Who co-starred as the "Egg Yolk"?

4178. Bob Hope and Bing Crosby took movie "roads" to seven destinations. How many can you name?

4179. Who wrote the scripts for his own films under pseudonyms that included Otis T. Criblecoblis and Mahatma Kane Jeeves?

Answers

4173. *Merle Oberon. Born Estelle Merle O'Brien Thompson, she went on to use a variation of her middle names for her professional name.*

4174. *In Italy, as Yvo Livi.*

4175. *Brummell was George; Geste, Michael.*

4176. *Peter Lorre.*

4177. *Sir John Gielgud.*

4178. *Singapore, Zanzibar, Morocco, Utopia, Rio, Bali, and Hong Kong.*

4179. *W. C. Fields.*

4180. What actor—and one-time New York Yankee batboy—portrayed Babe Ruth in the 1948 movie biography of the Sultan of Swat?

4181. What actor's profile was once compared to "the steely prehensile outline of an invariably victorious bottle opener"?

4182. Who provided Mickey Mouse's high-pitched voice in the early Walt Disney films starring the animated mouse?

4183. For what two films did Elizabeth Taylor win best actress Oscars?

4184. Who dubbed Miss Piggy's singing voice in "The Muppet Movie"?

4185. When British film companies buy a product called Kensington Gore, what are they purchasing?

4186. What American actress once described herself as "pure as the driven slush"?

4187. What was the name of the popular Broadway musical that was turned into the 1934 movie *The Gay Divorcée*?

4188. Who said: "A man in love is incomplete until he is married. Then he is finished"?

4189. What film did Ingrid Bergman make twice—first in Swedish and then in English for her Hollywood debut?

4190. What was the only horror film in which Humphrey Bogart appeared?

4191. What color was actor Yul Brynner's hair—when he had hair?

4192. Who was Gene Kelly's unusual dancing partner in an imaginative pas de deux in the 1945 film *Anchors Aweigh*?

4193. What entertainer boxed under the name Kid Crochet as a teenager?

4180. *William Bendix.*

4181. *George C. Scott's. Critic Kenneth Tynan made the comparison.*

4182. *Walt Disney, himself.*

4183. Butterfield 8, *in 1960;* Who's Afraid of Virginia Woolf, *in 1966.*

4184. *Johnny Matthis.*

4185. *Artificial blood, used for special effects.*

4186. *Tallulah Bankhead.*

4187. The Gay Divorce. *The Hollywood censors nixed that title, however, apparently finding it inappropriate to call a divorce happy.*

4188. *Oft-married Zsa Zsa Gabor.*

4189. Intermezzo: A Love Story.

4190. The Return of Dr. X. *Bogart played a zombie in the 1939 film.*

4191. *Dark brown.*

4192. *Jerry, the animated mouse from the* Tom and Jerry *cartoon.*

4193. *Dean Martin, was born Dino Crocetti.*

4194. How old was Shirley Temple when she appeared in her first film, *The Red-Haired Alibi* ?

4195. For what offense was Australian-born *Million Dollar Mermaid* Annette Kellerman, the first aquatic glamour girl, arrested in 1909?

4196. Who played Scorpio, the sadistic killer, in Clint Eastwood's 1971 film, *Dirty Harry* ?

4197. What British actor made his screen debut as a Mexican wearing a blanket in the very first Hopalong Cassidy movie?

4198. Who wrote the screenplay for *The Misfits*, the 1961 film that marked the last screen appearances of both Clark Gable and Marilyn Monroe?

4199. What 1977 movie was originally going to be called *Anhedonia*—a word that means the psychological inability to experience pleasure?

4200. Whose lengthy Oscar acceptance speech prompted the Academy of Motion Picture Arts and Sciences to set a time limit at later award ceremonies?

4201. What was the name of the dolphin that played Flipper in the movies?

4202. What famous American actress made her stage debut in 1966 as a silent Helen of Troy in *Dr. Faustus* ?

4203. In what film did tough guy actor Clint Eastwood first deliver his trademark line, "Make my day"?

4204. What was the first R-rated film produced by the Walt Disney studio?

4205. What was used to simulate blood in the famous shower scene in the 1960 Alfred Hitchcock chiller *Psycho* ?

4206. Comedian W.C. Fields' waterfront summer home in New York City was sold in 1980 so that an existing business could expand. What was the business?

4194. *Three years old.*

4195. *Indecent exposure—for wearing one of her newly created, one-piece bathing suits. The skirtless creation covered her legs all the way down to the calf.*

4196. *Andy Robinson, son of Edward G. Robinson.*

4197. *David Niven, who noted, "Of course they daren't let me open my mouth."*

4198. *Monroe's ex-husband, Pulitzer Prize-winning playwright Arthur Miller.*

4199. *Woody Allen's* Annie Hall.

4200. *Greer Garson's. She said her thanks for 5½ minutes at the 1943 ceremonies when she was honored for her starring role in* Mrs. Miniver.

4201. *Mitzi. For the TV series she was replaced by two other dolphins, Suzy and Cathy.*

4202. *Elizabeth Taylor. Her first speaking role in the theater came 15 years later when she appeared on Broadway in Lillian Hellman's* The Little Foxes.

4203. *In* Sudden Impact, *during his fourth appearance as Inspector "Dirty Harry" Callahan.*

4204. Down and Out in Beverly Hills, *starring Richard Dreyfuss, Bette Midler and Nick Nolte, in 1985.*

4205. *Hershey's chocolate syrup.*

4206. *The home of the man who reportedly once said, "Any man who hates children and dogs can't be all bad," was purchased by a nursery school.*

4207. In the 1952 hit musical *Singin' in the Rain*, who dubbed the splash dancing heard while Gene Kelly does his celebrated tap dance in the rain?

4208. What do Rudolf Nureyev's legs, Bette Davis' waistline and Jimmy Durante's nose have in common?

4209. What song was the musical theme of James Cagney's 1931 gangster classic *Public Enemy* ?

4210. What great American actor's first stage appearance was as a chorus girl in a show called *Every Sailor* ?

4211. What was Boris Karloff's real name?

4212. What was the real name of the elderly British schoolteacher in the James Hilton novel *Goodbye, Mr. Chips*, portrayed on the silver screen by Robert Donat?

4213. What famous Hollywood leading man appeared as Pinkerton in the 1932 non-musical film version of the Giacomo Puccini opera *Madame Butterfly* ?

4214. Actresses Mary Pickford and Alexis Smith were both born with the same name—and changed it for Hollywood. What was it?

4215. How many costume changes did Elizabeth Taylor make in the $37 million, 1963 motion picture extravaganza *Cleopatra* ?

4216. What were the first words spoken by Greta Garbo in a movie?

4217. What unusual pet did actor John Barrymore have?

4218. What 1939 James Stewart movie classic aroused Congressional threats against Hollywood and attempts to block its European release by U.S. Ambassador to England Joseph P. Kennedy?

4219. What actress changed her name from Edda van Heemstra for Hollywood?

4207. *Then-unknowns Gwen Verdon and Carol Haney.*

4208. *All were insured by Lloyd's of London.*

4209. *"I'm Forever Blowing Bubbles."*

4210. *James Cagney's, in 1920.*

4211. *William Henry Pratt.*

4212. *Mr. Chipping.*

4213. *Cary Grant. Sylvia Sidney was his Madame Butterfly.*

4214. *Gladys Smith.*

4215. *Sixty-five.*

4216. *"Gimme a vhiskey. Ginger ale on the side. An' don' be stingy, baby."*
The film was Anna Christie; *the year, 1930.*

4217. *A vulture named Maloney. It would sit on his knee and hiss.*

4218. *Frank Capra's* Mr. Smith Goes To Washington.

4219. *Belgian-born Audrey Hepburn.*

4220. What starring role did film stars Robert Redford, Steve McQueen and Paul Newman all turn down, despite a contract offer of $4 million?

4221. What was the nationality of Warner Oland, the actor who appeared as Charlie Chan in dozens of films?

4222. What 1935 movie was the silver screen's first Technicolor offering?

4223. Who dressed in Greta Garbo's clothes and doubled for her in a horseback-riding scene in her first American movie, the 1926 silent film *Torrent*?

4224. In the 1968 film *2001: A Space Odyssey*, what song did HAL, the computer, learn to sing?

4225. Who dubbed the voice of Darth Vader in the movies *Star Wars* and *The Empire Strikes Back*?

4226. What was the name of the Good Witch portrayed by Billie Burke in the 1939 film classic *The Wizard of Oz*?

4227. Who was Fred Astaire's first silver screen dancing partner?

4228. What was the name of the mechanical shark in the 1975 hit movie *Jaws*?

4229. What 1960 film classic is based on the Edward Gein murder case?

4230. What famous American playwright wrote the script for *The Cocoanuts* and several other Marx Brothers movies?

4231. What American actress was the first to have a theater named after her?

4232. What unusual insurance policy did silent-film slapstick comedian Ben Turpin take out?

4233. For starring roles in what two films did Jane Fonda win Oscars?

4220. Superman. *Christopher Reeve took the part—for $250,000.*

4221. *He was Swedish.*

4222. Becky Sharp, *a film adaptation of the William Makepeace Thackeray novel* Vanity Fair.

4223. *Actor Joel McCrea.*

4224. *"A Bicycle Built For Two."*

4225. *James Earl Jones.*

4226. *Glinda.*

4227. *Joan Crawford, in* Dancing Lady *in 1933. Later that year he teamed up with Ginger Rogers in* Flying Down to Rio.

4228. *Bruce.*

4229. *Alfred Hitchcock's* Psycho.

4230. *George S. Kaufman.*

4231. *Ethel Barrymore. The theater, in New York, opened in 1928.*

4232. *A $100,000 policy against the possibility that his trademark crossed eyes would straighten out.*

4233. Klute, *in 1971, and* Coming Home, *in 1978.*

4234. Who played Vincent Price's menacing mute assistant in the 3-D horror film *House of Wax* ?

4235. What Oscar-winning 1971 movie was based on the 1951 Broadway play *I Am a Camera* ?

4236. Robert Redford was paid $6 million for his role in the 1985 film *Out of Africa*. How much was leading lady Meryl Streep paid?

4237. A process called Smell-O-Vision was used in 1960 for one film and then abandoned forever. What was the odorous offering?

4238. How did Charlie Chaplin place when he entered a Charlie Chaplin lookalike contest in Monte Carlo?

4239. What movie's cast included 124 midgets?

4240. What movie series did Johnny Weissmuller star in after he outgrew his *Tarzan* loincloth?

4241. Who replaced Dorothy Lamour as the female lead in the last of the seven Bing Crosby-Bob Hope "Road movies?"

4242. What famous American movie star's ashes are in an urn that also contains a small gold whistle?

4243. Rudolph Valentino, the great lover, was married twice. How did he spend his wedding nights?

4244. What film star represented Scotland in the 1952 Mr. Universe contest?

4245. What was movie mogul Samuel Goldwyn's real name?

4246. How much was Marlon Brando paid for his brief appearance as Jor-el in the movie "Superman"?

4247. What is Dolly Parton's CB "handle"?

4248. What actress in what movie said, "How dare he make love to me and not be a married man"?

4234. *Charles Bronson, in 1953, before he changed his name from Charles Buchinski.*

4235. Cabaret, *starring Liza Minnelli and Joel Grey.*

4236. *She received $3 million.*

4237. Scent of Mystery, *produced by Mike Todd Jr.*

4238. *He came in third.*

4239. *The 1939 version of* The Wizard of Oz *starring Judy Garland. The midgets played Munchkins.*

4240. Jungle Jim, *in which he wore a bush jacket to cover his added weight.*

4241. *Joan Collins. Lamour, however, did make a cameo appearance in the 1962 film,* The Road to Hong Kong.

4242. *Humphrey Bogart's. His actress wife Lauren Bacall had the whistle inscribed, "If you need anything, just whistle"—words she spoke to him in their first film together,* To Have and Have Not.

4243. *His first, locked out by wife Jean Acker; his second, in jail for bigamy, unable to be with wife Natacha Rambova.*

4244. *Sean Connery.*

4245. *Samuel Goldfish. He took his new name from the company he formed with the Selwyn brothers.*

4246. *He received a reported $3.7 million, as well as another $15 million after suing for a share of the box-office take.*

4247. *Booby Trap.*

4248. *Ingrid Berman, speaking of Cary Grant in* Indiscreet.

4249. How much does the 13½-inch-tall Academy Award Oscar weigh?

4250. What famous passenger ship was sunk to provide the dramatic climax of the 1960 film, *The Last Voyage*?

4251. What actor claims he is never without his emerald-green socks?

4252. Can you name the three boxers Sylvester Stallone faced in the climactic scenes of his first four *Rocky* movies?

4253. What actress was the granddaughter of famed architect Frank Lloyd Wright?

4254. Who dubbed Lauren Bacall's singing voice in *To Have and Have Not*, her screen debut and first pairing with future husband Humphrey Bogart?

4255. In what three films did Doris Day sing "Que Sera Sera"?

4256. What two film classics did Victor Fleming direct in 1939?

4257. In what film did the star propose by saying, "Marry me and I'll never look at another horse"?

4258. What screen role did Telly Savalas, Donald Pleasance, Max Von Sydow and Charles Gray have in common?

4259. For her role of Rosie in the 1951 film classic *The African Queen*, who was Katharine Hepburn told to use as a model?

4260. In what film classic was the heroine advised: "You can't show your bosom 'fore three o'clock"?

4261. What was the first British sound film?

4262. What comedienne is a direct descendant of Edward Rutledge, the youngest signer of the Declaration of Independence?

4249. *The statuette weighs eight and a half pounds.*

4250. *The Ile de France, which was renamed Faransu Maru ("French Ship" in Japanese) for the occasion.*

4251. *Irish-born Peter O'Toole.*

4252. *Apollo Creed (Carl Weathers) in* Rocky *and* Rocky II; *Clubber Lang (Mr. T) in* Rocky III; *and Drago (Dolph Ludgren) in* Rocky IV.

4253. *Anne Baxter.*

4254. *A teenage Andy Williams.*

4255. The Man Who Knew Too Much *in 1956;* Please Don't Eat the Daisies *in 1960; and* The Glass Bottom Boat *in 1966.*

4256. Gone With the Wind *and* The Wizard of Oz.

4257. A Day at the Races. *Groucho Marx was popping the question to Margaret Dumont.*

4258. *All played SPECTRE chief Ernst Stavro Blofeld in James Bond films.*

4259. *Eleanor Roosevelt.*

4260. Gone With the Wind. *Hattie McDaniels gave the etiquette tip to Vivien Leigh.*

4261. Blackmail, *Alfred Hitchcock's 1929 masterpiece.*

4262. *Goldie Hawn.*

4263. At an MGM auction in 1970, two items went for the top price of $1,500. One was the full-sized boat used in the musical *Showboat.* What was the other?

4264. Clark Gable starred in the 1932 film *Red Dust* with Jean Harlow and Mary Astor. What was the name of the 1953 remake, featuring Gable in the same role with costars Ava Gardner and Grace Kelly?

4265. What filmmaker made a cameo appearance in *Close Encounters of the Third Kind*?

4266. What famous actor starred in two classic "Bridge" movies?

4267. Who appeared as a character named Alias in the 1973 Sam Peckinpah film *Pat Garrett and Billy the Kid*?

4268. What famous performer appeared in a movie riding Trigger before Roy Rogers rode him to silver-screen stardom?

4269. Who subbed for Claire Bloom in the dance sequences in the 1952 film *Limelight,* which also starred Charlie Chaplin?

4270. Who portrayed Snow White in a live-action movie to help Walt Disney's animators achieve realism in their cartoon feature film?

4271. What actress once sued a California animal breeder for naming a two-headed goat after her?

4272. Who was William Claude Dukenfield?

4273. What film did Alfred Hitchcock make twice?

4274. Where were the disco scenes in *Saturday Night Fever* shot?

4275. Who played *The Great Gatsby* in the 1949 film version of the F. Scott Fitzgerald novel?

4276. What film star won a special Oscar as "the most outstanding personality of 1934"?

4263. *Judy Garland's size-4½ red shoes from* The Wizard of Oz.

4264. Mogambo.

4265. *FranÁois Truffaut. He appeared as a UFO expert.*

4266. *William Holden. He was in* The Bridge on the River Kwai *and* The Bridges at Toko-ri.

4267. *Singer Bob Dylan.*

4268. *Olivia de Havilland, in* The Adventures of Robin Hood *in 1938. At the time, Trigger was known as Golden Cloud.*

4269. *Ballerina Melissa Hayden.*

4270. *Dancer Marge Champion, who was married to a Disney animator at the time. She also was the model for the Blue Fairy in* Pinocchio.

4271. *Hedy Lamarr.*

4272. *Comedian W.C. Fields.*

4273. The Man Who Knew Too Much—*in 1934 with Leslie Banks and Edna Best, and in 1956 with James Stewart and Doris Day.*

4274. *At the 2001 Odyssey Disco in Bay Ridge, Brooklyn.*

4275. *Alan Ladd. Robert Redford starred in the same role 25 years later.*

4276. *America's dimpled darling Shirley Temple, who was Hollywood's top box-office attraction from 1935 through 1938.*

4277. What actor launched his performing career as a public-address announcer for the Brooklyn Dodgers at Ebbets Field in 1938?

4278. In his first starring role in the 1935 film *The Phantom Empire,* what horse did Gene Autry ride?

4279. In what film did the heroine declare, "I've met the most wonderful man. Of course, he's fictional. But you can't have everything"?

4280. Who launched her film career at age 10 in a low-brow comedy called *There's One Born Every Minute,* which also featured former Our Gang star Carl "Alfalfa" Switzer?

4281. In the Walk Disney film, what was the profession of Snow White's friends, the seven dwarfs?

4282. Who paid $300 for 32 cotton sheets and 35 pillow cases—worth $50 new—at an auction of actor John Gilbert's personal effects following his death in 1936?

4283. Who was scheduled to star in the 1984 film *Beverly Hills Cop* before the role went to Eddie Murphy?

4284. Which of his almost 100 movies was Roy Rogers' favorite?

4285. For which Alfred Hitchcock film did artist Salvadore Dali design the graphics?

4286. Which profile did actor John Barrymore consider "the moneymaking side" of his face?

4287. What famous American author appeared in the 1976 movie comedy *Murder by Death* ?

4288. In Walt Disney's 1938 cartoon short *Mother Goose Goes Hollywood,* what star was caricaturized as Little Bo-Peep?

4289. Who starred in the title role in the 1977 film *Valentino* ?

4290. Two movies were named after the song "Red River Valley." Who starred in them?

4277. *John Forsythe.*

4278. *Tom Mix's horse Tony Jr.—not Champion.*

4279. The Purple Rose of Cairo, *starring Mia Farrow.*

4280. *Elizabeth Taylor.*

4281. *Bashful, Doc, Dopey, Grumpy, Happy, Sleepy and Sneezy were jewel miners.*

4282. *Marlene Dietrich.*

4283. *Sylvester Stallone, in a much more macho version written by Rocky-Rambo himself. And before Stallone, Mickey Rourke had been slated for the part.*

4284. My Pal Trigger.

4285. Spellbound, *in 1945. Dali created the graphics for amnesiac Gregory Peck's Freudian dreams.*

4286. *The left.*

4287. *Truman Capote.*

4288. *Katherine Hepburn.*

4289. *Another Rudolph—Rudolf Nureyev.*

4290. *Gene Autry in 1936; Roy Rogers in 1941. The song originated in New York at the turn of the century as "In the Bright Mohawk Valley."*

4291. Who said, "If I had as many love affairs as you have given me credit for, I would now be speaking to you from a jar in the Harvard Medical School"?

4292. When Eddie Cantor ducks to avoid a handful of mud in the 1932 film *Roman Scandals*, what Goldwyn girl gets it right in the face?

4293. Who coined the phrase "cameo role" to describe the appearance of a top movie star in a bit part?

4294. In what film did Jean Arthur make her last screen appearance?

4295. What Hollywood movie star's contract included a morals clause that forbade "adulterous conduct or immoral relations" with men other than her husband?

4296. Paul Newman took an ad in a newspaper to apologize for what movie, when the film was shown on TV?

4297. Whom did Fred Astaire name as his favorite dance partner?

4298. What American film classic did actor John Wayne call "the most un-American thing I've ever seen in my whole life"?

4299. Whom did actor Richard Dreyfuss portray in his first important film role—in the 1973 movie Dillinger?

4300. How old was actress Joan Collins when she posed semi-nude for Playboy in 1983?

4301. Italian film producer Carlo Ponti was considered for the title role of what 1972 blockbuster movie?

4302. Who played Watergate cover-up informant Deep Throat in the 1976 film *All The President's Men*?

4303. What struggling movie cowboy served as Gary Cooper's dialogue coach for his first all-talkie, the 1929 western classic *The Virginian*?

4291. Frank Sinatra.

4292. Lucille Ball.

4293. Showman Mike Todd, when he produced his Oscar-winning Around the World in 80 Days *in 1955. It featured Frank Sinatra, Marlene Dietrich, Buster Keaton, Noel Coward, Ronald Colman, Beatrice Lillie and others in unexpected walk-ons.*

4294. In Shane, *in 1953.*

4295. Gloria Swanson's.

4296. His 1954 screen debut, The Silver Chalice.

4297. Gene Kelly.

4298. The 1952 Gary Cooper western High Noon. Wayne's objection: *"The last thing in the picture is ole Coop putting the United States marshal's badge under his foot and stepping on it."*

4299. George "Baby Face" Nelson. Warren Oates was featured in the title role.

4300. 50. The issue sold out.

4301. The Godfather. Marlon Brando, the actor who finally got the role of Don Vito Corleone, won an Oscar for his performance.

4302. Hal Holbrook.

4303. Randolph Scott. Scott, a native Virginian, had a bit part in the film.

4304. What did actor Jack Lemmon use to strain spaghetti in the 1960 comedy classic *The Apartment?*

4305. What 1959 film ends with the heroine saying, "In spite of everything, I still believe that people are good at heart"?

4306. Actor Peter Fonda was once arrested and charged with disturbing the peace and destroying private property for slashing a sign. What did the sign say?

4307. What was the name of actress Elizabeth Taylor's childhood pet chipmunk, which she immortalized in a book written in 1946?

4308. A life-size statue of what Hollywood filmmaker has been erected in Puerto Vallarta, Mexico?

4309. What two tough-guy actors turned down the role of the avenging "Man with No Name" in Sergio Leone's spaghetti western *A Fistful of Dollars* before Clint Eastwood was offered the part?

4310. What popular movie was remade in 1981 under the title *Outland,* with Sean Connery in the lead role and the setting shifted from the Old West to the third moon of Jupiter?

4311. How many frames per second are projected in most animated films?

4312. Who dubbed the voice of the Beast in the animated 1991 Disney version of *Beauty and the Beast?*

4313. What famous actor's brother enjoyed a brief movie career as a child, appearing in a bit part in the 1939 Frank Capra classic *Mr. Smith Goes to Washington?*

4314. What was the name of the stray alley cat adopted by Holly Golightly, portrayed by Audrey Hepburn, in the 1961 movie *Breakfast at Tiffany's?*

4315. What 1977 R-rated hit movie was later re-released with a PG rating after seven minutes of footage had been removed?

4304. *A tennis racquet.*

4305. The Diary of Anne Frank.

4306. *"Feed Jane Fonda to the Whales." Charges against Fonda were dropped when two key witnesses to the 1981 incident at Denver's Stapleton International Airport failed to appear at his trial.*

4307. *Nibbles. Taylor wrote and illustrated the book Nibbles and Me when she was 14.*

4308. *Director John Huston—because of the number of tourists drawn to the picturesque seaside village by his 1964 hit The Night of the Iguana.*

4309. *James Coburn and Charles Bronson. Henry Fonda was the first choice, but he was too expensive.*

4310. High Noon.

4311. *24.*

4312. *Robby Benson.*

4313. *Dustin Hoffman's older brother Ronald.*

4314. *It had no name—she called it "cat."*

4315. Saturday Night Fever, *starring John Travolta. The cut footage featured some sex scenes and blue language.*

4316. What was the first name of Lt. Bullitt, the down-and-dirty San Francisco detective portrayed by Steve McQueen in the 1968 hit movie *Bullitt*?

4317. In what year did Hollywood start keeping the names of Oscar winners sealed and secret?

4318. What unusual message did actress Joan Hackett have inscribed on her grave marker?

4319. In what roles did Francis Ford Coppola's daughter, Sofia, appear in each of the Godfather movies?

4320. Which is the only airline "Rain Man" Dustin Hoffman says he would be willing to fly in the 1988 Academy Award-winning film?

4321. Under what pseudonym did strongman Arnold Schwarzenegger make his screen debut?

4322. Who wrote the 1975 Academy Award-winning song "I'm Easy" for the movie *Nashville*?

4323. What is comedian Chevy Chase's real first name?

4324. What movie star's trademark telephone greeting became the title of a popular 1965 movie comedy?

4325. What Cecil B. DeMille film was the first movie to include screen credits?

4326. By what name do we know the play and cult movie that was originally going to be called *They Came From Denton High*?

4327. What were the names of mad scientist Dr. Emmett Brown's dogs in *Back to the Future* and *Back to the Future II*?

4328. Who wrote and directed the 1984 "rockumentary" satire *This Is Spinal Tap* and the 1986 hit *Stand By Me*?

4329. In the 1953 film *Mogambo*, what did Clark Gable reply when Grace Kelly asked, "Who is this man Thomson that gazelles should be called after him?"

4316. *Frank.*

4317. *1940—the year after the Los Angeles Times broke its promise and published the names of the winners before they had been officially announced.*

4318. *"Go Away! I'm Sleeping."*

4319. *In* The Godfather *she was a baby; in* The Godfather, Part II, *she was a child immigrant; and in* The Godfather, Part III, *in her first speaking part, she played Godfather Michael Corleone's daughter, Mary.*

4320. *Qantas, because of its safety record.*

4321. *Arnold Strong. He starred in the 1970 Italian-TV film Hercules in New York.*

4322. *Actor Keith Carradine, who sang the song in the film and at the Oscar ceremonies.*

4323. *Cornelius.*

4324. *Warren Beatty's line "What's new, pussycat."*

4325. *His 1913 silent version of* Squaw Man—*the first of three versions DeMille made of the story.*

4326. The Rocky Horror Picture Show.

4327. *Einstein and Copernicus.*

4328. *Rob Reiner, who once played Mike "Meathead" Stivic on TV's* All in the Family.

4329. *Gable said: "He's a third baseman for the Giants who got a home run against the Dodgers once." Actually, the Thomson's gazelle is named for nineteenth-century Scottish explorer Joseph Thomson, who was the first European to visit many regions of East Africa.*

4330. Who were the only consecutive Best Actress Oscar winners to appear together in the first movie both made after receiving their awards?

4331. What movie introduced the song "Some Day My Prince Will Come"?

4332. What film star early in his career appeared in a series of movies as Singin' Sam, the silver screen's first singing cowboy?

4333. What Oscar-winning title role, rejected by both Marlon Brando and Albert Finney, brought stardom to the little-known actor who signed for the part?

4334. What was the name of Baby Jane's wheelchair-bound sister in the 1962 chiller *Whatever Happened to Baby Jane?*, starring Bette Davis and Joan Crawford?

4335. What four 1939 Hollywood classics were honored on 25-cent stamps issued by the U.S. Postal Service in celebration of their 50th anniversaries?

4336. What movie star couple, in a bid to discourage sightseers, once put a hand-painted sign in front of their Beverly Hills home that said "Please—They have Moved!—The Piersons"?

4337. Who appeared as God in the 1968 Otto Preminger film *Skidoo?*

4338. According to his Nazi dossier in the 1942 film classic *Casablanca*, what color are Rick's eyes?

4339. Who turned down the role of Bonnie in the 1967 hit movie *Bonnie and Clyde* before Faye Dunaway got the part?

4340. What unique money-saving attachments did Greta Garbo have installed in her Duesenberg automobile?

4341. How many films had Humphrey Bogart made when he co-starred with wife-to-be Lauren Bacall in her first movie, *To Have and Have Not*, in 1945?

4330. *Jessica Tandy, who won the Oscar in 1989 for* Driving Miss Daisy, *and Kathy Bates, who won it in 1990 for* Misery. *Their joint project was the 1992 film* Fried Green Tomatoes.

4331. *Walt Disney's 1937* Snow White and the Seven Dwarfs. *The song was written for the film by Frank Churchill and Larry Morey.*

4332. *John Wayne. He gave up the role because his singing and guitar-playing were dubbed, making personal appearances difficult if not impossible.*

4333. Lawrence of Arabia. *The role, of course, went to Peter O'Toole.*

4334. *Blanche. Davis played Jane; Crawford, Blanche.*

4335. Gone With the Wind, Beau Geste, Stagecoach *and* The Wizard of Oz.

4336. *Paul Newman and Joanne Woodward.*

4337. *Groucho Marx.*

4338. *Brown. In the film, Rick—played by brown-eyed Humphrey Bogart—asks Major Strasser, "Are my eyes really brown?" when he's handed a copy of his dossier.*

4339. *Jane Fonda.*

4340. *Safes—six of them.*

4341. *50.*

4342. Who played the parole officer of elderly ex-con train robbers Burt Lancaster and Kirk Douglas in the 1986 film comedy *Tough Guys*?

4343. Why has actor Robert Duvall named several of his pet dogs Boo Radley?

4344. What 1987 chiller was an expanded version of a 45-minute 1979 British film called *Diversion*?

4345. What line, delivered by Carole Lombard to William Powell in the 1936 comedy *My Man Godfrey*, inspired the trademark greeting of a popular cartoon character?

4346. What actress, asked to audition for a supporting role in a 1990 Hollywood movie, sat down at the casting director's desk, pulled two Oscars from a satchel and demanded, "Do you still want me to read for this part?"

4347. Who was listed as "Shakespearean Tutor to Mr. Newman" in the credits for the 1990 Paul Newman—Joanne Woodward film *Mr. and Mrs. Bridge*?

4348. What did Marilyn Monroe reply when a journalist asked her what she wore to bed?

4349. What famous actor worked at New York's Central Park Zoo—sweeping out the lion cages—to support himself while trying to make it in show biz?

4350. What hairy covering was used to make a 40-foot-high, 6 ½-ton mechanical ape look lifelike in the 1976 remake of the 1933 film classic *King Kong*?

4351. What do the initials RKO stand for in the theater company's name?

4352. In 1980, who were the Top 10 box-office stars in Hollywood, according to the nation's film exhibitors?

4342. *Comedian Dana Carvey, best known as the Church Lady on TV's* Saturday Night Live, *and as Garth Algar in the 1992 film* Wayne's World

4343. *In honor of his breakthrough film role as Boo Radley, the reclusive, retarded neighbor in the 1962 movie* To Kill a Mockingbird.

4344. Fatal Attraction. *The screenplays of both were written by James Dearden.*

4345. *"What's up, Duke?"—which Bugs Bunny's creator Bob Clampett borrowed and turned into "What's up, Doc?"*

4346. *Shelley Winters. The film was* ß. *The part she auditioned for—Robert De Niro's mother—went to actress Ruth Nelson.*

4347. *Senator Bob Dole. Newman, who played a Kansas lawyer in the film, had asked the Kansas senator to help him get the accent right by tape-recording part of the balcony scene from Romeo and Juliet (which Newman recites in the film).*

4348. *"Chanel No. 5."*

4349. *Sylvester Stallone.*

4350. *Argentine horse tails—2 tons of them.*

4351. *Radio-Keith-Orpheum. It was formed by the merger of the Radio Corporation of America (RCA) and the Keith-Orpheum theater chain in 1921.*

4352. *From 1 to 10: Burt Reynolds, Robert Redford, Clint Eastwood, Jane Fonda, Dustin Hoffman, John Travolta, Sally Field, Sissy Spacek, Barbra Streisand and Steve Martin.*

4353. Who played Nicky Jr., son of Nick and Nora Charles, in the last of the six films in the Thin Man series, *Song of the Thin Man*?

4354. Under the motion picture censorship code in effect from 1934 to 1968, how long did a screen kiss have to last to be judged "indecent"?

4355. What film role did actresses Theda Bara, Claudette Colbert and Elizabeth Taylor have in common?

4356. What did writer Somerset Maugham ask about Spencer Tracy's performance during a visit to the set of the 1941 film *Dr. Jekyll and Mr. Hyde*?

4357. On a movie set, what is the job of the "best boy"?

4358. Who was the youngest performer in history to win an Oscar?

4359. What was Sleeping Beauty's name in the 1959 Walt Disney film?

4360. What famous American actor made his screen debut portraying a paraplegic war veteran struggling to overcome his handicap?

4361. Jack Palance portrayed Cuban dictator Fidel Castro in the 1969 movie *Che!* Who appeared in the title role as revolutionary leader Che Guevara?

4362. Where did actress Sigourney Weaver—whose given name was Susan—find her unusual adopted first name?

4363. What line did Jean Arthur deliver to Cary Grant in *Only Angels Have Wings* that Lauren Bacall repeated to Humphrey Bogart in *To Have and Have Not* and Angie Dickinson said to John Wayne in *Rio Bravo*?

4364. Who once said, "I always wanted to do what my mother did—get all dressed up, shoot people, fall in the mud. I never considered doing anything else"?

4353. *Dean Stockwell.*

4354. *More than thirty seconds.*

4355. *Cleopatra. Each starred in a film entitled* Cleopatra—*Bara in 1917; Colbert in 1934; Taylor in 1963. Others who appeared as the Egyptian queen include Vivien Leigh, in* Caesar and Cleopatra, *1945;* Rhonda Fleming, *in* Serpent of the Nile, *1953; and Hedy Lamarr, in* The Story of Mankind, *1957.*

4356. *"Which one is he playing now?"*

4357. *Assisting the "gaffer," or chief electrician.*

4358. *Tatum O'Neal, who was 10 when she won an Oscar for best supporting actress as a chain-smoking, foul-mouthed young con artist in the 1973 film* Paper Moon.

4359. *Princess Aurora. The Good Fairies, however, called her Briar Rose.*

4360. *Marlon Brandon, in the 1950 film* The Men.

4361. *Egyptian-born Omar Sharif.*

4362. *In* The Great Gatsby *by F. Scott Fitzgerald. Sigourney is a minor character in the book.*

4363. *"I'm hard to get—all you have to do is ask me." All three films were directed by Howard Hawks.*

4364. *Actress Carrie Fisher, daughter of Debbie Reynolds.*

4365. Can you name Hollywood's Top 10 box-office stars of 1965—according to the nation's film exhibitors?

4366. What were the names of Bambi's rabbit and skunk friends in the 1942 Walt Disney film *Bambi*?

4367. What top Hollywood star co-scripted and co-produced *Head*, a 1968 psychedelic musical fantasy that starred the rock group the Monkees?

4368. By what stage names do we know father and son actors Ramon and Carlos Estevez?

4369. Three stars appearing in the 1953 Academy Award-winning film *From Here to Eternity* were nominated for best actor or best actress Oscars. How many won?

4370. Who won a job in Hollywood after appearing in a screen test wearing only a loincloth and sporting a rose behind his left ear?

4371. Russia permitted the 1940 American film classic *The Grapes of Wrath* to be shown because of the grim picture it painted of the American depression. Why was it later banned?

4372. Who played the tyrannical king in the movie *Anna and the King of Siam*—10 years before Yul Brynner starred in the musical version, *The King and I*?

4373. What was the name of the hard-nosed paratrooper colonel who blasted apart a Coca-Cola vending machine in Stanley Kubrick's 1964 film satire *Dr. Strangelove*?

4374. What distinguished English actor appeared as pirate William Kidd in the 1952 film *Abbott and Costello Meet Captain Kidd*?

4375. Can you name the four "Lucky H" movies that actor Paul Newman starred in during the 1960s?

4376. What unusual insurance policy did Anthony Quinn take out when he agreed to appear in the 1968 film *The Magus*?

4377. In 1940, what Hollywood stars were voted the Top 10 box-office attractions in the land by the nation's film exhibitors?

4365. *From 1 to 10: Sean Connery, John Wayne, Doris Day, Julie Andrews, Jack Lemmon, Elvis Presley, Cary Grant, James Stewart, Elizabeth Taylor and Richard Burton.*

4366. *The rabbit was Thumper; the skunk, Flower.*

4367. *Jack Nicholson.*

4368. *Ramon is Martin Sheen; Carlos is his son Charlie Sheen. The name was inspired by Roman Catholic Bishop Fulton J. Sheen.*

4369. *None. Burt Lancaster and Montgomery Clift lost to William Holden (Stalag 17) for best actor, and Deborah Kerr lost to Audrey Hepburn (Roman Holiday) for best actress. But Frank Sinatra won an Oscar for best supporting actor, and Donna Reed won one for best supporting actress.*

4370. *Clark Gable.*

4371. *Because Russian audiences were impressed that the poor, struggling Dust Bowl family depicted in the film was able to own an automobile.*

4372. *Rex Harrison, in 1946. His co-star was Irene Dunne.*

4373. *Bat Guano, who was portrayed by Keenan Wynn.*

4374. *Charles Laughton.*

4375. The Hustler, *1961; , 1963;* Harper, *1966; and* Hombre, *1967.*

4376. *Quinn, who shaved his head for his role, was insured against failing to grow back a healthy head of hair.*

4377. *From 1 to 10: Mickey Rooney, Spencer Tracy, Clark Gable, Gene Autry, Tyrone Power, James Cagney, Bing Crosby, Wallace Beery, Bette Davis and Judy Garland.*

4378. What comedy team appeared in more movies than any other in U.S. film history?

4379. In what film did Julie Andrews make her first appearance in a non-singing role?

4380. What historic figure has been portrayed on the silver screen by actors Errol Flynn, Clark Gable, Marlon Brando and Mel Gibson?

4381. Who played Mr. Smith in the 1937 Irene Dunne-Cary Grant comedy *The Awful Truth* and George in the 1938 Katherine Hepburn-Cary Grant comedy *Bringing Up Baby*?

4382. What was Marion Michael Morrison's screen name before he sought stardom as John Wayne?

4383. Rotund comedian Billy Gilbert, famous for his repertoire of violent sneezes, dubbed the voice of Sneezy in Walt Disney's *Snow White and the Seven Dwarfs*. Whose voice was used for Dopey in the 1937 cartoon classic?

4384. What cameo role did Charlie Chaplain play in his last movie, *A Countess from Hong Kong*, in 1967?

4385. What famous Hollywood star was married to Avrom Goldbogen?

4386. Who appeared in the 1957 Elvis Presley film *Loving You* as members of an enthusiastic audience?

4387. In the 1954 film *Her Twelve Men*, Greer Garson portrays a dedicated school teacher at a boys' school. How many boys were in her class?

4388. Who were the four artists of the silver screen who founded the United Artists film company in 1919?

4389. What Academy Award-winning title role was turned down by Hollywood heavy-hitters Burt Lancaster, John Wayne, Robert Mitchum, Lee Marvin and Rod Steiger?

4378. *The Three Stooges.*

4379. *In* The Americanization of Emily, *in 1964.*

4380. *Fletcher Christian, first mate on the Bounty. Flynn in* In the Wake of the Bounty, *in 1933; Gable in* Mutiny on the Bounty, *in 1935; Brando in* Mutiny on the Bounty, *in 1962; and Gibson in* The Bounty, *in 1984.*

4381. *Asta, the terrier who became a star in the Thin Man series.*

4382. *Duke Morrison.*

4383. *No one's—Dopey was a mute in the movie.*

4384. *He appeared as an elderly, seasick ship's steward in the film, which starred Marlon Brando and Sophia Loren.*

4385. *Elizabeth Taylor—long after Goldbrogen had changed his name to Mike Todd.*

4386. *Elvis' parents, Gladys and Vernon.*

4387. *Thirteen.*

4388. *Douglas Fairbanks, Mary Pickford, Charlie Chaplain and D. W. Griffith.*

4389. Patton, *in 1970. George C. Scott got the role.*

4390. Producer-director Otto Preminger paid Columbia Pictures $100,000 to use Kim Novak in the 1956 film *The Man with the Golden Arm*. How much was Novak paid?

4391. Why was popcorn banned at most movie theaters in the 1920s?

4392. Why was Mike Nichols fired as a busboy at a Howard Johnson's restaurant in New York, where he worked while taking drama lessons in the early 1950s?

4393. Under what name did a family named Blythe gain fame on stage and screen?

4394. On what planet did Abbott and Costello land in their 1953 film *Abbott and Costello Go to Mars* ?

4395. How much were Spencer Tracy and Katharine Hepburn paid for their last joint film appearance—in the 1967 film *Guess Who's Coming to Dinner* ?

4396. How much was paid at a 1987 auction for Charlie Chaplin's famous bowler hat and cane?

4397. What 1955 American movie was shown in Hong Kong under the title *The Heart of a Lady as Pure as a Full Moon Over the Place of Medical Salvation* ?

4398. What Hollywood great started his show business career on Broadway dancing in the background in Eskimo clothes as Mary Martin sang "My Heart Belongs to Daddy"?

4399. What now-famous actress had a bit part as Woody Allen's date at the end of his 1977 film *Annie Hall* ?

4400. What famous actor's Oscar was on display in the front window of his father's hardware store for 20 years?

4401. What symbol did Charlie Chaplin wear as a parody of the swastika in his 1940 film satire *The Great Dictator* ?

4402. What comic strip character does Whoopi Goldberg have tattooed above her left breast?

4390. *Her salary was $100 a week.*

4391. *It was considered too noisy.*

4392. *He claims he was canned "when somebody asked me the ice cream flavor of the week and I said, 'Chicken.'"*

4393. *Barrymore—as in John, Ethel and Lionel. Founding father Maurice, who had been disowned by his family in England for boxing professionally, took the name Barrymore from an aging poster on an old English vaudeville house in London before leaving for America to launch his acting career.*

4394. *Venus.*

4395. *Tracy was paid $300,000; Oscar-winner Hepburn, $200,000.*

4396. *$151,800.*

4397. Not as a Stranger, *starring Robert Mitchum as a young doctor and Olivia de Havilland as his nurse-wife.*

4398. *Gene Kelly. The year was 1938; the show, the Cole Porter hit* Leave It to Me.

4399. *Sigourney Weaver.*

4400. *James Stewart's. The Oscar was for his performance in the 1940 film* The Philadelphia Story; *the hardware store, founded by his grandfather in 1853, was in Indiana, Pennsylvania.*

4401. *Two "×" marks—the sing of the double cross.*

4402. *Woodstock, Snoopy's bird-buddy in the* Peanuts *comic strip.*

4403. Who made a cameo appearance as a man who thinks he's singer Ethel Merman in the 1980 film *Airplane!*?

4404. In the 1939 film classic *The Wizard of Oz*, what did the scarecrow, played by Ray Bolger, recite to prove he had a brain?

4405. What was actor Michael Keaton's name at birth?

4406. What popular actress once greeted Lauren Bacall by saying, "Hi, I'm the young you"?

4407. What famous Hollywood husband and wife once took out a half-page ad in *The Los Angeles Times* to deny rumors that they were splitting up?

4408. What famous actress helped pay her college tuition by modeling for a brochure promoting Washington's Watergate Hotel?

4409. Japanese filmmaker Akira Kurosawa's movies *The Seven Samurai* and *Yojimbo* were remade as the westerns *The Magnificent Seven* and *A Fistful of Dollars,* respectively. What American classic did his 1958 offering *The Hidden Fortress* inspire?

4410. In what popular 1975 film did teenager Carrie Fisher make her screen debut?

4411. Who dubbed the voice of the late Laurence Olivier when his previously cut, sexually suggestive Roman bathhouse scene with Tony Curtis was restored for the 1991 re-release of the 1960 biblical epic *Spartacus*?

4412. What vehicle did Arnold Schwarzenegger receive as partial payment for starring in *Terminator 2: Judgement Day*?

4413. What film star lives in a house that once served as a hideaway for gangster Al Capone?

4414. What role did director John Landis have his mother, Shirley Levine, play in his 1983 Eddie Murphy-Dan Akroyd comedy *Trading Places*?

4403. *Ethel Merman.*

4404. *The Pythagorean theorum: The square of the hypotenuse of a right-angled triangle is equal to the sum of the squares of the other two sides.*

4405. *Michael Douglas.*

4406. *Kathleen Turner.*

4407. *Joanne Woodward and Paul Newman. The ad cost $2,000.*

4408. *Susan Sarandon, who at the time was known as Susan Tomalin.*

4409. Star Wars, *in 1977.*

4410. Shampoo—*in which she seduces Warren Beatty.*

4411. *Anthony Hopkins.*

4412. *A Gulfstream G-III jet.*

4413. *Burt Reynolds—in Jupiter, Florida.*

4414. *A bag lady.*

4415. Who played John Wayne's young niece—orphaned, kidnapped and raised by Indians— in the great 1956 western saga *The Searchers*?

4416. Who portrayed artist Paul Gauguin in *Lust for Life*, the 1956 film biography of Vincent van Gogh?

4417. When the pedigree spaniel Lady had four puppies in the 1955 Disney film *Lady and the Tramp*, what name was given to the only one resembling papa-mutt Tramp?

4418. Who was originally cast as the bumbling Inspector Jacques Clouseau before Peter Sellers got the role in the 1963 film comedy *The Pink Panther*?

4419. What famous director featured his teenage daughter in a 1969 film, to the great dismay of reviewers, one of whom described her as having the face of "an exhausted gnu, the voice of an unstrung tennis racket, and a figure of no describable shape"?

4420. What was the wet stuff raining down on Gene Kelly in his famous splash-dance scene in the 1952 musical *Singing' in the Rain*?

4421. What was the most expensive silent film ever made?

4422. What popular 1973 movie was almost renamed *Another* Slow *Night in Modesto* because a studio executive feared the planned title would mislead filmgoers into believing it was an Italian movie?

4423. What is the only thing shown in color in Francis Ford Coppola's 1983 film *Rumble Fish*?

4424. Who is the only movie star to win the best actor Academy Award two years in a row?

4425. What does R2-D2—the name of the robot in the movie *Star Wars*—mean in film editing lingo?

4426. As a child, what famous actress shaved her head, wore pants and called herself "Jimmy" because she wanted to be a boy?

4415. *Natalie Wood.*

4416. *Anthony Quinn, who won an Oscar as best supporting actor for his performance. Van Gogh was played by Kirk Douglas.*

4417. *Scamp.*

4418. *Peter Ustinov. He bowed out at the last minute.*

4419. *John Huston—who cast his daughter, Anjelica, in a leading role in* A Walk with Love and Death. *It was her film debut.*

4420. *A mixture of water and milk. The milk was added to make the rain more visible.*

4421. Ben Hur. *The 1926 epic, which starred Ramon Novarro and Francis X. Bushman, cost $3.9 million.*

4422. American Graffiti.

4423. *Mickey Rourke's Siamese fighting fish.*

4424. *Spencer Tracy, in 1937 and 1938, for his performances in* Captains Courageous *and* Boy's Town.

4425. *Reel 2, dialogue 2.*

4426. *Katherine Hepburn.*

4427. What actress, using the name Rainbo, recorded a song entitled "John, You've Gone Too Far This Time," which gently chided John Lennon for appearing nude with wife Yoko Ono on the cover of the album *Two Virgins*?

4428. What was served in the 1981 film *My Dinner with Andre*?

4429. In what actress's marital split was Warren Beatty named corespondent and ordered to pay the divorce costs?

4430. What role did Dennis Hopper play in the 1957 western classic *The Gunfight at the O.K. Corral*?

4431. What was the name of singing cowboy Gene Autry's ranch in Placerita Canyon, northwest of downtown Los Angeles?

4432. Who turned down the role of the seductive and vindictive Mrs. Robinson in *The Graduate* before Anne Bancroft was offered the part in the 1967 hit film?

4433. What popular leading man dropped out of college to tour as Snow White's Prince Charming in the *Disney on Parade* ice show?

4434. How old was actor Jeff Bridges when he made his screen debut?

4435. How much was producer David O. Selznick fined by the Motion Picture Association of America for letting the word "damn" be used in *Gone With the Wind*?

4436. Before actor Clint Eastwood spent a record $25,000 on his winning 1986 campaign for mayor of Carmel, California, what had been the previous high for that town?

4437. How many doggie spots did Walt Disney animation artists draw for the 1961 cartoon feature *One Hundred and One Dalmations*?

4438. What now-famous entertainer's big break came when she jumped from the Broadway chorus of Zero Mostel's *Fiddler on the Roof* to the principal role of Tzeitel, the fiddler's eldest daughter?

4427. *Sissy Spacek. The record was a flop and Spacek turned her attention to acting.*

4428. *Potato soup, fish pâté and roast quail.*

4429. *Leslie Caron's, in 1965. British stage director Peter Hall obtained the divorce in London.*

4430. *Billy Clanton, the youngest of the outlaw Clanton gang.*

4431. *The Melody Ranch. Autry sold it in 1991 after the death of his horse Champion at age 41.*

4432. *Doris Day, who explained that she rejected the part because: "I can't picture myself in bed with someone, all the crew around us, doing what I consider so exciting and exalting when it is very personal and private."*

4433. *Patrick Swayze.*

4434. *Four months. He appeared as a crying baby in the 1950 film* The Company She Keeps.

4435. *$5,000.*

4436. *$750.*

4437. *6,469,952.*

4438. *Bette Midler.*

4439. What famous entertainer once told an interviewer, "I patterned my look after Cinderella, Mother Goose and the local hooker"?

4440. What was the name of the school that murderous teenager Carrie attended in the 1976 movie shocker *Carrie* ?

4441. Who was originally slated to play paraplegic Vietnam War veteran Ron Kovic in the anti-war epic *Born on the Fourth of July* ?

4442. What does actor E.G. Marshall reply when asked what his initials stand for?

4443. What leg did James Stewart have in a cast in the 1954 Alfred Hitchcock thriller *Rear Window* ?

4444. What famous actor won a part in the 1937 Cecil B. DeMille western *The Plainsman* by pretending to be a Cheyenne Indian with little knowledge of the English language?

4445. What was the name of the machine that replaced sex in Woody Allen's 1973 comedy *Sleeper*?

4446. Why did *Cleopatra*, the 1963 film extravaganza starring Elizabeth Taylor, Richard Burton and Rex Harrison, have to be color-corrected before its release?

4447. What did Nick and Nora Charles give their dog Asta as a Christmas present in the 1934 comedy classic *The Thin Man* ?

4448. When did former child screen star Shirley Temple stop believing in Santa Claus?

4449. What is the French equivalent of the Oscar?

4450. In 1928, what was the only word of dialogue in MGM's first picture with sound, *White Shadows in the South Seas* ?

4451. What unique weapon was featured in the movies *The Tenth Victim*, starring Marcello Mastroianni and Ursula Andress, and *The Ambushers*, with Dean Martin and Janice Rule?

4452. In what film did Brooke Shields make her screen debut?

4439. *Dolly Parton.*

4440. *Bates High—in homage to Alfred Hitchcock and his "Psycho" killer Norman Bates.*

4441. *Al Pacino, in 1978, but the financing fell through. The film was finally made in 1989 with Tom Cruise.*

4442. *"Everyone's Guess." Marshall generally refuses to reveal his given names—but has acknowledged that the initials stand for Edda Gunther, a name that reflects his Norwegian ancestry.*

4443. *Both. Most of the time, it was on the left leg. But in one scene with co-star Grace Kelly, the cast shifted to the right leg. And at the end of the movie, both legs were in casts at the same time.*

4444. *Anthony Quinn, who answered a casting call for an Indian who could do a war chant in native Cheyenne.*

4445. *The Orgasmatron.*

4446. *Because Taylor sunbathed while outdoor scenes were being shot in Italy and her skintones in those scenes didn't match those in footage shot earlier indoors.*

4447. *A toy fire hydrant.*

4448. *As she tells it: "When my mother took me to see him in a department store and he asked for my autograph."*

4449. *The César.*

4450. *"Hello." (It was also the first film to feature Leo the Lion's roar.)*

4451. *A shooting bra.*

4452. Holy Terror, *a 1977 horror movie also known as* Alice, Sweet Alice.

4453. What was Citizen Kane's full name in the 1941 Orson Welles film classic?

4454. The first film documentary was screened in 1922 and given a sound track in 1939. What was it?

4455. What is the "Tech" in Technicolor—the color process introduced in the Disney film *Flowers and Trees* in 1932?

4456. What role did Patty Duke play in *The Miracle Worker*?

4457. Leonard Slye and Frances Octavia Smith rode to fame under what show business names?

4458. Who portrayed Mighty Joe Young's mistress in the movie about the giant gorilla?

4459. In the film *The Day the Earth Stood Still*, what words did Patricia Neal utter to stop the robot Gort from destroying the world?

4460. Movie mogul Sam Goldwyn spent $20,000 to reshoot a scene in his first all-talking film, "Bulldog Drummond," because he didn't understand what word?

4461. In 1968, two movie stars won the Oscar for Best Actress. Who were they?

4462. The PATSY—Picture Animal Top Star of the Year—award was first given in 1951. Who won it?

4463. Who was the first actor to have a pie thrown in his face in a movie?

4464. Jack Nicholson played the title role in his first movie. What was it?

4465. What actress once confessed, "I used to be Snow White, but I drifted"?

4466. Buddy Ebsen was originally cast as the Tin Man in the movie *The Wizard of Oz.* Why did Jack Haley replace him?

4453. *Charles Foster Kane—who was modeled after publishing tycoon William Randolph Hearst.*

4454. *The Eskimo saga* Nanook of the North.

4455. *Inventor Herbert Kalmus's tribute to his alma mater, the Massachusetts Institute of Technology.*

4456. *She played Helen Keller, in the 1962 movie, and Keller's teacher-companion Annie Sullivan, in the 1979 made-for-TV movie.*

4457. *Roy Rogers and Dale Evans.*

4458. *Terry Moore.*

4459. *Klaatu barada nikto.*

4460. *"Din." He had it changed to "noise".*

4461. *Katherine Hepburn, for* The Lion in Winter, *and Barbra Streisand, for* Funny Girl.

4462. *Francis the Talking Mule.*

4463. *Cross-eyed comic Ben Turpin, in an early Keystone Kop film. Mabel Normand threw it.*

4464. The Crybaby Killer, *in 1958.*

4465. *Mae West.*

4466. *Ebsen's aluminum-dust makeup turned him bright blue and sent him to the hospital with serious respiratory problems. Different makeup was devised for Haley.*

4467. Where was King Kong's home?

4468. Gangster Al Capone enjoyed the 1932 film *Scarface* so much that he gave director Howard Hawkes a gift. What was it?

4469. In what movie did long-time Superman George Reeves make his screen debut?

4470. In the saucy 1953 comedy *The Moon is Blue*, starring William Holden, David Niven, and Maggie McNamara, what word made its movie debut and caused the film to be banned in several parts of the country?

4471. To whom did actor Ryan O'Neal mail a live tarantula?

4472. What was the name of the general played by Sterling Hayden in the movie *Dr. Strangelove*?

4473. Who played the title role in *Marty* when it was presented as a TV movie in 1953—three years before the Oscar-winning film starring Ernest Borgnine?

4474. Who starred in: *The Black Camel, Black Dragons, Black Friday, The Black Sheep,* and two films entitled *The Black Cat*?

4475. In the movie *Bananas*, who did the play-by-play on Woody Allen's wedding night with Louise Lasser?

4476. What British actress made her stage debut at age 33, when she appeared as a fairy with a long nose in a pantomime play called *Little Jack Horner*?

4477. What was the name of the sewer worker attacked by a 36-foot alligator in the 1980 monster movie, *Alligator*?

4478. Where did John Wayne get his nickname Duke?

4479. Who portrayed the dying sea captain who delivered the *Maltese Falcon* in the 1941 John Huston film classic?

4480. What actor started his career on Broadway in 1922 as one of the robots in Karel Capek's *R.U.R.*?

4467. *Skull Island.*

4468. *A miniature machine gun.*

4469. Gone With the Wind. *He played Brent Tarleton, one of the redheaded twins who wooed Scarlett O'Hara.*

4470. *"Virgin."*

4471. *Gossip commentator Rona Barrett.*

4472. *Gen. Jack D. Ripper.*

4473. *Rod Steiger.*

4474. *Bela Lugosi.*

4475. *Sportscaster Howard Cosell.*

4476. *Margaret Rutherford, who was 71 when she made her first Miss Marple movie and 80 when she died.*

4477. *Ed Norton, undoubtedly in deference to the character created by Art Carney in TV's* The Honeymooners.

4478. *From his favorite childhood dog, an Airedale called Duke.***4479.** *John Huston's actor-father, Walter.*

4480. *Spencer Tracy.*

4481. What foreign actress once earned a living as a model, working under the name Diana Loris?

4482. What actress once said, "Sometimes I'm so sweet, even I can't stand it"?

4483. Who played wise-guy dragster Bob Falfa in the movie *American Graffiti*?

4484. There were 291 words spoken in *The Jazz Singer*, the first motion picture feature with a sound track. What six are the most famous?

4485. What two people involved in the 1956 movie *The Invasion of the Body Snatcher*s had cameo roles in the 1978 remake?

4486. What actress had a daughter by Marcello Mastroianni and a son by Roger Vadim but married neither of them?

4487. How did HAL, the computer in *2001: A Space Odyssey,* get its name?

4488. What country was *The Mouse That Roared* in the Peter Sellers movie of that name?

4489. Who played the ancient lama in the 1937 movie *Lost Horizon* ?

4490. What actress performed topless in Las Vegas before breaking into the movies as an outer space sex siren?

4491. Robert Mitchum launched his film career playing bad guy bit parts in whose cowboy movies?

4492. What actor first went to Hollywood as a chaperon-bodyguard for a gangster's girlfriend?

4493. Who made her film debut in the 1948 film *Scudda-Hoo! Scudda-Hay!* ?

4494. What two Brooklyn comedians named Kaminsky gained fame under other names?

4481. *Gina Lollobrigida.*

4482. *Julie Andrews.*

4483. *Harrison Ford.*

4484. *Al Jolson's first: "You ain't heard nothing yet, folks!"*

4485. *Star Kevin McCarthy and director Don Siegel.*

4486. *Catherine Deneuve.*

4487. *Advance each letter by one and you have the answer—IBM.*

4488. *The Grand Duchy of Fenwick.*

4489. *Sam Jaffe.*

4490. *Valerie Perrine. Her film debut was as Montana Wildhack in* Slaughterhouse Five.

4491. *Hopalong Cassidy's.*

4492. *George Raft, who watched over nightclub singer Texas Guinan for his buddy Owney "the Killer" Madden.*

4493. *Marilyn Monroe. She was in the distant background rowing a boat.*

4494. *David Daniel Kaminsky, who became Danny Kaye; and Melvin Kaminsky, who became Mel Brooks. They are not related.*

4495. When Janet Gaynor won the first Academy Award for Best Actress in 1928, who won for Best Actor?

4496. What actor has to cover his arm with make-up when he performs in order to mask tattoos proclaiming his love for Mom and Dad and Scotland?

4497. Where was Francis Ford Coppola's Vietnam epic *Apocalypse Now* filmed?

4498. Who played Humpty Dumpty in the 1933 movie *Alice in Wonderland*?

4499. In what 1968 film did Marlon Brando play a long-haired Jewish guru; Ringo Starr, a Mexican gardener; Charles Aznavour, a hunchback; and Richard Burton, an alcoholic Welsh poet?

4500. What famous comedian played the Tin Woodman in the 1925 silent-movie version of *The Wizard of Oz*?

4501. Who was the first black performer signed to a long-term contract by a major Hollywood studio?

4502. Where did the Warner Brothers—Jack, Harry, Sam and Albert—get the 99 chairs they used in the first theater they opened in 1903 in New Castle, Pennsylvania?

4503. Where was Anthony "Zorba the Greek" Quinn born?

4504. Whose ashes does actor Marlon Brando keep in his home in Tahiti?

4505. What was the name of Hollywood's first 3-D movie, released in 1952?

4506. Who portrayed Mia Farrow's sister in Woody Allen's *Zelig* and *The Purple Rose of Cairo*?

4507. What famous funnyman co-authored the 1974 film comedy *Blazing Saddles* with actor-director Mel Brooks?

4508. In what film did actress Dorothy Lamour first don a sarong?

4495. *Emil Jannings.*

4496. *Sean Connery, best known for his James Bond portrayal.*

4497. *In the Philippines.*

4498. *W. C. Fields.*

4499. Candy, *based on Terry Southern's novel.*

4500. *Oliver Hardy, of Laurel and Hardy fame.*

4501. *Singer Lena Horne, in 1942. The studio was Metro-Goldwyn-Mayer.*

4502. *From the local undertaker. The chairs had to be returned whenever there was a funeral.*

4503. *In Chihuahua, Mexico.*

4504. *Those of his childhood friend, comedian Wally Cox, who died in 1973.*

4505. Bwana Devil.

4506. *Mia's sister, Stephanie Farrow.*

4507. *Richard Pryor.*

4508. *In her very first movie,* The Jungle Princess, *in 1936—four years before her first "Road" movie with Bob Hope and Bing Crosby.*

4509. What famous leading man turned down the role of Rhett Butler in *Gone With the Wind* and predicted it would be "the biggest flop in Hollywood history"?

4510. On what day of the week was actress Tuesday Weld born?

4511. Which two top Hollywood stars turned down the role of Professor Henry Higgins in the film version of *My Fair Lady* before Rex Harrison was offered the part?

4512. From what earlier stage name did actress-comedienne Whoopi Goldberg derive her current name?

4513. What two Frank Sinatra movie thrillers did Ole Blue Eyes own and order shelved for years because of their frightening political themes?

4514. Who played Robert Redford's laid-back rodeo pal and manager in the 1979 film *The Electric Horseman*?

4515. What actor was dropped by Universal Studios in the early 1950s because of his protruding Adam's apple and slow speech?

4516. What star—seven months pregnant with her first child—sang the Oscar-winning song "Once I Had a Secret Love" at the 1953 Academy Awards show?

4517. Ronald Reagan used a famous line from one of his movies as the title of his 1965 autobiography. What's the line?

4518. The family name of what famous fictional sleuth was Charalambides before it was anglicized by an immigration official on Ellis Island?

4519. What unusual stipulation was included in funnyman Buster Keaton's contract with MGM?

4520. What song does Kate Capshaw sing in broken Chinese in the opening scene of the 1984 film Indiana Jones and the *Temple of Doom*?

4509. *Gary Cooper.*

4510. *Friday—August 27, 1943.*

4511. *Cary Grant and James Cagney.*

4512. *Whoopi Cushion.*

4513. The Manchurian Candidate, *made in 1962, and* Suddenly, *made in 1954—both of which dealt with political assassinations.*

4514. *Country singer Willie Nelson.*

4515. *Clint Eastwood.*

4516. *Ann Blyth sang the song, which was from the movie* Calamity Jane.

4517. *"Where's the rest of me?"—words he delivered in the 1941 film "King's Row" when he woke up and discovered both his legs had been amputated.*

4518. *"The Thin Man" Nick Charles.*

4519. *He was not to smile in public.*

4520. *The Cole Porter classic* Anything Goes.

4521. Robert Redford turned down the lead role in *The Graduate* because he considered himself too old. How old was Dustin Hoffman when he took the part?

4522. The mother of what famous European actress once won a Great Garbo look-alike contest and a trip to Hollywood to work as Garbo's double?

4523. What actress changed her name to avoid seeking fame and fortune as Sarah Jane Fulks?

4524. Who played Gypsy Rose Lee's younger sister June in the 1962 movie *Gypsy* ?

4525. What Alfred Hitchcock classic was filmed but not released in 3-D?

4526. What was the last Hollywood film made by silver-screen legend Cary Grant?

4527. With whom did Dorothy live in the film classic *The Wizard of Oz* ?

4528. What was the name of the killer whale movie made in 1977 in a bid to cash in on the popularity of the killer shark shocker *Jaws* ?

4529. What actor, following his 1966 film debut as a bellboy in *Dead Heat on a Merry-Go-Round*, was told, "Kid, you ain't got it"?

4530. What was the name of the chimpanzee that starred with Ronald Reagan in the 1951 film *Bedtime for Bonzo* ?

4531. What popular 1982 film was banned in Sweden because it showed parents acting hostilely toward their children?

4532. What film so embarrassed star Katharine Hepburn that she offered to make another movie without salary if RKO withheld its release?

4533. How much was Jacqueline Onassis reportedly offered to portray herself in the 1978 film *The Greek Tycoon* ?

4521. *Thirty—the same age as Redford.*

4522. *Sophia Loren. But her mother never made the trip because her own mother (Sophia's grandmother) wouldn't let her.*

4523. *Jane Wyman.*

4524. *Ann Jillian.*

4525. *His 1954 chiller,* Dial M for Murder.

4526. Walk, Don't Run, *in 1966.*

4527. *Her Auntie Em and Uncle Henry.*

4528. Orca.

4529. *Harrison Ford.*

4530. *Peggy. The talented chimp also appeared in Johnny Weissmuller's* Jungle Jim *movies.*

4531. E.T

4532. Sylvia Scarlett. *Hepburn plays a young woman who dresses like a boy in the film, which was released in 1935. Her co-star was Cary Grant.*

4533. *$1 million. Jacqueline Bisset took the role for half that amount.*

4534. For what 1969 film did poet Rod McKuen write the popular Oscar-nominated ballad "Jean"?

4535. In what 1950 film classic did Cecil B. DeMille, Buster Keaton and Hedda Hopper all play themselves?

4536. The film version of what great novel had its title changed to *Lost Child in Foggy City* when it was shown in China?

4537. What condition does Roger Moore include in all his film contracts?

4538. Who played Major Major, the timid squadron leader, in the 1970 film *Catch 22* ?

4539. Under what title was the 1978 hit movie *Grease* released in Venezuela?

4540. Who was the highest paid star in the 1943 film classic *Casablanca* ?

4541. Who played Dirty Harry Callahan's cute rookie partner in Clint Eastwood's 1976 film *The Enforcer* ?

4542. Who played the female lead in *Satan Met a Lady*, the 1936 film version of Dashiell Hammett's *The Maltese Falcon* ?

4543. Who spoke only Sioux in portraying an Indian named Buffalo Cow Head in the 1970 film *A Man Called Horse* ?

4544. Who played the role of Jack Nicholson's bowling alley pickup in *Five Easy Pieces* ?

4545. What actor appeared in more Alfred Hitchcock thrillers than any other?

4546. What 1977 film included "first aid" in its list of credits?

4547. Who was the only female to appear in the 1954 film classic *Bad Day at Black Rock* ?

4548. What famous child star failed her screen test for a part in the *Our Gang movie comedies*?

4534. The Prime of Miss Jean Brodie.

4535. Sunset Boulevard, *starring Gloria Swanson and William Holden.*

4536. Oliver Twist, *by Charles Dickens.*

4537. *That he be provided with an unlimited supply of hand-rolled Cuban cigars while on location.*

4538. *Bob Newhart.*

4539. Vaselina.

4540. *Not Bogart, Bergman, Greenstreet, Raines, or Lorre—but Conrad Veidt. He was paid $5,000 a week to portray Major Strasser.*

4541. *Tyne Daly, who went on to become veteran cop Mary Beth Lacey on TV's* Cagney & Lacey.

4542. *Bette Davis.*

4543. *Dame Judith Anderson.*

4544. *Sally Struthers.*

4545. *Leo G. Carroll. He was in five—*Suspicion, Spellbound, The Paradine Case, Strangers on a Train *and* North by Northwest.

4546. The Gauntlet, *a chase film starring Clint Eastwood.*

4547. *Anne Francis, who played the young gas station operator who was one of the 37 residents of Black Rock. The male cast included Spencer Tracy, Robert Ryan, Dean Jagger, Walter Brennan, John Ericson, Ernest Borgnine and Lee Marvin.*

4548. *Shirley Temple.*

4549. Who was the first American movie star to headline in a film directed by Sweden's Ingmar Bergman?

4550. Who won the Oscar for best supporting actress in 1983—for her portrayal of a man?

4551. How old was actor Sydney Greenstreet when he made his screen debut?

4552. What actor appeared as a fig leaf in a Fruit of the Loom television commercial before he landed an Oscar-winning role?

4553. Can you name the four sets of brothers featured in *The Long Riders*, a 1980 film about the James gang?

4554. What size bra did Dustin Hoffman wear in the 1982 film *Tootsie*?

4555. What Oscar-winning actress placed a three-page thank you note in a movie trade paper listing all the people she had forgotten to mention in her 1987 acceptance speech?

4556. Who did James Cagney want to play the lead role in his life story?

4557. What was the name of the prince who woke up Sleeping Beauty with a kiss in the Walt Disney version of the popular fairy tale?

4558. Dudley Moore appeared in the 1984 film *Unfaithfully Yours*, about a conductor who suspects his wife is cheating on him. Who appeared in the same role in the 1948 film of the same name?

4559. Caryn Johnson is a well-known comedienne, but she performs under another name. What is it?

4560. What comic-to-be made his movie debut at age five as a little boy thrown from a moving train in the cliff-hanger serial *The Perils of Pauline*?

4561. What late Broadway and Hollywood entertainer is known by a grade school nickname he acquired because of his poor marks?

4549. *Elliott Gould, in 1971. The film was* The Touch.

4550. *Linda Hunt. The film was* The Year of Living Dangerously.

4551. *He was 62. The movie was John Huston's* The Maltese Falcon; *the year, 1941.*

4552. *Murray Abraham, who won a best actor Academy Award in 1984 for his portrayal of Salieri in* Amadeus.

4553. *Stacy and James Keach as the James brothers; David, Keith and Robert Carradine as the Younger brothers; Randy and Dennis Quaid as the Miller brothers; and Nicholas and Christopher Guest as the Ford brothers.*

4554. *Size 36C.*

4555. *Cher, who won the best actress Oscar for her performance in* Moonstruck.

4556. *Michael J. Fox.*

4557. *Prince Philip. (Sleeping Beauty's name was Princess Aurora.)*

4558. *Rex Harrison.*

4559. *Whoopi Goldberg.*

4560. *Milton Berle.*

4561. *Zero Mostel, who was born Samuel Mostel.*

4562. Who is seen hitting the jackpot at a slot machine in a brief cameo appearance in the 1956 film *Meet Me in Las Vegas*?

4563. Can you name the two students Actors Studio guru Lee Strasberg said stood out "way above the rest"?

4564. What was distinctive about the line of towels introduced as a commercial tie-in to the 1939 film extravaganza *Ben Hur*?

4565. How many rats were specifically bred for the film *Indiana Jones and the Last Crusade*?

4566. What famous comic once doubled for actress Dolores Del Rio by jumping from the second-story window of a Klondike saloon in a flowing black wig and can-can dress?

4567. Who appeared at the 1968 Academy Awards celebration in a see-through pants suit?

4568. What famous Hollywood husband and wife met when both were working as understudies for the 1953 Broadway production of *Picnic*?

4569. By what name is S.P. Eagle, the producer of *The African Queen*, better known?

4570. What woman sports figure appeared as a maid in John Ford's 1959 film classic *The Horse Soldiers*?

4571. What was the last line ever spoken by Marilyn Monroe on the silver screen?

4572. What famous American acting family has a town in New York named after it—thanks to an ancestor who settled there in the seventeenth century?

4573. What famous actress once said, "The less I behave like Whistler's mother the night before, the more I look like her the morning after"?

4574. What Steve Martin movie was shown in Spanish-speaking countries under the title *Better Alone Than Badly Accompanied*?

4562. *Frank Sinatra.*

4563. *Marlon Brando and Marilyn Monroe.*

4564. *They were marked "Ben-His" and "Ben-Hers."*

4565. *3,000.*

4566. *Lou Costello, the hefty half of the Abbott and Costello team. The silent movie was* The Trail of '98.

4567. *Barbra Streisand. The following year she showed up in what one writer described as a "nice pink bar-mitzvah mother dress."*

4568. *Joanne Woodward and Paul Newman.*

4569. *Sam Spiegel. The Polish-born producer of* The Bridge on the River Kwai, Lawrence of Arabia, *and* On the Waterfront *used the pseudonym S.P. Eagle until 1954.*

4570. *Tennis star Althea Gibson.*

4571. *"How do you find your way back in the dark?" The line, said to Clark Gable, came at the end of the 1961 film* The Misfits. *She died in 1962.*

4572. *The Fondas. Their ancestors emigrated from Italy to the Netherlands in the fifteenth century, and two centuries later one of their descendants— Douw Fonda—sailed to America and settled in upstate New York.*

4573. *Tallulah Bankhead.*

4574. Planes, Trains and Automobiles, *the wacky 1987 comedy in which he co-starred with John Candy.*

4575. What actor turned down the roles played by Humphrey Bogart in the movies *High Sierra*, *The Maltese Falcon* and *Dead End*?

4576. On what cliffs did silent film serial queen Pearl ("Perils of Pauline") White do her famous cliff-hanging?

4577. What African political leader portrayed a tribal chief in the 1935 British adventure film *Sanders of the River*?

4578. In Japan, they called this 1962 movie thriller *We Don't Want a Doctor*. What was its title in the United States?

4579. What famous playwright wrote the Oscar-winning screenplay for the 1976 movie *Network*?

4580. What Hollywood legend spent three days in jail in 1916 after being arrested by New York vice squad detectives on charges of blackmail?

4581. In what film do the two main characters meet when one asks the other, "Hey, boy, what you doin' with my momma's car?"

4582. What 1954 film classic was based on a series of prize-winning exposés published in a New York newspaper?

4583. In the 1939 Hollywood classic *The Wizard of Oz*, what directions did Glinda, the good witch, give Dorothy for getting back home to Kansas?

4584. How much was Dustin Hoffman paid for appearing in the title role of the 1967 hit *The Graduate*, which grossed $80 million?

4585. Why was famed opera singer Enrico Caruso's first film, *My Cousin*, a big flop and his second film, *The Splendid Romance*, never released?

4586. What 1957 film was based on the life of Christine Sizemore? Hint: an actress won an Oscar for her performance in the title role.

4587. Where did director Elia Kazan shoot *Splendor in the Grass*, the 1961 Natalie Wood-Warren Beatty hit film about hot-blooded teenage love in Kansas in the late 1920s?

4575. *George Raft.*

4576. *On the Pallisades—on the western shore of the Hudson River, across from New York City.*

4577. *Jomo Kenyatta, who went on to become president of Kenya.*

4578. Doctor No. *It was the first of the James Bond film series.*

4579. *Paddy Chayefsky, who earlier gave us* Marty.

4580. *Rudolph Valentino.*

4581. Bonnie and Clyde. *Bonnie (Faye Dunaway) asks the question of Clyde (Warren Beatty) as he's about to drive off with her mother's car.*

4582. On the Waterfront. *The articles, by Malcolm Johnson of the* New York Sun, *exposed waterfront crime.*

4583. *"Close your eyes and tap your heels together three times. And think to yourself, there's no place like home."*

4584. *He got $750 a week—for a total of about $20,000—and graduated to the big time.*

4585. *Both were silent movies—not a big box-office draw for a professional singer.*

4586. *The film was* The Three Faces of Eve; *the actress, Joanne Woodward.*

4587. *On Staten Island, the least populated of New York City's five boroughs.*

4588. Who created the role of finicky Felix Ungar in 1965 in the original Broadway production of *The Odd Couple* ?

4589. What aspiring actor changed his name in 1938 after a movie executive told him, "Beedle! It sounds like an insect!"

4590. John Wayne wore a variety of studio-issued military uniforms in the movies. Which did he wear in real life?

4591. What Alfred Hitchcock spy thriller was almost called *The Man on Lincoln's Nose* ?

4592. Who was crowned the first Artichoke Queen in Castroville, California, the self-proclaimed "artichoke capital of the world"?

4593. Who played Santini, the mentally retarded student, in the 1955 film classic *The Blackboard Jungle* ?

4594. Who turned down the movie role of Eliza's father, Alfred P. Doolittle, in *My Fair Lady* before Stanley Holloway got the part?

4595. In the 1961 film *Breakfast at Tiffany's,* what are stars Audrey Hepburn and George Peppard shown when they ask a Tiffany salesman for something in the $10 range?

4596. Why were 30 acres of old movie sets in Culver City, California, put to the torch in 1938?

4597. Jack Nicholson won an Oscar for his portrayal of Randle P. McMurphy in the 1975 film *One Flew Over the Cuckoo's Nest.* Who starred in the same role on Broadway in 1963?

4598. What performers were originally sought as co-stars for *The Road to Singapore*, the first of the popular "Road" films that featured Bing Crosby and Bob Hope?

4599. What popular actor worked as an efficiency expert for the Connecticut State Budget Bureau before pursuing his acting career?

4600. What was the name of Mickey Rooney's mythical hometown in the "Andy Hardy" film series?

4588. *Art Carney, best known for his portrayal of far-from-finicky sewer worker Ed Norton on Jackie Gleason's* The Honeymooners. *Walter Matthau played Oscar Madison.*

4589. *William Holden, who was named William Beedle at birth.*

4590. *None. He was granted an exemption from military duty during World War II as a father of four and the sole support of his widowed mother.*

4591. North by Northwest, *starring Cary Grant and Eva Marie Saint. The title that didn't make it referred to a key scene that takes place on Mount Rushmore in the 1959 film.*

4592. *Marilyn Monroe. The year was 1947 and Monroe was then a little-known Hollywood starlet.*

4593. *Jamie Farr, best known for his portrayal of nutty, cross-dressing corporal Maxwell Klinger on TV's* M*A*S*H. *He is listed in the movie credits under his given name, Jameel Farah.*

4594. *James Cagney.*

4595. *A sterling silver telephone dialer for $6.75. They don't buy it.*

4596. *To recreate blazing, battle-torn Atlanta for the 1939 film classic* Gone With the Wind.

4597. *Kirk Douglas.*

4598. *George Burns and Fred MacMurray. Hope and Crosby were signed up after MacMurray turned down the project.*

4599. *Peter Falk.*

4600. *Carvel.*

4601. What film star launched his Hollywood career as a $5-a-day extra, portraying a swarthy Mexican soldier in Douglas Fairbanks Sr.'s film "His Majesty, the American"?

4602. What famous character actor—best known for his sinister screen roles—was a tea planter in Ceylon before he turned thespian?

4603. What famous actress made her stage debut portraying a boy in Henrik Ibsen's *A Doll's House* ?

4604. What star-to-be appeared on Broadway in 1954 as the insolent homosexual Arab houseboy in André Gide's *The Immoralist* ?

4605. Who was the first movie star to deliver the oft-repeated line, "We could have made beautiful music together"?

4606. Who won the Oscar for best actress in 1950—beating out Bette Davis, who starred in *All About Eve*, and Gloria Swanson, who appeared in *Sunset Boulevard* ?

4607. Who sang the role of Prince Charming in the 1937 Walt Disney classic *Snow White and the Seven Dwarfs* ?

4608. What is the "Oscar" of the saddle-and-spurs set—the award given to entertainers branded the best in the world of movie and TV westerns?

4609. What were the names of the three good fairies in Walt Disney's 1959 movie *Sleeping Beauty* ?

4610. What voice do the movies *The King and I, My Fair Lady* and *West Side Story* have in common?

4611. What film star would have been known as Lucille Le Sueur if Hollywood hadn't changed her name after she was discovered in a Broadway chorus?

4612. Actor Sylvester Stallone appeared in a Japanese television commercial in 1989. What was he promoting?

4601. *Boris Karloff, in 1919.*

4602. *Sydney Greenstreet.*

4603. *Joan Collins.*

4604. *James Dean.*

4605. *Gary Cooper, in the 1936 film* The General Died at Dawn. *The line was delivered to Madeleine Carroll.*

4606. *Judy Holliday, for her performance in* Born Yesterday.

4607. *Harry Stockwell, actor-singer father of Dean Stockwell.*

4608. *The Golden Boot.*

4609. *Fauna, the fairy of song; Flora, the fairy of beauty; and Merryweather, the fairy of happiness.*

4610. *That of Marni Nixon. She dubbed the singing for Deborah Kerr, Audrey Hepburn and Natalie Wood.*

4611. *Joan Crawford.*

4612. *Processed ham. There was a stipulation in his contract that the commercial not be shown in the U.S.*

4613. Sales of what part of the male wardrobe dropped sharply after Clark Gable appeared in the romantic comedy *It Happened One Night* in 1934?

4614. Whose family planned to erect a headstone that was a two-ton, nine-foot-tall marble replica of the Oscar—until the Academy of Motion Picture Arts and Sciences complained that it would be a copyright infringement?

4615. In how many films did Katharine Hepburn and Spencer Tracy appear together?

4616. What actor was the first man to appear on the cover of *Playboy* magazine?

4617. Who cursed more—Elizabeth Taylor or Richard Burton—and by how much in the 1966 film *Who's Afraid of Virginia Woolf?*

4618. In how many of his 200 films did Hollywood legend John Wayne die?

4619. What Hollywood great was originally cast in the title role *The Adventures of Robin Hood*—the 1938 film that starred the dashing Errol Flynn?

4620. Who dubbed gagging noises for actress Vivien Leigh in the 1939 film classic *Gone With the Wind*?

4621. What all-American Hollywood leading man appeared in the movies *Arizona Bound, Nevada, The Virginian, The Texan* and *A Man from Wyoming*?

4622. Who portrayed Vito Corleone as a young man in the 1974 film *The Godfather II*?

4623. What 1972 movie won an Oscar for its theme song, "The Morning After"—a song that earned singer Maureen McGovern a gold record?

4624. For what film did Cary Grant delay his honeymoon with his second wife, Woolworth heiress Barbara Hutton, in 1942?

4613. *The undershirt. Gable didn't wear one in the film.*

4614. *Showman Mike Todd's.*

4615. *Nine*—Woman of the Year, Keeper of the Flame, Without Love, Sea of Grass, State of the Union, Adam's Rib, Pat and Mike, The Desk Set and Guess Who's Coming to Dinner?

4616. *Peter Sellers, in 1964.*

4617. *Burton, by two. It was Burton, 24; Taylor, 22.*

4618. *In eight*—Reap the Wild Wind, The Fighting Seabees, The Wake of the Red Witch, Sands of Iwo Jima, The Alamo, The Man Who Shot Liberty Valance, The Cowboys and The Shootist.

4619. *James Cagney. He quit the movie in a contract dispute with Warner Brothers.*

4620. *Actress Olivia de Havilland, who played Melanie in the movie. Leigh, in the starring role of Scarlett O'Hara, refused to make the unladylike sounds when she choked on a radish in her vegetable-garden scene.*

4621. *Gary Cooper—who also starred in* It's a Big Country.

4622. *Robert De Niro.*

4623. The Poseidon Adventure.

4624. Once Upon a Honeymoon, *in which he co-starred with Ginger Rogers.*

4625. Actor Matthew Broderick was offered the lead in the 1983 film *War Games* after Kevin Costner turned it down to take a lesser role in what other film?

4626. Who played Moses as a baby in the 1956 film spectacular *The Ten Commandments*, which starred Charlton Heston?

4627. What famous leading man appeared in drag in two Marlene Dietrich movies?

4628. What substance was used as fuel for the time-traveling car in *Back to the Future Part II* ?

4629. What famous entertainer turned down the role of Romeo in Franco Zeffirelli's 1968 version of Shakespeare's *Romeo and Juliet* before the part was given to teen unknown Leonard Whiting?

4630. According to Hollywood legend, what famous tradition was started in 1927 after actress Norma Talmadge tripped while walking along the street with Douglas Fairbanks Jr. and Mary Pickford?

4631. What was the name of the motorcycle gang led by Lee Marvin in the 1954 Marlon Brando biker movie *The Wild One* ?

4632. What 1937 film starring Humphrey Bogart, Edward G. Robinson, Bette Davis and Wayne Morris is shown on television under the title *Battling Bellhop* to avoid confusion with a 1962 Elvis Presley musical remake?

4633. Who did actor Steve McQueen replace when he was hired to appear in Frank Sinatra's 1959 war film *Never So Few*?

4634. How much per hour did Paramount Pictures pay the U.S. Defense Department for each of the $37 million F-14 jets used in the 1986 Tom Cruise film *Top Gun*?

4635. How much was actor Burt Reynolds paid for posing as *Cosmopolitan* magazine's first nude centerfold in April 1972?

4636. What physical feature did both Rudolph Valentino and George Raft have changed with plastic surgery?

4625. The Big Chill. *Costner signed up to play Alex, the character whose suicide leads to the reunion that provides the movie's setting, but he's not seen in the film. His part—a 15-minute flashback scene—ended up on the cutting room floor.*

4626. *Heston's son Fraser, who grew up to become a screenwriter and motion picture producer.*

4627. *John* Wayne—*in* Seven Sinners *in 1940 and* The Spoilers *in 1942.*

4628. *Miller beer. The car was a DeLorean.*

4629. *Paul McCartney.*

4630. *Having movie stars leave hand- or footprints on the sidewalk outside Grauman's Chinese Theatre. That's where Talmadge tripped and fell into wet cement.*

4631. *The Beetles.*

4632. Kid Galahad.

4633. *Sinatra's "rat pack" buddy Sammy Davis Jr., who was dropped from the cast following a quarrel with Sinatra.*

4634. *$7,600. The total paid to the Defense Department for equipment and assistance was $1.2 million.*

4635. *He got what he was wearing—absolutely nothing. He posed for free.*

4636. *Their bat ears.*

4637. What common location was used in filming the movies *The Graduate, Cocoon, Gross Anatomy, Shocker, The Paper Chase* and both the 1939 and 1982 versions of *The Hunchback of Notre Dame* ?

4638. Child actress Shirley Temple was famous for her long curls. How many did she have?

4639. What famous Hollywood character actor portrayed the evil ex-con Gruesome in a 1947 Dick Tracy film?

4640. What film did Notre Dame try to keep off the silver screen in 1965 by going to court?

4641. How did Elizabeth Taylor's rebellious brother, Howard, get out of the screen test—and acting career—his stagestruck mother had set up for him?

4642. What movie star was one of both *The Magnificent Seven* and *The Dirty Dozen*?

4643. What well-known Hollywood producer is the grandson of the man who developed a popular vegetable?

4644. The summer of 1989 was dubbed the "Summer of Sequels." Can you name the eight film sequels that were responsible for this?

4645. What Oscar-winning actor appeared on Broadway in the early 1960s as Rolf, the youth who sings "You Are Sixteen," in the Rodgers and Hammerstein hit musical *The Sound of Music*?

4646. What actors represented *The Good, the Bad and the Ugly* in the 1966 Sergio Leone epic about three drifters in search of a treasure?

4647. What is the name of the actress daughter of Jessica Tandy and Hume Cronyn?

4648. In what film did former television talk-show host Arsenio Hall make his movie debut?

4649. What is actor Michael J. Fox's real middle initial?

4637. *The campus of the University of Southern California, in Los Angeles.*

4638. *55—not counting the spit curl on her forehead.*

4639. *Boris Karloff.*

4640. John Goldfarb, Please Come Home. *In the movie, Richard Crenna plays a Jew forced by an Arab king to coach an Arab football team to beat Notre Dame because the king's son had been cut from its team.*

4641. *He shaved his head on the eve of the scheduled screen test.*

4642. *Charles Bronson.*

4643. *Albert "Cubby" Broccoli, whose grandfather developed the broccoli in Italy. The vegetable was introduced to America in the 1870s by Broccoli's uncle, Pasquale de Cicco.*

4644. Friday the 13th Part VIII: Jason Takes Manhattan; Ghostbusters I ; Indiana Jones and the Last Crusade; The Karate Kid III; Lethal Weapon II; License to Kill *(in the James Bond series);* Nightmare on Elm Street V: The Dream Child; *and* Star Trek V: The Final Frontier.

4645. *Jon Voight.*

4646. *Clint Eastwood was the Good; Lee Van Cleef, the Bad; and Eli Wallach, the Ugly.*

4647. *Tandy Cronyn.*

4648. Amazon Women on the Moon, *in 1987.*

4649. *A, for Andrew. He had to use an initial under Screen Actors Guild regulations because there was already an actor named Michael Fox, but he didn't want to use A. because of the word play it suggested. He opted for J. out of admiration for character actor Michael J. Pollard.*

4650. What actress once performed as a singer and keyboard player with an all-girl band known as Psychotic Kindergarten?

4651. What was the theme song of comics Laurel and Hardy?

4652. Who was the first American movie director to be paid $1 million to direct a single film?

4653. What did the makeup people do to actress Lana Turner during the filming of *The Adventures of Marco Polo* in 1938 that permanently altered her features?

4654. What is the name of the friendly skunk in Walt Disney's *Bambi*?

4655. The 1987 film *Three Men and a Baby*, starring Tom Selleck, Steve Guttenberg and Ted Danson, is the American version of what very successful French film that came out a year earlier?

4656. What two-time Oscar-winning actress played young Jane Eyre's saintly, consumptive friend in the 1944 film that featured Joan Fontaine in the title role?

4657. What was Pluto's name when he made his debut in 1930 in a Mickey Mouse film?

4658. How old was Orson Welles when he co-wrote, produced, directed and starred in the 1941 film classic *Citizen Kane*?

4659. As a toddler, what famous movie-star-to-be had his picture on packages of baby food?

4660. What popular actor is married to Melissa Mathison, the writer who provided the screenplay for *E.T.*?

4661. What actress appeared on a magazine cover in the late 1970s with director Louis Malle's name tattooed on her breast?

4662. In how many Alfred Hitchcock movies did James Stewart appear? What were they?

4663. Actor Gary Cooper's given name at birth was Frank. What inspired an agent to change it to Gary?

4650. *Daryl Hannah.*

4651. *"The Dancing Cuckoos."*

4652. *Mike Nichols, in 1967, for "The Graduate."*

4653. *For her role as a Eurasian handmaiden, they shaved off her eyebrows regularly for three weeks and replaced them with false slanting eyebrows. As a result, her eyebrows never grew back and she had to either draw them in or paste them on ever after.*

4654. *Flower.*

4655. Three Men and a Cradle.

4656. *Elizabeth Taylor, who was 12 at the time.*

4657. *Rover. The film was* Chain Gang, *a short, in which he had a small role as Minnie Mouse's dog.*

4658. *25.*

4659. *Humphrey Bogart. His mother, a commercial artist, used him as the model for a picture that was used on packages of Mellins baby food.*

4660. *Harrison Ford.*

4661. *Susan Sarandon. Malle was her boyfriend at the time.*

4662. *Four—*Rope *(1948),* Rear Window *(1954),* The Man Who Knew Too Much *(1956) and* Vertigo *(1958).*

4663. *The agent's hometown—Gary, Indiana.*

4664. Who was Thomas "Pop" Dennehy, the prototype for the unseen "Mr. Dennehy" in comedian Jackie Gleason's "Joe the Bartender" skits?

4665. What actor operated a hot-dog stand known as "Tiny's" before making it big in films?

4666. What Hollywood leading man was once a dancer with the Eliot Feld Ballet company?

4667. What Hollywood star turned down the Jack Nicholson role in *The Witches of Eastwick*, the Dustin Hoffman role in *Rain Man* and the title role in *Batman*?

4668. In the 1988 Oscar-winning movie *Rain Man*, the character portrayed by Dustin Hoffman memorizes a telephone book up to the names Marsha and William Gottsegen. Who are they?

4669. What film role was James Dean next scheduled to play when he died in 1955?

4670. Who accepted the Academy Award for best actress in a gown she made herself out of $100 worth of fabric?

4671. For what film did Hollywood hold its first nude screen tests?

4672. What are the names of the young husband and wife who own Lady in Walt Disney's 1955 animated classic *Lady and the Tramp*?

4673. How many years passed between Paul Newman's making of *The Hustler* and its sequel, *The Color of Money*?

4674. What was the size of Scarlett O'Hara's waist in the Margaret Mitchell classic *Gone With the Wind*?

4675. What Oscar-winning actress dubbed the hair-raising voice of the devil in the 1973 chiller *The Exorcist*?

4676. Why did actor Gary Cooper dress in a Yankee uniform with New York spelled backward during the filming of *The Pride of the Yankees*, the story of Lou Gehrig?

4664. *The superintendent of the apartment building Gleason lived in when he was growing up in Brooklyn, New York.*

4665. *Actor Alan Ladd, who was about 5 feet 6 inches tall.*

4666. *Patrick Swayze, who dazzled us with his dancing in the 1987 film* Dirty Dancing.

4667. *Bill Murray.*

4668. *Hoffman's mother- and father-in-law.*

4669. *Boxer Rocky Graziano, in* Somebody Up There Likes Me—*the role that set Paul Newman on the road to stardom.*

4670. *Joanne Woodward. She won her Oscar for* The Three Faces of Eve *in 1957.*

4671. Four for Texas, *a 1963 Western comedy starring Anita Ekberg and Ursula Andress, along with Frank Sinatra and Dean Martin. The screen tests proved unnecessary—censors cut all the nude scenes.*

4672. *He's "Jim, Dear"; she's "Darling."*

4673. *25.* The Hustler *was filmed in 1961;* The Color of Money *in 1986.*

4674. *13 inches.*

4675. *Mercedes McCambridge.*

4676. *Because Gehrig was a lefty and Cooper was a righty. Cooper had tried to bat and field lefty for the part, but looked too awkward. So he was filmed batting righty and fielding righty from third base. Then the negative was reversed to make it look like he was playing lefty. In reversing the negative, New York was no longer spelled backward.*

4677. What was actor Willem Dafoe's name at birth?

4678. What was the only film directed by Marlon Brando?

4679. What did costume designer Edith Head say she was going to do with her Oscar when she accepted the coveted award for her contribution to the 1953 film *Roman Holiday*?

4680. What two Oscar-winning movie stars tied as "least likely to succeed" when they were students at the Pasadena Playhouse acting school?

4681. Joanne Woodward won an Oscar for her first film, The Three Faces of Eve. How many films did her husband Paul Newman appear in before he won an Oscar?

4682. In what city were scenes of the Brooklyn waterfront filmed for the 1954 Academy Award-winning movie *On the Waterfront*?

4683. What was movie hero Indiana Jones's first name?

4684. What famous entertainer's 1980 autobiography is entitled *A View from a Broad*.

4685. Robert De Niro sported 37 tattoos as a vengeful ex-con in the 1991 remake of the thriller *Cape Fear*. How many were his own?

4686. In how many films did Alan Hale play Robin Hood's strapping sidekick Little John?

4687. In the 1974 film *Alice Doesn't Live Here Any More*, what now-famous actress played Audrey, the street urchin who tried to get Alice's son to drink Ripple?

4688. Whom did author Ian Fleming suggest for the role of Agent 007 in the 1962 movie *Dr. No*, the first of Hollywood's James Bond films?

4689. What famous actor once portrayed a character named Badass Buddusky?

4677. *William Dafoe. Willem is the name he adopted in high school to avoid being called Billy.*

4678. *The 1961 movie* One Eyed Jacks.

4679. *She said, "I'm going to take it home and design a dress for it."*

4680. *Dustin Hoffman and Gene Hackman.*

4681. *46. Newman, a frequent nominee, won the Best Actor Oscar for The* Color of Money *in 1986. (Two years earlier, he had been given the Cecil B. DeMille Award for "outstanding contributions to the entertainment field.")*

4682. *Hoboken, New Jersey.*

4683. *Henry.*

4684. *Bette Middler's.*

4685. *Only one—the black panther on his right shoulder.*

4686. *Three—in the 1922 silent film* Robin Hood, *starring Douglas Fairbanks; in the 1938 film* The Adventures of Robin Hood, *with Errol Flynn in the title role; and in the 1950 film* Rogues of Sherwood Forest, *featuring John Derek as the son of Robin Hood.*

4687. *Jodie Foster.*

4688. *Composer-entertainer Hoagy Carmichael. The role, of course, went to Sean Connery.*

4689. *Jack Nicholson, in the 1973 film* The Last Detail.

4690. How many purebred Large White piglets appeared in the title role of *Babe*, the 1995 movie about a piglet that yearns to be a sheepdog?

4691. In what two films did Peter O'Toole portray England's King Henry II?

4692. What popular actor did poet Carl Sandburg describe as "one of the most beloved illiterates this country has ever known"?

4693. Who dubbed the voice of Draco, the dragon hero, in the 1996 film *Dragonheart*?

4694. What is writer-director-actor Woody Allen's legal name?

4695. What are the names of actor River Phoenix's four siblings?

4696. What two-time Academy Award-winning actress announced her retirement from the movies in 1992 after she was elected to Parliament in England?

4690. *48—all 11 weeks old. It was necessary to change piglets regularly because pigs grow fast and the film took 5 months to shoot. The film also used one "animatronic" robot pig.*

4691. Becket, *in 1964, and* The Lion in Winter, *in 1968.*

4692. *Gary Cooper.*

4693. *Sean Connery.*

4694. *Heywood Allen. He changed it from his birth name, Allen Stewart Konigsberg.*

4695. *Summer, Rainbow, Liberty and Joaquin (once known as Leaf).*

4696. *Glenda Jackson. She won Best Actress Oscars for* Women in Love *in 1970 and* A Touch of Class *in 1973.*

4697. In what two pictures did British comic actor Peter Sellers play three roles?

4698. What actress's father was the first American to be ordained a Tibetan Buddhist monk?

4699. What actress thanked 27 people in her Oscar acceptance speech—more than anyone else ever has?

4700. Who is the only entertainer to have five stars on Hollywood's Walk of Fame, one in each of the walk's five categories—film, TV, recording, radio and theater?

4701. What was the name of the 1970 sequel to the 1966 movie Hawaii?

4702. What actress sisters starred in the 1991 TV remake of the 1962 film *Whatever Happened to Baby Jane?*, which starred Joan Crawford and Bette Davis?

4703. What role did director John Huston play in his 1966 film epic *The Bible*?

4704. In what field of study did actor James Stewart earn a degree at Princeton University?

4705. Who played Beau Geste as a boy in the 1938 film *Sons of the Legion,* which featured Gary Cooper in the adult role?

4706. What is the entertainment publication *Variety* referring to when it uses the word helmer?

4707. Who dubbed James Dean's voice for his climactic "last supper" monologue in the 1956 film *Giant*?

4708. What was the name of the white mongrel with a brown spot over one eye that appeared with Charlie Chaplin in *It's a Dog's Life* and scores of other films?

4709. What does actor Keanu Reeves's first name mean in Hawaiian?

4697. The Mouse That Roared *in 1959 and* Dr. Strangelove, or How I learned to Stop Worrying and Love the Bomb *in 1963.*

4698. *Uma Thurman's. Her father, Robert, later renounced the monastic life.*

4699. *Olivia de Havilland, when she accepted the Oscar for Best Actress for her performance in the 1946 film* To Each His Own.

4700. *Gene Autry.*

4701. *The Hawaiians. Both films were drawn from the James Michener novel* Hawaii.

4702. *Lynn and Vanessa Redgrave.*

4703. *Noah.*

4704. *He received a B.S. in architecture in 1932, but never practiced.*

4705. *Donald O'Connor, who is perhaps best known for his comic dancing in* Singin' in the Rain. *He was 13 years old when he played young Beau.*

4706. *A director.*

4707. *Nick Adams. Shooting of the scene was finished just three days before Dean died.*

4708. *Scraps.*

4709. *"Cool breeze over the mountains." Reeves's father, who is of Chinese-Hawaiian ancestry, named his son after his own father.*

4710. What top film star made an unbilled cameo appearance as a TV news anchor in the 1987 film *Broadcast News*?

4711. In the 1983 film *The Man With Two Brains*, what actress provided the voice of the brain that Steve Martin loves and wants to transplant into his wife's body?

4712. Which Woody Allen movie was the first in which neither the filmmaker nor one of his real-life romantic partners appeared?

4713. What is the entertainment publication *Variety* referring to when it uses the word chopsocky?

4714. What movie and its sequel both won Academy Awards for Best Picture?

4715. Barry Fitzgerald appeared as matchmaker Michaleen Flynn in the 1952 John Ford comedy classic *The Quiet Man*. What role was played by his younger brother, Arthur Shields?

4716. What actress wrote her autobiography, *Little Girl Lost,* when she was just 14 years old?

4717. What well-known movie critic wrote the screenplay for the widely panned 1970 film *Beyond the Valley of the Dolls*?

4718. What is Demi Moore's full first name?

4719. What popular actor, while a student at Oxford, sought but did not get the role of Tarzan in the 1984 movie *Greystoke: The Legend of Tarzan, Lord of the Apes*?

4720. What line did a survey find had been spoken in 81 percent of the Hollywood films produced between 1938 and 1985?

4721. What was the name of the movie Marilyn Monroe was making when she died, and who was her co-star?

4722. What record-breaking hit movie used "A Boy's Life" as a working title to conceal its real subject until the release date?

4723. Artanis was the movie/television production company of which entertainer?

4710. *Jack Nicholson.*

4711. *Sissy Spacek.*

4712. Bullets Over Broadway, *in 1994.*

4713. *A martial arts film.*

4714. The Godfather *(1972) and* The Godfather, Part II *(1974).*

4715. *Rev. Cyril Playfair, the Protestant minister with a dwindling congregation. Irish-born Fitzgerald was born William Joseph Shields but adopted a stage name for fear of losing his civil service job.*

4716. *Drew Barrymore.*

4717. *Roger Ebert.*

4718. *Demetria. Her name at birth was Demetria Guynes. Moore was her first husband's surname.*

4719. *Hugh Grant.*

4720. *"Let's get outta here."*

4721. Something's Got to Give, *with Dean Martin. The movie was later remade as* Move Over Darling, *with Doris Day and James Garner.*

4722. E.T.- the Extra-Terrestrial.

4723. *Frank Sinatra. "Artanis" is "Sinatra" spelled backwards.*

4724. What was the original title of Elvis Presley's 1956 movie debut, *Love Me Tender*?

4725. On what ship did Dr. Doolittle and his friends sail in the 1967 film, *Dr. Doolittle*?

4726. Who are the youngest male and female performers to win Oscars for acting?

4727. Susan Hayward was nominated for an Oscar for three movies in which she played an alcoholic. What were the films?

4728. Henry Winkler and Susan Dey both turned down leading roles in the 1978 film version of a Broadway play that went on to become a huge success—both at the box office and for the people who ultimately took the parts. What was the film?

4729. What bleak, futuristic 1982 movie was based on Philip K. Dick's story, *Do Androids Dream of Electric Sheep?*?

4730. What do Marilyn Monroe, Elizabeth Taylor, Grace Kelly and Brooke Shields have in common, besides their obvious charms?

4731. For what film was the admission price to a movie first raised to $1.00?

4732. Which well-known actress provided part of the speaking voice for the loveable alien, in the 1982 movie, *E.T.—The Extra-Terrestrial*?

4733. In what movie did ex-football player Alex Karras play Squash?

4734. Who was the lowest-paid contract player in Hollywood's history?

4735. Other than being film stars, what do Doris Day and Marlon Brando have in common?

4736. In 1965, John Wayne made a brief appearance in a movie, his only line being, "Truly, this was the Son of God." Name the film.

4724. The Reno Brothers.

4725. *The Flounder.*

4726. *Timothy Hutton, who won Best Supporting Actor for Taps at the age of 20; and Tatum O'Neal, who was awarded Best Supporting Actress for Paper Moon at the age of 10.*

4727. Smash-Up, the Story of a Woman *(1947),* My Foolish Heart *(1950), and* I'll Cry Tomorrow *(1956).*

4728. Grease, *starring John Travolta and Olivia Newton-John.*

4729. Blade Runner.

4730. *They have all had dolls modeled after them.*

4731. *For the silent film,* Quo Vadis, *in 1913.*

4732. *Debra Winger.*

4733. Victor/Victoria, *in 1982. Squash was his character's name.*

4734. *Robert Taylor, who signed a seven-year contract in 1934 for $35 a week.*

4735. *They were both born on April 3, 1924.*

4736. The Greatest Story Ever Told.

4737. The Oscar winners of Best Supporting Actress from 1978 to 1981 all had the same initials—M.S. Name all four of these talented ladies.

4738. What is Johnny Carson's only movie acting credit?

4739. Who is the only performer to have won Best Actor Oscars in consecutive years?

4740. In July 1978, what actor became the first male to appear on the cover of *McCall's* magazine in its 100-year-plus history?

4741. What popular 1965 comedy film was subtitled "Or: How I Flew From London To Paris In 25 Hours and 11 Minutes"?

4742. Who was the first child nominated for an Oscar?

4743. What 1977 hit movie featured a frantic search for Devil's Tower, Wyo., America's first national monument?

4744. During the shooting of what film did Grace Kelly meet her future husband, Prince Rainier of Monaco?

4745. Whose screen test was assessed as, "Can't act, can't sing, slightly bald, can dance a little"?

4746. Who was the butt of Constance Bennett's quip, "Now there's a broad with her future behind her"?

4747. What was the only word spoken in the 1976 Mel Brooks film, *Silent Movie*, and who said it?

4748. What was the only song from an Alfred Hitchcock movie ever to win an Oscar for Best Song?

4749. What future world leader appeared as an extra in the 1944 Esther Williams film, *Bathing Beauty*?

4750. Which actor turned down the role of Dr. Indiana Jones in the 1981 movie, *Raiders of the Lost Ark*?

4751. Who was the first American actress to be depicted on a postage stamp?

4737. *Maggie Smith (for* California Suite *in 1978), Meryl Streep (for* Kramer vs. Kramer *in 1979), Mary Steenburgen (for* Melvin and Howard *in 1980) and Maureen Stapleton (for* Reds *in 1981).*

4738. Looking for Love, *with Connie Francis, in 1965.*

4739. *Spencer Tracy, for* Captains Courageous *in 1937, and* Boy's Town *in 1938.*

4740. *John Travolta.*

4741. Those Magnificent Men In Their Flying Machines.

4742. *Jackie Cooper, nominated for Best Actor in 1930 for* Skippy.

4743. Close Encounters of the Third Kind.

4744. To Catch a Thief, *directed by Alfred Hitchcock, in 1955.*

4745. *Fred Astaire's.*

4746. *The young Marilyn Monroe.*

4747. *"No," spoken by mime Marcel Marceau.*

4748. *"Que Sera Sera" ("Whatever Will Be, Will Be") sung by Doris Day in the 1956 film,* The Man Who Knew Too Much.

4749. *Fidel Castro.*

4750. *Tom Selleck, citing his commitment to his TV series,* Magnum, P.I.

4751. *Grace Kelly, on a stamp in Monaco, (1956).*

4752. Who won an Oscar for Best Actor for portraying George M. Cohan, the composer of many patriotic tunes, including "You're a Grand Old Flag"?

4753. Which daughter of a U.S. President appeared with Elvis Presley in the 1964 film, *Kissin' Cousins*?

4754. Within five years of the 1961 release of the film *The Misfits*, three of its stars were dead. Who were they?

4755. From what monolithic building did the giant ape fall in the 1976 remake of the movie, *King Kong*?

4756. Who dubbed the speaking voices of the late actors Peter Sellers and David Niven in the 1983 movie, *The Curse of the Pink Panther*?

4757. Who narrated the 1943 World War II film, *Gung Ho*?

4758. Whose body was used as the model for Tinker Bell in Walt Disney's film, *Peter Pan* ?

4759. In what 1931 film did James Cagney push half a grapefruit into the face of Mae Clarke?

4760. What was the name of Luke Skywalker's home planet in the 1977 film, *Star Wars*?

4761. Who was the only performer in the sound era to win an Oscar for Best Actress without having uttered a word in the film for which she was nominated?

4762. Who was the first actor to appear on the cover of *Time* magazine?

4763. What was actor Stewart Granger's real name?

4764. What is the only X-rated film to win the Academy Award for Best Picture?

4765. Who is the only woman James Bond ever married?

4752. *James Cagney, for* Yankee Doodle Dandy, *in 1942.*

4753. *Maureen Reagan.*

4754. *Clark Gable, Marilyn Monroe and Montgomery Clift.*

4755. *From one of the twin towers of the World Trade Center.*

4756. *Rich Little.*

4757. *Newsman Chet Huntley.*

4758. *Marilyn Monroe's.*

4759. The Public Enemy.

4760. *Tatooine.*

4761. *Jane Wyman, as the deaf-mute in* Johnny Belinda, *in 1948.*

4762. *Charlie Chaplin, on July 6, 1925.*

4763. *James Stewart.*

4764. Midnight Cowboy, *in 1969 (the rating was later reduced to R).*

4765. *Teresa Draco in* On Her Majesty's Secret Service. *Miss Draco was killed soon after their marriage.*

4766. What was the first movie sequel to be filmed in the same year as the original?

4767. What movie record was set in the 1952 film, *Scaramouche*?

4768. James Cagney directed only one film. Name it.

4769. *Joliet Jake* was the working title of what 1980 film?

4770. Who was the only one of Snow White's seven dwarfs not to have a beard?

4771. Who is Ginger Rogers' famous red-headed cousin?

4772. For what 1959 film were some theater seats wired to give a mild shock to the audience?

4773. After the formation of their comedy team, what was the only film made by Lou Costello without Bud Abbott?

4774. Johnny Weismuller and Buster Crabbe, who both were Olympic swimming champions and played Tarzan in the movies, made only one film together. What was it?

4775. The famous advertisement, "Gable's back and Garson's got him," was used for what 1945 Clark Gable-Greer Garson film?

4776. Who was Barbra Streisand's first choice as her co-star in the 1976 remake of the movie, *A Star Is Born*?

4777. For what crime was Lucas Jackson (played by Paul Newman) convicted in the 1967 movie, *Cool Hand Luke*?

4778. Who is the only actor to win an Oscar for playing Santa Claus?

4779. The 1954 film *White Christmas*, starring Bing Crosby, was a remake of an earlier film in which he also starred, and which introduced the famous song. What was the title of the original film?

4780. What popular Hollywood actor calls his production company Oak Productions because of an early nickname?

4766. Son of Kong, *the sequel to* King Kong. *Both were filmed in 1933.*

4767. *The longest sword fight: Stewart Granger and Mel Ferrer dueled for six and a half nerve-racking minutes.*

4768. Short Cut To Hell, *in 1957.*

4769. The Blues Brothers.

4770. *Dopey.*

4771. *Rita Hayworth; their mothers were sisters.*

4772. The Tingler.

4773. The Thirty-Foot Bride Of Candy Rock, *in 1959.*

4774. Captive Girl, *in 1950.*

4775. Adventure.

4776. *Elvis Presley. (Kris Kristoferson got the part when Miss Streisand and Col. Tom Parker, Elvis's manager, couldn't agree on terms.)*

4777. *Cutting the heads off parking meters.*

4778. *Edmund Gwenn, who won the Best Supporting Actor award for his role as Kris Kringle in* Miracle on 34th Street, *in 1947.*

4779. Holiday Inn, *made in 1942, was the original vehicle for the song, "White Christmas."*

4780. *Muscleman Arnold Schwarzenegger, who was known as the Austrian Oak in his body-building days.*

4781. Where was horror-film star Bela Lugosi born?

4782. How was actor Walter Matthau listed in the credits for the 1974 film *Earthquake*, in which he had a recurring cameo role as a drunk?

4783. Who turned down the role of the marshal in the 1952 Western classic *High Noon* before Gary Cooper was offered the part?

4784. What baseball great did Ronald Reagan portray in the 1952 biopic *The Winning Team*?

4785. What actress appeared in the 1987 film *Made in Heaven* as Emmett, a red-headed male archangel who served as head administrator of heaven?

4786. What popular TV and movie star cut the first syllable— Bum—from his last name when he launched his acting career?

4787. The plaintive musical score of what British motion picture classic was performed on a zither?

4788. What are Captain Nemo's cigars made of in the 1954 Walt Disney version of Jules Verne's *20,000 Leagues Under the Sea*?

4789. How many days in jail did Zsa Zsa Gabor serve in 1989 for slapping a Beverly Hills policeman?

4790. What is the only fast-food chain left on the planet in Sylvester Stallone's 1993 film *Demolition Man*, which takes place in the year 2032?

4791. What top cover girl first came to the attention of American moviegoers as an enemy agent in the 1983 James Bond film *Never Say Never Again*?

4792. How many movies did tough-guy actors James Cagney and Edward G. Robinson appear in together?

4793. What 1984 film was involved in so much litigation before its release that its closing credits include the name of the winning law firm?

4781. *In Lugos, Hungary—as Bëla Blasko. He took his stage name from his hometown.*

4782. *He was listed under his real name—Walter Matuschanskayasky.*

4783. *Gregory Peck. Marlon Brando and Montgomery Clift also were considered for the part by producer Stanley Kramer, but his backer insisted on Cooper.*

4784. *Hall of Fame pitcher Grover Cleveland Alexander.*

4785. *Debra Winger, who agreed to take the role as long as she was not identified or listed in the credits.*

4786. *James Garner—whose name was originally James Bumgarner.*

4787. *The Third Man.*

4788. *Seaweed.*

4789. *Three. The judge also ordered Gabor to put her true age on her driver's license.*

4790. *Taco Bell, which won the "franchise wars" in the early 21st sentury. In copies of the film distributed in Europe, Taco Bell was replaced by Pizza Hut.*

4791. *Kim Bassinger.*

4792. *Only one—Smart Money, in 1931.*

4793. The Cotton Club.

4794. In the 1966 remake of *Stagecoach*, what famous entertainer made his last film appearance as the drunken doctor—the role created by Thomas Mitchell in the 1939 John Wayne classic?

4795. What is the name of Bacchus's donkey-unicorn in Fantasia, Walt Disney's 1940 animated spectacular?

4796. What popular actor's first film role was that of an accident-prone young man in a half-hour Army training film?

4797. The 1932 film *What Price Hollywood* was remade three times—under what much better known title?

4798. What famous actress dubbed the dialogue for Andie MacDowell when she appeared as Jane Porter in the 1984 film *Greystoke: The Legend of Tarzan, Lord of the Apes*?

4799. What 1990 movie was the first film released with an NC-17 rating?

4800. What 1963 movie Western starring John Wayne and Maureen O'Hara was based on William Shakespeare's *The Taming of the Shrew*?

4801. What famous film director invented false eyelashes?

4802. As a young man, what cowboy star was offered $100 a month to play shortstop for a professional baseball team?

4803. What film role did Eli Wallach give up in 1953—making way for a famous Oscar-winning performance by an entertainment world legend?

4804. What was the name of the jeep driven by Pat Brady, Roy Rogers's comic sidekick both in the movies and on television?

4805. What restaurant chain had a branch in the space station in the 1968 film *2001: A Space Odyssey*?

4806. In what film does actor Marlon Brando appear on ice skates?

4794. *Bing Crosby.*

4795. *Jacchus.*

4796. *Jack Lemmon.*

4797. A Star Is Born.

4798. *Glenn Close. MacDowell's Southern accent made her a very unconvincing British Jane.*

4799. Henry and June. *NC-17, which means "no children under 17," was created to replace the X rating.*

4800. *McLintock!*

4801. *D.W Griffith, in 1916. He wanted one of the actresses in his film* Intolerance *to have eyelashes that brushed her cheeks.*

4802. *Gene Autry. He turned down an offer from the Cardinal organization to play with its Tulsa farm team and kept his $150-a-month job as a railroad telegraph operator. Years later, Autry became the owner of the California Angels.*

4803. *The part of Private Maggio in* From Here To Eternity. *Wallach bowed out to appear on Broadway in* Camino Real, *paving the way for Frank Sinatra's show business comeback.*

4804. *Nellybelle.*

4805. *Howard Johnson.*

4806. *In the 1990 film,* The Freshman.

4807. What two umbrella-carrying characters are featured in Walt Disney movies?

4808. What country music star appeared in three teen movies in 1960—*Sex Kittens Go To College*, *Platinum High School* and *College Confidential*?

4809. What actor served as Ronald Reagan's best man when he married Nancy Davis in 1952?

4810. How many motion pictures did Elizabeth Taylor and Richard Burton make together?

4811. What fictional character has been portrayed at various times by actors Humphrey Bogart, James Garner, Elliot Gould, Robert Mitchum, George Montgomery, Robert Montgomery and William Powell?

4812. In film and advertising slang, what do the letters SFX represent?

4813. What 1991 film role went to Kevin Costner after it was turned down by both Harrison Ford and Mel Gibson?

4814. What popular movie thriller was the first Hollywood film to include footage of a flushing toilet?

4815. What now-famous comedienne had a small role as nightclub hostess Texas Guinan in the 1961 Warren Beatty-Natalie Wood film *Splendor in the Grass*?

4816. What actress once gave her dimensions as 20-20-20?

4817. What actresses were the first mother and daughter to be nominated for Oscars in the same year?

4818. Before making it big in Hollywood, what famous actress provided the background singing for Andy Warhol's 1968 film *Lonesome Cowboys* and appeared as an extra in Warhol's 1971 movie *Trash*?

4807. *Mary Poppins, in the film of the same name; and Jiminy Cricket in* Pinocchio.

4808. *Conway Twitty.*

4809. *William Holden.*

4810. *10—*Cleopatra, The VIPs, The Sandpiper, Who's Afraid of Virginia Woolf?, The Comedians, The Taming of the Shrew, Dr. Faustus, Boom, Under Milk Wood, *and* Hammersmith Is Out.

4811. *Philip Marlowe, the hard-boiled private eye created by writer Raymond Chandler.*

4812. *"Sound effects."*

4813. *The part of New Orleans district attorney Jim Garrison in the docudrama* JFK.

4814. *Alfred Hitchcock's* Psycho, *in 1960. A long-standing taboo was violated when Janet Leigh was filmed flushing scraps of paper down a toilet.*

4815. *Phyllis Diller.*

4816. *Mia Farrow.*

4817. *Laura Dern was nominated for best actress and her mother, Diane Ladd, for best supporting actress in 1991—both for performances in* Rambling Rose. *Neither won.*

4818. *Sissy Spacek.*

4819. Why did Italian movie director Federico Fellini call his 1963 autobiographical film *8½*?

4820. What 1988 film ends with 763 names—the longest list of credits on record?

4821. To what famous actress did Winston Churchill propose marriage?

4822. When did Charlie Chaplin's 1952 film *Limelight* win an Oscar?

4823. In the 1985 film *Back to the Future* starring Michael J. Fox, what does Marty McFly's mother-to-be mistakenly think his name is?

4824. For the 1981 Oscar-winning movie *Chariots of Fire*, where was the race around the Great Court of Trinity College at Cambridge filmed?

4825. Who provided the voice of Mufasa, Simba's father, in the 1994 movie, *The Lion King*?

4826. After demanding top billing over Katherine Hepburn in the 1949 film *Adam's Rib*, what did Spencer Tracy reply when someone asked if he'd ever heard of "ladies first"?

4827. What was the name of the 1986 sequel to the 1979 film *Alien*?

4828. What famous Hollywood legend—named Carol Jane Peters at birth—took her stage name from a New York City drugstore?

4829. What father and daughter were originally scheduled to star in the 1973 film *Paper Moon* in the roles that went to Ryan O'Neal and his daughter, Tatum?

4830. In what movie did burly character actor Rod Steiger make his singing and dancing debut?

4831. What Oscar-winning film included scenes shot on the River Kwai in Thailand?

4819. *He considered it his No. 8½ directorial effort—having completed seven full-length and three short (or half-length) features.*

4820. Who Framed Roger Rabbit? *The credits take 6½ minutes and don't include Kathleen Turner, who asked not to be listed as the voice of Jessica Rabbit.*

4821. *Ethel Barrymore.*

4822. *The movie won the Oscar for Best Original Dramatic Score in 1972, when it was first screened in Los Angeles.*

4823. *Calvin Klein. The reason, she tells him, is, "It's written all over your underwear."*

4824. *At Eton College. The dons at Trinity refused to have anything to do with the movie.*

4825. *James Earl Jones.*

4826. *"This is a movie, not a lifeboat."*

4827. Aliens.

4828. *Carole Lombard. The drugstore was the Carroll, Lombardi Pharmacy on Lexington Avenue and 65th Street in Manhattan.*

4829. *Paul Newman and his daughter Nell Potts. Their deal was called off when John Huston bowed out as director and Peter Bogdanovich took over.*

4830. *In the 1955 movie musical* Oklahoma!, *in which he portrayed "Pore Jud" Fry.*

4831. The Deer Hunter. *The 1978 film won five Oscars—including one for Best Picture.* Bridge on the River Kwai, *the 1957 Oscar winner for Best Picture, was filmed in Ceylon.*

4832. What disclaimer appears with the opening credits of the 1954 film *The Caine Mutiny*, which featured Humphrey Bogart as Captain Queeg?

4833. What actor, in describing his craggy appearance, once said, "I resemble a rock quarry that got dynamited"?

4834. What Oscar-winning movie role was turned down by TV newscasters Walter Cronkite and John Chancellor before it was given to an actor?

4835. Why did filmmaker George Lucas file suit against President Ronald Reagan?

4836. By what professional name do we know the actor who was born Walter Palanuik?

4837. In what film besides *Yankee Doodle Dandy* did James Cagney play the legendary George M. Cohan?

4838. What is the closing line in the credits for the 1974 film *The Taking of Pelham One, Two, Three*, about a hijacked New York City subway train?

4839. For which of Jimmy Stewart's films did his father publicly chastise the actor for making a "dirty picture"?

4840. What movie starring Robert Redford was an adaptation of a Broadway play in which he also appeared?

4841. In what film did Marnie Nixon, who dubbed the singing for stars in a number of popular movie musicals, finally make her screen debut?

4842. Which was the only Alfred Hitchcock film to win an Academy Award for Best Picture?

4843. What was the literary source of the title of the 1961 Warren Beatty-Natalie Wood film *Splendor in the Grass?*

4844. Of the banks shown in the 1967 film Bonnie and Clyde, how many were actually robbed by the notorious outlaw couple?

4832. *"There has never been a mutiny in the history of the United States Navy."*

4833. *Charles Bronson.*

4834. *The role of the crazed anchorman in* Network, *the 1976 film that starred Peter Finch and gave us the line, "I'm mad as hell and I'm not going to take it anymore."*

4835. *To get him to stop using the term Star Wars to describe his Strategic Defense Initiative, the outer space computer-controlled defense system.*

4836. *Jack Palance.*

4837. The Seven Little Foys.

4838. *"Made without any help whatsoever from the New York Transit Authority."*

4839. Anatomy of a Murder. *The actor's father found the 1959 film's frank treatment of rape offensive and took out an ad in his hometown paper urging people not to see it.*

4840. Barefoot in the Park. *Redford's co-star in the 1964 stage production of the Neil Simon play was Elizabeth Ashley; in the 1967 movie, Jane Fonda.*

4841. The Sound of Music—*in which she appears as Sister Sophia. She did the singing for Audrey Hepburn in* My Fair Lady; *Natalie Wood in* West Side Story; *and Deborah Kerr in* The King and I.

4842. *The romantic thriller Rebecca, his first American film, in 1940.*

4843. *William Wordsworth's* Ode: Intimations of Immortality from Recollections of Early Childhood. *It reads: "Though nothing can bring back the hour/Of splendor in the grass, of glory in the flower;/We will grieve not, rather find/Strength in what remains behind."*

4844. *Three. Although closed since the Depression, they were reopened briefly for the filming of the movie.*

4845. What movie classic takes place in a town called Hadleyville?

4846. How many women appeared in Stanley Kubrick's 1964 film *Dr. Strangelove, or How I Learned to Stop Worrying and Love the Bomb?*

4847. In the 1977 film *Star Wars*, what name was originally planned for Luke Skywalker, the character played by Mark Hamill?

4848. In what Cary Grant film is a tombstone shown inscribed with his real name—Archibald Leach?

4849. Mae West once said she liked two kinds of men. What were they?

4850. Elizabeth Taylor starred in 10 movies with husband Richard Burton. How many did she appear in with hubby Eddie Fisher?

4851. How much did a Masai chief offer for actress Carrol Baker in 1964, when the average Masai maiden was valued at $200 and 12 cows?

4852. In what town did the Martian landing in Orson Welles' 1938 radio broadcast of *War of the Worlds* allegedly take place?

4853. What was the name of the ancient souped-up spacecraft captained by Han Solo in the film classic *Star Wars?*

4854. What 1959 film spectacular was nominated for 12 Oscars— and won all but one of them?

4855. Who was originally cast to play the role of T.E. Lawrence in *Lawrence of Arabia*, the Academy Award winner for Best Picture in 1962?

4856. In what Academy Award-winning 1967 film did a teenage Richard Dreyfuss make his movie debut in a one-line role?

4857. Which American actress had the longest screen career on record?

4858. What was the source of the hundreds of authentic-looking early 19th-century tinware pieces used in the 1997 movie *Amistad?*

4845. High Noon, *starring Gary Cooper and Grace Kelly.*

4846. *Only one. Tracy Reed, daughter of British director Sir Carol Reed. She played a nubile Pentagon secretary.*

4847. *Luke Skykiller. The name was changed on the first day of filming.*

4848. *The black-comedy classic* Arsenic and Old Lace, *which was released in 1944.*

4849. *"Domestic and foreign."*

4850. *One.* Butterfield Eight, *in 1960—for which she won an Academy Award for Best Actress.*

4851. *He offered $750 along with 150 cows and 200 goats and sheep. She was in Kenya filming the movie* Mr. Moses.

4852. *Grovers Mill, New Jersey.*

4853. *The Millennium Falcon.*

4854. Ben-Hur. *The Oscar that got away was for Best Screenplay Based on Material from Another Medium.*

4855. *Marlon Brando. He had to bow out when the shooting schedule of* Mutiny on the Bounty *was extended by several months. The part went to a virtual unknown, Peter O'Toole.*

4856. The Graduate. *He appears in the rooming house scene. His breakthrough role in* American Graffiti *came six years later.*

4857. *Helen Hayes, whose career spanned 78 years. It started with her 1910 debut in* Jean and the Calico Doll, *when she was 10, and ended with her appearance in the 1988 religious docudrama* Divine Mercy, No Escape, *when she was 88.*

4858. *Old Sturbridge Village, a re-created 1830s New England community in Sturbridge, Massachusetts. The tinware was crafted in its tin shop.*

4859. What was the first black-and-white film to be converted to color electronically?

4860. For which performer did Hollywood greats Humphrey Bogart and Lauren Bacall name their daughter?

4861. What was the first name of Ensign Pulver—played by Jack Lemmon in the 1955 film, *Mr. Roberts* and by Robert Walker Jr. in the 1964 sequel *Ensign Pulve*r?

4862. What is the name of the writer-director Chris Columbus's production company?

4863. What was actor Robert Redford doing when he first saw the vast alpine canyon in Park City, Utah, that he later bought and turned into an artists' retreat, ski resort and family compound?

4864. What serious actor worked as a lion tamer during a summer break form the Professional Children's Acting School in New York City?

4865. What 1951 movie classic inspired the pilot for a TV series that never made it, despite a cast that featured James Coburn and Glynis Johns?

4866. What replaced Charlie, the pet dog, when the 1961 movie *The Absent-Minded Professor* was remade as *Flubber* in 1997?

4867. What 1946 American film classic was denounced as Communist propaganda in an FBI memo because of its "rather obvious attempt to denounce bankers"?

4868. What high-flying actor named his son Jett?

4869. What popular actress wrote a magazine article entitled *The Alien Inside Me*?

4870. How much did actor Arnold Schwarzenegger pay for John F. Kennedy's set of golf clubs at a 1996 auction?

4871. What two films share the dubious distinction of having 11 Oscar nominations and no Oscar wins?

4859. Yankee Doodle Dandy, *the 1942 biopic of George M. Cohan with James Cagney in the title role.*

4860. *Leslie Howard. Their daughter's name is Leslie Howard Bogart. The couple's son, Stephen, was named for the character Bogie played in their first movie together,* To Have and Have Not.

4861. *Frank. Lemmon's portrayal won him an Oscar for Best Supporting Actor.*

4862. *1492 Films, Inc.*

4863. *Hunting mountain lions. At the time, Sundance, his 5000-acre spread in the Wasatch Range, was a sheep ranch.*

4864. *Christopher Walken, in 1961. His job was with the Tarryl Jacobs Circus.*

4865. The African Queen. *The pilot was aired as an episode of* The Dick Powell Show *in March 1962.*

4866. *Weebo, the computer.*

4867. It's A Wonderful Life, *starring Jimmy Stewart. The FBI memo said the film attacked bankers "by casting Lionel Barrymore as a 'Scrooge-type' so that he could be the most hated man in the picture. . . a common trick used by Communists."*

4868. *John Travolta, who's a licensed pilot.*

4869. *Sigourney Weaver, who starred as Ellen Ripley in the 1979 high-tech horror movie* Alien *and its sequels* —Aliens, Alien3 *and* Alien Resurrection. *Her article appeared in* Premiere *magazine.*

4870. *$772,500. Schwarzenegger is married to JFK's niece Maria Shriver.*

4871. The Turning Point *in 1977 and* The Color Purple *in 1985.*

4872. Who won a Best Actor Oscar for a role he also played on Broadway and in a weekly TV series?

4873. For what role did actress Jodie Foster have to undergo psychiatric evaluation by the California Labor Board?

4874. What celebrity bought the first Hummer manufactured for civilian use?

4875. What Hollywood legend played the accordion in a tearoom before he was offered a bit role in a Broadway play?

4876. What well-known actress, early in her career, appeared in a low-budget 3-D horror film as a young woman menaced by giant slugs?

4877. What did Lauren Hutton use to seal the gap between her front teeth early in her modeling career?

4878. What popular actor made an 18-second cameo appearance as a body-pierced, heavy-metal fan at a rock concert in the 1997 Billy Crystal-Robin Williams film comedy *Father's Day*?

4879. What highly acclaimed 1966 movie won five Oscars—including one for Best Cinematography for a black-and-white film?

4880. What did Marilyn Monroe do to create her sexy walk?

4881. Who coined the nickname "Tinsel Town" for Hollywood?

4882. What three John Ford films starring John Wayne featured the Seventh Cavalry?

4883. What are the names of the two cats in the animated 1955 Walt Disney film, *Lady and the Tramp*?

4884. What job did 7-foot 2-inch Peter Mayhew return to after playing the "Wookie" Chewbacca in the 1977 film *Star Wars*?

4885. How many names appeared above Elvis Presley's in the screen credits for his first film, the 1956 drama *Love Me Tender*?

4872. *Yul Brynner. The role, of course, was the King of Siam, whom Brynner portrayed on Broadway in the musical* The King and I *in 1951, in the hit movie of the same name in 1956, and in an unsuccessful TV version called* Anna and the King *in 1972. He continued to play the role in a series of revivals until his death in 1985.*

4873. *Iris, the teen prostitute in the 1976 film* Taxi Driver. *Because she was a minor, the board had to determine whether she was emotionally capable of handling the controversial role.*

4874. *Arnold Schwarzenegger, in 1992. The 6,300-pound, 7-foot-wide vehicle is the civilian version of the military Humvee.*

4875. *Jimmy Stewart, who played the accordion in the 1955 movie* The Man From Laramie.

4876. *Demi Moore. The film,* Parasite, *was advertised as "the first futuristic monster movie in 3-D" when it was released in 1982.*

4877. *Undertaker's wax or candle wax. She later had a dentist make a removable cap she could use as needed to hide the gap.*

4878. *Mel Gibson.*

4879. Who's Afraid of Virginia Woolf? *Starring Elizabeth Taylor (Best Actress), Richard Burton, Sandy Dennis (Best Supporting Actress) and George Segal. Its other Oscars were for Best Art Direction-Set Decoration (black-and-white film), and Best Costume Design (black-and-white film).*

4880. *She sawed off part of the heel of one shoe.*

4881. *Oscar Levant, the pianist, composer and cynical Hollywood wit, who observed, "Strip the phony tinsel off Hollywood, and you'll find the real tinsel underneath."*

4882. Fort Apache *(1948),* She Wore A Yellow Ribbon *(1949) and* Rio Grande *(1950).*

4883. *Si and Am. They were Siamese, of course.*

4884. *Hospital porter in London.*

4885. *Two. He got third billing, after Richard Egan and Debra Paget.*

4886. What was the name of the sly fox in the Disney film version of *Pinocchio*?

4887. What was the only movie about the Vietnam conflict to be filmed while the war was going on?

4888. What was the name of the baby in the 1987 film *Three Men and a Baby*?

4889. In the original script for the 1931 film *The Public Enemy*, what was James Cagney supposed to rub in Mae Clarke's face?

4890. What part did Robert De Niro play in his elementary school production of *The Wizard of Oz*?

4891. On what movie soundtrack did Gene Autry's 1939 rendition of Back in the Saddle Again go platinum for the second time?

4892. What special-interest magazine featured a photo of Demi Moore on its cover with a line promoting a story on her "secret passion"?

4893. What special clause, relating to clothes, did actor James Stewart have included in all his movie contracts?

4894. What Oscar-winning film featured a scene with an estimated 300,000 extras?

4895. What are the only two films to have received Oscars for Best Actor, Best Actress, Best Picture, Best Director, and Best Writing (Adaptation)?

4896. In the 1989 film hit *Field of Dreams*, what major flub was made by actor Ray Liotta in portraying baseball great Shoeless Joe Jackson?

4897. Who provides the voice for Yoda in the *Star Wars* series?

4886. *Worthington Foulfellow.*

4887. *The 1968 film* The Green Berets, *starring John Wayne.*

4888. *Mary.*

4889. *An omelette. In the famous scene Cagney ended up squashing a grapefruit in her face.*

4890. The Cowardly Lion. *De Niro was 10 at the time.*

4891. *The 1993 hit* Sleepless in Seattle.

4892. Cigar Aficianado, *in its fall 1996 issue. Moore's secret passion, the magazine reported, is cigar-smoking.*

4893. *The right to select the hats he wore on camera.*

4894. Gandhi. *The scene in the 1982 film was a recreation of the Indian leader's massive funeral in New Delhi 40 years ago today.*

4895. It Happened One Night, *in 1934, and* One Flew Over The Cuckoo's Nest, *in 1975.*

4896. *He batted righty—Jackson was a lefty.*

4897. *Frank Oz,, also the voice of Muppets™ Cookie Monster, Fozzie Bear and Ms. Piggy.*

4898. Where did the clairvoyant in director Tim Burton's *Pee Wee's Big Adventure* tell Pee Wee he would find his bicycle?

4899. Who had a cameo playing the president of the United States in Mike Myers' psychedelic comedy, *Austin Powers: The Spy Who Shagged Me?*

4900. In the 1989 cult fairy tale *The Princess Bride*, for what did the initials R.O.U.S. stand?

4901. What movie heartthrob played the corpse in *The Big Chill*— but ended up on the cutting room floor?

4902. Who posed for *Cosmopolitan* magazine's first nude centerfold in April 1974?

4903. Until 1990, what was the only Western to have been awarded the Oscar for Best Picture?

Bonus Trivia

4904. Preston Foster, Joanne Woodward, Ernest Torrence, Olive Borden, Edward Sedgwick, Louise Fazenda, Ronald Colman and Burt Lancaster were the first stars in Hollywood's Walk of Fame, begun in 1958.

4905. Outlaw Jesse James has been portrayed on screen by many different actors, but the first person ever to play him in a movie was his own son, Jesse James Jr.—in *Jesse James Under the Black Flag* (1921) and *Jesse James as the Outlaw* (1921).

4906. It was escape artist Harry Houdini who gave the young vaudeville player, Joseph Keaton, the name by which he would be known throughout his long film career. Having seen the acrobatic youngster scramble and fall about in his parents' boisterous stage routine, Houdini re-christened him "Buster."

4898. *At the Alamo. In the basement.*

4899. *Tim Robbins.*

4900. *Rodents of Unusual Size.*

4901. *Kevin Costner.*

4902. *Burt Reynolds.*

4903. Cimarron, *in 1931. It would be nearly 60 years before another western-themed movie,* Dances with Wolves, *would win, in 1990. Two yeasr later Clint Eastwood's brooding wWestern,* The Unforgiven, *would also claim the award.*

4907. Lana Turner was not discovered at the now-defunct Schwab's Pharmacy in Hollywood, as movie legend has it. She was discovered across the street from Hollywood High in Top's Café by Billy Wilkerson of *The Hollywood Reporter*, in January, 1936.

4908. John Travolta's stand-in for *Saturday Night Fever* was Jeff Zinn. It was Zinn's legs that were shown walking down the street in the film's opening.

Miscellaneous

Questions

4909. In land surveying, how long—in feet—is a chain?

4910. What synthetic fabric, introduced in the 1970s, is made of Teflon?

4911. What shade results when the rhubarb plant is used in hair dye?

4912. How many square inches are there in an acre?

4913. According to the Greek philosopher Aristotle, what part of the body served as the seat of the emotions?

4914. What was the childhood nickname of Leslie Hornby, the English model and sometimes actress better known as Twiggy?

4915. How many sets of letters on the standard typewriter and computer keyboard are in alphabetical order—reading left to right, of course?

4916. How much water does a 10-gallon hat hold?

4917. What was the only wood used by famed London cabinetmaker Thomas Chippendale?

Answers

4909. 66 feet.

4910. Gore-Tex.

4911. Blond. Its principal active ingredient is chrysophanol.

4912. 6,272,640. It's the number of square feet in an acre (43,560) times the number of square inches in a square foot (144).

4913. The liver.

4914. Sticks. It's the nickname Twiggy was derived from, given to her because of her gangling appearance.

4915. Three sets—F-G-H, J-K-L and O-P.

4916. ³/₄ gallon—or 3 quarts.

4917. Mahogany.

4918. What are the six fields of endeavor for which Nobel Prizes are awarded?

4919. In the early days of English law, why did grand juries sometimes write the word ignoramus on the back of indictments?

4920. What is a well-trained horse expected to do when given the command "gee"?

4921. Where on the grounds of the Playboy Mansion West did Hugh Hefner propose to his wife Kimberley?

4922. How many acres are there in a square mile?

4923. How large was the fund bequeathed in 1896 by Alfred Nobel to establish the annual Nobel Prizes?

4924. Who wrote the first known book on cosmetics, recommending face packs of barley-bean flour, eggs and mashed narcissus bulbs for smoother skin and warning against "powder too thickly applied, or ointments spread to excess"?

4925. Who referred to her famous son as "my golden Ziggy"?

4926. Approximately how many grains of sand does a quart-size pail hold?

4927. What is the fuel capacity—in gallons—of a Boeing 747 airliner?

4928. How many feet per minute does the standard escalator move?

4929. What philosophy was expounded by the American League for Physical Culture, established in 1929?

4930. What was the original name of the Girl Scouts?

4931. Charles E. Weller is best known for a single sentence he created. What is it?

4932. Who is credited with saying, "The bigger they are, the harder they fall"?

4918. Physics, chemistry, physiology or medicine, literature, peace and economic science. Economic science was added in 1969.

4919. Ignoramus is Latin for "we do not know." Jurors wrote the word on indictments when they found insufficient evidence to indict.

4920. Turn to the right. The opposite command, "haw," means turn left.

4921. At the wishing well.

4922. 640.

4923. $9.2 million.

4924. The Roman poet Ovid, in 10 A.D.

4925. Sigmund Freud's mother, Amalie Freud.

4926. 8 million.

4927. 57,285 gallons.

4928. 120.

4929. Nudism.

4930. The Girl Guides.

4931. "Now is the time for all good men to come to the aid of their party." He invented it as a typing exercise.

4932. Heavyweight boxer Bob Fitzsimmons. He made the statement before fighting (and losing to) champion James J. Jeffries in 1902.

4933. When Elizabeth Cochrane traveled around the world in less than 80 days in 1890, she used another name to conceal her identity. What was it?

4934. Identify the following: It was insured for $140,000; Sime Silverman, founder of *Variety* gave it its nickname; and it measured 2⅝ inches from head to tip.

4935. Who was Alexander the Great's teacher?

4936. Exactly how long is one year?

4937. Who was the first inductee into the National Trivia Hall of Fame?

4938. "Uphold the Right" (Maintiens le Droit) is the motto of what law enforcement agency?

4939. What do the initials, M.G., stand for on the famous British-made automobile?

4940. When were vitamins first described, and who is credited with their discovery?

4941. What is the origin of the $64 question?

4942. Canadian stagecoach-robber Bill Miner (the Gentleman Bandit), is credited for creating what classic line in a holdup?

4943. What are the only two letters that are not on a telephone dial?

4944. On what type of product would you find a message signed, "P. Loquesto Newman"?

4945. On what date will the twenty-first century begin?

4946. The most common hat size for men is 7⅛ what is the most common size for women?

4947. In earlier times, what building material did most Eskimos use to build their homes?

4933. *Nellie Bly.*

4934. *Jimmy Durante's nose.*

4935. *Aristotle.*

4936. *365 days, 5 hours, 48 minutes and 46 seconds.*

4937. *Robert L. Ripley, who was inducted in 1980 into the honorary Hall sponsored by* Trivia Unlimited *magazine of Lincoln, Neb.*

4938. *The Royal Canadian Mounted Police.*

4939. *Morris Garage.*

4940. *In 1912; F. G. Hopkins and Casmir Funk.*

4941. *It was the highest prize ever paid to a winner on radio's* Take it or Leave it.

4942. *"Hands up."*

4943. *Q and Z.*

4944. *Actor Paul Newman's line of food products.*

4945. *January 1, 2001. (Strictly speaking, January 1, 2000 will be the first day of the last year of the twentieth century.)*

4946. *22. Although both are measured in inches, men's hats are sized according to diameter and women's according to circumference.*

4947. *Sod. Igloos, made of ice, were generally built only as temporary shelters.*

4948. How is Eleanor Thornton, secretary to British Lord Montagu of Beaulieu in the early twentieth century, part of automotive history?

4949. Who has requested that her gravestone epitaph read, "Big deal! I'm used to dust"?

4950. In 1937, sewing machine heiress Daisy Singer Alexander put her will in a bottle and tossed it into the Thames River near London. Where and when did it wash up?

4951. Who was Grace Toof and how has she been immortalized?

4952. What was the first word that the blind Helen Keller learned in sign language from her teacher Annie Sullivan?

4953. Annie Oakley, in a demonstration of her incredible marksmanship, once shot at 5,000 pennies tossed into the air. How many did she hit with her rifle fire?

4954. What did comic genius Ernie Kovacs have installed in his California driveway to make maneuvering easier for visitors?

4955. In what year was January 1 first used to mark the beginning of the new year?

4956. What Census Bureau category do you fall into if you are classified as a POSSLQ?

4957. The four-leaf clover is considered lucky because of its rarity and symmetry. What about the even rarer five-leaf clover?

4958. What is the size of the standard credit card?

4959. What group's motto is "Blood and Fire"?

4960. What do the following crayon colors have in common— maize, raw umber, lemon yellow, blue gray, violet blue, green blue, orange red and orange yellow?

4961. What was the original use of crinoline—the stiff fabric most commonly associated with women's petticoats?

4948. *She was the inspiration for the Flying Lady statuette—known as "The Spirit of Ecstasy"—that graces the radiator of the Rolls Royce. The original was created for Lord Montagu's Silver Ghost by sculptor Charles Sykes in 1911.*

4949. *Writer-humorist-homemaker Erma Bombeck.*

4950. *On a beach in San Francisco, 12 years later. Under the terms of the will, the lucky beachcomber who found it inherited half of Daisy's $12 million estate.*

4951. *She's the woman that Graceland, Elvis Presley's estate in Memphis, Tennessee, is named after. Presley bought it from Ruth Brown, who had named it for her Aunt Grace.*

4952. *Water.*

4953. *4,777—for an average of almost 96 percent.*

4954. *An asphalt turntable, which made U-turns unnecessary.*

4955. *In 153 B.C., by the Romans. Previously, New Year's Day was in March.*

4956. *Person of Opposite Sex, Sharing Living Quarters.*

4957. *The superstitious consider it bad luck if kept—but good luck to both parties involved if given away immediately upon finding.*

4958. *3⅜ by 2⅛ inches.*

4959. *The Salvation Army's.*

4960. *They were the first colors ever dropped from the Crayola crayon line. They were replaced in 1990 with bolder colors—cerulean, dandelion, wild strawberry, vivid tangerine, fuchsia, teal blue, royal purple and jungle green.*

4961. *Men's collars.*

4962. Nineteenth-century English physician Peter Mark Roget devised his famous thesaurus to help people find the right word. What equally useful tool did he develop for those searching for mathematical solutions?

4963. From what is rice paper made?

4964. What day is the middle day of the year—in non-leap years?

4965. Can you fill in the last word of this Victorian-era saying: "Horses sweat, men perspire, women . . ."?

4966. How much weight is saved when an airline doesn't paint an MD-11 jumbo jet?

4967. What did prospectors in ancient times use to collect grains of gold from streams?

4968. What was the average life span of a Stone Age cave dweller?

4969. What was used to erase lead pencil marks before rubber came into use?

4970. How many points are there on a Maltese cross?

4971. Why do federal park rangers working in the subtropical marshlands of south Florida wear snowshoes designed for use in subarctic climates?

4972. How many dust mites can a gram of dust hold?

4973. What inspired bareback rider Nelson Hower to introduce circus tights in 1828?

4974. What high-fashion clothing designer spent two years in medical school before deciding to find another career?

4975. What highly paid supermodel was valedictorian of her high school class and winner of a full college scholarship to study chemical engineering?

4976. An organization called SCROOGE was formed in 1979 in Charlottesville, Virginia. What does the acronym stand for?

4962. *A special (log-log) slide rule.*

4963. *The pith—the inner part of the trunk—of a small tree native to swampy forests of southern China and Taiwan.*

4964. *July 2nd. There are 182 days before it, and 182 after.*

4965. *". . .glow."*`

4966. *Almost 300 pounds.*

4967. *The fleece of sheep—unlike the '49ers and other prospectors who panned for gold.*

4968. *18 years.*

4969. *Pieces of bread.*

4970. *Eight.*

4971. *The web-footed, wood-framed shoes keep them from sinking into the silty marshes.*

4972. *500 (an ounce can hold 13,500).*

4973. *His regular costume was missing—so he performed in his long knit underwear. Hower and other performers with the Buckley and Wicks Show normally wore short jackets, knee breeches and stockings. When their costumes didn't arrive in time for a show, Hower improvised and changed circus fashions forever.*

4974. *Italian style-setter Giorgio Armani.*

4975. *Cindy Crawford. The college was Northwestern University. Crawford dropped out after just one semester to pursue a modeling career.*

4976. *Society to Curtail Ridiculous, Outrageous and Ostentatious Gift Exchanges.*

4977. For what magazine did Hugh Hefner serve as circulation manager while he was raising money to launch *Playboy*?

4978. What article of clothing is named for James Brudenell, the British major general who led his men "into the valley of death" in the Crimean War's famous "Charge of the Light Brigade"?

4979. Prior to his death in 1999, John F. Kennedy, Jr. founded what politically-themed magazine?

4980. What was the cost of the first tour arranged by travel entrepreneur Thomas Cook in 1841?

4981. What problem did Leonardo da Vinci, Winston Churchill, Albert Einstein, Thomas Edison and General George Patton have in common?

4982. What would the Barnie Doll's measurements be if she were life-size?

4983. What did All Nippon Airways do in an effort to prevent its planes from sucking birds into their engines?

4984. Where did the phrase "Let George do it" originate?

4985. What is the "Newgate Calendar"?

4986. What foreign form of transportation was invented by American Baptist missionary Jonathan Goble in 1871?

4987. What was the chief source of the shiny material used in making artificial pearls before the advent of plastics?

4988. What is the centerfold feature called in *Playboar*, a magazine for swine breeders?

4989. What were the names of the two dogs launched into space aboard Russia's Sputnik 5 and later returned to earth, becoming the first animals recovered from orbit?

4990. What English earl had both a coat style and a furniture style named for him?

4977. Children's Activities *magazine.*

4978. *The cardigan sweater. Brudenell was the seventh earl of Cardigan.*

4979. George.

4980. *The equivalent of fourteen cents. It was a 48-mile round trip by British rail between Leicester and Loughborough for a temperance meeting.*

4981. *All were dyslexic.*

4982. *39-21-33.*

4983. *It painted giant eyes on the engine intakes to discourage birds from approaching.*

4984. *With France's King Louis XII, who let his chief minister, Cardinal George d'Amboise, do it.*

4985. *The biographical record, first published in the late eighteenth century, of the most notorious criminals incarcerated at London's famous Newgate prison.*

4986. *The rickshaw. Goble, while serving as a missionary in Yokohama, had a Japanese carpenter build the rickshaw for his invalid wife.*

4987. *Fish scales.*

4988. *"Littermate of the Month."*

4989. *Belka and Strelka; they made their historic flight in 1960.*

4990. *Philip Dormer Stanhope, the fourth earl of Chesterfield. The Chesterfield coat and sofa are named for him.*

4991. Before the introduction of the hair dryer in 1920, what common household appliance was promoted for its hair-drying ability?

4992. Who was described in *Playboy* magazine as "Mary Poppins in Joan Collins' clothing"?

4993. How much hay was eaten daily by Jumbo, showman P. T. Barnum's famous 6½-ton elephant?

4994. What was the first living creature ever ejected from a supersonic aircraft?

4995. To whom did Mahatma Gandhi write for advice on diet and exercise?

4996. In 1964, a capsized freighter was refloated in Kuwait by filling its hull with polystyrene balls. Where did this idea originate?

4997. Where do these lines come from?
   "I always voted at my party's call,
   And never thought of thinking for myself at all."

4998. Why does the Bronx Zoo get blood daily from a local slaughterhouse?

4999. What famous Englishman's experiments with freezing meat in 1626 caused his death from exposure?

5000. What trade was Greek philosopher Socrates trained for?

5001. Who was billed as "The Human Mop" when he joined his family's comic acrobatic vaudeville act at age 3?

5002. What did Hyman Lipman do in 1858 that made life easier for students?

5003. Who went to New York City to launch her modeling career in 1966, after winning the Miss Rocket Tower beauty contest in California?

4991. The vacuum cleaner—which could be converted into a hair dryer by attaching a hose to the exhaust.

4992. Vanna White, of TV's Wheel of Fortune fame.

4993. Two hundred pounds.

4994. A bear, in 1962. It was parachuted from 35,000 feet to a safe landing on earth.

4995. Strongman Charles Atlas.

4996. In a 1949 Donald Duck comic, in which Donald and his nephews raised a yacht using ping pong balls.

4997. Gilbert and Sullivan's operetta, HMS Pinafore.

4998. To feed its vampire bats, part of its captive breeding collection of bats—the largest in the world.

4999. Sir Francis Bacon, philosopher, courtier, statesman, essayist.

5000. Stonecutting.

5001. Buster Keaton.

5002. He put pencil and eraser together.

5003. Cheryl Tiegs.

5004. How much did 16-year-old Edgar Bergen pay a woodcarver for Charlie McCarthy's head in 1925—and what size hat did it wear?

5005. The term "Siamese twins" originated with the birth of two brothers joined together at the chest. What were their names?

5006. What did Lizzie Borden, Napoleon, and Titian have in common?

5007. Gen. Tom Thumb, 3 feet 4 inches tall, was the first husband of Mercy Lavinia Bump, who measured 2 feet 8 inches. How tall was her second husband, Count Primo Magi?

5008. Who were actress-socialite Dina Merrill's super-rich parents?

5009. Who runs the Spirit Foundation, a charity dedicated to helping the aged, abused, and orphaned?

5010. In the words of the popular English nursery rhyme, "Who killed Cock Robin"—and how?

5011. By what name was Nobel Peace Prize winner Agnes Gonxha Bojaxhiu better known?

5012. How is Sir Benjamin Hall memorialized?

5013. Who was Apollos De Rivoire?

5014. Who was Pablo Ruiz?

5015. What reason did Yale University graduate student Edmund D. Looney give when he sought court permission in 1956 to change his name?

5016. What do the surnames Adler and Aguila have in common?

5017. What is the chief ingredient in the rich brown pigment we know as sepia?

5018. What was the response of England's White Chapel Foundry in 1970 when members of the Procrastinators Club of America demanded a refund for the Liberty Bell because it cracked in 1835?

5004. Cost, $36; hat size, 5⅞.

5005. Chang and Eng, born in 1811.

5006. They were all redheads.

5007. Her equal at 2 feet 8 inches.

5008. Financier E. F. Hutton and cereal heiress Marjorie Merriweather Post.

5009. Yoko Ono.

5010. "I," said the sparrow, "with my bow and arrow."

5011. Mother Teresa, India's "saint of the gutter."

5012. His nickname—Big Ben—was adopted for the 13½-ton hour bell in the clock tower of the British Houses of Parliament in London. Hall was London's chief commissioner of works in 1859, when the bell was installed.

5013. The French Huguenot father of American patriot Paul Revere. Rivoire changed his name to Paul Revere after immigrating to the colonies as a boy, and later passed that name onto his son.

5014. Pablo Picasso. Born Pablo Ruiz, the great artist chose to use Picasso—his mother's less common surname.

5015. He claimed the name Looney would interfere with the practice of his chosen profession—psychiatry.

5016. Both mean eagle—Adler in German; (guila in Spanish.

5017. The inky fluid secreted by the cuttlefish—which belongs to the genus Sepia.

5018. The British bell maker offered a full refund—but only if the defective product was returned in its original packaging.

5019. What was the first man-made object to reach the moon?

5020. What is daredevil Evel Knievel's real first name?

5021. On board a ship, what times would be indicated by seven bells?

5022. What is the standard width between rails on North American and most European railroads?

5023. What do the letters stand for in the acronym CARE—the name of the relief organization established in 1945?

5024. Why wasn't 10-year-old Eric, the orangutan at Chicago's Lincoln Park Zoo, sent to China for stud duty as planned in 1984?

5025. What was the name of Hugh Hefner's all-black private jetliner?

5026. For what highly valued commodity did one early seventeenth-century Dutch farmer trade 4 loads of grain, 4 oxen, 12 sheep, 8 pigs, 2 tubs of butter, 100 pounds of cheese, 4 barrels of ale, 2 hogsheads of wine, a bed with bedding, a chest of clothes and a silver goblet?

5027. How thick is the gold leaf used for lettering and gilding?

5028. Where did the countdown used in rocket and spaceship launchings originate?

5029. What is the telephone area code for a cruise ship in the Atlantic Ocean?

5030. Left to right, what are the seven letters on the bottom row of the standard typewriter or computer keyboard?

5031. What is the color of the "black box" that houses an airplane's voice recorder?

5032. What did former president Richard Nixon, striptease artist Gypsy Rose Lee, opera impresario Rudolph Bing and French novelist Simone de Beauvoir have in common?

5019. *Luna 2, an unmanned Soviet spacecraft that crashed onto the lunar surface in September 1959.*

5020. *Robert.*

5021. *3:30, 7:30 and 11:30—both A.M. and P.M.*

5022. *4 feet 8½ inches—about the width of cart tracks in ancient Rome, where that was found to be the most efficient width for a loaded horse-drawn vehicle.*

5023. *Cooperative for American Relief Everywhere. When the group was first formed, the letters stood for Cooperative for American Remittances to Europe, and then Cooperative for American Remittances Everywhere.*

5024. *"He" unexpectedly gave birth to a baby—and was renamed Erica.*

5025. *"Big Bunny."*

5026. *A single tulip bulb.*

5027. *Approximately ¹⁄₂₀₀,₀₀₀ inch.*

5028. *In a silent German science fiction film,* Die Frau in Mond (The Girl in the Moon) *in 1928. Director Fritz Lang reversed the count to build suspense.*

5029. *871.*

5030. *z, x, c, v, b, n, m*

5031. *It's orange—so it can be more easily detected amid the debris of a plane crash.*

5032. *Their birthday—January 9.*

5033. In a famous New Year's Day column, newspaperman Westbrook Pegler repeated the same sentence 50 times. What was it?

5034. If we saw the emblem known as a fylfot decorating a Byzantine structure, what would we most likely call it?

5035. How did the inch-long 2-penny (or 2d) nail get its name?

5036. Approximately how many blades of grass are there in an acre of lawn?

5037. What did Aristotle believe was the main purpose of the human brain?

5038. In medieval days, how much did the average suit of armor weigh?

5039. In the children's rhyme that begins "Ding, Dong, Bell," who put Pussy in the well and who pulled her out?

5040. How big is a cord of wood?

5041. Who was the first person to walk untethered in space?

5042. What did movie star Mary Pickford use to christen the first Hollywood-to-San Francisco bus in the early 1920s?

5043. In a bid to calm manic and psychotic juveniles, what color did California's San Bernardino County Probation Department paint its detention cells?

5044. Who said, "The great question . . . which I have not been able to answer despite my 30 years in research into the feminine soul, is 'What does a woman want'?"

5045. What was the first hurricane named after a man?

5046. What great feat made Isaac Van Amburgh a circus headliner in the late 1830s?

5047. What incredible adventure did British seaman James Bartley survive while whale hunting in 1891?

5033. *"I will never mix gin, beer, and whiskey again."*

5034. *A swastika. The Nazis adopted the ancient symbol as their emblem.*

5035. *It was the nail that was sold at the rate of 100 for 2 pennies, or pence, in Great Britain in the fifteenth century, when the sizing system for nails was first established. (The d in 2d is the British symbol for pence.)*

5036. *564,537,600—according to the Lawn Institute.*

5037. *To cool the blood.*

5038. *Between 50 and 55 pounds.*

5039. *Little Johnny Green put her in; Little Tommy Stout got her out.*

5040. *It is 128 cubic feet and usually measures 4 feet high, 4 feet wide and 8 feet long.*

5041. *Navy Captain Bruce McCandless II, 164 miles above the earth, from the space shuttle Challenger on February 7, 1984.*

5042. *A bottle of grape juice. Prohibition made champagne taboo.*

5043. *Bubble-gum pink.*

5044. *Sigmund Freud.*

5045. *Bob, in July 1979. He put in a brief, blustery appearance on the Louisiana coast and then turned into an offshore breeze.*

5046. *He was the first animal trainer to put his head in a lion's mouth.*

5047. *He spent two days in a whale's stomach after being swallowed alive— and then lived another 35 years to tell about it.*

5048. What was a 13.5-carat diamond used for on the Pioneer 2 space probe to Venus in 1978?

5049. Who was featured in the *Playboy* centerfold when the magazine made its debut in 1953?

5050. What did the R in Edward R. Murrow stand for?

5051. What is the source of the hair in most camel's hairbrushes?

5052. Several American zoos have put up signs indicating "The Most Dangerous Animal in the World." Where are they posted?

5053. What was the name of Smokey the Bear's mate?

5054. Where are the Islands of Langerhans?

5055. Why did the Smithsonian Institution develop a special perspiration and barnyard scent for one of their exhibitions?

5056. What unusual twosome spoke at ventriloquist Edgar Bergen's funeral in 1979?

5057. Why is the phrase "the quick brown fox jumps over a lazy dog" used to check typewriters?

5058. The highest surface wind speed ever recorded was at Mount Washington, New Hampshire, on April 24, 1934. What was it?

5059. What is the highest rating given a top quality diamond?

5060. What altitude does a vehicle have to exceed for its pilot and passengers to be officially recognized as spacemen?

5061. What did the Apollo 8 astronauts use to fasten down tools during weightlessness on their 1968 moon-orbiting voyage?

5062. In what kind of store are you most likely to find Chilean nylons and Australian bananas?

5063. What does a vamp have to do with a shoe?

5064. What did Shirley Temple, Enrico Caruso, Irving Berlin, and Gene Tunney have in common?

5048. *Instrument-viewing ports. It was the only substance that was both transparent to infrared light and also able to withstand the red-hot heat and tremendous pressure of the Venusian atmosphere.*

5049. *Marilyn Monroe.*

5050. *Roscoe.*

5051. *Squirrel tails.*

5052. *Next to full-length mirrors—for the viewing public.*

5053. *Goldie.*

5054. *In the human body—in the pancreas.*

5055. *To make their re-creation of a Maryland sharecropper's house more realistic.*

5056. *Muppet creator Jim Henson and Kermit the Frog.*

5057. *It's a pangram—it contains every letter in the alphabet at least once.*

5058. *It was 231 miles per hour. (Winds become hurricane force when they reach 74 miles per hour.)*

5059. *D-flawless.*

5060. *According to NASA 400,000 feet, or 75¾ miles, above the earth.*

5061. *Silly Putty.*

5062. *A fish store. They are species of shrimp.*

5063. *It's the upper front part of a shoe.*

5064. *When they married, their blue-blooded spouses were kicked out of the Social Register.*

5065. All told, how many children did Siamese twins Chang and Eng Bunker father?

5066. What is the maximum flight speed of a Boeing 747-300 jetliner?

5067. What was the greatest number of people ever carried in an airship?

5068. According to Aristotle, what determined whether a baby would turn out to be a girl or a boy?

5069. How many teaspoons are there in a cup?

5070. Why did local environmental officials spray-paint 108 pink plastic flamingos white and place them in groups around marshes in the Everglades?

5071. What was the symbolism behind flying a flag at half-mast as a sign of mourning when the custom was first introduced at sea in the seventeenth century?

5072. What are the names of the six Gummi Bears?

5073. How are the monkeys Mizaru, Kikazaru and Iwazaru better known to us?

5074. If all the water were drained from the body of an average 160-pound man, how much would the body weigh?

5075. What is the average life expectancy of a toilet?

5076. Which was the first Impressionist painting to be owned by the French government?

5077. How much does owning a typical dog cost over its average 11-year life span—not including the original purchase price?

5078. What famous medal depicts three naked men with their hands on each other's shoulders?

5079. What percentage of men are left-handed? How about women?

5065. 22. Chang had 10; Eng, 12.

5066. 583 miles per hour.

5067. 207. They were aboard the U.S. Navy's Akron in 1931. The trans-Atlantic record is 117—held by the ill-fated Hindenburg, which exploded in May 1937.

5068. Wind direction.

5069. 48. There are 3 teaspoons to a tablespoon and 16 tablespoons to a cup.

5070. To attract snowy egrets, white ibis and wood storks. The plastic flamingos were much cheaper than white egret decoys.

5071. The top of the mast was left empty for the invisible flag of death.

5072. Gruffi, Cubbi, Tummi, Zummi, Sunni and Grammi.

5073. As See No Evil, Hear No Evil and Speak No Evil, respectively.

5074. 64 pounds.

5075. 50 years.

5076. Edouard Manet's Olympia, which was bought through public subscription in 1890, seven years after his death. It is still owned by the Louvre.

5077. An average of $14,600—with food ($4,020) the biggest expense, followed closely by veterinary costs ($3,930).

5078. The Nobel Peace Prize.

5079. 10 percent of men; 8 percent of women.

5080. How many seats are there on the standard 747 jumbo jet?

5081. What gem was once considered a charm against drunkenness?

5082. In the late 1920s, who arranged 200 golf balls in neat rows in the hollow of a fallen tree at a public golf course in Winnipeg, Canada?

5083. How many grooves are there on the edge of a quarter?

5084. How many letters are there in the Hawaiian alphabet?

5085. In writing Roman numerals what does $\bar{V}$ represent?

5086. What is the only fifteen-letter word in the English language that can be written without repeating a letter?

5087. What is the largest amount of American currency one can hold without having change for a dollar?

5080. 420.

5081. The amethyst—which gets its name from the Greek amethystos—which means "remedy for drunkenness."

5082. A gopher, in the mistaken belief that they were eggs and would make appetizing wintertime eating.

5083. 119.

5084. Twelve: vowels A-E-I-O-U; consonants H-K-L-M-N-P-W.

5085. It represents 5,000. The bar is a multiplier, indicating 1,000 times the number below.

5086. Uncopyrightable.

5087. $1.19—three quarters, four dimes and four pennies.

CADILLAC DESERT

MARC REISNER

CADILLAC DESERT

The American West
and Its Disappearing Water

VIKING

VIKING
Viking Penguin Inc., 40 West 23rd Street,
New York, New York 10010, U.S.A.
Penguin Books Ltd, Harmondsworth,
Middlesex, England
Penguin Books Australia Ltd, Ringwood,
Victoria, Australia
Penguin Books Canada Limited, 2801 John Street,
Markham, Ontario, Canada L3R 1B4
Penguin Books (N.Z.) Ltd, 182–190 Wairau Road,
Auckland 10, New Zealand

First published in 1986 by Viking Penguin Inc.
Published simultaneously in Canada

Grateful acknowledgment is made for permission to reprint an excerpt
from "Talking Columbia," words and music by Woody Guthrie. TRO
—© Copyright 1961 and 1963 Ludlow Music, Inc., New York, N.Y. Used by
permission.

LIBRARY OF CONGRESS CATALOGING IN PUBLICATION DATA
Reisner, Marc.
Cadillac desert.
Bibliography: p.
Includes index.
1. Irrigation—Government policy—West (U.S.)—
History.   2. Water resources development—Government
policy—West (U.S.)—History.   3. Corruption (in
politics)—West (U.S.)—History.   I. Title.
HD1739.A17R45   1986   333.91'00978   85-40814
ISBN 0-670-19927-3

Printed in the United States of America by
R. R. Donnelley & Sons Company, Harrisonburg, Virginia
Set in Aster

Endpaper maps by David Lindroth

For Konrad and Else Reisner

OZYMANDIAS

I met a traveller from an antique land
Who said: Two vast and trunkless legs of stone
Stand in the desert . . . Near them, on the sand,
Half sunk, a shattered visage lies, whose frown,
And wrinkled lip, and sneer of cold command,
Tell that its sculptor well those passions read
Which yet survive, stamped on these lifeless things,
The hand that mocked them, and the heart that fed:
And on the pedestal these words appear:
"My name is Ozymandias, king of kings:
Look on my works, ye Mighty, and despair!"
Nothing beside remains. Round the decay
Of that colossal wreck, boundless and bare
The lone and level sands stretch far away.

PERCY BYSSHE SHELLEY

CONTENTS

Contents

CADILLAC DESERT

INTRODUCTION

A Semidesert
with a Desert Heart

One late November night in 1980 I was flying over the state of Utah on my way back to California. I had an aisle seat, and since I believe that anyone who flies in an airplane and doesn't spend most of his time looking out the window wastes his money, I walked back to the rear door of the airplane and stood for a long time at the door's tiny aperture, squinting out at Utah.

Two days earlier, a fierce early blizzard had gone through the Rocky Mountain states. In its wake, the air was pellucid. The frozen fire of a winter's moon poured cold light on the desert below. Six inches away from the tip of my nose the temperature was, according to the pilot, minus sixty-five, and seven miles below it was four above zero. But here we were, two hundred highly inventive creatures safe and comfortable inside a fat winged cylinder racing toward the Great Basin of North America, dozing, drinking, chattering, oblivious to the frigid emptiness outside.

Emptiness. There was nothing down there on the earth—no towns, no light, no signs of civilization at all. Barren mountains rose duskily from the desert floor; isolated mesas and buttes broke the wind-haunted distance. You couldn't see much in the moonlight, but obviously there were no forests, no pastures, no lakes, no rivers; there was no fruited plain. I counted the minutes between clusters of lights. Six, eight, nine, eleven—going nine miles a minute, that was a lot of uninhabited distance in a crowded century, a lot of emptiness amid a civilization whose success was achieved on the pretension that natural obstacles do not exist.

Then the landscape heaved upward. We were crossing a high, thin cordillera of mountains, their tops already covered with snow. The Wasatch Range. As suddenly as the mountains appeared, they fell away, and a vast gridiron of lights appeared out of nowhere. It was clustered thickly under the aircraft and trailed off toward the south, erupting in ganglionic clots that winked and shimmered in the night. Salt Lake City, Orem, Draper, Provo: we were over most of the population of Utah.

That thin avenue of civilization pressed against the Wasatches, intimidated by a fierce desert on three sides, was a poignant sight. More startling than its existence was the fact that it had been there only 134 years, since Brigham Young led his band of social outcasts to the old bed of a drying desert sea and proclaimed, "This is the place!" *This* was the place? Someone in that first group must have felt that Young had become unhinged by two thousand horribly arduous miles. Nonetheless, within hours of ending their ordeal, the Mormons were digging shovels into the earth beside the streams draining the Wasatch Range, leading canals into the surrounding desert which they would convert to fields that would nourish them. Without realizing it, they were laying the foundation of the most ambitious desert civilization the world has seen. In the New World, Indians had dabbled with irrigation, and the Spanish had improved their techniques, but the Mormons attacked the desert full-bore, flooded it, subverted its dreadful indifference—moralized it—until they had made a Mesopotamia in America between the valleys of the Green River and the middle Snake. Fifty-six years after the first earth was turned beside City Creek, the Mormons had six million acres under full or partial irrigation in several states. In that year—1902—the United States government launched its own irrigation program, based on Mormon experience, guided by Mormon laws, run largely by Mormons. The agency responsible for it, the U.S. Bureau of Reclamation, would build the highest and largest dams in the world on rivers few believed could be controlled—the Colorado, the Sacramento, the Columbia, the lower Snake—and run aqueducts for hundreds of miles across deserts and over mountains and through the Continental Divide in order to irrigate more millions of acres and provide water and power to a population equal to that of Italy. Thanks to irrigation, thanks to the Bureau—an agency few people know—states such as California, Arizona, and Idaho became populous and wealthy; millions settled in regions where nature, left alone, would have countenanced thousands at best; great valleys and hemispherical basins metamorphosed from desert blond to semitropic green.

On the other hand, what has it all amounted to?

Stare for a while at a LANDSAT photograph of the West, and you will see the answer: not all that much. Most of the West is still untrammeled, unirrigated, depopulate in the extreme. Modern Utah, where large-scale irrigation has been going on longer than anywhere else, has 3 percent of its land area under cultivation. California has twelve hundred major dams, the two biggest irrigation projects on earth, and more irrigated acreage than any other state, but its irrigated acreage is not much larger than Vermont. Except for the population centers of the Pacific Coast and the occasional desert metropolis—El Paso, Albuquerque, Tucson, Denver—you can drive a thousand miles in the West and encounter fewer towns than you would crossing New Hampshire. Westerners call what they have established out here a civilization, but it would be more accurate to call it a beachhead. And if history is any guide, the odds that we can sustain it would have to be regarded as low. Only one desert civilization, out of dozens that grew up in antiquity, has survived uninterrupted into modern times. And Egypt's approach to irrigation was fundamentally different from all the rest.

If you begin at the Pacific rim and move inland, you will find large cities, many towns, and prosperous-looking farms until you cross the Sierra Nevada and the Cascades, which block the seasonal weather fronts moving in from the Pacific and wring out their moisture in snows and drenching rains. On the east side of the Sierra-Cascade crest, moisture drops immediately—from as much as 150 inches of precipitation on the western slope to as little as four inches on the eastern—and it doesn't increase much, except at higher elevations, until you have crossed the hundredth meridian, which bisects the Dakotas and Nebraska and Kansas down to Abilene, Texas, and divides the country into its two most significant halves—the one receiving at least twenty inches of precipitation a year, the other generally receiving less. Any place with less than twenty inches of rainfall is hostile terrain to a farmer depending solely on the sky, and a place that receives seven inches or less—as Phoenix, El Paso, and Reno do—is arguably no place to inhabit at all. Everything depends on the manipulation of water—on capturing it behind dams, storing it, and rerouting it in concrete rivers over distances of hundreds of miles.

3

Were it not for a century and a half of messianic effort toward that end, the West as we know it would not exist.

The word "messianic" is not used casually. Confronted by the desert, the first thing Americans want to do is change it. People say that they "love" the desert, but few of them love it enough to live there. I mean in the real desert, not in a make-believe city like Phoenix with exotic palms and golf-course lawns and a five-hundred-foot fountain and an artificial surf. Most people "love" the desert by driving through it in air-conditioned cars, "experiencing" its grandeur. That may be some kind of experience, but it is living in a fool's paradise. To *really* experience the desert you have to march right into its white bowl of sky and shape-contorting heat with your mind on your canteen as if it were your last gallon of gas and you were being chased by a carload of escaped murderers. You have to imagine what it would be like to drink blood from a lizard or, in the grip of dementia, claw bare-handed through sand and rock for the vestigial moisture beneath a dry wash.

Trees, because of their moisture requirements, are our physiological counterparts in the kingdom of plants. Throughout most of the West they begin to appear high up on mountainsides, usually at five or six thousand feet, or else they huddle like cows along occasional streambeds. Higher up the rain falls, but the soil is miserable, the weather is extreme, and human efforts are under siege. Lower down, in the valleys and on the plains, the weather, the soil, and the terrain are more welcoming, but it is almost invariably too dry. A drought lasting three weeks can terrorize an eastern farmer; a drought of five months is, to a California farmer, a normal state of affairs. (The lettuce farmers of the Imperial Valley don't even *like* rain; it is so hot in the summer it wilts the leaves.) The Napa Valley of California receives as much Godwater—a term for rain in the arid West—as Illinois, but almost all of it falls from November to March; a weather front between May and September rates as much press attention as a meteor shower. In Nevada you see rainclouds, formed by orographic updrafts over the mountains, almost every day. But rainclouds in the desert seldom mean rain, because the heat reflected off the earth and the ravenous dryness can vaporize a shower in midair, leaving the blackest-looking cumulonimbus trailing a few pathetic ribbons of moisture that disappear before reaching the ground. And if rain does manage to fall to earth, there is nothing to hold it, so it races off in evanescent brown torrents, evaporating, running to nowhere.

One does not really conquer a place like this. One inhabits it like an occupying army and makes, at best, an uneasy truce with it. New England was completely forested in 1620 and nearly deforested 150 years later; Arkansas saw nine million acres of marsh and swamp forest converted to farms. Through such Promethean effort, the eastern half of the continent was radically made over, for better or worse. The West never can be. The only way to make the region over is to irrigate it. But there is too little water to begin with, and water in rivers is phenomenally expensive to move. And even if you succeeded in moving every drop, it wouldn't make much of a difference. John Wesley Powell, the first person who clearly understood this, figured that if you evenly distributed all the surface water flowing between the Columbia River and the Gulf of Mexico, you would *still* have a desert almost indistinguishable from the one that is there today. Powell failed to appreciate the vast amount of water sitting in underground aquifers, a legacy of the Ice Ages and their glacial melt, but even this water, which has turned the western plains and large portions of California and Arizona green, will be mostly gone within a hundred years—a resource squandered as quickly as oil.

At first, no one listened to Powell when he said the overwhelming portion of the West could never be transformed. People figured that when the region was settled, rainfall would magically increase, that it would "follow the plow." In the late 1800s, such theories amounted to Biblical dogma. When they proved catastrophically wrong, Powell's irrigation ideas were finally embraced and pursued with near fanaticism, until the most gigantic dams were being built on the most minuscule foundations of economic rationality and need. Greening the desert became a kind of Christian ideal. In May of 1957, a very distinguished Texas historian, Walter Prescott Webb, wrote an article for *Harper's* entitled "The American West, Perpetual Mirage," in which he called the West "a semidesert with a desert heart" and said it had too dark a soul to be truly converted. The greatest national folly we could commit, Webb argued, would be to exhaust the Treasury trying to make over the West in the image of Illinois—a folly which, by then, had taken on the appearance of national policy. The editors of *Harper's* were soon up to their knees in a flood of vitriolic mail from westerners condemning Webb as an infidel, a heretic, a doomsayer.

Desert, semidesert, call it what you will. The point is that despite heroic efforts and many billions of dollars, all we have managed to do in the arid West is turn a Missouri-size section green—and that conversion has been wrought mainly with nonrenewable groundwater. But a goal of many westerners and of their federal archangels,

5

the Bureau of Reclamation and Corps of Engineers, has long been to double, triple, quadruple the amount of desert that has been civilized and farmed, and now these same people say that the future of a hungry world depends on it, even if it means importing water from as far away as Alaska. What they seem not to understand is how difficult it will be just to hang on to the beachhead they have made. Such a surfeit of ambition stems, of course, from the remarkable record of success we have had in reclaiming the American desert. But the same could have been said about any number of desert civilizations throughout history—Assyria, Carthage, Mesopotamia; the Inca, the Aztec, the Hohokam—before they collapsed.

And it may not even have been drought that did them in. It may have been salt.

The Colorado River rises high in the Rockies, a trickle of frigid snowmelt bubbling down the west face of Longs Peak, and begins its fifteen-hundred-mile, twelve-thousand-foot descent to the Gulf of California. Up there, amid mountain fastnesses, its waters are sweet. The river swells quickly, taking in the runoff of most of western Colorado, and before long becomes a substantial torrent churning violently through red canyons down the long west slope of the range. Not far from Utah, at the threshold of the Great Basin, the rapids die into riffles and the Colorado River becomes, for a stretch of forty miles, calm and sedate. It has entered the Grand Valley, a small oasis of orchards and cows looking utterly out of place in a landscape where it appears to have rained once, about half a million years ago. The oasis is man-made and depends entirely on the river. Canals divert a good share of the flow and spread it over fields, and when the water percolates through the soil and returns to the river it passes through thick deposits of mineral salts, a common phenomenon in the West. As the water leaves the river, its salinity content is around two hundred parts per million; when it returns, the salinity content is sixty-five hundred parts per million—twenty-eight times higher.

The Colorado takes in the Gunnison River, whose waters have also filtered repeatedly through irrigated, saline earth, and disappears into the canyonlands of Utah. Near the northernmost tentacle of Lake Powell, where the river backs up for nearly two hundred miles behind Glen Canyon Dam, it receives its major tributary, the Green River. The land along the upper Green is heavily irrigated, and so is the land beside its two major tributaries, the Yampa and the White. Some of *their* tributaries, which come out of the Piceance Basin, are saltier than the ocean. In Lake Powell, the water spreads, exposing vast surface acreage to the sun, which evaporates several feet each year, leaving all the salts behind. Released by Glen Canyon Dam, the Colorado takes in the Little Colorado, Kanab Creek, the Muddy, and one of the more misnamed rivers on earth, the Virgin. It pools again in Lake Mead, again in Lake Mojave, and again in Lake Havasu; it takes in the Gila River and its oft-used tributaries, the Salt and the Verde, all turbid with alkaline leachate. A third of its flow then goes to California, where some of it irrigates the Imperial Valley and the rest allows Los Angeles and San Diego to exist. By then, the water is so salty that restaurants often serve it with a slice of lemon. If you pour it on certain plants, they will die.

Along the Gila River in Arizona, the last tributary of the Colorado, is a small agricultural basin which Spaniards and Indians tried to irrigate as early as the sixteenth century. It has poor drainage—the soil is underlain by impermeable clays—so the irrigation water rose right up to the root zones of the crops. With each irrigation, it became saltier, and before long everything that was planted died. The Spaniards finally left, and the desert took the basin back; for a quarter of a millennium, it remained desert. Then, in the 1940s, the Bureau of Reclamation reclaimed it again, building the Welton-Mohawk Project and adding an expensive drainage system to collect the sumpwater and carry it away. Just above the Mexican border, the drain empties into the Colorado River.

In 1963, the Bureau closed the gates of Glen Canyon Dam. As Lake Powell filled, the flow of fresh water below it was greatly reduced. At the same time, the Welton-Mohawk drain was pouring water with a salinity content of sixty-three hundred parts per million directly into the Colorado. The salinity of the river—what was left of it—soared to fifteen hundred parts per million at the Mexican border. The most important agricultural region in all of Mexico lies right below the border, utterly dependent on the Colorado River; we were giving the farmers slow liquid death to pour over their fields.

The Mexicans complained bitterly, to no avail. By treaty, we had promised them a million and a half acre-feet of water. But we hadn't promised them *usable* water. By 1973, Mexico was in a state of apoplexy. The ruin of its irrigated agricultural lands along the lower Colorado was the biggest issue in the campaign of presidential candidate Luis Echeverría, who was elected by a wide margin in that

7

year. Still, the United States continued to do nothing. But 1973 also saw the arrival of OPEC. Some new geologic soundings in the Bay of Campeche indicated that Mexico might soon become one of the greatest oil-exporting nations in the world. When Echeverría threatened to drag the United States before the World Court at The Hague, Richard Nixon sent his negotiators down to work out a salinity-control treaty. It was signed within a few months.

Once we agreed to give Mexico water of tolerable quality, we had to decide how to do it. Congress's solution was to authorize a desalination plant ten times larger than any in existence that will clean up the Colorado River just as it enters Mexico. What it will cost nobody knows; the official estimate in 1985 was $300 million, not counting the 40,000 kilowatts of electricity required to run it. Having done that, Congress wrote what amounts to a blank check for a welter of engineered solutions farther upriver, whose exact nature is still under debate. Those could cost another $600 million, probably more. One could easily achieve the same results by buying out the few thousand acres of alkaline and poorly drained land that contribute most to the problem, but there, once again, one runs up against the holiness of the blooming desert. Western Congressmen, in the 1970s, were perfectly willing to watch New York City collapse when it was threatened with bankruptcy and financial ruin. After all, New York was a profligate and sinful place and probably deserved such a fate. But they were not willing to see one acre of irrigated land succumb to the forces of nature, regardless of cost. So they authorized probably $1 billion worth of engineered solutions to the Colorado salinity problem in order that a few hundred upstream farmers could go on irrigating and poisoning the river. The Yuma Plant will remove the Colorado's salt—actually just enough of it to fulfill our treaty obligations to Mexico—at a cost of around $300 per acre-foot of water. The upriver irrigators buy the same amount from the Bureau for $3.50.

Nowhere is the salinity problem more serious than in the San Joaquin Valley of California, the most productive farming region in the entire world. There you have a shallow and impermeable clay layer, the residual bottom of an ancient sea, underlying a million or so acres of fabulously profitable land. During the irrigation season, temperatures in the valley fluctuate between 90 and 110 degrees; the good water evaporates as if the sky were a sponge, the junk water goes down, and the problem gets worse and worse. Very little of the water seeps through the Corcoran Clay, so it rises back up into the root zones—in places, the clay is only a few feet down—waterlogs the land, and kills the crops. A few thousand acres have already gone out of production—you can see the salt on the ground like a dusting of snow. In the next few decades, as irrigation continues, that figure is expected to increase almost exponentially. To build a drainage system for the valley—a giant network of underground pipes and surface canals that would intercept the junk water and carry it off— could cost as much as a small country's GNP. In 1985, the Secretary of the Interior put forth a figure of $5 billion for the Westlands region, and Westlands is only half the problem. Where would the drainwater go? The Westlands' drainwater, temporarily stored in a huge sump which was christened a wildlife preserve, has been killing thousands of migrating waterfowl; the water contains not just salts but selen- ium, pesticides, and God knows what else. There is one logical ter- minus: San Francisco Bay. As far as northern Californians are concerned, the farmers stole all this water from them; now they want to ship it back full of crud.

As is the case with most western states, California's very exis- tence is premised on epic liberties taken with water—mostly water that fell as rain on the north and was diverted to the south, thus precipitating the state's longest-running political wars. With the ex- ception of a few of the rivers draining the remote North Coast, vir- tually every drop of water in the state is put to some economic use before being allowed to return to the sea. Very little of this water is used by people, however. Most of it is used for irrigation—85 per- cent of it, to be exact. That is a low percentage, by western standards. In Arizona, 90 percent of the water consumed goes to irrigation; in Colorado and New Mexico, the figure is almost as high. In Kansas, Nevada, Nebraska, North Dakota, South Dakota, Oklahoma, Texas, Wyoming, Montana; even in Washington, Oregon, and Idaho—in all of those states, irrigation accounts for nearly all of the water that is consumptively used.

By the late 1970s, there were 1,251 major reservoirs in California, and every significant river—save one—had been dammed at least once. The Stanislaus River is dammed fourteen times on its short run to the sea. California has some of the biggest reservoirs in the country; its rivers, seasonally swollen by the huge Sierra snowpack, carry ten times the runoff of Colorado's. And yet all of those rivers and reser- voirs satisfy only 60 percent of the demand. The rest of the water comes from under the ground. The rivers are infinitely renewable, at least until the reservoirs silt up or the climate changes. But a lot of

9

the water being pumped out of the ground is as nonrenewable as oil.

Early in the century, before the federal government got into the business of building dams, most of the water used for irrigation in California was groundwater. The farmers in the Central Valley (which comprises both the Sacramento and the San Joaquin) pumped it out so relentlessly that by the 1930s the state's biggest industry was threatened with collapse. The growers, by then, had such a stranglehold on the legislature that they convinced it, in the depths of the Depression, to authorize a huge water project—by far the largest in the world—to rescue them from their own greed. When the bonds to finance the project could not be sold, Franklin Delano Roosevelt picked up the unfinished task. Today, the Central Valley Project is still the most mind-boggling public works project on five continents, and in the 1960s the state built its own project, nearly as large. Together, the California Water Project and the Central Valley Project have captured enough water to supply eight cities the size of New York. But the projects brought into production far more land than they had water to supply, so the growers had to supplement their surface water with tens of thousands of wells. As a result, the groundwater overdraft, instead of being alleviated, has gotten worse.

In the San Joaquin Valley, pumping now exceeds natural replenishment by more than half a trillion gallons a year. By the end of the century it could rise to a trillion gallons—a mining operation that, in sheer volume, beggars the exhaustion of oil. How long it can go on, no one knows. It depends on a lot of things, such as the price of food and the cost of energy and the question whether, as carbon dioxide changes the world's climate, California will become drier. (It is expected to become much drier.) But it is one reason you hear talk about redirecting the Eel and the Klamath and the Columbia and, someday, the Yukon River.

The problem in California is that there is absolutely no regulation over groundwater pumping, and, from the looks of things, there won't be any for many years to come. The farmers loathe the idea, and in California "the farmers" are the likes of Exxon, Tenneco, and Getty Oil. Out on the high plains, the problem is of a different nature. There, the pumping of groundwater is regulated. But the states have all decided to regulate their groundwater out of existence.

The vanishing groundwater in Texas, Kansas, Colorado, Oklahoma, New Mexico, and Nebraska is all part of the Ogallala aquifer, which holds two distinctions: one of being the largest discrete aquifer in the world, the other of being the fastest-disappearing aquifer in the world. The rate of withdrawal over natural replenishment is now roughly equivalent to the flow of the Colorado River. This was the region called the Dust Bowl, the one devastated by the Great Drought; that was back before anyone knew there was so much water underfoot, and before the invention of the centrifugal pump. The prospect that a region so plagued by catastrophe could become rich and fertile was far too tantalizing to resist; the more irrigation, everyone thought, the better. The states knew the groundwater couldn't last forever (even if the farmers thought it would), so, like the Saudis with their oil, they had to decide how long to make it last. A reasonable period, they decided, was twenty-five to fifty years.

"What are you going to do with all that water?" asks Felix Sparks, the former head of the Colorado Water Conservation Board. "Are you just going to leave it in the ground?" Not necessarily, one could reply, but fifty years or a little longer is an awfully short period in which to exhaust the providence of half a million years, to consume as much nonrenewable water as there is in Lake Huron. "Well," says Sparks, "when we use it up, we'll just have to get more water from somewhere else."

Stephen Reynolds, Sparks's counterpart in New Mexico—as state engineer, the man in charge of water, he may be the most powerful person in the state—says much the same thing: "We made a conscious decision to mine out our share of the Ogallala in a period of twenty-five to forty years." In the portions of New Mexico that overlie the Ogallala, according to Reynolds, some farmers withdraw as much as five feet of water a year, while nature puts back a quarter of an inch. What will happen to the economy of Reynolds's state when its major agricultural region turns to dust? "Agriculture uses about 90 percent of our water, and produces around 20 percent of the state's income, so it wouldn't necessarily be a knockout economic blow," he answers. "Of course, you are talking about drastic changes in the whole life and culture of a very big region encompassing seven states.

"On the other hand," says Reynolds, half-hopefully, "we may decide as a matter of national policy that all this agriculture is too important to lose. We can always decide to build some more water projects."

More water projects. During the first and only term of his presidency, Jimmy Carter decided that the age of water projects had come to a deserved end. As a result, he drafted a "hit list" on which were a couple of dozen big dams and irrigation projects, east and west, which he vowed not to fund. Carter was merely stunned by the reaction from the East; he was blown over backward by the reaction from the West. Of about two hundred western members of Congress, there weren't more than a dozen who dared to support him. One of the projects would return five cents in economic benefits for every taxpayer dollar invested; one offered irrigation farmers subsidies worth more than $1 million each; another, a huge dam on a middling California river, would cost more than Hoover, Shasta, Glen Canyon, Bonneville, and Grand Coulee combined. But Carter's hit list had as much to do with his one-term presidency as Iran.

Like millions of easterners who wonder how such projects get built, Jimmy Carter had never spent much time in the West. He had never driven across the country and watched the landscape turn from green to brown at the hundredth meridian, the threshold of what was once called the Great American Desert—but which is still wet compared to the vast ultramontane basins beyond. In southern Louisiana, water is the central fact of existence, and a whole culture and set of values have grown up around it. In the West, lack of water is the central fact of existence, and a whole culture and set of values have grown up around it. In the East, to "waste" water is to consume it needlessly or excessively. In the West, to waste water is *not* to consume it—to let it flow unimpeded and undiverted down rivers. Use of water is, by definition, "beneficial" use—the term is right in the law—even if it goes to Fountain Hills, Arizona, and is shot five hundred feet into 115-degree skies; even if it is sold, at vastly subsidized rates, to farmers irrigating crops in the desert which their counterparts in Mississippi or Arkansas are, at that very moment, being paid not to grow. To easterners, "conservation" of water usually means protecting rivers from development; in the West, it means building dams.

More water projects. In the West, nearly everyone is for them. Politicians of every stripe have sacrificed their most sacred principles on the altar of water development. Barry Goldwater, scourge of welfare and champion of free enterprise, has been a lifelong supporter of the Central Arizona Project, which comes as close to socialism as anything this country has ever done (the main difference being that those who are subsidized are well-off, even rich). Former Governor Jerry Brown of California attended the funeral of E. F. Schumacher, the English economist who wrote *Small Is Beautiful*, then flew back home to lobby for a water project that would cost more than it did to put a man on the moon. Alan Cranston, the leading liberal in the U.S. Senate, the champion of the poor and the oppressed, successfully lobbied to legalize illegal sales of subsidized water to big corporate farmers, thus denying water—and farms—to thousands of the poor and oppressed.

In the West, it is said, water flows uphill toward money. And it literally does, as it leaps three thousand feet across the Tehachapi Mountains in gigantic siphons to slake the thirst of Los Angeles, as it is shoved a thousand feet out of Colorado River canyons to water Phoenix and Palm Springs and the irrigated lands around them. It goes 444 miles (the distance from Boston to Washington) by aqueduct from the Feather River to south of L.A. It goes in man-made rivers, in siphons, in tunnels. In a hundred years, actually less, God's riverine handiwork in the West has been stood on its head. A number of rivers have been nearly dried up. One now flows backward. Some flow through mountains into other rivers' beds. There are huge reservoirs where there was once desert; there is desert, or cropland, where there were once huge shallow swamps and lakes.

It still isn't enough.

In 1971, the Bureau of Reclamation released a plan to divert six million acre-feet from the lower Mississippi River and create a river in reverse, pumping the water up a staircase of reservoirs to the high plains in order to save the irrigation economy of West Texas and eastern New Mexico, utterly dependent on groundwater, from collapse. Since the distance the water would have to travel is a thousand miles, and the elevation gain four thousand feet, and since six million acre-feet of water weigh roughly 16.5 trillion pounds, a lot of energy would be required to pump it. The Bureau figured that six nuclear plants would do, and calculated the cost of the power at one mill per kilowatt-hour, a tiny fraction of what it costs today. The whole package came to $20 billion, in 1971 dollars; the benefit-cost ratio would have been .27 to 1. For each dollar invested, twenty-seven cents in economic productivity would be returned. "That's kind of discouraging," says Stephen Reynolds. "But when you consider our balance-of-payments deficits, you have to remember that we send $100 billion out of this country each year just to pay for imported oil. The main thing we export is food. The Ogallala region produces a very large share of our agricultural exports."

More water projects. In the early 1960s, the Ralph M. Parsons Corporation, a giant engineering firm based in Pasadena, California, released a plan to capture much of the flow of the Yukon and Tanana rivers and divert it two thousand miles to the Southwest through the Rocky Mountain Trench. The proposal, called the North American Water and Power Alliance, wasn't highly regarded by Canada, which was the key to the "alliance," but in the West it was passionately received. Ten years later, as environmentalism and inflation both took root, NAWAPA seemed destined for permanent oblivion. But then OPEC raised the price of oil 1,600 percent, and Three Mile Island looked as if it might seal fission's doom. California was hit by the worst drought in its history; had it lasted one more year, its citizens might have begun migrating back east, their mattresses strapped to the tops of their Porsches and BMWs. All of a sudden the hollowness of our triumph over nature hit home with striking effect. With hydroelectricity now regarded by many as salvation, and with nearly half the irrigated farmland in the West facing some kind of doom—drought, salt, or both combined—NAWAPA, in the early 1980s, began to twitch again. The cost had doubled, from $100 billion to $200 billion, but by then we were spending that much in a single year on defense. The project could produce 100,000 megawatts of electricity; it could rescue California, the high plains, and Arizona and still have enough water left to turn half of Nevada green. The new Romans were now saying that it wasn't a matter of *whether* NAWAPA would be built, but when.

Perhaps they are right. Perhaps, despite the fifty thousand major dams we have built in America; despite the fact that federal irrigation has, for the most part, been a horribly bad investment in free-market terms; despite the fact that the number of free-flowing rivers that remain in the West can be counted on two hands; perhaps, despite all of this, the grand adventure of playing God with our waters will go on. Perhaps it will be consummated on a scale of which our forebears could scarcely dream. By encouraging millions of people to leave the frigid Northeast, we could save a lot of imported oil; by doubling our agricultural exports, we could pay for the oil we import today. As the ancient, leaking water systems and infrastructure of the great eastern cities continue to decay, we may see an East-West alliance develop: you give us our water projects, we'll give you yours. Perhaps, in some future haunted by scarcity, the unthinkable may be thinkable after all.

In the West, of course, where water is concerned, logic and reason have never figured prominently in the scheme of things. As long as we maintain a civilization in a semidesert with a desert heart, the yearning to civilize more of it will always be there. It is an instinct that followed close on the heels of food, sleep, and sex, predating the Bible by thousands of years. The instinct, if nothing else, is bound to persist.

The lights of Salt Lake City began to fade, an evanescent shimmer on the rear horizon. A few more minutes and the landscape was again a black void. We were crossing the Great Basin, the arid heart of the American West. The pilot announced that the next glow of civilization would be Reno, some six hundred miles away. I remembered two things about Reno. The annual precipitation there is seven inches, an amount that Florida and Louisiana and Virginia have received in a day. But even though gambling and prostitution are legal around Reno, water metering, out of principle, was for a long time against the law.

CHAPTER ONE

A Country of Illusion

The American West was explored by white men half a century before the first colonists set foot on Virginia's beaches, but it went virtually uninhabited by whites for another three hundred years. In 1539, Don Francisco Vásquez de Coronado, a nobleman who had married rich and been appointed governor of Guadalajara by the Spanish king, set out on horseback from Mexico with a couple of hundred men, driving into the uncharted north. Coronado was a far kinder conquistador than his ruthless contemporaries Pizarro and De Soto, but he was equally obsessed with gold. His objective was a place called Cibola, seven cities where, legend had it, houses and streets were veneered with gold and silver. All he found, somewhere in northwestern Arizona, were some savage people living in earthen hovels, probably descendants of the great Hohokam culture, which had thrived in central Arizona until about 1400, when it mysteriously disappeared. Crestfallen, but afraid of disgracing the Spanish crown, Coronado pushed on. Tusayan, Cicuye, Tiguex, Quivira—no gold. His fruitless expedition took him from the baking desert canyons of south-central Arizona up to the cool ponderosa highlands of the Mogollon Rim, then down again into the vast, flat, treeless plains of West Texas and Oklahoma and Kansas. He returned, miraculously, a couple of years later, having lost half his men and some of his sanity when a horse stepped on his skull during a fight with some Apaches. Since the climate of the American West is often compared, by those who don't know better, with that of Spain, it is in-structive to quote part of the letter Coronado wrote to Viceroy Mendoza as he was recovering along the Rio Grande:

> After traveling seventy-seven days from Tiguex over these bar-ren lands, our Lord willed that I should arrive in the province called Quivira [Kansas], to which the guides El Turco and the other savage were taking me. They had pictured it as having stone houses many stories high; not only are there none of stone, but, on the contrary, they are of grass, and the people are savage like all I have seen and passed up to that place. They have no woven fabrics, nor cotton with which to make them. All they have is tanned skins of the cattle they kill, for the herds are near the place where they live, a fair-sized river. [The Indian guides' reward for their misleading travelogue was to be garroted to death.] . . .
>
> The natives gave me a piece of copper which an Indian chief wore suspended from his neck. I am sending it to the viceroy of New Spain, for I have not seen any other metal. . . . I have done everything within my power to serve you, as your faithful sergeant and vassal, and to discover some country where God our Lord might be served by extending your royal patri-mony. . . . The best country I have discovered is this Tiguex River [the Rio Grande] and the settlement where I am now camping. But they are not suitable for colonizing, for, besides being four hundred leagues from the North Sea and more than two hundred from the South Sea, thus prohibiting all inter-course, the land is so cold, as I have informed Your Majesty, that it seems impossible for anyone to spend the winter here, since there is no firewood, nor any clothing with which the men may keep themselves warm, except the skins which the natives wear. . . .

The greatest irony of Coronado's adventure was that he must have passed within a few miles of the gold and silver lodes at Tomb-stone and Tubac, Arizona. A few of his party, on a side excursion, discovered the Grand Canyon, but they were unimpressed by its beauty, and guessed the width of the Colorado River far below them at eight feet or so. The Rio Grande, which would later sustain the only ap-preciable Spanish settlements outside of California, didn't impress them, either. When he returned to Guadalajara, Coronado was put on trial for inept leadership, which, though an utterly unfounded charge, was enough to discourage would-be successors who might have discovered the precious metals that would have induced Spain to lay a far stronger claim on the New World. His expedition also lost a few horses, which found their way into the hands of the native Americans. The two dominant tribes of the Southwest, the Apache and Comanche, soon evolved into the best horsemen who ever lived, and their ferocity toward incursionists made them formidable adversaries of the Spaniards who tried to settle the region later.

The Spanish did make a more than desultory try at establishing a civilization in California, which was more to their liking than the remainder of the West. (And, in fact, the huge California land grants doled out by the king established a pattern of giant fiefdoms that persists there to this day.) But they never found gold in California, so the territory didn't seem worth a fight. Challenged by the first American expeditionary force in 1842, the Spanish ceded the entire territory six years later—just a few months before a man named James Marshall was to discover a malleable yellow rock in the tailrace of Sutter's Mill on the American River above Sacramento.

In 1803, the United States of America consisted of thirteen states along the Atlantic Seaboard, three-quarters of which were still untrammeled wilderness, and a vast unmapped tract across the Appalachian Mountains—which would metamorphose, more quickly than anyone might have expected, into the likes of Cleveland and Detroit. In that same year, the new First Consul of France, Napoleon Bonaparte, sat in Paris wrestling with a question: what to conquer? France had recently acquired a million square miles of terrain in North America from Spain—Spain having gotten it originally from France— and the prospect of a huge colonial empire in the New World was tempting. On the other hand, here was Europe—settled, tamed, productive—waiting for civilized dominion by the French. For what would history remember him better—the conquest of Russia or the conquest of buffalo?

The new President of the United States was Thomas Jefferson, an ardent Francophile, but, above all, a practical man. Jefferson knew better than anyone that a French presence in the New World could only be considered a threat. Jefferson was also exceedingly clever, and he was not above a little ruse. "The day that France takes possession of Louisiana," he wrote in a message to his ministers in Paris, "we must marry ourselves to the British fleet and nation." Having said that, Jefferson, through the offices of a Franco-American gunpowder manufacturer named du Pont de Nemours, then inaugurated a hallowed presidential tradition known as the intentional leak. Reading the "intercepted" message, Napoleon lost his half-formed resolve to create an empire on two continents. The result was the Louisiana Purchase.

Napoleon had no idea what he had sold for $15 million, and Jefferson had no idea what he had bought. For fifteen years, however, he had been trying to send an expedition to the unknown country west of the Mississippi River, and now, for the first time, he was able to persuade Congress to put up the money. In 1804, Jefferson's personal secretary, a private, moody, and sensitive young man named Meriwether Lewis, together with a bluff and uncomplicated army captain named William Clark, left St. Louis with a party of fifty men. Poling, tugging, and, at times, literally carrying a fifty-foot bateau up the whipsawing braided channels of the Missouri River, they arrived at the villages of the Mandan tribe, in what has come to be North Dakota, in the early winter. When the ice broke in the spring, some of the party returned to St. Louis with the boat. The thirty-one others, accompanied by a Shosone Indian girl named Sacajawea, who had been captured and enslaved by the Mandans, and her newborn baby, continued westward on horseback and on foot. Guided by Sacajawea—whose usefulness as an interpreter was only a small part of the Lewis and Clark expedition's fabulous luck—they pressed across the plains to the beginning of the true Missouri at Three Forks, Montana. From there, they struggled over the Continental Divide and found the Salmon River, whose alternative name, the River of No Return, is an indication of the experiences they had trying to follow it. In despair, the party gave up and turned northward, finding the Clearwater River, which offered them an easier path westward. The Clearwater led them to the Snake, and the Snake led them to the Columbia—a huge anomaly of a river in the pale desert east of the Cascades. Entering the Columbia gorge, they made an almost instantaneous transition from arid grasslands to rain forest as the river sliced through the Cascade Range—a type of transition utterly fantastic to an easterner. From there, it was a short hop to the Pacific, where the party spent the winter, fattening on seafood. In August of 1806, they were back in St. Louis.

The country Lewis and Clark saw amazed, appalled, and enchanted them. Above all, it bewildered them. They had seen the western plains at their wettest—in the springtime of an apparently wet year—but still there were few rivers, and full ones were fewer. The sky was so immense it swallowed the landscape, but the land swallowed up the provenance of the sky. There was game—at times a ludicrous abundance of it—but there were no trees. To an easterner, no trees meant no possibility of agriculture. If the potential wealth of the land could be judged by the layers of fat on its inhabitants, it was worthwhile to note that the only fat Indians seen by Lewis and Clark were those on the Pacific Coast, sating themselves on salmon and clams. Reading their journals, one gets the impression that Lewis and Clark simply didn't know what to think. They had never seen a landscape like this, never guessed one could even exist. Each "fertile prairie" and "happy prospect" is counterweighted by a "forbidding plain." Louisiana, though penetrated, remained an enigma.

The explorers who followed Lewis and Clark were more certain of their impressions. In the same year the expedition returned, General Zebulon Montgomery Pike crossed the plains on a more southerly course, through what was to become Kansas and Colorado. There he saw "tracts of many leagues . . . where not a speck of vegetable matter existed" and dismissed the whole country as an arid waste. "These vast plains of the western hemisphere may become in time as celebrated as the sandy deserts of Africa," wrote Pike. Major Stephen Long, who followed Pike a decade later, had a similar impression. Long referred to the whole territory between the Mississippi and the Rocky Mountains as the Great American Desert—a phrase and an image that held for almost half a century. The desert might have sat there even longer in the public mind, ineradicable and fixed, had not a member of the Lewis and Clark expedition by the name of John Colter noticed, in the rivers and streams tumbling out of the Rocky Mountains, a plenitude of beaver.

The settlement of the American West owed itself, as much as anything, to a hat. The hat was made of beaver felt, and, during the 1820s and 1830s, no dedicated follower of fashion would settle for anything less. Demand was great enough, and beavers east of the Mississippi were scarce enough, that a cured plew could fetch $6 to $10—at the time, a week's wages. If one was reckless, adventurous, mildly to strongly sociopathic, and used to living by one's wits, it was enough money to make the ride across the plains and winters spent amid the hostile Blackfoot and Crow worth the danger and travail. The mountain men never numbered more than a few hundred, but their names—Bridger, Jackson, Carson, Colter, Bent, Walker, Ogden, Sublette—are writ large all over the American West. Supreme outdoorsmen, they could read important facts in the angle and depth of a bear track; they could hide from the Blackfoot in an icy stream, breathing through a hollow stem, and live out a sudden blizzard in the warm corpse of an eviscerated mountain sheep. As trappers, they were equally proficient— so proficient that within a few years of their arrival in the Rocky Mountain territory, the beavers had already begun to thin out. But that was all the more reason for the more restless of them, especially those backed by eastern money, to go off exploring unknown parts for more beaver streams. And no explorer in the continent's history was more compulsive and indefatigable then Jedediah Smith.

In 1822, when he joined the Rocky Mountain Fur Trading Company, Smith was twenty-two years old, and had never seen the other side of the Rockies. Within two years, however, he was in charge of an exploratory party of trappers heading into utterly unfamiliar territory along the Green River. They found beaver there in fabulous numbers, and Smith, feeling unneeded, decided to see what lay off to the north and west. With six others, he set a course across the Great Basin toward Great Salt Lake. The landscape was more desolate than anything they had seen. If the Great American Desert was on the other side of the mountains, then what would you call this? Game was pitifully scarce. The herds of buffalo had vanished, and the only creatures appearing in numbers were rattlesnakes and jackrabbits. The few human beings encountered were numbingly primitive. They built no lodges, used the crudest tools, made no art. They subsisted, from all appearances, on roots and insects; a live gecko made a fine repast. Mark Twain, encountering some of the last of the wild Digger Indians half a century later, called them "the wretchedest type of mankind I have ever seen." But they were, as Twain noted, merely a reflection of the landscape they found themselves in.

Smith's party skirted Great Salt Lake and continued westward, becoming the first whites, and probably the first humans, to cross the Bonneville Salt Flats—a hundred miles of horrifyingly barren terrain. They then struck across what is now eastern Oregon, eventually reaching a British fort near the Columbia River. Sensing something less than a generous welcome (the British still wanted at least a piece of this subcontinent), the party turned around, and was back on the Green River by July of 1825, in time for the trappers' first rendezvous.

The rendezvous was the first all-male ritual in the non-Indian West—a kind of Baghdad bazaar leavened by fighting, fornication, and adventure stories that would have seemed outlandish if they hadn't, for the most part, been true. Trappers arrived from hundreds of miles around with their pelts, which they traded for whiskey sold by St. Louis entrepreneurs at $25 the gallon, for ammunition, and for staples such as squaws. There was usually carnage, inhibited mainly by the water the traders had added to the whiskey. At the Green River rendezvous, however, Smith and two of his partners, David Jackson and William Sublette, forsook the festivities for serious business. They had decided to take over the Missouri Fur Trading Company from its owner, General William Ashley, who had amassed a substantial fortune in an astonishingly short time. When the deal was consummated, Smith was given the assignment he coveted—to be in charge of finding new sources of pelts.

Within days of returning from Oregon, Smith was already heading out with a party of fourteen men from Cache Valley, Utah, in search of virgin beaver streams. They followed the languid Sevier River through the red-and-blond deserts of southwestern Utah, then jumped across to the Virgin River, which led them to the Colorado above the present site of Hoover Dam. Unknowingly, they were breaking the Mormon Outlet Trail, by which the secrets of successful irrigation would migrate to California and Arizona and be applied with such ambition that, within a scant century and a half, there would be proposals to import irrigation water from Alaska along the same route. By the time they reached the Colorado River, winter was already near; they had trapped only a few beaver, and didn't feel like turning back. Anxious to find warmth and food, Smith decided to lead the party across the Mojave Desert toward the ocean coast. "A complete barrens" was his description, "a country of starvation." After several exhausting days (they had to carry all their water), the explorers sighted two tall ranges to the west. They crossed the pass between them and found themselves in the Los Angeles Basin, at Mission San Gabriel Archangel in Spanish California. The padres' reception was friendly, but the Spanish governor's was not. Ever since hearing about the expedition of "Capitán Merrie Weather," his attitude toward Yankees had tilted toward paranoia. Exiled from the basin, Smith led his party up the San Joaquin Valley and into the Sierra Nevada, where, along the Stanislaus River, they found beaver in urban concentrations. After a few weeks of trapping, Smith loaded hundreds of plews on horses, selected his two toughest men, and set off across the spine of the Sierra Nevada into what is now Nevada.

Of all the routes across the Great Basin, the one he chose is the longest and driest. U.S. Highway 6 now runs parallel and slightly south; the trip is so desolate and frightening that many motorists will not take it, even in an air-conditioned car loaded with water jugs; they go north, along Interstate 80, which stays reassuringly in sight of the Humboldt River. In six hundred miles of travel, Smith's party crossed three small inconstant streams. That they survived at all is a miracle. "My arrival caused a considerable bustle in camp," he wrote in his diary after arriving in time for the second rendezvous on the Bear River in Utah. "A small cannon, brought up from St. Louis, was loaded and fired for a salute. . . . Myself and party had been given up for lost."

Two weeks after the rendezvous, Smith was, incredibly, on the way to California again, anxious to relieve the men who had remained on the Stanislaus and to trap out the beaver of the Sierra Nevada before someone else discovered them. His route was pretty much the same as the time before. While crossing the Colorado, however, his party was ambushed by a band of Mojave Indians; nine of the nineteen men survived, among them Smith. Fleeing across the desert, they finally reached southern California, where Smith left three wounded men to recover. The rest of the party then joined the trappers they had left the year before. (How they managed to find each other is a subject Smith passes over lightly in his diary.) Both groups, by now, were bereft of supplies. Selecting his two friendliest surviving men, Smith rode across the Central Valley to the missions at Santa Clara and San Jose to barter plews for food, medicine, clothing, and ammunition. As soon as the members of the party were sighted, they were dragged off to jail in Monterey. Bail was set at $30,000, an amount calculated to ensure that they would remain there at the governor's whim. Smith's luck, however, seemed to ricochet between the abominable and sublime; a wealthy sea captain from New England, who was holding over in Monterey, was so impressed by Smith's courage that he arranged to post the entire amount.

Freed but banished forever from California, Smith gathered the remnants of his expedition, and they wandered up the Sacramento Valley, trapping as they went. It was by then the middle of winter, and the snowpack in the Sierra was twelve feet deep; crossing the range was out of the question. Smith decided to venture back toward the ocean. Crossing the Yolla Bolly and Trinity mountains, the party found itself in a rain forest dominated by a gigantic species of conifer they had never seen. Reaching the Pacific near the mouth of the river that now bears Smith's name, they slogged northward through country which can receive a hundred inches of rain during six winter months. At the mouth of the Umpqua River, they stopped to rest.

Smith went off to reconnoiter in an improvised canoe. While he was gone, a band of the Umpqua tribe stole into camp and murdered all but three of the men. Fleeing through the tangled forest beneath giant trees, two of the survivors found Smith, and they raced off together in the direction of Fort Vancouver on the Columbia River. They arrived there in August of 1828, emaciated and in shock. Their last surviving companion straggled in after them; he had found his way alone.

The British, by then well established in Oregon, considered the attack ominous enough to demand a reprisal. An expedition was dispatched for the Umpqua Valley, where the marauding band was cornered; thirty-nine horses and Smith's seven hundred beaver pelts were seized. Although the British were still smarting from the War of 1812, the commander refused to let Smith compensate him for his trouble; instead, he paid him $3,200 for the horses and pelts. He also offered the Americans a long rest at the fort, since it would take most of the winter for them to tell all their tales. In the spring of 1829, the assembled force of Fort Vancouver watched in disbelief as Smith and Arthur Black, the last of the four survivors who still retained their nerve, strode confidently through the gates and up the Columbia River, en route to the June rendezvous. "They are sporting with life or courting danger to madness," remarked the commander, who never went out with fewer than forty men. Within twelve weeks, Smith and Clark were back among their companions in Jackson Hole.

After six years of hair-raising adventures, Jedediah Smith decided to relax and devote a season to tranquil pursuits—trapping beaver on icy mountain streams in territory claimed by Indians and grizzly bears—and then returned to St. Louis to see what opportunity lay there. But civilization stank in his nostrils, and wilderness coursed through his blood. After a brief stay in the frontier capital, Smith was back on the Santa Fe Trail, guiding pioneers westward. It was there, at the age of thirty, that his life came to an abrupt end, a Comanche tomahawk embedded in his skull. He is memorialized today across a region the size of Europe, though modern explorers in a Prowler or a Winnebago may not realize that half a dozen Smith Rivers and a landscape of Smith Parks, Passes, Peaks, and Valleys in eleven states are mostly named after the same Smith.

The "useful" role ascribed to the mountain men is that they opened the door to settlement of the West. It might be more accurate, however, to say that they slammed it shut. The terrors they endured were hardly apt to draw settlers, and their written accounts of the region had to lie heavy on a settler's mind: plains so arid that they could barely support bunchgrass; deserts that were fiercely hot and fiercely cold; streams that flooded a few weeks each year and went dry the rest; forests with trees so large it might take days to bring one down; Indians, grizzly bears, wolves, and grasshopper plagues; hail followed by drought followed by hail; no gold. You could live off the land in better years, but the life of a trapper, a hunter, a fortune seeker—the only type of life that seemed possible in the West—was not what the vast majority of Americans sought.

There were those who believed, in the 1830s, that the Louisiana Purchase had been a waste of $15 million—that the whole billion acres would remain as empty as Mongolia or the Sahara. And then, just a generation later, there were those who believed a billion people were destined to settle there. It seemed there was only one person in the whole United States with the wisdom, the scientific detachment, and the explorer's insight to dissect both myths and find the truth that lay buried within.

John Wesley Powell belonged to a subspecies of American which flourished briefly during the nineteenth century and went extinct with the end of the frontier. It was an estimable company, one that included the likes of Mark Twain, John Muir, Abraham Lincoln, William Dean Howells, and Hamlin Garland. They were genuine Renaissance men, though their circumstances were vastly different from those of Jefferson or Benjamin Franklin. The founding fathers, the most notable among them, were urban gentlemen or gentlemen farmers who grew up in a society that, though it sought to keep Europe and its mannerisms at arm's length, had a fair amount in common with the Old World. They lived in very civilized style, even if they lived at the edge of a frontier. Powell, Howells, Lincoln, and the others were children of the real frontier. Most grew up on subsistence farms hacked out of ancient forests or grafted onto tallgrass prairie; they lacked formal education, breeding, and refinement. Schooled by teachers who knew barely more than they did, chained to the rigors of farm life, they got their education from borrowed books devoured by the embers of a fireplace or surreptitiously smuggled into the fields. What they lacked in worldliness and schooling, however, they more than made up in vitality, originality, and circumambient intelligence. John Wesley Powell may be one of the lesser-known of this group,

25

but he stood alone in the variety of his interests and the indefatigability of his pursuits.

Powell's father was a poor itinerant preacher who transplanted his family westward behind the breaking wave of the frontier. As a boy in the 1840s, Powell moved from Chillicothe, Ohio, to Walworth County, Wisconsin, to Bonus Prairie, Illinois. Nothing was paved, little was fenced; the forests were full of cougars and the streams full of fish. To Powell, the frontier was a rapturous experience. Like John Muir, he got a vagabond's education, rambling cross-country in order to become intimate with forests and fauna, with hydrology and weather. In the summer of 1855, Powell struck out for four months and walked across Wisconsin. Two years later he floated down the Ohio River from Pittsburgh to St. Louis. A few months later, he was gathering fossils in interior Missouri. The next spring he was rowing alone down the Illinois River and up the Mississippi and the Des Moines River to the middle of Iowa, then a wilderness. Between his peregrinations Powell picked up some frantic education—Greek, Latin, botany, a bit of philosophy—at Wheaton, Oberlin, and Illinois College, but he never graduated and he never stayed long. Powell learned on the run.

When the Civil War broke out, Powell enlisted on the Union side, fought bravely, and came out a major, a confidant of Ulysses Grant, and minus an arm, which was removed by a steel ball at the Battle of Shiloh. To Powell, the loss of an arm was merely a nuisance, though the raw nerve endings in his amputated stump kept him in pain for the rest of his life. After the war he tried a stint at teaching, first at Illinois Wesleyan and then at Illinois State, but it didn't satisfy him. He helped found the Illinois Museum of Natural History, and was an obvious candidate for the position of curator, but decided that this, too, was too dull an avenue with too visible an end. Powell, like the mountain men, was compulsively drawn to the frontier. In the United States of the late 1860s, there was but one place where the frontier was still nearly intact.

By 1869, the population of New York City had surpassed one million. The city had built a great water-supply aqueduct to the Croton River and was imagining its future subway system. Chicago, founded thirty years earlier, was already a big sprawling industrial town. The millionaires of San Francisco were building their palatial mansions on Nob Hill. New England was deforested, farms and settlements were spilling onto the prairie. However, on maps of the United States published in that year a substantial area remained a complete blank, and was marked "unexplored."

The region overlay parts of what is now Colorado, Utah, Arizona, New Mexico, and Nevada. It was about the size of France, and through the middle of it ran the Colorado River. That was about all that was known about it, except that the topography was awesome and the rainfall scarce. The region was known as the Plateau Province, and parties heading westward tended to avoid it at all costs.

Some of the Franciscan friars, who were as tough as anyone in the Old West, had wandered through it on the Old Spanish Trail. Otherwise, the Mormon Outlet Trail skirted the region to the west, the California and Oregon trails swung northward, and the El Paso–Yuma Trail went south. From a distance, one could see multicolored and multistoried mesas and cliffs, saurian ridges, and occasionally a distant snowcapped peak. There were accounts of canyons that began without reason and were suddenly a thousand feet deep, eroded more by wind than by water. A distance that a bird could cover in an hour might require a week to negotiate. The days were hot and the nights were often frigid, owing to the region's high interior vastness, and water was almost impossible to find. Lacking wings, there was only one good way to explore it: by boat.

On the 24th of May, 1869, the Powell Geographic Expedition set out on the Green River from the town of Green River, Wyoming, in four wooden dories: the *Maid of the Canyon*, the *Kitty Clyde's Sister*, the *Emma Dean*, and the *No Name*. For a scientific expedition, it was an odd group. Powell, the leader, was the closest thing to a scientist. He had brought along his brother Walter—moody, sarcastic, morose, one of the thousands of psychiatric casualties of the Civil War. The rest of the party was made up mostly of mountain men: O. G. Howland, his brother Seneca, Bill Dunn, Billy Hawkins, and Jack Sumner, all of whom had been collected by Powell en route to Green River. He had also invited a beet-faced Englishman named Frank Goodman, who had been patrolling the frontier towns looking for adventure, and Andy Hall, an eighteen-year-old roustabout whose casual skill as an oarsman had impressed Powell when he saw him playing with a boat on the Green River. There was also George Bradley, a tough guy whom Powell had met by accident at Fort Bridger and who had agreed to come along in exchange for a discharge from the army, which Powell managed to obtain for him.

For sixty miles out of the town of Green River, the river was sandy-bottomed and amiable. There were riffles, but nothing that could legitimately be called a rapid. The boatmen played in the currents, acquiring a feel for moving water; the others admired the scenery. As they neared the Uinta Mountains, they went into a sandstone canyon colored in marvelous hues, which Powell, who had a knack for naming things, called Flaming Gorge. The river bore southward until it came up against the flanks of the range, then turned eastward and entered Red Canyon.

In Red Canyon, the expedition got its first lesson in how a few feet of drop per mile can turn a quiet river into something startling. Several of the rapids frightened them into racing for shore and lining or portaging, an awful strain with several thousand pounds of boats, supplies, and gear. After a while, however, even the bigger rapids were not so menacing anymore—if, compared to what was about to come, one could call them big.

Beyond Flaming Gorge the landscape opened up into Brown's Park, but soon the river gathered imperceptible momentum and the canyon ramparts closed around them like a pair of jaws. A maelstrom followed. Huge scissoring waves leaped between naked boulders; the river plunged into devouring holes. The awestruck Andy Hall recited an alliterative verse he had learned as a Scottish schoolboy, "The Cataract of Lodore," by the English Romantic poet Robert Southey. Over Powell's objection—he did not like using a European name—the stretch became the Canyon of Lodore.

As they approached the first big rapid in the canyon, the *No Name* was sucked in by the accelerating current before anyone had a chance to scout. "I pass around a great crag just in time to see the boat strike a rock and rebounding from the shock career and fill the open compartment with water," wrote Powell in his serialized journal of the trip. "Two of the men lost their oars, she swings around, and is carried down at a rapid rate broadside on for quite a few yards and strikes amidships on another rock with great force, is broken quite in two, and then men are thrown into the river, the larger part of the boat floating buoyantly. They soon seize it and down the river they drift for a few hundred yards to a second rapid filled with huge boulders where the boat strikes again and is dashed to pieces and the men and fragments are soon carried beyond my sight."

The three crew members survived, but most of the extra clothes, the barometers, and several weeks' worth of food were gone. The next day the party found the stern of the boat intact, still holding the barometers, some flour, and a barrel of whiskey that Powell, who was something of a prig, did not realize had been smuggled aboard. When they finally floated out of Lodore Canyon into the sunlit beauty of Echo Park, Powell wrote in his journal that despite "a chapter of disaster and toil . . . the canyon of Lodore was not devoid of scenic interest, even beyond the power of the pen to tell." And O. G. Howland, who nearly lost his life in Disaster Falls, wrote haughtily that "a calm, smooth stream is a horror we all detest now."

Desolation Canyon. Gray Canyon. They were now in territory even Indians hadn't seen. The landscape closed in and opened up. Labyrinth Canyon. Stillwater Canyon. They shot a buck and scared a bighorn lamb off a cliff, their first fresh meat in weeks. Powell, climbing a cliff with his one arm, got himself rimmed and required rescue by Bradley, who got above him, dangled his long johns, and pulled Powell up.

The country grew drier and more desolate. Fantastic mesas loomed in the distance, banded like shells. The Grand Mesa, to the east, the largest mesa in the world, rose to eleven thousand feet from desert badlands into an alpine landscape of forests and lakes. Wind-eroded shiprocks loomed over the rubblized beds of prehistoric seas. Battlements of sandstone rose in the distance like ruins of empire. Deep in uncharted territory the Colorado River, then known as the Grand, rushed in quietly from the northeast, carrying the snowmelt of Longs Peak and most of western Colorado. The river's volume had now doubled, but still it remained quite placid. Was it conceivable that they were near the end of its run? Powell was tempted to believe so, but knew better. There were four thousand feet of elevation loss ahead. On the 21st, after a short stop to rest and reseal the boats, they were on the water again, which was high, roiled, and the color of cocoa. In a few miles they came to a canyon, frothing with rapids. They lined or portaged wherever they could, ran if they had no alternative. Soon they were between vertical walls and the river was roaring mud. Cataracts launched them downriver before they had time to think; waves like mud huts threw them eight feet into the air. The scouts would venture ahead if there was room enough to walk, and return ashen-faced. The canyon relented a little at times, so they could portage, but the river did not. In one day, they made three-quarters of a mile in Cataract Canyon, portaging everything they saw.

During the daytime, the temperature would reach 106 degrees; at night the men shivered in their dank drawers. Some became edgy, prone to violent outbursts. Bradley's incendiary moods lasted through most of a day, and he would run almost anything rather than portage.

Powell's instinctive caution infuriated Bradley, as did his indefatigable specimen gathering, surveying, and consignment of everything to notes. The pace was maddeningly uneven: they would do eight miles in a day, then a mere mile or two. Two months' worth of food remained, most of it musty bread, dried apples, spoiled bacon, and coffee. Once, Billy Hawkins got up in the middle of dinner, walked to the boats, and pulled out the sextant. He said he was trying to find the latitude and longitude of the nearest pie.

On the 23rd of July they passed a foul-smelling little stream coming in from the west; they called it the Dirty Devil. The big river quieted. The hunters took off up the cliffsides and returned with a couple of desert bighorn sheep, which were devoured with sybaritic abandon. The sheep were an omen. For the next several days, they floated on a brisk but serene river through a canyon such as no one had seen. Instead of the pitiless angular black-burned walls of Cataract Canyon, they were now enveloped by rounded pink-and-salmon-colored sandstone, undulating ahead of them in soft contours. There were huge arched chasms, arcadian glens hung with maidenhair ferns, zebra-striped walls, opalescent green fractures irrigated by secret springs. Groping for a name that would properly convey their sense of both awe and relief, Powell decided on Glen Canyon. On August 1 and 2, the party camped in Music Temple.

By the 5th of August, they were down to fifteen pounds of rancid bacon, several bags of matted flour, a small store of dried apples, and a large quantity of coffee. Other than that they would have to try to live off the land, but the land was mostly vertical and the game, which had never been plentiful, had all but disappeared. They met the Escalante River, draining unknown territory in Utah, then the San Juan, carrying in snowmelt from southwestern Colorado.

The river on which they were floating was made up now of most of the mentionable runoff of the far Southwest. They were in country that no white person had ever seen, riding the runoff of a region the size of Iraq, and they approached each blind bend in the river with a mixture of anticipation and terror. Soon the soft sandstone of Glen Canyon was replaced by the fabulous coloration of Marble Canyon. Then, on August 14, the hard black rock of Cataract Canyon reemerged from the crust of the earth. "The river enters the gneiss!" wrote Powell. Downriver, they heard what sounded like an avalanche.

Soap Creek Rapids, Badger Creek Rapids, Crystal Creek Rapids, Lava Falls. Nearly all of the time, the creeks that plunge down the ravines of the Grand Canyon will barely float a walnut shell, but the flash floods resulting from a desert downpour can dislodge boulders as big as a jitney bus. Tumbled by gravity, the boulders carom into the main river and sit there, creating a dam, which doesn't so much stop the river as make it mad. Except for the rapids of the Susitna, the Niagara, and perhaps a couple of rivers in Canada, the modern Colorado's rapids are the biggest on the continent. Before the dams were built, however, the Colorado's rapids were *really* big. At Lava Falls, where huge chunks of basalt dumped in the main river create a thirty-foot drop, waves at flood stage were as high as three-story houses. There was a cycling wave at the bottom that, every few seconds, would burst apart with the retort of a sixteen-inch gun, drenching anyone on either bank of the river—two hundred feet apart. To run Lava Falls today, in a thirty-foot Hypalon raft, wrapped in a Mae West life jacket, vaguely secure in the knowledge that a rescue helicopter sits on the canyon rim, is a lesson in panic. The Powell expedition was running most of the canyon's rapids in a fifteen-foot pilot boat made of pine and a couple of twenty-one-foot dories made of oak—with the rudest of life jackets, without hope of rescue, without a single human being within hundreds of miles. And Powell himself was running them strapped to a captain's chair, gesticulating wildly with his one arm.

The river twisted madly. It swung north, then headed south, then back north, then east—east!—then back south. Even Powell, constantly consulting sextant and compass, felt flummoxed. The rapids, meanwhile, had grown so powerful that the boats received a terrible battering from the force of the waves alone, and had to be recaulked every day. As they ran out of food and out of caulk, Powell realized that the men were also beginning to run out of will. There was mutiny in their whisperings.

August 25. They had come thirty-five miles, including a portage around a spellbinding rapid where a boulder dam of hardened lava turned the river into the aftermath of Vesuvius. (That, as it turned out, had been Lava Falls.) There were still no Grand Wash Cliffs, which would signal the confluence with the Virgin River and the end of their ordeal. They saw, for the first time in weeks, some traces of Indian habitation, but obviously no one had lived there in years. Occasionally they caught a glimpse of trees on the canyon rim, five thousand feet above. They were in the deepest canyon any of them had ever seen.

August 26. They came on an Indian garden full of fresh squash. With starvation imminent, they stole a dozen gourds and ate them ravenously. "We are three-quarters of a mile in the depths of the earth," wrote Powell. "And the great river shrinks into insignificance, as it dashes its angry waves against the walls and cliffs, that rise to the world above; they are but puny ripples and we but pigmies, running up and down the sands or lost among the boulders. . . . But," he added hopefully, "a few more days like this and we are out of prison."

August 27. The river, which had been tending toward the west, veered again toward the south. The hated Precambrian granite, which had dropped below the riverbed, surfaced again. Immediately came a rapid which they decided to portage. At eleven o'clock in the morning, they came to the worst rapids yet.

"The billows are huge," wrote Bradley. "The spectacle is appalling." It was, Jack Sumner wrote, a "hell of foam." The rapids was bookended by cliffs; there was no way to portage and no way to line. There wasn't even a decent way to scout.

After the party had had a meal of fried flour patties and coffee, O. G. Howland asked Powell to go for a walk with him. The major knew what was coming. It saddened him that if there was to be mutiny, the leader would be Howland. He was a mountain man by nature and experience, but, after Powell, still the most literate and scientific-minded of the group. Nonetheless, Howland had been plagued by bad luck; it was he who had steered the *No Name* to its destruction in Lodore Canyon; he who had twice lost maps and notes in swampings. He had tested fate enough. In the morning, Howland told Powell, he and his brother Seneca, together with Bill Dunn, were going to abandon the boats and climb out of the canyon.

Powell did not sleep that night. He took reading after reading with his sextant until he was as positive as he dared be that they were within fifty miles of Grand Wash Cliffs. At the most, they ought to be four days from civilization, with the only remaining obstacle in view a wild twenty-second ride through a terrific rapid. Powell woke Howland in the middle of the night and poured out his conviction, but it was too late. His immediate reaction was two laconic sentences in his journal, but later he offered this version of what took place:

We have another short talk about the morrow, but for me there is no sleep. All night long, I pace up and down a little path, on a few yards of sand beach, along by the river. Is it wise to go on? I go to the boats again, to look at our rations. I feel

32

satisfied that we can get over the danger immediately before us; what there may be below I know not. From our outlook yesterday, on the cliffs, the cañon seemed to make another great bend to the south, and this, from our experience here-tofore, means more and higher granite walls. I am not sure that we can climb out of the cañon here, and, when at the top of the wall, I know enough of the country to be certain that it is a desert of rock and sand, between this and the nearest Mormon town, which, on the most direct line, must be seventy-five miles away. True, the last rains have been favorable to us, should we go out, for the probabilities are that we shall find water still standing in holes, and, at one time, I almost con-clude to leave the river. But for years I have been contem-plating this trip. To leave the exploration unfinished, to say that there is a part of the cañon which I cannot explore, having already almost accomplished it, is more than I am willing to acknowledge, and I determine to go on.

August 28. Breakfast was as "solemn as a funeral." Afterward, Powell asked all of the men, for the last time, whether they planned to go ahead or climb out. The Howlands and Bill Dunn still intended to walk out; the rest would remain. The party gave the three some guns and offered them their equal share of the remaining rations. They accepted the guns. "Some tears are shed," Powell wrote. "It is rather a solemn parting; each party thinks the other is taking the dangerous course." Billy Hawkins stole away and laid some biscuits on a rock the mutineers would pass on their way up the cliffs. "They are as fine fellows as I ever had the good fortune to meet," declared taciturn George Bradley, blinking away a tear.

As the others rowed cautiously toward the monster rapids in their two boats, the Howland brothers and Bill Dunn had already begun climbing up one of the canyon arroyos. Powell felt himself torn between watching them and the approaching rapids. They plunged down the first drop. The hydraulic wave at the bottom inundated them, but the water was so swift that they were out of it before the boat could fill. They were launched atop a pillow of water covering a rock, slid off, then rode out a landscape of haystacks. As the *Maid of the Canyon* circulated quietly in the whirlpool at rapids' end, *Kitty Clyde's Sister* wallowed up alongside. The roar of the rapids was al-most submerged by the men's ecstatic shouts. They grabbed rifles and fired volley after volley into the air to show their erstwhile companions that it could be done. Unable to see around the bend in the river or to walk back up, they waited in the eddy for nearly two hours, hoping the others would rejoin them, but they never did.

A few miles below Separation Rapid, the party came to another rapid, Lava Cliffs, which, were it not now under the waters of Lake Mead, would perhaps be the biggest on the river. In a style so much like the man himself—exact and fastidious, yet felicitous and engaging—Powell wrote down what happened there:

[O]n [the] northern side of the canyon [is] a bold escarpment that seems to be a hundred feet high. We can climb it and walk along its summit to a point where we are just at the head of the fall. Here the basalt is broken down again, so it seems to us, and I direct the men to take a line to the top of the cliff and let the boats down along the wall. One man remains in the boat to keep her clear of the rocks and prevent her line from being caught on the projecting angles. I climb the cliff and pass along to a point just over the fall and descend by broken rocks, and find that the break of the fall is above the break of the wall, so that we cannot land, and that still below the river is very bad, and that there is no possibility of a portage. Without waiting further to examine and determine what shall be done, I hasten back to the top of the cliff to stop the boats from coming down. When I arrive I find the men have let one of them down to the head of the fall. She is in swift water and they are not able to pull her back; nor are they able to go on with the line, as it is not long enough to reach the higher part of the cliff which is just before them; so they take a bight around a crag. I send two men back for the other line. The boat is in very swift water, and Bradley is standing in the open compartment, holding out his oar to prevent her from striking against the foot of the cliff. Now she shoots out into the stream and up as far as the line will permit, and then, wheeling, drives headlong against the rock, and then out and back again, now straining on the line, now striking against the rock. As soon as the second line is brought, we pass it down to him; but his attention is all taken up with his own situation, and he does not see that we are passing him the line. I stand on a projecting rock, waving my hat to gain his attention, for my voice is drowned by the roaring of the falls. Just at this moment I see him take his knife from its sheath and step forward to cut the line. He has evidently decided that it is better to go over with the boat as it is than to wait for her to be broken

34

to pieces. As he leans over, the boat sheers again into the stream, the stem-post breaks away and she is loose. With perfect composure Bradley seizes the great scull oar, places it in the stern rowlock, and pulls with all his power (and he is an athlete) to turn the bow of the boat down stream, for he wishes to go bow down, rather than to drift broad-side on. One, two strokes he makes, and a third just as she goes over, and the boat is fairly turned, and she goes down almost beyond our sight, though we are more than a hundred feet above the river. Then she comes up again on a great wave, and down and up, then around behind some great rocks, and is lost in the mad, white foam below. We stand frozen with fear, for we see no boat. Bradley is gone! so it seems. But now, away below, we see something coming out of the waves. It is evidently a boat. A moment more, and we see Bradley standing on deck, swinging his hat to show that he is all right. But he is in a whirlpool. We have the stem-post of his boat attached to the line. How badly she may be disabled we know not. I direct Sumner and [Walter] Powell to pass along the cliff and see if they can reach him from below. Hawkins, Hall, and myself run to the other boat, jump aboard, push out, and away we go over the falls. A wave rolls over us and our boat is unmanageable. Another great wave strikes us, and the boat rolls over, and tumbles and tosses, I know not how. All I know is that Bradley is picking us up. We soon have all right again, and row to the cliff and wait until Sumner and Powell can come. After a difficult climb they reach us. We run two or three miles farther and turn again to the northwest, continuing until night, when we have run out of the granite once more.

August 30. At the confluence of the Colorado and the Virgin River, three Mormons and an Indian helper are seine-netting fish. They have been there for weeks, under orders from Brigham Young to watch for the Powell expedition. Since the members of the expedition have already been reported dead several times in the newspapers, the Mormons are really on the lookout for corpses and wreckage; they hope to salvage whatever journals and maps have survived in order that they might learn something about the unexplored portion of the region where they have banished themselves. Late in the morning, one of them flings a glance upriver and freezes. There are two boats coming down, and, unless they are ghosts, the people inside them seem to be alive.

It had taken three months and six days for the expedition to travel from Green River to Grand Wash Cliffs. Though wilder water than the Colorado is routinely run today, few river runners would dispute that the Powell expedition accomplished the most impressive feat of perilous river exploration in history. But the expedition ended, as fate would have it, on an ironically tragic note. While Powell and those who stayed with him were being fed and pumped for information by the Mormons, the Howland brothers and Bill Dunn were lying dead on the rim of the Grand Canyon, murdered by a band of Shivwits Indians. Later there were rumors that they had molested a Shivwits girl, but the Indian wars were raging and they may have been killed simply for taking the band by surprise. That the Shivwits shot Powell's companions full of holes contains a cold irony, for years later, after Powell had sat around many campfires with them, the Shivwits tribe would come to regard the one-armed major as their most faithful white friend.

When John Wesley Powell first left Council Bluffs, Iowa, in 1867, bound for Denver and the valley of the Green River, the region he crossed was virtually empty. It was like modern interior Alaska, after removing Fairbanks. Indians were more common than whites, and buffalo were much more prevalent than Indians. By the time he reached the ninety-eighth meridian, about two-fifths of the way across Nebraska, the light dusting of settlers' towns and farms had thinned out to nothing. Before him were another five hundred miles of virgin plains, almost uninhabited by whites; then there was Denver, a rowdy little town that owed its existence mainly to furs and gold, and not much else until one got to Salt Lake and California.

On each successive trip west the changes took away Powell's breath. The breaking wave of settlement was eating up half a meridian a year; from one season to the next, settlements were thirty miles farther out. By the late 1870s, the hundredth meridian had been fatefully crossed. There were homes sprouting in central Nebraska, miles from water, trees, and neighbors, their occupants living in sod dugouts suggestive of termite mounds. Farms began to grow up around Denver, where a type of agriculture thoroughly alien to America's farmers—irrigation—was being experimented with. (Horace Greeley, the publisher of the New York *Herald Tribune*—the publisher whose words "Go west, young man" galvanized the nineteenth century— was mainly responsible for this; he had dispatched his agricultural editor, Nathan Meeker, to a spot north of Denver to found a utopian irrigation colony which, not surprisingly, became Greeley, Colorado. The colony appeared to be a success, even forgetting the large annual contribution from Greeley.) On their way across the plains, travelers could see huge roiling clouds of dust on the southern horizon, caused by cattle drives from Texas to railheads at Dodge and Kansas City. The plains were being dug up; the buffalo were being annihilated to starve the Indians and make way for cows; the vanishing tribes were being herded like cattle onto reservations.

This enormous gush of humanity pouring into a region still marked on some maps as the Great American Desert was encouraged by wishful thinking, by salesmanship, that most American of motivating forces, and, most of all, by natural caprice. For a number of years after 1865, a long humid cycle brought uninterrupted above-average rainfall to the plains. Guides leading wagon trains to Oregon reported that western Nebraska, usually blond from drought or black from prairie fires, had turned opalescent green. Late in the 1870s, the boundary of the Great American Desert appeared to have retreated westward across the Rockies to the threshold of the Great Basin. Such a spectacular climatic transformation was not about to be dismissed as a fluke, not by a people who thought themselves handpicked by God to occupy a wild continent. A new school of meteorology was founded to explain it. Its unspoken principle was divine intervention, and its motto was "Rain Follows the Plow." Since the rains coincided with the headlong westward advance of settlement, the two must somehow be related. Professor Cyrus Thomas, a noted climatologist, was a leading proponent. "Since the territory [of Colorado] has begun to be settled," he announced in declamatory tones, "towns and cities built up, farms cultivated, mines opened, and roads made and travelled, there has been a gradual increase in moisture. . . . I therefore give it as my firm conviction that this increase is of a permanent nature, and not periodical, and that it has commenced within eight years past, and that it is in some way connected to the settlement of the country, and that as population increases the moisture will increase." Ferdinand V. Hayden, who was Thomas's boss and one of the most famous geographers and geologists of his time, also subscribed to the theory. (Hayden happened to be a notable rival of John Wesley Powell, who believed otherwise.) The exact explanations varied. Plowing the land exposed the soil's moisture to the sky. Newly planted trees enhanced rainfall. The smoke from trains caused it. Vibrations in the air created by all the commotion helped clouds to form. Dynamiting the air became a popular means of inducing rain to fall. Even the Secretary of Agriculture came out for a demonstration in Texas. "The result," he reported, "was—a loud noise!"

The notion that settlement was changing the climate on the flat, loamy, treeless plains rang irresistibly true to the subsistence farmer from the East who spent more time clearing his land of rocks and stumps than plowing and harvesting. Hamlin Garland, the writer, was the son of such a subsistence farmer, a man hounded out of Wisconsin by trees and hills. "More and more," Garland was to remember, "[my father] resented the stumps and ridges which interrupted his plow. Much of his quarter section remained unbroken. There were ditches to be dug and young oaks to be uprooted in the forest. . . . [B]itterly he resented his uptilted, horse-killing fields, and his complaining words sank so deep in the minds of his sons that for years thereafter they were unable to look upon any rise of ground as an object to be admired."

The Irish potato famine, a bad drought in the Ohio Valley, the reflexive restlessness which, Alexis de Tocqueville thought, set Americans apart from the Europeans they had recently been—all of these, too, were behind the flood. When Hamlin Garland's family settled in Iowa, they had no neighbors within sight. A year later, they were surrounded, fencepost to fencepost. "All the wild things died or hurried away, never to return," wrote Garland mournfully. "The tender plants, the sweet flowers, the fragrant fruits, the busy insects . . . prairie wolves [that] lurked in the grass and swales . . . all of the swarming lives which had been native here for countless centuries were utterly destroyed." If poor immigrants arrived in Iowa and found land too expensive, they could either return East and look for some hardscrabble farm they could afford—in West Virginia, perhaps, or New Hampshire—or continue on to Nebraska. Since rain was bound to follow the plow, they went to Nebraska. Merchants in St. Louis and other railhead cities, who dreamed of markets expanding in three directions at once, became cheerleaders for the New Meteorology. So did land speculators, who figured that even if it was nonsense, they could buy out the burned-out homesteaders for a pittance and convert their farms to rangeland. But nothing did away with the Great American Desert quite as effectively as the railroads.

In 1867, the Kansas Pacific did not reach the Pacific—few of the railroads which veiled themselves in oceanic mists ever did—but it did reach as far as Abilene, Kansas. The Atchison, Topeka, and Santa

Fe Railroad was already to La Junta, Colorado, and branching south to Santa Fe. The Union Pacific made Cheyenne, and two years later it met the Central Pacific at Promontory, Utah, spanning the continent. The Southern Pacific linked Texas to San Francisco. The Northern Pacific hitched Montana to Duluth. The initial result of such unparalleled expansion was an ocean of debt. The federal government had arranged the loans, but what was a loan worth if you didn't see how you could raise the income to pay it back? Of course, there was a way for the government to help with that problem: after all, it did own plenty of land.

During the four decades following the Civil War, 183 million acres went out of the public domain into railroad ownership. To call it a bonanza is to understate the matter significantly. The railroad land grants were a gift the size of California plus the major part of Montana. The deeded lands usually paralleled the railroad's track; reproduced on maps, they resembled jet streams flowing in reverse. Anyone who bought land from the railroads would be utterly dependent on them for getting his harvests to eastern markets and receiving supplies in return. When the time came to set rates, the railroads could charge pretty much what they pleased. But first they had to seduce the settlers who were still content to battle stumps in Kentucky or endure peonage in Germany and Ireland. J. J. Hill, the founder of the Great Northern, said as much himself. "You can lay track through the Garden of Eden," he told an acquaintance. "But why bother if the only inhabitants are Adam and Eve?" The upswing in precipitation, and the crypto-science that explained it, were exactly what was needed. From there it became a job for advertising.

The creative juices flowed. A publicist working for the Rio Grande and Western Railroad noticed, while gazing at a map of the territory of Deseret—now Utah—a faint resemblance to the cradle of civilization. The Rio Grande and Western promptly published a map of Deseret that contained an inset map of Palestine ("The Promised Land!"), calling attention to their "striking similarity." "Follow prairie dogs and Mormons," went a pamphlet of the Burlington line, "and you will find good land." (It failed to mention that prairie dogs, which build their homes underground, cannot do so in wet or soggy ground, and therefore loathe any place receiving a decent amount of rain.) A Northern Pacific circular proclaimed, with no evident sense of shame, that not a single case of illness had been recorded in Montana during the previous year, except for indigestion caused by overeating.

Many of the railroads published their own newspapers, full of

39

so-called testimonials from alleged Kansas farmers who were raising a hundred bushels of corn to the acre, from settlers who had traded rags for riches in five years. "Why emigrate to Kansas?" asked a testimonial in *Western Trail*, the Rock Island Railroad's gazette. "Because it is the garden spot of the world. Because it will grow anything that any other country will grow, and with less work. Because it rains here more than in any other place, and at just the right time." The railroads were careful to conceal their ties with the land-sales companies they owned, and with the journalists to whom they gave free passage and free meals, if not paychecks. One such journalist, Frederick Goddard, produced a popular publication entitled *Where to Emigrate and Why*. The Laramie Plains of Wyoming, he said, were a good place, "as ready today for the plow and spade as the fertile prairies of Illinois." (The Laramie Plains are five thousand feet higher than Illinois; the growing season is at least fifty days shorter; there is about a third as much rain.) Western Nebraska was also a delight. A few patches of drift sand, perhaps, but calling it a desert was preposterous. By drift sand, Goddard may have meant the Sand Hills, a fifteen-thousand-square-mile expanse of thirsty dunes which, to this day, remains mostly uninhabited and unfarmed.

"The utmost care has been exercised to admit nothing . . . that cannot be depended upon as correct." "All claims may be fully sustained, upon investigation." "If hard work doesn't agree with you, or you can't get on without luxuries, stay where you are. If you don't have enough capital to equip and stock a farm, if you are susceptible to homesickness, if you do not have pluck and perseverance, stay where you are." At a time when a five-course dinner in a fancy restaurant cost $1.25, the Union Pacific and the Burlington spent $1 million on advertising for Nebraska alone. Even so, sooner or later the railroads were bound to run out of settlers—long before they ran out of land. Then it became a problem of moving the more intrepid ones westward so that others could fill their places. The strategy used most often had to do with the effects of western climate on health. In 1871, the Union Pacific described the climate throughout eastern Kansas as "genial and healthy." With irresistible logic, the railroad asked, "What doth it profit a man to buy a farm . . . if he and his family lose their health?" That was enough to bring pioneers from the malarial swamps of Louisiana. Eleven years later, when eastern Kansas was filling up with settlers and five million acres of Union Pacific land remained unsold at the other end of the state, the climate in eastern Kansas suddenly turned unhealthy. For their own benefit, the railroad began advising settlers to "get to the higher elevations of the state."

Meanwhile, in Europe, an enormous harvest of souls was waiting to be converted. Western railroad agents frequently showed up in port cities, where they held court under striped awnings and dazzled groups of murmuring listeners with claims they wouldn't dare utter in the States. Swedes, who seemed to have a tendency toward home-sickness, were promised free passage back to Europe if they returned to port with a small quota of relatives in tow. The steamship companies, which were having trouble filling their expensive ships—partly because they had a chronic inclination to explode—were happy to cooperate. When a new ship docked in New York harbor, the mob of land-sales agents rushing aboard was like a migration in reverse. The terms of sale—10 percent down, 7 percent interest, interest alone required for the first three years—could have been regarded as usurious, since deflation was the chronic economic ailment of the time. But terms like this were not to be found in Europe. Neither, for that matter, was land.

The number-one allies of the railroads in their efforts to bring settlers to the West were the politicians, newspaper editors, and territorial jingoists who were already there. No one excelled William Gilpin in this role. Gilpin, who had been a member of John C. Frémont's expedition to Oregon in 1843, was the prototypical nineteenth-century Renaissance man of the American West: soldier, philosopher, orator, lawyer, geographer, governor, author, windbag, and booby. In an essay—"Geopolitics with Dew on It"—published in *Harper's* magazine in 1943, Bernard DeVoto called Gilpin's thinking typical of what passed, in nineteenth-century America, for science: "a priori, deduced, generalized, falsely systematized, and therefore wrong." He might have added "dotty." Imagining himself in space, Gilpin saw the North American continent as a "vast amphitheater, opening toward heaven"—an enormous continent-wide bowl formed by the Rockies and the Appalachian ridges which was ready, as far as Gilpin was concerned, "to receive and fuse harmoniously whatever enters within its rim." A capitalist-expansionist mystic as only the nineteenth century could offer up, Gilpin thundered to a meeting of the Fenian Brotherhood in Denver, "What an immense geography has been revealed! What infinite hives of population and laboratories of industry have been set in motion! . . . North America is known to our own people. Its concave form and homogeneous structure are revealed."

The hives of population of which Gilpin spoke were the 1,310,000,000 people who, he was convinced, could fit comfortably within his continental bowl—and because they *could* fit, then it was weakness of will to settle for anything less. Obviously, a desert had no place in such a galvanic vision. "The PLAINS are not *deserts*," Gilpin shouted in one of his books, which was modestly titled *The Continental Railway, Compacting and Fusing Together All the World's Continents*, "but the OPPOSITE, and the cardinal basis for the future empire now erecting itself upon the North American continent." Empire was a passion with Gilpin, as it was with his mentor, Senator Thomas Hart Benton of Missouri. Benton, in addition to being the father of John C. Frémont's wife, was the father of Manifest Destiny, which was to become the rationalization for those excesses that its companion doctrine, Social Darwinism, could not excuse.

While Benton sat in Missouri flogging pioneers westward, Gilpin stood in Colorado welcoming them and shrieking for more. And there was no scarcity of Bentons and Gilpins in the states between. Kansas's Board of Agriculture was reporting a statewide average of 44.17 inches of precipitation in 1888 and 43.99 inches in 1889. It has never rained that much in Kansas since. There was also a Kansas Bureau of Immigration, which announced that the climate in Kansas was, without exception, the most desirable in the United States. Summer might linger into November, and then "at the close of February we are reminded by a soft gentle breeze from the South, that winter is gone." At the same time, a story began to circulate among disillusioned settlers about a mule standing in a field of Kansas corn. It grew so hot that all the corn around him began to pop, and mistaking it for a blizzard, he froze to death.

Nebraska had its Bureau of Immigration, too, which specialized in isothermal belts. These were longitudinal and latitudinal bands within which, by natural laws, the most advanced muscular and mental development, as well as the most heroic achievements of invention and creative genius, were invariably produced. The most significant isothermal belt in America ran right through Nebraska. As evidence, you had only to look at Colorado, which was farther south and west and full of dirty Spaniards and Indians. Coloradans, of course, shrugged off this type of thing; they were busy describing their own miracles.

Capitalists, newspaper editors, lonely pioneers, local emperors of Gilpin's ilk—all had a stake in retreating deserts. But they were not the only ones. Abolitionists, for example, did, too. In the 1850s, when Kansas seemed likely to be the next state admitted to the Union, something approaching warfare broke out between those who would have made it a free state and those who would have tolerated slavery. Horace Greeley, an avowed abolitionist with considerable interest in the West, found the climate in Kansas wonderful and the rainfall abundant. In such a state, Greeley said in his influential editorials, a 160-acre homestead could produce an ample living. A plantation, of course, demanded more land—but if Kansas was full of yeoman farmers working 160-acre plots, plantations and slaves were not likely to intrude.

One hundred and sixty acres. If anything unifies the story of the American West—its past and its present, its successes and its dreadful mistakes—it is this mythical allotment of land. Its origins are found in the original Homestead Act of 1862, which settled on such an amount—a quarter-mile square, more often referred to as a quarter section—as the ideal acreage for a Jeffersonian utopia of small farmers. The idea was to carve millions of quarter sections out of the public domain, sell them cheaply to restless Americans and arriving immigrants, and, by letting them try to scratch a living out of them, develop the nation's resources and build up its character.

In the West, the Homestead Act had several later incarnations. The Desert Lands Act, the Timber Culture Act, and the Timber and Stone Act were the principal ones. Neither Congress nor the General Land Office, which was responsible for administering the acts, could ever comprehend that the relative success of the land program east of the Mississippi River had less to do with the perseverance of the settlers or the wisdom of the legislation than with the forgiving nature of the climate. In the East, virtually every acre received enough rainfall, except during years of extraordinary drought, to grow most anything that didn't mind the soil and the temperature. (Unlike much of the West, which suffers through months of habitual drought, the East gets precipitation year-round; in the spring and early summer, when crops need water most, much of the East is exceptionally wet.) Since the growing season, except in the extreme north, was at least five months long, even an ignorant or lazy farmer could raise *some* kind of crop.

In the West, even if you believed that the rainfall was magically increasing, you still had to contend with high altitudes (the western plains, the Snake River Valley, and most of the irrigable lands in the Great Basin would float over the tops of all but the highest Appalachian Mountains) and, as a result, chronic frost danger even in May and September. Then there were the relentless winds, hailstones bigger than oranges, tornadoes, and breathtaking thunderstorms. There were sandy lands that would not retain moisture and poorly drained lands that retained too much; there were alkaline lands that poisoned crops.

The General Land Office bureaucrats sat in Washington pretending that such conditions did not exist. Their job, as they perceived it, was to fill little squares with people. They extended no credit, provided no water, offered no services. And the permutations of the Homestead Act that found their way into the western versions of the law sometimes *added* to the farmers' burdens. Under the Timber Culture Act, for example, you had to plant one-quarter of your quarter section with trees, a stipulation inserted because it was thought that trees increased the rainfall. In West Texas, where, meteorologically speaking, all that is predictable is the wind, you would have to spend most of your time replanting your fallen-down trees. Under the Desert Lands Act, which applied to land so arid even the government realized that farming was hopeless without irrigation, you had to demonstrate "proof of irrigation" before you could own the land. Unless you owned reasonably flat land immediately adjacent to a relatively constant stream which did not, as most western rivers do for much of their length, flow in a canyon, complying with the Desert Lands Act was almost out of the question. A mutual irrigation effort by the inhabitants of a valley was, perhaps, a possibility. That was what the Mormons had done, but they were a close-knit society linked by a common faith and a history of persecution.

The members of Congress who wrote the legislation, the land office agents who doled out land, and the newspaper editors who celebrated the settlers' heroism had, in a great many cases, never laid eyes on the land or the region that enclosed it. They were unaware that in Utah, Wyoming, and Montana—to pick three of the colder and drier states—there was not a single quarter section on which a farmer could subsist, even with luck, without irrigation, because an unirrigated quarter section was enough land for about five cows. The Indians accepted things as they were; that is why they were mostly nomadic, wandering toward greener grass and fuller herds and flowing water. If whites were going to insist on living there—fixed, settled, mortgaged, fenced—the best they could do with the land was graze it. But in those three states, an economical grazing unit was, say, twenty-five hundred to five thousand acres, depending on the circumstances. To amass that much land you had to cheat—on a magnificent scale. If you didn't, you had to overgraze the land and ruin it, and many millions of acres were damaged or ruined in exactly this way. Many settlers were tasting property ownership for the first time in their lives, and all they had in common was greed.

Speculation. Water monopoly. Land monopoly. Erosion. Corruption. Catastrophe. By 1876, after several trips across the plains and through the Rocky Mountain states, John Wesley Powell was pretty well convinced that those would be the fruits of a western land policy based on wishful thinking, willfulness, and lousy science. And by then everything he predicted was happening, especially land monopoly, water monopoly, graft, and fraud.

Homesteads fronting on streams went like oranges aboard a scurvy-ridden ship. The doctrine of riparian rights, which had been unthinkingly imported from the East, made it possible to monopolize the water in a stream if you owned the land alongside it. But if the stream was anything larger than a creek, only the person who owned land upstream, where it was still small, could manage to build a dam or barrage to guarantee a summer flow; then he could divert all he wanted, leaving his downstream neighbors with a bed of dry rocks. Riparian doctrine alone, therefore, made it possible for a tiny handful of landowners to monopolize the few manageable rivers of the West. When their neighbors saw their predicament and sold out, they could monopolize the best land, too.

As for the Desert Land Act and the Timber and Stone Act, they could not have promoted land monopoly and corruption more efficiently if they had been expressly designed for that purpose. A typical irrigation scene under the Desert Land Act went as follows: A beneficiary hauled a hogshead of water and a witness to his barren land, dumped the water on the land, paid the witness $20, and brought him to the land office, where the witness swore he had seen the land irrigated. Then, with borrowed identification and different names, another land application was filed, and the scene was repeated. If you could pull it off six or seven times, you had yourself a ranch. Foreign sailors arriving in San Francisco were offered a few dollars, a jug of whiskey, and an evening in a whorehouse in exchange for filing a land claim under the Timber and Stone Act. Before shipping out, the sailors abdicated title; there were no restrictions on transfer of ownership. Whole redwood forests were acquired in such a manner.

Then there was the Swamplands Act, or Swamp and Overflow Act—a Desert Lands Act of the bulrushes. If there was federal land that overflowed enough so that you could traverse it at times in a flat-bottomed boat, and you promised to reclaim it (which is to say, dike and drain it), it was yours. Henry Miller, a mythical figure in the history of California land fraud, acquired a large part of his 1,090,000-acre empire under this act. According to legend, he bought himself a boat, hired some witnesses, put the boat and witnesses in a wagon, hitched some horses to it, and hauled the boat and witnesses over county-size tracts near the San Joaquin River where it rains, on the average, about eight or nine inches a year. The land became his. The sanitized version of the story, the one told by Miller's descendants, has him benefiting more from luck than from ruse. During the winter of 1861 and 1862, most of California got three times its normal precipitation, and the usually semiarid Central Valley became a shallow sea the size of Lake Ontario. But the only difference in this version is that Miller didn't need a wagon for his boat; he still had no business acquiring hundreds of thousands of acres of the public domain, yet he managed it with ease.

One of the unforeseen results of the homestead legislation was a high rate of employment among builders of birdhouses. In most instances, you were required to display an "erected domicile" on your land. The Congress, after all, was much too smart to give people land without requiring them to live on it. In a number of instances, the erected domicile was a birdhouse, put there to satisfy a paid witness with a tender conscience. It is quite possible that the greatest opportunity offered by the homestead legislation in the West was the opportunity to earn a little honest graft. By conservative estimates, 95 percent of the final proofs under the Desert Land Act were fraudulent. "Whole townships have been entered under this law in the interest of one person or firm," thundered Binger Hermann, a commissioner of the General Land Office, about the Timber and Stone Act. Not long afterward, Hermann himself was fired for allowing unrestricted fraud.

Mark Twain might have written it off to the human condition, but Powell, who subscribed to a more benevolent view of humanity, wrote it off to the conditions of the desert and the failure to understand them. Americans were making a Procrustean effort to turn half a continent into something they were used to. It was a doomed effort. Even worse, it was unscientific.

The document that Powell hoped would bring the country to its senses was called *A Report on the Lands of the Arid Region of the United States, with a More Detailed Account of the Lands of Utah*. Published in 1876, the volume was seven years in preparation—though Powell took time out for a second expedition down the Colorado, in 1871, and for his usual plethora of intermittent pursuits. Powell's *Report* is remarkably brief, a scant two hundred pages in all. Unlike many of his rivals, such as the bombastic Ferdinand V. Hayden, Powell was more interested in being right than in being long. But his portrait of the American West has revolutionary implications even today.

At the beginning, Powell reconfirmed his view, which he had already submitted to an unbelieving Congress, that two-fifths of the United States has a climate that generally cannot support farming without irrigation. On top of that, irrigation could reclaim only a fraction of it. "When all the waters running in the streams found in this region are conducted on the land," Powell said, "there will be but a small portion of the country redeemed, varying in the different territories perhaps from *one to three percent*" (emphasis added). Powell regarded the theory that increased rainfall accompanied human settlement as bunk, but, typically, he disposed of it in a sympathetic and felicitous way: "If it be true that increase of the water supply is due to increase in precipitation, as many have supposed, the fact is not cheering to the agriculturalist of the arid region. . . . Any sudden great change [in climate] is ephemeral, and usually such changes go in cycles, and the opposite or compensating change may reasonably be anticipated. . . . [W]e shall have to expect a speedy return to extreme aridity, in which case a large portion of the agricultural industries of these now growing up would be destroyed."

The whole problem with the Homestead Acts, Powell went on, was that they were blind to reality. In the West, a 160-acre *irrigated* farm was too *large*, while a 160-acre *unirrigated* farm was too *small*. Most western valley soil was fertile, and a good crop was a near certainty once irrigation water was applied; in the milder regions the growing season was very long and two crops were possible, so one could often subsist on eighty irrigated acres or less. That, in fact, was about all the irrigated land one family could be expected to work. Remove the irrigation water, however, and things were drastically different. Then even a whole section was too small a piece of land. Under most circumstances, Powell claimed, no one could make a living through dryland ranching on fewer than 2,560 acres—four full sections. And even with that much land, a settler's prospects would be dicey in times of drought, because the land might lie utterly bare. Therefore, every pasturage farm should ideally have a water right sufficient to irrigate twenty acres or so during emergencies.

Having thrown over the preeminent myths about agriculture in the American West, Powell went on to the truly revolutionary part of his report. Under riparian water law, to give everyone a water right for twenty irrigated acres was impossible if you gave everyone a neat little square of land. Some squares would contain much greater stream footage than others, and their owners would have too much water compared with the others. The property boundaries would therefore have to be gerrymandered to give everyone a sufficient piece of the stream. That was one way you could help avert the monopolization of water. Another way was to insist that people *use* their water rights, not hold on to them in the hope that cities would grow up and one could make a killing someday selling water to them. An unused water right should revert—let us say after five years—to the public trust so someone else could claim it.

Doing all this, Powell reasoned, might help assure that water would be used equitably, but not necessarily efficiently. Ideally, to get through drier months and times of drought, you needed a reservoir in a good location—at a low altitude, and on the main branch of a stream. That way you could get more efficient storage of water—a dam only twice as large, but lower down, might capture five times as much water as a smaller one upstream. Also, you could then irrigate the lower valley lands, which usually have better soil and a longer growing season. In any event, an on-stream storage reservoir was, from the point of view of irrigation, preferable to small shallow ponds filled with diverted streamwater, the typical irrigation reservoirs of his day; the ponds evaporated much greater amounts of water and displaced valuable cropland.

But who, Powell asked, was building on-stream reservoirs? Practically no one. Homesteaders couldn't build them at all, let alone build them right, nor could groups of homesteaders—unless perhaps they were Mormons. Such dams required amounts of capital and commitment that were beyond the limits of aggregations of self-interested mortals. Private companies probably couldn't build good irrigation projects, either, nor even states. Sooner or later, the federal government would have to get into the irrigation business or watch its efforts to settle the West degenerate into failure and chaos. Once it realized that, it would have to undertake a careful survey of the soil characteristics so as not to waste a lot of money irrigating inferior land with drainage problems. And (he implied rather than stated) the government ought to put J. W. Powell in charge; the General Land Office, which would otherwise be responsible, was, as anyone could see, "a gigantic illustration of the evils of badly directed scientific work."

Having gone this far, Powell figured he might as well go the whole route. Fences, for example, bothered him. What was the sense of every rancher enclosing his land with a barbed-wire fence? Fenced lands tended to be unevenly grazed, and fences were obvious hazards to cattle in winter storms. Fencing was also a waste of time and money, especially in a region where rainfall could skid from twenty to six inches in successive years and someone was lucky to survive at all, let alone survive while constantly repairing and replacing fences. Individually fenced lands were a waste of resources, too; it takes a lot more tin, Powell reasoned, to make five eight-ounce cans than to make one forty-ounce can. The sensible thing was for farms to be clustered together and the individually owned lands treated as a commons, an *ejido*, with a single fence around the perimeter.

States bothered Powell, too. Their borders were too often non-sensical. They followed rivers for convenience, then struck out in a straight line, bisecting mountain ranges, cutting watersheds in half. Boxing out landscapes, sneering at natural reality, they were wholly arbitrary and, therefore, stupid. In the West, where the one thing that really mattered was water, states should logically be formed around watersheds. Each major river, from the glacial drip at its headwaters to the delta at its mouth, should be a state or semistate. The great state of Upper Platte River. Will the Senator from the state of Rio Grande yield? To divide the West any other way was to sow the future with rivalries, jealousies, and bitter squabbles whose fruits would contribute solely to the nourishment of lawyers.

While Powell knew that his plan for settling the American West would be considered revolutionary, he saw a precedent. After all, what was the difference between a cooperative irrigation district and a New England barn-raising? One was informal, the other organized and legalized, but otherwise they were the same thing. Communal pasturelands might be a gross affront to America's preoccupation with private property rights, but they were common in Europe. In the East, where inland navigation was as important as irrigation was in the West, you already had a strong federal presence in the Corps of Engineers. If anything was revolutionary, it was trying to graft English common law and the principles and habits of wet-zone agriculture onto a desert landscape. There was not a desert civilization in the world where that had been tried—and most of those civilizations had withered even after following sensible rules.

Powell was advocating cooperation, reason, science, an equitable sharing of the natural wealth, and—implicitly if not explicitly—a return to the Jeffersonian ideal. He wanted the West settled slowly, cautiously, in a manner that would work. If it was done intelligently instead of in a mad, unplanned rush, the settlement of the West could help defuse the dangerous conditions building in the squalid industrial cities of the East. If it was done wrong, the migration west might go right into reverse.

The nation at large, however, was in no mood for any such thing. It was avid for imperial expansion, and the majority of its citizens wanted to get rich. New immigrants were arriving, dozens of boatloads a day, with that motive burning in their brains. To them America was not so much a democratic utopia as a gold mine. If monopolists reigned here, they could accept that; someday *they* would be monopolists, too. Forty years earlier, Alexis de Tocqueville had captured the raw new country's soul: "To clear, to till, and to transform the vast uninhabited continent which is his domain, the American requires the daily support of an energetic passion; that passion can only be the love of wealth; the passion for wealth is therefore not reprobated in America, and, provided it does not go beyond the bounds assigned to it for public security, it is held in honor." In Powell's day, that passion for wealth had if anything grown more intense. A pseudoscientific dogma, Social Darwinism, had been invented to give predatory behavior a good name. Darwin could not be taught in the schools; but a perversion of Darwin could be practiced in real life.

The unpeopled West, naturally, was where a great many immigrants hoped to find their fortunes. They didn't want to hear that the West was dry. Few had ever seen a desert, and the East was so much like Europe that they imagined the West would be, too. A tiny bit semiarid, perhaps, like Italy. But a desert? Never! They didn't want to hear of communal pasturelands—they had left those behind, in Europe, in order that they could become the emperors of Wyoming. They didn't want the federal government parceling out water and otherwise meddling in their affairs; that was another European tradition they had left an ocean away. Agricultural fortunes were being made in California by rampant capitalists like Henry Miller; acreages the size of European principalities were being amassed in Texas, in

Montana. If the federal government controlled the water, it could also control the land, and then the United States might become a nation of small farmers after all—which was exactly what most Americans *didn't* want. For this was the late nineteenth century, when, as Henry Adams wrote, "the majority at last declared itself, once and for all, in favor of the capitalistic system with all its necessary machinery . . . the whole mechanical consolidation of force . . . ruthlessly . . . created monopolies capable of controlling the new energies that America adored."

It was bad enough for Powell that he was pulling against such a social tide. He also had to deal with the likes of William Gilpin, who had traded his soapbox for the governor's mansion in Denver; he had to fight with the provincial newspapers, the railroads, and all the others who were already there and had a proprietary interest in banishing the Great American Desert; he had to deal with western members of Congress who could not abide anyone calling their states arid (although a hundred years later, when the Bureau of Reclamation had become their prime benefactor, members of Congress from these same states would argue at length over whose state was the *more* arid and hostile).

Powell seemed at first to have everything going in his favor. The West was coming hard up against reality, as more hundreds of thousands of settlers ventured each year into the land of little rain. His exploits on the Colorado River had made him a national hero, the most celebrated adventurer since Lewis and Clark. He was on friendly if not intimate terms with a wide cross-section of the nation's elite—everyone from Henry Adams to Othniel C. Marsh, the great paleontologist, to Carl Schurz, the Interior Secretary, to Clarence King, the country's foremost geologist, to numerous strategically placed members of Congress. By 1881, he was head of both the Bureau of Ethnology and the Geologic Survey, two prestigious appointments that made him probably the most powerful, if not the most influential, scientist in America. But none of this prestige and power, none of these connections, was a match for ignorance, nonsense, and the nineteenth century's fulsome, quixotic optimism. When he testified before Congress about his report and his irrigation plan, the reception from the West—the region with which he was passionately involved, the region he wanted to *help*—was icily hostile. In his biography of Powell, Wallace Stegner nicely characterized the frame of mind of the typical western booster-politician when he surveyed Powell's austere, uncompromising monument of facts:

51

What, they asked, did he know about the West? What did he know about South Dakota? Had he ever been there? When? Where? For how long? Did he know the average rainfall of the James River Valley? Or the Black Hills? . . . [Did he] really know anything about the irrigable lands in the Three Forks country in Montana? They refused to understand his distinction between arid and subhumid, they clamored to know how their states had got labelled "arid" and thus been closed to settlement. . . . [W]hat about the artesian basin in the Dakotas? What about irrigation from that source? So he gave it to them: artesian wells were and always would be a minor source of water as compared to the rivers and the storm-water reservoirs. He had had his men studying artesian wells since 1882. . . . If all the wells in the Dakotas could be gathered into one county they would not irrigate that county.

Senator Moody [of South Dakota] thereupon remarked that he did not favor putting money into Major Powell's hands when Powell would clearly not spend it as Moody and his constituents wanted it spent. We ask you, he said in effect, your opinion of artesian wells. You think they're unimportant. All right, the hell with you. We'll ask somebody else who will give us the answer we want. Nothing personal.

The result, in the end, was that Powell got some money to conduct his Irrigation Survey for a couple of years—far less than he wanted, and needed—and then found himself frozen permanently out of the appropriations bills. The excuse was that he was moving too slowly, too deliberately; the truth was that he was forming opinions the West couldn't bear to hear. There was inexhaustible land but far too little water, and what little water there was might, in many cases, be too expensive to move. Having said this, held to it, and suffered for it, Powell spent his last years in a kind of ignominy. Unable to participate in the settlement of the West, he retreated into the Bureau of Ethnology, where his efforts, ironically, helped prevent the culture of the West's original inhabitants from being utterly trampled and eradicated by that same settlement. On September 23, 1902, he died at the family compound near Haven, Maine, about as far from the arid West as he could get.

Powell had felt that the western farmers would stand behind him, if not the politicians themselves; there he made one of the major miscalculations of his life. "Apparently he underestimated the capacity of the plains dirt farmer to continue to believe in myths even while his nose was being rubbed in unpleasant fact," Stegner wrote. "The press and a good part of the public in the West was against him more than he knew. . . . The American yeoman might clamor for government assistance in his trouble, but he didn't want any that would make him change his thinking."

What is remarkable, a hundred years later, is how little has changed. The disaster that Powell predicted—a catastrophic return to a cycle of drought—did indeed occur, not once but twice: in the late 1800s and again in the 1930s. When that happened, Powell's ideas—at least his insistence that a federal irrigation program was the only salvation of the arid West—were embraced, tentatively at first, then more passionately, then with a kind of desperate insistence. The result was a half-century rampage of dam-building and irrigation development which, in all probability, went far beyond anything Powell would have liked. But even as the myth of the welcoming, bountiful West was shattered, the myth of the independent yeoman farmer remained intact. With huge dams built for him at public expense, and irrigation canals, and the water sold for a quarter of a cent per ton—a price which guaranteed that little of the public's investment would ever be paid back—the West's yeoman farmer became the embodiment of the welfare state, though he was the last to recognize it. And the same Congress which had once insisted he didn't need federal help was now insisting that such help be continued, at any cost. Released from a need for justification, released from logic itself, the irrigation program Powell had wanted became a monster, redoubling its efforts and increasing its wreckage, both natural and economic, as it lost sight of its goal. Powell's ideal was a future in which the rivers of the American West would help create a limited bounty on that tiny fraction of the land which it made sense to irrigate. It is hard to imagine that the first explorer of the Colorado River would have welcomed a future in which there might be no rivers left at all.

CHAPTER TWO

The Red Queen

While Los Angeles moldered, San Francisco grew and grew. The city owned a superb natural harbor—the best on the Pacific Coast, one of the best in the world. When gold was struck in the Sierra Nevada foothills, 150 miles across the Central Valley, San Francisco became the principal destination of the fortune seekers of the world. The names of the camps suggested the potency of the lure: New York-of-the-Pacific, Bunker Hill, Chinese Camp, German Bar, Georgia Slide, Nigger Hill, Dutch Corral, Irish Creek, Malay Camp, French Bar, Italian Bar. Those who found their fortunes were inclined to part with them in the nearest haven of pleasure, which was San Francisco. Those who did not discovered that they could do just as well providing the opportunities. With oranges going for $2 apiece at the mines, and a plate of fresh oysters for $20 or more, it was a bonanza for all concerned.

In 1848, the population of San Francisco was eight hundred; three years later, thirty-five thousand people lived there. In 1853 the population went past fifty thousand and San Francisco became one of the twenty largest cities in the United States. By 1869, San Francisco possessed one of the busiest ports in the world, a huge fishing fleet, and the western terminus of the transcontinental railroad. It teemed with mansions, restaurants, hotels, theaters, and whorehouses. In finance it was the rival of New York, in culture the rival of Boston; in spirit it had no competitor.

Los Angeles, meanwhile, remained a torpid, suppurating, stunted little slum. It was too far from the gold fields to receive many fortune seekers on their way in or to detach them from their fortunes on the way out. It sat forlornly in the middle of an arid coastal basin, lacking both a port and a railroad. During most of the year, its water source, the Los Angeles River, was a smallish creek in a large bed; during the few winter weeks when it was not—when supersaturated tropical weather fronts crashed into the mountains ringing the basin—the bed could not begin to contain it, and the river floated neighborhoods out to sea. (For many years, Santa Anita Canyon, near Pasadena, held the United States record for the greatest rainfall in a twenty-four-hour period, but it may be more significant to state that the twenty-six inches that fell in a day were nearly twice the amount of precipitation that Los Angeles normally receives in a year.) Had humans never settled in Los Angeles, evolution, left to its own devices, might have created in a million more years the ideal creature for the habitat: a camel with gills.

The Spanish had actually settled Los Angeles long before they ever saw the Golden Gate. It was more convenient to Mexico and, from an irrigation farmer's point of view, it was a more promising place to live. By 1848, the town had a population of sixteen hundred, half Spanish and half Indian, with a small sprinkling of Yankees, and was twice the size of San Francisco. A decade later, however, San Francisco had grown ten times as large as Los Angeles. By the end of the Civil War, when San Francisco was the Babylon of the American frontier, Los Angeles was a filthy pueblo of thirteen thousand, a beach for human flotsam washed across the continent on the blood tide of the war. One of the town's early pioneers, a farm boy whose family had emigrated from Iowa, described it as a "vile little dump . . . debauched . . . degenerate . . . vicious."

If anything could be said to have saved Los Angeles it was its reputation as a haven from persecution, a place where one could lose oneself. Since the ranks of the persecuted include those who are too virtuous for their fellow citizens, as well as those who are not virtuous enough, sooner or later the city was bound to attract the victims of mobocracy. And the most persecuted among the virtuous in nineteenth-century America were, besides peaceful Indians and runaway slaves and Mennonites and Quakers, the members of the Mormon faith.

After fleeing Illinois for Utah, the Mormons had always been obsessed with finding escape routes to the sea. The first irrigation canals were still being dug beside the Wasatch Range when Brigham Young dispatched a party of his most loyal disciples, in 1851, to follow

Jedediah Smith's old route to the coast. When they crossed the San Bernardino Mountains, they found themselves in a huge arid basin that reminded them of home and was only a day or two from the sea. The streams were less reliable than those in Utah—the southern mountains received a scantier snowpack that never lasted halfway through the summer—but the San Bernardinos got decent winter rain, and artesian wells below them flowed like geysers. With money earned by selling food and supplies at usurious prices to adventurers bound through Utah for the gold fields, the Mormons purchased a huge chunk of land from an old Spanish rancho. The soil was good, the climate was ideal, and no one was better at irrigation farming than Mormons. Before long they were supplying much of the basin with food. In 1857, the U.S. Cavalry marched on Utah and Brigham Young ordered all distant settlements abandoned, but the Mormons' achievement had left its mark. A Presbyterian colony was soon established nearby, then a Quaker colony, then an ethnic colony of Germans. In this freakish climate—semitropical but dry, ocean-cooled but lavishly sunny—you could grow almost anything. Corn and cabbages sprouted next to oranges, avocados, artichokes, and dates. The capitalists of San Francisco did not remain oblivious; the Southern Pacific ran a spur line to Los Angeles in 1867, finally linking it to the rest of the world. On this same line, huge San Bernardino Valencias found their way to the 1884 World's Fair in New Orleans, where they attracted crowds. No one could imagine *oranges* grown in the western United States. It was then and there, more or less, that the phenomenon of modern Los Angeles began.

They came by ship, they came by wagon, they came by horse. They came on foot, dragging everything they could in a handcart, but the real hordes came by train. In 1885, the Atchison, Topeka, and Santa Fe Railroad linked Los Angeles directly with Kansas City, precipitating a fare war with the Southern Pacific. Within a year, the cost of passage from Chicago had dropped from $100 to $25. During brief periods of mad competition, you could cross two-thirds of the continent for a dollar. If you were asthmatic, tubercular, arthritic, restless, ambitious, or lazy—categories that pretty well accounted for Los Angeles' first flood of arrivals—the fares were too cheap to pass up. Out came Dakota farmers with hopes and wills blasted by blizzards and droughts. Out came farmers who despaired at the meager profits they made growing wheat. *You could grow oranges.* Out came Civil War veterans looking for an easy life, failures looking for another chance, and the usual boom-town complement of the slick, the sharp, and the ruthless.

The first boom began in the early 1880s and culminated in 1889, when the town transacted $100 million worth of real estate—in today's economy, a $2 billion year in Idaho Falls. Fraud was epic. Hundreds of unseen, paid-for lots were situated in the bed of the Los Angeles River, or up the nine-thousand-foot summits of the San Gabriel Range. The boom was, predictably, short-lived. In 1889, a bank president, a newspaper publisher, and the town's most popular minister all fled to Mexico to spare themselves jail terms, and a dozen or more victims took their own lives. By 1892, the population had dropped by almost one-half, but the bust was followed quickly by an oil boom, and enough fortunes were being made (the original Beverly Hillbillies were *from* Beverly Hills, then a patch of jackrabbit scrub overlying an oil basin) to pack the arriving trains again. Los Angeles soon drew close to San Francisco in population and was crowing with glee. "The 'busting of the boom' became but a little eddy in the great stream," enthused the Los Angeles *Times*, "the intermission of one heartbeat in the life of . . . the most charming land on the footstool of the Most High . . . the most beautiful city inhabited by the human family." Only one thing stood in the way of what looked as if it might become the most startling rise to prominence of any city in history—the scarcity of water.

The motives that brought Harrison Gray Otis, Harry Chandler, and William Mulholland to Los Angeles were the same that would eventually bring millions there. Otis came because he had been an incontrovertible, if not quite an ignominious, failure. He was born in Marietta, Ohio, and as a young man held a series of unspectacular jobs—a clerk for the Ohio legislature, a foreman at a printing plant, an editor of a veterans' magazine. His one early taste of glory came during the Civil War, in which he fought on the Union side, acquired several wounds and decorations, and ultimately rose to the rank of captain. *Captain* Harrison Gray Otis. He liked the title well enough to think himself deserving of a sinecure, and after the war he drifted out to California in search of one. What he got was an appointment as government agent on the Seal Islands, some frigid, treeless, wind-blasted humps of rock in the Bering Sea. His chief duty there was to prevent the poaching of walrus and seals, an assignment that suited

Otis better than he knew, since he bore an odd resemblance to the former and had a disposition to match. He was a large blubbery man with an intransigent scowl, an Otto von Bismarck mustache and a goatee, and a chronic inability to communicate in tones quieter than a yell, whether he was debating the American role in the Pacific or telling someone to pass the salt. "He is a damned cuss who doesn't seem to feel well unless he is in a row with someone," one among his legion of enemies would later remark.

The Seal Islands post was a humiliation that Otis, who was more ambitious than he was clever, couldn't afford to pass up. But after three years he had had enough, and he returned, bilious and frustrated, to California, where he got a job as editor of a local newspaper in Santa Barbara. Otis hated Santa Barbara. It was a hangout of the privileged classes, smug, snobbish, and perfectly content to remain small. Otis despised inherited wealth and class, but he despised a town that was disdainful of growth even more. He believed in it, perfervidly, just as he believed in those who start with nothing and dynamite their way to success. "Hustlers . . . men of brain, brawn, and guts" were the people he admired most, even if he had less in common with them than he thought. Otis would pursue a sinecure as a greyhound chases a rabbit, and it was his rotten luck at it, more than anything else, that finally caused his success. Trying to get himself appointed marshal of California, he was offered the job of consul in Tientsin, an insult that was more than he could bear. In 1881, Otis quit the paper in Santa Barbara and moved his family to Los Angeles.

The city was still small when Otis arrived, but it was already served by several newspapers, one of which, the *Times and Mirror*, was owned by a small-time eastern financier named H. H. Boyce. Boyce was looking for a new editor, and, though the pay was a miserable $15 a week, Otis took the job. Perhaps because he was fuming about the pay, or perhaps because he knew that time was running out, Captain Otis then made one of the bolder decisions of his life. He took all of his savings and, to help offset the low pay, convinced Boyce to let him purchase a share in the newspaper. Privately he was thinking that someday, perhaps, he could force H. H. Boyce out.

Harry Chandler came to Los Angeles for his health. He grew up in New Hampshire, a cherubic child with cheeks like Freestone peaches. His falsely benign appearance, which stayed with him all his life, made him a popular boy model among advertisers and photographers. But cherubic Harry was a rugged individualist and a ferocious competitor, and if there was money involved he would rarely pass up an opportunity or a dare. While at Dartmouth College, he accepted someone's challenge and dove into a vat of starch—a display that nearly ruined his lungs. Advised by doctors to recuperate in a warm and dry climate, he bought a ticket to Los Angeles. Arriving there, he moved from flophouse to flophouse because none of his fellow tenants could endure his hacking cough. When he was thoroughly friendless and nearly destitute, Harry met a sympathetic doctor who suffered from tuberculosis and owned an irrigated orchard near Cahuenga Pass, at the head of the San Fernando Valley. Would Harry like a job picking fruit?

The work was hard but invigorating. Before long, Harry felt almost cured. The work was also surprisingly lucrative. The doctor was as uninterested in money as Harry was interested, and let him sell a large share of what he picked. In his first year, Harry made $3,000. It was a small fortune, and inspired in Harry an awed faith in the potential of irrigated agriculture and, most particularly, agriculture in the San Fernando Valley. With the proceeds, Harry began to acquire newspaper circulation routes, which, at the time, were owned independently of the newspapers and bought and sold like chattel. Before long, he was a child monopolist, owning virtually all the routes in the city.

By 1886, Harrison Gray Otis had finally managed to hound H. H. Boyce out of the Los Angeles *Times and Mirror*. It was a pyrrhic victory, however, because Boyce had immediately established a rival paper, the *Tribune*, and engaged Otis in an all-out circulation war. With the allegiance of whoever dominated the circulation routes, one or the other was certain to win. It was Otis's luck that he got to Harry Chandler first. Within days, the *Tribune* began to disappear mysteriously from people's doorsteps, and its delivery boys simultaneously contracted a contagion. Meanwhile, new subscribers began to flock, like moths scenting pheromones, to the *Times*. Boyce was broken within months. Before Otis had much chance to gloat, however, he learned that the defunct *Tribune*'s printing plant had secretly acquired a new owner, whose name was Harry Chandler, and that the tactics that they had used together against Boyce could just as easily be turned against the *Times*. Otis, who bore lifelong grudges over provocations infinitely smaller than this, was realistic enough to know when he was had. Besides, this mild-appearing young man was the embodiment of every quality he admired. As a result, the *Times* acquired a new circulation manager and guiding light, whose name was

Harry Chandler, and in 1894 Harry Chandler acquired a new father-in-law, whose name was Harrison Gray Otis.

William Mulholland came to Los Angeles more or less for the hell of it. He was born in 1855 in Dublin, Ireland, where his father was a postal clerk. At fifteen, he signed on as an apprentice seaman aboard a merchant ship that carried him back and forth along the Atlantic trade routes. By 1874 he had had enough, and spent a couple of years hacking about the lumber camps in Michigan and the dry-goods business in Pittsburgh, where his uncle owned a store. It was in Pittsburgh that Mulholland first heard about California. He had just enough money to get to Panama by ship, and after landing in Colón, he traversed the isthmus on foot and worked his way north aboard another ship, arriving in San Francisco in the summer of 1877. Being back on a ship had renewed Mulholland's taste for the sea, and, after a brief failure at prospecting in Arizona—where he also fought Apaches for pay—he decided to ship out at San Pedro, the port nearest Los Angeles. He had ten dollars to his name. Anxious to make a little extra money, he joined a well-drilling crew. "We were down about six hundred feet when we struck a tree. A little further we got fossil remains. These things fired my curiosity. I wanted to know how they got there, so I got hold of Joseph Le Conte's book on the geology of the country. Right there I decided to become an engineer."

In his official photograph for the Los Angeles Department of Water and Power, which was taken when he was nearly fifty, Mulholland still looks young. He is wearing a short-brimmed dark fedora and a dark pinstripe suit; a luxuriant silk cravat circumnavigates a shirt collar that appears to be made of titanium; from a thick, bushy mustache sprouts a lit cigar. The face is supremely Irish: belligerence in repose, a seductive churlish charm. Once, in court, Mulholland was asked what his qualifications were to run the most far-flung urban water system in the world, and he replied, "Well, I went to school in Ireland when I was a boy, learned the Three R's and the Ten Commandments—most of them—made a pilgrimage to the Blarney Stone, received my father's blessing, and here I am." He began his engineering career in 1878 as a ditch-tender for the city's private water company, clearing weeds, stones, and brush out of a canal that ran by his house. One day Mulholland was approached by a man in a carriage who demanded to know his name and what he was doing. Mulholland stepped out of his ditch and told the man that he was doing his goddamned job and that his name was immaterial to the quality of his goddamned work. The man, it turned out, was the president of the water company. Learning this, Mulholland went to the company office to collect his pay before being fired. Instead, he was promoted.

The Sierra Nevada blocks most of the weather fronts moving across California from the Pacific, so that a place on the western slope of the range may receive eighty inches of precipitation in a year, while a place on the east slope, fifty miles away, may receive ten inches or less. The rivers draining into the Pacific from the West Slope are many and substantial, while those emptying into the Great Basin from the East Slope are few and generally small. The Owens River is an exception. It rises southeast of Yosemite, near a gunsight pass that allows some of the weather to come barreling through, heads westward for a while, then turns abruptly south and flows through a long valley, ten to twenty miles wide, flanked on either side by the Sierra Nevada and the White Mountains, which rise ten thousand feet from the valley floor. The valley is called the Owens Valley, and the lake into which the river empties—used to empty—was called Owens Lake. Huge, turquoise, and improbable in a desert landscape, it was the shrunken remnant of a much larger lake that formed during the Ice Ages. Due to a high evaporation rate and, for its size, a modest rate of inflow, the lake was more saline than the sea, but it supported two species of life in the quadrillions: a salt-loving fly and a tiny brine shrimp. The soup of shrimp and the smog of flies attracted millions of migratory waterfowl, a food source whose startling numbers were partially responsible for inducing some of the valley's first visitors to remain. "The lake was alive with wild fowl," wrote Beveridge R. Spear, an Owens Valley pioneer. "Ducks were by the square mile, millions of them. When they rose in flight, the roar of their wings . . . could be heard . . . ten miles away. . . . Occasionally, when shot down, a duck would burst open from fatness which was butter yellow."

The greater attraction, however, was the river. When whites arrived in the 1860s, Paiute Indians who had learned irrigation from the Spanish were already diverting some of the water to raise crops. In traditional pioneer fashion, the whites trumped up some cattle-rustling charges against the Indians, which appear to have led to the murder of a white woman and a child. The pious Owens Valley citizens then murdered at least 150 Paiutes in retaliation, driving the last hundred into Owens Lake to drown. They then took over the

Indians' land, borrowed their irrigation methods, and began raising alfalfa and pasture and fruit. By 1899, they had established several ditch companies and had put some forty thousand acres under cultivation.

The huge new silver camp at Tonopah, Nevada, consumed most of what the valley grew. With prosperity, several thriving towns sprang up: Bishop, Big Pine, Lone Pine, Independence. The irrigated valley was postcard-pretty, a narrow swath of green in the middle of the high desert, with 14,495-foot Mount Whitney, the highest peak between Canada and Mexico, looming over Lone Pine and the river running through. Mark Twain came to visit, and Mary Austin, who was to become a well-known writer, came to live. But the entrance that most excited the valley people was that of the United States Reclamation Service (later renamed the Bureau of Reclamation). The Service was an unparalleled experiment in federal intervention in the nation's economy, and was being watched so closely by skeptics in Congress that it could not afford to have any of its first projects fail. To Frederick Newell, the first Reclamation Commissioner, the Owens Valley looked like a place where he could almost be guaranteed success. The people were proven irrigation farmers—a rarity in the non-Mormon West; the soil could grow anything the climate would permit; the river was underused; and there was a good site for a reservoir. Sixty thousand additional acres were irrigable, and all of them could be gravity-fed. In early 1903, just a few months after the Service was created, a team of Reclamation engineers was already trooping around the valley, gauging streamflows and making soil surveys. Sixty thousand new acres would even make it worthwile to run a railroad spur to Los Angeles. Los Angeles, everyone thought, was going to make the Owens Valley rich.

Fred Eaton thought differently. Eaton had been born in Los Angeles in 1856; his family had founded Pasadena. Most of the Eaton men were engineers, and when they looked around them it seemed that half of what they saw they had built themselves; it gave them an overpowering sense of pride-in-place. Fred had gone into hydrologic engineering, which is to say that he pretty much taught it to himself, and by the time he was twenty-seven, he was superintendent of the Los Angeles City Water Company. As San Francisco had bloomed into pseudo-Parisian splendor, Fred Eaton had chafed. When Los Angeles finally began to take on the appearance of a place with a future, he had been intensely proud. But he was one of the few people who understood that this whole promising future was an illusion. With artesian pressure still lifting fountainheads of water eight feet into the air, no one believed that someday the basin would run out of water. Few understood that the occasional big floods in the Los Angeles River were testimony to the *absence* of rain: that the basin was normally so dry there wasn't enough ground cover to hold the rain when it fell. The annual flow of the Los Angeles River (that which ran aboveground) represented only a fifth of 1 percent of the runoff of the state, and because of the pumping the flow was dropping fast, from a hundred cubic feet per second in the 1880s to forty-five cfs in 1902. If growth continued, the population and the water would fall hopelessly out of balance. Everyone was living off tens of thousands of years of accumulated groundwater, like a spendthrift heir squandering his wealth. No one knew how much groundwater lay beneath the basin or how long it could be expected to last, but it would be insane to build the region's future on it.

There was no other source of water nearby. Deserts lay on three sides of the basin, an ocean on the fourth. The nearest large rivers were the Colorado and the Kern, but to divert them out of their canyons to Los Angeles would require pumping lifts of thousands of feet—an impossibility at the time. It would also require a Herculean amount of energy.

But there was, 250 miles away, the Owens River. It might not be quite sufficient for the huge metropolis forming in Eaton's imagination, but it was large enough; there was water for at least a million people. Indeed, Eaton was one of the few Los Angeleans who knew the river even existed. Its distance from Los Angeles was staggering, but its remoteness was overshadowed by one majestically significant fact: Owens Lake, the terminus of the river, sat at an elevation of about four thousand feet. Los Angeles was a few feet above sea level. The water, carried in pressure aqueducts and siphons, could arrive under its own power. Not one watt of pumping energy would be required. The only drawback was that the city might have to take the water by theft.

During their years together at the Los Angeles City Water Company, Fred Eaton and Bill Mulholland became good friends, thriving on each other's differences. Eaton was a western patrician, smooth and diffident; Mulholland an Irish immigrant with a musician's repertoire of ribald stories and a temperament like a bear's. Eaton thought so much of Mulholland that he groomed him to be his successor, and when Eaton left the company in 1886 to pursue a career in politics and seek his fortune, Mulholland was named superintendent. In the years that followed, Fred Eaton would become messianic about the water shortage he saw approaching. The only answer, he told Mulholland, was to get the Owens River. At first, Mulholland found the idea preposterous: going 250 miles for water was out of the question, and Mulholland didn't much believe in surface-water development anyway. Damming rivers meant forming reservoirs, and in the heat and dryness of California, reservoirs would evaporate huge quantities of water. It made more sense to slow down the rainfall as it returned to the ocean and force more of it into the aquifer. Mulholland preached soil and forest conservation thirty years before its time. He wanted to seed the whole basin, and when he said that the deforestation of the mountainsides would reduce the basin's water supply, everyone thought he was slightly nuts. He had his men filling gullies and installing infiltration galleries and checkdams all over the place. Everything he did, however, was nullified by the basin's growth.

By 1900, Los Angeles' population had gone over 100,000; it doubled again within four years. During the same period, the city experienced its first severe drought. Even with lawn watering prohibited and park ponds left unfilled, the artesian pressure, as Eaton had predicted, began to drop. Gushes became gurgles, then dried up. Pumps were frantically installed. By 1904, the pressure was low enough to prompt Mulholland to begin shutting irrigation wells in the San Fernando Valley, which lay across the Hollywood Hills and fed both the aquifer and the river. The farmers were furious, and Mulholland began spending a lot of time in court. The Los Angeles City Water Company was eventually taken over by the city, and Mulholland was retained in command. (The city didn't have much choice in the matter. Mulholland was such a seat-of-the-pants engineer that the plan of the entire water system resided mainly in his head; the most elemental schematics and blueprints did not exist.) In late 1904, the newly created Los Angeles Department of Water and Power issued its first public report. "The time has come," it said, "when we shall have to supplement the supply from some other source." With that simple statement William Mulholland was about to become a modern Moses. But instead of leading his people through the waters to the promised land, he would cleave the desert and lead the promised waters to them.

There is a widely held view that Los Angeles simply went out to the Owens Valley and stole its water. In a technical sense, that isn't quite true. Everything the city did was legal (though its chief collaborator, the U.S. Forest Service, did indeed violate the law). Whether one can justify what the city did, however, is another story. Los Angeles employed chicanery, subterfuge, spies, bribery, a campaign of divide-and-conquer, and a strategy of lies to get the water it needed. In the end, it milked the valley bone-dry, impoverishing it, while the water made a number of prominent Los Angeleans very, very rich. There are those who would argue that if all of this was legal, then something is the matter with the law.

It could never have happened, perhaps, had the ingenuous citizens of the Owens Valley paid more attention to a small news item that appeared in the Inyo *Register*, the valley's largest newspaper, on September 29, 1904. The item began: "Fred Eaton, ex-mayor of Los Angeles, and Fred [*sic*] Mulholland, who is connected with the water system of that city, arrived a few days ago and went up to the site of the proposed government dam on the [Owens] River." The person who took them around, the story continued, was Joseph Lippincott, the regional engineer for the Reclamation Service. It wasn't so much this small piece of news that should have aroused the valley's suspicions. It was the fact that Lippincott had already taken Eaton around the valley twice before.

The valley had no particular reason to distrust J. B. Lippincott, although a search into his background would have dredged up a revelation or two. As a young man out of engineering school, he had joined John Wesley Powell's Irrigation Survey, the first abortive attempt to launch a federal reclamation program in the West, but had lost his job soon thereafter when Congress denied Powell funding. Embittered by the experience, Lippincott migrated to Los Angeles, where, by the mid-1890s, he had built up a lucrative practice as a consulting engineer. In 1902, when the Reclamation Service was finally created, its first commissioner, Frederick Newell, immediately thought of Lippincott as the person to launch its California program. He had a good reputation, and he understood irrigation—a science few engineers were familiar with. The post, however, meant a substantial cut in salary, and Lippincott insisted on being allowed to maintain a part-time engineering practice on the side. Newell and his deputy, Arthur Powell Davis (who was John Wesley Powell's nephew), were a little wary; in a fast-growing region with little water, a district engineer with divided loyalties could lead the Service into a thicket of conflict-of-interest entanglements. The centerpiece of the Service's program in California was to be the Owens Valley Project, and there were already rumors that Los Angeles coveted the valley's water. One of the Service's engineers, in fact, had raised this issue with Davis; with Lippincott, a son of Los Angeles, in charge, a collision between the city and the Service over the Owens River might leave the city with the water and the Service absent its reputation. But the Service's early leadership, unlike those who succeeded them, suffered from a certain lack of imagination. "On the face of it," Davis scoffed, "such a project is as likely as the city of Washington tapping the Ohio River."

The only person who seemed suspicious when Lippincott began showing Eaton and Mulholland around the Owens Valley again and again was one of his own employees, a young Berkeley-educated engineer named Jacob Clausen. His apprehensions had been aroused during Eaton's second visit, when Lippincott and Eaton had ridden up to the valley from Los Angeles by way of Tioga Pass and Clausen, at Lippincott's request, had met them at Mono Lake. On the way down the valley, Lippincott insisted that they stop at the ranch of Thomas Rickey, one of the biggest landowners in the valley. Rickey's ranch was in Long Valley, an occluded shallow gorge of the Owens River, hard up against the giant Sierra massif, which contained the reservoir site the Reclamation Service would have to acquire in order for its project to be feasible. Eaton had told Clausen that he wanted to become a cattle rancher and was interested in buying Rickey's property if he was willing to sell. As they visited the ranch, however, he seemed much more interested in water than in cattle. Clausen understood the dynamics of the Owens Valley Project—the stream-flows, the water rights, the interaction of ground and surface water—better than anyone, and Lippincott asked him to explain to Eaton how the project would work. Eaton hung on his every word, and that, Clausen was to testify later, "was exactly what Lippincott wanted." The two Los Angeleans were good friends, and Eaton had been the first to dream of Los Angeles going to the Owens Valley for water. Was it so farfetched, Clausen would remember thinking to himself, to believe that Lippincott was out to help Los Angeles steal the valley's water?

If Clausen's suspicions were aroused, those of his high superiors remained utterly dormant, even though they would soon have equal reason to suspect Lippincott of being a double agent for Los Angeles. In early March of 1905, Lippincott had sent his entire engineering staff to Yuma, Arizona, on the Colorado River, to move the Yuma Irrigation Project forward at a faster pace. Work on the Owens Valley

Project had been held up by winter and by the delayed arrival of a piece of drilling equipment which was on order. During the hiatus, the Reclamation Service received a couple of applications for rights-of-way across federal lands from two newly formed power companies in the Owens Valley. Each was interested in building a hydroelectric project, and Lippincott had to decide which, if any, of the plans could coexist with the Reclamation project. Unable or unwilling to look into the matter himself, Lippincott might have waited for one of his engineers to return later in the spring, but he wanted to dispose of the issue, so he decided to appoint a consulting engineer to look into the matter for him. And though there were dozens of engineers in Los Angeles and San Francisco among whom he could have chosen, he decided to turn to his old friend and professional associate Fred Eaton.

The news that Lippincott had hired Fred Eaton to decide on a matter that could affect the whole Owens Valley Project left his superiors stunned, but their response, typically, was one of bafflement rather than anger. "I fail to understand in what capacity he is acting" was the only response Arthur Davis managed to give.

Eaton himself had no questions about the capacity in which he was acting, though the public face he presented was very different. With his letter of introduction from Lippincott and an armload of freshly minted Reclamation maps, he strode into the government land office in Independence, claiming to represent the Service on a matter of vital importance to the Owens Valley Project. For the first three days, however, his investigations had nothing to do with the hydroelectric plans. Poring over land deeds in the office's files—deeds to which he might have had no access as a private citizen—Eaton jotted down a wealth of information on ownership, water rights, stream flows—things Los Angeles had to know if and when it decided to move on the Owens Valley's water. Handsome and charming, Eaton even managed to get the land office employees to help him, unaware that the information they were digging out had nothing to do with the matter that had allegedly brought Eaton there. When he finally had what he felt he needed, he turned to the official matter at hand.

The problem of the conflicting power-license applications was straightforward; there could only be one resolution. One of the two power companies, the Owens River Water and Power Company, held water rights senior to those of its competitor, the Nevada Power Mining and Milling Company. Its rights even predated those of the Reclamation Service, and if it was refused its application it might cause the Service some real legal embarrassment. In addition, its plan of development was far more compatible with the Reclamation project than the Nevada company's; Jacob Clausen had taken a cursory look at both and decided that the Nevada company's project could reduce the Long Valley reservoir to a glorified mudflat during the peak summer irrigation season, when water was needed most. To Clausen, the applications were hardly worth a second look, and he couldn't understand why Lippincott had even bothered to hire someone to review them so carefully. The Owens River company deserved a conditional go-ahead, the Nevada company decidedly did not. But Clausen was far too naive to understand the complexity of such matters: One of the founders of, and partners in, the Nevada Power Mining and Milling Company was a rancher named Thomas B. Rickey.

Eaton's baffling recommendation in favor of the Nevada Power Mining and Milling Company threw Clausen into a state of apoplexy. When Lippincott formally endorsed his judgment a few weeks later, Clausen finally understood that something was terribly wrong, but how wrong even he could not fathom. On the 6th of March, exactly three days after Lippincott had hired Eaton as his personal representative in the matter of the power company applications, the city of Los Angeles had quietly hired its own consultant to prepare a report on the options it had in its search for water. The report had taken only a couple of weeks to prepare—most of the information was in Mulholland's office, and the conclusion was foregone anyway—and the consultant had received an absurdly grandiose commission of $2,500, more than half his annual salary. It was not so much a commission as a bribe. The money, however, was well spent: the name of the consultant was Joseph B. Lippincott.

One other person besides Jacob Clausen had begun to follow the comings and goings of Eaton, Lippincott, and Mulholland with more than detached interest—Wilfred Watterson, the president of the Inyo County Bank. Wilfred and his brother, Mark, were the most popular citizens in the Owens Valley. Their family had founded the bank, and Wilfred and Mark, when still in their twenties, became president and treasurer. Both were attractive young men, but Wilfred in particular was strikingly handsome. He had clean-cut, perfect features, an absolutely even gaze, and the erect, confident air of a nineteenth-century optimist. In his elegant clothes, Wilfred could have passed easily for Bat Masterson instead of a small-town banker. The lending policies of the Inyo County Bank were as much of an aberration as its owners. The Wattersons rarely refused a loan and often stretched out debts;

they displayed a strong interest in the valley's survival and a casual, almost careless attitude toward money.

Wilfred's suspicions that Los Angeles was engineering a water grab had begun to simmer when word got around that Fred Eaton, the would-be cattle rancher, was offering some astonishingly generous sums for land with good water rights. There were stories that Eaton would make an offer that already seemed generous, and, if a landowner gambled and tried to raise him, Eaton would readily meet his terms. It was hard for Wilfred to nail any of this down, because no one wanted to let the Wattersons know that he was thinking of selling out—not after they had loaned money with such abandon up and down the valley—but the stories were enough to make Wilfred skeptical about Eaton's true intentions. Was he rich enough to pay those prices? Where did he get the money?

Watterson's suspicions became intensely aroused one day in the early summer of 1905 when an unidentified young man arrived in the valley, went directly to the Inyo Bank, and displayed a written order from Fred Eaton to pick up a parcel in a safe deposit box. As soon as he had it in his hand, the young man left with unseemly haste and stalked down the street in the direction of the post office. Watterson sprang up from his desk and asked the teller who the man was. He was Harry Lelande, the Los Angeles city clerk—the official legally charged with handling any transactions for the city that involved transfers of water or land.

Watterson burst out the door and ran down the street in the direction in which Lelande had disappeared. He found him across the street from the post office.

Watterson ambled up to Lelande, accosted him in his disarming manner, and said, "I'm sorry, Mr. Lelande, but there's a small formality we forgot to carry out at the bank."

Lelande looked perplexed. Watterson asked him to follow him back to the bank.

Once they were safely inside the president's office, Watterson offered the clerk a seat and some coffee, then walked casually to the door and locked it. "We want the deed back," he said.

Lelande looked stricken. "What deed do you mean?" he asked.

"The deed by which your city is going to try to rape this valley," Watterson answered.

"I haven't any idea what you're talking about."

"Maybe this will help," said Watterson. He opened his desk drawer, removed a revolver, and put it on top of the desk.

Lelande's mouth opened. "I can't give you something I don't have," he begged.

Watterson stood up and hovered menacingly over the clerk. "Take off your coat and trousers," he said.

Lelande, badly frightened, obliged.

Watterson turned all of his pockets inside out and found nothing. He ordered Lelande to get dressed and take him to his room at the Hotel Bishop.

"Eaton's been buying land in an underhanded way to secure water for the city of Los Angeles, hasn't he?" Watterson said to Lelande on the way over. He was inventing the theory as he walked, but Lelande's agonized expression told him he was right. "You've paid high prices not because you're dumb but because you're smart. You're masquerading as investors and all you're going to invest in is our ruin."

Lelande kept insisting that he didn't know what Watterson was talking about. At the hotel, Watterson nearly tore apart his room, but found none of the documents Lelande had extracted from Eaton's box. It was obvious that Lelande had been so fearful of being discovered that he had immediately run to the post office and mailed the deed. Without the document, Watterson had nothing to go on but his hunches, and he was forced to let Lelande go. But, his temper notwithstanding, he knew he would have had to let him go anyway; the clerk had done nothing against the law. Neither, from what he knew, had Eaton. Was it possible, Watterson asked himself, that a distant city could destroy the valley he and his family had worked so hard and gambled so recklessly to build up, and never step outside the law?

Meanwhile, the $2,500 contract accepted by Joseph Lippincott from Los Angeles was, if not exactly illegal, an apparent violation of the most basic ethical standards for government officials. Newell had let Lippincott off with another fatherly lecture, but everyone in the Reclamation Service had heard about it, and since the Service had been created as an answer to the epic graft and fraud associated with the General Land Office, some of Lippincott's associates were furious with him. By July of 1905, Newell realized that the whole thing might blow up in his face; he had to do something to contain the damage. As a result, he decided to appoint a panel of engineers to review the conflict between the Reclamation project and the water needs of Los Angeles and decide whether the Owens Valley Project should move forward, be put on hold, or be abandoned. Newell felt that Lippincott, as the senior engineer most familiar with the project, should sit on the panel. To his and Lippincott's astonishment, several Reclamation engineers said they would refuse to sit next to him. Lippincott now realized that he, too, would have to mount a damage-control operation in a hurry. On July 26, the night before the panel was scheduled to convene, he dashed off a telegram to Eaton that read, "Reported to me and publicly accepted that you had represented yourself as connected with Reclamation and acting as my agent in Owens Valley. As this is entirely erroneous and very embarrassing to me, please deny publicly or the Service will be forced to do so." The truth of Lippincott's denial can best be judged by Fred Eaton's reaction, which was incendiary. He received the telegram in the federal land office in Independence, where he was still trying to masquerade as Lippincott's agent. After reading it he felt compelled to vent his spleen on the nearest person available, agent Richard Fysh. "Eaton said he had a telegram from Mr. Lippincott and it was a damned hot one," said Fysh later in a deposition, "and he, Eaton, did not like it a little bit, as it put him in a wrong light."

Newell's panel of engineers was convened in San Francisco on July 27. After two days of hearing divided opinions (Clausen testified in favor of continuing, Lippincott in favor of abandonment), the panel reached a unanimous verdict. The Owens Valley Project should not be sedulously pursued, they recommended; the needs of Los Angeles had become too great an issue. But neither should it be formally abandoned until a more persuasive case could be made for doing so. Los Angeles would have to demonstrate that it had absolutely no choice but to go to the valley for water, and it would have to prove that it had the resources to carry out such a gigantic undertaking on its own. Such a recommendation, the panel added, was of course based on the assumption that the Reclamation project was still feasible.

Which, unbeknownst to anyone but Eaton and a select handful of Los Angeles officials, it was not. Four months earlier, after completing his consultant duties for Lippincott, Eaton had gone back to see the stubborn Thomas Rickey, who held the key piece of land in the valley—the land the city had to have in order to block the federal project—but who had refused to sell. In Eaton's hand was his recommendation that Rickey's hydroelectric company be allowed to usurp its competitor's claim on the main power sites on the river. That, Eaton thought, was the sweetener that would surely make Rickey sell. After hours of pleading and cajoling, however, the rancher still

71

held out. In disgust, Eaton finally stood up, roughly shook Rickey's hand, and stomped out the door. As he was standing at the railroad depot, waiting for the train that would take him back to Los Angeles, Rickey raced up in his carriage. He had had a sudden change of heart; for $450,000, he told Eaton, he would sell him an option clear on the ranch, including the Long Valley reservoir site.

Eaton's jubilation was so great he couldn't restrain himself. He ran to the telegraph office and shot off a cryptic message to Mulholland. "The deal is made," he wired. All it had required was "a week of Italian work."

Los Angeles now had most of what it needed, but Mulholland still wanted some additional water rights in order to kill the Reclamation project once and for all. Within hours of receiving Eaton's telegram, he was frantically organizing an expedition of prominent Los Angeleans to the Owens Valley, using the pretext that they were investors interested in developing a resort. The group included Mayor Owen McAleer and two prominent members of the water commission. For them to see the river firsthand was crucial, Mulholland reasoned, because he and Eaton would need more money to buy the last water rights they wanted, and the city could not legally appropriate money toward a project that hadn't even been described, let alone authorized. A group such as this could easily free up some money in the Los Angeles business community if they fathomed how much water there was.

It went exactly as planned. The group arrived in the valley on the cusp of spring, when even small tributaries of the Owens River were overflowing; days after they returned, Eaton and Mulholland had all the money they needed. They requisitioned an automobile and raced off to the valley by the shortest route, across the Mojave Desert—probably the first time anyone crossed it by car. After a week of frantic, furtive buying, the two men returned. "The last spike has been driven," Mulholland announced to the assembled water commissioners. "The options are all secured."

Like all the other newspaper publishers in the city, Harrison Gray Otis had been operating under a self-imposed gag rule. Although the publishers knew what was going on, not a word of Mulholland and Eaton's stealthy grab of water options had appeared in the papers. However, on July 29, the same day the Reclamation panel reached its verdict, Otis could no longer contain himself. Under a headline that read, "Titanic Project to Give the City a River," the whole unauthorized story spilled out in the Los Angeles *Times*.

Otis seemed to take particular satisfaction in the way Fred Eaton had hoodwinked the greedy but guileless rubes in the Owens Valley. "A number of the unsuspecting ranchers have regarded the appearance of Mr. Eaton in the valley as a visitation of Providence," the *Times* chortled. "In the eyes of the ranchers he was land mad. When they advanced the price of their holdings a few hundred dollars and he stood the raise, their cup of joy fairly overflowed. . . . The farmer folk in the Owens River Valley think that he has gone daffy on stock raising. To them he is a millionaire with a fad." The paper even admitted that the town of Independence, whose neighboring ranchers had been made offers they couldn't refuse, was faced with financial ruin, but it refused to let such a fact spoil its enjoyment of a good joke. The paper also recalled in excruciating detail Joseph Lippincott's career as a double agent, apparently thinking it was doing him a favor. "In the consummation of the great project that is to supply Los Angeles with sufficient water for all time, great credit is given to J. B. Lippincott," it said. "Without Mr. Lippincott's interest and cooperation, it is declared that the plan never would have gone through. . . . *Guided by the spirit of the Reclamation Act . . .* he recognized the fact that the Owens River water would fulfill a greater mission in Los Angeles than if it were to be spread over acres of desert land. . . . Any other government engineer, a nonresident of Los Angeles and not familiar with the needs of this section, undoubtedly would have gone ahead with nothing more than the mere reclamation of the arid lands in view" (emphasis added). It was praise that was to damn Lippincott for the rest of his life.

There was nothing quite as revealing in the *Times*'s story, however, as its very lead sentence: "The cable that has held the San Fernando Valley vassal for ten centuries to the arid demon," it gushed in a spasm of metaphorical excess, "is about to be severed by the magic scimitar of modern engineering skill."

There was something very strange about that sentence. All along, the Owens River had been portrayed as a matter of life or death to the city of Los Angeles. No one had ever said a word about the San Fernando Valley.

Sesquipedalian tergiversation was the strong suit of Harrison Gray Otis, along with slander, meanness, biliousness, and the implacable pursuit of a good old-fashioned grudge. Under his ownership, the *Times* was less a newspaper than a kind of mace used to bludgeon and destroy his enemies, who, and which, were many. (Otis often said that he considered objectivity a form of weakness.) The Democratic Party was "a shameless old harlot"; labor leaders were "corpse defacers," labor unions "anarchic scum"; California's preeminent reformer, Governor (later Senator) Hiram Johnson, was "a born mob leader—a whooper—a howler—a roarer." The newspaper owned by Otis's former partner, H. H. Boyce, was the "Daily Morning Metropolitan Bellyache," while Boyce himself was "a coarse vulgar criminal." William Randolph Hearst and his *Examiner*, more serious rivals than Boyce, were, interchangeably, "Yellow Yawp." Even innocent bystanders were vaporized by the General's ire. One morning Otis was greeted by a new neighbor who happened to mispronounce his name. "Good morning, General Ah-tis," said the man cheerily. "It's *O*-tis, you goddamn fool," the General bellowed back.

General Harrison Gray Otis. Otis's military coronation had come through the offices of President William McKinley as a reward for volunteering to send young men into the Philippine jungles during the Spanish-American War. By the time he returned to the States, the twentieth century had dawned, and Otis was utterly unprepared for it. Unions were organizing, the open shop was threatened, and even in Los Angeles the Socialists—the *Socialists*—were getting ready to run a candidate for mayor. Anti-unionism became breakfast fare for *Times* readers, as predictable as sunrise, and Otis was soon ordained public enemy number one by organized labor in the United States—no mean feat for a newspaper publisher in a remote western city. It was a notoriety he loved. To celebrate it, Otis commissioned a new headquarters that resembled a medieval fortress—it even had a parapet with turrets and cannon slots—and had a custom touring car built with a cannon mounted on the hood. The effect of all this on his enemies was inspirational. Hiram Johnson was addressing a crowd in a Los Angeles auditorium when someone in the audience, who knew that Johnson's talent for invective surpassed even the General's, yelled out, "What about Otis?" Johnson, all prognathous scowl and murderous intent, took two steps forward and began extemporaneously. "In the city of San Francisco we have drunk to the very dregs of infamy," he said in a low rumble. "We have had vile officials, we have had rotten newspapers. But we have had nothing so vile, nothing so low, nothing so debased, nothing so infamous in San Francisco as Harrison Gray Otis. He sits there in senile dementia with gangrene heart and rotting brain, grimacing at every reform, chattering impotently at all things that are decent, frothing, fuming, violently gibbering, going down to his grave in snarling infamy. This man Otis is the one blot on the banner of southern California; he is the bar sinister on your escutcheon. My friends, he is the one thing that all Californians look at when, in looking at southern California, they see anything that is disgraceful, depraved, corrupt, crooked, and putrescent—*that*," concluded Johnson with a majestic bawl, "that is Harrison Gray Otis!"

The vitriol that Otis and his rivals hurled at one another, however, could be turned off instantly if some more important matter was at hand. In the avaricious social climate of southern California, that usually meant an opportunity to make money; and in the dry climate of southern California, money meant water.

The first sign something was afoot came in the weeks following the *Times*'s disclosure of Mulholland and Eaton's daring scheme, when Otis's newspaper took time out from its usual broadsides to laud the future of the San Fernando Valley, an encircled plain of dry, mostly worthless land on the other side of the Hollywood Hills. "Go to the whole length and breadth of the San Fernando Valley these dry August days," the paper editorialized on August 1. "Shut your eyes and picture this same scene after a big river of water has been spread over every acre, after the whole expanse has been cut up into five-acre, and in some cases one-acre, plots—plots with a pretty cottage on each and with luxuriant fruit trees, shrubs and flowers in all the glory of their perfect growth. . . ." Again on October 10, a so-called news story began, "Premonitory pains and twitches: The San Fernando Valley has caught the boom. It appears just about ready to break. . . ."

What was odd about this was that there was as yet no guarantee—at least none publicly offered by Mulholland—that the San Fernando Valley was going to receive any of the Owens Valley water. In the first place, the route of the aqueduct had not yet been disclosed; it might go through the valley, but then again it might not. Secondly, the voters had not even approved the aqueduct, let alone voted for a bond issue to finance it. Mulholland had been saying that the city had surplus water sufficient for only ten thousand new arrivals. If that was so, and if the city was expected to grow by hundreds of thousands during the next decade, where was this great surplus for the San Fernando Valley to come from? In those days, the valley was isolated from Los Angeles proper; it sat by itself far outside the city limits. In theory, the valley couldn't even *have* the city's surplus water, assuming there was any—it would be against the law.

The truth, which only a handful of people knew, was that William

Mulholland's private figures were grossly at odds with his public pronouncements; it was the same with his intentions. Despite his talk of water for only ten thousand more people, there was still a big surplus at hand. (During the eight years it would take to complete the aqueduct, in fact, the population of Los Angeles rose from 200,000 to 500,000 people, yet no water crisis occurred.) The crisis was, in large part, a manufactured one, created to instill the public with a sense of panic and help Eaton acquire a maximum number of water rights in the Owens Valley. Mulholland and Eaton had managed to secure water rights along forty miles of the Owens River, which would be enough to give the city a huge surplus for years to come. But Mulholland was not saying that he would *use* any of the surplus; in fact, he seemed to be going out of his way to assure the Owens Valley that he would not. For example, the proposed intake for the aqueduct had been carefully located downstream from most of the Owens Valley ranches and farms, so that they could continue to irrigate; Mulholland would later tell the valley people that his objective was simply to divert their unused and return flows.

In truth, Mulholland planned to divert every drop to which the city held rights as soon as he could. Like all water-conscious westerners, he lived in fear of the use-it-or-lose-it principle in the doctrine of appropriative rights. If the city held water rights that went unused for years, the Owens Valley people might successfully claim them back. But where would he allow the surplus to be used?

Privately, Mulholland planned to lead the aqueduct through the San Fernando Valley on its way to the city. In his hydrologic scheme of things, the valley was the best possible receiving basin; any water dumped on the earth there would automatically drain into the Los Angeles River and its broad aquifer, creating a large, convenient, nonevaporative pool for the city to tap. It provided, in a word, free storage. That it was free was critically important, because Mulholland, intentionally or not, had underestimated the cost of building the aqueduct, and to build a large storage reservoir in addition to the aqueduct would be out of the question financially. Even had it been feasible, Mulholland was deeply offended by the evaporative waste of reservoirs; he was much more inclined to store water underground.

Mulholland had an even more important reason for wanting to include the San Fernando Valley in his scheme. Under the city charter, Los Angeles was prohibited from incurring a debt greater than 15 percent of its assessed valuation. In 1905, that put its debt limit at exactly $23 million, which was what he expected the aqueduct to cost. But the city already had $7 million in outstanding debt, which left him with a debt ceiling too low to complete the project. After coming this far—securing the water rights, organizing civic support—he wouldn't have the money to build it!

Mulholland, however, was clever enough to have thought of a way out of this dilemma. If the assessed valuation of Los Angeles could be rapidly increased, its debt ceiling would be that much higher. And what better way was there to accomplish this than to *add to the city*? Instead of bringing more people to Los Angeles—which was happening anyway—*the city would go to them*. It would just loosen its borders as Mulholland loosened his silk cravat and wrap itself around the San Fernando Valley. Then it would have a new tax base, a natural underground storage reservoir, and a legitimate use of its surplus water in one fell swoop.

Anyone who knew this, and bought land in the San Fernando Valley while it was still dirt-cheap, stood to become very, very rich.

The person who finally began to figure it all out was Henry Loewenthal, the editor of Otis's despised rival newspaper, William Randolph Hearst's *Examiner*. The *Examiner* had been skeptical of the aqueduct plan from the beginning, though it did not oppose it outright; Loewenthal's editorials merely made a point of questioning Mulholland's sense of urgency and, on occasion, his figures. But even such mild skepticism was more than enough to enrage Otis, who attributed Loewenthal's doubts to the fact that the *Times* had scooped the *Examiner* about the aqueduct story. "Anyone but a simpleton or a poor old has-been in his dotage would sing very low over a failure like that," snarled Otis in an editorial, "but the impossible Loewenthal insists on emphasizing his own incompetency."

Such invective simply instilled in Loewenthal a passionate urge to outscoop Otis, and, in the process, catch him with his hand in the till. There *must* be some hanky-panky, Loewenthal surmised. Otherwise why Otis's sudden interest in a desolate valley? And why did Otis's number-one enemy, E. T. Earl, rival publisher of the *Express*, seem as enthusiastic as Otis? In the past, Earl had opposed nearly anything Otis endorsed, and vice versa, as a simple matter of dignity. But now Otis, Earl, and virtually all the rival newspapers, except his own, were united on perhaps the most controversial issue Los Angeles had ever faced. Why? Loewenthal decided to send a couple of his top reporters to the courthouse in San Fernando to find out.

The co-conspirators hadn't even bothered to cover their tracks. They could have invented blind trusts, paper corporations, or some other ruse to conceal their identity; but there they were, caught in the open on an exposed plain.

On November 28, 1904—just six days after Joseph Lippincott was paid $2,500 to help steer his loyalties in the direction of Los Angeles—a syndicate of private investors had purchased a $50,000 option on the Porter Land and Water Company, which owned the greater part of the San Fernando Valley—sixteen thousand acres all told. Innocent enough. But the investors had then waited to consummate their $500,000 purchase until March 23, 1905—*the same day* that Fred Eaton had telegraphed the water commission that the option on the Rickey ranch in Long Valley was secured. On that day, as anyone who had access to Mulholland's thinking knew, Los Angeles was all but guaranteed 250,000 acre-feet of new water—an amount that would leave the city with a water surplus for at least another twenty years. And the only sensible place to use the surplus water was in the San Fernando Valley.

Was the timing mere coincidence? The names of the investors who made up the secret land syndicate strongly suggested that it was not. In fact, their identity had given Loewenthal the scoop of his dreams. The only way he could improve its impact was to wait for exactly the right moment to go to press.

Loewenthal knew that the San Francisco *Chronicle* was, in a vague way, on to the same story. He also knew the *Chronicle* was not nearly as methodical in its investigations as his paper, and would probably publish rumors without supporting facts. On August 22, just as Loewenthal supposed, the *Chronicle* ran a story, unsupported by evidence, to the effect that the Owens Valley aqueduct was somehow linked to a land-development scheme in the San Fernando Valley. Two days later, the *Times* derisively dismissed the allegations in an editorial which, to Loewenthal's delight, ran under the heading "Baseless Rumors." On that same morning, the *Examiner*'s story went to press.

The San Fernando land syndicate, the *Examiner* revealed, was composed of some of the most influential and wealthy men in Los Angeles. There was Moses Sherman, a balding school administrator from Arizona who had moved to Los Angeles and become a trolley magnate—one of the most ruthless capitalists in a city that was legendary for same. (By coincidence, Moses Sherman also sat on the board of water commissioners of Los Angeles; the syndicate could not have prayed for a better set of eyes and ears.) Then there was Henry Huntington, Sherman's implacable rival in the rush to monopolize the region's transportation system. There was Edward Harriman, the chairman of the Union Pacific Railroad and a rival of both Sherman and Huntington. There was Joseph Sartori of the Security Trust and Savings Bank, and *his* rival, L. C. Brand of the Title Guarantee and Trust Company. There was Edwin T. Earl, the publisher of the *Express;* William Kerckhoff, a local power company magnate; and Harry Chandler, Otis's son-in-law, the tubercular young man with the minister's face, the gambler's heart, and the executioner's soul. But Loewenthal reserved the best for last. The person who had signed the check securing the $50,000 option on the immense San Fernando property was the same person who, that very morning, had dismissed talk of such a nest of land speculators as lies—Brigadier General Harrison Gray Otis.

"This is the prize for which the newspaper persons . . . are working and the size of it accounts for their tremendous zeal," wrote Loewenthal, almost squealing with delight. "The mystery of the enterprise is how it happens that Messrs. Huntington and Harriman, who let no one into their [previous] land purchasing schemes, but who bought up everything for themselves, consented to let the others in." Loewenthal was, of course, enough of a cynic to know exactly why they had. The participants, taken together, represented the power establishment of southern California with an exquisite sense of proportion. Railroads, banking, newspapers, utilities, land development—it was a monopolists' version of affirmative action. Besides, William Kerckhoff was a prominent conservationist and friend of Gifford Pinchot, the chief of the U.S. Forest Service, whose influence with President Theodore Roosevelt could prove invaluable. Harriman's railroad owned a hundred miles of right-of-way along the aqueduct path that the city would need permission to cross, and Huntington owned the building that housed the regional headquarters of the Reclamation Service! Including Earl and Otis, the two feuding neighbors and publishers, was the master stroke. Like a couple of convicts bound together by a ball and chain, neither could betray the other without exposing himself.

The *Examiner*'s exposé had Harrison Gray Otis venting steam from both nostrils and ears, but he didn't dare look the accusations directly in the eye, so in the ensuing weeks he tried to hide behind "Mr. Huntington's" skirts, as if Huntington had been solely responsible for the syndicate and he—Otis—had been an innocent seduced into joining, as a fresh young wayward girl is seduced into sex. Where Otis couldn't weasel out, he blazed away. "Had Hearst's . . . yellow atrocity been the first to announce the plans of the Water Board, it would have claimed the project as its own conception and inauguration," he raved.

> Its front page would have shrieked in poster type about "The *Examiner*'s solution to the water problem," and the public would have been deafened with yawp about how the *Examiner* "discovered Owens River," laid out plans to bring the water to Los Angeles and showed the engineers how to build the aqueduct. The line would have been dubbed, "The Great Hearst Aqueduct," or "The *Examiner* Pipe-line," and Loewenthal the Impossible would have been the Moses of Los Angeles, who smote the rock of Mount Whitney with the rod of his egotism and caused the water to flow abundantly. Deprived of the opportunity for mendacious self-glorification . . . the foolish freak vents its impotent rage in snarling under its breath. . . . The insane desire of the *Examiner* to discredit certain citizens of Los Angeles has at last led it into the open as a vicious enemy of the city's welfare, its mask of hypocrisy dropped and its convulsed features revealed.

In the end, though, the broadsides between the rival papers were all sound and fury, signifying not much. Ever since their foremost minister had fled prosecution for land fraud, the citizens of Los Angeles had grown accustomed to scandal, and the city's temperamant was quite comfortable with graft. Henry Loewenthal would later speak of a "spirit of lawlessness that prevails here, that I have never seen anywhere else." Nature was also smiling on the Owens Valley scheme. On August 30, a week before the scheduled referendum on the aqueduct, the temperature climbed to 101 degrees. The city had gone its usual four months without rain, and there would likely be two rainless months to come. On September 2, Hearst himself rode down from San Francisco in his private railroad car for a quiet palaver with the city's oligarchs. As men of commerce, they understood each other, and Hearst had recently been bitten by the presidential bug; if he was truly serious about the White House, he could use their help. When the meeting was over, the publisher strode into the *Examiner*'s offices, barked Loewenthal into acquiescence, and personally wrote an editorial recommending a "yes" vote. Samuel T. Clover's *Daily News*, the only paper on record opposing the aqueduct, lobbed a potential bombshell when it reported that the city's workers, under cover of darkness, were dumping water out of the reservoirs into the Pacific to make them go dry, thus assuring a "yes" vote. But Mulholland's lame explanation that they had merely been "flushing the system" was widely believed.

On September 7, 1905, the bond issue passed, fourteen to one.

To the Los Angeles *Times*, it was a "Titanic Project to Give the City a River." To the Inyo *Register*, it was a ruthless scheme in which "Los Angeles Plots Destruction, Would Take Owens River, Lay Lands Waste, Ruin People, Homes, and Communities." That sensational headline actually belied the feeling in the valley somewhat. Few people thought, at first, that things would be so bad. A number of the ranchers had made out well selling their water rights, and they would be able to keep their water for years, until the aqueduct was built. The city had bought up nearly forty bank miles of the river and would probably dry up the lower valley, but the upper valley, except for Fred Eaton's purchase of the Rickey estate, had been left mostly intact. When Eaton moved up from Los Angeles as promised and began his new life as a cattle rancher, the valley people were reassured. After a while, they even began to fraternize with him.

Mulholland, meanwhile, had begun his own campaign to mollify the people of the valley, a campaign in which he was joined, somewhat more bellicosely, by the Los Angeles *Times*, which featured headlines such as "Ill-feeling Ridiculous" and "Owens Valley People Going Off at Half-Cock." Inyo County's Congressman, Sylvester Smith, was an influential member of the House Public Lands Committee, and since the city would have to cross a lot of public land it would have to deal with him. Meanwhile, Theodore Roosevelt, the bugaboo of monopolists, had just been elected to a second term. He would never let the Owens Valley die for the sake of Henry Huntington, Harrison Gray Otis, and their cronies in the San Fernando Valley syndicate. On top of all this, the Owens was a generous desert river, with a flow sufficient for two million people. It was laughable to think of Los Angeles growing that big, so even under the worst of circumstances there would be water enough for all. The reasoning was very sensible, the logic very sound, and it was fatefully wrong.

There was one person who knew that it was. She was Mary Austin, the valley's literary light, who had published a remarkable collection of impressionistic essays entitled *Land of Little Rain* that won her recognition around the world. In the course of her writing she had spent long hours with the last of the Paiutes, the Indians who had lived in the valley for centuries until they were instantly displaced by the whites. The Paiutes showed her what no one else saw— that order and stability are the most transient of states, that there is rarely such a thing as a partial defeat. In a subsequent book, a novella about the Owens Valley water struggle called *The Ford*, she wrote about what happens when "that incurable desire of men to be played upon, to be handled," runs up against "that Cult of Locality, by which so much is forgiven as long as it is done in the name of the Good of the Town." Mary Austin was convinced that the valley had died when it sold its first water right to Los Angeles—that the city would never stop until it owned the whole river and all of the land. One day, in Los Angeles for an interview with Mulholland, she told him so. After she had left, a subordinate came into his office and found him staring at the wall. "By God," Mulholland reportedly said, "that woman is the only one who has brains enough to see where this is going."

No sooner had the city gotten the aqueduct past the voters than it faced the more difficult task of getting it past Congress. Most of the lands it would traverse belonged to the government, so the city would have to appeal for rights-of-way. The Reclamation project, though moribund, was still not officially deauthorized, which was, at the very least, a nuisance to the city. But deauthorization could prove to be even worse, because tens of thousands of acres that the Service had withdrawn would return to the public domain and be available for homesteading. Homesteading in California was another name for graft; half of the great private empires were amassed by hiring "homesteaders" to con the government out of its land. If the withdrawn lands went back to the public domain, every available water right would be coveted by speculators for future resale to the city. Mulholland seemed to believe that the city would never require more water, but others, notably Joseph Lippincott, thought him wrong. The withdrawn lands had to be kept off-limits at all costs.

The instrument for achieving this wishful goal was a bill introduced at the behest of Mulholland's chief lawyer, William B. Matthews, by Senator Frank Flint of California, a strong partisan of Los Angeles and urban water development in general. The bill would give the city whatever rights-of-way it needed across federal lands and hold the withdrawn lands in quarantine for another three years, which would presumably give the city enough time to purchase whatever additional water or land it might need. Flint's bill reached the Senate floor in June of 1906, and flew through easily. Its next stop, however, was the House Public Lands Committee, where it crashed into Congressman Sylvester Smith. Smith was an energetic and charming politician, a former newspaper publisher from Bakersfield with a sense of public duty and enough money to maintain an ironclad set of principles. The idea of Harrison Gray Otis and Henry Huntington becoming vastly richer than they already were on water abducted from his district inflamed his well-developed sense of outrage. Smith knew what he was up against, however, and realized that his best defense was to appear utterly reasonable. As a result, he said that he was willing to acknowledge the city's need for more water, that he was willing to let it have a substantial share of the Owens River, and that he was willing to grant the aqueduct its necessary rights-of-way. He was not willing, however, to do any of this in the way the city wanted. He suggested a compromise. Let the Reclamation Service build its project, including the big dam in Long Valley—a dam that could store most of the river's flow. The water could then be used first for irrigation, and because of the valley's long and narrow slope, the return flows would go back to the lower river, where they could be freely diverted by Los Angeles. The city would sacrifice some of the water it wanted, the valley would sacrifice some irrigable land. It was, Smith argued, an enlightened plan: sensible, efficient, conceived in harmony. It was the only plan under which no one would suffer. He would add only two stipulations: the Owens Valley would have a nonnegotiable first right to the water, and any surplus water could not be used for irrigation in the San Fernando Valley.

Smith's proposal was obviously anathema to the San Fernando land syndicate, and to the city as well. The chief of the Geologic Survey doubted that it would work, and even if it did, for the West's largest city to settle for leftover water from a backwater oasis of fruit and cattle ranchers was, to say the least, humiliating. The city might have to beg for extra water in times of drought or go to court to try to condemn it. If the Owens Valley held on to its first rights and expanded its irrigated acreage, Los Angeles might soon have to look for water again, and the only river in sight was the Colorado, a feckless brown torrent in a bottomless canyon which the city could never afford to dam and divert on its own. Smith's proposal led directly to one unthinkable conclusion: at some point in the relatively near future, Los Angeles would have to cease to grow.

What was William Mulholland's response? He took a train to

Washington, held a summit meeting with Smith and Senator Flint, and decided to do what any sensible person would have done: he accepted the compromise.

If it was a smokescreen, as it appears to have been, it was a brilliant move. (Mulholland seems to have been a far better political schemer than he was a hydrologist and civil engineer.) For one thing, it put Sylvester Smith off guard, making him believe that the reconciliation he wanted to effect was a success. For another, it gave Los Angeles some critical extra time to plead its case before the two people who might help the city get everything it wanted: the President of the United States, Theodore Roosevelt, and the man on whom he leaned most heavily for advice—Gifford Pinchot.

Pinchot was the first director of Roosevelt's pet creation, the Forest Service, but that was only one of his roles. He was also the Cardinal Richelieu of TR's White House. Temperamentally and ideologically, the two men fit hand in glove. Both were wealthy patricians (Pinchot came from Pittsburgh, where his family had made a fortune in the dry-goods business); both were hunters and outdoorsmen. Though their speeches and writings rang of Thomas Jefferson, at heart Pinchot and Roosevelt seemed more comfortable with Hamiltonian ideals. Roosevelt liked the Reclamation program because he saw it as an agrarian path to industrial strength, not because he believed—as Jefferson did—that a nation of small farmers is a nation with a purer soul. Pinchot espoused forest conservation not because he worshiped nature like John Muir (whom he privately despised) but because the timber industry was plowing through the nation's forests with such abandon it threatened to destroy them for all time. Roosevelt was a trust-buster, but only because he feared that unfettered capitalism could breed socialism. (For evidence he only had to look as far as Los Angeles, where Harrison Gray Otis was whipping labor radicals into such a blind, vengeful froth that two of them blew up his printing plant in 1910 and killed twenty of their own.) The conservation of Roosevelt and Pinchot was utilitarian; their progressivism—they spoke of "the greatest good for the greatest number"— had a nice ring to it, but it also happens to be the progressivism of cancer cells.

On the evening of June 23, Senator Frank Flint left his offices on Capitol Hill for a late meeting with the President. It was a hot and muggy night, and Roosevelt seemed in an irritable mood. Behind him, however, stood a man who seemed a model of coolness and decorum, Gifford Pinchot. Flint, who had just received an intensive coaching from Matthews and Mulholland, began a passionate appeal.

Smith's so-called compromise, he said, was nothing less than capitulation. Los Angeles had agreed only in despair; it was going to run out of water any day and it couldn't afford to be filibustered to death in Congress. Smith's prohibition on using surplus water in the San Fernando Valley left the city no choice but to leave any surplus in the Owens Valley or dump it in the ocean. In the first case, water rights the city had purchased at great expense might revert to the valley under the doctrine of appropriative rights; in the second case, the city would violate the California constitution, which forbade "inefficient use" of water. The real estate bust of 1889 had depopulated the city by one-half. Imagine what a water famine would do! All of the city's actions in the Owens Valley had been legitimate. It had paid for its water, fair and square, and it wanted to let the valley survive. But there was only so much water, and it was a hundred-fold—a thousandfold, said Smith—more valuable to the state and the nation if it built up a great, strong, progressive city on America's weakly defended western flank instead of maintaining a little agrarian utopia in the high desert.

It was a rousing speech—the kind of speech that Roosevelt liked to hear. It was, in fact, just the kind of speech *he* would have made.

Roosevelt turned to his other visitor. "What do you think about this, Giff?"

"As far as I am concerned," Pinchot answered coolly, "there is no objection to permitting Los Angeles to use the water for irrigation purposes."

It was as simple as that. Roosevelt did not even bother to call in the Interior Department's lawyers or the Geologic Survey's hydrologists to ask whether Flint's argument was sense or nonsense. He never invited Sylvester Smith to give his side of the argument. He didn't even tell Smith or his own Interior Secretary, Ethan Hitchcock, about his decision; they found out about it secondhand a day and a half later. Hitchcock, a wealthy, principled man in the style of Sylvester Smith, had been profoundly embarrassed by the two-faced behavior of his employee J. B. Lippincott, and had been looking for a way to make amends to the Owens Valley. Flabbergasted and infuriated by the President's decision, Hitchcock raced over to the White House, where Roosevelt refused to hear him. Instead, he forced him to suffer the humiliation of helping him draft a letter explaining "*our* attitude in the Los Angeles water supply question." As Hitchcock stood by, impotent and enraged, Roosevelt wrote, "It is a hundred or a thousandfold more important to state that this water is more valuable to the people of Los Angeles than to the Owens Valley." The words could have come right out of William Mulholland's mouth.

The Otis-Sherman-Huntington-Chandler land syndicate was, potentially, enough of an embarrassment to Roosevelt's antimonopolist image that he felt compelled to add an amendment to Flint's bill prohibiting the city from reselling municipal water for irrigation use. In the opinion of the House Public Lands Committee, however, the stipulation was "meaningless." "This water will belong absolutely to Los Angeles," said the bill's sponsor, echoing the sense of the committee, "and the city council can do as it pleases. . . ." Which it would.

Roosevelt's support for Flint's bill was only the beginning of the aid and comfort he was to give to the most powerful city on the Pacific Coast. When the Reclamation Service officially annulled the Owens Valley Project in July of 1907, the hundreds of thousands of acres it had withdrawn were not returned to the public domain for homesteading, on Roosevelt's orders—just as Mulholland wished. It was a decision without precedent, and its result was that the handful of rich members of the San Fernando syndicate could continue using the surplus water in the Owens River that thousands of homesteaders might have claimed instead. Ethan Hitchcock had promised that such a decision, which he already foresaw when Roosevelt closed ranks behind Los Angeles, would be made over his dead body, but Roosevelt spared his life by firing him first. And when the city, immensely satisfied with the result, asked Pinchot whether he couldn't go a step further, the chief of the Forest Service decided to include virtually all of the Owens Valley in the Inyo National Forest.

The Inyo National Forest! With six inches of annual rainfall, the Owens Valley is too dry for trees; the only ones there were fruit trees planted and irrigated by man, some of which were already dying for lack of water. This didn't seem to bother Pinchot, nor did the fact that his action appears to have been patently illegal. The Organic Act that created the Forest Service says, "No public forest reservation shall be established except to improve and protect the forest . . . or for the purpose of creating favorable conditions of water flow, and to provide a continuous supply of timber for the use and necessities of the United States; but it is not the purpose of the these provisions . . . to authorize the inclusion . . . of lands more valuable for the mineral therein, *or for agricultural purposes*, than for forest purposes" (emphasis added). The valley's irrigated orchards were infinitely more valuable than the barren flats and scattered sagebrush that characterized the new national forest, so Pinchot's action was incontrovertibly a violation of the legislation that put him in business. He lamely countered that he was simply acting to protect the quality of Los Angeles' water; but since much of the treeless acreage he included in the Inyo National Forest lay *below* the intake of the aqueduct, it was a flimsy excuse. As a formality, Pinchot was obliged to send an investigator to the Owens Valley to recommend that he do what he had already made up his mind to do. He sent three before he found one who was willing to go along. "This is not a government by legislation," lamented Sylvester Smith on the Senate floor, "it is a government by strangulation."

In July of 1907, with the reclamation project in its grave and the Owens Valley imprisoned inside a national forest without trees, Joseph Lippincott resigned from the Reclamation Service and immediately went to work, at nearly double his government salary, as William Mulholland's deputy. He remained utterly unchastised. "I would do everything over again, just exactly as I did," he said as he departed.

The one thing that no one seems to have thought about in all this was that the people of Owens Valley were only human, and there was just so much they could take.

The aqueduct took six years to build. The Great Wall of China and the Panama Canal were bigger jobs, and New York's Catskill aqueduct, which was soon to be completed, would carry more water, but no one had ever built anything so large across such merciless terrain, and no one had ever done it on such a minuscule budget. It was as if the city of Pendleton, Oregon, had gone out, by itself, and built Grand Coulee Dam.

The aqueduct would traverse some of the most scissile, fractionated, fault-splintered topography in North America. It would cover 223 miles, 53 of them in tunnels; where tunneling was too risky, there would be siphons whose acclivities and declivities exceeded fifty-grade. The city would have to build 120 miles of railroad track, 500 miles of roads and trails, 240 miles of telephone line, and 170 miles of power transmission line. The entire cement-making capacity of Los Angeles was not adequate for this one project, so a huge cement plant would have to be built near the limestone deposits in the grimly arid Tehachapi Mountains. Since there was virtually no water along the entire route, steampower was out of the question and the whole job would be done with electricity; therefore, two hydroelectric plants would be needed on the Owens River to run electric machinery that a few months earlier had not even been invented. The city would have to maintain, house, and feed a work force fluctuating between two thousand and six thousand men for six full years. And it would have to do all this for a sum equivalent, more or less, to the cost of one modern jet fighter.

The workers would have to supply their own hard-shelled derby hats, since hard hats did not yet exist, and even if they had the city couldn't afford them. They would live in tents in the desert without liquor or women—although both were available nearby and ended up consuming most of the aqueduct payroll. They would eat meat that spoiled during the daytime and froze at night, since the daily temperature range in the Mojave Desert can span eighty degrees. Nonetheless, the men would labor on the aqueduct as the pious raised the cathedral at Chartres, and they would finish under budget and ahead of schedule. If you asked any of them why they did it, they would probably say that they did it for the chief.

The loyalty and heroics that Mulholland inspired in his workers were a perpetual source of wonder. For six years he all but lived in the desert, patrolling the aqueduct route like a nervous father-to-be pacing a hospital waiting room—giving advice, offering encouragement, sketching improvised solutions in the sand. In sandstorms, windstorms, snowstorms, and terrifying heat, his spirits remained contagiously high. Pilfering, which can add millions to the cost of a modern project, was almost unknown. Although the pay was terrible—Mulholland simply couldn't afford anything more—he initiated a bonus system that shattered records for hard-rock tunneling. (The men were in a race with the world's most illustrious tunnelers, the Swiss, who were digging the Loetchberg Tunnel at the same time.)

Throughout the entire time, Mulholland showed the better side of a complex and sometimes heartless character. If he wandered through a tent city and discovered that a worker's wife had just had a baby, he would stop long enough to show her the proper way to change a diaper. He would sit down and eat with the men and complain louder than anyone about the food. In lieu of newspapers, his wit was breakfast conversation. Once, when a landslide sealed off a tunnel with a man still inside, Mulholland arrived to check on the rescue effort.

"He's been in there three days, so I don't suppose he's doing so well," said the supervisor, a mirthless Scandinavian named Hansen.

"Then he must be starving to death," said Mulholland.

"Oh, no, sir," said the supervisor. "He's getting something to eat. We've been rolling him hard-boiled eggs through a pipe."

"Have you?" said Mulholland archly. "Well, then, I hope you've been charging him board."

"No, sir," said the flustered Hansen. "But I suppose I should, eh?"

And Los Angeles loved Mulholland even more than the men, because its reward would be infinitely greater than theirs—to the thirsty city, he was Moses. And he was that greater rarity, a Moses without political ambition. When a move was afoot a few years later to run him for mayor, Mulholland dismissed it with a typical bon mot: "I would rather give birth to a porcupine backwards than become the mayor of Los Angeles." But nothing that William Mulholland ever said or did quite matched the speech he gave when, on November 5, 1913, the first water cascaded down the aqueduct's final sluiceway into the San Fernando Valley. It had been a day of long speeches and waiting, and the crowd of forty thousand people was restless. Mulholland himself was exhausted; his wife was very ill, and he had slept only a few hours in several nights. When the white crest of water finally appeared at the top of the sluiceway and cascaded toward the valley, an apparition in a Syrian landscape, Mulholland simply unfurled an American flag, turned toward the mayor, H. H. Rose, and said, "There it is. Take it."

It was the high point of Mulholland's life and career.

Very little of the water that was, according to Theodore Roosevelt, a hundred or a thousandfold more important to Los Angeles than to the Owens Valley would go to the city for another twenty years. All through the teens and early twenties, the San Fernando Valley used three times as much aqueduct water as the city itself, the vast part of it for irrigation. During one particularly wet year, every drop of the copious flow of the aqueduct went to irrigate San Fernando Valley crops; the city took nothing at all. Understandably, this news enraged the people of the Owens Valley. For Los Angeles to take their water to fill their washtubs and water glasses was one thing. For it to turn their valley back to desert so that another desert valley, owned by rich monopolists, could bloom in its place was quite another.

The teens and early twenties, however, were extraordinarily wet years—the same wet years that caused the Reclamation Service to overestimate dramatically the flow of the Colorado River—and there was water enough for everyone. The irrigated acreage in the San Fernando Valley rose from three thousand acres in 1913—the year both the completion of the aqueduct and the annexation of the valley occurred—to seventy-five thousand acres in 1918. Even so, the Owens Valley lost few of its orchards and irrigated pasturelands, and the new railroad to Los Angeles and the silver mine at Tonopah fed in enough wealth to allow the town of Bishop to build a grand American Legion Hall and Masonic Temple, those cathedrals of the rural nineteenth century.

The same uncharacteristically engorged desert river that was keeping the Owens Valley green was responsible, in Los Angeles, for the most transfixing change. Santa Monica Boulevard, once a dry dusty strip, became an elegant corridor of palms; in Hollywood, where the motion picture industry had risen up overnight, outdoor sets resembled New Guinea; and since most Los Angeleans were immigrants from the Middle West, every bungalow had a green lawn. The glorious anomaly of a fake tropical city with a mild desert climate brought people from everywhere. Dirt farmers came from Arkansas; Aldous Huxley moved from England. The Chamber of Commerce, an Otis creation, kept them coming. They arrived on the Union Pacific, a Harriman railroad, and once they were there, the *Times*, an Otis and Chandler newspaper, urged everyone to settle in the San Fernando Valley, an Otis and Chandler property. Few could afford automobiles, so they got around on Sherman and Huntington trolley cars between Sherman-and-Huntington-built homes and Sherman and Huntington resorts in the San Gabriel and San Bernardino Mountains.

As Otis never tired of saying, this was the promised land. All things were possible; anyone could get rich; the cardinal sin was doubt. During the nadir of the Depression, when the city was invaded by homeless Okies so destitute they sat hollow-eyed in the parks and gnawed on the crusts thrown out for the pigeons, the *Times* sent them this holiday greeting: "Merry Christmas! Look pleasant! Chin up! A gloomy face never gets a good picture. The great battles are fought by Caesars and their fortunes, by Napoleons and their stars. Faith still does the impossible! Merry Christmas! Catch the tempo of the times. You have your life before you, and, if you are growing old, the greatest adventure of all is just around the corner. Earth may have little left in reserve, but heaven is ahead! Merry Christmas!" The only greater fraud than such blather from Otis and Chandler's newspaper was the overflowing desert river on which all depended.

In the West, drought tends to come in cycles of about twenty years, and the next drought arrived on schedule. The years 1919 and 1920 were a premonition; rainfall was slightly below average. It rose back to average—a measly fourteen inches—in 1921 and went slightly over that in 1922. Then it crashed. Ten inches in 1923; six inches in 1924; seven inches in 1925. In Florida, a seven-inch rainstorm may occur two or three times a year, but Los Angeles was trying to look like Florida, and grow even faster, on a fifth of its precipitation, and when the drought struck it kept going on a tenth. Mulholland had expected 350,000 people by 1925, but had 1.2 million on his hands instead. The city was growing fifteen times faster than Denver, eleven times faster than New York. And though the city at its core had become a metropolis, Los Angeles County led the nation in the value of its agricultural output. All of this agriculture depended on irrigation, which, together with the phenomenal urban growth, depended on a river draining Mount Whitney two hundred miles away.

As the drought intensified, the Owens River moved perilously close to overappropriation. The problem was not only that the river was small, but also that no carryover storage existed—nothing but some small receiving reservoirs around the basin and the snowfields in the Sierra. The Los Angeles Aqueduct was essentially a run-of-the-river project. If the river didn't run, the city collapsed.

If the city and the Owens Valley were to continue sharing the river, carryover storage would have to be built; otherwise, one place or the other would lose its water during a drought. Mulholland, of course, knew this, but still refused to build the dam at Long Valley. He blamed it on the city's fragile finances, but that was a poor excuse; the real reason was that he and his old friend Eaton had had a nasty falling-out.

Fred Eaton had not even bothered to attend the dedication of the aqueduct in 1913, though its existence was owed mainly to him. He had bought the initial water rights the city needed with his own money, taking a considerable risk; had the voters failed to approve the bond referendum, he would have been drowning in both unusable water and debt. The city had paid him quite adequately for the right, but it had not made him a multimillionaire. Originally, Eaton had hoped to operate the Owens Valley end of the aqueduct as a private concession, which could have made him incredibly rich, but Frederick Newell and Roosevelt had dashed that dream, insisting that the project be municipally owned from end to end. Eaton had also had some bad luck in the cattle business, and had to switch ignominiously to chickens. He was sixty-five years old; it was time things finally went right. The one item of real value Eaton owned was the reservoir site on the ranch he had purchased from Thomas Rickey. Ideally, a dam built at the site ought to be 140 feet high, the approximate depth of the gorge; that would create a reservoir large enough to provide for both the city and the valley during all but the worst droughts. A damsite of such importance to the city—a site which, if developed, would drown a good portion of his ranch—was worth a lot of money, as far as Eaton was concerned. When Mulholland asked him what his price was, Eaton said $1 million. Mulholland, who seemed personally indifferent to money (though he was reputedly the highest-paid civil servant in California), laughed him off. Time and time again he asked Eaton to accept a reasonable offer—$500,000, perhaps, or a little more—and each time his offer was more angrily refused. By 1917, the two old friends were no longer on speaking terms.

As the drought intensified, Mulholland begged the city fathers to end their abject deification of growth. The only way to solve the city's water problem, he grumbled aloud, was to kill the members of the Chamber of Commerce. When he was ignored, he began to regulate irrigation practices in the San Fernando Valley. First he forbade the irrigation of alfalfa, a low-value, water-demanding crop; then he prohibited winter planting. When these measures proved inadequate, he swallowed his disdain for surface storage and began building reservoirs in the basin—first the Hollywood Reservoir, then a much larger dam in San Francisquito Canyon, a deep fissure in the shaky, shaly topography of the Santa Paula hills.

With the tens of thousands of people pouring in each year, everything was a stopgap measure. By the early 1920s, Mulholland was already lobbying for an aqueduct from the Colorado River. This, however, put him on a collision course with Harry Chandler, who owned 860,000 acres in Mexico that relied on the Colorado, and who was so greedy that, despite his enormous wealth, he put the interests of his Mexican holdings above the welfare of the city he had created out of whole cloth. Chandler's opposition, together with fierce feuding among the Colorado River Basin states, kept the Boulder Canyon Project Act, which would create the storage reservoir that any Colorado River aqueduct would need, bottled up for years. Frustrated at every turn, Mulholland reached the end of his tether sometime in 1923. The only answer, he decided, was to do what Mary Austin had predicted the city would ultimately do—dry the Owens Valley up.

The trouble began where troubles usually begin, in the heart. Wilfred and Mark Watterson, the brothers who symbolized the Owens Valley's mortmain and its success, had a young uncle named George, only ten years older than Wilfred. George's attitude toward his nephews was less avuncular than competitive. Somehow, in competition, George always lost. When Wilfred and George had filed rival claims on a mining right, Wilfred won. George had always wanted to own the first automobile in the valley, but one day he looked down the street and saw Wilfred drive up in a yellow Stanley Steamer, mobbed by adoring crowds. Wilfred and Mark were treasurer of this, president of that; George Watterson was not even a has-been—he was a never-was.

George Watterson had an ally in bitterness. Some years earlier, a lawyer with an adventuresome bent named Leicester Hall had wandered into the Owens Valley from Alaska, taken one look at Wilfred and Mark's sister Elizabeth, and fallen helplessly in love. Elizabeth, however, had spurned him and married Jacob Clausen, Lippincott's former assistant—a symbol, like the Watterson brothers, of resistance to Los Angeles. The Owens Valley was a gossipy place, and the hatred that George Watterson felt for his nephews and the bitterness that Hall felt toward Jacob Clausen were well known. The city had its agents in the valley, and they had ears. When William Mulholland invited George Watterson, Hall, and their friend William Symons down for dinner at his club one evening, they were happy to come.

The tactic was the old reliable one: the lightning strike. Symons was the president of the McNally Ditch, which held the oldest and largest water right among all the irrigation cooperatives in the valley. Hall and George Watterson were officers in the Bishop Creek Ditch and the Owens River Canal Company. On March 15, 1923, the three men returned to the valley and went immediately to work. "Leave none of the ranchers out," Mulholland had told them. "We want them all." Within twenty-four hours, Watterson, Symons, and Hall owned options on more than two-thirds of the McNally Ditch's water rights. They had paid as much as $7,500 per cubic second-foot of water, and the total cost to the city was more than $1 million—the price Fred Eaton had wanted for access to his damsite.

The size and length of an irrigation ditch depend critically on the number of people who use it. Since all the irrigators must spend a substantial amount of time maintaining it—clearing out weeds, desilting it, repairing earthslides—losing just a few farmers can put a terrible burden of responsibility on those who remain. So many farmers who belonged to the McNally Ditch had sold out that the cooperative was quickly put out of its misery; those who remained couldn't possibly maintain it by themselves, so ultimately they would have to sell out, too. By the time the three men moved on the other ditch companies, however, pockets of resistance had formed, and they had to seek out the more avaricious or vulnerable souls. Hall had managed to raid the confidential files of the collective ditch companies, making off with critical information about who was in financial trouble, who was a poor farmer, who was inclined to move on. He and his collaborators, therefore, didn't waste much time on people who were unlikely to yield to temptation; they knew who would. But their strategy—a strategy of division and attrition—was especially cruel, not only because it placed an even larger burden of responsibility on the farmers and ranchers who held out, but because it pitted neighbor against neighbor, wife against husband, brother against brother.

Meanwhile, the master strategist, off in Los Angeles, was sixty-nine years old and a changed man. Thirty years earlier, Mulholland had spent his idle hours in a cabin at one of the city's outlying reservoirs, reading the classics and planting poplars. When the city had first talked about tapping the Owens River, his concern about the valley's welfare led him to suggest that the city plant millions of trees which the residents could sell for firewood to the barren mining camps in Nevada—until someone informed him that so many trees would suck up enough groundwater to bleed the river dry. In his later years, however, the William Mulholland who had read Shakespeare and quoted Alexander Pope was hardly recognizable. No person ever put his imprint on an agency as strongly as Mulholland left his on the Los Angeles Department of Water and Power, and that agency was now using secret agents, breaking into private records, and turning neighbors into mortal foes. And, worst of all, Mulholland was ignoring a solution that would have satisfied everyone—a dam at Long Valley—out of petty niggardliness and almost fanatical pride.

In 1980, there were few people still alive who remembered Mulholland, but one who did was Horace Albright, the director of the National Park Service under Herbert Hoover. Albright could no longer remember the year—he was eighty-two—but it was probably 1925 or 1926, and he was a young park superintendent invited to attend a testimonial dinner for Senator Frank Flint, the man who had engineered the dubious federal decisions that allowed the Owens Valley aqueduct to be built. Albright was seated at Mulholland's table, a couple of chairs away, and midway through dinner he felt a rough tap on his shoulder.

"You're from the Park Service, aren't you?" Mulholland demanded more than asked.

"Yes, I am," said Albright. "Why do you ask?"

"Why?" Mulholland said archly. "Why? I'll tell you why. You have a beautiful park up north. A majestic park. Yosemite Park, it's called. You've been there, have you?"

Albright said he had. He was the park's superintendent.

"Well, I'm going to tell you what I'd do with your park. Do you want to know what I would do?"

Albright said he did.

"Well, I'll tell you. You know this new photographic process they've invented? It's called Pathé. It makes everything seem lifelike. The hues and coloration are magnificent. Well, then, what I would do, if I were custodian of your park, is I'd hire a dozen of the best photographers in the world. I'd build them cabins in Yosemite Valley and pay them something and give them all the film they wanted. I'd say, 'This park is yours. It's yours for one year. I want you to take photographs in every season. I want you to capture all the colors, all the waterfalls, all the snow, and all the majesty. I especially want you to photograph the rivers. In the early summer, when the Merced River roars, I want to see that.' And then I'd leave them be. And in a year I'd come back, and take their film, and send it out and have it developed and treated by Pathé. And then I would print the pictures in thousands of books and send them to every library. I would urge every magazine in the country to print them and tell every gallery and museum to hang them. I would make certain that every American saw them. And then," Mulholland said slowly, with what Albright remembered as a vulpine grin, "and then do you know what I would do? I'd go in there and build a dam from one side of that valley to the other and *stop the goddamned waste!*"

"It was the tone of his voice that surprised me," Albright said. "The laughingly arrogant tone. I don't think he was joking, you see. He was absolutely convinced that building a dam in Yosemite Valley was the proper thing to do. We had few big dams in California then. There were hundreds of other sites, and there were bigger rivers than the Merced. But he seemed to want to shake things up, to outrage me. He almost *wanted* to destroy."

It was the same tone, the same bitter and unreasoning quarrel-someness, that Mulholland displayed when a reporter from the *Times* asked him why there was so much dissatisfaction in the Owens Valley. "Dissatisfaction in the valley?" said Mulholland mockingly. "Yes, a lot of it. Dissatisfaction is a sort of condition that prevails there, like foot and mouth disease." It was the same unreasoning rage that made him say, when his war of attrition against the Owens Valley had finally caused events to take a drastic turn for the worse, that he half regretted the demise of so many of the valley's orchard trees, because now there were no longer enough live trees to hang all the trouble-makers who lived there.

Trees or no trees, that George Watterson, Leicester Hall, and William Symons had not yet been lynched themselves said something about the valley's self-restraint. Symons and Watterson had prudently taken to carrying sidearms, but, aside from an occasional curse or jeer, they were left alone. The valley thought it had a better means of taking revenge on the city than assassinating its agents. Soon after the McNally Ditch coup was engineered, the ditch companies that still had control of their water began opening their headgates and letting water flood uselessly over their fields. Before long, only a trickle was reaching the intake of the aqueduct. Mulholland demanded that the diversions stop, but the farmers refused. In exasperation, he tried a bit of double psychology: he sent more purchasing agents to reinforce Watterson, Symons, and Hall, and at the same time sent his attorney, William Matthews, to meet with the ranchers to see if the matter could still come to an amicable settlement. Just hours before Matthews was scheduled to sit down with the ditch companies, however, Mulholland went into one of his sudden fits of anger and telephoned his main-tenance crews to demolish the intake of the largest diverter, the Big Pine Canal.

The reaction was instantaneous. The leaders of the Big Pine Com-pany were the worst people Mulholland could have chosen to antag-onize: the Watterson brothers, a resort operator and speculator named Karl Keough, and Harry Glasscock, the incendiary editor of the *Owens Valley Herald*. As soon as news arrived of what was happening, a posse of twenty men, bristling with guns, roared out to the canal intake. As guns were trained on Mulholland's crew, the rest of the men dumped their equipment into the Owens River. The valley mood veered sud-denly from bitterness to wild exuberance. "Los Angeles, it's your move now," exulted the Big Pine *Citizen*. And yet the Big Pine farmers were soon to prove as indifferent to the valley's fate as the members of the McNally Ditch. When Mulholland shrewdly responded with ever higher offers for the cooperative's water rights, a majority (not including the Watterson brothers) finally agreed to sell out for a price of $15,000 per second-foot, twice what the city had paid for the McNally Ditch rights. Mulholland was jubilant, but victory carried a heavy price. To satisfy his vendetta against his oldest friend, he had now spent twice what the Long Valley damsite would have cost, and made himself evil incarnate throughout an entire valley as well.

As the farmers who held out felt increasingly alone, their methods grew more and more violent. On May 21, 1924, a group of men "broke" into the Watterson brothers' warehouse, "stole" three cases of dynamite, and blew a large section of the aqueduct to smithereens. From that moment on, William Mulholland refused to refer to anyone in the Owens Valley by any other name than "dynamiter." Then, in August, Leicester Hall, who had been warned to stay away forever, returned to the valley and was abducted from a restaurant as he ate. He was driven blindfolded to a road's end, where he found himself facing a grim-looking group of men and a noose strung over a tree. Hall saved himself by uttering the Freemason's distress call; there were so many Masons among the valley population that one was in the gang of would-be lynchers, and he managed to talk the others out of murder. But the dynamitings continued. When the Department of Water and Power released a report that recommended "destroying all irrigation"—those were the exact words—in the valley, and it turned out that the main author was Joseph P. Lippincott, the response was a fresh series of blasts. Glasscock's paper was now openly counseling sabotage. The Ku Klux Klan, sensing a perfect battle stage between "Hollywood"—which was to say, cities, big business, liberalism, and Jews—and the small-town, revanchist values it cherished, was sending recruiters into the valley and getting good results. Even Fred Eaton, after holding himself aloof, finally entered the fray against the city of which he had been mayor. "Wherever the hand of Los Angeles has touched Owens Valley," he wrote in a letter to the editor, "it has turned back into desert."

Joseph Lippincott, whose one admirable quality may have been prescience, had said twenty years earlier that the Owens Valley was doomed as soon as Los Angeles obtained its first water right. Mulholland, however, kept insisting blindly that the valley could live on—he didn't say how—even as he turned life there into a kind of hell.

No one knew when his neighbor would be approached and persuaded to sell out; no one knew when the city would move to condemn; no one knew when the armed guards who patrolled the aqueduct would receive orders to shoot to kill. "Suspicions are mutual and widespread," a visitor from Los Angeles observed. "The valley people are suspicious of each other, suspicious of newcomers, suspicious of city men, suspicious, in short, of almost everybody and everything. . . . Owens Valley is full of whisperings, mutterings, recriminations. . . ." It seemed only a matter of time before the onset of real war.

On November 16, 1924, as the drought continued to hold Los Angeles in a deadly grip, a caravan of automobiles rumbled slowly southward through the town of Independence. In the first car, behind drawn blinds, sat the grim figure of Mark Watterson. The cars turned toward the Alabama Hills, a small range of barren rises at the foot of the Sierra escarpment. Weaving through the hills was the Owens River aqueduct, and somewhere along its course were the Alabama Gates. In wetter times, the gates had turned floodwaters in the aqueduct onto the desert to keep them from straining the capacity of the siphons below. They hadn't been used in years, but they still worked. When the caravan arrived at the gatehouse, a hundred men got out of the cars, walked up to the spillway, and turned the five huge wheels that moved the weirs. For the first time in many years, the Owens River flowed back across the desert into Owens Lake.

The effect of the seizure was electrifying. Mulholland was in a murderous rage. He dispatched two carloads of armed city detectives to take back the gates, but news of their imminent arrival prompted the local sheriff to go down to meet them. "If you go up there and start trouble," he told the detectives, "I don't believe you will live to tell the tale." They never went. Mulholland, in the meantime, secured a court injunction against the seizure, but when the papers were served to the men at the gates they threw them into the water.

And then, to everyone's surprise, what could easily have produced bloodshed turned into a picnic. Wives, children, grandmothers, and dogs joined the lawbreakers. Tom Mix was filming a movie nearby, and when he heard what was happening he sent over his salutations and his orchestra. By evening a huge cloud of smoke began to rise from the scene, but it came from a barbecue pit. After dinner, the sheriff arrived and joined in. The crowd was now seven hundred strong, and the strains of "Onward Christian Soldiers" filled the desert night.

Events were finally swinging to the Owens Valley's side. To Mulholland's disgust, even the Los Angeles *Times*, now that Otis was dead, was sympathizing with the lawbreakers. "These farmers are not anarchists or bomb throwers," it said in an editorial, "but in the main honest, hardworking American citizens. They have put themselves hopelessly in the wrong by taking the law into their own hands, but that is not to say that there has not been a measure of justice on their side." Meanwhile, as Mark Watterson led the seizure of the Alabama Gates, Wilfred had wisely gone to Los Angeles to closet himself with the Joint Clearinghouse Association, a roundtable of the city's bankers. After several hours, he emerged and sent Mark a telegram. "If the object of the crowd at the spillway is to bring their wrongs to the attention of the citizens of Los Angeles, they have done so one hundred percent," he wired. "I feel sure that the wrongs done will be remedied."

But such a simple happy ending could occur only on a Hollywood movie lot. As soon as the Alabama Gates were released and Wilfred Watterson had returned home, the bankers with whom he had met rejected his price for the consolidated valley water rights, to which he swore they had agreed. Meanwhile, Mulholland's public relations department was flooding the state with a booklet "explaining" the Owens Valley crisis. "Never in its history has the Owens Valley prospered and increased in wealth as it has in the past twenty years," it said. And it was true, as long as you looked at only the first nineteen of those years; in the twelve subsequent months, the city had almost brought the valley to its knees. Shops and stores were closing for lack of business—thousands of people had already moved out—but Mulholland dismissed pleas for reparations out of hand. If business was down, he said, the shopkeepers could move, too.

The first order to shoot to kill came on May 28, 1927, a day after the No Name Siphon, a huge pipe across a Mojave hill, lay in shards, demolished by a tremendous blast of dynamite. As city crews hauled in 450 feet of new twelve-foot pipe, another blast destroyed sixty feet of the aqueduct near Big Pine Creek. On June 4, another 150 feet went sky high. In response, a special train loaded with city detectives armed with high-velocity Winchester carbines and machine guns rolled out of Union Station for the Owens Valley. Roadblocks were erected on the highways; all cars with male occupants were searched; floodlights beamed across the valley as if it were a giant penitentiary. Miraculously, though the Owens Valley water war had gone on for more than twenty years, though it had turned violent during the past three, there were still no corpses. Harry Glasscock, however, was predicting in his editorial columns that the aqueduct would "run red with human blood," and no one was prepared to argue with him. But before it could happen fate cast a plague on both houses. First came the collapse of the Watterson banks, and the revelation that the Owens Valley's leading citizens were felons. Then, a few months later, came the collapse of the Saint Francis Dam.

The relationship between George Watterson and his two nephews had gone from one of competitiveness to one of bitterness to one of rancid hatred. In the early months of 1927, George saw his opportunity to invest in their final ruin. Four years of drought and rapidly declining business had left all five branches of the Inyo County Bank severely weakened. At the same time, the election of a new governor, Clement Young, on a huge infusion of campaign cash from A. P. Giannini and his Bank of Italy had resulted in the liberalization of the state banking laws, mainly to Giannini's advantage. It was no surprise, then, when George Watterson filed, in the name of the Bank of Italy, an application to launch a competitive bank in Inyo County. But it was no surprise either when the state banking commissioner voided the application on the strength of Wilfred Watterson's testimony that the bank was a front which Los Angeles would use to drive the valley into submission. Nor was it a surprise when, in response, an infuriated George Watterson, with considerable help from the Los Angeles Department of Water and Power, began a dirt-gathering investigation into his nephews' bank. The surprise was what they ultimately found.

To say that the Wattersons had played fast and loose with their investors' capital was an understatement. For at least the past two years, they had been using the amalgamated capital of the Owens Valley to shore up their failing financial empire—their resort, their mineral water company, their tungsten mine. They had recorded deposits in other banks that were never made, recorded debits that were already paid, entered balances that never existed on ledger sheets. They had loaned the entire life savings of their friends and neighbors to enterprises which were, at best, unlikely to succeed. When it was all tallied, there was a $2.3 million discrepancy between the bank books and reality. The brothers had always been the valley's best and last hope. Now they were going to go to jail for embezzlement and fraud.

They had done it, they said, for the good of the valley, and as outrageous as it sounded, it was probably true. None of the money had ever left Inyo County. With the irrigation economy dying at the hands of Los Angeles, the valley's only chance of surviving at all was to develop its minerals, its mining, its potential for tourism. During the trial, people who had lost everything nodded and agreed. Even as the Wattersons were being charged with thirty-six counts of embezzlement and grand theft, the citizens of Owens Valley were pledging $1 million to keep them in business.

It was too late. On August 4, 1927, all five banks were permanently closed. People wandered over to gawk at their final sign of defeat, a bitter message posted on the door: "This result has been brought about by the past four years of destructive work carried on by the city of Los Angeles."

The prosecuting attorney was a lifelong friend of both Wilfred and Mark. If he had not been the prosecutor, he said, he would have agreed to be a character witness. He cried openly as he made his final argument, and the judge and jury wept along with him. On November 14, the Wattersons were sent to San Quentin for ten years, later reduced to six. As the train taking them to San Francisco passed outside Bishop, someone was putting up a sign. It read, "Los Angeles City Limits."

William Mulholland had only four months to savor his triumph.

By refusing to pay Fred Eaton the $1 million he wanted for his reservoir site, Mulholland had left himself short of water storage capacity. It was a serious situation to begin with, and it was compounded by the drought, the dynamitings, and the phenomenal continuing influx of people. His power dams were also running day and night, spilling water into the ocean before it could be reused. The water he had obtained at such expense and grief was being wasted. As a result, he turned to the dam he had under construction in San Francisquito Canyon, and, ignoring the advice of his own engineers, decided to make it larger.

The reservoir behind the enlarged Saint Francis Dam reached its capacity of 11.4 billion gallons in early March of 1928, and immediately began to leak. Few dams fail to leak when they are new, but if they are sound they leak clear water. The water seeping around the abutment of the Saint Francis Dam was brown. It was a telltale sign that water was seeping through the canyon walls, softening the mica shale and conglomerate abutment.

It was also a sign that William Mulholland chose, if not exactly to ignore, then to disbelieve. After all, it was *his* dam. Would the greatest engineering department in the entire world build an unsafe dam? To reassure the public, Mulholland and his chief engineer rode out to the site on March 12 for an inspection. The last of the season's rains was falling, and muddy water was running from a nearby construction site. After a perfunctory look, Mulholland decided that the site was the source of the mud, and pronounced the dam safe. On the same night, at a few minutes before midnight, its abutment turned to Jell-O, and the reservoir awoke from its deceptive slumber and tore the dam apart.

There are few earthly phenomena more awesome than a flood, and there is no flood more awesome than several years' accumulation of rainfall released over the course of an hour or two. The initial surge of water was two hundred feet high, and could have toppled nearly anything in its path—thousand-ton blocks of concrete rode the crest like rafts. Seventy-five families were living in San Francisquito Canyon immediately below the dam. Only one of their members, who managed to claw his way up the canyon wall just before the first wave hit, survived. Ten miles below, the village of Castaic Junction stood where the narrow canyon opened into the broader and flatter Santa Clara Valley. When the surge engulfed the town, it was still seventy-eight feet high. Days later, bodies and bits of Castaic Junction showed up on the beaches near San Diego.

The flood exploded into the Santa Clara River, turned right, and swept through the valley toward the ocean. It tore across a construction camp where 170 men were sleeping, and carried off all but six. A few miles below, Southern California Edison was building a project and had erected a tent city for 140 men. At first, the night watchman thought it was an avalanche. As it dawned on him that the nearest snow was fifty miles away, the flood crest hit, forty feet high. The men who survived were those who didn't have time to unzip their canvas tents, which were tight enough to float downstream like rafts. Eighty-four others died.

When the flood went through Piru, Fillmore, and Santa Paula it was semisolid, a battering ram congealed by homes, wagons, telephone poles, cars, and mud. Wooden bridges and buildings were instantaneously smashed to bits. A woman and her three children clung to a floating mattress until it snagged in the upper branches of a tree. They survived. A rancher who heard the deluge coming loaded his family in his truck and began to dash to safety. As he stopped by his neighbors' house and ran to the door to warn them, the flood arrived and swept his family out to sea. A four-room house was dislodged and floated a mile downstream without a piece of furniture rearranged; when the dazed owners came to inspect it, they found their lamps still upright on their living-room tables. A brave driver trying to outrace the flood could not bring himself to pass the people waving desperately along the way; his car held fourteen corpses when it was hauled out of the mud. The flood went on, barely missing Saticoy and Montalvo, and, at five o'clock in the morning, went by Ventura and spent itself at sea.

Hundreds of people were dead, twelve hundred homes were demolished, and the topsoil from eight thousand acres of farmland was gone. William Mulholland, whose career lay amid the ruins, was still alive, but as he addressed the coroner's inquest he bent his head and murmured, "I envy the dead." After a feeble effort to put the blame on "dynamiters," he took full responsibility for the disaster.

But the great city his aqueduct had created was, for the moment at least, willing to forgive him. "Chief Engineer Mulholland was a pitiable figure as he appeared before the Water and Power Commission yesterday," the Los Angeles *Times* reported on March 16. "His figure was bowed, his face lined with worry and suffering. . . . Every commissioner had the deepest sympathy for the man who has spent his life for the service of the people of Los Angeles . . . his Irish heart is kind, tender, and sympathetic."

Nine separate investigations eventually probed the collapse of the Saint Francis Dam. No one is even sure how many lives were lost, but a likely total is around 450: it would become one of the ten worst disasters in American history. The precise cause of the collapse was never officially determined, but when an investigator dropped a piece of the rock abutment into a glass of water, it dissolved in a few minutes. It was also learned that Mulholland had ordered the reservoir filled fast—a violation of a cardinal engineering rule—because he didn't want Owens River water to go to waste.

The city took full responsibility for all losses and paid most of the claims without contest, which cost it close to $15 million. For much less than that, Mulholland not only could have bought the Long Valley site, but built the dam, too.

In the ensuing months, in hearing after hearing, Mulholland was dragged through an agonizing reappraisal of his career. It was learned that two other dams in whose design and construction he participated as a consultant eventually collapsed, and a third had to be abandoned when partially built. He was a bold engineer, an innovative engineer;

he was also a reckless, arrogant, and inexcusably careless engineer. His fall from grace was slow, awful, and complete. By the time he wearily resigned, in November of 1928, at the age of seventy-three, his reputation was sullied beyond redemption. His wit and his combativeness vanished in retirement, and even in the company of his perfervidly loyal children he often lacked the energy to speak. He told them, "The zest for living is gone."

The city finally settled with Fred Eaton, who lost almost everything in the collapse of the Watterson banks, for $650,000. A few weeks later, the two old and broken men moved to heal their twenty-year rift. Lost in despondency at home, Mulholland received a message that Eaton, who had since returned to Los Angeles, would like to see him. Without a word, he got his hat and strode out the door. Eaton had suffered a stroke; he needed a cane to walk, and he looked ancient. "Hello, Fred," said Mulholland as he approached Eaton's bedside. Then both of them broke down and wept.

T he dam in Long Valley was ultimately built, and the reservoir that formed behind it, which was named Lake Crowley in honor of a priest who devoted the latter part of his life to healing the rift between city and valley, was, in its day, one of the largest in the country. By then, however, all hope of fruitful coexistence had died. On a map, the Owens Valley was still there, but it had ceased to exist as a place with its own aspirations, its own destiny. By the mid-1930s, Los Angeles was landlord of 95 percent of the farmland and 85 percent of the property in the towns. In the town of Independence, the Eastern California Museum, which tells the story of the battle largely from the valley's side, sits on land leased from the city.

Los Angeles leased some of the land back to farmers for a while, but the unpredictability of the water supply discouraged most of those who tried to carry on. There might be enough for twenty or thirty thousand acres in wetter years; then there might be enough for only three or four thousand. As the city grew, the river became utterly appropriated; when that happened, the Department of Water and Power sank wells and began depauperating the aquifer, as would happen—as is happening—in so many places in the West. The last of the ranchers quit in the 1950s and the economy shifted to tourism; most of those who remain now pump gas, rent rooms, or serve lunch to the skiers and tourists driving through on Highway 395. By the

1970s, even that tenuous existence was threatened; the aquifer was so drawn-down that desert plants which can normally survive on the meagerest capillary action of groundwater began to die, and the valley went beyond desert and took on the appearance of the Bonneville Salt Flats. When the winds of convection blow, huge clouds of alkaline dust boil off the valley floor; people now live in the Owens Valley at some risk to their health. The city has refused every request that it limit its groundwater pumping, just as it has refused to stop diverting the creeks that feed Mono Lake to the north—another casualty of its unquenchable thirst. Some sporadic dynamitings began to occur again in the 1970s, and reporters arrived eager to cover the "second Owens Valley War," but the war was long since over—there was nothing left to win.

As for Otis, Chandler, Sherman, and the rest of the syndicate that called itself the San Fernando Mission Land Company, they became rich—phenomenally rich. While presiding over the San Fernando Valley's metamorphosis from desert to agricultural cornucopia, they used the profits to constantly acquire more land. In 1911, Chandler, Otis, and Sherman purchased another 47,500 acres nearby and began to develop them—the biggest subdivision in the world. Within a year, they were assembling the third-largest land empire in the history of the state, the 300,000-acre Tejon Ranch, straddling Los Angeles and Kern counties. (Besides the Los Angeles *Times*, the Tejon Ranch, undiminished in size, remains the principal local asset of the Chandler family.) In a speech given in 1912, Theodore Roosevelt singled out Otis as "a curious instance of the anarchy of soul which comes to a man who in conscienceless fashion deifies property at the expense of human rights." But Roosevelt, as much as anyone, was responsible for setting this anarchic soul loose. No one knows how great a profit the syndicate realized from the initial seventeen thousand San Fernando acres, but one writer, William Kahrl, estimates that Chandler was worth as much as $500 million when he died, and the San Fernando Valley was the soil from which this incredible fortune grew. It may not have been the most lucrative land scam in United States history, but it ranked somewhere near the top.

Between the arrival of William Mulholland and his death, Los Angeles grew from a town of fifteen thousand into the then most populous desert city on earth. Today it is the second-largest, barely surpassed by Cairo. Its obsessive search for more water, however, was never to end. While Lake Crowley was filling, the city was already completing its aqueduct to the Colorado River, whose construction almost precipitated a shooting war with Arizona, a rival as formidable as the Owens Valley was weak. And though the first Colorado River aqueduct was supposed to end its water famines forever—as was the Owens River aqueduct—the city was soon planning a second Colorado River Aqueduct and plotting to seize half of the Feather River, six hundred miles away, at the same time. No sooner had it managed to do all of that than the city fathers were secretly meeting with the Bureau of Reclamation, mapping diversions from rivers a thousand miles distant in Oregon and Washington. Like the Red Queen, Los Angeles runs faster and faster to stay in place.

No one says or remembers much about the Reclamation Service's involvement in the Owens Valley story, which is ironic, because nothing in its history may have affected the interests of the nation-at-large quite as much. Almost as soon as it was created—well before it metamorphosed into the mighty Bureau of Reclamation—the agency found itself working on behalf of the wealthy and powerful and against the interests of the constituency it was created to protect, the small western irrigation farmer. In California, to a surprising degree, it has done so ever since. Small farmers do not matter much in the worldly scheme of things; if they did, their numbers would not be declining by the tens of thousands every year. But large farmers do, and explosively growing desert cities do, too, and the Bureau of Reclamation, after learning this lesson in the Owens Valley, would remember it well. Its largest dam is San Luis in central California; its most magnificent dam is Hoover. Above all, the Bureau loves to build great dams, and were it not for Los Angeles, the odds are low that either Hoover or San Luis would exist.

The Owens River created Los Angeles, letting a great city grow where common sense dictated that one should never be, but one could just as well say that it ruined Los Angeles, too. The annexation of the San Fernando Valley, a direct result of the aqueduct, instantly made it the largest city in the world in terms of geographic size. From that moment, it was doomed to become a huge, sprawling, one-story conurbation, hopelessly dependent on the automobile. The Owens River made Los Angeles large enough and wealthy enough to go out and capture any river within six hundred miles, and that made it larger, wealthier, and a good deal more awful. It is the only megalopolis in North America which is mentioned in the same breath as Mexico City or Djakarta—a place whose insoluble excesses raise the specter of some majestic, stately kind of collapse. In *The Water Seekers*, Remi

Nadeau, a city historian, says, "They brought in so much water for so many people that few cared any more whether Los Angeles grew at all. . . . Indeed, one might say that . . . they have brought in too much water. For if California now has enough water to more than double in population, then much of California is doomed to be insufferable."

That, in any event, is the way it appears some days from atop Mulholland Drive.

CHAPTER THREE

First Causes

When archaeologists from some other planet sift through the bleached bones of our civilization, they may well conclude that our temples were dams. Imponderably massive, constructed with exquisite care, our dams will outlast anything else we have built—skycrapers, cathedrals, bridges, even nuclear power plants. When forests push through the rotting streets of New York and the Empire State Building is a crumbling hulk, Hoover Dam will sit astride the Colorado River much as it does today—intact, formidable, serene.

The permanence of our dams will merely impress the archaeologists; their numbers will leave them in awe. In this century, something like a quarter of a million have been built in the United States alone. If you ignore the earthen plugs thrown across freshets and small creeks to water stock or raise bass, then fifty thousand or so remain. These, in the lexicon of the civil engineer, are "major works." Even most of the major works are less than awesome, damming rivers like the Shepaug, the Verdigris, Pilarcitos Creek, Mossman's Brook, and the North Fork of the Jump. Forget about them, and you are left with two or three thousand really big dams, the thought of whose construction staggers the imagination. They hold back rivers our ancestors thought could never be tamed—the Columbia, the Tennessee, the Sacramento, the Snake, the Savannah, the Red, the Colorado. They are sixty stories high or four miles long; they contain enough concrete to pave an interstate highway from end to end.

These are the dams that will make the archaeologists blink—
and wonder. Did we overreach ourselves trying to build them? Did
our civilization fall apart when they silted up? Why did we feel compelled to build so many? Why five dozen on the Missouri and its
major tributaries? Why twenty-five on the Tennessee? Why fourteen on the Stanislaus River's short run from the Sierra Nevada
to the sea?

We know surprisingly little about vanished civilizations whose
majesty and whose ultimate demise were closely linked to liberties
they took with water. Unlike ourselves, future archaeologists will
have the benefit of written records, of time capsules and so forth. But
such things are as apt to confuse as to enlighten. What, for example,
will archaeologists make of Congressional debates over Tellico Dam,
where the vast majority ridiculed the dam, excoriated it, flagellated
it—and then allowed it to be built? What will they think of
Congressmen voting for water projects like Central Arizona and
Tennessee-Tombigbee—projects costing three or four billion dollars
in an age of astronomical deficits—when Congress's own fact-finding
committees asserted or implied that they made little sense?

Such debates and documents may shed light on reasons—rational or otherwise—but they will be of little help in explaining the
psychological imperative that drove us to build dam after dam after
dam. If there is a Braudel or a Gibbon in the future, however, he may
deduce that the historical foundations of dams as monumental as
Grand Coulee, of projects as nonsensical as Tennessee-Tombigbee,
are sunk in the 1880s, a decade which brought, in quick succession,
a terrible blizzard, a terrible drought, and a terrible flood.

The great white winter of 1886 came first. The jet stream drove northward, grazed the Arctic Circle, then dipped sharply southward, a
parabolic curve rushing frigid air into the plains. Through December
of 1886, the temperature in South Dakota barely struggled above zero.
A brief thaw intervened in January, followed by a succession of monstrous Arctic storms. Week after week, the temperature fell to bottomless depths; in the Dakotas, the windchill factor approached a
hundred below. Trapped for weeks, even for months, in a mind-warping
expanse of frozen treeless prairie, thousands of pioneers literally lost
their minds. As the last of the chairs were being chopped and burned,
settlers contemplated a desperate hike to the nearest town, unable
to decide whether it was crazier to stay or to leave. No one knows

how many lost their lives, but when the spring thaw finally came, whole families were discovered clutching their last potatoes or each other, ice encrusted on their eyes.

But the settlers' suffering was merciful compared to that of their cows. On the woodless plains, barns were rare. Cattle were turned out into blizzards to survive by their wits, which they don't have, and which wouldn't have done them much good anyway. They were found piled by the hundreds at the corners of fenced quarter sections, all facing southeast; even when a storm abated, the survivors were too traumatized to turn around, and they died a night or two later under a listless winter's moon. It was a winter not just of horrendous cold but of gigantic snows, horizontal broadsides that reduced visibility to zero and stung the cattle like showers of needles. Twenty-foot drifts filled the valleys and swales, covering whatever frozen grass was left to eat. At night families would lie awake listening to their cows' dreadful bawls, afraid to go out and have the wind steal their last resources of warmth. Anyway, there was nothing they could do.

The toll was never officially recorded. Most estimates put the loss of cattle at around 35 percent, but in some regions it may have been nearer 75 percent. In sheer numbers, enough cows died to feed the nation for a couple of years. Much of the plains' cattle industry was in financial ruin. The bankrupt cattle barons dismissed thousands of hired hands, who were forced to find new careers. When the snows of 1886 melted, Robert Leroy Parker, a young drover, cattle rustler, and part-time bank robber with a reputation, had more recruits on his hands than he knew what to do with. He organized them into a gang known as the Wild Bunch and called himself Butch Cassidy. The Wild Bunch and the scores of outlaw bands like them worked the banks, the railroads, and the Pinkerton agents into a murderous froth. To others, however, they were a moral weight on the mind. Many of the outlaws had been "good boys," former ranch hands and farmers, occupations that everyone hoped would domesticate the West and cure it of its cyclical agonies of boom and bust. But weather was the ultimate arbiter in the American West. Unless there was some way to control it, or at least minimize its effects, a good third of the nation might remain uninhabitable forever.

As if to confirm such a prophecy, the decade following the great white winter was a decade when the western half of the continent decided to dry up. Like most droughts, this one came gradually, building up force, nibbling away at the settlers' fortunes as inexorably as their cattle nibbled away the dying grass. The sun, to which the settlers had so recently offered prayerful thanks, turned into a despotic orb; as Hamlin Garland wrote, "The sky began to scare us with its light." In July of 1888, at Bennett, Colorado, the temperature rose to 118, a high that has never since been equaled in the state. It was the same throughout the West, as an immense high-pressure zone sat immobile across the plains. Orographic clouds promising rain formed over the Rockies, were boiled off in midair, and disappeared. The atmosphere, it seemed, had been permanently sucked dry.

By 1890, the third year of the drought, it was obvious that the theory that rain follows the plow was a preposterous fraud. The people of the plains states, still shell-shocked by the great white winter, began to turn back east. The populations of Kansas and Nebraska declined by between one-quarter and one-half. Tens of thousands went to the wetter Oklahoma territory, which the federal government usurped from the five Indian tribes to whom it had been promised in perpetuity and offered to anyone who got there first. Meanwhile, the windmills of the farmers who remained north were pumping up sand instead of water, and the huge dark clouds on the horizon were not rain but dust. The great cattle freeze of the white winter had been, in retrospect, a blessing in disguise. Had several million more cows been around to graze the dying prairie grasses to their roots, the Dust Bowl of the 1930s could have arrived half a century early.

When statistics were collected a few years later, only 400,000 homesteading families had managed to persevere on the plains, of more than a million who tried. The Homestead Acts had been a relative success in the East; west of the hundredth meridian, however, they were for the most part a failure, even a catastropic failure. Much of the blame rested on flaws in the acts themselves, and on the imperfections of human nature, but a lot of it was the fault of the weather. How could you settle a region where you nearly froze to death one year and expired from heat and lack of water during the next eight or nine?

The drought that struck the West in the late 1880s did not occlude the entire continent. In the spring of 1889, the jet stream that had bypassed the West was feeding a thoroughfare of ocean moisture into the eastern states. In the mountains of Pennsylvania, it rained more or less continuously for weeks. The Allegheny and Susquehanna rivers became swollen surges of molten mud. Above Johnstown, Pennsylvania, on the South Fork of the Conemaugh River, a tributary of the Allegheny, sat a big earthfill dam built thirty-seven years earlier by

111

the Pennsylvania Canal Company; it was, for a while, the largest dam in the world. Pounded by the rains, infiltrated by the waters of the rising reservoir, the dam was quietly turning into Cream of Wheat. On May 31, with a sudden flatulent shudder, it dissolved. Sixteen billion gallons of water dropped like a bomb on the town below. Before anyone had time to flee, Johnstown was swallowed by a thirty-foot wave. When the reservoir was finally in the Allegheny River, sending it far over its banks, the town had disappeared. Four hundred corpses were never positively identified. The number of dead was eventually put at twenty-two hundred—twice as many casualties as in the burning of the *General Slocum* on the East River in 1904; four or five times as many as in the San Francisco earthquake and fire; nine times as many as in the Chicago fire. The only single disaster in American history that took more lives was the hurricane that struck Galveston, Texas, eleven years later. The Johnstown flood was significant if only for this sheer loss of life; but it was also an indictment of privately built dams.

The rapid rise of the federal irrigation movement in the early 1890s was due in part to this succession of overawing catastrophes. But it had just as much to do with the fact that by the late 1880s, private irrigation efforts had come to an inglorious end. The good sites were simply gone. Most of the pioneers who had settled successfully across the hundredth meridian had gone to Washington and California and Oregon, where there was rain, or had chosen homesteads along streams whose water they could easily divert. Such opportunities, however, were quick to disappear. Groundwater wasn't much help either. A windmill could lift enough drinking water for a family and few cattle; but it would require thirty or forty windmills, and reliable wind, to lift enough water to irrigate a quarter section of land—a disheartening prospect to a farmer with no money in a region with no wood.

Even if their land abutted a stream with some surplus water rights, few farmers had the confidence, cooperative spirit, and money to build a dam and lead the stored water to their lands through a long canal. It was one thing to throw a ten-foot-high earthen plug across a freshet in order to create a two-acre stock pond—though even that taxed the resources of most farmers in the West, who had invested all their savings simply to get there from Kentucky or Maine. It was quite another thing to build a dam on a stream large enough to supply a year-round flow, and to dig a canal—by horse and by hand—that was long enough, and deep enough, and wide enough, to irrigate hundreds or thousands of acres of land. The work involved was simply stupefying; clearing a field, by comparison, seemed like the simplest, most effortless job.

The farmers' predicament, on the other hand, was an opportunity for the legions of financial swashbucklers who had gone west in pursuit of quick wealth. In the 1870s and 1880s, hundreds of irrigation companies, formed with eastern capital, set themselves to the task of reclaiming the arid lands. Almost none survived beyond ten years. At the eighth National Irrigation Congress in 1898, a Colorado legislator likened the American West to a graveyard, littered with the "crushed and mangled skeletons of defunct [irrigation] corporations . . . [which] suddenly disappeared at the end of brief careers, leaving only a few defaulted obligations to indicate the route by which they departed."

There was, indeed, a kind of cruel irony in the collapse of the irrigation companies. Most of them operated in the emphatically arid regions—the Central Valley of California, Nevada, Arizona, southeastern Colorado, New Mexico—where agriculture without irrigation is daunting or hopeless, but otherwise the climate is well suited for growing crops. The drought, on the other hand, struck hardest in the region just east of the hundredth meridian, where, in most years, a nonirrigating farmer had been able to make a go of it. Kansas was emptied by the drought and the white winter, Nevada by irrigation companies gone defunct. In the early 1890s, the exodus from Nevada, as a percentage of those who hung on, was unlike anything in the country's history. Even California, in the midst of a big population boom, saw the growth of its *agricultural* population come to a standstill in 1895.

California, the perennial trend-setting state, was the first to attempt to rescue its hapless farmers, but the result, the Wright Act, was another in the long series of doomed efforts to apply eastern solutions to western topography and climate. The act, which took its inspiration from the township governments of New England, established self-governing mini-states, called irrigation districts, whose sole function was to deliver water onto barren land. Like the western homestead laws, it was a good idea that foundered in practice. The districts soon buckled under their responsibilities—issuing bonds that wouldn't sell, building reservoirs that wouldn't fill, allocating water unfairly, distributing it unevenly, then throwing up their hands when anarchy prevailed. Elwood C. Mead, then the state engineer of Wyoming and probably the country's leading authority on irrigation, called the Wright Act "a disgrace to any self-governing people." George Maxwell, a Californian and founder of the National Irrigation Association, said "the extravagance or stupidity or incompetence of local [irrigation] directors" had left little beyond a legacy of "waste and disaster." Though the Wright Act was in most ways a failure, Colorado, thinking it had learned something from California's mistakes, adopted its own version, which added a modest subsidy for private irrigation developers in order to improve their odds of success. By 1894, under Colorado's new program, five substantial storage reservoirs had been built. Three were so poorly designed and situated that they stored no water at all; the fourth was declared unsafe and was never even filled; and the fifth was so far from the land it was supposed to irrigate that most of the meager quantity of water it could deliver disappeared into the ground before it got there.

In that same year—1894—Senator Joseph Carey of Wyoming, thinking he had learned something from California's and Colorado's mistakes, introduced a bill that offered another approach: the federal government would cede up to a million acres of land to any state that promised to irrigate it. But, by some elusive reasoning, the states were forbidden to use land as the collateral they would need to raise the money to build the irrigation works—and land, at the time, was the only thing of value most of them had. Sixteen years later, using a generous estimate, the Carey Act had caused 288,553 acres to come under irrigation throughout the entire seventeen-state West—about as much developed farmland as there was in a couple of counties in Illinois.

As the private and state-fostered experiments with irrigation lay in shambles, many of the western reclamation advocates heaped blame on the East and "Washington" for not doing more to help, just as their descendants, four generations later, would vilify Jimmy Carter, an easterner and southerner, for not "understanding" their "needs" when he tried to eliminate some water projects that would have subsidized a few hundred of them to the tune of hundreds of thousands of dollars apiece. In each case, the West was displaying its peculiarly stubborn brand of hypocrisy and blindness. Midwestern members of Congress were understandably uneager to subsidize competition for their own farmer constitutents, but they had little to do with making reclamation fail; the West was up to the task itself. Its faith in private enterprise was nearly as absolute as its earlier faith that settlement would make the climate wetter. John Wesley Powell, a midwesterner, knew that all the private initiative in the world would never make it bloom. Theodore Roosevelt, an easterner, had returned from the West convinced that there were "vast areas of public land which can be made available for . . . settlement," but only, he added, "by building reservoirs and main-line canals impractical for private enterprise." But the West wasn't listening. For the first time in their history, Americans had come up against a problem they could not begin to master with traditional American solutions—private capital, individual initiative, hard work—and yet the region confronting the problem happened to believe most fervently in such solutions. Through the 1890s, western Senators and Congressmen resisted all suggestions that reclamation was a task for government alone—not even for the states, which had failed as badly as the private companies, but for the national government. To believe such a thing was to imply that their constituents did not measure up to the myth that enshrouded them—that of the indomitable individualist. When they finally saw the light, however, their attitude miraculously changed—though the myth didn't—and the American West quietly became the first and most durable example of the modern welfare state.

The passage of the Reclamation Act of 1902 was such a sharp left turn in the course of American politics that historians still gather and argue over why it was passed. To some, it was America's first flirtation with socialism, an outgrowth of the Populist and Progressive movements of the time. To others, it was a disguised reactionary measure, an effort to relieve the mobbed and riotous conditions of the eastern industrial cities—an act to save heartless capitalism from itself. To some, its roots were in Manifest Destiny, whose incantations still held people in their sway; to others, it was a military ploy to protect and populate America's western flank against the ascendant Orient.

What seems beyond question is that the Reclamation Act, or some variation of it, was, by the end of the nineteenth century, inevitable. To resist a federal reclamation program was to block all further migration to the West and to ensure disaster for those who were already there—or for those who were on their way. Even as the victims of the great white winter and the drought of the 1880s and 1890s were evacuating the arid regions, the trains departing Chicago and St. Louis for points west were full. The pull of the West reached deep into the squalid slums of the eastern cities; it reached back to the ravined, rock-strewn farms of New England and down into the boggy, overwet farmlands of the Deep South. No matter what the

115

government did, short of erecting a wall at the hundredth meridian, the settlement of the West was going to continue. The only way to prevent more cycles of disaster was to build a civilization based on irrigated farming. Fifty years of effort by countless numbers of people had resulted in 3,631,000 acres under irrigation by 1889. There were counties in California that contained more acreage than that, and the figure included much of the easily irrigable land. Not only that, but at least half the land had been irrigated by Mormons. Each additional acre, therefore, would be won at greater pain. Everything had been tried—cheap land, free land, private initiative, local initiative, state subsidy—and everything, with a few notable exceptions, had failed. One alternative remained.

There seemed to be only one politician in the arid West who fathomed his region's predicament well enough to end it. He had emigrated to San Francisco from the East, made a fortune through a busy law practice and the inheritance of his father-in-law's silver mine, moved to Nevada, and in 1888 launched the Truckee Irrigation Project. It was one of the most ambitious reclamation efforts of its day, and it failed—not because it was poorly conceived or executed (hydrologically and economically, it was a good project) but because squabbles among its beneficiaries and the pettiness of the Nevada legislature ruined its hopes. In the process Francis Griffith Newlands lost half a million dollars and whatever faith he had in the ability of private enterprise to mount a successful reclamation program. "Nevada," he said bitterly as his project went bust in 1891, "is a dying state."

Newlands, who succeeded at everything else he tried, gave up on irrigation, ran for Congress, and won. For the remainder of the decade, he kept out of the reclamation battles, if only to give everyone else's solutions an opportunity to fail. All the while, however, he was waiting for his moment. It came on September 14, 1901, when a bullet fired by an anarchist ended the life of President William McKinley.

Theodore Roosevelt, the man who succeeded McKinley as President, was, like Francis Newlands, a student and admirer of John Wesley Powell. Infatuated with the West, he had traveled extensively there and been struck by the prescience and accuracy of Powell's observations. Roosevelt was first of all a politician, and had no interest in sharing Powell's ignominious fate; nonetheless, he knew that Powell's solutions were the only ones that would work, and he wanted a federal reclamation effort badly. A military thinker, he was concerned about Japan, bristling with expansionism and dirt-poor in

resources, and knew that America was vulnerable on its underpop-
ulated western flank. A bug for efficiency, he felt that the waste of
money and effort on doomed irrigation ventures was a scandal. Roosevelt was also a conservationist, in the utilitarian sense, and the
failure to conserve—that is, use—the water in western rivers irritated
him. "The western half of the United States would sustain a population greater than that of our whole country today if the waters that
now run to waste were saved and used for irrigation," he said in a
speech in December of 1901. For all his enthusiasm, however, Roosevelt knew that his biggest problem would be not the eastern states
in Congress but the myth-bound western bloc, whose region he was
trying to help. His second-greatest problem, ironically, would be his
chief ally, Francis Newlands.

As soon as Roosevelt was in the White House, Newlands introduced a bill creating a federal program along the lines suggested by
Powell. But the bitterness he felt over his huge financial loss was so
strong that he described his bill in language almost calculated to
infuriate his western colleagues, who were clinging to the myth that
the hostile natural forces of the West could be overcome by individual
initiative. In a long speech on the floor of the Congress, Newlands
said outright that the legislation he was introducing would "nationalize the works of irrigation"—which was like saying today that one
intended to nationalize the automobile industry. Then he launched
into a long harangue about the failures of state reclamation programs,
blaming them on "the ignorance, the improvidence, and the dishon-
esty of local legislatures"—even though many of his listeners had
recently graduated from such legislatures themselves. He even suggested that *Congress* should have no oversight powers, implying that
he distrusted that body as much as he did the thieves, opportunists,
and incompetents whom he saw controlling the state legislatures.

Newlands's bill, as expected, ran into immediate opposition. When
it came up for a vote in March, it was soundly defeated. Western
members then began to support a rival bill, proposed by Senator
Francis E. Warren of Wyoming, that contained none of the features
Newlands wanted. By February of 1902, Warren's bill was finally
passed by the Senate and seemed destined to become law. At that
point, however, fate and Theodore Roosevelt intervened. Mrs. Warren
became gravely ill, necessitating the Senator's return to Wyoming.
In Warren's absence, Roosevelt leaned on Newlands to tone down his
language, and before long the Congressman was describing his defeated measure, which he had already reintroduced, as a "conser-

vative" and "safe" bill. Roosevelt still wouldn't risk supporting it, but he came up with a brilliant ploy. Announcing his "sympathy with the spirit" of Warren's bill, he said he would support it with "a few minor changes." The person whom he wanted to make the changes and lead the bill through Congress was Wyoming's young Congressman-at-large, Frank Mondell, the future Republican leader of the House. Mondell had a weakness for flattery and a less than athletic mind, and Roosevelt was a master at exploiting both. Before long, he had persuaded Mondell to incorporate as "minor changes" in Warren's bill almost all of Newlands's language. Roosevelt then softened up his eastern opposition with some implied threats that their river and harbor projects might be in jeopardy if they did not go along—a strategy that has seen long useful service. By the time Warren returned from Wyoming, Newlands's bill, disguised as his own, had cleared both houses. On June 17, 1902, the Reclamation Act became law.

The newly created Reclamation Service exerted a magnetic pull on the best engineering graduates in the country. The prospect of reclaiming a desert seemed infinitely more satisfying than designing a steel mill in Gary, Indiana, or a power dam in Massachusetts, and the graduates headed west in a fog of idealism, ready to take on the most intractable foe of mankind: the desert. But the desert suffers improvement at a steep price, and the early Reclamation program was as much a disaster as its dams were engineering marvels.

The underlying problems were politics and money. Under the terms of the Reclamation Act, projects were to be financed by a Reclamation Fund, which would be filled initially by revenues from sales of federal land in the western states, then paid back gradually through sales of water to farmers. (It should be mentioned right away that the farmers, under the law, were exempted from paying interest on virtually all of their repayment obligations—a subsidy which was substantial to begin with, and which was to become breathtaking in later decades, as interest rates topped 10 percent. In some cases, the interest exemption alone—which is, of course, an indirect burden on the general taxpayer—has amounted to a subsidy of ninety cents on the dollar.) Section 9 of the Reclamation Act implied, if it didn't require, that all money accruing to the Reclamation Fund from sales of land in any given state should be spent in that state as well. Frederick Newell, the Service's first director, was particularly anxious to locate a few projects in each state anyway, because that might dispel some of the antipathy that had attended the Service's creation. By

1924, twenty-seven projects were completed or under construction. Of those, twenty-one had been initiated before the Service was even half a decade old.

The engineers who staffed the Reclamation Service tended to view themselves as a godlike class performing hydrologic miracles for grateful simpletons who were content to sit in the desert and raise fruit. About soil science, agricultural economics, or drainage they sometimes knew less than the farmers whom they regarded with indulgent contempt. As a result, some of the early projects were to become painful embarrassments, and expensive ones. The soil turned out to be demineralized, alkaline, boron-poisoned; drainage was so poor the irrigation water turned fields into saline swamps; markets for the crops didn't exist; expensive projects with heavy repayment obligations were built in regions where only low-value crops could be grown. In the Bureau of Reclamation's quasi-official history, *Water for the West*, Michael Robinson (the son-in-law of a Commissioner of Reclamation) discreetly admits all of this: "Initially, little consideration was given to the hard realities of irrigated agriculture. Neither aid nor direction was given to settlers in carrying out the difficult and costly work of clearing and leveling the land, digging irrigation ditches, building roads and houses, and transporting crops to remote markets. . . ."

Robinson also acknowledges the political pressures that have bedeviled the Reclamation program ever since it was born. The attitude of most western members of Congress was quaintly hypocritical: after resisting this experiment in pseudosocialism, or even voting against it, they decided, after it became law, that they might as well make the best of it. "The government was immediately flooded with requests for project investigations," Robinson writes. "Local chambers of commerce, real estate interests, and congressmen were convinced their areas were ideal for reclamation development. State legislators and officials joined the chorus of promoters seeking Reclamation projects. . . . Legislative requirements and political pressures sometimes precluded careful, exhaustive surveys of proposed projects. . . . Projects were frequently undertaken with only a sketchy understanding of the area's climate, growing season, soil productivity, and market conditions."

Congress's decision, in passing the act, to ignore much of John Wesley Powell's advice made things worse. Powell had proposed that in those inhospitable regions where only livestock could be raised, settlers should be allowed to homestead 2,560 acres of the public domain—but allocated enough water to irrigate only twenty. The Reclamation Act gave everyone up to 160 acres (a man and wife could jointly farm 320 acres), whether they settled in Mediterranean California or in the frigid interior steppes of Wyoming, where the extremes of climate rival those in Mongolia. You could grow wealthy on 160 acres of lemons in California and starve on 160 acres of irrigated pasture in Wyoming or Montana, but the act was blind to such nuances. And by building so many projects in a rush, the Reclamation Service was repeating its mistakes before it had a chance to learn from them.

All of these problems were compounded by the fact that few settlers had any experience with irrigation farming—nor were they required to. They overwatered and mismanaged their crops; they let their irrigation systems silt up. Many had optimistically filed on more acreage than they had resources to irrigate, and they ended up with repayment obligations on land they were forced to leave fallow. From there, it was a short, swift fall into bankruptcy. Fifty years earlier, the ancestors of the first Reclamation farmers had endured adversity by putting their faith in God and feeding themselves on game. But this was the twentieth century; the game was vanishing, and government was replacing God as the rescuer of last resort. As Michael Robinson wrote, "Western economic and social determinants were changing rapidly. Nineteenth-century irrigation pioneers were better suited to endure hardships than settlers who struggled to survive on Federal Reclamation projects after 1902. In the nineteenth century, wild game was plentiful, livestock could graze on the public domain outside irrigated areas, and the settlers were inured to privation." And so, after a few years of trial and a lot of error, the Reclamation Act began to undergo a long and remarkable series of "reforms."

The first reform was humble—a $20 million loan from the Treasury to the bankrupt Reclamation Fund to keep the program from falling on its face. It was approved in 1910, the same year that Section 9—the ill-advised clause promoting the construction of projects where they couldn't work—was repealed. New projects were also required to have the explicit consent of the President before they were launched. A paper reform, however, is not necessarily a reform in real life. Every Senator still wanted a project in his state; every Congressman wanted one in his district; they didn't care whether they made economic sense or not. The Commissioner of Reclamation and the President were only human. If Congress authorized a bad project and voted funding for it, a President might have good reasons not to veto the bill—

especially if it also authorized a lot of things the President *did* want. Congress caught on quickly, and was soon writing "omnibus" authorization bills, in which bad projects were thrown in, willy-nilly, with good ones. (Later, Congress would learn a new trick: attaching sneaky little amendments authorizing particularly wretched projects to legislation dealing with issues such as education and hurricane relief.) As a result, instead of weeding out or discouraging bad projects, the "reforms" began to concentrate on making bad projects work—or, to put it more bluntly, on bailing them out.

The first of these adjustments came in 1914, when the repayment period, which had been set in the act at a rather unrealistic ten years, was extended to twenty. It was quite a liberal adjustment, but failed to produce any measurable results. By 1922, twenty years after the Reclamation program began, only 10 percent of the money loaned from the Reclamation Fund had been repaid. Sixty percent of the irrigators—an astounding number—were defaulting on their repayment obligations, even though they paid no interest on irrigation features.

In 1924, Congress commissioned a Fact Finder's report on the Reclamation program, which recommended an even more drastic adjustment—raising the repayment period from twenty years to forty. No sooner was that done, however, than the most chronic and intractable problem of twentieth-century American agriculture began to appear: huge crop surpluses. Production and prices reached record levels during the First World War; when the war ended, production remained high, but crop prices did not. The value of all crops grown on Reclamation land fell from $152 million in 1919 to $83.6 million in 1922—as morose a statistic as the number of farmers in default. With their profits shriveling, the beleaguered farmers were reluctant to pay for water they were beginning to regard as rightful recompense for attempting to civilize the desert, especially when the Reclamation Service, in most cases, didn't dare shut it off when they refused to pay. So Congress took further steps to bail the Reclamation program out, rerouting royalties from oil drilling and potassium mining to the Reclamation Fund on the theory that the West, while being stripped of its mineral resources, ought to get something in return. But even after all these measures had been adopted a number of projects continued to operate at a hopeless loss.

Nonetheless, the psychic value of the Reclamation farms remained high. The only relief in a pitiless desert landscape, their worth was computed in almost ethereal terms, as if they were art. And their investment value to speculators remained high, too. An acre which in pre-project years was worth $5 or $10—if that—was suddenly worth fifty times as much. At such prices, many farmers found the temptation to sell out irresistible; by 1927, at least a third of the Reclamation farmers had. The buyers were usually wealthy speculators who figured they could absorb some minor losses for a while— especially if they could convince Congress to give them tax breaks —as long as they could make money when agricultural prices went back up. The Salt River Project in Arizona was notable for having been all but taken over by speculators. Elwood Mead, who succeeded Newell and Arthur Powell Davis as Commissioner of Reclamation, called speculation "a vampire which has done much to destroy the desirable social and economic purposes of the Reclamation Act." But the big, distant new owners were often better at paying their water bills than the stone-broke small farmers, so the Reclamation Service, in a number of instances, turned a blind eye toward what was going on. It was a case of lawlessness becoming de facto policy, and it was to become more and more commonplace.

Part of the reason the Reclamation Service (which metamorphosed, fittingly, into the *Bureau* of Reclamation in 1923) seemed so hapless at enforcing its social mandate had to do with the Omnibus Adjustment Act of 1926, one of those well-meaning pieces of legislation that make everything worse. Intended to clamp down on speculation, the act demanded that landowners owning excess amounts of land sign recordable contracts in which they promised to sell such lands within a designated period, at prices reflecting the lands' pre-project worth. But the contracts were to be signed with the local irrigation district acting as wholesaler of the Bureau's water—not with the Bureau itself. It was an ideal opportunity to camouflage acreage violations, since the same people who were in violation of the Reclamation Act often sat on the local irrigation district's board of directors.

A more important and insidious reason, however, had to do with the nature of the Bureau itself. "There was a tendency for some engineers to view public works as ends in themselves," admits Michael Robinson. "Despite official declarations from more sensitive administrators that 'Reclamation is measured not in engineering units but in homes and agricultural values' . . . the Service regarded itself as an 'engineering outfit.' "

That may have been the understatement of the year. To build a great dam on a tempestuous river like the Snake was terrifically exhilarating work; enforcing a hodgepodge of social ideals was hardly that. Stopping a wild river was a straightforward job, subjugable to logic, and the result was concrete, heroic, real: a dam. Enforcing repayment obligations and worrying about speculators and excess landowners was a cumbersome, troublesome, time-consuming nuisance—a nuisance without reward. Was the Bureau to abandon the most spellbinding effort of modern times—transforming the desert into a garden—just because a few big landowners were taking advantage of the program, just because some farmers couldn't pay as much as Congress hoped?

There were to be still more "reforms" tacked onto the Reclamation Act: reforms extending the repayment period to fifty years, setting water prices according to the farmers' "ability to pay," using hydroelectric revenues to subsidize irrigation costs. It wasn't until the 1930s, however, that the Reclamation program went into high gear. In the 1920s and early 1930s, the nation's nexus of political power still lay east of the Mississippi River; the West simply didn't have the votes to authorize a dozen big water projects each year. Western politicians who were to exercise a near-despotic rule over the Bureau's authorizing committees in later years, men like Wayne Aspinall and Bernie Sisk and Carl Hayden, were still working their way up the political ranks. (In 1902, the year the Reclamation program began, Arizona was still ten years away from becoming a state.) Presidents Harding and Coolidge were ideological conservatives from the East who sternly resisted governmental involvement in economic affairs, unless it was an opportunity for their friends to earn a little graft. And even Herbert Hoover, though a Californian and an engineer, was not regarded by the western water lobby and the Bureau as a particularly loyal friend.

All of this was to change more abruptly than the Bureau of Reclamation and its growing dependency could have hoped. The most auspicious event in its entire history was the election to the presidency in 1932 of a free-wheeling, free-spending patrician. The second most auspicious event was the passage, during the four-term Roosevelt-Truman interregnum, of several omnibus river-basin bills that authorized not one, not five, not even ten, but dozens of dams and irrigation projects at a single stroke. Economics mattered little, if at all; if the irrigation ventures slid into an ocean of debt, the huge hydroelectric dams authorized within the same river basin could generate the necessary revenues to bail them out (or so it was thought). It was a breathtakingly audacious solution to an intractable problem, and the results were to be breathtaking as well. Between Franklin Roosevelt and the river-basin approach—which, in an instant, could authorize dams and canals and irrigation projects from headwaters to river mouth, across a thousand miles of terrain—the natural landscape of the American West, the rivers and deserts and wetlands and canyons, was to undergo a man-made transformation the likes of which no desert civilization has ever seen. The first, and perhaps the most fateful, such transformation was wrought in the most arid and hostile quarter of the American West, a huge desert basin transected by one comparatively miniature river: the Colorado.

CHAPTER FOUR

An American Nile (I)

Ours was the first and will doubtless be the last party of whites to visit this profitless locale.

> —Lieutenant Joseph Christmas Ives,
> on sailing up the Colorado River
> to a point near the present location of Las Vegas, in 1857

The Colorado is neither the biggest nor the longest river in the American West, nor, except for certain sections described in nineteenth-century journals as "awful" or "appalling," is it the most scenic. Its impressiveness and importance have to do with other things. It is one of the siltiest rivers in the world—the virgin Colorado could carry sediment loads close to those of the much larger Mississippi—and one of the wildest. Its drop of nearly thirteen thousand feet is unequaled in North America, and its constipation-relieving rapids, before dams tamed its flash floods, could have flipped a small freighter. The Colorado's modern notoriety, however, stems not from its wild rapids and plunging canyons but from the fact that it is the most legislated, most debated, and most litigated river in the entire world. It also has more people, more industry, and a more significant economy dependent on it than any comparable river in the world. If the Colorado River suddenly stopped flowing, you would have two years of carryover capacity in the reservoirs before you had to evacuate most of southern California and Arizona and a good portion of Colorado, New Mexico, Utah, and Wyoming. The river system provides over half the water of greater Los Angeles, San Diego, and Phoenix; it grows much of America's domestic production of fresh winter vegetables; it illuminates the neon city of Las Vegas, whose

125

annual income is one-fourth the entire gross national product of Egypt—the only other place on earth where so many people are so helplessly dependent on one river's flow. The greater portion of the Nile, however, still manages, despite many diversions, to reach its delta below the Mediterranean Sea. The Colorado is so used up on its way to the sea that only a burbling trickle reaches its dried-up delta at the head of the Gulf of California, and then only in wet years. To some conservationists, the Colorado River is the preeminent symbol of everything mankind has done wrong—a harbinger of a squalid and deserved fate. To its preeminent impounder, the U.S. Bureau of Reclamation, it is the perfection of an ideal.

The Colorado has a significance that goes beyond mere prominence. It was on this river that the first of the world's truly great dams was built—a dam which gave engineers the confidence to dam the Columbia, the Volga, the Paraná, the Niger, the Nile, the Zambezi, and most of the world's great rivers. The dam rose up at the depths of the Depression and carried America's spirits with it. Its electricity helped produce the ships and planes that won the Second World War, and its water helped grow the food. From such illustrious and hopeful beginnings, however, the tale of human intervention in the Colorado River degenerates into a chronicle of hubris and obtuseness. Today, even though the Colorado still resembles a river only in its upper reaches and its Grand Canyon stretch—even as hydrologists amuse themselves by speculating about how many times each molecule of water has passed through pairs of kidneys—it is still unable to satisfy all the demands on it, so it is referred to as a "deficit" river, as if the river were somehow at fault for its overuse. And though there are plans to relieve the "deficit"—plans to import water from as far away as Alaska—the twenty million people in the Colorado Basin will probably find themselves facing chronic shortages, if not some kind of catastrophe, before any of these grandiose schemes is built—if, indeed, one is ever built.

One could almost say, then, that the history of the Colorado River contains a metaphor for our time. One could say that the age of great expectations was inaugurated at Hoover Dam—a fifty-year flowering of hopes when all things appeared possible. And one could say that, amid the salt-encrusted sands of the river's dried-up delta, we began to founder on the Era of Limits.

In terms of annual flow, the Colorado isn't a big river—in the United States it does not even rank among the top twenty-five—but, like a forty-pound wolverine that can drive a bear off its dinner, it is un-rivaled for sheer orneriness. The virgin Colorado was tempestuous, willful, headstrong. Its flow varied psychotically between a few thousand cubic feet per second and a couple of hundred thousand, sometimes within a few days. Draining a vast, barren watershed whose rains usually come in deluges, its sediment volume was phenomenal. If the river, running high, were diverted through an ocean liner with a cheesecloth strainer at one end, it would have filled the ship with mud in a couple of hours. The silt would begin to settle about two hundred miles above the Gulf of California, below the last of the Grand Canyon's rapids, where the river's gradient finally moderated for good. There was so much silt that it raised the entire riverbed, foot by foot, year by year, until the Colorado slipped out of its loose confinement of low sandy bluffs and tore off in some other direction, instantly digging a new course. It developed an affection for several such channels, returning to them again and again—Bee River, New River, Alamo River, big braided washes that sat dry and expectant in the desert, waiting for the river to return. The New and Alamo channels drove into Mexico, then veered back north into the United States, a hundred-mile semiloop, and ended at the foot of the Chocolate Mountains, where the delinquent river would form a huge evanescent body of water called the Salton Sea. After a while, the New and Alamo channels would themselves silt up and the Colorado would throw itself back into its old bed and return to the Gulf of California, much to the relief of the great schools of shrimp, the clouds of waterfowl, and the thousands of cougars, jaguars, and bobcats that prowled its delta. The Salton Sea would slowly evaporate and life would return to normal, for a while. The river went on such errant flings every few dozen years—a vanishing moment in geologic time, but long enough so that the first people who tried to tame it had no idea what they were in for.

The first of these tamers was an eastern developer with a grandiose imagination, a bulldog chin, a shock of steel-wool hair, and a name suggestive of his temperament. In 1892, Charles Rockwood saw the Colorado River for the first time and became obsessed. Sitting north of it, an appendage of the vast Sonoran Desert of southern California and Arizona, were hundreds of thousands of absolutely flat acres built by its ancient delta, fertile land where you could grow crops twelve months of the year. All that stood in the way of cultivation was an annual rainfall of 2.4 inches, about the lowest in the United States. Despite the imposing nature of the task, the temptation to play God with the river and turn this brutal desert green was too much for Rockwood to resist. After traveling halfway around the world for financial support, he seduced the most famous private irrigationist of his day, George Chaffey, into joining forces with him. By 1901, Rockwood and Chaffey had cut a diversion channel, and a good portion of the river was pouring over fields in what had once been called the Valley of the Dead (in grand nineteenth-century fustian tradition, Rockwood renamed it Imperial Valley). Within eight months, there were two towns, two thousand settlers, and a hundred thousand acres ready for harvesting.

By 1904, however, the artificial channel had already silted up, and a bypass had to be cut. It silted up. Another bypass was cut; it too silted up. Finally, after much negotiation, the developers persuaded the Mexican government to let them cut still another channel below the border. Because it was meant as a temporary expedient while the original channel was cleaned out in advance of the spring floods, the Mexican channel had the flimsiest of control gates. As luck would have it, the spring floods arrived two months early. In February, a great surge of snowmelt and warm rain spilled out of the Gila River, just above the Mexican channel, and made off with the control gate. For the first time in centuries, the river was back in its phantom channel, the Alamo River, heading for its old haunt, the Salton Sink. As the surge advanced across the Imperial Valley, it cut into the loamy soil at a foot-per-second rate, forming a waterfall that marched backward toward the main channel. Even as their fields were being eaten and as their homes swam away, the valley people came out by the hundreds to see this apparition, a twenty-foot falls moving backward at a slow walk. By summer, virtually all of the Colorado River was out of its main channel, and the Salton Sink had once again become the Salton Sea.

Chaffey had had some differences with Rockwood and got out of the California Development Company a short while earlier with his reputation intact, leaving his erstwhile partner ruined. But the Southern Pacific Railroad had already invested too much money in a spur line to the valley to watch it abandoned to fate, so it took Rockwood's company into receivership and set about trying to tame the river. For the next two years, Edward H. Harriman, the railroad magnate, and the Colorado River fought nose to nose. Southern Pacific trains crawled back and forth across the valley like caterpillars, carrying rock and gravel to plug the half-mile breach. But 1905, 1906, and 1907 were some of the wettest years in the Colorado Basin's history. In 1907, the river sent a record twenty-five million acre-feet—eight quadrillion gallons—to the gulf. The floods, one following another, casually ripped Harriman's brush weirs to shreds; his miles of driven piles were uprooted and washed away. Finally, in February of 1907, after laughing away the railroad's best efforts, the river decided to lull. With mad energy, the SP crews finally secured the breach. When the next surge came down, the weirs held, and the river, dumping silt ten times faster than the trains, began rebuilding its own confinement.

Victory or no, the Colorado River was a rampant horse in a balsa corral. The only way to control it effectively, and to give the farmers some insurance against its countervailing tendency to dry up, was to build a dam—a huge dam—to lop the peaks off the floods and provide storage during droughts. The problem with such a dam, from the point of view of the basin at large, was that California was then the only state in a position to use the water. Wyoming, Arizona, Nevada, and New Mexico were still mostly uninhabited. Colorado and Utah had a few hundred thousand people each, but they had scarcely begun to tap the Colorado River and its tributaries; most of Utah's irrigation had been developed in another basin. California, on the other hand, was gaining people like no place on earth, and most of the growth was occurring in the south. The Imperial Valley could have immediately used three or four million acre-feet of the river, the consumption of all the upper-basin states and then some. The Coachella Valley, farther north, and the Palo Verde and Yuma projects could swallow another million acre-feet. Los Angeles, growing like a gourd in the night, would soon overrun its Owens Valley supply; the next logical source of water—the *only* logical source—was the Colorado River. Under simple appropriative-rights doctrine, the water would belong to California as soon as it began to use it. If California perfected its rights in court, it would, in effect, monopolize a huge portion of the river for itself. And the *real* injustice in all of this was that California contributed nothing to the river's flow. Nearly half the runoff came from Colorado and another third from Wyoming and Utah. Arizona and New Mexico contributed very little; Nevada and California, nothing at all. California's efforts to get the dam authorized by Congress were soon beaten back. Finally, it realized that if it wanted the dam and a reliable share of the river, it would have to sit down with its neighbor states and divide it up.

The negotiation of the Colorado River Compact took place in 1922 under the guidance of Commerce Secretary Herbert Hoover at

Bishop's Lodge, a swank resort outside Santa Fe, New Mexico. For the time spent debating and drafting it—about eleven months—and its reputation as a western equivalent of the Constitution, the compact didn't settle much. Using the Reclamation Service's estimated average flow of 17.5 million annual acre-feet, the delegates from the seven states divided the river arbitrarily at Lee's Ferry, Arizona—a point just below the Utah border—into two artificial basins. California, Arizona, and Nevada were the lower basin; the other four states were the upper basin; pieces of New Mexico and Arizona were in both. Each basin was allotted 7.5 million acre-feet. How they were to divide that among themselves was their problem. Of the remainder, 1.5 million acre-feet were reserved for Mexico, and the final million acre-feet were apportioned, with extreme reluctance on the part of some, as a bonus to the lower basin, whose delegates had threatened to walk out of the negotiations if they didn't get a bettter deal.

The compact was signed by the delegates in November of 1922; they then took it home for ratification by the voters or legislatures of their respective states, which quickly tore it to shreds. California wouldn't ratify without a conjugal authorization of Boulder Canyon Dam and a new canal running exclusively through American territory to Imperial Valley, a demand that gave the upper basin fits. Arizona wanted to divide the lower basin's apportionment before it ratified anything. Harry Chandler, probably the most influential human being in the Southwest—he talked through his vast wealth and his newspaper—was delighted by the compact and the authorization of the dam, but he was too greedy to tolerate an All-American Canal, which would divert the river right above his 860,000 acres in Mexico, so he ended up opposing everything. George Maxwell, the head of the National Reclamation Association, should have been in favor of Boulder Dam, but out of principle he opposed anything Harry Chandler liked.

In 1928, after six years of paralysis, Congress took matters into its own hands. It authorized Boulder Dam and the All-American Canal on the condition that at least six of the seven states ratify the compact, and that California limit its annual diversion to 4.4 million acre-feet per year. That implied only 2.8 million for Arizona (Nevada got 300,000 acre-feet), which was less than it wanted. Arizona, as a result, became the one state that refused to ratify, an act of defiance that would muddle things for another thirty-five years. At the time, however, its vote wasn't needed, and the other states' ratification led forthwith to the California Limitation Act and, subsequently, to passage of the Boulder Canyon Project Act. All of this appeared to settle matters:

130

the basin could now embark on an orgy of growth the likes of which the West had never seen. And it did settle things, temporarily at least, except for one small matter: the average annual flow of the Colorado River was nowhere near 17.5 million acre-feet.

In 1930, the American West had a population of eleven million people, about the population of New York State. Half of the people were in California, by far the most populous and modern of the western states. When Californians traveled, however, they went mainly on dirt roads. The drive from San Francisco to Lake Tahoe, which is now done in three or four hours, was a two-day adventure or ordeal, depending on one's point of view. The city's great bridges had not yet been built. San Jose was a dumpy little town of fifteen thousand, Silicon Valley a stronghold of orchards and roaming mountain lions. In some of the other states, the usual means of locomotion was still a horse and wagon. Electricity and telephones were unknown in most rural communities, and didn't reach the more remote ones until the 1950s. In the midst of this same depopulated, untrammeled region, however, the engineering wonder of all time was about to rise.

In Oakland, California, an egomaniacal small-time construction tycoon named Henry J. Kaiser had followed the passage of the Boulder Canyon Project Act with consuming interest. Obsessed with his niche in history, Kaiser was still enough of a realist to know that he could not begin to build such a dam alone. So he called up his friend W. A. Bechtel to ask if he was interested in making a joint bid. Dad Bechtel was a horse-drawn Fresno-scraper kind of contractor; most of his business was road paving, his most noteworthy innovation a folding toothbrush which he carried on trips. Outside of northern California, and even there, the Bechtel Corporation was all but unknown. "I don't know, Henry" was Bechtel's response when Kaiser, flushed with excitement, got him on the phone. "It sounds a little ambitious to me."

A thousand miles away in Utah, two sheep-ranching Mormon brothers named W. H. and E. O. Wattis were as captivated by the Boulder Canyon Project as Kaiser, and just as unable to undertake it themselves. The Wattises' other business, the Utah Construction Company, specialized in something as mundane as Bechtel's paving contracts: laying railroad bed. Lately, however, they had taken on a new partner, a maverick Mormon banker with Keynesian leanings who talked about deficit financing while candidate Franklin Roosevelt was still promising a balanced budget. His name was Marriner

131

Eccles, and the reward he was about to receive for his ideological flexibility was an influential position on the Federal Reserve Board. The Wattises had also been in contact with Harry Morrison and Morris Knudsen, two engineers formerly with the Bureau of Reclamation who had gone into business together in Boise, Idaho. And they had spoken with Frank Crowe, another former Bureau engineer whose enthusiasm for Boulder Dam was as obsessive as Kaiser's. Morrison had just returned from a trip east, where he had tried to influence the financial community to back a bid on the dam. He was told by the eastern bankers that there wasn't a company west of the Mississippi they would trust to take on something like this. But one thing would lead to another. Before long, the Wattises were talking with Bechtel and Kaiser, and Henry and Dad were in touch with some other firms—J. F. Shea Construction of Los Angeles, McDonald and Kahn of San Francisco, General Construction of Seattle. In February of 1931, during a meeting at the Engineers Club in San Francisco, the first of the West's supercompanies was born. There were eight firms altogether, but Kaiser couldn't resist borrowing a name from the tribunal before which the tongs, the Chinese equivalent of the Mafia families, took their grievances. At his insistence, the executives agreed to call their joint venture Six Companies, Inc. Hocking everything but their shirts, they could barely scrape together the few million dollars they would need to buy enough equipment to begin the job. When the Bureau auctioned off the job, however, it was Six Companies' amazingly low bid, in the amount of $48,890,995.50, that won. Once again, sang the Los Angeles *Times*, the West had "laughed at logic and driven [its] destiny over obstacles that rational minds deemed insuperable."

The first eighteen months of work on Boulder Canyon Dam involved the contruction of a new Colorado River. Four diversion tunnels were blasted through the rock of the box canyon, two on the Nevada side and two on the Arizona side, each of them three-quarters of a mile long. Their diameter was spacious enough to accommodate a jumbo jet shorn of its wings—a capacity that was needed mainly as insurance against an errant flood of 200,000 cubic feet per second, or more. The task required the excavation of three and half million tons of rock with enough dynamite to level Toledo. On November 13, 1932, four tremendous explosions blew out the entrances and exits of the two Arizona tunnels. The dust had not yet settled when a caravan of trucks lumbered onto a trestle bridge built downstream from the tunnel entrances and began dumping rocks and earth in the river's path. Finding itself blockaded, the Colorado slowly roiled and rose in frustration; sensing an escape route, it rode off into the tunnels. In a matter of hours, the river had been lured out of a bed it had occupied since the Grand Canyon was formed.

No sooner was the Colorado flowing through the canyon walls than the crews began replacing the flimsy trestle dam with a far more substantial cofferdam; then, for good measure, they built another below. Made of earth and rock and faced with concrete, the upper cofferdam measured 450 by 750 by 96 feet. Half a century earlier, it would have been the largest dam in the world, but its usefulness was to be measured in months.

When the cofferdams were finished, the engineers turned to the next task—stripping the canyon abutments to expose fresh clean solid rock. Because the dam would rise more than seven hundred feet, there was no crane big enough to do the job; it would have to be done by hand. The four hundred men whose job it was to clean the walls were known as high-scalers. Those who persevered—seven were killed on the job—spent months hanging four or five hundred feet in the air, drilling holes in the rock, inserting dynamite, and praying they would be hauled to safety before it exploded. Because the canyon was so tight, they also had to blast out space for portions of the huge powerhouse, the intake towers, and the penstock headers. Some of the rock amphitheaters they created could have held an orchestra.

Besides the hazards of the construction work (the falling rock, the explosives, electrocution, behemoth machines); besides the hazards of off-hours (fist fights, drunken binges, social diseases from the whores who camped about); besides all this, there was the heat. The low-lying parts of the Colorado and Sonora deserts are the hottest corner of North America, and we are speaking of temperatures in open, ambient air. The Colorado's box canyon held heat like an oven with the door open about an inch. Workers sometimes sacrificed eggs to see if they would actually fry on a sun-fired rock. The first death from heat prostration occurred a few days after construction began, and so many men collapsed that some of the crews finally forced a shutdown, demanded a pay raise, and ultimately staged a strike. The strike, however, did no good. Next to Boulder City was an encampment of tents and shanties known as Ragtown, where the unemployed waited by the hundreds for someone to give up, be fired, or die. "One of the myths about the Depression," Arthur Miller, the playwright, once said, "is that it brought everyone closer together. Actually, it just made everyone more voracious." "They will work under our conditions, or they will not work at all," proclaimed W. H. Wattis. And they did, at a base pay of $4 per day.

It was in 1933 when the explosive din suddenly stopped and an eerie silence descended on Boulder Canyon. The canyon walls were finally clean, the abutments sculpted, the cofferdams in place. Nearly three years after work had begun, the dam was still a figment of the imagination. Now it was time to dig down to bedrock.

The bed of the Mississippi River is hundreds, even thousands, of feet deep in silt. The Columbia and the Missouri flow over alluvial wash as thick as Arctic glaciers. On the Colorado, however, to everyone's amazement, bedrock was struck at forty feet. A milled piece of sawtimber was found resting at the bottom of the muck, obviously of very recent origin. Since white men had begun to settle the region, perhaps eighty years before, a huge flood had evidently washed the entire channel clean. In the middle of the bedrock, however, the men found a narrow channel a hundred feet deep. It was the farewell trail of a glacier, a reminder that not many thousands of years ago, a large part of the parched Southwest lay under water and ice.

In June of 1933, the foundation was finally ready, and the first of the wooden forms that would be used to lay concrete was being built. The concrete—sixty-six million tons of it—created one of the most vexing problems the engineers had faced, a problem peculiar to large dams. The dam's size and weight would generate superpressures and insulating mass that would both generate and retain heat. Though the dam would appear solid, it would be, in reality, a pyramid of warm pudding. Left to its own devices, Boulder Dam would require 100 years to cool down. Moreover, the cooling would be uneven, and the resultant shrinkage and warping would leave the structure fissured and cracked. After weeks of wondering what to do, the engineers finally agreed on a solution. As each form was poured, one-inch pipe would be laid through it at five-foot intervals; frigid water from a cooling plant would then be run through the pipes until convection cooling had lowered the temperature of the concrete to forty-three degrees near the base and seventy-two degrees near the crest. Since the amount of pipe required, if it had been laid out in a straight line, would have reached to Big Sur on the central California coast, this was no mean refrigeration plant. Converted to ice-making, it could have produced several million cubes a day. Instead, it reduced a century of cooling time to something like twenty months.

When visitors were led to the canyon rim to watch Boulder Dam on the rise, there was usually a long moment of silence, a moment when the visitors groped for something appropriate to say, something that expressed proper awe and reverence for the dazzling, half-formed monstrosity they saw. The dam defied description; it defied belief. Standing on the upstream side of it, two on each flank, were the intake towers, marvelous fluted concrete columns rising 395 feet from platforms that had been blasted halfway up the canyon walls. The towers were as high as forty-story buildings, and someone who had never been to New York or Chicago or Philadelphia would never have seen a man-made structure that high. But the crest of the dam rose nearly to the tops of the towers, and its foundation was *hundreds of feet* below their base. Its seamless curve swept across the canyon and imbedded itself in each side, a gigantic but somehow graceful intrusion. The men working on top were not even ants; they hardly qualified as fleas. Stretching overhead, from canyon rim to canyon rim, was a thick cable on which hung suspended a sixteen-ton bucket that lowered fresh concrete into the forms. Although it was big enough to accommodate a Buick, the bucket seemed incapable of ever filling the dimensions of Hoover Dam—the name it was ultimately to acquire. But twenty-four hours per day, 220 cubic yards an hour, it did. After two years of pouring, the dam was finally topped out. On March 23, 1935, it stood 726 feet and 5 inches tall.

When the engineers surveyed what they had built, it seemed impossible to believe that anything so immense could fail to hold back the Colorado River under every conceivable circumstance. Between 1907 and 1917, however, the wettest period on record, the river had discharged nearly enough water to fill the reservoir during several years: twenty-four million acre-feet; twelve million; twenty-five and a half million; fourteen million; twenty million; nineteen million; twenty million. Hidden within the figures were big floods, periods when the river flowed at 100,000 or 200,000 cubic feet per second for weeks in a row. If such a flood happened to hit when the reservoir was full, the full force of it would have to be spilled; the penstocks leading to the power plant would never be able to handle it. But 200,000 cfs sent over the top of the dam could erode it like a seawall in a storm. The dam, therefore, required spillways on either side, and to allow for the unforeseen and the incredible they were to be built to handle 400,000 cubic feet per second—nearly twice the Columbia River's flow. The spillway troughs were excavated on the canyon sides of the intake towers and led into the vast diversion tunnels hollowed through the walls. Like everything else about the dam, they were designed curvilinear and graceful, with immense brass drum gates shaped like diamond heads. Set down in a spillway channel, the *Bismarck* would have floated clear. Some of the project engineers wistfully suggested that turbines be installed at the spillway outlets, even if they operated only during floods. With the penstocks and the outlet works both generating power, the dam, during brief periods, could have electrified the state of California.

Nothing, however, was more astonishing than the speed with which all of it was built. As the nation languished in the Depression, as plant after plant remained idle and company after company went bankrupt, Hoover Dam was being built at a breathtaking pace. The eyes of the country were fixed on it in awe. A landmark event—the completion of a spillway, the installation of the last generator—was front-page news. The initial excavations for the diversion tunnels had begun on May 16, 1931. The river was not detoured from its channel until November, and the cofferdams were not completed until April of 1933. But two years later, all the blocks in the dam were raised to crest elevation, and a year later everything was finished: spillways, powerplant, penstocks, generators, galleries, even the commemorative plaque in the frieze alongside U.S. Highway 93, which ran across the top. The first electrical power, from what was then the largest power plant in the world, was produced in the fall of 1936. The greatest structure on earth, perhaps the most significant structure that has ever been built in the United States, had gone up in under three years.

The difference in climate between the eastern and western United States—the fact that the East generally gets enough rainfall to support agriculture, while the West generally does not—is easily the most significant distinction between those two regions. It is also obvious that there are significant distinctions within each region as well. For example, oranges grow well in central Florida; they do not in South Carolina, a few hundred miles north. The climate in Duluth, Minnesota, is quite different from that in Chicago, a mere day's drive away.

In the West, however, climatic differences far more striking than these may occur within the same state, even within the same county. In the Willamette Valley of Oregon, a farmer can raise a number of different crops without irrigation; there is usually a summer drought, but it is short, and even if he decides not to depend entirely on rainfall, a few inches of irrigation water—instead of the hundred inches used by some farmers in California and Arizona—will usually do. Two hours away, on the east side of the Cascades, rainfall drops to a third of what the Willamette Valley ordinarily receives; not only that, but the whole of eastern Oregon is much higher than the section west of the Cascades, and lacks a marine influence, so the climate is far colder as well. It can be forty above zero in Eugene and ten below zero in Bend, a two-hour drive to the east. In eastern Oregon, not only must a farmer irrigate but he is extraordinarily limited, compared to his Willamette Valley counterpart, in the types of crops he can grow.

Around Bakersfield, California, an irrigation farmer can raise the same crops that one sees growing in Libya, southern Italy, Hawaii, and Iraq: pistachios, kiwis, almonds, grapes, olives, melons, crops whose value per cultivated acre is astonishingly high. An hour's drive away, across the Tehachapi Mountains, lies the Antelope Valley, a high-desert region with a cold interior climate that can bring frost in May, and where little but alfalfa and grass can be grown. Both Bakersfield and the Antelope Valley are within Kern County, whose climatic extremes are rather typical of California, and, for that matter, of many counties throughout the West. Air conditioners and furnaces in two relatively nearby towns—Phoenix and Flagstaff—may be running at the same time; one end of a county may be plagued by floods while another is plagued by drought.

The reason for all this is mainly topographic: the mountains that block weather fronts and seal off the interior from the ocean's summer cooling and winter warmth (the prevailing westerly winds of the northern hemisphere give the ocean a much wider influence in the West than in the East, reaching as far away as Idaho); the tectonic upheavals that pushed much of the interior West, even the flat mountainless sections, to elevations higher than a mile. The significance of it, from the standpoint of water development, is that it makes infinitely greater economic sense to build dams and irrigate in warmer regions than in colder ones—even if it makes infinitely greater *political* sense to do otherwise.

When John Wesley Powell explored the American West, he duly noted these bewildering extremes of climate. Powell knew that irrigation was an expensive proposition, and that a few inches of extra rainfall or a couple of thousand feet of elevation difference would mean a project that was worth developing or, on the other hand, a project that would require heavy subsidization. A farmer raising fruit

137

or two annual crops of tomatoes in the Imperial Valley might earn ten times more per irrigated acre than a farmer raising alfalfa at six thousand feet in Colorado; yet it might cost far more to deliver water to the Colorado farmer because his water might have to be pumped uphill, out of deep river canyons, while the Imperial Valley lay near sea level below Hoover Dam. The Imperial Valley farmer could pay enough for water to allow the government to recoup its enormous investment in dams, canals, and other irrigation works; the Colorado farmer might be able to repay, at best, a dime on every dollar.

What Powell did not foresee, however, was the Colorado River Basin arbitrarily divided, with each half given an equal amount of water. To him, such a false partitioning might have seemed absurd, for it made far better sense to irrigate in the lower basin than in the upper. But he could not imagine that the blind ambition of the Bureau and the political power of the upper basin would join forces to try to pretend that a mile of elevation difference, and the staggering climatic difference such a disparity implies, did not exist.

Simply stated, the problem with most of the upper basin was that it was too high, too dry, and too cold. Land that was well suited to irrigation in a topographic sense—meaning that a river flowed through a wide valley with good soil which lay below a natural dam-site somewhere in the mountains above—often sat at altitudes above five thousand feet. Virtually the whole state of Wyoming, for example, lies at an altitude of six thousand feet or higher. Much of Colorado is over a mile high; most of Utah is over four thousand feet. In Cheyenne, Wyoming, the frost-free season is barely four months. In such a climate, one can grow only low-value crops—alfalfa, irrigated pasture, wheat—which require much acreage to produce a meager income. Not only that, but some such crops—irrigated pasture in particular—require a lot of water, up to three times more than some high-value crops: oranges, tomatoes, nuts, even lettuce.

In 1915, it made sense to build a few economically ill-advised projects in the interior West anyway, in order to reduce its abject reliance on imported food and offer some economic stability to the region. And, in fact, dozens of marginal projects were built in the Rocky Mountain and northern plains states during the first thirty years of Reclamation's reign. But it began to make less and less sense by 1945, after tens of billions of dollars had been invested in an efficient transportation system that forever ended the isolation of places like Cheyenne and helped bring them into the nation's economic mainstream. And it made even less sense by 1955, when the nation was burying itself under mountains of surplus crops—often the same crops (wheat, barley, corn) that had to be grown in the high, cold intermountain West.

What all of this meant—to the taxpayers, anyway—was that the overwhelming share of the cost of any so-called self-financing project in the upper Colorado Basin would end up being subsidized by them. The cost of the projects would be so great, the value of the crops so low, and the irrigators' ability to pay for water so pitiful that to demand that they repay the taxpayers' investment in forty years, even allowing for the exemption from interest payments, would be to lead them into certain bankruptcy. Some of the older, *better* projects had already had some of their repayment contracts deftly extended by several decades, and there was absolutely no evidence that they could be repaid even then. But, on the other hand, to imagine Congress booting farmers off Reclamation projects because they couldn't meet their payment obligations was unthinkable. The taxpayers would have to bail them out, even if bailing them out meant a long-term bill of billions and billions of dollars.

How well the Bureau's leadership understood this is a good question—although the secret correspondence in the Bureau's files reveals that they knew a lot more than they let on in public. (In the 1920s, Frederick Newell, the former Reclamation commissioner, was already decrying the "sentimentality" of the federal irrigation program, through which, he said, money was "deftly taken from the pockets" of the taxpayers.) What is *true*, of course, does not necessarily *matter* in a political sense, and that was particularly the case in the American West, and even more so in the upper basin. By the 1950s, California was already using its full 4.4 million acre-foot entitlement to the Colorado River and planning a second aqueduct to Los Angeles that would allow it to suck up 700,000 acre-feet of surplus flows. The Bureau, having built Hoover Dam mainly for California's benefit, was now embarking on the Central Valley Project, a project of absolutely breathtaking scope that was exclusively for California. As far as the upper basin was concerned, it was time for some equity. And equity was only the half of it. If there was surplus water in the river—water which the upper basin owned but wasn't yet able to use—and California began "borrowing" it, would that imperial-minded state deign to give it back? The imperative for the upper basin was to develop its share of the Colorado River as fast as possible, whether the projects that could be built there made sense or not. And it was the basin's unbelievably good fortune that in the 1940s, Congress would give it a money-making machine that would allow it to do so—a machine that became known as the cash register dam.

A cash register dam was to be a dam with an overriding, if not a single, purpose: to generate electricity for commercial sale. The electricity would bring in many millions of dollars in annual revenues which could be used to subsidize irrigation projects that hadn't a prayer of paying back the taxpayers' investment. The dams were an invention spawned by something the Bureau of Reclamation called river-basin "accounting," which was itself spawned by something it called river-basin "planning."

River-basin planning, at least, made a certain amount of sense. A river like the Arkansas, which rises in the Colorado Rockies and empties into the Mississippi in an utterly different time zone and topography and climate, invites competing and potentially incompatible uses. Upstream, it is valuable for irrigation; downstream, it is valuable for inland navigation. If the Bureau diverts too much water for upstream irrigation, there won't be enough water available downstream to justify the Army Corps of Engineers' efforts to turn the lower river into a freeway for barges—an obsession it has been pursuing on virtually every large river in the country. The dilemma could also work in reverse; if the Corps got a head start on the lower sections of a river, the Bureau could find itself unable to get any upriver projects authorized. The creation of the Tennessee Valley Authority marked the first time a major river system was "viewed whole," even if the natural river virtually disappeared as a result. The TVA was regarded as such a success by the administration of Franklin Roosevelt that it began to demand, if not more quasi-dictatorial authorities like the TVA, then at least a coordinated plan of development between the Bureau and the Corps. This was river-basin "planning," and, except for the fact that no one ever spent more than a minute or two thinking about the value of a river in its natural state, it made some degree of sense.

River-basin "accounting" was a horse of a different color, though the Bureau developed a propensity to use "planning" and "accounting" interchangeably. With river-basin accounting, one could take all the revenues generated by projects in any river basin—dams, irrigation projects, navigation and recreation features—and toss them into a common "fund." The hydroelectric dams might contribute ninety-five cents of every dollar accruing to the fund, while the irrigation features might contribute only a nickel (and cost three times as much to build and operate as the dams), but it wouldn't matter; as long as revenues came in at a pace that would permit the Reclamation Act's forty-year repayment schedule to be met, the whole package could be considered economically sound. It was as if a conglomerate purchased a dozen money-losing subsidiaries while operating a highly profitable silver mine—a case of horribly bad management which, nonetheless, still leaves the company barely in the black.

Michael Robinson, the Bureau's semiofficial historian, exhibits no compunction about admitting any of this in the Bureau's authorized history, *Water for the West:*

> By the late 1930s, the high cost of projects made it increasingly difficult for Reclamation engineers to meet economic feasibility requirements. In the early 1940s, the Bureau devised the plan of considering an entire river basin as an integrated project. It enabled the agency to derive income from various revenue-producing subfeatures (notably power facilities) to fund other works not economically feasible under Reclamation law.
>
> Thus, by offsetting construction and development costs against pooled revenues the Bureau was able to demonstrate the economic feasiblity for the entire, pooled program. In 1942 this method was used for the first time in planning a basinwide development program for the Bighorn River in Wyoming. All benefits and income from producing units were lumped together to establish overall feasibility. In 1944, the Bureau's "Sloan Plan" for the development of the Missouri River followed the same formula . . . [and] encouraged the Bureau to *enthusiastically prepare basinwide plans for several western rivers*. . . . [Emphasis added]

"Enthusiastically" is a bit of an understatement. The beauty of river-basin "accounting," from the Bureau's point of view, was that it would be literally *forced* to build dams. The engineering mentality which, Robinson himself admits, came to dominate the Bureau's thinking in the 1930s and 1940s created an institutional distaste for irrigation projects. They were a necesary nuisance that provided the rationale for what Bureau men really loved to do: build majestic dams. In the past, however, the infeasibility of many projects put a damper on their ambitions, because if a project didn't make economic sense, they lost the rationale they needed to build a dam to store water. With river-basin accounting, the equation was stood on its head: a lot of bad projects—economically infeasible ones—created a rationale for building *more*, not fewer, dams. The dams—all with hydroelectric features, of course—would be required to compensate for the financial losses of the irrigation projects; the losses would miraculously vanish in the common pool of revenues.

River-basin "accounting," then, was a perversion of a sensible idea—that idea being to plan the "orderly" (a favorite Bureau word) development of a river basin from headwaters to mouth. But even if it subverted logic, economics, and simple common sense, it was essential to the Bureau's survival as an institution and to the continued expansion of irrigation in the high, arid West. On the other hand, it was something akin to a blanket death sentence for the free-flowing rivers in sixteen states.

What the upper basin of the Colorado lacked, because of its elevation, in feasible irrigation projects it more than made up—for the same reason—in sites for cash register dams. High and mountainous, geologically young, the basin had deep valleys and tight plunging gorges ideal for dams—gorges in which ran rivers that fed the main Colorado and could be included, under the bizarre new logic of river-basin accounting, in any grand basinwide scheme. The rivers, draining arid and semiarid regions, may not have held much runoff, but a very high dam on a small river can yield as much hydroelectricity as a low dam on a much larger one; that is the beauty of what dam engineers call hydrologic head: velocity of falling water does the work of volume, of mass. There was Glen Canyon on the main-stem Colorado, Powell's favorite riverine haunt, an ideal site for a seven-hundred-foot dam. There was Flaming Gorge on the Green, and Red Canyon— each a perfect site for a gigantic curved-arch, thin-wall dam approaching Hoover in size. There was the Black Canyon of the Gunnison, an almost sheer thousand-foot gorge with several sites for high dams. The Dolores, the Yampa, the White, even smaller streams like the Animas and San Miguel and Little Snake—each had at least one site for a cash register dam. Since the dams would have to be large compared to the meager river flows, they would be expensive to build. But that wouldn't matter; the Bureau had the Treasury at its disposal.

All the upper basin needed, then, was Congressional clout—that, and a Reclamation Commissioner who believed in dams for dams' sake. And it was the upper basin's further good fortune that, near the end of his third term, Franklin Roosevelt would appoint such a man as his Commissioner of Reclamation. His name was Michael Straus.

Mike Straus was the unlikeliest commissioner the Bureau ever had. For one thing, he was an easterner; for another, he was a newspaperman. On top of that, he was rich. By temperament, Straus was an exact opposite of the slide-rule engineers who had guided the Bureau during its forty-odd years. He was an anomaly down to his very genes. Straus had married into the Dodge family, and his brother-in-law was Eliot Porter; he had wealth and social connections, too. While typical Bureau of Reclamation families spent their vacations on houseboats cruising the reservoirs that Daddy built, Straus went to the family retreat at Spruce Head Island, on Maine's Penobscot Bay. It was their island—all of it. Straus could have spent his life clipping coupons, safari hunting, or writing the hyperventilating prose that was his second love. But there was nothing on earth that gave Mike Straus quite as much boyish, exuberant satisfaction as erecting dams. In eight years as Commissioner of Reclamation, he would become responsible for as many water projects as any person who ever lived.

Straus had been selected at the close of the war by Harold Ickes, himself a newspaperman, after the Roosevelt administration had endured twelve years of relatively plodding Bureau leadership under Elwood Mead, Harry Bashore, and John Page. Straus was Ickes's alter ego—a newspaperman, a liberal, a fighter, a curmudgeon. Franklin Roosevelt, who equated wealth with energy and idealism, heartily endorsed the appointment. It was a brilliant stoke. For all his man-of-the-people reputation, FDR felt paranoia about the common man. His secret fear was that the Depression would begin anew after the war, and the returning veterans would be unable to find jobs; ultimately, they might revolt. In the Bureau of Reclamation, FDR had a vast job-creating engine, an agency that remade the western landscape into a place where the dispossessed could go. In Mike Straus, he had a commissioner who would stoke the engine until the rivets began to pop.

Like a lot of people who inherit or marry wealth, Straus viewed money abstractly. A million was a number, budgets were a nuisance, feasibility reports were a waste of time. And, having abandoned a career that asked for a constant objective adherence to facts, he soon acquired an easygoing way with the truth. "Facts," said one of his successors as commissioner, Floyd Dominy, "didn't mean a goddamned thing to him."

Straus was a spectacle. He was shambling, big as a bear, a terrible dresser, and a slob. "The characteristic Mike Straus pose," remembered Dominy, "was for him to plant his feet on his desk, almost in your face, and lean back in his swivel chair flipping cigarette ashes all over his shirt. At the end of the day, there was a little mound of ash behind his seat. He was an uncouth bastard! He carried one white shirt with him on trips. I remember one night when Reclamation was throwing a party, and a cub reporter came by and asked me where to find Mike Straus. I just said, 'Go upstairs and look for the guy who reminds you of an unmade bed.' "

There was something else about Mike Straus: his arrogance. Once, in the very early 1950s, he got on a plane without reconfirming his reservation, which one was required to do in those days. The plane turned out to be overbooked, and since Straus had not reconfirmed, he was the one who was supposed to be bumped. The flight attendants invited him off the plane, but Straus refused to budge; he pretended not to hear. As a whole plane full of passengers cursed him under their breaths, Mike Straus sat there like a pig in goo. Finally, the captain had to ask for volunteers to bump themselves so that the plane could take off. There weren't a lot of flights in the early 1950s, and the passengers would have to wait a long time for another one. But Straus appeared unmoved; he wasn't even embarrassed. "It didn't faze Mike a bit," said a Reclamation man who was with him. "He thought he was performing the greatest work in the country, and he felt like the holiest bureaucrat in the land."

Cavalier, arrogant, mendacious, and whatever else he was, Mike Straus was also an idealist. A good stalwart liberal in the New Deal tradition, he believed in bringing the fruits of technology to the common man. He bore a ferocious grudge against the private utilities of the West, who denied reasonably priced power (or power at all) to rural areas struggling against adversity on every side, and who bought space in magazines and (he was convinced) bribed reporters to rail against the Bureau's public-power dams. Straus also made some tentative efforts to crack down on the big California growers who were setting up dummy corporations and trusts in order to farm tens of thousands of acres illegally with subsidized Bureau of Reclamation water. In so doing, he infuriated the growers' and the utilities' friends in Congress, and a group of them finally decided to get rid of him. Since Straus served at the President's whim and had Harry Truman's blessing, it was useless to demand he be fired, so the politicians tried another tack. In 1949, they pinned an obscure rider onto the public-works appropriations bill that specifically withheld the salaries of Michael Straus and his regional director in California, Richard Boke.

The independently wealthy Straus remained as commissioner—without pay. His enemies were upset, and that is putting it mildly. "Straus made them so mad I thought they might put out a contract on his life," says Floyd Dominy. "I have done what no good Republican has been able to do," Straus wrote to his friend Bill Warne, a former assistant commissioner then in Iran, "and that is to unite the Republican party on at least one platform and provide them with one program—to wit, who can fire Straus first."

However, as the big growers in California and the private western utilities were trying to get rid of Mike Straus, the upper basin was cultivating him just as assiduously. The population of the basin had grown substantially since the Colorado River Compact was signed, but the growth of irrigated agriculture had remained well behind. Most irrigation was by simple diversion, without benefit of reservoir storage. During droughts, the farmers were flirting with disaster; during floods, they watched millions of acre-feet escape to the lower basin unused. The farmers on the other side of the Front Range, on the perfectly flat expanse of the plains, had topography working for them; they could easily lead a diversion channel out of a river such as the Platte, fill a small offstream basin, and have a ready-made storage reservoir for a fraction of the cost of an on-stream dam. The West Slope farmers—those sitting in the Colorado River drainage— were at a terrific natural disadvantage, having no way to store their water and (in the case of some) being at a higher elevation besides. Meanwhile, California was now using up its entire entitlement and still growing by leaps and bounds. If the upper basin didn't hurry and begin using its own entitlement, California seemed certain to try to "borrow" it; if it succeeded, and millions of people then depended on that water, how would the upper basin ever get it back? But how, on the other hand, were Colorado, Utah, and Wyoming ever to use their share of the river if they couldn't afford to build dams themselves and if high-altitude Reclamation projects could never pay themselves back?

The answer, frantically conceived by Mike Straus's Bureau during the last days of his reign—much of it was laid out in the weeks after Eisenhower, who was certain to fire Straus, was already President-elect—was the Colorado River Storage Project. Behind the innocuous name was something as big as the universe itself. In a press release that accompanied the legislation's transmittal to Congress in early 1953—days before Ike's inauguration—Straus described it rather modestly as "a series of ten dams having a storage capacity of 48.5

million acre-feet." What he failed to mention was that 48.5 million acre-feet was more than all the existing reservoirs on the main-stem Colorado and all the tributaries could hold—more than the combined capacity of Lake Havasu, Theodore Roosevelt Lake, Apache Lake, Bartlett Reservoir, San Carlos Reservoir, Painted Rock Reservoir, plus the then largest reservoir on earth, Lake Mead. The ten dams would, according to Straus, capture "several times the total annual flow of the river." In fact, with the lower basin reservoirs already holding close to forty million acre-feet, between *five* and *eight* times the long-term annual flow of the river would be captured, depending on whose estimate you believed—a storage-to-yield ratio that was not approached by any other river in the world, no matter how used. The annual evaporation from all these huge, exposed bodies of water, languishing under the desert sun, would itself exceed the storage capacity of any existing reservoir except 28 million acre-foot Lake Mead.

It wasn't, however, the mere magnitude of the project that set it apart. What set it apart was the way irrigation and power production were linked. The earliest projects were designed exclusively as irrigation projects; if any power was incidentally generated, it was sold to project farmers at bargain rates. With Hoover Dam, the Bureau took a big plunge into public power; nearly two-thirds of its hydroelectricity went to light Los Angeles. However, when Los Angeleans paid their power bills, they weren't subsidizing the farmers in the Imperial and Coachella valleys who were irrigating with Lake Mead water; they were merely paying back the cost of the dam.

The Colorado River Storage Project would be utterly and fatefully different. Anyone who bought electricity at market rates from the dams—and 1,622,000 megawatts, an enormous amount at that time, was planned—would be subsidizing irrigation in the upper basin. *Eighty-five cents* of every dollar spent on irrigation features would be subsidized by power revenues. Every time they flicked a switch, electricity consumers in the region would be helping a farmer plant alfalfa at six thousand feet to feed a national surplus of beef.

The Bureau was strikingly candid about the dismal economics of irrigation in the upper basin. "The [upper basin] farmers can't pay a dime, not one dime," lamented the Bureau's chief of hydrology, C. B. Jacobsen, to a Congressional committee. And as if to demonstrate how far Congress had come in accepting the subsidization of an entire region, Jacobsen's words fell on sympathetic ears. Western members, even those whose districts were well outside the basin, lined up to support the bill—perhaps because they expected their own uneconomical projects to be supported in return. For the first time, a majority of eastern members seemed indifferent, neutral, or even sympathetic—perhaps because *they* had Corps of Engineers projects they wanted built which might require the western members' support. Even the Eisenhower administration decided to give the Colorado River Storage Project lukewarm support, though it violated every conservative principle Ike had ever espoused.

The most effective opposition, by far, came from Paul Douglas, the urbane Senator from Illinois, who, ironically, had played a pivotal role in the creation of the New Deal. When World War II broke out, Douglas was fifty years old, a former economics professor at the University of Chicago who had become a reform-minded Chicago alderman. He promptly enlisted in the Marines, talked himself out of a desk job, and got to the front lines of the Pacific theater. He was gravely wounded at Peleliu and again at Okinawa, and was lucky to return alive. Elected to the Senate after the war, Douglas brought all of his determination and iconoclastic, brilliant thinking to Washington with him. He was—perhaps because of his economics background—the first architect of the New Deal who seemed to sense that something had gone drastically wrong. And the worst perversion of the New Deal ideas that *he*, at least, had in mind was the Reclamation program, subsidizing high-altitude desert farmers so they could grow the same crops some of Douglas's farmer constituents were being paid *not* to grow—so serious had America's crop-surplus problem become now that Europe was back in production again.

In a series of memorable debates on the Senate floor, Douglas, tall, athletic, and white-haired, went after the Colorado River Storage Project hammer and tongs. At Glen Canyon Dam, he told his colleagues, the cost of hydroelectricity per kilowatt would be $463; at Echo Park Dam, it was over $600; at Central Utah, it was $765; at Flaming Gorge, it was more than $700. "Let us compare that cost with the average cost in the Tennessee Valley of $166 per kilowatt of capacity. At Bonneville, the average cost was only $115. At Hoover, the cost was only $112. At Grand Coulee, the cost was only $90. . . . [I]t is extraordinary that an administration which has declared public power to be creeping socialism, which has put the lid on additional dams on the Columbia, should go up into the mountains of Colorado and there locate public power projects where the cost will be three, four, or five times what they would be at these other locations. . . . I am not saying that the administration wishes to have this project

147

fail. But I will say that if the administration had wished to discredit the public power system, it could not have proceeded in any better fashion than it has done in this instance." And he couldn't help noticing, said Douglas sarcastically, that certain Senators who opposed public power in the Tennessee Valley and the Columbia Basin had suddenly emerged as great champions of public power when it was to come from cash register dams in the mountains of Colorado.

The power features, however, were, as Douglas knew, not the worst aspect of the storage project, but the best. The worst, by far, was the irrigation. "The original projects," he lectured his colleagues, "tended to be at low altitudes and in fertile soil, and to involve low costs. . . . Now we are being asked to irrigate land in the uplands, at altitudes between five thousand and seven thousand feet, where the growing season is short and the chief products will be hay, corn, livestock, and alfalfa. . . . There exists an interesting tendency for Senators in those States to congregate on the Committee on Interior and Insular Affairs and the Committee on Appropriations, which consider irrigation and reclamation bills. There is a sort of affinity, just as sugar draws flies." For the benefit of his colleagues and the Bureau, whose economists had labored mightily to put the CRSP in the best possible light, Douglas had sat down and figured out the per-acre costs of the various projects himself. The Silt River Project in Colorado, for example, would cost $674 per acre; the Paonia project, $873 per acre; the Central Utah Project, the most expensive of the lot, $1,757. If one calculated interest, Paonia would go up to $2,135 per acre, Central Utah to $3,953 per acre. These were the mid-1950s, when land prices in the West were still dirt-cheap. Most of the land whose conversion to irrigation would cost thousands of dollars an acre was not worth more than $50 an acre, and that, in many cases, was being generous. "In my state of Illinois," Douglas pointed out, "the price of the most fertile natural land in the world is now between $600 and $700 per acre. In the largest project of all, the Central Utah Project, the cost would be nearly $4,000 an acre—six times the cost of the most fertile land in the world."

If an investment of $2,000 an acre could create reclaimed land worth $2,000 an acre, that would be one thing. But even after being supplied with irrigation water, the upper-basin lands would be worth nowhere near that. "What is to be grown on the land?" asked Douglas. "Of the sixteen projects reported, eight of them were stated as being suitable for livestock only, through the raising of alfalfa and pasture.

Seven were stated as being primarily for livestock, but with some fruit and vegetable production . . . 95 percent of the projects contemplate the production of alfalfa or grain or are directly or indirectly for the feeding of cattle. As a consequence, this land, *after irrigation*, will not be worth very much, probably not more than from $100 to $150 per acre—$150 per acre at the outside. Yet we are being asked to make an average expenditure of $2,000 an acre on land which, when the projects are finished, will sell for only $150 an acre."

Douglas's western colleagues, of course, had no answer to this; his math was correct, his reasoning impeccable. All they could do was stand the rhetoric of their nineteenth-century predecessors on its head; instead of praising the fertile soil and glorious climate of the West, they talked about how miserable and uninhabitable their home states were. "The Senator from Illinois has correctly stated that we have little rain," said Joseph O'Mahoney of Wyoming. "I say to him, 'Pity us. Let us store the rainwater which for thousands of years has been rolling down the Colorado River without use. Please have some pity on the area, which is the arid land area of the country. It wants to conserve the great natural supply of water which the Almighty placed there, for man to use, if he has the intelligence and the courage to use it.' "

All of Paul Douglas's eloquence and logic, as it turned out, were a poor match for appeals such as O'Mahoney's and the growing Congressional power of the arid West. O'Mahoney and Clinton Anderson of New Mexico, representing Colorado Basin states, were powerhouses on the Senate Interior Committee; Carl Hayden of Arizona ruled Appropriations; Wayne Aspinall of western Colorado was the ascendant power at the House Interior Committee. The Colorado River Storage Project also enjoyed overwhelming public support, not just among the western farmers, but among their city brethren, too; conservatives, liberals, Democrats, Republicans—ideology meant nothing where water was concerned. The only serious public opposition came from southern California (which was expected) and from conservationists, who were horrified at the prospect of watching three of the most magnificent river canyons in the West filled by giant, drawn-down reservoirs: Glen Canyon on the main Colorado and Flaming Gorge and Echo Park on the Green. Each of these reservoirs would be as long as smaller eastern states; Glen Canyon would stretch back for nearly two hundred miles behind the dam, not even counting tentacles of water that would reach up side canyons and tributary streams. But in those days conservationists didn't count for much. The Sierra Club had just one full-time person, whose name was David Brower, on its paid staff.

The outcome was foreordained. California had gotten Hoover Dam, Parker Dam, Davis Dam, the Imperial and Coachella projects, and water and power for Los Angeles. Now the upper basin would get its share. After minimal debate on the floor, the CRSP bill passed both Houses and was signed into law by Eisenhower in April of 1956. The estimated cost of everything was around $1.6 billion, but it would, of course, be substantially more. Never in U.S. history had so little economic development been proposed at such an exorbitant public cost, for all the billions were buying, besides extremely expensive public power, were a few patches of new irrigated lands whose composite size was smaller than Rhode Island. The subsidies, it turned out later, would be worth as much as $2 million per farm, perhaps five times as much as the farms themselves were worth. But even if the Colorado River Storage Project seemed like utter folly, the Bureau of Reclamation and its sometime collaborator and rival, the Army Corps of Engineers, were on a binge.

CHAPTER FIVE

The Go-Go Years

The U.S. economy had fallen flat on its face several times before. In the years after the Great Crash, however, it could not pick itself back up. Things were worse in 1930 than in 1929, worse in 1931 than in 1930. By 1932, millions of people had lost all faith and hope—in the nation, in the capitalist system, in themselves.

The person whom Americans elected to pull the country out of the abyss came across as a genial aristocrat; in some ways, though, he was as close to being a benevolent despot as a democracy can allow. Franklin Roosevelt's own Treasury Secretary, Henry Morgenthau, said that the President never saw himself as "anything else but a ruler." Carl Jung met him and came away saying, "Make no mistake, he is a force—a man of superior but impenetrable mind, but perfectly ruthless, a highly versatile mind which you cannot see." But the President, a man of greater charm and persuasiveness than ruthlessness, was adored by most of the country no matter what he did. Had Gerald Ford or Lyndon Johnson tried to pack the Supreme Court, they probably would have been impeached; when Roosevelt tried it, nearly half the country thought it was a good idea. After seeing Roosevelt in action, Republicans who had voted for Hoover prayed to God to forgive them. Even God must have felt humbled by the new President; in a popularity contest conducted among New York City schoolchildren, Roosevelt outpolled Him.

Franklin Roosevelt said that he wanted to be remembered as the greatest conservationist and the greatest developer of all time. In a country with a population barely greater than Germany's and with fifteen times the landmass, it seemed possible to be both. FDR's conservation was not scientific, as his cousin Teddy's was to a great degree, but instinctive. At Hyde Park, he had spent afternoons planting thousands of little trees. Why not plant millions of them on the high plains to break the wind and conserve the soil? A lot of scientists laughed and said it would never work, but it did. FDR thought up the Civilian Conservation Corps, too, and it became the most popular of all his programs.

What TR and FDR did have in common was an acute awareness of the limits of capitalism. The former Roosevelt saw the seeds of capitalism's self-destruction in monopoly and rapacious business practice; the latter saw them in chronic depression and unemployment. In 1933, when he assumed the Presidency, nearly a quarter of the U.S. population was without visible means of support. Declaring a bank holiday was one way to arrest the widespread financial panic that was costing millions of workers their jobs, but the only thing that would make a real dent in the horrifying unemployment figures was to build public works: bridges, highways, tunnels, parks—dams.

The person whom Roosevelt put in charge of much of the apparatus of recovery was Harold Ickes, a stolid, round, owlish, combative ex-newspaperman who grew to love his nickname, "the old curmudgeon." (Because of Ickes's high-pitched squawk of a voice, Roosevelt, in private, called him Donald Duck.) Ickes ran not only the Interior Department—in which were the Bureau of Reclamation, the Civilian Conservation Corps, the National Park Service, and the Fish and Wildlife Service—but the Public Works Administration as well. The PWA was a catch basin of programs with a chameleon identity (it was also known as the Civil Works Administration and the Works Progress Administration) and interchangeable leaders (first Harry Hopkins, then Ickes, then Hopkins again). In a few years, it had overseen the building of the Lincoln Tunnel, the Washington Zoo, the Triborough Bridge, Fort Knox, Denver's water-supply system, a deepwater port at Brownsville, Texas, the huge Camarillo Hospital in southern California, and the causeway to Key West. It built a dozen fantasyland bridges along Oregon's coast highway. Above all, it built dams.

Under Roosevelt and Ickes, the Bureau of Reclamation underwent some fundamental changes, the most obvious of which was in size. From two or three thousand employees under Herbert Hoover— a very large federal agency in its day—the Bureau mushroomed into an elephantine bureacracy with a staff of nearly twenty thousand by the time Roosevelt died. Headquarters was the top floor of the gigantic new Interior building in Washington—the Bureau's offices were above those of the Interior Secretary himself—but the real work was done out of the Bureau's sprawling engineering complex in west Denver, where it designed its mighty dams. Then there were regional offices, field offices, project offices. When Jim Casey, who was to become deputy chief of planning in the 1960s, first went to work for the Bureau in Nebraska, he found himself amid nine hundred fellow employees. "This wasn't even a regional office," remembers Casey. "This was just a field office. I never had the faintest idea what everyone did, and neither did they." And very few of the Bureau's people had anything to do with the actual physical construction of the dams; that work was contracted out to the engineering firms, the Bechtels and Morrison-Knudsens, that had become instant giants after cutting their teeth on Hoover Dam. The Bureau's nineteen thousand–odd employees merely planned projects, supervised projects, and looked for new projects to build.

There were also some fundamental changes in the Bureau's approach, in its character. In the beginning, FDR was content to let it be run, as it had been in the past, by engineers. Elwood Mead, who, after John Wesley Powell, was the most illustrious reclamationist in America, headed the agency until his death in 1936. He was succeeded by John C. Page and Harry Bashore, engineers who had come up through the ranks. As commissioners, Mead, Page, and Bashore, remembering Congress's exasperation over the Bureau's early failures and cognizant that the nexus of power still lay east of the Mississippi River, tended to be somewhat modest in their ambitions. And if they lapsed from time to time, Ickes, at least in the beginning, was prepared to restrain them himself. "Commissioner Mead, of course, is always in favor of any new reclamation project," he wrote in a sarcastic memo to Roosevelt bemoaning a Bureau proposal. "That is his job." As the economics of reclamation played themselves out, however, and the salvation of the program lay in the construction of big public-power dams—which most of the electric utilities and much of the Republican Party regarded as anathema—the role of the commissioner abruptly changed. In the new reclamation era, a commissioner needed to be someone very much like Ickes: a fighter, a public-power ideologue, and, above all, a salesman. There was no better candidate than Ickes's close friend, fellow newspaperman, and faithful subordinate, Mike Straus.

153

Public relations and salesmanship, skills few engineers possess, were second nature to Mike Straus. "Born with a gold-plated irrigation shovel ready to be placed in her hands," reads a Straus press release dated June 5, 1952, "Reclamation's Golden Jubilee baby arrived at Washington's Yakima Memorial Hospital at 12:45 today, the daughter of Mr. and Mrs. Donald T. Dunn of Moses Lake, Washington. . . . The baby was born on the eve of the fiftieth anniversary of federal Reclamation, and the child has been adopted by the National Reclamation Association. . . .

"Michael W. Straus, Commissioner of the Bureau of Reclamation, declared in a congratulatory message that 'the Reclamation program must be pushed forward with utmost speed so the Dunn child and all the other kiddies born this year will have a happier and more secure life on the land through Reclamation development. . . . We should be starting today on [new] development so that there will be a Reclamation farm ready for baby Dunn.' "

Whether the cost of supplying water to baby Dunn's ex-desert was utterly beyond reason; whether she even wanted to spend her life on an irrigation farm; whether the country, already suffocating under mountainous farm surpluses by 1952, really needed her production—these were the kinds of questions which the Bureau, after eight years of Mike Straus, would rarely ask again.

To Mike Straus, millionaire dam builder, economic feasibility mattered little, if at all. Once, on a visit to the Bureau's regional office in Billings, Montana, Straus rented the town's only theater and demanded that all the employees show up in the evening for a "pep talk." The Billings office was in charge of the upper Missouri Basin, where the greatest concentration of physically possible but economically unfeasible projects happened to be located. When the employees had filed in and taken their seats, Straus slouched against a lectern on the stage and launched into a tirade against them for doing their jobs. "I don't give a damn whether a project is feasible or not," he thundered at his astonished staff. "I'm getting the money out of Congress, and you'd damn well better spend it. And you'd better be here early tomorrow morning ready to spend it, or you may find someone else at your desk!"

The Great Depression and the Roosevelt administration, together with the pyramid-scheme economics of the river-basin accounts, were more than enough to launch the federal dam-building program on a forty-year binge. It probably wouldn't have needed the Dust Bowl—but it helped.

Since the blizzards and drought of the 1880s and 1890s, the farmers of the western plains had been playing a game of "Mother May I?" with nature. When the isohyet of twenty inches of rainfall maundered westward, they advanced. When it moved eastward, they retreated— some of them, anyway. Through most of the first three decades of the twentieth century, the line stayed close to the lee side of the Rockies. The teens and 1920s, in particular, were years of extraordinary and consistent rainfall. Millions and millions of acres of shortgrass prairie west of the hundredth meridian, land already depauperated by live- stock overgrazing during the last century, were converted to the pro- duction of wheat, whose price had reached record levels during the war. "Everything in the country was going full blast," wrote Paul Sears in his book *Deserts on the March*. "It was the most natural thing in the world for the plains farmers, whose cattle business had pros- pered during the war and who had been encouraged to try dry farm- ing, to attempt the growing of wheat on a huge scale. The soil was loose and friable; the land was theirs to use as they saw fit." Even in the wettest years of the 1920s, the high-plains wheat rarely grew taller than someone's knee; sometimes it was ankle-high, and during a dry year it wouldn't come up at all. Everyone knew the wet years wouldn't last, and everyone knew that the loose soil, with the wheat stubble disked under, had nothing to hold it if drought and wind should coincide. But everyone was making money.

The first of the storms blew through South Dakota on Armistice Day, November 11, 1933. By nightfall, some farms had lost nearly all their topsoil. "Nightfall" was a relative term, because at ten o'clock the next morning the sky was still pitch-black. People were vomiting dirt. Machinery, fences, roads, shrubs, sheds—everything was cov- ered by great hanging drifts of silt. "Wives packed every windowsill, door frame, and keyhole with oiled cloth and gummed paper," Wil- liam Manchester wrote, "yet the fine silt found its way in and lay in beach-like ripples on their floors." As a gallon jug of desert floodwater, after settling, contains a quart and a half of solid mud, the sky seemed to be one part dust to three parts air. A naked human tethered outside would have been rendered skinless—such was the scouring power of the dirt-laden gales. Huge numbers of jackrabbits, unable to close their eyes, went blind. That was a blessing. It gave the human victims something to eat.

The storms, dozens of them, continued through the spring and summer of 1934. An old physician in southwestern Nebraska wrote

155

in his diary, "Wind forty miles an hour and hot as hell. Two Kansas farms go by every minute." With the temperature up to 105 degrees and the horizon lined with roiling clouds that seemed to promise ten inches of rain but delivered three feet of dirt, the plains took on a phantasmagorical dreadfulness. The ravenous storms would blow for days at a time, eating the land in their path, lifting dust and dirt high enough to catch the jet stream, which carried it to Europe. In 1934, members of Congress took time out from debating the Taylor Grazing Bill—designed to control overgrazing on the public lands—to crowd the Capitol balcony and watch the sky darken at noon. From the look of the western horizon, half the continent could have been on fire. The Taylor Act was passed in that year, despite efforts by some western members to weaken it even as their states were sailing over their heads. Between storms, when visibility sometimes increased to five or six miles, people in the Oklahoma and Texas panhandles, in Kiowa and Crowley counties in Colorado, in Texas's Gaines County on the New Mexico border, in 756 counties in nineteen states that were ultimately affected, watched their world turn into the Sahara.

The Dust Bowl was triggered by the same fatal congelation of hope and drought that caused the plains to empty half a century earlier. The longest severe drought in the nation's history—the one that Bureau of Reclamation planners, ever optimistic, now use as their "worst-case scenario"—began to descend over the West in 1928. For seven years in a row, precipitation remained below normal. The snow that fell on the plowed-up fields of the Dakotas was so light that the ground, bereft of insulation, froze many feet down; the snow evaporated without penetrating and the spring rains, those that came, slid off the frozen ground into the rivers, leaving the land bare. The virgin prairie, grazed well within its carrying capacity by thirty million buffalo, could probably have withstood the wind and drought; ravaged by too many cattle and plowed up to make way for wheat, it could not. If not the worst man-made catastrophe in history, it was, at least, the quickest.

By 1934, the National Resources Board reported that thirty-five million acres—Virginia and then some—had been essentially destroyed; 125 million acres—an area equivalent to Virginia plus Ohio plus Pennsylvania plus Michigan plus Maryland—were severely debilitated, and another hundred million acres were in marginal shape. "We're through," wrote a wheat baron from the shortgrass territory. "It's worse than the papers say. Our fences are buried, the house hidden to the eaves, and our pasture, which was kept from blowing by the grass, has been buried and is worthless now. We see what a mistake it was to plow up all that land, but it's too late to do anything about it." In the wake of the Dust Bowl, the short-term prospect was bankruptcy; the long-term prospect was the migration of three-quarters of a million itinerant paupers to California, Washington, and Oregon.

As the grizzled Okies advanced on California in their ancient LaSalles, Dodges, and Model T's, mattresses and washbasins strapped to the rooftops, they seemed to represent, as Arthur Schlesinger, Jr., wrote, "the threat of social revolution by a rabble of crazed bankrupts and paupers—a horrid upheaval from below . . . which could only end in driving all wealth and respectability from the state." Since the population of Hall County, Texas, to cite one example, had dropped from forty thousand to one thousand, and the states of North and South Dakota lost at least 146,000 people, the laws of probability demanded that there had to be at least a grain of respectability in the human tide—mayors and preachers were migrating along with toothless dirt farmers and petty thieves—but to those who were being invaded, the Okies were an appalling mob. They had to be settled somewhere; anywhere but here.

One of the more promising places to settle them was the Central Valley of California—more specifically, in the arid and morosely bleak southern two-thirds known as the San Joaquin Valley. The irrigation of the San Joaquin Valley—60 percent of all the prime farmland in a state made up mostly of mountains and high desert—had been an unrequited obsession with California for half a century. By the late 1800s, a few parts of it had been privately reclaimed by farmers and irrigation districts rich enough to build small dams, but most of the valley was a vista of wild blond grassland and wheat. Then came cheap oil, electricity, and the motorized centrifugal pump. Finally freed from all constraints but nature's (irrigation could last only as long as the finite aquifer held out), the farmers began pumping in the finest California tradition—which is to say, as if tomorrow would never come.

By 1930, a million and a half acres were under irrigation in the San Joaquin Valley, and a subterranean thicket of 23,500 well pipes had sucked up so much groundwater that the prognosis for irrigation was terminal within thirty to forty years. In some places, the water table dropped nearly three hundred feet. It was a predicament of their own making, but the farmers were not about to blame themselves; guilt-free life-styles took root in the San Joaquin Valley long before Marin County became a trendsetter. Having exhausted a hundred centuries' worth of groundwater in a generation and a half, they did what any pressure group usually does: run to the politicians they ordinarily despise and beg relief.

Thanks to the stunning wealth irrigation farming had produced, California came rolling out of the 1920s like Jay Gatsby in his alabaster phaeton. Agriculture *was* California; there was no defense and aerospace industry, there was no Silicon Valley. To give all of this up was unthinkable, even if it was the middle of the Depression. The rescue project which the legislature approved in 1933 not only was bold, it was almost unimaginable. If built, it would be by far the biggest water project in history. It would capture the flows not just of the San Joaquin River, which drained the southern half of the Sierra Nevada, but of the Sacramento, which drained the northern half and some of the Coast Range. It was planned to capture two-thirds of the runoff of the nation's second-largest state, and would move water through thousands of miles of canals and relocate rivers, quite literally, from one end of the state to the other. In normal times, California might even have had the means to begin building it. But this was the Depression, and California, rich as it was, still had to go to the New York bond markets for cash. The voters had no sooner approved a $170 million bond issue (a colossal sum considering the time and circumstances) than the bottom fell out of the market. No sooner had that happened, however, than Franklin Roosevelt landed in the White House.

On FDR's orders, the Bureau of Reclamation officially took over the Central Valley Project in December of 1935. By then the Great Plains had dissolved into the Dust Bowl and the first hundreds of thousands of Okies were rattling into California. In the face of such destitution and calamity, the dams going up were a thrilling sight. The grandest of them was rising in a wild madrone and digger pine canyon on the upper Sacramento River; 602 feet high, it would top out 124 feet lower than Hoover, but it would be half again as wide, an immense, curvilinear, gravity-arch curtain of concrete whose name would be Shasta. On the San Joaquin River, a big squat dam called Friant was being built at the same time; a third huge earth-and-rock structure would be erected later on the Trinity River, shoveling water from the Klamath drainage to the Sacramento. All together, the dams would give the project an annual yield of more than six million acre-feet of water, enough to irrigate a million and a half, two million, perhaps three million acres—depending on how much was supplemental irrigation for existing farms and how much was new land. But all of this effort would create, at most, jobs and farms for 100,000 displaced people. (Most of the refugees would actually become migrant workers—wetbacks with Oklahoma accents and white skin.) The biggest public-works project in the world, in other words, was not nearly big enough to soak up the huge tide of the dispossessed. FDR knew that, and that was why he had announced, before the Central Valley Project was even officially underway, "in definite and certain terms, that the next great . . . development to be undertaken by the Federal Government must be that on the Columbia River."

Daughter of ice, orphan of fire, the Columbia River emerged sometime within the relatively recent past, say twenty million years ago, and for most of its ancestral existence followed a course straight westward toward Seattle and Puget Sound. Seattle, of course, was not there when the Columbia first rose. Neither was Puget Sound. Neither was Washington. Most of what we call the Pacific Northwest is accreted terrain—a landmass of exotic origin that migrated up from somewhere around the Equator, riding the Pacific Plate, and glommed on. When the Pacific and North American plates began to collide millions of years ago, the Pacific plate was at first subducted into North America's basement. Down there, it encountered the large fraction of the planet that is still molten, and began to crowd it. The lava had nowhere to go but up.

To geologists, the age of the Columbia River Basalts was a particularly exciting time. The vulcanism lasted ten million years or so, and covered a broad area. You can see the evidence in the cindered lava beds of Idaho and eastern Oregon, in the columnar basalts of Devil's Postpile in the Sierra Nevada, in the smoking cones of the Cascades. The Cascade volcanoes, which formed recently—Mount St. Helens is probably no more than fifteen thousand years old—are the last embers of a giant bonfire which began to end, according to the available evidence, about seven million years ago. By then, the Pacific and North American plates had begun to equalize, grinding against each other like teeth and causing a chaos of earthquakes and volcanos beyond anything imaginable in our time. The Columbia River flowed during the whole period of eruption; constantly smothered by lava dams, it must have changed course hundreds of times. As the vulcanism subsided, the river began to enjoy the first quietude of its long existence, which lasted several million years—until the ice came.

The continents of snow that slid down from the North Pole during the Ice Ages stopped somewhere along a latitudinal line defined by Seattle, Spokane, and Great Falls, Montana. Where the topographic conditions were right, however, some of them went farther, huge peninsulas of ice that protruded a hundred or two hundred miles south. Near the present location of Lake Coeur d'Alene in western Idaho, an ice lobe laid itself across the path of the voluminous melt pouring from the mile-high glacial walls and blocked it, forming what may well have been history's most prodigious dam. Confronted by a wall of ice thousands of feet high, the runoff pooled and backed into a reservoir referred to by geologists as Glacial Lake Missoula. Frigid, ephemeral, hundreds of feet deep, the lake covered an area roughly the size of Lake Michigan and contained half as much water. At some point, as the lake deepened behind the ice dam, the dam must have begun to float—ice being lighter than a corresponding volume of water. The flood probably came in a sudden instantaneous release, like the collapse of Teton Dam, and emptied Lake Missoula within a couple of weeks. The volume of the flood is anyone's guess; Larry Meinert, a geologist at Washington State University at Pullman, says a reasonable estimate is ten times the combined flow of all the rivers in the world. The modern topography of the Northwest was pretty well formed by then; most of Lake Missoula searched out the main stream of the Columbia as its route to the sea. Inundated by a flood surge of 230 million cubic feet per second, the Columbia's spacious canyon was a thimble holding a dinosaur egg. In the upper stages the flood was probably twenty miles wide, confined by steeper valleys, but as it poured across the old lava plains of central Washington it spread into a flowing tumult as wide as Indiana. In places, the water excavated canyons overnight, extensive channels scoured through bedrock that remain such a dominant feature of the landscape that central Washington is more often referred to by geologists as "the channeled scablands." The big channels are known as coulees—Rocky Coulee, Lind Coulee, Esquazal Coulee. The biggest of all—seven hundred feet deep, five miles across, more than fifty miles long—is called the Grand Coulee.

Lake Missoula—greater and lesser incarnations of it—formed and reformed at least six times. The last time was about seventeen thousand years ago; by then there may have been humans living in the region. All of the land swept by the floods was stripped absolutely to bedrock. The glaciers, however, had left behind mountains of fine silt—the ground-up surface of Canada—and the winds distributed it around the region with a generous universality. The silt, known as loess, makes for extremely good farmland, and in some parts of Washington, such as the Palouse region below the Blue Mountains, it accumulated to depths of nearly two hundred feet. Rainfall is sparse behind the Cascades—ten to twenty inches is the norm—but loess has outstanding water-retentive qualities. Through this fortuitous coincidence, the soil neither washed away nor blew away—it grew a cover of blond grass and stayed put, waiting for the white man to arrive. That, in any case, is what white men thought. One spot in particular, around the Grand Coulee, was astonishingly suited for irrigation farming. There were more than a million acres of fine soil on the benchlands, a natural storage reservoir in the coulee itself, and, in the river canyon, a favorable site for a dam. A very, very large dam.

In 1933, the Columbia was by far the biggest river anyone had ever dreamed about damming. Bigger than the Colorado, bigger than the Snake, bigger than the Klamath, bigger than the Rio Grande—about twice as big, in fact, as all of those put together—it was the fourth biggest river in North America. Swelling out of the Purcell Range in Canada, it took off for the ocean like an express train on a route mapped by the Olympic Torch Committee: for three hundred miles it went straight for Alaska, until it picked up the melt from Columbia Glacier, an icefield the size of Chicago; then it turned south; then west; then south again; then east; then south; then west again to the sea. By the time it crossed the U.S. border, it was already so large that the Pend Oreille, a tributary larger than the Colorado, could be swallowed without appreciable effect. At Grand Coulee, the virgin Columbia had an average flow of 200,000 cubic feet per second, one of the largest rivers anywhere with enough of a drop to contain rapids. Such a volume and such a drop—all of it in a confined canyon—made the river ideal for hydroelectricity; it had a power potential out of proportion even to its vast size. In 1933, it could, if fully developed, have generated enough electricity for everyone living west of the Mississippi River.

For all its power potential, the idea of building a large hydroelectric dam at Grand Coulee was regarded by many people as insane. The Northwest had plenty of smaller rivers, much more easily dammed. The region, in 1930, had only three million inhabitants, and 70 percent of the rural people had no electricity. Even a tenth of its power

161

potential could not be used—especially with Bonneville Dam having just gone up downriver. The Bureau of Reclamation had surveyed the soils of the Grand Coulee benchlands in 1903 and found them excellent, but it had said nothing about building a dam. Major General George Goethals, with the Panama Canal under his belt, came to size up the task and backed off; he recommended a run-of-the-river irrigation diversion instead. Herbert Hoover, himself an engineer and an enthusiast about the dam that was to bear his name, said that construction of a dam at Grand Coulee was "inevitable," that it should be built "at the earliest possible date," but from the zeal with which he pursued the goal he might have been talking about the Second Coming. Even the Columbia's propensity to drown low-lying Portland and Vancouver—it could raise a flood of a million cubic feet per second without too much effort—left the Corps of Engineers unmoved. Only three institutions in the entire country seemed interested in Grand Coulee Dam: the Wenatchee (Washington) *Daily World*, the Bureau of Reclamation, and the new President of the United States.

Franklin Roosevelt first heard about Grand Coulee from Nat Washington, a descendant of George Washington's brother, who approached him about it at the Democratic National Convention in 1920, when FDR was James M. Cox's running mate. The future President was intrigued, but in a mild way; it would cost a fortune, and FDR, in those days, was still promising to balance the budget. By 1933, however, the Grand Coulee project would have been invented by Roosevelt if someone else hadn't thought of it first. It was colossal and magnificent—a purgative of national despair. It would employ tens of thousands. It could settle tens of thousands more on irrigated lands in a region whose inhabitants, in the late 1920s, consisted of a ferryman and a couple of hay farmers. It was loathed by the Republican conservatives and the private-power interests. Perhaps best of all, it was regarded by none other than the president of the American Society of Civil Engineers as "a grandiose project of no more usefulness than the pyramids of Egypt." To Roosevelt, that remark was as good a reason as any to build it.

And it was built on a foundation of deception.

In 1931, the Corps of Engineers finally pronounced the construction of a concrete dam at Grand Coulee feasible. What the Corps had in mind, however, was a low dam, rising two or three hundred feet from bedrock—a dam similar to its own Bonneville Dam downstream, useful only for regulating navigation flows and for hydroelectricity.

The Bureau, however, was not interested in a low dam. The pump lift from the reservoir surface to the canyon rim would be at least five hundred feet; such a lift was beyond the capacity of any pumps in existence at the time, and even if they *had* existed their enormous appetite for power would make any irrigation project infeasible in an economic sense. A high dam was absolutely necessary for an irrigation project, not only because it would knock twenty stories off the pump lift, but because it would produce a vast amount of surplus hydroelectricity to handle the still impressive pump lift and generate enough revenue to subsidize the cost of water so that the farmers could afford it.

The problem with a high dam, however, was Congress. Confronted on all sides by calamity and cries for relief, Congress was not about to appropriate $500 million (about twelve times as much in today's money) to build a white elephant of a dam in a remote corner of the country where hardly anyone lived. As it happened, however, Congress had undermined its own intention by giving FDR blanket authority, under the Public Works Administration and the National Industrial Recovery Act, to select and fund "emergency" projects that would assist the relief effort. Why not use some of that money to get started with a low dam—and then switch horses in midstream?

Nowhere is there absolute proof that this is the strategy FDR had in mind. The circumstantial evidence is merely overwhelming. In 1933, he designated $63 million, the greatest sum ever for any single purpose, from the Public Works Administration under Section 202 of the National Industrial Recovery Act to begin construction on a low dam at Grand Coulee. At that point, there was no question of intent; a low dam was specifically mentioned in the appropriation. A few months later, the construction contract for the dam was let to a consortium of engineering firms that went by the acronym MWAK. The contract also specified a low dam. The $63 million was spent in a hurry; by 1935, cofferdams were already in place and the permanent dam's foundation was rising in the riverbed. It was not, however, a foundation for a low dam—*it was the foundation of a high dam.*

In interviews, no engineer who worked on Grand Coulee Dam would admit that the Bureau and FDR had a high dam in mind all along and quietly decided to hoodwink a Congress which they knew would never authorize it. Nonetheless, no other explanation seems plausible. Charles Weil, the Bureau engineer who was in charge of concrete inspection, said that a "substantial" amount of the high dam foundation's concrete had already been poured before the Roosevelt administration went to Congress in 1935 with a request to change the authorization from a low dam to a high dam. Still, he insisted that the Bureau never tried to deceive anyone. "I wouldn't say that the Bureau tried to mislead Congress," Weil offered. "But it had to keep in mind what Congress was willing to fund." That, of course, is another way of saying that the Bureau chose to mislead Congress. In the beginning, before construction began, a high dam was out of the question. After $63 million had been spent building a foundation for it, however, a *low* dam was out of the question; at the very least, it wouldn't have made much sense. The Bureau had presented Congress with a *fait accompli* in the form of a gigantic foundation designed to support a gravity dam 550 feet tall. To build a two-hundred-foot dam on it would have been like mounting a Honda body on the chassis of a truck.

Phil Nalder, who rose from draftsman to manager of the entire Columbia Basin Project, was as circumspect as Weil about the Bureau's motives and strategy. According to Nalder, "The Bureau determined belatedly that a low dam would have been impractical at the site." But that, of course, is something the Bureau must have recognized all along. There was nothing "impractical" about building a low dam for power and navigation, but building a low dam for an irrigation project was hopelessly impractical. Nalder, at least, was a bit more candid about whether the evidence didn't suggest that Roosevelt and the Bureau had pulled a fast one on the Congress. "Well, if you look at the evidence superficially," he said, "it would certainly appear that way."

The issue of a high dam versus a low dam involved much more than power production and the fate of the irrigation project. It also involved the fate of the greatest spawning run of salmon in the world. During the Depression, salmon was the one high-protein food most people could afford; it was still so abundant that it cost about ten cents for a one-pound can. America's Atlantic salmon were almost wiped out by then; virtually all domestic salmon came from Alaska and the West Coast, and the greatest run—equal to or greater than all the streams and rivers in Oregon and California combined—went up the Columbia River. Some of the fish branched off into the lower tributaries to spawn, but the majority went far up the river into the higher tributaries, beyond Grand Coulee. Many salmon could probably have gotten past a low dam; today, tens of thousands manage to circumnavigate The Dalles, John Day, and Bonneville dams through fish ladders every year. A high Grand Coulee Dam, however, would block their passage forever. A fifty-story wall rising straight out of the river would form an ultimate obstruction—hopeless and forbidding. A fish ladder, built at a proper gradient, would have to run for many miles, cut into sheer canyon walls. No one was even talking about building it; the cost might approach the price of the dam. (Fish facilities at Bonneville Dam's second powerplant, built many years later, would end up costing $65 million, almost one-fourth the cost of the powerplant itself.) If the high dam spelled doom for most of the salmon in the Columbia River, however, it did perform a miraculous service which, at the time, was utterly unforeseen. It probably won the Second World War.

It is hard to imagine today, when big public-works projects such as New York's Westway are held up for fifteen years in the courts, what the go-go years were like. In 1936, the four largest concrete dams ever built—Hoover, Shasta, Bonneville, and Grand Coulee—were being erected at breakneck speed, all at the same time. In Montana, Fort Peck Dam, the largest structure anywhere except for the Great Wall—which took a third of the Chinese male population a thousand years to build—was going up, too. The age of dams reached its apogee in the 1950s and 1960s, when hundreds upon hundreds of them were thrown up, forever altering the face of the continent—but most of those dams were middle-sized, squat, utilitarian, banal. The 1930s were the glory days. No dam after Hoover has ever quite matched its grace and glorious detail. Shasta Dam looks rundown now—the Grecian pavilions are rotting, the face is water-stained—but it was nearly as majestic as Hoover when it was built, and quite a bit bigger.

Symbolic achievements mattered terribly in the thirties, and the federal dams going up on the western rivers were the reigning symbols of the era. A few years earlier it had been the great skyscrapers that served as the landmarks of American achievement. In the late 1920s, they were rising simultaneously, too—the Empire State Building, the Chrysler Building, the Bank of Manhattan, 70 Pine Street, the Lincoln-Leveque Tower in Columbus, and the Carew Tower in Cincinnati—but just as they were being finished, the capitalist engine that had built them fell into ruin. In a slip of time, the mantle of achievement passed from private enterprise to public works. The dams announced that America could still do remarkable things; they also said that the country would never be the same. The centralized welfare state that everyone decries, and nearly everyone depends on to some degree, is said to have emerged from the war, the Depression, and the Great Society. It might be more accurate to say that it was born in the rivers of the American West.

Hoover was big; Shasta was half again as big; Grand Coulee was bigger than both together. Many of the workers who came up to build it were those who had just finished Hoover. When they imagined it filling this huge U-shaped canyon, they were speechless. "When they worked on Hoover they thought it made everything else look like nothing," says Phil Nalder. "When they saw what we were going to build here they said it made Hoover look like nothing."

After a while, visitors being taken around the damsite became tired of the phrase "largest in the world." The mass (10.5 million cubic yards) and crest length (four-fifths of a mile) were, for a concrete dam, the largest and longest in the world. The cement-mixing plant, the spillway, the generators, the powerhouse, the pumps, the penstocks, and the pump lift from the reservoir to the irrigated benchlands would all be the largest in the world, and as the dam went up the engineers were still scratching their heads about how to lift such an immense volume of water thirty stories high. The turbines, the scroll casings, the conveyor belts, the forms, the cofferdams, and the concentration of brothels and bars within a five-mile radius were also the largest in the world. The dam's dimensions—height and length—were roughly those of the Golden Gate Bridge—it was not quite as high or long—but it was *solid*, and, at the base, five times as wide. Grand Coulee would use more lumber—130 million board feet—than any edifice ever built, but it was a tiny fraction of the dam's total mass, and none of it was even visible. Like Hoover, the dam was so massive it would ordinarily have required hundreds of years to cool down, and cooling pipe had to be laid through it at close intervals. Laid out in a straight line, the pipe would have connected Seattle to Chicago.

The astonishing thing about Grand Coulee—about the whole era—was that people just went out and built it, built anything, without knowing exactly how to do it or whether it could even be done. There were no task forces, no special commissions, no proposed possible preliminary outlines of conceivable tentative recommendations. Tremendous environmental impacts, but no environmental impact statements. When Chuck Weil applied for a job on Grand Coulee, he didn't know the first thing about concrete; before long, he was in charge of inspecting more concrete than anyone in history. Phil Nalder was trained as an electrical engineer; he started as a tracer (one rung below draftsman) and, later on, was put in charge of the whole project.

Once, well into construction, a mudslide the size of a small mountain came off one side of the canyon and threatened to cover the foundation of the dam. To stabilize it, the Bureau ran around the Northwest looking for the biggest refrigeration units it could find; then it ran supercooled brine through the slide and froze it while construction continued. No one had ever tried it before, but it worked. When one of the cofferdams sprang a huge leak, it was plugged with old mattresses. The dam was finished and in service by September of 1941, an unbelievable sight. The three largest ocean liners in the world could have sat atop its crest like bathtub toys.

Much of the country thought Grand Coulee was marvelous, but it was so gigantic a project that it had to invite some kind of attack. Private utilities, not quite brave enough to lambast so popular a creation, were suspected of bribing journalists to write diatribes against it. One writer, Walter Davenport, went out to see the dam for *Collier's* magazine; it was, he reported, in the middle of a "dead land, bitter with alkali," shunned "even by snakes and lizards," where "the air you breathe is full of the dust of dead men's bones." But Ickes and Mike Straus cooked up the idea of hiring Woody Guthrie as a "research assistant" to write some songs in praise of the dams. Guthrie, an itinerant Okie guitar picker, toured the Northwest like a prince in a chauffeured car, composing paeans to water and power like "Talking Columbia":

> You jus' watch this river 'n pretty soon
> E-everybody's gonna be changin' their tune. . . .
> That big Grand Coulee 'n Bonneville Dam'll
> Build a thousand factories f'r Uncle Sam. . . .
>   'N ev'rybody else in the world.
>   Makin' ev'rything from sewin' machines
>   To a-tomic bedrooms, 'n plastic . . .
>   E-everything's gonna be made outa plastic.
>
> Uncle Sam needs wool, Uncle Sam need wheat
> Uncle Sam needs houses 'n stuff to eat
> Uncle Sam needs water 'n power dams,
> Uncle Sam needs people 'n the people need land.
>   Don't like dictators none much myself,
>   What I think is the whole world oughta be run by
>   E-electricity. . . .

What Guthrie sensed, and what Franklin Roosevelt knew by 1939, was that America stood an excellent chance of going to war. It would

167

be a war won or lost not so much through strategy as through production. Germany had the greatest industrial capacity in Europe; Japan's was the greatest in the Orient. In the balance stood the United States. And since this would be a war of, more than anything, air power, the critical material was going to be aluminum. It would be, at least, until the critical material became plutonium.

In the nineteenth century, aluminum had a street value close to gold's—a function of the amount of energy needed to produce it and the type of energy required. It takes twelve times as much energy to produce raw aluminum as it does to make iron, and since the process is electrolytic, it has to be done with electricity. Until another process is invented, nothing else will do. The one-thousand-ounce aluminum Pope's cap installed in the pinnacle of the Washington Monument when it was completed in the mid-nineteenth century was the largest ingot of its day. After the First World War, aluminum became cheaper, though still not common. The raw material, the production flow, the manufacturing patent, and the end uses were pretty much controlled by the Aluminum Company of America, which was to vertical integration what William Randolph Hearst was to yellow journalism. Hearst, at least, had competition; Alcoa didn't— except from Adolf Hitler, who made Germany the world leader in aluminum production soon afer seizing power, for reasons the Allies did not immediately discern. When the first electricity began to flow out of Bonneville Dam, the Corps of Engineers' big power and navigation dam three hundred miles downriver, the government tried to induce Alcoa's potential competitors to build plants in the Northwest by offering them bargain rates, but nobody was particularly interested. By the time the Japanese bombed Pearl Harbor, however, the luxury of persuasion could no longer be afforded. The government simply went out and built the plants itself.

No one knows exactly how many planes and ships were manufactured with Bonneville and Grand Coulee electricity, but it is safe to say that the war would have been seriously prolonged at the least without the dams. Germany's military buildup during the 1930s gave it a huge head start on Britain and France. When Hitler invaded Poland and war broke out in Europe, the United States was, militarily speaking, of no consequence; we had fewer soldiers than Henry Ford had auto workers, and not enough modern M-1 Garand rifles to equip a single regiment. By 1942, however, we possessed something no other country did: a huge surplus of hydroelectric power. By June of that year, 92 percent of the 900,000 megawatts of power available from Grand Coulee and Bonneville dams—an almost incomprehensible amount at the time—was going to war production, most of it to building planes. One writer, Albert Williams, estimates that "more than half the planes in the American Air Forces were built with Coulee power alone." After France capitulated, England was left hanging by a thread. It was rescued by a European sky suddenly full of American planes. The Columbia River was a traffic jam of barges carrying baux-ite to the smelters in Longview, Washington. By the middle of the war, almost half of the aluminum production in the country was located in the Northwest—nearly all of it going toward the war effort. American planes were being downed almost as fast as they could be produced. German planes, however, were being downed faster than they could be produced. The Nazis had neither the raw materials nor the electricity to produce what they needed fast enough.

In late 1940, when Grand Coulee Dam was being completed, people had been saying that its power would go begging until the twenty-first century. Twenty-two months later, all of its available power was being used and the defense industries were screaming for more. As the first six generators were being installed, the next two units were still being manufactured and wouldn't be ready for power production for some weeks. The war was at such a critical juncture that some weeks was too long. The Bureau collected every outsize piece of transportation equipment it could find, took the two gener-ators waiting to be installed at Shasta Dam, and laboriously moved them to Grand Coulee instead. Shasta's generators were thirty thou-sand kilowatts smaller than Grand Coulee's, and the turbines re-volved in the wrong direction: Grand Coulee's went clockwise, Shasta's went counterclockwise. The Bureau solved the problem by installing the Shasta units in the wrong pits and excavating tunnels to the proper ones next door, so the water could surge in from the right side. After the war, the engineers had to invent some special tools and use a lot of dynamite to shoehorn them out.

The Westinghouse generators built for Grand Coulee were rated for a maximum output of 105,000 kilowatts each, which was the capacity of a good-sized oil power plant that could run, say, Duluth. For the entire duration of the war, they ran at 125,000 kilowatts, twenty-four hours a day, without a glitch. "We would shut one down only when it was absolutely necessary," says Phil Nalder. "You'd stand there in the powerhouse and feel that low vibration, that low but incredibly powerful vibration, and you'd feel certain that they were going to burn themselves up. And you'd think that maybe the course of history depended on these damned things. But they never overheated, so we just ran them and ran them. God knows, they were beautifully made. By the end of the war, at Grand Coulee, we were generating 2,138,000 kilowatts of electricity. We were the biggest single source of electricity in the world. The Germans and the Japanese didn't have anything nearly that big. Imagine what it would have been like without Grand Coulee, Hoover, Shasta, and Bonneville. At the time, they were ranked first, second, third, and fourth in the world. We had so much power at Grand Coulee that we could afford to use two generators just to run Hanford."

Although few of the people who lived there knew it at the time, the strange squat structures going up in 1943 at the Hanford Reservation, an ultrasecret military installation along the Columbia River near Richland, Washington, were intimately connected to the Manhattan Project. A lot of the history is well-known now: how Niels Bohr was smuggled out of Nazi-occupied Denmark in the wheel well of a British balsa-wood aircraft; how pacifistic Albert Einstein urged Franklin Roosevelt to build the bomb before the Nazis did; how thousands of technicians and scientists descended on the tiny mountain hamlet of Los Alamos, New Mexico, to figure out how to build their catastrophically explosive device. The key material was plutonium-239, an element virtually unknown in nature which has just the right fissile characteristics for an atomic bomb. The problem with plutonium—aside from its being fiendishly toxic—is that its production is energy-consumptive in the extreme. The amount of electricity used by the eight plutonium-production reactors at Hanford is still classified information, but a good guess is fifteen or twenty megawatts each—perhaps 160 megawatts in all. Nowhere else in a country involved in a gigantic war effort could one have found that kind of power to spare.

In the end, the Axis powers were no match for two things: the Russian winters, and an American hydroelectric capacity that could turn out sixty thousand aircraft in four years. We didn't so much outmaneuver, outman, or outfight the Axis as simply outproduce it.

The main stem of the Columbia River didn't have a single dam on it until 1933, when the Chelan County Public Utility District went out on its own and built a run-of-the-river dam called Rock Island, which produced 212,000 kilowatts of power—a mind-boggling amount in its day. Five years later, Bonneville Dam was finished and generated almost three times as much power. In 1941 came Grand Coulee; in 1953, McNary Dam; in 1955, Chief Joseph Dam; in 1957, The Dalles, contributing 1,807,000 kilowatts to the seven million or so that had already been wrung out of the river. In that same year, the Grant County Public Utility District finished Priest Rapids Dam, which added another 788,500 kilowatts. In 1961, the Chelan County PUD came back and built Rocky Reach Dam, with a capacity one million kilowatts greater than the dam by which it had gotten things off to a start twenty-eight years before. And it still wasn't over. In 1963, the Grant County PUD added Wanapum Dam and another 831,250 kilowatts. In 1967, the Douglas County PUD completed Wells Dam. The Corps of Engineers, which had built Bonneville and Chief Joseph and McNary and The Dalles, got back into the picture in 1968 with John Day Dam, whose 2,160,000 kilowatts were second only to Grand Coulee. In that year, the Canadians finally joined in, building Keenleyside Dam, whose sole purpose was to equalize the upper river's flow throughout the year for the benefit of navigation and power production. In 1973, they added Mica Dam, which formed the largest reservoir on the river in a remote wilderness not far from the Columbia's headwaters. Thirteen tremendous dams in forty years.

And these were just the *main-stem* dams. As they were going up, the Columbia tributaries were also being chinked full of dams. Libby Dam on the Kootenai River. Albeni Falls and Boudary dams on the Pend Oreille. Cabinet Gorge and Noxon Rapids dams on the Clark Fork. Kerr and Hungry Horse on the Flathead. Chandler and Roza dams on the Yakima. Ice Harbor Dam, Lower Monumental Dam, Little Goose Dam, Lower Granite Dam, Oxbow Dam, Hells Canyon Dam, Brownlee Dam, and Palisades Dam on the Snake. Dworshak Dam on the North Fork of the Clearwater. Anderson Ranch Dam on the South Fork of the Boise. Pelton and Round Butte dams on the Deschutes. Big Cliff, Foster, Green Peter, and Detroit dams on the three forks of the Santiam River. Cougar Dam on the South Fork of the McKenzie. Dexter, Lookout Point, and Hills Creek dams on the Willamette. Merwin Dam, Yale Dam, and Swift Dam on the Lewis

River. Layfield and Mossyrock dams on the Cowlitz. Thirty-six great dams on one river and its tributaries—a dam a year. The Age of Dams.

The Corps of Engineers and the region's public utilities played a big role in the damming of the Pacific Northwest because it had in abundance what the rest of the region lacked—water—so many of the dams were built for flood control, navigation, or power. Everywhere else in the West, however, where deserts were the rule and irrigation was the be-all and end-all of existence, the Bureau reigned supreme. Within its first thirty years, it had built about three dozen projects. During the next thirty years, it built nineteen dozen more. The Burnt River Project, the Cachuma Project, the Mancos Project, the Ogden River Project, the Collbran Project, the Gila Project, the Pine River Project, the Palisades Project, the Weber Basin Project, the Columbia Basin Project, and the Central Valley Project. Shasta Dam, Parker Dam, Friant Dam, Davis Dam, Laguna Dam, Canyon Ferry Dam, Cascade Dam, Flaming Gorge Dam. Cedar Bluff Lake, Paonia Reservoir, Kirwin Reservoir, Webster Reservoir, Pathfinder Reservoir, Waconda Lake, Clair Engle Lake, Lake Berryessa, Lake C. W. McConaughy, Enders Reservoir, Box Butte Reservoir. The Tucumcari Project, the Palo Verde Project, the San Angelo Project, the Canadian River Project, the Crooked River Project, the Kendrick Project, the Hubbard Project, the Hyrun Project, the Eden Project, the W. C. Austin Project, the Colorado–Big Thompson Project, the Pecos River Basin Water Conservation Project ("conservation" meaning, in this case, the virtual drying-up of the Pecos River), the Mercedes Division, the Middle Rio Grande Project. Trinity Dam, Keswick Dam, Folsom Dam, Morrow Point Dam, Blue Mesa Dam. The Oroville-Tonasket Unit of the Okanogan Similkameen Division of the Columbia Basin Project. Glen Canyon Dam. Lake Powell, Jewel of the Colorado.

By 1956, the Congress had voted 110 separate authorizations for the Bureau of Reclamation, some encompassing a dozen or more irrigation projects and dams. Of these, seventy-seven—nearly three-quarters—were authorized between 1928 and 1956, along with hundreds of projects built by the Corps of Engineers in the East and West. In that astonishingly brief twenty-eight-year period between the first preparations for Hoover Dam and the passage of the Colorado River Storage Project Act, the most fateful transformation that has ever been visited on any landscape, anywhere, was wrought.

It was profound change—profound and permanent. You can levee a river, dredge it, riprap it, channelize it, straighten it, do almost anything to it except build a dam on it, and, unless you maintain your works diligently, nature will soon take the river back. Simple diversion works of great ancient civilizations collapsed not long after the civilizations themselves did; for the most part, a remnant here and there is all that remains. Had the Assyrians built Grand Coulee Dam, however, it would sit exactly where it does today, looking exactly as it did when it was built. The only thing different is that the dam would no longer function as a dam. It would be a waterfall. The reservoir behind it would have long since silted up.

And the effects would go far beyond the natural world. In the Northwest, the dams produced so much cheap hydroelectricity that hundreds of thousands of people who flocked to the region during and after the war did not bother to insulate their homes. Insulation was expensive; electricity was dirt-cheap. In 1974, $196.01 worth of power from Con Edison in New York would have cost $24 if purchased from Seattle City Light. (For decades, the Northwest and British Columbia have had the highest rates of electricity consumption in the world.) The result was that by the 1970s, to everyone's amazement, the seemingly limitless hydroelectric bonanza was coming to an end; brownouts were being predicted for the 1980s. Since the good damsites were gone, the region's utilities and their federal power broker, the Bonneville Power Administration—another product of the go-go years—launched a program of coal and nuclear powerplant construction which, viewed in retrospect, seems more like dementia than the rational, orderly planning it was purported to be. Of the twenty-four thousand-megawatt plants that were to be built under the Washington Public Power Supply System—one a year—five were begun, only to be scrapped or mothballed, half-completed, a few years later, threatening to cause the biggest municipal bond default in history. The cost of their construction, driven by inflation and hyperactive interest rates, drove electricity rates up, which immediately drove demand down, which drove rates further up, which drove demand further down—a self-perpetuating vortex known among municipal bond traders and their hapless victims and the region's hollow-eyed utilities as "death spiral." No one knows where this fiasco—now referred to simply by the power consortium's onomatopoetic acronym WPPSS—may end, but more than $6 billion has been invested in nuclear plants that may never produce a watt of power. The blame for it—if it is worth laying blame at all—has to fall on the region's forty-year love affair with dams.

It was, of course, a love affair not limited to the Northwest or even the West. The whole country wanted more dams. In Appalachia, the Tennessee Valley Authority had an answer to poverty: dams. No river in the entire world has as much of its course under reservoirs as the Tennessee; by the late 1960s, it was hard to find a ten-mile free-flowing stretch between dams. The Missouri is a close second; about seven hundred miles in its middle reaches became a series of gigantic stair-step reservoirs. In Texas and Oklahoma, between 1940 and 1975, something like twelve million acres of land were submerged by artificial lakes. Much of this land was in the eastern part of those states; it was exceptionally fertile (as were the bottomlands along the Tennessee) and visited by adequate rainfall, making it some of the best farmland in the nation. No one seemed bothered by the spectacle of a government creating expensive farmland out of deserts in the West while drowning millions of acres of perfect farmland in the East. If there was a stretch of free-flowing river anywhere in the country, our reflex action was to erect a dam in its path.

There were legitimate reasons, of course, to build a fair number of those thousands of dams. Hydropower obviously was one; the Columbia dams helped prevent the horror of Nazism from blackening the entire world. Some new irrigation projects made economic sense, as late as the 1940s and 1950s (though virtually none did after then). The Tennessee and Red rivers were prone to destructive floods, as was the Columbia—as were many rivers throughout the country. A better solution, in many cases, would have been to discourage development in floodplains, but the country—least of all the Congress— wasn't interested in that. For a dam, whether or not it made particularly good sense, whether or not it decimated a salmon fishery or drowned a gorgeous stretch of wild river, was a bonanza to the constituents of the Congressman in whose district it was located—especially the engineering and construction firms that became largely dependent on the government for work. The whole business was like a pyramid scheme—the many (the taxpayers) were paying to enrich the few—but most members of Congress figured that if they voted for everyone else's dams, someday *they* would get a dam, too.

And this, as much as the economic folly and the environmental damage, was the legacy of the go-go years: the corruption of national politics. Water projects came to epitomize the pork barrel; they were the oil can that lubricated the nation's legislative machinery. Important legislation—an education bill, a foreign aid bill, a conservation bill—was imprisoned until the President agreed to let a powerful committee chairman tack on a rider authorizing his pet dam. Franklin Roosevelt had rammed a lot of his public-works programs through a Congress that was, if not resistant, then at least recumbent. A generation or two later, however, it was Congress that was writing omnibus public-works bills authorizing as much as $20 billion worth of water projects at a stroke and defying threats of presidential vetos. Most members who voted for such bills had not the faintest idea what was in them; they didn't care; they didn't dare look. All that mattered was that there was something in it for them. What had begun as an emergency program to put the country back to work, to restore its sense of self-worth, to settle the refugees of the Dust Bowl, grew into a nature-wrecking, money-eating monster that our leaders lacked the courage or ability to stop.

CHAPTER SIX

Rivals in Crime

O n the 16th of August, 1962, Major General William F. Cassidy, the director of civil works for the United States Army Corps of Engineers, gave a speech titled "The Future of Water Development" before a gathering of his peers in Davis, California. Considering what Cassidy had to say, the speech attracted surprisingly little attention in the press.

"Before white men came to North America," the General began, "it is estimated that about one million Indians inhabited the region between the Canadian border and the Gulf of Mexico. The streams were unpolluted, the forests still stood, and the plow had not broken the plains. They had the resources of a continent at their disposal, and about four hundred acres of arable land for every man, woman, and child. Yet they often starved—because they lacked the capacity to develop their resources.

"In the 1890s," Cassidy continued, "the United States had about seventy-seven acres of cultivated land per person. Before World War I, about four acres. Today, we have only about two acres of cultivated land per person. Yet the United States maintains the highest level of living known to history, it exports food to other nations, and it has even accumulated substantial surpluses of a few crops. This is the result of increasingly intensive resource development."

But all of this resource development had been a mere warm-up exercise compared with what was still to come. "During the next twenty years," Cassidy went on, "we estimate that we will have to provide some 320 million acre-feet of reservoir storage at a cost of about $15 billion; about thirteen thousand miles of new or improved inland waterways; about sixty new or improved commercial harbors; thirty million kilowatts of hydroelectric power-generating capacity; some eleven thousand miles of levees, floodwalls, and channel improvements; and recreational facilities for perhaps 300 million visitors at our reservoirs. . . ." If all of that seemed "unduly large or visionary," Cassidy admonished, "let us remember the responsibilities our nation is facing."

It is worth taking a moment to put some of these figures in perspective. In 1962, the total amount of federally built reservoir storage in the nation was somewhere around 300 million acre-feet. In twenty years, Cassidy wanted to more than double that. Every year, the Mississippi River carries about 355 million acre-feet of water out to sea, the runoff of most of the United States from Pennsylvania to Montana. In twenty years, according to the Corps of Engineers, we were going to put the equivalent of 90 percent of that water behind dams. In 1962, there were 37,342 megawatts of installed hydroelectric generating capacity in the United States; by 1982, that figure was nearly to double. By 1962, nearly all the major rivers in the United States—long reaches of the Mississippi, the Snake, the Columbia, the Illinois, the Missouri, the Sacramento, the Susquehanna, the Red, the Delaware, the Tennessee, the Apalachicola, the Savannah—had been dredged, realigned, straitjacketed, riprapped, diked, leveed, stabilized, and otherwise made over in order to accommodate barge and freighter traffic. In twenty years, we were going to add or "improve" thirteen thousand more miles.

And this Promethean agenda was going to be possible, according to the director of civil works, because we were "about to enter an era of unprecedented cooperation in planning water resource development to meet future needs. . . . The walls which formerly separated various spheres of interest are crumbling under the pressure of manifold needs."

Even allowing for the temper of the times, Cassidy's prophecy, in retrospect, seems one of derangement more than vision. Nineteen years later, the $15 billion which was to construct 320 million acre-feet of reservoir storage would barely suffice to build ten million acre-feet of new storage in California—had it been politically possible to do it. It was hard to imagine thirteen thousand miles of new or "improved" navigable waterways without envisioning barges bumping against the Rocky Mountains or poking into bulrushes at the headwaters of southern streams. Even had there been money to build all those reservoirs, there wasn't any room for them—as Cassidy was almost willing to admit. "In many intensively occupied river basins," he said, using the military jargon of which the Corps is inordinately fond, "we . . . face a very difficult task in finding sites for the reservoirs needed to support future growth"—thus raising the prospect of a nation requiring so many new dams to feed water and electricity into its hyperventilating economy that it would flood itself right off the land and find itself forced to go about its business aboard houseboats.

Actually, the General's vision was to mutate into irony as fabulous as the prophecy itself. He was right in one sense—you did not build such incredible works to carry water from areas of "surplus" to areas of "deficit" without intricate political compromises among the states involved and unprecedented collaboration between the agencies that would presumably do the job, the Bureau of Reclamation and the Corps. But he was dead wrong in predicting that such harmonious relations would ever be. And if a single entity could be blamed for this—because it schemed constantly against its would-be confederate, because it seized every opportunity to build any senseless project it could, because it worked diligently, if unwittingly, to give water development a bad name—it was none other than his own agency, the U.S. Army Corps of Engineers.

In California, where Cassidy gave his speech—at the very moment, in fact, when he was giving his speech—the Corps of Engineers was shamelessly trying to steal from the Bureau of Reclamation at least one major project the Bureau had intended to build for years. It had already done it several times before, in California and elsewhere. Across the entire West, the Corps, as opportunistic and ruthless an agency as American government has ever seen, was trying to seduce away the Bureau's irrigation constituency; it was toadying up to big corporate farmers who wanted to monopolize whole rivers for themselves; it was even prepared to defy the President of the United States. As a result, the business of water development was to become a game of chess between two ferociously competitive bureaucracies, on a board that was half a continent plus Alaska, where rivers were the pawns and dams the knights and queens used to checkmate the other's ambition. But the Corps and the Bureau played a little too well and a little too long for their own good. While they were fighting over a Lake Ontario–size reservoir in the middle of Alaska, and over countless squalid little projects desired by local interest groups, an unprecedented water crisis was gathering on the southern high plains—

a crisis tailor-made for their own limitless ambition which, in the end, they would do nothing about. The Corps and the Bureau wasted so much money on frivolous projects which didn't so much solve the nation's water situation as satisfy the greed of powerful interests and their own petty ambitions that in the 1980s, despite dozens of new dams and reservoirs built during the intervening years, a water crisis loomed larger than in 1962. Within the next half century, as much irrigated land is likely to go out of production—land that grows nearly 40 percent of our agricultural exports—as the Bureau of Reclamation managed to put *into* production during its entire career. And though projects to rescue those regions remain on the drawing boards, the age when they might have been built seems to have passed.

The Corps of Engineers, the construction arm of the United States Army, was baptized during the Revolutionary War, when a group of engineers in the Continental Army built a breastwork on Bunker Hill. In 1794, the Corps was officially christened with its current name and divided into a civilian and a military works branch. The civil works branch, which was to become by far the larger of the two, began modestly enough, clearing driftwood and sunken ships out of rivers and harbors and occasionally doing a bit of dredging. It also played a role in the early exploration and surveying of the nation. The Corps' great work—and its transmutation into one of history's most successful bureaucracies—began late in the nineteenth century, when it took upon itself the task of restyling America's largest rivers to accommodate barge traffic and, occasionally, deep-draft ships. At the same time, it found a role for itself in flood control, which it first accomplished by building levees and dikes, and then, after denying for years that reservoirs could control floods, by building flood-control reservoirs. And it built them at a pace that would have left the most ambitious pharaoh dazzled—something like six hundred in sixty years.

The Army Engineers have so many hands in so many different types of work that their various activities sometimes cancel each other out. The Corps drains and channels wetlands—it has ruined more wetlands than anyone in history, except perhaps its counterpart in the Soviet Union—yet sometimes prohibits the draining and dredging of wetlands by private developers and other interests. (This was a role forced on the Corps by the Congress, not one it undertook voluntarily.) Its dams control flooding, while its stream-channelization and wetlands-drainage programs cause it. Its subsidization of intensive agriculture—which it does by turning wetlands into dry land, so they may then become soybean fields—increases soil erosion, which pours into the nation's rivers, which the Corps then has to dredge more frequently.

Cynics say this is all done by design, because the Corps of Engineers' motto, "Building Tomorrow Today," really ought to be "Keep Busy." Its range of activities is stupendously broad: the Corps dams rivers, deepens rivers, straightens rivers, ripraps rivers, builds bridges across rivers, builds huge navigation locks and dams, builds groins on rivers and beaches, builds hatcheries, builds breakwaters, builds piers, and repairs beach erosion (finally fulfilling the first stage of a destiny conservationists have long wished on it: carrying sandpiles from one end of the country to the other and back again). The works for which the Corps is most famous—or notorious, depending on one's point of view—are the monumental inland navigation projects such as Red River, Tennessee-Tombigbee, and Arkansas River. However, though each of these may cost billions to begin with, and hundreds of millions to maintain, the opportunities for such work are pretty thin. Opportunities for serious work come most frequently in the form of flood-control and water-supply dams.

The Corps confined its activities mainly to the East and Middle West until the Great Depression—it is widely, and falsely, regarded as the "eastern counterpart" of the Bureau of Reclamation—but the temptations of the West ultimately proved too much to resist. Throughout much of the East, it is hard to find a decent spot for a dam. There are few tight gorges and valleys, or there are few natural basins behind them, or there are too many people along rivers who would have to be moved. (Not that uprooting and relocating people particularly bothers the Army Engineers; it is more a matter of expense.) The West, however, is a dam builder's nirvana, full of deep, narrow canyons and gunsight gaps opening into expansive basins. The West is also more sparsely populated, and has floods—enormous floods—because its precipitation tends to be both erratic and highly seasonal, and because of this, the groundcover, compared with the East, is spare. With little in the way of grass or forests or wetlands to hold it back, runoff during the storms is extreme. Small streams, even tiny creeks, have flowed at rates approaching the country's largest rivers. They rarely flow like this for long, but a few minutes is all it takes to float away a town. Bijou Creek in Colorado, nearly always dry, has gone over 400,000 cubic feet per second after an eight-inch rainstorm. California's Eel River peaked at 765,000 cfs—the flow of the Mississippi and the Columbia combined—during the Christmas flood of 1964.

On many rivers in the West a dam built for irrigation will incidentally control floods. But the equation also works in reverse: a flood-control dam, by evening out a river's flow year-round, makes it useful for irrigation. And if the Corps of Engineers builds the dam, and calls it a flood-control dam, the water is free.

The Kings, the Kaweah, the Tule, and the Kern are the southernmost rivers flowing out of the Sierra Nevada into the Central Valley of California. They are the only rivers that do not ultimately end up in either the Sacramento or the San Joaquin drainage, because a low rise of land in the upper San Joaquin Valley, south of Fresno, effectively divides the valley into two hydrologic basins. The southernmost one, which receives the runoff of the Kings, Kaweah, Tule, and Kern, is known as Tulare Basin. Historically, the four rivers of Tulare Basin went into two terminal lakes, Tulare and Buena Vista, which appeared and disappeared every year like phantoms. During the wet winters, the lakes would begin to fill; they would reach their largest size in May, after twenty feet of Sierra snow had melted into them in a matter of weeks; and, in all but the wettest years, they would evaporate so quickly under the glaring summer sun that they were dry again, or mostly dry, around September. Tulare, the more impressive of the two lakes, often grew larger than Lake Tahoe, though it was not more than a few feet deep. From year to year, its shoreline would shrink or grow by miles. It was a wonderful sight to see all of that water glimmering amid the merciless dryness of the San Joaquin Valley in summer, and the lakes were a stopover for millions of migrating ducks, geese, and sandhill cranes. But to those who wanted to get rich off the valley's fine soil the lakes were both unpredictable and land-consuming, and therefore a nuisance.

Before World War II, most of the agricultural lands around Tulare and Buena Vista lakes—and the lakes themselves—were owned by four private landholders. They were, in a sense peculiar to California, "family" farms. Buena Vista Lake and the land around it was the largest remnant of the million-acre domain amassed by Henry Miller, and later squandered by a succession of dissolute heirs. The property encompassed about eighty thousand acres, seven times the area of Manhattan Island. The adjacent Kern County Land Company, the estate originally put together by Miller's archenemies James Ben

Ali Haggin and Lloyd Tevis, was even larger. According to testimony by Senator Paul Douglas before the Senate Interior Committee in 1958, the company controlled some 1.1 million acres in 1939, of which 413,300 acres were in California—most of it in Kern County. (The Kern County Land Company later became the main agricultural holding of the Tenneco Corporation, one of the nation's largest conglomerates.) The Salyer and Boswell farming empires were in and around Tulare Lake, each of them comprising tens of thousands of acres. Since most large California growers also lease land, the total acreage under their control could only be guessed at; they may not have known themselves. Without a doubt, however, Salyer, Boswell, Kern County Land, and Miller and Lux were among the very largest and richest farmers in the entire world.

To the four companies, Tulare and Buena Vista Lake were both a convenience and a nuisance. Usually, as the lakes shrank, their exposed beds would be quickly planted with grains or row crops, which were irrigated by pumping back the remaining water. After particularly wet winters, however—and there had been a string of them in the 1940s—the Sierra snowmelt kept filling them into July and August, by which time it was too late to plant. Both water and available land were therefore unpredictable, and, though farmers around the world have learned to live with unpredictableness, it is something that California's big growers intensely dislike.

Although Tulare and Buena Vista lakes were privately owned, for the most part, the rivers that fed them were in the public domain. The four big farming companies held rights to a substantial amount of their water, but there were still big surpluses in all but the driest years—especially in the larger rivers, the Kings and the Kern. Had those surpluses been directed elsewhere in the valley, they could have created a great many small irrigated farms. If the rivers were going to be developed—if any agency of government was to develop them—it was a job for the Bureau of Reclamation. The only problem with that rationale was that the big growers wanted all of the water for themselves, they wanted the government to develop it for them, and they didn't want to have to pay for it.

Someday, if anyone has the inclination or the ability to penetrate the wall of secrecy behind which the Corps of Engineers has always managed to carry on its affairs, we may hear from its own mouth—from incriminating letters, memoranda, or confessions of its officials—why it was so eager to develop the Kings and the Kern—to ally itself unabashedly with a handful of huge land monopolies and,

Three godfathers of the newly reclaimed West.
AT LEFT: John Wesley Powell, who got things
moving. BELOW, LEFT: Michael Straus, the millionaire commissioner of reclamation, who under
FDR and Truman threw up thousands of dams.
BELOW, RIGHT: Floyd Dominy, the two-fisted commissioner who rode reclamation's falling star.

Mules lugging sections of the Los Angeles Aqueduct into place. At the time, no motorized vehicle existed that could haul anything so heavy.

(*Photo Department of the Los Angeles Department of Water and Power*)

The Owens Valley before the Los Angeles Aqueduct was completed.

(*Photo Department of the Los Angeles Department of Water and Power*)

The three main actors, from Los Angeles' standpoint, in the Owens Valley episode. AT RIGHT: Fred Eaton, the ex-mayor who ultimately felt betrayed by the city he helped create. BELOW, LEFT: J. B. Lippincott, who acted as a double agent in behalf of the city. BELOW, RIGHT: William Mulholland, the man who brought the water.

*(Photo Department of
the Los Angeles Department of Water and Power)*

ABOVE AND BELOW: Two views of Los Angeles—the squalid pueblo in 1869, and the megalopolis, at once tawdry and glitzy, that water built, in the late 1950s.
(*Photo Department of the Los Angeles Department of Water and Power*)

OPPOSITE: Rare photos of the Saint Francis Dam, before and after its collapse. After the disaster, the Los Angeles Department of Water and Power attempted to acquire and hoard as many photos as it could find; it didn't release them until many years later. A virtually identical dam, which creates the Hollywood Reservoir, was faced with earth and seeded with grass and trees so people living below it would be less inclined to think about the Saint Francis catastrophe, which killed more people than the San Francisco earthquake.
(*Photo Department of the Los Angeles Department of Water and Power*)

A section of the just-completed Los Angeles Aqueduct crosses the Mojave Desert.

(Photo Department of the Los Angeles Department of Water and Power)

Looking like a masterwork left by the Romans, Theodore Roosevelt Dam stands athwart the Salt River in Arizona. The Bureau of Reclamation's first great structure—and the prototype of all high, curved-arch dams—Roosevelt Dam was constructed entirely of huge stone blocks hewn from cliffs in the Salt River Canyon. *(Bureau of Reclamation)*

Still the architectural masterpiece among all the world's dams, Hoover rises seventy stories from the bed of the Colorado River. Though Hoover appears minuscule compared to Lake Mead, whose length is greater than a hundred miles—it widens considerably a few miles upriver—the dam may outlast the reservoir.

(*Bureau of Reclamation*)

Grand Coulee Dam under construction in June of 1938. Appearances are deceptive: the width of the dam is four fifths of a mile. *(Bureau of Reclamation)*

in the process, shove the Bureau off two made-to-order small-farm irrigation projects. The only obvious explanation (which is probably the correct one) is that it sensed the growing unpopularity of the acreage limitations of the Reclamation Act. Here was an unparalleled opportunity to establish a beachhead in a region where the natural topography and demand for water could give it new work for decades to come. No stranger to power politics, the Corps knew that its best hope of long-range success was a quick, dramatic demonstration of its abilities. The best way to ensure that was to pick a group of beneficiaries who were nearly as potent a political force as the Corps itself. If this was indeed its reasoning, then it reasoned well.

In 1937, the Bureau of Reclamation was just beginning its detailed feasibility investigations of the Kings and Kern River projects; it had, in fact, already been authorized to build the Kings River Project on the basis of cruder reconnaissance studies alone. In the very same year that the Bureau began its investigations, however, the Corps went to the House Flood Control and Appropriations Committees and extracted an authorization and some money to perform investigations of its own on these same two rivers—rivers which, in effect, had already been promised to the Bureau. It was a brazen act. The Bureau was incensed, and Harold Ickes, the Interior Secretary, was apoplectic. Nonetheless, neither the Bureau nor Ickes could do anything to stop the Corps; they were, in effect, in a race. The National Resources Planning Board, one of FDR's superagencies, pleaded with the agencies to plan a unified project, then practically ordered them to do so. But they refused. As a result, in 1940, Congress received two separate reports on developing the Kings and the Kern: one on a traditional Reclamation project, the other on a project that purported to be for flood control, but which, by controlling the rivers' runoff and drying up Tulare Lake, would irrigate a roughly equal amount of land.

It was a fierce bureaucratic battle that was to drag on for more than five years. Sympathies in California, where the Bureau had a lot of support from smaller farmers, were divided—as they were in Congress. The Roosevelt administration, however, was emphatically on the side of the Bureau of Reclamation. FDR felt so strongly about the matter that on the 5th of May, 1941, he wrote a personal letter to the chairman of the House Flood Control Committee, saying, "A good rule for Congress to apply in considering these water projects, in my opinion, would be that the dominant interest should determine which agency should build and operate the project." Obviously, Roosevelt said, the dominant interest was irrigation. "Not only that, but Kings River had already been authorized for construction by the Bureau of Reclamation; to [reauthorize] would only lead to needless confusion."

But the Flood Control Committee was practically married to the Corps of Engineers, and ignored Roosevelt's recommendation; the committee quickly authorized Kings River for construction by the Corps. With Ickes lobbying furiously on behalf of the Bureau, however, the full Congress refused to go along.

At that point, FDR made what would, in retrospect, look like a fateful mistake. The United States had by then entered the Second World War; to squander precious funds on a water project when there was still no demonstrable need for it seemed foolish. Even a few hundred thousand dollars would have given the Bureau enough of a head start, at least on the already-authorized Kings River project, to thwart the Corps' ambition. But Roosevelt refused to recommend any money in his budget.

To the Corps of Engineers, the Bureau's inability to move represented a last chance. In 1942, without any clear authorization from Congress, it began to construct an "emergency" flood diversion structure on the lower Kings. Although its action outraged those members who sided with the Bureau, and who saw what the Corps was trying to do, they could not bring the full Congress, now utterly preoccupied with the war, to waste its time debating such a trivial issue. Besides, the Corps' works didn't seem like much, a mere diversion gate. But it wasn't the size of the works so much as the fact that the Corps had established its beachhead in the Tulare Basin before the Bureau ever got to turn a shovelful of earth. The Corps also made sure the flood-waters were diverted where they could do some economic good— toward the lands of the big growers.

Nothing much happened with the Kings River and Kern River projects during the middle war years. By 1944, however, Europe's farmlands and economy were in ruins; overnight, the United States had become the breadbasket of the world. Now, at last, the two projects seemed to make some sense. In his budget request for fiscal year 1945, FDR included a request of $1 million to permit the Bureau to begin work on the Kings River. The House, dominated by the Flood Control Committee, immediately took the appropriation out; the Senate threw it back in. Finally, hearings had to be scheduled to try to resolve the matter.

It was at those hearings that the Corps of Engineers demonstrated where its true loyalty lay. Although the White House had left absolutely no doubt that it was strongly behind a Reclamation project, and expected the rest of the administration to support its position, the Corps of Engineers chose not to; instead, Chief of Engineers Raymond A. Wheeler displayed outright defiance of his commander in chief. Testifying at the hearings, Wheeler gave no support at all to the Roosevelt position, a breach of loyalty that made Harold Ickes, the ultimate Roosevelt loyalist, absolutely livid. Meanwhile, the deputy chief was busy undermining the administration's position back in California. In a speech to a group of business leaders in Sacramento, Major General Thomas Robins said that Californians were being denied "necessary flood control" by "a lot of arguments that are neither here nor there." If the state would only "wake up and get the water first and then decide what to do with it," he said, "she would be a lot better off." Otherwise, by the time the dams are built "we may all be dead." What Robins didn't say is that most Californians *wouldn't be able* to use the water in the Kings and the Kern if the Corps built the dams. It had already announced that it would build dams, but not aqueducts; therefore, the water couldn't go anywhere but down the river channels, and the big growers owned nearly all the land on both sides. The Corps had also announced that if its projects offered incidental irrigation benefits, it would not apply the Reclamation Act and its acreage laws. What all of this meant was that if the Corps built the Kings and Kern dams, nearly all of the water could be used by four agribusiness giants and a handful of oil companies owning land nearby—which were to become agribusiness giants themselves.

In the end, the hearings resolved nothing. Congress was still deadlocked. Sensing this, it came up with an inimitable solution to a paralysis of its own making: it authorized the Kings River Project for construction by *both* the Bureau and the Corps. Whichever could convince the appropriations committees to give it money first would end up building it.

The fight now began to get serious. In its budget request for fiscal year 1947, the Truman administration said that the War Department's earlier requests to begin construction on both the Kings and Kern rivers were to be considered "officially eliminated." There were to be no further requests from the Corps of Engineers pending "a decision by the President as to the course to be followed on these works." In his personal testimony during the appropriations hearings, however, the Chief of Engineers calmly announced that "we are ready to make a definite recommendation to undertake the construction"—

a remark that could only be interpreted as smug defiance once again of his commander in chief.

Had Roosevelt not died, the Corps might well have lost the battle. But Harry Truman lacked the romantic feeling about the Reclamation program that Roosevelt had, and he was from a state where the Corps was generally loved. Ickes, the old curmudgeon, was gone, too, replaced by the more conciliatory Cap Krug. In the end, the Corps simply played a waiting game, confident that the growers' friends in Congress would extract money with which it could begin work on both the Kings and the Kern—which they soon did. Truman was so angry that he impounded the first funds, but he gradually lost interest in the whole affair. By 1948, he and Krug had given up. The Kings and Kern rivers belonged to the Corps.

The Army Engineers did accede to Truman's request that they collect a one-time user fee from the growers. The figure settled on was $14,250,000, which covered just a third of the $42,072,000 cost of Pine Flat Dam. Considering the tens of thousands of new acres that would be opened to double-crop production when the floodwaters were stored in the Pine Flat and Isabella reservoirs, the "user fee" was more tokenism than anything else.

The covert liaison between the Corps of Engineers and the world's largest irrigation farmers was to live on. A few years later, the Corps added insult to injury by damming the Kaweah and the Tule rivers, which, by rights, should have been Reclamation rivers, too. But as an example of government subsidizing the wrong people, for the wrong reasons, nothing would quite equal its performance thirty-five years later in the Tulare Lake floods of 1983.

During the El Niño winter of 1983, when the eastern Pacific's resident bulge of high pressure migrated to Australia and the storm door was left open for months, much of California got double or triple its normal rainfall. The previous year hadn't been much different. By the early spring of 1983, all four Corps of Engineers dams were dumping hundreds of thousands of acre-feet over their spillways as the largest snowpack in the annals of official California weather records melted. Because the farmlands in what used to be Tulare Lake were now protected by dikes, most of the water couldn't enter its old basin and had to go elsewhere. When the floodwaters began encroaching on nearby towns, the Corps of Engineers spent $2.7 million in emergency funds to erect levees around them. There was nothing inherently wrong with that, except that 80,000 acres of old lake bottom—land that could have absorbed the floods—remained dry;

one need only have breached one of the levees that had since been built around the ex-lake. But the Tulare Lake Irrigation District, dominated by Salyer and Boswell, wouldn't have that, so the growers convinced the Corps to spend taxpayers' money on levees in order that their land, the natural catch basin for the floods, could remain in subsidized production.

However, El Niño was soon to prove too much even for the big growers and the Army Engineers. By March of 1983, the flooding rivers were out of control and one of the lake levees was breached, inundating thirty thousand acres of farmland. The Tulare Lake Irrigation District immediately applied to the Corps for a permit to pump out the water and send it over the Tulare Basin divide into the San Joaquin River, which feeds San Francisco Bay. There was nothing inherently wrong with that idea, either—the bay and the Delta normally can use all the fresh water they can get—except that at least one of the reservoirs upstream had been illegally planted with a species of fish called white bass, which got flushed down by the floodwaters and were already flourishing in the reincarnated Tulare Lake. White bass are a voracious, opportunistic, highly adaptable type of rough fish and love to eat young salmon and striped bass. (Salmon and white bass have never managed to coexist, anywhere.) Unless a fish screen below the pumps could guarantee that 100 percent of the white bass would be removed before entering the San Joaquin, the bay and Delta's two most valuable commercial and sports fish would be threatened with extinction. Just a handful of escaped white bass of opposite sexes could be enough to seal their doom.

Even though no fish screen has *ever* operated 100 percent effectively, the Corps of Engineers, ignoring a cacophony of protest from sportsmen in several states, issued another "emergency" permit on Friday, October 7, 1983, to allow the pumping to begin. The growers hadn't even waited for the permit; the pumps were all in place and ready to operate, and television reporters who arrived to take a look at things were scared away by armed guards. The pumps howled to life minutes after the permit was issued. The California Department of Fish and Game had strung a gill net across the river below the fish screen, just in case. On Saturday morning, not twenty-four hours after the pumping began, the net yielded four white bass. The pumps were shut off, and Fish and Game—as if to underscore the catastrophic consequences of releasing white bass—poured a thousand gallons of rotenone, a virulent pesticide, into six miles of river around the fish screens. Everything in that stretch of river—crappies, black bass, white bass, catfish, crayfish, ducks—died a ghastly death. A week later, Fish and Game performed a second mass poisoning. Then, satisfied that there was no danger to humans, it allowed the pumps to start up again. Every legal effort to stop them failed. Virtually all of the water was pumped out of the lake, and although there is no evidence yet that white bass got into the San Joaquin River and migrated down to the Delta and bay, they could just as well be there; no one knows. If they are—and some sportsmen think it is inevitable that white bass will reach the Delta—then the last remnant of central California's once prolific salmon fishery may soon be a thing of the past.

It would have been one thing, this whole game of Russian roulette with the most important anadromous fishery in the state, if the drowned lands in Tulare Lake were pumped out so they could grow valuable food. Most of them, however, have been planted in cotton for years. And as the lake was being pumped out, they were not even growing cotton. In March of 1983, just four days after the levee was breached and the floodwaters began to fill Tulare Lake, several of the big corporate farmers applied to the Department of Agriculture for enlistment in the Payment-in-Kind (PIK) program, which had recently been created to relieve the nation's chronic problem of surplus crop production. Thanks to PIK, they would receive free grain from bulging silos in exchange for not planting crops. The Boswell Company alone got $3.7 million worth of wheat in exchange for keeping fourteen thousand acres idle. (Boswell has consistently received more money from agricultural price support programs than any other farmer in the entire nation.) No one knows how much the other farmers got, but most of the eighty thousand acres of the old lake bed were registered in PIK—even as they were underwater.

In his personal epitaph on the Kings and Kern saga, written in 1951, Harold Ickes lambasted the Corps as "spoilsmen in spirit . . . working hand in glove with land monopolies." He called it a "willful and expensive . . . self-serving clique . . . in contempt of the public welfare" which had the distinction of having "wantonly wasted money on worthless projects" to a degree "surpassing any federal agency in the history of this country. . . . [N]o more lawless or irresponsible group than the Corps of Army Engineers," Ickes concluded, "has ever attempted to operate in the United States either outside of or within the law. . . . It is truly beyond imagination."

The Corps' success in bouncing the Bureau of Reclamation off a project it had already been authorized to build, and three other projects where it should have been the one to build, had the effect Ickes foresaw. An effort was immediately launched by the state's growers to repeal all the constraining features of the Reclamation Act—the acreage limitation, the prohibition on leasing, the requirement that farmers must live within fifty miles of their land—as it applied to the Central Valley Project. (Naturally, all the subsidies were to be retained.) Even though the campaign failed, the Corps' record in California made the irrigation lobby throughout the entire West sit up and take notice. The Bureau of Reclamation was a good thing, but the *Corps*—the Corps of Engineers was a dream come true.

A t the same time the Corps and the Bureau of Reclamation were fighting over the rivers of the southern Sierra Nevada, they were engaged in a battle of more epic proportions over the Missouri River. The historical significance of that battle would be greater, too—not only because the Missouri is a much bigger and more important river than the Kings or the Kern, but because, in defiance of common sense, economics, and even simple hydrology, the Missouri was an instance where *both* agencies managed to win.

The Missouri River is, after the Columbia, the biggest river in the American West, though it takes it a long time to grow to size. The Columbia, rising prodigiously out of the rain forests of the Purcell Mountains in Canada, is like a Clydesdale horse, big and powerful at birth. The Missouri, still small after going a distance in which the Columbia becomes huge, is a scavenger of a river, struggling to attain size. It isn't until the North Dakota border, nearly a thousand miles from its source, where the Yellowstone River adds a surge out of the Absaroka and Big Horn Mountains, that the Missouri begins to look impressive. The river turns south, capturing the Platte and the Niobrara and the Kansas and the James, and then east again. By the time it has gone two and a half thousand miles and joined the Mississippi, it is the twelfth-longest river in the world; however, because of the aridity of the basin it drains, the Missouri is only the seventh-ranking river in the country in terms of annual flow.

Meager for its huge watershed and length, the virgin Missouri also flowed erratic in the extreme. At Hermann, Missouri, the discharge to the Mississippi has been measured as low as forty-two hundred cubic feet per second and, in June of 1944, as high as 892,000 cubic feet per second, enough water in a day to satisfy New York City for seventy years. Its course was as unpredictable as its volume. Flowing across the glacial outwash of the plains, the Missouri is unconfined by a true canyon; it is held in check, more or less, by low bluffs as far apart as ten miles. Even these bluffs, in the river's days of freedom, existed pretty much at the Missouri's whim. Within its wide and crumbly confinement, the virgin Missouri writhed like a captive snake. Seemingly permanent islands and bottomlands covered by meadows and trees would seduce farmers down to the river; then they would disappear, never to return, when the river made a lateral migration of a half mile in a single day. Boats often marooned on what had been the main channel the day before; whole neighborhoods on the river bluff sometimes dropped in when the Missouri chewed its banks.

Until 1940, when the Corps of Engineers finished Fort Peck Dam and created, for reasons that were and still are less than obvious, a 140-mile-long reservoir in the middle of Montana, the Missouri River was almost completely uncontrolled. There were two reasons for this. One was that the river didn't show promise of carrying much barge traffic—at least compared to other big rivers like the Mississippi and the Illinois—so the Corps of Engineers didn't have a good reason to improve it for navigation. Even if it had wanted to, the task of making such an erratic, muddy, unconfined river suitable for navigation was overwhelming. The Missouri habitually flooded Kansas City and other towns along its course, but until a major federal flood-control act was passed in 1937—and until the Corps abandoned the doctrine, which it had held to with Ptolomeic rigidity, that reservoirs don't control floods—the Army Engineers had little interest in doing much about it.

The Bureau hadn't built much in the upper Missouri Basin, either, for the same reason that it hadn't built much along the upper Colorado and its tributaries: irrigation farming in cold, high-altitude terrain was usually a losing proposition. It had investigated the basin thoroughly, and by 1907 it had nine projects underway there, mainly for political reasons: the Missouri Basin states contributed a lot of money to the Reclamation Fund. But of the nine projects, not a single one was going to pay for itself within the forty-year term required by the amended Reclamation Act. The nine projects together owed the Treasury and the Reclamation Fund $55,755,000, but had repaid only $17,518,000, even though they were exempted from paying interest. At the rate that revenues—which depended more than anything else on the irrigators' meager ability to pay—were dribbling in, the projects wouldn't be repaid within two hundred years, if ever.

The only way to steer reclamation away from utter financial disaster in the Missouri Basin was to subsidize it with hydropower revenues. Hydroelectric output being a function of two variables—volume of water and height of drop—it made good sense, from the Bureau's point of view, to build high dams along the upper tributaries to generate as much power as possible. The stored water could then be used to irrigate adjacent agricultural land, and hydropower revenues would cover the inevitable losses. Glenn Sloan, an assistant engineer in the Billings office, had begun to draw the outlines of such a basinwide project in the late 1930s, and was reasonably close to finishing his report in 1943, when the Missouri decided to go on a rampage. It produced three big floods—in March, May, and June—and during the last one Omaha and Kansas City were navigable by boat. The Corps' regional office happened to be in Omaha, and its petulant director, Lewis Pick, who would later become the Chief of Engineers, was nearly chased by the river to higher ground. To a military man like Pick, it was an unforgivable insult. "I want control of the Missouri River!" he is said to have barked at his subordinates. Before the end of the year, Pick had dispatched to Washington a twelve-page report on harnessing the Missouri, which was to become known as the Pick Plan.

The trouble with the Pick Plan and the Sloan Plan—which was frantically completed after the Bureau learned about the Pick Plan—was that you could logically build one or the other, but not both. The Corps wanted to build a few dams on upriver tributaries, although, in locating them, it paid no attention at all to irrigation. It also wanted to erect fifteen hundred miles of new levees. All of that was dwarfed, however, by what the Corps planned to do to the river between Fort Peck Reservoir and Yankton, South Dakota. The plan called for five dams and reservoirs, all of them of monstrous size. Garrison Dam, in western North Dakota, was the largest, and would, as the Corps took pains to point out, contain twenty-five times as much material as the Great Pyramid of Cheops. Two and a half miles long, 210 feet high, the dam would be the second-biggest structure on earth (Fort Peck Dam was larger). The Washington Monument would stick out of it like a nail in a four-by-four. The other dams—Oahe, Gavins Point, Big Bend, Fort Randall—would be smaller, but large enough to dwarf almost anything else around. Eight hundred miles of the Missouri would be transformed into a chain of huge, turbid reservoirs. The six main-stem dams would back up almost ninety million acre-feet of water, sufficient to turn Pennsylvania into a shallow lake. The whole scheme—if one believed the Corps' figures, which have always been notoriously low—would cost $660 million, in 1944 dollars.

There was almost nothing about the Corps' plan that the Bureau liked. The dams were all too low or poorly situated to draw the power potential out of the river. (The Corps usually installed about as much public power as it felt the private power companies would tolerate, and it was no surprise to anyone that the Western Power Company became a champion of the Pick Plan, not the Sloan Plan.) The storage was, with a few exceptions, far downriver from the lands the Bureau wanted to irrigate, and a lot of it was in the middle of unirrigable wastelands, which made the Bureau furious. The Missouri's potential as a navigable waterway—that was one of the main justifications of the Pick Plan—was, as far as the Bureau was concerned, shamelessly overstated; to spend more than half a billion dollars on a river channel that would never carry more than a few hundred barges a year was a criminal waste of scarce money and water. It was wasteful in other ways as well. One of the reservoirs, Garrison, would drown the best winter cattle range in North Dakota. Although the Bureau had flooded its share of productive river bottomlands, this was an instance where it was troubled by the idea. As for flood control, Glenn Sloan, who understood the hydrodynamics of the Missouri River as well as anyone alive, said in Congressional testimony that "the 1943 flood could have been regulated to a safe capacity . . . at Sioux City, Omaha, and Kansas City with only two million acre-feet in storage." But the Corps was talking about creating *sixty million* acre-feet of new reservoir storage.

The Corps of Engineers' obsession with humbling the wild Missouri River seemed to derive mainly from the fact that Colonel Pick was mad at it. (Although, needless to say, in the wake of the war his agency, its staff swollen by the thousands, was eager for new work.) According to Henry Hart, a journalist and historian who covered the Pick-Sloan controversy in the 1940s and later wrote a book about the Missouri, the Corps "relied for justification entirely on the public sense of shock at the disruption caused by floods." Nonetheless, the Pick Plan went through the House Rivers and Harbors Committee without a hitch, and passed the full House in the spring of 1944, while still under consideration in the Senate. It seemed only a matter of weeks before it became law.

The Bureau of Reclamation, meanwhile, felt so threatened by the Pick Plan that it had quickly produced a plan of its own that was equally ambitious, and only slightly more susceptible to logic. Reconnaissance studies of reservoir and irrigation sites were conducted with such haste that, even within the Bureau, they were referred to as "windshield reconnaissance"—an allusion to $30 million reservoirs being plotted from behind the windshields of moving cars. The Bureau spewed out project recommendations like popcorn. The final Sloan Plan was a catch basin of ninety dams and several hundred individual irrigation projects; among other things, it called for fifteen reservoirs on three meager tributaries in the Dakotas. The Sloan Plan, however, soon acquired some powerful supporters, too. By the end of 1943, the Congress had two irreconcilable plans before it. The lobbies behind them were about equally matched. Under the circumstances, there was only one thing to do: adopt them both.

The impetus came from FDR himself, though the result was not exactly what he intended. With the Bureau and the Corps stalemated, Roosevelt decided to break the impasse by sending Congress a strongly worded letter saying that the solution to developing the Missouri Basin was to create a regional authority, similar to the TVA, and take development out of both agencies' hands. That was more than the Corps and the Bureau had bargained on. On October 15, 1944, Glenn Sloan and a representative of Colonel Pick (who had since gone off to build the Ledo Road in Burma) sat down in a meeting which is probably historic for what it accomplished in a given amount of time. On October 17, two days later, they emerged to announce that the Pick Plan and the Sloan Plan had been "reconciled." Had anyone taken a closer look—hardly anyone did—he would have seen that the reconciliation amounted to the adoption, virtually intact, of both agencies' plans. With the single exception of a dam at Oak Creek, South Dakota, originally proposed by the Corps of Engineers, the Pick-Sloan "compromise" included every dam and project in the original and separate plans, plus some additions which the agencies had somehow managed to overlook. Critics such as James Patton, the president of the National Farmers' Union, called it a "shameless shotgun wedding," and calculated that instead of saving the taxpayers money, it would cost them at least $250 million in redundant features. Henry Hart acidly observed that "reconciliation meant chiefly that each agency became reconciled to the works of the other."

The most significant aspect of the reconciliation was that the two agencies had agreed to spend $1.9 billion of the taxpayers' money (an estimate which would, as usual, turn out to be much too low) on a whole whose parts, according to their earlier testimony, would cancel out each other's usefulness. The second most significant aspect was that the Bureau agreed to let the Corps go ahead and build its huge main-stem reservoirs first. "The Corps got the here and now," says David Weiman, a lobbyist who would later be hired to fight several of the Bureau's projects by the same farmers who were supposed to benefit from their existence. "The Bureau got the then and later."

O ne of the least-known consequences of water development in America is its impact on the Indians who hadn't already succumbed to the U.S. Cavalry, smallpox, and social rot. Although many of the tribes had been sequestered on reservations that were far from the riverbottoms where they used to live, some tribes had been granted good riverbottom reservation land—either because the lands were prone to flooding, or because the government was occasionally in a generous mood.

The three tribes whom Lewis and Clark encountered along the Missouri River in North Dakota were the Mandan, the Hidatsa, and the Arikara. Perhaps because they were generally peaceful and had helped the explorers (Lewis and Clark spent their first winter with the Mandan, and their adopted Shoshone-Mandan interpreter, Sacajawea, probably saved their lives), the associated Three Tribes were later rewarded with some of the better reservation land in the West: miles of fertile bottoms along the serpentine Missouri, which they used mainly for raising cattle. These were the same lands that the Bureau of Reclamation considered the best winter cattle range in the state, and which it said ought never to be drowned by a reservoir. Under the Corps of Engineers plan, however, the Three Tribes' reservation would sit directly under the reservoir behind Garrison Dam.

The Corps had, of course, taken extraordinary care not to inundate any of the white towns that were situated along the river. The reservoir behind Oahe Dam, which would be more than 150 miles long, would stop just shy of Bismarck, North Dakota. Pierre, the capital of South Dakota, would sit safely inside a small reservoir-free zone between the tail end of Lake Francis Case and the upper end of Lake Oahe; were it not for the town, the two reservoirs would have virtually touched, nose to tail. Chamberlain, South Dakota, nestled between the reservoirs formed by Big Bend and Ford Randall Dams, was similarly spared. The height of Garrison Dam was reduced by twenty feet so that the surface level of the reservoir would be 1,830 feet above sea level, not 1,850 feet as originally planned. It was a loss of several million acre-feet of storage exclusively for the benefit of Williston, North Dakota, a small part of which could have been subject to inundation during wet years.

For the sake of the Fort Berthold Indian Reservation, where the Mandan and Arikara and Hidatsa lived, no such intricate gerrymandering of reservoir outlines was even attempted. Garrison Dam, which the Corps justified largely because of its flood-control benefits downstream, was going to cause horrific local flood damage the moment its reservoir began to fill. Virtually every productive acre of bottomland the tribes owned would go under.

Colonel Lewis Pick, the architect of the tribes' inundation, was the embodiment of a no-nonsense military man. Pick liked to punctuate his conversation with Cagney-style "See? See?"'s; these were not questions—they were commands. When first assigned to the Missouri River Division during the early part of the Second World War, he ordered all of his staff to work a series of continuous seven-day weeks. On the first Sunday after the order was given, Pick spied on all his top officers and summarily dismissed those who were not at their desks. Later, when he was in Burma, he fired a whole team of surveyors for laying out a technically perfect road which, in his opinion, would take too long to build. Instead, he designed a treacherous road that could be finished slightly sooner.

Since what Pick proposed to do to the Indians was the most calamitous thing that had happened to them in their history, he might have had the good grace to leave the proceedings through which the tribes would be compensated to someone else. But Pick was a take-charge type. He not only insisted on participating; he insisted on running them himself.

Initially, the Three Tribes pleaded with the government not to build Garrison Dam at all. "All of the bottom lands and all of the bench lands on this reservation will be flooded," wrote the business council of the Three Tribes in an anguished resolution condemning the plan.

> Most of it will be underwater to a depth of 100 feet or more. The homes and lands of 349 families, comprising 1,544 individuals, will be covered with deep water. The lands which will be flooded are practically all the lands which are of any use or value to produce feed for stock or winter shelter. We are

195

stockmen and our living depends on our production of cattle. . . . All of our people have lived where we now are for more than 100 years. Our people have lived on and cultivated the bottom lands along the Missouri River for many hundreds of years. We were here before the first white men stepped foot on this land. We have always kept the peace. We have kept our side of all treaties. We have been, and now are, as nearly self-supporting as the average white community. We recognize the value to our white neighbors, and to the people down stream, of the plan to control the River and to make use of the great surplus of flood waters; but we cannot agree that we should be destroyed, drowned out, removed, and divided for the public benefit while all other white communities are protected and safe-guarded by the same River development plan which now threatens us with destruction. . . .

However, when the Interior Department, the parent agency of the Bureau of Indian Affairs, threw itself behind the plan, the Three Tribes saw the futility of abject resistance. What they asked for as compensation, considering the agony they were about to be put through, was pitifully little. First, they wanted at least an equivalent amount of compensatory land. Since it would inevitably be poorer land, they also wanted twenty thousand kilowatt-hours per year of electricity, mainly to run the pumps they would need to bring water, once freely available from the river, up from depths of three hundred feet or more on the arid plains. They asked for permission to graze and water their cattle along the margins of the reservoir, and for first rights to the timber which the reservoir would flood. They wanted a bridge built across a narrow reach of the reservoir so their people could maintain contact with one another (the reservoir would effectively split the reservation in half). Otherwise, they would have to spend hours driving around its endless shore or brave violent winds and waves trying to cross its surface by boat.

One small faction of the Three Tribes, led by a flamboyant young radical named Crow Flies High, remained opposed to any compromise at all. As negotiations were already underway between the Interior Department, the Corps, and the Tribal Business Council, a delegation from the dissident faction burst into the room in ceremonial dress and began disrupting the proceedings. The leader of the group, who was probably Crow Flies High, went up to Colonel Pick and made an obscene gesture. Pick turned the color of uncooked liver.

It was an insult, he said lividly, that he would remember as long as he lived.

On the basis of that single insult, Pick stormed out of the negotiations, never to return. As far as he was concerned, all of the points of agreement that had already been reached were null and void. When Arthur Morgan, the first director of the Tennessee Valley Authority—and the one person who kept the memory of the Indians' tragedy alive—visited the Three Tribes some time later, however, he discovered a different sentiment as to why Pick had walked out. There was, he wrote, "a nearly unanimous opinion that the Corps welcomed the attack of the Crow Flies High group because it provided a semblance of justification for ignoring the clear terms of the law. . . ."

Before the negotiations were interrupted, the Corps had offered the Indians some scattered property on the Missouri benchlands to replace the bottomlands they would lose. ("I want to show you where we are going to place you people," a local Congregationalist minister quoted Pick as saying.) Under the law, all compensatory lands were to be "comparable in quality and sufficient in area to compensate the said tribes for the land on the Fort Berthold Reservation." It was up to the Secretary of the Interior, Cap Krug, to decide whether the criteria had been met. As Krug well knew, there was no land in North Dakota that could adequately compensate the tribes for prime winter cattle range in a river valley. He had decided, therefore, to accede to the Indians' other demands for water, at-cost hydroelectric power, and first timber and mineral rights. Since even this appeared to be too little, he also agreed to pay them $5,105,625 for the 155,000 acres they would lose. It was only $33 an acre, but it was better than nothing.

Colonel Pick, however, was still smoldering over the insult he had received, and he had his good friends in Congress. A few months after Krug announced that he was prepared to meet most or all of the Indians' terms, the disposition of their case was removed by Congress from Interior's hands and given to the Committee on Interior and Insular Affairs. The committee soon tore up Interior's version of the bill and wrote its own version exactly along the lines suggested by Pick. The Fort Berthold tribes would not even be permitted to fish in the reservoir. Their cattle would not be allowed to drink from it, or graze by it. The right to purchase hydroelectricity at cost was abrogated. The tribes were forbidden to use any compensatory money they received to hire attorneys. They were not even allowed to cut the trees that would be drowned by the reservoir, except in one case, and there, according to the new terms, *they were not permitted to haul them away*.

On May 20, 1948, Secretary Krug ceremoniously signed the bill disposing of the Fort Berthold matter in his office in Washington. Despite some intervention by the Interior Department, most of the Corps' vengeful provisions were still intact. Standing behind Krug, alongside a slouching Mike Straus of the Bureau of Reclamation and a scowling General Pick, was handsome George Gillette, the leader of the tribal business council, in a pinstripe suit. "The members of the tribal council sign this contract with heavy hearts," Gillette managed to say. "Right now the future does not look good to us." Then, as Krug reached for a bundle of commemorative pens to sign the bill, and as the assembled politicians and bureaucrats looked on embarrassed or stony-faced, George Gillette cradled his face in one hand and began to cry.

To eliminate any possibility that Congress or the President might succumb to a tender conscience and eliminate Garrison Dam from the Pick-Sloan Plan, the Corps had already begun work on it in 1945, three years before the agreement with the Indians was signed. In fact, it would spend $60 million on ambiguously authorized "preliminary" work on the dam between 1945 and 1948. A number of members of Congress protested that such work was, if not outright illegal, then certainly a moral wrong. But the one party that might have gone to court for a ruling—the Fort Berthold tribes—had been forbidden to spend any of their compensatory money on attorneys.

The Fort Berthold Indians have never recovered from the trauma they underwent. Their whole sense of cohesiveness was lost, and they adjusted badly to life on the arid plains and in the white towns. But no humiliation could have been greater than for them to see the signs that were erected around the reservoir as it slowly filled, submerging the dying cottonwoods and drowning the land they had occupied for at least four hundred years. In what looked to the Indians like a stroke of malevolent inspiration, the Corps of Engineers had decided to call the giant, turbid pool of water Lake Sacajawea.

As is the case with most schemes that involve a dazzling transmogrification of nature, this is a story without an end, and a later chapter will say something about the likely consequences of trapping most of the Missouri's silt behind six great dams. For now, it is worth looking briefly at what the Pick-Sloan plan has wrought.

The Corps' six Missouri River reservoirs, which cost $1.2 billion to build even then, have undoubtedly lowered the flood crests all the way down to New Orleans—though they did not prevent a disastrous flood in the early 1970s, when the Mississippi widened by several miles and caused tens of millions of dollars in damage. Barge traffic hasn't come close to the Corps' projections; in 1984, traffic on the entire navigable stretch of the Missouri amounted to only 2.9 million tons, an infinitesimal percentage of the 590 million tons carried by the Mississippi system. The small port of Lorain, Ohio, handled nearly five times as much. The worst natural damage was the flooding of some of the best riparian waterfowl habitat in the world. A former director of the U.S. Fish and Wildlife Service, John Gottschalk, remembers walking along the undammed middle Missouri for five miles and flushing countless flocks of pheasants and migrating ducks; today, one would be lucky to see anything at all. The birds thrived in the spacious, secluded bottomlands and oxbow pools and marshes, and those are almost entirely gone.

Had the Missouri been left to the Bureau of Reclamation exclusively, things wouldn't necessarily have turned out much better. However, because the projects would, for the most part, have been well upriver, the Fort Berthold Reservation wouldn't have been drowned, a lot of riparian waterfowl habitat in the heart of the Central Flyway wouldn't have been inundated, and the dams, being high rather than wide, would likely have produced a lot more hydroelectricity for their size. The irrigation projects the Bureau planned might have been losers in an economic sense, but the Missouri, if it had to be intensively developed, might have been more useful irrigating crops than providing free transit—at enormous public expense—for a handful of barges.

The Bureau, of course, was not to be denied, either, if it could help it. Ever since the 1950s, it has been trying, without too much success, to build the irrigation projects authorized by the Pick-Sloan Plan—the "then-and-later" dams over which the Corps' reservoirs took precedence. The O'Neill Project on the Niobrara River in Nebraska, the Narrows Dam on the South Platte in Colorado, the Garrison and Oahe projects in the Dakotas—projects that have become some of the most controversial in the nation—were all authorized by that same misbegotten act. The Bureau, of course, knew well enough that few, if any, of those projects made economic sense, and at least one of its officials, in private, was willing to admit it. In 1955, future commissioner Floyd Dominy, then chief of the Irrigation Division, received an angry letter from two old farmer friends from Nebraska, Claire and Donald Hanna. The Hannas were dryland farmers, and they were incensed that the Bureau's Ainsworth Project—one of the Pick-Sloan bunch—might literally force them into irrigation farming. "I am really not happy about the Ainsworth Project," Dominy confessed in his letter of reply of April 15, 1955. ". . . My views about the impropriety and damn foolishness involved in the construction of irrigation projects in relatively good dry land areas at the present state of the nation's economy at a cost in excess of $1,000 per acre have been repeatedly expressed. . . . As dear and honored friends I am troubled as to how to advise you," Dominy went on. "The local towns and businessmen wanted it [the Ainsworth Project]. They could see themselves growing fat on large-scale construction payrolls. They could see something to be gained by increasing the number of farm families in their service area. Like the usual selfish citizen they were willing to accept this increase to their personal larder without thought as to the burden to be placed on the Federal tax payer."

Predictably, Dominy managed to overcome such scruples after he was appointed commissioner. In the 1960s and 1970s, the Bureau launched a mighty effort to push forward the Garrison and Oahe projects, enormous diversions from Lake Sacajawea and Oahe Reservoir to compensate North and South Dakota (if not the dispossessed tribes) for the land drowned by the Corps. But the irrigation canals and local storage reservoirs would have consumed nearly as much productive farmland as the irrigation water would have created—in the case of the Garrison Diversion Project, 220,000 acres for canals and reservoirs versus 250,000 new acres irrigated. In addition, Garrison, in its original version, would have converted some 73,000 more acres of superb waterfowl habitat—prairie marshes and potholes used by hundreds of thousands of migrating ducks—into farm fields. Not only that, but it could easily have introduced parasites and competitive trash fish from the Missouri into streams emptying into Lakes Winnipeg and Manitoba, threatening very productive pike and lake trout fisheries. The Canadians, in fact, had been screaming objections into the deaf ear of the Bureau for years, and even sent a series of stern diplomatic protests to the State Department.

In the late 1970s, the Oahe Diversion Project, after reigning for years as the biggest political issue in South Dakota, was defeated by the very same farmers for whose alleged benefit it was to be built, and one of its principal champions, former Senator George McGovern, saw his political career buried with it. McGovern's surprising loss, according to local political insiders, had as much to do with his unwavering support for a suddenly unpopular Oahe Project as it did with the campaign mounted against him by the ultraconservative Right. Garrison, in 1985, was partly completed and still alive, and a bobtailed version of the project seems likely to be built, irrigating perhaps 130,000 acres (devoted mainly to surplus crops) at a cost of $1,650,000 per farm. Energy requirements for pumping, which totaled 288,000 kilowatts under the original plan, would also be reduced, but how the dams can pump water to 130,000 acres *and* sell power at market rates to subsidize the water costs is a question that no one, least of all the Bureau, can answer.

As for the other dozens of projects assigned to the Bureau, few have been built, but the Corps, despite the antipathy of the local citizenry, has tried to steal away even these. On May 9, 1963, Dominy's regional chief in Billings, Bruce Johnson, reported that the Corps "is not dismayed by the opposition" to two newly proposed dams on the Missouri, Fort Benton and High Cow Creek—nor, Johnson said, would "the highly preliminary stage of the basic investigations . . . deter them. . . . They will, I think, seek authority to build both dams." As a result, Johnson advocated "that we grit our collective teeth and decide to use the reconnaissance data that we have so we can go to the 'hill' just as quickly as the Corps does and ask for authority [to build] without additional investigation." If such "additional investigation" (reconnaissance data are usually based on a mere desultory look) disclosed that either dam would be a waste of money, that was the taxpayers' problem.

And, by now, it is, even if Fort Benton and High Cow Creek dams have not yet been built. Between the money-losing irrigation ventures in the Missouri Basin and the river's mediocre power potential, the Missouri Basin "Fund" appears to be in unhealthy financial shape. The problem is, no one knows exactly how bad things are. According to a Carter administration audit, Missouri Basin power is *already* vastly oversubscribed, and the Corps and the Bureau, employing some complex economic chicanery even the auditors couldn't quite decipher, may be borrowing on "anticipated" revenues from as far away as the next century, just as New York City did in the early 1970s before some of its elected officials almost went to jail. "Our conclusion is that the financial posture of Pick-Sloan is, at best, based on an uncertainty," the auditors wrote. "At worst, it is based on an unreality."

The "reconciliation" of the Pick Plan and the Sloan Plan had

201

taken a mere two days; the political fallout, the environmental damage, and the drain on the Treasury that have resulted seem likely to go on forever.

It was back in California, meanwhile, that the bitterest rivalry and the most vicious infighting between the Bureau and the Corps continued to occur. Awkward, expensive, and redundant as it was, Congress had at least come up with some kind of division of responsibilities in the Missouri Basin. The same applied to the Columbia Basin. In California, however, the two giant bureaucracies were left pretty much to fight it out among themselves. Their rivalry was a wonderful opportunity for the state's irrigation lobby; the growers could sit back and smile coyly as they were madly pursued by rival suitors in hard hats. But it was an equally wonderful opportunity in the 1960s for Governor Pat Brown, under whose leadership the state was trying, all by itself, to complete the most expensive water project ever built.

On Wednesday, January 27, 1965, a highly secret meeting was held in the office of California's resources secretary, Hugo Fisher. In attendance were most of the oligarchs of water development in California: Pat Brown's water resources director, Bill Warne; Robert Pafford, the Bureau of Reclamation's regional director; Brigadier General Arthur Frye of the Corps of Engineers; Ralph Brody, the chairman of the California Water Commission; state senator James Cobey; and assemblyman Carley Porter, the chief author of the bill that authorized the State Water Project in 1959. The purpose of the meeting was to discuss the future of Marysville Dam.

With all the big Sierra rivers developed close to their limits, precious few good damsites were left anywhere in the state except on the North Coast. There were, however, still three rather marginal sites in the Sierra foothills which the Bureau wanted to develop in order to augment the water supply of the Central Valley Project. One was New Melones on the Stanislaus River. Another was Auburn Dam on the American River. The third was Marysville Dam on the Yuba River. Of the three rivers, the Yuba, at the time, had the blackest reputation. It had devastated Yuba City and forced the evacuation of twenty thousand people during an awesome flood in 1955, and just a few weeks earlier it had flooded menacingly again during the great Christmas storm of 1964. The dam, therefore, was of interest not only to the Bureau but to the Corps of Engineers. No one, however, was more interested in it than the governor of California and his director of water resources, Bill Warne.

Brown and Warne had an unenviable dilemma on their hands, even if they had brought it on themselves. They had misrepresented, either unintentionally or by design, the cost of the State Water Project, and were left without the funds to finish it. The state had signed binding contracts to deliver 4,230,000 acre-feet of water; the $1.75 billion bond issue that the voters had approved, however, would not even suffice to build Oroville Dam, San Luis Dam, and the 444-mile aqueduct down the San Joaquin Valley and over the mountains to Los Angeles. All of those works could deliver a safe yield of only 2.5 million acre-feet of water. Somehow, the state had to come up with nearly two million additional acre-feet—quite an imposing agenda. The water was there, on any number of northern California rivers. But since the voters had just shouldered the most expensive state bond issue in history, the money to develop it was emphatically not.

Marysville Dam, therefore, was exactly the opportunity Brown and Warne were looking for, provided the State Project could gain rights to some or all of the water and contribute little or nothing to the cost of the dam. No federal dam could be built without the consent of the governor of the state. The question, then, was which of the potential builders would give the state what it wanted: the Bureau or the Corps.

The report on the meeting which Bob Pafford of the Bureau sent to his superior in Washington, Commissioner Floyd Dominy, began on a gloomy note. The state was very much inclined to let the Corps build Marysville, for obvious reasons. There would be no federal claim on the water in a purported flood-control reservoir and no strings attached to its use, as there would be if the Bureau built the dam. Pafford, however, held out one hopeful prospect to Dominy: "California might be willing to recommend changing their position from one of strong support for immediate construction and operation of Marysville Reservoir by the Corps of Engineers, with the State taking the conservation water via Title III, to one of support for immediate authorization of Marysville for early construction by the Corps, but with the project to be integrated fully with the Central Valley Project."

The Title III of which Pafford spoke referred to a section of the federal Water Supply Act of 1958, which allowed water from a federal dam to be sold to another political entity, such as a city or state,

provided the water was used only for municipal or industrial purposes—that is, not for irrigation. The provision, in fact, owed its
existence to the earlier battle on the Kings and the Kern rivers; there
was so much resentment over the fact that the state's biggest growers
had gotten an enormous supply of water virtually free from the Corps
that a number of Congressmen vowed never to let it happen again,
and the result was Title III. But Brown and Bill Warne's predicament
was that the State Water Project was first and foremost an *irrigation*
project. The specter of water famine in southern California gave the
project its moral justification, and Los Angeles offered the assessed
property wealth needed to guarantee the bonds, but the first deliveries
of water would go to the big corporate farmers in the San Joaquin
Valley. Los Angeles wasn't scheduled to receive its full entitlement
for many years—and, in fact, would take only a fraction of each year's
entitlement all through the 1970s and early 1980s, permitting most
of the water to be sold, at bargain prices, as "surplus" water to the
same big growers in the San Joaquin Valley.

Pafford told Dominy that he had cautioned Warne about the
inherent legal risks in trying to use the water from a federally built
reservoir to augment a state project whose main purpose, at least for
now, was irrigation. "I pointed out that authorization for the sale of
water under Title III . . . might severely limit the use of this water,
since the Act referred to the use of water only for municipal and
industrial purposes." In other words, if the Corps built the dam, the
whole arrangement would be quite naked—the Kings and the Kern
all over again—and probably enjoinable in a court of law. If the
Bureau built the dam, on the other hand, the water, in theory, would
have to go into the Central Valley Project and the State Water Project's main beneficiaries, the big San Joaquin growers, could not touch
a drop.

There had to be a way out of the predicament, and Bill Warne
was canny and cynical enough to come up with it. What if the Corps
built the dam on the promise that the water would "someday" flow
into the Central Valley Project? And what if, since there was still
plenty of surplus water sloshing around in the CVP, the Bureau let
the State Water Project "borrow" it for a while?

What Warne wanted to do, Pafford confided to Dominy (and he
apparently thought it wasn't a bad idea), was create exactly such an
arrangement as "a test of this Act"—by which he meant Title III of
the Flood Control Act of 1958. If the Corps built the reservoir and the
state took the water with no strings attached, they were risking a

head-on collision with existing law. But promising the water to the Bureau—eventually—might provide a legal out; Congress should have no objection to California's "borrowing" it for twenty or thirty years. That would give the state time enough to climb out from under the staggering pile of debt into which the construction of its huge water project had dumped it, and to build the necessary works to develop the full 4,230,000 acre-feet of water it was legally obligated to provide.

If the Bureau acceded to Bill Warne's plan, it wouldn't get to do what it loved best: build a dam. But at least it would get *something* out of it instead of being boxed out entirely, as it was on the Kings and the Kern and the Kaweah and the Tule.

That it was willing to let itself be so used is an indication of how desperate the Bureau had become since the Corps of Engineers began trying to muscle its way into its domain. If anything, Pafford ought to have been incensed by Warne's idea. After all, the Bureau, more than any other single entity, had made California into the wealthy and populous state it was. It built Hoover Dam for Los Angeles and the Imperial Valley, and Parker and Davis and Imperial dams as well. It built the Central Valley Project to rescue the growers from economic suicide by groundwater overdraft. It was paying nearly half the cost of the world's fourth-largest dam, San Luis, which would store water jointly for both the CVP and the State Project; without such assistance, the California project might have fallen on its face. And on top of this, the state's big farmers, when they began to receive cheap "surplus" water from the State Project, would be in a position to engage in cutthroat competition with the Bureau's constituency, the smaller farmers. From the point of view of many small farmers—and this would be borne out later in actual fact—the expansion of the State Water Project was one of the worst things that could happen.

Not only did outrage fail Bob Pafford, but he was willing to go the Corps one better—so badly did he want an opportunity to construct a new dam. Should the Bureau, instead of the Corps, be allowed to build Marysville Dam, he wrote Dominy, "I restated our offer to make water from Marysville available to the state on an interim basis *at a price no greater* than under a Title III arrangement with the Corps" (emphasis added). Then he added a cryptic, furtive remark: "It was concluded that it would not be necessary to include this possibility in the State's comments."

And no wonder! What Pafford was proposing was, if not illegal, then at the ragged margin of the law. Where did the Reclamation Act permit the Bureau to sell deeply subsidized water to a state on an "interim" basis, when the state would turn right around and resell it to some of the largest corporate farmers in the world? Where did it allow the Bureau to promise to match any price offered by the Corps *before it even knew what the cost of developing the water would be*?

The answer was, nowhere. But the Bureau was willing to sell subsidized water from one of its dams to California, which would turn around and resell it, at bargain "surplus" rates, to thirty- and forty-thousand-acre farmers who had the economic muscle to drive the Bureau's chief clients and dependents—the state's smaller farmers—out of business. And it was willing to do this, to play with federal law and forsake its small-farmer constituency, simply because its archrival might snatch away a damsite it wanted for itself.

Nineteen years later, Robert Pafford, then retired, never saw a bit of irony in this position. During an interview in 1983, he downplayed the rivalry between the Bureau and the Corps—"we had our points of contention, but it was nothing serious"—and said that he "didn't blame Bill Warne for playing both ends against the middle." After all, he said, "you might have done the same thing yourself." Warne, whom he referred to as a "great guy," had "a legal obligation to deliver water to his own constituency—those contracts with the San Joaquin farmers were valid contracts and he couldn't just ignore them." But why would the Bureau go out of its way to help a group of giant corporate farmers who might put the Bureau's little farmers out of business? "Our farmers had water at $3.50 an acre-foot. No way anyone is going to compete with that." Involuntarily, Pafford admitted what the Bureau has always tried to deny: that its cheap water gives its client farmers an unfair advantage over all the other farmers of the nation.

Two years after the secret 1964 meeting, however, no agreement had been reached on Marysville Dam; evidently, neither federal party would yield (Floyd Dominy, a proud man, privately loathed the Corps of Engineers, and probably refused to go along with Pafford's recommendation), and each had the power to hang the project up in Congress, which appropriated no money for construction by anyone. By 1966, in fact, Pat Brown and Bill Warne evidently realized that their strategy of pitting the Bureau against the Corps could backfire on them. If the agencies became *too* competitive, then nothing might get built, just as a pair of rutting bull elk can lock horns so hopelessly that both of them starve. As a result, that year saw the formation of a new suprabureaucratic entity called the California State-Federal Interagency Group—William E. Warne, chairman—which immediately issued a call for a Herculean amount of water development, most of it on the undammed rivers of the isolated, rainy North Coast. On a big wall map depicting what they wanted to build, one saw, traced in red, a Dos Rios Reservoir and an English Ridge Reservoir and a Sequoia Reservoir and an Etsel Reservoir and a Panther Reservoir and a Frost Reservoir and a Sebow Reservoir and a Mina Reservoir on the Eel—eight reservoirs on three forks of a middle-size river that was nearly dry from June to October. And that wasn't all. There was a Baseline and a Dinsmore Dam on the Van Duzen. There was a Butler Valley and an Anderson Ford and an enlarged Ruth Reservoir (a smaller one already existed) on the Mad River. Sounding like the Creator himself, Bill Warne, in his introduction to the report, described how the waters had been divided up: "The upper main Eel above the Middle Fork, as shown on attached Chart One, was assigned to the Bureau of Reclamation. . . . The main Eel between the Middle Fork and the South Fork was assigned to the Corps of Engineers . . . the Van Duzen River Basin to the Bureau, the Lower Eel to the Corps. . . ." Nothing was to be built by California itself, though it, of course, would reap the rewards, especially its big growers, who would receive millions of acre-feet of water via long tunnels drilled through the Coast Range. The whole scheme, said Warne in his introductory remarks, represented "a new chapter in California's illustrious history of water planning."

But it wouldn't quite work out that way. In fact, the feuding agencies were about to lock horns and starve over the first two dams on their priority lists.

The North Coast dam that the state and the Corps passionately wanted to build was Dos Rios, a seventy-three-story earthfill wall across the Middle Fork of the Eel that would capture twice as much water as Shasta Lake; it would create one of the biggest reservoirs in the West. The dam the Bureau wanted to build first was English Ridge, which would create a smaller reservoir on the main Eel a short distance away. Since each project required a hard-rock tunnel, about twenty miles long, to shunt the water to where it was allegedly needed, they would both be very expensive. To become economically feasible, a large proportion of their costs would have to be written off to flood control, which is nonreimbursable. The Corps of Engineers has always been vested with the authority to compute the flood-control benefits of federal dams. It was, as expected, quite generous in computing the flood-control benefits of Dos Rios; it was inexplicably niggardly in the case of English Ridge. David Shuster, who would become the operations manager for the Central Valley Project—and who would later be hounded out of the Bureau for being too fair-minded about Jimmy Carter's water projects "hit list"—would later insist that English Ridge was a perfectly feasible project. "There was nothing wrong with English Ridge," Shuster remembered. "A lot of the water would have gone to municipalities in the North Bay and to grape growers. Repayment-wise, it was in sound shape. The thing that killed us was the Corps wouldn't give us the flood-control benefits they gave to Dos Rios. It was like they were using two separate formulae."

Flood-control benefits for both dams, it would turn out, were largely a fraud. Even huge Dos Rios Dam would have reduced the thirty-five-foot crest of the monstrous 1964 flood by less than a foot—a fact which the Corps took pains to camouflage, but which its enemies, especially a local Dartmouth-educated rancher named Richard Wilson, who led the opposition, managed to bring out and make stick. It was Wilson, and Ronald Reagan—who, as governor, refused to approve the project—who ultimately killed Dos Rios Dam, but it was the infighting between the agencies that set the stage for its defeat—and for the ultimate collapse of the whole carefully orchestrated development push. By 1981, not a single one of the thirteen North Coast dams on the Corps' and the Bureau's priority lists had been built. In that year, moreover, all the major North Coast rivers were added to the federal Wild and Scenic Rivers system by the Carter administration—which, in theory, puts them forever off-limits to any dams.

The single cooperative achievement since the Marysville summit meeting a decade and a half earlier was the erection of New Melones Dam on the Stanislaus River. There, the Marysville formula was finally tried: the Corps built the dam, the Bureau gets to market the water—if it can. By 1985, seven years after the dam was completed, not a teacup of New Melones water had been sold, which was especially infuriating to those who despaired at watching the last wild stretch of the lower Stanislaus River drowned. One reason no water had been sold was lack of demand, no matter what the Bureau said about demand "being there." The other reason was that no canals had been built to carry water from the reservoir to the farmers' fields. Why had they not been built? The conspiracy theorists—who, by now, include a lot of people who have watched the progress of California water politics from the losers' side—thought they had an answer. As long as New Melones water remains unsold, it simply runs out, in carefully regulated and fully usable flows, to the Delta, where it can be sucked up by the State Water Project's battery of ten-thousand-horsepower pumps and conveyed either to the big San Joaquin growers or to Los Angeles. It is hard to argue with people who insist that this was the intention all along.

The relatively small yield from behind New Melones Dam, however, is scarcely enough to supply the Chandler family's Tejon Ranch or to satisfy two years' worth of subdivision growth in southern California. As a result, the State Water Project seems destined to remain chronically undersupplied, unless Californians do a remarkable about-face and approve $10 billion or $20 billion worth of new water development. The state, the Bureau, and the Corps have all heaped blame on environmentalism and "selfish" northern Californians for the fact that so little has been built, but if anyone was selfish it was the Bureau and the Corps, who coveted too much, and cooperated too little, for their own good. As for Pat Brown and Bill Warne and the California water lobby, they appear to have schemed themselves into a dry hole.

No one will ever know how many ill-conceived water projects *were* built by the Bureau and the Corps simply because the one agency thought the other would build it first. What is clear, thanks to long-hidden files from the Bureau that have come to light, is that the Corps of Engineers has kept a full-court press on the Bureau since it moved on the Kings and Kern rivers forty years ago. And it was during this period that by far the most objectionable projects were built.

A May 19, 1962, memorandum from Bruce Johnson, the Bureau's regional director in Billings, Montana, to Floyd Dominy offers a vivid illustration of how far things could go. Johnson's memo discussed a series of potential conflicts between the Bureau and the Corps in the upper Missouri Basin. One project which the Corps was talking about building at the time was Bowman-Haley, a dam on the Grand River in North Dakota—which is not much of a river, despite its name. "They will build [Bowman-Haley] if they get the money," Johnson warned Dominy. "I predict the state will see to it that they get the money unless steps are taken to have the Secretary of the Interior [that is, the Bureau] authorized to build it."

Would it make sense for the Bureau to build it, in that case? "We have reported on Bowman-Haley, always unfavorably, at various times for some thirty years," Johnson wrote. ". . . If we take this on we will be building another tributary dam with little to show in the way of repayment contracts. Benefits and repayment are based on a delivery of 3,000 acre-feet per year. However, some years delivery of this amount of water will not be possible." It was, in short, a perfectly miserable Reclamation project, a project whose yield was not only pitiable, but impossible to guarantee. But it made no better sense, Johnson quickly added, for the Corps to build the dam instead. Flood control was a poor justification; the damsite was so near the river's headwaters that most of the floods were raised downstream. That left municipal water supply as the sole conceivable justification. But "most of the municipal and industrial [water-supply] benefits," he continued, "are anticipatory of urban and industrial growth." And not only was North Dakota the one state in the union that was *losing* population, but the little town of Haley—the town that would presumably get the water— is so small it wasn't even listed in the American Automobile Association's road atlas for 1976. The water might be piped to Bowman, a considerable distance away, but even Bowman, a relative metropolis, had only thirteen hundred people. If the dam were justified on the basis of local water supply, then, it would give Bowman and Haley about two and a half acre-feet per person—twelve times as much water as average per-capita use.

It was difficult to conceive of a more worthless project, but in the 1950s and 1960s projects as dubious as Bowman-Haley had a way of getting built. The agency that ended up building it was, indeed, the Corps of Engineers; authorized by Congress in 1962, Bowman-Haley was finally completed eight years later. Seeing it there, on a piddling river snaking through the drought-bleached rises and swales of western North Dakota, one needn't be a hydrologist or an engineer to fathom why Bruce Johnson was right. The dam itself is huge: more than a mile across and seventy-nine feet high from the base, it has nearly half the bulk of the smaller of the Corps's main-stem Missouri dams. The reservoir, by contrast, is tiny and shallow, a puddle as reservoirs go; it holds only 19,780 acre-feet, while the smallest of the main-stem Missouri reservoirs holds ninety times more. A lot of tax money had gone for a thimbleful of water.

The Bureau's main problem throughout the Missouri Basin, Johnson added in a footnote to his secret memorandum to Dominy, was the indefatigable opportunism of the Corps of Engineers. "They [the Corps] will build projects that we may find unacceptable from a financial standpoint. The states are aware of this. . . . The Corps will gladly give us their 'bad' project proposals on the tributaries but do not intend to refuse Congress if money is appropriated to build either 'good' ones or 'bad' ones. I do not think they believe that the Memorandum [an informal division of responsibility Johnson and his counterpart in the Corps had recently signed] ends the historic game of the states playing the Army against the Bureau to get what is locally desired."

It was an incredible admission—although it was obviously not intended as such—since neither the Corps nor the Bureau would assert publicly that *any* federal water project, anywhere, had ever been a waste of tax dollars. As Johnson intimated, however, the ultimate blame for the bad projects had to be laid at the feet of the "local interests," the contractors and irrigation farmers and patriotic Chamber of Commerce types who haven't the slightest compunction about wasting the taxpayers' money on pointless dams. A perfect example was offered by the Bureau's area engineer in Salem, Oregon, John H. Mangan, who wrote a confidential letter—what the Bureau calls a blue-envelope letter—dated January 22, 1965, to Harold Nelson, the regional director in Boise, recalling a conversation he recently had with a member of the Oregon State Water Resources Board. "He expressed his feeling," Mangan wrote, "that the Corps of Engineers working through the Public Works Committee did not have the difficulties Reclamation has. . . . He did not feel that the Public Works Committee was concerned with legislation such as Public Law 9032 of the last Congress relative to reimbursement of recreation and fish and wildlife functions." Mangan said he told the man that any such environmental protection provisions would likely apply to the Corps as much as to the Bureau. But his derisive response, according to Mangan, was that he should watch what happened during the upcoming Congressional session. "If the Corps is able to secure rapid authorization of a number of projects and the Bureau is having trouble getting their projects authorized by the Interior and Insular Affairs Committee, [the man said], 'perhaps we should have the Corps building all our projects.' "

Harold Nelson forwarded Mangan's letter to Floyd Dominy, adding a postscript of his own. He had just spoken confidentially with the head of a local pressure group organized to support a new Bureau project in eastern Oregon. Nelson's confidant, a Mr. Courtright, said he was finding considerable sentiment that the group should switch its allegiances and push for rapid authorization by the Corps instead. "Courtright . . . stated quite frankly that the argument which they are having the greatest difficulty to counter is the one that authorization through channels available to the Bureau will be much more difficult and time-consuming than through Public Works Committee channels." Actually, Courtright told Nelson, he knew the real cause of the Bureau's difficulties. "He attributes [them] to field representatives of the Oregon Water Resources Board and to the Corps of Engineers" itself.

As Harold Nelson intimated, an unholy alliance of local economic interests and a powerful member of Congress was something the Bureau was at pains to resist. In 1967, the Johnson administration, preoccupied with the war in Vietnam and the chronic inflation Johnson's policy was creating, requested only a minuscule appropriation for Auburn Dam in California. Robert Pafford, the regional director, wrote a memo to Dominy discussing the options the Bureau had. The obvious one was to slow down the construction schedule on the dam itself, but this was "quite inconsistent with the urgent needs for flood control and power." Another was temporarily to stop work on the irrigation and conveyance facilities—the Forest Hills development and the Auburn-Folson South Canal. "However," Pafford wrote, "[Congressman] Bizz Johnson has made it quite clear that he wants Forest Hills moved rapidly, and I am sure you know how unhappy the East Side Association [the main local pressure group] is that we are not moving the Folsom South Canal even faster—they and [neighboring Congressman] Bernie Sisk would react violently if we cut the canal out in fiscal 1967." Pafford proposed a more palatable alternative: "[O]ur soundest course will be to reprogram Auburn funds internally to handle the urgently needed preconstruction program, and reduce our right-of-way program accordingly. . . . By reducing land acquisition from $900,000 to $135,000 we will be able to carry out a preconstruction program suitable to Denver's needs for design data. This will provide for some additional land acquisition, although not nearly as much as would be desirable."

The remarkable thing about this suggestion was that, first of all, it defied the will of Congress, which had specifically allocated money for land acquisition and expected it to be used that way. Secondly, its effect could only be to put the squeeze on landowners who sat in the path of the reservoir. It was critical to keep the land-acquisition program moving because of the rapid inflation in California land values, but now Pafford was proposing to do that with one-seventh of the money the Bureau had deemed necessary. This could only mean that people would be offered less money to sell out, and might well accede, since the Bureau could always hold the threat of condemnation over their heads. But it was typical of the way the Bureau operated. If it had a cash-flow problem, the losers would be the people who had had the bad judgment to own property in the valleys it wanted to flood with its reservoirs.

One might be tempted to feel a little sorry for the Bureau of Reclamation. It was, after all, operating at a great disadvantage compared to the Corps, which was unencumbered by social legislation and ostensibly built its reservoirs with the holiest of motives in mind, controlling floods. The available evidence also suggests that the Bureau was not quite as committed to self-perpetuation and self-promotion nor as inclined to trample its opposition. Under several Interior Secretaries—Ickes, Udall, Andrus, even Nixon's Walter Hickel— it had environmental constraints imposed on it that the Corps needn't have bothered with. But one's sympathies might be tempered if one were told that the Bureau, over the intense opposition of a local town, and on a pristine stretch of river up for inclusion in the Wild and Scenic Rivers system, was perfectly capable of proposing a dam which, by its own admission, was completely useless.

The fact that the Yellowstone River was one of the four or five remaining rivers of any size in the American West without a single major dam on it had made it attractive to the Bureau since the 1920s. At one point, according to a former director of the National Park Service, Horace Albright, it had even toyed with the idea of damming the river's outflow from Yellowstone Lake and turning the jewel of Yellowstone Park into a regulated reservoir, and Albright had ordered his rangers to take the drastic step of hiding the Park Service boats so the Bureau couldn't come in and survey. The original Pick-Sloan Plan included a dam lower down on the Yellowstone, which is a major tributary of the Missouri, but in twenty years of trying the Bureau hadn't been able to justify it. The farmers along the river had already built a number of small-scale diversion projects without the Bureau's help; there was plenty of irrigation going on. Flood control wasn't a good enough reason, either, since the damaging floods were all on the lower Missouri, and by the 1960s the Corps had that river completely under control. Power potential didn't amount to much, weighed against the cost of a dam. By 1965, the river had survived six and a half decades of the Bureau and nearly two centuries of the Corps without being dammed—a noteworthy feat of sorts. At about the same time, the conservation movement awoke to the fact that a river of great beauty and substantial size still flowed wild through the northern Rockies and plains, and began to push for official protection in the Wild and Scenic Rivers system. There seemed to be no earthly reason for the Bureau to resist such status—but it did.

The person assigned to take a last, long look at the Yellowstone River, in the light of the conservationists' effort, was dour, impassive Gil Stamm, a future commissioner, who had just been promoted to assistant commissioner by the man he admired and had served so well. In a long blue-envelope letter to Dominy, dated February 3, 1965, Stamm delivered his report. In general, Stamm wrote, "no storage regulation in the Yellowstone River is required . . . as Yellowtail Dam, now under construction, will provide regulation of the Bighorn River and this will insure dependable supplies [of water] below the mouth of the Bighorn," where most of the irrigation was. The only residual interest the Bureau could rightfully claim was "to provide electric power and flood control to the city of Livingston."

The problem was compounded by the fact that the Mission site, where the dam was originally planned, was now occupied by several miles of Interstate 90, which went right along the river below Livingston. Relocating the highway would cost more than it was worth. That left three other sites to select from. The best of them, in beautiful Yankee Jim Canyon above Gardiner, Montana, would back water into Yellowstone Park; Stamm decided to rule it out. The Wanigan site was more expensive to develop and, therefore, "can barely show a [benefit-cost] ratio of one to one." That left the Allenspur site, which was practically in the town of Livingston.

"There is intense local opposition to storage on the upper Yellowstone and particularly the Allenspur site," Stamm cautioned. "The dam would be very close to Livingston, in effect inundating valuable farm and ranch properties and a reach of outstanding stream fishing with national reputation. . . . [Both] ranchers and conservationists have expressed strong opposition to any storage development above the town of Big Timber, which is about 35 miles downstream from Livingston. . . . Findings of the Bureau of Sport Fisheries and Wildlife and the National Park Service show that a dam and reservoir in this area would be detrimental to both fishery and outdoor recreation." The reservoir, Stamm said, would inundate thirty miles of Class I trout fishery—8 percent of the outstanding trout habitat left in Montana. On top of that, it would create an ideal habitat for goldeneye, a rough fish highly competitive with trout; there was "a definite threat of eventual invasion of the streams of Yellowstone National Park by this generally unwanted fish."

As if that were not enough, Stamm said that "a single-purpose flood-control reservoir at Allenspur"—which is essentially what the Bureau was left with—"would cost more than presently estimated benefits." Designing it as a power project wouldn't help; "if the power were to be evaluated realistically in the light of present-day power values . . . Allenspur power would not be very attractive." But adding a hydroelectric plant might be necessary to win authorization, because "the only support for the potential project is from a few public power supporters."

In short, a miserable project: without irrigation benefits, without worthwhile power benefits, without demonstrable flood-control benefits, potentially disastrous to a long reach of the most productive trout river in the West (if not the entire country), and opposed by virtually everyone who stood to benefit from it—for once, by ranchers and conservationists alike. On top of this, an expensive project, projected to cost at least $128 million—say half a billion dollars today. Stamm's letter reads like an argument *for* giving the upper Yellowstone Wild and Scenic status—a conservationist couldn't have said it much better himself. But would the Bureau make such a recommendation? Would it at least not *oppose* such a recommendation?

Only if it was allowed to build the Allenspur Dam. "[F]uture events such as a disastrous local flood possibly could change local attitudes," Stamm concluded. Therefore, his recommendation to Dominy was that the Bureau try "to get the wild river determination altered . . . to accommodate the potential future construction of the Allenspur Unit." By doing so, it would ensure that "all foreseeable desirable future water resource developments would be protected." The Bureau was prepared to accept Wild and Scenic River status for the Yellowstone, in other words, as long as it could someday build the dam that would largely destroy it as a wild and scenic river.

Behind such nearly pathological unwillingness to let go of even *one* river stood, of course, the lurking shadow of the U.S. Army Corps of Engineers. The only conceivable justification for a dam on the Yellowstone was flood control. For now, the Bureau held the authorization to build the project. If it demurred, the Corps might waste no time in trying to build it instead.

If, by the late 1960s, the rivalry between the Bureau and the Corps of Engineers had degenerated into an ongoing squabble over needless projects instead of necessary ones; if each agency was reaching farther afield from its original mandate—the Bureau now talking about building a single-purpose flood-control dam, the Corps incessantly trying to steal the loyalty of the Bureau's irrigation constituency; if they were trying to move into geographic territory where they had no business being—the Bureau into the swamps of Louisiana (there are internal memos suggesting that even this wet state should perhaps be brought into the Bureau's orbit, per request of Senator Russell Long), the Corps into the middle of the Central Valley Project's service area—if all of this was true, then it was entirely fitting that the climactic battle between the Bureau and the Corps should be fought in, of all places, Alaska.

On April 7, 1961, Daryl Roberts, the head of the Bureau's Alaska District office, wrote a blue-envelope letter to Commissioner Dominy reporting on a luncheon conversation he had just had with C. W. Snedden, the publisher of the Fairbanks *Daily News-Miner*. Snedden, Roberts wrote, had told him that "the Corps of Engineers was cutting my throat and brainwashing the local people in favor of Rampart Dam." Snedden reported that the Corps had "held two meetings with the City Council, had met with the Chamber of Commerce, the National Resource Committee and others to sell them on holding off on the Devil's Canyon Project until the Corps completes their Rampart study." This news had so upset Roberts that he made a proposal to Dominy that, in all likelihood, no one had ever made before: the Bureau should enlist the same conservationists who had just defeated one of its most beloved dams, Echo Park, in a joint effort to make war on the Corps of Engineers.

What was ironic about the Bureau and the Corps staging their climactic battle in Alaska was that, strictly speaking, neither of them had any business being there. Alaska has very little agriculture— about the only place one can grow anything is in the Matanuska Valley north of Anchorage—and its few farmers employ little irrigation, if any. Besides, the state has more groundwater than one can dream of, most of it a few feet beneath the surface of the earth. The only navigable inland waterway is the Yukon River, and what the Corps was proposing to build would have put an end to that. Anchorage, Fairbanks, and the tiny towns along the Yukon sit on bluffs; none has ever had a serious flood—nor, for that matter, have any of the towns in rainy southeastern Alaska. Irrigation, flood control, navigation—none of those applied; yet those were the principal assignments of the Bureau and the Corps. Everything else—recreation, power, fish and wildlife "enhancement"—was supposed to be incidental to those activities. In Alaska, however, such "incidental" benefits were the only rationale they could come up with to build dams. And the dams they wanted to build were too monumental to pass up.

The Corps' dream project, Rampart Dam on the Yukon River, was, at last, an opportunity to show the world what it could really do. It wasn't its size that was so breathtaking—although, with a speculative height of 530 feet and a length of 4,700 feet, it had the dimensions of Grand Coulee—as the size of the reservoir that would form behind it. Lake Rampart would become the largest reservoir in the world. It would cover 10,800 square miles, making it almost exactly the size of Lake Erie. And it was the *power*—five million kilowatts of it, two and a half times more than the initial output of Grand Coulee. Rampart was, by far, the grandest virgin hydroelectric damsite under the American flag; there were only a dozen like it in the entire world.

The Bureau's project, Devil's Canyon Dam on the Susitna River, was, by contrast, almost invisible. But it was still huge: a high plug in a great canyon on the river which ranked sixteenth in the United States in terms of annual flow, Devil's Canyon would produce hundreds and hundreds of megawatts of power, depending on how high it was built. In Alaska, it was second only to Rampart as a hydropower site.

The Bureau's dam would drown Devil's Canyon, a remote stretch of almost unbelievable wildwater rapids about a hundred miles north of Anchorage. Even fish couldn't navigate those rapids, and no sane person would try—although in the mid 1970s, a group of kayakers led by Dr. Walt Blackadar, a fifty-three-year-old surgeon from Salmon, Idaho, did, and succeeded, at least in the sense that none of them died. Devil's Canyon's value was mere spectacle, even if it was the greatest spectacle of whitewater on the North American continent.

Rampart Dam, however, was an ecological disaster probably without precedent in the world. It would drown the entire Yukon Flats, a sightless plain of marshes, bogs, and small shallow lakes that nurtures more ducks than *all of the United States* below the Canadian border. In its report on the project, the U.S. Fish and Wildlife Service stated, "Nowhere in the history of water development in North America have the fish and wildlife losses anticipated to result from a single project been so overwhelming." At least a million and a half ducks were contributed to the North American flyways by the Yukon Flats, besides 12,500 geese, thousands of swans, an estimated ten thousand little brown cranes, eagles, sandhill cranes, osprey, and moose—thousands and thousands of moose, to which such boggy habitat was pure paradise. The ducks, the moose, the geese, and the swans all required

217

drowned lands, shallow wet habitat, and the Yukon Flats were the greatest continuous expanse of it in North America.

There were salmon. More than a quarter of a million salmon passed through Rampart Canyon every year, some of them destined to go through two time zones to spawning tributaries all the way across Alaska and into Canada. A high dam would end their migration, irrevocably. The Corps' plan to lift them out and carry them across the 250-mile reservoir in barges wouldn't help, because the tiny fry couldn't possibly navigate such a vast body of slack water on their way back to the sea.

There were also furbearing animals—wolverines, lynx, weasels, martins, muskrat, otter, mink, beaver—animals which were the livelihood, to greater or lesser degrees, of most of the Yukon people. Some forty thousand pelts, according to the Fish and Wildlife Service, could be taken from the area to be covered by the reservoir on a sustained-yield basis every year.

And there were people—twelve hundred of them in the taking area, another eight or nine thousand whose livelihoods would be drastically affected, by either the drowning of animal habitat or the end of the salmon runs. Many of those people were Canadian citizens, many others were American Indians and Eskimos who had been promised, by treaty, a land that could sustain them forever. The Corps was promising jobs building the dam, jobs in the tourist industry, jobs in the lake trout fishery that was supposed to replace the salmon. Those were promises; what was already there had sustained their ancestors for five hundred generations.

The whole idea behind Rampart Dam was to turn Alaska, overnight, into an industrial subcontinent. Five million kilowatts were enough to heat and light Anchorage and ten other cities its size, with power left over for a large aluminum smelter, a large munitions plant, a couple of pulp and paper mills, a refinery, perhaps even a uranium-enrichment facility tucked safely away in the wilderness—and even then, about half of the power would be left over for export. But that was the problem. Export where? The dam made sense only if all of the power could be immediately sold.

Realistically speaking, the dam made no sense at all. Neither did Devil's Canyon Dam. The last thing Alaska had to worry about was an energy crisis. It had 300,000 inhabitants; its population could fit inside a few square blocks of Manhattan. Even then, before the gigantic North Slope oil field was discovered, it had proven oil reserves estimated at 170 million barrels (the North Slope was to increase the figure by some ten billion more). It had 360 million board-feet of timber; the driftwood floating down the Susitna River seemed enough fuel to fulfill Anchorage's needs. It had, right around Anchorage, some of the most dramatic tidal variations in the world; the difference between high and low tide approached twenty feet, and a single tidal project taking advantage of similar conditions at De-Rance, France, was producing hundreds of megawatts, more than Anchorage (which held half of Alaska's population) would need for decades. Mainly, though, it had plenty of smaller hydroelectric sites scattered about, some of them practically at Anchorage's doorstep. They should be developed first—that was the "orderly" water development the water planners were always talking about.

The problem was simply that Alaska might have to build those itself.

Behind their fiercely independent stance, Alaskans, in the 1960s, were a people completely dependent on Washington, D.C. Their major industry, after fishing, was the U.S. military; their third major industry was the rest of the U.S. government. Alaskans spoke of their state as a "colony," but as colonies go they had themselves a pretty good thing, and they exhibited all the character traits of colonial people—which is to say that they wanted to exploit "their" resources for themselves, but expected the federal government to pay the cost.

Senator Ernest Gruening, formerly a governor of the state, was the main booster of Rampart; he lobbied for it with a zeal that bordered on the fanatic. Behind him were pressure groups like Yukon Power for America, or the more picturesque North of the Range association, which said in its brochures that Alaska's future depended on "coming forward with both guns blazing." What mattered most to the boosters was that Rampart was an opportunity—the first real opportunity—to leave mankind's mark on a place that held it in magnificent contempt. George Sundborg, Gruening's administrative assistant, dismissed the area to be drowned by the dam as practically worthless; there were "not more than ten flush toilets in it." Gruening went further: it was totally worthless. "[T]he Yukon Flats," he wrote, "—a mammoth swamp—from the standpoint of human habitability is about as worthless and useless an area as can be found in the path of any hydroelectric development. Scenically it is zero. In fact, it is one of the few really ugly areas in a land prodigal with sensational beauty."

And, since these were the 1960s, and since this was the army that wanted to build the project, there may have been a further consideration working behind Rampart Dam. Ernest Gruening had, he said, recently returned from Russia, where he had seen "hydroelectric power dams larger than the largest in America." The dam, then, was to be a monument against Communism; and if it made it any easier to build it, one might as well note that the ducks whose habitat would be drowned were Communist ducks—many of them migrated to Siberia. Did it make sense, a director of Yukon Power for America asked, "to mollify these feathered defectors"? It is hard to judge whether or not he was serious.

It is also hard to say, in retrospect, how close Rampart Dam ever came to being built. The odds are, moderately close. But Floyd Dominy killed it.

If the dam was built, the Bureau would have no future in the last place where there were still plenty of big damsites left. Congress wouldn't authorize another dam there for decades; the power probably wouldn't be needed for two hundred years. That was the argument Dominy used, and used brilliantly. With Stewart Udall's enthusiastic blessing, Dominy had the Bureau turn all of its guns on Rampart Dam—the planning division, the hydroelectric division, the demographics branch: everyone who had some expertise that could cripple Rampart's chances was enlisted in the cause. In 1967, the Interior Department produced its Rampart report, a document nearly a hundred pages long, complete with appendices and reams of supporting documentation in the files. The report demonstrated that Rampart power had to be sold immediately or the project would be a financial fiasco of the first order. But it also showed that the power market projected by the Corps and the local boosters couldn't possibly develop within the state—not in twenty years, not in fifty, perhaps never. Shipped to the nearest market—the Pacific Northwest—the power couldn't possibly sell at competitive prices; the cost of *transmission alone* would be more than people were paying, more even than nuclear electricity.

In the end, Dominy was asked to testify on Rampart Dam, and it was one of the most brilliant performances of his career. Without anger, without malice, he tore the Corps' justification to shreds. Even the pedestrian rhetoric of his successors—of a Gil Stamm or a Keith Higginson—might have demolished Rampart's prospects, but Dominy spared nothing in his presentation. When he was finished, Rampart Dam lay pretty much in ruins. The project surfaced a few more times during the 1970s, then floated under and hasn't been seen since.

Devil's Canyon Dam, however, was seemingly dead, too—at least as far as the Bureau was concerned. (Late in the 1970s the state of Alaska announced plans to build the dam itself; it will be interesting to see whether it can without falling into the kind of financial hole that the $18 billion Itaipu Dam dug for Brazil.) And there the irony of the whole long fight between the Bureau and the Corps of Engineers came full circle. Had they really cooperated—as General William Cassidy had stated they would, and must—there is no telling what they might have built. Their rivalry prevailed, and grew more intense, during one of history's truly unique periods—a time when we had the confidence, and the money, and, one might say, the compulsion to build on a fantastically grand scale. The money invested in the dozens of relatively small projects each agency built—in many cases because the other threatened to build first—would have sufficed to build the great works they insisted were necessary, but which required extraordinary determination, cooperation, and raw political clout in order to be authorized. Fifty million here, eighty million there, a hundred million here, and soon one was talking about real money. In the 1960s, Dos Rios Dam could have been built for $400 million; today it might cost $3 billion or more. A diversion from the Columbia River to the Southwest could have been built for $6 billion or so in the sixties, and there was so much surplus energy in the Northwest that a few million acre-feet of water removed from a river that dumps 140 million acre-feet into the sea might not have been missed. Today the cost seems utterly prohibitive, and Washington and Oregon would probably resist the engineers with tanks. The opportunity was there. But the Corps of Engineers and the Bureau squandered their political capital and billions in taxpayers' money on vainglorious rivalry, with the result that much of what they *really* wanted to build does not now exist, and probably never will.

CHAPTER SEVEN

Dominy

When Emma Dominy, writhing and shrieking, finally evicted her son Floyd, the doctors dumped him on a scale and whistled. Floyd Elgin Dominy, ten pounds, four ounces, at birth. Floyd Elgin Dominy, larger than life. All of Floyd's siblings were born huge. His brother Ralph weighed twelve pounds. Emma's six giant babies were a cross she was to bear through the rest of her life. Her uterus became distended, causing her horrid pain. She developed a nervous condition. Her temper became explosive, her outbursts hysterical. Strong-willed, French-Irish, and beautiful, Emma May Dominy was a handful anyway. Charles Dominy and his wife fought day and night. They had what is referred to as a "difficult" marriage, cemented precariously by children, religion, and a pious wheatbelt condemnation of divorce. Life, remembers Floyd, was like living on an earthquake fault. There was never any peace. "They fussed and fumed from morning to night. We'd lie awake at night and listen to them tearing into each other." He is seventy when he says this, but his childhood is still a bad memory; you can read it in the turned-down corners of his mouth. "I remember what a relief it was to get away from home. It bugged me right through college. When everyone else was having nightmares about missing exams, I was having nightmares that my parents were murdering each other."

Hastings, Nebraska, is a long way from paradise: Libya in the summer, Siberia in the winter; too wet for the Bureau of Reclamation, too arid for trees. Hard up against the hundredth meridian, Hastings occupies America's agricultural DMZ. Neither God nor government has taken it under its wing. Disaster is Hastings's stock-in-trade—that and dullness. "The capriciousness of nature is the one thing that livens that place up," says Dominy. "When they aren't talking crop prices or tattling on their neighbors, all anyone talks about is the weather." Hastings is tornado country (one of the few double-funneled tornadoes ever seen was photographed near there), baseball-size-hail country, banshee blizzard country, drought-without-end country. The region's whole economy can be drained by a summer's drought, dashed by an afternoon's hailstorm. The anarchy of nature may be one reason why most of Hastings's residents—Republican or Democrat, dry farmer or irrigation farmer, city dweller or country dweller—devoutly believe that man should exercise as much dominion over the earth as he can. Hastings, Nebraska: birthplace of Floyd Dominy, future Commissioner of Reclamation.

Floyd was headstrong and impulsive—"an independent cuss from the beginning." He was an above-average but somewhat uninterested student, and his intelligence was more obvious than evident in his grades. His distinguishing characteristic was self-reliance. Floyd had great confidence in himself. At the age of eleven, he could manhandle a neighbor's two-thousand-pound Belgian draft horses as if they were a pair of pygmy ponies. He fixed things, ran things, organized things. Other children respected and feared him. To most children, the home is a refuge from a dangerous world; in Floyd's case, it was the other way around. Compared to home, shadowed by gloom and rumbling with thunder, the world was a sunlit place.

"I always felt there was a contradiction between my parents' fussing and fuming and their Christian piety," he says. "It seemed inconsistent to me. As a boy, I was very moral. I was president of my Sunday school class. I thought money was the root of evil. If someone had offered me a job paying $300 a year for life, I would have taken it. When I first married Alice, I made her take off her lipstick if we went out for the evening.

"I'm an enigma, even to myself."

At seventeen, Floyd fell in love. Her name was Alice Criswell. She was sweet, demure, and very pretty, a little heroine out of Willa Cather. They met at a state convention; he was Master Counsellor for the Order of DeMolay, and she was the Queen of Job's Daughters. Alice's family lived in western Nebraska, near Chappell, a good two hundred miles away. Floyd was mad for her, but his father refused to let him borrow the car. Floyd had $30 to his name. He spent $25 of it on a beat-up one-cylinder motorcycle that, with luck, would take him to Alice. "It was a helluva trip out there. The roads were all dirt in those days. I wore out a pair of boots balancing that one-lunger, but I made it. When I got ready to go back home, the damn thing wouldn't fire up. Alice's father looked at it and said, 'Your magneto's shot.' I said, 'Can we fix it?' He spent two hours trying, but the son-ofabitch was beyond repair. I had to sell it for what I could get, which was five bucks, and start hitchhiking home. Hitchhike, hell. You hardly saw a car in western Nebraska in those days. I'd walked about three miles when I came upon an old guy with his head stuck under the hood of his truck. I said, 'What's the matter?' and I looked in and saw that *his* magneto was shot. Well, in the last two hours I'd learned about magnetos. I took his apart, saw right away what was wrong with it, and fixed it then and there. That old geezer was so impressed that he offered me a job on the spot. I never went home again."

Floyd and Alice married secretly in Georgia, where Floyd had gone after two years at Hastings College to work on a gas pipeline being built across the South. They spent their three-day honeymoon in Florida. Floyd signed in ahead for three days of work and they took off. A supervisor, his heart warmed by a young couple in love, covered for him. "I was nineteen," Floyd says. "I think that was the first lie I ever told in my life."

When his stint in Atlanta was up, Floyd and Alice went back to Hastings. For $15 a week, he drove a truck between Hastings and Lincoln. Driving anything—a team of horses—was a dream job to many a farm boy, but Floyd found it excruciatingly dull. "I finally said to myself, 'Hell, $15 a week is nothing. I'll go out to western Nebraska with Alice.' I got myself a job on Fred Smith's place. Man, that was a badly run operation. They had new weeding tractors and their wheat fields were still being run over by weeds. They only ran the tractors during the daytime—they were too lazy to run them at night. This land was dry-farmed, and those weeds were using precious rainfall that was needed by the wheat. There were lights on the trac-tors. They should have been running the goddamned machines twenty-four hours a day. So I finally said, 'This is a helluva way to run a farm!' Fred Smith thought I was quite an upstart. He said to me, 'How would *you* run it?' and I said, 'I'll show you.' I climbed on one of those tractors and I ran it till ten o'clock at night. Then I went to bed, got up at three in the morning, and finished the job by four the next afternoon. Cleared out every weed on that farm. I was hell-for-leather. I didn't stop to take a leak. Old Fred Smith came up to me later as I was changing clothes and said, 'With that kind of drive, you're wasting yourself. You ought to go back to college.' "

The sensible thing for a mechanically gifted farm boy who didn't particularly like farming to major in was engineering. At Hastings College, Dominy had given it a brief go and quit. "I didn't like the preciseness," he says. In 1930, he entered the University of Wyoming at Laramie, choosing economics as a major. He was captain of the hockey team. He stayed on and won a master's degree in 1933. By then the country's economy was in a screaming nosedive and the West was five years into the Great Drought. The ranchers around Laramie couldn't sell their cattle—first because no one had money to buy them, second because the cattle weren't worth buying anyway. They were thirsty and starving, vacant-eyed beasts with bellies bloated from hunger and protruding ribs. Stupefied by the intensity of the disaster, Wyoming's people were in the same condition, mentally if not physically. Campbell County, two hundred miles north of Laramie, was typical of the places that had plummeted through FDR's safety net of relief. Roosevelt couldn't launch a federal dam project there because Campbell County had no river worth a dam. It had no highway project because no one went there and it hardly had cars. It had no writers' projects, no hospital projects, no dog census. All it had was the cattle liquidation program. The Agriculture Department's county agent paid the ranchers $8 a head for their scrawny cattle, then shot them. The farmers took the $8 and spent it on horse feed and rifle shells, then headed into the uplands in search of deer and rabbits. During the Depression, Campbell County reverted substantially to the hunter-gatherer existence of the Crow and northern Cheyenne who had forfeited the territory. The two things it had going for it were reasonably abundant herds of game and the county agent, Floyd Dominy.

At eleven o'clock one morning in the spring of 1980, Dominy, floating on three gin and juices and powered by two cigars, was in a mood to talk about his Campbell County days. "We had a drought, grasshoppers, crickets. I tell you it was something else. It looked as if nothing could live. Under the federal regulations, five thousand cattle were to be bought in the whole state of Wyoming. Fifty thousand were dying in Campbell County alone. I called up Washington and said, 'This is worse than you can believe. Send me another vet, dammit.' They sent me three vets. That got me some attention. The range improvement program, though, really put me on the map. That

225

took creativity and force. The government was paying farmers fifteen cents a cubic yard to move dirt. Hell, I wasn't going to pay fifteen cents if it cost ten. I said to those ranchers, 'I'm gonna pay you cost—nothing more.' Naturally, they bellyached. But with my relief allotment stretched further I could build a lot more dams."

Campbell County is drier than crisp toast, but it does get some rain. There are mountains around that produce orographic clouds, and some of them produce rain—not much, but enough to make it worth trying to store the runoff that occasionally pours down the creeks. "I said to myself, 'It's stupid to let a drop of that stuff escape. We've got to capture that water.' I'd take these ranchers out to where I wanted them to build a dam, some godawful-looking dry creek somewhere, and they'd say, 'A dam's no good. There's no water to take.' And I'd say, 'Goddamn it, a ten-minute downpour in this de-vegetated moonscape and you'll see a nice little surge come through here.' The one good thing about Wyoming is there's not enough groundcover to soak up the rain where it falls. I said to the farmers, 'You capture that water and at least your cows won't die of thirst. You get a little extra for irrigation and you can grow some grass on it. What do you want to do—just sit here and starve?'

"So I got them building dams. I practiced myself with a little four-horsepower Fresno scraper. The county surveyor and I developed our own set of regulations. We said it's got to have ten-foot width and five feet of freeboard. The federal regulations said the Soil Conservation man had to approve the damsite. The Forest Service guy was supposed to have his say-so, too. I said to hell with it. I cut all that red tape. The extension director and the Wyoming dean of agriculture finally got wind of what I was up to. They said to me, 'Floyd, you can't *do* that. You've got to play by the *rules*.' I said, 'The Democrats would have a really black eye if they announce a program that doesn't work.' "

Dominy took a swig of gin and juice, leaned back in his black easy chair, and chuckled. "That was the end of 'prior approval.' Henry Wallace took the phrase right out of the law.

"We built three hundred dams in my county. That was more than in the whole rest of the West. I was a one-man Bureau of Reclamation. We were moving! I was twenty-four years old, and I was king. Campbell County was my demesne. They still talk about me out there. I saved a lot of cattle from dying and a lot of farmers from going on relief. After that, I started getting job offers from Washington. But I had already psychoanalyzed myself as a strong starter who got bored easily. I figured I'd have to watch that if I wanted to succeed in life. So I had made up my mind to stay in Campbell County five years."

For Floyd and Alice, the first two and a half years in Campbell County meant a life-style a cut above that of his ancestors when they arrived in Nebraska in 1873. They lived in a stone dugout built into a hillside; they had a gasoline lantern and a coal-burning stove, but no windows. "The place had been abandoned for thirty years. It was vandalized. The house had a leaning chimney and big holes in the floor. I was being paid $130 a month, plus five cents a mile for the car. The guy who owned the hovel was named Mr. Bartles. He was as bald as a billiard ball. I said, 'What's the rent?' He said, 'You're crazy wanting to live there in the first place. I'm not going to let you live there *and* charge you rent.' "

Dominy didn't quite achieve his goal of staying five years in Campbell County; he finally succumbed to an offer from the Agricultural Adjustment Administration to help administer the nation's increasingly complex farm program, working as a field agent for the western states. In 1942, he transferred to the Inter-American Affairs Bureau, working under Nelson Rockefeller. The war effort demanded immense quantities of bauxite, rubber, and chincona, most of it coming out of the Caribbean and South America. Tens of thousands of miners and loggers were dumped in the middle of the jungle without enough to eat. Instant farms became Dominy's specialty. He set them up in nine Central and South American countries, and, later, on the islands of Saipan, Tinian, Iwo Jima, and Peleliu as they were recaptured from the Japanese.

In March of 1946, Dominy was back from the Pacific. Reviewing his career on a homebound ship, he decided that nothing had been as satisfying as building all those dams in Campbell County. It was one thing to hack a farm out of a jungle clearing—that was brutal and monotonous work, requiring neither brains nor talent. It was quite another thing to build a dam, store the water, and make the desert bloom. That, in a small way, was changing the order of the universe. On the same day he returned to Washington, Dominy went to a phone booth and put in a call to the Bureau of Reclamation. He had a job in three hours.

As a land-development specialist for the Bureau, Dominy proved his mettle quickly. His experience helped, as did his prodigious energy, but Dominy also had something a great many of the Bureau's engineers lacked—a knack with people. "It was two things," he says. "First, I cared about making these projects work. The engineers would build the dam and the irrigation features and walk away from it. They felt the projects were supposed to work out by themselves. When I got there, we had projects failing all over the place. The Bureau would send a threat out to the farmers to shape up, then forget about them for five years. No one took us seriously. Well, by God, they took *me* seriously. I was tough, but they saw I cared about their problems. That was number two. I proved myself right away. One of our early projects in big trouble was Milk River in Montana. The regional director, Ken Vernon, had revised the repayment contract under political pressure and it was a complete giveaway. I had moved up to Allocation and Repayment then, and I sent him a blistering letter about it. Vernon was several ranks above me and he couldn't believe it. He called up Goodrich Lineweaver, my superior, and made himself hoarse chewing him out. 'Who is this goddamned upstart?' Lineweaver thought he could put me in my place by sending me to negotiate a better deal. He was sure I'd fail. So I went out to Montana. I saw these old farmers lined up in a room like a country church. They were hostile as hell. I demanded that tables and chairs be brought in. I gave them all pencils and a scratch pad and something to drink. Now they could put their feet under something, light up a smoke, and we could have a serious goddamn discussion. We got a whole new package out of this."

Floyd Dominy's rise to power in the Bureau of Reclamation was astonishingly fast. From dirt sampler to waterlord of the American West took just thirteen years, and he might as well have been commissioner during the last three. Like a chess master, Dominy leaped and checked his way to the top, going from Land Development to an entirely different branch, Allocation and Repayment, then sidelong to Operation and Maintenance, then to the Irrigation Division, and finally to assistant, associate, and full commissioner. His strategy was simple. He would settle in a branch with a weak man as chief and learn as fast as he could. Then he would flap up to the ledge occupied by the chief and knock him off. The first to go was Bill Palmer, who headed Operation and Maintenance and was there largely because he was a Mormon and had an influential constituency. "Mike Straus was totally unsatisfied with Palmer," says Dominy, "so I told Lineweaver that they ought to replace him with me. He said, 'I can't do that.' I said, 'Well, what *can* you do?' Lineweaver said, 'We can make you acting director and not tell Palmer about it.' I said, 'How long acting?' He said, 'Well, I don't know, until we can work something out.' I said, 'Let's make it sixty days.' Lineweaver mumbled and grumbled, 'I don't know, Floyd, that's awfully short.' I said, 'It's long for me.' Well, I got him to agree. There I was, 'acting director,' and Palmer doesn't even know it. The first thing he does is start making a fuss about having to train me, because he'd just trained some other guy. So I walked into his office late one day and said, 'Bill, I think you've got a bad attitude. I hear you've been complaining about having to train me. Well, you don't have to. Dominy can train Dominy.' He looked up at me and said, 'What do you mean by that, Floyd?' I looked him *cold* in the eye and said, 'I mean I'm about to run this division, Bill. It's you or me, and I can guarantee you it's going to be me. So maybe what you ought to do is request a transfer. Maybe you should go out West.' " Mimicking his tone of voice then, Dominy sounds like a Mafia shakedown artist running a recalcitrant store owner out of the neighborhood. "Well, he took my cue. Next thing I know Bill Palmer is requesting a move to Sacramento and I'm chief of Allocation and Repayment. It took exactly sixty days, just like I said. I brought him back, though. Ultimately, I made him an assistant commissioner. Bill was a good man."

In his new position, Dominy had an opportunity to learn anything he wanted about the three-hundred-odd Reclamation projects in existence. He read every project history, reserving for special attention the "bad elements"—the projects that were failing. "Half of our projects were insolvent. I was fascinated: why some and not others? I said to myself, 'Whoever figures this out and starts to haul Reclamation out of this financial ooze is going to be the next commissioner.' The reasons were complicated. In the early days, Reclamation made some bad mistakes—we miscalculated water availability, we laid out canals that didn't work right, we had drainage problems that we should have anticipated. Soil, altitude, crop prices, markets—they all made a difference. On top of that, there were practically no requirements. Straus and Warne let any idiot get into a Reclamation project. You didn't have to demonstrate that you had capital, farming skills, anything. Any fool could sign up and get on a Reclamation farm and use whatever intelligence he had cheating the government. When the projects began to go bankrupt, Straus and Warne were afraid to expose them. They covered the goddamn things up and that got us in a hell of a lot of trouble with Congress. We were illegally delivering water all over the place. Payments were way in arrears and no one was doing a damn thing about it. I think we were violating the law at least as often as we were not violating it."

Dominy approached the problem in a somewhat schizophrenic way. Privately, he was appalled by the lassitude of the Reclamation program, by the indifference of the engineers to its problems, and by the hypocrisy of members of Congress who voted for bad projects as special favors to colleagues and then griped about the money they were losing. At the same time, he was, in public, the program's most belligerent defender after Mike Straus. His defenses were so eloquent he even came to believe them himself.

Once a prominent Senator from South Dakota, Chan Gurney, sent Straus a copy of an article that was witheringly critical of the Belle Fourche project in his own state, implying that he agreed with it. For years, Belle Fourche had been perhaps the Bureau's preeminent fiasco. Streamflow calculations and reservoir carryover capacity were based on nine months of gauging during a wet year; when the drought of the 1930s came, the reservoir was dry within months. No investigation had been made of the need for drainage, which was turning out to be a terrific problem the farmers could not begin to pay to solve. Farmers settling the project were not selected on the basis of character, aptitude, or available capital, and the vast majority of them were bankrupt within a few years. Even with the Bureau forgiving almost all their obligations, many of the farmers were going broke. They were still receiving water, however, so the project was technically in violation of the law. Congressmen hostile to the Reclamation program loved to crucify Belle Fourche at appropriations time; it was like stoning a flightless auk. Even blustery Mike Straus was going to send Gurney a milquetoast letter in response. When he reread the draft that had been prepared by an aide, however, he couldn't bear to do it. So Dominy volunteered.

Of course the project was in deep trouble, Dominy wrote. It was planned at the turn of the century, one of the first large-scale irrigation ventures since the Fertile Crescent. There was hardly any experience to go on. Records of North America's climate scarcely existed. But it was *Congress*, not the Bureau, that had been especially anxious to get the Reclamation program underway—that was the main reason Belle Fourche was undertaken on such a paucity of data. It was *Congress*, not the Bureau, that had established impossibly short repayment periods, that had failed to appropriate funds for demonstration projects. It was *Congress* that demanded projects in areas where the value of agriculture wasn't worth the cost of irrigation, making subsidies inevitable. The point was the project was there. Thousands of South Dakotans depended on it; they had helped feed the country when the state's dryland farmers were utterly ruined. What would the Senator do? Shut it down? Tear down the dam? Kick defaulting farmers off their lands and onto the relief rolls? Or would he help the Bureau come up with solutions to put the Reclamation program on a sound foundation? After all, if anyone was embarrassed by the Belle Fourche Project, it was the Bureau. Did the Senator believe that the greatest amalgamation of professional talent in the government was *glad* when its projects became financial disasters? "Straus read that letter and loved it so much he read it twice again," Dominy chuckled. "He didn't change one word. I was in thick with him from that point on. We really blew smoke up that Senator's ass."

Dominy had the instincts of a first-rate miler. He could pace himself beautifully, moving on the margin of recklessness but always with power in reserve. He knew when to cut off a runner, when to throw an elbow, when to sprint. He also knew that there was nothing like a grudge to make him run harder.

If Dominy harbored a lifelong grudge, it was against engineers. Away from their drafting tables, he thought, engineers could be inexcusably stupid. On the other hand, they had a mystical ability to erect huge structures along exact lines, using bizarre formulas he could not even read. They could map a river basin, analyze some abutment rocks, measure the streamflow, and build a dam of precisely the shape, size, and structure to suit it. They had labored through the trigonometry, the calculus, the chemistry, the topology, and the geology that he had backed away from—the one time in his life he had given up on anything. The problem was, they couldn't explain their own work or its importance, couldn't understand human relations, couldn't see a political problem about to smack them in the face. He could do all of that—brilliantly. Dominy needed them, and he knew it, and they needed him—and didn't know it. It made him furious. In the mid-1950s, after mastering Operation and Maintenance and Repayment and Irrigation, Dominy felt he should move on to the second most important job in the Bureau—the assistant commissioner for legislative liaison. He should be the one working Congress—explaining new projects, justifying the problem ones, tantalizing members with grandiose plans, horse trading, cajoling, threatening. After all, if the Republicans held to their "no new starts" policy, the Bureau would soon have nothing to do.

The position, however, had never gone to a non-engineer, and the person Commissioner Wilbur Dexheimer wanted to appoint was Ed Neilson. Dominy had warned Dexheimer about Neilson. He was, he told Dex, just like him: good-natured, somewhat bumbling, uninterested in politics, and therefore inept. Neilson was the last person who should be sent up to explain the Bureau's work to Congress. "He had already admitted that he didn't even know the names of most of the projects, and if someone mentioned one to him he wouldn't be able to say what state it was in. For Christ's sake!"

The Public Works Subcommittee of the House Appropriations Committee, which authorized every penny the Bureau spent, had been reorganized after the 1954 election in a way that was profoundly inauspicious for the Bureau. Only two Congressmen sympathetic to Reclamation still sat on it, and one of them, Mike Kirwan, was from Ohio, whose farmers were beginning to raise hell about subsidized competition from Reclamation lands. Everyone else on the subcommittee was hostile or indifferent to the Bureau.

The Appropriations Committee hearings began in April of 1955, and, as Dominy had predicted, the roof caved in. "Dexheimer had gone off for two weeks to watch an atomic bomb test in Nevada. It was utterly inexcusable. The assistant commissioners, Neilson and Crosthwait, and the regional directors were all there, but they were the most tongue-tied bunch of engineers you ever saw. They muffed answers to the simplest questions. It was the biggest fiasco. But Neilson and Crosthwait kept telling me my presence 'wasn't required,' because the subcommittee was only allowing five witnesses to be present at one time. Actually, they were scared I would upstage them. On the tenth day, I was invited to lunch by Senator Gale McGee of Wyoming. Word was getting around about how unbelievably inept Reclamation's witnesses were, and like every other member from the West, he was concerned. He said, 'Floyd, can you do something?' See, I already had a reputation as the most knowledgeable person in the Bureau. After lunch, I called in for my messages.

"My secretary told me I'd gotten a telephone call from Neilson up on the Hill. 'He needs you desperately,' she said. I was madder than hell. I stalked into that hearing room and went up to Neilson and said, 'You got your chestnuts burned pretty good and now you want me to pull them out of the fire.' You should have seen the look on his face. He said, 'Are you being insubordinate?' I said, 'Hell, no, I'm being loyal. I'm here to save your can. But you introduce me first.'

"Rudy Walters, the regional director from Denver, was up there at that moment testifying about the Kendrick Project. I knew all about the Kendrick Project—it was in Wyoming. Rudy was totally tongue-tied. You could read the exasperation on those committee members' faces. Neilson ran up to the front of the room and said, 'Mr. Chairman, Mr. Chairman, Floyd's here.' '*Floyd*'s here.' No introduction, no last name, nothing. I was mad as a bull with a spear in his back, but I know how to channel anger. I walked to that witness dock and said, 'Mr. Chairman, my name is Floyd Elgin *Dominy*. I am not an engineer. I'd be happy to tell you about the Kendrick Project. In the first place, the Kendrick Project would never have been built if it hadn't been for Senator Kendrick. If our engineers had been left solely with the decision, they probably wouldn't have built it.' That kept them from dozing off. Then I told them everything they wanted to know.

"For the first hour I was standing up, resting my hands on the chair of the official reporter. Neilson didn't even give me a goddamned seat in his pew. Then the committee wanted me to testify about some other projects, and the chairman directed Neilson to make room for me. I went on all afternoon, and they invited me right back the next day. I ended up testifying for a week. The committee publicly reprimanded the Bureau for inexcusable lack of preparedness and unwillingness to provide facts, but they specifically mentioned *Dominy* as the one exception. From then on, if a Congressman wanted to know anything about Reclamation, he came to *me*. Before long, they were asking me about the Corps of Engineers projects, too. I became the person they trusted. I wasn't afraid of any of them, either. I chased one out of my office once.

"What I did on Fred Smith's farm got me my start in life. What I did in Campbell County got me to Washington. Those hearings made me commissioner."

"I liked Floyd. I trusted him. I thought he would be loyal to me as secretary."

"I liked Stewart. He was a bad administrator, but he had marvelous instincts. He also had guts. He wouldn't bite a chainsaw, but he had guts."

"Dominy despised Stewart Udall, and Udall regarded him like a rogue elephant. Dominy used to come storming out of Udall's office and say, 'Who does he think he is?! The Commissioner of Reclamation?' "

"Dominy was the most able bureaucrat I've ever known."

"I was amazed by him. He had the constitution of a double ox. He'd be dead drunk at a party at three a.m. and he'd be testifying at eight-thirty the next morning and you couldn't tell."

"He was merciless to the people around him. He could be hell on his assistant commissioners. He was horrible to some of the regional directors. If you made a stupid mistake he was all over you and he wouldn't quit."

"When we went on tours abroad, Dominy was treated like the President of the United States."

"He was a magician with Congress. His friends there would do anything for him. They believed every word he said."

"When he testified he spouted numbers like a computer. He spoke with absolute self-assurance. It was all hogwash. If he didn't know a number, he made one up."

"When Dominy was ousted the Bureau of Reclamation fell apart. It will never recover. The disarray over there now is ridiculous."

"When you worked for Dominy you were always terrified of the page-eight syndrome. If you handed him a memorandum and page eight was missing, he'd call your supervisor and say, 'Get that asshole off the job. Put him in a hole someplace.' Guys ruined their careers because they stumbled on the rug when they entered his office."

"Basically, he was a terrorist."

"All the wives were disgusted with him. Some of them refused to come to parties when he was going to be there, because he'd start propositioning them all."

"We played a game of golf once. Floyd was a below-average golfer and I'm an above-average golfer, but he beat me with psych. On the second or third hole, I sliced a ball. He spent the rest of the game ridiculing my slice. I didn't know whether I was madder at him or at myself. He got me all worked up and nervous. Ordinarily, when one grows up and becomes successful, one learns not to let silly mistakes or ridicule become bothersome. But I was so bothered I felt like a little kid on the verge of tears. He psyched me out. He won the game."

"He was one of the best gamblers I ever saw. I was on an airplane with him once and watched him play a game of high-stakes bridge. He won $1,200 in a couple of hours. He took the money and bought himself a tractor."

"If Dominy were commissioner today, he'd be killed."

Nominally, the Bureau of Reclamation is a part of the Interior Department. The commissioner is, in theory, directly responsible to the Interior Secretary and the President, and carries out the wishes of whatever administration occupies the White House—whether that administration appointed him or not. Actually, everyone who has watched the Bureau in action over the years knows it doesn't work that way. The Bureau is a creature of Congress, and most Presidents have not been able to control it any better than they could control the weather or the press. The role of the Bureau vis-à-vis the White House and Congress might be likened to that of a child placed in a foster home by a doting pair of unstable parents. The child may tell lies, throw tantrums, wreck the house, and eat everything in the icebox, but if his foster parents finally decide to give him a thrashing, his real parents materialize out of nowhere and wrest the paddle from their hands. Jimmy Carter lost the momentum of his presidency, and a chance at a second term, through a hapless effort to bring the Bureau and the Corps of Engineers under control. Eisenhower, Johnson, Nixon, and Ford all tried to dump or delay a number of projects the Bureau and Corps wanted to build, and failed in almost every case. Congress simply tossed the projects into omnibus public-works bills, which would have required that the President veto anything from important flood-control projects to fish hatcheries to job programs in order to get rid of some misbegotten dams.

The peculiar relationship between the Bureau and the two leading branches of government—in which it can defy the wishes of the branch that supposedly runs it and is largely subservient to the wishes of the other—is something relatively new. Mostly it is a development of the postwar era. In the past, the President often had to champion the Reclamation program *against* the objections of an eastern-dominated Congress, which found the whole idea a waste of money. Teddy Roosevelt, Franklin Roosevelt, and even Herbert Hoover all fought with Congress over Reclamation dams they wanted built. As the dams octupled the population of the West, however, and as long-lived members of Congress from the South and West rose into important committee chairmanships, the character of Congressional leadership changed, and its attitudes followed. With Wayne Aspinall and Carl Hayden running the Interior and Appropriations committees, Ike could no more enforce a "no new starts" policy than Jimmy Carter could bounce a $40 million Corps of Engineers dam whose sole beneficiary was to be a private catfish farm in the district of an influential Congressman from Oklahoma. As far as public works were concerned, by the 1950s it was Congress, not the White House, that ran the government. We had become a plutocracy of the powerful and entrenched.

No one in government recognized this earlier, or exploited it more brilliantly, than Floyd Dominy. Dominy cultivated Congress as if he were tending prize-winning orchids. Long before he became commissioner, on almost any day you would find him eating lunch with some powerful or promising Congressman or Senator who needn't necessarily represent a western state. Not only would Dominy have lunch with him, but often Dominy would pick up the tab. If a Congressman broke his toe, he might receive a nice letter of condolence. Dominy sent out reams of condolence letters, often to acquaintances who could only be described as casual, though he didn't write too many himself; much of his underlings' work had nothing to do with dams. Favored Congressmen like Mike Kirwan (an easterner) might receive an expensive, custom-crafted set of bookends in the shape of Flaming Gorge and Hoover dams, which they could use to contain the public works bills that were flooding the country in a tide of red ink.

Dominy was a meticulous list-keeper. In his files he kept lists of the Bureau's friends on Capitol Hill, arranged in categories: close friends, reliable supporters, occasionally wayward supporters. Those on the "A" list were handsomely rewarded. "Dominy yanked money in and out of those Congressmen's districts like a yo-yo," says a former associate assistant Interior Secretary who admired Dominy so much he was assigned to tell him he was fired, and whose name was James

Gaius Watt. "If some Senator was causing him trouble, money for his project could disappear mighty fast. It went right into projects for the politicians who were Dominy's friends." All Dominy had to do was order his engineering department to say that it simply couldn't spend the money any faster. A memorandum dated April 10, 1967, from Dominy's chief of public affairs, Ottis Peterson, put together, at Dominy's request, a list of Senators whose terms were about to expire and whom, in Peterson's words, "we should make a particular effort to protect and give as many news breaks as possible." The list of thirteen names—among which were McGovern of South Dakota, Morse of Oregon, Church of Idaho, and Magnuson of Washington—was for "very special attention and protection," although "we can fatten our batting average by taking care of everyone to the best of our ability." Small wonder that George McGovern became so blindly wedded to the Bureau's Oahe Diversion Project that his constituents voted him out of office thirteen years later when they turned against it.

Dominy's power and influence with Congress were so extraordinary that all he usually had to do to change his superiors' minds—whether they were contemplating his dismissal or merely a stretch of Wild and Scenic River where he wanted to put a dam—was make a few phone calls to Congress. At worst, he simply had to threaten to resign.

Talk of resignation was Dominy's ace in the hole. "Dominy threatened to resign so many times I lost count," says his onetime regional director in Sacramento, Pat Dugan. Early in the 1960s, Stewart Udall's Under Secretary, Jim Carr, a voluble pro-Californian who loathed Dominy at least half as much as Dominy loathed him, ordered Dugan to fire his chief of planning, Pat Head, for allegedly causing delays in the preconstruction work for Auburn Dam—delays that Dominy may very well have instigated himself. Dugan was in Washington at the time, and he and Dominy went out to lunch. After they had consumed two big steaks and several belts of whiskey, Dugan told Dominy about Carr's order, and suggested self-effacingly that maybe *he* had better resign, since he was Pat Head's superior. Dominy was enraged. "Hell, let's *both* resign!" he boomed in a voice that stopped conversation cold. And, in fact, he made his customary threat, which wouldn't have worked so well if Udall hadn't suspected that he was mercurial enough to carry it out. But it did work, and neither Dominy, nor Dugan, nor even Pat Head left his job, and Jim Carr died without watching a bucket of concrete poured for his favorite dam. Small wonder Dominy used the threat of resignation so much—after all, it had made him commissioner.

Floyd Dominy was furious when Dexheimer failed to appoint him assistant commissioner, and he believed in carrying a grudge. After Dexheimer's designee, Ed Neilson, failed so miserably before the Appropriations Committee in 1955, only to be rescued by Dominy, the chief of the Irrigation Division went to see the commissioner after he returned from watching his atomic bomb blast. "Today I told the Commissioner that in eighteen years on government payroll . . . I had never seen an agency perform so ineptly," Dominy confided in his diary on June 7, 1955. "I went on to tell him that I thought it was a crime to personally absent himself from the City through practically all of the hearings. . . . I concluded that I was prepared to move up to strengthen the front office . . . I had made my speech and if he wished to think it over I would be available. With this I terminated the discussion." Contempt dripped from every word. Obviously, Dominy no longer thought he should be assistant commissioner; he thought he should be commissioner. Over the next several months, he lobbied assiduously on his own behalf with Congress. He was only forty-five, and he had been in the Bureau less than half as long as others who were eminently qualified to replace Dexheimer. Not that this was about to deter Dominy—after all, they were merely engineers.

The campaign worked. Dominy fastidiously made a notation in his diary every time he won a Congressman over. Once, after going to see Congressman Keith Thomson of Wyoming only to find him preparing to pay a visit to Interior Secretary Douglas McKay, Dominy wrote approvingly, "His purpose in seeing McKay was to urge the appointment of Floyd E. Dominy as Commissioner." By 1957, Fred Seaton, who had replaced McKay as Secretary, was so besieged with requests to make Dominy commissioner that he had to do something. Seaton's solution was to appoint Dominy "associate commissioner"—a position that, as Seaton conceived it, would be about as meaningful as Vice-President. It had never before existed in the Bureau, and it has never existed since. Seaton, however, thought Dominy would be satisfied with a fancy title, and there he badly misjudged the man. Dominy wanted power. When, after several months, he still didn't have enough of it to suit him, he began making his wish plain to his friends in Congress—and threatening to quit. Fortunately, his wish was their wish, too. One day, Seaton called Dominy into his office for a chat. "The Secretary . . . advised me that he had been getting almost unanimous demands from Senators and Congressmen that I be put in charge of the Bureau's budget presentation and other works with the Congress," Dominy typed in his diary. "He went on to make it plain that he desired to carry out these changes in the Associate Commissioner role with as little discomfort to Commissioner Dexheimer as possible. He asked me to guard against any reaction that would tend to belittle the Commissioner. . . . I assured him that I would be as careful as possible in that connection."

That was hardly the way it was to be. "The whole thing was pathetic to watch," says an old Interior hand who was there. "Dexheimer was like an old bull who's been gored by a young contender and has lost his harem and is off panting under a tree, licking his wounds." The associate commissioner was now in substantial charge of the Reclamation Bureau—Dominy knew it, Dexheimer knew it, nearly everyone in the Bureau could see it. But Dexheimer had nowhere else to go. His whole life had been dams, and now he had reached the pinnacle of the dam-building profession. Any move would have been a step down, a terrible loss of face. One could hardly blame the commissioner for absenting himself as much as possible to deal with "important business" abroad. It was during one such trip—a month in Egypt—that Dominy decided to make his move. The day Dexheimer returned, Dominy walked into his office and demanded all the authority he had been asking for. If he didn't get it, he would resign. Dexheimer said he would "think about it," and in the weeks that followed he continued to hedge and waffle, relinquishing as little power as he could but relinquishing it anyway, afraid that his popular associate commissioner would really deliver on his threat. Dominy was effectively in command when Congress put poor Dex out of his misery. A number of higher Reclamation officials—Dexheimer included—had been moonlighting at consulting jobs, and when the news reached Congress some members were furious about it. (These were the days when Cabinet members still resigned over ethical transgressions which, today, would be considered almost innocent.) When the commissioner refused to produce a list of offenders, Congress demanded that Eisenhower force him out. On May 1, 1959, Dexheimer, "for personal reasons," announced his resignation as Commissioner of Reclamation. "My decision was not arrived at easily," he said. Floyd Dominy landed in his seat a few days later with a terrific thump.

Most Commissioners of Reclamation were dull, pious Mormons—or, if not Mormon, and pious, then at least dull. Floyd Dominy was a two-fisted drinker, a gambler; he had a scabrous vocabulary and a prodigious sex drive. In interviews, Bureau men tend to be careful, guarded, and obviously suspicious of reporters. Dominy was candid and amazingly open. Most commissioners like to operate within carefully defined parameters, always going by the book. Dominy was freewheeling and reckless, racing yellow lights and burning rubber in three gears. He could be methodical, he worked incredibly hard, he always did his homework—those were the qualities that sustained him through four successive administrations. But he had a self-destructive impulse, a violent temper, and a compulsion to tempt fate. He could, for example, make a lifelong enemy of a very powerful politician over lunch.

The governor of Utah during the early 1960s, George Dewey Clyde, personified, as far as Dominy was concerned, the hypocrisy of conservative Mormons—a faith he privately detested—where the Reclamation program was concerned. Clyde wanted the government to build as many dams as there were sites in his state, but he wanted private utilities to be able to sell the power. Dominy knew the Bureau needed the power to make the projects appear feasible, and besides, he was a Harry Truman Democrat—a warm, if not quite passionate, public-power man. At the National Reclamation Association's annual convention in Portland in 1962, Clyde gave a ringing speech calling for unity among the western states in support of the Reclamation program. He deplored the fact that 40 percent of the members of Congress from the seventeen western states had failed to vote for two big projects the Bureau wanted built. However, Clyde said, the West had a duty to veto "counterfeit" reclamation projects—dams whose purpose was not irrigation but public power. He then went on to single out "a current example in a state neighboring Utah, where a project continues to be pushed by public-power interests which has no reclamation values, whatever." The project which he alluded to, but did not name, was the Bureau's Burns Creek Project in Idaho, which would occupy a hydroelectric site that the company of which Clyde was a puppet, Utah Power and Light, wanted to own itself.

Clyde might as well have impugned the morals of Dominy's daughter. Edward Weinberg, the Interior Department's solicitor, was sitting with Dominy as Clyde spoke. "Dominy just turned maroon," Weinberg recalls. "He said, 'Eddie, you keep me out of jail, but I gotta attack this guy.' Over lunch, he hunkered in a back room redrafting his prepared speech. He showed it to me after lunch, and I said, 'Jesus Christ, you can't say that! They'll crucify you!' 'Let them try' was all he said."

By the time Dominy was scheduled to give his speech, the three thousand conventioners already had an inkling that something portentous was likely to occur. "The title of my speech is 'Crosses Reclamation Has to Bear,'" Dominy began in a sarcastic voice. After making some desultory remarks about the Bureau's routine difficulties, he turned with relish to the subject at hand. "Only yesterday, my good friend, the governor of Utah, preached the gospel of unity to this association. He warned the West that if it did not unite, the cause of reclamation was in danger. I want to underscore the governor's warning. It is timely and it is true, but apparently the governor's warning fell on some deaf ears. Among those deaf ears, I regret to say, were those of Governor George D. Clyde of Utah." Dominy then tore into Clyde for attacking the Burns Creek Project—"a counterfeit reclamation project," he said acidly, "that was first proposed by those well-known foes of private power, Dwight Eisenhower and his Secretary of the Interior, Fred Seaton." As Clyde sat in the audience red-faced, Dominy's attack became more and more bitter. The delegates were absolutely stunned. "Which is the greater counterfeit?" Dominy asked. "The Burns Creek Project or the governor of Utah?" At the end, he thundered, "Among all the many crosses Reclamation has to bear, I would say there is none greater than the hypocritical attitudes of people like my friend George Dewey Clyde!"

Nineteen years later, Weinberg was still shaking his head. "No one could believe it," he said. "George Dewey Clyde sat there like he'd been hit by a Buck Rogers ray. Dominy just stood up there smiling serenely. I've never known such nerve. It took the audience thirty seconds to decide whether it dared applaud him at the end of his speech.

"You'd probably have to go back to Andrew Jackson's administration," said Weinberg, his tone full of wonder, "to find another instance where a bureaucrat attacked a sitting governor like that."

Going after a sitting governor was one thing. Going after an entire profession was another, especially if it was a fraternity to which 95 percent of your immediate colleagues belonged. But Dominy was quite capable of that, too.

When the American Society of Civil Engineers held its annual meeting in 1961, they asked Stewart Udall to be the keynote speaker. Udall had a prior engagement and had to decline, and the natural person to speak in his stead was Floyd Dominy. This was the same society, however, whose president had twice written a letter to the President asking that Dominy not be appointed Commissioner of Reclamation—first when Eisenhower appointed him, then when Kennedy reconfirmed his appointment. The reason was both simple and gratuitous: Dominy was no engineer. "When Udall said I should speak in his place," Dominy remembers, "I told him, 'The hell I will!' I wasn't going to speak to a bunch of people who didn't think I deserved my job. I told Stewart, 'You make them send me a personal invitation to give the address. Then I will *consider* whether my schedule permits me to appear.' I didn't think they'd invite me, but damned if they didn't."

When he was introduced and took the lectern, the assembled engineers should have known what was coming. "I'm never fully at ease before so large a group," Dominy began, "but in this one instance I am at ease. I'm at ease because *I* know that *you* know that *I* know that I would never have been appointed commissioner if two Presidents had listened to your organization's advice. Be that as it may," Dominy went on, "I'm here to offer you gentlemen a little edification. I think that both you and your honorable president should go back and read the Reclamation Act, the document that has provided so many of you with jobs. I've read the act many times, and nowhere do I see evidence that it was set up as a job security program for engineers. The act is a land settlement program, and if land settlement were left solely to engineers I think we would still be hunters and gatherers, because it's a lot sexier to design a better mace than it is to plant a garden.

"I'll make you a solemn vow here tonight," Dominy concluded after another few minutes of this. "I promise never to refuse to promote anyone in the Bureau of Reclamation just because he happens to be an engineer."

A few weeks after his speech, Floyd Elgin Dominy was inducted as an honorary member into the American Society of Civil Engineers.

If attacking the governor of Utah took nerve, if taking on the entire engineering profession took gall, then waging ceaseless war against one's superiors would have to be regarded as slightly nuts. But Dominy continually attacked and defied all three of his immediate superiors in the Interior bureaucracy—the Secretary, Under Secretary, and Assistant Secretary—and won nearly every time.

Stewart Udall, who served as Interior Secretary during the Kennedy-Johnson reign, was an enigmatic man. A jack Mormon—a lapsed member of the faith—who hailed from a desert state but assumed office on the threshold of the conservation era, he spent his entire term trying to reconcile his conflicting views on preservation and development, especially when it came to water projects. A smooth politician, handsome, vigorous, and diffident, he was a favorite of Jack Kennedy and a darling of the press; he was continually getting his picture in the papers. There was Stew Udall rafting rivers, Stew Udall climbing Alaskan peaks, Stew Udall and his sometime friend Dave Brower trekking through one of the National Parks. This was the same Stew Udall who wanted to build a nuclear-powered desalination plant off Long Beach to slake Los Angeles' giant thirst; the same Udall who secretly plotted aqueducts carrying water from the Columbia River to the Southwest; the Udall who gave his official, if not private, blessing to plans to dam the Grand Canyon. However, what was to Udall a delicate reconciliation of divergent instincts was to Dominy—who held the conservation movement in contempt—a Hamlet-like ambivalence or, even worse, outright capitulation to "posy-sniffers."

To make a strained relationship worse, Udall appointed as his Under Secretary James Carr, a brash, opinionated young Irish Catholic from California who could not help inflaming the ire of a brash, opinionated, and older Floyd Dominy, who happened to be a Celtic-Irish Protestant. To make matters still worse, Udall appointed as his Assistant Secretary for Water and Power a big, dour South Dakota Swede named Kenneth Holum, a man whose very essence and style found their exact opposites in Floyd Dominy.

Dominy's battles with Udall were, for the most part, due to disagreements on issues; personally, when neither had the other's goat, they liked each other tolerably well. On the other hand, his battles with Holum and Carr had more to do with the fact that Dominy despised them both as much as they despised him. Carr had been the legislative assistant of someone Dominy hated: Congressman Clair Engle of California, who tried repeatedly to get him removed from his job for not favoring California enough. (When Engle died of brain cancer, Dominy told his inner circle, half seriously, that he was responsible. "That cancer in his head was something I put there. He got it arguing with me all the time." Twenty years later, the commissioner still loved to tell about the time he booted the Congressman out of his office.) Personal dislike soon escalated into all-out war: Holum was trying to prevent Dominy from giving a speech; Carr was ordering him not to make a trip; Carr and Holum were trying to give the commissioner a new secretary who Dominy suspected was their personal spy. By late 1962 or 1963, the feud had grown so intense that it kept the denizens of the Interior building coming to work just to see what would happen next. Before long, Dominy, to the amazement and exasperation of Udall, had established a firm policy on dealing with Holum: the commissioner would no longer walk downstairs to speak with the assistant secretary. If the big dumb sonofabitch wished to speak with the commissioner, he could walk upstairs to see *him*. "As his superior I simply had to rein him in from time to time," muttered Holum during a telephone interview, and declined to discuss the subject further. The truth was, however, that Dominy made a fool of Holum much more frequently than Holum made a fool of him. The one time he did—when he and Carr managed to freeze the commissioner off the Presidential airplane during one of Kennedy's western tours—Udall returned to his office only to find powerful Congressman Wayne Aspinall on the other end of the telephone, waiting to chew off his ear. After that, Dominy not only got to ride on Air Force One, but he had his *own* fancy aircraft—and his own building.

For years, the world's great amalgamation of engineering talent had been housed in a complex of warehouses, military depots, and glorified barracks outside Denver known today as Federal Center. Then, it was simply known as the Ammo Depot. Thrown up hastily during the war, the Bureau's headquarters, a two-block-long hangar called Building Fifty-four, had neither air conditioning nor many windows. The only source of heat was some undersized radiators spaced many yards apart. Chunks of ceiling calved like icebergs; water dribbled from a hundred leaks. The plumbing sounded as if a team of Russian weightlifters were banging wrenches against the pipes.

Mike Straus and Dexheimer had tolerated this travesty of a headquarters, but Dominy would not. He wouldn't keep his cows in there. He was going to get Congress to appropriate money for a new building—a new building that would, in time, become known as the Floyd E. Dominy Building. Under his tutelage, the Bureau's public relations department produced a picture book called *Inside Building Fifty-four*.

In it were photographs of rusting pipes, of rotting ceilings suspended over bowed heads, of huddled secretaries typing in overcoats. Accompanying the pictures was a text that might have described the Sheraton Maui. It was, especially from engineers, a high-class piece of wit. The results, however, were negligible. Udall was frightened of a new building's cost; a few Congressmen even wondered out loud why such a brochure should be produced at public expense. That was enough to make Dominy mad, but not half as mad as he was when he learned that the General Services Administration, run by a close friend of James Carr—the same Jim Carr who had told Dominy that the Bureau's headquarters were adequate—erected a new building next door to house the complex's garbage cans.

The federal code stated things plainly enough: the construction of new federal edifices, unless Congress voted otherwise, was left to the discretion of the GSA. Dominy asked his lawyer, Eddie Weinberg, to give him the exceptions to the rule. There were none, Weinberg said—except that, obviously, the GSA had no say-so over the Bureau's dams. "Well, then, it's simple," he told Weinberg, "we'll get the goddamned thing authorized as a dam."

It was a quintessential Dominy solution, brilliant in its simplicity, splendid in its insolence. The building would be authorized as a dam. The Senate Appropriations Committee—Carl Hayden, chairman—would approve money for Dominy Dam, and the dam would metamorphose into a building. Then it was only a matter of getting the House to agree.

Fascinated by the outcome of this thing, Weinberg was finally persuaded to go along. Later that year, there was Dominy, with Hayden's blessing already in hand, testifying before his counterpart on the House Appropriations Committee, chairman Clarence Cannon of Missouri. Dominy was eloquent in his blunt Harry Truman style. "I've got a building where icicles practically form in winter," he complained, "and a plane where ice *does* form, right in the carburetor. My people need a decent place to work, and I need a plane that isn't going to fall out of the sky so I can live to see them enjoy it."

Cannon asked, "Do you have any idea when your plane might fall out of the sky?"

"Probably on the very next flight," said Dominy.

"Well, you let me know, then, when you plan to arrange it," said Cannon. "I've got a list of passengers for you."

Then, without further questioning, Cannon approved both of Dominy's requests.

When Carr's friend, the GSA administrator, found out that Dominy had sneaked a new building into a bill that nominally authorized only dams, he was apoplectic. When Carr found out soon thereafter that Dominy had immediately signed a $250,000 design agreement without his approval, *he* was beside himself. Carr forgot, however, that Dominy had been clever enough to make a friend in every strategic place; and there was no more strategic place in the Interior Building than the mailroom.

Stewart Udall was out of town, making a speech, but he was indignant when he learned from Carr how Dominy had operated behind his back. With the Secretary's approval, Carr wrote and signed a letter agreeing to hand the $250,000 back to the Treasury. "When I found out about that," says Dominy, "I called my man in the mailroom. I said, 'I'll take the rap and you'll keep your job—don't you let that letter out of the building.' He promised me he wouldn't. Then I called up Udall that night in his hotel room. I dialed him every fifteen minutes so he wouldn't get away from me. When I got through to him, I said, 'Stew, dammit, you can't do that. It's not $250,000 cash. It's $250,000 credit with the Appropriations Committee. I promised them I'd save that amount of money in the rest of the program. It's their money, not yours. You do this and you're going to run smack into Senator Carl Hayden and Congressman Clarence Cannon.'

"That did it," Dominy chortled. "There was nothing he could do. I got my building. I got my airplane, too. When the GSA chief found out the building was going to be a high-rise, he really squeaked. He sent me three letters of complaint. I didn't bother to answer one."

For years, the Dominy Building—a name it has not yet officially received—was the only high-rise anywhere around Denver. You could see it from far across the Platte River, rising significantly behind the thrusting skyline of downtown. Without knowing what it was, you knew it was a monument to something or someone powerful. "I want it functional, dammit!" Dominy barked at his architects. "I want a building like a dam." What he got is a lot worse. Square as a cinder block, thuddingly banal, it is done in the Megaconglomerate style of the 1960s and 1970s—a J. Edgar Hoover Building without the grotesque semicantilevered overhangs. Despite the cold, the heat, and the feeling of marcescence, Building Fifty-four had a refreshing air of purposefulness, a MASH-like crisis atmosphere. The Dominy Building, by contrast, is fixed, solid, and sealed, as impervious to a rose's scent as to a typhoon—rather like a dam. When it was finished, thousands of Bureau engineers could leave their climate-controlled suburban homes, climb into their climate-controlled cars, and drive to their climate-controlled, windowless new offices, never once encountering the real world.

It is probably pure coincidence that, at about the same time, the mid-1960s, the Bureau—especially its chief—began losing touch with other types of reality.

In the early days, Floyd Dominy had been something of a crusader, if only because he hated being pushed around by politicians and big farmers. Bureau water was by far the cheapest in the West, sold at a fraction of its free-market worth, and if you could manage to irrigate enough land with it you could not only prosper, you could grow rich. Legally, under the Reclamation Act, you could irrigate 160 acres and no more. "We didn't even want them to irrigate that much land," says Dominy. "The law was created to pack as many farmers as possible in a region with limited water. If they could make a living on forty acres, we gave them water for forty. We were talking about subsistence." However, many farmers in Bureau projects were irrigating 320 acres, the result of a liberal interpretation of the act that permitted joint ownership and irrigation of 320 acres by a man and wife. (Married men, it was discovered, made more reliable farmers than bachelors.) In all but the highest and coldest regions of the West, you could make a good living on 320 acres irrigated by subsidized water. If you were in California and raised two cash crops a year with water that cost a quarter of a cent per ton, you could make more money than a lawyer. In 1958, the Fresno Chamber of Commerce published a brochure whose purpose was to lure more farmers to the Central Valley, and which estimated the number of irrigated acres one had to plant in various crops to support a family. The figure for oranges was twenty to thirty acres; for peaches, thirty to forty acres; for grapes and raisins, forty to fifty acres; for figs, sixty to eighty acres. Even a hundred and twenty acres of cotton and alfalfa, comparatively low-value crops, could support a family if you had Reclamation water.

Rumors abounded, however, of corporate farmers illegally irrigating thousands of acres with the super-subsidized water—by inventing complicated lease-out lease-back arrangements, by controlling excess land through dummy corporations, by leasing from relatives, and so on. It is unclear how much the Bureau knew about this and how exact its knowledge was; what *is* clear is that it did little or nothing to end it. Even a self-proclaimed populist like Mike Straus

247

was afraid to tangle with the giant California farming corporations and the politicians they helped elect. "Straus huffed and puffed about the acreage limit," Dominy said later, "but he didn't do a damn thing to enforce it." (This is largely but not completely true. One of Straus's worries, which turned out to be well founded, was that the Corps of Engineers, unencumbered by social legislation or much of a social conscience, would gladly step in and replace the Bureau as the major water developer of the West if the Bureau began cracking down too hard on violators.)

At first, Dominy was self-righteous about enforcing the Reclamation Act. In 1954, when the Corps of Engineers, with the acquiescence of Interior Under Secretary Clarence Davis, tried to do exactly what Mike Straus feared—let water from its two biggest California reservoirs run free of charge onto the lands of two gigantic farming corporations, the J. G. Boswell Company and the Salyer Land Company—he was apoplectic. "Special Assistant Frye showed the [Under Secretary's] letter [of acquiescence] to me confidentially," Dominy wrote in his professional diary on February 4, 1955. "I blew my top and stated emphatically the detrimental effect that would have on Reclamation's ability to conclude repayment contract negotiations . . . with other groups of water users. [A] very plausible legal basis can be made that Congress has directed that irrigation water available as a result of Army construction should be sold pursuant to Reclamation law."

Later, Dominy, now chief of the Irrigation Division, paid a visit to the Boise regional office and learned, he wrote in his diary, "that there is apparently a rather widespread evasion of the incremental land provisions of the Columbia Basin Project Act." (According to the incremental-land-value provisions of the act, beneficiaries newly supplied with Bureau water are supposed to sell their excess lands at a price reflecting their worth *before* the Bureau water arrived. Otherwise, speculation would be as rampant as in the old days of the Homestead Acts; people with an insider's knowledge of future projects could buy land in the project area for $10 or $20 an acre and sell it later for fifty times as much.) "I made it plain," Dominy wrote, "that it was the Bureau of Reclamation's responsibility to either (a) energetically enforce the law or (b) ask Congress to repeal it." When Assistant Interior Secretary Aandahl privately expressed extreme reluctance to prosecute the violators, Dominy wrote, "I am happy to report that this is the first time in my 24 years of Government work that I have heard a top administrator say that he was unwilling to take action to enforce a law which he was sworn to uphold and which comes under his jurisdiction." Ultimately, there was an FBI investigation, a prosecution, and a conviction in the Columbia Basin case. The sentence was a fine of $850. "The sentence made you feel like a fool," says Gil Stamm, who worked on the case with Dominy and was ultimately to succeed him as commissioner.

It did gross injury to Floyd Dominy's image to be made to look like a fool. That may be the main reason why, as commissioner, his indignation over violations of the Reclamation Act appeared to evaporate like a summer cloud. Under Dominy's tenure, the one serious example of enforcement in the Bureau's career did take place: the breakup of the huge DiGiorgio Company holdings in California after it was proved that the lands were illegally receiving subsidized water. But the main instigator in that action was not Dominy but Frank Barry, the first Interior solicitor under John Kennedy. And though it is true, as Dominy insists, that the record of enforcement during his reign was at least as good as any other commissioner's, that isn't saying much, because the record of enforcement over eighty years has been almost nil. No only that, but the violations had become more frequent and worse by the time Dominy was appointed. It wasn't until the administration of Jimmy Carter that a serious attempt was even made to find out how bad the violations were. The conclusion was that they had multiplied considerably after the Second World War and reached their apogee about the time Dominy became commissioner. As it happened, the Carter investigation found that the vast majority of illegalities were occurring in California and Arizona. But the senior Senator from Arizona was Dominy's best friend in Congress, Carl Hayden. In California, the Congressmen who represented the region where most of the acreage violations were taking place were three Dominy stalwarts: Bizz Johnson, John McFall, and Bernie Sisk. None of those gentlemen ever showed much interest in enforcing the acreage limitations of the Reclamation Act. They did, however, display a passionate interest in new dams, and their attitudes became Floyd Dominy's attitudes the longer he remained in office. He had begun as a crusader, a person who at least appeared to possess a sense of fairness and justice, a non-engineer whose outlook was basically agrarian. He ended his term as a zealot, blind to injustice, locked into a mad-dog campaign against the environmental movement and the whole country over a pair of Grand Canyon dams.

The fact is that Dominy *knew* that scandalous violations of the acreage limit were occurring right around Los Angeles—for example, that the Irvine Ranch, one of the largest private landholdings in the entire world, was illegally receiving immense amounts of taxpayer-subsidized Reclamation water—and did absolutely nothing to stop it. When he was shown the list of violators, compiled during a months-long secret investigation, he put it in his desk drawer and never looked at it again. Though he went to great lengths to try to disprove it, Dominy knew that the Bureau was opening new lands for crops which farmers were paid not to grow back east—cotton being the prime offender. The Bureau could easily have refused to supply new water to a region until it could demonstrate that its crop patterns would not make the nation's agricultural surpluses worse, but its response, under Dominy, was to launch a belligerent campaign to deny that the problem existed.

What Dominy appeared *not* to realize was that these three syndromes, often occurring at once—farmers illegally irrigating excess acreage with dirt-cheap water in order to grow price-supported crops—were badly tarnishing the Bureau's reputation. By the 1960s, the Reclamation program was under attack not only from conservationists but from church groups (who objected to its tacit and illegal encouragement of big corporate farms), from conservatives, from economists, from eastern and midwestern farmers, and from a substantial number of newspapers and magazines that had usually supported it in the past—even from the Hearst papers in California. Dominy was not so blind that he didn't see this; his fatal mistake was in believing that the protest and indignation amounted to sound and fury, signifying nothing: Dominy had a peculiar adeptness at denying reality. And the conservation movement was the reality he liked least of all.

Throughout its history, the conservation movement had been little more than a minor nuisance to the water-development interests in the American West. They had, after all, twice managed to invade National Parks with dams; they had decimated the greatest salmon fishery in the world, in the Columbia River; they had taken the Serengeti of North America—the virgin Central Valley of California, with its thousands of grizzly bears and immense clouds of migratory waterfowl and its million and a half antelope and tule elk—and transformed it into a banal palatinate of industrial agriculture. The Bureau got away with its role in this partly because its spiritual fathers, John

Wesley Powell and Theodore Roosevelt, happened to be two of the foremost conservationists of their day—a heritage which, in the right hands, might have all but immunized it against more modern conservationists' attacks.

The Bureau's response to the rising tide of conservation, however, was to let them eat cake. It might have learned some valuable lessons from the Corps of Engineers, which at least knew how to build a Trojan horse. While the Corps was preoccupied with such mightily destructive wonders as the Tennessee-Tombigbee Waterway and its county-size reservoirs in the South, it was proclaiming the 1970s the "Decade of the Environment," publishing a four-color magazine devoted to wild rivers and fish and swamps, and holding regular palavers with its environmental adversaries to throw them off guard. General John Woodland Morris, who became chief of the Corps in 1970, is regarded by many conservationists as the most brilliant and effective adversary they ever met. Some of the same adjectives are used to describe Dominy—tough, brilliant, formidable—but it is odd how seldom anyone refers to him as "effective."

Dominy's problem stemmed from a fatal sin—pride—and a fatal misjudgment: that his despised adversary, David Brower, was the corporeity of the conservation movement—its unanimous voice, its unified soul. To Dominy, anyone who objected to any single thing the Bureau wanted to do was "a Dave Brower type." He failed utterly to understand that Brower had always been a fringe figure in the conservation movement—respected, admired, but not necessarily followed or trusted or believed. Jack Morris of the Corps understood that, as a rule, conservationists enjoyed widespread public respect—that an endorsement from one conservation organization was worth the endorsements of a hundred Chambers of Commerce. He knew that when it came to a conflict between nature and civilization, millions of Americans automatically turned to the conservation groups for guidance. If such an organization endorsed a compromise proposal, general opposition could die like a puff of wind.

But the last thing Floyd Dominy was going to do was seek a compromise with conservation groups. If he went out of his way at all, it was to antagonize them. On February 13, 1966, he gave a speech in North Dakota lambasting the principle that certain rivers, or portions of rivers, ought to be set aside as "wild and scenic." Calling the undammed Colorado River "useless to anyone," Dominy harrumphed, "I've seen all the wild rivers I ever want to see." The speech elicited a furious letter from the state's fish and game commissioner (who was hardly a Dave Brower type) to Stewart Udall, suggesting that Dominy badly needed some edification about changing American values—not to mention the importance of rivers and wetlands to waterfowl. "Floyd, it seems to me that Commissioner Stuart has a point," Udall wrote in a short memo with a copy of the letter attached. "My Secretary's becoming a Dave Brower type," Dominy sneered to his comrades in arms. A few months later, ignoring his advice, Congress passed the Wild and Scenic Rivers Act.

Under Dominy, the Bureau lost touch with reality so completely that it developed an uncanny knack for snatching defeat from the jaws of victory. At the northern end of Lake Havasu, a few miles south of Needles, California, it had inadvertently created a large freshwater wetland known as Topock Marsh. Migrating ducks and geese that were evicted from the Central Valley soon discovered the marsh and descended on it by the tens of thousands during their winter sojourns. By the late 1940s, Topock Marsh had become one of the most important man-made attractions on the Pacific Flyway, and the Bureau, had it had any sense, would have graciously accepted its share of credit and basked in it. The grasses and duckweed, however, were phreatophytes, and consumed valuable water that could have been sold to Imperial Valley farmers for $3.50 an acre-foot. As a result, the Bureau began trying to dredge the marsh in 1948; when at first the dredging didn't work, it spent millions of dollars and stepped up its efforts and pursued them so relentlessly that by the 1960s about 90 percent of the food grasses were gone. The marsh's visiting waterfowl soon diminished from forty or fifty thousand a year to a few hundred or thousand at most.

Dominy's Bureau regarded the operation as a "success," failing utterly to recognize the public relations catastrophe into which it had happily stepped. Even Imperial Valley farmers, who had so much water to waste that some of them applied ten or twelve feet per year to their crops, were opposed to the dredging because they liked to shoot ducks. Ben Avery, a widely read outdoor columnist for the *Arizona Republic*—a newspaper never known to oppose water development unless it was California's—adopted Topock Marsh as his personal crusade and made a point of savaging the Bureau several times a year. In June of 1966, one of his columns finally caught Dominy's attention. "I believe we will have to take Avery on," he wrote to his regional director, Arleigh West, "or face up to the realities [sic] that there is a great deal of truth in what he is saying." In other words, Dominy *knew* Avery was right. He *knew* that Topock Marsh was pitiful compensation for all the habitat the Bureau and Corps had ruined. He *knew* that the marsh would reappear unless the Bureau continued to spend millions of dollars trying to annihilate it. But which course of action did he choose? The Bureau, he decided, was going to deny everything Ben Avery said and continue demolishing the marsh.

Stewart Udall was upset over the Topock Marsh situation, and since the marsh was being eradicated for the sake of California—not Arizona—he ordered Dominy to do something about it. In typical fashion, Dominy's response was to try to make an end run around Udall, through the Congress. Though he was nominally Dominy's boss, Udall didn't like tangling with his two-fisted commissioner; that was the reason he had John Carver on his staff. Tough, profane, built like a nose guard, Carver had been hired to be Udall's all-purpose troubleshooter. Manhandling Dominy, however, was turning into his full-time job.

"The summit meeting was to take place in Udall's office," remembers John Gottschalk, who was then the director of the Fish and Wildlife Service. "It was a good choice—the Secretary was absent, but the trappings of authority would impose themselves. I was a little late in arriving, and as I was walking down the hall I could already hear Carver and Dominy at each others' throats. God Almighty! Were they screaming at each other! When I walked in they were standing at opposite sides of Udall's desk just like a couple of football players facing off. They were pounding the table with their fists. Dominy's face was beet-red. I remember him yelling, 'What do you want me to do? Resign my fucking job?' And Carver was shouting back, 'We want you to get on the *team*, Floyd! We don't want you to resign. We want you to stop throwing tantrums and get on the goddamned *team*!'

"I just stood there transfixed," says Gottschalk. "I didn't know whether to try to break it up or slink out the door. It went on like that for another fifteen minutes until Dominy gave up. I remember exactly what he said. He yelled, 'You realize you're asking me to go against every sound precept of water management for a bunch of goddamned birds and fish!' And then he barged out the door like a Sherman tank."

By the mid-sixties, Dominy finally had realized that the conservation movement was a serious enough threat to the Reclamation program that he would have to acknowledge not only its existence, but its political power. At first he had paid it as much attention as he would a flea, but now he began to go after the flea with a hydrogen bomb. In one issue of *Audubon* magazine—which had a circulation far smaller than it does today—the magazine's bird-watching columnist, Olin Pettingill, made a derogatory reference to the Bureau in an article which, for the most part, was about curlews and gallinules. Pettingill remarked that the Bureau's Nimbus Dam, on the American River east of Sacramento, "has ruined what once were spawning grounds for salmon and steelhead rainbow trout"—an observation that happens to be entirely true. That was the sum total of Pettingill's criticism: one sentence in a two-thousand-word article about birds. However, as far as Dominy was concerned, the magazine was guilty of delivering "a gratuitous slap in the face." He wrote to his regional director, "We think it would be opportune and worthwhile to work with the Sacramento newspaper in the development of a feature story on the lengths to which Reclamation has gone . . . to enhance the fishery and wildlife resources of the Central Valley. An ideal situation would be for such a story to be used in the *Bee* on the opening day of the Audubon Society convention in Sacramento, to be followed up by an editorial."

Two interesting questions are raised by Dominy's response. One is whether he really had enough influence with the Sacramento *Bee* to enlist it in an orchestrated campaign to perfume the Bureau's reputation. One also wonders what he had in mind when he spoke of Reclamation projects "enhancing" fish and wildlife habitat in the Central Valley. By the mid-1960s, nearly 90 percent of the valley's wetlands habitat was gone, almost entirely because of irrigation farming, and wetlands were by far the most important natural feature in all its five-hundred-mile length; the valley was once the winter destination of at least ten million waterfowl cruising the Pacific Flyway, and now their numbers were reduced to four million or fewer, jammed onto refuges or forced to scrounge a meal in unwelcoming farmers' fields. The Sacramento–San Joaquin river system once had six thousand miles of salmon spawning streams, but by the mid-1960s there were perhaps six hundred miles left, and it was the Bureau's dams, cemented across rivers low down in the foothills, that blocked the salmon most effectively. So what had the Bureau done to "enhance" fish and wildlife resources? At best, it had created a series of slackwater reservoirs that were host to such rough fish as catfish, crappie, and bass, plus some trout and an occasional landlocked salmon. The reservoirs were useless to ducks and geese, which couldn't feed in their deep waters and would be driven mad by the powerboats anyway.

Those reservoirs, however, were the only thing Dominy could

have had in mind, unless he had completely lost touch. To him, it seemed, nothing in nature was worthwhile unless it was visited by a lot of people. If it was a pristine river, accessible only by airplane or jeep or on foot, navigable only by whitewater raft or kayak or canoe, populated by wily fish such as steelhead that were difficult to catch, then it was no good. But if the river was transformed into a big flatwater reservoir off an interstate highway, with marinas and house-boats for rent—then it was worth something after all.

There was, for example, Lake Powell. Before Glen Canyon Dam had been built, that stretch of the Colorado River was one of the remotest, most inaccessible places in the United States. Only a few thousand people had seen it. Utterly unlike the turbulent reaches of the Grand Canyon, Glen Canyon was a stretch of quiet water drifting sinuously between smooth, rainbow-colored cliffs. Labyrinthine and cool, some of the canyons were as lush as a tropical forest, utterly incongruous in the desert. All of this was drowned by Lake Powell, but to demonstrate how nature had actually been improved, Dominy decided to publish a book called *Lake Powell: Jewel of the Colorado*. He even decided to take the photographs and write the text himself. "Dear God," he wrote on the inside cover, "did you cast down two hundred miles of canyon and mark: 'For poets only'? Multitudes hunger for a lake in the sun." He went on:

> How can I describe the sculpture and colors along Lake Pow-ell's shores? Over eons of time, wind and rain have carved the sandstone into shapes to please 10,000 eyes. The graceful, the dramatic, the grand, the fantastic. Evolution into convolution and involution. Sharp edges, blunt edges, soaring edges, spires, cliffs, and castles in the sky. . . . Like a string of pearls ten modern recreation areas will line Lake Powell's shores, with names that have the tang of the Old West. . . . Feel like ex-ploring? Hundreds of side canyons—where few ever trod be-fore the lake formed—are yours. . . . You have a front-row seat in an amphitheater of infinity. . . . Orange sandstone fades to dusky red—then to blackest black. . . . There is peace. And a oneness with the world and God. I know. I was there.

Dominy's war against the conservationists may have given him some satisfaction, but, from his point of view, it was hardly time well spent. No public figure would be as hated by the environmental movement until James Watt came along a decade later. His blind insistence on building dams in the Grand Canyon—not just dams, but cash register dams whose purpose was to generate income to build *more* dams—won him the wrath of *Reader's Digest* and *My Weekly Reader;* his habit of making end runs around federal laws and regulations by begging special relief from Congress did not endear him to those whose laws he was circumventing; and hundreds of well-placed officials in Washington, many within his own building, were laying for him.

Despite all this, in the late 1960s Dominy was as entrenched as any bureaucrat in Washington. The main reason was his relationship with Senator Carl Hayden of Arizona, the chairman of the Appropriations Committee, the most powerful man in legislative government. It was the relationship of a fawning nephew and a favorite uncle—the kind of relationship young Lyndon Johnson enjoyed with Sam Rayburn—and it gave Dominy an authority, an insolence, an invulnerability scarcely anyone else enjoyed.

When Carl Hayden was in his late eighties, senile, half blind, half deaf, confined to a hospital bed half the time, Floyd Dominy all but served as chairman of the Appropriations Committee when dam authorizations came around. He managed this by telling Hayden exactly what he wanted him to say—by actually writing dialogue for the two of them to recite. He would go to Hayden's office, sit down with his legislative aide, Roy Elson, and write the questions he wanted Hayden to ask him; then he would go back to his own office and write the answers. It is unclear whether he did the same for other witnesses. The Hayden-Dominy scripts were of dubious enough ethical propriety for Dominy to keep them locked in the Bureau's sensitive files, their existence known to only a handful of aides. Old, frail, and sick as he was, Hayden was still a man no one wanted to cross, and Dominy, knowing this, basked as long as he could in his failing light. "When you walked into Dominy's office," says John Gottschalk, "the first thing you saw was a huge framed picture of Hayden and Dominy getting off a plane in Hawaii all decked out in leis. Hayden's inscription went something like this: 'As this photograph was being taken I was thinking to myself that Floyd Dominy is the greatest Reclamation Commissioner who ever lived.'

"It was powerful medicine," says Gottschalk. "There's no member of Congress today who's nearly as powerful as Hayden was then. You'd walk in there to complain about something the Bureau did and see that picture and say to yourself, 'How the hell am I going to go up against this man and win?' "

Dominy was, of course, much too canny to put all of his eggs in

Carl Hayden's basket. In the House, he maintained the most cordial of relations with Wayne Aspinall, the chairman of the House Interior Committee. Aspinall, a former schoolteacher from Palisade, Colorado, with a nasty disposition and a religious conviction that only the Bureau of Reclamation stood between the West and Armageddon, would say that Floyd Dominy was "not only the best Reclamation Commissioner I have ever known, but the *only* good Reclamation Commissioner I have known." Besides cultivating the powerful, Dominy, for the most part, did a marvelous job of concealing his political prejudices from the world. He could get on famously with Frank Church, the liberal Senator from Idaho, and get on just as famously with William Egan, the right-wing governor of Alaska. If a Congressman didn't get on famously or even politely with him, Dominy had little compunction about taking revenge: a dam project in his district might suddenly become unfeasible, a weather modification program might move somewhere else. "He pulled money in and out of those Congressmen's projects like a yo-yo." Loved by some, feared by many, respected by all, Dominy seems to have had only one enemy of consequence in the whole Congress—Senator Henry Jackson of Washington. But Jackson knew better than to take his enmity too far.

And Dominy could be jovial, amusing, a lot of fun. Reclamation parties were legendary in Washington—hardly what one would expect in a hotbed of Mormon engineers. He could beat the conservationists at their own game. When the Sierra Club and the Wilderness Society and others complained bitterly that a finger of Lake Powell would extend to Rainbow Bridge, a spectacular natural arch in Utah, leaving a stagnant, fluctuating, man-made pool of water under one of the nation's scenic wonders, Dominy went to see the place himself—on foot, with a mule. It was a grueling twenty-mile hike in desert heat to the arch, a trek so tough the mule almost didn't make it. Later, he flew a bunch of conservationists in by helicopter so they could see it themselves, taking care to ask each one whether he had been there before. Almost none had. Dominy used that fact to great advantage in testimony before Congress. Not only had they never seen what they so passionately wanted to protect, he said acidly, but they wanted him to erect a *dam* to keep the waters out. A dam! After regaling the committee with his story, Dominy got a special exemption from the federal law prohibiting significant man-made intrusions in national monuments. Today Rainbow Bridge is visited mainly by overweight vacationers clambering out of houseboats and trudging up to stare briefly at the arch.

He had a politician's way with names. On visits to the Bureau's dams, he greeted maintenance people whom he had met briefly years before, and he even knew the names of people he had never met. When the University of Wyoming awarded him an honorary degree, he was invited to dinner at the home of Gene Gressley, the director of its American Heritage Center. He had never met Gressley, nor his family, but when he walked in the door he knew all of Gressley's children by name. When, during an interview, I reminded Dominy of the incident and told him how impressed Gressley said he had been, his response seemed somehow predictable: "Who's he?"

One of his former aides said Dominy liked people the way we like animals—we like them, but we eat them. His employees laughed at his antics, admired his guts, profoundly respected his abilities, and were scared half to death. He could be sadistic, and he would carry a grudge to his grave. As soon as he became commissioner, he tried to fire all of his regional directors—not on the basis of incompetence, necessarily, but because they had been appointed by Dexheimer. But he couldn't dislodge the one whose head he wanted most, Bruce Johnson in the Billings office, because Johnson had strong political support. The reason he wanted to fire Johnson so badly is that he had refused to arrange a "date" for Dominy with his secretary, whom Johnson was courting himself. Unable to depose him, Dominy tried to hound Johnson out—ridiculing him mercilessly, intimidating him, humiliating him. Johnson took it for several years and finally quit.

He hated weakness, but he needed a weak person to serve as his whipping boy, and he had one in Arleigh West, his regional director in Boulder City. "Arleigh was his Sancho Panza," says Pat Dugan, one of the few whom Dominy didn't cow. "He had a rough life. He brought out everything that was sadistic in Floyd." When West was in Washington, Dominy commandeered his hotel room as his trysting spot, and there were evenings when poor Arleigh found himself out window-shopping, waiting for Dominy to finish. He had someone in Denver—another weak man, a top-level aide—whom everyone referred to as the "Official Pimp." His responsibilities went beyond procurement. When a public relations flack leaked the story of how Dominy had gotten Congress to give him a new airplane, thinking he was doing Dominy a favor—after all, he was always telling those kinds of stories on himself—the commissioner was beside himself. He was in the middle of a meeting with some Colorado bureaucrats at the time. "You fire that son of a bitch," he yelled to the Official

Pimp in the presence of the astonished bureaucrats. "We can't fire him," said the Pimp, "he's civil service." "You fire him," roared Dominy," or I'll can your goddamned ass, too!"

It wasn't his blindness, his stubbornness, his manipulation of Congress, his talent for insubordination, his contempt for wild nature, his tolerance of big growers muscling into the Reclamation program—in the end, it wasn't any of this that did Dominy in. It was his innate self-destructiveness, which manifested itself most blatantly in an undisguised preoccupation with lust. His sexual exploits were legendary. They were also true. Whenever and wherever he traveled, he wanted a woman for the night. He had no shame about propositioning anyone. He would tell a Bureau employee with a bad marriage that his wife was a hell of a good lay, and the employee wouldn't know whether he was joking or not. He preferred someone available, but his associates say he wasn't above paying cash. "The regional directors were expected to find women for him," says one former regional director. "It always amazed me how he carried on in the light of day. He was opening himself up to blackmail, but somehow he always seemed immune." The Bureau airplane was known, by some, as the "Winged Boudoir in the Sky."

As he bullied weak men, Dominy preyed on women whom he considered easy marks. According to one regional director, Felix Sparks, the head of Colorado's Water Conservation Board, was married to a woman who occasionally overindulged, so Dominy went right after her. In time, an indignant Mary Sparks refused to attend any party where Dominy threatened to show up. Sparks, one of the most decorated veterans of World War II, might have been expected to punch Dominy in the jaw. Everyone, however, seemed to humor him. "He's just being *Floyd*," they would say. "You know how *Floyd* is." "He's just a little drunk. Ignore him."

Alice Dominy must have known. Her life was insulated, she rarely went with him on trips, but for years everyone suspected that she knew. And there came a day when she had to find out for sure. She drove into town to the hotel where, according to the rumors, he liked to conduct his trysts. She took the elevator upstairs, mustered her courage, and knocked on the door. A woman opened up. Floyd Dominy, her husband, was in the back of the room. "He just told her to go home and mind her own business," says one of Dominy's confidants. "And she was of that era where that's what women did. I don't know how he rationalized it. He probably said, 'Well, lots of people commit adultery.' He had a talent for rationalizing anything.

"Alice was sweet. She was a dear lady. It broke your heart to see her treated that way."

Dominy did not even aspire to discretion. He bragged about his exploits. He taunted his assistants with remarks about their wives. He ordered them to find him women. It seemed as if he simply couldn't help himself. He could testify before Congress on a half bottle of bourbon and two hours of sleep, he could throw Representative Clair Engle out of his office, he could learn more about the Reclamation program than any person alive—he was tough, ferociously disciplined, indomitable. But he was also compulsive, addicted, a fool for lust—and exposed himself quite recklessly to full view. "I'm not sure what Dominy is better remembered for," says one Washington lawyer who knew him well, "having been Commissioner of Reclamation or having been the greatest cocksman in town."

"I've tried to psychoanalyze him," says Pat Dugan, "and I don't think he ever believed that his playing around would get him in real trouble. He got away with so much that after a while he must have decided he was immune."

But he wasn't.

The man assigned to tell Floyd Dominy that he was fired was a young, intense, middle-level Interior bureaucrat barely thirty years old, a born-again Christian from Wyoming named James G. Watt. The order came directly from the newly inaugurated President of the United States, Richard M. Nixon. At Nixon's behest, the FBI had run its customary investigation of top federal officials to look for improprieties, and had come back with a file on Dominy that was inches thick. ("The FBI knows every woman I've ever fucked," Dominy once confessed to an interviewer.) "He didn't act surprised when I told him," Watt remembers. "I think he knew it was coming. We had decided to let him stay on a while longer so his pension could vest, and he acted grateful about that. I was in awe of this man. Everyone was. I was half his age. But he took the news very mildly. I can remember feeling very, very relieved."

When Dominy was himself relieved, he retired to his cattle ranch in the Shenandoah Valley, leaving his twenty-five-year Reclamation career behind him as if it had never occurred. "When I quit something," he said, "I really quit it." Once in a while he could be enticed into a lucrative consultancy—in 1981, he was hired by Egypt to help draft a solution to the grotesque drainage problems created by the Russian-built Aswan High Dam—and he drove to Capitol Hill now and then to testify against the likes of a Hells Canyon National Monument (which would preclude more dams on the lower Snake River); mostly, though, he preoccupied himself with enshrining his reputation and with his cows. In 1979, he was named Virginia Seed Stockman of the Year, a fitting title: he had been proclaimed the state's preeminent stud expert.

Dominy's reputation and legacy are more problematical—at least as complex as the man himself. In *Encounters with the Archdruid*, John McPhee portrays him as a commissioner who led Reclamation on a terrific binge, plugging western canyons as if they were so many basement leaks. His reputation, even today, is outsize; he is often talked about in Washington, and in the conservationists' annals of villainy he remains a figure as large as, if not larger than, James Watt. Watt, however, hopped around so much with his foot in his mouth that he didn't really have a chance to do much that the environmental movement regarded as awful. But Dominy presided over Glen Canyon Dam, over Trinity Dam, over a dozen other big dams, over the federal partnership with California in that state's own water project, which dammed the Feather River and allowed Los Angeles' explosive growth to continue, and with it its appetite for even more water. Those enamored of such giant engineering works were at least as sorry to see Dominy go as the conservationists were thrilled; no successor, they believed, could ever hope to equal him as a master tactician in Congress, as a fiercely committed believer in the cause of reclaiming the arid West.

On balance however, Floyd Dominy probably did the Bureau of Reclamation and the cause of water development a lot more harm than good. That, at least, is Daniel Dreyfus's assessment. Brilliant and hardheaded, the Bureau's house intellectual—and a native New Yorker—Dreyfus was the only person it had who could sit down with an influential Jewish Congressman from New York City, trade some urban banter and rabbi jokes, and convince him that he ought to vote for the Central Arizona Project. He left, in part, because of Floyd Dominy. "You could take so much of him," Dreyfus remembered one day in 1981, sitting in his office at the Senate Energy Committee, where he had gone to become staff director. "He got to be like a stuck record. The same damn stories about himself, the same fights with the same people over and over again. The mood of the country was changing, but Dominy refused to let the Bureau change. You got the feeling that you belonged to the Light Brigade." The loss

261

of Dreyfus was especially ironic, because the chairman of the Senate Energy Committee was Henry Jackson, Dominy's one powerful enemy from a western state. In Dreyfus, Jackson had acquired the one person on earth who knew as much about the Bureau and its work as its commissioner.

Jim Casey, the Bureau's deputy chief of planning, worked under Dreyfus and also left in disgust. Like Dreyfus, Casey had become cynical about the whole Reclamation program, but he couldn't help retaining his loyalty to the Bureau. Once, in the early 1970s, when a friend sent a young engineering graduate over for job advice, Casey suggested that he apply at the Bureau, and the young man made a sour face. "He told me that the Bureau of Reclamation was a disgrace," Casey remembered. "And I got mad at him for saying that, but here was a guy fresh out of one of the top engineering schools— the kind of guy who once would have loved to work for the Bureau —and he said it was nothing but a bunch of nature-wreckers out to waste the taxpayers' money. It was Floyd Dominy who gave it that reputation. You couldn't convince him that the Bureau's pigheadedness about things like Marble and Bridge Canyon dams was turning the whole country off. After he'd told me his Rainbow Bridge story for the seventh time and how he'd licked the conservationists, I said, 'Well, you won that one, but you haven't won too many others lately.' He said, 'What haven't I won?' And I said, 'Well, they licked you pretty good on Marble and Bridge Canyon.'

"You know what his answer was? 'My Secretary turned chickenshit on me.' The man was blind. He went completely blind."

These are mere opinions, but the record speaks for itself. The Central Arizona Project which Dominy finally managed to build is a pitiful dwarf compared with the Pacific Southwest Water Plan he had planned, and he had to sacrifice the last years of his career to the effort to get it authorized. Today, few of the other grand projects conceived under him exist. There is no Devil's Canyon Dam on the Susitna River, no Texas Water Plan, no Auburn Dam, no Kellogg Reservoir, no English Ridge Dam, no Peripheral Canal, no additional dams in Hells Canyon on the Snake River, no Oahe and Garrison diversion projects. Dominy wanted to move the Bureau's activities into the eastern United States, because he came to believe that irrigation often makes better sense in wetter regions than in emphatically dry ones, and also because he wanted to invade the Corps of Engineers' domain in order to retaliate for the Corps having encroached on the Bureau in the West. But all of those plans—for irrigation projects in Louisiana, for a series of reservoirs in Appalachia set around new industrial towns—came to naught. The legacy of Floyd Dominy is not so much bricks and mortar as a reputation—a reputation and an attitude. The attitude is his—one of arrogant indifference to sweeping changes in the public mood—and it is probably the foremost obstacle in the Bureau of Reclamation's way as it tries to play a meaningful role in the future of the American West.

Actually, there is one more legacy, one of flesh and blood. In Dominy's office at his Shenandoah farm, next to his huge commissioner's desk, is a photograph of him with his son on a boat speeding across Lake Powell, arms around each other. Remove the film of thirty years and Floyd could be Charles Dominy's twin—they look that much alike. In 1984, Charles was the chief of the southeastern district of the Army Corps of Engineers. He was turning the Savannah River into a continuous reservoir, channelizing countless miles of meandering streams and creeks, draining the last wild swamp and forest lands of the wet Southeast for soybean farms. He was also plotting to revive the cross-Florida barge canal—a casualty of the same administration that deposed his father.

A couple of hours earlier Dominy had been lambasting the Corps, saying it "has no conscience." As he saw his guest look at the photograph, however, he broke into a proud grin. He said, "That boy is going to be Chief of Engineers someday."

CHAPTER EIGHT

An American Nile (II)

Nineteen twenty-eight, the year the Hoover Dam legislation was passed, was a milestone year in Arizona in another sense. The population went past 400,000—the largest number of people who had lived there in approximately seven hundred years.

The original 400,000 Arizonans (that is an outside estimate; the number may have been somewhat smaller) were, for the most part, members of the Hohokam culture, a civilization that thrived uninterrupted near the confluence of the Gila, Salt, and Verde rivers for at least a thousand years, until about 1400, when it disappeared. The confluence of Arizona's only three rivers occurs in the hottest desert in North America, a huge bowl of sun now occupied by modern Phoenix and environs. Average summer temperature is 94 degrees; average annual rainfall is just over seven inches. There are far more hospitable places in the state, such as the cool Ponderosa-clad Mogollon Rim, but archaeologists surmise that the inhabitants of Arizona's higher and wetter regions drifted down to join the Hohokam in the latter days of their realm; something about the desert proved irresistibly attractive. The lure was probably food, which the Hohokam rarely lacked. They were the first purely agricultural culture in the Southwest, if not all of North America. Midden remains, well preserved by the desert's dryness and heat, suggest that the Hohokam rarely hunted, or even ate meat; their copious starch and vegetable diet was supplemented only occasionally by a bighorn sheep, antelope, raven, or kangaroo rat. Sometimes they ate sturgeon. That sturgeon bones have been found amid the Hohokam ruins suggests a Gila River considerably fuller and more constant than the ghost river whites have known—a river that, even before its headwaters were dammed, usually ran underground. And this, in turn, suggests a possible reason for the Hohokam's demise: that the climate was considerably wetter during the centuries their civilization flourished, then turned suddenly dry.

Whatever happened, the Hohokam, by A.D. 800, had already established a civilization that rivaled the Aztec, Inca, and Maya farther south. They were good builders, using rafters for houses and I-beams to create ancestral skyscrapers four stories high. They lived in small cities; the ruins of one of them, Pueblo Grande, occupied a large piece of land just about where downtown Phoenix is today. Superb flint and stone masons and excellent potters, they also worked beautifully with shells; they may have traded with people living on the Mexican coasts. For sport, they built enclosed ball courts very much like those of the Maya, who probably gave them the idea.

When it came to irrigation, however, the Hohokam were in a league by themselves. The largest of the canals they dug was fifteen miles long and eleven yards wide from bank to bank; like the other main canals, it had a perfectly calibrated drop of 2.5 meters per mile, enough to sustain a flow rate that would flush out most of the unwanted silt. There were dozens of miles of laterals and ditches, implying irrigation of many thousands of acres of land. Because of the dry climate and the provenance of the irrigated land, the Hohokam should have enjoyed good health; they made superior weapons; they were more populous than any culture around. Why then should they disappear? It is hard to imagine a civilization covering thousands of square miles and comprising hundreds of thousands of people just vanishing, but, according to Emil Haury, an archaeologist who became fascinated by their demise, they apparently did. "We are almost totally ignorant of Hohokam archaeology . . . after 1400," writes Haury in *Snaketown*, an archaeological record of the impressive Hohokam artifacts he and his colleagues unearthed. The relatively few Pima Indians whom whites found living in central Arizona in the 1800s were presumably descended from the Hohokam—which, in Pima language, means "those who have gone"—but they offered no explanation as to what happened to them. Drought remains a possibility—perhaps a twenty-year drought the likes of which they had never seen—but an equally plausible explanation is that they irrigated too much and waterlogged the land, leading to intractable problems with salt buildup in the soil, which would have poisoned the crops. In either case, the mysterious disappearance of Hohokam civilization seems linked to water: they either had too little or used too much.

And that is exactly the problem that Arizona faces today.

When Franklin Roosevelt came out to dedicate Hoover Dam on September 30, 1935, the one important dignitary who refused to attend the ceremony, which drew some ten thousand people, was the governor of Arizona, B. B. Moeur.

Though the dam had been built to safeguard the future of the entire Southwest—that was what FDR said in his speech—Moeur, like many Arizonans, looked on it more with trepidation than with satisfaction and awe. The Colorado River Compact hadn't really given Arizona anything; it had just promised the lower basin 7.5 million acre-feet. In passing the Boulder Canyon Project Act, Congress had implied that Arizona's share was at least 2.8 million acre-feet, but this, Moeur felt, was only a paper guarantee. For one thing, the guarantee had probably been jeopardized, in a legal sense, by Arizona's refusal to sign the compact. Even if it wasn't, Arizona's water rights would become exceptionally vulnerable the moment the Bureau of Reclamation completed its giant canal to the Imperial Valley and California built the mammoth aqueducts headed for the Coachella Valley, San Diego, and Los Angeles. Southern California was growing much too fast to be satisfied with 4.4 million acre-feet of the river's flow—its compact entitlement. In all likelihood, its demand for water would overtake its allotment in another twenty years. Suppose, then, that California began "borrowing" some of Arizona's unused entitlement, which it could probably do. Would Arizona ever get it back, if millions of people depended on it? For the foreseeable future, Arizona was in no position to use its share of the river, because most of the people and most of the irrigated lands were in the central part of the state, nearly two hundred miles away. Rich, urban Los Angeles had the money to build an aqueduct that long, but Arizona, still mostly agricultural, did not. And yet California had vowed to blockade any effort by Arizona to have a federal aqueduct authorized unless the major issue that still divided the two states—the Gila River—was resolved in California's favor.

The Gila, with its tributaries, the Salt and the Verde, was Arizona's only indigenous river of consequence. In the historic past, it evaporated so quickly as it meandered through the scorching Sonoran desert that all that reached the Colorado River at Yuma was an average flow of 1.1 million acre-feet. However, the Salt River Project, by erecting dams in the mountain canyons east of Phoenix, had increased storage and reduced evaporation enough to give the state 2.3 million acre-feet to use. Which of those figures ought to be deducted from Arizona's 2.8-million-acre-foot share of the Colorado watershed? Arizona said neither, or, at most, 1.1 million acre-feet, which was the historical flow. California said 2.3 million acre-feet—the amount which the dams effectively conserved for Arizona's use. If California's reasoning prevailed, Arizona would be left with a paltry 500,000 acre-feet of compact entitlement, which was hardly enough to sustain growth. But if Arizona's reasoning prevailed, California had vowed that a Central Arizona Project would never be built.

To Moeur, a showman politician in the grand carnival style, California's threats were worse than an outrage. In the arid West, denying one's neighbor water was a virtual declaration of war. But Moeur had his own response to such a challenge. He would begin waging a *real* war.

The advance expeditionary force consisted of Major F. I. Pomeroy, 158th Infantry Regiment, Arizona National Guard, plus a sergeant, three privates, and a cook. Their instructions, issued personally by the governor, were to report "on any attempt on the part of any person to place any structure on Arizona soil either within the bed of said river [the Colorado] or on the shore." Moeur knew full well that such an attempt had already been made, for the Bureau was doing some test drilling at the site of Parker Dam—a smaller regulation dam downriver from Hoover—from a barge, and the barge was secured against the current by a cable whose eastern end was anchored in Arizona soil.

When the newspapers caught wind that an army had actually been dispatched, they were ecstatic. The Los Angeles *Times* promptly inducted its military correspondent to cover the hostilities. He made it to the Parker Dam site on his state's fast macadam roads before the expeditionary force even arrived. When it did, exhausted from the heat, dust, and twelve fords across the ooze of the Bill Williams River, Major Pomeroy requisitioned a ferryboat from the town of Parker, and the force was instantly renamed the Arizona Navy. After a full inspection of the offending cable, Pomeroy tried to steam up the Colorado to the mouth of the Bill Williams to reconnoiter, but the ferry was too high to sneak under the cable, and it got hung up.

It was a harbinger of how things were to turn out that the occupants were finally delivered to their campsite by the Los Angeles Department of Water and Power's fast motor launch.

Pomeroy stayed at the site for seven months, sending daily dispatches to the governor by radio. When the Bureau finally began to lay a trestle bridge to the Arizona shore, Moeur decided to demonstrate that he meant business. He declared the whole Arizona side of the river under martial law and sent out a hundred-man militia unit in eighteen trucks, some with mounted machine guns. According to residents of the town of Parker, who were watching a good joke turn sour in a hurry, the guardsmen seemed eager for a fight. By now, however, the imbroglio had became national news and a source of embarrassment to Interior Secretary Harold Ickes. Well aware that Arizona had at least a moral case to make, Ickes ordered construction halted on the dam while the dispute was settled in the courts. To its own surprise as much as everyone else's, Arizona, which had already lost twice in the Supreme Court in its efforts to block Boulder Dam, was upheld. Parker Dam, ruled the Court, was technically illegal because it had not been specifically authorized by Congress. (That the Bureau could begin to put up a big dam without even asking Congress for formal approval says a lot about how far it had come in the intervening years.) Four months later, however, California's Congressional delegation pushed a bill through Congress that specifically authorized the dam, and Arizona was left without recourse, unless it wanted to declare war on the United States.

A few years later, in 1944, Secretary of State Cordell Hull formally promised Mexico the 1.5 million acre-feet that had been set aside for it by the Colorado River Compact. Feeling itself the odd man out, Arizona finally gave in and signed the compact in disgust; it also signed a contract with the Interior Secretary to purchase 2.8 million acre-feet of water. A few years after that, in 1948, the upper-basin states apportioned their 7.5 million acre-feet among themselves, and only two major issues involving the river remained unresolved: how much of her allocated 2.8 million acre-feet Arizona could take out of the main-stem Colorado, and whether California could invoke prior appropriation and deny Arizona most of that. These, at any rate, were the last *legal* issues left to be resolved. The *real* issues had much more to do with nature and economics than with law, and they were just beginning to make themselves felt.

The 1940s and 1950s were boom years in Arizona. Phoenix—population in 1940, 65,000; population in 1960, 439,000—grew overnight from outsize village to big city. Between 1920 and 1960, the state's population doubled twice, and millions of irrigated acres came into production. One of the revelations of the postwar period was that, given the opportunity, people were happy to leave temperate climates with cold winters for desert climates with fierce summers, provided there was water to sustain them and air conditioning to keep them from perishing (Phoenix, in the summer, is virtually intolerable without air conditioning). Not that the migrants had bothered to ask whether there was enough water before they loaded their belongings and drove west. They simply came; no one could stop them. How they were to fill their pools and water their lawns was Arizona's problem.

Arizona's solution was the same most other western states relied on: it began sucking up its groundwater, the legacy of many millennia, as if tomorrow would never come. By the 1960s, despite the Bureau's big Salt River Project—which captured virtually the entire flow of the Gila drainage—four out of every five acre-feet of water used in the state came out of the ground. The annual overdraft—the difference between pumping and replenishment by nature—went past 2.2 million acre-feet a year, which was more than the historic yearly runoff of all the rivers in the state. In dry years, it approached four million acre-feet. In the early days, artesian wells flowed around Phoenix. By the 1960s, some farmers could drill to two thousand feet and bring up nothing but hot brine. Parts of Maricopa County, which includes metropolitan Phoenix, literally began to subside as the water below was pumped out and the aquifers collapsed. Drivers heading toward Tucson on Interstate 10 learned to watch for fissures opening in the highway as a vast block of land sank several inches and the one next to it stayed put. Arizona had reversed the pattern of some western states—it had fully developed its surface water first, and *then* began to overdraft its groundwater. Except for its Colorado River entitlement—whatever it was—it literally had nothing left.

Arizona's politicians reserved their most grandiloquent and apocalyptic imagery for speeches about the state's water dilemma. "Without more water," Congressman John Rhodes liked to say, "we are all going to perish." Morris Udall, Rhodes's ideological opposite on most matters, sounded no less like John the Baptist. Arizona, he said, was "returning to desert, to dust." As far as Senator Carl Hayden was concerned, "the survival of our dear state is at stake."

In 1952, when Los Angeles began planning a second aqueduct to the river and California's diversion climbed toward 5.3 million acre-feet—900,000 more than its entitlement—Arizona, in desperation, went to the Supreme Court a third time to try to get the issue resolved. The case, *Arizona* v. *California*, was to become one of the longest-running lawsuits in the annals of the Court, and the Justices appointed a "Special Master," the New York lawyer Simon Rifkind, to review the case. (Rifkind found the lawsuit and the constant commuting to San Francisco, where the trial was held, so taxing that he suffered a heart attack halfway through; he was still in his early fifties.) The performance of California's chief attorney, Northcutt Ely, is still studied by lawyers interested in the high art of dilatory obfuscation; one expert witness complained that Ely spent three days cross-examining him about a matter that could have been settled in a minute and a half. California, of course, had a vested interest in delay, since each year of irresolution meant 300 billion more gallons of water for the state.

In 1963, the Supreme Court finally ruled. To California's astonishment, it upheld Arizona on virtually all counts. The Salt-Verde-Gila watershed was exclusively Arizona's except for a small portion that belonged to New Mexico. Its use of that water would not be counted against its 2.8-million-acre-foot main-stem Colorado entitlement, which remained intact. That Los Angeles had built a second aqueduct that might soon go empty, and that a California-born Interior Secretary, Ray Lyman Wilbur, had contracted to sell it 5,362,000 acre-feet of water, mattered not in the least. The real zinger, though, came at the end of the decision, and had nothing to do with the immediate issues at hand. If, during a natural calamity or a drought, the river could not begin to satisfy all the claims on it, then, according to the Court, it was up to the Interior Secretary to decide who got how much. From that moment on, the genealogy of each Secretary became a matter of high importance to all the basin states. But there was another matter of even greater importance. The one exception to the rule it had just established, said the Court, was when someone had water rights that predated the Colorado River Compact. Those rights had to be satisfied first, no matter what.

There was an exquisite irony in this. Most of the Indians of the Southwest were hunter-gatherers when whites arrived; a purely agricultural culture such as the Hohokam no longer existed. When the whites came and killed off the buffalo and antelope and ran the Indians onto reservations, their old way of life perished, and they had no choice but to become farmers or wards of the state. The reservation land they got, however, was, for the most part, land no one else had wanted. Much of it was terrible farmland, too sandy or infertile or high in elevation to grow anything well. Because it was such poor land, it required a lot of irrigation water, and the government had implicitly attached large water rights to it—rights that were confirmed in 1908 by the Supreme Court under the *Winters* doctrine. The Navajo Reservation in Arizona carried implicit rights to nearly 600,000 acre-feet, about one-fifth of the natural runoff of the state. Now, according to the Supreme Court, the Navajo could use every drop of that water during an extended drought even as people in Phoenix and Tucson were being allocated five gallons per day, even as millions were fleeing Los Angeles and leaving it the largest ghost town in the world. It probably wouldn't come to that, but the Indians, where water was concerned, clearly had the upper hand. The white man's cavalry had made beggars of them; now his courts had made them kings.

Things looked pretty bleak for southern California after the Supreme Court decision. At some point it would presumably have to give up the 600,000 acre-feet of Arizona's entitlement it was diverting, enough water for the city of Chicago. But things looked bleak for Arizona, too, because the Central Arizona Project, which was supposed to deliver the water to Phoenix and Tucson and the dying farmland in between, was neither built nor even authorized, and California could be counted on to try to achieve politically what it hadn't been able to achieve in court. Only the Indians were satisfied with what they had won. As it would turn out, however, things were even worse for California and Arizona—white man's Arizona—than they looked.

The 17.5-million-acre-foot yield that the Compact negotiators had ascribed to the Colorado River was based on about eighteen years of streamflow measurement with instruments that, by today's standards, were rather imprecise. During all of that period, the river had gone on a binge, sending down average or above-average flows three out of every four years. Not once had the flow dropped below ten million acre-feet, as it had repeatedly during the Great Drought of the 1930s. But all it takes to make statisticians look foolish is a few very wet or very dry years. In San Francisco, precipitation records have been kept for more than a hundred years—a log which, one might think, is good enough for a highly accurate guess. But 1976 and 1977, two unprecedented drought years, lowered the average rainfall figure from 20.66 to 19.33 inches. In a marginal farming region such as the Great Plains, an inch less precipitation can mean all kinds of trouble. In a desert region such as the Southwest, utterly dependent on one river, a difference of a couple of million acre-feet can spell disaster.

The first serious doubts about the 17.5-million-acre-foot figure were raised by Raymond Hill, a distinguished hydrologic engineer, at a conference in Washington, D.C., in 1953. "The discharge of the Colorado River at Lee Ferry [near the Arizona-Utah border]," Hill told his disbelieving audience, "has averaged only 11.7 million acre-feet since 1930." As Hill pointedly noted, the Colorado Basin states had not only been counting on 17.5 million acre-feet per year; they had been building and planning as if they thought that figure was *conservative*. But during the period from 1930 to 1952, the river's annual average had fallen nearly six million acre-feet shy of the accepted safe yield. He didn't need to tell his audience that this was enough water for thirty million people or a couple of million acres of irrigated farmland, maybe more.

As it would do on innumerable occasions, the Bureau refused to believe any expert who told it what it didn't want to hear. Three years later, it was frantically lobbying the Colorado River Storage Project through Congress, as if it considered Hill's figures bunk (if he was right, some of the upper-basin reservoirs it wanted to build might never fill). Then, despite mounting evidence that Hill was more right than wrong, it began planning the Central Arizona Project, which would divert another two million acre-feet from the lower basin to Phoenix and Tucson and the sinking farmland in between. Even as it continued to hold forth for 17.5 million acre-feet, however, the Bureau was beginning to develop some serious internal doubts— doubts which it would attempt to conceal for several more years, but which, in the meantime, would lead it on the most ambitious quest for water in U.S. history.

On August 18, 1965, the Bureau's resident expert on the Colorado River, Randy Riter, forwarded a long letter to Commissioner Floyd Dominy by blue envelope. Blue-envelope mail was meant to be seen by only the commissioner, the regional directors, and a small handful of top assistants. It was the Bureau's version of a diplomatic pouch, and the contents usually meant trouble.

Riter, a gruff engineer and a bishop in the Mormon church, had just attended a meeting of the Colorado Water Conservation Board, a group whose purpose is to prevent a single drop of water from leaving that state's borders without first having been put to beneficial use. The featured speaker at the closed-door meeting was Royce Tipton, a consulting hydrologist in whom the Bureau placed considerable stock. Tipton's reluctant conclusion, Riter told Dominy, was that "there is not enough water in the Colorado River to permit the Upper Basin to fully use its apportionment of 7.5 million acre-feet and still meet its compact obligations to deliver water at Lee Ferry." Tipton's estimate of the river's flow was a lot more optimistic than Hill's had been, but even he felt that it should be set no higher than fifteen million acre-feet. In that case, if one divided the shortage equally between the two basins, each would be left with 6.3 million acre-feet. After you deducted another 1.5 million acre-feet or so for evaporation, and another 1.5 million acre-feet for Mexico, you had a figure low enough to throw seven states into panic.

The implications were enough to make the Bureau panic, too. The Colorado River Storage Project, which it had begun to build—Glen Canyon Dam was already completed—and the Central Arizona Project, which it dearly wanted, were both predicated on the availability of 7.5 million acre-feet to each basin. What if it invested billions in both projects only to find that there wasn't nearly enough water in the river to operate them? The upper-basin projects, in particular, were critically dependent on the full volume of water flowing through the dams; that was the only way the Bureau could generate enough hydroelectric income to give them the illusion of being economically "viable." A shortfall of nearly two million acre-feet could initiate a chain of bankruptcies among thousands of farmers or else force the Bureau to appeal to Congress for rescue. It would also open up a ghastly can of worms involving water rights. Would the shortages come equally out of each basin's hide, or would the earlier projects invoke seniority and try to keep their water under the doctrine of appropriative rights? Obviously, the new figures could knock the whole painstakingly constructed edifice of the Colorado River Compact into rubble. And what would happen when someone discovered that the Bureau had been ignoring warnings such as Hill's and Tipton's for years?

As far as Riter was concerned, there was only one way to face it. "It is futile to argue about an inadequate water supply," he wrote to Dominy. "[F]uture development in the Colorado River Basin is dependent upon the future importation of water to augment the dependable supply in the basin." He suggested that, "as a minimum," the Central Arizona Project legislation pending before Congress be rewritten to contain "a conditional authorization of an import plan of at least 2.5 million acre-feet." Riter didn't say where 2.5 million acre-feet of water from outside the basin should come from. But he knew, and Dominy knew, that there were only a few places where it *could* come from. That much unappropriated water couldn't be found within eight hundred miles. It could come from the rivers of far-northern California. It could come from the Pacific Northwest. Or it could come from Canada.

The idea of relocating distant rivers into the depletion-haunted Colorado Basin—"augmentation" was the euphemism of choice—was really nothing new. One of its earliest and most relentless proponents was William E. Warne, who was brought into the Bureau by Mike Straus and later built the California Water Project under Governor Pat Brown. As a young boy, Warne had moved from Indiana—average precipitation, thirty-six inches per year—to the Imperial Valley of California—average rainfall, 2.4 inches per year—and Warne seems never to have gotten over the shock. A smooth, handsome, genial sort (though even some of his fellow Bureau men considered him water-mad), Warne in his later years would raise his voice to shouting pitch over just one issue: the "ridiculous waste" that was condoned by continuing to allow the rivers of northern California to spill practically unused out to sea. It was unconscionable, Warne would say, that those rivers were so near—"within striking distance," as he put it—and still undammed. Warne was haunted not only by the desert, but by the desert's growth. As a boy in the Imperial Valley, he heard stories about how it had been when not a soul lived there, ten years before. By the time his family arrived, forty thousand people had already moved in. Five years later, another forty thousand had come, and the valley was appropriating about 20 percent of what was then considered to be the Colorado's flow. In the same period, the population of Los Angeles had gone from 100,000 to 500,000 people. "It was the wonder of the world," Warne mused, "how that city grew." By the time he became Assistant Secretary of the Interior for Water and Power in 1949, Bill Warne had developed an obsession: rerouting the fabulous amount of water that spilled into the Pacific from Eureka on north.

The engineering study that would determine how best to do it was called the United Western Investigation. It is, to this day, the best-kept secret in the history of water development in the West; people who have been in the business all their lives have never heard of it. Since it would involve the movement of unprecedented flows of water over unprecedented distances at unprecedented expense, the investigation would need someone of unusual vision and character to lead it, and Mike Straus and Bill Warne would have to go outside the Bureau to locate him. They found him in Bogotá, Colombia, building dams for the descendants of conquistadors. His name was Stanford P. McCasland.

Stan McCasland had worked in the planning division of the Bureau for some years. He quit, evidently, because the predictable tedium of designing small projects on small rivers was something which he considered beneath him. In South America, where you could find unnamed tributaries of the Amazon bigger than the Colorado, he at last found the landscape of his dreams. Like a lot of Bureau engineers, McCasland had only a faint interest in irrigation; it was damming rivers that got his juices flowing. An irascible Scot, he viewed rivers not so much as challenges or opportunities but as willful monsters to be beaten into submission. In the likes of him, the rivers had an unlikely foe. "He was as skinny as a rail," says Pat Dugan, a longtime Bureau engineer who worked with him, "and he had a shock of flaming red hair that made him look as if the top of his head had ignited. He always wore a tweed suit that was about three sizes too big. He looked like he could turn around 180 degrees in that suit while the suit stood still."

The investigation took two years to complete. Its conclusions filled several volumes with descriptions, economic analyses, appendices, and maps. To Clarence Kuiper, a young engineer recruited from the Corps of Engineers, "it was the closest I ever came to feeling omnipotent. We were looking at ideas even Mike Straus hadn't thought of yet." The UWI team raced around the Pacific rim like Rommel's army, concocting schemes to put deserts to flight. They dinged rock samples out of canyon walls. They traced future reservoir basins by air. They floated rivers and explored by jeep. They spread contour maps across the floors of rooms and built tunnels and aqueducts with pencils. They spread oceans of theoretical water over horizons of potential farmland; on paper, they turned half the Southwest green. "Straus told us to look at every possibility," Kuiper would recall years later. "He said, 'Don't you laugh at a goddamn thing.' Well, we

275

didn't. We looked over every harebrained idea that ever came up. We looked at an undersea pipeline from the mouth of the Columbia to Los Angeles. Lord, we found every conceivable place where you could divert the Columbia. We looked into jumping the Willamette out of its bed at Oregon City and turning it right around in an aqueduct to California. Southern Oregon is a big mess of mountains, so we plotted a tunnel that would have been 135 miles long. We had one guy in the Bureau who thought you could keep wall-to-wall tankers moving between the mouth of the Columbia and L.A., so we looked at that, too."

If anything, the United Western Investigation suffered from a surfeit of choices. "Numerous possibilities exist for the interbasin transfer of supplies into water-deficient regions," wrote McCasland in the cover document, which bore the splendidly militaristic title *United Western Investigation, Interim Report on Reconnaissance, Report of the Chief*. You could, for example, take a few million acre-feet out of the Snake River at Twin Falls, Idaho, pump it up the south side of the Snake River in fifteen-foot siphons, and drop it into the Humboldt River, the only constant river in the state of Nevada, meandering small and forlorn beside Interstate 80 for three hundred miles until it disappears in shallow, salty Humboldt Lake. Then you could move the suddenly prodigious Humboldt straight across seamless desert to the Owens Valley, two hundred miles away. You could tunnel thirty miles under the White Mountains and just dump it in. Then you could quadruple the size of everything Los Angeles had built to divert the Owens River, and move the mingled waters of the Snake and the Humboldt and the Owens to L.A., to San Diego, to the Mojave Desert, and dump the surplus in the Colorado to satisfy our treaty with Mexico, leaving the other basin states with the whole Colorado to hoard for themselves.

Alternatively, you could build a whole series of dams at a more or less equal elevation on the bigger rivers of coastal Oregon and, at a level approximate to the elevation of the upper Sacramento Valley, run a gravity-diversion aqueduct from reservoir to reservoir, picking up half-million-acre-foot increments as a bus picks up passengers, then run the aqueduct beneath the Siskiyou Mountains and plop the water into Shasta Lake, then lead it south from there. You could take millions and millions of acre-feet out of the Pend Oreille in Washington, an obscure river bigger than the Wabash or the Hudson or the Sacramento, and move it by gravity—aqueduct-tunnel-aqueduct-tunnel-aqueduct-tunnel—from Albeni Falls, near the Canadian border, across the deserts of eastern Washington and central Oregon all the way to California, passing by the Rogue and the Illinois and picking up some surplus flows, with the end result that California's developed water yield would be increased by nearly one-half. "The total length of the aqueduct . . . would be about 1,020 miles, of which about 290 miles would be tunnel and 40 miles in siphon. No estimates of cost were made for this plan because the necessary length of aqueduct causes it to appear unattractive." Most or all of these diversions, the *Report of the Chief* implied, would *have* to be built, sooner or later. "Regardless of magnitude, scope, and timing of the undertaking, if it can be shown that moving surplus waters of the Northwest to water-deficient areas elsewhere is in the realm of sound public interest, it is, in Reclamation's opinion and half century of experience, only a matter of time before exhaustion of nearer water supplies forces the undertaking of a suitable project for that purpose." All of this, however, might still be fifty years in the future. For now, the immediate need was in the Colorado Basin and its parasitic appendage, southern California, and the obvious river of rescue was the Klamath.

Remote, wild, half-forgotten, the Klamath was a perfect example of how God had left the perfection and completion of California to the Bureau of Reclamation. The second-largest river in the state—three times the size of the third-largest river—it was imprisoned by mountains and hopelessly remote from Los Angeles. Spilling out of Klamath Lake in southern Oregon, a huge shallow apparition cradled between mountains and desert, the river drops across the California border and bends its way westward toward the coast. Then it dips suddenly southward toward populated California, and, as if recognizing covetous intent, immediately doubles back on itself and flees to Oregon through the plunging topography of the Siskiyou Range. Diverting the Klamath would be easy along the first half of its course, but it doesn't contain much water yet. A hundred miles from the Pacific, however, rainfall shoots up to a hundred inches, the Trinity and Scott and Salmon rivers pour in, and the Klamath is suddenly huge. On a random day late in February of 1983, after a week of rain, the Klamath was flowing at four thousand cubic feet per second below Klamath Lake and at 148,000 cfs near its mouth, a Niagara-size flow in a canyon you can bat a ball across. Small tributaries were tumbling oven-size rocks like ice cubes. To the Bureau, the Klamath's huge and reliable winter surges were only its second greatest attraction—the first was its availability. The Klamath was wasting twelve

277

million acre-feet to the sea with hardly a claim on it. Its principal appropriators were salmon, steelhead, and bears.

To capture the Klamath, you had to dam it twelve miles from the Pacific, then move the water in reverse across, or under, a hundred miles of the most rugged topography in the United States. The dam, which would be called Ah Pah, would occupy the river's last gorge. It would stand 813 feet high. The Pan Am Building in New York City stands 805 feet high. A man-made El Capitán, it would pool water seventy miles up the Klamath and forty miles up the Trinity to form a reservoir with 15,050,000 acre-feet of gross storage. (The reservoir that obliterated Johnstown, Pennsylvania, held fifty thousand acre-feet.) The Klamath, both forks of the Trinity, and the Salmon River would, for all practical purposes, disappear; 98 percent of the salmon and steelhead spawning grounds would be lost; at least seven towns would vanish, including the main settlements of the Hoopa tribe, from whose language the dam's name was borrowed, and whose reservation it would drown. "Only minor improvements [i.e., towns] exist in this [the reservoir] area," said the United Western report. The site, in a dense metasandstone formation, was presumed to be safe, although it "probably contains minor faults."

Trinity Tunnel, which would spin water out of the bottom back side of the reservoir and carry it to the Central Valley, would be sixty miles long. Its shape would resemble a horseshoe, and its diameter would be thirty-seven feet. There would be no tunnel remotely like it anywhere in the world. The Delaware Aqueduct, stretching from the Catskill Mountains to Westchester County, is eighty-five miles long, but its diameter is only fourteen feet. Trinity Tunnel could hold four passenger trains operating on two levels. It alone would cost nearly half a billion dollars, in 1951, and it was merely the longest and biggest of numerous tunnels. The Tehachapi Tunnel, forty miles long, would move the water through the Transverse Ranges, which cordon off Los Angeles from the rest of the state. Seven known fault zones would be crossed along the aqueduct route, and one of them, the San Andreas Fault, would present a fracture zone at least two miles wide in the middle of the Tehachapi Tunnel which could pose "unusual construction problems." An ordinary tunnel would shear if the fault slipped—it slipped nearly twenty feet in the 1906 quake—leaving Los Angeles unwashed and unquenched. "Extra-heavy supports would be required throughout this zone."

The cost of everything—Ah Pah Dam, the other dams, the tunnels, the aqueducts, the pumps, the canals, the receiving reservoirs, and an item called a Peripheral Canal, which would be built to carry the Sacramento's hugely increased flow around California's Delta—would be $3,293,050,000. It was an incredible bargain; today, a couple of nuclear power plants cost much more than that. Had the Bureau reckoned how expensive life was going to become, the Klamath Diversion might well have been built. "In those days, almost everything the Bureau proposed was being built," Kuiper says. "But Straus decided to move cautiously on this one. If you read the report, you'll see that we were always talking about 'orderly development.' That's code talk for building at a deliberate pace, taking care to butter everyone's bread, instead of going gung-ho, which is what they did on the Missouri. In California, you had two choices: you could build a lot of little projects on tributaries of the Sacramento and the San Joaquin, or you could build one huge project on the Klamath. I don't know whether it made better sense to do one or the other. What I do know is that Mike Straus was constitutionally incapable of seeing that the clock was already running out on these tremendous projects. He thought it was the other way around—that the Bureau would keep building bigger and bigger things. The only way Mike knew how to think was bigger and bigger. He and Bill Warne were sure the Klamath Diversion was going to be built someday, so they didn't try to railroad it through."

McCasland didn't help. Arrogant and prickly, he may have been a fine engineer, but he was the public relations equivalent of Sherman's march to the sea. Without asking clearance from the commissioner's office, he wrote an article describing the Klamath Diversion for *Civil Engineering* in 1952. Northern California's thirty-five years of passionate opposition to southern California's diversion plans can be traced directly to that article. McCasland would not even say that this huge, incredibly disruptive project would take care of the southland's needs for all time: "The plan described as the Northern California Diversion," he wrote, "would not by any means constitute a complete water supply for the Southwest. It would meet the most imminent demands . . . but it would more probably constitute the initial stage of a large plan to serve much wider markets a future economy might dictate." Clarence Kuiper says, "What I remember about that time is the phone ringing off the hook with reporters from Oregon and Washington asking me if it was true that the Bureau was planning to divert the Columbia River." But the outrage cascading down from the Pacific Northwest was the least of the Bureau's problems. Its main problem was that Los Angeles, for whose benefit the

Klamath Diversion had mainly been conceived, was unalterably opposed to it, too.

The idea of the city it was trying to save vilifying the project it had planned in order to save it left the Bureau of Reclamation speechless. Had its engineers known a thing or two about law and psychology, however, they wouldn't have been the least surprised. Los Angeles, in the middle of an epic feud with Arizona over Colorado River water rights, saw the Klamath Diversion as a ploy to encourage it to relinquish its claim on the share of the river that it wanted to consider its own. In fact, if any Californian even *mentioned* the idea of going north for water, Los Angeles came down on him like Thor. When Republican Congressman Richard J. Welch of San Francisco did just that, the Los Angeles *Daily News* denounced his idea as "the kiss of Judas." "This San Franciscan," it fumed, "is trying not to succor but to sucker us." As Carey McWilliams wrote in *California: The Great Exception*, "To suggest that Colorado River water was not the only water which might be made available in southern California was, of course, an act of treason, a betrayal." The Republican Party of the state, with its center of power in Los Angeles and Orange County, went so far as to mount an effort to excommunicate poor Welch, who, as bewildered as the Bureau by then, said he was only trying to help.

The Bureau was flummoxed. Copies of the UWI report were buried in the archives in the regional office in Salt Lake City, where they sat under lock and key. Before he could do more damage, McCasland was transferred to a desk job in Washington, and young Kuiper was left with the job of repairing the wreckage his boss had created. The Klamath Diversion, potentially the greatest engineering scheme of all time, was dumped on the scrapheap of human dreams. "The whole thing kind of backfired on them," said Kuiper in 1981, still wryly amused after all those years.

The Eisenhower era put transbasin diversions into the Colorado on hold for at least another eight years. Ike's Interior Secretary, Douglas McKay, a Chevrolet dealer from Portland, Oregon, followed the honorable Republican tradition of using the office as a vending machine for timber and minerals, but recoiled at the idea of an activist government marketing water and power. Ike's water-development policy, announced shortly after his inauguration, was that there would be "no new starts" during his administration, especially if the production of power was involved. His own Republican allies from the western states would soon make him eat his words, but his immediate

problem, after his inauguration, was finding a Reclamation Commissioner who would do his bidding—an exact opposite of Mike Straus.
Since the Bureau had been stuffed with liberals, public-power advocates, and super-engineers of the McCasland ilk during the previous
thirty years of Democratic reign, he wouldn't be easy to find within
the Bureau—whence commissioners traditionally came. After leaving
the post vacant for several months, the Republicans finally came up
with Wilbur Dexheimer, the Bureau's assistant chief construction
engineer. Dexheimer was handsome, amiable, and a competent engineer, but he was, as Winston Churchill said of Clement Attlee, a
modest man with much to be modest about. He had spent his entire
career in the Denver engineering headquarters, and he was an ingenue
at politics, which was the breath of life to Mike Straus. Dexheimer
was the first to admit that he was the consummately wrong choice
for the job. As soon as he was appointed, he called his regional commissioners to Washington, gathered them in his office, and blurted
out, "I don't have to tell you guys that I'm the least likely person in
Creation to be sitting at this desk. I'm ignorant as hell about what
goes on in this town, but by God they made me commissioner and
here I am and now you've got to follow my orders even if you and I
think they stink."

To the routed myrmidons of the New Deal, the golden age of
water development seemed truly over. But Republican principles would
prove to be no match for the stark imperative of the American desert.
In 1956, Ike would end up signing the Colorado River Storage Project
Act against his better judgment, and the budgets of both the Bureau
and the Corps of Engineers would increase dramatically during his
administration. In the lower Colorado Basin, however, Eisenhower
had an excuse to do nothing. Until the Central Arizona Project was
given final shape—and that couldn't happen until the legal battle
had ended and it was determined who had rights to what water—
the river's looming deficit would remain an inconsequential fact.
Once the lawsuit was settled, however, the Bureau would face two
seemingly insuperable problems at once: how to build the most expensive water project of all time; and, even worse, how to authorize
an even *more* expensive augmentation scheme that would give the
Colorado Basin enough water for everything it was planning to build.

On a map of Arizona, the Colorado River can be seen making a wide
circle around the northern and eastern half of the state. At every point
along that six-hundred-mile sojourn, the populated center of the state

is walled off from the river by mountains. In the north, the river flows in a bottomless canyon, a mile below its southern rim; to lift it out of there and lead it to Phoenix would be out of the question—even though the water, once out of the Grand Canyon, could flow downhill all the way. Closer to its mouth, the river escapes its canyon confines and flows across broad sandy wastes, but numerous ranges stand between the river and Tucson and Phoenix—the Aquarius Cliffs, the Black Mountains, the Maricopa Mountains, the Saucera Range. Regardless of where one located the point of diversion, to move a portion of the Colorado River to Tucson and Phoenix would involve a pump lift of at least twelve hundred feet. Pumping irrigation water there would be like taking it out of the Hudson River and lifting it over the World Trade Center in order to water lawns on Long Island. The CAP was to be, first and foremost, an *irrigation* project, a rescue project to save the dying farmlands between Phoenix and Tucson; the cities would also get some water, but the farmers would receive the overwhelming share. Hardly anywhere on earth, however, is water lifted that high in order to irrigate crops, unless the water flows nearly as far downhill somewhere along its route as it was lifted uphill, so that much of the energy required to lift it can be recovered. Even then, the Second Law of Thermodynamics exacts a heavy toll: for every hundred units of energy expended to lift the water, only seventy or so can be recovered on the way back down. Using the most optimistic set of circumstances—high-value crops, unprecedented crop prices, dirt-cheap power from preexisting dams—the Central Arizona Project was likely to be an economic catastrophe.

A simple matter of physics, then, made the Central Arizona Project even worse, in an economic sense, than the Colorado River Storage Project. But politics demanded that it be built, and in the 1960s, Arizona had power. Barry Goldwater was the presidential candidate of the Republican Party; Carl Hayden was the chairman of the Senate Appropriations Committee. He could, if he wanted, hold up every other water project in the country until his state was satisfied. And there was the issue of equity. California had its water, Nevada had its water, the upper basin was developing its water, and Arizona still had nothing. What were a couple of billion dollars in the face of these other, more important concerns?

Still, something would have to be done about the project's horrifically poor economic rationale. And something would ultimately have to be done about the fact that the river now seemed certain to dry up if the CAP was built. Something—but what? The obvious answer was a couple of big cash register dams that could generate enough power, and enough money, to give Arizona's irrigation farmers the 90-percent subsidy they would probably need. If the dams were big enough, there might be enough revenue left over to begin a fund that, in the future, could help build the gigantic augmentation project that the basin would require.

But where could one locate the dams? There were no sites for big dams left in Arizona, and besides, the Gila River system didn't have nearly enough water to develop the kind of power the Bureau had in mind. California still had a lot of undeveloped hydroelectric potential, but it wouldn't think of allowing dams to be built within its borders whose revenues would allow Arizona to divert water it was then using. The Colorado River Storage Project was cementing dams in all the best hydroelectric canyons in the upper basin. New Mexico's rivers had neither the sites nor the water flows. There was only one place in the entire Southwest where reliable water flowed through a section of river with a thousand-foot drop—the Grand Canyon.

The proposal for Grand Canyon dams was officially revealed on January 21, 1964, with the release of something called the Pacific Southwest Water Plan. One had only to read the title to see that, now that another New Deal Democrat was in the White House (Lyndon Johnson had just beaten Barry Goldwater with 60 percent of the popular vote), the Bureau had happily returned to the mode of thinking prevalent during the FDR and Truman years. The plan was majestic. It contemplated two huge new dams on the Colorado River in Marble Gorge and Bridge Canyon, at opposite ends of Grand Canyon National Park. Both had been carefully situated so as not to flood the park itself—except for what the Bureau called "minor" flooding that would drown lower Havasu Creek, the canyon's most beautiful side stream, and submerge Lava Falls, the river's most thunderous rapid. But the park would sit inside a dam sandwich: Bridge Canyon Dam would back up water for ninety-three miles below it, entirely flooding the bottom of Grand Canyon National Monument, and Marble Gorge Dam would create a reservoir more than forty miles long right above it. The dams had one purpose—hydroelectric power—and a single objective: lots and lots of cash. They would not conserve any water, because there was none left to conserve; in some years, they would cause a net *loss* to the river through evaporation. They were there only to take advantage of the thousand feet of elevation loss between

Glen Canyon and Hoover dams. Together, they would generate 2.1 million megawatts of peaking power, marketable at premium rates. Later, the power revenues would finance an artificial river of rescue; for now it would pay for the other features of the plan.

One of those features—actually, it was the centerpiece of the plan— was a pair of big dams on the Trinity River, in far-northern California, and a long hard-rock tunnel that would turn their water into the Sacramento River, where it would begin its journey to Los Angeles. That city and its burgeoning suburbs would thus receive a huge surge of high-quality water from northern California to replace the salty Colorado. The San Joaquin Valley would siphon off a considerable portion along the way; it was going to be rescued, for the *third* time, from its suicidal habit of mining groundwater. New Mexico would get Hooker Dam, which would inundate yet another scenic monu- ment—the Gila Wilderness—and Utah would get two more projects. In the middle of the list, camouflaged under "water salvage and re- covery programs," was the most expensive item of all: the Central Arizona Project. It was the same multibillion-dollar shell game that the United Western Investigation had proposed: new water from northern California would take care of southern California's needs so that the Colorado could be conserved for the upper basin and Arizona.

Curiously, the United Western Investigation did not even rate a passing mention in the report, though it dwelled at some length on earlier plans to solve the Southwest's water dilemma. Evidently, the UWI was still so closely associated with a raid on the Columbia River that the framers of the Pacific Southwest Water Plan would rather have pretended that it never existed. Another name hard to find in the report was that of the Interior Secretary, Stewart Udall. There were three possible explanations for this. One—the one conserva- tionists wanted to believe—was that the plan did not really have Udall's support. He was, after all, being described by them as the best Interior Secretary since Harold Ickes. How could the best Interior Secretary since Harold Ickes wish to inundate the most stunning feature of the American landscape? How could he talk about the "minor" intrusion of a reservoir into a national park? Another ex- planation was that Udall, as a native of Arizona, felt that he had to distance himself from a plan whose ultimate purpose was to deliver a couple of million acre-feet to his home state. A third explanation— the one conservationists least wanted to believe—was that Udall sup- ported the plan but didn't want to admit it.

The most interesting curiosity about the plan, however, was the obvious discrepancy between the amount of new water the Trinity River could deliver and the looming shortfall in the Colorado River. At the moment the plan was released, the second-largest reservoir in California, Clair Engle Lake, was beginning to fill on the upper reaches of the Trinity. Its capacity of 2,448,000 acre-feet was not much less than the river's annual flow of 3,958,000 acre-feet. Clair Engle Lake was a main feature of the Central Valley Project; its water, therefore, was exclusively for California's use. According to the Pacific Southwest Water Plan, only 1.2 million acre-feet would be left in the Trinity to augment the Colorado River—and that was assuming the Trinity, one of the world's great salmon and steelhead rivers, would be bled virtually dry before reaching the sea. But the shortfall which the Bureau was projecting in the Colorado Basin, privately if not publicly, was at least 2.5 million acre-feet. Where would the other 1.3 million acre-feet come from? The Pacific Southwest Water Plan said nothing about it. It only hinted that it "does not provide an overall solution for the region's water needs," then failed to mention what such an ultimate solution would be. The Bureau's maps had other reservoirs all over the place, drawn in gray—several on the Eel River, one on Cache Creek, the huge Ah Pah reservoir on the Klamath—but referred to these as "alternative storage possibilities," as if they might substitute for, but not augment, the Trinity dams. Where, then, was water for six million people to come from?

In the Pacific Northwest, there was a lot of suspicion that the Pacific Southwest Water Plan was merely a smokescreen for a much larger plan, long a gleam in the Colorado Basin's eye, to tap the Columbia River. Such paranoia was inflamed by occasional speeches delivered to sympathetic ears by some of the Bureau's engineers, insisting that this was the final solution that would someday have to be built to allow continued growth in the parching Southwest. Officially, however, the Interior Department went to great lengths to reassure the Northwest that it had no such designs. Udall publicly scoffed at the notion of diverting the Columbia, and Floyd Dominy, the Bureau commissioner, sharply reprimanded his underlings if they even mentioned the idea. But the truth of the matter was that the Pacific Southwest Water Plan *was* a smokescreen. The Columbia was on Udall's and Dominy's minds the entire time.

On December 15, 1964, less than a year after the Pacific Southwest plan was revealed, a four-hour-long meeting quietly took place at the regal new offices of the Metropolitan Water District of Southern California. (Built on a hill at one end of Sunset Boulevard, the MWD headquarters had a splendid view of the immense sprawl and traffic congestion it had helped create—four freeways converged right below its windows—but it was walled off from same by a forest of fountains and, fittingly, a moat.) The participants in the meeting were Udall, Dominy, Interior solicitor Edward Weinberg, Los Angeles Congressman Chet Holifeld (whose twin passions were water diversion and nuclear power), and seven carefully selected members of the MWD. Officially, this was a meeting that never took place, but as the chairman of the MWD, Joe Jensen, enthused in a "Confidential Report to MWD Directors," it was "one of the most constructive conferences we have attended." Udall, he reported, "expects to discuss with Senator Jackson of Washington a feasibility study and the eventual taking of ten to fifteen million acre-feet of water from the Columbia River. He would hope to have Senator Jackson lead off with the statement that the export program would be possible according to such guidelines as Jackson felt necessary for such an export program."

"Mr. Dominy," Jensen continued, "explained that a group in Denver had been working for thirty days on a preliminary study to bring water from the Columbia River, and that by March he should be able to give a definite answer as to the route and the general features of the project; as well as a comparison of cost of this project and the cost of delivering water from California and desalting. . . . Washington may need a stepped-up reclamation program," Jensen quoted Dominy as saying, *"in order to offset the adverse effects of closing down several federal installations in that state"* (emphasis added).

"The Secretary stated two courses appeared to be possible at the present time," Jensen wrote his fellow board members. "(1) Have a study made and defer action on authorization while the study is done right; (2) Introduce a bill which would authorize the import program, Bridge and Marble Canyon Dams, Central Arizona Project, and a few of the other projects. By March more definite information should be available and it should be possible to have the Committee report a bill to authorize the study and authorize the construction of the import program. . . . Dominy indicated the first six months of any presidential term was the best time to hit Congress. *He stated that the Bureau had never had any trouble getting funds once a project had been authorized*, but it frequently had trouble getting projects authorized" (emphasis added).

Udall and Dominy, in other words, wanted to study the feasibility of the Columbia diversion *after* it was already authorized, on the assumption that even if it wasn't economically sound, it would be too late to stop it. Their real concern seemed to be lining up the political firepower that would let them succeed. And the plan, as Jensen described it, included so many gifts to so many states that it certainly *ought* to succeed. It contemplated numerous new irrigation projects in both Oregon and Nevada, some more projects in the upper Colorado Basin, and the stepped-up reclamation program in Washington that would make up for the mysterious "facilities" that might have to be shut down. Even then, Jensen said, "up to 7.5 million acre-feet of [Columbia River] water" would still reach Lake Mead every year. The plan, then, had to be far more expensive and ambitious than anything ever contemplated—more so, by far, than the Pacific Southwest Water Plan, more so even than the Klamath Diversion studied by the Bureau twelve years earlier. That was remarkable enough. What was *really* remarkable, however, was that the water would be available *"at the present price of Colorado River water."*

To charge no more for Columbia River water delivered to Los Angeles or Arizona than was being charged for water from nearby Hoover Dam would be a feat as astonishing as Moses' bifurcation of the Red Sea. The water would have to come a thousand miles by aqueduct; Hoover water came only a couple of hundred miles, and the immense power output of the dam subsidized the big pump lift to L.A. Hoover Dam was financed with Depression-era interest rates and built by workers earning $4 a day; this project would be financed by Vietnam-era interest rates and built by unionized labor earning at least $6 an hour. There would be little, if any, hydroelectric power produced, but a lot of power might be required for pumping; the water had to go over or through two major mountain ranges! The difference in cost, per acre-foot, ought to be at least 800 percent, probably much more. But, according to Joe Jensen, Stewart Udall was offering it at the same price the MWD paid for water from Lake Mead. Somewhere, there was an immense subsidizing engine, but where?

In his memorandum, Jensen merely hinted at an answer; it may have sounded so good he didn't believe it himself. "The cost of such Columbia River supply," he wrote, "is to be paid out of the first power revenues. The remaining power revenues would be available for assisting in the payment of the main program or project, and water revenues would pay part of the cost." Apparently, Jensen was promised by Udall and Dominy that the power revenues generated by the dams that would be part of the import scheme were going to subsidize the price of water before they even began to pay back the cost of the facilities! Before the dams were paid for; before the aqueducts were paid for; before the tunnels were paid for; before the siphons and canals were paid for—before a penny went to all of that, the power revenues were going to go directly into the pockets of water consumers in southern and central California and Arizona, subsidizing the price of their water. How else *could* Udall be promising the Southwest water—water that probably wouldn't be available until the 1980s—at 1935 prices? If this was what it took to get the Central Arizona Project built—and Jensen, a leading foe of that project, did not say an unkind word about it in his memorandum—Udall and Dominy were prepared to *give* the water away.

In an economic sense, what the backers of the Pacific Southwest Water Plan were proposing was unprecedented. It violated every principle of economics, even the fast and loose principles of Reclamation economics. If the lion's share of the power revenues were going to subsidize not only irrigation but *municipal* water costs—municipal water whose revenues had usually subsidized *irrigation* in the past— the project could not possibly be paid back for hundreds of years, if ever. The cost, which had to be in the many billions, would simply be borne on the backs of the taxpayers. From a national perspective, it was a stunningly ill-conceived idea; but from a regional perspective, it was a wonderful idea—an offer none of the basin states could refuse. At a price guaranteed to be affordable—not only affordable but dirt-cheap—the yield of the Colorado River would be increased by one-half. Oregon would get a slew of new irrigation projects, as would Nevada. California's irrigators would be relieved of their most desperate worry, the self-inflicted groundwater overdraft. And it could all be accomplished by taking a mere 10 percent of the flow of the Columbia River and turning it southward.

Behind the proposal was a spectacular gamble—that Congress and the public would go along with the idea; or, even if they didn't, that the Southwest had the political power to persuade them to. But how could one sell the public on a program that was supposed to remain a tightly guarded secret? On December 31, 1964, two weeks after learning of the Columbia plan, Joe Jensen sent his New Year's greeting to Stewart Udall, expressing "very great appreciation" for Udall's decision to support the project that had always been Jensen's dream. Then he added, "Since your program is to be kept confidential there is little that we can do except give you assurance of our support and our desire to assist in every way." It must have been frustrating for Jensen. The Metropolitan Water District had the mightiest propaganda apparatus in the entire West, and he didn't dare push the button to fire it up.

Maintaining a self-enforced silence about the proposal was actually the least of the proponents' problems. By 1965, the war in Vietnam was consuming an ever-larger bite of the federal budget, and LBJ's antipoverty programs also promised to cost a tremendous amount. No price had been put on the Columbia diversion, but the Trinity River version of the Pacific Southwest Water Plan was expected to cost $3,126,000,000; going as far as the Columbia for much more water could easily cost three times that much. The federal budget in 1965 was only $118.4 billion; to persuade the Congress to authorize perhaps $10 billion for a single water project would take some doing. But the biggest and most unyielding obstacle would not even be the enormous cost. It would be the man who, Udall foolishly felt, he could persuade to lead the bill through Congress—a pugnacious, five-foot-ten-inch, third-term Senator and fellow Democrat from Washington state named Henry Jackson.

In June of 1965, with no discernible opposition, Senator Henry Jackson tacked an innocent-looking rider onto an innocuous-seeming bill that established standardized guidelines for the allocation of costs to fish and wildlife enhancement. What the rider did, in a couple of brief sentences, was prohibit the Bureau of Reclamation from undertaking feasibility studies that Congress did not approve in advance. The effect of the manuever, which few recognized at first, was the same as if Jackson had strung a six-hundred-volt electrified fence along the entire south bank of the Columbia River. Without a feasibility study, the Bureau couldn't approach Congress for authorization. Without a Congressional authorization, it couldn't build. Explaining his amendment to a couple of reporters who were smart enough to see what it meant, Jackson made no mention of the Columbia River. He was annoyed, he said, by the Bureau's habit of "working up local interest and enthusiasm for projects in the field before presenting its case to Congress." Such tactics, he said, put Congress in a "take it or leave it position" when the Bureau came to authorization hearings with a gaggle of local politicians and noisy project boosters in tow. His amendment was nothing for the Bureau to get upset about; "the Corps of Engineers has operated under similar provisions for many years."

It was true that the Corps operated under a similar restriction; it was also true that it rarely paid much attention to it. But Jackson's rider had made illegal the feasibility study that Dominy had quietly ordered on the Columbia diversion. Jackson, who obviously had heard rumors of the secret plan, was out to kill it in its embryonic state. The Northwest had water to spare, but it no longer had power to spare, and nearly all of its electricity came from dams. To remove ten million acre-feet from the Columbia River meant a reduction of several billion kilowatt-hours in power output, unless one diverted the water below the dams. The Bureau would undoubtedly want to do that; but suppose the pumping cost of a diversion from low elevation would add tremendously to the project's cost, and it made much more sense to divert above the dams? If the enormous momentum that could develop behind the diversion scheme really got rolling, the Northwest would look awfully selfish refusing to part with some of its superabundant water just because it insisted on paying one-fourth the average national price for electricity.

"I told Jackson that we ought to let them study the idea," recalled Daniel Dreyfus, who was then the Senator's closest aide. "There was no way it was going to be economically feasible. Twenty years earlier, maybe. In the sixties, absolutely not. 'Let's let 'em study it,' I told Jackson. 'Study the damned thing and it will slay itself. It's a crazy idea.' But his reasoning was that there'd been other crazy projects that got built just because they were studied. I still never thought it could get built, but he was right on that point."

Without a feasibility study—which Jackson, as chairman of the Senate Interior Committee, would never allow—the Columbia diversion was stillborn. What is more interesting is how quickly the Trinity Diversion died with it, even though Jackson had not publicly opposed it. One reason may have been that Los Angeles viewed it, as it had viewed the United Western Investigation, as a threat—an implied source of water that wasn't the Colorado River (it didn't mind the Columbia because that source was *really big*). But another and better reason was that it didn't make any economic sense. The Trinity River offered too little water at too great an expense. No matter what the cost or opposition, the Colorado Basin had to get its hands on the Klamath, the Snake, or the Columbia; those were the only rivers left in the American West that were worth thinking about.

It was actually the upper Colorado Basin states, not the lower, that were pursuing the water importation idea with particularly feverish interest. California wasn't worried. The Imperial Valley had so much water it was almost drowning in it, and Los Angeles had more on the way from the State Water Project, then just being built. Through the

CAP, Arizona might soon receive most of its entitlement to the river through a single diversion. The upper-basin projects, however, were small and spread all over the map, and few of those authorized by the Colorado River Storage Project had yet been built. Several, in fact, had been denied startup funds in Congress—partly because their backers lacked the awesome Appropriations Committee clout of the California delegation or a Carl Hayden, partly because they were beginning to be regarded by some members of Congress as a scandalous waste of taxpayers' money, especially with a war going on. Floyd Dominy had told Joe Jensen that he always got funds for projects that had been authorized, but the upper basin was learning that, indeed, this was *not* always the case. At the languid rate its projects were being built, the upper basin would be the last to develop its full entitlement to the river. And when the overappropriated river was played out, the compact might not mean a thing. Whoever was using the most water would end up keeping the most water; the various Congressional delegations—especially the powerful one from California—would see to that. No one was going to turn off the spigot to Los Angeles, Arizona, or the Imperial Valley for the sake of a few marginal irrigation projects in the upper basin—especially if they hadn't even been built.

Exactly how adamant the upper basin was on this issue became apparent, for the first time, at a secret summit meeting attended by representatives of the four states at Denver, Colorado, on January 18 and 19, 1966. The subject of the meeting was the CAP legislation that Dominy, Udall, and the Arizona and California delegates had coalesced behind, HR 4671. HR 4671 was a drastically trimmed-down version of the Pacific Southwest Water Plan. It authorized only the Central Arizona Project, Bridge Canyon Dam (Marble Gorge, the other Grand Canyon dam, had been dropped because its meager power output didn't seem worth the inevitable fight), and a new aqueduct to Las Vegas. The bill also authorized something called a "development fund"—a receptacle for revenues from the power dams that, in the future, would help finance the augmentation scheme everyone knew would be needed. The legislation, in other words, authorized the projects that would ensure the Colorado River's early exhaustion; it also authorized the means of financing the basin's rescue. What it did not authorize—what it didn't even *mention*, let alone describe—was the importation plan itself. Udall and Dominy had evidently concluded that the development fund would be enough to mollify the upper basin. Only after Dominy's regional director in Salt

Lake City, Dave Crandall, sent him his report on the Denver meeting did they see how utterly wrong they were.

Of the four upper-basin states, the one that seemed most intent on a specific authorization for the rescue project was Colorado, within whose borders half the river's flow originates. This, from Udall and Dominy's point of view, was most unfortunate. Colorado's delegation was headed by Felix Sparks, the head of its Water Conservation Board. Sparks had won the Medal of Honor in World War II, among many other medals, for single-handedly storming a machine-gun nest with a sidearm and a jacketful of grenades and killing half a platoon of Germans. According to those who knew him, he was not afraid of God, man, or the devil. He was also stubborn, vindictive, and a bully, but in Colorado, where water was concerned, he was king.

According to Dave Crandall, Sparks had terrorized the Colorado delegation into asserting that "a feasibility study of import must be a part of the [CAP] bill, otherwise they would not support it. They would prefer an authorization of import but recognize the impracticality of seeking such authorization at this time." Wyoming, he said, took a similar view: "It feels that import is an absolute necessity for their future development and protection and they desire conditional authorization. . . . Studies of importation are an absolute minimum and anything else would result in opposition to the bill." Utah was slightly less adamant than Colorado and Wyoming, but not much. New Mexico would accept a bill that only authorized a feasibility study, but nothing less than that. Between them, as Dominy well knew, the four states had the power in Congress to kill any bill they didn't like. Wayne Aspinall of Colorado was the autocratic chairman of the House Interior Committee, which would have to report out the bill in order for it to reach the floor of Congress; he could bottle it up forever if he desired. Clinton Anderson of New Mexico had similar power in the Senate, Carl Hayden notwithstanding. And there were plenty of others in both houses to be reckoned with.

However, for all their insistence on an augmentation project that might be viewed as something akin to a military invasion by northern California or the Pacific Northwest, the upper-basin representatives were curiously ambivalent about the one item *already authorized* in HR 4671 that would generate the billions that would allow such a rescue project to be built—Bridge Canyon Dam. "New Mexico observes that its inclusion could be untimely and unwise," reported Crandall to Dominy. Even the choleric Felix Sparks, he wrote, was inclined "to defer to the lower-basin states on this question." Wyoming's and Utah's positions were "not materially different than the position of Colorado and New Mexico." And yet if Bridge Canyon Dam were not built, with its promise of huge amounts of high-priced peaking power, how could the rescue project they insisted on be self-financing? It couldn't. But no Reclamation project had ever been built that didn't at least create the *illusion* that it was self-financing.

For the moment, however, the upper-basin states were not worried about that. They were much more worried about a former magazine editor and amateur lepidopterist from Berkeley, California, named David Brower.

David Brower's passionate opposition to dams has its origins in his teeth. Brower's childhood, spent in that most tolerant of American cities, had not been happy. He had an awkward case of shyness and, to boot, a row of missing teeth, and his schoolmates taunted him mercilessly about both. In his midteens he departed for the only place in California where he felt he would be left alone or at least find better company: the Sierra Nevada. In those days—the late 1920s—backpacking and mountaineering were considered the oddest of preoccupations, the province of slightly deranged British peers. The Sierra Nevada, which is invaded by so many hikers today that it feels like a zoo, was virtually devoid of humanity. The rapture Brower experienced there transported him to a mystic state; it became a dependency, a drug. He had food and supplies cached all over the place; he could return to one weeks after laying it in and it would still be there. Like his hero John Muir, Brower grew intimate with vast portions of that range. He would return to Berkeley, work at odd jobs for a while, make enough money to quit, and leave for the mountains again. By his late twenties, Brower had become the sort of person the water-development lobby cannot fathom: someone who puts unspoiled nature above the material aspirations of mankind. For his part, by the time he became the first paid executive director of the Sierra Club, in 1952, Brower had decided that no work of man violated nature as completely, as irrevocably, as a dam.

Relatively late in life, Brower had discovered the sublime emptiness of the plateau and red canyon country of the Colorado River Basin. It was the same terrain that had enchanted John Wesley Powell eighty years before, and it was almost as unpeopled and unspoiled as it had been then. Brower loved everything about it: the bottomless dry wind-sculpted canyons, beginning suddenly and leading nowhere; the rainbow arches, overhangs, and huge stately monoliths (an expert rock climber, Brower had pioneered the route up the most impressive of them, Shiprock in New Mexico); the amphitheater basins ringed by great hanging rock walls; the chiaroscuro desert sky, with its promise of rain that rarely came. Above all, he loved the desert rivers. Brower's favorite place in the Colorado Basin was Echo Park. Near the confluence of the Green and the Yampa rivers, Echo Park was a pure indulgence in the most austere of deserts. In autumn, its groves of cottonwood and yellowing willow gave it a New England air. In the spring, the swollen Green would flood the canyon bottom and leave lush meadows as it went. Echo Park was probably the most beautiful canyon flat in all of Utah, part of Dinosaur National Monument. It was also an ideal site for a dam.

Echo Park Dam was to have been a part of the Colorado River Storage Project—one of the first of the giant cash register dams. David Brower loathed it as he had never loathed something before. Brower had no training as an engineer, but he was the son of an engineer, and he led the fight against Echo Park Dam in the late 1950s, going after the Bureau with its own favorite weapon—statistics. Brower liked to quote Disraeli about the three kinds of lies: lies, damned lies, and statistics. The Bureau had confidently proclaimed that Echo Park would conserve 165,000 acre-feet of water over any alternative site; Brower demonstrated convincingly that it would conserve nineteen thousand acre-feet at most. The Bureau said it would add to the basin's water supply; Brower argued, with evaporation figures, that the basin might well lose water if Glen Canyon, the other big cash register dam, was also built. He demonstrated that a coal-fired powerplant would produce power for less money. It would be a great mistake, he told an incredulous Congressional subcommittee composed mainly of westerners, to rely on the Bureau's figures "when they cannot add, subtract, multiply, and divide." The Bureau reacted to such challenges with a mixture of bafflement and contempt, especially after Brower admitted that he had only made it through the ninth grade. But he had been secretly coached by Walter Huber, then the president of the American Society of Civil Engineers—for someone who had limited skill with people, Brower had an amazing ability to marshal expertise—and his calculations were largely supported by General Ulysses S. Grant of the Corps of Engineers. (Sometime later, the Bureau's regional director in Salt Lake City, Olie Larson, was presented with a rubber slide rule by a group of fellow engineers; it was his award for stretching the truth at Echo Park.)

In the end, Brower and a handful of conservationists managed to bring about the biggest defeat the western water lobby had suffered until then: a denial of funds to build Echo Park Dam. To pull it off, though, they had had to compromise; for the sake of victory at Echo Park, they had agreed to leave Glen Canyon Dam alone. Later, when the dam was already under construction, Brower floated this then almost inaccessible reach of the Colorado River in a dory much like Major Powell's. He was astonished by the beauty of the place, as were most of the handful of people (a few thousand perhaps) who managed to see Glen Canyon before it was drowned. When the reservoir filled, Brower's friends actually wondered whether he might shoot himself. In the forward to a Sierra Club book called *The Place No One Knew*, he flagellated himself over the loss. "Glen Canyon died in 1963," he wrote, "and I was partly responsible for its needless death. So were you. Neither you nor I, nor anyone else, knew it well enough to insist that at all costs it should endure." Never again, Brower vowed, was he going to compromise over such a dam.

The battle over the Grand Canyon dams was the conservation movement's coming of age. Only the upper basin had wanted Echo Park built; the lower-basin states had either remained neutral or opposed it. But now everyone knew the river was overallocated, and everyone wanted to see it replenished by water from somewhere else, so all the basin states were in favor of the Grand Canyon dams. Never before had conservationists challenged the collective will of seven states. Brower and the Sierra Club led the fight. As in the Echo Park battle, he managed to recruit heavyweight expertise. Luna Leopold, one of the country's leading hydrologists and the son of Aldo Leopold, the famous ecologist, was willing to take a swipe at the Bureau's flow calculations. Brower found some nuclear engineers from M.I.T. and Bechtel who were eager to demonstrate why nuclear reactors were a cheaper alternative. (Brower would later become one of the leading opponents of nuclear fission.) His most valuable discovery, however, was an utterly unknown thirty-year-old mathematician from New Mexico named Jeffrey Ingram. Ingram was a self-described fanatic about two things: the Grand Canyon, and numbers. He loved playing with figures, and above all he loved exposing figures as frauds. In particular, pyramid schemes fascinated him, and in the Bureau's payback scheme for the Pacific Southwest Water Plan, he thought he had discovered the greatest pyramid scheme anyone ever saw.

In order to finance the CAP and Bridge and Marble Gorge dams, Ingram discovered, the Bureau planned to capture the revenues from Hoover, Parker, and Davis dams, after their power sales had paid them off in the late 1980s, and reroute them into the new projects. For one thing, the Bureau, under Reclamation law, had no business doing this. All surplus power revenues were supposed to revert to the Treasury, in order to compensate the taxpayers for having forgiven interest obligations on the irrigation features of the projects. But that was not the half of it. The whole rationale for the Grand Canyon dams was that the river would have to be augmented someday, and power dams were the only means of raising the money for an importation project. The new dams, however, would be terrifically expensive compared to their predecessors. Hoover had been built for the incredibly low sum of $50 million; Bridge Canyon would likely cost close to $1 billion. Because of their enormous cost, the new dams would see their revenues tied up for years, for decades, repaying their own costs and subsidizing the CAP—a subsidy that was crucial if the Bureau was to find anyone to buy its water. Even if revenues from Hoover, Parker, and Davis dams were added, all of that money would be consumed for a seemingly endless period paying for the new works and the CAP subsidy. It would be financing the *depletion* of the river; there would be no money for *augmentation* until long after the basin was predicted to run out of water. In fact, according to Ingram's calculations, if you *didn't* build the Grand Canyon dams, money would start flowing into the development fund sooner than if you *did*. Ultimately, the dams would generate a lot of money—perhaps enough to finance most of the cost of diverting a distant river, if one could be found. But by then it would be too late. The Colorado River would have long since run dry.

It was a formidable argument, and it forced the Bureau of Reclamation to redirect its creative energies toward convincing the Bureau of the Budget that it wasn't really so. In the meantime, David Brower was free to do what he did best: publicity. With the help of two San Francisco advertising men, Jerry Mander and Howard Gossage, the Sierra Club took out full-page advertisements attacking the dams in the Washington *Post*, the New York *Times*, the San Francisco *Chronicle*, and the Los Angeles *Times*. One of the Bureau's arguments for building the dams, an argument which it would later regret, was that tourists would better appreciate the beauties of the Grand Canyon from motorboats. "Should we also flood the Sistine Chapel," asked one advertisement, "so tourists can get nearer the ceiling?"

The response was thunderous. Dan Dreyfus was still with the Bureau of Reclamation then, in charge of planning projects like the CAP. "I never saw anything like it," remembers Dreyfus. "Letters were arriving in dump trucks. Ninety-five percent of them said we'd better keep our mitts off the Grand Canyon and a lot of them quoted the Sierra Club ads."

"Jerry Mander and Howard Gossage were both geniuses," Brower would later reminisce. "We did a split run of one ad. I wrote one, which went, 'Who Can Save Grand Canyon—An Open Letter to Stewart Udall.' Jerry Mander's said, 'Now Only You Can Save Grand Canyon from Being Flooded for Profit.' We arranged to have a split run because I thought my ad was saying the right things and he thought his ad was. The upshot of it all was that Jerry Mander's ad outpulled mine two to one. The Sistine Chapel line was suggested by a Sierra Club member from Princeton. I wasn't sure about it. Jerry Mander jumped at it. He was right. That ad was dynamite. It was the ad the Internal Revenue Service cited when they revoked our tax-deductible status."

Who persuaded the IRS to revoke the Sierra Club's tax-deductible status is a question still debated today. Brower is convinced that Congressman Morris Udall, Stewart's brother, was behind it. He insists Udall even confessed to him once in an unguarded moment. Others suspect Stewart. Everyone wanted to lay the blame with Dominy, but private memoranda from Dominy's files suggest that he was as perplexed as everyone else; he wanted to locate the culprit so he could congratulate him. It was, obviously, a purely political strike. Other tax-deductible groups were at least as active in trying to influence legislation as the Sierra Club, and nothing happened to them. Whoever was responsible, the Sierra Club suddenly found itself tilling fund-raising soil as arid as the West, and had a close brush with bankruptcy. Brower, for his part, would soon find himself without a job, fired by the club's board of directors for fiduciary irresponsibility. But, in the end, none of it was to make much difference. The ads had been published; the public was outraged; the Grand Canyon dams were doomed to defeat. Everyone knew it except Floyd Dominy, the Bureau of Reclamation, and the Colorado Basin states.

At the same time that Lyndon Johnson was telling himself and anyone who would listen that the opponents of his war in Vietnam were a handful of draft-dodgers, the proponents of the Grand Canyon dams were telling themselves that their opposition was limited to the Sierra Club. The real problem, Wayne Aspinall, Carl Hayden, and

Floyd Dominy would fume, was Dave Brower's "lies." Once people understood that Bridge Canyon Dam would only flood Grand Canyon National Monument, and not the park itself, they would come around and support the dams. They believed, in other words, that the fate of the dams hinged on a technicality. They couldn't fathom that a sea change in public feeling toward the natural world was taking place, one of those epochal shifts that guarantee that things will never be the same. But it was, and people didn't care whether the dams flooded the monument or the park, or whether they drowned a mile or a hundred miles of the canyon, or whether they submerged the bottom fifty feet or the entire chasm. They wanted no dams—period.

In 1966, the National Reclamation Association held its annual meeting in Albuquerque, and Brower, to his considerable surprise, was invited to speak. To the NRA's surprise, he showed up. So did Wayne Aspinall, the chairman of the House Interior Committee, and when a photographer spied them twenty feet apart he tried to arrange a picture. Aspinall glared at Brower and shouted, "No picture of mine is being taken with that liar!" When a reporter asked the Congressman how Brower had lied, he responded that the dams would in no way flood the national park. They would merely flood 120 miles of the Grand Canyon. As far as Aspinall was concerned, that was a distinction of the utmost significance.

As for Dominy, facing the prospect of a major defeat for the first time in his life, he not only believed that Brower was a liar—h. was convinced he wasn't worth worrying about. "If you even suggested to Dominy that Brower was winning," says a former Bureau man, "he would have fired you on the spot." Finally, when even his allies in the Southwest began to have misgivings about Bridge Canyon Dam, Dominy began to take his nemesis a little more seriously. He ordered employees to stalk Brower, showing up at his speaking engagements to report on what he said and get in a little heckling on the side. But Dominy's men either were poor judges of audience response or were so afraid of their chief that they told him exactly what he wanted to hear. "Mr. Brower's talk . . . was highly emotional," wrote a Bureau man in a blue-envelope report on a Brower address. "It was completely lacking in any kind of substantiating data, and he appeared a far less formidable opponent than anticipated. It is my opinion from this encounter that the Bureau should encourage face-to-face discussions with Mr. Brower before unbiased audiences because any reclamationist, armed with basic facts, could adequately defend the Bureau's position against his pure emotionalism."

In that particular speech, Brower had said that he wouldn't mind dams in the Grand Canyon as long as the Bureau built a comparable canyon somewhere else. He received a standing ovation—in Denver.

The handwriting was on the wall by March of 1966, when the *Reader's Digest* ran an article attacking Marble Gorge and Bridge Canyon dams in a tone that could almost be described as enraged. "Right after the *Reader's Digest* article, *Life* ran a big goddamned diatribe," remembered Dan Dreyfus. "Then we got plastered by *My Weekly Reader*. You're in deep shit when you catch it from them. Mailbags were coming in by the hundreds stuffed with letters from schoolkids. I kept trying to tell Dominy we were in trouble, but he didn't seem to give a damn. It was kind of surprising, because Dominy could be very flexible when it came to the smaller projects. He made some big concessions here and there and wasn't bothered by it. On this one he was an utter maniac. In a way you can't fault the man, though, because even though Dominy was a good liar when he had to be, here he was a prisoner of his own intellectual honesty. A lot of people figured that no one was going to let the Southwest run out of water, and if the time came when it wanted more the country would just pay for it, whatever the cost. I mean, New York City was full of immigrants, criminals, minorities, so who gave a damn if it went bust? But Phoenix and irrigated farmland—that was America! So it may have been a correct assumption. But Dominy said, 'No way— this project is going to include those dams.' "

By 1967, it had become obvious to everyone but Dominy and Carl Hayden that the Grand Canyon dams would have to go. Rescue for the Colorado Basin might never come without them, but the Central Arizona Project would never be built with them. The problem, for Stewart Udall, was how to sneak the amended legislation past Hayden and Dominy. Hayden might not be too much of a problem; he was old and senile and in the hospital half the time, and he was desperate to see the CAP authorized before his death, which might come at any time. It was Dominy—bullheaded, willful, obsessed with defeating Brower—who somehow had to be handled. The opportunity came fairly soon. With the Bureau now helping to build dams all over the world, the commissioner had to make an annual global inspection of projects-in-progress; it was a condition imposed by the Agency for International Development, which was pumping billions of dollars into dam construction, and even as the Colorado River battle raged away Dominy had to absent himself for a few weeks. In early 1967, the commissioner grabbed his hat and was gone. Almost as soon as his plane left the runway at Dulles Airport, Udall was telling his Assistant Secretary, Ken Holum, to take Bridge Canyon Dam out of the CAP legislation and come up with an alternative before Dominy returned. The main objective was to find enough power to pump the water to central Arizona. The means of financing a rescue project would simply have to be put off. A Dominy representative would, of course, have to sit on the task force, and Udall had just the person in mind—Daniel Dreyfus. Publicly, Dreyfus could write a good rah-rah speech for Dominy about Marble Gorge and Bridge Canyon dams. Privately, he believed neither in them nor, for that matter, in the CAP. He wasn't even sure he believed in the Bureau of Reclamation anymore.

"The hardest part for me was getting the regional commissioners to go along," Dreyfus would recall in his Senate office in 1981. "Dominy had them all so scared that when I told them what we were up to, they wanted to crawl in a hole. 'Oh, no, *Floyd's* got to be here!' 'You know what *Floyd* would think of this.' '*Floyd* will shit a brick.' One regional director was so terrified I had to fly out to Phoenix to put some fiber in his backbone. The solution itself was kind of clumsy, but it was simple. We decided to buy a share of the Navajo Powerplant in northern Arizona. For the first time, the Bureau was going to own something it always hated—a piece of a great big smoke-belching coal-fired powerplant. It didn't solve a damn thing except that it gave us the power to pump water to central Arizona. The fact is we were licked. The conservationists and the press and ultimately the public licked the Bureau of Reclamation, and the last person in the world to admit it was Dominy. He wouldn't admit it, but I can't believe he didn't know what was coming. By the time he took off to go overseas he was fighting a rearguard action, and he knew it. Maybe being out of the country was a way for him to save his honor. When he returned, I was the one who had to go see him with a copy of the agreement we'd worked out. I thought he was going to go through the roof, but Dominy always had a way of catching you off guard. His reaction was complete and total lack of interest. He already knew all about it. He just said, 'I don't even want to hear about it,' and told me to get the hell out of his office. He didn't even look up from what he was reading on his desk."

Like the westbound wagons that had to jettison furniture, food, even water in order to plow through the desert sands, the Central Arizona Project was finally light enough to move. The Colorado River Basin

Project Act was signed into law by Lyndon Johnson on September 30, 1968—the most expensive single authorization in history. Besides the CAP, it authorized Hooker Dam in the Gila Wilderness of New Mexico, the aqueduct from Lake Mead to Las Vegas, the Dixie Project in Utah, and the Uintah Unit of the Central Utah Project—the first piece of a water-diversion scheme that promised to be nearly as grandiose as the CAP. It also authorized the San Miguel, Dallas Creek, West Divide, Dolores, and Animas La Plata projects in Colorado, and it authorized a Lower Colorado Development Fund, still penniless, to build an augmentation project that hadn't yet been defined, let alone approved. Almost unnoticed alongside everything else, the bill made deliverance of Mexico's 1.5 million acre-feet of water—of tolerably sweet water—a *national* responsibility, whatever that meant. Loosely interpreted, it might mean a pipeline from Lake Superior to Mexicali.

The five Colorado projects—which could easily add a cool $1 billion to the cost of everything else—were an object lesson in the workings of the Congressional pork barrel. They were put into the bill at the insistence of Wayne Aspinall, the black-eyed former schoolteacher with a principal's testy disposition who had climbed from a little western Colorado town to become the chairman of the House Interior and Insular Affairs Committee. Aspinall distrusted urban, expansionist California with all the recondite loathing of a small-town mind, and he didn't trust Arizona much more. The overallocated river ran right under the window of his expensive home on Aspinall Drive in Palisade, Colorado, and he figured that Colorado had better extract every drop of its rightful share or California and Arizona would take it and never give it back. If the CAP was to get past the chairman of the House Interior Committee, Colorado was going to be satisfied first.

The problem was that by 1968, there wasn't a single irrigation project left on the West Slope of the Rockies that was economically feasible. The best ones—or, to put it more accurately, the least outrageous ones—had already been authorized by the Colorado River Storage Project Act in 1956. If Colorado had a need for more water, and a place where a new project might actually make sense, it was on the eastern plains, where both the growing cities of the Front Range and the farms atop the Ogallala aquifer were facing water famine thirty or forty years down the road. One of the Bureau's most successful projects, Colorado–Big Thompson, was already delivering Colorado River water across the Continental Divide through a tunnel to the East Slope; the power produced by the steep drop down the Front Range was enough to justify the expense of the tunnel, and the additional water diverted from the upper Colorado to tributaries of the Platte River was welcomed by everyone from canoeists to whooping cranes to irrigators in Colorado and Nebraska. There was no reason why another such transbasin diversion project couldn't be built. No reason, that is, except Wayne Aspinall. The eastern plains were in someone else's district.

During an interview in 1979, Felix Sparks, who selected the five projects at Aspinall's behest, conceded as much. "Twenty years ago, we already saw urbanization as ineveitable," Sparks said. "So I looked around for a place where we could keep a viable agricultural industry going. *We didn't want* to let cities and industry have the water. We picked those projects on the basis that it would be impossible, physically impossible, for Denver to get its hands on that water." It was an extraordinary admission. All that Sparks failed to mention was the fact that he was likely to benefit personally from new projects on the West Slope. Though a modestly paid public servant, Sparks was a fairly wealthy man, the result of some shrewd and highly secretive business investments across the Front Range. He was widely rumored to own a large interest in a food-processing plant on the West Slope— a plant that could use a fresh supply of locally grown fruit nurtured on taxpayer-subsidized water. Of course, Felix Sparks, like a lot of western farmers, didn't believe in such a thing as federally subsidized water. "This business of federal Reclamation subsidizing irrigation water," he snorted, "is absolute, utter, unmitigated crap."

Subsidy, however, was exactly what Aspinall and Sparks's five projects would require, subsidy on a scale that made even the Bureau cringe. It fell to Dan Dreyfus, the Bureau's house magician, to invent enough benefits to make them pass muster. "Those projects were pure trash," said Dreyfus in an unusually candid interview in 1981, as he prepared to retire from public service. "I knew they were trash, and Dominy knew they were trash. The way they got into the bill was, Aspinall called up Udall one day and said, 'No Central Arizona Project will ever get by me unless my five projects get authorized, too.' When Udall passed the word on to us, we were appalled. The Office of Management and Budget had just bounced Animas–La Plata. Now we had to give it back to them and make them reverse themselves. I had to fly all the way out to Denver and jerk around the benefit-cost numbers to make the thing look sound.

"As a last resort," Dreyfus continued with a grim smile, "Dominy and I went to see Aspinall and tried to talk him out of it. Dominy said, 'Look, Congressman, these projects won't work as irrigation projects. We can't afford to pump water from the reservoirs to the irrigable lands because we haven't got any surplus power in the river, and the alternative is to follow the land contours with canals that are going to be ungodly long and expensive. They'll cost so much you might run into some real problems getting appropriations for these things.' What Dominy suggested was to build the dams and forget the rest. He said, 'What you really want is to capture your entitlement. The dams alone will do that. California will never see that water, and you'll cut the cost in half.'

"Dominy could be the most persuasive man I ever met," Dreyfus said, "but Aspinall wouldn't budge. He liked to think of himself as almighty principled, so he got huffy and said, 'The Reclamation program knows no such thing as a project without beneficiaries. The answer is no.' "

Those kinds of principles usually end up costing the taxpayers a lot of money, but in this case they may have cost Aspinall his projects. If he had thought about it longer, he would have seen that the Colorado River Basin Project Act was solely an authorization bill. It appropriated no money for any of the projects; that could only be done in the annual appropriations bills. But it wouldn't make sense for California's and Arizona's Congressional delegations, which outnumbered Colorado's ten to one, to vote appropriations for five projects which would mean surrendering water their own constituents were using. Since the projects made so little sense, and were so expensive, the rest of Congress might follow their lead. Aspinall, however, had already succumbed to the twin delusions that affect so many committee chairmen—that he would be reelected forever, and that he would live nearly that long. As long as he sat in his committee chair, he could deny California and Arizona whatever he pleased unless they voted in favor of his projects. It was a reasonable argument, until he was bumped out of office four years later by a virtually unknown law professor named Alan Merson—a candidate who had campaigned heavily on the environmental principles that Aspinall often scorned. By 1984, only one of the five Colorado projects was underway. The others were receiving no funding at all, or just enough to let them die a lingering death.

However, twelve years and more than $2 billion after the passage of the Colorado River Basin Project Act, the Central Arizona Project was nearly built.

A political mirage for three generations of Arizonans, the Central Arizona Project is now a palpable mirage, as incongruous a spectacle as any on earth: a man-made river flowing uphill in a place of almost no rain. To see it there in late 1985, just being filled, induces a kind of shock, like one's first sight of Mount McKinley or the Great Wall. But it is an illusion that works both ways. Up close, the Granite Reef Aqueduct seems almost too huge to be real. Where will all the water come from? From the air, however, the aqueduct and the river it diverts are reduced to insignificance by the landscape through which they flow—a desert that seems much too vast for the most heroic pretensions of mankind. The water the aqueduct is capable of delivering is more than Cleveland, Detroit, and Chicago consume together. Pour it on Arizona, however, and it would cover each acre with two hundredths of an inch. In the summer, when the temperature reaches 135 degrees at ground level, that much water would evaporate before you had a chance to blink.

To build something so vast—an aqueduct that may stretch eventually to 333 miles, pumps that will lift the water 1,249 feet, four or five receiving reservoirs to hold the water when it arrives—at a cost that may ultimately reach $3 billion, perhaps even more, would seem to demand two prerequisites: that there be a demand for all the water, and that it be available in the first place. In Arizona, all of this has been an article of blind faith for more than half a century. Build the CAP, and the aqueduct will be forever filled because of Arizona's Compact entitlement; fill the aqueduct, and the water will be put to immediate use—that is what every politician who ever aspired to sainthood in Arizona has said. But there are a number of reasons why this will not be the case—perhaps not remotely the case. If anything, the Central Arizona Project may make the state's water crisis *worse* than ever before.

When the Colorado River Basin Storage Act was bottled up in the House Interior Committee in the mid-1960s, it wasn't just the Sierra Club and the Grand Canyon dams that were responsible. The dams, it was feared, might drag the bill down to defeat on the floor of Congress, but it had to get out of committee first, and the bill's major hurdle there—a hurdle that seemed about fifty feet high—was California. California had five members on the committee and a powerful ally in John Saylor, the senior Republican committee member, who was from Pennsylvania. Saylor was as antagonistic toward the Bureau of Reclamation as anyone in Congress; he especially loved to pick a fight with Floyd Dominy; and he was unalterably opposed to the CAP. He was so valued in office by California that tens of thousands of dollars poured into his campaign coffers from that state to keep him there.

What California demanded as the price for acquiescence was simple—devastatingly simple. Before Arizona received a drop of its entitlement, it wanted its full 4.4-million-acre-foot entitlement guaranteed. As far as California was concerned, there would be no equitable sharing of shortages, no across-the-board cuts in times of drought; it wanted satisfaction no matter what. In fact, what it was really asking was a legislative reversal of the lawsuit it had lost in the Supreme Court. It was an outrageous demand from Arizona's point of view, and few believed that its Congressional delegation would swallow it. But, in the end, they did.

"How do I explain it?" asked Sam Steiger, then a junior committee member from Arizona, repeating the question just asked of him. "I can't. Obviously a deal was struck. I was too junior to be in on it. Mo Udall, Stewart's brother, and John Rhodes were the ones in a position to do it. *Why* did they do it? The only answer I can think of is that they didn't really believe the river was overallocated—that, or else they really believed we were going to get an augmentation project, even without Bridge Canyon Dam. The Bureau of Reclamation wasn't running around Capitol Hill crying, 'The river's overallocated! The river's overallocated!' I don't know what figures they were using, but we sure as hell weren't hearing the ones that came out a few years later. They made like there was plenty of water for everyone."

And so, before a real fight even developed over California's imperious demand, the CAP legislation became saddled with what is known as the California Guarantee: 4.4 million acre-feet or bust. Come drought, come calamity, California must be satisfied first.

A few years later, the Bureau was finally forced to admit that its estimate of 17.5 million acre-feet a year was a convenient fiction, and amended it to around fifteen million acre-feet. A few years after that, even the latter figure looked optimistic; independent hydrologists were putting the Colorado's average flow at somewhere around thirteen million acre-feet, perhaps a little more. Southern California was diverting its full 4.4 million acre-feet as it had for years. The upper basin had a diversion capability that had moved past 3.6 million acre-feet and was still building moderately. Evaporation varies from year to year, but averages close to two million acre-feet from

305

all the reservoirs on the main stem and tributaries; and Mexico must get its 1.5 million acre-feet.

Work these figures out and the Colorado River is almost used up if its flow is as low as some say. If the higher estimates are used, there are two to two and a half million acre-feet left. Now consider the projects that are authorized and, in some cases, nearly built or being built. The Central Utah Project. The Animas–La Plata Project. The Dolores Project. The Fruitland Mesa Project. The West Divide Project. The Dallas Creek Project. San Miguel, Savery Pot Hook, Paonia, Florida, and the largest of them all, the CAP. Three or four of these could send the Colorado River into "deficit"; the rest will merely make the deficit hopeless. Everything has turned out exactly as could have been predicted twenty years ago—everything, that is, except the rescue project that was supposed to save the basin states from a Sumerian fate.

The prospects that an augmentation project would be built were already dim in the mid-1960s, before double-digit inflation, before double-digit interest rates, before environmentalism, before deficits that have grown larger than the federal budget was then. Meanwhile, northern Californians have grown so jealous of their "underused" rivers that in a 1982 referendum they emphatically refused to release more water even to the desperate supplicants in the southern half of their own state. The Klamath River alone has nearly as much water in it as the Colorado, and flows to the ocean almost entirely unused, and one could build a reservoir on it two-thirds the size of Lake Mead, but the odds of the Klamath River being rerouted to southern California so the Colorado Basin states can have more water are about the same as the odds of being bitten by a rattlesnake while crossing the street in Washington, D.C. If that is unthinkable, then the odds that Oregon's rivers will be turned southward are even less so. As for the Columbia River diversion, it still has at least one champion, a Los Angeles supervisor named Kenneth Hahn who introduces a resolution calling for it every year, but his resolution cannot even make it past the board of supervisors of one of the most water-starved cities in the world, and that, with luck, is about as far as it will get.

The Colorado Basin, then, is a few years away from permanent drought, and it will have to make do with whatever nature decrees the flow shall be. If the shortages were to be shared equally among the basin states, then things might not be so bad for Arizona. But this will obviously not be the case; there is that fateful clause stipulating that California shall always receive its full 4.4-million-acre-foot entitlement before Phoenix and Tucson receive a single drop. What began as an Olympian division of one river's waters emerged, after fifty years of brokering, tinkering, and fine-tuning according to the dictates of political reality, as an ultimate testament to the West's cardinal law: that water flows toward power and money.

Despite one of the most spellbinding and expensive waterworks of all time, Arizonans from now until eternity will be forced to do what their Hohokam ancestors did: pray for rain. During wet cycles, when Lake Mead and Lake Powell are sending water down the spillways as they were in 1983, the Granite Reef Aqueduct may be delivering something close to peak yield. During drought cycles, the aqueduct may run half empty, if that, and the odds are extremely high that it will run progressively more empty as the years go by. It would be foolish, at this stage, to surmise that all or even most of the upperbasin projects are going to be built, but a few of them are likely to be, and each one will cut into the CAP's supply. The Colorado River, to which Arizona decided to marry its future hopes, will prove no more trustworthy than a capricious mistress, delivering a million acre-feet one year, 400,000 the next.

And this, in turn, raises a bizarre possibility, as unthinkable to modern Arizona as it was to the planners of the CAP: the people of Arizona may not even *want* the modest amount of precious water this $3 billion project is able to deliver.

In early 1980, Phoenix experienced a series of damaging winter floods. The Salt River goes through the center of town and is usually an utterly dry bed of pebbles and rocks; therefore, city streets are laid right across the river, as if it had long since gone extinct. In 1980, however, it rolled cars like boulders—cars whose owners were so used to driving through the riverbed that, despite repeated warnings on the radio, they didn't bother to detour and cross on a bridge as the waters began to rise. Even if they had, it wouldn't have done them much good. Only two of Phoenix's bridges were designed to withstand a flood flow greater than twenty-five thousand cubic feet per second. In February of 1980, the Salt River peaked at 180,000 cfs.

Phoenix owes its existence to this ephemeral desert river, but even so it doesn't seem to hold the Salt in high esteem. On both banks, the floodplain is encroached on by industrial parks, trailer parks, RV parks, but no real parks. The flood channel itself has been developed to a degree, playing host to establishments which are, by nature, transient: topless-bottomless joints, chop shops, cock-fighting emporia. Paris built its great cathedral by its river, Florence its palaces of art; Phoenix seems to have decided that its river is the proper place to relegate its sin. When the Bureau of Reclamation performed a cost-benefit analysis for Orme Dam, once a central feature of the Central Arizona Project, it included as a benefit the flood protection the dam would offer to the cock-fighting and striptease establishments downstream.

That particular dam—a $400 million structure intended to store Colorado River water shipped over in the Granite Reef Aqueduct, and to hold back the occasional flood surge—was one of the main topics of conversation in 1980. On February 27, just after the biggest flood hit, the *Arizona Republic* ran a huge editorial that read, "Are you fed up sitting in traffic, creeping to work, because floods have taken out all but two of the major bridges crossing the Salt River? Are you fed up with reading stories about a new study and more hearings into whether construction of Orme Dam would interrupt the nesting habits of bald eagles . . . of this community playing second fiddle to high-and-dry special pleaders who shed tears over nesting eagles, but can't find compassion for the thousands of families who endure hardship, fear, and ruin as flood waters rampage through the valley?

"I'm mad!" continued the editorial, which was signed by the *Republic*'s editor-in-chief, Patrick Murphy. "I'm mad as hell that high-and-dry Washington bureaucrats have been dilly-dallying for at least ten years over approval of Orme Dam. . . . Now, dammit, give us our dam!"

The "special pleaders" Murphy referred to numbered among them the Yavapai Indians, whose remnant population of three hundred or so lives on a reservation near the confluence of the Salt and Verde rivers, and who would lose their homes to the reservoir. The Yavapai, who appear to be some of the most peaceful, sweet-natured souls on earth—many of them are old and still weave baskets for a living—had won a lot of well-placed sympathy, which was apparently what Murphy was complaining about. Cecil Andrus, then the outgoing Secretary of the Interior—and someone who spent a good part of his term trying to stop the Bureau from carrying out its plans—vowed that the tribe would be relocated over his dead body, and one local attorney who was preparing to fight Orme Dam on their behalf was Stewart Udall—the man who, as much as anyone, had made the CAP and Orme Dam possible. (In later years, Udall, unlike the Bureau, was to rue much of what he said and did in the 1960s; he even spoke at a testimonial dinner, in 1982, celebrating the seventieth birthday of his old nemesis, David Brower.) The dam was in the news so often that one could almost imagine the dancers in the bars debating the pros and cons between acts. What was most striking about the debate, however, was that practically no one seemed to be asking the more fundamental question about Orme Dam. As a $400 million flood-control structure, it made little economic sense; it would be much cheaper to move the relatively few threatened structures and reinforce the bridges. Only if it received and stored a substantial amount of Colorado River water—which implied not only a decent flow in the river but a demand for the water, and an ability to pay for it—did Orme Dam make any sense. Would the water arrive, and arrive predictably and often enough, and be economical enough, so that anyone would want to buy it?

In 1980, one of the few people in the state who seemed to be asking this question was William Martin, an economist at the University of Arizona at Tucson. For having done so, and answering negatively, Martin had been accused in local newspapers of being a paid agent of California, where he was born. The dean of his department denied him merit raises for eight years, and even led a campaign to discredit his academic qualifications, though he wouldn't go quite so far as to try to have him fired outright.

Large and bearded, inclined toward jeans, cowboy boots, and western shirts, Martin looks as if he would feel more at home in the cockpit of a Peterbilt than at a professor's desk, even if his writings are nationally known. His first notoriety came in 1973, when he and a colleague, Robert Young—who was so wounded by the hounding he got that he opted to leave the state—published a book called *Water Supplies and Economic Growth in an Arid Environment*, an innocuous-sounding little tract which, in Arizona, was almost as revolutionary as *Das Kapital*. They first asked, as a matter of speculation, what might happen if the Central Arizona Project was *not* built. The underground aquifers, Young and Martin reckoned, would undoubtedly be depleted as the farmers continued to pump them out (in the 1960s, the rate of overdraft—use over replenishment—climbed as high as four million acre-feet per year). As pumping costs rose due to the dropping water table, some farmers would begin to go out of business. But there was still enough water so that the decline would be very slow. Arizona's farm income, by Young and Martin's calculations, would be reduced by about one-fifth of 1 percent per year. The reason the decline in income would be so modest was self-evident: as pumped water got more expensive, the farmers would conserve it better and switch to higher-value crops, and they would do more with less. The way to see if the Central Arizona Project was worth building, then, was to see if each acre-foot of water it brought in would be cheaper than the value (in lost farm income) of each disappearing acre-foot from the aquifers. Martin and Young figured that every acre-foot that was being mined was causing a loss of $5.35 in farm income—a conservative estimate, as far as they were concerned. Could the CAP deliver water cheaper than that? By the Bureau's own calculations, CAP water would cost at least $10 per acre-foot—without even figuring the cost of distributing it. As a result, the farmers would make *more* money if they continued pumping groundwater than if they bought water from the CAP. In fact, if the price of distribution systems—which the farmers would presumably have to build themselves—was as high as it promised to be, buying CAP water might be a ticket into bankruptcy.

Twice since then, Martin has repeated the analysis, and his results confirm his earlier conclusions—only far more emphatically. By 1977, the projected canalside price of CAP water had reached $16.67 per acre-foot. Add the cost of a distribution network, and farmers growing any kind of low-value crops—alfalfa, small grains, perhaps even the state's main crop, cotton—could not afford it. In 1980, he and another colleague from the University of Arizona, Helen Ingram, did a detailed study, region by region, of the likely cost of distribution systems, and were amazed by what they found out. In one irrigation district, Maricopa-Stansfield, the price of the distribution system—hundreds of miles of canals and laterals, headgates, and people to operate them—would likely come to $160 million, leaving each farmer a bill of $100 per acre-foot of water *per year* just for distribution. The Bureau's canalside estimate for CAP water had, by then, risen to around $30 per acre-foot, so the total price of CAP water would be $130 per acre-foot, per year. The price of pumped groundwater *was nearly $100 less* per acre-foot at Maricopa-Stansfield—around $39. It was an extreme case, but Ingram and Martin couldn't find a single irrigation district where CAP water promised to be cheaper than groundwater. In most of them, it would cost half again or twice as much, sometimes more. One of the main arguments the farmers had always made for the CAP was that they couldn't all switch to high-value crops as the groundwater table went lower and pumping costs became intolerable. The American consumer, they said, could only eat so many lemons and oranges. But if Martin's figures were right, farmers who signed contracts to buy CAP water might not even be able to raise oranges on it. In 1980, about the only crop you could raise with water that cost $130 per acre-foot was marijuana.

But that was the *good* news. The bad news was that during periods of drought, with California guaranteed its full entitlement before Arizona received a drop, this incredibly expensive water might often not arrive. The Bureau's own projections showed "firm" CAP water dwindling from 1.6 million acre-feet at the beginning to 300,000 acre-feet or less in fifty years; only during wet years, or if the upper-basin projects are never built, will there be more. To think of the Central Arizona Project as salvation, then, is not just to stretch things a bit. For those groundwater-dependent farmers who will have to build distribution systems, at least—and there are a lot of them—the Central Arizona Project could spell economic ruin.

Did Arizona's farmers realize any of this? One of William Martin and Helen Ingram's graduate students, Nancy Laney, traveled around the state to find out. To her astonishment, most of the farmers didn't. One of the farms Laney visited was the Farmers' Investment Corporation, a huge pecan-growing operation south of Tucson that is about as far from the diversion point on the Colorado River as one can be. If it arrives, CAP water will have surmounted a lift of well over a thousand feet and traveled more than three hundred miles to get there. Meanwhile, there is still plenty of water immediately under the farm, less than two hundred feet down. Despite the huge subsidies written into the CAP—as with any Reclamation project, the farmers are excused from paying interest costs—the groundwater is certain to be much cheaper, at least until the aquifer drops several hundred more feet. (The worst areawide decline in Arizona's water table has been around two hundred feet, and that took decades to happen.) But the farm manager at Farmers' Investment expressed to Laney his unalterable belief that "CAP water will be cheaper than pumping." "Water is essential," he said with religious conviction, adding that he "would back any plan where more water would be available." He had no idea what CAP water would cost him, but planned to sign contracts to buy it anyway. His state of knowledge and level of blind faith were not unusual. One farmer thought that the water was going to arrive by gravity instead of being pumped many hundreds of feet uphill. One believed that there was still enough surplus water in the Colorado River to turn the entire Grand Canyon into a reservoir—something he devoutly wished. Only two of the farmers Laney interviewed seemed to have a sense of things as they really were. One realized that Arizona's Colorado River water was jeopardized and

311

thought it was high time we "took" Canada's surplus water to replenish it. The other said that even if it turned out he couldn't afford CAP water, he was going to sign a contract to buy it anyway, because "contracts are made to be broken."

"Contracts are made to be broken." There, in a simple phrase, was perhaps the worst legacy of the Bureau of Reclamation's eighty years as the indulgent godfather of the arid West. The irrigation farmers not only had come to expect heavily subsidized water as a kind of right, allowing them to pretend that the region's preeminent natural fact—a drastic scarcity of that substance—was an illusion. They now believed that if it turned out they couldn't afford the water, the Bureau (which is to say, the nation's taxpayers) would practically *give* it away. These farmers were about the most conservative faction in what may be the most politically conservative of all the fifty states. They regularly sent to Congress politicians eager to demolish the social edifice built by the New Deal—to abolish welfare, school lunch programs, aid to the handicapped, funding for the arts, even to sell off some of the national parks and public lands. But their constituents had become the ultimate example of what they decried, so coddled by the government that they lived in the cocoonlike world of a child. They remained oblivious to what their CAP water would cost them but were certain it would be offered to them at a price they could afford. The farmers had become the very embodiment of the costly, irrational welfare state they loathed—and they had absolutely no idea.

In 1984, Congress began to demonstrate why the farmers might not be so foolish after all. Early that year, it voted to lend them $200 million to help build distribution systems—an interest-free loan, as one might have expected, but the sum was only about half of what they would need, and there was a lot of resistance to lending them the rest. But they still weren't out of the woods. For one thing, the Indian water-rights issue was still substantially unresolved. There was a good chance that the white farmers would have to lease water from the Indians, who could well end up with most of the water in the CAP. The Ak Chin and the Papago tribes had recently settled with the Interior Department for 300,000 acre-feet, about the consumption of Phoenix. The Papago tribe's water will come directly out of the Tucson Aqueduct—water which the farmers, most of whom had conveniently ignored the Indian water-rights question, had always expected to get. More and more, the CAP was metamorphosing from an agricultural rescue project into an expensive atonement for travesties visited on the Indians, and, perhaps, into a municipal water supply project for Phoenix and Tucson—if *they* feel they can afford it.

"The cities in Arizona are going to get hit even worse than the farmers," Bill Martin told an interviewer in 1984. "The farmers at least get the interest-free subsidy, which is worth a fortune to them. They also get interest-free loans on things like the distribution systems. The cities get none of that. They pay full fare.

"Here in Tucson, we're already drawing groundwater out of neighboring basins because we've depleted ours, and we pay around $430 per household, which seems like a lot. But most of that, I'd say around $400, is to pay off the water mains, the infrastructure, the bureaucracy. It's a distribution cost. It only costs us $30 or a little more to pump the water. But to pump CAP water all the way from the Colorado River to Tucson is going to cost at least $250 per acre-foot; that's what the water is worth when you get rid of all the interest subsidies and so forth. Add $250 to $400, the distribution cost, and people are going to be paying $650 for water. There are families around here who only earn ten or fifteen times that much in a year. So what's obviously going to happen is people are going to conserve, and use a lot less water, and there will be less and less of a need for the CAP.

"It's already happening," Martin continued. "We've all gotten water-conscious, even if we weren't before. Tucson uses a third less water than Phoenix, because up there they still get cheap water from the Salt River Project. Once Phoenix starts paying $600 a year, though, they're going to conserve just like we are."

But if the farmers can't afford the water, and the cities can't afford the water, then who is going to buy it and justify the whole expense?

"Damned if I know" was Martin's response.

If it seems implausible that Arizona's farmers will buy here-today, gone-tomorrow water that costs three times what farm economics suggests they can pay; if it seems implausible that cities will want to waste millions of dollars a year buying turbid, alkaline water from the Colorado River when they can pump cheaper, fresher groundwater instead—if all of this seems unlikely, what is even *less* likely is that Arizona and the Bureau of Reclamation will permit a giant

313

concrete aqueduct to sit empty in the desert, a ruin before its time. For the aqueduct to remain full as long as it can, however, the farmers must receive most of the water; their collective thirst is much greater than that of the cities. (And in 1985, work on the extension aqueduct to Tucson, the only big potential urban buyer besides Phoenix, had not even begun.) What this in turn implies is subsidy, more than is already there in the form of cheap electricity and interest exclusion—subsidy on a rather heroic scale. The question is, how will it be done?

One person who thought he had it figured out was Sam Steiger, a former Congressman from Prescott, a small city up in north-central Arizona. In the 1960s, Steiger was a prototypical Arizona Republican—crew-cut, jut-jawed, archconservative—who nonetheless had little trouble voting for the CAP. "Of course I was for it. Any Arizona politician who wanted any kind of political future had to be for it. Besides, I was on the Interior Committee, which authorized the thing—one of two Arizonans versus five Californians on the committee. If I had voted against it, I would probably have been shot." In the 1980s, however, Steiger, no longer in office, had gotten into the water-brokering business, which was becoming a cottage industry in western states whose laws permitted some degree of free market in water rights. Suddenly Steiger had an economic interest in the very condition the CAP would pretend to relieve—scarcity—because he was earning a living helping people with good water rights—mainly farmers—sell those rights to people who could pay top dollar for them—usually subdevelopers and cities. If the CAP suddenly brought in a big volume of water to be sold at vastly subsidized rates—or if CAP water was somehow forced on cities that didn't really want to buy it—it would create an artificial glut and hurt his business. But that was exactly what Steiger thought would happen: subsidy and political coercion were going to create a "demand" for CAP water which, even in this third-driest state in the country, would otherwise not exist.

"In the first place," Steiger said during an interview in 1985, "we passed a strict groundwater law here in 1980, one that was supposed to have been passed ten years earlier. The CAP legislation we passed in 1968 demanded it—what was the point of approving the project if the farmers kept sending the aquifer down to hell anyway? When the Carter people threatened to withhold funds for the CAP until the law was passed, it finally went through the state legislature. What that law does, besides restrict pumping, is demand that any developer who sells a new home guarantee the buyer a hundred-year supply of water. Otherwise, he can't sell. Hell, I can sell you a home and guarantee you that in a hundred years I'll give you desalted water from the ocean. I'll be dead then anyway—that's how ridiculous the provision is. But the way it's being interpreted by the Department of Water Resources is this: no developer gets his certificate unless he's signed up for CAP water, and without that certificate he can't sell his house. The odds that there'll be water in the Granite Reef Aqueduct in a hundred years are probably lower than the odds we'll be getting water from the ocean, but the developers are stuck. So are the cities. If a city wants to grow, it has to buy water from the Central Arizona Project."

That, by Steiger's reasoning, was how the cities would be forced into the hand. The farmers, he felt, would be corralled by the new law's restrictions on groundwater pumping; at some point, they would have to rely more on surface water, and the only available surface water would be the CAP. The problem with the farmers, though, is that their demand is, to use that economists' word, inelastic: charge them too much and they'll go belly up. So the farmers, according to Steiger, will be brought in with the carrot rather than the stick. In 1984, the first fifty-year contracts for cheap Hoover Dam power expired—the dam was finally paid off. The new contracts negotiated by the Interior Department didn't raise the rates much, but they did tack on a surcharge of four mills per kilowatt-hour which is to go as a direct subsidy to the CAP. Four mills per kilowatt-hour—a few cents per day—may not sound like much, but multiply it by a couple of million users and it is a fair piece of change: millions of dollars per year. It is an almost poetic irony that most Hoover power is sold in southern California; at last, Arizona was going to get its pound of flesh from California, after involuntarily "loaning" that state water for so many years. A similar, smaller subsidy applies to power sold by the Navajo Power Plant. On top of *that*, the Central Arizona Conservancy District—the imperium created to receive and distribute CAP water—is permitted, by law, to buy cheap Hoover power and resell it at market rates, funneling the profits directly into the project to subsidize the water.

"Add all this nonsense to Congress's interest-free loan for distribution systems and some other things they're bound to cook up, and it's all of a piece," Steiger said with palpable disgust. "They'll skin the cat twenty ways if they have to, but they're going to make the water affordable. Congress will go along, because it will be goddamned embarrassing for Congress to have authorized a multibillion-dollar water project when there's no demand for the water because no one can afford it. The CAP belongs to a holy order of inevitability. Will Congress bail out the big banks that pushed all those loans on Latin America, when the countries finally default? Of course. Will it make water affordable for Arizona's farmers? Of course.

"The sensible thing would have been for the farmers to move," Steiger said. "There are hundreds of thousands of acres of good farmland right along the Colorado River where you'd only have to build short diversion canals and maybe pump the water uphill a few hundred feet. But the farmers got established in the central part of the state because of the Salt River Project. The cities grew up in the middle of the farmland. The real estate interests, the money people—they're all in Phoenix and Scottsdale and Tucson. They didn't want to move. So we're going to move the river to them. At any cost. We think."

CHAPTER NINE

The Peanut Farmer and
the Pork Barrel

At the restaurant in the Dillard Motor Hotel in Clayton, Georgia, a little town in a mountainous northern corner of that state, a yellowed old newspaper clipping has been posted by the telephone for years. The story includes a photo showing two men in an open canoe going through Bull Sluice, a Class V rapids on the Chattooga, one of the South's preeminent whitewater streams. According to the official classification system of the American Whitewater Affiliation, a Class V rapids consists of "extremely difficult, long, and very violent rapids with highly congested routes which nearly always must be scouted from shore. Rescue conditions are difficult and there is significant hazard to life in event of a mishap." In the photo, the man in the stern of the canoe looks scared to death, but the man in the bow has a look of grim, Annapolis determination on his face—as if he were smoking out a nest of wasps. According to the story, which is dated sometime in 1972, this was the first run of Bull Sluice in an open canoe, ever. Others have their doubts about that—which is, of course, to be expected on a river with this sort of reputation—but most everyone acknowledges that even if they were not the very first, they were among the first.

The man in the stern is Claude Terry, an expert local river runner. The man in the bow is the governor of Georgia, Jimmy Carter.

The lore of the South could not survive without rivers any better than the human body could survive without blood. Rivers wind through Twain's and Faulkner's and James Dickey's prose; they flow out of Stephen Foster's lyrics. Yet it is the South, more than any region except California, that has become a landscape of reservoirs, and southerners, more than anyone else, are still at the grand old work of destroying their rivers. With one hand they dam them; with the other they channelize them; the two actions cancel each other out—the channelized streams promote the floods the dams were built to prevent—and the whole spectacle is viewed by some as a perpetual employment machine invented by engineers.

The reasons behind the South's infatuation with dams are somewhat elusive. Precipitation in the South is uniformly ample, the rivers run well and often flood, and good damsites are, or were, quite common. But the same applies to New England, and there the landscape contains relatively few dams. There are water-supply reservoirs and small power dams, but only a handful of mammoth structures backing up twenty-mile artificial lakes, which are encountered everywhere in the South. Whatever the reasons, it is an article of faith in the South that you send a politician to Washington to bring home a dam. The first southern politician of national stature who went on record opposing one may have been Jimmy Carter.

Carter's misgivings about dams appear to have been rooted in metaphysics, flintiness, and a sense of military honor. As a businessman, a state legislator, and the chairman of the Middle Flint River Planning and Development Council, he was at first enthusiastic when the Army Corps of Engineers announced plans to erect Spewrell Bluffs Dam, a $133 million structure on the Flint, which is one of Georgia's larger rivers. However, some of Carter's personal friends belonged to the state's environmental community, and at about the same time he was running for governor, they introduced him to canoeing and river rafting, a sport with which he immediately fell in love. Caught between political expediency—many of the state's business and labor interests were equally in love with Spewrell Bluffs Dam—and the appeals of close friends and his own changing values, Carter decided to make up his mind purely on the facts. He got a copy of the Corps' general plan and environmental statement, closeted himself in a room, and, displaying that passion for detail that was to contribute to his political undoing, read it from cover to cover. He cross-checked its assertions with a number of experts; he did his own math; he graded the Corps' hydrology (Carter had graduated from Annapolis as an engineer). In the end, he wrote a blistering eighteen-page letter to the Corps accusing it of "computational manipulation" and of ignoring the environment; then, exercising his gubernatorial discretion, he vetoed the dam. According to friends, Carter was deeply incensed by the Corps' reliance on deception to justify the dam; as an Annapolis graduate, he didn't believe a military unit would do such a thing. And, perhaps because he did go to Annapolis instead of West Point, he took it personally. "The Corps of Engineers lied to me," he told his friends. He said it as if a stranger had wandered into his house, eaten everything in the icebox, and then, on leaving, chopped down his favorite tree.

Carter also possessed something rare among American politicians—a sense of history—and, according to those close to him, he began to wonder what future generations would think of all the dams we had built. What right did we have, in the span of his lifetime, to dam nearly all the world's rivers? What would happen when the dams silted up? Fixed, huge, and permanent, dams were also oddly vulnerable. What if the climate changed? What if there were floods which the dams, their capacity drastically reduced by silt, couldn't hold? What if there were terrible droughts, and farms and desert cities that owed their existence to dams faced economic ruin? Besides, having already built fifty thousand of them, what were we getting for our investment now? By the time Carter became President, the cumulative federal debt was approaching a trillion dollars and inflation had already visited double digits, but the federal water bureaucracies were still going through $5 billion every year. One of the first things he was going to chop out of the federal budget was dams.

To a degree that is impossible for most people to fathom, water projects are the grease gun that lubricates the nation's legislative machinery. Congress without water projects would be like an engine without oil; it would simply seize up. If an influential southern member of Congress didn't much like a program designed to aid a certain part of the Northeast, then it would not be unheard-of for the Congressional delegation from that region to help him get a dam built in his state. If a Senator threatened to launch a filibuster against a particular program, perhaps the program's advocates could muster support for the Senator's favorite water project.

In the Congress, water projects are a kind of currency, like wampum, and water development itself is a kind of religion. Senators who voted for drastic cuts in the school lunch program in 1981 had no compunction about voting for $20 billion worth of new Corps of Engineers projects in 1984, the largest such authorization ever. A jobs program in a grimly depressed city in the Middle West, where unemployment among minority youth is more than 50 percent, is an example of the discredited old welfare mentality; a $300 million irrigation project in Nebraska giving supplemental water to a few hundred farmers is an intelligent, farsighted investment in the nation's future.

(The phrase "pork barrel" derives from a fondness on the part of some southern plantation owners for rolling out a big barrel of salted pork for their half-starved slaves on special occasions. The near riots that ensued as the slaves tried to make off with the choicest morsels of pork were, apparently, a source of substantial amusement in the genteel old South. Sometime in the 1870s or 1880s, a wag decided that the habitual efforts by members of Congress to carry large loads from the federal treasury back to their home districts resembled the feeding frenzies of the slaves. The usage was quite common by the late 1880s; and in 1890 it showed up in a headline in the New York *Times*, assuring its immortality.)

Among members of Congress, the intricate business of trading favors is commonly referred to as the "courtesy" system, or, more quaintly, the "buddy" system. Among its critics—a category that extends to include anyone who has not yet benefited from it—it is called log-rolling, back-scratching, or, most often, the pork barrel. Members of Congress who believe in the system—there are many who fervently do, and probably an equal number who dislike it but go along—argue that it benefits the nation as a whole by distributing public-works money to all the fifty states in more or less equal proportion. It doesn't. Anyway, to say the Congress cannot function without the "courtesy" system is to say that it cannot conduct its business without indulging in bribery, extortion, and procuring.

Ideology is the first casualty of water development. Senator Alan Cranston of California, who is well out on the left of the Democratic Party, spearheaded the successful effort to sextuple the maximum acreage one could legally own in order to receive subsidized Reclamation water. Having accomplished that, Cranston, heavily financed by big California water users, launched his presidential campaign, railing against "special interests." Senator Ernest Gruening of Alaska, who built a reputation as one of the more ardent conservationists in Congress, also campaigned mightily for Rampart Dam, which, if built, would have destroyed more wildlife habitat than any single project ever built in North America. In 1980, Steve Symms of Idaho, a right-wing small businessman, ran against and defeated Senator Frank Church, one of the Senate's most respected liberals; the one thing they ever agreed on was that the Bureau of Reclamation ought to build Teton Dam.

"New Age" politicians who strive to disassociate themselves from the old Left or the old Right seem to fall into the same old habits where the pork barrel is concerned. Senator Gary Hart of Colorado is a neoliberal and a self-proclaimed expert on how to trim the federal budget; he has also supported, consistently, a couple of billion dollars' worth of unbuilt Colorado reclamation and salinity-control projects, most of them sporting costs far greater than benefits. Former Governor Edmund G. Brown, Jr., of California flew to London at his own expense to attend the funeral of his hero E. F. Schumacher, who wrote *Small Is Beautiful*, then returned to promote what could turn out to be the most expensive single public-works project ever built, the expansion of the California Water Project.

Politicians beach themselves in such ideological shallows for various reasons: the power of money, the selfishness of their constituents, or their own venality. The system thrives as it does, however, largely because of the power and nature of the committee system in Congress. The leadership of the appropriations and public-works committees that approve and fund water projects traditionally comes from the South and West, where water projects are sacrosanct. In 1980, for example, Congressman Jamie Whitten of Mississippi was chairman of the House Appropriations Committee; Congressman Tom Bevill of Alabama was chairman of its Subcommittee on Public Works; Congressman Ray Roberts of Texas was chairman of the House Public Works Committee; Jennings Randolph of West Virginia was chairman of the Senate Environment and Public Works Committee; Mike Gravel of Alaska was chairman of its Subcommittee on Water Resources; Mark Hatfield of Oregon was chairman of the Senate Appropriations Committee. In that same year, 1980, 288 individual projects were included for funding in the omnibus Public Works Appropriations bill. Only eight got more than $25 million. All but one of the eight were located in the South or West. The most expensive item on the menu was the $3 billion Tennessee-Tombigbee Waterway, which was to receive $243 million—in a single year. The waterway is in the districts of Bevill, Whitten, and the immortal John Stennis, who was second in seniority on the Senate Appropriations Committee that year.

Together, the House and Senate committees and the water-development agencies run a remarkably efficient operation. They work in concert, rewarding those who vote for water projects and punishing those who do not, sometimes to the point of stopping virtually any federal money from going into their districts. They would, of course, much rather use the carrot than the stick. In 1978, before he had even set foot in Washington, Senator-elect Alan Simpson of Wyoming was paid a special visit by three high-ranking officers in the Corps of Engineers asking if there was anything they could "do" for him. Once in Washington, Simpson was approached again, this time by the leaders of the appropriate committees, who made him the same offer. Every freshman Senator and Congressman got the same treatment, even Bob Edgar. "The old-boy network comes to you," says Edgar, who was elected to the House of Representatives in 1974, at the age of thirty-one. "They say, 'You've got a water project in your district? You want one? Let us take care of it for you.' Then they come around a few months later and get their pound of flesh. You actually risk very little by going along. You get a lot of money thrown into your district for a project that few of your constituents oppose. In return, you vote for a lot of projects your constituents don't know about or care about. Not many of my constituents are going to base their vote for or against me on whether or not I supported Stonewall Jackson Dam in West Virginia. Then everyone wonders why we're running such big federal deficits, and they cut the social programs, which must be the culprit."

As it turned out, Edgar did not support Stonewall Jackson Dam in West Virginia, nor did he support dozens of other projects ear-marked for funding in the Appropriations Committee that year. He has even made a concerted effort to have them taken out, year after year. For this, Edgar has become a virtual pariah among his colleagues and a hero among conservation groups. By general consensus, no one among the 535 members of Congress has been quite as willing to risk his political career attacking the pork-barrel system. The reason may have something to do with the fact that Edgar is a former Methodist minister who became a Congressman almost by accident. Well-built, handsome, a picture of rectitude in repose, he was, in the early 1980s, perhaps the most stubbornly principled person in that legislative body, a distinction that has worked against him at every turn. "Some of my colleagues come up to me and say, 'Bob, I wish I had your guts,' " says Edgar. "Then they attack me on the floor." Actually, Edgar has a built-in advantage in his district. He represents suburban Philadelphia, and it would be difficult for the Corps of Engineers to tantalize his constituents with a water project—where would one build one in the suburbs?—and then see to it that the appropriations committees deny him funds (a strategy which, according to a number of Congressional staff aides, has been used on numerous occasions, with good results). Still, federal public-works money has, in recent years, tended to detour around Edgar's district. His colleagues have also subjected him to threats. "Tim Lee Carter of Kentucky came up to me once after I fought to remove Paintsville Lake from the appropriations bill," says Edgar. "He was blazing mad. He punched a finger in my chest and said, 'I know nothing about the Philadelphia shipyard, *but I will*.' Another Congressman told me he hopes I *am* successful in knocking off his project, because then hundreds of his constituents will walk into my district and work for my defeat."

After a while, it is difficult to remain principled in such an atmosphere, let alone be effective. "Congress as an institution is pretty sick," says Bob Eckhardt, who was a liberal Congressman from Houston until his defeat in 1980. "It has two diseases: special interestitis and parochialism. My opponent made a big issue out of the fact that I was too generous to the Northeast. He said I voted to guarantee New York City's loan when the money could have been spent in Texas. He boasted about *not* being a candidate with a national perspective. New Yorkers are just as parochial in their own way. Liz Holtzman of New York feels the question of the Concorde landing at Kennedy Airport is as important as the Equal Rights Amendment. People like Pat Moynihan [the Democratic Senator from New York] oppose western dams but want to waste even more money on a crazily expensive project like Westway. If New York City *had* gone bankrupt in 1975 it would have been a terribly serious blow to the bond markets of many other cities, including places like Boise, Idaho, and Jackson, Mississippi. I didn't detect that many members recognized that fact, or cared about it if they did. They mainly didn't want to be accused of spending their constituents' money on a lousy place like New York."

"We are a tyranny presiding over a democracy," says Edgar. "Congressman Floyd Fithian of Indiana has a water project planned for his district which he doesn't want. He wants it out of the bill, deauthorized. I don't know whether a majority of his constituents support him or not, but that should be his problem and their problem. He should be able to take a project out of his own district and if his constituents don't like it they can vote him out of office. But he hasn't been able to remove the project from the appropriations bill. Congressman John Myers sits on the Appropriations Committee and its Energy and Water Development Subcommittee. He has some big construction people in his district, which is next door to Floyd's, who would get some big contracts if the project is built. So every time Fithian tries to remove the project, Myers puts it back in.

"It's pathetic to watch what can happen to grown men here. One guy had a good project—I thought it was good—in the 1978 appropriations bill, but Ray Roberts yanked it out because he was upset over a couple of votes the guy had cast. He had the poor Congressman crawling up to him on his hands and knees for a year. He finally got his project back. Ray jerked him around like a beaten dog."

It was against this system that Jimmy Carter, a rube from Georgia who had never been elected to public office outside the state, decided to declare war.

Carter's appointments alone probably got him off on the wrong foot; in their own way, they were like Ronald Reagan's chemical-industry people taking over the EPA. His Interior Secretary, Cecil Andrus, had been governor of Idaho and, before that, a sawmill owner. Andrus was a stranger to Washington, and he had made a reputation in Idaho as an unusually conservation-minded governor from a state full of millionaire sheep ranchers and irrigation farmers. Andrus's Assistant Secretary, Guy Martin, looked like a bearded logger, but he was a lawyer and made a reputation as a politically canny resources director under another conservationist governor, Jay Hammond of Alaska. The first head of Carter's Council on Environmental Quality was Charles Warren, probably the most active conservationist in the California legislature. One of the other members, later chairman, was Gus Speth, a lawyer from the archconservationist Natural Resources Defense Council. Speth was a Yale-educated Rhodes Scholar from Orangeburg, South Carolina, who had a dense drawl, resplendent southern charm, and Carter's ear on water projects and nuclear energy, which he had fought relentlessly at NRDC. Katherine Fletcher, a scientist with the equally archconservationist Environmental Defense Fund, became a natural resource specialist under Stuart Eizenstat, the head of Carter's domestic policy staff. In the Environmental Protection Agency and the Interior Department were a dozen more high- and middle-level appointees pulled off the environmental organizations' staffs. All of the conservation groups were, of course, beside themselves with glee to lose so many people to Carter. In view of the astonished anger that greeted the appointments among the entrenched committees in Congress, however, they may have been one of the worst mistakes Carter made.

Long before the inauguration, Carter's domestic policy staff, under Eizenstat, was working up alternatives to the Ford budget it had inherited for fiscal year 1978. Since Carter's most dramatic campaign promise had been to balance the federal budget by the end of his first term, he needed to make substantial cuts right away; besides that, like many new Presidents, he wanted to inaugurate his term by doing something bold. In a series of memoranda, Eizenstat gave him his options. There weren't many. Most of the budget was soaked up by defense and the entitlement programs, and it seemed impossible to touch the discretionary part of the budget without ruffling the feathers of some large interest group. In February of 1977, on a working weekend, Carter flew to Georgia for the first time aboard the "Doomsday plane"—the jet from which the President is supposed to run the country, or what is left of it, in the event of a nuclear war. His reading material was the Eizenstat issue paper on water projects. Sitting there, imagining himself running an incinerated nation from an airplane, Carter worked himself into a negative mood. As he flipped through Eizenstat's memo, which was written largely by Kathy Fletcher, Carter began to smolder. "There is no coherent federal water resources management policy," he read. ". . . extensive overlap of agency activities . . . several million acres of productive agricultural and forest land and commercial and sport fisheries [have been ruined] while [other] large expenditures have been made to protect these resources . . . overlapping and conflicting missions . . . large-scale destruction of natural ecosystems . . . 'the pork barrel' . . . obsolete standards . . . self-serving . . . pressure from special interests." By the time he returned from Georgia, according to one of his aides, he knew how he was going to make his big splash. He called up his chief lobbyist, Frank Moore, and told him to put Congress on notice that he wanted to cut all funding for nineteen water projects. That same day, Cecil Andrus, who knew nothing of this, stepped on a plane and flew off to Denver for a western governors' conference on that year's severe drought.

The incident demonstrated a characteristic that was to plague the Carter administration for the rest of its term—a capacity for mind-boggling political naiveté. That the news of the hit list got out before Andrus was even notified was soon attributed to a "leak" within the White House, and the culprit was identified, by sly innuendo, as Kathy Fletcher. According to one of Carter's own legislative aides, however, the source of the news was none other than Carter himself. "He told Frank Moore to put the Hill on notice that he wanted those projects cut," says the aide. "The projects had been selected at a meeting attended by Andrus, but he didn't know they were actually going to go ahead with the idea. He was opposed to it from the start."

Whatever the case, the timing was miserable. It was 1977 and California was in the midst of its driest year on record—the year before had been the third-driest—and Auburn Dam was on the hit list. Though Auburn's existence would hardly have helped the state a bit, no one was about to notice that during a drought. Colorado, whose mountains were so bereft of snow that many of the ski slopes were closed in February, had three projects on the list, the most of any state. None of them would have helped much, either, but reason is the first casualty in a drought. The Central Arizona Project was already half-built, but it, too, was on the hit list. The western governors, who saw, by Andrus's own embarrassed and baffled reaction, the hopeless disarray of the Carter administration, milked the incident for all it was worth. Governor Richard Lamm of Colorado had to plumb the depths of his emotions to convey properly his deep and profound sense of outrage and shock. "We're not going to be satisfied," Lamm shouted at a huge crowd of scribbling reporters, "until we get our projects back." Governor Raul Castro of Arizona was "stunned and angry." The ever-opportunistic Jerry Brown of California, who had won over the state's powerful environmental community by publicly opposing the only two federal dams then being built in California—Auburn and New Melones—made one of his deft about-faces and said, "We want to build more dams."

The reaction from Congress was even stronger. Congressman Morris Udall of Arizona immediately dubbed the incident the "George Washington's Birthday Massacre," a term that stuck. Interestingly, Udall was one of several dozen Congressmen who had written a much publicized letter to Carter only five days earlier, saying, "During your campaign you stated many times that as President you would halt the construction of unnecessary and environmentally destructive dams. . . . We support . . . your efforts to reform the water-resources programs of the Army Corps of Engineers and the Bureau of Reclamation." Reminded of this, Udall was gracious enough to admit that "one man's vital water-resources project is another man's boondoggle." His colleagues were not so gracious. Words like "infamous," "dastardly," "incredible," "incomprehensible," and "mind-boggling" peppered the pages of the *Congressional Record*.

If Carter was counting on help from anyone, it was the press. After all, newspapers had been criticizing other regions' public works projects since the nation's founding, and the national press was nothing if not cynical about Congress. The press, however, found Carter a better target than the projects themselves. Even principled David S. Broder wrote in the Washington *Post*, "That Carter would let something like the Red River Project put him at odds with the man [Senator Russell Long] whose cooperation is essential for passage of all the vital economic, energy, health, and welfare legislation on the administration's agenda is so unlikely that some observers conjured up a theory that made the President seem much shrewder." Evidently Broder couldn't fathom a stand of principle on something as inconsequential as a new $900 million artificial waterway a few jumps away from the Mississippi River. *Newsweek* and *Time* made a desultory effort to explain the projects to their readers, then implied that people, not surplus crops (as was the case), were using most of Arizona's water. *Time* unquestioningly accepted Morris Udall's prediction that without the CAP, "Tucson and Phoenix are going to dry up and blow away." There was good coverage in *Science*, *National Journal*, and *Congressional Quarterly*, but those were publications few read.

The intensity of the reaction from Congress and the affected regions was so white-hot that Carter had to move much more quickly than he had reckoned toward conciliation. In a letter to Congress, he chastised its members for authorizing projects that made so little sense, but promised regional hearings on every project in question and invited the leadership to the White House for a talk. It was hardly the kind of talk he had in mind. "All they did was tell him what an idiot he was for doing this," said Carter's House lobbyist, Jim Free. "It was like a lynch mob. He was the sheriff throwing calm facts back at them, but they kept yelling at him to release the projects. One Congressman kept banging his fist on the table. They compared him to Nixon—the Imperial Presidency line. They were rude. They interrupted him. And most of them belonged to his own party."

Despite its best efforts, Congress couldn't budge Carter. He may have been naive, but he was adamant. Seeing this, Congress, as the

New Republic remarked, began "breaking out the high-minded rhetoric that Congressmen reserve for their grubbiest and most cynical
undertakings." Majority leader Jim Wright of Texas, for example,
wrote a letter to his colleagues urging them "to help defend the Constitutional prerogative of Congress. The White House," Wright said,
"in trying to dictate [budgetary] line items, is reaching for powers
never granted any Administration by Congress." (This was the same
Jim Wright who was one of the key backers of the constitutionally
dubious Gulf of Tonkin resolution; it was the same Jim Wright who,
in defiance of his own constituents—who had decisively rejected a
bond issue to help finance the proposed Trinity River Project—kept
sticking money for it back into the public-works appropriations bills.)
Senator Edmund Muskie of Maine picked up Wright's Imperial Presidency line in the Senate—the same Edmund Muskie who was pushing the Corps' $800 million Dickey-Lincoln Dam on the St. John River
even as it was opposed by both the president and minority leader of
the Maine senate, by Maine's two U.S. Representatives, by most of
the local newspapers, and, according to several opinion polls, by a
majority of the people in the state. Senator Robert Byrd of West
Virginia said, "A project is not 'pork barrel' to someone who has to
shovel black mud . . . or see his home swept away." The most recent
flood disaster in Byrd's state, which killed more than sixty people,
was caused by the collapse of a dam, and the West Virginians most
immediately threatened by flooding were the homeowners who lived
in the valley behind Stonewall Jackson Dam.

Notwithstanding Congress's threats, Carter continued to move
his water reforms along. Simply applying a reasonable discount, or
interest, rate of 6¾ percent—still too low, but reasonable—the hit
list easily swelled to eighty projects. Vice-President Walter Mondale,
who regarded the hit list as a terrible idea from the start, told Carter
that a stand against eighty projects would be his last. With reluctance,
he and his water-policy staff began a deliberate effort to winnow it
down. The Tennessee-Tombigbee Waterway would devour more money,
for a more illusory purpose, than anything on the list, but it had to
be left alone; even the NAACP was for it. The Red River Project was
also to survive; Carter had evidently read David Broder's column.
Animas–La Plata in New Mexico and Colorado offered something to
the local Indian population; it would survive. In most cases, Carter
was going against his own deeper instincts when he let a project slip
by. Once, in the midst of a string of rank political judgments, he
called Charlie Warren of the Council on Environmental Quality over

to his office. "He spent the first half hour telling Charlie about how outrageously wasteful and harmful some of the projects were," says one of Warren's aides. Then, together, he and Warren reduced the final hit list to eighteen projects.

On April 18, Carter announced his final, unalterable decision on the projects. It was obvious to anyone that the administration had tried to steer around states from where powerful committee chairmen came; nonetheless, it couldn't help crashing into some formidable egos and interest groups along the way. There were three projects in Colorado—Dolores, Fruitland Mesa, and Savery–Pot Hook—which was home to the second-largest Congressional delegation in the West and a Democratic governor, Dick Lamm, who hadn't hesitated to attack Carter before. The Dayton, Paintsville, and Yatesville projects were all in Kentucky, a swing state in an election year. There were Cache Basin in Arkansas, Grove Lake in Kansas. The Harbor Project and the Bayou Boeuf, Chene, and Black Channel were both in Louisiana, Russell Long notwithstanding. There was Dickey-Lincoln in Maine; Merremac Park in Missouri; Lukfata Lake in Oklahoma— peanuts as such projects go, but irresistible because the only real beneficiary of a $39 million investment would be a private catfish farm. And then, to make the whole effort financially worthwhile, there were five immense projects, none of them worth less than $500 million, two of them likely to end up costing six or seven times that much, all conceived by the Bureau of Reclamation: Garrison in North Dakota; Oahe in South Dakota; Auburn Dam in California; the Central Utah Project; and then—one could almost sense the administration crunching the bullet between its teeth—the most expensive project the West had ever seen, the rival of Tennessee-Tombigbee itself, the Central Arizona Project. Carter said he wanted all of the projects terminated. Not just unfunded—terminated.

As Carter had by then come to expect, the decibel level was highest from within his own party. Republicans, of course, stood up for their own threatened projects, but the Minority Leader in the House, Congressman Robert Michel of Illinois, said privately—and sometimes not so privately—that he thought the hit list was a pretty good idea. It was the Democratic leadership, their values and spending habits unchanged since the New Deal, that gave Carter fits. In a lectern-thumping floor speech, Jim Wright said that Carter was carrying his environmental ideas so far he threatened to become "a laughingstock." Then, to show that he, too, was an environmentalist, Wright held up a glass of water to extol its goodness. Public Works

Committee chairman Ray Roberts said Carter was a captive of "environmental extremists and budget hackers." House Speaker Tip O'Neill took the highly unusual (and, for Carter, embarrassing) step of arranging a meeting with the New York *Times* to complain that Carter was "not listening" to Congress. Senators Gary Hart and Floyd Haskell of Colorado began to pepper the administration with Freedom of Information Act requests, ostensibly to learn how their projects were selected. ("They implied that we were practicing some kind of secret skulduggery," a Carter staff member complained bitterly later on. "The skulduggery was when the Bureau justified those dams, not when we reevaluated them.") Even Mondale began undermining Carter's effort—whether he knew it or not—by going around the country privately assuring Democrats that it was all a phase, that Carter meant well, of course, but that he was certainly subject to reason.

On June 13, the House Appropriations Committee, studded with Democrats, reported out its own version of the 1978 Public Works Appropriations bill. If Carter had hoped it would heed his request and delete the eighteen projects, he was mistaken. The committee bill represented not only outright but vindictive defiance of his wishes. Only one of the projects he wanted to abandon—Grove Lake in Kansas, which lacked firm support even in the district where it was to be built—was omitted. Everything else was generously funded, some with minor conditions attached (Auburn Dam wouldn't receive more money until there was a better idea whether or not an earthquake would destroy it). On top of that, money was included for a dozen new projects nowhere to be found in the administration's budget. And on top of *that*, there was a section of the bill that rejuvenated the Cross-Florida Barge Canal, which was anathema to environmentalists, and which Richard Nixon himself decided to halt in 1971.

Publicly, Carter said nothing. Privately, he was seething. "The only way now is a veto," one of his aides was quoted as saying. "We're in a game of chicken." A quick head count, however, showed that the Senate could muster the two-thirds majority required to override a veto. If he was serious about vetoing the bill, Carter would have to shore up his support in the House. With moral support from the administration, and perhaps some rewards—to his chagrin, Carter was learning that he might have to resort to the pork barrel to win his fight against the pork barrel—the House was a distinct possibility. It would only take one branch of Congress to win.

Carter's lobbyists, Frank Moore and Jim Free, worked the House furiously, joined by the railroads (which were being undercut by competition from federally subsidized barge traffic), lobbyists from the conservation groups, and every dissident farmer, businessman, rancher, and mayor from a project region whom they could get to come to Washington to help them. Vote by vote, the frailest of margins was stitched together. On the straight head count, Carter would surely lose; the problem was holding Congress's margin below the two-thirds necessary for an override. Many Congressmen, especially those whose support would take great political courage—South Carolina's Butler Derrick, for example, who had opposed Richard Russell Dam in his own district, or Philip Burton of California, who leaned heavily on labor support—demanded absolute assurances that Carter would veto the bill. If they voted not to override and he signed it anyway, their embarrassment would be acute. Meanwhile, the administration was fighting insubordination within its own ranks. The Bureau of Reclamation was widely suspected of feeding numbers to Capitol Hill that made the administration's figures appear suspect. The Corps, which had more than once disregarded the wishes of its commander in chief, was suspected by Carter's people of doing the same thing. Once, as Jim Free was passing by the Public Works committee room, he noticed several high-ranking officers of the Corps talking with Ray Roberts. Free stopped and eavesdropped long enough to capture the gist of the conversation. "They were laughing about how they were going to beat us at our own game," he says.

By fall, as the showdown approached (the Senate had already passed a close equivalent of the House bill), Moore and Free were finally convinced they had the votes to stop an override in the House. Tip O'Neill, the House Speaker, who wanted to avoid such an outcome at all costs, was apparently sure of it, too. At the last minute, he decided to play his trump card. "Tip called Ham Jordan," the President's top aide, remembers Free, "and made him a bargain. Something would be worked out on Clinch River [the demonstration breeder reactor which Carter wanted to stop even more than the water projects]. A few projects would be deleted, and Tip would help the President get a reform process going.

"It was a nice piece of work," Free grudgingly admits. "They went right to Hamilton because he was the closest thing we had to a good ol' boy. He was also in a little trouble for not returning people's phone calls and things like that. If he worked out a compromise, it would make him look good, and they knew it."

331

O'Neill's offer was actually far less than it seemed. Although he had gotten Tom Bevill to agree to take nine projects out of the 1978 bill, he had not secured a firm promise that he would not put them back in next year. The same applied to Clinch River: the compromise might slow it down, but there was no commitment to stop it, even for a couple of years. Bevill had also agreed to a 3-percent across-the-board cut in funding, but that did not affect the ultimate cost of the projects; if anything, it made them more expensive in the long run.

No one knew exactly what had been discussed except O'Neill and Jordan and Carter themselves. Had O'Neill promised that the projects were out for good, or had Carter simply accepted that on faith? Did he really believe he had stopped the Clinch River reactor? No one who was intimately familiar with Bevill, or with Congress, believed they were in a mood to make such an offer. Andrus and Guy Martin were still urging Carter to veto the bill; now that he had gone this far, they argued, he couldn't abandon the fight unless he got nearly everything he had asked for. There was no indication from the White House that Carter felt otherwise. "Up until the last moment," says Free, "I was being told, and was telling everyone, that he was going to veto." Then, with no advance word to anyone, Carter signed the bill.

Carter's allies in Congress were thunderstruck. No one had been forewarned. Butler Derrick, according to his staff, was white with anger. Silvio Conte, the one senior Republican member on the House side who vociferously supported the administration, said that he would never trust Carter again on anything. His own lobbyists were furious. Even Andrus, who had opposed the hit lists from the beginning, was mad. Free, a young Tennessean, had had a local-boy-makes-good pro-file published about him in his hometown newspaper, which hap-pened to be in the district where Columbia Dam was to be built, and his parents had received so much verbal abuse because he was lob-bying against the dam that they unlisted their phone number and took their name off their mailbox. "It hardly seemed worthwhile after that," Free said dejectedly.

Even though Carter protested that the compromise was a good one—it was still unclear exactly what it meant, and would remain so for over a year—one thing was becoming abundantly clear: Carter was already in a mood to retreat. He had underestimated Congress's passion for dams and overestimated his ability to move the rest of his legislative program forward. In January of 1977, Cecil Andrus told the New York *Times*, "Thank God, there'll be no more hit lists." A lot of fence-mending was obviously being done. Later that month, Lou Cannon, the Washington *Post*'s correspondent in San Francisco, could write that "the West's Democratic governors have been offered unconditional surrender by the Carter administration, [which] has backed away from nearly every position" on water projects. An "options paper" drafted shortly thereafter and leaked, to Carter's chagrin, to the environmental groups made no mention of several of the main water-policy reforms Carter had spoken of earlier.

Having reversed himself once, however, Carter was perfectly capable of reversing himself again. In October of 1978, his second big challenge on water projects came around. The fiscal year 1979 public-works appropriations bill that emerged from the House and Senate conference committee did exactly what most of Carter's advisers said it would. To begin with, it restored money for every one of the nine projects deleted the previous year. Carter, in his innocence, evidently believed that the projects had been killed for good, and he was livid. On top of that, the bill contained money for a number of new starts, despite the fact that inflation was well into double digits, interest rates were topping 15 percent, and a balanced budget was slipping out of Carter's grasp.

Once again, Jim Free began making his rounds on Capitol Hill, urging support of a presidential veto when the vote came—even though the administration's allies were still seething over Carter's performance with the previous year's bill. Whatever doubts they had about Carter's courage, however, were soon stilled. A few days later, after making a terse, angry statement denouncing it, Carter vetoed the entire appropriations bill.

The timing of the veto, as it happened, coincided neatly with the passage of Proposition 13 in California, a draconian measure which effectively held the annual increase in property taxes to about 1 percent. Everyone knew the public was fed up with government spending; this was the first sign that it was *really* fed up. The main sponsor of the measure, a real estate lobbyist named Howard Jarvis, instantly became something of a celebrity. And though the rest of the country felt that California was more than slightly daft, everything that happened there had an odd way of spreading eastward.

One of the people who realized this right away was Larry Rockefeller, the nephew of Nelson and son of his elder brother Laurance. Rockefeller, who was then a staff attorney at the Natural Resources Defense Council, was thirty-six, almost neurotically shy, and a strikingly gifted propagandist and politician. Almost single-handedly, he pieced together the Alaska Coalition, the vast umbrella organization that was responsible, two years later, for passage of the Alaska Lands Act—which created, in an instant, as much federal parkland as the country had set aside in more than a hundred years. The full-page advertisements run by the Alaska Coalition were written and often paid for by Rockefeller, and they were astute; mostly, they talked about how much resource development and fabulous economic growth the Alaska Lands Act would still allow.

The Alaska campaign was based on persuasion. To make Congress sustain Carter's veto of the appropriations bill, however, a campaign would have to be based on fear. There was too little time to try any other tack, and fear seemed to be the one universal motivator on Capitol Hill. At that particular moment, Rockefeller reasoned, Congressmen feared no one more than Howard Jarvis.

Getting Jarvis's cooperation was surprisingly easy. Although the value of real estate in his hometown, Los Angeles, depended entirely on aqueducts bringing water from three directions, they were already built. Besides, an opportunity to take on Congress was more than the feisty old man could resist. Rockefeller recalled some of Jarvis's speeches, shut himself in his office, and imagined what sort of advertisement Jarvis might write. When he finished a draft, he read it to him over the phone. Jarvis was stunned. "That's just what I would have said," he answered.

On the morning of October 5, with a vote to override Carter's veto just hours away, four hundred-odd members of the House opened their copies of the Washington *Post* and the New York *Times* and saw the scowling visage of Howard Jarvis staring back at them. "IT'S AN OUTRAGE," he croaked. "THE PUBLIC WORKS APPROPRIATIONS BILL IS THE BIG TAX, BIG GOVERNMENT, BIG SPENDING, BIG WASTE BILL OF THE YEAR." During the debate that day, the "spirit of Howard Jarvis" was invoked several times. When the vote was taken, the attempt to override Carter's veto had barely failed.

As the dam saboteurs in Carter's administration were to discover, however, victories over the Congressional pork-barrel system tend to be short-lived. They are especially short-lived if they come thirteen months before an election year.

In July of 1979, a group of California's wealthiest irrigation farmers, many of them from the Westlands Water District, played host to Rosalyn Carter at a big Democratic fund-raiser in Fresno. Soon thereafter, a number of big growers from the nominally conservative San Joaquin Valley were making hefty campaign contributions to the Carter-Mondale reelection campaign. Their reward was a new water contract obligating them to pay only $9.10 an acre-foot—well below cost, and a subsidy worth $60 million over the term of the contract.

Westlands, which the Bureau had illegally expanded back in the 1960s at the behest of the farmers, was the one place where Carter could put one of his most ballyhooed reforms, realistic water pricing, to work, because the illegal expansion had technically voided the original contract. He not only failed to do that, but, by caving in on an issue he could easily have won—Westlands had no other source of water except groundwater, which was running out, and therefore had little choice but to accept the administration's terms—he sent a signal to Congress that he was prepared to do business with them.

It was just the beginning. Carter had entered office convinced that the 160-acre land limitation in the Reclamation Act was a sound principle. But in Congress there was talk of removing the acreage limitation altogether, and of allowing unlimited leasing (which was, in effect, the same thing as removing the limitation). The more "moderate" proposals called for a limit of 1,260 acres, an eightfold expansion. Most of Carter's advisers were telling him that he had to hang tough on the acreage issue: if subsidized water suddenly became available to the biggest growers in the West, it would not only be an outrageous subsidy of the wealthy, but it would intensify pressure for even more projects. Assistant Interior Secretary Guy Martin, the administration's canniest strategist on western water policy, says he recommended a revised acreage limit of perhaps six hundred acres—a compromise which, he felt, the administration could sell. By late 1979, however, Martin's boss, Cecil Andrus, was suddenly agreeing with Jerry Brown, another lapsed champion of the 160-acre limit, on a new limit of 1,260 acres. (It wasn't clear whether that meant 2,520 acres for a man and wife.) In California, with 1,260 acres and subsidized water costing between $3.50 and $9 per acre-foot, a halfway ambitious farmer could become a millionaire—which was not exactly the intention of the Reclamation Act.

And then, on top of everything else, there was Tellico Dam.

Tellico was a dam the Tennessee Valley Authority had conceived as early as the 1930s and hadn't gotten around to proposing seriously until the 1960s—which was mute testimony to the kind of project it was. The dam itself would produce no power—it would merely raise and divert the Little Tennessee River about a mile from its confluence with the main Tennessee so some extra water could be run through the turbines of nearby Fort Loudon Dam. The result would be twenty-three megawatts of new power, about 2 percent of the capacity of one of the nuclear and coal plants the TVA was simultaneously building. There were no flood-control benefits; there were hardly recreational benefits (the region had more reservoirs than it knew how to fill with boats); there were no fish and wildlife benefits. On the other hand, the Little Tennessee was about the last fast-flowing coldwater stream in the state. It was dammed only once upriver, while most tributaries of the Tennessee were dammed several times. It had a large and healthy population of trout. It was a splendid canoeing stream. It flowed through a beautiful valley, one of those happy places that contain both farms and bears. The Cherokee Indian Nation had had its pick of all the rivers of central Appalachia, and it chose the valley of the Little Tennessee as its home. There were hundreds of archaeological sites, some probably yet to be discovered. With its pretty white clapboard houses and its well-tended little farms, the valley was a beautiful anomaly, a place more at home in the nineteenth century. Tellico Dam would put all of this under eighty feet of water.

After wrestling with its lack of a *raison d'être* for a while, the TVA decided that the only way it could justify the new dam was to change the whole character of the region in which it would be. The solution, it finally decided, was to create an entirely new town around the reservoir, a chrome-and-steel headquarters for a major branch of the Boeing Corporation which would go by the somewhat ironic name Timberlake. (Actually, the TVA may have come up with the idea because the Bureau of Reclamation had thought of it first. In the 1960s, it was no secret that the Bureau, boxed out of much of its historical domain by the Corps of Engineers, was looking to expand its activities eastward, and Appalachia was the first place it planned to give things a try, building exactly the kind of sterile, reservoir-centered new towns of which Timberlake would be a first example.) It was like deciding to put a fifty-thousand-seat Superdome in the middle of Wyoming and then building a city of 150,000 people around it to justify its existence. And there was no real guarantee by Boeing that it would establish itself there; it had merely expressed interest in the idea. But that was enough to get the project moving. By 1969, Tellico Dam was well on the way to being built.

As it was going up, however, two entirely new hurdles were thrown in Tellico's path. One was the National Environmental Policy

Act of 1969, which requires an environmental-impact statement and a discussion of alternatives before any major federal project can proceed. (The TVA claimed it was exempt from NEPA and had to be taken to court before it complied.) The other hurdle, which no one paid much attention to at first, was the Endangered Species Act of 1973.

In that same year, 1973, a professor of zoology from the University of Tennessee was snorkeling around in the Little Tennessee when a small fish, resembling a dace, darted out from under a rock in front of his face and gulped a snail. The zoologist, whose name was David Etnier, followed the fish until he could get a good look at it. He had never seen one like it before. After some taxonomic investigation, the fish was identified as a snail darter—a species that appeared to inhabit only a portion of the Little Tennessee, mainly the taking area of Tellico Dam. Its numbers estimated to be in the low thousands, its habitat apparently confined to one place, the darter seemed eligible for classification as an endangered species. Before the act, that would have meant merely that the fish was probably doomed. Now it meant, by law, that "protection of habitat . . . critical to [its] continued existence" was the federal government's number-one priority.

The TVA tried to get around the act by attempting, without much success, to transplant the darter to other nearby streams. Meanwhile, instead of suspending construction, it redoubled its efforts to complete the dam in a hurry, a time-honored strategy employed by the public-works bureaucracies—but one which, this time, resulted in its being hauled into court by the Environmental Defense Fund. The federal district court essentially found for the EDF, but ruled that the Endangered Species Act was never intended by its framers to stop a project which was already 80 percent built. On appeal, however, the district court's decision was overturned, and completion of Tellico was stopped cold.

The national media, which had covered the story with yawning lack of interest up to then, were suddenly tearing each other's clothes trying to get onto the Tellico site. Half the newspapers in the country seemed to run the story on page one, under some variation of the same headline: "Hundred-Million-Dollar Dam Stopped by Three-Inch Fish." In most cases, the coverage went little deeper than that. Some editorial writers couldn't even see humor in the impasse; the Washington *Star* harrumphed that it was "the sort of thing that could give environmentalists a bad name."

Had the editorialists and reporters taken a longer look, they might have seen that the big story was not the dam at all but the TVA itself, an agency that had evolved from a domestic variation on the Job Corps into the biggest power producer, biggest strip miner, and single biggest polluter in the United States. Unaccountable to the public, largely unaccountable to Congress, the TVA was a elephantine relic of the age of public works; it had undoubtedly done its region some good, but by the 1970s it had passed the uncharted point in an agency's career—twenty years, thirty years, sometimes much less—when it confronts new challenges with barnacled precepts and, in a sense, turns on the constituency it was created to help. Had they looked around them, the reporters might have seen that Appalachia, the godchild of this benevolent agency for four decades, still looked socially depressed; physically, it looked horrifying. The single most important reason was the TVA's purchase of immense quantities of strip-mined coal. It still clung to the discredited notion that the salvation of Appalachia lay in cheap power, and strip-mined coal was the cheapest fuel. But the strip-mining, besides eliminating thousands of jobs in deep-mined coal, was creating a scene of gruesome devastation. The denuded mountains seemed covered with a reddish-brown rash, and rivers that were once pristine were running with what looked like old blood. Meanwhile, the TVA's older coal-fired power plants were creating pollution traps in the valleys where they were situated, and its newer ones, with smokestacks a thousand feet high, were wafting sulfur and nitrogen oxides up to New York State and Canada, where they fell as acid rain.

This same obsession with cheap electricity had, of course, resulted in the TVA's having built thirty-odd major dams in the Tennessee Basin over the course of thirty-odd years. The dams, mostly built during the Depression and the war with low-interest money and by workers earning a few dollars a day, were the cheapest source of power around, and TVA's rates were as low as those in the Northwest. As in the Northwest, a complement of energy-intensive industries had moved in—aluminum, uranium enrichment, steel—and now the TVA was afraid they would move right back out if it raised its rates. It was a fear whose end result, rational or not, was Tellico Dam.

In June of 1978, the Supreme Court upheld the injunction against the dam on the basis of the Endangered Species Act, as written. Legally, the Court had little choice, even though, by then, the dam was more than 90 percent built. Chief Justice Warren Burger, who wrote the decision, was clearly offended by the whole situation, and all but invited Congress to amend the act. Congress required no such prompting. The legislative hopper began to spin with amendments to weaken or gut the act. Through the leadership of Senator John Culver of Iowa, however—and of Senator Howard Baker of Tennessee, whose only real interest was completing the dam—a less drastic amendment was passed, by which an endangered species review committee would be created to resolve any case where a major project such as Tellico ran up against the act. It was to be a Cabinet-level committee, composed of the Secretaries of Interior, Agriculture, and the Army, in addition to the administrators of the Environmental Protection Agency and the National Oceanic and Atmospheric Administration, the chairman of the Council of Economic Advisers, and a representative from the affected state. According to the language of the amendment, the committee, which some began to call the God Squad, could grant exemptions to the act where no "reasonable and prudent" alternative exists, where the project is of national significance, or where the benefits of building it "clearly outweigh" any other course of action.

The makeup of the interagency committee suggested a predisposition toward completing stalled projects, especially in the case of a dam. At best, Tellico's opponents were hoping for a four-to-three split in favor of construction, which might seem like enough of a hung jury to let them try another tack. They were wondering what such a tack might be when the committee's decision was announced. No one was prepared for the outcome: a unanimous decision that held for the snail darter and against the dam. In so doing, the committee skipped over metaphysics, transcendentalism, and evolutionary philosophy and ruled solely on the basis of economics. Tellico was a terrible investment—even worse, if the committee was to be believed, than the environmentalists had said. "Here is a project that is 95 percent complete," said Charles Schultz, the chairman of the Council of Economic Advisers, "and if one takes just the cost of finishing it against the benefits . . . it doesn't pay." Cecil Andrus added, "Frankly, I hate to see the snail darter get the credit for delaying a project that was so ill-conceived and uneconomic in the first place." God, in his new bureaucratic incarnation, had spoken. Tellico was a loser—it didn't deserve to be finished.

The dam's two main Congressional defenders, Senator Howard Baker and James Duncan, a Republican Congressman whose district encompassed both the dam and the TVA's headquarters, still tried to blame everything on the snail darter. "Should a worthless, unsightly, minute, unedible minnow outweigh a possible injustice to human beings?" groused Duncan on the floor of the House—ignoring the injustice to the thousand-odd people who would be evicted from their homes. Nonetheless, the finale had been written. Baker and Duncan had been beaten, fair and square—beaten, through some oddly poetic reprise, by Howard Baker's own amendment. The only thing for them to do was to accept defeat gracefully.

June 18, 1979, was a dull day on the floor of the House, even duller than most. Little was going on, so hardly anyone was there. Bob Edgar was one of the many who were absent, and he still hates himself for it. He was one of the few Congressmen who might have been suspicious enough to stop what was about to take place. "Duncan walked in waving a piece of paper," Edgar recalls. "He said, 'Mr. Speaker! Mr. Speaker! I have an amendment to offer to the public-works appropriations bill.' Tom Bevill and John Myers of the Appropriations Committee both happened to be there. I wonder why. Bevill says, 'I've seen the amendment. It's good.' Myers says, 'I've seen the amendment. It's a good one.' And that was that. It was approved by voice vote! No one even knew what they were voting for! *They were voting to exempt Tellico Dam from all laws.* All laws! They punched a loophole big enough to shove a $100 million dam through it, and then they scattered threats all through Congress so we couldn't muster the votes to shove it back out. I tried—lots of people tried—but we couldn't get that rider out of the bill. The speeches I heard on the floor were the angriest I've heard in elective office. For once, a lot of my colleagues were properly outraged. Senator Baker and Representative Duncan couldn't have cared less. They got their dam."

A few days later, the House passed the appropriations bill with the Tellico rider still in it. The Senate followed suit, 48–44, despite two earlier votes against the dam. "That," said Edgar with sardonic disgust, "is the democratic process at work."

There was, of course, still the possibility of a presidential veto. If anything, it seemed inevitable. Here, in the case of one dam, was everything that was rotten in Denmark: a bad project proposed by a dinosaurian bureaucracy; needless destruction of one of the last wild rivers in the East; usurpation of a quiet valley; and a cynical Congress sneaking around one of its own laws. Guy Martin and Cecil Andrus were both urging a veto in the strongest possible terms. Gus Speth, by then chairman of the Council on Environmental Quality, was privately talking of resignation if Carter backed down. Few in Carter's conservationist constituency even entertained the possibility that he wouldn't veto the bill. Congress, however, had taken care of everything. Carter was in the midst of negotiating a treaty that would give the Panama Canal back to Panama, and he was meeting stubborn resistance in Congress. The votes were lined up closely enough to put the President in a position of wretched vulnerability. The threats were quite naked. If Carter vetoed the bill, there would be no treaty; his education bill might suffer the same fate. In both cases, his embarrassment would be extreme—worse, perhaps, than if he swallowed the Tellico exemption. The gulp was almost audible. On the night he signed the bill, the President telephoned Zygmund Plater, the young law professor from the University of Tennessee who handled the case before the Supreme Court, and performed a *mea culpa*. Plater was taken aback. He was, in fact, speechless, and he wasn't even sure why. Was it having the President on the other end of the phone, or was it the fact that a dam was now dictating foreign policy?

When the gates closed on Tellico Dam a year or so later, Carter's humiliation was just about complete. Not a vestige of his water-policy reforms remained. Everything he had asked for was out; everything he wanted out was in. Congress had made a mockery of one of its own laws, and even of an amendment weakening that law, for the sake of a water project so bad it made better sense to abandon than to finish it. The Tellico vote was one of the things that prompted the normally restrained Elizabeth Drew, the *New Yorker*'s Washington correspondent, to write a devastating series on Congress's capitulation to money and power. To those familiar with water projects, though, it was nothing new.

With the benefit of hindsight, some of Carter's own people are scathingly critical of how the administration handled the water-projects issue. Guy Martin, his Assistant Interior Secretary, is one. "He blundered from the word go," says Martin. "He might as well have gone up to the Hill with a six-pound codfish and slapped it across their faces. Andrus begged him not to come out with a big long hit list, but he did it anyway, and from that point on the merits of the whole issue got lost. It became 'Congressional prerogative,' the 'Imperial Presidency.' He was his own worst enemy. He had a great big chip on his shoulder about water projects, that was his problem. It made him focus way too much on the environmental issue, when the only way he could win was with the economic one. Most Congressmen don't really care about wild rivers. The New Deal mentality is entrenched up there—even the right-wingers believe in it. Carter loved wild rivers, and in the end they thought he was just plain kooky.

341

"What Carter *could* have done," Martin continues, "is pick the three or four worst projects instead of nineteen, or thirty-two—that was another problem, he kept changing the numbers on them—and get rid of them. He could have done it. In war, you don't take two dozen beachheads on the same day. You can't, for God's sake. But he could have won some big ones. Auburn Dam, for instance. If that dam failed, it would be the worst peacetime disaster in American history. He had them there. Garrison and Oahe were awful. The farmers didn't even *want* Oahe. The Tug Fork Project is so ridiculous it strains belief. I can't help believing that if Carter had focused on a few he could have eliminated them. Then he would have had a small victory, but a real one. Then there's next year."

Having said all this, Martin added, almost apologetically, "Carter was right, though. The projects are as bad as he said, most of them. The environmental damage is bad. The economics are bad. The politics are bad. The agencies are out of control. If the Corps and the Bureau built everything they wanted to, we'd hardly have any flowing water left. His instincts were good."

M any western members of Congress, not to mention the water lobby and the bureaucracies, were overjoyed when Ronald Reagan was elected President after Jimmy Carter. Reagan might talk like a fiscal conservative, but surely he wouldn't be against water development. After all, he was a westerner. He owned a ranch in dry country. His Interior Secretary, James Watt of Colorado, was the environmentalists' anti-Christ. Most of his other key domestic advisers were westerners, too—James Baker, Ed Meese, William Clark, Paul Laxalt. All of them, and Reagan, too, certainly *talked* as if they believed in water development.

No sooner had Reagan taken office, however, than his budget director, David Stockman, was talking about recovering 100 percent of the costs of new navigation projects from the beneficiaries—not just the capital costs, but the operating costs, too. (In 1985, the Corps of Engineers spent around $1 billion on project operation and maintenance alone.) There was also talk of forcing states to pay a large share of the costs of flood-control dams—something Carter had never seriously proposed. Even Watt was suggesting that the states should contribute to Reclamation projects—up front. It wasn't exactly clear how large a share the administration had in mind, but privately Watt was suggesting that 33 percent might be a reasonable amount. Since that would preclude practically all new water development, the water lobby didn't know quite how to react. Jan van Schilfgaarde, the director of the Agriculture Department's Salinity Control Laboratory, was speaking one day with William Johnston, the manager of the Westlands Water District in California, and he asked, "Why do you think Reagan is your friend if he wants you to pay a third of the fare? Carter only wanted 10 percent." As van Schilfgaarde recalls it, Johnston was silent for a moment, then said, "Well, Reagan understands us." "You can get cheaper understanding from a psychiatrist" was van Schilfgaarde's response.

As expected, Reagan's original proposals were slowly nibbled away by Congress, but meanwhile, year after year, no new authorization bills managed to clear the floor—partly because the federal government was suffocating under its own mass, but also because Reagan, like Carter, was threatening to veto. In 1984, the entire $20 billion water-projects authorization in the public-works bill—three hundred projects' worth—was taken out due to such a threat. A year later, when an almost identical bill reached the floor of the House, environmentalists, who had formed a discreet alliance with Stockman and other fiscal conservatives in the administration, had managed to sneak in amendments and conditions requiring local cost-sharing on the order of 10 to 30 percent—even for flood control. If the amendments and conditions stayed in the bill, only a handful might get built; when a state sees that it has to put up $50 million toward construction of a dam, its enthusiasm is apt to wilt like a plucked blossom. As for the Bureau, one of its largest projects, Central Utah, had been burdened with a supplemental repayment contract that absolutely guarantees recovery of all costs before the CUP receives any further funding. That provision, which could stop the project dead in its tracks, also had Reagan's private blessing. No one could predict how much of this would remain in the bill when it cleared Congress and reached the President's desk—and the Tellico experience led some to think, not much—but the pork barrel seemed finally to have lost its anchorings, and to be adrift on the very thing it helped produce: an uncontrollable tide of national debt.

CHAPTER TEN

Chinatown

Everyone knows there is a desert somewhere in California, but many people believe it is off in some remote corner of the state—the Mojave Desert, Palm Springs, the eastern side of the Sierra Nevada. But inhabited California, most of it, is, by strict definition, a semidesert. Los Angeles is drier than Beirut; Sacramento is as dry as the Sahel; San Francisco is only half as wet as Mexico City. About 65 percent of the state receives under twenty inches of rainfall a year. California, which fools visitors into believing it is "lush," is a beautiful fraud.

California is the only state in America with a truly seasonal rainfall pattern—stone-dry for a good part of the year, wet during the rest. Arizona is much drier overall, but has two distinct rainy seasons. Nevada is the driest state, but rain may come at any time of year. If you had to choose among three places to try to grow a tomato relying on rainfall alone, South Dakota, West Texas, or California, you would be wise to choose South Dakota or West Texas, because it rains in the summer there. California summers are mercilessly dry. In San Francisco, average rainfall in May is four-tenths of an inch. In June, a tenth of an inch. In July, none. In August, none. In September, a fifth of an inch. In October, an inch. Then it receives eighteen inches between November and March, and for half the year looks splendidly green. The reason for all this is the Pacific high, one of the most bewildering and yet persistent meteorological phenomena on earth—a huge immobile zone of high pressure that shoves virtually all precipitation toward the north, until it begins slipping southward to Mexico in October, only to move back up the coast in late March. More than any other thing, the Pacific high has written the social and economic history of California.

Actually, San Francisco looks green all year long, if one ignores the rain-starved hills that lie disturbingly behind its emerald-and-white summer splendor, but this is the second part of the fraud, the part perpetrated by man. There was not a single tree growing in San Francisco when the first Spanish arrived; it was too dry and wind-blown for trees to take hold. Today, Golden Gate Park looks as if Virginia had mated with Borneo, thanks to water brought nearly two hundred miles by tunnel. The same applies to Bel Air, to Pacific Palisades, to the manicured lawns of La Jolla, where the water comes from three directions and from a quarter of a continent away.

The whole state thrives, even survives, by moving water from where it is, and presumably isn't needed, to where it isn't, and presumably is needed. No other state has done as much to fructify its deserts, make over its flora and fauna, and rearrange the hydrology God gave it. No other place has put as many people where they probably have no business being. There is no place like it anywhere on earth. Twenty-seven million people (more than the population of Canada), an economy richer than all but seven nations' in the world, one-third of the table food grown in the United States—and none of it remotely conceivable within the preexisting natural order.

For all its seasonal drought, its huge southern deserts, and its climatic extremes, there is plenty of water in California for all the people who live there today. If, God forbid, another twenty-five million arrive, there will still be plenty for them. The only limiting factor will be energy: to get to where the people are likely to settle, a lot of the water has to be lifted over mountains. Take any ten of the largest reservoirs—Shasta, Bullard's Bar, Pine Flat, Don Pedro, New Melones, Trinity, a few others—and you have enough water for the reasonable needs of twenty-five million people; enough for their homes, their schools, their offices, their industries, even (in all but the driest times) their swimming pools and lawns. As for the other 1,190 California dams and reservoirs, their purposes are twofold: power, and, above all, water for irrigation. What few people, including Californians, know is that agriculture uses 85 percent of all the water in this most populous and industrialized of states.

California's $15 billion agricultural industry—and it is a gigantic, complex, integrated industry—is the largest and still the most important in the state, Silicon Valley notwithstanding. That figure, $15 billion, only begins to convey what agriculture really means to California. A great proportion of its freight traffic is agricultural produce. A disproportionate amount of the oil and gas mined in the state is used by agriculture. California agriculture supports a giant chemicals industry (it uses about 30 percent of all the pesticides produced in the United States), a giant agricultural-implements industry, an unrivaled amount of export trade. Because it relies on irrigation—and therefore on dams, aqueducts, and canals—there is a close symbiotic relationship with the construction industry, which is why politicians who lobby hard on behalf of new dams can count on great infusions of campaign cash from the likes of the Operating Engineers Local No. 3 and the AFL-CIO. And, more than any other state, California has been a source of opportunities for the Bureau of Reclamation and the Corps of Engineers.

All of this production, all of these jobs, all of these concentric rings of income-earning activity nourish California's awesome $300 billion GNP. It is a gross *state* product, obviously, but everyone seems to refer to it as the "California GNP," as if the state were a nation unto itself—which it really is, and nowhere more so than in the example of water. California has preached and practiced water imperialism against its neighbor states in a manner that would have done Napoleon proud, and, in the 1960s, it undertook, by itself, what was then the most expensive public-works project in history. That project, the State Water Project, more than anything else, is *the* symbol of California's immense wealth, determination, and grandiose vision—a demonstration that it can take its rightful place in the company of nations rather than mere states. It may also be the nation's foremost example of socialism for the rich.

In the 1850s, when the California gold rush was at full flood, the Great Central Valley traversed by the miners on the way to the mother lode was an American Serengeti—a blond grassland in the summertime, a vast flourishing marsh during the winter and spring. The wildlife, even after a century and a half of Spanish settlement, was unbelievable: millions of wintering ducks, geese and cranes, at least a million antelope and tule elk, thousands of grizzly bears.

The winter of 1861 and 1862 was the beginning of the end for this scene of wild splendor. Relatively few of the Forty-niners found enough gold to pay their fare back home, let alone retire in the style of which they dreamed. An astonishing number fell so ill or suffered so badly on the trip out—five months by ship or by land, with a roughly equal dose of hardship either way—that they never even made it to the Sierra foothills. San Francisco in the 1850s was full of broken men, searching for whatever day labor they could find. Many of them, having given up on returning home, decided to make a try at farming or ranching in the Central Valley. Most of the pioneers who followed the miners in wagon trains had farming on their minds, too, and by the 1860s the Central Valley was already a vista of cows. Because of the rainless summers, no important crop except wheat could be raised without irrigation, which was an alien form of agriculture to Americans. But the valley's chronic scarcity of moisture was suddenly reversed in 1861. A prodigious snowpack fell on the Sierra Nevada that year—somewhere around fifty feet—and a fast melt in May left the valley half submerged, a shallow sea the size of Lake Ontario. The floods would have been bad anyway, but their destructiveness was greatly intensified by the incredible amount of spoil—whole sides of hills—which hydraulic mining had sent down the rivers to the lowlands. The beds of the valley rivers were raised several feet, and could not begin to contain the torrential runoff; downtown Sacramento was under seven feet of water. The 1861 flood marks the beginning of the valley's obsession with bringing the rivers under control. Meanwhile, farther south, in the San Joaquin Valley, Henry Miller was using the same flood to acquire hundreds of thousands of acres of ephemerally drowned lands under the Swamp and Overflow Act. Miller's acquisitive nature, combined with the serendipity (in his case) of the flood, made him enough money to construct a large dam, and he soon had his hundreds of thousands of acres under irrigation. Before he died, he was likely the richest farmer in the United States.

When the valley ranchers saw how rich one could become through irrigation farming, they began to switch from cows and dryland wheat to crops. Few had Miller's ambition or wealth, however, and even when organized into irrigation districts they couldn't duplicate his dam, so they irrigated with primitive sluiceways cut from the rivers, much as did the farmers along the Nile. As for the state and federal governments, they wanted nothing to do with publicly financed irrigation projects, which were widely regarded as socialistic.

Everything changed with the invention, shortly after World War

347

I, of the centrifugal pump. Suddenly able to draw hundreds of gallons per minute out of the valley's shallow aquifer, the irrigation farmers no longer had to worry about building expensive canals, about cleaning them of silt; they no longer had to dream of regulating the rivers with dams to ensure summer flows. By the mid-1920s, thanks to irrigation pumping, California had surpassed Iowa as the richest agricultural state in the country; the Central Valley was the largest semicontinuous expanse of irrigated farmland in the world. The aquifer, which had collected over many thousands of years, was prodigious; before pumping began, it may have held three-quarters of a billion acre-feet. With the expansion of irrigation farming from a few thousand to millions of acres, however, the water table began to drop sharply. By the end of the Great Drought of the 1930s, the farmers had so badly depauperated the groundwater that the depletion curves were precipitous. Twenty thousand acres had already lost their groundwater and gone out of production; hundreds of thousands more overlay a groundwater table that was becoming dangerously low. Suddenly, the valley's reserve of groundwater, which had so recently seemed limitless, had only a few more decades of economic life.

The farmers could look in two directions for help: Sacramento and Washington, D.C. The Bureau of Reclamation, which was just completing Hoover Dam, had such a hold on the public imagination and the Roosevelt administration that it could build almost anything it pleased. On the other hand, it was supposed to create new subsistence farms in the West, not rescue the farmers who were already there from the consequences of their short-sighted avarice. Besides, Hoover Dam had been a great gift to California, and the other western states were waiting in line.

Sacramento, then, was the better bet, even if it couldn't dip into the federal treasury to finance the farmers' rescue. In 1933, the state legislature succumbed to heavy lobbying from the growers—who had become its biggest source of campaign contributions—and passed the Central Valley Project Act. The legislation was a striking display of ambition for a single state, proposing as it did the control, through dams and reservoirs, of the largest and third-largest rivers in California. The project bonds, however, could not be sold in the middle of the Depression, so the state was forced to let the Bureau of Reclamation take over the Central Valley Project; it was such a gargantuan scheme that the completion of its main features, including four big dams, required eighteen years.

The Central Valley Project was without question the most magnificent gift any group of American farmers had ever received; they couldn't have dreamed of building it themselves, and the cheap power and interest exemption constituted a subsidy that would be worth billions over the years. It is interesting, therefore, that originally many of the farmers *hadn't wanted* the Bureau to build the CVP.

The wedding between the Bureau of Reclamation and the Central Valley farmers was never more than a marriage of convenience, and, like many such marriages, it was soon on the rocks. As a starlet trades a virile but impecunious husband for a wealthy old tycoon, the farmers had, in effect, traded whatever hope they had of becoming agricultural grandees like Henry Miller for a secure supply of water. The Reclamation Act, which would apply, in theory, to the CVP even though it only delivered supplemental water to most, required a farmer owning more than 160 acres of land (320 for a man and wife) to sign recordable contracts to dispose of the excess holdings in order to continue receiving subsidized water. Since a great many farmers owned far more than that, the CVP looked as if it might become the first real land-redistribution device in U.S. history. Leasing acreage above and beyond the 320-acre limit was also prohibited under the act, and all excess holdings were supposed to be sold at their pre-project worth— which, in a valley where no crop could be raised without irrigation, was very little. On top of all this, farmers receiving Reclamation water were required to live on their land, not farm from Fresno or San Francisco, as many of them did. (The Bureau stopped enforcing the residency provision in 1916, but a federal court later determined that it was still valid.) The whole idea was to keep speculators away, and to open up arid land to as many new farmers as possible. "We weren't even supposed to give them 160 acres if they could make a living on less," says former commissioner Floyd Dominy. "And in warm states like California you could make a living on a lot less. We were talking about subsistence—nothing more."

The CVP, in short, was fundamentally different from every earlier Reclamation project. It did not create many new irrigated farms. It rescued thousands of farms that were already there, including a good many that were far larger than the law allowed. One of the "farmers" whose land lay within the service area of the Central Valley Project, and who was scheduled ultimately to receive its water, was the DiGiorgio Corporation, whose lands grew more commercial tomatoes than any state except Florida. Another was the Southern Pacific— not a mere railroad, but the largest private landowner in California, and the eventual owner of 109,000 acres in the Westlands Water

District, which was scheduled to become the largest single recipient of CVP water. The roster of landlords within the San Joaquin Valley was a Who's Who in corporate agriculture. Figures for 1946, published in a Senate report on the acreage limitation, reveal that Standard Oil owned 79,844 acres in the probable CVP service area; Will Gill and Sons owned 29,926 acres: the Bellridge Oil Company owned 30,120 acres; the Tidewater Associated Oil Company owned 25,554 acres; the Richfield Oil Company owned 10,718 acres; the Anderson and Clayton Company owned 19,144 acres; and the J. G. Boswell Ranch Company, which, among others listed, was already receiving Kings River water virtually free courtesy of the Army Corps of Engineers, owned 16,760 acres—part of a worldwide land empire later estimated at some 860,000 acres minimum. If such growers availed themselves of the Bureau's water, which they would doubtless want to do, the law was quite clear about the disposition of their cases: they would have to sell all lands in excess of 160 (or, more likely, 320) acres that received the subsidized water. The Reclamation Act's chief sponsor in the House, Frank Mondell, had said on introducing the bill that this divestiture provision "was drawn with a view to breaking up any large landholding which might exist in the vicinity of Government works." It was hard to imagine it stated more emphatically than that.

The threat of divestiture gave the big growers in the CVP service area fits, even if the Bureau was far more interested in building more dams than in trying to enforce such an unpopular law—especially when the Interior Department's lawyers, few of whom were legal stars, had to go up against some of the craftiest legal talent in the state. One modest example of how the farmers managed to deceive the Bureau was provided by the case of Russell Giffen, one of the big landowners in the Westlands district. A Fresno rancher who stitched together seventy-seven thousand acres of valley property—about seven times the acreage of Manhattan Island—Giffen was the largest cotton grower in the world: nationally, he also ranked just behind Boswell and one other farming company in the combined federal farm subsidies he received. In the 1970s, Giffen decided to clean up his estate for probate, and sold most of the land for $32.5 million. One of the buyers was a New York–based company called Jubil Farms, in which a Bakersfield couple, William and Judith Rogers, owned an 80 percent interest. The Rogerses, five other couples (most of them Rogers employees), the trusts of four Rogers children, and a mail-order denture company took title to 1,812 acres, all of it in parcels of 160 acres or less. All the new landowners then leased their property back to Jubil

Farms. Financing for the whole deal, in the amount of $3.5 million, was provided by the Nissho Iwai American Corporation, the subsidiary of a Japanese conglomerate, which happened to own the other 20 percent of Jubil Farms.

On paper, and in the Bureau's recordable contracts file in Sacramento, the requirements of the Reclamation Act were satisfied. In reality, the whole business was a translucent sham. One company, Jubil Farms, with its headquarters in New York City, was farming eleven times as much California land as the law allowed, with water it bought from the government for a few dollars per acre-foot—probably one-tenth of its worth on the free market, had there been such a thing. But this phony transaction, cynical as it was, was at least a gesture of compliance with the Reclamation Act. Other farmers chose to stonewall the Bureau in court, moving into compliance a centimeter at a time. Any self-respecting lawyer could drag such a case out for years, while his client continued to receive subsidized water the whole time. Others were being granted special exemptions by the Interior solicitor's office. No one has ever produced hard evidence, but there has been speculation that such exemptions bore a more than casual relationship to the size of a campaign contribution—and these were growers who could easily contribute $50,000 to a candidate's coffer. Rita Singer was a lawyer in the Interior solicitor's office through the 1960s and early 1970s, until she resigned and joined the legal staff of California's Department of Water Resources. "We'd be working on a case for months," Singer recalled during an interview in 1984, "and then my supervisors would send down an interpretation of the law that nullified our cause of action. Some of the subterfuges would be allowed. Others would be disallowed. There wasn't any rhyme or reason. In most cases we never got an explanation. It was legal hairsplitting. The solicitor's office would recognize 'distinctions' in cases that were identical.

"In effect, we were telling the growers, 'Go ahead. Do whatever you want.' When we moved for enforcement, it was always inconsistent. We never gave them a serious message that we meant business." In public, Singer says, the growers cursed the Bureau, calling it "dictatorial" and using epithets far stronger than that. "In private, they regarded the federal government as a laughingstock."

The Bureau knew full well that numerous violations were taking place in California. In 1965, Interior Secretary Stewart Udall ordered Commissioner Floyd Dominy to investigate the number of violations occurring within the service area of the Metropolitan Water District of Southern California—presumably to use the information as a weapon to force the Met to drop its campaign of divide and delay against the Central Arizona Project. Dominy's regional director in Boulder City, Arleigh West, hired an investigator from Phoenix named Ralph O. Baird to conduct a surreptitious hunt for violators, learning what he could through deed records and word of mouth. According to a December 30, 1964, blue-envelope memo sent to Dominy by West, "extreme caution was required"—apparently Baird thought he had some reason to fear for his safety. In three months, he managed to document ninety-nine violations of the excess-lands provision, totaling 105,229 acres. Several growers were irrigating thousands of acres with federally subsidized water wholesaled to them by the Met; the largest of them was the Irvine Ranch, which, in 1980, was the eleventh-largest landowner in California, with 28,257 acres of cropland, 82,344 acres all told, and $140 million in annual sales, according to the California Department of Corporations and Dun and Bradstreet. The list of violators has apparently been destroyed; not a trace of it could be found in Dominy's files or Bureau records in Boulder City. But West would admit in retirement that the violations had indeed occurred, that they might still be occurring, that in his estimation it was a clear-cut illegality under Reclamation law, and that—for reasons he "wasn't privy to"—nothing was done. "I didn't even dare mail the list to Dominy," he said. "I hand-carried it to him on a plane. He looked it over and put it away. He told me never to talk about it—and he said it in that tone of voice of his that meant you'd better obey—and I never saw it again. There were some pretty powerful people on that list."

In eighty-two years, the Bureau would see the breakup of only one major illegal landholding through to the end. That was the DiGiorgio Company, and it was stripped of its excess lands only because John Kennedy's Interior Department solicitor, Frank Barry, was relatively serious about enforcing the act. Later, when Jimmy Carter began making noises about enforcing the letter of the law again, the growers managed to lobby through (in 1982) the most extensive and, in the view of those who had watched in frustration as large growers evaded the Reclamation Act not just for years but for decades, the least justifiable revision of the law in its eighty-year history. The 160-acre limit was raised to 960 acres, and the leasing and residency restrictions were all but eliminated. In return, the growers are supposed to pay "full cost" for water delivered to all lands beyond the 960-acre limit, if anyone can figure out what full cost is; the Bureau has captured so much water in the West that no free market exists, and no one knows what the price of water should really be. (The chief author of the so-called Reclamation Reform Act was, not surprisingly, California Senator Alan Cranston.) Ironically, a Carter administration investigation a couple of years earlier—the first serious effort to gauge the degree of compliance with the law—had established that more than 90 percent of the acreage violations were occurring in California and Arizona, whose hot climate permits high-value crops and two-crop seasons—exactly the kind of climate where the original 160-acre limit is eminently fair. In Colorado, or Montana, or Wyoming, where most farms are at altitudes of at least four thousand feet, where the freeze-danger period runs to eight months, and where farmers are lucky to raise one good crop of low-value corn or wheat, a revision of the acreage limit was probably in order. But California's farmers, having received the gift of subsidized water not long before, were now awarded with a so-called reform whose chief result was to legalize wholesale noncompliance with federal law.

Even if the farmers sensed that, ultimately, such a "reform" was inevitable, the Reclamation law was at the very least a nuisance to the big growers in the CVP service area. And to many of the *really* big growers who owned huge acreages toward the southern end of the valley, between Fresno and Bakersfield, the Central Valley Project meant nothing at all. Nearly all of its water deliveries stopped at Fresno, and most of it went to the valley's east side. The biggest owners were south of Fresno, and a number were on the west side, where they had amassed fiefdoms of dirt-cheap scrubland, which they were either irrigating or hoping to irrigate someday. Not a single substantial stream drains the lee side of the Coast Range south of San Francisco—precipitation is barely six inches a year—so most of the west-side growers were utterly dependent on groundwater. It was fossil water, water that had accumulated over hundreds of thousands of years but which, at the rate it was being pumped, evaporated, and transpired by plants, would barely last another fifty, if that.

The Central Valley Project was, in fact, to have an interesting—a startling—effect on the groundwater table of the San Joaquin Valley. In Tulare County, at one test well, the aquifer dropped sixty feet between 1920 and 1960, the year the first CVP water arrived. Thanks to the flood of new surface water, the water table then rose twenty feet in nine years. Just three years later, however, it had dropped another thirty-three feet. In Kern County, where the depth to groundwater is much greater, farmers who had pumped from 275 feet during

World War II were pumping from 460 feet by 1965. The reason was obvious: the CVP and the Corps of Engineers projects on the Kings, the Kaweah, the Tule, and the Kern had delivered a lot of surface water throughout the valley, but they had encouraged so much agricultural expansion that they hadn't really relieved the pressure on the aquifer at all. For a while things were better; *then the projects actually made things worse.* Half the agricultural water used in the state was still coming out of the ground—even farmers who got cheap federal water continued to pump from their own wells in order to irrigate as much land as possible—and with three times as much irrigated land in production as there had been thirty years before, the big projects, besides depriving San Francisco Bay of half of its historical outflow, were just encouraging more pumping.

If there were no controls over groundwater pumping, a lot of farming in the southern half of the San Joaquin Valley faced extinction. By the late 1950s, the land was producing the greatest agricultural bounty in the world. Four counties—Fresno County, Kings County, Kern County, Madera County—that were consistently among the six wealthiest agricultural counties in the nation now looked as if they might topple like a row of dominoes. The farmers were like addicts, oblivious to their self-destructive ways; they were making so much money they wouldn't think of groundwater regulation, and any politician who so much as uttered the phrase was instantly marked as a threat. (A hand-picked Fresno legislator named Ken Maddy once referred to groundwater regulation as "World War III.") The only answer, then, was to try once more to have the citizens of the nation's richest state build them a huge project to bring in more water from somewhere else.

A Himalaya of obstacles, a series of seemingly insurmountable crests, stood between the San Joaquin Valley and its goal. Cities could afford to build dams and aqueducts, because urban water was at least ten times more valuable than irrigation water. And urban property was worth much more than agricultural land—the richest acre of valley land couldn't be traded for a fifty-by-one-hundred plot in Beverly Hills—so a big urban aqueduct would have billions in assessed valuation standing behind its bonds. But without the fabulous subsidies written into the Reclamation Act—the "ability to pay" clause, the exemption from interest, the hydropower profits shoveled right back to the farmers—few irrigation projects could be built anywhere. The only feasible ones were at perfect sites—where a first-class river with a first-class gunsight canyon lay right above some first-class irrigable land. If one had to build a huge dam on a middling river or an aqueduct hundreds of miles long, or if the water had to be pumped uphill, any nonfederal project was out of the question.

Unfortunately, the San Joaquin Valley had every one of those problems. Much of the land in need of rescue was second- or third-class, even fifth-class, with vast depths to groundwater or drainage problems or alkaline deposits in the soil. Some of the barren acreage held for speculative purposes by oil companies at the southern extremity of the valley had no usable groundwater at all. The big rivers were all in the north, so an aqueduct hundreds of miles long would have to be built. And since the San Joaquin Valley slopes imperceptibly upward as one travels south, most of the land lay several hundred feet above sea level. The water would have to go to sea level in order to cross the Delta, in the middle of the state; then it would have to be pumped three to five hundred feet uphill.

One thing was clear: the growers, rich as they were, could never finance such a project themselves, as cooperative irrigation districts had financed a few smaller projects on the east side. The state would have to build it. But California had become highly urbanized since World War II; the votes had shifted toward the cities on the coast. Those urban voters would be crucial in getting the project through the legislature. In fact, they would probably demand a public referendum, and a referendum cannot be bought as easily as an act of legislation. The urban voters would obviously have to subsidize the growers, too. Between the astronomical cost of building such a project *and* the cost of pumping the water uphill, the farmers could never afford it—not as long as CVP water was being sold to farmers next door for $3.50 an acre-foot. Not as long as their cotton-farming competitors in Georgia and Texas and Louisiana (cotton was the main crop in the southern San Joaquin) got their water free from the sky. And that meant only one thing: urban Californians would have to get some of the water. If they didn't, they wouldn't vote for the project.

Only one major city could logically be tied into the project, and that was Los Angeles. Water on its way from northern California to Los Angeles would, of course, pass right through the San Joaquin Valley. With its meager and erratic rainfall, Los Angeles had always been haunted by drought; the thought of more water always set off a Pavlovian response. On the other hand, the metropolitan region didn't really *need* the water. The city of Los Angeles proper was getting virtually all its needs fulfilled by its Owens River Aqueduct, and its countless suburbs, together with San Diego, had recently gotten the first of their 550,000-acre-foot entitlement from the Colorado River. By the early 1950s, Los Angeles was extending its aqueduct into Mono Basin, where it planned to divert the streams tumbling out of Yosemite that feed Mono Lake. Meanwhile, the Metropolitan Water District, the area-wide water imperium serving most of southern California, was already planning a *second* aqueduct to the Colorado River, which would double that supply. (This was water that southern California planned to "borrow" from Arizona's entitlement for as long as Arizona—stymied by southern California's Congressional delegation—was unable to build the Central Arizona Project.) Six million new people could settle in southern California before a water famine developed.

What made matters worse was that in order to deliver northern California water to Los Angeles, you would have to contend with the Tehachapi Mountains, which separate southern California from the San Joaquin Valley. Either you had to tunnel through that brutish, barren summit, or you had to pump the water up and over, two-thirds of a vertical mile. Since the Tehachapis sit on two major active earthquake faults, the Garlock and the San Andreas, tunneling would be risky. An earthquake could crush the aqueduct inside the mountains and shut off the water for months or years. That meant you would have to pump the water uphill, and the energy requirements would simply be awesome.

Why, then, would Los Angeles, which had most of its water arriving entirely by gravity from the Owens River, and the rest of the South Coast region, which got its water pumped by subsidized electricity from Hoover Dam, vote for a project that would sell them expensive water they wouldn't need for decades?

There were two possible reasons. One was Arizona's lawsuit against California over its Colorado River entitlement. If California lost, and the Central Arizona Project was built, southern California would have to forfeit a vast quantity of water, on whose promise much of its expected growth was based—water enough for three million people. With such stakes, its smug confidence that it would win the lawsuit had to be at least *somewhat* shaky.

The other reason southern California might go along was simply that opportunities to find water did not arise every year. Ten or twenty years would be required to complete the project; by the time it was finished, if the region continued its spellbinding growth, there would be millions of new people there. Los Angeles was growing so fast that it might not want to pass up *any* opportunity to find more water—whether it made good sense or not.

If one thought about it this way, and thought about it long enough, it all began to seem inevitable. Los Angeles would resist, it would drag its feet and fret, but once the project began to roll through the legislature it would climb aboard. Since southern California was, financially speaking, the key to the whole plan, it simply *had* to be dragged along. Southern California would sign on—out of fear, out of simple ignorance if nothing else. And southern Californians would get some of the water. But not too much.

During the winter of 1955, California was hit by the biggest floods since the monumental deluges of 1861 and 1862. After weeks of almost continuous rain, the rivers of the Sierra Nevada and the North Coast were tumultuous. The Eel River in the coastal mountains, which nearly dries up during the late summer and fall, was carrying the flow of the Yukon, the St. Lawrence, and the Missouri combined. The flood that spilled out of the mouth of the Eel—550,000 cubic feet per second—could have driven a fleet of battleships to Japan. The Sacramento River, despite the enormous bulk of Shasta Dam in its path, also rose to monstrous heights. But it was the Feather River, the Sacramento's main tributary in the northern Sierra, that was the killer.

At the end of December, as a series of huge, slow-moving cloud-masses wrung themselves out against the western wall of the range, the Feather River rose with hurricane suddenness. Swelling toward a crest of 250,000 cubic feet per second, it burst out of its canyon and flooded over Yuba City and Marysville, two small cities on the flood-plain below, near the confluence with the Sacramento. Within hours, a parade of houses, some wrecked and some nearly intact, was floating toward San Francisco. Yuba City was substantially destroyed, first by water and then by mud. More than twenty people died.

The San Joaquin growers would never have admitted to feeling relief, but the Marysville and Yuba City disaster was the best news they had heard in years. If there had to be floods, the Feather River's wrath was a serendipitous one, for it had already been chosen as their river of rescue.

The origins of the rescue project went back to the Bureau of Reclamation's United Western Investigation, the two-year study of transcontinental water-diversion schemes, completed in 1951, that had been the swan song of Commissioner Mike Straus. Having looked at the possibility of diverting the Columbia, the Snake, and all the larger rivers of the Northwest to the desert Southwest, the Bureau had settled on the Klamath, which it wanted to run in reverse, through a sixty-mile tunnel, back into the Sacramento River and then south. The plan had collapsed under the weight of its own ambition, and the Eisenhower administration had administered the *coup de grâce* by firing Straus. But the idea of a transbasin water diversion had quickened the pulse of California's state engineer, A. D. Edmonston, an unreconstructed, gung-ho, New Deal water-development type. In 1951, Edmonston, backed by the agricultural lobby, persuaded the legislature to give him enough money to undertake an "inventory" of the state's water resources—where water was in surplus, where it might be needed. What emerged three years later was something else entirely. The "inventory" had metamorphosed into something called the California Water Plan—a scheme for moving water southward that virtually duplicated the Bureau's plan. Only two things were different. There would be no Martian aqueduct leading from the Klamath River to Lake Mead; the remote Klamath was, in fact, out of the picture, replaced by the smaller but much more accessible Feather River. The other distinction was that the plan, as envisioned by Edmonston, would not be a federal project in any sense. It did not come right out and say so (perhaps because it hoped to get some federal help), but if one read between the lines, the state, or at least Edmonston, was now contemplating something this monumental on its own, just as it had originally planned the CVP. In fact, no sooner was the California Water Plan released than a new agency, the Department of Water Resources, was created out of a jumble of fifty-two agencies that had previously dealt with water, and given administrative powers to match.

Edmonston's scheme was mesmerizing. The largest water project ever built by a state or local government was New York City's Delaware water system, completed during World War II. The Delaware Aqueduct was eighty-five miles long and entirely underground—by far the longest hard-rock tunnel in the world. But the California Water Plan, in its first phase alone, contemplated the movement of four times more water over a distance six times as long. What was even more startling was that most of the water would go to irrigation. The Delaware Aqueduct had left New York, a Babylon of wealth, up to its ears in debt. But since each average household paid around a hundred dollars an acre-foot for water, and because the city had a huge commercial and industrial sector sharing the cost, the bonds would be paid off unless the city, for some reason, saw its growth curve go drastically into reverse. In the mid-1950s, the most that irrigation farmers could pay for water was, by a generous average, about $15 an acre-foot—less than a fifth as much as New Yorkers paid. And New York City's water arrived by gravity; California's farmers would have to pay for several hundred vertical feet of pumping, and Los Angeles would have to buy water pumped more than three thousand feet if the aqueduct went over instead of through the Tehachapi Mountains. (The United Western Investigation had already concluded that tunneling was too risky because of earthquake hazards). How could anyone afford it?

What passed for an answer provides an insight into the thinking of Edmonston and the water lobby and a good many politicians at the time. It was also as remarkable a statement as any certifiably sane person ever made. "It is believed that the cost of water *will not be a limiting factor* in ultimate development of the water resources of California," Edmonston's report read. "It is indicated that urban communities will always be able and willing to pay the cost of water to meet their municipal needs. Furthermore, it is considered probable that under pressure of future demands for agricultural produce, *the water necessary for greatly expanded irrigation development will be provided, at whatever cost may be required....* Many works financially infeasible today will undoubtedly be financed and constructed in the future" (emphasis added).

If anyone found such a statement preposterous—it was really like saying that, because of population pressure, we were bound to settle Mars—he kept his opinions to himself. The nearest thing to a publicly expressed doubt was the somewhat timorous suggestion of the Stanford Research Institute, which was asked to comment on the report, that a "definite price policy" would be required for "more realistic estimates of probable water sales," and that these, in turn, might well decide "the financial outcome of the project"—that is, whether or not it would end in the greatest bankruptcy of all time. The prevalent mood was more accurately reflected in a remark by the director of California's new Department of Water Resources, Harvey Banks—a remark he used in a great many of the speeches he gave to drum up support for the plan. "We must build now," Banks would say, "and ask questions later."

Meanwhile, the financial foundation of this most recklessly ambitious of plans was quietly being laid.

In the 1940s, some petroleum deposits were discovered off the southern Californian coast, near Long Beach. A few years later, when several major oil companies announced that they planned to begin exploiting the reserve, California decided to impose a severance, or extraction, tax, and agreed to give the revenues to Long Beach. After all, the money wouldn't amount to all that much, and Long Beach would need it to enlarge its harbor and cope with the mini-boom that would inevitably result. But after the tidelands oil revenues had been promised to Long Beach, in a contract duly signed by the city and state, the amount of oil offshore was discovered to be far greater than the initial estimates had indicated. The severance tax, if these estimates were correct, would amount to hundreds of millions of dollars over the years. As a result, the attorney general of California decided that there was only one sensible course of action: he nullified the contract.

The attorney general, whose name was Edmund G. Brown, was at the time a politician of less than starlit promise. Of middle height, a little squat, Pat Brown was a cheery Irish ward-heeler kind of politician—hale, earthy, utterly lacking in the complexity and awkwardness of his future rival, Richard Nixon. At about the same time he voided Long Beach's tidelands oil contract, Pat Brown developed an obsession, one that would remain with him for the rest of his life: water. As his water czar, Bill Warne, was to describe it later on, Bob Edmonston, the state engineer, had corralled him one day in the capitol and implored him to do something about "the water crisis." Brown, who grew up in San Francisco, said he wasn't aware there was any. Hadn't Los Angeles built its Colorado River aqueduct? Hadn't the Bureau just built the Central Valley Project? Yes, answered Edmonston, and that was precisely the problem. When you added a couple of lanes to a freeway or built a new bridge, cars came out of nowhere to fill them. It was the same with water: the more you developed, the more growth occurred, and the faster demand grew. California was now hitched to a runaway locomotive. At the rate the state was growing in both population and irrigated agriculture, it ought to be developing 750,000 new acre-feet each year. It was developing nothing. It had no major plans. Even if it started today, it would take twenty years to get a big project authorized, financed, and built. By then, California could have another seven or eight million people. "When we finally come to our senses," Edmonston told Brown, "the biggest bandwagon in history is going to come rolling through with water written all over it. If you want to be elected governor, you jump on it early—now."

It was a moment of epiphany, Brown told his friends. The thought of all those people arriving to no water, perhaps even to a Biblical drought, suddenly left him staggered. He would never be the same. Edmonston was right—water was worth developing at whatever cost. Nearly twenty-five years later, in 1979, he still believed it. In an interview he granted to the University of California's Oral History Program, Brown said, "No, I don't think it [cost] has any validity because you need water. Whatever it costs you have to pay it. It's like oil today. If you have to have oil, you've got to pay for it. What's the value of oil? What's the value of water? If you're crossing the desert and you haven't got a bottle of water, and there's no water anyplace in sight and someone comes along and says, 'I'll sell you two spoonfuls of water for ten dollars,' you'll pay for it. The same is true in California."

In 1958, after campaigning for and winning the governorship of the state, Pat Brown turned to the task of building his new dream, Edmonston's water plan, with an energy few of his friends had ever seen. He wheedled, cajoled, and mule-traded like a home-grown Lyndon Johnson, trying to accomplish something which, in its own way, was as daunting as Johnson's Great Society agenda: uniting a state divided into wet and dry parts, into sophisticated cities and hundreds of mean little farm towns, on a breathtaking agenda of water development. An Irish Catholic, Brown came across like a missionary preaching to the damned when he spoke to Californians of their water crisis. But he was also ruled, at times, by a Catholic's impulse to confess, and later he would tell an interviewer about his other, more prosaic motivation. "I loved building things," he blurted in an unguarded moment of candor. "I wanted to build that goddamned water project. I was *absolutely determined* I was going to pass this California Water Project. I wanted this to be a monument to *me*."

It must have been frustrating for Brown that the most implacable opposition did not at first come from northern California, as expected. It came from the corner of the state whose cooperation was essential if the project was ever to be built: metropolitan Los Angeles.

The stubborn resistance of the Metropolitan Water District of Southern California to a plan that would give it more water, at one stroke, than it had ever received was perfectly understandable from its point of view, even if it was baffling on its face. The water it had been counting on to meet its future growth was water that Arizona felt it rightfully owned, and was at issue in a seemingly endless lawsuit then before the Supreme Court. The Met's case, which was based largely on Arizona's initial refusal to sign the Colorado River Compact, was somewhat flimsy; it wasn't so much a legal argument as a game of chicken with the Supreme Court. In effect, the Met was daring the Court to take away water for three million people just as they were coming to depend on it. Because of the weakness of its legal position, southern California had at least as great a stake in thwarting bills that would have authorized the Central Arizona Project—something which its Congressional delegation had accomplished for twenty years. But the key to victory, in Congress if not in the Supreme Court, too, was demonstrating that the contested water was crucial to its growth, if not its very survival.

From the Met's point of view, then, the Feather River Project, which it ought to have viewed as salvation, was in a more immediate sense a threat. If it was built, it could wash away the strategic foundation of its legal and moral argument. It was an absurd position to be in, but the Met was committed—it had to pretend that no water was available from anywhere else.

As a result, the chairman of the Met's board of directors, Joe Jensen, decided to oppose the Feather River Project at all costs. The Met also disliked the idea of subsidizing the growers in the southern San Joaquin, who would receive half of the water but pay less than a third of the cost, and that was the argument it trundled out for public consumption. "If an urban area is to help carry this agricultural load," Warren Butler, the Met's vice-chairman, told the Los Angeles *Times* on August 10, 1960, "the urban area of Kern County should." (As Butler well knew, that urban area—Bakersfield—couldn't possibly afford to.) If any project bringing water to the South Coast was going to be built, the Metropolitan Water District was going to build it on its own. While Pat Brown thumped his Feather River Project up and down the state, Joe Jensen was talking about water from the Eel River, from the Trinity, from the Columbia—in due time (which was to say, *after* it had won its lawsuit with Arizona). While Brown talked of water famine in apocalyptic tones, the Met board issued a statement that "these forecasts of disaster are without foundation in fact." To the utter consternation of the growers, who were frantically lobbying for the project under the auspices of the Feather River Project Association, the Met went after the idea hammer and tongs, arguing against it on every conceivable ground: cost, need, feasibility, practicality, even morality. In 1957, the board of directors staged an opulent victory dinner in honor of several legislators who had successfully crushed the project's hopes in the last legislative session. "They refused to listen to reason," Bill Warne, Brown's water chief, would recall. "I must have gone down to talk to them a dozen times, but all they could think about was that they might weaken their case before the Supreme Court. I didn't think they would. As a matter of fact, I didn't think they had much of a case to begin with. But *they* thought they did."

Pat Brown was wise enough to see that eventually the Met would be brought into the fold. "I remember Norman Chandler saying he was going to oppose the project in the Los Angeles *Times* unless we went along with the Metropolitan's viewpoint," Brown recalled later in an interview. "I told Norman, 'Then you just oppose the project, Mr. Chandler. The people will look at you with scorn as the years go on.' So he walked out and I didn't know whether he was going to support it or not. . . . But they *had* to do it. I knew we had them. I knew that if they didn't get this bond issue over, they'd never get water in southern California."

Actually, though, the Met's opposition wasn't Pat Brown's thorniest problem, even if it may have been his most frustrating one. The thorniest problem was the cost.

Brown knew that a lot of voters will vote reflexively against any bond issue, even one to hire police and build jails in the midst of a crime wave. They would rather not pay taxes and buy guns, rather not pay taxes and dig wells. This was especially true in southern California, the home turf of the John Birch Society and the Liberty Lobby. Northern Californians were sure to be violently opposed, even if they were promised some of the water. Northern Californians had always resisted sending *their* water to L.A. Between metropolitan San Francisco, Sacramento, San Jose, Oakland, Stockton, and Contra Costa County, there were four million people and at least a million voters (out of three million who might vote statewide) who were certain to go against him. Those votes had to be counterbalanced by "yes" votes in southern California. But when those good Republican migrants from the Middle West down there saw how much the project would cost, they would blanch. How could he possibly win? There was only one way, Brown decided. It was to lie.

"Lie" is a strong word, but in this case it is advised, because one day Pat Brown would all but admit it himself.

It was, to begin with, hard to say how much the project would cost, except that it would cost a bundle. Oroville would be not only the world's tallest dam, but its fourth most massive. San Luis, in the Coast Range foothills farther south, would be the *fifth* most massive dam in the world, nearly two miles long. Two of the world's biggest dams; the world's longest aqueduct; the world's highest pump lift, surmounted by the world's most powerful pumps—five full batteries of pumps; a chain of smaller dams and reservoirs strung out to receive the water—all of this would be incredibly expensive. The Department of Water Resource's feasibility report, known as Bulletin 78, offered an estimate of $1,807,000,000, but an economist for the RAND Corporation, Jack Hirschleifer, immediately tore it to shreds. Reading between the lines, Hirschleifer noticed that though the report mentioned Oroville Dam, its cost estimate *failed to include the expense of building it*. It was an extraordinary omission, to say the least. The DWR explained that the dam wouldn't be needed right away and might be built later. (It would be built right away.) The estimate also failed to include the cost of branch aqueducts to San Luis Obispo and Santa Barbara, although the DWR had promised those cities water and Pat Brown was counting on their votes. And there was no "cross-Delta facility," later known as the Peripheral Canal, on the price list, though without it the project could never deliver its full annual yield of 4,230,000 acre-feet. In fact, it was unclear how the above-mentioned facilities, immense as they were, and assuming all were built, could deliver that much water every year. Even ignoring that, Hirschleifer wrote in his report, "the correct figure, for capital costs only and accepting official estimates, is certainly in excess of $3 billion." Three billion dollars in 1959 was the equivalent of $12 billion in 1985. What state would vote for a $12 billion bond issue today? Not one. Pat Brown knew that very well. That was why he decided to say that the project would cost $1.75 billion—just over half of what he knew, or should have known, the estimate should have been.

Years later, a conversation with an unthreatening interviewer from Berkeley's Oral History Program finally brought out the truth. "We were questioning, could we even pass a bond act of $1.75 billion," Brown told his interviewer, Malca Chall. "We didn't know exactly the cost of the project. We hadn't priced it out to any exactitude. As a matter of fact, we thought it would cost *more* than the $1.75 billion, probably in the neighborhood of $2.5 billion. . . . We had to scrape and pull to put this project together. I mean don't kid yourself. [Laughs.] It was a close fit and $1.75 billion was about all that we felt we could get a bond issue [*sic*]. We were afraid to make it $2 billion. It was like $1.99 instead of $2. We thought that just sounded better to the people.

"I remember someone telling me how Huey Long operated in Louisiana where the legislature wouldn't give him money to build a road," Brown added. "He started at one end, built it to here, and left a great big gap."

$1.99 instead of $2. Like many of the New Deal politicians of his era, Brown had a habit of dropping the last few zeroes from his figures. These were *billions*, not pennies, that were being talked about, back when a billion was still real money. Brown's $750 million lie (and, if Hirschleifer was right, it was considerably more than that) was a $3 billion lie in modern money. And it would set the stage for a monumental predicament, one that the governor's son, ironically, would be the first to have to face. In order to embark on building the project, the DWR would have to have contracts in hand to sell water. That was the whole idea—demand before supply. Those contracts would ultimately demand that the state deliver 4,230,000 acre-feet of water. But if the initial bond issue failed to deliver the full amount, and the voters subsequently rejected bonds to expand the project, the state would expose itself to a torrent of crippling lawsuits from cities and farmers who had planned their growth and invested their money on the promise of water it could never deliver. The damage claims might cost more than the project itself. Back in 1959, however, all of that still seemed far in the future.

One of the reasons Pat Brown felt confident with his misleading cost estimate had to do with the tidelands oil contract between Long Beach and the state which, as attorney general, he had abrogated in 1954. Long Beach was understandably outraged, and immediately filed suit against the attorney general's office. To its amazement, the California supreme court sided with the state. It was a remarkable legal opinion. The attorney general had nullified a signed contract to let a city have some revenues, and the court had upheld it even though the state had no demonstrable need for the revenues. It didn't even have a plan to use them. What kind of court was this?

An answer—a speculative one—popped up in another part of the governor's long 1981 interview with Malca Chall. Actually, they were discussing something else—Brown's decision to try to use the old Central Valley Project bonds which the voters had authorized in

1933 to scrape together another $170 million in cash. That, in its own right, was a matter of peculiar legality: using a bond issue passed twenty-seven years earlier—a bond issue that was meant to finance the Central Valley Project—in order to construct an *entirely different water project*. But, mystifyingly, the California supreme court had okayed that, too. "That was Phil Gibson, the chief justice, with whom I worked very closely," Brown told his interviewer. Then, according to the transcript, he laughed. "He was a great chief justice and it was great to validate those bonds. . . . The chief justice worked very, very closely with me in all of those decisions. You see the supreme court didn't have to take original jurisdiction in those cases. But I would call the chief justice and say, 'Chief, this is very important. I want you to take it.' And invariably he did."

Phil Gibson died before he could be interviewed for this book, and Pat Brown, in a personal interview, hotly denied ever having tried to influence the court's decisions. But Gibson's obituary in the San Francisco *Chronicle* described him as perhaps the most powerful and influential chief justice in the history of the court, and he was, after all, Pat Brown's bosom friend. All of this leaves at least a *suggestion* that, in California, where an issue as important as water was concerned, strict legality, separation of powers, honesty, and other niceties of governmental conduct could easily be ground into mush.

In 1959, after intensive lobbying by Pat Brown, the California state legislature agreed to allot the tidelands oil money for the water project—an annual interest-free loan of $25 million, repayable . . . whenever. It was an open-ended deal; the Tidelands Oil Fund could keep feeding the project until the oil ran out, which might take a hundred years. Even Brown would admit in yet another startling little confession to Malca Chall that "it was another subsidy to the big farmers." But it was not just any old subsidy. It was a subsidy that had an architectural elegance, a wonderful symmetry to it. Several of the "big farmers" who would get much of the water from the Feather River Project were oil companies—the same oil companies that were paying into the Tidelands Oil Fund. In exchange for a modest extraction tax—quickly offset by the billions they would make on the easily accessible oil—they would have their barren, worthless acreages in the San Joaquin Valley turned opalescent green. *And* they would get the growth, and the cars, and the freeways, that would increase the demand for—and the cost of—the oil!

In the last days of the legislative session in 1959, the legislature

gave final approval to the Burns-Porter Act, which authorized the
Feather River Project—now rechristened the California Water Project—subject to a statewide referendum on the bond issue scheduled
for November of the following year. Once again Pat Brown had shown
what great Irish politician's instincts he possessed. One of the two
sponsors, Hugh Burns, was a northern Californian who had made a
reputation *opposing* water diversions from the north. Brown, among
whose attributes modesty was notably absent, would later boast,
"The fact that I selected Hugh Burns to carry the bill in the Senate . . . that was political *genius* if I do say so myself." Cyril Magnin,
"Mr. San Francisco," was persuaded to serve as campaign chairman
there. The supporters put on prominent display in southern California
were fiscal conservatives and Republicans. Everyone would get a little
water, too: Napa County, Alameda County, the Santa Clara Valley.
But the Kern County Water Agency alone would get thirty times as
much as all of California north of San Francisco.

Only in December, *after* the legislature had already authorized
the project, did the Department of Water Resources make a stab at
an economic justification, in a report called *An Investigation of Alternative Aqueduct Systems to Serve Southern California*. Instead of
trying to justify the project by weighing costs against benefits—which
is what the Bureau of Reclamation did, or went through the motions
of doing—it compared the cost of the project to the most expensive
alternative: desalinating seawater. On that basis, it concluded that
the project made sense. But as Jack Hirschleifer disdainfully com-
mented in his RAND Corporation report, you can justify *anything* if
you compare it to a more expensive alternative.

The critics were too few and too late. On Friday, November 4,
1960, just four days before the referendum was scheduled, the Metropolitan Water District capitulated and signed the contracts that
indicated its support. The Los Angeles *Times* was now in favor. The
only widely read newspaper that adamantly opposed the plan was
the San Francisco *Chronicle*. When the votes finally came in, forty-
eight of the fifty-eight counties in the state had voted against the
bonds. But the populous counties in the artificial paradise of southern
California all went heavily for the project. It was, after all, early
November, and they hadn't seen real rain since April. November—
the last days before the rainy season began. That was another little
bit of subtlety from Pat Brown. The bond issue passed by 174,000
votes.

———

The California Aqueduct begins at Oroville Dam, a man-made pyramid of such improbable dimensions—the height of the Pan Am Building, the width of the Golden Gate Bridge—that it appears much smaller than it actually is. In February of 1980, in the midst of a long spell of wet Pacific fronts, Oroville Reservoir, despite its capacity of something like a trillion gallons, was full, and the dam was spilling—seventy thousand cubic feet per second, the Hudson River in full flood, roaring down the spillway at forty miles per hour, sending a plume of mist a thousand feet in the air.

Below the dam and the Thermalito Afterbay the Feather River joins the Sacramento, which flows through the Delta out to San Francisco Bay. In the winter of 1980, the Delta, a huge reclaimed marsh protected by weakening dikes made of peat, was in danger of being reclaimed by nature; the levees were being repeatedly breached by the flood, and farmed tracts of three thousand acres were disappearing under twenty feet of water. From a chartered Piper Cub, the odd vulnerability of this Brobdingnagian contrivance was manifest: the levees keep intruding seawater from mingling with southern California's water as it traverses the Delta on its way to the California Aqueduct, which begins south of there. The Delta is the system's weakest link, and one could see why from an airplane: below was the water on which a million-plus acres and ten million people depend; a few miles west, lapping hungrily at the first phalanx of levees, was the tongue of a salty ocean that humbles all.

At the south end of the Delta, the Clifton Court Forebay appeared below us—a receiving reservoir big as a Minnesota lake that rises and falls like the Bay of Fundy in rhythm with southern California's thirst. A wide canal leads out of the forebay toward a rectangular building resembling the nonnuclear end of a very large nuclear power plant. The building houses the delta pumps—a battery of ten-thousand-horsepower machines that suck Feather River water thirty miles across the Delta before it can escape to sea, then lift it the first three hundred feet toward its ultimate thirty-four-hundred-foot rise over the Tehachapi Mountains. The water disappears inside and reappears thirty stories up the hill, at the beginning of the California Aqueduct. From overhead one could see the water spurting out of the siphons, each one wide enough to consume a freight car, as if shot from a water cannon. The aqueduct wound southward through the pale foothills, as level as a railroad grade, and disappeared in valley heat. It is 444 miles long, the longest river, if you can call it that, in California, and it is entirely man-made.

Interstate 5 parallels the aqueduct for two hundred fifty miles through the San Joaquin Valley. Not many years ago this was utterly barren land: it sprouted some patches of green during the winter, then lay dead during summer's drought. Now it is a wide swath of cotton and orchards growing billions of new dollars in agricultural wealth. A hundred miles south of the Clifton Court Forebay the water arrives at San Luis Dam, now the ninth-largest dam in the world, a structure almost as immense as Oroville. What is bizarre about San Luis is that its basin, in the rain shadow of the Coast Range, is devoid of constant streams. Nearly all the water in the huge reservoir, eight miles across, is Feather River and Sacramento River water, pumped uphill. San Luis adds stability and security in a state inclined toward unpredictable weather and tectonic upheaval; in such a theater of disaster, a state utterly dependent on reservoirs needs to store its water in as many places as possible. The penalty for this added security is the giant jolt of electricity required to lift the water another three hundred feet. It is a Sisyphean lift, for the water comes right back down again when the San Joaquin Valley and Los Angeles call for more. You recapture some of the expended energy in turbines when you release it from San Luis, but the overall loss is around 33 percent. More than anyplace else, California seems determined to prove that the Second Law of Thermodynamics is a lie.

This whole hydrologic ballet, this acrobatic rise and fall of megatonnages of water performed on a stage twice the length of Pennsylvania, is orchestrated by a silent choreographer in the Water Resources building in Sacramento: a Univac Series 904 computer punched and fed floppy disks by a team of programmers. At the south end of the valley, the aqueduct arrives at its moment of truth. The Sierra escarpment curves westward and the Coast Range bends eastward and they mate, producing a bastard offspring called the Transverse, or Tehachapi, Range. The Tehachapis stand between the water and Los Angeles, which sits in the ultramontane basin beyond.

The water is carried across the Tehachapis in five separate stages. The final, cyclopean one, which occurs at the A. D. Edmonston Pumping Plant, raises the water 1,926 feet—the Eiffel Tower atop the Empire State—in a single lift. To some engineers, the Edmonston pumps are the ultimate triumph, the most splendid snub nature has ever received: a sizable river of water running uphill. At their peak capacity, if it is ever reached, the Edmonston pumps will require six billion kilowatt-hours of electricity every year, the output of an eleven-hundred-megawatt power plant. Moving water in California requires more electrical energy than is used by several states.

Having surmounted the Tehachapis, the water charges downhill again through closed siphons and a battery of turbines that steal some of its energy back. Soon it is in an open aqueduct again, which ultimately forks like an interstate highway: the West Branch goes straight to Los Angeles, and the East Branch continues southward across the high Mojave Desert to the vicinity of Riverside, where it terminates in Lake Perris—a reservoir. Lake Perris is six hundred miles from Oroville Dam.

Walking along the West Branch Aqueduct, you see people strolling, bicycling, and fishing as if this were a river through a city park instead of a concrete highway of water under a blazing sun in a shadeless desert where it rains seven or eight times a year. The Department of Water Resources stocks the aqueduct with fish—that way it can write off a fraction of the project's cost to recreation—but fish seem to find their way in there anyway. In fact, sections of the aqueduct have respectable fishing for striped bass, which cannot easily tolerate the pollution of Chesapeake Bay or spawn in the freakish cross-Delta currents that the project pumps have caused, but which don't seem to mind a three-hundred-foot lift in a pressurized elevator of water. This turbid, computer-controlled, concrete-walled river is the unlikeliest habitat imaginable for striped bass—as fitting a symbol of wild, fecund nature as one could find. The water project seems as make-believe as California itself, in its relentless quest to deny its desert heart.

Aside from lying about the true cost of the State Water Project, Pat Brown and his water resources chief, Bill Warne, had been less than candid about another matter of supreme importance: how much water the initial bonds would actually buy. Most Californians, it seems, believed they were buying four million acre-feet or more. But, as early as October of 1960, Joe Jensen had predicted that the bonds would never suffice to develop that much, and he was right. The initial facilities, it turned out, could deliver around 2.5 million acre-feet, perhaps three to three and a third million in wetter years—at least a million acre-feet less than the various cities and irrigation districts had signed up to buy. Meanwhile, population projections for southern California continued their horrifying march; in 1961, the Los Angeles

Department of Water and Power was estimating that forty million people would live in the South Coast area by 1990. By February of 1962, Alfred Golze, Bill Warne's chief engineer, was already calling for new reservoir construction on the North Coast as early as 1972; Warne himself said that "new reservoirs, dams, tunnels, and diversion projects must be undertaken somewhere in the North Coast area within the next twenty years."

As it turned out, a splendid opportunity to do just that arrived sooner than Warne dared hope. In December of 1964, California was hit by floods that were even wilder than the great floods of 1955. In three days, from December 21 to 24, Blue Canyon on the American River recorded twenty inches of rain. All the rivers were roaring, from Big Sur to the Oregon border and beyond. But the river that rampaged most was the Eel. The Eel rose seventy-two feet from its bed. It snapped bridges with surgical precision; it uprooted three-hundred-foot redwoods; it swept fifty million board feet of timber out to sea—driftwood which, for the most part, is still piled along California's beaches. At Scotia, near its mouth, the Eel was carrying the Mississippi River in a garment bag; 765,000 cubic feet of water were going by each second. Every town along the river was damaged—some were never seen again. The high-water mark can still be seen along the Avenue of the Giants, displayed on a number of redwood trees. It is about three stories above the road.

The Christmas flood—the second "hundred-year" flood in just nine years—had Brown, Warne, and the Army Corps of Engineers issuing statements expressing profound dismay while they privately rubbed their hands with glee. Within months, the Corps, the Bureau, and the Department of Water Resources had locked arms as the State-Federal Interagency Task Force, ready, once and for all, to choke California's untamed rivers into submission. Every river on the North Coast, except the Smith and the Klamath, was to get at least one big dam; the various forks of the Eel were to get eight. But the Bureau and the Corps kept getting into scraps over who was to build what first, and Pat Brown's term was running out, so, one by one, the dams fell into obscurity. By 1966, when Ronald Reagan became governor, the only dam in which strong interest was still being expressed was the largest, Dos Rios, on the Middle Fork of the Eel. With twice the storage capacity of Shasta Lake, Dos Rios was the ideal addition to the State Water Project; it could deliver another 900,000 acre-feet, almost enough to bring the total yield, in normal years, up to the 4,230,000 acre-feet the state had promised to deliver. The site was reasonably close to the Central Valley; all one had to do was dig a twenty-one-mile tunnel through the Yolla Bolly Mountains and dump the water into Stony Creek, a tributary of the Sacramento.

Dos Rios had three things going against it, though the Eel had acquired such a black reputation that none seemed likely to prevent its being built. One was the fact that it would do nothing to control the Eel. During the Christmas flood, more than 500,000 cubic feet per second had poured out of the South and North forks and the main Eel, which would all remain undammed. What did it matter if one's house was under twelve feet of water or eleven feet four inches? Those eight inches at Scotia were the sum total of the flood crest that Dos Rios would contain; a local rancher, Richard Wilson, who had a degree in agricultural engineering from Dartmouth, proved it, and the Corps could only wish him wrong.

Another drawback was that the reservoir would drown an Indian reservation and the town of Covelo—population two thousand—but that sort of thing had been done many times before. (The Corps had included the flooding of the reservation in its benefit-cost analysis, but had it down as a *benefit* because the Indians would get a "nicer" town somewhere else.) The third drawback was that the new governor of California, Ronald Reagan, wasn't particularly interested.

Reagan, as a westerner, should have been a friend of dams, but he was growing more conservative by the hour, and true conservatives tend to dislike great public works. He also distrusted the Corps of Engineers—a feeling which the Corps, if anything, seemed to reinforce. Reagan's resources secretary, Norman Livermore, remembers asking the Corps to do two cost-benefit analyses—one using the $3\frac{1}{4}$ percent interest rate which the Corps planned to use, the other using the $6\frac{1}{2}$ percent rate that reflected economic reality. "When they gave it to me," remembers Livermore, "I looked at the two columns, and the bottom line was exactly the same. I took it into a cabinet meeting and really got a laugh."

For four and a half years, Reagan stalled on Dos Rios while the water lobby was practically battering down his door. The head of his Department of Water Resources, Bill Gianelli, a short, square man with a Vince Lombardi temperament and an American flag perpetually stuck in his lapel, was, according to Richard Wilson—who was the leader of the ragtag opposition—an "absolute zealot" in favor of building the dam. So was Don Clausen, the Republican Congressman representing the North Coast. But Wilson was a friend of Norman

Livermore's, and Livermore had Reagan's ear. According to Wilson, when the governor realized he finally had to say yes or no, he asked Livermore to give him every argument he could think of against the dam. When Livermore was finished, he emerged from Reagan's office and almost fell into the arms of Don Clausen, who was waiting to give Reagan his arguments *for* the dam. Clausen was a voluble and persuasive man, but later he confided to his intimates what had really happened during the meeting. Halfway through it, Clausen said dispiritedly, the governor had fallen asleep.

Wilson insists he got the story from Livermore himself, though Livermore, still a Reagan loyalist in 1984, said he "couldn't remember" it. Whatever the case, in 1969, Reagan finally announced that he would not support Dos Rios Dam. In the press release explaining his reasoning, he talked about costs, poor economics, the frailty of the flood-control rationale. Privately, though, Reagan was upset about flooding the Round Valley reservation. "We've broken enough treaties with the Indians already," he is reported to have said.

By the time Reagan left Sacramento, in 1974, the Department of Water Resources was predicting that the dreaded shortfall—demand for water greater than supply of water—might be as little as fifteen years away. To plan the final phase of the State Water Project, get it approved and funded, and build it would easily require fifteen years. Through an irony some found delicious, then, the person who took it upon himself to complete the project that Pat Brown had left unfinished was none other than the apostle of the "era of limits," the first politician to proclaim that "small is beautiful" and "less is more": Jerry Brown—Pat Brown's son.

"He did it for the old man" was how Jerry Brown's last loyalists explained the spectacle of the younger Brown promoting what seemed certain to become the most expensive water project in the history of the world. Depending on which of the Brown administration's estimates one believed—and a new one seemed to appear every six months or so—the cost of completing the project was either astonishing or flabbergasting. What Pat Brown hadn't foreseen, when he underfunded the bond issue to ensure that the voters would pass it, was inflation. Because of inflation, it would cost two to five times more to deliver the project's last 1,730,000 acre-feet than it had cost to deliver the first 2.5 million. The most detailed estimate, released by the DWR in 1980, pegged the cost at $11.6 billion. Interest on the bonds—based on a rate of 9 percent, which was then three points too low—would add another $12 billion. It was unheard-of. The only comparable project anywhere in the world was Itaípu Dam, which would end up costing $19 billion and help Brazil dig itself a bottomless financial hole. But Itaípu would at least generate 12,500 megawatts of electricity to help pay for itself. Brown's Phase Two water plan would *consume* an awesome amount of power, because the water, cubic miles of it, would be pumped not just uphill but over a mountain range.

Jerry Brown's dilemma—which was insoluble, but which he thought he could solve anyway—was trying to please the water lobby and his large environmental constituency at the same time. He wanted a project, but he wanted it to be "environmentally sound." To be environmentally sound, there could be no on-stream storage—no dams or reservoirs on any significant wild streams. The North Coast rivers, with 28 percent of the state's runoff, were therefore off limits. Instead, Brown wanted to skim high "surplus" flows from the Sacramento River during the winter and spring and store them. But all the natural storage basins were at elevations well *above* the river. His Department of Water Resources engineers, acting on orders some of them considered insane, finally settled on a basin in the foothills of the Yolla Bolly Mountains, near Red Bluff, which had a stream running through it and a couple of small preexisting flood-control dams. They would run a twenty-mile aqueduct up there, up a thousand-foot slope, and dump the Sacramento surplus flows in. The reservoir, to be called the Glenn "Complex," would be as large as San Francisco Bay. It would submerge both preexisting reservoirs and a couple of small towns. There would be some contribution from Stony Creek, but not much; a tremendous amount of energy would be required to pump water uphill. A second off-stream reservoir—smaller, but still a third the size of Shasta Lake—would be created farther south, in the foothills near Mount Diablo. Below there, water was already being pumped three hundred feet uphill for storage in San Luis Reservoir—another off-stream site—and farther south it was being lifted to improbable heights by the Edmonston Pumps. If it was all built, the California Water Project would require about as much electricity as both units of the $5.4 billion Diablo Canyon nuclear reactor could produce, and Brown *didn't* want that built. Where, then, would the energy come from? The DWR set loose a bewildering flurry of "soft path" proposals—geothermal plants, wind machines, solar-generating ponds. The meanest of the governor's critics, taking note of his interest in Buddhism, said it was all going to be powered by yak dung.

George Gillette, chairman of the Fort Berthold Indian Tribe Business Council, weeps as he watches Secretary of the Interior J. A. Krug sign a contract whereby the tribe sells 155,000 acres of its reservation's best land in North Dakota to the government for the Garrison Dam and Reservoir Project on May 20, 1948. Gillette said of the sale: "The members of the Tribal Council sign the contract with heavy hearts. . . . Right now, the future does not look good to us." *(AP–Wide World Photos)*

For more than fifty years, the tiny man-made river in the foreground, the Granite Reef Aqueduct of the Central Arizona Project, has been viewed by Arizonans as the one thing that can save them from oblivion. In the next century, however, as seven states suck up their full share of the feckless and overappropriated Colorado River, the aqueduct may run as empty as the diversion canal on the right. *(Bureau of Reclamation)*

Teton Dam, just as the flood abated. Hours earlier, the flow of four Mississippi Rivers was thundering through the breach. The big concrete structure on the left is the spillway, whose outlet works hadn't been completed and which couldn't be used to begin emptying the reservoir when the first signs of trouble appeared. The height from river level to the crest of the remnant of the dam is about thirty stories; at the spot from which the photo was taken, boiling waves were more than one hundred feet high. *(Bureau of Reclamation)*

The remains of Teton Dam, as seen from the air, hours after the flood.
(Bureau of Reclamation)

The three main antagonists in the Narrows Dam controversy. To Colorado Governor Richard Lamm (AT LEFT) the dam was an offer he couldn't refuse. To water lawyer Glenn Saunders (BELOW, LEFT) the dam symbolized a spendthrift society clinging to obsolete hopes. Former Colorado State Engineer C. J. Kuiper (BELOW, RIGHT) still believes the dam could fail catastrophically, as Teton did.

A section of the spillway at Glen Canyon Dam completely destroyed by raging floodwaters spilled during the very wet El Niño winter of 1982–83. Although the Glen Canyon spillways run directly beneath the dam through rock that is mainly sandstone, the Bureau of Reclamation insists that the structure itself was never threatened. *(Bureau of Reclamation)*

OPPOSITE, ABOVE: The desert blooms on the Gila Project near Yuma, Arizona. Not far from here, the Hohokam, one of the world's great irrigated civilizations, went extinct.

(Bureau of Reclamation)

OPPOSITE, BELOW: The Control Room of the California Water Project, where the man-made flow of nearly a trillion gallons a year is orchestrated. *(© Peter Menzel, 1986)*

The California Aqueduct winds through Lost Hills, turning nearby desert, once considered worthless, into a billion-dollar agricultural bonanza. (© *Peter Menzel, 1986*)

The A. D. Edmonston pumps, which send water from the Feather River over the 3,400-foot summit of the Tehachapi Range, consume the electrical output of a nuclear power plant and stand between Los Angeles and disaster. *(© Peter Menzel, 1986)*

Mono Lake, an inland sea in eastern California desert country, is slowly dying. Most of the water that used to flow into the lake is now being diverted and piped to Los Angeles, three hundred miles away. As the lake's depth has decreased, natural calcium formations called tufa towers have been exposed. *(© Peter Menzel, 1986)*

Salt deposits cover ruined farmlands in the San Joaquin Valley. A million acres in California alone may ultimately be affected.

(© Peter Menzel, 1986)

Brown was so sympathetic to environmentalists in other ways that a lot of them were hesitant to oppose the plan. (The California Sierra Club's leadership first endorsed it, only to be overturned in a referendum taken to the members at large.) After all, his director of water resources was Ron Robie, a smart, elfin, fast-talking lawyer who had been instrumental, while on the Water Resources Control Board, in writing decision 1422, a decree requiring minimum fresh-water flows through the state's most important estuary, the Delta. Robie's assistant director was Gerald Meral, a former staff scientist for the Environmental Defense Fund. Meral, a gaunt, bearded zool-ogist, was a great fan of wild rivers, an expert whitewater kayaker—there was even a falls and pool on the Tuolumne River named for him. How could people like Jerry Brown, Ron Robie, and Gerry Meral propose anything really bad?

One answer came from Tom Graff, a lawyer for the Environ-mental Defense Fund and Meral's former colleague. The centerpiece of Brown's plan was called the Peripheral Canal, an outsize channel to be constructed around the collapsing Delta. The Peripheral Canal had been a top priority of the water interests for forty years. What Brown wanted to do to win the environmentalists' and northern Cal-ifornia's support was guarantee minimum releases to the Delta from the canal—a big surge of water would be let out every few miles, turning the Brown Canal, in effect, into a giant sprinkler hose. Robie and Meral argued that their plan would mimic the primordial river inflows and eliminate the cross-flows caused by the Delta pumps; in so doing, it would help salmon and striped bass spawn and actually improve the fishery. In fact, if one listened to them long enough, the whole $11.6 billion scheme was mainly for the sake of the Delta fish. But Graff pointed out that the Peripheral Canal would remove an-other couple of million acre-feet of water from the Delta and San Francisco Bay, water that normally went through at high flows. Delta outflows had already been reduced from 35 million acre-feet to around 17 million, and the fresh water that still managed to escape the project pumps was needed to wash pollution out of the bay; besides, the whole bay ecosystem had grown dependent on large seasonal fresh-water flows over tens of thousands of years. Who was to say that the bay, having already seen its fresh-water outflow decline by 55 percent, wasn't on the brink of ecological ruin?

Besides, what if the legislature, dominated by southern Califor-nia and the agricultural lobby, decided to overrule the Delta outflow guarantees? And what if it decided to dam the North Coast rivers?

With the canal in place—it was, after all, to be four hundred feet wide, and would be capable of containing most of the Sacramento River—the water could finally be moved. The Glenn Reservoir site, curiously, was at the receiving end of the proposed Grindstone Tunnel, which was to have carried water from Dos Rios Reservoir through the Coast Range. The Peripheral Canal, according to Graff, was a "loaded gun pointed at the North Coast."

Brown's answer to that, in 1981, was yet another set of environmental guarantees. When his first canal legislation failed to pass the legislature, he supported a new package known as Senate Bill 200, which included an amendment to the state constitution keeping the North Coast rivers wild and scenic forever—which meant no dams. All of the larger ones had had such designation since 1972, but it was state, not federal, protection, and the legislature could annul it at will. Brown's constitutional amendment would have made it impossible to develop the Eel and the other rivers unless the state's voters, by a two-thirds majority, decided at some point to repeal it.

Jerry Brown was quite sure his proposal would mollify the environmentalists, but it had a totally different result. Until then, feeling about the Peripheral Canal—a term that became shorthand for everything else in the plan—had sloughed along traditional lines: northern Californians were mostly against it, the valley and the South Coast were mostly for it. But his decision to include constitutional protection for the North Coast rivers in S.B. 200 created a stranger alliance than Brown and the growers. It was, in the minds of some, the oddest alliance since the Hitler-Stalin Pact. All of a sudden, two of the mightiest, wealthiest growers in California were on the side of Friends of the Earth.

The two retrograde growers were the J. G. Boswell Corporation and the Salyer Land Company, which had long dominated affairs at the valley's southern end. Salyer and Boswell were two of the main beneficiaries of the Corp of Engineers' Kings River and Kern River dams, which gave them year-round irrigation water that was nearly free and tens of thousands of new acres in the old bed of Tulare Lake. They had figured prominently in the Feather River Project Association, which helped get the State Water Project authorized in the first place. In 1980, Boswell owned 206,021 acres in California, plus hundreds of thousands of acres elsewhere; it was the biggest grower in the state. Salyer's holdings were smaller, about 77,000 acres, more than the five boroughs of New York. In one year, Boswell's private political action committee, or PAC, ranked among the top ten in the nation in the amount of money it showered around. For all their power and money, however, Boswell and Salyer had a problem. They were located in the part of the valley with the severest groundwater overdraft. Someday, if pumping wasn't to become prohibitively expensive, more surface water would have to be brought in—a lot more water, since the valley's groundwater overdraft was projected to surpass the yield of the State Water Project by 1999. Boswell and Salyer felt there was only one place it could come from—the Middle Fork of the Eel. The idea of making the North Coast rivers wild and scenic seemed like a prescription for their economic demise; they were also incensed, as a Salyer spokesman put it, that "the Delta fish come before we do" —an allusion to the minimum Delta outflow guarantees in S.B. 200.

By the end of 1981, to everyone's amazement, Boswell and Salyer had poured $406,000 into the campaign against the Peripheral Canal, outspending the thirty-three largest contributors on the pro-canal side—which included Shell Oil, Getty Oil, Southern California Edison, Lockheed, the Fluor Corporation, and Walt Disney Enterprises— by $73,689. It helped, but not enough. Later that year, the legislature passed S.B. 200, subject to ratification by the voters in a special election to be held in June of 1982. The planning meetings among the canal's opponents, as they prepared for the referendum, must have been something to behold. Environmentalists and northern Californians were there because they thought S.B. 200 was too weak. Boswell and Salyer were there because they thought it was too strong. Delta interests didn't much care one way or the other; they just wanted to keep getting their irrigation water free. (As water on the way to the federal and state aqueducts flows between their levees, they simply slurp it out; they would have to pay to get it out of the canal.) After a series of ferocious catfights, the strategy that the canal opponents and Russo-Watts, the public relations firm handpicked by Salyer and Boswell, agreed on was to hammer away at the cost.

It wasn't a bad idea. The votes the canal would need were in southern California, and those voters would be saddled with most of the cost. About 70 percent of the original works of the State Water Project were being financed by the Metropolitan Water District's customers. Actually, they paid for the project twice: through daily water rates, and through an assessment of twelve cents on every $1,000 of property value in the service area, which they paid whether they got water or not. (The city of Los Angeles still got 93 percent of its water from the Owens Valley and Mono Basin, but paid the assessment like everyone else because it was subsumed under the MWD.) Using simple arithmetic, one could divide the number of Metropolitan customers into the $11.6 billion that Phase Two was supposed to cost, multiply that by .70, and come up with a figure of $3,000. That was the average cost of S.B. 200 to each household in southern California. If one added the $12 billion in interest that would have to be paid on the bonds, the figure doubled. As if that weren't bad enough, the California Energy Commission was predicting that energy, in the year 2000, would cost thirty-three cents per kilowatt-hour, which was six times what it cost in 1981. At those rates, it would cost at least $50 just to pump one average family's share over the Tehachapis. And that share was only a fraction of the family's *annual use,* because the MWD's full entitlement to State Project water amounted to less than a third of all the water used in southern California. People would also be paying for water pumped sixteen hundred vertical feet from the Colorado River; they would be paying for water pumped from the ground. If one added it all together, the cost of water in southern California would be . . .

The estimates varied about as wildly as estimates can. State Senator Reuben Ayala, the chief sponsor of the Peripheral Canal bill, said it would cost the average family only $5 extra per year. The Met said $50 per year. Dorothy Green, the leader of the opposition in southern California and the founder of an organization whose acronym had somehow been tortured into spelling WATER, was saying that a year's worth of water would cost $1,400 in the year 2000 if the canal and everything else were built. The public remained utterly confused by all of this, which, as far as both sides were concerned, was fine. The campaign could then be run on fear. Magazine spreads began appearing in southern California showing a child's upturned tricycle at the edge of a dried-up reservoir. Northern California billboards were papered with huge letters (courtesy of Salyer and Boswell, who ended up spending $1 million on the campaign) that simply read, "It's Just *Too* Expensive." Everyone knew what "It" was, just as everyone knew what horrible fate the abandoned tricycle was supposed to represent. One leader of the stop-the-canal campaign, a businessman, talked off the record about how dirty a war over water in California can get:

"The business community in southern California has got the business community in northern California scared half out of its wits. Crown Zellerbach, the big San Francisco paper company, has been told it better not take an anticanal position if it wants to sell any more paper south of San Jose. They've stayed neutral. The San Francisco Chamber of Commerce is staying neutral, too, even though an informal plebiscite among its members showed 92 percent of them opposed to the Peripheral Canal. The chamber's board of directors has refused to share those results with the membership. *We're* going to have to tell them. The chairman of the board is opposed to the canal—he *hates* it—but he won't say so in public. These guys are representing the interests of their own corporations, not of northern California, or even the Chamber of Commerce. They're scared to death. It's hard for us to raise any money, because contributions are iden-tifiable and everyone is scared they're going to be found out and blacklisted down south. It's like a banana-republic election where the houses of the opposition candidates all catch fire."

Nineteen seventy-six and 1977 were the third-driest and the driest years, respectively, in California history. Shasta Lake, the reservoir on which billions of dollars in farm income depend, was nearly dry, down to an eighth of its capacity; water rationing was imposed all over the state. But 1978, which looked as if it might herald the be-ginning of California's end, was, to everyone's surprise, a wet year; 1979 was even wetter. In 1980, Los Angeles was clobbered by a succes-sion of subtropical Pacific storms that threatened to float it out to sea. By then, memories of the drought—which had panicked almost everyone in California, even environmentalists in Marin—were grow-ing dimmer. 1981 was drier than normal, but not by much. 1982 marked the beginning of what climatologists called the "El Niño episode," when parts of the state got three times their normal rainfall and relentless storms caused $1 billion worth of property damage. It would be excessive to say that a string of five rain-laden years de-termined the outcome of the vote on the Peripheral Canal, but it would probably be true. Had the referendum been held in October of 1977, when most of the state had barely seen rain in a year and a half, Californians might have voted for anything, even dragging icebergs down from the North Pole. Memories of the drought had grown faint, but memories of inflation hitting 15 percent in 1980 were strong. Houses that had cost $35,000 in 1974 were being snapped up for $200,000. The referendum on the Peripheral Canal carried southern California by two to one. But in counties around San Francisco it lost nine to one. When the final tally was in, the Peripheral Canal had gotten around 40 percent of the vote. It was trounced.

As it turned out, however, the big San Joaquin growers would have plenty of water—miraculously cheap water—for a long, long time.

Twenty-two years earlier, after Californians had voted in favor of building the State Water Project, the Department of Water Resources began to circulate water sales contracts in the San Joaquin Valley. Few of the farmers were willing to sign. The irrigation water would be relatively unsubsidized—the main subsidy being the $25 million annual contribution from the Tidelands Oil Fund, which was called a "loan" even though virtually none of it has been repaid—and it would be expensive. The development cost would be around $20 per acre-foot, plus the price of delivery, so most irrigation water would cost anywhere from $25 to $45 per acre-foot. And that was actually a discount price, held low by cheap power rates and a drawn-out repayment schedule, so that the farmers could afford to build laterals, headgates, and all the other appurtenances they would need to shift from groundwater to surface irrigation, or from no irrigation to irrigation. Eventually, the cost would shoot up dramatically to recover the initial discount. Farther north and east in the valley, farmers were buying water from the Bureau of Reclamation for $2.50 to $3.50 an acre-foot. The most anyone paid for Bureau water was $7.50. In a lot of places you could still pump groundwater for $15 an acre-foot. How could the State Project's customers compete? The difference between water at $3.50 an acre-foot and water at $30 an acre-foot—if you irrigated 320 acres and used four feet on your crops— was $33,920. That was more than the net income of a typical small farmer in a year.

There was, however, a way to make the water affordable. The phenomenal growth rate that California had sustained since the turn of the century was finally slowing down. (In 1969, for the first time ever, the state registered a net loss of a few thousand people.) The Metropolitan Water District wouldn't need its full entitlement for a good while—that was common knowledge—and now it looked as if it could do without it for even longer than expected. But water projects do not make more water available in small increments. Once Oroville Dam was completed, an immense amount of water would suddenly be available. The system was likely to have a big surplus sloshing around in it for years. What was wrong with letting the growers have that water for the energy cost of delivery?

The growers made their case to Bill Warne and found him sympathetic. Naturally, he said, there ought to be some restrictions. The surplus water should go only to lands that overlie the aquifer (the extreme southern part of the San Joaquin has no usable groundwater at all). Otherwise it would bring a lot of land into production that would be stranded when the surplus deliveries ended, creating even more pressure for new water development. The water would have to be sold on an interruptible basis, from one year to the next, and it ought to irrigate only pasture or alfalfa, not permanent crops such as orchards. Otherwise, when the surplus ran out, the farmers, having invested a lot of money in trees, would begin pumping groundwater like crazy to protect their investment, and demand still more dams, and the vicious cycle the State Water Project was intended to stop would begin all over again.

If Warne was amenable to the idea, Joe Jensen, the thin-lipped, mercurial Mormon chairman of the Metropolitan Water District, was not. The growers, he told Warne, were self-interested, avaricious cutthroats who wanted a free ride on the Met's customers. They—the urban users—would be paying capital and interest costs on each acrefoot developed, whether it was delivered to them or not. In fact, they would be paying higher development costs on the surplus water, without seeing a drop of it, than the growers would pay to have it delivered to them. Why, shouted Jensen, should *not* receiving water cost more than receiving water? The whole idea was an outrage. The Met, Jensen said, would never stand for it.

Jensen held his board of directors under "an almost absolute dictatorship"—those were Warne's words—so the prospect that the growers would get anywhere were slim. When Warne tried intervening on the growers' behalf with some friendlier members of the Met's board, they spurned him. One day, however, an old colleague of Warne's from his Interior days, who had since become chief counsel for the Kern County Water Agency—which owns the largest entitlement of all in the State Project, 788,409 acre-feet—called. The lawyer, Stanley Kronick, told him that the issue of cost-of-delivery surplus water was extremely important to the growers, and could jeopardize the whole future of the project, because without it the growers might not be able to pay their way, and the project could default. Kronick wondered whether he shouldn't go down to Los Angeles and speak with the board himself.

Warne remembers being faintly amused. "Sure, Stan," he said. "You're welcome to try. But you aren't going to get anywhere, you know. Joe Jensen is adamant, and the rest of them have got their heels dug in. I've been over it with them a dozen times already."

Nonetheless, Kronick said, he was going to try. A few days later, Warne received another call from him. When he picked up the telephone, he felt sure that he knew what he was going to hear.

"Well," said Kronick, "they agreed."

The fifty-two members of the board of directors of the Metropolitan Water District are protected, by charter, against conflict-of-interest disclosures. No one has to release information on stock ownership, business connections, or anything else that might provide a clearer picture of where their true interests lie. As a result, no one knows much about them—though many have tried to find out—except what is obvious: most are white, male, middle-aged or older, wealthy, and passionately committed to water development.

Therefore, the most cynical interpretation of the Met's decision to let the San Joaquin growers have its customers' unused water cannot be proved. They did it, this argument goes, because when they realized what a bonanza it would be to the growers they all invested in valley agriculture themselves. After all, if they had their customers' interests truly at heart they should have held out for a higher price, forcing the growers to share at least some of the capital and interest costs. The people who make this argument usually take their listeners on a guided tour through California's verdant history of public graft to reinforce their point. Bill Warne, for his part, doesn't share such paranoid suspicions. In his mind, they did it because they knew they would need the valley's help when the time came to get more water from the north. "With the environmental opposition to new development, the Met realized it had to stop fighting with the valley and close ranks," he says. "Maybe this was their way of making peace."

Whatever the answer, the first of the surplus water was delivered to the San Joaquin Valley in 1973. Precipitation stayed near or above normal for the next ten years, except for the two freak years of the drought, and consumption in southern California remained well below predictions. As a result, there was a literal flood of surplus water in the valley, sold at an average price of $3.50 per acre-foot—the same incredibly low price the Bureau charged. Even in 1976, the beginning of the drought, the state inexplicably let go of 580,110 acre-feet of "surplus" water that it might well have husbanded for the near-catastrophe waiting around the corner. The Kern County Water Agency, whose clients include many of the biggest and wealthiest growers in the state, took 442,250 acre-feet of that amount, setting a pattern: since 1973, it has gotten between one-half and three-quarters of the share. By the end of 1981, it had received a total of 1.8 million acre-feet of surplus water. It got it for around $6 million—the alleged cost of delivery. Meanwhile, according to Richard Walker and Michael

Storper, two economists at the University of California, the Met's customers had been assessed about $170 million for the same water—water they never received. The growers had gotten a $164 million gift.

After peaking at 524,247 acre-feet in 1979, Kern County's surplus deliveries began to diminish as the Met called on more of its entitlement, but it was virtually guaranteed hundreds of thousands of acre-feet for years. Meanwhile, as the Peripheral Canal debate was raging on, and the Met was saying that without the canal southern California would perish, an internal study, not intended for release, predicted that "as much as 750,000 acre-feet [of unused water] in the MWD service area" would be available if the canal was built. In other words, the Peripheral Canal would not so much save Los Angeles as allow the growers to keep using hundreds of thousands of acre-feet of surplus water while metropolitan Los Angeles paid for it. The farmers, for their part, seemed to be counting on it, for they were using surplus water to expand their acreage well beyond a leval sustainable with contract water alone. According to at least one agricultural economist at UC-Davis, they were also using it to irrigate permanent crops—exactly what Bill Warne had said they must not do. It would have been very foolish of them to do so unless they expected to have a lot of surplus water for a long time.

It was the same old story again. The big farmers had managed to get something (a lot of water) for next to nothing. People in Los Angeles, meanwhile, were being taught a different lesson: that you can get nothing for something.

All of this raises a further question: who, exactly, are the farmers getting most of the water?

In 1981, Les Melville had been growing olives for nearly fifteen years on his fifty-acre farm near Oroville, the town that grew up alongside the Water Project's monumental dam. He bought the farm in the 1960s, and through innovation, and a lot of lavish care, he raised the previous owner's average yields from around thirty tons a year to 250 tons a year. It was a remarkable effort. Then, having finally accomplished what he set out to do—prove you can make a good living on a fifty-acre farm—he began to go broke.

"When we started here in 1967," Melville told an interviewer, "we ended up with some $500 per ton of fruit. In 1980, we were down to $350 a ton. We're getting less for our fruit now than we were getting in 1946." Melville's costs, meanwhile, were constantly rising, and his disposition and his health were failing. The problem wasn't competition from imported olives; it was the California Water Project.

At the other end of the valley, the Prudential Insurance Corporation was farming more acres of olives than all four-hundred-odd olive growers in Tehama County, where Les Melville's farm is. Prudential had five thousand acres planted in olives on its McCarthy Joint Venture A ranch near Bakersfield, in which it owned a 75 percent interest, and those five thousand acres were only about a quarter of the entire ranch. Its olive trees were planted very close together, like hedgerows—not because the country wants more olives than anyone can produce, but because the fruit can then be harvested by machine. Machine harvesting wastes fathomless numbers of olives, but saves a substantial amount of labor. The olive-harvesting machinery was developed, in large part, by the taxpayers of California, who finance the agricultural experimentation programs of the University of California's extension service—which are largely devoted to inventing and perfecting labor-saving machinery. (One of its star creations, the tomato harvester, is said to have displaced twenty thousand agricultural workers.)

When Prudential's olive trees matured in 1978, they began producing all at once. California's production of olives increased by 46 percent in that year—a single year—and olive prices fell like overripe olives. Of all the state's growers, however, only one was relatively unaffected by the drastic drop in wholesale prices: the Prudential Insurance Corporation. The company was well aware that its prolific production would cause the collapse of the market, and therefore decided to write an unusual contract with Early California Industries, the state's largest independent olive processor. In exchange for an opportunity to defer the purchase price of $1 million, Early Cal agreed to buy Prudential's entire harvest. Previously, it had bought from many small growers around the state, like Les Melville, who now had to look elsewhere to sell their production. The deferred payment, Early Cal proudly remarked in its annual report, "bears no interest and is repayable only on termination of the contract." It was what labor unions like to call a "sweetheart" deal. With a single stroke, a New Jersey–based insurance corporation had, in its first year of competition, with a single gigantic orchard, pretty much captured the olive market of the United States.

Like a number of other corporations, holding companies, and investor cartels, Prudential got into farming in the 1960s, when Congress passed legislation allowing investors to deduct all expenses on a number of crops (chiefly orchard fruits and nuts) while the trees or vines are maturing and bearing no fruit. All of a sudden, a lot of land that wasn't worth very much was worth a great deal—in an inverted sense. According to economists at the University of California at Davis, the new tax provisions amounted to a tax break of $346 on an acre of land for persons in the 70 percent bracket. For corporations it was less of a break, but still a good one. With its 75 percent share of the McCarthy Ranch, Prudential could realize a tax saving of around $1 million per year, farming the government. Then, when the trees were mature, it could begin earning at least that much income every year. It was all made possible by the State Water Project.

The land on the far southwestern side of the San Joaquin Valley, where the McCarthy Ranch sits, is underlain by a brackish, boron-poisoned aquifer. The quality of the water ranges from execrable to unusable. The climate is so dry—around six inches of rainfall a year—that the few small freshets barely trickle during the rainy season. Until the late 1960s, when the first deliveries from the California Water Project arrived, $50 an acre would have been a good price. Now it is worth at least $2,000 an acre.

In August of 1981, the California Institute for Rural Studies released a report on property ownership in five water districts within the service area of the State Project. Most of the districts are in Kern County; most of the farms are neighbors of the McCarthy Ranch. Together they accounted for two-thirds of all the entitlement water delivered to the San Joaquin Valley by the project. However, because the Kern County Water Agency, the region's main water broker, had been receiving a flood of surplus water (1.8 million acre-feet) as well, the five districts had actually received about half of *all* the water the State Project had delivered throughout the state.

The CIRS report corroborated what the Department of Water Resources had taken unusual pains to point out: that the majority of farmers receiving project water were small farmers. Of 479 identifiable owners in the five water districts, 291, more than half, had farm holdings of 160 acres or less. Nine out of ten worked farms smaller than 1,281 acres. But those farmers owned less than a third of the total acreage; the other two-thirds, which amounted to 227,545 acres, was owned by eight companies.

The largest of the farmers was Chevron USA, the main subsidiary of the Standard Oil Company of California. Chevron owned 37,793 acres in the immediate vicinity, in addition to 42,000 acres scattered elsewhere in the valley. In second place, with 35,897 acres, was the Tejon Ranch, one of the great land empires of California—272,516 acres all told. The principal stockholders of the Tejon Ranch are members of the Chandler family, which owns the Los Angeles *Times*— the strongest voice for water development in California for the past eighty years.

In third and fourth place were two more oil companies, Getty and Shell, which owned 35,384 and 31,995 acres, respectively. The presence of Getty (and Chevron USA) in the service area of the California Water Project again pointed up the architectural brilliance with which the project was conceived. They pay a severance tax to California on oil they pump off Long Beach, which is immediately put into a fund that makes annual interest-free "loans" of $25 million a year to the State Water Project, which delivers doubly subsidized irrigation water to their formerly worthless land.

Fifth place belonged to Prudential's McCarthy Ranch, whose total acreage was 25,105. (If these numbers are bewildering, it helps to know that a good-size Illinois farm consists of six hundred to a thousand acres.) In sixth place was the Blackwell Land Company, whose 24,663 acres are part of a burgeoning U.S. land empire being assembled by a company of foreign investors, among them S. Pearson and Sons of England, Mitsubishi of Japan, and Les Fils Dreyfus of Switzerland, an offshoot of Lazard Frères.

Tenneco, the huge chemicals and food conglomerate, was seventh among the eight largest owners, with 20,180 acres. A few years before, Tenneco executives had been making some unusually candid statements to the effect that small family farms are the most efficient food-producing units human beings could ever create, and said it might give up farming altogether. When the State Water Project became operational, the company began singing a different tune. In the early 1970s, it bought the old James Ben Ali Haggin–Lloyd Tevis estate, the Kern County Land Company—300,000 acres of prime valley land—and metamorphosed into one of the most ardently competitive agribusiness growers in the world.

In last place, with 16,528 acres—a plot of land that is still considerably larger than Manhattan Island—was the Southern Pacific Railroad, the largest private landowner in California. In 1981, besides owning 700,000 acres of California forest and range land, Southern Pacific owned a large portion of downtown San Francisco and 109,000 acres in the Westlands Water District, where, between the good graces of the Bureau of Reclamation and the dilatory expertise of its battery of lawyers, it was still receiving subsidized federal water for $7.50 an acre-foot.

In California, when the issue is water, the ironies seem to string out in seamless succession. Bill Warne, the man who built the California Water Project, was in government service nearly all his life, and never made a great deal of money. In his mid-seventies, Warne was still doing consulting work; he also owned a small almond orchard outside of Sacramento. The consulting work was lucrative, but unpredictable. The almonds, on the other hand, were a good, reliable source of income. Or they were until Tenneco, by far the largest almond grower in the state, made a bid in 1981 to control the market—the same kind of power play that Prudential made with olives. "The bastards really went for our throats," Warne admitted ruefully during an interview early in 1982. "They beat the hell out of the rest of us in the market, and that includes me." Of course, one could just as well have said that Warne beat the hell out of himself. It was *his* project that irrigated Tenneco's almond orchards; it was *his* aqueduct that flowed practically within view of his small almond ranch, destined for the huge factory farms in the desolate southern reaches of the valley. Because of the hot climate down there, the crops grown on irrigation water have always been, in large part, specialty crops: almonds, pistachios, grapes, olives, kiwis, melons, canning tomatoes. And because the national acreage given over to such crops is comparatively small (California accounts for most of it), a single big grower who doesn't mind being a little ruthless can whiphand the market pretty much as he pleases.

Bill Warne's project had become a Frankenstein's monster. But its maker still refused to turn against his creation. "The moment we began settling California, we overran our water supply," he said. "We've never gotten to the point where you could just stop. And we never will."

Whether or not that is true, it was hard to imagine, by 1985, how the State Water Project would ever be completed. The old warhorses, the Bill Warnes and Pat Browns, might still be talking about the "unconscionable waste" of water flooding down the Eel River each winter (as Warne did, to whoever would listen), or saying that "the Columbia doesn't need all that water that flows down there—it's ridiculous, between you and me" (as Pat Brown did during an interview in 1979), but those who followed them in public office and were faced with the nitty-gritty problem of diverting the Eel, or the

Columbia, or any so-called "surplus" water that could be found, discovered that it was like uncovering a nest of killer bees. Jerry Brown's successor, George Deukmejian, was elected with large infusions of cash from the growers in the San Joaquin Valley, where he is from. As expected, Deukmejian, a deeply conservative Republican, proved himself ideologically double-jointed on the issue of water development; while wading through the state budget with a machete, he made a wide circle around the Peripheral Canal, which he wanted to build but call something else, and he spoke approvingly of plans to send a lot more water southward. The reaction from northern California politicians, who, in the meantime, had managed to seize control of the speaker's chair in the legislature, and, through Congressman George Miller (who represents the Delta) of a key committee in Congress that can probably thwart much of what Deukmejian hopes to build, was so intemperate that the governor, after a year in office, was hardly mentioning the canal anymore.

Deukmejian may merely have decided to lie low, but by 1985 the people who will feel the impending shortages most acutely—the growers and the cities of the South Coast—appeared to have given up on the idea; either that, or they were mollifying their opposition while they stealthily plotted some hydrologic equivalent of Pearl Harbor. In June, the State Water Contractors, an organization representing all the customers of the State Water Project, issued a report predicting a shortfall, by the year 2010, of 4.9 million acre-feet statewide—the domestic consumption of twenty million people. The deficit within the State Project service area alone would be about 1.9 million acre-feet. Without more construction, the San Joaquin Valley would receive 733,000 fewer acre-feet than it was counting on. The South Coast cities and irrigation districts, which signed contracts to buy 2,497,500 acre-feet from the State Water Project, could be guaranteed a firm yield of only 1,120,000 acre-feet. Only in wet years could each region hope for more; during extended droughts they would receive even less. Meanwhile, a state report on groundwater pumping was describing the overdraft as "potentially critical" in eleven subregions of the Central Valley, most of which were in the service area of the State Water Project. What made things worse was that the valley's ancient saltwater aquifer, lying below the fresh water, could eventually rise to take its place.

Those figures, if they were accurate, bespoke calamity from both regions' points of view. What was startling, therefore, was the fact that the report said virtually nothing about sending more water from northern California southward. Its solutions—which it admitted were only halfway solutions—were for the most part the same ones that had been proposed by the environmental lobby, and which the water lobby had scorned just a few years earlier. The Imperial Valley farmers, according to the report, could conserve about 250,000 acre-feet if they lined their earthen canals and improved their irrigation practices; the water could then be sold to Los Angeles. The occasional surplus Colorado River flows below Parker Dam, as long as they lasted, could be stored in groundwater basins near Los Angeles and San Diego. Reusing treated sewage water (the report didn't go so far as to advocate drinking it) could save a few tens of thousands of acre-feet. Delta channels could be widened and levees rebuilt to allow slightly greater flows. The state could buy the surplus water in the Central Valley Project, for as long as that lasted. It was nickel-and-dime stuff, no heroics; the water savings might amount to 1.6 million acre-feet, which would only make up a third of the projected statewide shortfall. Only two new reservoirs, both off-stream and judiciously located south of San Francisco, were even mentioned, and the report didn't even advocate that they be built; it merely called for "investigations." (Initial investigations by the Department of Water Resources suggested a per-acre-foot price range of $310 to $400 from one of the reservoirs, Los Banos Grande; since that was fifteen to twenty times the cost of Oroville water, it was hard to imagine who in his right mind would buy it, at least as long as there was groundwater to overdraft.) Not a word was said about the Peripheral Canal.

Ironically, the State Water Contractors' report was accompanied by a rather lengthy history of the State Water Project, written by the first head of the Department of Water Resources, Harvey Banks, which called the project "a high water mark symbolizing the results of the collective efforts of people of many points of view to resolve their differences equitably through the political process and to move forward with a program of statewide benefit." Reviewing the history of the project, it was hard for some to see how Banks managed to arrive at such a conclusion. To begin with, Californians had been sold a pig in a poke: a project whose cost was deliberately and extravagantly understated, and whose delivery capability was much less than they had been led to believe. Completing just the first phase of construction had required federal cost-sharing at San Luis Dam, nearly half a billion dollars in tidelands oil subsidies, and several hundred million dollars in scavenged new revenue bonds. Then, when spectacular agricultural and urban growth had occurred on the promise of water the project couldn't deliver, a new leadership of "new age" politicians had tried to sell the voters an even bigger and more expensive pig, which they had spurned. Los Angeles had fought with the growers, then formed an alliance with them, then fought again, then formed another alliance; two of the biggest growers had been instrumental in launching the project, then played an indispensable role in the defeat of the Peripheral Canal; and, all the while, the state had remained bitterly divided along the geographic and climatologic lines the project was supposed to supersede. This was "cooperation"?

As for the "statewide benefit" Banks wrote about, the California Water Project may have been necessary if the state was to continue to grow at its historical, breathtaking rate. But that was the point. The growth it created was not "orderly" growth, to use that buzzword of which the water developers are so fond. It was giantism. It was chaotic growth. In southern California, project water is allowing some four hundred acres to be subdivided, malled, and paved over each day, transforming what could have been a Mediterranean paradise into one of the twentieth century's urban nightmares. In Kern County, it created, solidified, and enriched land monopolies that are waging economic war against the small farmers who are so important to the state's economic stability, and who give its agricultural regions what little charm they have. To drive from east to west across the San Joaquin Valley, from a pretty little palm-colonnaded city such as Chowchilla, made prosperous by the Central Valley Project and surrounding small farms, to a shabby town such as Huron, surrounded by endless tracts of irrigated land farmed by distant corporate owners, is to fathom the sorry social impact agricultural monopoly can have.

And what is worse, the State Water Project fostered growth in the desert, willy-nilly, without a secure foundation of water. Twenty million people may live between Santa Barbara and San Diego in 2010; the current outlook, according to the State Water Contractors, is that five million of them won't have water unless some drastic conservation steps are taken and surpluses are scavenged from every available source. Even if the groundwater overdraft in the San Joaquin Valley continues to increase—and the chairman of the California Water Commission said recently that it may become "intolerable" by the year 2000—a shortfall of nearly a million acre-feet looms ahead there. The likeliest "solution" to the shortages, as things now stand, will be a lot of land going out of production. The farmers who are apt to give up first are those who are wholly dependent on farming for their livelihood. The ones likely to continue are those to whom farming is a sideline to oil refining or banking or running a railroad, or a tax writeoff—a way to accumulate a little judicious financial loss.

When Pat Brown's two terms as governor were over, he opened a lucrative law practice in Beverly Hills. One of his firm's most important clients became the Berrenda Mesa Water District, where the lands of several of the biggest corporate growers are located. The Blackwell Land Company, for example, owns 16,000 acres within Berrenda Mesa and co-owns 4600 more; Getty and Shell both farm thousands of acres there; one company, Mendiburu Land and Cattle, controls some 250,000 acres statewide. Thanks to his beloved Oroville Dam and the Governor Edmund G. Brown California Aqueduct—it was finally given that name by his son, in 1982—he had an opportunity to build up a tidy nest egg for his retirement.

But in his later years Pat Brown remained unrepentant about his firm's client relationships, which some might have considered unseemly, and he was as proud of his project as ever. Another thing that hadn't changed about him, curiously, was his candor. During his interviews for the Bancroft Library's Oral History Program, he allowed himself some final thoughts about the meaning of the State Water Project in California's history. "This project was a godsend to the big landowners of the state of California," he confessed to Malca Chall. "It really increased the value of their property tremendously. . . . But also the ordinary citizen has been helped by it, too." When his interviewer asked if enriching the big landowners of the state at public expense was really the result he had in mind, Brown responded, "It was the extreme liberals who wanted to break up the big farms in the state of California. They felt that the device of the delivery of water would do it. I was never convinced that the small farmer could succeed or would be good for the economy of the state and I don't know today as I talk to you whether that's true or not."

Having said that, Brown suggested another motive that had made him, a northern Californian by birth, want so badly to build a project which would send a lot of northern California's water southward: "Some of my advisers came to me and said, 'Now governor, don't bring the water to the people, let the people go to the water. That's a desert down there. Ecologically, it can't sustain the number of people that will come if you bring the water project in there.'

"I weighed this very, very thoughtfully before I started going all out for the water project. Some of my advisers said to me, 'Yes, but people are going to come to southern California anyway.' Somebody said, 'Well, send them up to northern California.' I knew I wouldn't be governor forever. I didn't think I'd ever come down to southern California and I said to myself, 'I don't want all these people to go to northern California.' "

CHAPTER ELEVEN

Those Who Refuse to Learn . . .

E arly in September of 1965, the Bureau of Reclamation's newest dam, Fontenelle, on the Green River in southwestern Wyoming, sprang a leak. A big leak.

Eighteen years later, Pat Dugan remembered it as vividly as if it had been yesterday. Dugan was then regional director in Denver; he was the person who held the keys to the Bureau's airplane. "Barney Bellport, the chief engineer, called me up at four A.M.," Dugan remembers. "He said, 'We've got to get that plane in the air quick. We've got a dam that's about to go.' Barney was a self-confident guy— a little bit of an arrogant bastard—so I figured if *he* was worried, we were in plenty of trouble. We were."

Fontenelle was an earthfill dam of moderate size on a troublesome site; it stored water for the Seedskadie Project. That the site had geologic problems was apparent from the very beginning, but the Bureau, as it would do in a number of cases, built it anyway, for the simple reason that it was running out of good places to erect its dams. "I think I was the first person who ever did up a detailed cross section of that site," Dugan remembers. "I didn't like it from the beginning. The left abutment was fine, but for some reason we had a lot of trouble with the right one. It was shaly and just generally lousy. I figured it would take a lot of grout." Asked what he thought of the Seedskadie Project itself, Dugan said, "It was one of the few lemons we could find in Wyoming that didn't make your mouth pucker completely shut."

Wyoming has had its share of powerful politicians in recent decades, from Senator Joseph O'Mahoney, who stopped FDR's plan to pack the Supreme Court, to Senator Gale McGee, Lyndon Johnson's most articulate ally on the subject of Vietnam. What the economy of their high, harsh, hot, arid, and bitterly cold state could not produce on its own, they could produce for it out of the national treasury. The growing season in the region is extremely short: the altitude is between six thousand and seven thousand feet, and there is frost nine months of the year, sometimes even in August. The land is useless for growing anything but cattle browse. To build an expensive dam, a spillway, an outlet works, and canals in order to grow grass or alfalfa is not generally an economically rewarding proposition. It can, however, be a politically rewarding one. To paraphrase what someone said about pleasure and pain, economics are an illusion, while politics are real. Besides, as Wyoming's politicians never tired of pointing out, their state had contributed substantial mineral royalties to the Reclamation Fund, and they were supposed to get some projects in return. If they didn't, Wyoming's share of the Colorado River—all of it contained in its biggest tributary, the Green—might disappear down California's maw.

The leak began as a wet spot on the downstream face of the dam which first appeared on the 3rd or 4th of September and grew steadily larger. By the evening of the 6th it was a small waterspout cascading out of the earthen monolith. Then it became a large waterspout. A waterspout is a signal that water is piping inside the dam—forming placer-nozzle velocities and excavating channels which allow the dam to be eaten from within. By the time Barney Bellport flew overhead, Fontenelle Dam was firehosing water from its downstream face. It appeared too late to save it.

"We left as soon as it was light enough to see," Bellport remembered. "Wyoming seems like a mighty big state when you're flying across most of it to inspect a leaking dam. After we made a pass over the dam, I didn't need to make another. I was really worried that we were going to lose it." The Bureau plane landed at nearby Kemmerer, the improbable site of the first J. C. Penney store. The chief engineer then roared overland toward the Green River, wondering whether he could get there in time to save his reputation.

It would have been one thing if the dam were newly completed and the reservoir pool just forming behind it. But Fontenelle had, oddly enough, held water for some weeks; filling the reservoir had given no indication that some serious trouble lay inside the dam or bedrock. The reservoir was therefore full, and had to be emptied fast.

"My project engineer hadn't begun emptying it because the contrac-tor was downstream fixing the apron of the power plant," Bellport recalled, sounding still disgusted with the man. "I asked him if he would rather wash away the contractor's equipment or the town of Green River." With the dam hemorrhaging across a wide section of its face—huge burps of muddy water were gushing out of it, as if it were gagging on the reservoir and vomiting it up—Bellport ordered both outlet works opened full-bore. The water that was being stored to irrigate the surrounding high desert began flooding uselessly over it, reverting a large piece of Wyoming to something it had not been since the last Ice Age: a swamp. The outlet works carried off so much water so fast that the reservoir could be seen dropping visibly, like a bathtub. A crowd of tiny figures watched tensely from the canyon rim. Forty miles downriver sat the town of Green River, exposed and vulnerable, right on the riverbank. "You felt like you do when you're passing another car and suddenly there's an oncoming car coming right at you," Bellport recalled. "You've got to keep passing but your heart's fluttering and you wonder why you didn't buy a car with more pickup." Only in this case the almost unbearable tension was to last for hours instead of seconds. The outlet works could empty the res-ervoir only so fast; the dam was still belching out great surges of muddy water; its downstream face was steadily eroding under the force. Downriver, there were already reports that the rising Green was inundating the town golf course. Volunteers were furiously sand-bagging the river's banks.

The Bureau was lucky. By early evening, the force of the huge leak finally began to expire. As the flow subsided, one could see the frightening gouges and gullies that the exit of superpressurized water had caused in the downstream face. The dam looked as if it had been pounded by artillery shells. But, miraculously, it had held.

In 1983, sitting at home in Rossmoor, California, Barney Bellport still echoes the attitude of the Bureau of Reclamation during the whole affair. When speaking of the crisis itself, he allows himself an excursion into melodrama. "It was damn serious," he says. *"We really thought we were going to lose it."* But then, having talked himself through the incident, he jumps to his own and the Bureau's defense, like the sinner who avoided being caught and therefore believes he didn't sin. "We repaired it, and it held," he says. "It's been holding water ever since. The Bureau has built hundreds of dams, and they've all held beautifully, except Teton." That, it is suggested, was a pretty large exception. Bellport pauses, looks ironically at his wife, and lets his gaze drink in his surroundings. "Teton," he says firmly, "was either an act of God or human error. You do not blame an organization with a single blemish on its record for the mistakes—if they were mistakes—of a handful of employees who didn't live up to its reputation."

There is not now—there was not then—much evidence of soul-searching on the part of the Bureau's leadership, old or new. They did not seem to be asking themselves what they were doing building potentially dangerous dams like Fontenelle to serve demonstrably wasteful projects like Seedskadie. No one seemed to be wondering whether a bad project might not, through some Shakespearean inevitability, lead to a worse end.

Actually, that is not quite true. Pat Dugan was wondering, and so was Dave Crandall, the regional director in Salt Lake, whose office had to deal with the Fontenelle aftermath. Judging from the correspondence he carried on with his superiors in the wake of the near-disaster—correspondence that traveled the blue-envelope route—Crandall seemed to sense what the others did not: that the Bureau had committed the sin of pride. In a letter to Bellport, he mentioned a demand by some local citizens—people who would have to spend their lives immediately below a dam that had almost failed—asking that the Bureau convene a major investigation before rebuilding the dam. "I do not accede to threats," Crandall wrote, "but since there is this feeling in the local area, and also to preserve our position of impartiality and objectivity, I urge that you consider a Board of Review to appraise the repairs at Fontenelle." Such a board, Crandall pointedly added, should include "qualified non-Bureau non-federal professionals."

To this, Bellport's response was a peremptory harrumph. Ignoring Crandall, he took the matter directly to Commissioner Floyd Dominy. "As you know, the principal competence in earth dam design and construction lies within the Bureau," Bellport wrote to Dominy. "I strongly suspect that a review of the competent earth dam people in consulting firms throughout the country would reveal that a considerable portion of them have either Bureau or Corps background. I also take a very dim view," Bellport offered, "of a professor of geology from a university sitting in judgment on the Bureau."

However, what Bellport's "professor" might have told him, had he and the Bureau felt like listening, was that it had just about run out of good damsites. As Fontenelle was an inferior site compared with Flaming Gorge, as Glen Canyon was inferior to Hoover, as Auburn was vastly inferior to Shasta (but six times as expensive, even allowing for inflation), the Bureau was now being forced to build on sites it had rejected forty, fifty, or sixty years earlier. It was building on them because while the ideal damsites had rapidly disappeared, the demand for new projects had not. The demand for new projects had, if anything, increased, especially now that the Reclamation Act had been amended and re-amended to such a degree that federally supplied water was the closest thing left to a free good. The West and the Congress wanted more projects, and the Bureau wanted more work, but the good damsites were gone. The Bureau, of course, rationalized its decision to keep on building by claiming that advances in engineering were keeping up with the challenges. Even though it was now building dams on rotten foundation rock, between spongy sandstone abutments, in slide-prone canyons, and close to active earthquake faults, the dams held—for now.

"The country around Fontenelle is trona country," Barney Bellport says. "It's full of sodium carbonate—soda ash. The stuff speeds up the setting of concrete. We finally figured out that it had made the concrete we poured for the grout curtains set too fast. Somewhere it left a fissure where the water got through and entered the dam. After that we knew to mix and pour concrete in trona country that wouldn't set so fast."

Pat Dugan essentially agrees. "There hasn't been an ideal damsite since 1940," he says. "Every site we've built on since then would probably have scared hell out of a nineteenth-century engineer. But you wouldn't feel safe going a hundred miles per hour in a Model T, either, if you could get it going that fast down a hill. You might feel perfectly safe in a Porsche." That might be true, except that the dams built at less than ideal locations are usually larger than those built at the earlier, better sites, and with so many dams now in place one dam's failure could conceivably cause other dams to fail, resulting in a domino of disasters unlike anything the country has ever seen. The failure of one large, strategically placed dam (Glen Canyon, for example, which would surely take out Hoover as it went) could undo much of what the Bureau of Reclamation has built up over seventy years, leaving southern California a desert underwater and the economy of the Southwest in ruins.

A modest version of that is what might have happened when Teton Dam collapsed. What actually happened was bad enough.

When Bob Curry got his first look at a cross section of the Teton damsite, his reaction was much like Pat Dugan's when he looked at his finished cross section of Fontenelle. "Holy Christ!" Curry, a geologist, remembers thinking to himself. "What a terrible site for a dam!" By then, however, the dam was already one-quarter completed.

The French colonizers of what is now Chad informally divided their hollow prize into two separate nations. The south was *Chad utile*—"useful Chad"—and the north was *Chad inutile*. In the south, which delved into the fringes of the Central African rainbelt, you could raise a crop; there was wildlife. Northern Chad was deep in the Sahara, as barren as Antarctica. One's first impression of Idaho is much the same, only the polarity is reversed. Northern Idaho is green and welcoming; it is beautiful. Close enough to the Pacific to be influenced by its storehouse of winter warmth, mountainous enough to wring moisture out of passing weather, northern Idaho is the banana belt of the Rockies—warmer than the mountains of New Mexico a thousand miles to the south, wetter than eastern Oregon and Washington to the West. Wild rivers pour out of the mountains—the Salmon, the Clearwater, the Lochsa, the Boise, the Pend Oreille. Apple and cherry orchards thrive in the valleys. In the middle is a vast wilderness, the Salmon River breaks—the most expansive roadless area in the conterminous United States.

Northern Idaho, however, doesn't count much in the economic scheme of things. Real Idaho, serious-minded Idaho, is in the south, along the desolate reaches of the Snake River's old volcanic plain. Like barnacles on an anchor chain, Idaho's cities, its most productive farmland, and much of its wealth are strung along the Snake as it loops around the southern half of the state. Thanks to irrigation, it is a useless place made rich; nowhere except in Arizona and California's Central Valley has such an utter transformation been wrought in the West. Twenty miles from either side of the Snake there is little but desert, and more desert, and rockpiles of basaltic tuff. It was exactly this sort of landscape that appealed to early Mormons, who found a place attractive in exact proportion to its ability to repel anyone else. Drifting up from Salt Lake Basin, the Mormons glimpsed the Snake, incongruously big in the desert, and immediately saw a future. Diverting the few smaller streams, they made a tentative beachhead; then the Bureau of Reclamation arrived and built Jackson Lake and Minidoka and American Falls dams, and the beachhead became an invasion. Within the forty-mile corridor along the Snake River now exists an irrigation economy that has given Idaho a higher percentage of millionaires than any other state in the nation. The best-known crop is potatoes, which like their soil loose, friable, a little sandy, and well drained—the exact conditions of the Snake River Plain. One of the problems of Idaho irrigation farming, in fact, is that water, in places, tends to drain through the soil too quickly, requiring annual waterings in excess of ten feet. That, in part, is how Teton Dam came to be built.

The fountainhead of southern Idaho's agricultural wealth lies to the northeast, where the Yellowstone plateau and the Grand Teton Mountains produce enough water to engorge the Snake to substantial size before it enters the state. On a bright day, the Grand Tetons are visible from the eastern reaches of the plain; a huge buttress wall facing north-south, ninety miles long and thirteen thousand feet high, the range wrings a lot of water out of passing Pacific storms. On the western side the runoff gathers into two rivers, the Henry's Fork and the Teton, which ultimately join the Snake above Idaho Falls. The Teton is, or was, the prettier river; for thirty miles, it whipsawed through a low, U-shaped canyon amid cottonwoods along the bottom and conifers that walked up the canyon's collapsed slopes. An oasis stream in a landscape that is at best austere, the Teton was coveted by the deer that wintered in its canyon, by the fat trout darting from pool to pool, and by the humans who thought it could be put to better use. Since the 1920s and before, there was talk of a dam somewhere on the river, but the dam was never built. One reason can be seen in the granular rock of the canyon's steep slopes. The geology of the region is ultravolcanic: the rock is fissured, fractionated, cavitated, and crisscrossed by minor faults. The neighboring farmland, meanwhile, though productive enough, requires inordinate amounts of water. Those two drawbacks add up to poor economics, and though a Teton Dam was studied and restudied through the 1940s and 1950s, it was never built—until the 1960s.

The impetus, as in the case of many dams, was disaster, or what was called disaster—first a drought, then a flood. The drought occurred in 1961 and 1962, the flood the winter after. The flood caused some few hundred thousand dollars worth of damage, most of it because ice jams occurred at a couple of bridges during a sudden early melt. The drought was mainly a misnomer, nothing like the early thirties or the drastic rainless period in California in the mid-1970s; farm income remained high. In the West, however, a drought and a flood together set off a strong Pavlovian response. The first thing that enters anyone's mind is a dam.

For a project that had spent three or four decades in the pupa stage, Teton was authorized and built in a great hurry. The main reason was Willis Walker, a crotchety Mormon farmer and president of the Fremont-Madison Irrigation District, who managed to organize all of southwestern Idaho behind it. His task was not that difficult. This, after all, was the Mormon West. The closest thing to opposition was indifference. Years later, speaking with a reporter, Walker reminisced, "One of the arguments we used back there was that in '60 and '61 we had a lot of potatoes and a lot of sugar beets around here that didn't have enough water to finish them out. I figured I had better find that water or quit farming." The argument conjured images of crops wilting on the vine, of families ruined on the eve of harvest for want of water to bring their crops to ripeness. Everyone bought it, even though it was nonsense, for the most part. Years later, a graduate student writing a thesis discovered that production of some crops had actually *increased* during the drought. In Fremont and Madison counties, for example, the yield of potatoes in 1961, the worst year of the drought, was 212 hundredweight per acre. Between 1956 and 1959, a stretch of more or less normal years, the average yield was only 184 hundredweight per acre.

Even had the drought threatened ruin, there was a solution much simpler and cheaper than a dam, the same solution that California's farmers would fall back on during their far more apocalyptic drought of 1976 and 1977: groundwater. Idaho may have more groundwater in storage than any other state except Alaska. The Snake River Aquifer, lying directly beneath the Teton River, is still prodigious. During the 1960s, when the drought occurred, thousands of pumps were already operating, supplementing the diversion ditches. Pumping, of course, can be expensive, especially if one's crops require nine or ten feet of water a year. The answer then might be to grow something that requires less water, or to install more efficient irrigation systems. But the farmers of Fremont and Madison counties, good upstanding Mormon conservatives, wanted things their way—and they wanted the descendants of the people who had chased them out of Ohio and Illinois and Iowa to pay 90 percent of the cost. "Mormons get burned up when they read about someone buying a bottle of mouthwash with food stamps," says Russell Brown, one of the dam's most persistent critics. "But they love big water projects. They only object to nickel-and-dime welfare. They love it in great big gobs."

With the entire Congressional delegation from Idaho behind the dam, authorization was a snap, and in the later years the appropriations came fast and furious. However, the project had a little trouble getting going; it received only $3 million during the first six years following authorization, probably as a result of the Vietnam War. During that same period, Congress passed the National Environmental Policy Act of 1969, and the Bureau was forced for the first time to make a public assessment of the environmental effects of its new dams. Before it learned to flood its critics with a tide of ink, the Bureau merely went through the motions of writing an environmental-impact statement; in the case of Teton, it ran to fourteen pages and didn't say much of anything. The exercise, however, drew some attention to the project; both the *Idaho Statesman*, the state's preeminent newspaper, and the Idaho Environmental Council began to take a closer look at it, and liked little that they saw. Published in Boise, on the other side of the state, the *Statesman* could afford to be objective, but even had the project been next door, the paper's maverick young editor, Ken Robison, was not the sort who parrots the views of the local Chamber of Commerce. The Environmental Council, which included a number of scientists from the Department of Energy's Nuclear Testing Station at Idaho Falls, was unusually sophisticated for a tiny organization, and fed Robison a steady diet of statistics worked out on a federal computer.

The statistics, on their face, were quite damaging. The project benefits had been calculated by the Bureau on the basis of the worst drought on record, outrageously stacking the deck in the project's favor. The figures it used to calculate the annual value of flood prevention were about 200 percent higher than historical losses to floods. Of the thirty-seven thousand "new" acres to be opened to irrigation, twenty thousand acres were *already* being irrigated by groundwater pumping; the project would simply substitute surface water for sprinklers, which is a lot different from bringing new land into production.

No statistic, however, was as startling as one freely provided by the Bureau itself. According to its own report, on the 111,000 already cultivated acres that were to receive supplemental water from the Teton project, the average annual irrigation amounted to *132 inches;* the project would simply give the farmers, on the average, another five. One hundred and thirty-two inches is five times the annual rainfall of farmland in Iowa; it is ten times what prudent farmers in the

Ogallala region of arid West Texas put on their crops. It is the precipitation of tropical forests. In fact, according to the Bureau, a common method of irrigating on the Rexford benchlands is subirrigation, which means literally what it implies: water is dumped on the ground in such prodigious quantities that the water table rises up into the root zones of the crops. In one of the driest zones of North America, the Bureau was going to sell dirt-cheap irrigation water to irrigators practicing the equivalent of hydroponic gardening.

The Teton project could be justified only by using an interest, or discount, rate of 3¼ percent. Even with that rate, which was unrealistic in the hyperinflationary 1970s, the best it could manage was a benefit-cost ratio of 1.2 to 1. After getting rid of the phony flood-control figures, the phony "new" irrigated land, and the more implausible fish and wildlife and recreation benefits, the Idaho Environmental Council came up with a benefit-cost ratio of .73 to 1.00. Using a 6 percent discount rate, which was more realistic, the ratio dropped to .41 to 1. Taking, for the sake of compromise, the midway point between the Environmental Council's more flattering figure and the Bureau's, the Teton project was exactly worthless as an investment of tax dollars: it would destroy a beautiful river for the sake of nothing in return.

Such arguments, persuasive though they might have been in an objective sense, seemed only to solidify the local support for Teton Dam. Since Willis Walker had won authorization for the project, the man who emerged as its chief propagandist was Ben Plastino, the political editor of the local newspaper, the Idaho Falls *Post-Register*. Plastino was the sort of small-town editor Twain or Mencken would have loved. It wasn't just his appearance, though that certainly helped. He was short, middle-aged, and pudgy, and his sartorial tastes ran to combat clashes of checks and plaids—vivid figurine shirts, loud polyester ties, acetate houndstooth-checked pants, multicolor Dacron-polyester jackets. Plastino felt a newspaper had two important roles. One was to bring as much federal money as possible into its region, especially in the form of a dam. The other was to rail against big government and creeping socialism. The late Senator Roman Hruska's immortal words during the Watergate hearings—"Don't confuse me with the facts"—were words Ben Plastino had gratefully taken to heart. As recently as 1979, he insisted that Teton was primarily a flood-control project (it wasn't, or it would have been built by the Corps of Engineers), maintained that none of the farmers put anywhere near ten feet of water on their crops (some used up to thirteen), and insisted that every water project pays for itself, regardless of cost.

The *Post-Register* was magnanimous enough to publish an occasional letter opposing the dam, but in its news stories the opposition was usually referred to as "extreme environmentalists." Covering one meeting of dam supporters, Plastino wrote obsequiously about their efforts in behalf of Teton, describing the "warm thanks" and "warm applause" that greeted each self-congratulatory testimonial. The paper, however, was a lot more objective than some of its readers. "Those who would cramp and belittle America's dream and who labor to stalemate needed natural development," stated one letter to the newspaper, "have plans for a singularly small and feeble nation, a blueprint for weakening our nation in a time when enemy nations are straining to develop their resources and strengths." Another asked, "I for one would like to know who is the power behind these so-called environmentalists? Why are they so radical about condemning anything that would improve Idaho's irrigation?"

Jerry Jayne, who was then president of the Idaho Environmental Council, hardly looks like the communist many of his neighbors seemed to think he was. Crew-cut, strong-jawed, erect as a cabinet, he bears a strong resemblance to Mike Nomad, in the *Steve Roper* comic strip, and one might expect to find him at the controls of a nuclear power plant—which is exactly where one would find him, since he works for the Department of Energy's nuclear testing facility at Idaho Falls. "I don't know what it is about these Mormon irrigation farmers," Jayne said. "I can talk to the loggers, I can talk to the ranchers. I can talk to the mining companies. I can say nothing to the irrigation farmers. They're not reasonable. They don't listen. They're true believers. *They're* like communists—only in reverse."

Idaho has had one of the most convulsive recent geologic histories of any state. Only a few million years ago, it was an almost continuous cataclysm of volcanic eruptions, earthquakes, and lava flows. The Yellowstone plateau, two hundred miles off to the northwest, still exhibits the remnants of such activity, as do the Cascade Ranges to the West. (In the fall of 1983, one of the biggest earthquakes in recent U.S. history struck a remote part of Idaho less than two hundred miles from the Teton site.) The whole eastern Snake River Plain, including the Teton site, is a vast bed of basaltic rock. The hazards of building a dam in such terrain, however, became an issue almost entirely by accident. In 1973, Robert Curry was teaching geology at the University of Montana; he did some occasional consulting work for the Sierra Club, mostly on the effects of logging and mining operations. Though he was quite familiar with the geological firmament of southern Idaho, and knew it was anything but firm, he always assumed the Bureau knew how to build a safe dam in such a locale. He also assumed it would have the sense not to build one at an absolutely terrible site. "The first time I heard anyone question the safety of Teton Dam," Curry remembers, "is when some people with the Idaho Environmental Council called me up in 1973. They had been sitting around drinking beer with some guys from the Geologic Survey and one of the Survey guys said—I guess he didn't even mean to let it out—'Well, the Bureau's going to have a hell of a time building Teton Dam.' An IEC member asked him what he meant, and the Survey guy said, 'Well, it's really a crummy spot to put a dam.' I was one of the few geologists around who had much sympathy for the environmental side, so they called me up and asked me what I knew. I didn't know anything. I figured, well, they'd built American Falls Dam down there and some other ones, so they must know what they're doing. But I asked the Survey if I could see their cross section anyway. I looked at it and that's when I said, 'Holy Christ!'

"The stuff they were going to build the dam on—all those ash-flows and rhyolitic rock—may look solid to you, but it's really a veneer, sort of like the wood veneer on a cheap desk. It's brittle, it's cracked. It could peel off just like the veneer on the desk. They were going to scrape away the worst of it and then say that they were anchoring the dam in bedrock. But it isn't really what most geologists would call bedrock. The dam was not going to have a true bedrock foundation.

"It was such an obviously lousy site to a trained geologist," Curry added, "it makes you wonder what happens to human judgment inside a bureaucracy."

Accompanying the Geologic Survey's schematic of the Teton foundation was a report to the Bureau of Reclamation written by four geologists in its regional office, which—in its first version—raised "certain questions about the fundamental safety of the Teton Dam. . . . Despite the incompleteness of the data," the geologists cautioned, "we feel obliged to bring them to your attention now, while they may still be useful and on the chance that some factors may not have been adequately considered in design of the project."

From reading the memorandum, it was clear that the four geologists considered the possibility of an earthquake to be the greatest hazard associated with the dam. "Young ashflows and associated rhyolitic volcanics like those being used as buttresses for the dam," they wrote, "are cut by very young block faults." Often, they said, undetected faults with substantial destructive capability can exist in such terrain. "The Seismic Risk Map of the conterminous United States assigns southeastern Idaho to Zone 3," the code for highest seismic risk. Although the geologists—Steven Oriel, Hal Prostka, Ed Ruppel, and David Schleicher—stopped just short of urging the Bureau to abandon its plans to build on the Teton site, they asked that their observations "be given the serious consideration we believe they merit."

Actually, the tone of the memorandum was mild and rather conservative compared with an earlier internal draft prepared by Dave Schleicher, who had made the initial observations. In his draft, which was addressed to his colleagues instead of the Bureau itself and written in early December of 1972, Schleicher, besides mentioning all the risks that were included in the later memorandum, expressed amazement over the fact that the Bureau appeared oblivious to them. "Within the last five years five earthquakes less than 30 miles from the proposed Teton damsite have been detected," he wrote. "At least two of them had Richter magnitudes greater than 3.

"I find no recognition of this . . . in any of the documents for the project and no indication that the dam and reservoir would be designed to withstand seismic damage and prevent serious secondary damage. There is no recognition . . . that reservoirs have actually caused earthquakes.

"The[se] points appear to be significant enough," Schleicher warned, "that they should be presented to the Bureau as soon as possible—certainly within a month or two. I'd plead that we need a firm deadline on this: we've been aware that there's some need for concern for nearly three months, and we're being seriously delinquent if we don't pass this information on."

At the end of his memorandum, almost as an afterthought, Schleicher included a remark which, in retrospect, would take on a chillingly prophetic overtone. "A final point," he said, "is that flooding in response to seismic or other failure of the dam—probably most likely at the time of highest water—would make the flood of February 1962 look like small potatoes. *Since such a flood could be anticipated, we might consider a series of strategically-placed motion-picture cameras to document the process . . .*" (emphasis added).

Most, but not all, of the urgency in Schleicher's tone was gone

405

by the time his three colleagues had redrafted his remarks. But even their toned-down version was never to be sent. The letter that finally arrived on the desk of the Bureau's Teton engineer, Robbie Robison, had the quality of weak tea. In place of Schleicher's remark about installing movie cameras at the site, the final paragraph of the delivered memorandum read, "We believe that the geologic and seismic observations, though preliminary, bear on the geologic setting of the Teton Basin Project. We are presenting them to you as promptly as possible for your consideration." The rest of the letter could have been lifted from a treatise on local geology—it did not warn of anything. Though Schleicher had made his initial remarks in December of 1972, the final version was dated April 3, 1973. By the time it had been routed through Boise and off to Denver, where any decision affecting the dam's fate would have to be made, it was already July. By then, the dam foundation was already being readied, and another $10.5 million had been appropriated for construction.

The metamorphosis of the report was mainly the work of the director of the Geologic Survey, Vincent McKelvey, but not all of the responsibility could be laid on him. It had just as much to do with the historic relationship between the Bureau and the Survey. Like an awkward older sibling who watches a younger one grow up to letter in four sports, the Survey held the Bureau in a certain awe. In 1902, when the Reclamation Service was newly fledged, the Survey, in a legal sense, became its parent. For the next couple of decades the Service and the Survey were more like sister agencies in pursuit of a common goal—the Survey mapping the West and its geology, the Reclamation Service taking the maps and transforming it. Since then, however, Reclamation had ridden a rising star; transformed from a mere Service into a *Bureau*, it had expanded its staff to as many as nineteen thousand, commanded half a billion dollars a year, and built half the wonders of the modern world. The Survey's great work, the mapping of North America, was essentially complete; it was now a rather small collegium of scratchers, samplers, and scientific scriveners. Who was *it* to tell the almighty *Bureau* what to do?

The Bureau, inflated by a sense of its own accomplishments, must have asked itself the same question. Steve Oriel, the most senior and diplomatic of the four USGS scientists, would later observe that "we got no feedback at all from the Bureau" after the Survey's letter was sent. The earliest evidence of a reaction—any reaction—from the Bureau was a confidential note by one of its geologists, J. D. Gilbert, concerning a telephone conversation he had with Oriel in

October, seven months later. Regarding some continuing investigations at Teton by Hal Prostka, Oriel's colleague, Gilbert wrote, "Steve said that Prostka had found numerous recent faults on the Snake River Plain in the general Teton area, but Steve had no information on the right-abutment 'fault' at Teton. [Even though the Survey strongly suspected it had found a hidden fault right at the damsite, Gilbert was inclined not to believe it.] . . . Steve said that a 'Sierra Club' type individual [one of the Idaho Environmental Council people] involved in the Teton litigation had looked him up in the field to discuss the USGS work in the area."

What *really* had Gilbert worried, it seems, was the fact that "the Washington office [of the Survey] has published (or will publish shortly) the material contained in the USGS letter to the Bureau on Teton . . . in their 'Short Contributions.' Several other reports of a preliminary nature will also be publiished shortly on this portion of the Snake River Plain." Gilbert had gone back and underlined those last two sentences. Hand-scrawled next to them was a margin note which read, "We better develop our ideas on points in the GS 'prel.' rpt. and present some constructive criticism and make effort to get some hard data on 'rt. abutment' fault."

In the mind of a good Bureau man, the first priority was to attack—"constructively"—anyone who questioned his agency's judgment. The second priority was to see whether there was some truth in what he said.

In the opinion of Steven Oriel, the Bureau's response was "disappointing." The Bureau would not listen to the Survey, he was to tell a Congressional committee, "because they were already committed to the project politically." Bob Curry agrees. "You could have told them that they were building a dam on top of an active volcano," he says, "and they would have had a hundred guys out there trying to prove you wrong. I tried to get some more information out of them and eventually I gave up. All I got was Mickey Mouse. No one was listening."

It is irrelevant, but irresistible nonetheless, to point out that while Curry was getting what he called "Mickey Mouse" out of the Bureau, its acting director of dam design and construction was named Donald J. Duck.

Meanwhile, for an entirely different set of reasons, the Nixon White House was beginning to take a closer look at Teton Dam. It wasn't so much the cost—compared to, say, the Central Arizona Project, Teton was small potatoes—as it was panic over the OPEC-spawned

inflation that had suddenly exacerbated the Vietnam-spawned inflation that already was. Also, an organization called Trout Unlimited,
made up substantially of rich Republican fly-fishermen who had donated to Nixon's reelection campaign, was quite audibly upset about
the loss of yet another blue-ribbon wild trout stream. Nixon's Council
on Environmental Quality and the Environmental Protection Agency
were similarly upset about the project, and their skepticism had partially infected the closest approximation of an environmentalist in
the inner White House, Presidential adviser John Erlichman.

The strongest official opposition came from Nathaniel Reed, a
wealthy Floridian whom Nixon had appointed Assistant Interior Secretary for Fish, Wildlife, and Parks. Reed, tall, intense, and witty, a
blazered social lion from the Gold Coast, was to clash repeatedly with
the prosaic engineers upstairs in the Interior building, and for a while
rivaled Dave Brower as the Bureau's public enemy number one. "They
took me on a tour of the engineering headquarters in Denver once,"
recalls Reed, "and I walked by some guy's office with a dartboard
that had my smiling face on it. There was a dart stuck in each of my
eyes. I didn't think anyone there even knew who I was."

Reed had the ear of Interior Secretary Rogers Morton, another
wealthy southeasterner, and, together with Robert Cahn of the Council on Environmental Quality, slowly brought Morton around. The
result was that on October 7, 1971, with contractors from across the
country gathered in Idaho Falls to bid on the major construction
contract for the dam, Morton suddenly gave instructions to postpone
the opening for thirty days. His explanation was that he wanted to
reevaluate the project one more time to see if its benefits would truly
exceed its costs. Morton, of course, was already pretty well convinced
that this was not the case. More likely, what he really wanted to do
was gauge the reaction to something as moderately drastic as he had
just done.

In the words of Nat Reed, "The shit hit the fan." The whole Idaho
Congressional delegation was up in arms, and almost every Idaho
newspaper carried an indignant editorial. In a matter of hours, an
obscure project no one had heard of in a remote western state had
become a main topic of discussion in the Nixon White House.

For a westerner and an ex-Congressman, Nixon himself had surprisingly little interest in water projects. It wasn't that he was a
conservationist in his secret heart; he had almost no interest in nature, either. Nixon was interested almost exclusively in politics, and
mainly in foreign affairs. Domestic policy bored him; public works

were especially deadly. Nonetheless, Nixon was an outstanding politician, and he knew as well as Lyndon Johnson how to use the budget
process to further his ends. "At the time, Nixon was about to open
the gates to China," John Erlichman recalled in 1983. "Then there
was the international monetary agreement, the SALT talks, détente
with the Soviets. He couldn't get anywhere on those without Congressional support, and Congress knew that, and the Idahoans in Congress
wanted that dam." Erlichman professed to remember little of the
Teton Dam episode, though rumors at the time made him the principal point man at the White House. Whoever it was, someone in the
White House turned Rogers Morton around very quickly. Eleven days
after he postponed the contract opening, he announced that Teton
was a sound project after all. Groundbreaking was to begin within
weeks.

There was only one person who could have jerked a President
and an Interior Secretary around so fast, and that was retiring Idaho
Senator Len Jordan. When Nat Reed went out to Idaho soon thereafter
to dedicate the Birds of Prey removal lands—a new national monument along the Snake River where hawks and golden eagles live in
remarkable numbers—Jordan was with him, all smiles and cama-
raderie, posing for photographers. "As soon as the photogs went off,"
Reed remembers, "Jordan got crude and angry. He yanked me aside
and said, 'Listen, Nathaniel Reed, *we're* going to build this fucking
dam and *you're* going to come out to dedicate it. I've used every chip
I've got on Teton Dam. What do you think I'm doing here dedicating
this goddamned vulture site?' " At least, Reed added ruefully, Jordan
was honest.

Without the support of Rogers Morton or Idaho's governor, Cecil
Andrus—who, if his later record on water projects as Interior Secretary is any clue, probably thought Teton was a bad project but
didn't dare come out against it—the only hope left for the dam's
opponents was the courts. There they went up not so much against
the Bureau as against Fred Taylor, the presiding judge of the federal
district court for Idaho—a man with deep local roots and a sense of
religion about water development. Was *he* going to preside over the
demise of the Teton project? Evidently not. Taylor refused to allow
any discussion of economics, or of safety, during the trial, using as
crabbed an interpretation of the National Environmental Policy Act
as he could get away with without inviting a reversal by the court of
appeals. The matter of safety did come up, once, as Sierra Club Legal
Defense Fund attorney Tony Ruckel tried unsuccessfully to introduce

some testimony to the effect that the dam might leak more than the Bureau admitted. Judge Taylor had a ready response. "Matter of fact," he told Ruckel, evidently thinking this was funny, "if the dam won't hold water, I don't think the fish and wildlife are going to be hurt." Then he disallowed Ruckel's testimony on grounds of irrelevance.

Ruckel had wanted to introduce testimony from Shirley Pytlak, a professional geologist who had worked briefly on the Teton project during the summer of 1973, drilling test holes at the damsite and injecting water into them. The idea was to see how fast the holes filled up, which would allow the Bureau to gauge—"guess" is a better word—the extent to which the surrounding rock was fissured and fractured and concomitantly leak-prone. For weeks, Pytlak said, the boreholes had been pumped with water at a rate of three hundred gallons per minute, which was like sticking a fire hose in them and turning it on full-blast. The holes never filled. If test holes leaked at such a rate, Pytlak asked her superiors, how much water would seep out of the reservoir and try to get around the dam?

Actually, none of this should have come as a surprise. Three years earlier, the Bureau had conducted a similar test-drilling program, and three deep holes—numbers 301, 302, and 303—turned out to be particularly thirsty. Injected with as much as 440 gallons of water per minute, all of them refused to fill. The three holes were all drilled in the right canyon wall. Number 303 was only 250 feet from what would be the dam's embankment. Clifford Okeson, the Bureau's regional geologist and the person supervising the drilling program, reported to his superiors: "The three deep drill holes which were completed on the right abutment of Teton Dam during 1970 encountered cracks capable of transmitting much more water than the cracks encountered in previous drill holes." This led Okeson to conclude that some reservoir leakage was inevitable. "Probably some of the reservoir water will leak around the ends of the dam, through cracks in the bedrock, and emerge from cracks at lower elevations of the bedrock surface downstream from the dam. The water would be under artesian pressure so it would gradually wet the thick cover of soil, thus turning [it] into a loblolly or quagmire. Loblolly conditions could also develop in places *within the impervious section of the dam* if one or more cracks is poorly grouted" (emphasis added).

Although he was loath to say so—using an adjective like "serious" is regarded by some engineers as unwarranted emotionalism—loblolly conditions inside the dam would be a serious occurrence, one under which the dam could conceivably be lost. The key to preventing them was proper grouting. Grouting, a commonly used technique in the dam builders' art, involves injecting liquid concrete under high pressure into drill holes in the abutment walls on either or both sides of a dam; the concrete moves like water, filling all the fissures, shear zones, and holes, and then hardens, leaving a supposedly impervious barrier against seepage. The plan at Teton was essentially the same as at Fontenelle—several grout curtains would be extended outward from the site, into the abutments, to block any flow of water trying to move around the dam. The grouting might be done improperly under three sets of conditions: if the engineers were inexperienced or otherwise incompetent; if the rock was so hopelessly fractured and fissured that a near-perfect job of grouting was impossible; or if the canyon wall surprised the engineers by taking so much more grout than expected that, at some point, they declared the job done and quit.

In 1969, the year before the water-injection tests, the Bureau had taken the rather unusual step of performing a test-grouting program, so unsure was it of the conditions at the Teton site. Holes were drilled in the rock, and grout was pumped in under high pressure; then the job was tested to see how well it worked. As far as the Bureau was concerned, it had worked fine. "Once we decided that the cracks in the abutments could be sealed with grout," Harold Arthur, then head of dam design and construction, told a reporter from the Los Angeles *Times*, "we never reconsidered the suitability of the Teton site, despite the difficulties we experienced later in construction."

Only one thing had been wrong with the Bureau's test-grouting program. There was a road leading to the damsite from Sugar City, a few miles to the southwest, but none from the north. All of the test grouting was performed on the south abutment of the dam. None whatsoever was performed on the north side, the right abutment of the dam—the side where three hundred gallons of water per minute injected into holes had simply disappeared, day after day after day.

With the defeat of the environmentalists in court, there was no way to stop the dam. From an appropriation of $1,575,000 in 1971, funding for Teton jumped to over $10 million in 1972 and went even higher for the next four years, reaching an apogee of $15,217,000 for fiscal year 1976, when the $85 million dam was completed. Or, to be more accurate, when the Bureau's engineers thought it was completed.

In his 1970 memorandum, Clifford Okeson, the Bureau geologist, had said that the largest cracks he could find after extending a miniature television camera and light down the length of a thirty-five-hundred-foot borehole were about an inch and a half wide. That was a small crack, easily grouted—nothing to worry about. In February of 1974, however, as the Bureau's main contractors, Morrison-Knudsen of Boise and Peter Kiewit of Omaha, were excavating the huge keyway foundation trench—which would replace the worst of the fractured surface rock with a man-made concrete foundation—they came on the right abutment's great secret. It was a discovery that five years of boring, injecting, and test grouting had failed to reveal. What they found, Robbie Robison, the Bureau's project engineer, wrote his superiors in a memo, were "unusually large" fissures in the rock of the right canyon wall.

"Unusually large" was hardly apt. The fissures were gigantic. They were *caves*. One of them was eleven feet wide and a hundred feet long. Another was nine feet wide, in places, and 190 feet long. One by one, other fissures were discovered. The whole right canyon wall was full of them.

If Robison's description of what had to be considered an appalling discovery was understated in the extreme—even if the fissures weren't a safety problem, it was astonishing that they had been missed—his recommendation of a course of action displayed an arresting mental paralysis. "We do not recommend to grout these voids at this time," Robison wrote Harold Arthur in Denver. "The claims situation [by the contractor] . . . makes us hesitant to cause any delays. . . . Furthermore, grouting of these voids is not critical at this time as they are located outside the dam area and could be grouted at a later date if you should so desire."

Robbie Robison, barely thirty years old, was on his first big project. It had been a troublesome project from the beginning, racked by delay. Costs were up; schedules were behind. For four years the Teton project had been officially underway, and now, in 1974, there was still nothing to show for it but a huge amount of excavation at the bottom of the canyon and some trailer sheds and a lot full of earthmoving equipment. The two biggest voids alone would eat a trainload of grout. Who knew what others would be found? The important thing, Robison figured, was that they were *beyond* the keyway trench; they were *beyond* the point where the Bureau had arbitrarily decided no further grouting was required; they were, therefore, beyond the limits of reasonable concern. After all, if you wanted to be *really* secure, you could have extended the keyway trench all the way to Ashton, which was twelve miles out from the north abutment of the dam. That was what Robie Robison sarcastically told a reporter, later on. It might not have been a bad idea.

Though the airy caves in the rock were a shocking discovery, no one besides Robison, the contractors, Harold Arthur, and a small circle of Bureau officialdom knew about them. Gil Stamm, the commissioner, was probably never told. The people of Rexburg and Sugar City, the two towns lying directly in the Teton River floodpath, were entirely in the dark, as were the politicians who had so assiduously promoted the dam. Of course, had they known about the voids, it probably wouldn't have mattered to them anyway. After all, the *Bureau* knew what it was doing.

The dam was finished, more or less, on October 3, 1975, when the flow of the river was interrupted for the first time. Even with the biggest voids left unfilled, the job had taken 503,000 cubic feet of grout—more than twice as much as the Bureau predicted it would have to use. That winter, a series of Pacific storms bashed into the Teton Mountains, depositing a big snowpack. As spring was about to arrive, Robbie Robison had two worries: how he was going to settle with the contractors over the cost of the extra grouting, and how he was going to capture the snow that was about to melt out of the Grand Tetons without violating the Bureau's time-honored rule about filling reservoirs behind earthfill dams.

The rule is simple: the rate of fill is to be kept at or below one foot a day measured vertically along the reservoir walls. That way, if problems develop with the dam or the abutments, or back along the reservoir itself—where rising water sometimes loosens rock and causes landslides, or causes the bedrock to shift under its weight, producing the same result—they can be dealt with. At a slow rate of fill, such problems are less likely to develop in the first place. It was a sensible rule, and, like most sensible rules, it had already been violated on a number of occasions. Why not dispense with it again, with all that precious water coming down from the Teton Range? On March 3, 1976, Robison wrote Harold Arthur formally requesting permission for a two-foot-per-day filling rate. Ironically, one of the arguments he used in support of his request was that a faster rate of fill would permit the Bureau to observe how effective its grouting program had been. It was, in a way, like arguing for a hundred-mile-per-hour speed limit on the grounds that motorists would spend less time on dangerous highways if they drove twice as fast. But on March 23, Arthur readily acceded to Robison's request.

Actually, the whole business—formal request, formal permission granted—was a meaningless charade. The main outlet works—the tunnel and appurtenances that would carry water out of the reservoir and into the adjacent canals—were not yet finished. The auxiliary outlet works were, but they were designed to carry a maximum flow of 850 cubic feet per second. Engorged by a snowpack half again as deep as normal, the Teton River was about to peak at several thousand cfs. Without a functioning main outlet works, the reservoir would rise as fast as the Teton River felt like filling it. It was likely to rise a lot faster than two feet per day.

Harold Arthur was unconcerned about such a fast rate of fill because he had ordered a series of observation wells to be drilled around the dam, which would—in theory—inform the Bureau of any developing problems. The water table around a damsite will often show a rise as the reservoir fills, because a certain amount of seepage into outlying terrain is inevitable. If the water table rises precipitously, however, and if wells far from the reservoir are affected—especially wells downstream—it could mean that the reservoir is seeping excessively. The only other possibility is a pressure response, where the adjacent water table rises out of proportion to the actual rate of seepage because of hydrologic pressure, much as the constriction of a hose nozzle turns a placid gurgle into a sixty-foot jet.

From what Arthur had heard from Robbie Robison, the observation wells in the vicinity of the dam were showing what he termed a "predictable buildup"; that was the term he used in his March 23 memo. Obviously, he had not yet seen, or even been told about, a Bureau report written almost exactly at the same time, which disclosed the startling fact that "the rate of travel of the rising water table north of the reservoir is over 1,000 times that calculated for predicted movement of water." The memo came from Gordon Haskett, the Bureau geologist who had been monitoring the observation wells. To engineers who had spent their lives working with microtolerances, who considered almost any adjective hyperbolic, something as extreme as a thousandfold increase should have leaped off the printed page. Haskell's report, however, was routinely routed through the Boise regional office, from where it went to Denver, where it reached Harold Arthur's in-box on April 13, three weeks after he had already consented to the faster rate of filling.

It probably wouldn't have mattered if it had arrived the day after it was written. After looking Haskett's memo over, Arthur filed it away. In a way, he cannot be blamed. Having reported the bizarre thousandfold increase in the predicted rise of the groundwater table, Haskell had felt obliged to explain it. It was, he said, *too excessive* to be attributable to seepage. "Therefore," he concluded, "[it] must be a pressure response."

Actually, a relatively simple and inexpensive piece of gauging equipment, a piezometer, could probably have told the Bureau whether something drastic was going on or whether the inexplicably rapid rise of the adjacent groundwater table was merely a pressure response. Forty miles across the Rexford Bench, on Willow Creek, the Corps of Engineers had just erected Ririe Dam, and all forty-nine of its observation wells were equipped with piezometers. Their use had been routine practice for years. The closest thing to an official explanation as to why they weren't used at Teton came from Richard Saliman, the chief of the Bureau's design division. "We do use them on other dams," Saliman told a reporter, "but basically, we had such an excellent foundation we didn't feel it necessary. . . . With the rock types we had we just didn't see the need for it." For his part, Harold Arthur doesn't think the piezometers would have detected anything "unless one of them happened to be exactly where the leakage was occurring. It would have been a matter of luck." But even if luck had been on the Bureau's side, it might not have made a difference. The Bureau didn't believe in luck—it believed in itself. "Suppose we'd gotten a reading from a piezometer that there was massive seepage from the dam," Arthur told an interviewer in 1983. "We might not have believed it. We had a perfect record up to then. We might have thought the thing was giving us a wrong reading."

By mid-May of 1976, the Teton River was a frigid deluge. Square miles of snowfields were melting into it under a hot, high sun, and the reservoir was rising much faster than it ought to have been, approaching four feet a day. As the reservoir filled, the emergency outlet works were the only real insurance against catastrophe. If the dam gave evidence that it was going to fail, the outlet works would permit a rapid but controlled drawdown of the reservoir. But the outlet works were still not operational; they were completely sealed off by a huge metal barrier and in the process of being painted. On May 14, Robison was finally concerned enough about the rapid filling to write his superiors. "Request your comments for flood control operations," he said in a terse memo. It was a pro forma exercise: the Bureau, by then, was completely in the river's hands.

On the 3rd of June, a Thursday, the first equipment operator arriving at the damsite early in the morning noticed a small leak pouring out of the canyon wall about a third of a mile below the dam. From the canyon rim, three hundred feet above the river, the leak looked like nothing; one could barely hear it bubbling above the quiet rush of what was left of the river flowing out of the auxiliary outlet works. The leak was coming out of the north abutment—the right canyon wall. The water was clear. Five hundred feet closer to the dam was another leak, even smaller, also clear. The next day there was still another. All three leaks were coming out of the right canyon wall.

Robbie Robison stood on the canyon rim watching the leaks for a while. Looking back at him impassively was his masterwork, Teton Dam: an average-size modern dam, but a monument that would have made a pharaoh reel. Although Robison was, as he later put it, "just a cog in a great big wheel," it was *his* monument. The reservoir was sitting quietly behind the dam, looking utterly serene. Suddenly set free, it would have a calculable energy release approximating that of a quarter-megaton bomb.

Robison returned to his office in the trailerlike project building. Then, restless, he went outside and watched the leaks again. Finally, he went down into the canyon and crossed the river by boat. The dam loomed above him, 305 feet high. Robison jumped over the rocky bed and climbed up the fifty-degree slope to the first leak and measured it. Sixty gallons a minute, about a seventh of a cubic foot per second. The second leak was flowing at about forty gallons a minute, the third—the one closest to the dam—at about twenty.

Robison went back across the river, climbed to the Bureau's trailers, and wrote a brief memo to Harold Arthur telling him about the leaks. At the end of the memo, he said, "I'll keep you advised."

Off and on during the day, Robison's men monitored the leaks through binoculars. By nine o'clock in the evening it became too dark to see, and they went home.

Saturday, June 5, dawned pellucid and bright, a warm and somnolent day. The first Morrison-Knudsen man arrived at the Teton site at seven in the morning. In the shadowy postdawn light, the downstream embankment, facing west, was still dark. He looked at it and saw nothing. Sometime around seven-thirty he looked again and saw something. There was a roiling creek of muddy water emerging from the right abutment adjacent to the dam.

The construction man immediately phoned Robison, who drove out at eighty miles an hour. By the time he arrived another leak had developed, almost exactly at the contact point of the dam with the abutment. Robison quickly ordered one of his men to try to divert the flow away from the powerhouse with a bulldozer. Then, at last, he decided to call his superiors in Washington, Denver, and Boise.

A Bureau report later said, "The project supervisors did not believe at this time that the safety of the dam was jeopardized."

At about nine-thirty, one of the men noticed an odd-looking shadow on the downstream face of the dam, twenty feet or so out from the right abutment. He looked at the sky. There was no cloud anywhere. The shadow was a wet spot. In a few more minutes it was a spring. Then it was a creek. Then it was a sizable torrent washing away the embankment of the dam. Robbie Robison called the sheriffs of Madison and Fremont counties and told them to prepare to evacuate twelve thousand people.

Watching the unprecedented spectacle beneath him, Robison was biting his lip until it almost bled. He thought of the main outlet works and did a quick mental calculation of how long it would take to open it. He decided hours, maybe a day, maybe two. He told his men to try anyway. Then he ordered a second bulldozer down to try to shove material into the widening hole. The two big Caterpillars crawled across the dam face like flies on a wall. As fast as they could plug the hole, the torrent swept away what they had filled in. The hole was now a crater, as large as a swimming pool. It was vomiting muddy water in rapid heaves.

At that same moment, a family of tourists was driving up the access road from Sugar City to take a look at the newly completed dam. It was just an unplanned side trip, prompted mainly by the sign at the junction of the access road with Highway 33 that proudly announced the existence of the dam. Through such a chance excursion, David Schleicher's wish was about to be fulfilled. On the seat of the car was a movie camera, loaded with film.

Nothing could plug the hole in the downstream face. After twenty minutes one of the Caterpillars fell halfway into it. Terrified as he was, the operator of the other dozer frantically tried to winch it out. Meanwhile, on the other side of the dam, a more ominous phenomenon was occurring. A whirlpool had begun to develop in the reservoir a few yards away from the face of the dam. Like the whirlpool over the outlet of an emptying bathtub, the vortex could only mean that water was leaving the reservoir in a hurry, and was sluicing directly through the dam. Two more dozer operators crawled down the canyon slope and onto the upstream side of the dam, shoving riprap from the embankment into the swirling hole. One of them was named Jay

Calderwood. Jay Calderwood, like almost everyone else in the area, was a Mormon. "Every pass I made I wondered whether it would be my last," he recalled later. "I thought, 'Well, Jay old boy, this is it. I'm going to go. Have I lived the righteous life my parents taught me?' I felt very close to the Lord at this time. I had Him on my mind all the time, when I was trying to stop the leak and save the dam. 'This is it, I can't do a bit of good at what I'm doing. But I'll go out fighting. I'll not be a coward.' "

Meanwhile, on the downstream side of the dam, the two bull-dozers were still trying to plug the huge spring gushing out of the embankment. It was now regurgitating the dam's insides by the cubic yard. The audience on the canyon rim, which had grown to include a couple of local radio reporters, was helplessly spellbound. At almost exactly eleven-thirty, the sides of the hole suddenly collapsed some more, widening it by twenty feet. The Caterpillars began to drop as if through a trapdoor, two huge yellow machines in slow-motion aerial freefall. Both drivers launched themselves out of their seats and ran for safety along the dam's crest and up the canyon slope.

Now one could only watch. Robbie Robison, trembling and licking blood off his punctured lip, may still have been telling himself it couldn't happen. The dam was too big, too solid. It could not be moved. At eleven fifty-five, the crest of the dam fell into the reservoir as if a sword had whacked it off. Two minutes later, as the movie camera whirred in the hands of a speechless tourist, the second-largest flood in North America since the last Ice Age was heading out the Teton River Canyon.

The dam went almost noiselessly. It didn't so much break as melt. One second there was a dam, three hundred feet high and seventeen hundred feet wide at the base; the next minute it was gone. Actually, two-thirds of it was somehow left standing as the flood roared through the bombed-out hole on the right side. The reservoir spilled out in a great, fat, smooth, probing tongue; then, a couple of hundred yards downstream, it suddenly erupted into a boil about fifteen stories high. For a moment, the spectators on the canyon rim thought it might consume them; then it boomed off in a heart-stopping chaos of boils, whirlpools, and fifty-foot waves. The initial rapids resembled Lava Falls on the Colorado River, a Colorado River with two million cubic second-feet of water. The color was an awful brown.

Six miles beyond the dam, the Teton Canyon abruptly comes to an end; below there, flat as a slightly inclined board, lies the Snake River Plain. Two towns, Wilford and Teton, sat at the terminus of the canyon, four or five miles apart. Teton was south of the river and above it; it would be spared, barely. Wilford was just north of the river at bank elevation. A few miles beyond Wilford was Sugar City, and six miles farther down was Rexburg, a community of eight thousand people. Another sixty river miles beyond was Idaho Falls, population 35,776, the third-largest town in Idaho. All four towns were going to absorb a direct hit, but none would be hit like Wilford. When road atlases were republished a year later, Wilford would not be listed among Idaho's cities and towns.

The leading wave arrived twenty-five minutes after the dam broke. It was twenty feet high. The fastest egress to safety was the road north to St. Anthony, even though it went straight across the plain in sight of the river for three miles before it began to climb. As the last refugees from Wilford roared up the highway in their cars, they could see the flood approaching out of the east. It looked like a dust storm, until they saw the dust snapping huge cottonwoods in half. One of the first homes hit was Alice Birch's. The day before, she had celebrated living in the same house for fifty years. The twenty-foot wall crashed into it, tore it off its foundations, and lifted it onto a power line, which snapped in half. The shooting voltage ignited a ruptured propane tank and Alice Birch's house blew to smithereens.

Glen Bedford's aging parents-in-law, the Liedings, lived in Wilford. When the first radio announcements about the dam came around ten o'clock, he raced up to their house from Parker, on the Henry's Fork of the Snake, to help them get out. Roaring by his sister-in-law's home in St. Anthony, five miles before Wilford, Glen Bedford saw his mother-in-law already unloading a pickup with a few belongings. Her husband was nowhere in sight. Believing that he was still at home in Wilford, Bedford drove his foot into the accelerator pedal. His father-in-law, who had been behind the house and out of view, read Bedford's mind and roared off after him. When he got to Wilford he could already see the flood pouring out of the canyon. From a mile and a half away, he said, it looked fifty feet high. When Lieding caught up with his son-in-law at his house he screamed at him to turn back to St. Anthony. "I'll be there in four minutes!" Bedford yelled and ran upstairs to collect a last armload of valuables and mementos. They found him eleven days later, twisted almost beyond recognition amid a pile of trees and torn-up trailers.

Wilford went in an instant. The flood left only the two-story

Mormon meetinghouse, and of that it left only the brick shell. The other 154 houses were intact or in pieces, riding the fifteen-mile-an-hour crest.

As the flood swept southwestward it spread to a width of two miles, but it had enough churning power to strip the topsoil off thousands of acres of first-class farmland. When it hit Sugar City the flood was no longer liquid, but semisolid.

There was a trailer park outside of Sugar City, and, according to witnesses in airplanes overhead, the flood hit town tumbling trailers like ice cubes, smashing houses off their foundations. Like Wilford, Sugar City was motionless one minute and moving fifteen miles an hour the next. Somehow, one of the victims there was killed by a shotgun blast.

In their desperation to flee Sugar City, Betty and Rodney Larson flooded their car's engine so badly that it wouldn't start. With the flood bearing down on them, it was too late to escape on foot. They ran upstairs with their three children and draped themselves over mattresses, hoping they would float. For three hours, their house felt as if a turbine generator were rattling itself loose in their basement. The house eventually came right off its foundation, but, miraculously, it did not move. Like a dud missile, it floated two feet off its pad and settled back down exactly where it had been. To pass the time, they counted dead cows.

Since eleven o'clock in the morning, the Rexburg police and civil defense had been herding people to higher ground. The Rexburg benchlands rise up from the eastern edge of the town, and on top of the first hill stood Mormon Ricks College, its dormitories recently emptied. Seven thousand people streamed up College Hill like the Hebrews during the Exodus, dragging whatever cars, wheelbarrows, and muscle could carry. By the time the flood hit Rexburg, the radio said, the crest would be only two to four feet deep. They saw the dust first, a four-mile-wide roiling cloud, then they saw the wall of water. It came just like a lava flow: five feet in front of it everything was dry, and then came the wave, seven feet high. Just before it hit town, the radio station went dead. The first thing the wave hit was the lumberyard outside of town. All the logs, thousands of them, were set loose. Dozens of them smashed against a bulk gasoline storage tank a few hundred yards away. The tank went off like a firebomb, setting flaming slicks adrift on the racing water. When the wave hit the front line of houses a hundred windows were instantaneously shattered. Witnesses said it sounded just like a rifle shot. Then the flaming gasoline poured into windows and set Rexburg on fire, like a floating-island dessert.

The throng on College Hill watched speechlessly as the wall of water washed their town away, burning it down as it went. A big white frame house floated over to the base of the hill below them and settled down in shallow water in the middle of a street. The water itself, moving only ten miles an hour now but engorged with a cubic quarter mile of topsoil, had force enough to separate homes from their foundations, but the real damage to Rexburg was done by Sugar City and Wilford. Reduced to giant pieces of flotsam—silos, walls, automobiles, telephone poles, pianos, trees—Wilford and Sugar City were a battering ram afloat, smashing Rexburg to pieces. When the flood passed after dusk, it had left six inches of silt on everything, as if it had snowed mud. A Greyhound bus sat on someone's lawn.

A hundred miles downriver on the Snake was American Falls Reservoir, holding four times as much water as Teton had held. American Falls was one of the Bureau's oldest dams. The dam was, in fact, unsafe—something the Bureau knew as early as 1966, but hadn't bothered to correct. (In 1967, chief engineer Barney Bellport wrote Floyd Dominy that "the need for replacement of American Falls Dam is largely governed by structural reasons, although the deterioration of the concrete due to alkali-aggregate reaction contributes to the poor condition of the structure. The lack of bond between constriction joints and the fact that the dam was not designed for ice pressures are of great significance." By 1976, however, the dam had been neither replaced nor fixed.)

If the dam was too weak to withstand the strain of the Teton flood coming on top of high flows in the Snake, the resulting calamity could only be guessed at. Instead of spreading out, the water would remain largely confined by the canyon of the Snake until it hit the Boise. Below, beyond Hells Canyon, the dams were lined up like dominoes: Ice Harbor, Little Goose, Lower Granite, Lower Monumental; then the Columbia River and McNary, The Dalles, John Day, and Bonneville dams. The bigger Columbia dams would have seen such a flood before, perhaps, but those on the Snake, unless their reservoirs could be emptied in time, might meet flows they were never designed to handle. There was only one course of action: empty American Falls. Over two days, the archaic dam would have to release more water than it ever had before, and its reservoir would receive more at one time than it ever got.

By nightfall on Saturday, Rexburg was a silhouette of wreckage, carnage, and flaring fires. The lower half of the town was a total loss. As Rexburg finally became a vast, slowly shrinking pool of standing water, the flood was washing up against the Menan Buttes, some low hills off to the west. Now six miles wide, it split suddenly into two streams. The one veering northward around the buttes struggled upward against the inclined plain and fell back into a channel it quickly dug down to bedrock. Within minutes, it was a replica of the chocolate-brown Colorado River at high water. Then, beyond the buttes, the two channels rejoined, and the flood went into Idaho Falls.

Two things saved Idaho Falls. One was the geologic bedrock and soil which had made Teton such a bad project, physically and economically. By the time the flood poured itself into the Snake River twenty miles above the town, a lot of it had drained off into the porous soil and deeply fractured bedrock beneath it. The other salvation was a night and a day spent by thousands of volunteers sandbagging the levees along the river, which goes through the dead center of town. The flood built toward a crest all day Sunday and finally peaked, at just over 100,000 cubic feet per second, at ten o'clock at night. As logs, fiberboard, and bales of hay crashed up against the Broadway Bridge, which retained only inches of freeboard, a reservoir began to form behind it. Nine pounds of dynamite and a sixty-foot dragline could not dislodge the debris. It was only after an escape channel was dug that officials decided they wouldn't have to blow up the bridge. It survived, looking as if it had been chewed by a hundred-foot shark. The town escaped with two hundred flooded homes.

At American Falls Dam, water was bursting furiously out of the outlet works. Ten thousand Bureau people and three million more downstream, all the way to the Pacific, held their collective breath as the reservoir began to fill early Monday morning. But the remains of the flood did not even overtop the spillway.

Eleven people died in the Teton flood, but the dam could just as easily have gone at two in the morning, in which case the toll could have risen into the thousands. Power and telephone lines between Sugar City and Rexburg were cut as soon as the flood struck, so the odds are there would have been no warning. The Bureau had installed no sensors below the dam to warn the towns if a flood was on the way.

Four thousand homes were damaged or destroyed; 350 businesses were lost. Damage estimates climbed to $2 billion, though settlements were to fall substantially short of that. Nothing, however, was as startling as what the flood had done to the land. The topsoil was gone from tens of thousands of acres—stripped off as if a plow a mile and a half wide had come along, scraping the earth down to bedrock. According to one estimate, more land was destroyed—permanently, made incapable of ever growing anything again—than would have been opened to irrigation by the dam.

That was merely the first in a long string of ironies that followed in the wake of the tragedy. As it turned out, the farmers on the Rexburg bench, the rich irrigators for whose benefit the dam was mainly built, were entirely spared. Their riverbottom neighbors, whose means of livelihood vanished with the flood, would have to search the region, the state, even the country to find a decent farm they could afford with their settlement money. But the farmers on the Rexburg bench could relax; they might not even miss the water they would now never receive. "A lot of wells have been drilled up on the bench," explained Agriculture Commissioner Bill Kellogg, confirming what the dam's opponents had been saying all along, "and the dam was only intended for supplemental water." This same supplemental water—a life-or-death matter three days before—had suddenly become something they could do without. The dam's opponents had argued that, too. But even had the irrigators on the benchlands been ruined for want of water, there were only a handful of them. There were thousands of victims on the floodplain below.

The politicians who had fought hardest for Teton Dam, such as Frank Church, were the first to pounce on the Bureau after the dam failed, the first to search the disaster for whatever political refuge could be found. Church castigated the Bureau for being "a prisoner of stale engineering ideas"; he made no apology for the stalest idea of all, the Congressional pork barrel. "No one told me the dam was going to break," Church blustered when the local people, most of whom had wanted the dam as badly as he, tried to hold him responsible. Actually, Bob Curry had suggested just that to him three years earlier, when he wrote Church about the geologic defects of the site. Curry claims he never got a decent response.

As for the Bureau, it said as little as it could. Its reputation suddenly in shambles, it tried not to make a wretched situation worse. Its press releases after the catastrophe were a dry recitation of events. They were honest, but there was no hint of responsibility, not even sympathy for the flood's victims, and no suggestion that perhaps the dam shouldn't have been built.

None of Teton's principal designers and builders were fired. Harold Arthur voluntarily retired—he had reached retirement age anyway—and started up a lucrative consulting business in Denver. Though he never publicly entertained a doubt about the dam, though he approved every major decision during its construction, though he vetoed a plan to install three grout curtains instead of one, not once during interviews in 1982 and 1984 did Arthur display a hint of remorse. "One minute I hear the dam is fine and the next minute it's failed," Arthur told me. "There wasn't anything *I* could do about it." Donald Duck was twice passed over for promotion, took early retirement, and moved to Chicago, where he became a vice-president of the Harza engineering firm, which builds dams. Robbie Robison drifted off and disappeared; in 1984, no one seemed to have any idea where he was. Commissioner Gil Stamm was, as always, wooden as a cigarstore Indian. "I ran into Stamm in Washington after the dam went," his old friend Floyd Dominy said. "I said to him, 'Jesus Christ, haven't you committed suicide yet?' He just smiled," said Dominy. "He just smiled."

To this day, no one is exactly sure what caused the collapse of Teton Dam, though several million dollars were spent on four independent investigations to figure it out. It might have been a leaky joint between the foundation and the dam. It might have been a flaw in the impervious core of the dam itself. It might have been poor filler material. It might have been expansion and contraction caused by ice that formed during winter construction. The theory Harold Arthur maintained is "incredible, virtually impossible"—that water drifted around the grout curtain on the right side and immediately went back into the dam, turning it to mud—is the one that one former Bureau engineer, who would rather not be named, believes is the likeliest explanation. "With the other theories, you can blame it on the contractors," he says. "With the grout-curtain theory, you're saying it was a lousy design. But that's why it failed. All the other theories are so much b.s."

However, among all the ironies that piled up in the aftermath of the Teton tragedy, everything pales beside one: there are a lot of voices in Idaho calling for the dam to be rebuilt. When a plague of locusts struck Utah after the first Mormons arrived, huge flocks of migrating seagulls flew in and ate them up. When clouds of disease-ridden flies and mosquitos appeared in the wake of the Teton debacle, the same thing happened again, so the Mormon irrigation confederacy of southern Idaho has apparently decided that God, all evidence to the contrary notwithstanding, is still on its side. On December 10, 1976, only half a year after the disaster, the Idaho Water Users' Association issued a resolution calling for a "safe" Teton Dam to be rebuilt at or near the same site. Harold Arthur still believes he could design a dam at the Teton site that would not collapse, though no one seems inclined to let him try. His suggestion, offered in muted tones, came as close to an apology as anything he said.

The economics of the project are worse than ever, and with so much of the arid West screaming for more projects—projects that, for whole regions, are really a matter of life or death, at least if irrigation is to continue—it would be hard to justify an irrigation project for farmers still putting ten feet of water on their land. None of this is to suggest, however, that the tragedy of Teton Dam might not be repeated somewhere else. Colorado, for example.

Flowing through Denver, the South Platte River appears so insignificant it is hard to believe it is the city's main water supply, let alone the sustenance of hundreds of thousands of irrigated acres downstream in Colorado and Nebraska. The South Platte is a mere fork of the main Platte, itself a tributary of the Missouri, itself a child of the Father of Waters. From a plane climbing up from Stapleton Airport, the South Platte is seen to meander forlornly out of town until it is quickly swallowed, as everything is, by the surreal endlessness of the Great Plains. Viewed from a low bluff two hundred miles downriver, it still appears of no consequence. The bottomlands are a tangle of shrubs and barbed wire interspersed with cottonwoods, and they are grazed bare by cows, which stare uncomprehendingly from the muck. It is a river without pretensions, haggard and used-looking, like a bag lady. In August, near the Nebraska border, the river dries up completely; all that reaches Nebraska is the underground flow. The Platte is one of the most hungrily used rivers in the entire world, surpassing even the Colorado. However, as far as Colorado is concerned, it is not used enough.

The South Platte is one of two rivers left in Colorado that isn't utterly and irrevocably appropriated, now and forever. To a state which is second to California in the arid West in population, industry, and irrigated acreage—but which has at its disposal about one-tenth as much water—the fact that some 7 percent of its share of the river still escapes to Nebraska is a fact of overarching significance. That the Bureau of Reclamation has offered to build an enormous dam across it to attempt to correct that situation is another. This last glimmering promise, in the face of a hopeless, nonnegotiable finality, has been enough to lead the members of Colorado's political establishment into a world of fantasy, leaving both their senses and their principles behind.

Don Christenson's crew cut stands up about an inch and a half, like a brush. A three-hundred-pound bear could nest down in that hair for the night and in the morning, after the bear lumbered off, it would spring right back up. The rest of Christenson fits the hairstyle: he is lean, weathered, bronzed as a Comanche. His jaw is made of cast iron. The one anomaly in his all-American countenance is a thick, voluptuous set of lips. In 1979, at the annual Conference on Rivers and Water Policy in Washington, D.C.—better known as the Damfighters' Conference—Christenson, surrounded by longhairs, environmental lawyers, bureaucrats, and kayakers, stood out like the man from Mars.

Christenson's presence at the Damfighters' Conference was a signal event. Unofficially, he was the first verifiable irrigation farmer who had ever attended the conference. He was probably one of the first who had ever opposed a dam, but he had a good reason. The Bureau of Reclamation, having nearly run out of decent damsites, had finally decided to turn the Reclamation Act inside out. It was going to flood out a bunch of small farmers so it could give supplemental water to a bunch of bigger farmers, several of whom would be in violation of the Reclamation Act. Christenson was one of the small farmers, and he was the one with the biggest mouth, so the Bureau wanted to drown him with a vengeance.

When Don Christenson's father settled in the Weldon Valley in 1926, there was already talk of a big dam at the Narrows of the South Platte, four or five miles downstream from his land. The first serious proposal seems to have emerged in 1908. The farm, the whole town of Weldona, and everything else from bluff to bluff for thirteen miles was to go under, but the elder Christenson refused to let the prospect faze him. "Dad would tell us, 'Maybe they are gonna build it. But maybe they're not gonna build it. Maybe they're gonna build it but they're not gonna build it for thirty years. I'm not going to sit here and let the goddamned government worry me to death. We're gonna farm our land and live a normal life and keep our property up, and to hell with them.' " His prophecy was remarkable. Finally authorized in 1944 as one of three-hundred-odd projects in the Pick-Sloan Act, the Narrows Project had still not been built forty years later.

The senior Christenson's attitude managed to infect all three of his sons, who raise their crops, paint their houses, fix their equipment, and otherwise carry on as if the threat of a dam did not exist. The same cannot be said, however, for the Weldon Valley as a whole. Weldona has the look of a town losing hope: houses unpainted, shutters askew, eerily quiet. "The people who've just decided to let their ol' house decay may be the smart ones," Christenson says bitterly. "Why spend $15,000 to fix up your property when you know the Bureau of Reclamation"—he pronounces it "*Bee*-yoor-o"—"is gonna tell you your house is a slum anyway when they make you an offer?"

The Weldon Valley was settled in the 1870s, only forty years before the first proposal for a Narrows Dam; for most of its existence it has been threatened with extinction. Any day, any hour, someone might appear on one's front lawn to survey; someone might amble up one's walk with a sheaf of papers and an offer to sign or else. It is bad enough to live like this; it is worse to live under the shadow of a project as nonsensical as the Narrows Dam. And it becomes almost ludicrous if there is a distinct possibility that the dam, once built, may not hold water and could conceivably collapse, rendering seventy-five years of worry, agony, and divisiveness for naught. This has been Don Christenson's fate since the day he was born.

The dam will be immense—an earthen monster. Twenty-two thousand four hundred feet long, it would stretch, if laid across Washington, D.C.—which is where Christenson suggests it ought to be built—from outer Georgetown to the Capitol. In New York, it would stretch from the Empire State Building to the Staten Island Ferry. For all its length, it would be only 147 feet high, and the reservoir behind it would be drawn down much of the time, which has prompted its critics to rename the project "the Shallows." How anything this monumental—one of the largest dams on earth, longer even than the main dam of Itaípu, longer than Fort Peck—could be built for $226 million (the official cost estimate as of 1980) is anyone's guess. Actually, a great part of that expenditure—probably half—wouldn't even be used to build the dam. It would go to 844 landowners to pay compensation for the ninety-five farms, twenty-eight businesses, two churches, and elementary school that would be put underwater. It would also be used to relocate twenty-six miles of the Union Pacific's track and twenty miles of State Route 144. The remainder of the money would somehow erect a four-mile-long dam.

The Narrows Reservoir would submerge fourteen thousand to seventeen thousand acres of productive, privately irrigated farmland, none of which has ever received the kind of subsidy the beneficiaries of Narrows would automatically get. (This is some of the oldest continuously irrigated land in the West; the Weldon Valley ditch was dug by human and horse muscle in 1881.) Another forty thousand acres of unirrigated grazing land would also be drowned or affected. Some waterfowl habitat would be affected, but the real damage to nature would be downstream. Flows in the hugely depleted South Platte, which are already critically low for the three-quarters of a million ducks and geese and the migrating whooping and sandhill cranes—the entire surviving U.S. population—for which the river is a crucial feeding and resting spot, would be further reduced. Although the amount of water diverted would not be much—for a dam of such size and cost, it would be pathetic—its absence would be sorely felt by the waterfowl. On top of this, the concentration of fertilizers, pesticides, and sewage—Denver's and Fort Collins's—in the river would become worse.

The main benefit of building Narrows, on the other hand, would be supplemental irrigation water for 287,000 acres of land downstream from Don Christenson's farm, most of it between the towns of Brush and Sterling. There would only be enough water for inches per acre, and one could reasonably question whether, during the occasional severe drought whose ravages Narrows is supposed to make less severe, so little water would do any real good. In fact, the continued profitability of the farms making up those 287,000 acres through dry years and wet ones makes one wonder why the water is needed at all. The other benefits claimed for Narrows are recreation and flood control.

The high plains are home to some of the most freakish and violent weather in the world. Once, in Spearfish, South Dakota, thermometers leaped from two below to thirty-eight above zero in two minutes. A rutting ground for Canadian and Caribbean airflows, the plains are also known as tornado alley. Something like 85 percent of the world's tornados occur in North America, most of them between the Rockies and the Mississippi River. A much more frequent natural phenomenon, however, is the tornado's weaker sister, the hell-raising, rambunctious, exhilarating Great Plains thunderstorm.

One has to experience such a thunderstorm, preferably while lying scared to death in a ditch, to fathom the magnificent power of creation. In Texas, where the tropical flows are still saturated with moisture when they clash with colder air, a parade of thunderstorms dumped thirty inches of rain in twenty-four hours in the spring of

1978, far more rain than West Texas normally receives in a year. In Colorado, six- and seven-inch storms have been known on the plains, and since the natural groundcover is sparse, the flooding that results is spectacular. In 1964, such a flood occurred in the Bijou Creek watershed eighty miles east of Denver. Most of the time, Bijou Creek is less a creek than a dry wash; one has to search to find a puddle. During that storm, however, the Bijou became the second-largest river in the United States, carrying 465,000 cubic feet per second off the barren plains. Don Christenson was there. "It was the most unbelievable son of a bitch you ever saw," he says. The Bijou rose in a few hours and was almost dry a day later: a phantom monster. But the damage downstream was done.

Bijou Creek enters the South Platte from the south, exactly at the site of Narrows Dam. Upriver, the Platte is well controlled; the main untamed tributary below Fort Collins, and the main cause of damage downstream, is Bijou Creek. The damsite is flexible enough so that one can more or less choose to put the dam in front of the Bijou confluence or behind it. If the dam goes in upstream from the Bijou confluence, obviously, most of the flood-control benefits are lost.

Originally, the Bureau was intent on capturing the Bijou behind Narrows Dam because the economics of the project would automatically improve: greater flood-control benefits could be claimed, and a much larger proportion of the dam's cost would be nonreimbursable. Flood control, however, has always been the province of the Corps of Engineers, and the Corps, not the Bureau, would have to decide whether capturing the Bijou was worth it—or, for that matter, whether it was even safe to try to contain it.

The decision was to be made in 1965, shortly after Narrows was reauthorized by Congress and the Bureau began to push it seriously. On July 14, 1965, in a confidential letter to Commissioner Dominy, Pat Dugan, who had just left California to become the Bureau's regional director in Denver, described his efforts to ensure a decision that controlling the Bijou was worthwhile. Having just attended a meeting of the Colorado Water Conservation Board, Dugan reported, "I stressed the necessity for an early answer from the Corps of Engineers on the benefits to be provided for control of Bijou Creek by extension of the dam. The Board strongly expressed themselves as being in favor of this facet of the Narrows Project, and *I am confident that the Corps will be under continued pressure to provide the necessary answer*" (emphasis added). Unfortunately for the Bureau, the pressure to provide the "necessary" answer came to naught. The Bijou flooded mightily, but it flooded most infrequently, the Corps decided, so controlling it wasn't worth the extra cost. There was also some question as to whether another 450,000-cfs flood might not take out the dam.

With most of its flood-control rationale gone, Narrows went into eclipse during the remainder of the 1960s. In the early 1970s, however, the tide of fortune changed. Wayne Aspinall, the chairman of the House Interior Committee, was growing old and politically vulnerable, and Narrows, it seemed, was to be his swan song. The imperious old schoolteacher began pushing it so relentlessly that he even refused to let the project's opponents testify before his House Interior Committee. At the same time, the first OPEC oil crisis hit, and everyone began eyeing Colorado's huge reserves of oil shale. Some Coloradans seemed to want to turn the state into an energy colony and grow rich off it; others wanted to lock up as much water as possible so the oil, coal, and uranium industries would be forced to remain relatively small and the state's rural character, what was left of it, would remain fairly intact. One of the main adherents of the latter view was the new governor, Richard D. Lamm; an even stronger adherent was his commissioner of natural resources, Harris Sherman. The fact that Narrows was nowhere near the shale oil and uranium was somehow lost. What mattered was giving the state's unappropriated water to agriculture and locking it up, as best one could, now and forever.

As Midas turned everything he touched into gold, the Narrows Project had a miraculous ability to turn everyone it touched into someone else. It turned a crew-cut, rawboned young farmer like Don Christenson into an environmentalist. It turned a handsome young environmentalist like Senator Gary Hart into an avid water developer. Above all, it turned perhaps the three most powerful men in Colorado into bitter enemies.

One of the three was Glenn Saunders, the chief counsel for the Denver Water Board. A brilliant man with a silver tongue, Saunders had, for more than thirty years, been *the* water lawyer in a state where water lawyers wield power that makes them objects of profound respect. Under his tutelage, the Denver Water Board had become a kind of understudy of the Metropolitan Water District of Los Angeles: a well-oiled, well-funded suprapolitical machine trying to purloin water from every corner of the state, all in the interest of turning Denver into the Los Angeles of the Rockies—a goal which has been largely achieved. In a strictly legal sense, of course, the Water Board didn't steal water. But cross the Front Range and go into the mountains, where most of Colorado's water originates, and the response to a mention of the Denver Water Board is likely to be an oath.

Saunders was the perfect symbol of this rough-and-tumble political machine. With his Dickensian visage, in his checked suits and pastel shirts and vivid ties, he was the city sharpie making ruthless inroads into the virgin old West—terrifying witnesses in the docket, shouting down citizens at public hearings, and always scheming, pushing, plotting for more dams.

The second of the three men was Clarence J. Kuiper, who, through most of the 1970s, served as Colorado's state engineer. In a state such as Colorado, where both ground and surface water are regulated and everyone wants more than there is, the state engineer is a combination of judge, jury, and cop. He decides what is a reasonable diversion to each farm; he decides who can put in a well and how much he can pump; he decides when a diverter can no longer divert during a drought and when a pumper can no longer pump; he makes sure enough water reaches neighboring states to satisfy compact agreements; and, in the course of making such decisions, he wins the wrath and, if he does his job honestly and well—as Kuiper did—the grudging admiration of every water user in the state. Kuiper's whole life had been spent in water development: first as a young engineer for the Corps and the Bureau mapping some of the most farfetched water-diversion schemes ever concocted; then as a construction engineer in Turkey, for whose government the Bureau was building dams; later as a consulting engineer for the state of Wyoming, for which he drew up a water plan; and, finally, as Colorado's viceroy of water. A gigantic man whose ponderous gait and basso profundo voice bely a quick and encompassing intellect, Kuiper was light-years from being a conservationist. He was a water developer and an admirer of Ronald Reagan; he was enough of a westerner to call Jimmy Carter's water-projects hit list an "act of war," even if, in private, he referred to most of the projects in question as "dogs." Kuiper never stood in the path of a water project, unless it was a project in another state that threatened his own state's supply. But that would change.

The third man was the governor of Colorado, Richard Lamm. Young, humorless, thoughtful, intense, prematurely silver-haired, Lamm was a prototype of the New Age politician. As a state legislator he had made a name as an environmentalist, and a rather bold one— he was the leader of the successful effort to keep the lucrative Winter Olympics out of Denver. In 1978, the *Almanac of American Politics* described him as "far-out." He flew periodically to Chicago or New

York to hobnob with people like Garrett Hardin, the ecologist, and Hazel Henderson, the "futurist," who served with him on the national board of the Council on Population and Environment. He staffed his administration with left-leaning people in their twenties and thirties—people like Harris Sherman, his resources secretary, who had served as counsel to the Environmental Defense Fund. Lamm was the sort of politician one could imagine drinking Red Zinger tea amid the whiskey-swillers in the smoke-filled rooms; he had backpacks and bicycles in his garage, and his wife, Dottie, was a well-known feminist. From every Chamber of Commerce in every mean little Colorado town there arose a collective groan. Dick Lamm—the *governor*?

But Lamm already had a reputation, in some circles, as a rather shameless opportunist. And even at the apogee of his alleged radicalism, he never was known as someone who didn't like water projects.

In 1975, when Don Christenson and his Weldon Valley landowners' group went shopping for a lawyer to represent them in what they were sure could culminate in a legal battle with the Bureau of Reclamation, they decided they had better choose well. "Everyone we talked to said, 'You want the best, go hire Glenn Saunders,'" Christenson remembers. "I said, 'Glenn Saunders, hell! Name one dam he's ever opposed. He isn't going to bother with a bunch of farmers like us.' Well, we went to see him anyway. At first he looked like he couldn't wait for us to go back out the door. But we served it up to him straight, and that man listened to us. You could watch his prejudices dissolve. I mean, he was a lawyer, first and foremost, and he knew we had a case."

"Here was this bunch of farmers marching in here saying they wanted to stop Narrows Dam," a raspy-voiced Saunders recounted. "I said to them, 'Stop Narrows Dam! We don't want that. We want to get everything we can built!' But they kept throwing facts at me, and they finally had me convinced Narrows is a boondoggle. When I took a closer look it was an even bigger boondoggle than they said."

"Old Saunders had sort of half agreed to represent us," Christenson recalls. "But I think he still wanted to hear what the Bureau had to say. So he ups and says, 'Get your coats! We're going out to see the Bureau.' Just like that! We drove out there to the Bureau's big box of a headquarters, Mr. Saunders and Marvin Etchison, our president, and me. Saunders knew just the man to see. We walked into the bureaucrat's office—I can't remember who he was—and sat down like we owned it. I was tickled—mad as I was at the Bureau,

I never would have done something like that. And Mr. Saunders and this Bureau guy got into an argument right away. I don't even know about what, but the Bureau guy said, 'Well, Mr. Saunders, *you* of all people should know that.' " Christenson is given to explosions of laughter, and the recollection makes him almost giddy. " '*You* should know the answer to that!' Saunders doesn't say another word. He was *mad*! He gets up and kind of calmly says to Marvin and me, 'Come on, Marvin and Don. We can accomplish nothing further here.' And out we went, just like we came in. In the car, Saunders says, 'I want you to go back to the Weldon Valley and start raising a kitty of a hundred thousand dollars. That's what it's going to cost you to fight your government.'

"A hundred thousand dollars! You could have licked me if I thought we could raise that kind of money from a little old bunch of farmers."

In plotting their strategy, the Weldon Valley landowners' group had made one crucial mistake. They had always assumed that their main fight would be with the Bureau, the Colorado Water Conservation Board—a chamber of commerce for dams—and the Lower South Platte Conservancy District, which was scheduled to receive water from Narrows. The Lower South Platte Conservancy District was led by two brothers, Dave and Don Hamel, both influential in state and national politics; Dave Hamel had run unsuccessfully for governor and was a former administrator of the Rural Electrification Administration. (If Narrows was built, the Hamels would probably be the chief violators of the Reclamation Act in its service area, for they owned several thousand acres there.) But, as it turned out, the Bureau and the Lower South Platte people were merely a major and a minor irritant. The really tough opposition came from the person they had originally counted on for help: Colorado governor Dick Lamm.

What had happened to Lamm, the onetime radical environmental legislator? His former friend Alan Merson, who beat Wayne Aspinall in the Democratic primary in 1972, lost the general election, and ended up as regional administrator for the EPA, thought he had his finger on it. "Lamm got religion rather late in life," Merson told an interviewer. "Once a political aspirant gets elected, he finds he has this strange new dilemma: rather than worrying about what people want to *hear*, he has to worry about what they want to *have*. There's a big difference. People move out here because of the Rocky Mountains, but if some huge hand came down and swept away the Rocky Mountains a lot of them wouldn't even notice. They're too busy getting rich. Well, Dick Lamm was elected in the middle of the biggest boom in this state's history. He saw that the great big capitalist machine creating all the filth and ugliness and pollution was also making his constituents fat and sleek and happy. He came to feel that he had slighted the capitalist machine, which suddenly seemed to him to be working miracles. I mean, you look out from the capitol dome and all you see is brown inhospitable plains on the one side and ice-covered mountains on the other. It looks like a tough place. But the capitalist machine was scratching phenomenal wealth out of it. At some point Lamm realized that the whole damned machine runs on the impoundment of water. So he said, 'By God, we'd better impound some more water.'

"It isn't just Lamm," Merson went on disgustedly. "The whole Congressional delegation, except for Pat Schroeder"—a young Democratic Congresswoman from Denver—"is on the run from the irrigators—not even all the irrigators, but just those who are lucky enough to be sucking off the big federal teat. Gary Hart, Floyd Haskell, Tim Wirth—I like them all, they're my friends, but they're all scared to death of not liking water enough. This state is booming like crazy, and we're running out of water. So politicians tend to go blind in office. They're for *any* water project—they don't care how bad it is.

"At EPA, we tried to start a permit program for salinity discharges," Merson went on. "Some of these irrigators are poisoning rivers all the way to the ocean, returning water that's twenty times saltier than when they take it out. I explained it to Dick and he said, 'You're right. It's a good plan. But I can't support it. The legislature will kill me over it. Goddamn it, this could be another Interstate 470. I'll lose!' That was what really bothered him," Merson said, " 'I'll lose!' I took it to Harris Sherman and he said, 'It's unconstitutional, illegal, and immoral—*and* it will hurt agriculture.' "

Agriculture was key in Lamm's and Sherman's thinking, because what they wanted even more than growth was *stable* growth. In 125 years, Colorado's economy has boomed and busted more than that of any other state except, perhaps, Nevada. Nevada had introduced stable industries: gambling, prostitution, marriage, divorce. In Colorado, the only industry that had filled the fearful troughs between the boom cycles, when it looked as if the state might be virtually abandoned, was agriculture. It represented stability. Late in the twentieth century, it had also come to represent something else. Unlike eastern states, which can keep out development only by passing laws, western states have a natural means of halting industries they don't want at their gates: a scarcity of water. In the early 1970s, Colorado became the first western state that actually wanted to keep an industry out, or at least keep it from overwhelming its economy and way of life. The industry was energy—especially oil shale. And the means of holding back its growth was to try to put the remaining water in agriculture's hands and let the energy companies worry about wresting it away—or let them import water from somewhere else, as Exxon was proposing to run an aqueduct from Oahe Reservoir in South Dakota.

C. J. Kuiper, on the other hand, was charged with putting water to beneficial use, and it seemed silly to him to waste tens of thousands of acre-feet on crops with a low economic return—crops which were subsidized by the Reclamation program and, in the case of some, federal price supports—when half of America's oil was now coming out of the Middle East. Privately, Kuiper believed oil shale development was necessary: philosophically, he believed in the doctrine of highest use. Water had become so scarce in Colorado that whoever could pay the most should get what remained. Reclamation farmers paid the least of anyone.

Such thinking, however, was ultimately to have very little to do with the position Kuiper took on the Narrows Project. His position rested on his growing conviction that Narrows, if built, wouldn't even be able to *hold* water; that it would never be able to deliver the water it promised; and that there was a very real possibility the dam would collapse.

Never, since Narrows was first authorized in 1944, had anyone suggested that it might sit on an unsafe site. How much on-site testing the Bureau did prior to the 1970s is unknown; its main concern seemed to be drumming up enough local support to overwhelm the opposition. But by 1976 it had its first sizable appropriation in hand, and finally decided it ought to learn something about the geology of the Narrows site.

One morning in the summer of that year, Corky Tomky, a neighbor of Don Christenson's and a leader in the battle against the dam, noticed that the Bureau had a man with a drilling rig down by the South Platte. Tomky wandered over to say hello. The man announced that he was drilling core samples to see what the foundation of the dam was like. Tomky asked him what he had found so far.

"Well, don't quote me," the driller answered, "but this site has big problems."

435

"Big problems?"

"*Big* problems. There's bedrock down there somewhere, but I can't find it. I've drilled two hundred and fifty feet down and still haven't hit it. All I get is gravel and loose rock, and sand."

"What do you suppose that means?" Tomky asked.

"It means," the Bureau man drawled, "that this dam is going to have a hell of a time holding water. The foundation is like a coffee filter. But don't tell 'em I told you that."

Tomky swore that he wouldn't, then he walked casually back to his truck and gunned it over the bumpy road toward Don Christenson's place.

"As soon as Corky told me what he heard," Christenson recalled, "we called up our Congressman, Jim Johnson. He was one hundred percent for the dam, but we figured *this* was a piece of news. We got his assistant on the line—I can't even remember what his name is. Well, he sounded real concerned on the phone. He told me, 'I'll talk to the Congressman and get right back to you.' I wished I'd had a tape recorder on that damn line. He never got back to me. No, sir. And the next day, wouldn't you believe it, that well driller was *not* back on the job. They handcuffed him to a desk in Denver somewhere. He never came back again. It was about then," Christenson said, "that we decided to see the state engineer."

The point at which Christenson decided to pay a call on the state engineer coincided nicely with the collapse of Teton Dam. Teton, as Kuiper put it, "scared the living bleep out of Lamm and Harris Sherman." Both of them watched poor Cecil Andrus face the reporters on the news, and saw his hapless water-resources director, Keith Higginson, blamed for a tragedy he had had little to do with. Andrus had been lukewarm at most about the Teton Project. What if a dam Lamm and Sherman strongly backed wiped out a string of Colorado towns? After Teton Dam went, Sherman decided he had better review the safety questions surrounding any imminent project planned for Colorado.

"When Sherman called his meeting, I was just leaving on a trip," Kuiper recalls. "I had never paid much attention to the Narrows— I'm not required to in the case of a federal project. I knew the ancient Platte River left a great big alluvial bed and that the Bureau would have to get through a lot of alluvial wash to anchor the dam on anything solid. But I figured they knew what to do. I could have walked into Sherman's meeting and said, 'Well, I know of a few problems with the site but I defer to the Bureau's expertise.' After *Teton*—good Lord, I didn't imagine that the Bureau was going to let something *that* stupid happen again." But, Kuiper figured, he was the state engineer; if a dam failed, and he had assayed the site, he would share in the blame no matter who deserved it. Besides, Sherman had asked for his opinion, and he might as well give an informed one. Therefore, as he left to go on his trip, he asked his assistants, in his absence, to prepare a schematic of the Narrows site, superimposing the dam over a big color diagram of what was known of the geologic conditions. When he got back he had only a few minutes to look over the schematic; a few minutes was all he needed. "I looked at that schematic," Kuiper said, "and in thirty seconds I saw why that test driller was right. The old alluvial bed of that ancient river is huge. There are about ten stories of gravel out there sitting on five stories of cobblestones. Way off on the south end of the site the alluvial bed is almost three hundred feet deep. Well, they can't clean all that stuff out—it would be much too expensive and God knows where they'd even put it. So they were just going to let the dam sit on top of the alluvium, not really anchored to rock except at the abutments. And the alluvium ran *under* the south abutment. To prevent seepage under the dam, they had a cutoff trench planned down to bedrock, sort of like the keyway trench they built at Teton. But basically they were just going to hang it under the dam like a curtain.

"Hell, that alluvium is so wide they've got to run that trench out on the south side, way beyond the dam, or water is going to creep around it—exactly the way it did at Teton. It looked to me, from the schematic, that they were going to have to extend it out a mile. Well, no way they were planning to do that—it would cost too much.

"I sat there staring at the schematic," Kuiper said, "and I said to myself, 'Here we go again. Doesn't the Bureau even know how to learn from a disaster?'"

Even if the seepage didn't reenter the dam immediately—which was what apparently happened at Teton—Kuiper guessed that the rate of water seepage would be so enormous that the reservoir would more or less disappear and emerge somewhere downriver, as a swamp. But where? The water would back up behind the dam, penetrate the porous reservoir bottom, and sneak around the cutoff trench, underground. Then, following the downslope of the plains, it would have to resurface at about the same elevation. That elevation coincided approximately with the town of Fort Morgan, population eight thousand, which lay fifteen miles downriver. "If they build the dam," Kuiper said sardonically, "those Fort Morganites had better learn how to swim."

When Kuiper walked into Harris Sherman's meeting, he was surprised to see his sometime nemesis Glenn Saunders smiling at him. Saunders had somehow caught wind of the gathering and had demanded admittance; Sherman, who could hardly have wanted him there, hadn't dared bar him. One did not invite the antipathy of the preeminent water lawyer in Colorado.

Sherman opened the meeting by asking each of the assembled members to state flatly whether they had any misgivings about the Narrows site.

"The site's fine," said the Bureau geologist.

"The site's fine," said Felix Sparks, the head of the Colorado Water Conservation Board.

"The site's fine," said the state geologist.

Everyone else had the same answer, except Kuiper.

"Well," said Kuiper, "I might have agreed with you until ten minutes ago, when I saw the schematic my staff prepared for me. Maybe you should have a look at it, too."

Sherman looked pained. "What are you saying, Kupe?" he demanded.

"I'm saying that looking at that schematic gave me some serious reservations about the Narrows site," Kuiper said. "From the looks of it there could be major leakage right under the dam. If it were a nonfederal project, I'd never approve it."

Sherman, watching Saunders and Don Christenson, whom the lawyer had brought with him, cackling silently behind closed lips, was incensed. "On what basis do you say that? Why do you say that?"

Kuiper then laid out what the schematic had told him. Sherman acted as if he hadn't heard a word of it. "I don't care about your schematic," he finally interrupted. "I want to see a lengthy memo on all of this. You've made some very serious charges in the presence of two people who will obviously use them against this dam. You had better be right."

Kuiper stood up to his full six feet six and glowered at Sherman, who was at least twenty-five years younger. "Young man, you'll get your lengthy memorandum," he growled. "But don't you tell me what I'd 'better' be." Then he stalked out of the room.

Kuiper had hardly finished his memorandum later that day when he received calls from both Saunders and the *Rocky Mountain News*, which had obviously been put onto the story by Saunders, asking whether they could have a copy. The *News* reporter also wanted to take a look through his Narrows file. As a public servant, Kuiper had no other choice than to keep his files open, except on matters involving national security. He was also legally obligated to make public any document he wrote, including the Sherman memo. He invited both Saunders and the reporter to come over. The reporter from the *News* was just taking the file to an empty desk when Sherman stalked into Kuiper's office.

"What is *he* doing here?" Sherman demanded, pointing at the reporter.

Kuiper said he had given him permission to look through the file.

Sherman was aghast. "*I* haven't even had a chance to look at it," he protested.

"Well, he asked first," said Kuiper. Sherman looked as if he were ready to throw a punch. He walked over to the reporter and grabbed the sheaf of files. "I'm looking through these first," he said, plopping the stack on an empty desk as the reporter stood by dumbfounded.

In Kuiper, Sherman had a messenger whom he couldn't kill, and when he tried he seemed only to wound himself. After the incident with the reporter, the state attorney general removed Kuiper's Narrows file for safekeeping because of the lawsuit pending over the issue. Kuiper insists he did not ask him to do it, but Sherman evidently thought he had; the whole thing reflected badly on him, because it looked as if the attorney general thought someone might pilfer materials from the file, and the person who would have seemed to have the best motive—the person most ardently in favor of Narrows—was Sherman himself. Sherman was enraged. He immediately wrote Kuiper a long memorandum impugning, implicitly or explicitly, his integrity, his motives, his sense of judgment, and even his competence as an engineer. Because he was about to leave town, Sherman dictated the memo and asked his assistant, Jerry Sjaagstad, to sign it. After reading the memo, Kuiper sat down and wrote a blistering one of his own, which he walked downstairs and threw on Sjaagstad's desk. Ten minutes later, Sjaagstad rushed into his office and demanded that he retract what he had said. Kuiper refused. When Sherman returned and heard what had happened, *he* came storming into Kuiper's office.

"You are being insubordinate," he yelled at Kuiper. "I'm going to take disciplinary action against you. You are going to regret this."

Kuiper stood up and went chest to nose with Sherman, who was a full head shorter. "I'm civil service," he thundered. "You *can't* discipline me without cause. But I hope you try. I'll blow you right out of the water, young man."

It seemed that *nothing* could change Dick Lamm's and Harris Sherman's minds about Narrows: not the plight of the Weldon Valley; not the state engineer's misgivings about the safety of the damsite; not the Teton disaster; not even the fact—which became an issue again after Kuiper's skepticism was reported in the press—that there was an alternative to the Narrows site. It was an alternative that appeared to be safer, that would inundate a cow feedlot instead of homes, churches, and graves, and that made as little or as much economic sense as the Narrows Project.

Twenty-five miles upriver toward Greeley, the Hardin site had been under consideration for years as an alternative to Narrows. It was not authorized by Pick-Sloan mainly because it would have cost slightly more to build. In other, highly important respects, however, it was the superior site. The main "improvement" within the taking area was the Joseph Monfort feedlot, the largest cattle-feeding operation in the world. Qualifying "improvement" is especially advised here, because the Monfort feedlot—100,000 cows on a couple of thousand acres—was an insult to all five senses. Its downwind neighbors found themselves wishing wistfully that they could replace it with a paper mill. One of the largest sources of nonpoint pollution in the country, the feedlot would sooner or later run into the Clean Water Act, and might be shut down for good. Rumor had it that Joe Monfort would be happy to have someone pay him to take it off his hands.

But the Hardin site, if it was substituted for Narrows, would have to be authorized all over again. At its authorization hearings, it would run into cost-conscious members of Congress and the environmental movement, which hadn't existed when Narrows was first authorized. Worse still—far worse—was the fact that it would have to be justified with a discount, or interest, rate twice as high. Since Narrows was the cheaper site, and *it* could barely pass muster at a 3¼ percent discount rate, it was hard to see how a Hardin dam could ever be authorized.

Now that the Hardin site had reemerged as an alternative, however, it could only be viewed as a threat. The Bureau of Reclamation, therefore, decided that there was only one course open to it. It had to break ground on the Narrows project quickly, and the first step was to move the people out of the way.

The history of "relocation"—removing people in the way of a project from their land and compensating them for what they lost—started early in the century with the Los Angeles Department of Water and Power, and was embellished a short while later by the New York City Water Department when it drowned the Catskill valleys to create a new water supply. These were the first times in our history—except, of course, for the indignities visited on the Indians—when thousands of people were dispossessed for the crime of impeding progress. What the TVA did in the 1930s, what the Corps of Engineers did along the Missouri in the later 1940s, and what the Bureau tried to do in the Weldon Valley in the 1970s followed the same script. They sniffed through the community, smelling out its most avaricious members, those most susceptible to an offer. They spread rumors; they spread lies. They offered extravagant settlements to the first few who bit, then grew less and less spendthrift with the holdouts, both to punish them and to balance the initial extravagance. They played on the social conscience of communities, accusing them of selfishness, of denying the greatest good to the greatest number. And in the final resort—judiciously at first, then more threateningly, then like a defensive line blitzing a quarterback—they invoked the prospect of eminent domain.

They did all this without a sense of shame, because they told themselves they were serving an ultimate good—they were preventing floods, feeding the hungry world, offering power and light to schools and heat and air conditioning to hospitals. They denied—to themselves as to their would-be victims—that the real reason they were doing it was that they couldn't bear the thought of no longer building dams. And the very majesty of their great works made it easier for them to do it. It may be easier to sweep hundreds of people out of the way than ten or twelve, as if a project important enough to call for the removal of so many must be worth building.

George Kyncl, an employee of the Colorado Department of Social Services, who witnessed firsthand the trauma the Bureau's relocation effort was causing in the Weldon Valley, was always struck by its indifference to its victims' fate. "They were like Jekyll and Hyde," Kyncl says. "When you met them on the street or in meetings or the coffee shop in Fort Morgan they'd smile and joke with the same people they were trying to throw off their land. They were in here for so long they almost felt like members of the local community. You had to keep reminding yourself of the real reason they were here."

When the Bureau's men approached Ben Schatz, a South Dakota farmer whose land it wanted for the Oahe Diversion Project, they said, "To us you're just a dot on the map. When you get in the way, we move you."

When you get in the way, we move you. Don Christenson was sitting at home one day in 1976 when the phone rang. Don's wife, Karen, picked it up. It was a neighbor, someone the Christensons did not see regularly. Don could see from Karen's expression that it was something bad. Karen kept saying, "No, no, no. No, it's ridiculous. It's crazy." When she hung up, she looked at Don with a pained expression—half laughing, half anguished. "The talk they hear is that we've sold out."

Don and Karen Christenson cannot prove that it was the Bureau that spread the rumor. Could it have been Felix Sparks? Harris Sherman? "The frustrating thing was we didn't know where the rumor came from," said Karen. "It was so evil, so nasty a thing to do. You feel so helpless, but you feel so mad. When I heard that rumor I just wanted to scream." It might have been the Lower South Platte Conservancy District. The district was not above some rather sneaky tactics. In the full-color brochure it was still using in 1981 as a propaganda piece for Narrows, it showed Bijou Creek coming in *behind* the dam, not in front of it, even though that plan had been dead since 1965. Called on this point, Gary Friehauff, its young executive director, offered what seemed like a lame explanation: "We're still going through the old stock of brochures."

It was not the first rumor, and by no means would it be the last. At the Damfighters' Conference in Washington, Christenson had been warned by someone who had watched the Corps of Engineers in action in the Middle West that divisive rumors spread innocuously in neighboring towns would be a prime tactic when the Bureau began trying to buy the land in the reservoir area. Not long afterward, Don got a call from a neighbor who had just gone to Fort Morgan to get a haircut. The man in the next chair had been talking about all the people who, according to scuttlebutt he had heard, were thinking of selling out early. He represented himself as a real estate broker from out of town. No one had ever seen him before.

The Bureau knew exactly whom to go after. Sandy Desmond (a pseudonym) was, for a time, one of the leaders of the Regional Landowners group. Everyone liked Sandy—he was amiable, a teddy bear, a sort of irrepressibly cheerful Mr. Micawber. His weakness was also Micawber's—Sandy loved money, and he liked to make a fast buck. Nonetheless, people didn't really worry too much about Sandy. He was, after all, a leader of the opposition. To hear him rave against the Bureau was almost an embarrassment—small children had to be kept out of earshot. "We're going to kick their goddamned butts out of here in six months," he said in 1975, after the Bureau set up its first project office since the 1940s.

One Weldon Valley resident remembers how she found out about Sandy. "My husband walked in the house one day," she says. "I think it was late in the afternoon. I was sitting right here at the kitchen table. I could tell from the look on my husband's face that something was really wrong. All the things that it could be flashed through my mind in a second and I just lighted on Sandy. I said, 'Sandy went over.' And he said, 'Yup. Sandy went over. They made him an offer he couldn't refuse.'

"They poisoned the atmosphere in this community something dreadful," said the woman. "They went after the people they thought were more likely to sell, but they also spread lies about the leaders of the Regional Landowners organization. We just heard the rumors. We didn't know who was spreading them, we didn't know if they were true. When I heard that rumor about Don Christenson selling out, I thought, 'Well, that's the end.' They created such an atmosphere of distrust it took years before we got over it. I'm not sure we have completely yet.'

Another weapon in the Narrows lobby's repertoire was the old strategy of feint and dodge. "Every time we read one of their new reports the figures were different," says Don Christenson. "In one document they said they were going to have 100,000 acre-feet available from the reservoir each year. Then they said 120,000 acre-feet. At one point they were up to 150,000. They never gave an explanation. They just changed the numbers on us all the time, so we had to get out the old calculator and prove them wrong again. All the while I'm trying to raise a thousand acres of corn and worry about a few hundred head of cattle. It was no picnic, I'll tell you. One thing about the Bureau, though," Christenson added grimly. "They sure know how to make a person mad."

Meanwhile, as the Bureau was doing battle with the Weldon Valley (or "poverty valley," as Gary Friehauff of the Lower South Platte organization described it to me) on the one hand and with the newly elected Carter administration on the other—one of Carter's

first actions was to put Narrows on his initial water-projects hit list—
the state engineer, C. J. Kuiper, thought he had discovered yet another
fatal flaw in the scheme. It was one of those details that dwell in a
special kind of obscurity reserved for the perfectly obvious. What if
the water couldn't possibly get to where it was intended to go?

"At first I never thought much about the channel losses," the
state engineer would remember later on. "But one of the biggest
headaches of my job had always been getting water down to the senior
irrigators along the South Platte. All the groundwater pumpers who
came along during the fifties and sixties and seventies had been depauperating the aquifer on both sides of the river. Some guy would
call on fifty second-feet that were his rights and my river master
would cut off the junior diverters and the pumpers upstream so he
could get it. Nothing would arrive. He'd call on another fifty cfs and
we'd send it to him and it still wouldn't arrive. I said to myself, 'What
the hell's going on here?' Then we figured out that it was all being
captured by the aquifers. The pumpers had emptied those aquifers
so bad that *they* were acting like pumps. The water we sent down
went right through the bottom of the Platte and migrated laterally
and went into the aquifer. It was like it had a great big hole in it.

"So I went to the Bureau and told them their water was going
to disappear on the way down from Narrows to the South Platte
Conservancy District, and they said, 'Hogwash!' I said, 'Hogwash?
We're cutting junior diverters up and down the river by four hundred
cfs so the seniors at Julesburg can get twenty cfs and they're still not
getting a goddamned drop!' The Bureau was saying that if they released a hundred thousand acre-feet out of Narrows Reservoir, maybe
ninety thousand acre-feet would arrive at the headgates of the guys
they'd contracted to sell water to. Well, they were full of baloney.
They'd be lucky to get twenty-five thousand acre-feet.

"I kept telling the Bureau and Felix Sparks and Harris that I
didn't care if they built their dam or not," Kuiper said. "But I'm the
one who has to see to it that every irrigator gets the water he's entitled
to. Well, if the Bureau promises them ninety thousand acre-feet, and
I can only deliver twenty thousand, I'm the one who gets blamed. I
can't give them ninety thousand unless I cut off others who have
senior rights, and that's illegal. The Bureau was making a bunch of
outlandish promises and I was the one who was supposed to keep
them."

The Bureau, Dick Lamm, Felix Sparks, and Harris Sherman naturally refused to believe a word Kuiper said. Even so, his reputation

was good enough, and his statements were colorful enough, that the newspapers listened to him, and soon the issue of channel losses—of the Bureau planning to build a $226 million project that might not be able to deliver water—was all over the local press. Sensing yet another impasse, the Bureau decided that it had better get someone else's opinion. "Someone else" turned out to be Woodward-Clyde.

A huge engineering firm of considerable reputation, Woodward-Clyde has enjoyed a comfortable relationship of long standing with the Bureau. The Bureau often relies on Woodward-Clyde to perform independent assessments of its plans; then it often rewards it with lucrative construction contracts. It was no surprise, therefore, when Woodward-Clyde's estimate of channel losses in the Platte coincided nicely with the Bureau's. Kuiper, however, continued to insist that both of them were wrong. "Their whole calculation was based on average *annual* channel losses," he said. "Well, they may be right on an annualized basis, but an annualized basis doesn't mean a damn thing. Most of those channel losses occur in the summertime, when the Platte Valley aquifer has been pumped out. That's when it acts like it has a hole in it and the water going down the river just disappears into it. But summertime is when the Narrows customers are going to need their water. That's the irrigation season. They're going to call on it and it won't get there."

The Woodward-Clyde study was interesting in other respects, for it went on to examine the other questions that were being raised about the Narrows. It concluded that "a safe dam can be built at the Narrows site," but, as Kuiper pointedly noted, declined to say at what cost. In stark contrast to the conclusions of the U.S. Fish and Wildlife Service, it said that the project "would have no adverse effect on sandhill cranes." And even though, fifty miles away, the Badger and Beaver irrigation districts were pioneering an alternative to on-stream and off-stream reservoirs, groundwater storage, it concluded that groundwater storage was "not an economically feasible" alternative to the Narrows.

Nothing was more striking, however, than its conclusion that the Bureau's claimed benefits for recreation "remain valid"—even though "primary production biomass in the reservoir will exceed levels that are usually indicative of eutrophy." In that remarkable juxtaposition of irreconcilable conclusions, Woodward-Clyde was tacitly agreeing with the Environmental Protection Agency, which was convinced that Narrows Reservoir, touted by the Bureau as a fine new recreational "lake," would quickly turn into a fetid, grossly polluted agricultural sump. Between the partially treated sewage of nearly two million people, the untreated runoff of hundreds of thousands of cows (some of them defecating right in the river), and pesticides and fertilizers washing in from thousands and thousands of acres of intensively farmed land—between this, and the fact that the reservoir would be shallow and warm, with an evaporation rate of four feet a year, the water quality was going to be absolutely awful. The EPA was suggesting that it would not be fit for *contact*, which meant no swimming or water skiing without a waterproof covering over every inch of one's body. Woodward-Clyde seemed to agree—it said biomass would *exceed* the levels that produce eutrophication, which is when a body of water begins turning into an algae pool. But it also agreed, implicitly if not explicitly, with the Bureau and Dick Lamm when they said that this aspiring swamp was destined to become the most popular reservoir in the entire state.

If one believed the brochure of the Lower South Platte Conservancy District, as many people would be drawn to fetid, shallow, bath-warm Lake Narrows as are drawn to Yellowstone National Park.

Here was a dam that the state engineer said would deliver only a third of the water it promised and could conceivably collapse; a project whose official cost estimate—if what two officials of the Union Pacific had privately suggested was correct—would barely suffice to relocate twenty-six miles of railroad track; a project whose real cost, whatever it turned out to be, would therefore be written off, in substantial measure, to "recreation," though the water would be unsafe to touch; a project whose prevailing interest rate (crucial to justifying the whole scheme) was one-fifth the rates banks were charging in the late 1970s; a project many of whose beneficiaries owned more land than the law permitted in order to receive subsidized water (even *after* the acreage limit was stretched to 960 acres in 1981); a project that might, if the state engineer was correct, seep enough water to turn the town of Fort Morgan into a marsh; a project that would pile more debt onto the Bureau's Missouri Basin Account; a project that would generate not a single kilowatt of hydroelectric power and would be all but worthless for flood control.

And yet, on top of all this, there was to be still another development, one that ought to have finished off the Narrows Project once and for all: *Most of the farmers who were supposed to be the beneficiaries said they didn't want the water.*

The farmers, it turned out, were not as ingenuous as the Bureau wished them to be. During the years it had pushed for the Narrows Project, the Bureau had never quoted them a firm price for the water nor guaranteed them a fixed amount. Why, in that case, should they obligate themselves to buy it for the next forty years?

In a letter to the Denver *Post*, Jacob Korman, the president of the Irrigationists' Association, Water District Number One—the preexisting water district over which the Lower South Platte Conservancy District was trying to impose itself as a superagency—explained the farmers' position. "There are fifteen irrigation districts in our association from Kersey near Greeley to Balzac below Brush," Korman wrote. "If built, the dam would be in the heart of our district. These ditch companies provide irrigation water to 125,000 acres of land. Twelve of these ditch companies representing farmers irrigating 105,350 acres have taken positions *opposing* the Narrows. One, representing 1,100 acres, has indicated support. At the last report, two, involving 19,100 acres, have taken no position."

Although many of the ditch companies in his district were initially enthusiastic about the project, Korman said, "those which have been offered specific contracts by the Lower South Platte Conservation District have found these contracts to be unacceptable." The main reason was that the contracts demanded that the farmers pay for water released *at the dam*. The Bureau refused to guarantee delivery of the water at the farmers' headgates—as if to demonstrate that it knew all along that Kuiper's theory about channel losses was correct. The farmers might be a trusting lot, but they weren't dumb.

"The office of our state engineer," Korman concluded, "is the only office . . . which has both the data and the technical staff to make a professional assessment as to what the real impact of the Narrows would be on providing water for irrigated agriculture in northeastern Colorado. . . . Actually, most of the ditch companies in the association feel . . . that the unadjudicated water which we need to supplement our reservoirs and decreed waters *would in all probability be lost if Narrows were built*" (emphasis added).

That a majority of the farmers for whose benefit Narrows was to be constructed finally decided they would *lose* more water than they would gain from the dam was fascinating. The "unadjudicated" water of which Korman spoke were those high flows which, after every Colorado farmer had taken his water right and Nebraska had been guaranteed its share, the farmers could skim off for themselves. As of now, no one "owned" these occasional surpluses in the river; anyone could divert them for storage in offstream reservoirs or in the aquifer beneath his farm. But with Narrows Dam in place, all but the most extraordinary high flows—the fifty-year floods—would be captured and they would belong to the Bureau of Reclamation. The Bureau would charge money for them—charge even if it refused to guarantee that the water would ever arrive. The Bureau wasn't even offering the farmers a pig in a poke; it was offering them a poke without a pig.

In 1982, at the behest of Senator Gary Hart, Woodward-Clyde did yet another study of the Narrows problem—it was now a "problem" as often as it was a "project"—and reversed its earlier conclusions as innocently as if they had never been held. Its estimate of water available for annual delivery was now down from more then eighty thousand acre-feet to thirty-four thousand acre-feet, almost in line with Kuiper's estimate and fathoms below the Bureau's. The effects on the sandhill and whooping cranes and other migratory wildlife downstream were now regarded as "moderately negative" instead of insignificant. But the most startling reversal came when the firm recalculated the worthiness of the project in simple economic terms. Using an interest rate of 7½ percent, but retaining the doubtful flood-control benefit of $800,000 a year and a highly optimistic view of the recreational potential, Woodward-Clyde came up with a benefit-cost ratio of only .10 to 1.0—for every dollar invested, *ten cents* would be returned. Even with an interest rate of 3¾ percent, Narrows was a loser.

Like most water projects, though, Narrows refused to roll over and die. In 1983, Congress, at the urging of local Representative Hank Brown, voted it another $475,000 appropriation. It wasn't enough to build anything, but it was enough to keep it alive. The latest unofficial cost estimates, in 1984, were in the neighborhood of $500 million. If they are correct, each acre-foot (assuming 34,000 acre-feet is the annual yield) will cost $14,500 to develop. Few Colorado farmers can afford to pay more than $50 an acre-foot for water, and the Bureau has never charged any of its client farmers half that much (most get it for $7.50 or less). The taxpayers, presumably, will make up the difference, buying a couple of hundred farmers about the most expensive water on earth.

And yet, in early 1984, the politicians who had always been for the Narrows were still for it. Senator Gary Hart, a neoliberal, was for it; liberal Congressman Tim Wirth was not against it; Senator Bill Armstrong, a budget-conscious conservative Republican, supported it. But no one was for it as much as Dick Lamm—although Dick Lamm was the one politician honest enough to admit, discreetly, that it wasn't worth building. Once, at a Denver Broncos football game, Karen Christenson's sister and her husband found themselves sitting a few seats away from the governor, sporting their big, bright "Stop the Narrows" buttons. Lamm noticed the buttons, came over, and asked who they were. Then, in an odd small burst of candor, the intense young forward-thinking governor delivered himself of a private opinion about the project he had championed so relentlessly. "I know Narrows isn't the best project in the world. I'd much rather use the money to build up the state's economy in a more efficient way. But when Washington offers you that kind of economic impetus, a governor can't just turn it down."

Repeating the story, Don Christenson mused, "If that's the way they run a railroad, then this country hasn't got any hope."

Meanwhile, in Denver, Clarence Kuiper had taken early retirement. "The Narrows thing got so annoying to me I couldn't stand it, so I retired," Kuiper says. "I've lived too long to put up with that sort of nonsense." Early in 1984, he was no less convinced than ever that Narrows, if built, stood a respectable chance of collapsing like Teton—an issue that had become all but lost in the minutiae of the debate. "Unless they extend that grout curtain a hell of a lot farther than they plan to, they're going to get seepage, just like they did at Teton. Seepage is one of the worst things that can happen to an earthfill dam. I'd rather have water going over the top in a waterfall than chewing away at my abutments. That's still the number-one issue as far as I am concerned."

Neither the Lamm administration nor the Bureau was ready to listen to Kuiper. Lamm, however, had finally found a way to get even. The firm with which Kuiper now serves as a consultant, the Harza Engineering Company of Chicago, was the other contender, with Woodward-Clyde, for the lucrative South Platte Basin Alternatives study in 1982. Because of Kuiper's relationship with Harza, it didn't get it. Suave Bill McDonald, who relieved the intemperate Felix Sparks of his command of the Colorado Water Conservation Board, put it right into his letter. Unless Harza dumped Kuiper as a consultant, it stood no chance of getting the contract. As far as Kuiper is concerned, he is being blackballed throughout the state. "They've stolen a man's livelihood," he says. "My pension isn't enough to live on. I know this state as well as anyone, but they've made my name mud."

If one were to put an epitaph on this story, one might do no better than to quote Glenn Saunders, the man who championed water development for fifty years in Colorado and then, in the end, came up against a project he wanted to kill—and couldn't. As he readily admits, it changed his whole way of looking at things.

To Glenn Saunders, Narrows Dam was not so much a dam as a symbol of a senescent society clinging to archaic hopes. "What that dam represents," he said, "is, first of all, the fact that there are very few really honest people in the world. Ninety-eight percent of humanity cannot admit when it's made a mistake. This applies especially to politicians. A politician for some reason thinks it is political suicide to admit that he was wrong. Dick Lamm cannot bring himself to admit that he has been in error about Narrows. He has one of the finest minds in Colorado, his thinking on some subjects is some of the best thinking any politician in this age is capable of—but he cannot bring himself to say, 'I was wrong on the Narrows Dam.'

"The Bureau is the same way," Saunders went on. "It cannot admit when it has made a mistake. It has also run out of good projects. *And* on top of that it has all of these bizarre cash-register funds—the Missouri Basin Fund, which is behind the Narrows—that are supposed to make these projects self-financing. They do not, but no one understands that. The Bureau is like one of these crooks with money earning interest in twenty different banks—it has to spend the money on something. It is all *borrowed* money—it belongs to the people of the United States—but the people of the United States don't know that. The whole thing is a machine, a perpetual-motion machine that keeps churning out dams, which the politicians and most westerners are reflexively in favor of, and the whole business is running the country into the ground.

"The people who support these boondoggle projects are always talking about the vision and principles that made this country great. 'Our forefathers would have built these projects!' they say. 'They had vision!' That's pure nonsense. It wasn't the vision and principles of our forefathers that made this country great. It was the huge unused bonanza they found here. One wave of immigrants after another could occupy new land, new land, new land. There was topsoil, water— there was gold, silver, and iron ore lying right on top of the earth. We picked our way through a ripe orchard and made it bare. The new generations are going to go down, down, down. With projects like the Narrows, we're trying to pretend that things are as they always were. 'Let's just go out and find some money and build a dam and we'll all be richer and better off.' We've been so busy spending money and reaping the fruits that we're blind to the fact that there are no more fruits. By trying to make things better, we're making them worse and worse."

CHAPTER TWELVE

Things Fall Apart

O n a hydrographic map, the outline of the Ogallala Aquifer resembles the South American and African continents—broad and bulbous to the north, tapering to a narrow cape at the southern end. Driving its entire length—from southern South Dakota down into the heart of West Texas, where it feathers out just above the Pecos River—takes two long days and feels almost like a transcontinental trip, the more so because the landscape is relentlessly the same: the same flatness, the same treelessness, the same curveless thirty-mile stretches of road. All that changes is the crops: sorghum, then corn, then sorghum, then corn, then alfalfa, wheat, cotton—enough cotton, one would think, to clothe all humanity.

This was the country that Coronado traversed, looking for the gold cities of Cibola; it is the country that cost him half his men, his reputation, and nearly his life. In Coronado's time, it grew nothing but short grass, on which millions of buffalo feasted; feasting on them were grizzly bears, prairie wolves, vultures, and an unknown number of Sioux, Comanche, and Cheyenne. The tribes, widely regarded as ferocious, merely reflected the landscape itself. Even the Indians used the open plains mainly for seasonal hunting, retreating to river valleys when the weather became extreme—which was a good part of the time. The southern high plains, from Colorado south to the hill country of Texas, never knew a permanent civilization, as far as archaeologists can tell. There was a Llano culture as early as 10,000 B.C., followed by others that came and went like snow. Around 1300 B.C., Pueblo Indians occupied the region, but abandoned it less than a century later. The Comanche, superb horsemen, may have shunned the open plains as much as possible because there was no tree where one could tie up one's mount. A place where one couldn't even secure a horse was no place to try to anchor a civilization.

White men were to learn that lesson, repeatedly, after the buffalo and the Indians were vanquished and gone. During the 1860s and 1870s the plains hosted great cattle drives from Texas to Kansas, but those ended in drought, overgrazing, and falling meat prices. Depauperated of much of its grass and invaded by mesquite and weeds, the region emptied out. But a decade of wet weather and demand for bread during and after the First World War sparked a repopulation, and the plains became a sea of wheat. Then came the Dust Bowl. After each calamity, a residual population managed to remain, surviving on a few cattle, some defiant wheat, the government, and, finally, oil and natural gas. It was one of those survivors who sank a water well, hooked up a new invention—a diesel-driven centrifugal pump—and discovered the region's bounteous secret: underneath it, confined in a closed-basin aquifer, was enough fresh water to fill Lake Huron.

Everyone had always known there was water below. If you sank a well and erected a windmill-driven pump, you got enough for a family and a few head of stock. But windmills could bring up only a few gallons a minute and offered no clue as to how much water was actually down there. The centrifugal pump, which could raise eight hundred gallons a minute or more, did, and when geologists took a closer look they confirmed the evidence offered by the pumps. Under the plains was the trapped runoff of several Ice Ages, all nicely confined within gravel beds. The thickness of the aquifer varied; along the periphery it feathered to a few feet, but in the middle portions under Nebraska there were saturations of seven hundred feet. All in all, there were probably three billion acre-feet in confinement.

A flow of eight hundred gallons a minute will fill an Olympic swimming pool in just over an hour. It will also conveniently irrigate a hundred or more acres of crops. A hundred acres of irrigated land on the plains is worth five hundred acres unirrigated; actually, it is worth more, because a farmer need never again worry about going bankrupt during a drought. The water was free; all you needed in order to make money, real money—to watch your net income rise from $8,000 to $40,000 a year—was cheap fossil fuel or electricity, a big mobile sprinkler, and pumps.

The irrigation of the Ogallala region, which has occurred almost entirely since the Second World War, is, from a satellite's point of view, one of the most profound changes visited by man on North America; only urbanization, deforestation, and the damming of rivers surpass it. In the space of twenty years, the high plains turned from brown to green, as if a tropical rainbelt had suddenly installed itself between the Rockies and the hundredth meridien. From an airplane, much of semiarid West Texas now appears as lush as Virginia. Where one saw virtually nothing out the window forty years ago, one now sees thousands and thousands of green circles. From thirty-eight thousand feet, each appears to be about the size of a nickel, though it is actually 133 acres—a dozen and a half baseball fields. The circles are created by self-propelled sprinklers referred to by some as "wheels of fortune." A quarter-mile-long pipeline with high-pressure nozzles, mounted on giant wheels which allow the whole apparatus to pass easily over a field of corn, a wheel of fortune is man-made rain; the machines even climb modest slopes which would ordinarily defeat a ditch irrigation system. Wheels of fortune are superefficient, but intolerant: they don't like trees, shrubs, or bogs. Therefore, the millions and millions of shelterbelt trees planted by the Civilian Conservation Corps have come down as fast as the region's fortunes have risen. All that now holds the soil in place is crops and water which cannot last.

In 1914, there were 139 irrigation wells in all of West Texas. In 1937, there were 1,166. In 1954, there were 27,983. In 1971, there were 66,144. Nebraska irrigated fewer than a million acres in 1959. In 1977, it irrigated nearly seven million acres; the difference was almost entirely pumping from the Ogallala. By that year, there were, depending on whose estimate one believed, somewhere around twelve million acres irrigated by the Ogallala Aquifer. One of the poorest farming regions in the United States had metamorphosed overnight into one of the wealthiest, raising 40 percent of the fresh beef cattle in America and growing a huge chunk of our agricultural exports. As West Texas sprouted corn, a water-demanding crop that had never been known there, Lubbock and Amarillo sprouted skyscrapers, most of them erected by the banks that ecstatically financed the farmers' road to wealth. On Fridays, the farmers cruise into town from eighty miles away, behind the wheels of their Cadillacs and big Buick Electras. After a conference with a deferential banker, they go off for drinks and a dinner of steak and lobster, then to watch a Texas Tech football game from fieldside seats. Since 1950, Lubbock's population has increased at about the same rate as Texas's irrigated land—7.5 percent a year. Anything growing at that rate doubles in size in a decade.

There is, however, a second set of statistics which offers a more meaningful depiction of what is going on. By 1975, Texas was withdrawing some eleven billion gallons of groundwater—per *day*. In Kansas, the figure was five billion; in Nebraska, 5.9 billion; in Colorado, 2.7 billion; in Oklahoma, 1.4 billion; in New Mexico, 1.6 billion. In places, farmers were withdrawing four to six feet of water a year, while nature was putting back half an inch. The overdraft from the Ogallala region in 1975 was about fourteen million acre-feet a year, the flow of the Colorado River; it represented half the groundwater overdraft in the entire United States. The Colorado is not a big river, but it would be big enough to empty Lake Huron in a reasonably short time.

The Ogallala region supports not so much a farming industry as a mining industry. If the pumping has been reckless, as some believe, it is an example of carefully planned recklessness, for all the states regulate the pumping of groundwater; their choice was to allow its exhaustion within roughly thirty to a hundred years after the pumping began in earnest back in the early 1960s. Except for petroleum and natural gas and coal, most mining industries affect a rather small area. This is one that affects an area larger than California. Actually, it affects the entire world, for the product of mining the Ogallala is a prodigious amount of food, much of it consumed overseas.

It is a dead certainty that the Ogallala will begin to give out relatively soon; the only question is when. Everything hinges on one constant—the weight of water—and two variables: the cost of energy and the price of food. As anyone knows who has ever carried a full pail up five flights of steps, water is one of the heaviest substances on earth; pumping it a hundred or two hundred feet out of the ground consumes a lot of energy. The Ogallala farmers do not benefit, as do many groundwater pumpers throughout the West, from hydroelectricity generated at Bureau of Reclamation dams and sold to them at discount rates. For the water table to drop fifteen or twenty feet during a period when the price of energy increases sevenfold is a catastrophe. This, however, is precisely what happened throughout much of Kansas, Oklahoma, and West Texas between 1972 and 1984. During the same period, the price of most farm commodities barely doubled, if that.

The odds are high, therefore, that long before all the water runs out, the farmers will no longer be able to afford to pump. In 1969, a study performed by Texas A and M University projected that the West Texas aquifer would decline to forty-four billion acre-feet by the year

2015, down from 341 billion acre-feet before the Second World War. Irrigated acreage would, by then, have fallen to 125,000 acres from a mid-sixties peak of 3.5 million acres. Sorghum yields would be down 90 percent; cotton would be down 65 percent; total agricultural value in the region would diminish by 80 percent. In those figures lay the makings of a Dust Bowl–sized exodus, a social calamity, and a huge rash of bankruptcies that could ripple through the nation's economy. In 2015, the study predicted, there would be 300,000 fewer people in the region than there were in 1969. A new set of figures compiled in 1979 by the Texas Department of Water Resources was somewhat more optimistic, but the planning director of that same agency did not sound as if he subscribed to the optimism himself. "It's pretty easy to conjure up a disastrous series of events," said Herbert Grubb in 1980. "We're sort of assuming that a lot of the farmers will stay in business raising dryland cotton or wheat. But with interest rates high as they are, and dryland yields down 70 or 80 percent from irrigation yields, I really don't see how the farmers are going to carry their debts. The older ones, maybe. But the younger ones, the newer ones, are up to their ears in debt. So you could just as easily assume that millions of acres suddenly go fallow. Then along comes a drought, some eighty-mile-an-hour winds, and you've got another Dust Bowl. The shelterbelt trees are gone. A lot of those farmers are milking every cent out of the land while the water lasts. The conditions are ripe for something downright catastrophic."

The decision of the Ogallala states to treat the aquifer as if it were a coal mine, thereby setting themselves up for a long, long fall, is ironic in an extreme sense. Their economies—as the states recognized and lamented long ago—are vulnerable to forces they can do little to control. What supports Colorado besides irrigated agriculture? Mainly minerals—coal, uranium, molybdenum, oil—and tourism, logging, and ranching. Every one of those industries is subject to someone else's whim: world supply and demand, international cartels, the price of oil, the Federal Reserve Board, or, the ultimate caprice of all, nature. Much the same applies to New Mexico. Oklahoma, Nebraska, and Kansas are farm states whose prosperity or ruin, before irrigation, depended on whether the isohyet of twenty-inch rainfall moved westward toward the Rockies or eastward toward the Mississippi River. Once they became dependent on a huge irrigation economy, all of the states knew they would be in the same position as a junkie. Texas with its vanishing oil and gas; Kansas astride the hundredth meridian; Colorado depending so much on tourists who, if oil prices doubled or there was no snow, would stay home—each state knew that when the water ran out, they would again face the same awful vulnerability that had haunted them since the first settlers arrived.

Strictly regulated, the Ogallala could have been made to last hundreds of years instead of decades. Irrigation farming could have been slowly phased in, kept at a lower level, and gradually phased out. In such a case, hundreds of thousands of people who became dependent on it overnight wouldn't face ruin, and the states' economies wouldn't go into sudden osmotic shock when the pumps began bringing up air. The states had begged the government to build them dams for irrigation, and they had lobbied to keep the price of water artificially low, arguing that agriculture was the only stability they had. The opportunity for economic stability offered by the world's largest aquifer, however, was squandered for immediate gain. The only inference one can draw is that the states felt confident that when they ran out of water, the rest of the country would be willing to rescue them.

A s deputy chief of planning for the Bureau of Reclamation in the mid-1960s, Jim Casey saw things from a fundamentally different perspective than the farmers, or, for that matter, most of his eleven thousand colleagues. The main concern of the typical Bureau engineer is building a bigger and grander project than the last one. It was Casey's job to think about what few of them did, or dared to: reservoirs silting up, river-basin funds drying up, salts building up—all the problems consigned through some unwritten conspiracy between politicians and bureaucrats to an amorphous, distant, and politically unrewarding future. Casey was, by definition, the Bureau's Cassandra. Peering into the future, he saw no place headed for deeper trouble than the Ogallala region. If surface water can be compared with interest income, and non-renewable groundwater with capital, then much of the West was living mainly on interest income. California was milking interest and capital in about equal proportion. The plains states, however, were devouring capital as a gang of spendthrift heirs might squander a great capitalist's fortune. To Casey's amazement, few of the farmers seemed to realize it. "They thought the water would last until the Second Coming," he says. Frustrated by the farmers' blindness, he finally decided that he had better address the one group that might listen to him: the region's bankers.

"I think it was about 1966 when I went out to give my speech," Casey says. His voice, after twenty years in Washington, is still thickly gravied with West Texas drawl. "You wouldn't believe how many bankers there are in Lubbock. I said to them, 'Look, you're all riding high out here and it's a great thing and we all like to pretend that great things are going to last. But no aquifer can sustain this rate of pumping. I don't know when you're going to run out of water, but I'd bet you're going to run out at about the same time you start running out of oil and gas. If that gets too expensive the farmers won't be able to pump, anyway. There goes your whole economy. This corner of the world is going to be an Appalachia without trees unless you get off your fannies and try to save it. I don't know if you *can* save it; I frankly don't know if it makes any sense for the nation to invest billions of dollars in a rescue project to keep a few million acres irrigated and a few hundred thousand people employed out here. I don't know where the water would come from, but you'd better start thinking about it now, because it will take forty years to get a rescue project this big authorized and built, and you haven't got a lot of time left."

The effect of Casey's speech was remarkable. "I gave them religion. A few months hadn't gone by before I heard they were setting up a big new lobby to fight for a rescue project. They called it Water, Incorporated." Ambitious, perhaps even incredible, as its goal was—a project to rescue even a modest portion of the irrigated plains would be a project more grandiose than any yet built—Water, Inc., had a number of things going for it. California's voters had just approved the most ambitious and expensive public-works project ever attempted by a single state in order to save its own agricultural industry. Would *Texans* countenance that upstart state building something they lacked the nerve to attempt themselves? In the mid-1960s, the age of limits had not yet dawned; a high-plains rescue project was seen by many people as the next logical step in "orderly" water development, something that might even capture the fancy of the nation at large. The generation of politicians then running the country had been suckled and reared on public works. And an astonishing number of them came from Texas.

The President of the United States, for example. As Robert Caro demonstrated in the first volume of his biography of Lyndon Johnson,

The Path to Power, Johnson owed his political career largely to the Marshall Ford Dam. Begun under an emergency appropriation during the Depression—begun, just like Grand Coulee and Garrison dams, before it was even authorized, and built on land the government didn't even own—the dam was to make a reputation and ultimately a huge fortune for a couple of struggling small-time contractors named Herman and George Brown. At the time, however, it was just a big Bureau of Reclamation dam on Texas's Colorado River a few miles from Austin, a project which had run through its emergency appropriation before it was half built. To anyone else this didn't matter much—no one doubted that the dam would be completed someday— but to the brothers Brown it was a calamity. They had invested every nickel they owned and scraped together all the collateral they could in order to purchase one and a half million dollars' worth of construction equipment they needed and didn't have. (Until then, most of the Browns' contracts had been for road-paving jobs; what they owned in construction equipment didn't amount to more than a few fresno scrapers.) If more funds were not approved immediately, they would go bankrupt. But everyone was crying for relief funds, and an unauthorized project with a serious land-title problem in a remote corner of Texas was at a distinct disadvantage among its competition. In desperation, Herman Brown, the fiercely archconservative entrepreneur, pleaded for help from the district's most important politician, a newly elected twenty-nine-year-old liberal New Deal Congressman whose name was Lyndon Baines Johnson. Using his connections among the White House inner circle and his absolutely shameless flattery of FDR, Johnson managed to get Herman and George Brown a formal authorization, a resolution of the land-title dispute, and another $5 million to finish the dam as their lenders were about to smash down their barricaded door. Profoundly grateful, the brothers Brown poured enough money into Johnson's subsequent campaigns to catapult him into the Senate at a tender age. Their company, Brown and Root, was to grow into one of the largest construction firms in the world, mining the government just as Johnson mined the profits of their work—a symbiotic relationship that not only transcended ideology but subverted it, as public works are wont to do. And it all began with a dam.

Johnson was not the only local politician who had climbed to political power up the wall of a dam. There was Robert Kerr of Oklahoma, one of the princes of the United States Senate until he died in 1963. Besides unabashedly using his Senate seat to make himself rich—he was a cofounder of the Kerr-McGee Corporation—Kerr helped authorize a number of very large reservoirs in his native state which kept Oklahoma's construction industry perpetually busy, not only building new dams, but rerouting major highways around the ever-larger reservoirs that constantly formed in their path. Perusing a map of eastern Oklahoma, one would think that Kerr's ultimate goal was to put the state under water.

Then there was Jim Wright, who began representing Fort Worth in 1954 and was to become Majority Leader of the House in the late 1970s, a position he used to defy his own party's President in his attempt to knock off a few billion dollars' worth of water projects—including Wright's own favorite, the Trinity River Project, which was to turn Dallas and Fort Worth, sitting four hundred miles from the ocean, into seaports. Wright's dedication to water projects struck some of his colleagues as fanatical. He took time out in the late 1960s to write a book called *The Coming Water Famine*, in which he said, "The crisis of our diminishing water resources is just as severe (if less obviously immediate) as any wartime crisis we have ever faced. Our survival is just as much at stake as it was at the time of Pearl Harbor, or the Argonne, or Gettysburg, or Saratoga. . . . Pure water, when and where you need it, is worth whatever it costs to get it there."

There was also Ray Roberts, who represented Sam Rayburn's old district, and whose interest in water projects would elevate him to chairman of the House Public Works Committee. There was George Mahon, the chairman of the House Appropriations Committee in the 1960s and one of the five most powerful men in Congress, who happened to represent the district around Lubbock. There was John Connally, the governor of Texas, a Johnson protégé whose enthusiasm for grandiose undertakings, big-game hunting, and gigantic limousines made him into an unselfconscious parody of ambitious, super-affluent Texas.

With such men in power during an era of no limits, anything seemed possible—even a project to rescue the southern half of the Ogallala region by rerouting a substantial portion of the Mississippi River.

The origins of the project went back to 1958, when a U.S. commission—chaired by George Brown of Brown and Root—was appointed to come up with a systematic plan for developing the river basins of the state. The proposal called for eighty-three storage reservoirs and some water-conveyance works to be built by the year 2010, all of which, the commission modestly suggested, could be completed for around $4 billion. The great omission in the plan, however, was an aqueduct to West Texas. The reason for that appears self-evident: West Texas sits at an elevation more than three thousand feet higher than East Texas, where most of the state's water is, and nearly four thousand feet higher than Louisiana or Arkansas, the two states with enough of a water surplus to suggest themselves as the ultimate source. Pumping enough water to rescue several million acres that far uphill, over a distance of a thousand miles or more, would require a fantastic amount of energy. The commission did not say this in those exact terms, but its omission of any proposal to rescue the Ogallala over-draft region spoke volumes.

There followed, however, one of those peculiar metamorphoses in which a plan, as it evolves, conforms less and less to the constraints of nature, economics, and thermodynamics and more and more to the stridency of certain constituents and the desires of certain elected officials. John Connally saw in an Ogallala-region rescue project an opportunity to become a pharaoh in a pinstripe suit. George Mahon, subjected to merciless lobbying by Water, Inc., enjoyed the power of the purse by virtue of his being chairman of the Appropriations Committee; it was unthinkable that he would give East Texas and South Texas dozens of dams if West Texas got nothing in return. As a result, Connally, as governor, pointedly disregarded the Brown Commission's report and decided to draw up a proposal of his own. Its title was to be the Texas Water Plan.

The idea was for several million acre-feet of water to be diverted from the Mississippi River below New Orleans—a point from where, presumably, Louisiana wouldn't mind its being taken—and moved across the marshlands and swamp forests of the state in an aqueduct built to the dimensions of an airplane hangar. A river approaching the Colorado in size, running in reverse, the water would climb up to Dallas and Fort Worth, which sit at an elevation of 750 feet, by way of a series of stairstep reservoirs. A generous portion would head toward those two cities in a spur aqueduct; some of it would go to South Texas; but most of it would head toward Amarillo and Lubbock in the Trans-Texas Canal. There would be seventeen pumping stations en route lifting the water up the imperceptible slope of the plains; there would be nine terminal reservoirs waiting to receive it. Nearly a million acre-feet a year would be fed into the Pecos River; another half million would head toward Corpus Christi; 6,480,000 acre-feet would arrive on the Texas high plains, having climbed thirty-six hundred feet and traveled twelve hundred miles since New Orleans; 1.5 million acre-feet would perhaps go on to New Mexico. Two million acre-feet, the consumption of New York City and then some, would evaporate en route. It would take 6.9 million kilowatts of electricity to run it—about 40 percent of the electricity consumption of the entire state.

As a politician from a neighboring state put it after hearing of the plan, "If those Texans can suck as hard as they can blow, they'll probably build it."

Without knowing anything but the vaguest outlines of the plan—without knowing whether the farmers could afford the water, whether its acid character was compatible with the plains' alkaline soils, whether Texas water law didn't exempt the farmers from paying a dime once the water had percolated to the aquifer, whether the powerplants to move it could be financed and built, whether Louisiana had any intention of parting with one molecule of it—the voters of Texas suddenly found themselves, in August of 1969, being asked to appropriate $3.5 billion toward the Texas Water Plan's construction. Actually, the question was couched much more circumspectly than that. The proponents of the measure, which became known as Amendment Two, insisted that the voters were merely being asked to guarantee $3.5 billion in bonds to establish a "repayable loan fund" which any city or region in the state could tap in order to meet its water needs—an argument which was greeted by the referendum's opponents with catcalls. The fact was, they said, that the Texas Water Development Board, which could arbitrarily and peremptorily decide who got how much of the money, was deeply committed to a rescue project for West Texas. Governor Preston Smith, who was trumping Amendment Two up and down the state, was a native of West Texas. If the hidden agenda wasn't to build, or at least begin (since the $3.5 billion would never complete a project of such magnitude), the rescue project, why had the referendum been scheduled for August in an off-year election, when voter turnout was certain to be light, and organized elements behind the measure could affect the outcome much more dramatically than during a regular election year? The one place where turnout was likely to be heavy was in West Texas, because the farmers would be at home, busy with their crops, while a lot of East Texans would be off on vacation, escaping the humid heat. Why were the backers trying to distance themselves from the Texas Water Plan when that was the only plan that could absorb such a stupendous amount of money? This was, after all, 1969; in 1984, its equivalent would be $10 billion.

"We were being sold a bill of goods," recalls Ronnie Dugger, the publisher of the *Texas Observer*, virtually the only newspaper in the state that opposed Amendment Two. "It was actually $7 billion, not $3.5 billion, when you factored in the interest. Seven billion for what? No one was saying. No one knew. It was the biggest blank check in the history of the United States."

All such objections notwithstanding, the proponents of the measure had managed to amass as formidable a group of sponsors as Texans were ever likely to see. The backers included nearly everyone who was anyone in the state. Three former governors—John Connally, Allan Shivers, and Price Daniel—served as cochairmen. The editors or publishers of the San Antonio *Light*, the Austin *American-Stateman*, the Houston *Chronicle*, the Dallas *Times Herald*, the Fort Worth *Star-Telegram*, the Wichita Falls *Times-Record-News*, the Lubbock *Avalanche-Journal*, the Corpus Christi *Caller-Times*, the Beaumont *Enterprise-Journal*, the Port Arthur *News*, the El Paso *Times*, and the San Angelo *Standard-Times* were on it, not to mention dozens of smaller papers like the Bonhom *Favorite* and the Waxahachie *Times*. The mayors of Midland, Dallas, Bay City, Corpus Christi, Austin, San Antonio, Laredo, Dallas, Lubbock, Fort Worth, and Arlington were on it. Presidents, chancellors, and regents of Texas universities were represented: Baylor, Texas Tech, the University of Texas, Texas A and M, Southern Methodist University. A hundred and forty-three of the 150 members of the Texas House of Representatives were on it. Twenty-eight of the thirty-one members of the Texas Senate were on it. The head of the Texas Parks and Wildlife Commission; lobbyists for railroads and manufacturers and municipalities; grocery-store magnates; retired Congressmen; Texas kingmakers such as Robert Strauss (later the head of the Democratic National Committee) and Leon Jaworski (later the Watergate special prosecutor)—the list read more like the sponsors of the United Way than a plan that appeared likely to end up dumping the Mississippi River on the expiring plains.

As an accident of geography made the rescue of West Texas so difficult and expensive, however, an accident of migration made passage of the referendum at least as difficult. In California, the conservative and reactionary factions of the state's electorate are concentrated mainly in the sprawl south of Los Angeles, in San Diego, and in the hard-bitten little cities of the San Joaquin Valley. Every one of those places is a desert or semidesert, haunted by extinction, and every one of them saw the State Water Project as salvation. An unknown number of people whose antipathy to government runs to things such as fluoridated water and Social Security voted enthusiastically for the most expensive public-works project in California's history. In Texas, the ultraconservative faction of the electorate tends to be spread more around the state. If it has a center, it is probably Houston, which stood to gain virtually nothing from the Texas Water Plan. The mayor of Houston, in fact, was conspicuously absent among those big-city mayors who had enlisted as members of the Committee of 500. Dallas, another conservative bastion, was to get water, but felt no sense of desperate need. Aside from that, Texas's population as a whole is skewed to the east, where the main problems with water tend to come in the form of thunderstorms, hurricanes, and floods. In California, two-thirds of the population resides in the drought-ridden south. "The opponents of Amendment Two were strange bedfellows," says Ronnie Dugger. "You had the Sierra Club voting with the little old ladies in tennis shoes." When the final count was in, the Texas Water Plan had lost, by sixty-six hundred votes.

About a year before the referendum on Amendment Two was held, Congressman George Mahon, the chairman of the House Appropriations Committee, had asked Jim Casey over for a chat between fellow West Texans. Mahon came from Lubbock, and was old enough to remember it as a one-horse town. "He had a fear that things could return to that," Casey remembers. "It haunted him." As Casey expected, the conversation immediately came around to the Texas Water Plan. "He asked me what my gut reaction was," Casey remembers. "Did I think it would fly? I told him, 'I hate to tell you this frankly, but my gut reaction is that it's crazy.' I'll never forget the look on his face. It was like I was a doctor telling him his daughter was going to die." Casey's pessimism notwithstanding, Mahon was adamant about studying the plan. He even had an amendment ready for the appropriations bill giving the Bureau whatever money it needed to perform a feasibility report. "I told him that a feasibility report on a plan this big was going to consume a hell of a lot of man-hours and money. But I told him if he insisted we'd do it, because this plan made more sense to me than some of the other cockamamie ideas that were floating around. If it turned out to be infeasible, then we'd all better get ready to kiss irrigation on the high plains goodbye."

The figures Casey's staff began toting up over the next three years were appalling. Routing the aqueduct across wet Louisiana and southeastern Texas would be a costly nightmare, even if the Bureau didn't have to pay for bodyguards to protect its construction crews. "The Louisiana legislature told us to go ahead and study it, because the numbers would kill us anyway," Casey remembers. "But if we'd actually gone ahead and tried to build the thing God knows what might have happened. I felt like taking out a new life insurance policy before going into the bayous down there." The aqueduct would have to go underneath four major rivers by siphon; 142 minor streams would be siphoned under it. But what encumbered the Mississippi diversion most of all was its gluttonous appetite for energy. "Carry two buckets of water up the Washington Monument, take the elevator back down, and do it five more times. That was the lift we had to overcome to West Texas. We were talking billions of buckets. We were talking *trillions* of buckets," says Casey. There was not nearly enough surplus power in Texas, so the project would have to build its own generating plants. The Bureau decided to go the nuclear route, on the widely held belief that nuclear electricity would soon be dirt-cheap. "We took the most pie-eyed projections we could find from the Atomic Energy Commission. We figured the plants would cost $250 million apiece. The plan required about twelve of them. Twelve nuclear plants of a million kilowatts each. You couldn't build *one* nuclear plant in 1985 for the price we thought we were going to pay for twelve in 1971."

Notwithstanding power price estimates that were beyond the realm of fantasy, the Texas Water Plan—which, in the Bureau's version, was somewhat larger than Texas's own—would consume $325 million worth of power every year, in 1971 dollars. The West Texas farmers would end up with a water bill of $330 an acre-foot, all because of the relentless upslope of the plains. The most they could possibly pay, the Bureau decided, was $125 ("and that was hocus-pocus," says Casey). Taxpayers, therefore, would subsidize the rest. The benefit-cost ratio ultimately worked out to .27 to 1.00—for every dollar invested, there would be twenty-seven cents' worth of economic return. "The disparity between primary benefits and costs is so great that there is no reasonable prospect that any plan for transporting Mississippi River water to West Texas or eastern New Mexico would [become] favorable," the Bureau's report read. And it continued, "It is unlikely that the project described . . . could be completed in time to prevent virtual cessation of groundwater irrigation on the Texas High Plains and large-scale reduction of such irrigation in eastern New Mexico." If there was any justification for it at all, it was that "the project could contribute significantly to population dispersion in the 21st century, if this becomes a national objective."

In the Ogallala region, the Bureau's conclusions were met initially with discouragement, but not despair. Everyone knew that the Bureau and the Corps had built projects which made little better sense; they were merely smaller. The real issue, as far as Texas and Kansas and Oklahoma and Colorado and New Mexico were concerned, was that one couldn't simply abandon millions of acres of farmland to the desert from which it had so recently been saved. One couldn't let another Dust Bowl occur. The economics might look bad now, but who knew how they would look in thirty years? By the turn of the century, according to projections, there would be ten billion people, maybe more, on the planet. Who would feed them? Who still had land? The Russians did, but they couldn't feed themselves. Neither could Europe. Asia was thick with humanity; in Java, people would kill for enough land to raise a couple of cows. Australia was not only a desert, but, unlike the American West, a desert without rivers. Could anyone imagine Africa feeding the world? Canada was too cold to grow much of anything besides wheat and cattle. The only place left was South America, but when you chopped down rain forests and tried to grow crops the soil turned to laterite, hard as stone.

On the high plains, you still had five or ten feet of loamy topsoil. You had 1 percent of the farmers on 6 percent of the nation's agricultural land growing 15 percent of the wheat, corn, cotton, and grain sorghum. You had American technology, American know-how. You had the most productive region of the nation that was the food larder of the world. You had cities of 100,000, 200,000 people which depended utterly on irrigation farming and oil and gas. Could the nation just *abandon* them to fate, like the Leadvilles and Silver Cities and Bodies of a hundred years ago?

From the looks of things, it would. After the Bureau's report was released, one heard little about the Texas Water Plan for a number of years. In 1976, and again in 1981, Texans rejected water bonds that appeared likely to set the plan in motion. Arkansas and Louisiana began to talk of their water as if it were their daughters' chastity. The farmers, meanwhile, were still in business.

By the late 1970s, however, the Ogallala had dropped several more feet while energy prices had gone up sevenfold in a decade. The first farmers began going bankrupt—in Texas, in Colorado, in Kansas, in New Mexico. Tens of thousands of acres began reverting to dryland. The press, tantalized by the prospect of an imminent catastrophe, finally took some interest; newspaper and magazine stories appeared by the dozen. The result of all this was a predictable welter of federal studies, the most important of which was the 1982 Six-State High Plains–Ogallala Area Study, coordinated by the Economic Development Administration of the Department of Commerce. The study, as expected, predicted calamity, but decided it would not arrive as soon as most people thought. By the year 2020—which was as far ahead as it looked—Texas's share of the Ogallala would be down to 87.2 million acre-feet from 283.7 million in 1977. New Mexico's would be all but used up. Colorado and Kansas would be somewhat better off. Irrigation in those states would increase over the near term, then begin to decline early in the twenty-first century. The real reckoning would come after 2020. Nebraska, however, would still overlie 1.9 billion acre-feet by then, and would be irrigating 11.5 million acres— far more than any state in the nation. Irrigation farming would simply move northward, leaving Lubbock, Clovis, and Limon behind. In Texas, according to the report, oil and gas production would be down to 7 percent of its 1977 level—a double blow that could make the fate of cities such as Buffalo appear benign. The economy of the southern plains would be a three-legged stool with two legs gone, unless some miraculous rise in agricultural prices, or some new source of cheap energy, or some revolution in DNA plant genetics came along, permitting corn to get by on fourteen inches of rain. The region would be, to use Jim Casey's phrase, an Appalachia without trees. The only commodities in abundance would be sun and wind.

Is it possible that the 1982 report's conclusions are overly optimistic? "It's possible," says Herbert Grubb, the planning director of the Texas Water Development Board. "When I saw the rate of increase they used for energy costs, I thought it was much too low. In the late seventies, I'd been hearing estimates of oil costing as much as $295 a barrel by the end of the century. It turns out now that they were pretty much on target, at least so far. A lot of us didn't expect an oil glut to materialize in the early 1980s. But no one can say how long it will last. If in ten years we get another series of price jolts like we did in the seventies, I don't see how the irrigators can keep pumping."

From a national perspective—forgetting about the farmers' plight— whether irrigation on the southern plains ends in thirty years, or in seven, or even in fifty years does not matter; the fact is, it will mostly end. The more important issue, from that same perspective, is what will happen then—not just to the farmers and the cost of food and the balance of payments deficits, but to the land.

When thousands of farmers on millions of irrigated acres can no longer afford to pump vanishing water, the dilemma they face will be universal: how to survive on a finite amount of acreage that has suddenly become one-fifth to one-eighth as productive as it was. The answer is foreordained: they cannot. Many of them, therefore, will sell out to more stubborn neighbors and head for the cities for work or relief. Those who remain on enough acreage to offer them a glimmer of hope will ponder their brief list of choices: they can try to raise dryland cotton or wheat or some desert crop—jojoba or guayule, perhaps—or they can try to revert their plowed fields to shortgrass prairie, and raise cattle.

Raising cattle, perhaps even buffalo—which outperform cattle in arid country—might seem the thing to do. However, it is hard to see how it will happen without billions of dollars' worth of federal support. To convert from, say, wheat to grassland, a farmer first needs to plant some fast-growing annual, such as rye, to develop a litter cover for the soil and build up its organic content; it will cost him perhaps $15 an acre and require a year. Then he has to seed grama grass; this costs him even more and takes another year. Finally, if the grass manages to take hold—a lot of it won't—he can begin grazing a few cattle and reseeding those areas that failed to propagate. If he owns a thousand acres, he will probably have spent $30,000 to $50,000 (valued circa 1984); it has taken him three years, and he hasn't earned a dime. He still has his living expenses to cover, and, unless he is a well-established farmer, a small mountain of unpaid debts. Once his grass is growing, he may still have to wait years for his cattle to mature. After seven years or so, he will finally begin to earn some income. But by then he will have fallen into a bottomless hole.

Farmers may therefore resist the temptation to raise cattle and do the economically sensible thing: raise a dryland crop. As Paul Sears wrote in *Deserts on the March*, "So long as there remains the most remote possibility that the drier grasslands, whose sod has been destroyed by the plow, can be made to yield crops under cultivation, we may count upon human stubbornness to return again and again to the attack...." And in that effort lurks the likelihood of a recurrence of the catastrophe that inspired Sears's book: the Dust Bowl.

When a $1 million home perched on a fifty-degree slope above Malibu is clobbered by a mudslide after three weeks of rain—as thousands of houses throughout California were during the El Niño winters of 1982 and 1983—their owners tend to think of themselves as the victims of a "natural" disaster. The Dust Bowl of the 1930s is commonly regarded as such a "natural" disaster, because seven dry years in a row were accompanied by fierce winds, which scoured up the topmost layer of Oklahoma and blew it as far as Norway. The climate of the plains has remained relatively unchanged for hundreds of years, however, and there is no convincing evidence that such a disaster ever occurred before white men plowed up the sod and brought in cattle or, much worse, sheep to graze it down. Even after seven years of drought, the Dust Bowl would probably not have occurred had not man created the conditions for it. By 1932, in Texas alone, seventy million acres of land that had once been covered with a blanket of grass were growing mesquite and thorny weeds, which are poor at holding soil in place. The weeds had no business there; they were native to the ultramontane basins several hundred miles west. As Paul Sears wrote, "Weeds, like wild-eyed anarchists, are the symptoms, not the real cause, of a disturbed order. When the Russian thistle swept down across the western ranges, the general opinion was that it was a devouring plague, crowding in and consuming the native plants. It was no such thing. The native vegetation had already been destroyed by the plow and thronging herds—the ground was vacated and the thistles took it over."

The Dust Bowl occurred after a profitable wheat market had coincided for years with, by plains standards, a spell of abundant moisture. Prices were high enough to inspire greed; the farmers began plowing up everything in sight. Millions of acres of fragile, highly erodable land, from New Mexico all the way up to the Dakotas, had their sod pierced and replaced by wheat. The farmers actually began going bust before the drought even began; a glutted market, international competition, high tariffs, and the impoverished condition of postwar Europe conspired to do them in. The Dust Bowl was the *coup de grâce*.

The second Dust Bowl is apt to result from hardship rather than 1920s-style prosperity, though the pattern of land abuse will be pretty much the same. As the Ogallala aquifer steadily runs out and the surviving farmers watch their debts mount and their living standards decline, they will be forced by financial need to acquire and dry-farm as much new land as they can. Unless they can still afford to pump irrigation water on an emergency basis during droughts—if there is any water left to pump under their land—they will no longer be

469

guaranteed a respectable harvest every year. Because of the high profits of irrigation, the plains farmers took a lot of marginal farmland *out* of production over the past few decades. They could afford to. Now it is likely to be returned to the plow. In the East, marginal land usually means rocks or swamps or steep hillsides. On the rockless, swampless, tabletop plains, it usually means fine sand. Most of western Nebraska is sand; so is a lot of eastern New Mexico and West Texas. In western Kiowa County, Colorado, 150,000 acres of sandy Class VI land (Class I is the best) are *already* in production, losing twenty tons of topsoil or more a year. There is also a lot of marginal land in production in the Portales region of eastern New Mexico.

The winds blow hardest on the southern plains in late winter and early spring—days of sixty-mile-per-hour gusts ripping across empty space, powered by convoluted airflows battling one another. On February 23, 1977, some of those winds blew into Portales country and began raising dust. A dust storm works on the principle of an avalanche: wind scours up some loose soil and forms a dense, stinging cloud of fine particles, which scours up more loose soil, and more, and more, until the horizon is filled by an advancing wave several thousand feet high, churning and swirling millions of tons of suspended matter. When these storms were first sighted in the 1930s, farmers ran inside their houses, fearing torrential rain. When they went back outside, their homes had lost their paint and their chickens were featherless. The Portales storm, which lasted only about a day and a half, removed forty tons of topsoil per acre from parts of Roosevelt and Kiowa counties—as much topsoil loss as rainfall causes in a year in the most erosion-prone parts of the East, and about three centuries' worth of topsoil formation on the arid plains. Early in 1984, the same thing happened in parts of West Texas, south of Lubbock. One reason the storms did not grow out of control was that a lot of the surrounding irrigated land was being prepared for planting, and was wet.

Wayne Wyatt, the manager of the Texas High Plains Underground Water Conservation District in Lubbock—a man now presiding over the most desperate water-conservation effort in the United States—does not believe irrigation will end on the southern plains in a spectacular cloud of dust. "In the thirties," says Wyatt, "most of the farmers were still plowing with mules. They had power to dig down about four or five inches. Now they have hundred-horsepower tractors, which can easily bring up soil from two feet. It's either wet or it's clayey enough to hold against the wind. The only way I can see another Dust Bowl is if we have a real long drought. If it goes on for years in a row and the farmers can't even manage one crop in between, and if it affects this whole country and not just a piece of it, then maybe it could happen again. But this region has never known a drought like that. Even during the big one, there were a couple of years when you could raise a dryland crop." I asked Wyatt how far back climatic records go on the southern plains. "They go back to about the 1880s" was his response.

Wyatt, a courtly ex-farmer ("I beat my brains out trying to make a go of it") who speaks in an almost opaque drawl, is rather optimistic about the future of the plains. "Half of the land around Lubbock is still dry-farmed. Farmers have been getting crops for forty, fifty years. Their costs are that much lower that they can make a profit, somehow. And I'm not sure the aquifer is going to run out so fast. Conservation is a religion around here now. We have farmers who've cut their water use in half. Anyone who doesn't conserve tends to lose his friends fast. We've begun experimenting with capillary water—the water that the soil draws up from the aquifer and that saturates the layer above it. You can't pump it, but by injecting compressed air into the soil there, you squeeze it out like a sponge and it drains into the aquifer. Our economist thinks capillary water could be available for $25 to $50 an acre-foot. The farmers can lease air compressors from the oil industry as their reserves give out. Then you still have to pump the water up, but with enough conservation I think they can afford it. Capillary water could prolong the life of the Ogallala by another twenty to forty years."

This, then, is the plains region today—a place that is reverting, slowly and steadily, into an amphitheater of natural forces toying with its inhabitants' fate. Besides the constant threat of drought and wind, there are half a dozen other swords suspended over their heads. They are as vulnerable to nuclear powerplant fiascos in Washington State as they are to the debt crisis in Latin America. A couple of percentage-point increases in interest rates coupled with a collapse of the nuclear industry (which would put a premium on oil and gas), all of it occurring when rainfall drops from eighteen inches to twelve, could send them into a death spiral of debt, cost, and dust that might seal their fate. Meanwhile, the promise of water arriving from somewhere else when the aquifer begins running out is slipping almost out of view. Touring the region and speaking with farmers and politicians and bankers, one doesn't hear much of rescue anymore, though the subject is on everyone's mind. According to Steve Reynolds, the

471

state engineer of New Mexico, the odds against a rescue project being built "have gone from maybe fifty-fifty twenty years ago to eighty-twenty against today." Reynolds says he "frankly doesn't see how society will make this kind of investment in our behalf"—this despite his region's "tremendously important contribution to America's agricultural export production, the only thing that lets us pay for all we import." But then he spreads his lanky frame out in his chair, scratches a plaster of mud off his boot (one of Steve Reynolds's leisure activities is walking along his state's meager rivers and pulling phreatophytes out by their roots), and begins to veer toward one of his favorite subjects: microwave energy stations in space. "One of those microwave satellites could produce ten thousand megawatts of power. That's enough to power the whole project. I've never felt that we should give up on space. It's our last frontier, and we need one. One of these microwave satellites would be a way to make space exploration economically useful."

Even the economists who have looked into a water-importation project for the plains and pronounced it absurd seem unable to give up on the idea—such is our reluctance to let nature regain control, to suffer the fate of nearly all the irrigated civilizations of antiquity. In 1982, the High Plains–Ogallala Aquifer Region study projected an impossible cost of $300 to $800 per acre-foot for water imported into the region. But then it added: "The only long-term solution to declining groundwater supplies and maintaining a permanent irrigated agricultural economy in most of the High Plains region is the development of alternate water supplies. . . . Although emerging technologies for local water supply augmentation offer some potential for alleviating the overdraft of the aquifer, none can provide sustained and replenishable supplies to meet the region's needs. [Therefore] regional water transfer potentials . . . should be *continued and expanded to feasibility and planning levels*" (emphasis added).

Such investigations, the authors added in a cryptic sentence whose meaning will become clear later on, "should be international as well as national in scope."

The overdraft of groundwater on the high plains is the greatest in the nation, in the world, in all of human history—but it is merely an enormous manifestation of a common phenomenon throughout the West. On the east side of the San Joaquin Valley in California, enough groundwater disappears every year to supply Illinois. The overdraft is projected nearly to double in eighteen years. Tucson and El Paso have fewer than eighty years of water left even after raiding neigh-boring basins; they will have to get more from somewhere else. The overdraft in Arizona is rapidly forcing the state into an urban econ-omy. There is a serious overdraft in parts of central and eastern Oregon, which pales so much beside the Ogallala, Arizona, and Cal-ifornia overdrafts one hardly hears it mentioned outside the state. Groundwater overdraft is, moreover, a phenomenon not limited to the West. Long Island, sitting atop a closed-basin aquifer, is both depleting it and poisoning it with chemical wastes; where it could go for more water is an interesting question, since there isn't any available within four or five hundred miles that anyone seems willing to give up.

Of all these places, the only one that now appears likely to bring its use of water in balance with its supply is Arizona, mainly because it has little choice. The probable result, of course, is that irrigation farming will largely disappear unless Colorado River water, brought in through the Central Arizona Project, is sold to the farmers at in-credibly subsidized rates. It was in Arizona, by ironic coincidence, that the only great desert civilization ever established in North Amer-ica in earlier times disappeared—either for want of water, or, perhaps more likely, because of a surfeit of salt.

A few hundred million years ago, the waters of the oceans were still fresh enough to drink. It is the earth that contains the mineral salts one tastes in seawater. The salts are in all runoff, leached out of rock and soil. The runoff concentrates in rivers, which end up in the oceans—or, as in the case of Mono Lake and Great Salt Lake, in closed-basin sumps up to seven times saltier than the sea. Once in the ocean, the salts have no place to go; the seas are stuck with them. When water is evaporated, the salts remain behind; when the water falls as rain and becomes runoff again, a fresh batch of salts washes in.

Like DDT in pelican egg shells, the salts in the oceans are tes-timony to the effects of concentration. As the evaporative cycle is repeated, day after day, year after year, millennium after millennium, eon after eon, the oceans grow saltier all the time. On March 24, 1984, the dissolved salt content in ocean water off San Francisco was about thirty-five thousand parts per million, perhaps a fraction of a ppm higher than it was ten thousand years ago. The process is so incredibly slow and immense that, for once, no act of man seems capable of affecting it by the tiniest measurable iota. What *is* changing—what has changed drastically in the very recent past—is the concentration of salts in some of the world's rivers, and in some of its preeminent agricultural land.

Explaining the collapse of ancient civilizations is a cottage industry within the anthropological and archaeological professions, like the riddle of the dinosaurs. The explanations vary considerably. Some blame their demise on chronic human failings: degeneracy, conflict, war. The decline of Rome, according to some, was the result of the Romans' use of lead in their eating and drinking utensils; since lead causes irreversible brain damage if eaten or ingested in fairly small amounts, the theory offers a tempting explanation for the obviously demented behavior of certain Roman leaders. (It does not, however, explain why most Romans were demonstrably sane, or why there was so much genius about.) Because most of the great civilizations rose in deserts or semideserts, a popular explanation has always been drought—a drought beyond any that modern mankind has known, perhaps caused by aberrant sunspot cycles or some huge volcanic eruptions that changed the climate.

The most fruitful of the ancient cultures grew up at the southeastern end of the Fertile Crescent, the broad valley formed by the Tigris and Euphrates rivers in what is now Iraq. From there civilization appears to have spread eastward into Persia, and on to Afghanistan, Pakistan, India, and China. Later, it spread to the west. Most of the Romans' fabled feats of hydrologic engineering were borrowed from the Assyrians, who borrowed them from their predecessors, the Sumerians. In the seventh century B.C., the Assyrians, under Sennacherib, built an inverted siphon into the Nineveh Aqueduct, a feat of hydrologic engineering which was not really improved upon until New York City built a pressurized siphon into its second Croton Aqueduct in the 1860s. For all its precocious brilliance and innovation, however, the southern part of the Fertile Crescent went into eclipse around the year 2000 B.C. When Babylon rose in the eighteenth century B.C., many impressive Sumerian cities lay in ruins around it, as Babylon itself would lie desolated centuries later.

The story was repeated nearly everywhere, even in the New World, where a number of remarkable civilizations arose and prospered independently. One of the most impressive was the Hohokam civilization, in central Arizona, which left as its legacy some seven hundred miles of irrigation canals. Sometime around the fourteenth century, however, the Hohokam vanished—reason unknown. The Inca, Aztec, and Maya used irrigation, too, though they didn't rely on it as absolutely as the Hohokam. Their fate was sealed by European invaders, so it is perhaps idle speculation whether they would ultimately have gone the route of their predecessors in Mesopotamia and elsewhere. Whatever the answer, it appears that only one civilization completely dependent on irrigation managed to survive uninterruptedly for thousands of years. That civilization was Egypt—but Egypt was fundamentally different from the others in one way.

The survival of a civilization depends mainly on sufficient food. But what makes a civilization great? Traveling across the United States, Lewis and Clark saw few fat Indians until they had arrived at the mouth of the Columbia River, where the Chinook were gorging themselves on salmon, oysters, and clams. With plenty of time for leisure, the Northwest Indians were making exquisite crafts and living in impressive lodges. Farther north, the Haida, similarly well fed, had ample time and energy to commit cruel depredations on fellow tribes in magnificent war canoes carved from whole trees. When we think of a great civilization, however, we think of great cities, of sublime architecture and monuments, of intricate governmental and social structures, of engineering ability which startles even the jaded modern observer. By that standard, neither the Chinook nor any of the other cultures in North America—except the Hohokam—was great. Individually, the Indians could be incredibly skillful—as horsemen, warriors, hunters, artisans—but their high achievement was just that: individual. Even where Indians shared a common language, they broke up into small, separate tribes that, for the most part, went their own way. In contrast to the collectivism of the great Mediterranean, Indus Valley, or Mayan city-states, North American Indian culture was fragmented, atomized, ephemeral.

Most of the great Mediterranean civilizations arose in a region notable for its benign weather. But the climate in California is very similar to that of southern Italy and Greece, and California was a gastronomical paradise on earth, with salmon in the rivers, acorns for the taking, whales grounding themselves on beaches, and enormous herds and flocks of game. But the Hurok and Miwok and Paiute tribes were living in caves and under trees when the Greeks and Romans were building aqueducts and the Parthenon.

An answer to this riddle begins to emerge when one considers that nearly all the great early civilizations were irrigated ones. That single act—irrigation—seems inextricably linked to their ascendance, as well as to their demise. Any people who, for the first time, managed to divert a river and seduce a crop out of wasted land had tweaked the majestic indifference of the universe. To bring off the feat demanded tremendous collective will: discipline, planning, a sense of shared goals. To sustain it required order, which led to the creation of powerful priesthoods, of bureaucracies. Irrigation invited large concentrations of people because of all the food; it probably demanded such concentrations because of all the work. Out of this, cities grew. Work became specialized. There had to be engineers, builders, architects, farmers—probably even lawyers, for the disputes over water rights among upstream and downstream irrigators could not have been much different from today's. The ample supply of food may have helped in the keeping of slaves; in California, during the mission days, some of the Indians signed themselves into absolute servitude with the padres in exchange for the certitude of being fed.

Once established, irrigated civilizations in the desert were incredibly well off. Before modern weapons, sheer numbers meant power, so they were formidable in war. Oases in hostile deserts, they would have been difficult to approach and attack. The desert was also a healthy place to live. There was no tsetse fly, no malarial swamp, no raging cold and chilling wind. Because everyone was out of doors much of the time, the spread of disease was much less of a risk than in colder climates. Famine was an almost forgotten nemesis. Food was also a wonderful commodity for trade. Mesopotamia had virtually no metals, but it produced enough food to trade not only for iron and bronze but for a phenomenal wealth of gold. Trade was also a way of exchanging ideas; it was through contact with the Assyrians and Greeks that the Romans learned to build aqueducts.

There were, of course, problems. Canals could silt up or wash out in floods. A rigid bureaucratic order could spawn revolution. Any disruption of the water supply—by an earthquake, a drought—would be catastrophic. But those were not the kinds of problems likely to crush civilizations as ingenious as these. They might take their toll, along with wars and plagues, but it seems unlikely they would have sent them into permanent eclipse or, as in the case of the Hohokam, cause a whole civilization simply to vanish off the face of the earth. There had to be another enemy—something subtle, unseen, subversive. It was likely to be something they could do little or nothing about, something which they may not even have understood, and thus might have been inclined to ascribe to vengeance from gods.

Contemplating the list of enemies, natural and man-made, that might fit such a description, more and more anthropologists and archaeologists are concluding that the one that fits it best is salt.

Irrigation is a profoundly unnatural act. It hardly occurs in nature, and that which does occur is mostly along the rare desert rivers, like the Nile, that produce a reliable seasonal flood. In Africa and a few other places, there are natural depressions where runoff collects during rainy seasons, greening the land when it recedes. For every one of those, however, there are dozens of dead saline lakes or lake beds where the same thing used to happen and where, today, nothing can grow. They are common in Nevada—Groom Lake, Newark Lake, Goshute Lake, Winnemucca Lake, China Lake, Searles Lake, Cuddleback Lake—big saucers of salt left over from shallow Pleistocene seas, when the climate of Nevada was more like Szechuan. The waters that filled those lakes came down from ranges a short distance away, but in that brief intimacy with soil and rock had already accumulated enough salts to spell death for the basin below.

Man-made irrigation faces the same problem. In the West, many soils are classified as saline or alkaline. Irrigation water percolates through them, then returns to the river. It is diverted downstream, used again, and returned to the river. On rivers like the Colorado and the Platte, the same water may be used eighteen times over. It also spends a good deal of its time in reservoirs which, in desert country, may lose eight to twelve feet off their surface to the sun every year. The process continues—salts are picked up, fresh water evaporates, more salts are picked up, more fresh water evaporates. The hydrologist Arthur Pillsbury, writing in *Scientific American* in July of 1981, estimated that of the 120 million acre-feet of water applied to irrigated American crops the previous year, ninety million acre-feet were lost to evaporation and transpiration by plants. The remaining thirty million acre-feet contained virtually all of the salts.

Above a heavily irrigated strip of land along the Pecos River in New Mexico, water taken from the river has a measured salinity level of about 720 parts per million. Thirty miles beyond, salinity levels have shot up to 2,020 parts per million, almost entirely because of irrigation; 2,020 parts per million spells death for many crops. Near its headwaters in the Colorado Rockies, the Arkansas River shows only a trace of salts. A hundred and twenty miles downriver, it contains 2,200 parts per million. The Colorado, a river whose importance is absurdly disproportionate to its size, has the worst problem with salt of any American river. There are small tributaries flowing out of the salt-ridden Piceance Basin with measured concentrations of as much as ninety thousand parts per million—three tablespoons in a cup—so it is plagued by natural sources to begin with. In the Grand Valley of Colorado, irrigation water runs through sedimentary salt formations on its subterranean return to the river, reaching saline levels thirty times higher than at the diversion point. Below there are two huge reservoirs, Powell and Mead, evaporating a million and a half acre-feet of pure water each year—at least a tenth of the river's flow. It should come as no surprise, then, that by the time the Colorado River has entered Mexico, its waters are almost illegal.

Behind Jan van Schilfgaarde's desk in his office at the Department of Agriculture's Salinity Control Laboratory is a plaque proclaiming him a member of the Drainage Hall of Fame. Drainage seems like a pedestrian business, and van Schilfgaarde is an uncommonly so-phisticated and witty man, so one wonders what odd fortune married him to this issue. As he explains it, however, drainage becomes the most difficult aspect of irrigation—rather like fine-tuning a racing car. In fact, on the face of things, drainage would appear a more challenging problem than building dams. On the Columbia River, Grand Coulee Dam is in place, impassive and content. Next door, in the Columbia Basin Project, the battle against poor drainage and salts is still going on.

"When you apply irrigation water," says van Schilfgaarde, "it has to go somewhere. If it drains back off into the river, quickly, then that's fine. If it drains down to an underlying aquifer, fine—at least for a while. If it doesn't drain or drains too slowly, then you have problems. Salts build up in the root zones. The soil becomes water-logged. Ultimately you can damage the structure of soil, ruining it forever. So you have to get rid of it. How? Where? These are tremen-dous problems in places with lots of poorly drained land that apply tens of millions of acre-feet of water per year, like the American West. Basically, you can take the macro or the micro approach. You can build big drain systems, desalination plants, and so on, but you are still left with saline wastewater or pure salt to dispose of. Or you can tune your crop mix and your irrigation system to the reality of poor drainage and saline water and keep the problem at bay. That is what we have been doing here, with considerable success. I keep telling people this but they don't want to listen to me."

"Here" is the Department of Agriculture's Salinity Control Laboratory, of which van Schilfgaarde was director in 1982. It sits in the shadow of a hulking butte near the city of Riverside, California, surrounded by the very last agricultural land in the Los Angeles Basin. Sixty years ago, this was, acre for acre, the richest farming region in the world. Los Angeles County led the nation in farm income. Today, the main crop in the basin is tract housing. Displaced by ten million people, agriculture moved eastward and northward into the San Joaquin Valley, which has one of the worst drainage problems in the world.

"Salinity is the monkey on irrigation's back," says van Schilfgaarde. "The good water goes up in the sky and the junk water goes down, so the problem gets worse and worse. Victor Kovda of the University of Moscow says the amount of land going out of production due to salinity now surpasses the amount being brought into production through new irrigation. In this country, we have lost a few tens of thousands of acres—actually a few hundreds of thousands if you include the Wellton-Mohawk Project in Arizona, on which we later spent a fortune in order to bring salted-out land back into production. But that figure is projected to increase drastically in the decades ahead. The problem is an abstraction to most people, like projections of declining oil reserves were back in the 1960s. If you want to see how bad it can get, go to Iraq."

Thousands of years before the birth of Christ, the Sumerians in the Fertile Crescent were already getting some experience with salinity firsthand. Counts of grain impressions in excavated pottery from sites in what is now southern Iraq—pottery that has been carbon-dated back to 3500 B.C.—suggest that at the time, the amount of wheat grown was roughly equal to the amount of barley. A thousand years later, wheat production had dropped by 83 percent. It wasn't that the Sumerians suddenly developed an insatiable craving for barley; they were forced to switch because wheat is one of the least salt-tolerant crops. Between 2400 B.C. and 1700 B.C., barley yields in Sumeria declined from twenty-five hundred per hectare (a highly respectable yield even today) to nine hundred liters per hectare. Not long afterward, massive crop failures began. "Sodium ions tend to be adsorbed by colloidal clay particles, deflocculating them," reads an article in *Science* magazine from 1958—the first authoritative report linking the demise of Sumeria to salt. "[This] leaves . . . the resultant structureless soil almost impermeable to water. In general, high salt concentrations obstruct germination and impede the absorption of water and nutrients by plants. Salts accumulate steadily in the water table, which has only very limited lateral movement to carry them away. Hence the groundwater everywhere [in southern Iraq] has become extremely saline. . . . New waters added as excessive irrigation, rains, or floods can raise the level of the water table very considerably under the prevailing conditions of inadequate drainage. With a further capillary rise when the soil is wet, the dissolved salts and exchangeable sodium are brought into the root zone or even to the surface," killing the crops. As the authors—Thorkild Jacobsen and Robert Adams—suggested, Iraq is still struggling with its most ancient nemesis. It can feed itself mainly because it exports oil. At least 20 percent of its arable land (which doesn't amount to much) is permanently destroyed and can never be returned to cultivation. "Probably there is no single explanation," the authors wrote, "but that growing soil salinity played an important part in the breakup of Sumerian civilization seems beyond question."

Van Schilfgaarde's approach to the salinity problem is not the one favored by the farmers, the Bureau of Reclamation, and members of Congress in whose districts the problem lies. "The Bureau says we've analyzed the solutions I am talking about and they've been discredited, which is utter nonsense. Nobody has had the guts to implement them. I'm an outcast at every meeting I go to." The solutions favored by van Schilfgaarde belong to a kind of jiujitsu style; the prevailing wisdom is to attack the problem with tanks and planes. "I have been saying for years that the solution to this problem is better management—very careful management," he says, his urbane Dutch manner giving way to rising exasperation. "Certain crops can take high salinity levels. At our experimental plots in the San Joaquin Valley, we have been growing cotton for six years with fifty-nine hundred parts per million water *and* getting 50-percent-higher yields. The salt stress seems to stunt the plants but doesn't affect their production of cotton flowers. The water also has boron in it—an average irrigator wouldn't touch it. This shows that you can use water on one crop, then on one that tolerates salt better, then bring it back and use it again on a still more salt-tolerant crop before letting it go. You use a lot less, which means that you have less to get rid of in poorly drained areas such as the San Joaquin Valley. The cost is low—about $10 an acre. The cost of the Yuma Desalination Plant is *officially* up to $300 million."

The Yuma Desalination Plant, now nearing completion, is an example of the tanks-and-guns approach. In the 1940s, with the Central Arizona Project deadlocked in Congress, the Bureau of Reclamation was anxious to build *something* in that state, not only to mollify its citizenry and the increasingly powerful Carl Hayden but also to give its regional office, suffering existential malaise after the completion of Hoover Dam, something new to do. Along the lower Gila River were several tens of thousands of prime irrigable acres which had been irrigated off and on by Spanish, Indians, and Americans for the past three hundred years. Unfortunately, the region, named Wellton-Mohawk after two desert hamlets located there, is plagued by poor drainage. The Bureau revived the region by installing, at considerable expense, an elaborate drainage system to carry the wastewater away. Perforated tiles were laid several feet beneath the land, which led into a master drain that emptied into the Colorado River above the Mexican border. The project was completed in the early 1960s, just as the Bureau was closing the gates of Glen Canyon Dam.

The effect of those two actions—a sudden surge of water containing sixty-three hundred parts per million of salts accompanied by a drastic reduction of fresh surplus flows from above—gave the Mexicans fits. Below the border, the salinity of the Colorado River shot up from around eight hundred to more than fifteen hundred parts per million. The Mexicali region is the most productive in the entire country, which suffers not only from frightening population growth but from a woefully archaic, unbalanced, and inefficient agricultural sector. All the irrigation around Mexicali is utterly dependent on the river. Only a well-managed irrigation system, which the Mexicans did not have, could tolerate such levels of salt, and even then under some duress. Predictably, crop yields went into abject decline. The Mexicans were all the more incensed because the United States seemed so unconcerned about their plight. We had promised them 1.5 million acre-feet of water a year, which they were still getting. The Compact, U.S. officials pointed out, contained no guarantees about water quality, as long as there was enough. President Luis Echeverría campaigned heavily on the issue, and, after winning the election, threatened to keep his promise to haul the United States before the World Court at The Hague. In 1973, for reasons which are still obscure—but which might conceivably have had something to do with the fact that Mexico showed some promise of owning a great deal of oil—President Richard Nixon appointed a former U.S. Attorney General, Herbert Brownell, to work out a hasty solution. Signed six months later, in August of 1974, the agreement, known as Minute 242, calls for the United States to deliver Mexico water whose salt content is not more than 115 parts per million (plus or minus thirty ppm) higher than measured levels at Imperial Dam in 1976—a level that turned out to be 879 parts per million. As a result, salinity levels at the border of a thousand ppm or above—and they have almost reached such levels—are a violation of international law.

The simplest and cheapest way to solve Mexico's salinity crisis would have been for the U.S. government to buy out the Wellton-Mohawk farmers and retire their lands. Even today, a generous settlement probably would not cost more than a couple of hundred million dollars, and a tremendous source of salts would be removed. Retiring some additional irrigated lands in the Grand Valley of Colorado, another prodigious source of salts, would be further insurance against the problem getting out of hand. None of this has, of course, happened. The solution of choice at Wellton-Mohawk has been the construction of a reverse-osmosis desalination plant—ten times larger than any in the world—which, while consuming enough electricity to satisfy a city of forty thousand people, will treat the wastewater running out the drain canal. The solution of choice in the Grand Valley is at least as expensive but more prosaic—lining irrigation canals to prevent seepage through subsurface salt zones is the main one. The legislation authorizing all of these works belongs in a class of Congressional sacred cows—whatever it costs to keep salinity levels down without retiring an acre of salt-ridden land is what Congress is willing to spend. The Yuma plant is now supposed to cost $293 million, a figure hardly anyone outside the Bureau believes, and the upper-basin works could cost another $600 million, perhaps much more. Energy costs could easily push the Yuma plant's cost to $1 billion or more over fifty years.

What Congress has chosen to do, in effect, is purify water at a cost exceeding $300 an acre-foot so that upriver irrigators can continue to grow surplus crops with federally subsidized water that costs them $3.50 an acre-foot.

"If the farmers at Wellton-Mohawk adopted efficient irrigation methods," says Jan van Schilfgaarde, "you could solve the problem without even retiring the lands. It would be quite possible to reduce their return flows from 220,000 acre-feet a year to 45,000 acre-feet. I'm not even talking about installing drip irrigation. I'm talking about laser-leveling fields and reusing water on salt-tolerant crops and not doing stupid things like irrigating at harvest time, which our neighboring farmer in the San Joaquin Valley did one year. A lot of these guys are actually absentee owners farming by telephone from their dentists' offices in Scottsdale. They hire some manager who may be competent or incompetent and they don't care. They're not in this business to farm crops, or even to make a profit. They're farming the government. They're growing tax shelters. But even if you *do* have a highly competent farmer who wouldn't mind reducing his waste-water flows, he has no incentive to conserve. Federal water is so cheap it might as well be free. What's the point of hiring a couple of additional irrigation managers to save free water? It's wrong to say the farmer is the culprit. He is being *forced* to consume water."

Van Schilfgaarde's outspokenness on this subject may well have had something to do with his departure from the USDA laboratory in 1984. Meanwhile, as his salinity-management approach is almost universally ignored and the Bureau's expensive solutions receive several hundred times more money than his laboratory does, salinity levels in the Colorado River continue to rise. According to the Bureau, the levels at Imperial Dam could reach 1,150 parts per million as early as the year 2000 and keep rising even if its desalination plant operates effectively—a prospect open to considerable doubt. New projects in the upper basin, oil shale development, the continued leaching of saline soil—all will contribute to salinity's inexorable march. This is bad news for the Mexicans, but it is bad news for Los Angeles, too. Each additional part per million of salts in the city's Colorado River supply is estimated to cause $300,000 worth of damage, basin-wide, to the things the water comes in contact with: pipes, fixtures, machinery, cars. A rise in salinity levels at Imperial Dam from 900 to 1,150 parts per million, then, will cost the citizens of southern California about $75 million a year.

The Bureau's answer to all of this appears on a chart which it has available for distribution. The answer is simply described as "further salinity-control projects under study." Adopting these unnamed solutions, at whatever cost, is supposed to hold salinity levels at about 1,030 parts per million at Imperial Dam, *still* too high to meet our Compact obligation to Mexico—which, since 1974, has become one of our three most important foreign suppliers of oil. The Bureau's answer to *that* appears on the graph as "future additional measures"—whatever those are.

In the Colorado Basin, the effects of wastefully irrigating saline lands are not, for the most part, being felt by those doing the irrigating. Thanks mainly to the taxpayers, the farmers who are contributing the lion's share of the salts to the river have had drainage facilities built which flush the problem down to someone else. In the San

Joaquin Valley, it is a different story. The San Joaquin's problem is unique—an ingenious revenge by nature, in the minds of some, on a valley whose transformation into the richest agricultural region in the world was wrought at awesome cost to rivers, fish, and wildlife. Several times in the relatively recent geologic past—within the last couple of million years—the valley was a great inland sea, thick with diatomaceous life and tiny suspended sediments which settled near the middle of the gently sloping valley floor. Compressed and compacted, the stuff formed an almost impervious layer of clay that now underlies close to two million acres of fabulously productive irrigated land. In the middle of the valley, the clay membrane is quite shallow, sometimes just a few feet beneath the surface soil. When irrigation water percolates down, it collects on the clay like bathwater in a tub. In hydrologists' argot, it has become "perched" water. Since the perched water does not have a chance to mingle with the relatively pure aquifer beneath the clay, it may become highly saline, as in Iraq. The more the farmers irrigate, the higher it rises. In places, it has reached the surface, killing everything around. There are already thousands of acres near the southern end of the valley that look as if they had been dusted with snow; not even weeds can grow there. An identical fate will ultimately befall more than a million acres in the valley unless something is done.

For years, the planners in the state and federal water bureaucracies have talked about the need for a "master drain" to carry the perched water out of the San Joaquin Valley. It is more accurate to say that their *reports* have talked about it, while the officials, whose main concern was building more dams to satisfy the demands of the irrigators, ignored the need for drainage because neither they nor (they guessed) the public and the farmers could face the cost. "In the early and mid-1970's," says van Schilfgaarde, "the state's position was that no drainage problem exists. The early reports all said that the State Water Project makes no sense without a drain, because it would add inevitably to the perched water problem. But the public doesn't read reports, so no one mentioned them. Then, a few years ago, when the problem began threatening to become critical, there was suddenly an awful drainage problem that threatened the future of agriculture in California."

Today, three decades after the first reports spoke of the need for a huge, valley-wide drainage system, no such system exists. A modest-sized spur, called the San Luis Drain, is being completed as a part of the Westlands Water District, which, by introducing a prodigious

amount of new surface water into a relatively small area, threatened
to waterlog the lands downslope. But the water carried off by the
San Luis drain has nowhere to go until a master drain is built. For
the time being, it is being dumped into a man-made swamp called
Kesterson Reservoir, near the town of Los Banos, which slowly fills
and evaporates according to the intensity of the valley heat and the
irrigation cycle. From the air, the reservoir, when it is full, is an
attractive sight to migrating waterfowl, which descend on it by the
tens of thousands as their ancestors once descended by the many
millions on the valley's primordial marshes and shallow lakes. The
presence of all of those coots, geese, and ducks at Kesterson Reservoir
gave the Bureau an idea about how to solve one of the most daunting
problems associated with the master drain: its enormous cost. By the
time the San Luis Drain, a modest portion of the proposed master
drain, is completed, its price tag will be more than $500 million. In
1984, Interior Secretary William Clark made an offhand projection
that solving the drainage problem valley-wide could end up costing
$4 to $5 billion. That comes to about $5,000 an acre to rescue the
affected lands, which is more than most of the land itself is worth.
The farmers, a number of whom are corporations or millionaires, are
understandably loath to pay the bill. If one wrote off a third of the
cost as a wildlife and recreational benefit, however, it would be easier
to swallow. That is exactly what the Bureau and California's Department of Water Resources, in a 1979 interagency study entitled
"Agricultural Drainage and Salt Management in the San Joaquin
Valley," proposed to do in the case of the master drain, which, in
that report, was projected to cost $1.26 billion in 1979 dollars. As-
cribing annual benefits of $92 million to the master drain, the Bureau
and the state's Department of Water Resources elected to write off
about a third of that total, or $31.7 million, as a nonreimbursable
benefit, payable by the taxpayers, for the creation of artificial marshes.
If one were to divide the number of ducks which might reasonably
be expected to use those man-made wetlands into $31.7 million, they
would become very expensive ducks indeed. When the Bureau's dams
went up, regulating the rivers and allowing the marshlands to be
dried up—about 93 percent of the Central Valley's original wetlands
are gone—it virtually ignored the economic value of the millions of
ducks it was about to displace. Now, suddenly, they have become
almost priceless.

Due to a distressing twist of fate, however, the Bureau and California may consider themselves lucky if they succeed in writing off

any part of the master drain to wildlife benefits. Sometime in 1982, hunters and biologists around Kesterson Reservoir began to observe that many overwintering birds seemed lethargic and sick—so ravaged by some strange malady that they could not even float on the water, and often drowned. At first, duck hunters and conservationists put forth an explanation that the farm lobby had always pooh-poohed—that pesticides and other chemical wastes in the sumpwater were making the birds die. By 1984, however, biologists were quite certain that the main cause of the ducks' awful fate was selenium, a rare mineral, toxic in small doses, that occurs in high concentrations in southern Coast Range soils—exactly those soils which, washing down from the mountains over aeons, formed the Westlands Water District. The San Francisco *Chronicle*, which has carried on a long, bitter battle against water exports to the valley and southern California, has played the story for all it is worth. But none of its news stories and editorials had quite the impact of a poignant front-page photograph of a gorgeous dying male pintail duck at Kesterson Reservoir, a duck about to sink like a doomed boat to the bottom of the poisoned man-made marsh its presence is to subsidize.

Since there can be only one ultimate destination for the wastewater carried by the master drain—San Francisco Bay—the spectacle at Kesterson has infuriated many of the five million people who reside in the Bay Area. They may pollute the bay badly enough themselves, even if they do not admit it; but to have a bunch of farmers grown wealthy on "their" water, and subsidized by their taxes, sending it back to the bay full of toxic wastes, selenium, boron, and salt—that is intolerable. The farmers, the Bureau, and the Department of Water Resources might reject such reasoning as simplistic and emotional. But the fact is that the people of the Bay Area appear to have the political clout to prevent the drain from ever reaching there, and they seem determined to use it. It matters little that the salts in the wastewater (the selenium and boron and pesticides are another matter) would hardly affect the salinity of a great bay into which the ocean rushes twice a day. What matters is that the San Joaquin Valley farmers asked for water and got it, asked for subsidies and got them, and now want to use the bay as a toilet. To their urban brethren by the ocean, living a world apart, all of this smacks of a system gone mad.

The one irrigated civilization of antiquity that remained intact for thousands of years was Egypt, and we are now reasonably certain why. Every year, the Nile, the world's most reliable river, would engorge itself in a spring flood and cover most of Egypt's agricultural land. The floods would both carry off the salts and deposit a fresh layer of silt. The farmers would then rush to plant their crops, which grew lavishly on the residual moisture and the perfect soil. In the 1960s, however, the Egyptians, pumped up with a sense of grandiose destiny by Gamal Abdel Nasser, decided to build a high dam on the Nile at Aswan. The Soviet Union helped them do it against the United States' advice. The result has been described as the worst ecological mistake committed in one place by mankind. The spring floods are gone; the nutrient-rich silts no longer come; the Nile sardine fishery in the Mediterranean is going extinct; bilharzia, or schistosomiasis, a gruesome disease borne by a snail that thrives in slack waters in Africa, is rampant; the reservoir is silting up quite rapidly due to erosion from primitive agriculture upriver; irrigation canals, meanwhile, are being scoured by the silt-free water released by the dam; and the salts have arrived. With their copious new supply of year-round irrigation water, the Egyptian farmers have been irrigating madly, and the water table, increasingly poisoned by salts, is rising dangerously. Recently, Egypt hired a group of American engineers and agronomists, among whom was former Reclamation Commissioner Floyd Dominy, to help them figure out a solution. "Goddamned crazy Russians" was Dominy's response when I asked him what things were like over there. "Anyone should have seen that Egypt wouldn't be able to handle the effects of that dam." The Egyptians now have no choice other than to install drainage, which they can ill afford—partly because schistosomiasis has become a national epidemic costing them some $600 million a year. The hydrologic engineer Arthur F. Pillsbury, writing in *Scientific American* in 1981, noted that Egypt, having avoided the fate of its sister civilizations all these centuries, "is now faced with the universal problem of keeping salts from accumulating in the irrigated fields."

In that same article, Pillsbury also wrote:

> In order to maintain and ensure the long-term viability of irrigated agriculture and to provide enough water to carry the salts to the ocean or some other natural sink, the development of water resources *should be intensified.* . . . Before man began harnessing the rivers, the seasonal floods were highly effective in carrying salts to the ocean and keeping the river basin in reasonably good salt balance. Today, with river flows being

regulated by storage systems, and with high consumptive use of the released water, there is not enough waste flow left to achieve anything approaching balance. The salt is being stored, in one way or another, within the river basins. . . . Unless the lower rivers are allowed to reassert their natural function as exporters of salt to the ocean, today's productive land will eventually become salt-encrusted and barren.

In the end, Pillsbury concluded, there is only one answer. "Eventually, some grand-scale water diversion concept will be needed. . . . "

In 1946, after participating in a conference involving twenty-four eminent hydrologists and engineers, Dr. Charles P. Berkey had a moment of epiphany. Berkey was, at the time, one of the foremost hydrologists in the world. Newbury Professor Emeritus of Geology at Columbia University, he had been a consultant to the city of New York on its Catskill and Neversink water supply projects, and had a list of accomplishments and credentials four times as long as his arm—a list which had kept him so busy he never had a chance to contemplate the implications of his life's work until he was well into advanced age. Then it came to him—a sunburst of perception, a giant semantic leap.

What prompted Berkey's enlightenment was a talk delivered at the conference by J. C. Stevens, then the president of the American Society of Civil Engineers. Berkey was so dumbstruck by what Stevens had to say that he drafted a response as soon as he got back to his desk at Columbia—a response which reads more like a confession of blindness or an admission of personal failing than anything else. This is part of what he had to say:

Although the principles involved in the paper by Mr. Stevens are well known, it is not certain that the implications are fully appreciated by many even in responsible relation to them. The Factual Data had been long known to the writer, but no statement before this one had brought so forcibly to mind their importance and bearing on long-range planning. . . . The United States has virtually set up an empire on impounded and redistributed water. The nation is encouraging development, on a scale never before attempted, of lands that are almost worthless except for the waters that can be delivered to them by the works of man. There is building up, through settlement and new population, a line of industries foreign to the normal resources of the region. . . .

Effort to use water on desert lands is not a new adventure by any means; but a program involving development of a great region—inviting thereby a large new population under conditions that carry elements of certain future destructive encroachment in limited and computable time—that is new. Not only is it new, but in some of the implications it is fairly astonishing. . . . The nearest thing in that respect was the settlement of the western high plains in earlier days by people who believed that these dust-bowl lands could be farmed in the same manner as those they came from in the Central Mississippi Valley, and no voice was raised to warn them. That was to be a vast and prosperous empire, too.

For the first time, after reading this paper, the long-range significance of the suffocating effect produced by accumulating silt in all these reservoirs was borne down on the writer. He had been so much taken with the fine things being done that he had not fully appreciated the fact that the program carried elements of destruction sure to bring some kind of ending. It was always evident, of course, that there were severe limitations, but it was too easy to overlook or belittle this element of damage from within.

The experience of founding, in difficult surroundings, settlements which finally grew into influence and power is not new; and neither is their decline, and even their ending. In the past, however, none of them carried, along with the agents that built them up, such relentless elements of destruction as in the present reclamation of arid lands. The astonishing thing is that the life of these relief works promises to be so short. One could forget it if the time vista were indefinite, or if there were promise of a thousand years. In that time most human subsistence and economic lines take new turns and become adjusted; but in some of these projects, typical of the average more or less, the beginnings of decline loom already and will certainly grow into a serious problem in three or four generations. One wonders how many settlers gathering around these projects appreciate what it means.

Of course, if one is able to divorce his interest from the future, there is nothing to worry about. In this generation, and the next and the next, an upgrade can be maintained. One can claim (and it is true) that much has been added to the world; but the longer-range view in this field, as in many others, is threatened by apparently incurable ailments and this one of slowly choking to death with silt is the most stubborn of all. There are no permanent cures.

The conference Berkey and Stevens had attended, "The Future of Lake Mead and Elephant Butte Reservoir," was, more precisely, a summit meeting on the subject of mud. Before Hoover and Elephant Butte dams were built, the Rio Grande and the Colorado River ran chocolate-brown in the spring and anytime a cloudburst occurred somewhere in the watershed. Now, the water emanating from the penstocks and spillways below the dams was an opalescent blue-green, colored only by the minerals and algae in it. Each year, millions of cubic yards of silt were coming to a dead halt behind both dams.

For all their breathtaking immensity, dams are oddly vulnerable things—a vulnerability that is shared and greatly intensified among the millions of people who depend on them. The engineers who have built them have gone to great lengths to make them safe from earthquakes, landslides, and floods. But their ultimate vulnerability, as Berkey wrote, is to silt. Every reservoir eventually silts up—it is only a matter of when. In hard-rock terrain with a lot of forest cover—the Sierra Nevada, the Catskill Mountains—a dam may have a useful life of a thousand years. In some overpopulated nations whose forests are nearly gone and whose farmlands are moving up mountains and whose rivers are therefore thick with silt, reservoirs built after the Second World War may be solid mud before the century is out. The Sanmexia Reservoir in China, an extreme case, was completed in 1960 and already decommissioned by 1964; it had silted up completely. The Tehri Dam in India, the sixth-highest in the world, recently saw its projected useful life reduced from one hundred to thirty years due to horrific deforestation in the Himalaya foothills. In the Dominican Republic, the eighty-thousand-kilowatt Tavera Hydroelectric Project, the country's largest, was completed in 1973; by 1984, silt behind the dam had reached a depth of eighteen meters and storage capacity had been reduced by 40 percent. In countries suffering from overpopulation, deforestation, which is the primary cause of reservoir siltation, can only be expected to grow worse.

As a matter of principle, any place where vegetation is relatively sparse, where soils are erodable, but where six inches of rain in a day or twenty inches in a month are not unknown is a less than ideal place to situate a dam. Those conditions, however, apply to a large part of the intermountain West—and, since the arrival of intensive agriculture, to a great portion of the Middle West as well. The Eel River in California is the most rapidly eroding watershed in North America—partly because the topography is ridden with erodable sediments, partly because of rampant clear-cutting earlier in the century from which the forests may never recover, partly because of stubble grazing by cattle and sheep that is still going on. There is no major dam on any branch of the Eel—at least not yet—but talk of building one there says a lot about what people are willing to ignore. Meanwhile, erosive forces are hard at work in the watersheds of the Missouri River, the Colorado, the Rio Grande, the Platte, the Arkansas, the Brazos, the Colorado of Texas, the Sevier, the Republican, the Pecos, the Willamette, the Gila—rivers on which there are dozens of dams.

Earlier in the century, it was thought by some that irrigation in those watersheds might actually slow the rate of erosion by creating more groundcover to hold the soil in place. In the 1920s, however, no one foresaw interest rates so high that farmers, pushed to the brink, would almost be forced to abandon careful husbandry of the soil for maximum profit. No one foresaw cheap fertilizers that allow land to be plowed year after year, never going fallow. No one foresaw six-ton tractors that tear up the soil and make it more apt to be carried off. No one foresaw a demand for U.S. agricultural exports that makes it profitable to farm Class VI land. As a result of all this—and because it was inevitable anyway—the dams are silting up.

Black Butte Reservoir, Stony Creek, California. Capacity in 1963: 160,009 acre-feet. Capacity in 1973: 147,754 acre-feet.

Conchas Reservoir, Canadian River, New Mexico. Capacity in 1939: 601,112 acre-feet. Capacity in 1970: 528,951 acre-feet.

Alamagordo Reservoir, Pecos River, New Mexico. Capacity in 1936: 156,750 acre-feet. Capacity in 1964: 110,655 acre-feet.

Lake Waco, Brazos River, Texas. Capacity in 1930: 39,378 acre-feet. Capacity in 1964: 15,427 acre-feet.

Elephant Butte Reservoir, Rio Grande River, New Mexico. Capacity in 1915: 2,634,800 acre-feet. Capacity in 1969: 2,137,219 acre-feet.

Hoover Dam, Colorado River, Arizona-Nevada. Capacity in 1936: 32,471,000 acre-feet. Capacity in 1970: 30,755,000 acre-feet.

San Carlos Reservoir, Gila River, Arizona. Capacity in 1928: 1,266,837 acre-feet. Capacity in 1966: 1,170,000 acre-feet.

Howard Brothers Stock Dam, Driftwood Creek, McDonald, Kansas. Capacity in 1959: 26.58 acre-feet. Capacity in 1972: 14.18 acre-feet.

Ocoee Dam Number 3, Ocoee River, North Carolina. Capacity in 1942: 14,304 acre-feet. Capacity in 1972: 3,879 acre-feet.

Guernsey Reservoir, North Platte River, Wyoming. Capacity in 1929: 73,810 acre-feet. Capacity in 1957: 44,800 acre-feet.

Wilson Dam, Tennessee River, Tennessee. Capacity in 1928: 687,000 acre-feet. Capacity in 1961: 641,000 acre-feet.

Clouse Lake, Center Branch of Rush Creek, Ohio. Capacity in 1948: 234 acre-feet. Capacity in 1970: 142 acre-feet.

In thirty-five years, Lake Mead was filled with more acre-feet of silt than 98 percent of the reservoirs in the United States are filled with acre-feet of water. The rate has slowed considerably since 1963, because the silt is now building up behind Flaming Gorge, Blue Mesa, and Glen Canyon dams.

The Bureau of Reclamation has an Office of Sedimentation, which was being run in 1984 by a cheerful fellow named Bob Strand. One wonders whether his good cheer stems from the fact that sedimentation is the one problem the Bureau hasn't really been forced to deal with yet. "All of our bigger reservoirs were built with a sedimentation allowance," says Strand. "There's enough surplus capacity in them to permit most of the projects to operate according to plan over their payout lifetime. In most cases that's fifty to a hundred years. After that, silt will begin to cut into capacity. It hasn't happened yet to any significant degree." What will the Bureau do when it does happen? "We're working on it," says Strand.

"The dams are wasting assets," says Raphael Kazmann, a retired professor of hydrology from Louisiana State University and one of the world's foremost authorities on water. "When they silt up, that's it." Can't the mud be removed somehow? "Sure," says Kazmann, "but where are you going to put it? It will wash right back in unless you truck it out to sea. The cost of removing it is so prohibitive anyway that I can't imagine it being done. Do you understand how many coal trains it would take to haul away the Colorado River's annual production of silt? How would you get it out of the canyons? You can design dams to flush out the silts nearest to the dam, but all you get rid of is a narrow profile. You create a little short canyon in a vast plateau of mud. Most of the stuff stays no matter what you do."

The one place with some experience at desilting dams is Los

Angeles, which has built a number of small retention reservoirs around the basin whose capacity it can ill afford to lose. Between 1967 and 1977, the Metropolitan Water District and the Department of Water and Power removed 23.7 million cubic yards of mud from behind those dams. The cost was $29.1 million. At that rate, it would cost more than a billion and a half dollars, in modern money, to remove the silt that accumulated in Lake Mead over thirty years—if one could find any place to put it.

"The average politician," says Luna Leopold, another hydrologist who seems to have some appreciation of the magnitude of the problem, "has a time horizon of around four years. The agencies are tuned to Congress, so theirs is about the same. No one has begun to think about this yet. But keep in mind that thousands of big dams were built in this country during a very brief period—between 1915 and 1975. Many are going to be silting up at the same time. There already are some small reservoirs in the East that are mud up to the gunwales. These are little manageable reservoirs—nothing like the big canyon reservoirs we've built in the West. But I haven't heard of anything being done about them."

The silt that is now accumulating behind the dams used to settle near the mouths of the rivers. The Mississippi-Atchafalaya Delta, which is bigger than New Jersey, is made up entirely of silt from the West and Middle West. About half of the sediment that used to reach it every year no longer does. Raphael Kazmann, who made a career of studying the Delta and may understand it better than anyone else alive, is convinced that a third to half of it will disappear within the next few decades; a significant percentage already has. He also believes the Mississippi will change course—probably by the year 2000—and begin pouring down the Atchafalaya Basin, wiping out many miles of interstate highway and several of the nation's largest gas pipelines. "The river has been straitjacketed and robbed of its silt," says Kazmann. "It's a much more powerfully scouring river than it was. It's just a matter of time before it eats away one of its bends and seeks out a completely new course." Kazmann also believes that, in an economic sense, such an event could be the greatest peacetime disaster in American history. The only thing that might eclipse it is the silting up of the dams.

"The answer I have always heard from bureaucrats," says Kazmann, "is that scientific and technological progress has accelerated at such a tremendous rate that some solution will come along. I don't know what they think—that we're going to have fusion energy pumping out the dams? The only answer I can see is to make the dams higher or build new ones. Right now I can think of few places where it would make economic sense to do that, even if it were feasible."

I n his book *Modern Hydrology*, Raphael Kazmann has written:

> [T]he reservoir construction program, objectively considered, is really a program for the continued and endless expenditure of ever-increasing sums of public money to combat the effects of geologic forces, as these forces strive to reach positions of relative equilibrium in the regime of rivers and the flow of water. It may be that future research in the field of modern hydrology will be primarily to find a method of extricating ourselves from this unequal struggle with minimum loss to the nation. . . . The forces involved . . . are comparable to those met by a boy who builds a castle on the sandy ocean beach, next to the water, at low tide. . . . [I]t is not pessimism, merely an objective evaluation, to predict the destruction of the castle. . . .

A Civilization,
if You Can Keep It

I n May of 1958, while testifying at Senate hearings on the acreage provisions of the Reclamation Act, the then Associate Commissioner of the Bureau of Reclamation, Floyd Dominy, departed both from the issue at hand and from his prepared remarks to lecture some critical eastern Senators on what the federal irrigation program has meant to the American West.

"My people came here as farmers and settled in East Hampton, Long Island, in 1710," Dominy began. "As the generations progressed they moved westward as public lands were opened up and as the West was developed, until my grandfather, Lafayette Dominy, in 1845, was born on a farm in LaSalle County, Illinois, carved from the wilderness by his own father and grandfather. When Lafayette Dominy reached maturity and married and had his first child, who was my father, he wanted a farm of his own but discovered that within his means he could not acquire one in Illinois. . . . He borrowed $2,000 from a preacher in 1876 and migrated with his small family to Nebraska and took one of the 160-acre homesteads about which we have been speaking.

"Now as to the adequacy of that homestead I would like to have you know that they lived in a sod house. They lived out beyond medical attention, without any of the modern facilities that we feel are desirable for all Americans today. They lost all the girl children in the family to diphtheria. The three male children survived, or else I would not be here.

"I want you to know that on that 160-acre homestead it took

that man from 1876 to 1919 to pay off the $2,000 that he borrowed. . . . [W]hen my father reached maturity he took a homestead in the same area, 160 acres. On that farm six of us children were born and six of us reached maturity on the substance of that 160-acre homestead. We had outside plumbing. We did not have deep freezers, automobiles, school buses coming by the door. We walked to school in the mud. We maybe had one decent set of clothes to wear to town on Saturday. . . .

"You take 160 acres that has to provide automobiles, modern school facilities, taxes for school buses, for good roads, to provide deep freezers, electric stoves, electric refrigerators, the modern conveniences that the farm housewife ought to have and deserves, it puts a much greater demand on the income of that land than was necessary to support us at a subsistence level, prevailing for my father or grandfather. . . .

"[When] I became a county agricultural agent . . . I saw the results of people who had decided 'this is the Utopia for which we seek,' and they had left Missouri and Iowa and other places where land was not available—they put their belongings in immigrant cars, and they went to Wyoming and Montana. They took out what was promised to them as an abundant chance for a great family living, 640 dryland acres. I want everyone in this room and I want this committee to know that most of those 640 acres could not sustain a family under any reasonable economic conditions that have prevailed then or now. I saw family after family, after devoting fifteen or twenty years of valiant effort . . . forced to sell out and start anew."

Considering all this, Dominy went on, how could you view the federal Reclamation program as anything less than the salvation of the West? The same 160 acres of flinty, stubbled, profoundly unwelcoming land that couldn't support a family, couldn't create a tax base, couldn't provide even dietary subsistence during drought years was magically transformed when water was led to it. Could one imagine what the West would be like if there *hadn't* been a Bureau of Reclamation? If the rivers hadn't been turned out of their beds and allowed to remake that pitless landscape?

It is a question worth thinking about. Nevada is the one western state without any mentionable rivers at all, and perhaps the closest approximation of how things could have remained if the landscape had suffered no improvement: its settlements a hundred miles apart, its economy rooted, for lack of a better alternative, in what used to be called sin, its ghost towns as numerous as those that managed to survive. Of course, in the states with rivers there was plenty of irrigation going on before the Bureau arrived on the scene, but an appalling number of those private ventures were destined to collapse. There were, as Dominy said, tens of thousands of heart-rending farm failures, and catastrophic overgrazing on the dryland ranches; irrigation helped put an end to both. There were all those rivers just *wasting* water to the Gulf and Pacific; there was the virgin Colorado, as Dominy liked to say, "useless to anyone." Did one prefer the tawdry mirage of Las Vegas to the palpable miracle of the Imperial Valley? Did one prefer a wild and feckless Colorado to one that measures out steady water and power to ten million people? Should we *not* have built Hoover Dam?

There are those who might say yes, who would argue that the West should have been left pretty much as it was. At the distant other end of the spectrum are the water developers and engineers who cannot rest while great rivers like the Yukon and the Fraser still run free, for whom life seems to hold little meaning except to subjugate nature, to improve it, to engage it in a contest of wills. For the rest of us, contemplating the modern West presents a dilemma. We mourn what has been lost since Lewis and Clark—the feast of wilderness, the mammoth herds of buffalo, the fifty thousand grizzly bears and the million antelope that roamed California, the coastal streams that one could cross on the backs of spawning salmon. On the other hand, to see a sudden unearthly swath of green amid the austere and mournful emptiness of the Mojave Desert or the Harney Basin is to watch one's prejudices against mankind's conquering instinct begin to dissolve. So we want to know, even if it seems an academic matter now, what it all amounts to that we have done out here in the West. How much was sensible? How much was right? Was it folly to allow places like Los Angeles and Phoenix to grow up? Were we insane or farsighted to build all the dams? And even if such questions seem academic, they lead to an emphatically practical one: What are we going to do next?

It isn't easy to get people to think along these lines, at least not yet, because the vulnerable aspect of our desert empire remains for most people, even most westerners, an abstraction, like the certainty of another giant earthquake along the San Andreas Fault. Drive through Los Angeles and see the millions of lawns and the water flowing everywhere and the transformation seems immutable: everything rolls along nonstop like the seamless ribbons of traffic; it all seems permanent. But then catch a flight to Salt Lake City and fly over Glen Canyon Dam at thirty thousand feet, a height from which even this magnificent bulwark becomes a frail thumbnail holding back a monstrous, deceptively placid, man-made sea, and think what one sudden convulsion of the earth or one crude atomic bomb or one five-hundred-year flood (which came close to occurring in 1983 and nearly destroyed a spillway under the dam) might do to that fragile plug in its sandstone gorge, and what the sudden emptying of Lake Powell, with its eight and a half quadrillion gallons of water, would do to Hoover Dam downstream, and what the instantaneous disappearance of those huge life-sustaining lakes would mean to the thirteen million people hunkered down in southern California and to the Imperial Valley—which would no longer exist. But the West's dependence on distant and easily disruptible dams and aqueducts is just the most palpable kind of vulnerability it now has to face. The more insidious forces—salt poisoning of the soil, groundwater mining, the inexorable transformation of the reservoirs from water to solid ground—are, in the long run, a worse threat. If Hoover and Glen Canyon dams were to collapse, they could be rebuilt; the cost would be only $15 billion or so. But to replace the groundwater being mined throughout the West would mean creating an entirely new Colorado River half again as large as the one that exists.

Like so many great and extravagant achievements, from the fountains of Rome to the federal deficit, the immense national dam-construction program that allowed civilization to flourish in the deserts of the West contains the seeds of disintegration; it is the old saw about an empire's rising higher and higher and having farther and farther to fall. Without the federal government there would have been no Central Valley Project, and without that project California would never have amassed the wealth and creditworthiness to build its own State Water Project, which loosed a huge expansion of farming and urban development on the false promise of water that may never arrive. Without Uncle Sam masquerading from the 1930s to the 1970s as a godfather of limitless ambition and means, the seven Ogallala states might never have chosen to exhaust their groundwater as precipitously as they have; they let themselves be convinced that the government would rescue them when the water ran out, just as the Colorado Basin states foolishly persuaded themselves that Uncle Sam would "augment" their overappropriated river when it ran dry. The government—the Bureau and the Corps of Engineers—first created a miraculous abundance of water, then sold it so cheaply that the mirage filled the horizon. Everywhere one turned, one saw water, cheap water, inexhaustible water, and when there were more virgin rivers and aquifers to tap, the illusion was temporarily real. But now the desert is encroaching on the islands of green that have risen within it, and the once mighty Bureau seems helpless to keep its advance at bay; the government is broke, the cost of rescue is mind-boggling, and the rest of the country, its infrastructure in varying stages of collapse, thinks the West has already had too much of a good thing.

There were excesses of both degree and style. For thousands of years Egyptian farmers irrigated by simple diversions from the Nile and nothing went badly wrong; then Egypt built the Aswan High Dam and got waterlogged land, salinity, schistosomiasis, nutrient-starved fields, a dying Mediterranean fishery, and a bill for all of the above that will easily eclipse the value of the irrigation "miracle" wrought by the dam. In the American West, the Bureau and the Corps fostered a similar style of water development that, though amazingly fruitful in the short run, leaves everyone and everything more vulnerable in the end. Only the federal government had the money to build the big mainstem reservoirs, which will end up being choked by silt or, at the very least, will require billions of dollars' worth of silt-retention dams to keep the main reservoirs alive (these smaller reservoirs will, of course, silt up fairly quickly themselves, even assuming it makes economic sense to build them). It was through the federal government that millions of acres of poorly drained land not only were opened to farming but were sold dirt-cheap water; the farmers flooded their fields with their cheap water and made the waterlogging and salt problems even worse; now that the lands are beginning to succumb to salt it looks as if the farmers will, in many cases, have to solve things on their own, and a lot of land that cost a fortune to bring into production is going to be left to die.

We didn't *have* to build main-stem dams on rivers carrying vast loads of silt; we could have built more primitive offstream reservoirs, which is what many private irrigation districts did—and successfully—but the federal engineers were enthralled by dams. We didn't *have* to mine a hundred thousand years' worth of groundwater in a scant half century, any more than we had to keep building 5,000-pound cars with 450-cubic-inch V8's. We didn't have to dump eight tons of dissolved salts on an acre of land in a year; we could have foresworn development on the most poorly drained lands or demanded that, in exchange for water, the farmers conserve as much as possible. But the Bureau still sells them water so cheaply they can't *afford* to conserve; to install an efficient irrigation system costs a lot more. The Israelis, who have far too little water to waste any of it, are stunned when they see the consumption of a typical western farm. And it is no coincidence that most of the water-saving innovations of the past years, such as drip irrigation, originated in Israel instead of here.

But the tragic and ludicrous aspect of the whole situation is that cheap water keeps the machine running: the water lobby cannot have enough of it, just as the engineers cannot build enough dams; and how convenient that cheap water encourages waste, which results in more dams. If federal water were realistically priced, the unholy alliance between the pseudo-conservative water lobby and those pseudo-socialist relics of the New Deal, the Bureau and the Corps, would soon collapse. Only a government that disposes of a billion dollars every few hours would still be selling water in deserts for less than a penny a ton. And only an agency as antediluvian as the Bureau of Reclamation, hiding in a government as elephantine as ours, could successfully camouflage the enormous losses the taxpayer has to bear for its generosity.

Recently, the magnitude of these losses has finally begun to come to light. In August of 1985, the Natural Resources Defense Council (NRDC) released a report on the Central Valley Project that it commissioned from a team of economists supported by a Ford Foundation grant. Through that report, a window was thrown open for the first time on the kinds of liberties the Bureau has been taking with public funds and the law in order to perpetuate the myth of abundance and keep up the demand for more dams.

According to the report, the Bureau not only has been giving its California clients—the nation's richest farmers—cheap water; it has been inventing a whole new realm of subsidies, which are quite possibly illegal, in order to keep the price from going up. For one thing, it adopted, years ago, a completely unwarranted interpretation of the principle of "ability to pay," which is one of the main instruments by which water prices are set. Originally, adjusting water rates according to the farmers' "ability to pay" meant that the price of water could vary from good years to bad ones, as long as the momentum of the fifty-year repayment schedules was maintained. But the Bureau undercharged its client farmers so regularly that the CVP repayment schedule had fallen drastically into arrears by 1985. By that year—some three decades after the project was essentially completed—the farmers had repaid a mere $50 million of the $931 million in capital costs that they are obligated to pay back. (Remember that the farmers are exempted from paying interest on this amount, a subsidy worth at least a couple of billion dollars in its own right.) What is worse, since 1982, payments for water and power have not been sufficient even to cover the operation and maintenance costs of the project, and the Bureau has been cannibalizing the capital-cost fund to keep it from running out of operating funds. This, of course, is robbing Peter to pay Paul, and according to the NRDC it is perfectly illegal. It would have been perfectly *legal* for the Bureau to raise its water rates—it may even have been required by law—but that was never done.

A multibillion-dollar interest exemption, a repayment schedule allowed to slip drastically toward default, an amazingly magnanimous interpretation of "ability to pay"—that would seem to be subsidy enough; but the Bureau wouldn't even stop there. A substantial chunk of the project's cost has been written off to fish and wildlife "benefits," even though the main impact on fish and wildlife has been a huge reduction in salmon and waterfowl populations. In addition, the NRDC report disclosed, the Bureau has for years been selling power to the farmers for considerably less than it pays to wheel it down from the dams in the Pacific Northwest.

The effect of everything, according to the economists, is that a few thousand farmers will, over the course of fifty years, receive a billion and a half dollars' worth of taxpayer generosity that was never supposed to be theirs. (The value of the interest exemption isn't included in this figure; that was their right.) And the result, according to the NRDC, is that "the repayment of [capital] costs of the CVP is likely to be *zero* by the time most of the water contracts expire in the 1990s." The farmers, who were entitled to incredibly cheap water, have ended up getting it nearly free.

Who are the beneficiaries of this vast unintended largess? The report found that the biggest subsidies, on a farm-by-farm basis, are going to the Westlands Water District, which is where the biggest farmers in the CVP service area happen to reside. (The Westlands, in fact, consumes about 25 percent of the water the project has for sale, enough to supply all of New York City.) By the economists' calculations, the true cost of delivering water to Westlands has now reached $97 per acre-foot; the farmers are being charged between $7.50 and

$11.80. Taking the average farm size in the district, this translates into a subsidy of around $500,000 per farm.

That sounds bad enough, but it is even worse than it sounds. Spread across the district, the subsidy to Westlands amounts to something like $217 per acre per year; the average annual *revenue* produced by an acre of Westlands land is only $290. This means that 70 percent of the profit on what is supposed to be some of the richest farmland in the world comes solely through taxpayer subsidization—not crop production. Not only that, but the main Westlands crop is cotton, which in the 1980s has become very much a surplus crop. So the same subsidies that are helping to enrich some of the wealthiest farmers in the nation are at the same time depressing crop prices elsewhere and undoubtedly driving unsubsidized cotton farmers in Texas and Louisiana and Mississippi out of business.

It was these same Westlands farmers, incidentally, who, with the help of their good friends Senator Alan Cranston and Representative Tony Coelho, led the successful effort to expand the acreage limitation from 160 to 960 acres in 1982. Even so, when their ten-year "grace" period expires in 1992, many will still be in violation of the law unless they sell off their excess lands; farms of 2,000 and 3,000 acres are commonplace; "farms" of 30,000 acres are not unknown; not a *single* 160-acre farm exists within its borders. (Why such a group of farmers should have received subsidized water in the first place is a good question.) After saying all this, it hardly seems worth mentioning that the Westlands Water District's irrigation return flows are the main source of the valley's high levels of selenium, which have been poisoning tens of thousands of waterfowl in valley wildlife refuges and, from the available evidence, all the way into San Francisco Bay.

There, in a nutshell, is how one of the nation's preeminent examples of reform legislation is stood completely on its head: illegal subsidies enrich big farmers, whose excess production depresses crop prices nationwide and whose waste of cheap water creates an environmental calamity that could cost billions to solve. And what was the response of the Bureau to the NRDC report? It quibbled about the actual size of the subsidies but, strikingly enough, didn't deny that they are occurring or even that they are illegal, and it didn't deny that the Central Valley Project is at least hundreds of millions, if not billions, of dollars in debt. Its response was a strange, calm, qualified agreement, as if to say, "Of course this is what has been going on. But it isn't really our fault."

In a sense, the Bureau is right. If blame is laid anywhere, it ought to be laid at Congress's door. Congress authorized the Central Valley Project; Congress approved the Westlands contract; Congress persistently refused to reform the Reclamation Act in any way except to enlarge the subsidies and to permit subsidized water to be sold to bigger farms; Congress, instead of offering incentives to conserve water, issued a multibillion-dollar license to waste it in the form of more and more dams. What cynic can blame it? To Congress, the federal water bureaucracy has been the closest thing to a schmoo, the little creature out of "Li'l Abner" that reproduced mightily and lived only to be eaten by us. The dams created jobs (how efficiently is another matter) and made the unions happy; they enriched the engineering and contracting firms, from giants like Bechtel and Parsons to small-time cement pourers in Sioux Falls, and made them happy; they subsidized the irrigation farmers and made them happy; they offered enough water to the cities to make them happy; they gave free flood protection to the real estate developers who ran the booming cities of the West out of their pockets and made them happy; and as a result of all this, the politicians were reelected, which made them happy. No one lost except the nation at large.

What federal water development has amounted to, in the end, is a uniquely productive, creative vandalism. Agricultural paradises were formed out of seas of sand and humps of rock. Sprawling cities sprouted out of nowhere, grew at mad rates, and ended up as Frank Lloyd Wright's sanitary slums; while they were being rescued from the tyranny of the desert they gave themselves over as slaves to the automobile. Millions of people and green acres took over a region that, from appearances, is unforgivingly hostile to life. It was a spectacular achievement, and its worst critics have to acknowledge its positive side. The economy was, no doubt, enriched. Population dispersion was achieved. Land that had been dry-farmed and overgrazed and horribly abused was stabilized and saved from the drought winds. "Wasting" resources—the rivers and aquifers—were put to productive use.

The cost of all this, however, was a vandalization of both our natural heritage and our economic future, and the reckoning has not even begun. Thus far, nature has paid the highest price. Glen Canyon is gone. The Colorado Delta is dead. The Missouri bottomlands have disappeared. Nine out of ten acres of wetlands in California have vanished, and with them millions of migratory birds. The great salmon runs in the Columbia, the Sacramento, the San Joaquin, and dozens

503

of tributaries are diminished or extinct. The prairie is civilized and is dull; its last wild features, the pothole marshes in the Dakotas, could all but disappear at the hands of the Garrison Diversion and Cendak projects, if they are ever built. And it didn't happen only in the West. Much the same thing happened in the East, especially in the South, where an incredible diversity and history and beauty in the old river valleys lies submerged under hundreds of featureless reservoirs. The vast oak and cypress swamps of the old South have been dried up, courtesy mainly of the Corps of Engineers, and converted to soybean fields (another crop of which we have an enormous glut). In fact, the Corps of Engineers is responsible for creating a lot more artificial farmland, wisely or unwisely, than the Bureau of Reclamation; by its own estimate, it has converted some 26 million acres of marshy or flood-threatened land, most of it in the East, into permanent crops. Depending on one's point of view, this achievement has been a monstrous travesty against nature, a boon to the local economies, or—the viewpoint most likely held by the Corps of Engineers—a fine opportunity to keep building more drainage projects and dams in order to protect what is only a precarious foothold against the forces of nature.

As we discover afresh each day, those forces can only be held at bay, never vanquished, and that is where the real vandalism—the financial vandalism of the future—comes in. Who is going to pay to rescue the salt-poisoned land? To dredge trillions of tons of silt out of the expiring reservoirs? To bring more water to whole regions, whole states, dependent on aquifers that have been recklessly mined? To restore wetlands and wild rivers and other natural features of the landscape that have been obliterated, now that more and more people are discovering that life is impoverished without them?

We won't have to. Our children probably won't have to. But somewhere down the line our descendants are going to inherit a bill for all this vaunted success, and between a $2 trillion national debt (a good bit of it incurred financing the dams) and the inevitability of expensive energy, it will be a miracle if they can pay it.

None of this is to say that we shouldn't have gone out and tried to civilize the arid West by building water projects and dams. It is merely to suggest that we overreached ourselves. What we achieved may be spectacular; in another sense, though, we achieved the obverse of our goals. The Bureau of Reclamation set out to help the small farmers of the West but ended up making a lot of rich farmers even wealthier at the small farmers' expense. Through water development, the federal government set out to rescue farmers from natural hardships—droughts and floods—but created a new kind of hardship in the form of a chronic, seemingly permanent condition of agricultural glut. We set out to tame the rivers and ended up killing them. We set out to make the future of the American West secure; what we really did was make ourselves rich and our descendants insecure. Few of them are apt to regret that we built Hoover Dam; on balance, however, they may find themselves wishing that we had left things pretty much as they were.

Suppose, though, that it were possible to solve at one stroke all the West's problems with water. Suppose you could import into the American West enough water to allow irrigation to continue, even to expand, for another three or four hundred years—to continue even after the great dams built during this century have largely silted up. Suppose you had enough surplus water to flush all the accumulated salts out to sea, thereby avoiding the hoary fate of almost every irrigated civilization. Suppose that, in the process of storing all this water behind great dams, you could create between 50,000 and 80,000 megawatts of surplus power—power that would be available for general consumption even after all of the irrigation water had been moved to where it was needed. (In 1978, the total installed electrical generating capacity of the United States was 515,000 megawatts, so if we take the higher figure we are talking about increasing the U.S. electrical output by nearly one-sixth.) This would be clean hydroelectric power—no pollution, no CO_2, no acid rain. The cost would be stupendous, but perhaps not much greater than the $300 billion the Pentagon managed to dispose of in 1984.

Physically, such a solution appears within the realm of possibility. In a $2- or $3-trillion economy, it may even be affordable, disregarding the question of whether it makes economic sense. In the West, many of the irrigation farmers who are threatened by one catastrophe or another regard it as a matter of life or death, and it has long been an obsession to no small number of engineers and hardhat politicians. Its main drawbacks are that it would largely destroy what is left of the natural West and it might require taking Canada by force.

Larger than California and Oregon and Washington stitched together, flooded by up to two hundred inches of rain annually, bisected by big rivers whose names few people know, British Columbia is to water what Russia is to land. Within its boundaries are, in whole or in part, the third-, the fourth-, the seventh-, the eighth-, and the nineteenth-largest rivers in North America. It is debatable how much of the world's accessible and renewable fresh water the province holds, but the usual estimates are between 4 and 10 percent. The Fraser River alone gathers nearly twice the runoff of California; the Skeena's flow approaches the runoff of Texas; both run to sea all but unused. The Talchako River, the main branch of the Bella Coola, which empties into the Pacific halfway between Vancouver and Prince Rupert, is fed by ice fields the size of eastern counties, and in the early summer the river runs like the Mistral, a riverine expressway in a Yosemite canyon that would make a dam-builder gasp. Among the larger rivers of British Columbia it barely rates a passing mention.

The relative proximity of so much water to so much arid land has been a source of compulsive longing in the American West for years. It wasn't until the late 1950s, however, that anyone began thinking seriously about moving some of that water south. It is undoubtedly the grandest scheme ever concocted by man, and it was conceived, rightfully enough, in an engineering office in Los Angeles.

NAWAPA—like the mouth of the Amazon River or Itaípu Dam, it is a thing one has to see to comprehend, and since it hasn't been built, even its architects may undervalue its brutal magnificence. Visualize, then, a series of towering dams in the deep river canyons of British Columbia—dams that are 800, 1,500, even 1,700 feet high. Visualize reservoirs backing up behind them for hundreds of miles— reservoirs among which Lake Mead would be merely regulation-size. Visualize the flow of the Susitna River, the Copper, the Tanana, and the upper Yukon running in reverse, pushed through the Saint Elias Mountains by million-horsepower pumps, then dumped into nature's second-largest natural reservoir, the Rocky Mountain Trench. Humbled only by the Great Rift Valley of Africa, the trench would serve as the continent's hydrologic switching yard, storing 400 million acre-feet of water in a reservoir 500 miles long. The upper Columbia and Fraser, which flow in opposite directions in the Rocky Mountain Trench, would disappear under it. Some of the water would travel east, down the Peace River—which would be remade and renamed the Canadian–Great Lakes Waterway—all the way to the Great Lakes and the Mississippi. It would be enough to raise the level of all five lakes, double the power production at Niagara Falls and down the St. Lawrence (New York, after all, has a large Congressional delegation), and allow some spillover into the Illinois River and the Mississippi, permitting ocean freighters to reach St. Louis and providing a fresher drinking supply for the cities now withdrawing carcinogenic wastes from the river. The rest of the water would go south.

Imagine the Sawtooth Lifts, a battery of airplane-hangar siphons shooting 30,000 cubic feet per second through tunnels in the Sawtooth Range of Idaho and on to California, Nevada, Arizona, and Mexico. Imagine Lake Nevada. Imagine the Columbia-Fraser Interchange, by which the West's two largest rivers would be merged; a Pecos River Reservoir the size of Connecticut (the feckless Pecos having received a huge jolt of water from the north); another giant reservoir in Arizona which, through some probably unintended irony, would be called Lake Geneva. Imagine 19 million acre-feet of new irrigation water for Saskatchewan and Alberta. Imagine 2.3 million acre-feet for Idaho, 11.7 million acre-feet for the Texas high plains, 4.6 million for Montana, 13.9 million for California (under the NAWAPA plan, water would, as usual, flow uphill toward political power and money). Imagine the Mojave Desert green. Imagine, on the other end of the continent, a phalanx of hydroelectric dams across the bigger rivers pouring into James Bay, the lower appendage of Hudson's Bay. Actually, those dams are the one part of the NAWAPA plan one needn't imagine. Over the past fifteen years, at a cost of $16 billion, Canada has gone ahead and built the James Bay Project itself.

NAWAPA—the North American Water and Power Alliance—was conceived in the early 1950s by Donald McCord Baker, a planning engineer for the Los Angeles Department of Water and Power. Baker took the idea to Ralph M. Parsons, the head of the Pasadena-based firm bearing his name, who instantly fell in love with it, as, he would later insist, "everyone who has worked on it has fallen in love with it." Before his death, Parsons created the NAWAPA Foundation, a tax-exempt receptacle for surplus profits from his company—which had fed on dams and aqueducts until it became the third- or fourth-largest engineering firm in the world—and dedicated it to enlightening the ignorant and converting the unappreciative about the project that was to become the obsession of his twilight years. In the 1960s, when anything big and brutish got at least a passing nod of attention, the

NAWAPA scheme excited a considerable spasm of interest. Stewart Udall was able to declare, as Interior Secretary, "I'm for this kind of thinking." Some exploratory discussions were apparently held between Canada and Secretary of State Dean Rusk. Groups of dignitaries began making excursions into Canada under the auspices of the NAWAPA Foundation and the Wenatchee, Washington, *Daily World*, whose publisher, Wilfred Woods, was as enchanted by NAWAPA as Parsons.

In the 1970s, however, as the environmental movement and Canadian nationalism waxed, NAWAPA's fortunes waned. Udall, having become a conservationist in office, began ridiculing the idea. Even the Bureau of Reclamation, which had been secretly assisting the NAWAPA lobby along with the Corps of Engineers, began to hold it at arm's length. (In April of 1965, Commissioner Floyd Dominy went so far as to deliver a mild reprimand to an overenthusiastic Bureau engineer who had spoken too loudly and fondly of NAWAPA. "While I agree that . . . potential interregional water transporation . . . is a subject in which the Bureau is intensely interested and with which, I hope, the future will find us closely identified," Dominy wrote his subordinate, whose name was Lewis Smith, "I do not believe the time is ripe for us . . . we should, however, be prepared to move quickly should we have the opportunity.") But the idea was kept alive by diehard believers: former Utah Democratic Senator Frank Moss (who in 1985 was still being kept on retainer by the Parsons company as a NAWAPA lobbyist), Hawaii Senator Hiram Fong, the late Governor Tom McCall of Oregon (proving that one could be a conservationist and a NAWAPA booster, too). "This is a plan that will not roll over and die," Moss lectured anyone who would listen. "It may be fifty years or it may be a hundred years, but something like it will be built."

By the late 1970s, Frank Moss was beginning to feel vindicated. People were gunning each other down in gas lines. California had just come through the worst drought in its history by a gnat's eyelash. Nuclear power seemed on the verge of collapse. The Islamic revolution was the latest threat to America's imported oil. Thousands of lakes and whole forests were dying from acid rain, a consequence of sulfur and nitrogen emissions from fossil-fuel power plants. Suddenly, the monster project that had been all but given up for dead began to twitch again. In October of 1980, at a California conference on "A High-Technology Policy for U.S. Reindustrialization" sponsored by the Fusion Energy Foundation—an offshoot of the U.S. Labor

Party, which despises the Soviet Union but envies its inveterate commitment to gargantuan public works—Dr. Nathan W. Snyder of the Parsons Company reintroduced NAWAPA to a large and enthusiastic audience. "Ultimately, the decision to build NAWAPA—or a project similar to it—will determine, in some part, the future economic well-being in North America," said Snyder. "Water is the most basic of all resources. Civilizations grew or withered depending on its availability."

The Canadians, for their part, have viewed all of this with a mixture of horror, amusement, and avarice. Few seem to believe that NAWAPA will ever be built, but anyone important who mentions it on either side of the border usually rates several column-inches in the Vancouver *Sun*. A number of times in the past several years, Canadian television crews have trooped into the United States to film the sputtering irrigation pumps in West Texas, the salt-encrusted lands in the San Joaquin Valley, and the ghostly abandoned orchards in central Arizona. In western Canada, at least, paranoia about NAWAPA seems to be the reigning state of mind. A few years ago, a British Columbia television journalist named Richard Bocking wrote a blistering book entitled *Canada's Water—For Sale?* which attacked not only NAWAPA but the huge and, as far as Bocking is concerned, pointless dams and reservoirs being built and planned by the provincial utility, B.C. Hydro—reservoirs that, as Bocking pointedly noted, could serve someday as off-the-shelf storage basins for a water-exportation scheme. The more conspiratorially minded in Canada's environmental community are convinced that an intimate confederacy exists among water developers—a kind of freemasonry of engineers—which makes them willing, even eager, to aid one another's grandiose ambitions at the expense of their own nation's interests. It happens to be true that in Canada most of those favorably disposed toward NAWAPA belong to the water-development fraternity. A Canadian professor of hydrologic engineering, Roy Tinney, has even proposed a somewhat less stupefying version of the plan, nicknamed CeNAWP, that would divert the Peace and Athabasca rivers and some of the water in Great Slave Lake to southern Alberta and the American high plains. Every now and then a British Columbia politician has dropped a coy hint that his province (which is, politically speaking, far more independent of Ottawa than an American state is of Washington) might be open to some mutually profitable continental water scheme—someday. Moira Farrow, a reporter for the Vancouver *Sun* who has covered water policy for years, says that some of the province's leading political figures are privately awed by the NAWAPA plan—as if they wished they had thought of it themselves.

There is, in fact, a great deal in the plan for Canada, as there is for Mexico, which has a surplus of oil but a chronic, and grim, and worsening shortage of food. Canada would get more hydroelectric power than the United States—some 38 million kilowatts under one version of the plan; Mexico would get 20 million acre-feet of water, enough to triple its irrigated acreage. Canada would also get a great deal of irrigation water, and, if the contemplated navigation canals are built, a shipping route between its mineral-rich northland and the Mississippi and Great Lakes.

It is Canada, however, that would have to suffer the worst of the environmental consequences, and they would be phenomenal. Luna Leopold, a professor of hydrology at the University of California at Berkeley, says of NAWAPA, "The environmental damage that would be caused by that damned thing can't even be described. It could cause as much harm as all of the dam-building we have done in a hundred years."

Every significant river between Anchorage and Vancouver would be dammed for power or water, or both—the Tanana, the Yukon, the Copper, the Taku, the Skeena, the Stikine, the Liard, the Bella Coola, the Dean, the Chilcotin, and the Fraser. All of these have prolific salmon fisheries, which would be largely, if not wholly, destroyed. (Since the extirpation of around 90 percent of the Columbia's salmon runs, the Fraser, the Stikine, and the Skeena have become the most important salmon rivers on earth.) In the western United States, the plan would drown or dry up just about any section of wild river still left: the Flathead, the Big Hole, the Selway, the Salmon, the Middle Fork of the Salmon, the Yellowstone, the Madison, the Lochsa, and the Clearwater would largely disappear. In Canada and the U.S. alike, not just rivers but an astounding amount of wilderness and wildlife habitat would be put under water, tens of millions of acres of it. Surface aqueducts and siphons—not to say hundred-mile reservoirs—would cut off migratory routes. Hundreds of thousands of people would have to be relocated; Prince George, B.C., population 150,000, would vanish from the face of the earth. In general, though, the project's proponents display a peculiar blindness to the horrifying dislocation and natural destruction it would cause. They are far more comfortable talking about how NAWAPA is our only hope of averting worldwide famine.

Because of its unprecedented destructiveness, and due to a natural reluctance on the part of Canadians to let go of so much water
for the sake of their paternalistic and overambitious neighbors, the
tours organized by the Wenatchee *Daily World* in the 1960s encountered pickets at every airstrip in the bush carrying signs that read
WATER THIEVES BEWARE. By 1981, anti-NAWAPA sentiment in British
Columbia had, if anything, intensified. Everyone seemed to have heard
of it, and nearly everyone was against it—"nearly," because here and
there one finds someone who is for it, at least for some smaller version
of it. Declining emphatically to be identified, a fairly well known
professor at a major university said, "The thing is too big and destructive as is, but a smaller version is worth considering. Compared
to the damage the loggers are inflicting on the coast, a few big new
reservoirs and canals might appear harmless. The water is worth a
lot of money to us, potentially. We wouldn't have to go out and fell
whole forests for income. Besides that, I think Canadians are being
very narrow-minded about the whole thing. We depend on you for
food, and why *shouldn't* we help our neighbor when she is running
out of water if we have far more than we can ever use?"

The logging of which the professor spoke is by far the largest
source of income in the province of British Columbia, and is being
conducted with a careless abandon that might make even the U.S.
Forest Service wince. Logging is also a cyclical industry, expanding
and contracting in rhythm with such imponderable forces as U.S.
deficits and housing starts. Agriculture is more stable, and water
could be sold through forty-year contracts like those of the Bureau
of Reclamation, ensuring a steady, predictable income every year.

Derreck Sewall, who teaches at the University of Victoria and is
widely acknowledged as the foremost authority on water in Canada,
says that Canada has its own water shortages looming, particularly
in the Okanagan region of southern British Columbia—western Canada's fruitbasket—and on irrigated parts of the Alberta plains, where
the farmers are overdrafting groundwater as determinedly as their
American counterparts. For the foreseeable future, he sees no possibility of NAWAPA's being built unless Canada itself broaches the idea.
"There's a xenophobic, *dirigiste* mood in this country today," Sewall
says. "Canadians feel like a colony of the U.S., which is in a certain
sense justified. You own 95 percent of our oil industry, for example.
So the mood is against exporting our most vital natural resource. But
eventually Canada will approach the United States and say, 'You
want some of our water? O.K. Here's the price to be paid. We'll deal

with you in realistic terms. Water will be part of an overall program of resource development and protection. You want our water, then don't build the Garrison Diversion Project, or keep the return flows out of Lake Winnipeg. We'll give you a certain amount of water for each certain percent reduction in acid rain.' Canadians will eventually come to realize that, as far as the U.S. is concerned, water has a value far beyond that which prevails today. You could almost say that we've got you over a tub."

So what, all things considered, are the odds that NAWAPA will be built?

"We're going to solve the water problem through conservation," says one venerable U.S. hydrologic engineer. "We're not going to build any NAWAPA projects, even if the Canadians invite us in. The Bureau of Reclamation is going to have to start charging realistic rates for water and the farmers are going to live with them by saving a lot of water. We're going to solve the energy problem with coal. I don't know what we're going to do about salinity—put it off into the future, probably. I don't know if we're even going to build any more big water projects in this country. The economics went sour forty years ago. A lot of irrigated land will go out of production and we'll just watch it go out."

"NAWAPA is the kind of thing you think about when you're smoking pot," says another. "People who say it will be built are crazy. Ralph Parsons himself told me he wasn't really serious about it. He just needed the foundation as a tax dodge."

"We won't build the big NAWAPA," says a third. "But I'd bet we'll build a baby NAWAPA. No one knows how much money water will be worth in the future, but it's going to be worth a lot. When we see we're about to lose millions of acres of the most productive farmland in the country and thousands of towns are going to go bust, it will just be a tremendous shock. If we stop talking about water importation for a while, the Canadians will bring it up themselves."

Recently the Soviet Union decided, after many years of planning, to shelve a scheme that would divert the Ob River, three-quarters the size of the Mississippi, from its northerly course into the Arctic Sea and send it fifteen hundred miles or so deep into the steppes of central Asia. A second diversion, which would shunt the Sukhona River into the Volga, has not yet been shelved, but remains in doubt. Together, the two projects are about as ambitious as a NAWAPA scheme built to two-fifths scale. As a result of the decision, the Aral Sea will continue to decline indefinitely at its current rate of eleven and a half feet per year, due to irrigation withdrawals. "Central Asia will simply have to get along with more rational use of its own resources," said a group of Soviet water planners in an official statement. Then they added, "At least until the 21st century."

On April 21, 1981, the premier of British Columbia, Bill Bennett, on a tour of California, gave a speech at San Francisco's Commonwealth Club. Castigating those who wanted to stop building dams, Bennett told his audience that a way must be found to harness and preserve the fresh water pouring out of British Columbia to the ocean. "Dams are more than hydro," he explained. "They preserve our greatest resource and control wild runoff." A questioner then asked whether, since British Columbia at the moment had no plans to use the water Bennett wanted to "conserve" for anything other than hydroelectric power, his call for more dams meant that his government was considering the exportation of water to the United States. The answer was no, Bennett said firmly. Then he added, "But come and see me in twenty years."

Shortly after Bennett's speech, Canada was smacked particularly hard by the worldwide recession that followed in the wake of the Reagan economic policy. In British Columbia, the timber industry went moribund, and plans for several huge hydroelectric dams on the Peace, Liard, and Stikine rivers were indefinitely shelved. The provincial utility, B.C. Hydro, cut its staff force from 11,000 to 6,000, and unemployment went into double digits throughout the country. As a severely chastened Canada began crawling, slowly and unsteadily, out of the deepest economic morass it had seen since the Depression, one could detect a strikingly different attitude on the part of some of its prominent politicians toward a NAWAPA-style water-diversion scheme. Early in 1985, the leader of Quebec's Liberal Party, Robert Bourassa, began to push an eastern Canadian version of NAWAPA, the GRAND Canal (for Great Replenishment and Northern Development Canal Concept), which would turn James Bay into a freshwater lake by constructing a tremendous dike across its northern side. The big rivers feeding the bay would pool below the dike, forming a freshwater reservoir nearly the size of Lake Ontario. The water would then be led by aqueduct into the Great Lakes, and from there, according to engineers from the Bechtel Corporation—which was spending a million dollars to study the plan—to the American high plains. The estimated cost would be $100 billion.

"I don't think the people of the province would stand for it," said Frank Miller, the premier of neighboring Ontario.

"On the whole I find more interest in the idea than opposition," said Robert Bourassa.

"I view the prospect with enthusiasm," said Brian Mulroney, Canada's new Prime Minister.

There was, for the time being, no word from the Reagan administration on what it thought of the plan.

ACKNOWLEDGMENTS

It would have been absolutely impossible for me to write this book without the love, support, and indulgence of my wife, Dorothy Lawrence Mott.

Second only to hers was the faith and support of my agent and dear friend F. Joseph Spieler, who talked me out of quitting several times, and not for selfish reasons; and of my parents, Konrad and Else Reisner, who rescued me from insolvency more than once.

I must also acknowledge and thank my brother-in-law, Roald Bostrom, who convinced me that I should try to write for a living in the first place.

This book managed to consume three editors in the process of being written. Alan Williams liked the idea, bought the book, and provided much encouragement at the beginning. William Strachan offered moral support and advice along the way. I am most grateful, however, to Dan Frank, who replaced Bill Strachan when the book was nearly completed but treated it as if he had been with it from the beginning. His aesthetic sensibility, resonant judgment, and clear thinking rescued many parts of the book that had managed to beach themselves on the shoals of muddleheadedness, and he wouldn't have tolerated a hackneyed metaphor like that if I'd showed it to him first.

I owe a tremendous debt to the Alicia Patterson Foundation, which got me going; to E. Philip LeVeen and Robert Wolcott of Public Interest Economics, who helped keep me going; to Robert Rodale and the Rodale Foundation, who helped keep me going a while longer; and to the now-defunct American Edition of *Geo* magazine, whose generous expense policy helped fund a good bit of the research.

I can't imagine how the book could have been written had it not been for a handful of people who were extraordinarily generous with their time, candid in their observations, and forthcoming with memoranda, anecdotes, documents, and private letters. I would especially like to thank C. J. Kuiper for many hours of his time and a superb memory and storytelling flair. I am much in debt to Floyd Dominy, another great storyteller, who believes in open files and is as fearless of consequences as his reputation suggests. H. P. Dugan, Daniel Dreyfus, and Jim Casey, all former high officials of the Bureau of Reclamation, were also exceptionally candid and helpful.

Peter Carlson of the Environmental Policy Institute is as knowledgeable as anyone alive on the subject of water projects, and answered countless questions over the telephone. John Leshy of the Arizona State University Law School and Tom Graff of the Environmental Defense Fund were also especially helpful, not only in answering questions but in reviewing portions of the manuscript. A lot of thanks are also owed to James Flannery, Jim Free, Guy Martin, Robert Edgar, Alan Merson, Patrick Porgans, Robert Smythe, David Shuster, Jim Cook, and Jan van Schilfgaarde.

Among the hundreds of others I interviewed, I want to single out a few dozen for special thanks. They are Philip Bowles, Helen Ingram, Frank Welsh, Robert Witzeman, Don and Karen Christenson, Richard Wilson, James Watt, Tom Barlow, John Gottschalk, Gilbert White, Bill Martin, Sam Steiger, Stewart Udall, David Brower, Dorothy Green, Phil Nalder, Steven Reynolds, Herbert Grubb, Arleigh West, former Governor Edmund G. Brown, Sr., John Erlichman, Nathaniel Reed, Pete van Gytenbeek, Derrick Sewell, Wayne Wyatt, William Gookin, Mohammed El-Ashry, Richard Madson, the late Horace Albright, Jack Burby, Willoughby Houk, George Baker, Jeffrey Ingram, Ronald Robie, Oliver Houck, Lynn Ludlow, Joe Moore, Barney Bellport, Kendall Manock, John Lawrence, George Ballis, Michael Catino, Keith Higginson, Peter Skinner, Edwin Weinberg, Ben Yellen, Samuel Hayes, Myron Holburt, Don Maughan, Moira Farrow, Bob Weaver, Sandy White, Felix Sparks, Russell Brown, Terry Thoem, Glenn Saunders, Robert Curry, Gus Norwood, Mason Gaffney, John Bryson, Bill Dubois, Mark Dubois, Alex Pesonen, the late Paul Taylor, Gilbert Stamm, Daniel Beard, Irving Fox, Lorelle Long, Stanford P. McCasland, John Newsom, Mary Ellen Morbeck, Brant Calkin, Carolina Butler and W. R. Collier.

The American Heritage Center at the University of Wyoming is a hospitable, if not luxurious, place to work and contains a monstrous trove of archives relating to the settlement of the West and water development; I would like to extend special thanks to Gene Gressley and his staff. The Lyndon Baines Johnson Library at the University of Texas, Austin, the Bancroft Library at the University of California, Berkeley, the main library at the University of California, Los Angeles, and the Interior Department Library in Washington, D.C., were also most helpful in providing source material.

For many favors and services rendered I am grateful to Tom Turner, the staff of *Not Man Apart*, and the now-defunct San Francisco office of Friends of the Earth. Thanks also to Donna Wilcox and the Washington office of the Natural Resources Defense Council; to John Adams for many favors; to Elyse Axell and Janice Cornwell for indenturing themselves as underpaid and underemployed typists; to Gail Liss for the index; to Joe Kane; and to Il Fornaio, Edible Delights, and the Howard Johnson's in Mill Valley for providing thousands of coffee refills and a pleasant place to go to write.

NOTES AND BIBLIOGRAPHY

CHAPTER ONE: **A Country of Illusion**

Wallace Stegner's *Beyond the Hundredth Meridian*, the preeminent source for this chapter, remains one of the finest biographies in print. It covers not only the life of John Wesley Powell but the lives of those in his circle— some of the most interesting Americans of the nineteenth century; how such things as laws and climatic aberrations influenced the settlement of the West in the nineteenth century; and the ideas that formed much of our present policy regarding natural resources. There are several Powell biographies, but Stegner's is the best.

Hamlin Garland's *A Son of the Middle Border* is as good a portrayal of life on the plains and the imperative that drove people there as has been written. See also O. E. Rolvaag's *Giants in the Earth* and Fred Shannon's *The Farmer's Last Frontier*.

Bernard De Voto, along with Stegner, is probably the finest of the modern western historians. *The Course of Empire* and *Across the Wide Missouri* were both a great help.

Walter Prescott Webb's *The Great Plains* is scholarly, prickly, readable, and as clean a dissection of the huge body of myth that has been built up around this region as anyone ever wrote. Fascinating visual imagery of the virgin West is contained in *Artists and Illustrators of the Old West*, edited by Robert Taft.

An interesting biography—really a hagiography, which makes it all the more interesting—of Henry Miller, the most acquisitive land baron in California history, is Edward Treadwell's *The Cattle King*. Though he is remembered mainly for his 1,090,000 acres, much of it acquired through a dubious legality, Miller's real contribution to history is *Lux* v. *Haggin,* a legal case which, to a considerable degree, formed the doctrine of western water law. The lawsuit pitted Miller and his lifelong partner, Charles Lux, against Lloyd Tevis and James Ben Ali Haggin, two rival land barons with a fiefdom of their own near the Kern River, who were prevented from irrigating when Miller tried to invoke his riparian water rights. Haggin and Tevis argued, unsuccessfully, that riparian doctrine would doom most of California's best land to dryland ranching, and that landowners with river frontage should not be allowed to hog all the water. Public reaction against Miller and Lux's victory was so strong that most western states who hadn't already opted strongly for the "appropriative"-rights doctrine, soon did. (This doctrine awarded water rights to anyone who used them first, even if his acreage did not border water.) California, for its part, has modified its legal code to allow a complex coexistence of riparian- and appropriative-rights doctrine.

The Education of Henry Adams, one of the most peculiar books ever written by an American, is interesting, in the context of this chapter, for its depiction of the mood of empire that swept the nation in the late nineteenth century.

Powell's journal—actually an embellished and edited version published for public consumption—is a very lively account of his Colorado River adventure and is worth reading, as is his original *Report on the Arid Lands.* Few, if any, bureaucrats since Powell have written as well.

A. B. Guthrie's *The Big Sky,* though a work of fiction, is the most compelling and realistic portrait of the mountain men I have seen. It is one of the few great American novels. Harrison Clifford Dale's account of the Ashley-Smith expeditions is a fairly rich account of some astonishing exploratory feats.

BOOKS

Adams, Henry. *The Education of Henry Adams.* Boston: Houghton Mifflin, 1918.

Athearn, Robert G. *High Country Empire.* Lincoln: University of Nebraska Press, 1971.

Boulton, Herbert Eugene. *Coronado: Knight of Pueblos and Plains.* New York: Whittlesey House, 1949.

Dale, Harrison Clifford. *The Ashley-Smith Expeditions and the Discovery of a Central Route to the Pacific, 1822–1829.* Glendale, Calif.: Arthur H. Clark, 1941.

De Voto, Bernard. *Across the Wide Missouri*. Boston: Houghton Mifflin, 1947.

———. *The Course of Empire*. Boston: Houghton Mifflin, 1952.

Dodge, Richard. *The Plains of the Great West*. New York: Archer House, 1959.

Dunne, John Gregory. "Eureka! A Celebration of California." In Jonathan Eisen and David Fine, eds., *Unknown California*. New York: Macmillan, 1985.

Garland, Hamlin. *A Son of the Middle Border*. New York: Macmillan, 1917.

Guthrie, A. B. *The Big Sky*. New York: Sloane, 1947.

Hafen, Leroy. *Mountain Men and the Fur Trade*. Glendale, Calif.: Arthur H. Clark, 1969.

Hoffman, Wilbur. *Sagas of Western Travel and Transport*. San Diego: Howell North Books, 1980.

Hollon, W. Eugene. *The Great American Desert, Then and Now*. New York: Oxford University Press, 1966.

Ise, John. *Sod and Stubble*. Lincoln: University of Nebraska Press, 1936.

Lewis, Meriwether, and William Clark. *The Journals of Lewis and Clark*. Edited by Bernard De Voto. Boston: Houghton Mifflin, 1953.

———. *The Journals of the Lewis and Clark Expedition*. New York: Dodd, Mead, 1906.

Lilley, William, and Lewis Gould. "The Western Irrigation Movement 1878–1902: A Reappraisal." In Gene Gressley, ed., *The American West: A Reorientation*. Laramie: University of Wyoming Publications, 1966.

Robinson, Michael. *Water for the West*. Chicago: Public Works Historical Society, 1979.

Rolvaag, O. E. *Giants in the Earth*.

Roosevelt, Theodore. *The Winning of the West*. Reprint. Fawcett House, 1963.

Shannon, Fred A. *The Farmer's Last Frontier*. New York: Farrar and Rinehart, 1945.

Smith, Henry Nash. *Virgin Land*. Cambridge, Mass.: Harvard University Press, 1950, 1970.

Stegner, Wallace. *Beyond the Hundredth Meridian*. Boston: Houghton Mifflin, 1953.

Taft, Robert. *Artists and Illustrators of the Old West*. New York: Scribner's, 1953.

Treadwell, Edward. *The Cattle King*. Fresno, Calif.: Valley Publishers, 1931.

Webb, Walter Prescott. *The Great Plains*. New York: Ginn, 1931.

Winship, George Parker. "The Coronado Expedition, 1540–1542." Washington, D.C.: U.S. Bureau of American Ethnology, Fourteenth Annual Report, 1892–93.

Winther, Oscar Osburn. *The Transportation Frontier: Trans-Mississippi West, 1865–1890*. New York: Holt, Rinehart and Winston, 1964.

CHAPTER TWO: **The Red Queen**

The story of how Los Angeles went to the Owens Valley for water has been told now and then, though not too accurately. The movie *Chinatown*, which came out in the mid-1970s, is a great film that may be responsible for misinforming a lot of people who consider it completely factual. (Oddly, Mulwray, the character whose name is a play on "Mulholland," comes across as a hero in the movie—and is murdered for his honesty—so the film may actually have polished Mulholland's reputation, which it probably did not intend to do.)

The most thorough and believable account, by far, of the whole Owens Valley–Los Angeles episode is William Kahrl's *Water and Power*, which was not published until 1982. Kahrl's prodigious research shows in the text. Remi Nadeau's *The Water Seekers* is considerably less exhaustive than Kahrl's book and is biased fairly heavily, in the end, in favor of Los Angeles. Nonetheless, it does contain some good anecdotal material, which I used in the chapter.

For a critical appraisal of Harrison Gray Otis, Harry Chandler, and the Los Angeles *Times* (the old *Times*, not the unrecognizably superior newspaper published by the third-generation Chandler, Otis), William Bonelli's *Billion Dollar Blackjack* is recommended. David Halberstam's *The Powers That Be* is also very good, though it deals more with the post-Otis newspaper. Anyone really interested in the mentality of the Los Angeles power structure at the turn of the century should peruse some old issues of the paper on microfilm; though more temperamental than most of his peers, Otis was no aberration.

Robert Matson's *William Mulholland: A Forgotten Forefather* provides some interesting personal detail about a very complicated man. Originally written as a thesis, the monograph is not easy to find in libraries.

Carey McWilliams's *California: The Great Exception* has to be considered required reading for anyone seriously interested in how California came to be the state and culture that it is. In fiction, James M. Cain may have captured southern California best, especially in *Mildred Pierce*; his essay "Paradise" is singular.

Important interviews for this chapter: Horace Albright, Jack Burby, Dorothy Green, David Kennedy, William Warne, Samuel P. Hays, and William Kahrl.

BOOKS

Bain, Joe S., et al. *Northern California's Water Industry.* Baltimore: Johns Hopkins University Press, 1966.

Beck, Warren A., and David A. Williams. *California: A History of the Golden State.* Garden City, N.Y.: Doubleday, 1972.

Bonelli, William G. *Billion Dollar Blackjack.* Beverly Hills, Calif.: Civic Research Press, 1954.

Carr, Harry. *Los Angeles: City of Dreams.* New York: Appleton-Century, 1935.

Chalfant, Willie Arthur. *The Story of Inyo.* Privately printed. Chicago, 1922.

Cooper, Erwin. *Aqueduct Empire.* Glendale, Calif.: Arthur H. Clark, 1968.

Dunne, John Gregory. "A Celebration of California." In Jonathan Eisen and David Fine, eds., *Unknown California.* New York: Macmillan, 1985.

Fogelson, Robert M. *The Fragmented Metropolis: Los Angeles 1850–1930.* Cambridge, Mass: Harvard University Press, 1967.

Gottlieb, Robert, and Irene Wolt. *Thinking Big: The Story of the Los Angeles Times, Its Publishers, and Their Influence on Southern California.* New York: Putnam, 1977.

Halberstam, David. *The Powers That Be.* New York: Knopf, 1979.

Hays, Samuel P. *Conversation and the Gospel of Efficiency.* New York: Atheneum, 1975.

Jorgenson, Lawrence C. *The San Fernando Valley, Past and Present.* Los Angeles: Pacific Rim Research, 1982.

Kahrl, William. *Water and Power.* Berkeley: University of California Press, 1982.

Kahrl, William, ed. *The California Water Atlas.* Sacramento: Department of Water Resources, 1979.

Keffer, Frank. *History of the San Fernando Valley.* Glendale, Calif.: Stillman, 1982.

Longstreet, Stephen. *All Star Cast: An Anecdotal History of Los Angeles.* New York: Thomas Y. Crowell, 1977.

McWilliams, Carey. *California: The Great Exception.* Santa Barbara: Peregrine Smith, 1949, 1976.

Matson, Robert W. *William Mulholland: A Forgotten Forefather.* Stockton,

Calif.: University of the Pacific, Pacific Center for Western Studies, 1976.

Nadeau, Remy. *The Water Seekers*. Santa Barbara: Peregrine Smith, 1974.

Outland, Charles F. *Man-made Disaster: The Story of Saint Francis Dam*. Glendale, Calif.: Arthur H. Clark, 1963, 1977.

Watkins, T. H. *California: An Illustrated History*. Palo Alto: American West Publishing, 1973.

ARTICLES

Amaral, Anthony. "A Struggle in the Owens Valley." *American Forests*, August 1964.

Hayden, Frederick. "Los Angeles Aqueduct." *Building and Engineering News*, August 15, 1915.

Hoffman, Abraham. "Joseph B. Lippincott and the Owens Valley Controversy: Time for Revision." *Southern California Quarterly*, Fall 1972.

———. "Origins of a Controversy: The United States Reclamation Service and the Owens Valley–Los Angeles Water Dispute." *Arizona and the West*, Winter 1977.

Lippincott, Joseph B. "William Mulholland: Engineer, Pioneer, Raconteur." *Civil Engineering*, February/March 1941.

Los Angeles Times, 1898–1928. (Author's note: So many issues of the newspaper were reviewed for this chapter that it seems pointless to list them all here. Most of the citations in the chapter are dated. The newspaper is well indexed for anyone who wishes to review its coverage of the water issue during the period.)

"Mulholland Retires after 50-Year Service at Los Angeles." *Engineering News-Record*, November 22, 1928.

Wood, R. Coke. "Owens Valley as I Knew It." *Pacific Historian*, Summer 1972.

Yonay, Ehud. "How Green Was My Valley." *New West*, March 28, 1977.

CHAPTER THREE: **First Causes**

The chronicle of the political events leading to the passage of the Reclamation Act is based largely on William Lilley and Lewis Gould's "The Western Irrigation Movement 1878–1902: A Reappraisal," in Gene Gressley, ed., *The American West: A Reorientation*. The essay is revisionist history at its best—provocative yet sturdy—and few people seem to know of it. The chronicle of natural events that helped lead to passage of the

Act is taken largely from Wallace Stegner's *Beyond the Hundredth Meridian*.

Samuel Hays's *Conservation and the Gospel of Efficiency* is a very good account of the early conservation movement and its utilitarian tenets.

Michael Robinson's *Water for the West* contains some good material on the failures of private irrigation ventures and contrasts vividly with William Smythe's supremely glorified view in *The Conquest of Arid America* (which was written much earlier). Eugene Hollon's *The Great American Desert, Then and Now* provided outstanding general background for this chapter, as did National Land for People's "Reclamation History" (three-part series).

BOOKS

Delano, Alonzo. *Life on the Plains and Among the Diggings.* Ann Arbor, Mich.: University Microfilms, 1966.

Gaffney, Mason. *Diseconomies Inherent in Western Water Laws.* Riverside, Calif.: January 1961 (unpublished monograph).

Hawgood, John A. *America's Western Frontiers.* New York: Knopf, 1967.

Hays, Samuel P. *Conservation and the Gospel of Efficiency.* New York: Atheneum, 1975.

Hollon, W. Eugene. *The Great American Desert, Then and Now.* New York: Oxford University Press, 1966.

Ise, John. *Sod and Stubble.* Lincoln: University of Nebraska Press, 1936.

Lilley, William, and Lewis L. Gould. "The Western Irrigation Movement 1878–1902: A Reappraisal." In Gene M. Gressley, ed., *The American West: A Reorientation.* Laramie: University of Wyoming Publications, 1966.

Robinson, Michael. *Water for the West.* Chicago: Public Works Historical Society, 1979.

Smythe, William E. *The Conquest of Arid America.* New York: Macmillan, 1905.

Warne, William. *The Bureau of Reclamation.* New York: Praeger, 1973.

CHAPTERS FOUR AND EIGHT: **An American Nile (I) and (II)**

These chapters (and the subsequent ones in the book) are drawn mostly from interviews, hitherto unseen files from the Bureau of Reclamation, and articles and reports. Anyone wishing to consult a single source for more background on the Colorado River and the conflicts over its use should read Philip Fradkin's *A River No More.*

Empires in the Sun, by Robert Gottlieb and Peter Wiley, contains an interesting account of how Kaiser, Bechtel, Morrison-Knudsen, and other firms that built Hoover Dam became instant giants through its construction. A detailed account of the actual construction work is in the Bureau of Reclamation's "Hoover Dam".

Helen Ingram's book, *Patterns of Politics in Water Resource Development,* is the best account I have seen of the political jockeying and compromising that led to passage of the Colorado River Basin Project Act. Dean Mann's *The Politics of Water in Arizona* is also helpful.

The Congressional debates over the Colorado River Storage Project (the 1956 act), especially those involving the late Senator Paul Douglas, one of the brainiest, wittiest, and most eloquent Senators we have ever had, are well worth reading. Economists were some of the earliest critics of water projects, but Douglas was even ahead of most economists.

Anyone who wishes to see how desperately Arizona wanted the Central Arizona Project built should review articles and editorials in the *Arizona Republic* and other state newspapers, particularly from the mid-1960s (prior to passage of the CAP legislation) and the late 1970s (the dread Carter years). Frank Welsh's *How to Create a Water Crisis* is a slightly dry but devastating dissection of the CAP and Arizona's perceived shortage of water, written by a former engineer with the Corps of Engineers and past president of the Phoenix chapter of the American Society of Civil Engineers.

David Brower's interviews for the Bancroft Library's Oral History Program (University of California, Berkeley) contain a lot of interesting anecdotal material about the battles over Echo Park, Glen Canyon, Marble Gorge, and Bridge Canyon dams. The Dominy archives at the University of Wyoming reveal what a pest Brower was to the water developers and make for an interesting dig.

In the 1980s it is striking to read the matter-of-fact tone with which the Pacific Southwest Water Plan and United Western Investigation propose monumental engineering works with staggering environmental consequences, and for what reasons. Both are in the author's files; they have become extremely difficult to find, though the Interior Department Library in Washington, D.C., ought to have them.

George Sibley's "The Desert Empire" is the best magazine article on the Southwest since Bernard De Voto's earlier essays in *Harper's.*

Important interviews for this chapter: Helen Ingram, John Leshy, Wesley Steiner, Daniel Dreyfus, David Brower, Jeffrey Ingram, Robert Young, William Martin, C. J. Kuiper, Stanford P. McCasland, William Warne, Myron Holburt, William Gookin, Daniel Beard, Nancy Laney, Robert Witzeman, Frank Welsh, Sam Steiger, Floyd Dominy, Tom Graff, Steven Reynolds, Patrick Dugan, Donald Maughan, Stewart Udall, Wayne Aspinall, Arleigh West.

BOOKS

Brower, David. *David R. Brower—Environmental Activist, Publicist, and Prophet*. Berkeley: Bancroft Library Oral History Program, University of California, 1980.

Fradkin, Philip L. *A River No More*. New York: Knopf, 1981.

Gottlieb, Robert, and Peter Wiley. *Empires in the Sun*. New York: Putnam, 1982.

Hollon, W. Eugene. *The Great American Desert, Then and Now*. Lincoln: University of Nebraska Press, 1985.

Holmes, Beatrice Hort. *History of Federal Water Resources Programs and Policies, 1961–70*. Washington, D.C.: U.S. Department of Agriculture Publication 1379, 1979.

Howe, Charles W., and K. W. Easter. *Interbasin Transfers of Water*. Baltimore: Johns Hopkins University Press, 1971.

Ingram, Helen M. *Patterns of Politics in Water Resource Development*. Tucson: University of New Mexico Press, 1969.

Mann, Dean. *The Politics of Water in Arizona*. Tucson: University of Arizona Press, 1963.

Ten Rivers in America's Future. Washington, D.C.: The President's Water Resources Policy Commission, 1950.

Trimble, M. *Arizona: A Panoramic History of a Frontier State*. Garden City, N.Y.: Doubleday, 1977.

U.S. Bureau of Reclamation. *Critical Water Problems Facing the Eleven Western States*. Washington, D.C.: U.S. Department of the Interior, 1975.

U.S. Water Resources Council. *The Nation's Water Resources*. Washington, D.C., 1968.

Welsh, Frank. *How to Create a Water Crisis*. Boulder, Colo.: Johnson, 1985.

ARTICLES

"Agency Mismanagement Responsible for Colorado River Flooding." Friends of the Earth, June 18, 1983.

Notes and Bibliography

"Alarm Over Deep 'Cracks' in Arizona." *San Francisco Chronicle*, July 4, 1982.

"All You Ever Wanted to Know About the CAP." Citizens Concerned About the Project (undated).

"Alternative to Orme Could Save Millions." *Phoenix Gazette*, June 2, 1979.

Animas–La Plata Project (feasibility data). U.S. Bureau of Reclamation, 1961.

"Arizonans Pushed Sierra Club Probe." *Phoenix Gazette*, July 1, 1966.

"Aspinall Raps Opposition to Project" and "Solon Blasts Detractors." *Albuquerque Journal*, November 11, 1966.

"Babbitt Appoints Water 'Czar.' " *Arizona Republic*, September 16, 1980.

"Battle Against Central Arizona Project Grows." *Rocky Mountain News*, March 30, 1966.

Boslough, John. "Rationing a River," *Science 81*, June 1981.

Bradley, Richard C. "Attack on Grand Canyon." *The Living Wilderness*, Winter 1964–65.

Brooks, Donald. "Testimony of Donald Brooks, Director of Planning, Metropolitan Water District of Southern California" (undated).

Brown, Howard. Memorandum to Senator Paul Fannin, "Wellton-Mohawk," May 5, 1975.

———. "The Central Arizona Project." Congressional Research Service, April 20, 1976.

"Build Orme Dam!" *Arizona Republic*, February 28, 1980.

"CAP Allocation Plan Criticized from All Sides." *Scottsdale Daily Progress*, October 28, 1980.

"Captured Flood Water Seen Aiding City Supply." *Phoenix Gazette*, December 16, 1978.

Casserly, J. J. "Andrus Is Maneuvering to Cement His Anti-West Water Policy." *Arizona Republic* (undated).

Central Arizona Project, Environmental Statement (Final). U.S. Bureau of Reclamation, Washington, D.C. (undated).

"Colorado River, Vital to Southwest, Travels Ever Rockier Course." *Wall Street Journal* (undated).

Congressional Record, April 18, 1955. Senate debate on Colorado River Storage Project Act.

Dallas Creek Project (feasibility data). U.S. Bureau of Reclamation (undated).

Dallas Creek Project. U.S. Department of the Interior, Water Projects Review, April 1977.

Dams in Grand Canyon—A Necessary Evil? Sierra Club, August 1965.

"Debate Roils over Utah's Troubled Waters." *High Country News*, April 4, 1980.

"Dr. Strangelove Builds in the Desert." Maricopa Audubon Society, 1976.

"Dolores Project." Private papers of Roger Morrison.

Dolores Project (feasibility data). U.S. Bureau of Reclamation (undated).

"The Echo of Echo Park." Colorado River Water Conservation District, Glenwood Springs, Colorado, July 1981.

Etter, Alfred G. "Reservoir of the Unknown." *Defenders of Wildlife News*, April 1965.

———. "The Reclamation Machine." *Defenders of Wildlife News*, 1967.

"Excerpts from Memoirs of E. W. McFarland." Arizona Water Commission hearings, February 22, 1977.

Facts About the Proposed Grand Canyon Dams and the Threat to Grand Canyon. Colorado Open Space Coordinating Council, March 15, 1967.

"Farm Interests Lose Battle over Ground Water." *Arizona Republic*, May 22, 1979.

"Farmers Face Dilemma on Water Usage." *Deseret News* (undated).

"Farmers See Little Help in CAP." *Phoenix Gazette*, October 28, 1980.

"Farms Called Big Losers in Water Battle." *Arizona Republic*, October 19, 1980.

"Fed Up? Here's a Way to Tell Washington." *Arizona Republic*, February 27, 1980.

"Flow Figures Suggest Orme as Inadequate." *Phoenix Gazette*, September 23, 1980.

"GAO: Colorado Basin in Trouble." *Rocky Mountain News*, May 22, 1979.

"GAO Glum on River Yield." *Denver Post*, May 22, 1979.

"Groundwater Balance Sought Early." *Arizona Daily Star*, March 20, 1982.

Hanson, Dennis. "Pumping Billions into the Desert." *Audubon* (undated).

Holburt, Myron. "California's Stake in the Colorado River." Colorado River Board of California, August 1979.

Ingram, Helen, et al. "Central Arizona Project: Politics and Economics in Irrigated Agriculture." John Muir Institute for Environmental Studies, August 1980.

Ingram, Helen, et al. "Water Scarcity and the Politics of Plenty in the Four Corners States." *The Western Political Quarterly*, September 1979.

"Interior Studying CUP Survival." *Deseret News*, February 23, 1977.

"Irrigation Costs in Upper Colorado Basin." Private papers of Roger Morrison.

Kennedy, John F. "Special Message to Congress on Natural Resources," February 23, 1961. *Public Papers of the Presidents.*

Khera, Sigrid. "The Yavapia: Who They Are and from Where They Come."

Notes and Bibliography

Lichtenstein, Grace. "The Battle over the Mighty Colorado." *New York Times Magazine*, July 31, 1977.
McCasland, S. P. *United Western Investigation: Interim Report on Reconnaissance.* Bureau of Reclamation, Salt Lake City, January 1951.
———. "Water from Pacific Northwest for Deserts of Southwest." *Civil Engineering*, February 1952.
McCaull, Julian. "Wringing Out the West." *Environment*, September 1974.
"New Colorado Water Fight." *Arizona Republic*, March 31, 1966.
"North Water Plan Detailed." *Sacramento Union*, March 17, 1965.
Ognibene, Peter. "Water Wasteland." *Washington Post*, May 3, 1978.
"The 160-Acre Limit and the 1902 Reclamation Act." Citizens Concerned About the Project, November 1977.
"Orme Still Needed." *Arizona Republic*, March 4, 1978.
"Panel Urges Land to Be Set Aside to Conserve Water." *Arizona Gazette*, December 14, 1978.
"Proposed Arizona Water Commission Staff Allocations of CAP Water." Arizona Water Commission (undated).
"Rio Salado, Not Orme." *Scottsdale Daily Progress*, March 8, 1978.
Riter, J. R. "Colorado River Basin Project," Memorandum to Chief Engineer, Bureau of Reclamation, February 13, 1967.
"River Plan Introduced by Kuchel." *Denver Post*, April 23, 1964.
Salisbury, David. "Managing Arid Lands." *Christian Science Monitor*, February 28, 1979.
San Miguel Project (feasibility data). U.S. Bureau of Reclamation, January 1966.
"Senate OKs Funds for CAP." *Arizona Republic*, September 11, 1980.
"Sen. Jackson Seeks More Congressional Authority over Bureau of Reclamation." *Medford Mail Tribune*, July 1, 1965.
Sibley, George. "The Desert Empire." *Harper's*, October 1977.
"Suit Seeks to Block CAP Dam." *Phoenix Gazette*, June 11, 1975.
"Thirsty Tucsonans Soaking the City Dry." *Arizona Daily Star*, February 7, 1982.
"Two Solons Decry Signing Reclamation Opponent." *Salt Lake Tribune*, October 23, 1966.
Udall, Morris. "Arizona and Water," February 1982.
"Udall Infuriated at Meet." *Arizona Republic*, March 31, 1966.
"Udall's Water Plan Shaky." *Arizona Republic*, January 24, 1964.
U.S. Department of the Interior. "Colorado River Storage Project." Washington, D.C.: U.S. Government Printing Office, 1964.
U.S. Department of the Interior. *Pacific Southwest Water Plan Report*, January 1964.

"Water Allocations: Central Arizona Project." William Gookin and Associates, March 3, 1975.

"Water and Politics." *Arizona Republic*, August 29, 1980.

"Water Code to Slow Growth." *Scottsdale Daily Progress*, June 6, 1980.

"Water from the Colorado Drawn into Arizona as Big Project Opens." *New York Times*, November 16, 1985.

Welsh, Frank. "Arizona Loses Water with CAP." *Arizona Reviews and News*, December 23, 1976.

———. "Sell Water to California." *Arizona Reviews and News*, March 3, 1977.

"Who, if Anybody, Is to Blame for Floods Along the Colorado?" *Wall Street Journal*, July 12, 1983.

Witzeman, Robert. "Consumers Ripped Off." *Arizona Republic*, October 19, 1978.

LETTERS, MEMORANDA, MISCELLANEOUS

Aspinall, Wayne. Letter to David Brower, November 22, 1966.

Beaty, Orren. Memorandum for S. Douglass Cater, Jr., The White House, February 10, 1967.

Bellport, Barney. Blue envelope letter to Commissioner Dominy, "Augmentation of critical water needs of major river basins," January 30, 1968.

———. Blue envelope memorandum to Commissioner of Reclamation, "Colored Dams," June 2, 1966.

———. Blue envelope memorandum to Commissioner Dominy, "Sierra Club," April 1, 1966.

Brower, David. Letter to Congressman Wayne Aspinall, November 19, 1966.

———. Letter to Congressman Wayne Aspinall, November 28, 1966.

———. Testimony, Colorado River Storage Project Hearings (undated, in files).

———. Letter to Interior Secretary James Watt, July 25, 1983.

Bureau of Reclamation, "Responses to Questions on Colorado River Water and Potential Raids on Pacific Northwest Water," internal memorandum, December 1975.

Clinton, Frank. Blue envelope memorandum to Floyd Dominy, Commissioner of Reclamation, "Eden Project, Wyoming," August 12, 1963.

Crandall, David. Blue envelope letter to Commissioner of Reclamation, "Incidental Scuttlebutt," April 4, 1968.

———. Blue envelope memorandum to Commissioner of Reclamation,

Notes and Bibliography

"Summary of Upper Basin discussions concerning H.R. 4671 held in Denver January 18 and 19, 1966," January 20, 1966.

———. Blue envelope memorandum to Commissioner, "Wyoming items for possible inclusion in Colorado River project legislation," January 27, 1967.

Dick, James. "Water Pricing Policy of the Bureau of Reclamation." Memorandum to John Leshy of Natural Resources Defense Council (undated, in files).

Dickenson, Philip. Letter to Stanford P. McCasland, July 21, 1972.

———. Memorandum to Congressman Clair Engle, April 9, 1964.

Director, Resources Program Staff. Memorandum to Secretary of the Interior, "Pacific Southwest Water Plan—briefing material for meeting with President," January 21, 1964.

Dominy, Floyd. Letter to Ellis Armstrong, January 6, 1967.

———. Speech before the Southern California Water Conference, Los Angeles, December 14, 1964.

Gordon, Kermit. Memorandum to President Lyndon Johnson, April 22, 1968.

Graff, Tom. Letter to Gray Davis, Governor's Executive Secretary (California), January 8, 1980.

Harvey, Dorothy. Letter to Nelson Plummer, Regional Director, Bureau of Reclamation, July 19, 1978.

Hearings on Colorado River Storage Project Act, House of Representatives, *Congressional Record*, July 14, 1955.

Hilliard, E. H. Open Letter to Wayne Aspinall, May 1966.

Hogan, Harry. Handwritten memo from associate solicitor, Department of the Interior, to "Floyd," "Columbia River Compact Will Block Diversion of Col. R. Water to the Southwest," February 20, 1964.

Jensen, Joseph. Letter to Stewart Udall, December 31, 1964.

Jukes, Thomas H. Letter to George Marshall, President, Sierra Club, September 2, 1966 (and several others by same author).

Kuchel, Thomas. Remarks on Senate floor, "Protecting the Present Users of Lower Colorado River Water," *Congressional Record*, April 25, 1964.

McCasland, Stanford P. Letter to Philip Dickenson, August 10, 1972.

Manatos, Mike. Memorandum to Lawrence O'Brien, The White House, May 11, 1964.

Mitchell, A. L. Memorandum to Chief Engineer, Bureau of Reclamation, "Attendance at meeting on the Colorado River sponsored by the Colorado Mountain Club and the Sierra Club—Phipps Auditorium, March 22, 1966," March 23, 1966.

Palmer, William. Memorandum to Commissioner of Reclamation, "Water resource development in the Lower Colorado River Basin," August 3, 1962.

Peterson, Ottis. Blue envelope letter to Commissioner Floyd Dominy, March 29, 1964.

Pugh, C. A. Blue envelope letter to Commissioner Dominy, "Reply to Aspinall letter to Colorado River Basin Governors regarding Central Arizona Project water supply," June 3, 1965.

———. Blue envelope memorandum to Regional Director, Bureau of Reclamation, "Report on debate with Mr. David Brower of the Sierra Club relative to Bridge Canyon and Marble Canyon Dams, February 10, 1965," March 30, 1965.

Riggins, Ted. Memorandum to F. Dominy, G. Stamm, N. B. Bennett, "Status Report: Central Arizona Project legislation," October 5, 1967.

Riter, J. R. Memorandum to Chief Engineer, Bureau of Reclamation, "Special Meeting of Colorado Water Conservation Board," August 18, 1965.

Robins, J. W. Memorandum to Project Manager, U.S. Bureau of Reclamation, Grand Junction, Colorado, "Colorado Water Conservation Board meetings of September 7 and 8, 1967," September 13, 1967.

Rorke, H. B. Note to Ottis Peterson, Director of Public Information, Bureau of Reclamation, "IntRevService clamp on the Sierra Club," June 21, 1966.

Schultz, Charles. Memorandum to President Lyndon Johnson, "1968 new construction starts for the Corps of Engineers," December 31, 1966.

Straus, Michael. Letter to William Warne, December 30, 1952.

Udall, Stewart. Memorandum to President Lyndon Johnson, "Senator Hayden and the Lower Colorado Project," August 9, 1967.

Warne, William E. Letter to Harry Bashore, November 12, 1963.

———. Letter to Senator Carl Hayden, March 4, 1964.

West, Arleigh. Blue envelope letter to Commissioner of Reclamation, "Randy Riter's latest 'ciphering' on the Lower Colorado River Basin water supply," June 17, 1965.

Witzeman, Dr. Robert. Letter to Cecil Andrus, Secretary of Interior, May 23, 1980.

———. Letter to Governor Jack Williams of Arizona, August 29, 1977.

———. Memorandum to Lee Thompson, January 24, 1980.

CHAPTER FIVE: **The Go-Go Years**

William Manchester's *The Glory and the Dream* is anecdotal history at its best, and contains much fascinating stuff on the Roosevelt years and the New Deal's glorification of public works.

Donald Worster's and Paul Bonnifield's books give strikingly different impressions of the Dust Bowl. To Bonnifield, it was a natural event that would have happened even if the plains hadn't been overgrazed and plowed up; to Worster, it was almost entirely a man-made disaster. Paul Sears's *Deserts on the March* is still the classic book on the subject, and Sears's conclusions land much closer to Worster than to Bonnifield (who, interestingly, is an Oklahoman).

George Sundborg's *Hail Columbia* is the story of the damming of the river from the viewpoint of an ardent New Deal water developer (he was administrative assistant to the late Senator Ernest Gruening, who wanted to dam the Yukon, too, and became exasperated that the Soviet Union was building bigger dams than ours). Albert Williams's book is more balanced, but not as detailed.

Daniel Jack Chasan's *The Water Link* and Anthony Netboy's *The Columbia River Salmon and Steelhead Trout: Their Fight for Survival* both contain mournful accounts of the fabulous fisheries destroyed by dams and logging in the Northwest.

Considerable information on the WPPSS fiasco, an indirect result of the huge dam-construction program in the Northwest (and something which I passed over rather lightly in the chapter), is in the files of the Natural Resources Defense Council in San Francisco.

Important interviews for this chapter: Phil Nalder, Frank Weil, Larry Meinert, Floyd Dominy, Ralph Cavanagh, Jim Casey, Horace Albright, Samuel Hays, Gilbert Stamm, C. J. Kuiper, Gus Norwood, A. J. Voy, Daniel Dreyfus.

BOOKS

Bonnifield, Paul. *The Dust Bowl.* Albuquerque: University of New Mexico Press, 1979.

Chasan, Daniel Jack. *The Water Link.* Seattle: University of Washington Press, 1981.

Columbia Basin Irrigation Project Report. Washington, D.C.: House Committee on Irrigation and Reclamation, 1928.

The Columbia River: A Comprehensive Report. Washington, D.C.: U.S. Bureau of Reclamation, 1947.

Holbrook, Stewart. *The Columbia River.* New York: Holt, Rinehart, and Winston, 1965.

Ickes, Harold. *The Secret Diary of Harold Ickes.* New York: Simon and Schuster, 1953.

Johanson, Dorothy O., and Charles M. Gates. *Empire of the Columbia.* New York: Harper and Row, 1957.

Jones, Fred O. *Grand Coulee from "Hell To Breakfast."* Portland, Ore.: Binfords and Mort, 1947.

Lavender, David. *Land of Giants.* Garden City, N.Y.: Doubleday, 1958.

Lowi, Theodore. *The End of Liberalism.* New York: Norton, 1969.

———. *Legislative Politics U.S.A.* (esp. "How the Farmers Get What They Want"). Boston: Little, Brown, 1962.

Manchester, William. *The Glory and the Dream.* New York: Bantam, 1975.

Netboy, Anthony. *The Columbia River Salmon and Steelhead Trout: Their Fight for Survival.* Seattle: University of Washington Press, 1980.

Neuberger, Richard. *Our Promised Land.* New York: Macmillan, 1938.

Schad, Theodore, and John Kerr Rose. *Reclamation: Accomplishments and Contributions.* Washington, D.C.: Library of Congress Legislative Reference Service, 1958.

Sears, Paul. *Deserts on the March.* Norman: University of Oklahoma Press, 1935.

Sheridan, David. *Desertification of the United States.* Washington, D.C.: Council on Environmental Quality, 1981.

Sundborg, George. *Hail Columbia: The Thirty-Year Struggle for Grand Coulee Dam.* New York: Macmillan, 1954.

Ten Rivers in America's Future. Report of the President's Water Resources Policy Commission. Washington, D.C., 1950.

Warne, William E. *The Bureau of Reclamation.* New York: Praeger, 1973.

Williams, Albert N. *The Water and the Power.* New York: Duell, Sloan and Pearce, 1951.

Worster, Donald. *Dust Bowl.* New York: Oxford University Press, 1979.

ARTICLES AND REPORTS

Case, Robert Ormond. "Eighth World Wonder." *Saturday Evening Post,* July 13, 1935.

Davenport, Walter. "Power in the Wilderness: Grand Coulee and Bonneville." *Collier's,* September 21, 1935.

George W. Goethals and Company. *Columbia Basin Irrigation Project,*

State of Washington: A Report. Washington State Department of Conservation and Development, 1922.

"Grand Coulee Dam Is Again the Biggest." *Seattle Post-Intelligencer*, August 17, 1980.

Marshall, Jim. "Dam of Doubt." *Collier's*, June 19, 1937.

"Salmon Shortage Cited as Eagles Shun Stream." *New York Times*, December 5, 1982.

Taylor, Frank. "The White Elephant Comes into Its Own." *Saturday Evening Post*, June 5, 1943.

Tucker, Ray. "Interior's Adventures in the Missouri Basin." *Public Utilities Fortnightly*, July 17, 1952.

"Washington's Power Problem." *New York Times*, February 15, 1983.

"What's Happening on the Ainsworth Project?" *Nebraska Farmer*, January 1964.

"Where's the Limit on Reclamation Projects?" *Nebraska Farmer*, March 1964.

"WPPSS Preparing to Sell What Remains of Two Huge Nuclear Units, Piece by Piece." *Wall Street Journal*, August 4, 1983.

LETTERS, MEMORANDA, MISCELLANEOUS

Bellport, Barney. Blue envelope memorandum to Commissioner Dominy, "Delegation of design and specifications work and contracting authority for drains—Columbia Basin Project," May 27, 1966.

Dominy, Floyd. Letter to Claire and Donald Hanna, April, 15, 1955.

———. Memorandum to Chief of Allocation and Repayment Division, "Delay in amendatory repayment contract material review," November 2, 1949.

Dugan, H. P., et al. Blue envelope memorandum to Commissioner Dominy, "OBE-ERS Presentation," March 30, 1965.

Dugan, Patrick. Blue envelope letter to Commissioner Dominy, April 22, 1966.

Lineweaver, Goodrich. Letter to Floyd Dominy, September 2, 1949.

———. Memorandum to E. D. Eaton, September 2, 1949.

Nelson, Harold. Memorandum to Commissioner Dominy, "Extension of Columbia River Basin Account Benefits to Older Projects," February 19, 1968.

Pafford, Robert. Letter to Brigadier General Arthur H. Frye, Jr., November 8, 1963.

Peterson, E. L. Letter to Secretary of the Interior, "Garrison Diversion Project," November 20, 1957.

Saylor, John. "Is Power Really Reclamation's Paying Partner? Or Hominy

Dominy Sat on the Wall." Extended remarks in *Congressional Record*, February 11, 1965.

Straus, Michael. Memorandum to regional director, Billings, Montana, "Proposed Repayment Contracts, Milk River Project," July 12, 1949.

Straus, Michael, Lewis Pick, J. A. Krug, and Kenneth Royall. Letter to the President, April 11, 1949.

CHAPTER SIX: **Rivals in Crime**

The account of the Corps of Engineers' coup on the Tulare Basin rivers in California is taken mainly from Arthur Maass's *Muddy Waters*. For the story of Garrison Dam and the drowning of the Three Tribes, I have relied largely on Arthur Morgan's *Dams and Other Disasters*.

The competition between the Corps and the Bureau is something of which I was completely unaware (as most conservationists are, too) until I came across the Bureau's secret "blue envelope" files. Spokesmen for the Corps of Engineers were of no help in corroborating this information. The Marysville Dam episode, however, was largely corroborated in interviews with Robert Pafford, one of the chief actors. The self-defeating competition on California's North Coast rivers was similarly corroborated by David Shuster, formerly operations manager of the Central Valley Project, and to a lesser degree by William Warne.

Some of the Rampart Dam story is based on interviews with Floyd Dominy and John Gottschalk.

Other important interviews for this chapter: David Weiman, Richard Madson, George Piper, Ed Green, General John Woodland Morris (ret.), H. P. Dugan, Peter Carlson, John Marlin, Tom Barlow, Jim Cook, Norman Livermore, Richard Wilson, Jim Casey, Edmund G. Brown, Sr., Ronald B. Robie, Gerald Meral, James Flannery, Brent Blackwelder, Anthony Wayne Smith, Raphael Kazmann, Guy Martin.

BOOKS

Frank, Bernard, and Anthony Netboy. *Water, Land and People*. New York: Knopf, 1950.

Hart, Henry C. *The Dark Missouri*. Madison: University of Wisconsin Press, 1957.

Maass, Arthur. *Muddy Waters: The Army Engineers and the Nation's Rivers*. Cambridge, Mass.: Harvard University Press, 1951.

Morgan, Arthur. *Dams and Other Disasters*. Boston: Porter Sargent, 1971.

Notes and Bibliography

Schad, Theodore, and John Kerr Rose. *Reclamation: Accomplishments and Contributions*. Washington, D.C.: Library of Congress Legislative Reference Service, 1958.

Terral, Rufus. *The Missouri Valley*. New Haven: Yale University Press, 1947.

Williams, Albert N. *The Water and the Power*. New York: Duell, Sloan and Pearce, 1951.

ARTICLES AND DOCUMENTS

"Audit reveals Pick-Sloan poorly run, loss of funds." *Lincoln Sunday Journal and Star*, 1977.

"Audits Show Unbusinesslike Management of Western Basin Accounts." Environmental Policy Center, Washington, D.C. (undated).

"Budget includes funds for CENDAK planning." *Huron* (S.D.) *Daily Plainsman*, February 1, 1983.

Brooks, Paul. "The Plot to Drown Alaska." *The Atlantic Monthly*, May 1965.

"CENDAK benefits might not offset costs, new study says." *Huron* (S.D.) *Daily Plainsman*, December 9, 1981.

"Conflicts Among Agencies Peril Water Development." *Willows* (Calif.) *Daily Journal*, July 27, 1965.

De Roos, Robert, and Arthur Maass. "The Lobby That Can't Be Licked: Congress and the Army Engineers." *Harper's*, May 1949.

"Friction Periling Vast Water Plan." *Willows* (Calif.) *Daily Journal*, July 27, 1965.

"Garrison: The Canadian Concern." Manitoba Department of Natural Resources, Winnipeg, Canada (undated).

Garrison Diversion: Opposing Views. A compendium published by the Red River Valley Historical Society, March 1981.

Gruening, Ernest. "The Plot to Strangle Alaska." *The Atlantic Monthly*, July 1965.

Jacobs, Mike. "The Garrison Diversion Project is North Dakota's history, and destiny." *High Country News*, September 17, 1984.

Oakes, John. "Pork—U.S. Prime." *New York Times*, July 29, 1981.

A Review of the Environmental, Economic, and International Aspects of the Garrison Diversion Unit, North Dakota. Committee on Government Operations, U.S. Congress, 1976.

U.S. Department of the Interior. "Alaska Natural Resources and the Rampart Project," June 1967.

LETTERS, MEMORANDA, MISCELLANEOUS

Bellport, Barney. Blue envelope letter to Commissioner, "Determination of optimum size of power plant—Auburn Dam," March 21, 1968.

Bureau of Reclamation. "Need for an Accelerated Water Resources Development Program, North Coast Project, California" (undated).

Cassidy, General W. F. Speech at Topical Conference on Hydraulics, Davis, California, August 16, 1962.

Chief, Division of Project Development, Bureau of Reclamation. Memorandum to Commissioner, "GAO Report on Central and Southern Florida Project," Corps of Engineers, December, 24, 1964.

Dickinson, Phil. Letter to J. A. Krug, Secretary of the Interior–designate, March 28, 1946.

Dominy, Floyd E. Blue envelope letter to Pat Dugan, April 13, 1960.

———. Letter to Claire and Donald Hanna, April 15, 1955.

———. Memorandum to Kenneth Holum, "Understandings with the Corps—Columbia River Basin," December 20, 1961.

Holum, Kenneth. Letter to Elmer Staats, "Coordination of Bureau of Reclamation and Corps of Engineers investigations programs," November 14, 1961 (includes report on subject).

Jennings, Robert. Blue envelope letter to Floyd Dominy, Associate Commissioner of Reclamation, March 5, 1959.

Johnson, Bruce. Blue envelope memorandum to Commissioner of Reclamation, "Joint Study Missouri River, Fort Peck to Great Falls," May 9, 1963.

———. Blue envelope memorandum to Floyd Dominy, Commissioner of Reclamation, "Memorandum of Agreement with the Corps of Engineers," May 19, 1962.

———. Blue envelope letter to Floyd Dominy, Commissioner of Reclamation, "Oahe Unit Feasibility Report," April 18, 1960.

Mangan, John. Memorandum to Regional Director, Bureau of Reclamation, Boise, Idaho, "Conversation with Mr. Don Lane, Oregon State Water Resources Board," January 22, 1965.

Nelson, H. T. Blue envelope memorandum to Commissioner of Reclamation, "Relationships with the Corps of Engineers—Umatilla River Basin, Oregon," April, 24, 1962.

Nelson, Harold. Blue envelope memorandum to Commissioner, "Army-Bureau relationships in the Northwest states," November 30, 1961.

———. Blue envelope memorandum to Commissioner, Bureau of Reclamation, "Interior and Insular Affairs Committee vs. Public Works Committee approach to water resource development authorizations," February 9, 1965.

————. Blue envelope memorandum to Floyd Dominy, Commissioner of Reclamation, "So-called 'Information Bulletin' issued by Corps of Engineers re: Rogue River Basin, Oregon," February 20, 1962.

————. Blue envelope memorandum to Floyd Dominy, Commissioner of Reclamation, "Subcommittee on Public Works visitation to flood disaster areas—California-Oregon," January 22, 1965.

Pafford, Robert. Blue envelope letter to Floyd Dominy, Commissioner of Reclamation, February 4, 1966.

————. Blue envelope letter to Floyd Dominy, Commissioner of Reclamation, August 4, 1966.

Project Manager, Bureau of Reclamation, Bismarck, North Dakota. Blue envelope memorandum to Commissioner, "Meeting with Local Interests in Minot," July 10, 1959.

A [Missouri] *River Basin Management Post-Audit and Analysis.* Arthur O. Little, Inc., Cambridge, Massachusetts, May 1973.

Roberts, Daryl L. Blue envelope letter to Floyd E. Dominy, April 7, 1961.

Roosevelt, Franklin Delano. Letter to Harold Ickes, May 29, 1940.

————. Letter to Harold D. Smith, June 1, 1940.

Sanders, Barefoot. Memorandum to Jim Jones, the White House, July 29, 1968.

Spencer, John. Blue envelope letter to Floyd Dominy, February, 19, 1960.

Stamm, Gilbert. Blue envelope memorandum to Floyd Dominy, Commissioner of Reclamation, "Establishment of a wild river on Yellowstone River above Emigrant, Montana," February 3, 1965.

White, Lee C. Memorandum to President Lyndon Johnson, "Meeting with Alaska Congressional Delegation," March 31, 1964.

CHAPTER SEVEN: **Dominy**

The most important source for this chapter was Floyd Dominy himself. He regaled me with exploits and achievements that made for irresistible listening. Anyone who has ever worked with Dominy has a story or tale to relate—and I've tried to select the best.

John McPhee's *Encounters with the Archdruid*, in which Floyd Dominy and David Brower raft the Colorado River together, arguing nearly all the way, is some of the best journalism published in years.

BOOKS

McPhee, John. *Encounters with the Archdruid.* New York: Farrar, Straus and Giroux, 1970.

Robinson, Michael. *Water for the West.* Chicago: Public Works Historical Society, 1979.

Warne, William. *The Bureau of Reclamation.* New York: Praeger, 1973.

LETTERS, MEMORANDA, AND ARTICLES

Anonymous. "Ode to Domine Dominy," April 18, 1955.

Bellport, Barney. Blue envelope memorandum to Commissioner, Bureau of Reclamation, "Criticism for development of irrigation projects," February 18, 1965.

———. Blue envelope memorandum to Commissioner, Bureau of Reclamation, "Replacement of American Falls Dam," May 24, 1967.

Buckman, H. H., President, National Rivers and Harbors Congress. Letter to Floyd Dominy, April 19, 1962.

"The Crisis in Water: Its Sources, Pollution and Depletion," *Saturday Review,* October 23, 1965.

Crandall, David. Blue envelope letter to Commissioner, Bureau of Reclamation, "Wyoming items for possible inclusion in Colorado River Project legislation," January 27, 1967.

———. Memorandum to Commissioner, Bureau of Reclamation, June 23, 1967.

Director, Columbia Basin Project. Blue envelope letter to Commissioner Floyd E. Dominy, January 28, 1969.

Dominy, Floyd. Blue envelope letter to B. P. Bellport, Bureau of Reclamation, August 13, 1965.

———. Blue envelope letter to Clyde Spenser, Regional Director, Bureau of Reclamation, Sacramento, July 12, 1954.

———. Blue envelope letter to Gilbert Stamm, November 7, 1952.

———. Blue envelope memorandum to Assistant Commissioner and Chief Engineer, "Escalation in Construction Contracts," March 15, 1960.

———. Blue envelope memorandum to Assistant Secretary for Water and Power, Department of the Interior, "Proposed employment of Robert J. Pafford, Jr., as Regional Director, Region II," December 11, 1962.

———. Blue envelope memorandum to Chief Engineer, "Bureau of Reclamation Flag," April 25, 1966.

———. Blue envelope memorandum to Regional Director, Bureau of Reclamation, Sacramento, "Audubon Society Convention," August 4, 1966.

———. Blue envelope memorandum to Secretary of the Interior, "Planned engagements and related travel for Commissioner of Reclamation," May 8, 1962.

———. Letter to Alfred Etter, November 23, 1965.

———. Letter to Senator Carl Hayden, September 6, 1966 (with attachments).

———. Personal memorandum to files, "Meeting with Commissioner Dexheimer et al.—Columbia Basin anti-speculation and excess land problems—February 28, 1956," March 12, 1956.

———. Professional Diary (miscellaneous items, 1954–55).

"Dominy Foresees Water Sharing Need After Northwest Meets Requirements," *Idaho Daily Statesman*, January 22, 1965.

"Dominy's Appointment Tipoff to Repayment," *Columbia Basin Herald*, January 18, 1961.

Dugan, H. P. Blue envelope memorandum to Commissioner, Bureau of Reclamation, "January 18 meeting of Nebraska Mid-State Reclamation District Board." January 20, 1965.

Etter, Alfred G. "How Reclamation Can Kill the West," *Defenders of Wildlife News*, April/May/June 1966.

Frantz, Joe B. *Floyd E. Dominy Oral History*. Lyndon Baines Johnson Library Oral History Program, University of Texas, Austin, November 14, 1968.

Holum, Kenneth. Blue envelope memorandum to Commissioner of Reclamation, "Briefing Session—House Interior Committee—January 28," January 28, 1965.

Nelson, H. T. Blue envelope memorandum to Commissioner, Bureau of Reclamation, "Interest of the Idaho Water Resources Board in Middle Snake River Development Program," October 20, 1967.

Nelson, Harold. Blue envelope memorandum to Commissioner, Bureau of Reclamation, "Relationships with the Corps of Engineers—Umatilla River Basin," April 24, 1962.

Peterson, Ottis. Memorandum to Mr. Dominy, March 30, 1967.

———. Blue envelope letter to George N. Pierce, District Manager, Bureau of Reclamation, Juneau, Alaska, June 1, 1965.

Pettingill, Olin. "Convention Country," *Audubon*, 1966.

"Reclamation Boss Chides Utah Chief," *Arizona Daily Star*, October 20, 1962.

Regional Directors, Bureau of Reclamation, Boise and Denver. Blue envelope letter to Commissioner, "Meeting with the Governor of the State of Wyoming," April 3, 1962.

Stamm, Gilbert. Blue envelope letter to Floyd Dominy, Director of Irrigation, Bureau of Reclamation, April 26, 1954.

Stuart, Russell. Letter to Stewart Udall, February 18, 1966.

Udall, Stewart. Personal memorandum to Floyd Dominy, Commissioner of Reclamation, February 26, 1966.

"Udall Effects Troubled Truce in Two-Year Carr-Dominy Feud," *Pueblo* (Colo.) *Chieftain*, February 25, 1963.

"Warning to Interior," *Pueblo* (Colo.) *Chieftain*, September 3, 1962.

West, Arleigh. Blue envelope memorandum to Commissioner, Bureau of Reclamation. "Excess Lands—Imperial Irrigation District—Boulder Canyon Project, California" (undated).

———. Blue envelope memorandum to Commissioner Dominy. "CONFIDENTIAL: Excess land survey in areas served by Metropolitan Water District, Southern California," December 30, 1964.

CHAPTER NINE: **The Peanut Farmer and the Pork Barrel**

This chapter is based mainly on interviews and newspaper reporting. Sources who should be mentioned are Robert Smythe, Richard Ayres, J. Gustave Speth, Jane Yarn, Claude Terry, James Flannery, Peter Carlson, David Conrad, Jim Free, Guy Martin, John Leshy, Laurence Rockefeller, Tom Barlow, David Weiman, Ronald Robie, Richard Ayres, Congressman Robert Edgar, Brent Blackwelder, former Congressman Robert Eckhardt, Congressman Tom Bevill, John Lawrence, Congressman John Myers, Ruth Fleischer, William Dubois, Daniel Beard, and Steven Lanich.

Congressman Jim Wright's *The Coming Water Famine* makes for interesting reading if one wishes to understand how thoroughly a basically self-interested politician can delude himself into thinking he is serving the commonweal.

The Tellico story is drawn partly from Fred Powledge's *Water*. A good critical appraisal of the TVA's record in Appalachia is William Chandler's *The Myth of TVA*.

BOOKS

Chandler, William U. *The Myth of TVA*. Cambridge, Mass.: Ballinger, 1984.

Powledge, Fred. *Water*. New York: Farrar, Straus and Giroux, 1982.

Reid, T. R. *Congressional Odyssey*. San Francisco: W. H. Freeman, 1980.

Wright, Jim. *The Coming Water Famine.* New York: Coward-McCann, 1966.

ARTICLES AND REPORTS

"Accord Reached in Westlands Pact." *Sacramento Bee,* 1979.

American Rivers, December 1977 (entire issue).

"Andrus, Governors Weigh Drought." *Denver Post,* February 21, 1977.

"Andrus Sees No Major Shifts under Successor." *New York Times,* November 18, 1980.

"Andrus's Popularity Washes Away in West." *New York Times,* February 20, 1978.

"Belly Up to the Trough, Boys!" *New Republic,* October 14, 1978.

Broder, David S. "A Most Puzzling Maneuver." *Washington Post,* March 16, 1977.

"California Farmers' Clout Preserves Federal Water Subsidy." *Washington Post,* August 19, 1979.

Carter, President Jimmy. "To the Congress of the United States," February 21, 1977.

Carter, President Jimmy. "To the Congress of the United States," June 6, 1978.

"Carter in Full Retreat in 'War on West.'" *Washington Post.* January 1978.

"Carter Opts to Sidestep Fight on 160-Acre Limit." *Sacramento Bee,* June 22, 1979.

"Carter Water Policy Hurt." *Washington Post,* March 31, 1978.

"Carter Will Ask Hill to Halt Aid for 18 Major Water Projects." *Los Angeles Times,* April 18, 1977.

"Carter Won't Seek Cut in Big Projects." *New York Times,* January 14, 1978.

"Carter Yields on Water Projects." *Philadelphia Inquirer,* January 15, 1978.

"Carter's Water Policy: Furor in an Election Year." *Washington Post,* June 11, 1980.

"CEQ Releases Summary of Water Resource Project Deletions." Council on Environmental Quality, February 23, 1977.

"Congress' Going Away Gifts." *Washington Post,* December 10, 1980.

"Congress Makes Waves over Carter's Water Policy." *National Journal,* July 1, 1978.

"Devastating Blow Dealt Water Projects Pork Barrel." *Science,* October 27, 1978.

"Energy and Public Works Appropriations Bill." *Congressional Record*, October 5, 1978.

"Energy and Water Development Appropriations for 1981." Hearings, House Appropriations Committee, 1981.

"Environmentalists Slam Carter." *Rocky Mountain News*, March 31, 1978.

"Executive Summary: Water Resources Option Paper." Carter Domestic Policy Staff (internal document, undated).

Gardner, Don. "The Trinity River: Water and Politics." *Texas Observer*, May 20, 1977.

"Governors Assured by Andrus on Water." *New York Times*, June 24, 1979.

"Hart, Haskell Demand Data on Water Projects." *Denver Post*, 1977.

"House Sustains Veto of Public Works Bill." *Wall Street Journal*, October 6, 1978.

"Issue Paper: Federal Water Resources Policy." Carter Domestic Policy Staff (internal document), January 28, 1977.

Lamm, Richard D., and Scott M. Matheson. "Deficits: A Noose," *New York Times* (undated).

"Louisiana Girding to Save Waterway from the 'Hit List.'" *Washington Post*, March 28, 1977.

"Plan to Share Water Project Costs Is Gaining in West Under Reagan." *New York Times*, September 12, 1982.

"President Is Warned by House Democrats." *New York Times*, May 23, 1977.

"Roll Out the Barrels, We'll Have a Barrel of Funds, Folks Say." *Wall Street Journal* (undated).

"Senate Vote Defies Carter." *Washington Post*, March 11, 1977.

"Senators, White House Wrangle over Powers." *Washington Post*, March 1977.

"A Threat to Block Valley Water Pact." *San Francisco Chronicle*, October 4, 1979.

"Top Western State Officials Blast Water Project Cuts." *The Missoulian*, February 21, 1977.

"Turning Off the Water." *Newsweek*, April 4, 1977.

U.S. Department of the Interior, Water Projects Review. "Auburn-Folsom-South Project, California," April 1977.

"Water Policy: Battle over Benefits." *Congressional Quarterly*, March 4, 1978.

"Water Policy Reforms Going down the Drain?" Environmental Policy Center, *Resource Report*, May 1978.

"Water Project Budget Remains Virtually Untouched." American Rivers Conservation Council, March 1980.

Notes and Bibliography

"Water Projects Dispute: Carter and Congress Near a Showdown." *Science*, June 17, 1977.
"Watt Studies Sharing of Costs for Western Water Projects." *New York Times*, June 19, 1983.
"Watt Wading into Water Policy." *Washington Post*, April 18, 1981.
"Watt Would Lift Irrigation Limit, Reduce Subsidy." *Washington Post*, December 10, 1981.
"Westlands Hearings Not Likely to Bring Immediate Decisions." *San Francisco Examiner*, March 20, 1980.

LETTERS, MEMORANDA, MISCELLANEOUS

Dugan, Patrick. Blue envelope letter to Floyd Dominy, Commissioner of Reclamation, "Folsom South Unit," November 23, 1962.
Gordon, Kermit. Memorandum for the President, "Policies for Handling Navigation Projects," March 8, 1965.
Green, John A., Environmental Protection Agency. Letter to David Crandall, Regional Director, Bureau of Reclamation, Salt Lake City, November 28, 1976.
Kirwan, Michael, et al. Letter to the President, April 26, 1966.
Udall, Morris, et al. Letter to the Honorable Jimmy Carter, February 14, 1977.
Watson, Marvin. Memorandum to the President, March 24, 1965.
Wright, Jim. Letter to the President, April 7, 1966.

CHAPTER TEN: Chinatown

All the quotations from former Governor Pat Brown are in *California Water Issues, 1950–1966*, a bound volume of interviews conducted by Malca Chall of the University of California's Bancroft Library Oral History Program. The Bancroft Library has also conducted interviews with William Warne, Ralph Brody, and some of the other important participants in California's recent water-development history that are well worth reading.

Lynn Ludlow of the *San Francisco Examiner* has done an excellent job of chronicling abuses of the Reclamation Act in California. So has George Baker of the *Sacramento Bee*, whose coverage of the Peripheral Canal wars was also the best in the state.

Patrick Porgans of Red Tape Abatement, Inc., a private research and consulting firm, provided considerable assistance in understanding the financial aspects of the State Water Project. E. Philip LeVeen and Rob Stavens of Public Interest Economics have also published much useful material, as has Dorothy Green of WATER and the Contra Costa County Water Agency. Anyone trying to fully understand the project should also consult the annual reports of the Department of Water Resources.

Carey McWilliams's *California: The Great Exception* is highly recommended for its portrayal of how agribusiness, banking, food processing, the university extension system, cheap imported labor, and publicly subsidized water have created a huge economic juggernaut in the state. It may be the best general book written about California. The best essayist rooting around where California culture and politics meet, in my opinion, is not Joan Didion, but her husband, John Gregory Dunne. His "Eureka! A Celebration of California" is especially fine, though Didion's more famous essay, "Holy Water," is not to be missed.

A sense of the concentration of agricultural wealth in California can be gained from "Getting Bigger", by the California Institute for Rural Studies, which profiles the 211 largest farming companies in the state (the smallest of the 211 is a 5,000-acre operation). The study, a superb piece of research, reveals a good deal about interlocking directorates, holding companies, vertical integration in the food market, parent companies, hidden partnerships, market penetration, and so on. Most of the information on the big growers benefiting from the State Water Project comes from CIRS.

It is almost impossible to understand water and California history without consulting the *California Water Atlas*, a huge (in dimension), beautifully produced work that really does deserve to be called unique. To anyone with a keen interest in the subject, the LANDSAT photos and graphs (depicting river flows, rainfall records, floods, droughts, irrigation deliveries, pumping energy consumed, etc.) will be fascinating. The text is persistently neutral when discussing the political wars.

For thirty or forty years, a Berkeley professor named Paul Taylor kept up a largely futile but unflagging effort to reform the enforcement of the Reclamation Act (rather than "reform" the Act). His essays on the subject are meticulous and readable, especially when they delve into the social effects of agricultural giantism. Much useful information on the acreage limitation, and violations thereof, has also been published by National Land for People; though it is portrayed by the growers as a "radical" organization, its only real goal is enforcement of one of the most poorly enforced laws in the nation.

Important interviews for this chapter: Ronald Robie, Dorothy Green,

Notes and Bibliography

Lorelle Long, Tom Graff, George Ballis, Kendall Mannock, Edmund G. Brown, Sr., Gerald Meral, Ellen Stern Harris, Lawrence Swenson, Patrick Porgans, E. Philip LeVeen, Myron Holburt, Jack Burby, Willoughby Houk, Paul Taylor, David Weiman, H. P. Dugan, Robert Pafford, Michael Catino, David Shuster, Jim Cook, Kenneth Turner, Richard Wilson, Philip Bowles, David Kennedy, James Flannery, John Bryson, John Leshy, Ben Yellen.

BOOKS

Bakker, Edna. *An Island Called California.* Berkeley: University of California Press, 1971.

Berkman, Richard, and W. Kip Viscusi. *Damming the West.* New York: Grossman, 1973.

Caughey, John, and Laree Caughey. *California Heritage.* Itasca, Ill.: F. E. Peacock, 1971.

Chall, Malca. *California Water Issues, 1950–1966.* Berkeley: Bancroft Library Oral History Program, 1981.

Eisen, Jonathan, and David Fine, eds. *Unknown California.* New York: Macmillan, 1985.

Fogelson, Robert. *Fragmented Metropolis.* Cambridge, Mass.: Harvard University Press, 1967.

Haslam, Gerald, and James Houston. *California Heartland.* Santa Barbara: Capra, 1978.

Hawgood, John A. *America's Western Frontiers.* New York: Knopf, 1967.

Kahrl, William, ed. *California Water Atlas.* Sacramento: California Department of Water Resources, 1979.

Lavender, David. *California.* Norton, 1976.

McWilliams, Carey. *California: The Great Exception.* Santa Barbara: Peregrine Smith, 1976.

Nadeau, Remi. *The Water Seekers.* Santa Barbara: Peregrine Smith, 1974.

Rogers, G. L. *A History of the Canal System of the Central California Irrigation District Prior to 1940.* Privately published, 1920; archives of G. M. Bowles.

Taylor, Paul. *Essays on Land, Water, and the Law in California.* New York: Arno, 1979.

Treadwell, Edward. *The Cattle King.* Fresno, Calif.: Valley Publishers, 1931.

ARTICLES AND REPORTS

Acreage Limitation, Interim Report. U.S. Department of the Interior, Washington, D.C., March 1980.

Acreage Limitation Review. Hearings Before the Subcommittee on Irrigation and Reclamation, Committee on Interior and Insular Affairs, United States Senate, April and May 1958.

Allman, T. D. "Jerry Brown: Nothing to Everyone." *Harper's,* July 1979.

"Association Notes These Are Difficult Times for Water Development." *Sacramento Bee,* September 23, 1979.

Baker, George. "An icy reception ahead for the state's new water plan." *California Journal,* August 1977.

Barnum, J. D. "What Shall I Say More Than I Have Inferred?" Unpublished monograph, 1969.

"Big Money for Delta Canal Votes." *Oakland Tribune,* July 13, 1980.

"Bill OK Stops Flow of Funds for Mid-Valley Canal Study." *Sacramento Bee,* June 20, 1979.

"Billions Urged to Tap North Coast Rivers." *Los Angeles Times,* March 11, 1965.

"Brown Turnaround." *Fresno Bee,* November 10, 1977.

"California Canal Plan to Divert River South Stirs a Flood of Protest." *Wall Street Journal,* February 12, 1981.

The California State Water Project—1977 Activities and Future Management Plans. Department of Water Resources, Sacramento, November 1981.

The California State Water Project—1978 Activities and Future Management Plans. Department of Water Resources, Sacramento, November 1979.

The California Water Project in 1964. Department of Water Resources, Sacramento, June 1964.

"California's Coming Water Famine." California Water Resources Association, Burbank, California, September 17, 1979.

Cannon, Lou. "High Dam in the Valley of the Tall Grass." *Cry California,* Summer 1968.

"City Wants MWD to Stop Overcharging." *Los Angeles Times,* February 10, 1982.

"Cost of Water Will Eliminate Need for Peripheral Canal." Working Alliance to Equalize Rates, Los Angeles, April 3, 1980.

Delta Water Facilities. Department of Water Resources, Sacramento, July 1978.

"Early Obstacle to Water Plan." *San Francisco Chronicle,* February 15, 1984.

"Environmentalists Split over Water Projects." *San Francisco Chronicle,* January 23, 1978.

Fact Sheet: Delta Alternatives. Department of Water Resources, Sacramento (undated internal draft).

"Farmers, Ecologists Argue 160-Acre Limitation." *San Francisco Examiner,* November 8, 1977.

Notes and Bibliography

"Federal Water Limitation Issue Revived in Westlands." *Sacramento Bee* (undated).

Flaxman, Bruce. *The Metropolitan Water District of Southern California: California's Billion Dollar Hidden Empire*, June 1978.

———. *The Price of Water: Who Pays and Who Benefits?* Public Policies Studies, Claremont Graduate School, Claremont, California, May 1976.

Hagan, Robert, and Edwin Roberts. *Energy Requirements of Alternatives in Water Supply, Use, and Conservation: A Preliminary Report.* California Water Resources Center, Davis, December 1975.

How "Firm" Is the "Risk" of a Water Shortage in California—An Important Aspect of the California Water Debate. Meyer-Sangri Associates, Davis, February 1982.

"Is the Canal a Disaster for Everybody?" *San Francisco Examiner*, February 10, 1980.

Is There Water for California? Bank of America Economics Department, San Francisco, September 1955.

"Kern Farms Bloom with State Water." *Sacramento Bee*, March 20, 1980.

Kirsch, Jonathan. "Politics and Water." *New West*, September 10, 1979.

Koch, Kathy. "Senate Water-Use Bill Pits Big Firms Against Small Farms." *Congressional Quarterly*, September 29, 1979.

"Liberalization of Federal Water Subsidy Law Sought." *Sacramento Bee*, July 3, 1980.

McCabe, Charles. "The 160-Acre Law." *San Francisco Chronicle*. November 21, 1977.

———. "Reactive Politics." *San Francisco Chronicle*, November 23, 1977.

———. "Small Is Ugly?" *San Francisco Chronicle*, December 19, 1977.

———. "That Damned Canal." *San Francisco Chronicle*, 1982 (series of four articles).

"MWD Consistently Exaggerates Water Needs." Contra Costa County Water Agency, California, January 9, 1980.

"MWD Subsidizes Agriculture at Expense of Urban Taxpayer." Contra Costa County Water Agency, California, December 5, 1980.

"MWD Water Charges Are Highly Inequitable." Contra Costa County Water Agency, California, December 11, 1980.

"North Coast Program Is Bared." *Sacramento Bee*, March 11, 1965.

"Offshore Oil May Bring State $1 Billion." *Los Angeles Times*, March 2, 1962.

"Oil, Water, and Boom: Will They Mix?" *New York Times*, October 28, 1980.

"Overview of Future Water Supply Available to Metropolitan." Metropolitan Water District of Southern California, Los Angeles, January 4, 1979.

People, Land, Food. National Land for People, Fresno, November 1977.

"Peripheral Canal Proponents' Solid Front Starts Crumbling." *Sacramento Bee*, May 25, 1981.

Phase II: Alternative Courses of Action. Department of Water Resources, Sacramento, March 1976.

Porgans, Patrick. *The State of the State Water Project.* Red Tape Abatement, Inc., Chico, California.

"Powerful Groups Battle over Peripheral Canal." *Sacramento Bee*, March 18, 1980.

"Projected Electric Power Costs for the California State Water Project." Department of Water Resources, March 20, 1980.

"Reclamation History" (three-part series). National Land for People, Fresno, California, 1979.

"Report: Westlands Violates 160-Acre Law." *Fresno Bee*, November 5, 1977.

Report of Activities of the Department of Water Resources. Department of Water Resources, Sacramento, February 2, 1980.

Responses to Analysts' Questions and Comments Prepared by the Staff of the Metropolitan Water District of Southern California. Metropolitan Water District, Los Angeles, January 27, 1981.

Review of the Central Valley Project. U.S. Department of the Interior, Department of Audit and Investigation, Washington, D.C., January 1978.

Robie, Ronald. "Statement on SB 200." Department of Water Resources, Sacramento, February 27, 1980.

"Santa Barbara Defeats $102 Million Water Issue." *San Francisco Chronicle*, March 8, 1979.

"Scare Tactics Issue." *Waterlog*, October 31, 1981.

"Senate OKs $3.4 Billion Water Projects Measure." *Sacramento Bee*, June 24, 1977.

"Senators Agree to Increase Historic Farm Acreage Limit." *Sacramento Bee*, June 21, 1979.

"South State Keeps Up Search for Water." *Sacramento Bee*, April 16, 1980.

State Water Project—Status of Water Conservation and Water Supply Augmentation Plans. Department of Water Resources, Sacramento, November 1981.

Stead, Frank M. "California's Cloaca Maxima." *Cry California*, Spring 1969.

Storper, Michael, and Richard Walker. *Subsidy and Uncertainty in Financing the State Water Project* (undated).

Taylor, Paul. "Evasion of Federal Acre Limit Laws," April 1967.

"Ten Farmers Who Astound Experts." *San Francisco Examiner*, May 6, 1979.

Thomes-Newville and Glenn Reservoir Plans: Engineering Feasibility, Department of Water Resources, Sacramento, November 1980.

"Top Cash Farm Products in California—1980." *San Francisco Examiner*, October 4, 1981.

Turner, Kenneth, and Steven Kasower. *Drought in Northern California: Implications for Water Supply Management*, December 1978.

"$23 Billion Tag for Water Project." *Sacramento Bee*, February 14, 1980.

"U.S. Aides Tread Water over Peripheral Canal." *Sacramento Bee*, March 16, 1980.

"Valley May Not Need the Water." *San Francisco Examiner*, January 22, 1978.

Villarejo, Don. *New Lands for Agriculture: The California State Water Project*. California Institute for Rural Studies, Davis, California, 1981.

Vizzard, James L. "The Water Poachers." *America*, February 13, 1965.

"The War over the Peripheral Canal." *San Francisco Chronicle*, June 26, 1980.

"Water Crisis in Year 2000?" *Sacramento Bee*, June 9, 1977.

"The Water Miners" (three-part series). *San Francisco Examiner*, March 26–28, 1979.

"Water Plan Leaks." *Sacramento Bee*, June 29, 1977.

"Westlands Hit in UC Report." *Fresno Bee*, June 12, 1980.

Westlands Water District, A Study of the Proposed Contract with the Bureau of Reclamation. Department of Water Resources, Sacramento, September 17, 1975.

Will the Family Farm Survive in America? (Federal Reclamation Policy: Westlands Water District). Joint Hearings Before the Select Committee on Small Business and the Committee on Interior and Insular Affairs, United States Senate, July 17 and July 22, 1975.

Willey, W. R. Z. *Economic and Environmental Aspects of Alternative Investments in California's Water System*. Environmental Defense Fund, Berkeley, California (undated).

LETTERS, MEMORANDA, MISCELLANEOUS

Dugan, H. P. Blue envelope letter to Commissioner of Reclamation, November 23, 1960.

———. Blue envelope letter to Commissioner of Reclamation, January 30, 1962.

———. Blue envelope memorandum to Commissioner of Reclamation,

"Discussion of Region 2 Activities under Secretary Carr," May 4, 1961.

Frandsen, L., of Southern Pacific Company. Letter to Harvey O. Banks, California Department of Water Resources, and Clyde Spencer, Regional Director of Bureau of Reclamation, October 1, 1956.

Harris, Ellen Stern. Memorandum to Carl Kymla, Metropolitan Water District, "MWD's Proposed 1979–80 Budget," June 4, 1979.

Interview between Lawrence W. Swenson and Donald Sandison, Department of Water Resources, and Patrick Porgans, Red Tape Abatement, Inc., August 4, 1981.

Lineweaver, Goodrich W., Senate Committee on Interior and Insular Affairs. Letter to William E. Warne, Commissioner of Agriculture, State of California, January 20, 1960.

McDiarmid, John M. Letter To Ronald Robie, May 30, 1980.

Pafford, Robert. Blue envelope memorandum to Commissioner of Reclamation, "Eel River Basin Planning and Interagency Coordination on Route Selection," January 19, 1968.

———. Blue envelope memorandum to Commissioner of Reclamation, "Proposed Alternative to Kellogg Unit, Central Valley Project," December 24, 1968.

———. Blue envelope memorandum to Commissioner of Reclamation, "Subsidence in the Westlands Water District" (undated).

Regional Director, Sacramento. Memorandum to Commissioner of Reclamation, "Westlands Water District—Ground water pumping and excess lands," March 16, 1964.

Robie, Ronald, Department of Water Resources. Letter to Thomas Graff, Environmental Defense Fund, July 19, 1977.

Robie, Ronald B. Letter to Michael Storper (undated; circa May 1979).

Staats, Elmer. Letter to Lee C. White, The White House, "The Westlands Distribution System," September 19, 1964.

Stamm, Gilbert. Memorandum to Commissioner of Reclamation, "Excess Land Problem of the Imperial Irrigation District," October 1, 1965.

West, Arleigh. Blue envelope memorandum to Commissioner of Reclamation, "Excess Lands—Imperial Irrigation District—Boulder Canyon Project, California," April 15, 1965.

———. CONFIDENTIAL. Blue envelope memorandum to Commissioner Dominy, Bureau of Reclamation, "Excess land survey in areas served by Metropolitan Water District, Southern California," December 30, 1964.

CHAPTER ELEVEN: **Those Who Refuse to Learn . . .**

The main sources for the Fontanelle story were H. P. Dugan, Barney Bellport, Floyd Dominy, and a series of blue envelope memoranda discussing the near-disaster.

The chronicle of the Teton disaster was put together largely from excellent reporting by the *Idaho Statesman*. Coverage in the *Los Angeles Times* was also exceptionally good. John Erlichman, Pete van Gytenbeek, and Nathaniel Reed provided much of the political background.

Major sources for the Colorado and Narrows Dam section of the chapter were C. J. Kuiper, Don and Karen Christenson, Glenn Saunders, Felix Sparks, Guy Martin, Robert Weaver, Gary Friehauff, Daniel Beard, Alan Merson, Sandy White, and Wayne Aspinall.

BOOKS

Athearn, Robert G. *High Country Empire*. Lincoln: University of Nebraska Press, 1960.

Gottlieb, Robert, and Peter Wiley. *Empires in the Sun*. New York: Putnam, 1982.

McPhee, John. *Basin and Range*. New York: Farrar, Straus, and Giroux, 1981.

Thomas, Janet, et al., eds. *That Day in June*. Rexburg, Idaho: Ricks College Press, 1977.

ARTICLES AND REPORTS

Actions Needed to Increase the Safety of Dams Built by the Bureau of Reclamation and the Corps of Engineers. Government Accounting Office, Washington, D.C., June 3, 1977.

"Analyst: Narrows benefit distorted." *Rocky Mountain News* (undated).

Arthur, Harold. *Preliminary Report on Failure of Teton Dam*, Denver, U.S. Bureau of Reclamation, June 7, 1976.

"Avid Environmentalists Castigated for Tactics." *Idaho Falls Post-Register*, June 4, 1972.

"B of R Eyed, Rejected Aerial Survey of Leaks." *Idaho Statesman*, July 29, 1976.

"B of R Left Fissure Unfilled to Avoid Delay of Dam Work." *Idaho Statesman* (undated).

Brown, Russell. Testimony, Teton Dam Hearing, Senate Interior Committee, Idaho Falls, Idaho, February 21, 1977.

"Bruised Teton Dam Wins Another Political Fight." *Idaho Falls Post-Register*, October 20, 1971.

Bureau of Reclamation. *The Fryingpan-Arkansas Project*, June 1977.

"Bureau of Reclamation Won't Fight Teton Report Criticizing Agency." *Idaho Statesman*, January 7, 1977.

"Bureaucratic Gamble Ended in Disaster." *Idaho Statesman*, September 6, 1976.

"Charge of Scapegoating." *Idaho Statesman*, May 20, 1977.

"Colorado, Carter, and the Dams." *Rocky Mountain News*, February 23, 1977.

"Colorado Water Projects—Impacts and Alternatives." *Denver Post*, April 17, 1977.

Committee on Government Operations. *Teton Dam Disaster*, Washington, D.C., 1976.

"Currents of Argument Swirl over Poudre River." *Denver Post*, May 24, 1981.

"Dam Opposition Said Obstructionism." *Idaho Falls Post-Register*, October 10, 1971.

"Dam Safety: No National Answer." *ENR News*, May 8, 1980.

"Devastation in Eastern Idaho Boggles Mind." *Idaho Statesman*, June 8, 1976.

Engstrom, Jay. *The Policy of Disaster: The Decision to Build the Teton Dam*, November 15, 1976.

"Environment Aims Cloud Idaho Industrial Role." *Idaho Falls Post-Register*, October 10, 1971.

"Fissures Made Teton Difficult." *Idaho Statesman*, July 9, 1976.

"Groundwater Rise Preceded Collapse." *Idaho Statesman*, July 17, 1976.

"Grout Curtain Failure May Have Triggered Teton Dam Collapse." *Engineering News Review*, June 10, 1978.

"He Protests Too Loudly." *Rexburg Standard*, September 14, 1971.

"Idaho Dam Disaster—New Blame." *San Francisco Chronicle*, December 27, 1979.

Idaho Environmental Council. *The Fraud of Teton Dam*, 1972.

Idaho Environmental Council. *The Teton Dam Symposium*, June 4, 1972.

"Impossible Dam Failure Spurs Study of Liability," *Idaho Statesman*, June 10, 1976.

"Lamm Reaffirms Narrows Support." *Denver Post*, August 4, 1976.

"Looters Hit Chaotic Rexburg." *Idaho Statesman*, June 9, 1976.

"Memos Tell of Teton Project Deficit." *Idaho Statesman*, July 13, 1976.

Notes and Bibliography

"More state water projects likely." *Rocky Mountain News*, July 23, 1979.

"Narrows Dam Gets 'Clean Bill of Health.' " *Denver Post*, August 17, 1968.

The Narrows Unit, Colorado. Lower South Platte Water Conservancy District, Sterling, Colorado.

Narrows Unit, Pick-Sloan Missouri Basin Project. U.S. Department of the Interior, Water Projects Review, April 1977.

"New Dangers confront victims of Idaho flood." *Deseret News*, June 8, 1976.

Odell, Rice. "Silt, Cracks, Floods, and Other Dam Foolishness." *Audubon*, September 1975.

"Officials Dispute Time of First BOR Warning."*Idaho Statesman*, June 9, 1976.

"Opposition to Teton Dam Hurts Environmentalists," *Idaho Falls Post-Register*, June 6, 1971.

Regional Landowners Group. *Narrows Fact Sheet*, March 1978.

Regional Landowners Group. *"The Narrows and Its Alternatives—A Benefit-Cost Comparison,"* March 1978.

Regional Landowners Group. *Response to the Bureau of Reclamation's "Special Report—Narrows Unit,"* February 1978.

Reed, Scott. Untitled monograph for Snake River Regional Studies Center Conference, April 1, 1977.

"Safety questions scarcely raised by opponents of ill-fated dam." *Denver Post*, June 8, 1976.

Saunders, Glenn. *Colorado Water Rights—A Briefing Paper* (undated).

"State Engineer on Narrows" (three-part series). *Fort Morgan Times*, April 5, 6, and 7, 1978.

"Sunset for the Narrows." *Empire Magazine (Denver Post)*, January 11, 1976.

"Team Says Teton Dam Eaten Away from Within." *Rocky Mountain News*, July 16, 1976.

"Teton: Background of the Dispute." *Intermountain Observer*, June 10, 1972.

"Teton Dam: The Sorry Lesson." *High Country News*, June 18, 1976.

"Teton Dam Collapse: How Disaster Struck." *Los Angeles Times*, July 18, 1976.

"Teton Dam Designers Called 'Stale.' " *Idaho Statesman*, February 22, 1977.

"Teton Meets Economic Test, Asserts Walker." *Idaho Falls Post-Register*, October 17, 1971.

"Teton Project Impresses Andrus, Safeguards Eyed." *Idaho Falls Post-Register*, May 17, 1971.

"Teton River Dam Stirs Controversy." *High Country News*, June 11, 1971.

556

"Teton Served as Battleground." *Idaho Statesman*, September 8, 1976.

"Teton Dam Termed Non-Political Issue." *Idaho Falls Post-Register*, October 20, 1971.

U.S. Bureau of Reclamation. Statement Before the Subcommittee on Conservation, Energy, and Natural Resources of the Committee on Government Operations, August 6, 1976.

U.S. Bureau of Reclamation. "Teton Dam Failure," press release, June 9, 1976.

U.S. Department of the Interior, Water Projects Review. *Fruitland Mesa Project, CRSP*, April 1977.

U.S. Fish and Wildlife Service. *Comments of the Fish and Wildlife Service on the Bureau of Reclamation's Special Report, Narrows Unit, February 1978* (undated).

U.S. Water Resources Council. *Manual of Procedures for Evaluating Benefits and Costs of Federal Water Resources Projects*, Washington, D.C., February 9, 1979.

"USGS Response to Queries About Teton Dam." U.S. Geologic Survey, Reston, Virginia, June 15, 1976.

"Warm, Lazy day in Rexburg, then crash." *Deseret News*, June 7, 1976.

"Water Project 'Hit List': A View from the West." *Denver Post*, March 27, 1977.

"Water Projects' Need Debated." *Denver Post* (undated).

"Water Users Support Rebuilding Teton." *Idaho Statesman*, December 11, 1976.

"Water Won't Stretch for Western Cities' Growth." *High Country News*, October 7, 1977.

"Welcome to Wrecksburg." *Sundowner*, Winter 1977.

Williams, Philip. "Dam Design: Is the Technology Faulty?" *New Scientist*, February 2, 1978.

LETTERS, MEMORANDA, MISCELLANEOUS

Acting Chief Geologist, Bureau of Reclamation. Memorandum to D. J. Duck, "Seismic Monitoring Program—Teton Dam and Reservoir," June 20, 1973.

Bellport, Barney. Blue envelope memorandum to Commissioner of Reclamation, "Fontanelle Dam and Reservoir—Seedskadee Project, Wyoming," May 11, 1965.

———. Blue envelope memorandum to Commissioner, Bureau of Reclamation, "Replacement of American Falls Dam," May 24, 1967.

Crandall, David. Blue envelope letter to Chief Engineer, Bureau of Reclamation, "Fontanelle Dam," September 30, 1965 (with response; undated).

Curry, Robert. Letter to V. E. McKelvey, U.S. Geologic Survey, July 6, 1976.

Green, John, Regional Administrator, Environmental Protection Agency. Letter to Keith Higginson, Commissioner of Reclamation, July 13, 1977.

Kosman, Jacob, Irrigationists' Association of Water District No. 1. Letter to President Jimmy Carter, et al., April 1, 1978.

Kuiper, C. J. Personal correspondence, November 21, 1979.

Kyncl, George. "A New Look at the Narrows," January 15, 1977.

McCabe, Joseph, Environmental Protection Agency. Letter to Daniel Beard, U.S. Department of the Interior, February 23, 1978.

McDonald, William, Colorado Conservation Board. Letter to Frank M. Scott, Harza Engineering Company, May 15, 1980.

McKelvey, V. E. Letter to Robert Curry, Department of Geology, University of Montana, July 21, 1976.

———. Letter to Senator Henry Jackson, June 11, 1976.

Nelson, Harold. Blue envelope letter to Commissioner of Reclamation, "Expedited processing of interim reports—Fremont Dam, Lower Teton Division: Ririe Dam; and raising Blackfoot Reservoir," February 24, 1962.

Oriel, Steven, et al. Unaddressed memorandum, "Preliminary Report on Geologic Investigations, Eastern Snake River Plain and Adjoining Mountains," June 1973.

Parenteau, Patrick A., National Wildlife Federation. Letter to Cecil D. Andrus, February 23, 1977.

Phipps, E. Personal correspondence, September 25, 1979.

Schleicher, David. Unaddressed memorandum, "Some geologic concerns about the Teton Basin Project," December 26, 1972.

Sparks, Felix. Memorandum to Colorado Water Conservation Board, "Consideration of FY 1980 Funding Requirements for Colorado Reclamation Projects," March 6, 1979.

CHAPTER TWELVE: **Things Fall Apart**

Most of the background on the Texas Water Plan comes from coverage in the *Texas Observer* and from "You Ain't Seen Nothing Yet" in *The Water Hustlers*.

The Ogallala situation is well described in the Economic Development Administration's report and in an excellent series of articles that ran in the *Denver Post* in 1979 (see bibliography). Desertification and its potential consequences are thoroughly covered in David Sheridan's *Desertification of the United States* and in Paul Sears's *Deserts on the March*. Sheridan's book, though not as eloquent, is considerably more up-to-date and crammed with information.

The Department of Agriculture's Salinity Control Laboratory in Riverside, California, is a great source of information on salinity, its consequences, and its avoidance. A good compendium on irrigation in general is Cantor's *World Geography of Irrigation*.

Information, much of it not so up-to-date, on reservoir siltation is available from both the Corps of Engineers and the Bureau of Reclamation. Most libraries are almost devoid of literature on this gigantic problem. This section of the chapter draws heavily on interviews with Raphael Kazmann and Luna Leopold, and on Kazmann's book *Modern Hydrology*, one of the few exceptions to the above statement.

Other important interviews for this chapter: Jan van Schilfgaarde, Jim Casey, Daniel Dreyfus, C. J. Kuiper, Joe Moore, Steven Reynolds, Herbert Grubb, Ronnie Dugger, Mary Ellen Morbeck, Bob Strand, Wayne Wyatt, Floyd Dominy, Jay Lehr, Philip Williams, Mohammed El-Ashry, George Pring, W. R. Collier.

Books

Cantor, Leonard Martin. *A World Geography of Irrigation.* New York: Praeger, 1970.

Goldsmith, Edward, and Nicholas Hildyard. *The Social and Environmental Effects of Large Dams.* Cornwall, England: Wadebridge Ecological Center, 1985.

Graves, John. "You Ain't Seen Nothing Yet." In Robert Boyle, et al., eds., *The Water Hustlers.* San Francisco: Sierra Club, 1971.

Kazmann, Raphael. *Modern Hydrology.* 2nd ed. New York: Harper and Row, 1972.

Peterson, Dean F., and A. Berry Crawford, eds. *Values and Choices in the Development of the Colorado River Basin.* Tuscon: University of Arizona Press, 1978.

Peterson, Elmer T. *Big Dam Foolishness.* New York: Devin-Adair, 1954.

Sheridan, David. *Desertification of the United States.* Washington, D.C.: Council on Environmental Quality, 1981.

Notes and Bibliography

ARTICLES, REPORTS

Adams, Daniel B. "Last-Ditch Archaeology." *Science 83*, December 1983.

Agricultural Drainage and Salt Management in the San Joaquin Valley. San Joaquin Valley Interagency Drainage Program, Fresno, California, June 1979.

Ambroggi, Robert P. "Underground Reservoirs Control the Water Cycle," *Scientific American*, May 1977.

"Arid West Is Trying Drip Irrigation." *New York Times*, June 28, 1983.

"Back to Basics: Mining Water Deep Below Heart of Texas." *New York Times*, July 27, 1980.

Began, Ann. "National Public Water Policy: The Colorado River." Environmental Policy Center, Washington, D.C., August 1977.

Briggs, Jean A. "There's no synwater industry to bail us out." *Forbes*, March 16, 1981.

Brown, Howard. "Wellton-Mohawk." Memorandum to Senator Paul Fannin, Library of Congress Congressional Research Service, May 5, 1975.

"Critics Call Billion-Dollar Water Project in Arizona Wasteful." *Washington Post* (undated).

"Department of State Sells U.S. Taxpayers and Mexico Down the Drain," Environmental Policy Institute (undated).

"Desalting Needs Reduced by Water-Savings Program." *Denver Post*, November 20, 1978.

"The Drying Out of America." *Discover*, April 1981.

Elephant Butte Reservoir, 1980 Sedimentation Survey, U.S. Department of the Interior, July 1983.

"Ground water levels dip in 10 Oregon farming areas." *Oregonian*, April 10, 1983.

"The High Plains: Depleting the Ogalalla" (series of six articles). *Denver Post*, December 16–21, 1979.

Holburt, Myron. "The 1973 Agreement on Colorado River Salinity Between the United States and Mexico." Presented at the National Conference on Irrigation Return Flow Quality Management, Fort Collins, Colorado, May 1977.

The Hydrologic History of the San Carlos Reservoir, Arizona, 1929–1971. Geological Survey Professional Paper 665-N, 1977.

Jacobsen, Thorkind, and Robert M. Adams. "Salt and Silt in Ancient Mesopotamian Agriculture." *Science*, November 1958.

Kuiper, C. J. "The Ground Water Rush of 1978." Office of the Colorado State Engineer, February 5, 1979.

Kuiper, C. J., Floyd Dominy, et al. *Nile River Irrigation System Rehabilitation and Improvement Program.* Report of the Scope Team.

"Lamm Calls 'Water Grab' Time Bomb in Constitution." *Denver Post,* April 3, 1979.

Lehr, Jay H. "Groundwater—in the Eighties." *WATER Engineering and Management,* March 1981.

LeVeen, E. Philip. *A Political-Economic Analysis of the Prospects for Irrigated Agriculture in California,* Berkeley, California, November 1984.

———. "Toward a New Food Policy." Public Interest Economics—West, Berkeley, California.

"Losers all around in irrigation battleground." *Fresno Bee,* November 25, 1984.

"Mexico Won't Pay for Texas Oil Spill Mess." *San Francisco Chronicle* (undated).

The 1964 Sedimentation Survey of Boysen Reservoir, Wyoming. U.S. Bureau of Reclamation, November 1965.

"Ogallala Overdraft Could Start Big Battle over Rescue Strategies." *World Water,* September 1982.

Pillsbury, Arthur F. "The Salinity of Rivers." *Scientific American,* July 1981.

"Plans to Hold Down Colorado River's Salt Content and Avoid Irking Mexico Are Hit by Rising Costs." *Wall Street Journal,* June 21, 1979.

"The Price of a Sweet River." *Boston Globe,* May 27, 1979.

Rates of Sediment Production in Midwestern United States. U.S. Department of Agriculture, Soil Conservation Service, Washington, D.C., December 1948.

"Representative Brown Calls Colorado River Desalting Plant 'Boondoggle,' Fights to Halt Project." *Los Angeles Times,* May 8, 1979.

Rhodes, J. D., and R. D. LeMert. "Use of San Joaquin Valley Saline Drainage Waters for Irrigation of Cotton." USDA Salinity Control Laboratory, Riverside, 1981.

Risser, James. "Worse Than the Dust Bowl." *The New Farm,* February 1983.

"Running Dry: Huge Area in Midwest Relying on Irrigation Is Depleting Its Water." *Wall Street Journal,* August 6, 1980.

Russell, Dick. "Ogallala—Half Full or Half Empty?" *The Amicus Journal,* Fall 1985.

S. 496, "A Bill to increase the appropriations ceiling for title I of the Colorado River Basin Salinity Control Act." U.S. Senate, February 22, 1979.

Sedimentation Report of Buffalo Bill Reservoir, Shoshone Project." U.S. Bureau of Reclamation, May 24, 1949.

Notes and Bibliography

Sedimentation Study, Glen Canyon Dam, Colorado River Storage Project, U.S. Bureau of Reclamation, May 1962.

"Seventy-six Tons of Tomatoes per Acre with Subsurface Trickle Irrigation." *USDA Agriculture Research Service News,* November 4, 1982.

Shaw, Gaylord. "The search for dangerous dams: a program to head off disaster." *Natural History.*

Shoji, Kobe. "Drip Irrigation." *Scientific American.*

Skogerboe, Gaylord V. "Agricultural Impact on Water Quality in Western Rivers." Department of Agricultural Engineering, Colorado State University, Fort Collins.

"SPLAT! Clements belly-flops over Arkansas water." *Texas Monthly,* May 1981.

"State's Bold Plan to Create Power, Drinking Water." *San Francisco Chronicle,* August 14, 1984.

Sudman, Rita Schmidt. "Salt in the San Joaquin." *Western Water,* May/June 1982.

Texas Observer, 1966–1981. (Author's note: Most of the material relating to the Texas Water Plan was gleaned from excellent reporting in this publication over some fifteen years. Unfortunately, this file was lost or misplaced. However, the *Texas Observer* maintains a good index for those who wish to read more about water and Texas. Reprints of many issues are available.)

Theodore Roosevelt Lake—1981 Sedimentation Survey. U.S. Department of the Interior, July 1983.

"Upper Colorado River Basin Energy Development Project Water Needs and Water Supplies." Unpublished Interior Department Discussion Draft, May 23, 1974.

"The Valley's Dangerous Drain Problem." *San Francisco Examiner,* May 20, 1979.

Van Schilfgaarde, Jan. "Water Conservation Potential in Irrigated Agriculture." *USDA* Salinity Control Laboratory, Riverside, California, August 1979.

"Water resource mismanagement brewing crisis." *Oregonian,* March 20, 1983.

"What to Do When the Well Runs Dry." *Science,* November 14, 1980.

Williams, Philip. "Dam Design: Is the Technology Faulty?" *New Scientist,* February 2, 1978.

Worster, Donald. "Water and the Flow of Power." *The Ecologist,* Vol. 13, No. 5, 1983.

LETTERS, MEMORANDA, MISCELLANEOUS

Adams, Mark. Blue envelope memorandum to Floyd Dominy, Commissioner of Reclamation, "Tenor of comments by a few members of Texas Congressional Delegation concerning Reclamation program in Texas," June 12, 1962.

Gessel, Clyde, and William Culp. Memorandum to Chief, Division of River Control, Bureau of Reclamation, "Sediment Deposition—Blue Mesa Reservoir Site—Curecanti Unit—Colorado River Storage Project," March 29, 1961.

Hill, Leon. Blue envelope memorandum to Commissioner, Bureau of Reclamation, "Texas Water Situation," September 1, 1966.

Mermel, T. W. Memorandum to Commissioner Dominy, "USSR Breaks Records—Earth and Arch Dams," November 19, 1968.

Nelson, Harold. Blue envelope memorandum to Commissioner of Reclamation, "Possible Leakage, Yellowtail Reservoir," April 20, 1966.

Oka, James N. Memorandum to Chief, Special Studies Branch, Bureau of Reclamation, "Sediment Study, Morrow Point Reservoir," March 28, 1962.

EPILOGUE: **A Civilization, if You Can Keep It**

Information on the North American Water and Power Alliance is readily proffered by the Parsons Company in Pasadena, California. Background on the project was also provided by Jim Casey, Barney Bellport, C. J. Kuiper, Stanford McCasland, Derrick Sewall, Frank Moss, and Irving Fox. Derrick Sewall, Irving Fox, and Moira Farrow were my main sources regarding the Canadian water situation.

BOOKS, ARTICLES, REPORTS, LETTERS, MEMORANDA, MISCELLANEOUS

"Actual Price of High Dams Also Includes Social Costs." *New York Times*, July 10, 1983.

"Alaska to Mexico Canals Urged to Water Deserts." *Denver Post*, February 27, 1977.

"Audits Show Unbusinesslike Management of Western Basin Accounts." Environmental Policy Center, Washington, D.C.

"Billion Dollar Plot Alleged: U.S. 'Wants Canada's Water.'" *Vancouver Sun*, June 27, 1981.

Bocking, Richard. *Canada's Water—For Sale?* James Lewis and Samuel, Toronto, 1972.

Notes and Bibliography

"Damage to Glen Canyon Spillways Complicates Plans for Spring Run-off." *Salt Lake Tribune*, December 14, 1983.

Dominy, Floyd. Untitled monograph (response to U.S. Chamber of Commerce report on adverse effects of expanding government), October 25, 1957.

Dominy Foresees Water Sharing Need After Northwest Meets Requirements." *Idaho Statesman*, January 22, 1966.

"Great Lakes States Seek to Keep Their Water." *New York Times*, June 13, 1982.

Kierans, Thomas W. *The Grand Canal: A Water Resources Planning Concept for North America*. Alexander Graham Bell Institute, Sydney, Nova Scotia.

King, Laura B., and Philip E. LeVeen. *Turning Off the Tap on Federal Water Subsidies* (Volume I: *The Central Valley Project: The $3.5 Billion Giveaway*). Natural Resources Defense Council, San Francisco, August 1985.

"Next B.C. Megaproject Looms." *Vancouver Sun*, September 29, 1985.

Pearce, Fred. "Fall and Rise of the Caspian Sea." *New Scientist*, December 6, 1984.

Rada, Edward L., and Richard J. Berquist. *Irrigation Efficiency in the Production of California Crop Calories and Proteins*. California Water Resources Center, Davis, California, May 1976.

Sewall, Derrick. *Water: The Emerging Crisis in Canada*. Canadian Institute for Economic Policy, Ottawa, 1981.

Snyder, Nathan. *Water from Alaska*. Ralph M. Parsons Company, October 15, 1980.

A Summary of Water Resources Projects, Plans, and Studies Relating to the Western and Midwestern United States. Senate Committee on Public Works, Washington, D.C., 1966.

Tunison, M. C. Letter to Senator William King of Utah, December 15, 1938.

"U.S. Demands Say in Stikine Dams." Telkwa Foundation *Newsletter*, May/June 1981.

Van der Leeden, Frits. *Water Resources of the World*. Water Information Center, Port Washington, New York, 1975.

Water Crisis. Ralph M. Parsons Company, Pasadena, 1980.

"Water Diversion Proposals." Idaho Water Resources Board, July 1969.

Water Use on Western Farms: An Examination of Irrigation Practices and Ways They Can Be Improved. INFORM, New York City, Spring 1982.

INDEX

Index

Index

Index

Index

Index

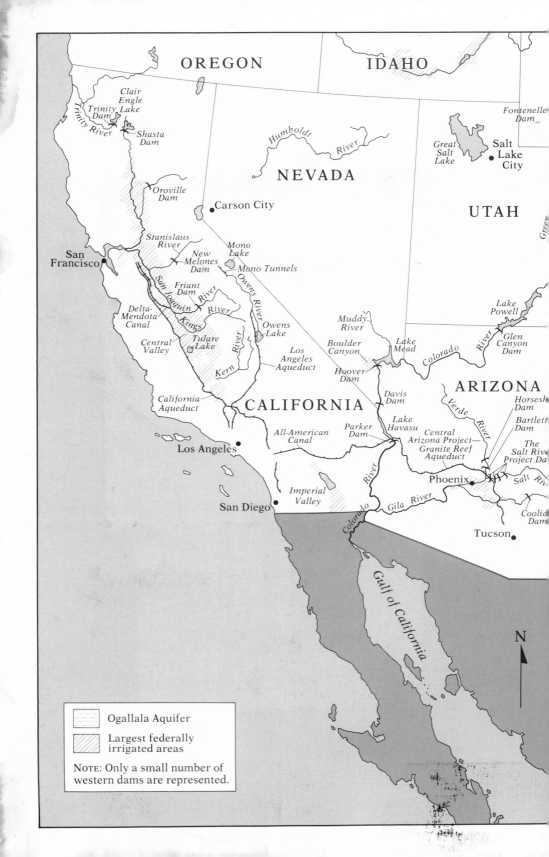